International Series in Operations Research & Management Science

Volume 323

Series Editor

Camille C. Price
Department of Computer Science, Stephen F. Austin State University,
Nacogdoches, TX, USA

Associate Editor

Joe Zhu
Foisie Business School, Worcester Polytechnic Institute, Worcester, MA, USA

Founding Editor

Frederick S. Hillier
Stanford University, Stanford, CA, USA

More information about this series at https://link.springer.com/bookseries/6161

Zhi-Long Chen • Nicholas G. Hall

Supply Chain Scheduling

 Springer

Zhi-Long Chen
Department of Decision,
Operations & Information Technologies
Robert H. Smith School of Business
University of Maryland
College Park, MD, USA

Nicholas G. Hall
Department of Operations
and Business Analytics
Fisher College of Business
Ohio State University
Columbus, OH, USA

ISSN 0884-8289 ISSN 2214-7934 (electronic)
International Series in Operations Research & Management Science
ISBN 978-3-030-90372-5 ISBN 978-3-030-90374-9 (eBook)
https://doi.org/10.1007/978-3-030-90374-9

© Springer Nature Switzerland AG 2022
This work is subject to copyright. All rights are reserved by the Publisher, whether the whole or part of the material is concerned, specifically the rights of translation, reprinting, reuse of illustrations, recitation, broadcasting, reproduction on microfilms or in any other physical way, and transmission or information storage and retrieval, electronic adaptation, computer software, or by similar or dissimilar methodology now known or hereafter developed.
The use of general descriptive names, registered names, trademarks, service marks, etc. in this publication does not imply, even in the absence of a specific statement, that such names are exempt from the relevant protective laws and regulations and therefore free for general use.
The publisher, the authors and the editors are safe to assume that the advice and information in this book are believed to be true and accurate at the date of publication. Neither the publisher nor the authors or the editors give a warranty, expressed or implied, with respect to the material contained herein or for any errors or omissions that may have been made. The publisher remains neutral with regard to jurisdictional claims in published maps and institutional affiliations.

This Springer imprint is published by the registered company Springer Nature Switzerland AG
The registered company address is: Gewerbestrasse 11, 6330 Cham, Switzerland

This book is dedicated to our families and friends.

Foreword

Scheduling of activities are ubiquitous processes. Scheduling takes place on a regular basis in many application areas at multiple levels, at operational levels as well as at strategic levels. I have been interested in the general area of scheduling for more than four decades and have been continuously amazed by the variety of application domains in which these processes play a critical role. One of the more important application areas is the scheduling that takes place in supply chains, which is the topic that is being covered in this book. The importance of this application area has become even more to the forefront in the pandemic period of 2020–2021, during which many global supply chains have been hurt considerably, requiring significant amounts of rescheduling.

I have known both Zhi-Long Chen and Nick Hall for more than three decades, and at every conference that we attend, either in the USA, in China, or anywhere else, we have been looking forward to our discussions on the topics we are working on. Zhi-Long and Nick have been working on the area of supply chain scheduling already for quite a while, and this monograph is the culmination of their and other people's work in this area.

While classical scheduling has been studied since the mid-1950s, the integration of scheduling with the coordination and competition issues that arise ubiquitously in supply chains dates back about 20 years. Some of the foundational works on this topic were written by the two authors of this book. This work has become highly influential within the operations research community. At the time of writing, an online search on the book title reveals 3300 published works. To my knowledge, however, this book represents the first attempt to synthesize the main research directions within supply chain scheduling into a single source.

Supply Chain Scheduling addresses the coordination and competition of scheduling and other operational decisions in supply chains from two perspectives. The first perspective is that of a single decision maker faced with multiple types of operational decisions—for example, production and distribution, or production and pricing. The second perspective is that of multiple self-interested decision makers whose decisions collectively determine the performance of a supply chain—for example, a supplier and a manufacturer, or multiple suppliers in an assembly system.

The problems studied are identified as centralized under the first perspective, and decentralized under the second one. Each perspective addresses a wide variety of applications and theoretical issues. A consistent focus of the book is the value added by the coordinated decision-making of scheduling and other functions, relative to local or even decentralized decision-making for different parts of a problem.

The book consists of two parts. Part I consists of Chaps. 3 through 6. These chapters study centralized problems in supply chain scheduling. Chapters 3 and 4 address the integration of production scheduling and outbound distribution decisions in both offline and online settings. Chapter 5 studies the coordination of production and pricing decisions, and Chap. 6 discusses the joint consideration of subcontracting and scheduling decisions. A wide variety of optimization methodologies are employed in Part I, including dynamic programming, integer optimization, branch-and-bound, heuristic design, and worst-case and asymptotic performance analysis.

Part II consists of Chaps. 7 through 9. Chapter 7 uses classical scheduling techniques and dynamic programming to identify the cost of conflict when individual players make self-interested decisions in supply chains. The works discussed in this chapter have been strongly motivational for the development of supply chain scheduling research. Chapter 8 views supply chain scheduling problems as cooperative games, and within that context studies application to sequencing and scheduling games, as well as capacity allocation and subcontracting problems. Chapter 9 uses the perspective of noncooperative games, and studies applications with complete information as well as others where some information is private.

This monograph will undoubtedly serve as a solid basis for future research on this important topic. I feel privileged to be allowed to write a foreword to this book and put this area in a proper perspective. I am confident that this text will become an indispensable foundation on which many researchers in academia and industry will rely.

New York University, New York, NY, USA   Michael L. Pinedo
August 2021

Preface

The topic of this book is decision-making at the interface of supply chain management and production scheduling. These are both very active research areas with profound practical impact through diverse applications. An essential component of such decision processes is coordination. In this book, coordination is studied in two different environments. We first study the coordination of multiple operational functions by a single centralized decision maker. This work generalizes the classical scheduling environment that typically addresses a single operation. We also study the coordination of the decisions of multiple decentralized decision makers who are self-interested but may be either cooperative or noncooperative. This work translates classical supply chain research into more detailed operational planning. The study of these topics within the book ranges broadly through the research areas of classical scheduling, combinatorial optimization, computational complexity, algorithm design, heuristic performance analysis, and cooperative and noncooperative game theory.

The book begins with two introductory chapters. Chapter 1 provides historical background on the research areas that support this work and identifies numerous applications that fall within our scope. Chapter 2 provides a concise overview of essential concepts and mathematical tools that are applied in the main body of the book.

The remainder of the book has two parts. Part I consists of Chaps. 3 through 6 on centralized supply chain scheduling problems, that is, those with a single decision maker who controls multiple operational functions. Chapter 3 studies offline versions of various integrated production and outbound distribution scheduling problems, whereas Chap. 4 is focused on online versions of such problems. Chapter 5 considers problems in which product pricing and production scheduling decisions are made together. Chapter 6 discusses situations where subcontracting and scheduling decisions are made jointly in order to optimize the overall system performance. In each chapter, we present solution algorithms and heuristics, analyze their performance, and evaluate the benefit of joint optimization.

Part II of this book consists of Chaps. 7 through 9. These chapters study decentralized problems, that is, those with multiple entirely or predominantly self-interested players, in supply chain scheduling. Chapter 7 uses optimization models to study the cost of conflict that arises from unequal supply chain power and the benefit that results when players coordinate their schedules. Chapter 8 uses cooperative games to study the stability of coalitions between supply chain members and various schemes for compensating them using the gains from cooperation. Chapter 9 uses noncooperative games to study equilibrium solutions, their system performance, and possible ways to enhance that performance including by incentivizing the truthful reporting of private information.

Our motivation for writing this book arises in part from our consistent research interest in scheduling and related problems over more than 20 years. A second motivating factor is the influence of supply chain management which focuses on the coordination issue mentioned above, but typically does not relate it to the level of detailed scheduling decisions. We believe that the integration of these two research areas has both theoretical interest and practical value. In addition, because many scheduling problems have a simple structure that offers easily obtained insights, we have observed that such problems are used in numerous works to develop results within cooperative and noncooperative game theory. Those works naturally fall within the scope of our book.

Our writing process for the book has been an evolutionary one. It began with a broad concept of a supply chain, which includes, for example, a traditional vertical supply chain such as a supplier and a manufacturer, where a single decision maker coordinates multiple operational functions, and a horizontal supply chain such as multiple suppliers competing for the capacity of a manufacturer, where there are multiple decision makers at the same level. Additional generality was provided by the flexibility to model decision makers as either jobs that require scheduling or machines that schedule the jobs. The focus on intensified competition, which has been a major motivation for the development of supply chain management, has also motivated the many supply chain scheduling applications we discuss. We have been inspired by the growing variety of applications enabled by e-commerce that can be modeled as supply chain scheduling problems. A challenge that we have faced during our 4-year development of the book has been keeping up with the rapid pace of new research.

Scheduling research, which began more than 65 years ago, remains very active with many theoretical developments and innovative new applications appearing each year. Some trends that support increasing interest in this work in the future include the ever more important role scheduling plays in a supply chain, the widespread implementation of computer-based scheduling systems, and the increasing use of online platforms to schedule work among decentralized decision makers. Indeed, it is the potential growth of such applications that convinces us of the timeliness of our book project.

The intended audience of this book is researchers and graduate students who are interested in supply chain planning, extensions of classical scheduling, combinatorial optimization generally, and emerging applications of cooperative and noncooperative game theory. The book does not provide a comprehensive exposure to supply chain management, classical scheduling, combinatorial optimization, or cooperative or noncooperative game theory. All these research topics are well supported by many excellent existing books, which can effectively prepare readers without previous background in these five topics. For students who are in possession of such background, this book could provide an extensive tour of those topics centered around the simple but highly intuitive paradigm of scheduling. We cite more than 400 references, which can be used as assigned readings in support of the content of the book. The book also contains more than 100 fully worked numerical examples that illustrate the broad range of mathematical techniques that model and solve supply chain scheduling applications.

Much of this book is based on work which we have done together or with other co-authors. For example, most of the content of Chap. 7 is based on four works which we originally wrote and which (based on the number of citations received) are viewed as foundational to the topic of supply chain scheduling. We have rewritten these works to make them more accessible and present the results in a unified way. However, we have also used parts of various works by other authors from the published open literature. In each case, we introduced some reorganization and rewriting, and of course appropriately referenced the work and where necessary (as advised by our publisher) obtained copyright permission. Under these guidelines, we have reproduced a number of proofs, especially mathematical proofs, without substantial changes. We have also contacted the most frequently cited authors to ensure that they believe that their work has been appropriately attributed. In several cases, they also suggested improvements to the presentation, which we appreciate.

This book has also benefited greatly from reading by several expert colleagues, including Alessandro Agnetis (Università di Siena), Zhixin Liu (University of Michigan-Dearborn), Daniel Ng (The Hong Kong Polytechnic University), Xiangtong Qi (The Hong Kong University of Science and Technology), Bingling She (Imperial College London), George Vairaktarakis (Case Western Reserve University), Shuling Xu (Jiangnan University), and Zijin Zhang (University of Michigan). Their detailed and helpful comments are much appreciated, as are more general conversations with our many co-authors referenced within the book. We also thank our helpful and efficient editor at Springer, Jialin Yan. Finally, we thank our respective academic institutions for providing support for several summers, during which much of the writing of the book was completed.

College Park, MD, USA Zhi-Long Chen

Columbus, OH, USA Nicholas G. Hall
August 2021

Contents

1 Introduction 1
  1.1 Supply Chain Scheduling 1
  1.2 Applications 5
    1.2.1 Centralized Applications and Models 7
    1.2.2 Decentralized Applications and Models 14
  1.3 Limitations to Scope 20
  1.4 Overview of the Book 21

2 Solution Methods for Supply Chain Scheduling Problems 23
  2.1 Common Elements in Scheduling Problems 23
  2.2 Computational Complexity 25
  2.3 Solution Methods 28
    2.3.1 Dynamic Programming Algorithms 28
    2.3.2 Branch-and-Bound Algorithms 31
    2.3.3 Integer Programming Based Algorithms 33
    2.3.4 Approximate Solution Methods 39
    2.3.5 Cooperative Game Theory 43
    2.3.6 Noncooperative Game Theory 46

Part I Centralized Supply Chain Scheduling

**3 Integrated Production and Outbound Distribution
  Scheduling: Offline Problems** 53
  3.1 Introduction 53
  3.2 Problem Definition and Classification 55
    3.2.1 Model Parameters and Notation 55
  3.3 Problems with Individual and Immediate Delivery 60
    3.3.1 Maximum Delivery Time Problems with a
           Sufficient Number of Vehicles 61
    3.3.2 Maximum Delivery Time Problems with a Limited
           Number of Vehicles 66
    3.3.3 Multi-Machine Problems 70

xiii

3.4		Problems with Batch Delivery to a Single Customer	72
	3.4.1	Optimality Properties	73
	3.4.2	Single-Machine Maximum Lateness and Transportation Cost Problem	75
	3.4.3	Single-Machine Total Weighted Delivery Time and Transportation Cost Problem	77
	3.4.4	Parallel-Machine Total Delivery Time and Transportation Cost Problem	79
	3.4.5	Problems with a Limited Number of Vehicles	85
3.5		Problems with Batch Delivery to Multiple Customers	88
	3.5.1	Single-Machine Maximum Lateness and Transportation Cost Problems with Direct Shipping	89
	3.5.2	Parallel-Machine Total Delivery Time and Transportation Cost Problem with Routing	96
	3.5.3	Problems with a Limited Number of Vehicles and Direct Shipping	99
3.6		Problems with Fixed Delivery Departure Dates	102
	3.6.1	Problems with Homogeneous Vehicles	103
	3.6.2	Problems with Heterogeneous Vehicles	106
3.7		Problems with Multiple Plants	117
	3.7.1	Minimizing Total Delivery Time and Transportation Cost	119
	3.7.2	Minimizing Maximum Delivery Time and Transportation Cost	122
3.8		Problems with Two Stages of Delivery	125
	3.8.1	Optimality Properties	127
	3.8.2	Solving the Total Delivery Time Problem	129
	3.8.3	Solving the Maximum Delivery Time Problem	131
3.9		Future Research	134

4 Integrated Production and Outbound Distribution Scheduling: Online Problems ... 137

4.1		Introduction	137
4.2		Online Problems with Individual and Immediate Delivery	139
	4.2.1	Single-Machine Maximum Delivery Time Problem and Some Variants	140
	4.2.2	Parallel-Machine Maximum Delivery Time Problem	145
4.3		Online Problems with Batch Delivery to a Single Customer	147
	4.3.1	Maximum Delivery Time Problems	147
	4.3.2	Maximum Delivery Time and Transportation Cost Problems	156
	4.3.3	Total Delivery Time and Transportation Cost Problems	160

Contents   xv

4.4   Online Problems with Batch Delivery to Multiple Customers 168
    4.4.1   Maximum Delivery Time and Transportation Cost
        Problems 168
    4.4.2   Total Delivery Time and Transportation Cost Problems..... 173
4.5   Online Problems with Two Stages of Delivery 175
4.6   Online or Offline Algorithms?.. 181
4.7   Future Research 183

5   Coordinated Product Pricing and Scheduling Decisions 185
5.1   Introduction 185
5.2   Single-Period Product Based Problems 187
    5.2.1   Exact Algorithms... 190
    5.2.2 NP-Hardness Proofs.. 194
    5.2.3   Fully Polynomial Time Approximation Schemes........... 197
    5.2.4   Heuristics 203
    5.2.5   Computational Results and Managerial Insights............. 207
5.3   Single-Period Order Based Problems 210
    5.3.1   Discrete Allowable Prices..................................... 211
    5.3.2   Continuous Allowable Prices 214
5.4   Multi-Period Problems... 220
    5.4.1   Exact Algorithms... 225
    5.4.2 NP-Hardness Proofs.. 228
    5.4.3   Approximation Algorithm 233
    5.4.4   Computational Results and Managerial Insights............. 236
5.5   Future Research 239

6   Joint Subcontracting and Scheduling Decisions 241
6.1   Introduction 241
6.2   Problem with a Lead Time Performance Guarantee.................. 243
    6.2.1   Problem Definition 244
    6.2.2   Complexity and Heuristic Analysis 245
    6.2.3   Computational Results 256
    6.2.4   A Related Problem 258
6.3   Value of Subcontracting 260
    6.3.1   Value of Subcontracting in the Total Cost Problem.......... 261
    6.3.2   Value of Subcontracting in the Weighted Sum of
        Makespan and Total Cost Problem 262
6.4   Problems with a Subcontracting Budget Constraint.................. 269
    6.4.1   The Total Completion Time Problem........................ 270
    6.4.2   The Maximum Tardiness Problem........................... 273
    6.4.3   The Total Tardiness Problem 274
6.5   Problems with a Flowshop Environment............................. 276
    6.5.1 NP-Hardness Proof... 278
    6.5.2   Polynomially Solvable Cases 281
    6.5.3   Proportionate Flowshop...................................... 282

xvi Contents

6.6 Problems Requiring Delivery of Subcontracted Jobs 284
    6.6.1 Single In-House Machine and Single
            Subcontractor's Machine 284
    6.6.2 Two-Stage Flowshop 289
6.7 Problems with a More Complex Subcontracting Cost Structure 292
    6.7.1 Problem Description 292
    6.7.2 Analysis of Problems with Incremental Discount 294
6.8 Future Research 298

Part II Decentralized Supply Chain Scheduling

7 Optimization and Conflict 303
7.1 Introduction 303
7.2 Scheduling and Batching in a Supply Chain 307
    7.2.1 Preliminaries 309
    7.2.2 The Supplier's Problem 316
    7.2.3 The Manufacturer's Problem 319
    7.2.4 The Combined Problem 324
    7.2.5 Cooperation 331
7.3 Sequencing in an Assembly System 335
    7.3.1 Notation and Assumptions 336
    7.3.2 Conflicts Between Suppliers and Manufacturer 338
    7.3.3 Suppliers Dominate and Manufacturer Negotiates 354
    7.3.4 Manufacturer Dominates and Suppliers Negotiate 360
    7.3.5 Manufacturer Dominates and Suppliers Adjust 362
    7.3.6 Suppliers and Manufacturer Cooperate 367
    7.3.7 Cost Saving from Cooperation 370
    7.3.8 Extensions 376
7.4 Manufacturer and Distributor 377
    7.4.1 Problem Descriptions 378
    7.4.2 Cost of Conflict 381
    7.4.3 Supply Chain Dominance 389
    7.4.4 Benefit of Cooperation 397
7.5 Resequencing in a Supply Chain 404
    7.5.1 Notation and Classification 405
    7.5.2 Manufacturer's Problems 407
    7.5.3 Supplier's Problems 420
    7.5.4 Combined Problems 424
7.6 Future Research 427

8 Cooperative Supply Chain Scheduling 431
8.1 Introduction 431
8.2 Cooperative Game Solutions 434
8.3 Sequencing Games 442
    8.3.1 General Related Games 443
    8.3.2 Linear Costs 446

	8.3.3	Regular Costs	453
	8.3.4	Rescheduling Games	456
	8.3.5	Relaxed Sequencing Games	463
	8.3.6	Batch Sequencing Games	467
	8.3.7	Proportionate Flowshops	471
	8.3.8	Openshops	476
	8.3.9	Multi-Stage Sequencing Games	480
	8.3.10	Balancedness in Generalized Games	485
8.4	Scheduling Games		489
	8.4.1	Artificial Initial Sequence: Tail Game	490
	8.4.2	Artificial Initial Sequence: Probabilistic Game	493
	8.4.3	No Initial Sequence: Penalty	497
	8.4.4	No Initial Sequence: Penalty and Subsidy	499
8.5	Project Games		503
	8.5.1	Project Planning Games	504
	8.5.2	Project Execution Games	513
8.6	Capacity Allocation Games		520
	8.6.1	Supply Chain Scheduling Problems	521
	8.6.2	Uncoordinated Supply Chain	522
	8.6.3	Coordinated Supply Chain	534
8.7	Outsourcing Games		537
	8.7.1	Common Third-Party Facility	537
	8.7.2	Concurrent Outsourcing	541
8.8	Future Research		545

9 Noncooperative Supply Chain Scheduling 549

9.1	Introduction		549
9.2	Complete Information Games		552
	9.2.1	Noncooperative Game Concepts	552
	9.2.2	Finding and Evaluating an Equilibrium	563
9.3	Enhanced Complete Information Games		589
	9.3.1	Sequential Games	589
	9.3.2	Leader–Follower Games	597
	9.3.3	Altruistic Games	606
	9.3.4	Central Authority Manipulation	614
9.4	Private Information: Mechanisms Without Payments		616
	9.4.1	Design Concepts	617
	9.4.2	Deterministic Truthfulness	620
	9.4.3	Randomized Mechanisms	623
9.5	Private Information: Mechanisms with Payments		630
	9.5.1	Design Concepts	630
	9.5.2	Deterministic Truthfulness	641

	9.5.3	Universal Truthfulness	645
	9.5.4	Truthfulness in Expectation	647
	9.5.5	Bayes–Nash Incentive Compatibility	650
9.6	Future Research		655

References 661

Index 679

Chapter 1
Introduction

Abstract This chapter introduces supply chain scheduling, the topic of this book. Our study of supply chain scheduling contains two main parts. In the first part, we consider decision making by a single *centralized agent* who evaluates tradeoffs between different operational decisions and their related profits or costs within a supply chain. In the second part, we consider decision making by two or more *decentralized agents* and study the combined effect of their self-interested decisions on the quality of overall supply chain solutions. A common theme throughout both these environments is how to achieve coordination among the various operational functions and decisions within the supply chain, in order to improve its overall performance. In this chapter, we first position supply chain scheduling relative to the literature of classical scheduling and that of supply chain management. For both centralized and decentralized supply chains, we then discuss a wide variety of applications that motivate the modeling and methodological developments which are studied in later chapters. Limitations to our scope are also discussed. Finally, we provide an overview of the book.

1.1 Supply Chain Scheduling

Scheduling is a natural and everyday economic activity. It organizes the fulfillment and completion of *work*. In many applications discussed in this book, work is defined as consisting of a given set of discrete *jobs*. However, in other applications, it consists of a single given *workload* or *workflow* that needs to be divided between available resources for processing. This work may arise in a manufacturing, service, logistical, or general business context, and we discuss a wide variety of such *supply chain* applications where it does. The focus of our book is on *scheduling decisions* about how the work is processed, rather than details of its actual execution or implementation. The success of scheduling decisions is measured by the quality of overall supply chain performance. However, the connection between decisions and performance is not always direct. For example, in decentralized scheduling, the decisions of an individual agent are subject to reactions by other agents. Even in

© Springer Nature Switzerland AG 2022
Z.-L. Chen, N. G. Hall, *Supply Chain Scheduling*, International Series
in Operations Research & Management Science 323,
https://doi.org/10.1007/978-3-030-90374-9_1

centralized scheduling, finding the best combination of scheduling decisions is a problem that is difficult to solve in many applications.

Scheduling involves the making and implementing of decisions that affect the efficiency of operating systems. Scheduling decisions focus on detailed planning at the individual job or workload level. Typically, higher level decisions such as production planning, capacity planning, and materials requirements planning have already taken place before scheduling decisions are made. Pinedo (2016) provides an overview of the planning context within which scheduling takes place. Input to scheduling decisions includes job data, such as processing time, release date (i.e., the time when a job is first available for processing), due date (i.e., the time when the customer expects completion), and a weight or value representing job importance. The other main input is the set of resources for processing the work, for example, the number and configuration of available machines. Typical scheduling decisions include the allocation of the jobs to available resources, the sequencing of the jobs, and the timing of their processing.

We provide a brief overview of the history of scheduling. The representation of scheduling decisions can be formalized by a Gantt chart, as developed in 1917 by Henry L. Gantt, which shows the progress of work and resource usage over time. The Gantt chart is still used extensively today and incorporated into scheduling and project management software. It is an important visualization tool for monitoring schedule progress, although it does not directly make scheduling decisions.

The challenge of making effective scheduling decisions is addressed through the mathematical analysis of scheduling which began in the 1950s. Initially, work was focused on simple problems with a single resource. This resource is modeled as a single machine that is continuously available over time. Jackson (1955) and Smith (1956), for example, develop scheduling rules that find optimal solutions for simple scheduling problems in this environment. In these early works, the objective of minimizing cost is viewed from the perspective of a single *centralized decision maker*. This perspective is natural when all scheduling decisions are being made over a single operation and within a single organization. This perspective also defines much of the work within classical scheduling, which has been an extremely active research area in the following decades.

Besides work on optimal algorithms, this research area includes the documentation of numerous high value applications, the development of heuristic or approximate solution methods along with their performance analysis, and the development of results that define limits to problem tractability. Within this work, the study of the single-machine environment has been extended to include a variety of more general and more practical production systems with multiple resources for processing, including parallel machines, flowshops, jobshops, and openshops. In addition, a wide variety of cost functions, motivated by incentives in delivery contracts or by internal costs incurred by manufacturers, has been considered. Pinedo (2016) provides a highly readable introduction to the classical scheduling literature. Other useful references on scheduling theory and applications include Leung and Anderson (2004), Brucker (2013), Project Management Institute (2019), and Sokolov et al. (2020). The research impact of the scheduling field has been vast. A bibliometric study by Calma et al. (2021) identifies scheduling as the second most studied problem within the journal *Operations Research* over the period 1952–2019, with almost twice as many published articles as any other problem except inventory management.

In the past four decades, concurrently with the growth of the scheduling literature, a substantial body of research literature has developed around various coordination and competition issues faced either by a centralized decision maker across *multiple functional areas* or by multiple *decentralized decision makers* within a supply chain. This research area is *supply chain management*. Topics studied within this area include the coordination of network design and allocation decisions, coordination of production, inventory and distribution, coordination of pricing and inventory, multi-echelon inventory management, information sharing in the supply chain, and the development of contracts that coordinate the decisions of different decision makers. However, most of this existing research focuses on coordination and competition issues at the strategic and tactical planning levels, rather than at the operational level where most scheduling decisions are needed. Many books (e.g., de Kok & Graves, 2003; Simchi-Levi et al., 2004; Tayur et al., 1999) and survey papers (e.g., Chen & Simchi-Levi, 2012; Erengüç et al., 1999; Goetschalckx et al., 2002; Sahin & Robinson, 2002) describe the extensive research on issues which arise at these levels of production planning.

By contrast, research on supply chain coordination and competition issues at the detailed scheduling level is more recent; most of the research in this area was performed within the last 15 years. Our study considers both *vertical* and *horizontal* supply chains. A vertical supply chain includes more than one level, for example, a supplier which sends parts to a manufacturer which sends finished products to retailers. In a horizontal supply chain, the supply chain includes functions or agents at the same level, for example, multiple suppliers to the same manufacturer. The field of supply chain scheduling approaches these problems from a global system perspective, while considering (a) the tradeoffs faced by the decision maker in the centralized case and (b) the motivations and incentives faced by individual agents in the decentralized case. In doing so, supply chain scheduling connects and integrates multiple traditional topics that have been studied independently for decades, such as production scheduling, vehicle routing, outsourcing, and capacity planning, among others.

Our work is apparently the first book that focuses specifically on scheduling within a supply chain context. We apply the following definition for the topic of this book.

Definition 1.1 *Supply chain scheduling* unifies the topics of scheduling and supply chain management, by developing and solving coordinated scheduling models that include scheduling and other related decisions made by either a single centralized decision maker or by multiple decentralized decision makers.

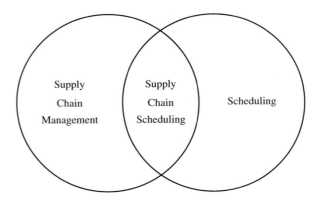

Fig. 1.1 Positioning of supply chain scheduling

In doing so, supply chain scheduling:

1. Integrates centralized scheduling decisions with issues that affect overall supply chain performance, for example, batching of jobs, inbound and outbound delivery, coordinated delivery of components, management of inventory buffers, pricing, and subcontracting
2. Integrates decentralized scheduling decisions with issues that influence supply chain performance, for example, cooperation between manufacturers to negotiate access to outside resources, partial central control of a scheduling system, coordination of production sequences, and mechanisms to encourage cooperation and to ensure truthful reporting of private information.

Our integrated perspective on supply chain scheduling is a relatively new one. Among the earliest works is Hall and Potts (2003), which discusses optimal scheduling and batching decisions for jobs in a three-stage supply chain. Since that time, research on supply chain scheduling has been growing rapidly within the operations research, operations management, industrial engineering, and computer science communities. As of August 2021, the academic literature contains more than 3300 works that study supply chain scheduling. Figure 1.1 provides an overview of the positioning of supply chain scheduling within the related literature.

As shown in Fig. 1.1, supply chain scheduling stands at the intersection of supply chain management and scheduling. Most supply chain management models do not contain a scheduling component, typically due to their focus on higher level planning issues. Conversely, classical scheduling research has focused predominantly on narrower optimization models without the consideration of supply chain coordination issues.

A more detailed perspective on the components of supply chain scheduling appears in Fig. 1.2, which shows examples of several application areas and methodologies that support supply chain scheduling. As described in more detail in Sect. 1.2 below, these applications fall naturally into two categories: *centralized applications* where a single decision maker or organization needs to evaluate tradeoffs between conflicting costs or other performance metrics and *decentralized applications* where

1.2 Applications

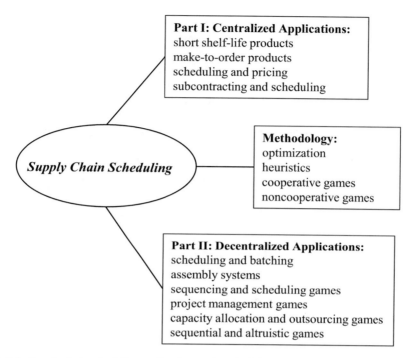

Fig. 1.2 Supply chain scheduling applications and methodology

multiple, typically self-interested, decision makers make decisions that affect each other's outcomes as well as the performance of the overall supply chain. On the methodology side, supply chain scheduling is strongly influenced by several central methodologies within operations research and mathematical economics, especially discrete optimization, computational complexity analysis, heuristic analysis, and cooperative and noncooperative game theory. The interaction of these important applications and strong methodologies presents many interesting research developments and future research opportunities that are the topic of this book.

1.2 Applications

In this section, we first discuss applications with only a single decision maker, i.e., centralized supply chain scheduling problems. Even here, there are multiple and potentially conflicting definitions of what constitutes a successful schedule. This occurs under various scenarios. For example, it may be necessary to trade off production scheduling and distribution costs. An efficient schedule may process many short jobs first, which minimizes work in process at a manufacturing plant. However, if the short jobs are for many different customers, then the delivery of those jobs is likely to require multiple batches and be expensive. Alternatively, in order to control distribution costs, it may be efficient to produce a batch of jobs that can all be delivered at once to the same customer. However, doing so may lead to inefficiencies in production scheduling, for example, if the jobs are of dissimilar types and require substantial production setups between their processing. The centralized supply chain scheduling problem involves optimization of the overall system cost. In many cases, the optimal supply chain scheduling solution is very different from the optimal solution for any subset of the supply chain's revenue or cost components. Moreover, finding it may require the solution of a more complex planning problem that is potentially less computationally tractable.

An alternative scenario that also defines supply chain scheduling problems is that more than one decision maker is involved in scheduling decisions, which defines decentralized supply chain scheduling problems. Typically, the interests of the decision makers are not well aligned. Even if the decision makers belong to the same organization, they may be incentivized differently. For example, a production manager may be compensated based on the efficiency of the production schedule. Whereas, a distribution manager may be compensated based on the ontime service rate. Problematically, the production manager's preferred schedule may provide a poor service rate for the distribution manager. Similarly, following the distribution manager's preferred delivery schedule may impose major inefficiencies on the production schedule. This is an example of a typical conflict in decentralized supply chain scheduling.

These conflicts are often exacerbated when two or more decision makers belong to different organizations. For example, a supplier and a manufacturer within the same supply chain may have different objectives that create conflicts. The supplier may wish to batch similar orders, to reduce setup time and cost. However, the manufacturer may need to receive a diverse collection of products at the same time, to meet the ongoing needs of its customers. In numerous practical supply chains, some parties have more commercial or other bargaining power than others, for example, in the case of large national retailers when dealing with their suppliers. This power asymmetry may enable one decision maker to influence another to modify its planning decisions. These typical conflicts require analysis within supply chain scheduling that goes beyond the boundaries of classical scheduling.

Several reasons explain the increasing importance of supply chain scheduling in both practice and research. The first is an increased understanding of the losses that can arise from poor scheduling coordination within the supply chain. A second reason is changes in the marketplace. These include greater pressure on time-to-market performance and increased demand for customized products in highly competitive industries such as consumer electronics. These developments place more emphasis on the scheduling function which is fundamentally concerned with improving efficiency with respect to time. Another change within this context is greater complexity of supply chains, for example, due to globalization of markets, increased product variety, and increased subcontracting of specialized work. A third reason is increased availability of data and of high speed computing power.

1.2 Applications

These reasons motivate and enable the modeling and solution of typically complex and even formally intractable supply chain scheduling problems. A final reason is methodological advances in cooperative and noncooperative game theory that enable the modeling of decisions by parties with incentives that are not necessarily well aligned. All these reasons strongly motivate our writing of this book.

The remainder of this chapter begins with a review of the literature of supply chain scheduling applications, classified into centralized ones with a single decision maker and decentralized ones with multiple decision makers. Then, we discuss the limitations to scope of supply chain scheduling for the purposes of our work. Finally, we provide an overview of the content of our book.

1.2.1 Centralized Applications and Models

Single decision maker, or centralized, applications of supply chain scheduling typically involve multiple functions within a centralized supply chain that may have locally optimal solutions that are contradictory. A common application involves the production and outbound distribution functions. The linkage between those two functions is provided by inventory of finished products, which may be expensive to carry, limited by storage capacity, or even impossible to carry in the case of perishable products. Because of these issues, finished goods inventory cannot be used as a flexible buffer between production and distribution; instead, scheduling decisions that affect the performance of those two functions need to be tightly coordinated. This creates complex issues that define supply chain scheduling problems which are in many cases financially significant.

1.2.1.1 Production–Distribution Scheduling for Short Shelf-Life Products

Several products have a short shelf-life, due to their rapid physical deterioration. Most obviously, these include fresh food and beverage products. They also include blood, plasma, and various other medical supplies. Some chemicals also fall within this definition. Other products have a short shelf-life because of their rapidly deteriorating market value due to timing or competitive issues or seasonal variations in demand. These include newspapers, mail, and specifically seasonal items such as Christmas cards. For all such products, delivery to customers must be accomplished within a strictly limited time after production. As a result, the production and distribution schedules need to be closely coordinated. This defines a fundamental supply chain scheduling problem.

An example of the coordination of production and outbound transportation arises in ready-mix concrete operations. Since the product being mixed in the vehicle has a life of about two hours, it can only be delivered within a limited area. An unusual feature of this problem is that the vehicle is both a production resource and a transportation resource. Also, deliveries are subject to precise time-of-day due dates imposed from the customer side. A natural objective is to maximize the value of orders served, a problem that can be solved using classical techniques from fixed interval scheduling (Arkin & Silverberg, 1987; Kroon et al., 1995). An alternative objective is to maximize the number of orders served using the minimum number of vehicles. For this problem, a heuristic based on swapping orders in and out of the current solution performs well on problem instances with up to 100 orders (Garcia & Lozano, 2004b). Also for this problem, Naso et al. (2007) use a metaheuristic approach to minimize the cost of meeting all orders and apply their methodology to an industry problem with 49 trucks in the Netherlands.

In a typical direct computer order system, there are many product configurations available for a customer to choose from when ordering. It is thus impractical to carry sufficient inventory based on forecasts of each configuration. As a result, assembly and packaging operations occur only after customer orders arrive. However, in highly competitive markets such as the one described, it is necessary to deliver to customers within a short lead time, such as two or three business days. Motivated by such applications in the computer and food processing industries, Chen and Vairaktarakis (2005) study an integrated model of production and distribution operations. They provide exact algorithms where possible and in other cases heuristic methods supported by computational experiments. Similar characteristics are also observed in a typical direct order system for food catering services.

Similar problems arise in the manufacture of industrial chemicals. In particular, an adhesive that is used for making plywood panels has a lifespan of only 7 days. The delivery process is complicated by the presence of two types of customers. One-time customers typically specify a short delivery time. Regular order, or periodic, customers require frequent delivery of partial orders. Geismar et al. (2008) consider the problem of determining the minimum time needed to produce and deliver a given set of orders to the regular order customers, subject to a given product lifespan, a given production rate, and the capacity of a single truck, while also meeting the expectations of one-time customers. This problem requires coordinated planning of product sequencing and vehicle routing issues. The specific decisions to be made include production quantities at different points in time, vehicle trip origination and delivery times to various customers, and vehicle routes. Because of the intractability of this complex problem, a heuristic solution procedure is developed. The heuristic uses a genetic algorithm to find feasible solutions and is capable of solving problems with up to 50 customers. The solutions delivered by the heuristic typically have cost that is within a small percentage of a lower bound. However, instances with a larger production capacity or faster production rate are more difficult to solve accurately. Even with a fixed customer sequence, this problem is challenging, as discussed by Armstrong et al. (2008). They develop a computationally efficient enumerative algorithm. They also describe a similar supply chain scheduling application for a manufacturer of home textile products such as linens, bedding, bathroom furniture, and window treatments. As in the other examples they discuss, there is no inventory of customized products.

1.2 Applications

The production and distribution of perishable food products is another important application for short shelf-life products. The main tradeoff in the problem is that frequent delivery not only improves the freshness of the products for customers but also increases delivery costs. This is an example of a fundamental supply chain scheduling problem. Farahani et al. (2012) study this problem, as faced by a catering company in Denmark. This highly intractable problem is first simplified by batching the fixed orders according to similar cooking temperature requirements. Once the batches are created, a solution procedure is developed, iterating between distribution schedules and production schedules. This procedure continues until it fails to deliver improved results. The results of the iterative procedure are compared with those from a benchmark approach used at the company, which involves a single pass through production and then distribution planning steps. For problem instances with 200 customers, a 40.9% reduction in product decay is achieved relative to the benchmark, but at an increased cost of 18.7%. For items that are more quickly perishable, the relative reduction in decay is even greater.

Another example of a short shelf-life product that naturally imposes coordination constraints between production and distribution is injectable chemotherapy medications, which are packaged into pouches and delivered to patient locations. These medications are only stable for a short amount of time. Beyond this time, the drug becomes ineffective or even dangerous. Hence, the time between the start of production and administration of the medication to the patient is strictly limited. On the other hand, the patient's treatment schedule cannot be changed to suit the stable period of a pouch of medication. Because of these constraints, production and outbound distribution of the pouches of medication need to be closely coordinated. This is another example of a fundamental supply chain scheduling problem. Kergosien et al. (2017) develop an optimization model for this problem, with the objective of minimizing the maximum tardiness of any delivery to the patient's location. They develop heuristics and lower bounds based on Benders decomposition. They are able to solve instances with up to 40 jobs and three machines that produce the medication, which is larger than problems that are solvable using standard software. However, the gap between upper and lower bounds remains large for some instances.

1.2.1.2 Production–Distribution Scheduling for Make-to-Order Products

Due to increased consumer demand for customization, an increasing number of products are made to order. Under a make-to-order business model, final products are not processed until customer orders arrive. This typically means that customers need to wait to receive the products which they ordered. However, in order to be competitive, companies often promise a very short delivery lead time, e.g., three to five business days. This means that orders have to be delivered right after they are processed, which requires that the order processing and order delivery systems are closely coordinated. Furthermore, some products are inherently difficult to store in inventory because of their physical characteristics. For example, they may be large or difficult to handle. Alternatively, they may require expensive maintenance while in inventory, for example, strict temperature, humidity, bacteria-free or dust-free control. For these products, while their time in inventory is not strictly limited like those described in Sect. 1.2.1.1, the expense and inconvenience involved in storing them or the physical space required to do so implies a high priority for inventory reduction. This is only achievable if the production and transportation schedules are closely coordinated.

A problem of this type arises in the production and delivery of computer assemblies. These products are customized for the make-to-order requirements of customers and shipped all over the world by air. At the time of order acceptance, based on order quantity and agreed due date, components are transferred from inventory to the assembly line. Air transport capacity is limited and has two types. First, normal capacity is reserved in advance, consistent with the company's production plan. Second, special capacity is available for immediate transportation; however, this is substantially more expensive than normal capacity. Delivery is time-sensitive, due to penalty costs for delivery either before or after the due date agreed for the order. Also, storage of the large computer assemblies is expensive. The two main decision problems are allocating accepted orders to flight capacities and scheduling assembly to match detailed schedules with minimum inventory. For these problems, Li et al. (2005b) develop heuristic procedures that outperform standard scheduling heuristics for planning periods up to 48 days. Li et al. (2006) report several performance statistics that show an improvement over industry benchmark procedures for problem instances with up to 100 orders and 20 flights.

Consider a make-to-order manufacturer that agrees to pay shipping cost when it accepts orders and delivery dates. In order to meet those due dates, multiple shipping modes—for example, overnight, 1-day, 2-day, and so on—are available. Shipping cost is typically more expensive for faster shipping. Orders have different processing times and may, in various situations, be processed either preemptively or nonpreemptively. An important question, addressed by Stecke and Zhao (2007), is how to schedule production so as to minimize shipping cost, while meeting agreed delivery dates. A significant characteristic of this problem is whether partial delivery of an order is allowed. If so, and shipping cost is a convex decreasing function of shipping time, then scheduling production in earliest due date order is optimal. However, if partial delivery of an order is not allowed, then the problem is intractable. For this case, a heuristic procedure is designed and shown to provide solutions that average within 6% of optimal shipping cost for problem instances with up to 500 orders. Many major online retailers face similar problems; see, for example, Schubert et al. (2018) and Zhang et al. (2018).

Appliance manufacturers face similar issues, when serving a mixture of domestic and international customers. Delivery to those customers is performed by several third-party logistics providers. Whereas domestic orders can be consolidated or split for shipping purposes, the same is not true for international customers. Companies may use a predetermined replenishment policy for many materials. As a result, trucks that are used for inbound delivery are available for reuse for outbound delivery at predictable times, although with additional cost in the event of a holding delay for the truck. Additional trucks may need to be obtained from a third-party logistics provider. In this case, the company faces a supply chain scheduling problem that requires coordination on three levels, insofar as both inbound and outbound deliveries need to be coordinated with the production process. Considering the objective of minimizing the total cost, Toptal et al. (2014) study myopic, hierarchical, and coordinated solutions. Using a numerical study, they compare these three approaches to quantify the benefit of coordination. They conclude that this benefit is significant, especially in situations where holding costs for inventory and vehicles are relatively small compared to other costs. A tabu search implementation of the coordinated approach finds solutions with costs that routinely come within 1% of a lower bound.

As a major worldwide industry, steel manufacturing presents similar problems, for example, in the shipment of make-to-order steel coils to customers. Each order has a specified time window that may vary between 1 and 5 days in length and is agreed at the time of order acceptance. Given a set of orders that need to be processed and delivered, the problem is to find a schedule for processing the orders, managing finished goods inventory when necessary, and delivering to customers within the time window. The objective is to minimize the total inventory and delivery cost. Li et al. (2017) study various cases of the problem, depending, for example, on whether orders are splittable or non-splittable and whether idle time is needed between the production of orders. The solvability of the different problems varies substantially, depending on those problem characteristics. They provide optimal algorithms or intractability results for the various cases.

When both offline and online scheduling of products are required, meaning that new orders are constantly being introduced, this problem becomes even more challenging. In this context, Tang et al. (2019) extend the work of Li et al. (2017) to consider both offline and online scheduling of products that require two stages of shipping, for example, from the manufacturing plant to a pool point such as a distributor and then from there to a customer site. For these intractable problems, they propose efficient heuristics and analyze their asymptotic performance. They use data from a Baosteel plant to validate the quality of their heuristic results for an offline version of the problem. Their results also provide managerial insights that are of value to the company and to other manufacturers.

1.2.1.3 Scheduling and Pricing

The coordination of scheduling decisions (which are typically made by an operations department) and pricing decisions (which are typically made by a marketing department) is central to supply chain scheduling. In studying this problem in a make-to-order environment, Chen and Hall (2010) cite several papers that discuss applications of joint production planning, inventory, and pricing models for catalog sales (Kunreuther & Schrage, 1973), multiple constant-priced goods (Gilbert, 2000), and multiple customers with price discrimination (Charnsirisakskul et al., 2006). An objective of the work of Chen and Hall (2010) is to motivate the consideration of decisions for these applications at the scheduling level, rather than at the production planning level. Thus, the applications are similar, but the decisions modeled are more detailed. They consider three alternative scheduling costs and the maximization of net profit which is defined as revenue less scheduling cost. They develop computationally efficient optimal algorithms for these three problems, accompanied where available by intractability results. This analysis enables estimation of the value of coordinating the pricing and scheduling decisions to various degrees, including a partially coordinated approach using information typically known to a marketing department, as well as an optimal algorithm and a simple heuristic for the fully coordinated problem. The main insight obtained is that the benefit of coordination is significant even if the pricing and scheduling decisions are only partially coordinated.

Consider a situation where a manufacturer quotes prices for a set of order inquiries. Each inquiry is either canceled or confirmed by its owner following a certain probability distribution that depends on the quoted price. The manufacturer then incurs a production scheduling cost for processing each firm order. Two types of price quotation schemes, simultaneous and sequential quotations, are investigated in Liu et al. (2012). Lu et al. (2013) discuss a fundamental tradeoff that arises in many organizations, where pricing decisions are made by the marketing department for the purpose of maximizing sales, whereas manufacturing cost issues that can be addressed by effective scheduling are made by the production department, a classic conflict within supply chain scheduling. A related case study by Respício and Captivo (2008) develops a decision support system for Portucel, a major Portuguese paper producer, for coordinating order acceptance, capacity planning, and scheduling decisions.

Finally, consider the coordination of pricing and production scheduling decisions in the context of a make-to-order environment. At the beginning of each period in a planning horizon, the manufacturer sets the price of the base product, which in turn sets the prices for the customized products accordingly. Given the chosen prices, orders for the products arrive. In each period, together with the pricing decision, the manufacturer needs to make a production scheduling decision for processing accepted orders on a single production line. Yue et al. (2019) provide a detailed description of this operation at Kuyin, a make-to-order manufacturer in China.

1.2.1.4 Subcontracting and Scheduling

Retail products with a short selling season present issues related to subcontracting. Such products include toys, fashion apparel, computer games, and other electronics. Because of the significant markdowns that are often taken on unsold products, retailers strongly prefer to delay placing orders until as much information is available as possible, which is typically right before the start of the selling season. This creates substantial problems due to limited production capacity. This in turn motivates the use of subcontracting, an alternative that is often substantially more expensive than in-house production. Chen and Li (2008) study this fundamental supply chain scheduling problem, where scheduling decisions need to be coordinated with

1.2 Applications

subcontracting decisions. They develop an analytical model to study this type of coordinated decision making. The objective is to minimize total production and subcontracting cost, subject to a constraint on the maximum completion time of the orders. They provide both worst-case and asymptotic analyses of a heuristic for the problem and study the value of the subcontracting option. A computational study reveals that subcontracting provides the manufacturer with a significant cost reduction.

A related problem arises in the manufacture of liquid crystal displays. LCD panels are purchased from subcontractors when production capacity or inventory level is insufficient. Lee and Choi (2011) address this problem. Similarly, in the steel industry, slabs are frequently purchased from subcontractors. These applications can be modeled as a two-stage production process, where the first stage is highly capital-intensive, and the second stage is an assembly process where there is an option to produce the needed components in-house or to outsource them. The decision maker needs to decide which operations to subcontract out and which to process in-house and also to determine a production schedule for the in-house items. The authors apply the natural objective of minimizing the sum of an internal scheduling cost and an outsourcing cost. They discuss the solvability of various special cases of the problems and describe and analyze a heuristic solution procedure.

1.2.1.5 Other Applications

The coordination of scheduling and transportation in the steel industry is an important application. Steel ingots are transported by a crane to a heating machine that operates in batch mode and then transported by a vehicle to a rolling mill. The objective is to minimize the total of makespan and setup cost of the batches. This work differs from most of the related literature in that it considers the transportation of semi-finished jobs and finished jobs as well as the scheduling of the batching machine. The key tradeoff here is as follows. Batching more jobs together reduces the setup cost incurred, but the delays that result from the batching process may increase the makespan of the schedule. The problem of minimizing the above combined objective is intractable. Tang and Gong (2008) develop a heuristic that makes extensive use of the rule of filling all batches except the first to a predetermined capacity, which permits a theoretical worst-case analysis. This heuristic also performs well on randomly generated problem instances. For problems with 50 jobs, relative errors can be more than 10%, but for problems with 1000 jobs they are typically less than 1%. However, performance degrades when the capacity of the batch processing machine is larger, apparently because the vehicle becomes the bottleneck resource which is not efficiently utilized.

The need for coordination of decisions at the tactical, operational, and transportation levels generates interesting problems. The design and implementation of a planning system for supply chain scheduling at Carlsberg Denmark, a high volume beer brewer, are described by Kreipl and Pinedo (2004). The overall challenge issue here is coordination of decisions for (a) medium term planning with a strong focus on production costs and capacities, (b) complex scheduling issues in supply chain operations, and (c) transportation decisions to provide a good customer service level. Viewed at a high level, the system generates its decisions hierarchically. First, the medium term planning system generates its results. Then, these are used as input to the short-term scheduling system. Finally, the results of the short-term planning system are used for transportation planning. Besides delivering a fully implemented solution to the company, this work illustrates how scheduling decisions fit within multi-functional centralized supply chains.

1.2.2 Decentralized Applications and Models

Multiple decision maker, or decentralized, planning problems arise everywhere in supply chains. The substantial body of supply chain management addresses many coordination issues in this environment. However, our focus here is on decisions which, at least in part, involve scheduling. One example is a manufacturer which works with a distributor. The manufacturer may face what it views as a production scheduling problem, whereas from the distributor's perspective the main issues are batching and vehicle routing. A second example would be a group of manufacturers who, either individually or in coalitions, are working with outsourced resources owned by one or more self-interested third parties. One distinction between the supply chain scheduling environments discussed in Sect. 1.2.1 and those discussed here is that, in the present case, administratively enforced coordination is not possible across different organizations. As a result, the design of incentives and the use of modeling with cooperative and noncooperative game theory are more prevalent for decentralized supply chain scheduling applications than for centralized ones.

1.2.2.1 Scheduling and Batching

A central supply chain scheduling problem is the coordination of scheduling, batching, and delivery decisions. Hall and Potts (2003) consider a variety of such problems that arise in an arborescent supply chain where a manufacturer delivers to several customers. They use the assumption of batch availability, under which a job only becomes available for subsequent processing or delivery to a customer when the entire batch that includes it has been processed. The need to coordinate scheduling, batching, and delivery decisions defines a fundamental supply chain scheduling problem. The objective considered is minimization of the total of scheduling and delivery cost, where the scheduling cost is measured in various practical ways. Each problem is either solved by the development of a computationally efficient dynamic programming algorithm or shown to be formally intractable. A computational study shows that cooperation between a supplier and a manufacturer has the potential to reduce the overall supply chain cost by 20% or more, depending on how the scheduling cost is measured. Incentive mechanisms that show how these cost savings can be distributed in order to encourage cooperation are also described.

Similar issues arise in just-in-time production lines with two products, as used, for example, in automobile manufacturing at Toyota, Nissan, and Chrysler. Here, the distributor batches the manufacturer's finished goods and delivers them to the retailers. Manoj et al. (2008) develop mathematical models for individual optimization of the manufacturer's problem and of the distributor's problem and for optimization of the overall supply chain problem. A computational study shows that substantial savings can be achieved by optimization at the supply chain level. They also study the cost of conflict, which is the additional cost incurred by one party when the other party imposes its optimal solution. From a computational study, the cost of conflict is found to be significant. However, coordinated decision making generates sufficient additional profit to encourage the cooperation of the parties.

1.2.2.2 Capacity Allocation

In industries that are capital-intensive and facing volatile demand for their products, several supply chain scheduling issues arise. These issues include vulnerability to capacity shortfalls (Durango-Cohen & Yano, 2006). Iyer et al. (2003) identify several practical examples in the fashion goods, telecommunications, and electricity supply industries. When faced with orders which they cannot meet, manufacturers apply capacity allocation mechanisms. However, these mechanisms need to be coordinated with scheduling decisions. This topic is studied by Hall and Liu (2010). This is a fundamental supply chain scheduling problem, in that it extends across multiple functions that include scheduling. Analysis of this problem requires the use of cooperative game theory to study the stability of coalitions of distributors that combine their orders. Hall and Liu (2010) consider a multiple product supply chain where a manufacturer receives orders from several distributors. If the orders cannot all be met from available production capacity, then the manufacturer allocates capacity and provides a set of resubmittable orders to the distributors. The distributors may then share their allocated capacity before submitting their orders. The distributors' problem is modeled as a cooperative game, and optimal algorithms are developed for all the models described. This work studies the benefit to the manufacturer from taking into account scheduling costs in capacity allocation decisions, the benefit to the distributor from sharing their capacity, and the value to the supply chain of coordination between the manufacturer and the distributors. The exact evaluation of decisions about the appropriate coordination level improves managers' ability to make those decisions.

Third-party reservation systems for outsourced capacity define another important supply chain scheduling problem. One example is SPADE, which provides a group of specialized support facilities to semiconductor companies. Capacity can be booked by those companies at rates which depend on the time when the capacity is needed. A second example, UMC, is Taiwan's leading semiconductor foundry, which provides information sharing and real-time capacity reservation to its customers. This process is supported by a full-service information portal. Cai and Vairaktarakis (2012) model this situation for a group of manufacturers which outsource their work to a third party that owns a specialized production facility. Manufacturers reserve capacity on a first-come first-served basis. Overtime capacity can be reserved, but it is substantially more expensive. There is a lateness cost penalty for jobs that are not delivered on time. The objective of each manufacturer is to minimize the total of booking, overtime, and lateness costs. A cooperative game model is developed for the problem, where the third party designs a savings scheme under which it is better for the manufacturers to cooperate than to reserve capacity individually. A mechanism that incentivizes the manufacturers to report their data truthfully is also designed. A computational study shows that the savings from cooperation increase with the number of manufacturers.

1.2.2.3 Sequencing and Scheduling Games

Cooperative games defined over sequencing problems have application to numerous service systems. Consider a situation where several customers need to be served by a single server. Each customer has a cost function that depends on his or her completion time, i.e., the waiting time before service begins plus the service time. The cost is a nondecreasing function of the completion time. In these situations, it is important to consider two problems. The first problem is how to find a sequence of the customers that minimizes the total cost. The second problem is how to allocate the total cost among the customers in a way that is stable, meaning that no pair of customers will agree to interchange their positions within the sequence. Within this class of problems, we discuss several variations of sequencing games.

In most sequencing games (Curiel et al., 1989), each customer may have a different service time. An assumption that is common but not universal is that the customer's cost is a linear function of the completion time. Under this assumption, it is easy to derive an indexing rule that minimizes the total cost, equivalently with a result in classical scheduling theory (Smith, 1956). Curiel et al. (1989) also derive a rule to divide the cost savings from changing the sequence to reduce the overall system cost and characterize this rule axiomatically. It is also shown that simple sequencing games are a proper subset of convex games and therefore have a stable allocation of savings. Scheduling games are an extension of sequencing games where the jobs do not have an initial sequence. Examples include passengers who arrive on the same flight at an immigration process and arriving mail orders.

1.2.2.4 Manufacturing and Distribution

An interesting everyday application that requires the coordination of manufacturing and distribution arises in the production of newspapers, a highly perishable product. A complication that arises with many major city newspapers is that several different editions are published, with content that includes locally relevant information and advertising for each of several "zones," for example, suburbs of a city. The distribution process involves transportation from the print facility to a few distribution centers, then to many drop-off points, and finally to customers' homes. Hurter and van Buer (1996) take the perspective that the printer and distributor are both parts of the same organization.

However, Dawande et al. (2006) discuss a similar problem in an equally natural decentralized context where the printer and the distributor are independent organizations. Complications and tradeoffs arise in the sequencing of different editions and varying travel times between locations. The manufacturer and the distributor each has an ideal schedule, which is determined by cost and capacity considerations. Lack of coordination between these two schedules results in poor overall system performance. The authors study two problems where the manufacturer focuses on minimizing unproductive time, while the distributor minimizes customer cost measures in the first problem and minimizes inventory holding cost in the second problem. Several practical scenarios about the level of cooperation between the manufacturer and the distributor are studied, leading to the development of algorithms for solving the related scheduling problems. The cost saving provided by cooperation between the decision makers is usually significant. This work has implications for how manufacturers and distributors negotiate, coordinate, and implement their supply chain schedules in practice.

1.2.2.5 Subcontracting Games

An important application of outsourcing is eHub, which is used by Cisco Systems as a private trading e-marketplace. This portal provides planning and execution functions for tasks across a company's extended supply chain, as described by Grosvenor and Austin (2001). Orders from Cisco's customers are communicated to its related manufacturing partners over a private network. The production schedules of all parties are visible to everyone with access to the portal. As a result, opportunities for coordinated capacity planning and scheduling abound within this network. Aydinliyim and Vairaktarakis (2010) consider a set of manufacturers that outsource their operations to a third party, based on published prices that vary with production times. The manufacturers minimize the total of reservation and work-in-process costs. After all reservations have been made, the third party finds a schedule that minimizes the total cost for the manufacturers as a whole, but not necessarily for all subsets of manufacturers. The third party then designs a savings sharing scheme to coordinate the manufacturers. Aydinliyim and Vairaktarakis (2010) develop an algorithm for the manufacturers and a savings scheme for the third party. A computational study shows that the overall supply chain cost can be reduced by an average of 32% if the third party agrees to cover a share of the work-in-process cost.

A well publicized and heavily subcontracted project is the design and construction of the Boeing 787 Dreamliner aircraft. Most of the top level component suppliers selected for this product are long-standing suppliers of Boeing. Because of short lead times for delivery, many of those suppliers subcontract part of their work to smaller companies, some of which then became overloaded due to the size of the overall project. As a result, each supplier needs to decide the amount of workload to be subcontracted, so as to minimize the completion time of the in-house and subcontracted workloads. Vairaktarakis (2013) considers a set of manufacturers that can outsource their jobs to a third party with production resources. The third party gives priority to manufacturers whose subcontracted workload is relatively small. This encourages manufacturers to compete for position in the processing sequence of the third party. Under various possible assumptions about what production sequences are feasible, equilibrium schedules are described. In an equilibrium solution, no decision maker has an incentive to change its decisions unless another decision maker does so first.

1.2.2.6 Multi-Stage Production with Setups

During the manufacture of kitchen furniture, a large number of different slabs of wood are cut, painted, and assembled to build the furniture. In different departments of the plant, items are grouped according to different attributes. In the cutting department, parts are grouped according to their shape and material; whereas, in the subsequent painting department, parts are grouped according to their color, and finally the assembly of the furniture is organized on the basis of kitchen models. In both departments, a setup occurs when the attribute of a new part changes. If a part must be cut with a different shape from the previous one, cutting blades and machinery must be reconfigured. Similarly, in the painting station, when a new color is used, the equipment as well as the pallets must be thoroughly cleaned in order to eliminate all the residue of the previous color. Hence, in both cases, costs in time and manpower are incurred. The limited availability of interstage buffering between the two stages forces the sequences in which the items are processed in the two stages to be coordinated. Agnetis et al. (2001) study this problem. Each department aims to minimize its own total setup cost, but the objectives of the two departments fundamentally conflict because their ideal schedules conflict. Relevant objectives include minimizing the total number of setups and the maximum number of setups by either of the two departments. While these problems are intractable, it is possible to design an efficient heuristic that finds an optimal solution in 887 out of 900 instances of the problem.

In many sequencing problems, a variety of products in various stages of development pass through multiple workstations, as occurs in automobile plants. Boysen et al. (2012) provide a survey of research on mixed-model assembly lines and a particular example of physical resequencing where trucks may violate efficient sequencing rules due to their different sizes which impact the limited available physical space. As a result, an automated storage and retrieval system with a buffer capacity of 118 places is used for resequencing. As a second example, they mention virtual resequencing, where in order to maintain production efficiency the model sequence is unchanged, but the assignment of completed products to customer orders may be changed in order to satisfy just-in-time delivery constraints.

1.2.2.7 Other Applications

Consider a multiple decision maker system for terminal management at a container port. The financial impact of this problem is considerable: an average cargo liner spends 60% of its time in port and incurs a cost of about $1000 per hour while it does so. There are five classes of decision makers: ship agents who schedule loading and unloading, stevedore agents who manage the loading and unloading of all the ships, service agents who distribute the containers within the terminal, transtainer agents who optimize the use of loading and unloading machines, and gate agents who interact with incoming and outgoing land transport. Rebollo et al. (2000) design a communication system under which the decision makers initiate requests and queries and receive information. The entire system is supported by a platform that is accessible to all.

Another important supply chain scheduling problem involves the operations of a supply chain consisting of a textile company that supplies fabrics to an apparel company. Retail buyers are typically located in a different country, and they impose due date requirements for orders. Meeting these due dates may require the fashion company to use expensive delivery methods. The short selling season for the fashionable apparel products imposes a time window for the production of materials, for example, yarn, by the supplier, and production and delivery time windows for the apparel company. The observed supply chain performance is suboptimal, due to double marginalization. For this problem, Yeung et al. (2011) develop a computationally efficient procedure to optimize the overall supply chain. They also describe two simple and practical profit sharing schemes that coordinate the supply chain.

Another important high value scheduling problem is the allocation of scarce radio spectrum among customers who submit bids for channels. Centralized auction mechanisms for this problem are known to have drawbacks, due to a lack of reliability and computational ability at the central planner. They are also vulnerable to problems with communication issues. As a potentially more robust alternative, Yang et al. (2019) focus on the design of *distributed mechanisms*. They design two such auction mechanisms, both of which are truthful, in the sense that it is in the interest of the bidding customers to bid their true value for the open channels. One of these mechanisms results in an overall optimal allocation, whereas the other is heuristic but computationally more efficient.

For many of the applications discussed above, additional details are provided in later chapters. For example, Sect. 3.5 provides more information about the work of Chen and Vairaktarakis (2005) on the production and distribution of short shelf-life products.

1.3 Limitations to Scope

We discuss various limitations to the scope of this book and provide some examples of valuable and interesting work that falls outside that scope. Our main focus is on the benefit that arises from coordinated decision making, either between production scheduling and other functions under the control of a single decision maker or between the decisions of multiple self-interested decision makers. Therefore, problems that involve some related issues but are reducible to a classical single decision maker scheduling problem, for example, by the addition of some constraints, fall outside our scope. The main reason for this is typically that the reduced problem is mathematically similar to the classical scheduling problem. This makes such problems of less interest within the context of our work. We now provide five examples of research that makes valuable and interesting contributions to the scheduling or supply chain literature, but nonetheless falls outside the scope of this book.

Sarmiento and Nagi (1999) provide an extensive review of the literature of integrated analysis of production–distribution systems. They describe numerous applications where coordinated decision making across functions provides improved performance relative to sequential decision making. However, the production problems considered are at the level of aggregate planning and therefore do not fit within our definition of scheduling. As a result, many of the works cited in their review are not within the scope of supply chain scheduling for the purposes of our book.

Wang et al. (2005) study the problem of how to process incoming mail in order to match a fixed outbound delivery schedule. Arriving mail has various destinations in different proportions and is delivered by trucks with limited capacity. The problem involves finding a processing sequence for the mail that maximizes the unused truck capacity. Since the outbound delivery schedule merely imposes due date constraints on the processing schedule and classical scheduling allows modeling of such issues, this problem does not fall within the scope of supply chain scheduling for the purposes of this book. Indeed, the authors model and solve the problem using classical scheduling methodology.

Lejeune (2008) studies the maintenance of cycle service levels in a multi-stage supply chain. The problem requires the development of integrated replenishment plans that satisfy various performance measures related to stockouts across multiple periods over a planning horizon. He derives a deterministic reformulation of the stochastic planning problem. Based on the results of a computational study for a chemical supply chain, practical problems can be solved using this approach. However, since this work does not consider scheduling decisions at the individual job level, it falls outside the scope of our book.

A comprehensive treatment of multi-agent scheduling can be found in Agnetis et al. (2014b). In a multi-agent environment, there is a single decision maker. However, multiple agents or customers each owns a (not necessarily disjoint) subset of the jobs. The reward or cost of each agent depends only on the performance of the jobs which it owns. The decision problem is substantially complicated by the

1.4 Overview of the Book

fact that the jobs share common resources. Agnetis et al. (2014b) describe several applications. This work focuses on the development of Pareto-optimal solutions for the agents, within classical scheduling environments. However, this topic contains no issues that arise directly from supply chains, and hence it does not fall within our scope.

Ivanov et al. (2014) consider an integrated multi-stage scheduling and job routing problem with nonpreemptive operations, which has application to process industries. They perform a dynamic decomposition of the problem and propose an integrated solution. Again, because the decisions considered, including the routing of jobs within flexible production environments, all fall within the range of classical scheduling problems, this work is outside the scope of supply chain scheduling for our purposes.

1.4 Overview of the Book

We provide an overview of the remainder of this book. Chapter 2 describes common elements shared by the scheduling problems to be discussed. It also contains some useful mathematical background including a discussion of computational tractability and an overview of a variety of optimization and game theory techniques that are applied in modeling and solving supply chain scheduling problems. Our main focus throughout the book is on the *value added* by the coordinated decision making of scheduling and other functions, relative to local or even decentralized decision making for different parts of a problem.

After the two introductory chapters, the book is divided into two parts. Part I consists of Chaps. 3 through 6. These chapters study centralized problems, i.e., those with a single decision maker, in supply chain scheduling. Chapter 3 considers integrated production scheduling and outbound distribution problems where decision making is offline, i.e., all the necessary data is available at the start of the planning horizon, including both single and multiple machine problems. The topics covered include delivery with a limited number of vehicles, batch delivery to single and also to multiple customers, problems with fixed delivery dates, problems with multiple manufacturing plants, and those with two stages of delivery.

Chapter 4 considers a similar set of problems to those studied in Chap. 3, but in an online environment, i.e., one where new information arrives after some decisions have already been made. This new information is typically about a new job or order, the parameters of which only become known when it becomes ready for processing. An interesting and practical issue that is also discussed here is when should a planning problem be modeled as offline, possibly with a rolling horizon approach, and when should it alternatively be modeled as an online problem.

Chapter 5 considers problems where production scheduling decisions are coordinated with pricing decisions. The topics covered include product- and order-based problems within a single period and also multi-period pricing and scheduling problems. Several of these problems are intractable, as we discuss. In some cases, the intractability of the problems considered motivates the design and performance analysis of approximation algorithms.

Chapter 6 concludes Part I with a discussion of joint subcontracting and scheduling decisions. One topic is the study of problems with a lead time performance guarantee. We also study the value of subcontracting and how to make scheduling decisions subject to a budget for subcontracting. The more general production environment of scheduling in a flowshop is also discussed, as well as problems that involve delivery of subcontracted jobs. Finally, we consider problems with generalized subcontracting structures such as volume discounts.

Part II consists of Chaps. 7 through 9. These chapters study decentralized problems in supply chain scheduling, i.e., those with multiple entirely or predominantly self-interested decision makers. Chapter 7 considers four foundational problems in the supply chain scheduling literature, where conflict and cooperation issues are addressed through optimization. These are (a) the coordination of schedule formation with the quantity and timing of batch deliveries, (b) the coordination of the delivery schedules of parts suppliers with a manufacturer's final assembly schedule, (c) the coordination of a manufacturer's production schedule with a downstream distributor's delivery schedule, and (d) the coordination of sequences involving setup costs between consecutive stages of a supply chain. In all cases, the benefit of coordinated *vs.* separate optimization is discussed and analyzed.

In Chap. 8, we consider various problems that require cooperative supply chain scheduling solutions. The first topic is cooperative sequencing games which, given an initial arrival order, model the priority system of a typical service process and include many practical variations. The second topic, scheduling games, assumes no initial order and allows us to study mechanisms for enabling cooperation between the agents when it does not occur spontaneously. Achieving cooperation within the globally important business process of project management is also discussed. In addition, the coordination of scheduling and capacity allocation decisions, and of scheduling and outsourcing decisions, is considered.

Chapter 9 concludes our work with a study of problems that require noncooperative supply chain scheduling solutions. For noncooperative games with complete information, we study a variety of methods for finding and evaluating an equilibrium solution. We discuss enhanced complete information games where sequential decision making improves the quality of an equilibrium, games with leaders and followers, and games with partially altruistic behavior by the agents. For situations where the agents have private information, we first consider mechanisms without payments that can be used to achieve truthful reporting and either optimal or approximately optimal supply chain performance. Finally, under algorithmic mechanism design, we consider several important supply chain scheduling applications which motivate a wide variety of algorithms and payment scheme specifications to achieve truthful reporting.

Each chapter in Parts I and II concludes with a section on future research topics of importance. These topics are motivated by applications that arise from changing marketplaces and also define challenging theoretical problems.

Chapter 2
Solution Methods for Supply Chain Scheduling Problems

Abstract In this chapter we describe some common elements shared by all scheduling problems, introduce some basic concepts related to computational tractability of a problem, and summarize several commonly used solution methods for solving supply chain scheduling problems. These solution methods include dynamic programming, branch-and-bound, integer programming, and approximation procedures. We also provide a brief introduction to both cooperative game theory and noncooperative game theory, which are often used to model decentralized supply chain scheduling problems. Several classical scheduling problems and supply chain scheduling problems are used as examples to illustrate the concepts and solution methods presented.

2.1 Common Elements in Scheduling Problems

Both classical and supply chain scheduling problems share some common characteristics. Most scheduling problems share four basic elements: (1) a set of jobs or orders $N = \{1, \ldots, n\}$, (2) a set of machines or production lines $M = \{1, \ldots, m\}$ where the jobs are processed, (3) a set of rules or constraints that must be followed or satisfied, and (4) one or more objective functions representing the performance criterion or criteria of the decision maker(s). Most studies on classical scheduling use the terms *jobs* and *machines*, whereas some studies on centralized supply chain scheduling use the terms *orders* and *production lines*, and some studies on decentralized supply chain scheduling use the terms *agents* and *resources*. While different terms are used to reflect the diverse application settings studied, for consistency, we use the terms jobs and machines throughout this chapter.

There are several commonly used *machine environments* or configurations where jobs are processed. Three most common machine environments are:

- *Single Machine*: all the jobs are processed on a single machine.
- *Parallel Machines*: all the machines perform the same function such that each job only needs to be processed on one of the machines. The machines can be *identical* if they have the same processing speed, *uniform* if they have different

© Springer Nature Switzerland AG 2022
Z.-L. Chen, N. G. Hall, *Supply Chain Scheduling*, International Series
in Operations Research & Management Science 323,
https://doi.org/10.1007/978-3-030-90374-9_2

23

speeds which are job independent, and *unrelated* if they have different speeds which are both job and machine dependent.

- *Flowshop*: the processing of each job consists of m operations, one on each machine, performed in a pre-specified sequence which is identical for different jobs. If the sequence of operations is job dependent, the resulting more general machine environment is called a *jobshop*. If the different operations of each job can be performed in any sequence, then the resulting machine environment is called an *openshop*.

It is assumed in almost all scheduling problems that the machine environment is known precisely in advance. However, the jobs and their parameters may or may not be known in advance depending on the nature of the application. In an *offline* scheduling problem where every parameter of the problem is known in advance, the job set N as well as all the parameters about each job are given before scheduling decisions are made. In an *online* or *stochastic* scheduling problem, however, not all the parameters of the problem are known in advance. Typically, in a stochastic scheduling problem, the job set N and some parameters of the jobs are known with certainty, but only probability distributions of some other parameters of the jobs are known. In an online scheduling problem, even the job set may not be known, and little or nothing may be known about the parameters of a job until it arrives.

Typical parameters of a job j and the commonly used notation include:

- *Weight* (w_j): the importance weight or priority factor of job j, or cost of job j.
- *Processing time* (p_j or p_{ij}): the time needed for processing job j on a single machine or one of the multiple identical parallel machines (p_j), or that on a specific machine i in other machine environments (p_{ij}).
- *Release time* (r_j): the nonnegative time when job j arrives at the system, i.e., the earliest time the job can start processing.
- *Due date* (d_j): the time when job j should complete processing, or be delivered to its destination. If the due date must be met, then it is referred to as the *deadline* of the job. Otherwise, there is typically a cost for not meeting it.

Two of the most fundamental decisions involved in a scheduling problem are assigning jobs to machines and sequencing the jobs on each machine. Most classical scheduling problems involve these two decisions only. However, besides these decisions, supply chain scheduling problems usually involve other decisions, such as capacity allocation, delivery, subcontracting, and pricing. There are many different objective functions that are motivated by practice and have been studied in the literature. Some commonly used objective functions include:

- *Makespan*, $C_{\max} = \max_{j \in N}\{C_j\}$ or $D_{\max} = \max_{j \in N}\{D_j\}$, where C_j denotes the completion time for processing job j, and D_j the delivery time of job j. The makespan represents the elapsed time during which work is being completed.
- *Total (weighted) completion time of the jobs*, $\sum_{j \in N} C_j$ ($\sum_{j \in N} w_j C_j$). This represents the total work-in-process inventory holding cost of the jobs.

- *Total (weighted) delivery time of the jobs*, $\sum_{j \in N} D_j$ $(\sum_{j \in N} w_j D_j)$. This measure, if divided by n, represents the average (weighted) delivery lead time of the jobs.
- *Maximum lateness*, $L_{\max} = \max_{j \in N} L_j$, where $L_j = C_j - d_j$, or $D_j - d_j$ (depending on whether C_j or D_j is used as the time when the work for job j is completed), denotes the lateness of job j. This measures the worst-case lateness of the jobs.
- *Total (weighted) tardiness of the jobs*, $\sum_{j \in N} T_j$ $(\sum_{j \in N} w_j T_j)$, where $T_j = \max\{0, L_j\}$ denotes the tardiness of job j. This measure, if divided by n, represents the average (weighted) tardiness of the jobs.
- *Total (weighted) number of tardy jobs*, $\sum_{j \in N} U_j$ $(\sum_{j \in N} w_j U_j)$, where $U_j = 1$ if $L_j > 0$ (i.e., job j is late), and 0 otherwise. This is similar to, but easier to measure than, the total (weighted) tardiness objective function.

In addition to the terms and notation defined above, in later chapters of this book where specific supply chain scheduling problems are discussed, new parameters and new objective functions are introduced whenever necessary. A three-field notation $\alpha|\beta|\gamma$ proposed by Graham et al. (1979) is commonly used to represent a classical scheduling problem, where the α field describes the machine environment such that single-machine, parallel-machine, and flowshop are represented as "1", "P_m", and "F", respectively. The β field describes constraints of the problem. For example, if jobs arrive over time (i.e., have non-zero release times), then "r_j" is entered in this field. The γ field describes the objective function to be minimized. Using this notation, for example, the problem of scheduling jobs on a single machine with the objective of minimizing total weighted tardiness can be represented as $1||\sum w_j T_j$, and the problem of scheduling jobs on m parallel machines with the objective of minimizing the makespan can be represented as $P_m||C_{\max}$.

To represent a class of supply chain scheduling problems involving both job processing and outbound delivery of completed jobs, Chen (2010) proposes a five-field notation, extended from the above three-field notation. This is described in Chap. 3.

2.2 Computational Complexity

The theory of computational complexity (Garey & Johnson, 1979) is a useful framework for understanding the tractability of combinatorial optimization problems, including scheduling problems. Generally speaking, the complexity or tractability of a problem is determined by the time complexity of the fastest possible (or most efficient) algorithm for finding an optimal solution to any instance of the problem. The *time complexity of an algorithm* for a given problem is the worst-case computational time of the algorithm for the problem, measured by the required number of basic operations as a function of the problem input length. The *problem input length* is the number of symbols, strings, or bites needed to describe an instance of the problem under a concise encoding scheme such as binary encoding which uses $\log_2 X$ bits to represent an integer number X. For example, consider the classical single-machine scheduling problem of minimizing the total tardiness $1||\sum T_j$ (Koulamas, 2010). Any instance of this problem consists of n jobs, a processing time p_j and a due date d_j for each job j, and a threshold Y for the total tardiness. The problem input length (or input size) under a binary encoding is thus $\sum_{j=1}^{n}(\lceil \log_2 p_j \rceil + \lceil \log_2 d_j \rceil) + \lceil \log_2 Y \rceil$.

There are three types of algorithms as classified by time complexity: polynomial-time algorithms, exponential-time algorithms, and pseudo-polynomial time algorithms. They are defined as follows.

Definition 2.1 Given an algorithm for a problem, it is said to be a *polynomial-time algorithm* if the worst-case computational time of the algorithm is bounded by a polynomial function of the problem input length. Otherwise (i.e., if the worst-case computational time is in the scale of an exponential function of the problem input length), the algorithm is said to be an *exponential-time algorithm*. A polynomial-time algorithm can further be called a *strongly polynomial-time algorithm* if its worst-case computational time depends on the number of items in the input data (e.g., number of jobs and machines), but not on the input lengths of items (e.g., input lengths of job processing times and weights). A special class of exponential-time algorithms is called *pseudo-polynomial time algorithms*, which have worst-case computational time that is polynomial in both the problem input length and the largest number in the problem input data.

For example, a simple algorithm that schedules the jobs in earliest due date first (EDD) sequence has a time complexity of $O(n \log n)$ for the above cited problem $1||\sum T_j$. Since this computation time is a polynomial function of the problem input length, this algorithm is a polynomial-time algorithm for the problem involved. However, this algorithm does not always find an optimal solution for the problem.

The set of all problems that can be solved by polynomial-time algorithms is denoted as set P. There is another set of problems, denoted as NP, which includes every problem such that given any solution, it takes polynomial time to check whether this solution is feasible or not for the decision version of the problem. It is known that $P \subseteq NP$, but it is a long-standing open question in computer science whether $P = NP$ (e.g., Kleinberg & Tardos, 2006). The general belief is that $P \subset NP$.

Based on complexity theory, we can divide scheduling problems into several categories:

- Polynomially solvable problems (or tractable problems), which can be solved by polynomial-time algorithms
- NP-hard problems, which are intractable in theory, i.e., cannot be solved by any polynomial-time algorithm unless $P = NP$. Such problems can further be divided into two classes:

2.2 Computational Complexity

- Ordinarily NP-hard problems (or NP-hard problems in the ordinary sense), which are NP-hard but can be solved by pseudo-polynomial time algorithms which are quite efficient computationally in many cases
- Strongly NP-hard problems (or NP-hard problems in the strong sense), which are intractable and cannot be solved by any pseudo-polynomial time algorithm unless $P = NP$

The above problem classification is based on the assumption that a concise encoding scheme such as binary encoding is used to represent problem input data. Hence, NP-hard problems are also known as *binary NP-hard* because they are NP-hard under a binary encoding scheme. If a unary encoding scheme is used to describe the input data, an ordinarily NP-hard problem would become polynomially solvable because the pseudo-polynomial time algorithm that solves the problem would become polynomial under a unary encoding scheme. However, strongly NP-hard problems would remain NP-hard even when a unary encoding scheme is used. Thus, strongly NP-hard problems are also called *unary NP-hard*.

The above discussed problem $1||\sum T_j$ is ordinarily NP-hard because it is intractable (Du & Leung, 1990), i.e., there is no polynomial-time algorithm that can solve this problem unless $P = NP$, but there is a pseudo-polynomial time $O(n^4 P)$ algorithm that can solve the problem to optimality (Lawler, 1977), where $P = \sum_{j=1}^{n} p_j$.

If 1 day it is shown that $P = NP$, then all NP-hard problems will become solvable in polynomial time. However, if $P \subset NP$, as commonly believed, then it becomes mathematically valid to say that no polynomial-time algorithms can solve NP-hard problems.

To clarify the complexity of a given problem, the concept of polynomial reducibility can be very useful. It is defined as follows.

Definition 2.2 Given a problem A. Suppose that some algorithm solves problem A. Another problem B is said to be *polynomially reducible* or simply *reduces* to problem A if problem B can be solved by transforming it to inputs for problem A in polynomial time and calling the algorithm that solves problem A a polynomial number of times.

If problem B is polynomially reducible or reduces to problem A, then problem B is no harder than problem A, and hence the following hold: (1) if A is polynomially solvable, then B is also polynomially solvable; (2) if B is ordinarily (or strongly) NP-hard, then A is at least ordinarily (or strongly) NP-hard.

To show a problem to be polynomially solvable, one needs to find a polynomial-time algorithm that can solve the problem to optimality, or show that the problem reduces to another problem that can be solved in polynomial time. To show a problem to be strongly NP-hard, a commonly used approach is to show that a known strongly NP-hard problem reduces to the problem under study. Intuitively, to show problem B reduces to problem A, one needs to show that problem B is a special case of or equivalent to problem A. Finally, to show a problem to be ordinarily NP-hard, one can first show that a known ordinarily NP-hard problem reduces to the given problem, and then find a pseudo-polynomial time algorithm that solves the given problem to optimality. Readers are referred to the classical books by Garey and Johnson (1979) and Papadimitriou and Steiglitz (1998) to learn a variety of techniques for proving NP-hardness of combinatorial optimization problems.

Supply chain scheduling problems are in general less tractable (i.e., more difficult to solve) than the corresponding classical scheduling problems. If a classical machine scheduling problem is ordinarily (strongly) NP-hard, then a corresponding supply chain scheduling problem is at least ordinarily (also strongly) NP-hard. In many cases, a corresponding supply chain scheduling problem becomes NP-hard even if the underlying classical machine scheduling problem is polynomially solvable. For example, the classical scheduling problem $1|r_j|C_{\max}$ is polynomially solvable; it is optimal to schedule the jobs by nondecreasing order of their arrival times. However, consider the corresponding supply chain scheduling problem where each job is delivered to its customer individually and immediately after its completion and the objective is to minimize the makespan $D_{\max}$, which is defined as the time when all the jobs are delivered to their destinations. This problem is strongly NP-hard (Chen, 2010, and discussed in Sect. 3.3.1). For another example, the classical machine scheduling problem $1||\sum w_j C_j$ is polynomially solvable; it is optimal to schedule the jobs in nondecreasing order of p_j/w_j. Now consider the following corresponding supply chain scheduling problem: there are pricing decisions that need to be made jointly with scheduling decisions such that the number of incoming jobs for each product type is determined by the price set for this product, and the objective is to maximize the total revenue of the jobs minus the total weighted completion time of the jobs. This problem is ordinarily NP-hard (Chen & Hall, 2010, and discussed in Sect. 5.2).

2.3 Solution Methods

We discuss several generally applicable solution methods for supply chain scheduling problems. Figure 2.1 provides an overview of the various solution methods discussed in this section.

2.3.1 Dynamic Programming Algorithms

Dynamic programming (DP) plays an important role in solving many scheduling problems including many supply chain scheduling problems. Most scheduling problems that are tractable can be solved either by a simple rule or by a polynomial-time DP algorithm. Many ordinarily NP-hard scheduling problems can be solved by a pseudo-polynomial time DP algorithm.

DP solves an optimization problem by breaking it down into a collection of simpler subproblems based on some optimality properties, solving each of those

2.3 Solution Methods

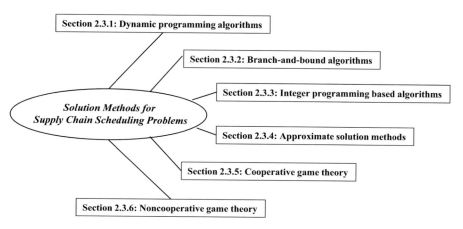

Fig. 2.1 Solution methods for supply chain scheduling problems

subproblems just once, and storing the solutions of the subproblems solved. When a previously solved subproblem occurs later as a part of another subproblem, instead of recomputing its solution, one simply looks up the previously computed solution. This saves computation time at the expense of some storage space that is needed to keep the solutions of the solved subproblems.

While some optimization problems cannot be decomposed in this way, many scheduling problems satisfy certain optimality properties which can be used to break the problems into smaller subproblems that are nested recursively inside larger subproblems. Consequently, there is a relation between the objective value of a larger subproblem and the objective values of the smaller subproblems. In DP, this relationship is called a *recurrence relation*. In addition to a recurrence relation, each DP algorithm is characterized by *states*, each corresponding to a subproblem, a *value function*, which maps a given state to a value, and *initial conditions*, which define the values of some initial states of the DP. Recurrence relations define how the value of a state is calculated based on the values of other states.

We illustrate below a DP algorithm for a classical machine scheduling problem and a DP algorithm for the associated distribution scheduling problem for delivering the completed jobs to their destinations, given the production schedule for the earlier machine scheduling problem.

We first consider the classical two-parallel-machine scheduling problem $P_2 || \sum w_j C_j$. This problem is ordinarily NP-hard (Bruno et al., 1974) and can be solved by the following pseudo-polynomial time DP algorithm.

Example 2.1 (DP Algorithm for $P_2 || \sum w_j C_j$)

Initialization Reindex the jobs in nondecreasing order of p_j/w_j (called SWPT order). Define $P_j = \sum_{k=1}^{j} p_k$.

Value Function Define $f(P^1, j)$ as the minimum total weighted completion time of a partial schedule containing the first j jobs where the completion time of the last job on the first machine is P^1 (and hence that on the second machine is $P_j - P^1$).

Boundary Conditions $f(0, 0) = 0$.

Recurrence Relation For $j = 1, \ldots, n$, and $P^1 = p_1, \ldots, P_j$:

$$f(P^1, j) = \min\{f(P^1 - p_j, j - 1) + w_j P^1, f(P^1, j - 1) + w_j(P_j - P^1)\}.$$

Optimal Solution $\min\{f(P^1, n) \mid P^1 = p_1, \ldots, P_n\}$.

The idea of the DP algorithm given in Example 2.1 is that in an optimal schedule, the jobs processed on each machine follow a SWPT order, which enables us to compute the value of the state (P^1, j) based on the values of the states $(P^1 - p_j, j - 1)$, if job j is scheduled on machine 1, and $(P^1, j - 1)$, if job j is scheduled on machine 2. Since the recurrence relation compares these two state transition possibilities and always chooses the least-cost possibility, it ensures that the solution generated by the algorithm is optimal. There are $O(n P_n)$ states in the DP, and the value function for each state is calculated in constant time. Therefore, the time complexity of this DP algorithm is $O(n P_n)$.

Now, consider the problem of scheduling the delivery of completed jobs to a single destination, given the production schedule generated by the DP algorithm in Example 2.1, with the objective of minimizing the sum of the total delivery time and total distribution cost, i.e., $\sum w_j D_j + TC$, where D_j is the delivery time of job j and TC is the total distribution cost. Let τ denote the transportation time from the plant to the destination. Each delivery shipment can carry up to b jobs, and costs Π. This problem can be solved by the following polynomial-time DP algorithm.

Example 2.2 (DP Algorithm for Delivery Scheduling, Given the Production Schedule from Example 2.1)

Initialization Reindex the jobs in the order they are completed under the schedule generated by the algorithm given in Example 2.1. Let their completion times be $C_1, \ldots, C_n$, respectively.

Value Function Define $g(j, k)$ as the minimum objective value of a partial schedule containing the first j jobs which are delivered in k shipments.

Boundary Conditions $g(0, 0) = 0$.

Recurrence Relation For $j = 1, \ldots, n$, and $k = 1, \ldots, j$:

$$g(j, k) = \min_{u=1,\ldots,\min(j,b)} \left\{g(j - u, k - 1) + u(C_j + \tau)\right\} + \Pi.$$

Optimal Solution $\min_{k=\lceil n/b \rceil, \ldots, n}\{g(n, k)\}$.

2.3 Solution Methods   31

The idea of the DP algorithm in the above example is that the value of the state (j, k) can be computed based on the values of the states $(j - u, k - 1)$, for $u = 1, \ldots, \min\{j, b\}$, and the contribution by the last delivery shipment containing u jobs. Since the recurrence relation compares all feasible state transitions and always chooses the least-cost possibility, it ensures that the solution generated by the algorithm is optimal. There are $O(n^2)$ states in the DP, and the value function for each state is calculated in $O(b)$ time. Thus, the time complexity of this DP algorithm is $O(n^2 b)$.

Remark 2.1 We observe that to prove the optimality of a DP algorithm, one usually needs to show that the recurrence relation of the DP compares all feasible state transitions and always chooses the transition that yields the minimum (maximum) objective value for the state being considered for a minimization (maximization) problem. In addition, to make a DP algorithm work, there are often some initial and boundary conditions that need to be set properly.

Now, we discuss the overall supply chain scheduling problem that combines the problems in Examples 2.1 and 2.2 with the same objective function as that in the latter problem. This supply chain scheduling problem is known to be strongly NP-hard even with a single machine (Hall & Potts, 2005, also discussed in Sect. 3.4.3). This means that the combined problem is more difficult to solve optimally than the production scheduling problem or the delivery scheduling problem involved alone. Similar results hold for many supply chain scheduling problems.

2.3.2 Branch-and-Bound Algorithms

Branch-and-bound (B&B) is a widely used solution framework for finding optimal solutions for NP-hard combinatorial optimization problems, including scheduling problems. B&B solves a problem by implicitly searching the entire feasible solution space of the problem in a divide-and-conquer fashion through its branching and bounding procedures. One often needs to exploit special structures of the under-lying problem in order to develop efficient branching and bounding procedures. Nemhauser and Wolsey (1988) provides detailed descriptions of various branching and bounding techniques for a variety of problems. We briefly discuss how branch-and-bound can be used for solving scheduling problems to optimality.

A good B&B algorithm should only explicitly search a small fraction of the feasible solution space by eliminating the vast majority of the space from consideration using structural results of the problem. A B&B algorithm is usually implemented using a search (or branching) tree which starts from a single node as the root node of the tree and grows as the algorithm progresses. The root node represents the original problem, and every other node in the tree represents a subproblem. Suppose we are solving a minimization problem. At each iteration, first an active node in the tree, say node A, is chosen. Then two procedures, branching and bounding, are performed on this node. Branching is the process of partitioning the problem associated with node A into several subproblems. For example, if the problem of node A is the original problem with the constraint that job 1 is sequenced as the first job on machine k, then one possible way of branching on node A is to divide the problem of this node into $n - 1$ subproblems, each being the same problem as that of node A with an additional constraint that job j is sequenced as the second job on machine k, for $j = 2, \ldots, n$, where n is the total number of jobs in the problem. A new node is added to the search tree corresponding to each such problem and is linked to node A by a new branch.

Bounding is the process of deriving a lower bound on the minimum objective value of each subproblem generated in the branching process. One possible approach to compute a lower bound of a problem is to use an integer programming based algorithm described in Sect. 2.3.3. There are four possible outcomes after bounding is performed on a node, as follows.

- The first possible outcome is that the problem associated with the node is shown to be infeasible. For example, if the LP relaxation of the IP formulation for the problem associated with a node is infeasible, then this problem is infeasible. In this case, this node is eliminated.
- The second possible outcome is that the problem associated with the node is solved to optimality. For example, if the solution of the LP relaxation of the IP formulation for the problem associated with this node is integer, then this problem is solved to optimality. In this case, this node is also eliminated and the incumbent solution of the original problem is replaced by the solution of this node if the optimal objective value of this node is less than that of the incumbent solution.
- The third possible outcome is that the lower bound on the objective value of the problem of this node is greater than or equal to the objective value of the incumbent solution of the original problem. In this case, none of the subproblems generated by branching down this node contains an optimal solution of the original problem, and hence this node is eliminated.
- The last possible outcome is that the lower bound on the objective value of the problem of this node is less than the objective value of the incumbent solution of the original problem. In this case, subproblems generated by branching down this node can contain an optimal solution of the original problem, and hence this node is kept as an active node to be considered in future iterations. The algorithm repeats the above steps until there is no active node in the search tree.

All three activities at each iteration of a B&B algorithm, namely node selection, branching, and bounding, can influence the performance of the algorithm in a significant way. There are several different node selection strategies (Nemhauser & Wolsey, 1988), including depth-first-search (selecting a node at the deepest level of the tree), and best-lower-bound (selecting a node with the lowest lower bound). Branching and bounding strategies are highly problem dependent. Special structures and optimality properties associated with a problem need to be fully exploited in order to derive effective branching and bounding strategies that make the underlying B&B algorithm efficient. For example, as described in Sect. 2.3.3,

2.3 Solution Methods

some scheduling problems have a certain structure that enables us to formulate them as set partitioning type of problems, possibly with additional constraints. Solving the LP relaxation of this type of formulation may provide a very tight lower bound within a B&B framework.

2.3.3 Integer Programming Based Algorithms

Integer programming (IP) is another useful tool commonly used for solving scheduling problems. IP is particularly useful to find tight lower bounds for NP-hard scheduling problems. Lower bounding is a necessary part of exact branch-and-bound algorithms (see Sect. 2.3.2), which are often used to solve NP-hard scheduling problems for which no faster exact algorithms, such as pseudo-polynomial time dynamic programming algorithms, exist. Lower bounding is also necessary in evaluating the performance of an approximate solution algorithm (see Sect. 2.3.4).

There are several different ways of formulating a scheduling problem into an integer programming formulation and computing a lower bound based on this formulation. We discuss two promising integer programming approaches for scheduling problems: (1) time-indexed formulations, and (2) column generation. They are discussed in Sects. 2.3.3.1 and 2.3.3.2, respectively.

2.3.3.1 Time-Indexed Formulations

Time-indexed formulations have been widely adopted for formulating and solving classical machine scheduling problems (e.g., Berghman & Spieksma, 2015; Sousa & Wolsey, 1992). To create a time-indexed formulation for a given scheduling problem, one needs to first discretize the time horizon of the problem, and then introduce time-indexed decision variables, and define the constraints and the objective function accordingly. A major advantage of time-indexed formulations is that the LP relaxation of such formulations tends to generate tighter bounds than other commonly used formulations. However, a clear disadvantage of such formulations is that they involve a large number of variables, especially when the total processing times of the jobs are large.

We give two examples below to illustrate how a classical scheduling problem and a supply chain scheduling problem can be formulated using time-indexed variables, respectively. We first consider problem $1|r_j| \sum C_j$. In this problem, there are n jobs $N = \{1, \ldots, n\}$ to be processed on a single machine. Each job $j \in N$ is associated with a release time r_j and a processing time p_j. The objective is to minimize the total completion time of the jobs. This problem is known to be strongly NP-hard (Lenstra et al., 1977).

Example 2.3 (Time-Indexed Formulation for Classical Scheduling Problem $1|r_j|\sum C_j$) Let $T = \max_{j\in N}\{r_j\} + \sum_{j\in N} p_j$. Clearly, in an optimal schedule, all the jobs are processed within the time horizon $[0, T]$. Define $x_{jt} = 1$ if job j starts processing at time t, for $t = r_j, \ldots, T - p_j$, and 0 otherwise. The problem can be formulated as the following integer program:

$$\min \sum_{j\in N} \sum_{t=r_j}^{T-p_j} (t + p_j)x_{jt} \tag{2.1}$$

subject to

$$\sum_{t=r_j}^{T-p_j} x_{jt} = 1, \quad \forall j \in N \tag{2.2}$$

$$\sum_{j\in N} \sum_{s=\max\{r_j,t-p_j+1\}}^{t} x_{js} \le 1, \quad \forall t = 0, \ldots, T - 1 \tag{2.3}$$

$$x_{jt} \in \{0, 1\}, \quad \forall j \in N; \ t = 0, \ldots, T - 1. \tag{2.4}$$

In this formulation, the objective (2.1) is to minimize the total completion time of the jobs, where $t + p_j$ is the completion time of job j if it starts processing at time t. Constraint (2.2) ensures that each job is processed once. Constraint (2.3) ensures that each time interval $[t, t+1)$ is occupied by at most one job, for $t = 0, \ldots, T-1$.

We observe that the formulation in Example 2.3 involves a pseudo-polynomial number of variables and a pseudo-polynomial number of constraints because both these numbers depend on the length of the time horizon. Thus, the size of the formulation grows with both the number of jobs and the average processing time of a job.

Now, we consider an extension of problem $1|r_j|\sum C_j$ where completed jobs are delivered to a single customer site in batches. Each delivery shipment can carry up to b jobs. The transportation time and cost of a delivery shipment from the plant to the customer site are τ and Π, respectively. Let D_j be the delivery time of job j. The objective of the problem is to minimize the sum of the total delivery time of the jobs, $\sum_{j\in N} D_j$, and the total transportation cost.

Example 2.4 (Time-Indexed Formulation for Supply Chain Scheduling Problem that Combines $1|r_j|\sum C_j$ and Delivery of Completed Jobs) In addition to the parameter T and variables x_{jt} defined in Example 2.3 above, we define two additional sets of variables, for $t = 0, \ldots, T$, and $j \in N$: $z_t = 1$ if there is a shipment that departs at time t, and 0 otherwise; $y_{jt} = 1$ if job j is assigned to the shipment that departs at time t, and 0 otherwise. The problem can be formulated as the following integer program:

2.3 Solution Methods

$$\min \sum_{j \in N} \left(\tau + \sum_{t=r_j+p_j}^{T} t y_{jt} \right) + \sum_{t=1}^{T} \Pi z_t \tag{2.5}$$

subject to

$$\sum_{t=r_j}^{T-p_j} x_{jt} = 1, \quad \forall j \in N \tag{2.6}$$

$$\sum_{j \in N} \sum_{s=\max\{r_j, t-p_j+1\}}^{t} x_{js} \leq 1, \quad \forall t = 0, \ldots, T-1 \tag{2.7}$$

$$\sum_{j \in N} y_{jt} \leq b, \quad \forall t = 1, \ldots, T \tag{2.8}$$

$$\sum_{t=r_j+p_j}^{T} y_{jt} = 1, \quad \forall j \in N \tag{2.9}$$

$$\sum_{s=r_j}^{t-p_j} x_{js} \geq y_{jt}, \quad \forall t = r_j + p_j, \ldots, T, j \in N \tag{2.10}$$

$$x_{jt} \in \{0, 1\}, \quad \forall j \in N; \ t = 0, \ldots, T-1. \tag{2.11}$$

$$y_{jt}, z_t \in \{0, 1\}, \quad \forall j \in N; \ t = 1, \ldots, T. \tag{2.12}$$

In this formulation, the objective (2.1) minimizes the total delivery time of the jobs and the total transportation cost. Constraints (2.6) and (2.7) are exactly the same as (2.2) and (2.3), respectively. Constraint (2.8) ensures that each shipment carries at most b jobs. Constraint (2.9) ensures that each job is assigned to exactly one shipment. Finally, constraint (2.10) represents the relationship between x and y variables, ensuring that a job assigned to a shipment with a departure time t is completed no later than t.

To solve time-indexed formulations, valid inequalities and other solution techniques such as column generation (discussed in Sect. 2.3.3.2) are often used (Berghman et al., 2021; Van den Akker et al., 2000). We refer the reader to Sect. 4.3.3.3 for a discussion of the online version of the problem illustrated in Example 2.4.

2.3.3.2 Column Generation

Column generation based algorithms have been widely applied to tackle difficult NP-hard combinatorial optimization problems (e.g., Barnhart et al., 1998; Desaulniers et al., 2010). Column generation is a decomposition approach where a given problem is decomposed into subproblems which are less difficult to solve than the entire problem. The idea of this method for an optimization problem can be described as follows. The given problem is first formulated as a set packing or set partitioning type of binary IP formulation, where each column represents a feasible solution to a part of the problem (or a subproblem) which involves a number of decisions, instead of a single decision. In this formulation, the decision variable corresponding to a column is 1 if the solution to the subproblem corresponding to the column is adopted, and 0 otherwise.

The optimal objective value of the linear programming (LP) relaxation of this formulation is a valid lower bound on the optimal objective value of the original problem. However, it is not efficient to solve the LP relaxation problem directly even using the fastest commercial LP solver available, since it typically contains a very large number of columns. Instead, the LP relaxation is solved using the Dantzig-Wolfe decomposition approach (Dantzig & Wolfe, 1960) in which the LP relaxation is decomposed into a master problem consisting of only a much smaller subset of columns and one or more subproblems. An iterative procedure can then be used where in each iteration, the master problem is first solved by a commercial LP solver directly. Based on the dual variable values of the master problem, the subproblems are solved next to generate new columns with a minimum reduced cost. One or more new columns with a negative reduced cost are added to the master problem for the next iteration. The LP relation problem is solved when, in an iteration, no new columns with a negative reduced cost can be found.

Below, we apply the column generation lower bounding technique to a classical scheduling problem and a supply chain scheduling problem, respectively. We first consider problem $P_m || \sum w_j C_j$. The column generation approach is first applied to this and other parallel-machine scheduling problems by Chen and Powell (1999a,b) and Van den Akker et al. (1999).

Example 2.5 (Column Generation for Classical Scheduling Problem $P_m || \sum w_j C_j$) Let Ω denote the set of all feasible partial schedules on a single machine. For any $s \in \Omega$, define f_s to be the total weighted completion time of the jobs in s, and a_{js} to be 1 if job j is in s and 0 otherwise. Define variable $y_s = 1$ if schedule $s \in \Omega$ is used and 0 otherwise. Then, the problem $P_m || \sum w_j C_j$ can be formulated as the following set partitioning problem with a side constraint:

$$\min \sum_{s \in \Omega} f_s y_s \tag{2.13}$$

subject to

$$\sum_{s \in \Omega} a_{js} y_s = 1, \quad \forall j \in N \tag{2.14}$$

$$\sum_{s \in \Omega} y_s = m \tag{2.15}$$

$$y_s \in \{0, 1\}, \quad \forall s \in \Omega, \tag{2.16}$$

2.3 Solution Methods

where the objective (2.13) is to minimize the total weighted completion time of the jobs in the chosen single-machine schedules, constraint (2.14) ensures that each job is included in one of the single-machine schedules chosen, and the side constraint (2.15) means that exactly m single-machine schedules are chosen.

This formulation contains an extremely large number of columns because the set Ω is exponentially large. Applying the column generation technique to solve the LP relaxation of this formulation, the LP relaxation problem is decomposed into a master problem which has the same form as the LP relaxation problem but with only a small subset of the columns, and a single-machine subproblem. Let π_j denote the dual variable value corresponding to job j, for each $j \in N$, in constraint (2.14) of the master problem, and σ denote the dual variable value corresponding to constraint (2.15) of the master problem. The subproblem is to find a single-machine schedule $s \in \Omega$ with the minimum reduced cost r_s defined as:

$$ r_s = f_s - \sum_{j \in N} a_{js}\pi_j - \sigma. \qquad (2.17) $$

The subproblem is shown to be ordinarily NP-hard, but it can be solved by a pseudo-polynomial time DP algorithm (Chen & Powell, 1999b). It is shown that the lower bound generated by the above column generation method is extremely tight; it is within 0.001% of the optimal objective value of the original problem for all the problems tested by Chen and Powell (1999b).

Next, we consider a problem that integrates the classical scheduling problem $1 || \sum w_j D_j$ and delivery scheduling of completed jobs to a single customer site. The objective is to minimize the total weighted delivery time of jobs and the total transportation cost, i.e., $\sum w_j D_j + TC$, as in the problem of Example 2.2 discussed in Sect. 2.3.1. Following the notation defined above, we assume that each delivery shipment can carry up to b jobs and is associated with a transportation time τ and a transportation cost Π for delivery to the customer site.

This problem is known to be strongly NP-hard (Hall & Potts, 2005, and discussed in Sect. 3.4.3). We are not aware of any existing integer programming based algorithm or lower bounding scheme for this problem.

Example 2.6 (Column Generation for Supply Chain Scheduling Problem that Combines $1 || \sum w_j D_j$ *and Delivery of Completed Jobs)* To apply the column generation approach to compute a lower bound for this problem, we formulate the problem based on the fact that every solution of the problem consists of some individual delivery batches, where each batch of jobs is processed consecutively in arbitrary order with delivery departure time equal to the completion time of the last job in it. Let Ω denote the set of all feasible production and delivery schedules of a single batch of jobs. Given a single-batch schedule $s \in \Omega$, the following parameters are all specified:

(i) The starting time of the first job in it, denoted as $L(s)$
(ii) The completion time of the last job in it, denoted as $R(s)$

(iii) Whether each job j is in s, which is represented by parameter a_{js} with its value being 1 if job j is in s and 0 otherwise, for all $j \in N$

(iv) Whether a specific time slot $[t - 1, t)$ is occupied by s, which is represented by parameter b_{ts} being 1 if $L(s) + 1 \leq t \leq R(s)$, and 0 otherwise, for all $t = 1, \ldots, P$, where $P = \sum_{j \in N} p_j$

The total cost of a schedule $s \in \Omega$ is then $f_s = (\sum_{j \in N} a_{js} w_j)(R(s) + \tau) + \Pi$, where Π is the delivery cost per batch, and τ is the delivery time from the plant to the customer.

Define variable $y_s = 1$ if schedule $s \in \Omega$ is used, and 0 otherwise. Then, the problem can be formulated as the following set partitioning problem:

$$\min \sum_{s \in \Omega} f_s y_s \tag{2.18}$$

subject to

$$\sum_{s \in \Omega} a_{js} y_s = 1, \quad \forall j \in N \tag{2.19}$$

$$\sum_{s \in \Omega} b_{ts} y_s = 1, \forall t = 1, \ldots, P \tag{2.20}$$

$$y_s \in \{0, 1\}, \quad \forall s \in \Omega, \tag{2.21}$$

where the objective (2.18) minimizes the total cost of the jobs in the chosen single-batch schedules, constraint (2.19) ensures that each job is included in one of the single-batch schedules chosen, and constraint (2.20) means that each time slot between 1 and P is occupied exactly once.

Following the column generation scheme, the LP relaxation of this formulation is decomposed into a master problem which has the same form as the LP relaxation formulation but with a small subset of the columns, and a single-batch subproblem. Let π_j denote the dual variable value corresponding to job j, for each $j \in N$, in constraint (2.19), and σ_t denote the dual variable value corresponding to time t in constraint (2.20). The subproblem is to find a single-batch schedule $s \in \Omega$ with the minimum reduced cost r_s given by:

$$r_s = f_s - \sum_{j \in N} a_{js} \pi_j - \sum_{t=L(s)+1}^{R(s)} \sigma_t. \tag{2.22}$$

This subproblem is more general than the subproblem involved in Example 2.5 and hence is at least ordinarily NP-hard. We observe that, given a single-batch schedule $s \in \Omega$, for given dual variable values π_j and σ_t, the reduced cost r_s given in (2.22) is determined by the specific jobs contained in the batch, and $L(s)$ and $R(s)$. The reduced cost r_s is independent of the processing sequence of the jobs. Thus, we can

2.3 Solution Methods

assume without loss of generality that the jobs in a batch are always processed in shortest processing time first (SPT) order.

The subproblem can be solved by a pseudo-polynomial DP algorithm as follows.

Initialization Reindex the jobs in non-increasing order of p_j.

Value Function Define $g(L, R, k, j)$ as the minimum total cost of a partial schedule containing k of the first j jobs $\{1, \ldots, j\}$, where the completion time of the last job is R, and the starting time of the first job is L.

Boundary Conditions $g(R, R, 0, 0) = 0$, for $R = 1, \ldots, P$.

Recurrence Relation For $j = 1, \ldots, n$, $k = 1, \ldots, b$, $L = 0, \ldots, R-1$, $R = 1, \ldots, P$:

$$g(L, R, k, j) = \min \begin{cases} g(L, R, k, j-1), \\ g(L + p_j, R, k-1, j-1) + w_j(R + \tau) - \pi_j - \sum_{t=L+1}^{L+p_j} \sigma_t. \end{cases}$$

Optimal Solution First, for fixed $R = 1, \ldots, P$, compute

$$G(R) = \min\{g(L, R, k, n) + \Pi \mid 1 \le k \le b, L = 0, \ldots R-1\}.$$

Then, compute $\min\{G(R) \mid 1 \le R \le P\}$.

In the recurrence relation, two possible cases are considered: (1) job j is either not included in the batch (in this case, $g(L, R, k, j) = g(L, R, k, j-1)$), or (2) it is included in the batch (in this case, job j is scheduled in the time slot $[L, L + p_j)$ and hence $g(L, R, k, j)$ is equal to $g(L + p_j, R, k-1, j-1) + w_j(R + \tau) - \pi_j - \sum_{t=L+1}^{L+p_j} \sigma_t$. The time complexity of this DP algorithm is $O(bnP^2)$.

2.3.4 Approximate Solution Methods

Most supply chain scheduling problems are strongly NP-hard. To solve a strongly NP-hard problem to optimality, one has to resort to exponential-time algorithms such as branch-and-bound and integer programming. One may be able to construct such algorithms to find optimal solutions for small instances of strongly NP-hard supply chain scheduling problems in a reasonable amount of computational time. However, for large instances of such problems, any exact algorithm is likely to be very time-consuming. Consequently, practitioners and academic researchers have a strong interest in developing approximate solution methods, also known as heuristic algorithms, for such problems. A *heuristic algorithm* or *approximation algorithm* (or simply called *heuristic*) for a problem does not guarantee an optimal solution but is much simpler and easier to implement in practice and typically requires much less computational time than an optimal algorithm.

Aarts and Lenstra (2003) and Voss et al. (1999) describe several types of heuristics for a variety of combinatorial optimization problems, including some scheduling problems. We summarize below some commonly used heuristics in the literature for solving supply chain scheduling problems.

- Rule based heuristics that generate a solution using simple rules (e.g., scheduling jobs in nondecreasing order of their processing times), or more sophisticated rules (e.g., a schedule is constructed iteratively based on multiple problem parameters).
- Local search heuristics such as Tabu Search, Simulated Annealing, and Genetic Algorithms (Aarts & Lenstra, 2003) which start with one or more initial solutions and then iteratively generate new solutions by searching the neighborhoods of existing solutions.
- Dynamic programming based heuristics which use DP algorithms to solve a problem approximately by searching only part of the solution space.
- Integer programming based heuristics which formulate a problem as an integer program and solve the formulation approximately by applying an incomplete branch-and-bound procedure or a decomposition technique such as Lagrangian relaxation or column generation (described in Sect. 2.3.3) to find a good, but generally not optimal, feasible solution.

The performance of a heuristic can be evaluated through computational tests using real or randomly generated data sets (Hall & Posner, 2001). The solutions generated by a heuristic are typically compared to either true optimal solutions or bounds (a lower bound in the case of a minimization problem or an upper bound in the case of a maximization problem). Simple (but often loose) bounds can be derived following some optimality properties. However, to obtain tighter bounds, one may have to resort to sophisticated methods such as integer programming, as described in Sect. 2.3.3.

2.3.4.1 Worst-Case and Average-Case Analysis

The performance of a heuristic can also be evaluated theoretically (e.g., Hochbaum, 1996). Two types of theoretical analysis are commonly conducted, *worst-case performance analysis* and *asymptotic performance analysis*. Given an optimization problem, let $\mathscr{I}$ be the set of all feasible instances of the problem, and $I \in \mathscr{I}$ any instance of the problem. Given a heuristic H for a minimization problem, let $Z^H(I)$ be the objective value of the solution obtained by the heuristic for the instance, and $Z^*(I)$ the optimal objective value of the instance. Then, we can define the following.

Definition 2.3 The *worst-case performance ratio* of heuristic H for the given problem is defined as

$$R^H = \sup_{I \in \mathscr{I}} \{Z^H(I)/Z^*(I)\}. \tag{2.23}$$

2.3 Solution Methods

Definition 2.4 The *asymptotic performance ratio* of heuristic H for the given problem is defined as

$$R_\infty^H = \inf\{r \geq 1 \mid \text{there exists } Y \text{ such that } Z^H(I)/Z^*(I) \leq r,$$
$$\text{for all instances } I \in \mathscr{I} \text{ with } Z^*(I) \geq Y\}. \tag{2.24}$$

For scheduling problems, asymptotic performance ratio may also be defined in terms of a threshold on the problem size, instead of a threshold on the objective value (e.g., Chou et al., 2006), as follows:

$$R_\infty^H = \inf\{r \geq 1 \mid \text{there exists a positive integer } n_0 \text{ such that } Z^H(I)/Z^*(I) \leq r,$$
$$\text{for all instances } I \in \mathscr{I} \text{ with number of jobs } n \geq n_0\}. \tag{2.25}$$

Clearly, for a minimization problem, the performance ratios R^H and R_∞^H of any heuristic H must be at least 1. The closer to 1 these ratios are, the better a given heuristic is. In conducting worst-case or asymptotic performance analysis, a lower bound is often used to replace $Z^*(I)$. The performance ratio obtained this way is then an upper bound on the true performance ratio. In this case, if an instance I_0 can be found such that $R^H = Z^H(I_0)/Z^*(I_0)$, then it is said that the worst-case performance bound is *tight*, meaning that R^H is exactly equal to the bound obtained.

Definition 2.5 If $R_\infty^H = 1$, the heuristic is then said to be *asymptotically optimal*, meaning the heuristic solution converges to an optimal solution when the objective value (or size) of the problem instance becomes infinitely large.

However, both R^H and R_∞^H represent performance of a heuristic in the worst case; they typically do not represent the *average-case performance* of the heuristic. Unfortunately, it is very difficult to conduct average-case performance analysis (also known as *probabilistic analysis*) of even simple heuristics theoretically (Coffman and Lueker, 1991). There are few existing average-case performance analysis results for scheduling problems, and to our knowledge, most such existing results are asymptotic (e.g., Kaminsky, 2003; Kaminsky & Simchi-Levi, 1998). That is, most existing average-case analysis results for scheduling problems that we are aware of are derived when the problem size goes to infinity. Such analysis is also known as *asymptotic probabilistic analysis*, which is often conducted under the assumption that some of the problem data follows a certain probability distribution (Simchi-Levi et al., 2013).

Definition 2.6 If we let $\varXi$ be a probability measure on the set of instances $\mathscr{I}$ (i.e., the problem instances are generated randomly from $\varXi$), a heuristic H is said to be *asymptotically optimal* for the problem defined on $\varXi$ if the ratio $Z^H(I)/Z^*(I)$ converges to 1 (or equivalently, the ratio $[Z^H(I) - Z^*(I)]/Z^*(I)$ converges to 0) with probability one (or equivalently, *almost surely*), when the problem size goes to infinity.

Remark 2.2 The *strong law of large numbers* (e.g., Ross, 1998) is often used to prove almost sure convergence of a random sequence. The strong law of large numbers states that given a sequence of n independently and identically distributed random variables, $X_1, X_2, \ldots, X_n$, with mean μ, $(X_1 + X_2 + \cdots + X_n)/n$ converges to the mean μ almost surely, when n goes to infinity.

2.3.4.2 Fully Polynomial Time Approximation Schemes

For many ordinarily NP-hard problems, there are heuristics called polynomial time approximation schemes or fully polynomial time approximation schemes.

Definition 2.7 For a given minimization problem, a heuristic is called a *polynomial time approximation scheme* (PTAS) if for any fixed accuracy requirement $\varepsilon > 0$, the heuristic is a polynomial-time algorithm with worst-case performance ratio bounded by $1+\varepsilon$. A heuristic is called a *fully polynomial time approximation scheme* (FPTAS) if (i) it is a PTAS, and (ii) its time complexity is bounded by a polynomial-time function of both the problem input length and $1/\varepsilon$.

We observe that a PTAS is required to have a polynomial-time complexity for any fixed ε, but its time complexity may be exponential in $1/\varepsilon$. Thus, there is a major difference in running time between an FPTAS and a PTAS, especially when ε is close to 0. For example, if we compare an FPTAS with a running time $O(n^2(1/\varepsilon)^3)$ and a PTAS with a running time $O(n2^{1/\varepsilon})$, when ε is relatively large, the FPTAS can be slower than the PTAS. However, when ε approaches 0, the PTAS becomes exponentially slower than the FPTAS.

An FPTAS is the strongest possible result one can achieve for a NP-hard problem unless $P = NP$ (e.g., Vazirani, 2001, p. 68). An FPTAS can be constructed for many ordinarily NP-hard scheduling problems. For such problems, there are usually pseudo-polynomial time dynamic programming algorithms, and such algorithms can in most cases be used to construct FPTAS (Woeginger, 2000). However, for strongly NP-hard scheduling problems, there is no FPTAS unless $P = NP$, but there can exist a PTAS.

2.3.4.3 Competitive Analysis

For online problems including online supply chain scheduling problems where jobs arrive over time and the parameters associated with a job are unknown until it arrives, online algorithms may have to be used to derive a solution. An *online algorithm* is one that can only process its input piece-by-piece in a serial fashion, i.e., in the order that the input is fed to the algorithm, without having the entire input available from the beginning. In contrast, an *offline algorithm* is given the whole problem data from the beginning and is required to output an answer which solves the problem at hand. *Competitive analysis* is often used to analyze the performance of an online algorithm. In such an analysis, the performance of an

2.3 Solution Methods

online algorithm is compared to the performance of an optimal offline algorithm that knows the sequence of job arrivals and their data in advance. The *competitive ratio* and *asymptotic competitive ratio* of an online algorithm H for an online problem are defined the same as in (2.23) and (2.24) or (2.25) for the worst-case performance ratio and asymptotic performance ratio of an offline algorithm, respectively, except that I is a specific realization of the problem input data, and $Z^*(I)$ is the optimal objective value of the offline problem corresponding to I. In competitive analysis, one typically imagines that there is an "adversary" who deliberately chooses difficult problem input data to maximize the ratio of the objective value generated by the online algorithm being studied and the optimal objective value of the offline problem which has the entire input data known from the beginning. For a given online problem, any online algorithm with the smallest possible competitive ratio is called a *best possible algorithm*, or an *optimal online algorithm*.

Online classical scheduling problems have been quite extensively studied in the past 20 years (Pruhs et al., 2004; Tan & Zhang, 2013). However, there are relatively few existing results on online supply chain scheduling problems.

2.3.5 Cooperative Game Theory

In a centralized scheduling environment, there is a single decision maker whose objective is to schedule jobs in a way that optimizes a system-wide criterion. The optimal solution generated this way is optimal collectively over all the jobs and all the supply chain stages or functional areas involved. However, in many supply chain environments, the jobs to be processed may come from different clients, and different stages or functions that serve the jobs may belong to different companies or decision makers. Different clients and functional areas may have conflicting objectives and may be interested only in a solution that optimizes their own objective. A solution that is optimal to one party in the supply chain is unlikely to be optimal for another party or for the overall system, and vice versa.

Game theory is often used to model and analyze problems involving multiple decision makers (or agents, or players). There are generally two types of games, *cooperative games* and *noncooperative games*, that can be used to model problems with multiple players with conflicting objectives. There are many comprehensive books on game theory (e.g., Myerson, 1997; Peleg & Sudhölter, 2007) that provide detailed descriptions of various aspects of these types of games. In this and the following section, we briefly describe some key concepts associated with these types of games using scheduling problems as examples. We describe other necessary concepts and provide further discussion about the games defined here in Chaps. 8 and 9.

When players cooperate and agree to adopt some solution π^* of the problem (e.g., a global or system-wide optimal solution), they may collectively achieve a higher cost saving (or a higher value, a lower cost, etc.), as compared to the case when the players act independently and use their own solutions $\pi_1, \pi_2, \ldots$.

However, some individual players may be worse off by using such a solution π^*. Such players must be compensated in a fair way in order for them to agree to the solution π^*. Cooperative game theory provides essential concepts and tools for designing compensation schemes that allocate the cost saving (or value, benefit, etc.) among the individual players.

We use a one-machine sequencing game (Curiel et al., 1989; Hamers et al., 1996) as an example to describe the concept of a cooperative game. There are n players, denoted by $N = \{1, \ldots, n\}$, each having one job to be processed on a given machine. Player j's job has a processing time requirement of p_j units, and player j's cost is a linear function $f_j(t) = w_j t$ of its completion time t on the machine. There is an initial processing sequence σ_0, which is the sequence the players use if they do not cooperate. This sequence can be given by the owner of the machine based on some rules, or it may result from the random arrival process of the jobs, and is typically not globally optimal. That is, the total cost of all the players under σ_0 may not be the minimum possible.

A cooperative game is defined by specifying a *characteristic function* v that maps any subset of players, also known as a *coalition*, to a real number, $v : 2^N \rightarrow R$ satisfying $v(\emptyset) = 0$. The characteristic function $v(S)$ represents the total cost saving (or the total value) the players in coalition $S \subset N$ can achieve if they cooperate by rearranging the positions of their jobs in the initial sequence σ_0, under the constraint that these players must use an admissible processing sequence for their jobs if they want to rearrange them. Admissible sequences can be defined in different ways. One example (Curiel et al., 1989) is to define any rearrangement of the jobs in σ_0 as an admissible sequence if only the jobs of the players in coalition S that are consecutively sequenced in σ_0 are rearranged among themselves.

Let $A(S)$ denote the set of all admissible sequences for the jobs of players in coalition S. The characteristic function $v(S)$ can be defined as

$$v(S) = \max_{\sigma \in A(S)} \sum_{i \in S} [f_i(C_i(\sigma_0)) - f_i(C_i(\sigma))], \qquad (2.26)$$

where $C_i(\pi)$ is the completion time of player i's job under schedule π.

When all the players cooperate to form a *grand coalition*, they together achieve a total cost saving or value $v(N)$, which is defined as

$$v(N) = \sum_{i \in N} \left[f_i(C_i(\sigma_0)) - f_i(C_i(\sigma^*)), \right], \qquad (2.27)$$

where σ^* is the sequence among all admissible sequences $A(N)$ with the lowest possible total cost of the jobs.

One of the main questions studied in cooperative game theory is: how to allocate the total cost saving or value $v(N)$ among the players such that no subset of players can be better off by separating themselves from the grand coalition and acting on their own behalf. Mathematically, this is equivalent to finding an allocation scheme, represented by $(x_1, \ldots, x_n)$, where x_i is the cost saving or value allocated to player i, such that

2.3 Solution Methods

$$\sum_{j\in N} x_j = v(N) \tag{2.28}$$

$$\sum_{j\in S} x_j \geq v(S), \quad \text{for all } S \subset N. \tag{2.29}$$

Equation (2.28) ensures that the total allocation to all the players is equal to $v(N)$, and inequalities (2.29) require that for any subset of players, the total allocation they receive is greater than or equal to the total cost saving or value if they form a coalition, which guarantees that no players have an incentive to leave the grand coalition.

One of the most fundamental concepts in cooperative game theory is the *core*. This, along with some related concepts, is defined below.

Definition 2.8 Any feasible solution x to (2.28)–(2.29) is *stable* or a *core allocation*. The collection of all feasible solutions to (2.28)–(2.29) is called the *core* of the game. Not every cooperative game has a nonempty core. A game with a nonempty core for all instances is *balanced*. A nonempty core often contains an infinite number of solutions.

A cooperative game as defined above is sometimes known as a cost savings game, a value game, or a profit game. Alternatively, if the characteristic function $v(S)$ represents the minimum total cost that can incur for the players in coalition S if they cooperate, then the game is known as a cost game. In this case, if an allocation scheme $(x_1, \ldots, x_n)$, where x_i is the cost allocated to player i, satisfies (2.28) and the opposite relation of (2.29) (i.e., the "$\geq$" in (2.29) becomes "$\leq$"), then this allocation is a core allocation.

Another fundamental concept in cooperative game theory is a *convex game*, which is defined below.

Definition 2.9 A cost savings game (N, v) is called a *convex game* if its characteristic function v is supermodular, i.e., $v(S\cup T)+v(S\cap T) \geq v(S)+v(T)$, $\forall S, T \subseteq N$. Conversely, a cost game (N, v) is called a *convex game* if its characteristic function v is submodular, i.e., $v(S \cup T) + v(S \cap T) \leq v(S) + v(T)$, $\forall S, T \subseteq N$.

The supermodularity of v is equivalent to

$$v(S \cup \{i\}) - v(S) \leq v(T \cup \{i\}) - v(T), \quad \forall S \subseteq T \subseteq N \setminus \{i\}, \forall i \in N,$$

and the submodularity of v is equivalent to

$$v(S \cup \{i\}) - v(S) \geq v(T \cup \{i\}) - v(T), \quad \forall S \subseteq T \subseteq N \setminus \{i\}, \forall i \in N.$$

This implies that the incentive for joining a coalition increases as the coalition grows (Shapley, 1971), leading to a so-called snowball effect. Convex cooperative games have many useful properties including the property that any convex game is balanced. However, a game does not have to be convex in order to be balanced.

Curiel et al. (1989) show that the one-machine sequencing game discussed above is a convex game. They propose an allocation rule called Equal Gain Splitting (EGS) which divides the cost saving obtained in an interchange of two neighboring jobs equally between the two players involved, and show that EGS is a core allocation. Curiel et al. (1994) consider a more general version of the sequencing game where each player j's cost is a weakly monotonic function of its completion time t. This is more general than the version discussed above where the cost function is linear in t. More details are provided in Sect. 8.3.3.

In addition to the concepts introduced above, there are several other commonly used concepts in cooperative game theory. One such concept is the *Shapley value* (Shapley, 1953). The Shapley value is a unique allocation solution that satisfies some valuable properties. Chapter 8 introduces this concept, along with some other single-point solution concepts. We refer the reader to Chap. 8 for those concepts and their applications in supply chain scheduling.

The sequencing game and variants discussed above use some assumptions that may be overly simplifying from a practical point of view. In these and many other scheduling related games studied in the literature, it is assumed that an initial schedule σ_0 of the jobs is predetermined (e.g., jobs are scheduled in first-come first-served order), and a characteristic function is defined as the cost saving or value improvement relative to this initial schedule if the members of a coalition work together. In practice, however, an initial schedule may not exist. There are several studies that consider games related to scheduling without an initial sequence (e.g., Hall & Liu, 2016).

There are also other practical issues that may need to be considered. For example, there can be more than one machine, a player may have more than one job, there can be a cost for using a particular period of the machine time, more general admissible sequences may be allowed when rearranging the job positions, the players may hide some information about their jobs, and in addition to being processed, the jobs may need to be delivered to their destinations after processing. Chapter 8 discusses models with some of these and other practical issues.

2.3.6 Noncooperative Game Theory

In large and complex decision making environments, especially those conducted online through commercial platforms, achieving cooperation is unrealistic. Difficulties in doing so arise from the competition of the players, lack of trust between them, and lack of information. In such situations, a more realistic model of the decision process is a noncooperative game.

In noncooperative game theory, individual players are typically assumed to maximize their own utility after considering how other players may react to their strategy. Based on the availability of information about the players, noncooperative

2.3 Solution Methods

games can be classified into *games with complete information*, where individual players do not have private information, and *games with private information*, where individual players have private information that is not known to other players.

Different research questions are studied in the literature for different types of noncooperative games. For games with private information, major research issues include the design of truthful algorithms and the design of mechanisms that guarantee that no player has an incentive to report false information, regardless of what is shared by other players. These, along with some other issues, are discussed in detail in Chap. 9 of the book. For this reason, we do not elaborate on these topics here.

In the following, we briefly discuss some of the key concepts and issues for noncooperative games with complete information. A key concept for noncooperative games with complete information is a *Nash equilibrium* (NE) in which no player in the game has anything to gain by changing only his or her own strategy. If each player has chosen a strategy and no player can benefit by changing his or her strategy while the other players keep theirs unchanged, then the current set of strategy choices and the corresponding payoffs constitute a Nash equilibrium.

We use a parallel-machine scheduling model (Heydenreich et al., 2007; Immorlica et al., 2005) as an example to describe the concept of noncooperative games and Nash equilibrium. There are n players, denoted as $N = \{1, \ldots, n\}$, with each player j having one job with a processing time of p_j. There are m identical parallel machines, $M = \{1, \ldots, m\}$. Each player needs to choose a machine to process its job. Let x_i denote the strategy or solution that player i chooses (i.e., the machine to process its job). Let X_i be the set of all feasible strategies associated with player i. Hence, $X_i = M$ for all $i \in N$. Each player i has a utility or payoff function $u_i(x)$ which is generally a function of the specific strategies used by all the players together, $x = (x_1, \ldots, x_n)$, as well as the underlying game rule or policy. Suppose the game rule is that the jobs assigned to a machine are processed in shortest processing time first (SPT) order where ties between any two jobs are broken in favor of the job with a smaller index. Consider the following utility function:

$$u_i(x) = -p_i - \sum_{j:x_j=x_i,p_j<p_i} p_j - \sum_{j:x_j=x_i,p_j=p_i,j<i} p_j, \quad x_i \in X_i, \text{ and } i \in N.$$

$$(2.30)$$

With the utility function defined this way, the utility of strategy x_i for player i is the negative completion time of his or her job.

Definition 2.10 A strategy vector of profile $x = (x_1, \ldots, x_n)$, where each $x_j \in X_j$, is called a *pure strategy Nash equilibrium* if, for every player $j \in N$,

$$u_j(x) \geq u_j(x_1, \ldots, x_{j-1}, x'_j, x_{j+1}, \ldots, x_n), \quad \text{for all } x'_j \in X_j. \qquad (2.31)$$

In addition to using one specific strategy (which is also called a *pure strategy*), a player j can sometimes also use a *mixed strategy*, which is a probability distribution over the set of pure strategies X_j. Under a mixed strategy, a player uses one of its pure strategies chosen randomly following the given probability distribution. Denote the set of all feasible mixed strategies of player j as $\Delta(X_j)$. Each element $\delta_j \in \Delta(X_j)$ is a specific probability distribution that player j can follow. Given a mixed strategy vector of profile $\delta = (\delta_1, \ldots, \delta_n)$, where each $\delta_j \in \Delta(X_j)$, let $u_j(\delta)$ be the expected utility of player j.

Definition 2.11 A given mixed strategy vector of profile δ is called a *mixed strategy Nash equilibrium* if, for every player $j \in N$,

$$\mathbb{E}u_j(\delta) \geq \mathbb{E}u_j(\delta_1, \ldots, \delta_{j-1}, \delta'_j, \delta_{j+1}, \ldots, \delta_n), \quad \text{for all } \delta'_j \in \Delta(X_j). \tag{2.32}$$

Not every game has a pure strategy Nash equilibrium. However, every game with a finite number of players in which each player can choose from finitely many pure strategies has at least one mixed strategy Nash equilibrium (Nash, 1951). Even a mixed strategy Nash equilibrium may not exist if the set of choices is infinite and non-compact. Given a noncooperative game, an interesting question is the existence of pure strategy Nash equilibria, and if they exist, then one needs to design efficient algorithms to compute pure or mixed strategy Nash equilibria.

For the above discussed noncooperative game defined on a parallel-machine scheduling model, there exist pure strategy Nash equilibria. Immorlica et al. (2005) prove that the set of pure strategy Nash equilibria is precisely the set of solutions found by the Ibarra-Kim algorithm (Ibarra & Kim, 1977).

Another commonly investigated question in dealing with noncooperative games is the *price of anarchy* (Koutsoupias & Papadimitriou, 1999).

Definition 2.12 Given a noncooperative game, the *price of anarchy* is the worst-case ratio of the value of a given objective function at a Nash equilibrium solution over the value of the same objective function at the system-wide optimal solution which can be obtained by a central agent who makes decisions for all the players.

The price of anarchy measures the worst-case performance deterioration due to the lack of coordination among independent self-interested players. Heydenreich et al. (2007) show that for the objective of minimizing the makespan in the parallel-machine scheduling model discussed above, the price of anarchy of pure strategy Nash equilibria is $2 - 2/(m + 1)$.

In the definitions and concepts described above, it is implicitly assumed that the underlying noncooperative game is a *simultaneous game* (also known as *static game*), where all the players make their decisions simultaneously without any knowledge of other players' decisions. However, in many practical settings, players make their decisions sequentially rather than simultaneously. A game where players make their decisions at different times or in turn is called *sequential game*. Players who move later in such a game have additional information about the actions of other players or states of the world. For sequential games, there is an important concept that extends from a Nash equilibrium.

Definition 2.13 For a sequential game, a set of strategies is called a *subgame perfect equilibrium* if the strategies constitute a Nash equilibrium for all subgames of the original game.

Chapter 9 provides more detailed discussions of the concepts and issues covered here, as well as other related topics motivated by several supply chain scheduling applications.

Part I
Centralized Supply Chain Scheduling

Part I consists of Chaps. 3 though 6 on centralized supply chain scheduling problems. Chapters 3 and 4 study various integrated production and outbound distribution scheduling problems that arise in supply chains for make-to-order or time-sensitive products. Chapter 3 is focused on offline problems where all the input data to a problem are known in advance. In this chapter, we discuss problem tractability, present optimal algorithms and heuristics, and analyze the performance of those heuristics. Chapter 4 is dedicated to online problems where information about a job is not known until it arrives. In this chapter, we present online algorithms for the problems studied and analyze their worst-case performance. Chapter 5 considers problems where product pricing and production scheduling decisions are made together in a coordinated way. We present optimal and approximation algorithms and heuristics and discuss their performance and related managerial insights. Chapter 6 discusses situations where there are subcontractors available that can be used to process some jobs, and the decision maker needs to make subcontracting and scheduling decisions jointly in order to optimize the overall system performance. We present solution algorithms for a variety of problems and investigate the value of subcontracting in various settings.

Chapter 3
Integrated Production and Outbound Distribution Scheduling: Offline Problems

Abstract In this chapter, we discuss various integrated production and outbound distribution scheduling problems that arise frequently in supply chains for make-to-order or time-sensitive products. We first briefly discuss background, motivations, and the current status of research on these problems. We then classify such problems into several different classes based on some of their major characteristics. We next focus on several representative problems in each class by discussing their tractability, algorithms for solving them, and some other related results.

3.1 Introduction

Production and distribution operations are the two most fundamental functions in a supply chain. In order to maximize customer service at the lowest cost, it is critical to integrate these two functions, and plan and schedule them jointly, in a coordinated manner. In the past three decades, many research studies have been conducted on various integrated production-distribution models at all levels—strategic planning, tactical planning, and operational scheduling. Many survey articles on such models have appeared, see, e.g., Sarmiento and Nagi (1999), Erengüç et al. (1999), Goetschalckx et al. (2002), Bilgen and Ozkarahan (2004), Chen (2004, 2010), and Wang et al. (2015). At a strategic or tactical planning level, production and distribution decisions are typically made based on estimated aggregate production and distribution capacity and customer demand over a relatively long period of time (e.g., 6 months, 1 year, or longer) as input. These decisions are often made jointly with location, network design, capacity, and inventory decisions. By contrast, at a scheduling level, production and distribution decisions are often made with actual machine availability and actual customer orders over a much shorter period of time (e.g., several hours, 1 day, or 1 week) as input. Such decisions are usually made jointly with customer service decisions such as order acceptance and on-time delivery performance.

Detailed scheduling level integration of production and distribution operations is necessary in many practical situations. Increased competition in today's global

© Springer Nature Switzerland AG 2022
Z.-L. Chen, N. G. Hall, *Supply Chain Scheduling*, International Series
in Operations Research & Management Science 323,
https://doi.org/10.1007/978-3-030-90374-9_3

53

marketplace, and heightened expectations of customers, have forced companies to invest aggressively to reduce inventory levels across the supply chain on one hand and be more responsive to customers on the other. Reduced inventory results in closer linkage between production and distribution operations, which makes the joint scheduling of these operations both necessary and possible. Joint scheduling of multiple operations enables firms to optimize the tradeoffs between various costs, total revenue, and delivery timeliness. It is especially critical to integrate production and outbound delivery schedules in the supply chain of many short-shelf-life or make-to-order products. Chapter 1 provides several examples of such products for which production scheduling and delivery scheduling need to be considered jointly.

In this book, we dedicate two chapters—this one and the next—to integrated production and outbound distribution scheduling (IPODS) models. This chapter is focused on offline problems where all parameters associated with jobs are known in advance, whereas Chap. 4 considers online problems where some or all of the parameters associated with jobs are not known until they arrive.

To the best of our knowledge, Potts (1980) is the first paper on an IPODS problem. The problem studied by Potts involves processing jobs on a single machine and delivering them to multiple customer sites individually and immediately after their completion, with the objective of minimizing the maximum delivery time of the jobs. Most of the work on IPODS models has been performed in the past 20 years. A detailed review on IPODS models is given in the survey paper by Chen (2010). Most of the IPODS papers with the individual and immediate delivery method are inspired by Potts (1980). Cheng and Kahlbacher (1993) is the first paper that considers batch delivery (i.e., multiple jobs are delivered together, as opposed to the case of individual delivery) and transportation costs. Almost all the IPODS problems studied prior to 2001 assume that there are always sufficient number of delivery vehicles such that whenever there is a delivery need, there is always a vehicle available. Lee and Chen (2001), which considers a variety of IPODS problems with batch delivery, is apparently the first paper that addresses problems where the number of delivery vehicles is limited. Their paper has motivated the study of a variety of such models. Although a large body of literature on IPODS problems has appeared, research interest in this area is still growing. We believe that the strong interest in this area is mainly motivated by the following facts: (1) historically, supply chain management (SCM) research has been almost exclusively focused on planning level decisions; (2) an increasing number of applications (as described in Chap. 1) require coordinated decision making at a detailed scheduling level; and (3) IPODS models fill the gap between traditional SCM research and new applications.

This chapter is organized as follows. Section 3.2 introduces necessary notation, defines IPODS problems, classifies them into several classes based on the characteristics of job delivery, and presents a representational notation scheme for describing most IPODS problems. Most existing problems involve a single production plant and a single stage of delivery of completed jobs from the plant to the customer sites. Such problems can be classified into problems with individual and immediate delivery, problems with batch delivery to a single customer, problems with batch delivery to multiple customers, and problems with fixed delivery departure times.

3.2 Problem Definition and Classification

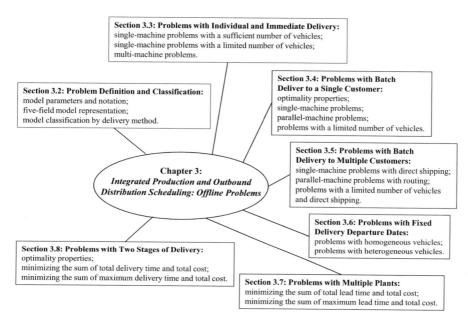

Fig. 3.1 Overview of the topics covered in Chap. 3.

Several representative problems from each of these classes are discussed in detail in Sects. 3.3 through 3.6, respectively. A few problems with multiple plants are discussed in Sect. 3.7, and a few problems with two stages of delivery are discussed in Sect. 3.8. Finally, Sect. 3.9 discusses some possible topics for future research.

Figure 3.1 provides an overview of the topics discussed in this chapter.

3.2 Problem Definition and Classification

Most existing IPODS problems involve a single production plant where all the job processing activities take place, and a single stage of delivery of completed jobs from the plant to the customer sites. In this section, we use the notation, definitions, and classification scheme given in the survey paper of Chen (2010) to describe and classify such IPODS problems.

3.2.1 Model Parameters and Notation

We first describe a general IPODS problem with a single plant and single stage of delivery. At the beginning of a planning horizon, a manufacturer receives a set of orders for n jobs $N = \{1, 2, \ldots, n\}$ from k customers $K = \{1, 2, \ldots, k\}$, which may be at different locations. Let $N_i \subset N$ be the subset of the jobs ordered by customer i, and $n_i = |N_i|$ for $i \in K$, where $N = N_1 \cup \cdots \cup N_k$, and $n = n_1 + \cdots + n_k$. The manufacturer needs first to process these jobs and then to deliver the processed jobs to the customers by $v \geq 1$ delivery vehicles (e.g., vans, trucks, air flights). Each job $j \in N$ needs to be processed by one or multiple machines, depending on the specific machine environment involved (see Sect. 2.1), and may be associated with a number of parameters, including:

- A processing time p_j if only one machine is needed, or a processing times p_{hj} on the hth machine if multiple machines are needed.
- An importance weight w_j.
- A release date (a.k.a. release time, ready time, and arrival time) r_j, which is the time when job j arrives and is ready for processing.
- A delivery due date d_j, such that a penalty may apply if the order is not delivered to its customer by this time.
- A delivery deadline $\bar{d}_j$, by which the order must be delivered to its customer.
- A size q_j, which is the units of capacity needed to carry job j by a delivery vehicle.
- A revenue R_j if job j is processed and delivered to its customer at a desired time (e.g., before or at the deadline, or within a specific time window).

The delivery vehicles may be homogeneous (i.e., they can go to the same customer destinations, and have the same delivery capacity, travel speed, and cost rate) or heterogeneous (i.e., one or more parameters are vehicle dependent). The number of available vehicles may be limited or infinite, and vehicle capacity may be limited (i.e., can only carry a subset of orders in a shipment) or infinite (i.e., can carry any number of orders in one shipment). There are generally nonzero transportation times and nonzero variable transportation costs for traveling between different locations. There may also be a fixed transportation cost associated with each shipment or each vehicle. Specific notation related to transportation times and costs is defined later where necessary.

A *schedule* (i.e., solution) of a given IPODS problem consists of a *production schedule* which specifies when and where each order is processed and a *delivery schedule* which specifies how many shipments (or batches) are used, the departure time and traveling route of each shipment, which jobs are in each shipment, and when each job is delivered to its customer. Using the same notation and definitions given in Sect. 2.1, we let C_j, D_j, and T_j denote the completion time, delivery time, and tardiness of order j, and U_j be a binary indicator for whether order j is tardy or not.

The objective of the manufacturer is to optimize one or a combination of the time-based, cost-based, and revenue-based performance measures defined below. The time-based measures have the same functional forms as the ones used in the production scheduling literature, except that they are functions of job delivery times D_j instead of completion times C_j used in the production scheduling literature. Commonly used time-based performance measures are defined in Sect. 2.1, including *makespan* or *maximum delivery time* $D_{\max}$, *total (weighted) delivery time*

3.2 Problem Definition and Classification

of the jobs $\sum D_j$ (or $\sum w_j D_j$), *total (weighted) tardiness of the jobs* $\sum T_j$ (or $\sum w_j T_j$), *maximum lateness* $L_{\max}$, and *total (weighted) number of late jobs* $\sum U_j$ (or $\sum w_j U_j$).

The most commonly studied cost-based performance measure is *total transportation cost*, denoted as TC, which includes all the fixed and variable total transportation costs incurred for delivering all the jobs. Since the total production cost for processing a given set of jobs is typically fixed independently of the job processing schedule used, total production cost is rarely considered in making scheduling decisions.

When not every job can be accepted for processing, e.g., when jobs have deadlines, but not every job can be processed and delivered by its deadline due to limited production and transportation capacity, a revenue-based performance measure is relevant. In this case, we denote the *total revenue of accepted jobs* to be $\sum R_j$ (which is $\sum_{j \in A} R_j$, where A is the set of accepted and successfully delivered jobs).

3.2.1.1 Five-Field Model Representation

We use the five-field notation $\alpha|\beta|\pi|\delta|\gamma$ proposed in Chen (2010) to represent an IPODS problem with a single plant and single distribution stage. The α, β, and γ fields describe the same components of a problem as are used in the well-known three-field $\alpha|\beta|\gamma$ notation for production scheduling problems (e.g., Graham et al., 1979, also discussed in Sect. 2.1). The reader is referred to Sect. 2.1 for commonly considered machine environments (field α) and commonly used time-based objective functions (field γ). Other commonly used objective functions, including cost-based and revenue-based performance measures, are discussed above. The other two fields π and δ specify the characteristics of the delivery process and the number of customers, respectively. Below, we describe some commonly studied constraints and restrictions (field β), number of customers (field δ), and delivery characteristics (field π), associated with IPODS problems.

Restrictions and Constraints (β)   Below are the symbols used in field β for some commonly used restrictions and constraints in IPODS problems.

- r_j: Jobs have unequal release dates (without this, it is assumed that all the jobs arrive and are ready for processing at time 0).
- $d_j = d$: Jobs have a common due date d.
- $\bar{d}_j$: Each job j has a deadline, before or at which job j must be delivered to its customer.
- fd_j: Each job j has a fixed delivery time fd_j such that if the job is accepted, it then must be delivered to its customer exactly at this point of time (i.e., $D_j = fd_j$ for $j \in N$).
- *pmtn*: Job processing can be preempted and resumed later.
- *no-wait*: Each job needs to be processed without idle time from one machine to the next in a flowshop environment.

Number of Customers (δ) There are three possible cases for the number of customers:

- A single customer (use symbol "1" in field δ).
- Multiple customers (use symbol "k" in field δ).
- n customers, such that each order belongs to a different customer (use symbol "n" in field δ).

It is assumed without loss of generality that each customer has a distinct location so that under certain circumstances (e.g., under a direct shipping strategy) only orders destined for the same customer can be consolidated for delivery.

Delivery Characteristics (π) Field π consists of two parts: vehicle characteristics (the number and capacity of delivery vehicles), and the delivery or shipping method used. Vehicle characteristics are represented by symbol $V(x, y)$ if all vehicles are homogeneous, or $V_{het}(x, y)$ if vehicles are heterogeneous, where x represents the number of delivery vehicles available, and y represents the capacity of each vehicle. The commonly studied cases of x and y are as follows:

- $x = 1$: There is a single delivery vehicle available.
- $x = v$: There are v vehicles available, where $v < n$ and is finite.
- $x = \infty$: There is a sufficient number of vehicles available, such that vehicle availability is not a constraint. This is applicable when the delivery is handled by a third-party logistics provider which typically owns a large number of vehicles.
- $y = 1$: Each vehicle can only deliver one job at a time.
- $y = c$: Each vehicle can deliver up to c jobs at a time, where $c < n$ and is finite. This is applicable when each job occupies an equal amount of vehicle capacity, such that vehicle capacity can be represented by the maximum number of jobs that a vehicle can carry.
- $y = \infty$: Each vehicle can deliver any number of jobs at a time. This is applicable when the jobs are all small in weight or volume, such that there is no vehicle capacity issue.
- $y = Q$: Each vehicle can deliver at most Q capacity units (weight or volume) at a time (in this case, each job j occupies a generally different size of q_j units of the vehicle capacity). This is the most general way of modeling the vehicle capacity constraint.

Commonly studied delivery or shipping methods and the corresponding representation symbols include the following:

- *Individual and immediate delivery* (symbol *"iid"*): Each job is picked up for shipping individually and immediately after it completes processing (i.e., $D_j = C_j + t_j$ for $j \in N$, where t_j is the transportation time from the plant to job j's destination). This delivery method is often used for products with an extremely short life span such that a job, once it has completed processing, must be delivered immediately.
- *Batch delivery by direct shipping* (symbol *"direct"*): Only jobs going to the same customer can be delivered together in the same shipment. This shipping

3.2 Problem Definition and Classification

method is often used for products with a short life span and for situations where customers do not want to share shipments with other customers, for example due to commercial confidentiality or possible contamination risk.

- *Batch delivery with routing* (symbol *"routing"*): Jobs going to different customers can be delivered together in the same shipment (where vehicle routing is a part of the decision).
- *Shipping with fixed delivery departure dates* (symbol *"fdep"*): Each vehicle has a fixed delivery departure date at which time exactly the vehicle must depart from the plant, which is pre-specified as a given parameter. This delivery method is applicable when delivery is performed by a third-party logistics service provider that picks up customer orders at fixed times in a day (e.g., 10:00 am, 3:00 pm), which cannot be changed by the user of the service.
- *Splittable delivery* (symbol *"split"*): A job is allowed to be split and delivered in multiple batches. This delivery method may be used in situations where customers do not require their jobs to be delivered in one shipment.

Below we give three examples to illustrate how the five-field representation scheme $\alpha|\beta|\pi|\delta|\gamma$ can be used to describe an IPODS problem precisely.

Example 3.1 (Problem $1|r_j|V(v,c),direct|1|\sum D_j+TC$) In this problem, there is a single machine available for processing all the jobs, which belong to a single customer. The jobs have different release times and are delivered by v vehicles, each capable of carrying up to c jobs at a time. The direct shipping method is used. The objective is to minimize the sum of total delivery time of the jobs and total transportation cost.

Example 3.2 (Problem $P_m||V(\infty,Q),routing|k|TC$) There are m identical parallel machines for processing the jobs, which belong to k different customers. Jobs have generally different sizes. There is a sufficient number of vehicles, each capable of carrying up to Q units total job size. Jobs destined for different customers can be delivered together; vehicle routing is part of the decision. The objective is to minimize the total transportation cost.

Example 3.3 (Problem $F_m|fd_j|V(v,1),iid|n|\sum R_j-TC$) There are m flowshop machines for processing the jobs. Each job belongs to a different customer and has a fixed delivery time at which the job must be delivered to its customer if it is accepted. Not every job needs to be accepted for processing and delivery. Accepted jobs are delivered individually and immediately after processing to the respective customers by v vehicles. The objective is to maximize the total revenue of the accepted jobs minus the total transportation cost.

3.2.1.2 Model Classification

The IPODS problems with a single plant and a single delivery stage can be classified into the following five classes by the delivery method used.

60 3 Integrated Production and Outbound Distribution Scheduling: Offline Problems

- *Models with individual and immediate delivery.* In these models, each job has to be delivered individually and immediately upon its completion. This class of models includes all the models with the "*iid*" delivery method.
- *Models with batch delivery to a single customer by direct shipping method.* The jobs come from a single customer and can be batched together for delivery. This class of models includes all the single-customer models with the "*direct*" shipping method.
- *Models with batch delivery to multiple customers by the direct shipping method.* This class of models is similar to the second class described above except for one major difference; that is, there are multiple customers such that batching is confined to the jobs from the same customer. This class of models includes all the multi-customer models with the "*direct*" shipping method.
- *Models with batch delivery to multiple customers by the routing method.* There are multiple customers, and the jobs destined to different customers can be delivered together by the routing method. This class of models includes all the multi-customer models with the "*routing*" shipping method.
- *Models with fixed delivery departure dates.* In these models, each delivery vehicle has a fixed delivery departure date that is pre-specified and not a part of the decision. This class of models includes all the models with the "*fdep*" shipping method.

We note that some models with fixed delivery departure dates allow batch delivery of orders from the same customer and hence could also be viewed as models with batch delivery with the direct shipping method.

In addition to the above five classes of models, which all involve a single production plant and a single delivery stage, there are two other classes of IPODS problems that have also been studied in the literature (e.g., Chen & Pundoor, 2006; Tang et al., 2019):

- *Models with multiple plants located at different locations.* These problems may involve decisions of assigning jobs to plants, which do not exist in other classes of problems.
- *Models with two stages of job delivery*, e.g., from a plant to a distribution center, and from the distribution center to customer sites. These problems may involve different transportation modes and different delivery methods in different delivery stages.

3.3 Problems with Individual and Immediate Delivery

As defined in Sect. 3.2, the class of problems with individual and immediate delivery share a common constraint, that is, each job, once it has completed processing, must be delivered immediately to its customer by a vehicle, and the delivery cannot be shared with any other jobs. For all the problems discussed in this section, we use t_j to denote the transportation time from the plant to job j's destination, for $j \in N$.

3.3 Problems with Individual and Immediate Delivery 61

In Sects. 3.3.1 and 3.3.2 below, we consider, respectively, two representative problems with a sufficient number of vehicles $1||V(\infty, 1), iid|n|D_{\max}$ and $1|r_j|V(\infty, 1), iid|n|D_{\max}$, and two representative problems with a limited number of vehicles $1||V(1, 1), iid|n|D_{\max}$ and $1||V(v, 1), iid|n|D_{\max}$. Several related problems involving multiple machines, including $P_m|fd_j|V(v, 1), iid|n|\sum R_j$, are discussed in Sect. 3.3.3.

3.3.1 Maximum Delivery Time Problems with a Sufficient Number of Vehicles

In this section, we consider two related single-machine $D_{\max}$ problems with a sufficient number of delivery vehicles, $1||V(\infty, 1), iid|n|D_{\max}$ and $1|r_j|V(\infty, 1), iid|n|D_{\max}$. The classical scheduling problems without delivery corresponding to these two problems are $1||C_{\max}$ and $1|r_j|C_{\max}$, respectively. These two classical problems are quite easy to solve. Any schedule without inserted idle time is optimal for $1||C_{\max}$, whereas scheduling the orders in nondecreasing sequence of their release dates is optimal for $1|r_j|C_{\max}$.

In the following, we first show that any problem $\alpha|\beta|V(\infty, 1), iid|n|D_{\max}$ is equivalent to the classical scheduling problem $\alpha|\beta|L_{\max}$, for any machine environment $\alpha \in \{1, P_m, F\}$, and any restrictions and constraints on the jobs, β. Based on this, we show that problem $1||V(\infty, 1), iid|n|D_{\max}$ can be solved easily following a simple rule, but problem $1|r_j|V(\infty, 1), iid|n|D_{\max}$ is strongly NP-hard. All these results are described in Chen (2010).

Theorem 3.1 *For any machine configuration $\alpha \in \{1, P_m, F\}$, and any restrictions and constraints β, the problem $\alpha|\beta|V(\infty, 1), iid|n|D_{\max}$ is equivalent to the classical problem $\alpha|\beta|L_{\max}$.*

Proof Given problem $\alpha|\beta|V(\infty, 1), iid|n|D_{\max}$, we define a corresponding classical problem $\alpha|\beta|L_{\max}$ involving the same set of jobs, where each job j has a due date $d'_j = M - t_j$, where M is a sufficiently large constant, e.g., $M = \max\{t_j|j \in N\}$. In any feasible schedule π for problem $\alpha|\beta|V(\infty, 1), iid|n|D_{\max}$, since $D_j = C_j + t_j = C_j + M - d'_j$, we have $D_{\max} = M + \max\{C_j - d'_j|j \in N\} = M + L'_{\max}$, where $L'_{\max} = \max\{C_j - d'_j|j \in N\}$ is the maximum lateness of jobs for the classical problem $\alpha|\beta|L_{\max}$. Therefore, minimizing $D_{\max}$ in the earlier problem is equivalent to minimizing the maximum lateness in the latter problem. □

Corollary 3.1

(i) *Problem $1||V(\infty, 1), iid|n|D_{\max}$ is solved optimally in $O(n \log n)$ time by scheduling the jobs in a nonincreasing order of transportation times t_j.*
(ii) *Problem $1|r_j|V(\infty, 1), iid|n|D_{\max}$ is strongly NP-hard.*

Proof

(i) By Theorem 3.1, problem $1||V(\infty, 1), iid|n|D_{\max}$ is equivalent to the classical problem $1||L_{\max}$ when the due date of job j is defined as $d'_j = M - t_j$, where M is a sufficiently large constant. It is known (Jackson, 1955) that for $1||L_{\max}$, scheduling the jobs in nondecreasing sequence of their due dates is optimal. By the definition of d'_j, a nondecreasing order of the due dates for problem $1||L_{\max}$ is equivalent to a nonincreasing order of transportation times t_j for problem $1||V(\infty, 1), iid|n|D_{\max}$. This shows result (i).

(ii) Similarly, by Theorem 3.1, problem $1|r_j|V(\infty, 1), iid|n|D_{\max}$ is equivalent to the classical problem $1|r_j|L_{\max}$, which is known to be strongly NP-hard (Lenstra et al., 1977). Thus, problem $1|r_j|V(\infty, 1), iid|n|D_{\max}$ is also strongly NP-hard.

$\square$

There are heuristics for problem $1|r_j|V(\infty, 1), iid|n|D_{\max}$ with a constant worst-case performance bound. In the remainder of this subsection, we describe the heuristic proposed by Potts (1980) and analyze its worst-case performance. The proofs are adapted from Potts (1980) and Hall and Shmoys (1992).

We first define some terms. In any given schedule π for the problem, suppose that the jobs are processed in the following sequence: $j_1, j_2, \ldots, j_n$, and that job j_c is delivered to its destination last in the schedule. Let j_a be the earliest-processed job such that no idle time exists between the processing of jobs j_a and j_c. Clearly, the maximum delivery time in this schedule, denoted as $D_{\max}(\pi)$, is given as

$$D_{\max}(\pi) = r_{j_a} + \sum_{h=a}^{c} p_{j_h} + t_{j_c}. \tag{3.1}$$

We call the sequence of jobs $j_a, \ldots, j_c$ a *critical sequence* for the given schedule π, and job j_c the *critical job* of this sequence. Among the jobs in this critical sequence, let job j_b, where $a \leq b < c$, be the latest-processed job satisfying $t_{j_b} < t_{j_c}$. If such a job j_b exists, we call it an *interference job*.

The heuristic of Potts (1980) utilizes a simple scheduling rule and applies it multiple times. We first state this simple rule, denoted as Rule S, below and show some properties of any schedule generated by this rule.

Rule S Whenever the machine is free and one or more jobs are available for processing, schedule an available job with the largest transportation time.

Let $\pi(S)$ be a schedule generated by applying this rule to the given job set N. Suppose that $j_a, \ldots, j_c$ is one of the critical sequences in schedule $\pi(S)$. Hence, job j_c is the critical job of this sequence. We observe the following facts: (i) $r_{j_a} \leq r_{j_h}$, for $h = a + 1, \ldots, c$; (ii) if there is an interference job j_b, then $t_{j_b} < t_{j_h}$ and $r_{j_b} < r_{j_h}$, for $h = b + 1, \ldots, c$; and (iii) if there is no interference job in this critical sequence, then schedule $\pi(S)$ is optimal. Facts (i) and (ii) follow immediately from the definitions of a critical sequence and an interference job and the fact that $\pi(S)$

3.3 Problems with Individual and Immediate Delivery

is generated by Rule S. Fact (iii) can be proved as follows. By Fact (i), the optimal maximum delivery time, denoted as $D_{\max}^*$, is at least $r_{j_a} + \sum_{h=a}^{c} p_{j_h} + \min\{t_{j_h} \mid h = a, \ldots, c\}$. If there is no interference job in this critical sequence, then $t_{j_h} \geq t_{j_c}$, for $h = a, \ldots, c$. This implies that $\min\{t_{j_h} \mid h = a, \ldots, c\} = t_{j_c}$, and hence $D_{\max}^*$ is greater than or equal to the right-hand side of (3.1). This implies that $D_{\max}^* = D_{\max}(\pi(S))$.

There are some other useful properties associated with the schedule $\pi(S)$. We state them in the following lemma.

Lemma 3.1 *Let $j_a, \ldots, j_c$ be a critical sequence for the schedule $\pi(S)$ generated by Rule S, and suppose that j_b is the interference job for this critical sequence. Then, $D_{\max}(\pi(S)) - D_{\max}^* < p_{j_b}$ and $D_{\max}(\pi(S)) - D_{\max}^* \leq t_{j_c}$.*

Proof Let S_{j_b} be the time at which job j_b is started processing in schedule $\pi(S)$. Then, from (3.1) and the fact that there is no idle time between the jobs $j_a, \ldots, j_c$, we have

$$D_{\max}(\pi(S)) = S_{j_b} + \sum_{h=b}^{c} p_{j_h} + t_{j_c}. \tag{3.2}$$

Since $\pi(S)$ is generated by Rule S, by Fact (ii) discussed above, at time S_{j_b}, none of the jobs $j_{b+1}, \ldots, j_c$ is available. Thus, in any optimal schedule, jobs $j_{b+1}, \ldots, j_c$ are all started after time S_{j_b}. This implies that

$$D_{\max}^* > S_{j_b} + \sum_{h=b+1}^{c} p_{j_h} + t_{j_c}. \tag{3.3}$$

Comparing (3.2) and (3.3), we have $D_{\max}(\pi(S)) - D_{\max}^* < p_{j_b}$. From Fact (i), $D_{\max}^* \geq r_{j_a} + \sum_{h=a}^{c} p_{j_h}$. This, along with (3.1), implies that $D_{\max}(\pi(S)) - D_{\max}^* \leq t_{j_c}$. $\qquad\square$

The heuristic of Potts (1980) applies Rule S repeatedly. Every time this rule is applied, a critical sequence is identified; if an interference job exists, then the release time of this job is reset to that of the critical job, such that in the next iteration this interference job will be processed after the critical job, which may improve the schedule.

We now present the heuristic formally.

Algorithm H3.1
Repeat Steps 1 and 2 n times or until there is no interference job in Step 2. The schedule with the minimum $D_{\max}$ is adopted.

Step 1: Apply Rule S to the given n jobs.
Step 2: Find a critical sequence in the schedule created in Step 1. Let job j_c be the critical job of this sequence. If an interference job j_b exists, then reset r_{j_b} to be r_{j_c} and go to Step 1. Otherwise, stop.

64   3 Integrated Production and Outbound Distribution Scheduling: Offline Problems

We illustrate the steps of this algorithm by the following numerical example.

Example 3.4 (Application of Algorithm H3.1)   Consider the following instance of problem $1|r_j|V(\infty, 1), iid|n|D_{\max}$ shown in the following table.

j	1	2	3	4	5
r_j	3	3	10	11	13
p_j	6	1	5	3	2
t_j	6	7	1	5	7

Step 1: Applying Rule S, we get job schedule $\sigma_1 = (2, 1, 3, 5, 4)$, with the starting time S_j, completion time C_j, and delivery time D_j shown in Table 3.1.

Step 2: The entire sequence of σ_1 is a critical sequence. Job 4 is the critical job. Job 3 is the interference job. Reset $r_3 = r_4 = 11$.

Step 1: Applying Rule S to the revised instance, we get job schedule $\sigma_2 = (2, 1, 4, 5, 3)$, with S_j, C_j, and D_j shown in Table 3.1.

Step 2: In σ_2, (4, 5) is a critical sequence. Job 5 is the critical job and job 4 is the interference job. Reset $r_4 = r_5 = 13$.

Step 1: Applying Rule S to the revised instance, we get job schedule $\sigma_3 = (2, 1, 3, 5, 4)$, with S_j, C_j, and D_j shown in Table 3.1.

Step 2: In σ_3, (3, 5, 4) is a critical sequence. Job 4 is the critical job and job 3 is the interference job. Reset $r_3 = r_4 = 13$.

Step 1: Applying Rule S to the revised instance, we get job schedule $\sigma_4 = (2, 1, 5, 4, 3)$, with S_j, C_j, and D_j shown in Table 3.1.

Step 2: In σ_4, (5, 4, 3) is a critical sequence. Job 3 is the critical job. There is no interference job. Stop.

Among the four schedules generated, schedule σ_2 has the minimum $D_{\max}$, which is 23. Thus, the final solution generated by the heuristic is σ_2 with $D_{\max} = 23$. It can easily be verified that σ_2 is in fact an optimal schedule for the given instance.

The following theorem provides the worst-case performance ratio of Algorithm H3.1.

Theorem 3.2 *For problem* $1|r_j|V(\infty, 1), iid|n|D_{\max}$, *Algorithm H3.1 generates a schedule* π *with* $D_{\max}(\pi) \leq (3/2)D_{\max}^*$.

Proof We establish the theorem by comparing the schedule π generated by Algorithm H3.1 with an optimal schedule, denoted as π^*. There are two cases to consider.

Case 1: All precedence constraints introduced due to the resetting of release times of some jobs in the algorithm are consistent with the optimal schedule π^*. If the algorithm stops because no interference job exists, then by Fact (iii), the schedule generated in the last iteration is optimal. Otherwise, the algorithm runs for n iterations. In this case, we prove the theorem by contradiction. Suppose that

3.3 Problems with Individual and Immediate Delivery

Table 3.1 Schedules generated

σ_1	2	1	3	5	4
S_j	3	4	10	15	17
C_j	4	10	15	17	20
D_j	11	16	16	24	25
σ_2	2	1	4	5	3
S_j	3	4	11	14	16
C_j	4	10	14	16	21
D_j	11	16	19	23	22
σ_3	2	1	3	5	4
S_j	3	4	11	16	18
C_j	4	10	16	18	21
D_j	11	16	17	25	26
σ_4	2	1	5	4	3
S_j	3	4	13	15	18
C_j	4	10	15	18	23
D_j	11	16	22	23	24

the schedule generated in every iteration has a maximum delivery time greater than $3D_{max}^*/2$, and hence the theorem does not hold. It can then be shown by Lemma 3.1 that the processing time of the interference job in every iteration is greater than $D_{max}^*/2$. Since the same job can be the interference job in at most $n - 1$ of the n iterations, there are at least 2 jobs with a processing time greater than $D_{max}^*/2$, which is a contradiction.

Case 2: At some iteration, an incorrect precedence constraint is introduced. Consider the first iteration when a precedence constraint that violates the sequence in π^* is introduced. Let j_b and j_c be the interference job and critical job found in this iteration, respectively. Suppose that the maximum delivery time of the schedule generated in this iteration is greater than $3D_{max}^*/2$. Then by Lemma 3.1, $p_{j_b} \geq D_{max}^*/2$, and $p_{j_c} \geq D_{max}^*/2$. The fact that the precedence constraint is inconsistent implies that job j_b precedes job j_c in the optimal schedule π^*. Thus in schedule π^*, $D_{max}^* > r_{j_b} + p_{j_b} + p_{j_c} + t_{j_c} > D_{max}^*$, which is a contradiction. This implies that the maximum delivery time of the schedule generated in this iteration is less than $(3/2)D_{max}^*$.

$\square$

There are other heuristics for problem $1|r_j|V(\infty, 1), iid|n|D_{max}$. Hall and Shmoys (1992) propose a modified heuristic based on Algorithm A with a tighter worst-case performance ratio of $4/3$. Hall and Shmoys (1992) and Mastrolilli (2003) propose polynomial time approximation schemes for this problem.

3.3.2 Maximum Delivery Time Problems with a Limited Number of Vehicles

In this section, we consider two single-machine $D_{\max}$ problems with a limited number of vehicles, $1||V(1, 1), iid|n|D_{\max}$ and $1||V(v, 1), iid|n|D_{\max}$. We first observe that the individual and immediate delivery (iid) method, together with a limited number of delivery vehicles, means that in these problems, (1) each vehicle may have to make multiple trips, and (2) the processing of a job cannot begin if there is no vehicle available to pick it up immediately after it has completed processing. For ease of presentation, we assume that in these problems the transportation time from a job's destination back to the plant is the same as that from the plant to this job's destination. Thus, the round-trip transportation time between the plant and job j's destination is $2t_j$, for $j \in N$. All the results in this section still apply without this assumption.

Before we analyze these problems, we first show that several problems with the "iid" delivery method and a limited number of delivery vehicles are identical to some two-stage no-wait flexible flowshop problems.

Theorem 3.3 *Problem* $1||V(v, 1), iid|n|f(D)$ *is equivalent to the two-stage no-wait flexible flowshop scheduling problem* $F(1, v)|no - wait|f(C)$, *for any* $f(D) \in \{\sum w_j D_j, \sum w_j T_j, \sum w_j U_j, L_{\max}\}$, *defined based on the job delivery times* $D = (D_1, \ldots, D_n)$, *where in the latter problem there are one machine at the first stage and* v *parallel machines at the second stage, and* $C = (C_1, \ldots, C_n)$ *is the vector of job completion times.*

Proof This equivalence is established when we view the v delivery vehicles in the earlier problem as the v parallel machines in the second stage in the latter problem. The iid constraint in the former problem is then equivalent to the $no - wait$ constraint in the latter problem. If we view the round-trip transportation time for each job j, i.e., $2t_j$, in the earlier problem as the processing time of the job in the second stage in the latter problem, then any schedule for the latter problem that satisfies the no-wait constraint corresponds to a schedule for the earlier problem that satisfies the iid constraint, and vice versa. For each job j, its delivery time D_j in the schedule for the earlier problem and its completion time C_j in the corresponding schedule for the latter problem satisfy $D_j = C_j - t_j$. This implies that when $f(D) \in \{\sum w_j D_j, \sum w_j T_j, \sum w_j U_j, L_{\max}\}$, our problem $1||V(v, 1), iid|n|f(D)$ is equivalent to the corresponding problem $F(1, v)|no - wait|f(C)$. For the case with $f(D) = \sum w_j D_j$, the equivalence of the two problems follows directly because $\sum w_j D_j = \sum w_j C_j - \sum w_j t_j$, which means that minimizing $\sum w_j D_j$ is equivalent to minimizing $\sum w_j C_j$. For the other objective functions, the equivalence is established when given the due date of job j, d_j in the former problem, we specify the due date of job j for the latter problem to be $d_j + t_j$. $\quad\square$

For results on no-wait flowshop and flexible flowshop problems, see the survey articles by Hall and Sriskandarajah (1996) and Bagchi et al. (2006).

3.3 Problems with Individual and Immediate Delivery

Remark 3.1 Although $1||V(v, 1), iid|n|D_{\max}$ and $F(1, v)|no - wait|C_{\max}$ are closely related, they are not equivalent because the fact that $D_j = C_j - t_j$ and the t_j's are generally different implies that minimizing $D_{\max}$ is not equivalent to minimizing $C_{\max}$.

We first focus on problem $1||V(1, 1), iid|n|D_{\max}$. For this problem, it is easy to see that in an optimal schedule for this problem, jobs processed earlier are picked up earlier. This means that once a schedule for job processing is given, the delivery schedule of the only vehicle involved is specified accordingly. Consequently, we only need to find an optimal schedule for job processing. Below, we give an optimal polynomial time algorithm for this problem. The algorithm considers n cases of the problem, where the kth case of the problem is to find an optimal schedule where job k is processed and picked up last, for $k = 1, \ldots, n$. For each case, the problem is formulated as a special case of the traveling salesman problem (TSP) solvable by the algorithm of Gilmore and Gomory (1964). The best among the n optimal sequences for the n cases of the problem is then optimal.

Algorithm A3.1

Step 0: Let $k = 1$.

Step 1: Reindex the jobs in $N \setminus \{k\}$ as $[1], \ldots, [n - 1]$. Formulate the problem with k being the last job in the schedule as a TSP in the following complete graph: there are n nodes $0, 1, \ldots, n - 1$ in the network, where node 0 corresponds to job k, and nodes $1, \ldots, n - 1$ correspond to jobs $[1], \ldots, [n - 1]$, respectively; the distance matrix (τ_{ij}) is defined as $\tau_{ij} = \max\{2t_{[i]}, p_{[j]}\}$ if $i \neq 0$ and $j \neq 0$; $\tau_{i0} = \max\{2t_{[i]}, p_k\}$ if $i \neq 0$; and $\tau_{0j} = p_{[j]}$ if $j \neq 0$.

Step 2: Solve the TSP by the Gilmore–Gomory algorithm. Let the optimal TSP tour be denoted as $\pi_k = (0, h_{k1}, h_{k2}, \ldots, h_{k,n-1}, 0)$, where $(h_{k1}, h_{k2}, \ldots, h_{k,n-1})$ is a permutation of nodes $1, \ldots, n - 1$. Let z_k denote the total distance of π_k.

Step 3: If $k < n$, let $k = k + 1$ and repeat Steps 1 and 2. Otherwise, stop. Find j such that $z_j + t_j = \min\{z_k + t_k \mid k = 1, \ldots, n\}$. The job sequence $([h_{j1}], \ldots, [h_{j,n-1}], j)$ corresponding to the TSP tour π_j is optimal.

We use the following numerical example to illustrate the central idea of Algorithm A3.1.

Example 3.5 (Application of Algorithm A3.1) Apply Algorithm A3.1 to the following instance of problem $1||V(1, 1), iid|n|D_{\max}$. There are 4 jobs with the parameters shown in the table below.

j	1	2	3	4
p_j	3	4	5	6
t_j	2	3	1	4

Applying Algorithm A3.1 to this instance, four solution cases are considered, each with one of the jobs scheduled last (i.e., both processed and delivered last).

68   3 Integrated Production and Outbound Distribution Scheduling: Offline Problems

As an illustration, we consider one of the cases, where job 3 is scheduled last. For this case, Step 1 of the algorithm creates a complete graph with nodes 0, 1, 2, and 3 corresponding to jobs 3, [1], [2], and [3], respectively, where reindexed jobs [1], [2], and [3] correspond to the original jobs 1, 2, and 4, respectively. The distance matrix (τ_{ij}) is shown in the following table, where for ease of reference, the corresponding job with its original index for each node is also shown. Each entry in the table τ_{ij} is the distance from node i to node j, as defined in Step 1 of the algorithm, where $\tau_{0j} = p_{[j]}$ for $j = 1, 2, 3$, $\tau_{ij} = \max\{2t_{[i]}, p_{[j]}\}$ for $i, j = 1, 2, 3$, and $\tau_{i0} = \max\{2t_{[i]}, p_3\}$ for $i = 1, 2, 3$.

		Job 3	Job 1	Job 2	Job 4
		Node 0	Node 1	Node 2	Node 3
Job 3	Node 0	–	3	4	6
Job 1	Node 1	5	–	4	6
Job 2	Node 2	6	6	–	6
Job 4	Node 3	8	8	8	–

Step 2 solves the TSP problem in the constructed network. The optimal TSP tour for the given network is $\pi = (0, 1, 2, 3, 0)$ with total distance $z = \tau_{01} + \tau_{12} + \tau_{23} + \tau_{30} = 21$. Tour π corresponds to job schedule $(1, 2, 4, 3)$ with $D_{\max} = z + t_3 = 21 + 1 = 22$.

Theorem 3.4 *Algorithm A3.1 solves the problem $1||V(1, 1), iid|n|D_{\max}$ optimally in $O(n^2 \log n)$ time.*

Proof For a fixed $k \in N$, reindex the jobs in $N \backslash \{k\}$ as $[1], \ldots, [n-1]$, as in Step 1 of the algorithm. Given a sequence of jobs $([u_1], \ldots, [u_{n-1}], k)$ for the problem, where $([u_1], \ldots, [u_{n-1}])$ is a permutation of $\{1, \ldots, n-1\}$. Define $\Delta([u_i], [u_{i+1}])$ to be the difference between the pickup times of the neighboring jobs $[u_i]$ and $[u_{i+1}]$. It can easily be shown that $\Delta([u_i], [u_{i+1}]) = \max\{2t_{[u_i]}, p_{[u_{i+1}]}\}$ for $i = 1, \ldots, n-1$, and that

$$D_{\max} = D_k = p_{[u_1]} + \sum_{i=1}^{n-1} \Delta([u_i], [u_{i+1}]) + t_k. \tag{3.4}$$

See Fig. 3.2 for an illustration, where a directed line represents either a delivery or a return trip of the vehicle.

Now consider a TSP tour $(0, u_1, \ldots, u_{n-1}, 0)$ for the TSP problem defined in Step 1, where node 0 corresponds to job k and nodes $u_1, \ldots, u_{n-1}$ correspond to jobs $[u_1], \ldots, [u_{n-1}]$, respectively. By definition of the distance matrix in Step 1, it can be seen that $\tau_{0,u_1} = p_{[u_1]}$, $\tau_{u_i, u_{i+1}} = \Delta([u_i], [u_{i+1}])$, for $i = 1, \ldots, n-2$, and $\tau_{u_{n-1}, 0} = \Delta([u_{n-1}], [u_n])$. Therefore, the total distance of this TSP tour, denoted as q_k, is given by

3.3 Problems with Individual and Immediate Delivery

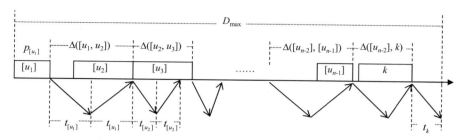

Fig. 3.2 Schedule $([u_1], \ldots, [u_{n-1}], k)$

$$q_k = \tau_{0,u_1} + \sum_{i=1}^{n-2} \tau_{u_i,u_{i+1}} + \tau_{u_{n-1},u_n} = p_{[u_1]} + \sum_{i=1}^{n-1} \Delta([u_i],[u_{i+1}]) = D_k - t_k. \quad (3.5)$$

Thus, any solution π to the problem $1||V(1,1), iid|n|D_{\max}$ with job k scheduled last corresponds to a solution σ to the TSP defined in Step 1. Also, (3.4) and (3.5) imply that the objective values of the solutions π and σ differ by a constant t_k. Therefore, the problem $1||V(1,1), iid|n|D_{\max}$ with job k scheduled last can be solved by solving the corresponding TSP. This shows the optimality of the algorithm.

For fixed $k \in N$, the TSP defined in Step 1 has a special structure. The distance parameters can be expressed as $\tau_{ij} = \max\{\lambda_i, \mu_j\}$ for all $i, j = 0, 1, \ldots, n-1$ with $i \neq j$, where $\lambda_0 = 0$, $\mu_0 = p_k$, and $\lambda_j = 2t_{[j]}$ and $\mu_j = p_{[j]}$, for $j \geq 1$. A distance matrix with this characteristic is called a *large matrix*, and the TSP with such a distance matrix can be solved by the Gilmore–Gomory algorithm in $O(n \log n)$ time (Van Dal et al., 1993). Because the algorithm solves n such TSP problems, the overall complexity is $O(n^2 \log n)$. □

Next, we show that problem $1||V(v,1), iid|n|D_{\max}$ is more difficult to solve.

Theorem 3.5 *Problem* $1||V(v,1), iid|n|D_{\max}$ *is strongly NP-hard even when there are two delivery vehicles.*

Proof As discussed above, this problem is closely related, but not equivalent, to the two-stage flexible flowshop problem $F(1,v)|no-wait|C_{\max}$. We prove the theorem for problem $1||V(2,1), iid|n|D_{\max}$ by a reduction from $F(1,2)|no-wait|C_{\max}$, which is known to be strongly NP-hard (Sriskandarajah & Ladet, 1986). The recognition version of $F(1,2)|no-wait|C_{\max}$ can be described as follows: Given h jobs $1, \ldots, h$ with processing times $a_1, \ldots, a_h$ in the first stage and $b_1, \ldots, b_h$ in the second stage, and a threshold value C_0, does there exist a feasible schedule with the makespan $C_{\max} \leq C_0$? We assume without loss of generality that all the parameters are even numbers.

Given an instance of $F(1,2)|no-wait|C_{\max}$, we construct an instance of $1||V(2,1), iid|n|D_{\max}$ as follows. There are $n = h+2$ jobs, $N = \{1, \ldots, h+2\}$, with processing times and transportation times: $p_j = a_j$ and $t_j = b_j/2$, for $j =$

1, ..., h, and $p_{h+1} = p_{h+2} = 0$, and $t_{h+1} = t_{h+2} = M$, where $M \geq C_0 + 1$. The threshold value for $D_{\max}$ is $D_0 = C_0 + M$. We show below that there exists a feasible schedule to the constructed instance of $1||V(2, 1), iid|n|D_{\max}$ with $D_{\max} \leq D_0$ if and only if there exists a feasible schedule to the instance of $F(1, 2)|no-wait|C_{\max}$ with $C_{\max} \leq C_0$.

($\Rightarrow$) Given a feasible schedule $\pi = (\pi_1, \pi_{21}, \pi_{22})$ for $F(1, 2)|no-wait|C_{\max}$ with makespan $C_{\max}(\pi) \leq C_0$, where π_1 is the schedule at the first stage and π_{21} and π_{22} are the schedules on the first and second machine at the second stage, respectively, we construct a schedule σ for $1||V(2, 1), iid|n|D_{\max}$ as follows. Process the jobs $1, ..., h$ using the same schedule as π_1, and process jobs $h + 1$ and $h + 2$ last starting at time $C_{\max}(\pi)$. Deliver the jobs in π_{21} and π_{22} by the two vehicles, respectively, with the pickup time of a job equal to the starting time of the job in π_{21} or π_{22}. Deliver jobs $h + 1$ and $h + 2$ by the two vehicles, respectively, with the same pickup time at $C_{\max}(\pi_1)$. Clearly, the constructed schedule σ is feasible for $1||V(2, 1), iid|n|D_{\max}$ with $D_{\max} = C_{\max}(\pi) + M \leq C_0 + M = D_0$.

($\Leftarrow$) Given a feasible schedule σ for $1||V(2, 1), iid|n|D_{\max}$ with makespan $D_{\max}(\sigma) \leq D_0$, we can conclude that jobs $h + 1$ and $h + 2$ respectively must be delivered last by the two vehicles. This is because if a vehicle delivers some job $j \in \{1, ..., h\}$ after delivering one of these two jobs, then the vehicle has to spend $2M$ units of time delivering j and returning to the plant, which will result in a makespan larger than D_0. Furthermore, since $t_{h+1} = t_{h+2} = M$, the pickup times of $h + 1$ and $h + 2$ must be $D_{\max}(\sigma) - M$. Therefore, by time $D_{\max}(\sigma) - M$, all the jobs $1, ..., h$ have been delivered and the vehicles have returned to the plant after the last jobs among $1, ..., h$ are delivered. Now, consider the part of schedule σ that spans from time 0 to $D_{\max}(\sigma) - M$. Denote this partial schedule as σ_0. Evidently, σ_0 covers jobs $1, ..., h$. Based on σ_0, we construct a schedule for $F(1, 2)|no-wait|C_{\max}$ as follows. Process the jobs in the first stage following the schedule in the processing part of σ_0. Process the jobs that are delivered in the two vehicles in σ_0 by the two machines in the second stage, respectively, with the starting time of a job equal to the pickup time of the job in σ_0. Clearly, this schedule is feasible for $F(1, 2)|no-wait|C_{\max}$ with makespan no larger than $D_{\max}(\sigma) - M \leq C_0$. $\qquad\square$

3.3.3 Multi-Machine Problems

All the problems discussed in Sects. 3.3.1 and 3.3.2 involve a single machine only. When there are multiple machines, these problems become more difficult to solve. Since the classical problem $P_m||C_{\max}$ is ordinarily NP-hard (Karp, 1972), any problem $P_m||V(x, 1), iid|n|D_{\max}$, for $x \in \{1, v, \infty\}$, is at least ordinarily NP-hard. Since $1|r_j|C_{\max}$ is strongly NP-hard (Lenstra et al., 1977), any problem $P_m|r_j|V(x, 1), iid|n|D_{\max}$ and $F_m|r_j|V(x, 1), iid|n|D_{\max}$, for $x \in \{1, v, \infty\}$, is also strongly NP-hard. It can also be shown that any problem $F_m||V(x, 1), iid|n|D_{\max}$, for $x \in \{1, v, \infty\}$ is strongly NP-hard. Woeginger

3.3 Problems with Individual and Immediate Delivery

(1994) proposes a heuristic for $P_m||V(\infty, 1), iid|n|D_{max}$. Hall and Shmoys (1989) and Mastrolilli (2003) give a PTAS and Gharbi and Haouari (2002) give a branch-and-bound exact algorithm for $P_m|r_j|V(\infty, 1), iid|n|D_{max}$. Kaminsky (2003) provides asymptotically optimal heuristics for $F_m||V(\infty, 1), iid|n|D_{max}$ and $F_m|r_j|V(\infty, 1), iid|n|D_{max}$.

Some "iid" problems studied in the literature have a delivery time window for each job. Either each job j has a fixed delivery time fd_j at which time exactly the job must be delivered to its customer, or each job j has a time window $[a_j, b_j]$ during which the job must be delivered. With such a constraint, it may not be possible to accept all the jobs. Therefore, all such problems involve job acceptance decisions and the objective function typically involves maximization of the total revenue of the accepted jobs. In a problem with a fixed delivery time for each job, if a job is accepted, both the processing starting time and the pickup time are then fixed. Thus, no sequencing decision is involved, and the only decisions are determining which jobs to accept, and which machine to process and which vehicles to deliver the accepted jobs. It is then easy to see that problem $P_m|fd_j|V(\infty, 1), iid|n|\sum R_j$, where the delivery part is not a bottleneck, reduces to a fixed interval scheduling problem (without the delivery), which can be solved as a min-cost network flow problem (Garcia & Lozano, 2004a).

For problem $P_m|fd_j|V(v, 1), iid|n|\sum R_j$, where the delivery part can be a bottleneck, Chen (2010) provides a dynamic programming algorithm with a polynomial running time when m and v are fixed constants. However, the complexity of this problem with arbitrary m and v is unknown (Chen, 2010). We present Chen's algorithm in the following. His algorithm utilizes the following optimality property of the problem. The property is straightforward and hence we do not give a proof.

Lemma 3.2 *In an optimal schedule for problem $P_m|fd_j|V(v, 1), iid|n|\sum R_j$, accepted jobs assigned to each machine are processed in nondecreasing sequence of their required completion times $fd_j - t_j$, and accepted jobs assigned to each vehicle are delivered in the same sequence.*

Chen's dynamic programming algorithm for problem $P_m|fd_j|V(v, 1), iid|n|\sum R_j$ considers jobs in nondecreasing sequence of $fd_j - t_j$, and in each iteration determines whether to accept or reject a job, and assigns the job to one of the machines and one of the vehicles if the job is accepted.

Algorithm A3.2
Reindex the jobs such that $fd_1 - t_1 \leq \cdots \leq fd_n - t_n$.

Value Function $F(j; x_1, \ldots, x_m; y_1, \ldots, y_v) = $ the maximum total revenue of the jobs scheduled so far, given that jobs $1, \ldots, j$ have been considered, and among these jobs, x_i is the last job processed by machine i, for $i = 1, \ldots, m$, and y_k is the last job delivered by vehicle k, for $k = 1, \ldots, v$.

Initial Condition $F(0; 0, \ldots, 0; 0, \ldots, 0) = 0$.

Recurrence Relation For $j = 1, \ldots, n$; $x_i = 0, \ldots, j$, for $i = 1, \ldots, m$; and $y_k = 0, \ldots, j$, for $k = 1, \ldots, v$:

$$F(j; x_1, \ldots, x_m; y_1, \ldots, y_v)$$

$$= \begin{cases} G_1, & \text{if } j > \max\{x_1, \ldots, x_m\} \text{ and } j > \max\{y_1, \ldots, y_v\} \\ G_2, & \text{if } j = x_i = y_k \text{ for some } 1 \leq i \leq m \text{ and } 1 \leq k \leq v \\ 0, & \text{otherwise} \end{cases}$$

where

$$G_1 = F(j; x_1, \ldots, x_m; y_1, \ldots, y_v)$$

$$G_2 = R_j + \max\{F(j - 1; x_1, \ldots, x_m; y_1, \ldots, y_v) \mid$$

$$0 \leq h \leq j - 1 \text{ with } fd_h - t_h + p_j \leq fd_j - t_j$$

$$\text{and } 0 \leq e \leq j - 1 \text{ with } fd_e + t_e + t_j \leq fd_j\}.$$

Optimal Solution Value
$\max\{F(n; x_1, \ldots, x_m; y_1, \ldots, y_v) \mid x_i = 0, \ldots, n, \text{ for } i = 1, \ldots, m, y_k = 0, \ldots, n, \text{ for } k = 1, \ldots, v\}$.

Chen (2010) shows the following result about Algorithm A3.2.

Theorem 3.6 *Algorithm A3.2 solves problem $P_m | fd_j | V(v, 1), iid | n | \sum R_j$ optimally in $O(n^{m+v+3})$ time.*

Proof The recurrence relation considers all three possible cases associated with each state $(j; x_1, \ldots, x_m; y_1, \ldots, y_v)$:

(i) If job j is not accepted (and hence $j > \max\{x_1, \ldots, x_m\}$), then the value function is equal to G_1.
(ii) If job j is accepted (and hence it must be scheduled last among all the jobs scheduled so far, i.e., $j = x_i = y_k$ for some i and k), then the value function is equal to G_2. The equation for G_2 maximizes the revenue over all possible h and e such that the resulting schedule is feasible. Feasibility is ensured by the two conditions involved: $fd_h - t_h + p_j \leq fd_j - t_j$ and $fd_e + t_e + t_j \leq fd_j$.
(iii) If the state is not feasible, then the value function is set to 0.

This shows the optimality of the algorithm. There are at most $O(n^{m+v+1})$ states in the dynamic program, and for each state the recurrence relation spends at most $O(n^2)$ time considering all possible values of h and e. Therefore, the overall time complexity of the algorithm is $O(n^{m+v+3})$. $\qquad\square$

3.4 Problems with Batch Delivery to a Single Customer

We first provide, in Sect. 3.4.1, some optimality properties shared by many problems with batch delivery to a single customer. We then discuss in Sects. 3.4.2, 3.4.3, 3.4.4, and 3.4.5, respectively, several representative problems

3.4 Problems with Batch Delivery to a Single Customer

$1||V(\infty, c), direct|1|L_{\max} + TC$, $1||V(\infty, \infty), direct|1|\sum w_j D_j + TC$, $P_m||V(\infty, c), direct|1|\sum D_j + TC$, $1||V(v, c), direct|1|D_{\max}$, and $1||V(v, c), direct|1|\sum D_j$.

In all the problems, we use t to denote the one-way transportation time between the plant and the customer site, and f the transportation cost of a shipment from the plant to the customer site, which includes both fixed and variable costs.

3.4.1 Optimality Properties

There are a number of structural properties shared by many problems with batch delivery to a single customer. Below we state some key properties that are needed in order to develop the solution algorithms provided below. The proofs for these results are quite straightforward and hence are not shown here. The reader is referred to Lee and Chen (2001) and Hall and Potts (2003, 2005) for proofs of Lemmas 3.3, 3.4 and 3.6, and Chen (2010) for a proof of Lemma 3.5.

Lemma 3.3 *For problems $\alpha||V(v, c), direct|1|\gamma$ and $\alpha||V(\infty, c), direct|1|\gamma$, where $\alpha \in \{1, P_m\}$ and $\gamma \in \{f(D), f(D) + TC\}$ with $f(D)$ being any nondecreasing function of $D = (D_1, \ldots, D_n)$ (including $D_{\max}, \sum(w_j)D_j, \sum(w_j)T_j, \sum(w_j)U_j$, and $L_{\max}$), there exists an optimal schedule that satisfies all of the following properties:*

(i) There is no idle time between the jobs processed on any machine.

(ii) For each delivery batch, all the jobs in the batch that are processed on the same machine are processed consecutively on that machine.

(iii) For each machine, jobs that are processed earlier on the machine are delivered no later than those processed later on the same machine.

(iv) For problem $\alpha||V(\infty, c), direct|1|\gamma$, for each delivery batch, its departure time is equal to the completion time of the last job in it. For problem $\alpha||V(v, c), direct|1|\gamma$, for each delivery batch, its departure time is equal to the maximum of the following two times: the completion time of the last job in it, and the time when the vehicle for this delivery becomes available.

Lemma 3.4 *Problem $\alpha||V(\infty, c), direct|1|\gamma$ with a nonzero transportation time from the plant to the customer is equivalent to the same problem with a zero transportation time, for $\alpha \in \{1, P_m, F_m\}$ and $\gamma \in \{f(D), f(D) + TC\}$ with $f(D) \in \{D_{\max}, \sum(w_j)D_j, \sum(w_j)T_j, \sum(w_j)U_j, L_{\max}\}$.*

Lemma 3.4 implies that for problems with a sufficient number of vehicles, we can assume without loss of generality that delivery can be performed instantaneously. We further observe that in an optimal solution to the problem $\alpha||V(\infty, c), direct|1|f(D)$ where no transportation cost is considered, each job is delivered individually and immediately upon its completion. Thus, problem $\alpha||V(\infty, c), direct|1|f(D)$ reduces to the classical problem $\alpha||f(C)$.

74 3 Integrated Production and Outbound Distribution Scheduling: Offline Problems

By Lemma 3.4, problem $1||V(\infty, c), direct|1|L_{\max}$ reduces to the classical problem $1||L_{\max}$, for which an EDD sequence is optimal. However, for the same problem but with transportation cost included in the objective function, i.e., problem $1||V(\infty, c), direct|1|L_{\max} + TC$, Pundoor and Chen (2005) give the following example to show that EDD sequence is not optimal.

Example 3.6 (EDD Is Not Optimal for $1||V(\infty, c), direct|1|L_{\max} + TC$) Consider four jobs 1, 2, 3, 4 with $p_1 = 1$, $p_2 = 5$, $p_3 = 1$, $p_4 = 5$; $d_1 = 2, d_2 = 12, d_3 = 13, d_4 = 14$. There is a sufficient number of vehicles, each with capacity $c = 2$, and the travel time and travel cost of a shipment are $t = 0$ and $f = 10$, respectively. Clearly, in any schedule at least two shipments are needed. Thus, the objective value cannot be less than 20. The following schedule has an objective value of 20, and hence is optimal: process the jobs in sequence $(1, 3, 2, 4)$ and deliver jobs 1 and 3 in one shipment at time 2, and jobs 2 and 4 in another shipment at time 12. Any schedule where the EDD sequence is used for processing jobs has an objective value greater than 20 because it has either a positive $L_{\max}$ and at least two shipments, or a zero $L_{\max}$ but more than two shipments.

The following lemma shows that a problem with a limited number of vehicles is in general more difficult to solve than the corresponding problem with a sufficient number of vehicles. The *polynomial reducibility* concept is defined in Sect. 2.2 of the book.

Lemma 3.5 *Problem $\alpha||V(\infty, c), direct|1|\gamma$ is polynomially reducible to $\alpha||V(1, c), direct|1|\gamma$, which is polynomially reducible to $\alpha||V(v, c), direct|1|\gamma$; and problem $\alpha||V(v, \infty), direct|1|\gamma$ is polynomially reducible to $\alpha||V(v, c), direct|1|\gamma$, where $\alpha \in \{1, P_m, F_m\}$ and $\gamma \in \{f(D), f(D) + TC\}$ with $f(D) \in \{D_{\max}, \sum(w_j)D_j, \sum(w_j)T_j, \sum(w_j)U_j, L_{\max}\}$.*

Lemma 3.6

(i) *For problem $1||V(x, y), direct|1|f(D) + TC$ with $x \in \{1, v, \infty\}$, $y \in \{c, \infty\}$, and $f(D) \in \{D_{\max}, \sum D_j\}$, there exists an optimal solution where jobs are processed in nondecreasing sequence of their processing times (also called SPT sequence).*

(ii) *For problem $1||V(x, \infty), direct|1|L_{\max} + TC$ with $x \in \{1, v, \infty\}$, there exists an optimal solution where jobs are processed in nondecreasing sequence of their due dates (also called EDD sequence).*

(iii) *For problem $1||V(x, \infty), direct|1|f(D) + TC$ with $x \in \{1, v, \infty\}$ and $f(D) \in \{\sum U_j, \sum w_j U_j\}$, there exists an optimal solution where on-time jobs are processed earlier than late jobs and are processed in nondecreasing sequence of their due dates.*

We note that for problems with a limited number of vehicles and a due-date related objective, including problems $1||V(x, c), direct|1|\gamma$ with $x \in \{1, v\}$ and $\gamma \in \{L_{\max}, L_{\max} + TC, \sum U_j, \sum U_j + TC\}$, scheduling jobs (or early jobs in cases with $\sum U_j$ in the objective function) in EDD sequence may not be optimal.

3.4   Problems with Batch Delivery to a Single Customer

Chen (2010) gives the following example of problem $1||V(v, c), direct|1|L_{\max}$, for which EDD sequence is not optimal.

Example 3.7 (EDD Is Not Optimal for $1||V(v, c), direct|1|L_{\max}$) Consider two jobs 1 and 2 with $p_1 = 4$, $d_1 = 7$, $p_2 = 1$, $d_2 = 8$, one vehicle with capacity $c = 1$, and one-way travel time between the plant and the customer $t = 2$. It can be seen that sequence $(2, 1)$ has $L_{\max} = 0$, whereas the EDD sequence $(1, 2)$ has $L_{\max} = 2$.

3.4.2   Single-Machine Maximum Lateness and Transportation Cost Problem

In this section, we consider problem $1||V(\infty, c), direct|1|L_{\max} + TC$. As shown in Example 3.6, scheduling jobs in EDD order may not be optimal for this problem. Fortunately, this problem can still be solved in polynomial time. Before we present the polynomial-time algorithm proposed by Pundoor and Chen (2005) for this problem, we first discuss two related problems that can be solved more easily.

First, for the problem with no vehicle capacity constraint, i.e., problem $1||V(\infty, \infty), direct|1|L_{\max} + TC$, it can easily be shown that processing jobs in EDD sequence is optimal. For this problem, Hall and Potts (2003) give an $O(n^3)$ dynamic programming algorithm for finding an optimal solution. The idea of their algorithm is based on the following observation: If the number of delivery batches to the customer in the final schedule is given, then the total transportation cost is fixed, and an optimal schedule can be found by comparing all possible ways of splitting the jobs (sequenced in their EDD order) into a desired number of batches.

Second, for the special case of problem $1||V(\infty, c), direct|1|L_{\max} + TC$ with agreeable job processing times and due dates, i.e., if $p_u \leq p_v$, then $d_u \leq d_v$ for all jobs $u, v \in N$, processing the jobs in EDD order is also optimal, as shown by Pundoor and Chen (2005). The above-mentioned DP algorithm of Hall and Potts (2003) can be modified by incorporating the vehicle capacity constraint to solve this problem to optimality.

Now, we describe the algorithm of Pundoor and Chen (2005) for the problem $1||V(\infty, c), direct|1|L_{\max} + TC$ with a general vehicle capacity constraint and a general relationship between job processing times and due dates. Their algorithm utilizes two auxiliary problems, AP1 and AP2. Suppose that each job $j \in N$ has a deadline e_j, which is defined below as the due date d_j plus some allowed lateness. Problem AP1 schedules the production and distribution of the jobs such that a minimum number of delivery shipments are used and all the jobs are delivered to the customer before or at their deadlines. Problem AP2 schedules the production and distribution of the jobs to minimize their maximum lateness $L_{\max}$, subject to the constraint that no more than a certain number of delivery shipments is used.

We solve our problem $1||V(\infty, c), direct|1|L_{\max} + TC$ by solving AP2 multiple times, where each application of AP2 is solved by solving AP1 multiple times. We

76   3 Integrated Production and Outbound Distribution Scheduling: Offline Problems

focus on AP1 first. The following algorithm solves this problem. The algorithm schedules jobs backwards and forms the delivery shipments from last to first.

Algorithm A3.3

Step 0: Let the set of unscheduled jobs be $U = N$. Set the departure time of the current last shipment to be $Q = \sum_{j \in N} p_j$. Let $k = 1$.

Step 1: Find the subset of the jobs that can be delivered in the kth last shipment without violating their deadlines, $S = \{j \in U | Q + t \leq e_j\}$. If S is empty but U is not, then stop, and the problem is infeasible.

Step 2: If $|S| > c$, select the c jobs with the largest processing times from S. Otherwise, select all the jobs from S. Let X and P be the set of the selected jobs and the total processing time of these jobs, respectively. Process the selected jobs consecutively without idle time in the time period $[Q - P, Q]$. Deliver them together in the kth last shipment with departure time Q. Update $Q = Q - P$, and $U = U \setminus X$. If U is empty, then stop, and we have a feasible schedule that uses exactly k batches. Otherwise, let $k = k + 1$, and go to Step 1.

To illustrate Algorithm A3.3, we apply it to an instance of problem AP1 generated based on the instance given in Example 3.6, as follows.

Example 3.8 (Application of Algorithm A3.3) Consider four jobs 1, 2, 3, 4 with $p_1 = 1, p_2 = 5, p_3 = 1, p_4 = 5; d_1 = 2, d_2 = 12, d_3 = 13, d_4 = 14$. There is a sufficient number of vehicles, each with capacity $c = 2$. The travel time of a shipment is $t = 0$. Suppose that the allowed lateness is 2 units. This implies that the deadlines of the jobs are: $e_1 = 4, e_2 = 14, e_3 = 15, e_4 = 16$. Thus, problem AP1 is to find a production and distribution schedule with a minimum number of shipments that deliver all the jobs by their deadlines.

We apply Algorithm A3.3 to this instance. Initially, $U = \{1, 2, 3, 4\}$, and $Q = p_1 + p_2 + p_3 + p_4 = 12$. Let $k = 1$. Step 1 finds $S = \{2, 3, 4\}$. Step 2 selects jobs 2 and 4 because they have the larger processing times than job 3. The total processing time of the selected jobs $P = 10$. Jobs 2 and 4 are processed from time 2 to 12. Update $Q = 12 - 10 = 2$ and $U = \{1, 3\}$.

Let $k = 2$. Step 1 finds $S = \{1, 3\}$. Step 2 selects all the jobs in S. The total processing time of the selected jobs $P = 2$. Jobs 1 and 3 are processed from time 0 to 2. U becomes empty. Stop. In the solution generated, $k = 2$, i.e., two shipments are used.

Pundoor and Chen (2005) show that Algorithm A3.3 finds an optimal solution to problem AP1 in $O(n^2 \log n)$ time. Next, we consider the second auxiliary problem AP2 which schedules the production and distribution of the jobs to minimize $L_{\max}$, subject to the constraint that no more than h delivery shipments are used, for a given integer h, where $\lceil n/c \rceil \leq h \leq n$. It can be seen that the value of $L_{\max}$ is nonincreasing in the value of h in the optimal solution of this problem. Based on this observation, Pundoor and Chen (2005) propose the following line search algorithm to find the optimal value of $L_{\max}$, given h.

3.4 Problems with Batch Delivery to a Single Customer

Algorithm A3.4

Step 0: Let LB and UB denote a lower bound and an upper bound on the maximum delivery lateness of jobs, $L_{\max}$, respectively. Initially, let LB be the maximum lateness of jobs if they are processed in EDD order and each job is delivered separately, and let UB be the maximum lateness of jobs if they are processed in EDD order and all are delivered in full shipments, except possibly the last several jobs which may be delivered in a partial shipment. Clearly, $LB \geq 0$ and $UB \leq t + P$, where $P = \sum_{j \in N} p_j$.

Step 1: Let $L^0 = (LB + UB)/2$. Define auxiliary problem AP1 by imposing a deadline on each job $j \in N$, $e_j = d_j + L^0$. Solve this problem by Algorithm A3.3, and let k be the optimal number of shipments used.

Step 2: If $k > h$, let $LB = L^0$. Otherwise, let $UB = L^0$. If $UB - LB < 1$, stop. The only integer in the interval $[LB, UB]$ is adopted as the solution value of $L_{\max}$. Otherwise, go to Step 1.

Pundoor and Chen (2005) show that Algorithm A3.4 finds an optimal solution to problem AP2 in $O(n^2 (\log n)(\log(P + t)))$ time, where $P = \sum_{j \in N} p_j$.

Based on Algorithm A3.4, Pundoor and Chen (2005) propose the following algorithm for solving problem $1||V(\infty, c), direct|1|L_{\max} + TC$.

Algorithm A3.5

Step 1: For $h = \lceil n/c \rceil, \ldots, n$, do the following: Define an auxiliary problem AP2 with the number of delivery shipments no more than h. Solve the problem by applying Algorithm A3.4. Let π_h and $L_{\max}(\pi_h)$ be the optimal schedule and its maximum lateness found by the algorithm.

Step 2: Find $u \in \{\lceil n/c \rceil, \ldots, n\}$ that minimizes the total cost $L_{\max}(\pi_u) + uf$. Then schedule π_u is optimal for problem $1||V(\infty, c), direct|1|L_{\max} + TC$ with objective value $L_{\max}(\pi_u) + uf$.

Pundoor and Chen (2005) show that Algorithm A3.5 finds an optimal solution to problem $1||V(\infty, c), direct|1|L_{\max} + TC$ in $O(n^3 (\log n)(\log(P + t)))$ time, where $P = \sum_{j \in N} p_j$. Since the input size of the problem is at least $\sum_{j \in N}(\lceil \log p_j \rceil + \lceil \log d_j \rceil) + \lceil \log t \rceil \geq n + \log(P + t)$, this means that Algorithm A3.5 runs in polynomial time.

3.4.3 Single-Machine Total Weighted Delivery Time and Transportation Cost Problem

Hall and Potts (2005) show that the single-machine problem $1||V(\infty, \infty), direct|1| \sum w_j D_j + TC$ is strongly NP-hard. However, when the jobs have identical weights, i.e., $w_1 = \cdots = w_n$, the corresponding problem even with a limited vehicle capacity, i.e., problem $1||V(\infty, c), direct|1| \sum D_j + TC$ can be solved in polynomial time (Chen & Vairaktarakis, 2005).

78   3 Integrated Production and Outbound Distribution Scheduling: Offline Problems

We first present the NP-hardness proof from Hall and Potts (2005) for problem $1||V(\infty, \infty), direct|1| \sum w_j D_j + TC$.

Theorem 3.7 *Problem* $1||V(\infty, \infty), direct|1| \sum w_j D_j + TC$ *is strongly NP-hard.*

Proof We use a reduction from 3-Partition, a known strongly NP-hard problem (Garey & Johnson, 1978). This problem can be described as follows.
3-Partition: Given $3u$ elements, $S = \{1, \ldots, 3u\}$, each with an integer size a_j, where $\sum_{j \in S} a_j = uz$ and $z/4 < a_j < z/2$ for some integer z, for $j \in U$, does there exist a partition of $S_1, \ldots, S_u$ of S such that $|S_i| = 3$ and $\sum_{j \in S_i} a_j = z$ for $j = 1, \ldots, u$?

Construct an instance of $1||V(\infty, \infty), direct|1| \sum w_j D_j + TC$ as follows: $n = 3u$, $N = S$, $p_j = w_j = a_j$ for $j \in S$, $t = 0$, $f = z^2/2$, and a threshold value $F = u(u + 2)z^2/2$. We prove that there exists a schedule to this instance of our problem with the objective value no greater than F if and only if there exists a solution to 3-Partition.

($\Rightarrow$) Given a solution $S_1, \ldots, S_u$ to 3-Partition, we assume without loss of generality that $S_i = \{3i - 2, 3i - 1, 3i\}$ for $i = 1, \ldots, u$. Consider the following schedule for the instance of our problem: Process the jobs in sequence $(1, \ldots, n)$ and deliver the three jobs in S_i together in one shipment at the completion time of job $3i$, which is iz, for $i = 1, \ldots, u$. This yields

$$\sum w_j D_j + TC = \sum_{i=1}^{u} z(iz) + uf = z^2 u(u + 1)/2 + uz^2/2 = F.$$

($\Leftarrow$) We first show that for the instance of our problem, the objective value of any schedule with h delivery shipments is minimized only when the total processing time of the jobs in each shipment is equal to uz/h. Suppose that x_i is the total processing time of the jobs in shipment i, for $i = 1, \ldots, h$. Finding the minimum possible objective value of a schedule with h shipments can be formulated as the following optimization problem with $x_1, \ldots, x_h$ as decision variables:

$$\text{minimize} \quad x_1^2 + (x_1 + x_2)x_2 + \cdots + (x_1 + \cdots + x_h)x_h + hz^2/2 \quad (3.6)$$

$$\text{subject to:} \quad x_1 + \cdots x_h = uz. \quad (3.7)$$

The objective function (3.6) can be rewritten as

$$\left(\sum_{i=1}^{h} x_i\right)^2 \Big/ 2 + \sum_{i=1}^{h} x_i^2/2 + hz^2/2 = u^2 z^2/2 + \sum_{i=1}^{h} x_i^2/2 + hz^2/2,$$

where the first term is a constant and the second term is minimized under the constraint (3.7) only when $x_1 = \cdots = x_h = uz/h$. Thus, the objective value of any schedule with h shipments is greater than or equal to $u^2 z^2/2 + \sum_{i=1}^{h} x_i^2/2 + hz^2/2$. This expression is minimized with respect to $h \geq 1$ only at $h = u$, and this minimum

3.4 Problems with Batch Delivery to a Single Customer

value is equal to F. This implies that in any schedule for the instance of our problem with the objective value less than or equal to F, there must be u shipments with the total processing time of the jobs in each shipment equal to z. This shows the existence of a solution to 3-Partition. □

Clearly, a more general problem with limited vehicle capacity, $1||V(\infty, c), direct|1| \sum w_j D_j + TC$, is also strongly NP-hard. Next, we consider a special case of this problem where the jobs have identical weights, i.e., problem $1||V(\infty, c), direct|1| \sum D_j + TC$. By Lemma 3.3, processing the jobs in SPT order is optimal for this problem. The problem is thus reduced to finding an optimal delivery schedule given the SPT job processing sequence. Chen and Vairaktarakis (2005) provide the following dynamic programming algorithm to solve this problem.

Algorithm A3.6

Reindex the jobs in SPT order so that $p_1 \leq p_2 \leq \cdots \leq p_n$. The completion time of each job $j \in N$ on the machine is thus $C_j = p_1 + \cdots + p_j$.

Value Function $F(j) = $ the minimum total cost contribution of a schedule for the first j jobs $\{1, \ldots, j\}$.

Initial Condition $F(0) = 0$.

Recurrence Relation For $j = 1, \ldots, n$,

$$F(j) = \min\{F(j - h) + h(C_j + t) + f | h = 1, \ldots, \min(c, j)\}.$$

Optimal Solution Value $F(n)$.

Chen and Vairaktarakis (2005) show that Algorithm A3.6 finds an optimal schedule for problem $1||V(\infty, c), direct|1| \sum D_j + TC$ in $O(n \log n + nc)$ time.

In addition to the two problems discussed above, several special cases of these problems are also studied in the literature. For example, Ji et al. (2007) show that problem $1||V(\infty, \infty), direct|1| \sum w_j D_j + TC$ with a constraint that the number of shipments cannot exceed a given constant is ordinarily NP-hard, and provide a pseudo-polynomial time dynamic programming algorithm for their problem.

3.4.4 Parallel-Machine Total Delivery Time and Transportation Cost Problem

In this section, we consider problem $P_m||V(\infty, c), direct|1| \sum D_j + TC$. Chen and Vairaktarakis (2005) show that this problem is ordinarily NP-hard even if there are only two machines (i.e., $m = 2$), give a polynomial-time heuristic algorithm, and show that this heuristic has a worst-case bound of $2 - 1/m$ and it is asymptotically optimal under certain conditions.

80   3   Integrated Production and Outbound Distribution Scheduling: Offline Problems

We describe Chen and Vairaktarakis' heuristic in the following. Their heuristic is developed based on the idea that a feasible schedule for the problem (which has m parallel machines) can be constructed from a feasible schedule for a closely related problem with a single machine ($m = 1$). They call this single-machine problem the *auxiliary problem* and denote it as AUX. This auxiliary problem can be solved by a modified version of Algorithm A3.6 given in Sect. 3.4.3. The optimal solution of the auxiliary problem is then transformed into a feasible solution for problem $P_m||V(\infty, c), direct|1| \sum D_j + TC$. Problem AUX is defined as follows: Find a way to partition the job set N into subsets $S_1, S_2, \ldots$ such that the number of jobs in each subset S_q is no more than c, and deliver each subset of jobs S_q in one shipment with the departure time d_q equal to the maximum of the following two terms: (i) and (ii), so as to minimize the objective function $\sum D_j + TC$.

(i) The maximum processing time of the jobs delivered in all the shipments so far (i.e., $\max\{p_j | j \in S_1 \cup \ldots \cup S_q\}$)
(ii) The sum of the processing times of all the jobs delivered in the shipments so far divided by m (i.e., $\sum_{j \in S_1 \cup \ldots \cup S_q} p_j / m$)

It can be seen that AUX is the same as the single-machine problem $1||V(\infty, c), direct|1| \sum D_j + TC$, except that the departure time of a shipment is calculated differently. Problem AUX uses the maximum of (i), (ii) while the latter problem uses the completion time of the job completed last in a shipment. Chen and Vairaktarakis (2005) show that AUX can be solved by a modified version of Algorithm A3.6 given in Sect. 3.4.3, where the recurrence relation is replaced by the following:

$$F(j) = \min \left\{ F(j - h) + h\left(\max \left\{ p_j, \sum_{l=1}^{j} p_l/m \right\} + t \right) \right.$$

$$\left. + f \mid h = 1, \ldots, \min\{c, j\} \right\}.$$

Building on this result, Chen and Vairaktarakis (2005) provide the following heuristic for problem $P_m||V(\infty, c), direct|1| \sum D_j + TC$. In this heuristic, an LPT (largest-processing-time-first) order of a given set of jobs denotes that the jobs are sequenced in nonincreasing order of their processing times p_j. Also, the first available machine (FAM) rule is used, where the first unscheduled job is scheduled to the earliest available machine of the processing facility until all the jobs are scheduled.

Heuristic H3.2

Step 1: Solve the auxiliary problem AUX using Algorithm A3.6 with the modified recurrence relation described above. Let π_{AUX} be the solution obtained, L be the number of shipments in this solution, and $S_1, \ldots, S_L$ be the set of jobs in these shipments.

3.4 Problems with Batch Delivery to a Single Customer

Step 2: Sort the jobs in every shipment S_q in LPT order for $q = 1, \ldots, L$. Assign the jobs to the machines for processing by applying the FAM rule to the jobs in $S_1, \ldots, S_L$ in this order. Let $C_{[q]}$ be the completion time of the last job in S_q and deliver the jobs in S_q in one shipment (the qth shipment) departing at time $C_{[q]}$, for $q = 1, \ldots, L$.

It is easy to see that Step 1 of the heuristic is more time-consuming than Step 2. Hence, the overall time complexity of Heuristic H3.2 is the same as that of Algorithm A3.6, which is $O(n \log n + nc)$.

Example 3.9 (Application of Heuristic H3.2) We apply Heuristic H3.2 to the following instance of problem $P_m || V(\infty, c), direct | 1 | \sum D_j + TC$: There are 6 jobs and 2 parallel machines with vehicle capacity $c = 3$, transportation time $t = 0$, transportation cost per batch $f = 10$, and the processing time p_j and the parameter $\max\{p_j, \sum_{l=1}^{j} p_l / m\}$ (denoted as δ_j) for each job j are shown in the following table, where the jobs are indexed in SPT order.

j	1	2	3	4	5	6
p_j	2	6	8	10	11	13
δ_j	2	6	8	13	18.5	25

Step 1: By the definition of the auxiliary problem AUX, if a shipment contains job j as the last job, then its departure time is δ_j. Solve this problem and find an optimal solution as follows: There are 3 shipments with $S_1 = \{1, 2, 3\}$, $S_2 = \{4, 5\}$, $S_3 = \{6\}$ with departure times 8, 18.5, and 25, respectively. The corresponding total cost of the solution is $(3(8) + 10) + (2(18.5) + 10) + (25 + 10) = 116$.

Step 2: Sort the jobs in each shipment S_i in LPT order, and assign these jobs to the machines by the FAM rule, for $i = 1, 2, 3$. We obtain the following solution: job sequence on machine 1: (3, 5) with completion times $C_3 = 8$, $C_5 = 19$, and job sequence on machine 2: (2, 1, 4, 6) with $C_2 = 6$, $C_1 = 8$, $C_4 = 18$, $C_6 = 31$. Use the same shipment formations as before, i.e., S_1, S_2, S_3. Their departure times are now 8, 19, and 31, respectively. The total cost of this solution is $(3(8) + 10) + (2(19) + 10) + (31 + 10) = 123$.

It can be verified that an optimal solution for this instance is as follows: job sequence on machine 1: (1, 4, 6) and job sequence on machine 2: (2, 3, 5); form three shipments, $S_1 = \{1, 2\}$, $S_2 = \{3, 4\}$, $S_3 = \{5, 6\}$ with departure times 6, 14, and 25, respectively. The total cost is $(2(6)+10)+(2(14)+10)+(2(25)+10) = 120$.

We note that as shown above, for the instance given here, the optimal objective value of problem AUX is a lower bound on the optimal objective value of problem $P_m || V(\infty, c), direct | 1 | \sum D_j + TC$. This is true for every instance, as shown below in Lemma 3.7.

82 3 Integrated Production and Outbound Distribution Scheduling: Offline Problems

Next, we analyze the worst-case and asymptotic performance of Heuristic H3.2. Given a solution π to the auxiliary problem AUX, we denote the total delivery time of jobs, total delivery cost, and the sum of these two by $D_{AUX}(\pi)$, $TC_{AUX}(\pi)$, and $Z_{AUX}(\pi)$, respectively. Similarly, given a solution π to the problem $P_m||V(\infty, c), direct|1|\sum D_j + TC$, these three values are denoted as $D(\pi)$, $TC(\pi)$, and $Z(\pi)$, respectively. Let π^* be an optimal solution of the problem with the optimal objective value Z^*. Then, $Z_{AUX}(\pi) = D_{AUX}(\pi) + TC_{AUX}(\pi)$, $Z(\pi) = D(\pi) + TC(\pi)$, and $Z^* = Z(\pi^*) = D(\pi^*) + TC(\pi^*)$.

Lemma 3.7 $Z_{AUX}(\pi_{AUX}) \leq Z^*$.

Proof Given an optimal solution π^* to problem $P_m||V(\infty, c), direct|1|\sum D_j + TC$, suppose that there are V shipments, $B_1, \ldots, B_V$, where B_v also represents the subset of jobs in the vth shipment, for $v = 1, \ldots, V$. Let E_v be the processing completion time of the last job in B_v, for $v = 1, \ldots, V$. Without loss of generality, we assume that the shipments $B_1, \ldots, B_V$ are indexed in nondecreasing order of E_v. Then,

$$E_v \geq \max \left\{ \max\{p_j | j \in B_1 \cup \cdots \cup B_v\}, \sum_{j \in B_1 \cup \cdots \cup B_v} p_j/m \right\} \quad (3.8)$$

and the total delivery time of the jobs is

$$D(\pi^*) = \sum_{v=1}^{V} |B_v|(E_v + t). \quad (3.9)$$

The solution π^* is feasible for the auxiliary problem AUX if we set the departure time of each shipment B_v, for $v = 1, \ldots, V$, to be

$$e_v = \max \left\{ \max\{p_j | j \in B_1 \cup \cdots \cup B_v\}, \sum_{j \in B_1 \cup \cdots \cup B_v} p_j/m \right\}$$

instead of E_v. By (3.8), $E_v \geq e_v$, for $v = 1, \ldots, V$. By (3.9), the total delivery time of the jobs in π^* for AUX satisfies

$$D_{AUX}(\pi^*) = \sum_{v=1}^{V} |B_v|(e_v + t) \leq D(\pi^*). \quad (3.10)$$

Clearly, solution π^* incurs the same transportation cost for problem $P_m||V(\infty, c), direct|1|\sum D_j + TC$ and AUX, i.e., $TC(\pi^*) = TC_{AUX}(\pi^*)$. Together with (3.10), this implies that $Z^* \geq Z_{AUX}(\pi^*)$. Since π_{AUX} is an optimal solution for AUX, $Z_{AUX}(\pi^*) \geq Z_{AUX}(\pi_{AUX})$. Thus, $Z^* \geq Z_{AUX}(\pi_{AUX})$. $\square$

Lemma 3.7 is quite intuitive. The way the departure time of a shipment in problem AUX is defined guarantees that each shipment in a solution to problem

3.4 Problems with Batch Delivery to a Single Customer

AUX always departs earlier than or at the same time as this same shipment if it is in a solution to problem $P_m||V(\infty, c), direct|1| \sum D_j + TC$.

Lemma 3.7 enables us to prove the following result about Heuristic H3.2.

Theorem 3.8 *The worst-case performance ratio of Heuristic H3.2 for problem $P_m||V(\infty, c), direct|1| \sum D_j + TC$ satisfies $Z(\pi)/Z^* \leq 2 - 1/m$, where π is the solution generated by H3.2 for problem $P_m||V(\infty, c), direct|1| \sum D_j + TC$.*

Proof The solution π constructed for $P_m||V(\infty, c), direct|1| \sum D_j + TC$ in Step 2 of Heuristic H3.2 has the same shipments $S_1, \ldots, S_L$ but with different shipment departure times from the solution π_{AUX} for the auxiliary problem. Therefore,

$$TC(\pi) = TC_{AUX}(\pi_{AUX}). \tag{3.11}$$

The total delivery time of jobs in π_{AUX} for the auxiliary problem is

$$D_{AUX}(\pi_{AUX}) = \sum_{l=1}^{L} |S_l| \left(\max \left\{ \max_{j \in S_1 \cup \cdots \cup S_l} p_j, \sum_{j \in S_1 \cup \cdots \cup S_l} p_j/m \right\} + t \right), \tag{3.12}$$

and the total delivery time of the jobs in π for problem $P_m||V(\infty, c), direct|1| \sum D_j + TC$ is

$$D(\pi) = \sum_{l=1}^{L} |S_l|(C_{[l]} + t), \tag{3.13}$$

where $C_{[l]}$ is the processing completion time of the jobs in shipment S_l, for $l = 1, \ldots, L$. For $l = 1, \ldots, L$, let v_l be the job that is completed last among all the jobs in $S_1 \cup \cdots \cup S_l$ in Step 2 of H3.2. Due to the FAM rule in Step 2, we have, for $l = 1, \ldots, L$,

$$C_{[l]} \leq \left(\sum_{j \in S_1 \cup \cdots \cup S_l} p_j - p_{v_l} \right) /m + p_{v_l}$$

$$= \left(\sum_{j \in S_1 \cup \cdots \cup S_l} p_j \right) /m + \frac{m-1}{m} p_{v_l}$$

$$\leq \left(\sum_{j \in S_1 \cup \cdots \cup S_l} p_j \right) /m + \frac{m-1}{m} \max_{j \in S_1 \cup \cdots \cup S_l} p_j. \tag{3.14}$$

From (3.12), (3.13), and (3.14), we have

$$D(\pi) \leq \sum_{l=1}^{L} |S_l| \left[\left(\sum_{j \in S_1 \cup \cdots \cup S_l} p_j \right) / m + \frac{m-1}{m} \max_{j \in S_1 \cup \cdots \cup S_l} p_j + t \right] \qquad (3.15)$$

$$\leq D_{AUX}(\pi_{AUX}) + \frac{m-1}{m} D_{AUX}(\pi_{AUX}) = \left(2 - \frac{1}{m} \right) D_{AUX}(\pi_{AUX}). \qquad (3.16)$$

This, together with (3.11) and Lemma 3.7, implies that

$$Z(\pi) = D(\pi) + TC(\pi) \leq \left(2 - \frac{1}{m} \right) D_{AUX}(\pi_{AUX}) + TC_{AUX}(\pi_{AUX})$$

$$\leq \left(2 - \frac{1}{m} \right) Z_{AUX}(\pi_{AUX}) \leq \left(2 - \frac{1}{m} \right) Z^*.$$

$\square$

Chen and Vairaktarakis (2005) also show that Heuristic H3.2 is asymptotically optimal under some mild conditions. Their result, along with a proof, is described below.

Theorem 3.9 *The schedule π generated by Heuristic H3.2 is asymptotically optimal for problem $P_m||V(\infty, c), direct|1| \sum D_j + TC$, as n approaches ∞, i.e., $\lim_{n \to \infty} \frac{Z(\pi) - Z^*}{Z^*} = 0$, under the assumption that m is fixed, and the processing time p_j of each job $j \in N$ is within a finite interval $[X, Y]$, where $0 < X < Y < \infty$.*

Proof From (3.12), we have

$$D_{AUX}(\pi_{AUX}) \geq \sum_{l=1}^{L} |S_l| \left(\sum_{j \in S_1 \cup \cdots \cup S_l} p_j / m \right)$$

$$\geq \frac{X}{m} \sum_{l=1}^{L} \left[|S_l| \left(\sum_{i=1}^{l} |S_i| \right) \right]$$

$$= \frac{X}{m} \left\{ \left(\sum_{l=1}^{L} |S_l| \right)^2 - \sum_{l=1}^{L} \left[|S_l| \left(\sum_{i=1}^{l-1} |S_i| \right) \right] \right\}$$

$$\geq \frac{X}{m} \left\{ \left(\sum_{l=1}^{L} |S_l| \right)^2 - \frac{1}{2} \left(\sum_{l=1}^{L} |S_l| \right)^2 \right\}$$

$$= \frac{X}{2m} \left(\sum_{l=1}^{L} |S_l| \right)^2$$

$$= \frac{n^2 X}{2m}. \qquad (3.17)$$

3.4 Problems with Batch Delivery to a Single Customer

Furthermore, from (3.12) and (3.15), we have

$$D(\pi) - D_{AUX}(\pi_{AUX}) \le \frac{m-1}{m} \sum_{l=1}^{L} \left[|S_l| \left(\max_{j \in S_1 \cup \cdots \cup S_l} p_j \right) \right] \le \frac{(m-1)n}{m} Y,$$

which, together with (3.17), implies

$$\lim_{n \to \infty} \frac{D(\pi) - D_{AUX}(\pi_{AUX})}{D_{AUX}(\pi_{AUX})} = 0. \qquad (3.18)$$

Since $Z_{AUX}(\pi_{AUX}) = D_{AUX}(\pi_{AUX}) + TC_{AUX}(\pi_{AUX})$ and $Z(\pi) = D(\pi) + TC(\pi)$, from (3.11) and (3.18), we have

$$\lim_{n \to \infty} \frac{Z(\pi) - Z_{AUX}(\pi_{AUX})}{Z_{AUX}(\pi_{AUX})} = \lim_{n \to \infty} \frac{D(\pi) - D_{AUX}(\pi_{AUX})}{Z_{AUX}(\pi_{AUX})} = 0.$$

This, along with Lemma 3.7 and the fact that $Z(\pi) \ge Z^*$, implies that $\lim_{n \to \infty} \frac{Z(\pi) - Z^*}{Z^*} = 0$. $\qquad\square$

Chen and Vairaktarakis (2005) conduct computational tests on the performance of Heuristic H3.2 based on randomly generated test instances of problem $P_m || V(\infty, c), direct|1| \sum D_j + TC$ and show that the heuristic is capable of generating near-optimal solutions quickly.

In addition, Chen and Vairaktarakis (2005) study several other related problems, including the extension of the problem discussed above to a multi-customer setting with vehicle routing, i.e., $P_m || V(\infty, c), routing|k| \sum D_j + TC$. This more general problem is discussed below in Sect. 3.5.2.

3.4.5 Problems with a Limited Number of Vehicles

In this section, we consider two problems with a limited number of delivery vehicles, $1 || V(v, c), direct|1| D_{\max}$ and $1 || V(v, c), direct|1| \sum D_j$, and present the algorithms proposed by Lee and Chen (2001) for solving these problems. There are two major differences between these problems and the corresponding problems with a sufficient number of vehicles. In problems with a limited number of vehicles, (i) each vehicle may have to make multiple delivery trips, each carrying one shipment; and (ii) after all the jobs to be delivered together in a shipment have completed processing, they have to wait if there is no available vehicle.

We first note that the corresponding problems with a sufficient number of vehicles, $1 || V(\infty, c), direct|1| D_{\max}$ and $1 || V(\infty, c), direct|1| \sum D_j$, are trivial. For the first problem, it is optimal to process the jobs in any order and deliver each job individually and immediately after it completes processing. For the second problem, it is optimal to process the jobs in SPT order and deliver each job

86   3 Integrated Production and Outbound Distribution Scheduling: Offline Problems

individually and immediately after it completes processing. Even with a more general objective function that includes the total transportation cost, these problems are still relatively easy to solve. For problem $1||V(\infty, c), direct|1|D_{\max} + TC$, Chen and Vairaktarakis (2005) show that the following $O(n)$ time algorithm finds an optimal solution: Process the jobs in an arbitrary sequence, and deliver the jobs in $\lceil n/c \rceil$ shipments, where all the shipments but at most one are full. For problem $1||V(\infty, c), direct|1| \sum D_j + TC$, Algorithm A3.6 described in Sect. 3.4.4 finds an optimal solution.

We now consider problem $1||V(v, c), direct|1|D_{\max}$. By Lemma 3.6, we only need to consider the SPT job processing sequence. Suppose that the jobs are reindexed in nondecreasing order of their processing times. For this problem, Lee and Chen (2001) show the following property.

Lemma 3.8 *There exists an optimal schedule for problem $1||V(v, c), direct|1|D_{\max}$ that satisfies the following: (i) there are $q = \lceil n/c \rceil$ delivery shipments; and (ii) If n is not an integer multiple of c (i.e., $n < qc$), then the first shipment contains $n - (q - 1)c$ jobs, and each of the other $q - 1$ shipments contains c jobs. Otherwise, all the q shipments contain c jobs.*

By this property and Lemma 3.6, we know exactly the jobs contained in each shipment and the time by which the jobs in each shipment have completed processing. Let $B_1, \ldots, B_q$ denote the q shipments and r_h denote the completion time of the last job in shipment B_h on the machine, for $h = 1, \ldots, q$. Let $P(j) = \sum_{k=1}^{j} p_k$. Then, there are two cases.

- Case 1: If $n < qc$, then $B_1 = \{1, \ldots, u\}$, where $u = n - (q - 1)c$, $r_1 = P(u)$; and $B_h = \{u + (h - 2)c + 1, \ldots, u + (h - 1)c\}$, $r_h = P(u + (h - 1)c)$, for $h = 2, \ldots, q$.
- Case 2: If $n = qc$, then $B_h = \{(h - 1)c + 1, \ldots, hc\}$, and $r_h = P(hc)$, for $h = 1, \ldots, q$.

With the delivery shipments $B_1, \ldots, B_q$ and their completion times on the machine as described above, problem $1||V(v, c), direct|1|D_{\max}$ reduces to the problem of dispatching v vehicles to deliver these batches so that the time when the last shipment gets to the customer is minimum. It is not difficult to see that, if we view a vehicle as a machine and delivering a shipment as a job, then this vehicle dispatching problem is similar to the classical parallel-machine makespan problem with generally different job arrival times and identical job processing times, i.e., $P_v|r_j, p_j \equiv p|C_{\max}$, where there are q jobs and v identical parallel machines, the arrival time of job j is r_j, for $j = 1, \ldots, q$, and the processing times of jobs are all equal to $2t$, which is the round-trip travel time between the plant and the customer site. Clearly, for problem $P_v|r_j, p_j \equiv p|C_{\max}$, the following solution is optimal: Sorting the jobs in nondecreasing order of their arrival times and assigning available jobs in this order to the earliest available machines. This implies that our problem $1||V(v, c), direct|1|D_{\max}$ can be solved by assigning the shipments to the earliest available vehicles in the order of their completion times on the machine.

3.4 Problems with Batch Delivery to a Single Customer

Based on the above discussions, we can see that problem $1||V(v,c), direct|1|D_{\max}$ can be solved by the following algorithm.

Algorithm A3.7

Step 1: Reindex the jobs in nondecreasing order of their processing times. Process the jobs on the machine in this order without any idle time.

Step 2: Let $q = \lceil n/c \rceil$. For q shipments $B_1, \ldots, B_q$ and calculate the completion time r_h of the last job in each shipment B_h, for $h = 1, \ldots, q$, following the two cases described above.

Step 3: Consider the shipments $B_1, \ldots, B_q$ one by one in this order. Whenever a shipment B_h is considered, assign it to the earliest vehicle that returns to the plant. The departure time of B_h is $\max\{r_h, \tau\}$, where τ is the time when the earliest vehicle returns to the plant.

It can be seen that the time complexity of Algorithm A3.7 for solving problem $1||V(v,c), direct|1|D_{\max}$ is $O(n \log n)$.

Next, we consider problem $1||V(v,c), direct|1|\sum D_j$. Utilizing the properties stated in Lemmas 3.3 and 3.5, Lee and Chen (2001) develop a dynamic programming algorithm for this problem. Since the jobs should be processed in SPT order, the problem reduces to finding an optimal delivery schedule, given the SPT processing schedule. Lee and Chen (2001) show that all possible departure times for a shipment can be calculated in advance by the following procedure.

Procedure DepTime

Step 1: Reindex the jobs in nondecreasing order of their processing times. Process the jobs on the machine in this order without idle time. Denote the completion time of job j on the machine by C_j, for $j \in N$.

Step 2: Possible departure times of a shipment are $C_j + kt$, for $k = 0, 1, \ldots, n-1$, and $j \in N$. Index the distinct time points among all these possible departure times by $1, 2, \ldots, T$, where $T \le n^2$, such that an earlier time point has a smaller index. Let $\tau(h)$ denote the hth time point, for $h = 1, 2, \ldots, T$ and let $\tau(0) = 0$.

Lee and Chen's dynamic programming algorithm for solving $1||V(v,c), direct|1|\sum D_j$ is given below.

Algorithm A3.8

Initialization Calculate possible departure times for shipments using Procedure DepTime. Define $G(k; j; s_1, \ldots, s_v)$ to be the minimum total delivery time of jobs $j, \ldots, k$, provided that these jobs are delivered in v shipments that depart at times $\tau(s_1), \ldots, \tau(s_v)$ from the plant, respectively. The value of $G(k; j; s_1, \ldots, s_v)$ can be calculated in $O(v)$ time as follows:

Let $A = \{j, \ldots, k\}$. Repeat the following procedure with $h = 1, \ldots, v$. Let A_h be the subset of jobs in A that complete processing before or at time $\tau(s_h)$. If there are more than c jobs in A_h, then assign the first c jobs of A_h to the shipment that departs at time $\tau(s_h)$. Otherwise, assign all the jobs in A_h to this shipment. The total delivery time of the jobs in this shipment can be calculated accordingly. Update A by removing the jobs delivered in this shipment.

Value Function $F(k; j; s_1, s_2, \ldots, s_v)$ is the minimum total delivery time of a partial schedule containing the first k jobs $1, \ldots, k$, provided that the current last v shipments contain jobs $j, j+1, \ldots, k$ and depart at times $\tau(s_1), \ldots, \tau(s_v)$ from the plant, where $\{s_1, \ldots, s_v\} \subseteq \{0, 1, \ldots, T\}$ and $0 \le s_1 < \cdots < s_v \le T$.

Boundary Conditions $F(0; 0; 0, \ldots, 0) = 0$.

Recurrence Relation
For $k = 1, \ldots, n$; $j = \max(1, k - vc), \max(1, k - vc) + 1, \ldots, \max(1, k - v)$; and $0 \le s_1 < \cdots < s_v \le T$,

$$F(k; j; s_1, \ldots, s_v)$$
$$= \min\{F(j - 1; i; b_1, \ldots, b_v) + G(k; j; s_1, \ldots, s_v) \mid i, b_1, \ldots, b_v$$
satisfy the following conditions (i) and (ii)$\}$

(i) $0 \le j - i \le vc$.
(ii) $0 \le b_1 < \cdots < b_v$, and $\tau(s_h) - \tau(b_h) \ge 2t$, for all $h = 1, \ldots, v$.

Optimal Solution $\min\{F(n; j; s_1, \ldots, s_v)\}$ over all possible states $(j; s_1, \ldots s_v)$.

Lee and Chen (2001) show that Algorithm A3.8 has time complexity $O(c^{v+2}v^{v+3}n^{2v+1})$, which is polynomial when v is fixed. When there is only one vehicle, i.e., $v = 1$, the complexity of this algorithm is $O(n^3)$. The complexity of problem $1||V(v, c), direct|1| \sum D_j$ with arbitrary v apparently remains open (Lee & Chen, 2001).

3.5 Problems with Batch Delivery to Multiple Customers

As discussed in Sect. 3.2, to deliver jobs to multiple customers in batches, there are two possible delivery methods, i.e., batch delivery by direct shipping, under which only jobs from the same customer can share a shipment, and batch delivery with routing, under which jobs from different customers can share a shipment and hence vehicle routing becomes a part of the decision. In this section, we discuss multi-customer extensions of some of the problems considered in Sect. 3.4, i.e., problems $1||V(\infty, c), direct|k|L_{\max} + TC, P_m||V(\infty, c), routing|k| \sum D_j + TC, 1||V(v, c), direct|k|D_{\max}$ and $1||V(v, c), direct|k| \sum D_j$. Section 7.2 studies several other problems with batch delivery by direct shipping.

We recall that, as defined in Sect. 3.2.1, in a problem with multiple customers, the set of customers is denoted as $K = \{1, \ldots, k\}$, and the number of jobs and set of jobs from customer i are denoted as n_i and N_i, respectively, where $n = n_1 + \cdots + n_k$ and $N = N_1 \cup \cdots N_k$. We introduce some additional notation and define some new terms relevant to the problems discussed in this section. We denote the jth job from customer $i \in K$ as (i, j) and its processing time and due date as p_{ij} and d_{ij}, respectively. Hence, $N_i = \{(i, 1), \cdots, (i, n_i)\}$, for $i \in K$. If direct shipping is used, the delivery time and cost of a shipment from the plant to customer i are denoted

3.5 Problems with Batch Delivery to Multiple Customers   89

as t_i and f_i, respectively. If vehicle routing is involved, the delivery time and cost of a shipment depend on the specific route used, and are defined below wherever necessary.

3.5.1 Single-Machine Maximum Lateness and Transportation Cost Problems with Direct Shipping

We consider problem $1||V(\infty, c), direct|k|L_{\max} + TC$ and the special case of this problem with no vehicle capacity limit, i.e., $1||V(\infty, \infty), direct|k|L_{\max} + TC$. Pundoor and Chen (2005) show that when the number of customers k is arbitrary, both problems are at least ordinarily NP-hard (Pundoor & Chen, 2005). Hall and Potts (2003) give an $O(n^{2k+1})$ dynamic programming algorithm for solving the latter problem with a fixed k. However, the complexity of the former problem with a fixed k apparently remains open. Pundoor and Chen (2005) propose an asymptotically optimal polynomial time heuristic algorithm for the former problem. In the following, we discuss these results in detail.

3.5.1.1 NP-Hardness Proof

We first present the NP-hardness proof given by Pundoor and Chen (2005) for problem $1||V(\infty, c), direct|k|L_{\max} + TC$ with an arbitrary k.

Theorem 3.10 *Problem $1||V(\infty, c), direct|k|L_{\max} + TC$ with an arbitrary number of customers is at least ordinarily NP-hard.*

Proof We prove the theorem by a reduction from the Subset Sum problem, a known ordinarily NP-hard problem (Garey & Johnson, 1979). The Subset Sum problem, denoted as SS, can be stated as follows:

SS: Given a set of $q + 1$ positive integers $\{a_1, \ldots, a_q\}$ and B, does there exist a subset $U \subseteq Q = \{1, \ldots, q\}$ such that $\sum_{i \in U} a_i = B$?
   Define $A = \sum_{i \in Q} a_i$ and $H = 3q + B$. We construct a corresponding instance of our problem as follows:

- Number of customers: $k = q$.
- Number of jobs from each customer i: $n_i = 3$, and the jobs are $(i, 1), (i, 2), (i, 3)$, for $i = 1, \ldots, k$.
- Processing times: $p_{i1} = 1, p_{i2} = a_i, p_{i3} = Ha_i$, for $i = 1, \ldots, k$.
- Due dates: $d_{i1} \equiv d_1 = q + B, d_{i2} \equiv d_2 = q + B + (H + 1)(A - B)$, and $d_{i3} \equiv d_3 = q + (H + 1)A$, for $i = 1, \ldots, k$.
- Vehicle capacity: $c = 3$.
- Transportation times and costs: $t_i = 0$, and $f_i = 1$, for $i = 1, \ldots, k$.
- Threshold cost: $Z = 2q$.

90   3 Integrated Production and Outbound Distribution Scheduling: Offline Problems

For ease of presentation, we call the jobs $\{(i, 1) \mid i = 1, \ldots, k\}$ type-1 jobs, $\{(i, 2) \mid i = 1, \ldots, k\}$ type-2 jobs, and $\{(i, 3) \mid i = 1, \ldots, k\}$ type-3 jobs. We first prove the following properties. In any schedule π to the constructed instance of our problem with objective value no greater than Z,

- (i) No shipment contains both a type-1 job and a type-3 job.
- (ii) There are exactly $2k$ shipments.
- (iii) There are no late jobs.
- (iv) Any type-3 job is processed later than any type-1 job.
- (v) Any type-2 job is in a shipment of size 2.

The proof for each property is given below.

- (i) If a type-1 job is shipped together with a type-3 job, then the lateness of the type-1 job is at least $1 + H - d_1 = 2q + 1$, which means that π has an objective value greater than Z, a contradiction.
- (ii) If there are more than $2k$ batches, the objective value would be greater than Z. Property (i) implies that at least $2k$ shipments are needed. Thus, there are exactly $2k$ shipments.
- (iii) Property (ii) means that the contribution from the total shipment cost to the objective value is already equal to Z. Thus, $L_{\max} = 0$, and there is no late job.
- (iv) If a type-3 job is processed before a type-1 job, then the completion time of the type-1 job is at least $H + 1 > d_1$, implying that the type-1 job is late, leading to a contradiction with Property (iii).
- (v) This follows directly from Properties (i) and (ii).

To complete the proof, we show that there is a solution to the constructed instance of our problem with total cost less than or equal to Z if and only if there is a solution to SS.

($\Rightarrow$) Given a subset $U \subseteq Q$ such that $\sum_{i \in U} a_i = B$, we construct a schedule for the instance of our problem as follows: First, process all the type-1 jobs from customers in $Q \setminus U$ in any order and deliver each of these jobs in a separate shipment; next, process the type-1 and type-2 jobs from each customer $i \in U$ consecutively and deliver the two jobs from each customer $i \in U$ together; next, process the type-2 and type-3 jobs from each customer $i \in Q \setminus U$ consecutively and deliver the two jobs from each customer $i \in Q \setminus U$ together; finally, process the type-3 jobs from the customers in U and deliver each of the jobs separately. Let the cardinality of set U be u. The cardinality of $Q \setminus U$ is thus $q - u$.

In the above constructed schedule, the delivery time of the last shipment containing type-1 and type-2 jobs is

$$T_1 = q + \sum_{i \in U} a_i = q + B = d_1.$$

Hence, all the type-1 jobs are delivered before or at their due date. Similarly, the delivery time of the last shipment containing type-2 and type-3 jobs is

3.5 Problems with Batch Delivery to Multiple Customers

$$T_2 = T_1 + (H+1) \sum_{i \in Q \setminus U} a_i = q + B + (H+1)(A-B) = d_2.$$

Thus, all the type-2 jobs are delivered before or at their due date. Similarly, the delivery time of the last type-3 job in the schedule is

$$T_3 = T_2 + H \sum_{i \in U} a_i = q + B + (H+1)(A-B) + HB = q + (H+1)A = d_3$$

Thus, all the jobs are delivered on time. The number of shipments in this schedule is $(q-u) + u + (q-u) + u = 2q = Z$. Hence, the objective value of the schedule is equal to Z.

($\Leftarrow$) In a given schedule for the instance of our problem with an objective value less than or equal to Z, let u be the number of shipments that contain type-1 and type-2 jobs, and U be the set of the corresponding type-2 jobs in these shipments. Since no late jobs exist in the schedule (from Property (iii) proved above), all these jobs should be delivered no later than $d_1 = q + B$. Since the delivery time for the last type-1 job is at least $X_1 = q + \sum_{i \in U} a_i$, we have $X_1 \le d_1 = q + B$, which implies that

$$\sum_{i \in U} a_i \le B. \tag{3.19}$$

Similarly, the delivery time of the last shipment containing type-2 and type-3 jobs should not be greater than d_2. By Property (iv) proved above, the completion time of the last shipment containing type-2 and type-3 jobs is at least $X_1 + (H+1) \sum_{i \in Q \setminus U} a_i$. Thus,

$$X_1 + (H+1) \sum_{i \in Q \setminus U} a_i \le d_2,$$

which implies that

$$q + \sum_{i \in U} a_i + (H+1) \sum_{i \in Q \setminus U} a_i = q + A + H \sum_{i \in Q \setminus U} a_i$$

$$\le q + B + (H+1)(A-B).$$

Thus, $\sum_{i \in Q \setminus U} a_i \le A - B$, i.e.,

$$\sum_{i \in U} a_i \ge B. \tag{3.20}$$

From (3.19) and (3.20), we have $\sum_{i \in U} a_i = B$, and hence U is a solution to SS. $\square$

92   3 Integrated Production and Outbound Distribution Scheduling: Offline Problems

Remark 3.2 Since in the proof of Theorem 3.10, the constructed instance of problem $1||V(\infty, c), direct|k|L_{\max} + TC$ involves three jobs for each customer, this proof still works if in this instance the vehicle capacity c is changed to any number greater than 3. Thus the proof also works for problem $1||V(\infty, \infty), direct|k|L_{\max} + TC$, and hence this problem is also at least ordinarily NP-hard.

3.5.1.2 DP Algorithm

We describe the dynamic programming algorithm of Hall and Potts (2003) for problem $1||V(\infty, \infty), direct|k|L_{\max} + TC$. Their algorithm is based on a straightforward property of this problem: There is an optimal schedule where (i) the jobs from each customer are processed in EDD order, and (ii) the jobs delivered in a shipment are processed consecutively, and the departure time of the shipment is equal to the completion time of the last job in this shipment.

Algorithm A3.9

Initialization Reindex the jobs of each customer in EDD order.

Value Function
$F(j_1, \ldots, j_k; h_1, \ldots, h_k)$ = the minimum value of the maximum lateness in a partial schedule that processes the first j_i jobs of each customer i, i.e., jobs $(i, 1), \ldots, (i, j_i)$, and delivers them using h_i shipments, for $i = 1, \ldots, k$.

Boundary Condition
$F(0, \ldots, 0; 0, \ldots, 0) = -\infty$.

Optimal Solution Value
$\min_{h_1, \cdots, h_k} \left\{ F(n_1, \ldots, n_k; h_1, \ldots, h_k) + \sum_{i=1}^{k} f_i h_i \right\}$, where the minimization is over $1 \leq h_i \leq n_i$ for $i = 1, \ldots, k$.

Recurrence Relation
For $j_i = 0, 1, \ldots, n_i$ and $h_i = 0, 1, \ldots, j_i, i = 1, \ldots, k$:

$$F(j_1, \ldots, j_k; h_1, \ldots, h_k) = \min_{\substack{i=1,\ldots,k; \\ \min\{j_i,1\} \leq l_i \leq j_i}}$$

$$\left\{ \max \left\{ G_i(l_i), \sum_{i=1}^{k} \sum_{u=1}^{j_i} p_{iu} + t_i - d_{i,l_i} \right\} \right\},$$

where $G_i(l_i) = F(j_1, \ldots, j_{i-1}, l_i - 1, j_{i+1}, \ldots, j_k; h_1, \ldots, h_{i-1}, h_i - 1, h_{i+1}, \ldots, h_k)$.

The recurrence relation in the above algorithm compares the cost of having the current last $j_i - l_i + 1$ jobs from customer i, i.e., $(i, l_i), \ldots, (i, j_i)$, as the last

3.5 Problems with Batch Delivery to Multiple Customers 93

shipment, for $i = 1, \ldots, k$. Hall and Potts (2003) show that this algorithm solves problem $1||V(\infty, \infty), direct|k|L_{\max} + TC$ to optimality in $O(n^{2k+1})$ time.

3.5.1.3 Heuristic

Finally, we discuss the heuristic by Pundoor and Chen (2005) for problem $1||V(\infty, c), direct|k|L_{\max} + TC$. We first define some new terms. The *shipping due date* of job (i, j), denoted as d'_{ij}, is defined as $d'_{ij} = d_{ij} - t_i$, which is the latest time that the shipment containing this job must leave the plant in order for the shipment to arrive at its destination by this job's due date. We define the *SEDD sequence* for a given set of jobs as the nondecreasing order of their shipping due dates, where in defining SEDD, in case of a tie, we arrange the jobs in nondecreasing order of their processing times. If both the shipping due dates and the processing times are the same, we then arrange them by their customer index, followed by their job index. Clearly, the above tie-breaking rule defines a unique SEDD sequence for a given set of jobs. Also, in the SEDD sequence, jobs from the same customer are sequenced in EDD order.

The heuristic of Pundoor and Chen (2005) is based on an optimality property of the problem, which is described below.

Lemma 3.9 *There exists an optimal schedule for problem* $1||V(\infty, c), direct|k|L_{\max} + TC$ *where*

(i) *The jobs that are delivered in the same shipment are processed consecutively in EDD sequence.*

(ii) *The first job from each shipment together forms an SEDD sequence.*

(iii) *For any given shipment, let u denote the first job processed in this batch. All the jobs that come before u in the SEDD sequence for all the jobs are processed before this batch of jobs.*

The heuristic generates a schedule that satisfies the properties in Lemma 3.9 by (i) first solving a single-customer *auxiliary problem* for each customer independently in such a way that the contribution due to the other customers is taken care of indirectly, and (ii) then combining the schedules for individual customers to obtain a single schedule.

The single-customer auxiliary problem for customer $i \in K$, denoted as AUX_i, is defined as follows: Schedule the processing and delivery of the jobs from N_i subject to the following two constraints:

(i) The jobs are processed in EDD order on the machine.

(ii) The departure time of each delivery shipment B containing (i, j) as the first job is required to be the sum of C_{ij}^{SEDD} and the total processing time of the remaining jobs in the batch, i.e., $\sum_{(i,u)\in B} p_{iu} - p_{ij}$, where C_{ij}^{SEDD} is the completion time of job (i, j) when all the jobs in N are processed in SEDD sequence.

94 3 Integrated Production and Outbound Distribution Scheduling: Offline Problems

The objective of problem AUX_i is to minimize the maximum delivery lateness of the jobs given that the jobs are delivered in a pre-specified number of batches. Due to constraint (ii), a feasible schedule to AUX_i may contain idle time between the processing of the last job in one batch and the first job in the next batch.

Each auxiliary problem AUX_i can be solved to optimality by the following dynamic programming algorithm.

Algorithm A3.10

Value Function $F(j, m)$ is the minimum maximum delivery lateness for the first j jobs $\{(i, 1), (i, 2), \ldots, (i, j)\}$ when they are delivered in m shipments.

Boundary Condition $F(0, 0) = 0$.

Recurrence Relation For $j = 1, \ldots, n_i$, and $m = \lceil j/c \rceil, \ldots, j$,

$$F(j, m) = \min_{1 \le q \le \min\{c, j\}} \left\{ \max \left\{ F(j - q, m - 1), \right. \right.$$

$$\left. \left. \max \left(0, C_{i, j-q+1}^{SEDD} + \sum_{u=j-q+2}^{j} p_{iu} + t_i - d_{i, j-q+1} \right) \right\} \right\}.$$

Optimal Solutions For any $m = \lceil n_i/c \rceil, \ldots, n_i$, $F(n_i, m)$ is the minimum maximum lateness for AUX_i when the jobs of customer i are delivered in m shipments.

In the recurrence relation of the above algorithm, the current last delivery shipment contains q jobs $(i, j - q + 1), \ldots, (i, j)$, and all possible values of q, $1 \le q \le \min\{c, j\}$, are considered. The second max operator calculates the maximum lateness of the jobs in the current last shipment.

Let $L_{max}^i(m)$ be the optimal maximum lateness and $\Lambda_i(m)$ denote the corresponding batch configurations in the optimal solution of AUX_i with m delivery shipments. Let $\Gamma_i = \{L_{max}^i(m) | m = \lceil n_i/c \rceil, \ldots, n_i\}$, and $\Gamma = \Gamma_1 \cup \Gamma_2 \cup \cdots \cup \Gamma_k$. Then, $|\Gamma| \le \sum_{i=1}^{k} (n_i - \lceil n_i/c \rceil + 1)$.

Next, we present the heuristic of Pundoor and Chen (2005) for problem $1||V(\infty, c), direct|k|L_{max} + TC$.

Heuristic H3.3

Step 1: Create an auxiliary problem AUX_i, as described above, for each customer $i \in K$. Solve AUX_i by the above Algorithm A3.10, for all $i \in K$.

Step 2: For each value $x \in \Gamma$, and each customer $i \in K$, define $m_i(x)$ to be the minimum number of shipments $m \in \{\lceil n_i/c \rceil, \ldots, n_i\}$ that satisfies $L_{max}^i(m) \le x$. If such an m does not exist, then define $m_i(x) = \infty$. Find $x^* \in \Gamma$ such that

$$x^* + \sum_{i \in K} f_i m_i(x^*) = \min_{x \in \Gamma} \left\{ x + \sum_{i \in K} f_i m_i(x) \right\}. \tag{3.21}$$

3.5 Problems with Batch Delivery to Multiple Customers

With x^* thus identified, for each customer $i \in K$, the corresponding number of delivery shipments $m_i(x^*)$ and the corresponding batch configurations $\Lambda_i(m_i(x^*))$ in the optimal solution of AUX_i with $m_i(x^*)$ delivery shipments are all known.

Step 3: Sequence all the batches of jobs determined by the batch configurations $\{\Lambda_i(m_i(x*))|i \in K\}$ obtained in Step 2 such that the first job from each of these batches together forms an SEDD sequence. This gives a feasible schedule π for the original problem. Calculate the objective value of π.

We note that in Step 2, the selected value of maximum lateness x^* optimizes the overall objective when each customer is considered separately. The schedule π generated in Step 3 satisfies the properties of Lemma 3.9.

Pundoor and Chen (2005) show that the overall complexity of Heuristic H3.3 is $O(n^2 c + nk \log n)$, and that the heuristic is asymptotically optimal for problem $1||V(\infty, c), direct|k|L_{\max} + TC$ as n goes to infinity, with k and c fixed.

They also conduct computational tests by comparing the solutions generated by the heuristic and lower bounds generated by solving the LP relaxation of an integer programming formulation of the problem. They use randomly generated test instances with a relatively small size involving 20, 30, or 40 jobs, 2 or 4 customers, and a vehicle capacity 2 or 4. The heuristic solves every test problem within 1 CPU second. The average gap between the objective value generated by the heuristic and the lower bound is less than 5%.

We give a numerical example below to illustrate the steps of Heuristic H3.3.

Example 3.10 (Application of Heuristic H3.3) Consider an instance of problem $1||V(\infty, c), direct|k|L_{\max} + TC$ with 5 jobs and 2 customers. The problem parameters are given as $n_1 = 3, n_2 = 2, c = 2, t_1 = 3, t_2 = 5, f_1 = 1, f_2 = 1.5$, and the processing times p_{ij}, due dates d_{ij}, and shipping due dates d'_{ij} shown in the following table, where the jobs from each customer are indexed in EDD order. The SEDD sequence of all the jobs together is $((1, 1), (2, 1), (1, 2), (2, 2), (1, 3))$ with $C_{11}^{SEDD} = 4, C_{21}^{SEDD} = 7, C_{12}^{SEDD} = 8, C_{22}^{SEDD} = 10, C_{13}^{SEDD} = 12$.

Job (i, j)	(1, 1)	(1, 2)	(1, 3)	(2, 1)	(2, 2)
p_{ij}	4	1	2	3	2
d_{ij}	3	6	12	7	9
d'_{ij}	0	3	9	2	4

Step 1: For each customer $i = 1, 2$, solve the auxiliary problem AUX_i using Algorithm A3.7 as follows. Since it is a small instance, we can simply enumerate all possible delivery batches that can be involved in AUX_i.

For AUX_1, there can be either 2 or 3 batches (i.e., $m \in \{2, 3\}$). When $m = 2$, there are two possible batch formations, $B_1 = \{(1, 1), (1, 2)\}, B_2 = \{(1, 3)\}$ or $B_1 = \{(1, 1)\}, B_2 = \{(1, 2), (1, 3)\}$. Let $L_{\max}(B)$ denote the maximum lateness of the jobs in a given batch B. Based on how the departure time of a batch is defined for the auxiliary problem, it can be calculated that in the first case of batch formation, $L_{max}(B_1) = \max(0, C_{11}^{SEDD} + p_{12} + t_1 - d_{11}) = 5$, and $L_{max}(B_2) = \max(0, C_{13}^{SEDD} + t_1 - d_{13}) = 3$, which means that the maximum lateness of all the jobs together is 5. Similarly, in the second case of batch formation, $L_{max}(B_1) = \max(0, C_{11}^{SEDD} + t_1 - d_{11}) = 4$, and $L_{max}(B_2) = \max(0, C_{12}^{SEDD} + p_{13} + t_1 - d_{12}) = 7$, which means that the maximum lateness of all the jobs together is 7. Thus, the first case of batch formation is optimal for AUX_1 with $m = 2$, and the associated maximum lateness is 5.

For AUX_1, when $m = 3$, there is only one possible batch formation, $B_1 = \{(1, 1)\}$, $B_2 = \{(1, 2)\}$, $B_3 = \{(1, 3)\}$. It can be calculated that $L_{max}(B_1) = 4$, $L_{max}(B_2) = 5$, and $L_{max}(B_3) = 3$, which means that the maximum lateness of all the jobs together is 5.

For AUX_2, there can be 1 or 2 batches, i.e., $m \in \{1, 2\}$. When $m = 1$, the only possible batch formation is $B = \{(2, 1), (2, 2)\}$ with $L_{max(B)} = \max\{0, C_{21}^{SEDD} + p_{22} + t_2 - d_{21}\} = 7$. When $m = 2$, the only possible batch formation is $B_1 = \{(2, 1)\}$, $B_2 = \{(2, 2)\}$ with $L_{max}(B_1) = 5$ and $L_{max}(B_2) = 6$, which means that the maximum lateness of all the jobs together is 6.

Step 2: $\Gamma = \{5, 6, 7\}$. It can be seen from the results derived above that for $x = 5$, $m_1(x) = 2$ and $m_2(x) = \infty$; for $x = 6$, $m_1(x) = 2$ and $m_2(x) = 2$; and for $x = 7$, $m_1(x) = 2$ and $m_2(x) = 1$. By (3.21), we find that $x^* = 7$ with $x^* + \sum_{i=1}^{2} f_i m_i(x^*) = 10.5$, and the corresponding batch formation consisting of $\{(1, 1), (1, 2)\}, \{(2, 1), (2, 2)\}, \{(1, 3)\}$ is used.

Step 3: Schedule the batches generated in Step 2 so that the first jobs in them follow an SEDD sequence. This gives the final sequence of the jobs on the machine: $(1, 1), (1, 2), (2, 1), (2, 2), (1, 3)$, which are delivered in batches as specified in Step 2. This is the final solution generated by the heuristic for the given instance. This solution has $L_{max} = 8$ and a total cost of $8 + 2f_1 + f_2 = 11.5$.

It can be verified that an optimal solution for this example is the following: Use the same sequence to process the jobs as in Step 3, but use four delivery batches instead as follows: $\{(1, 1), (1, 2)\}, \{(2, 1)\}, \{(2, 2)\}, \{(1, 3)\}$. This solution gives $L_{max} = 6$ and a total cost of $6 + 2f_1 + 2f_2 = 11$.

3.5.2 Parallel-Machine Total Delivery Time and Transportation Cost Problem with Routing

In this section, we consider problem $P_m||V(\infty, c), routing|k| \sum D_j + TC$, where because the delivery method of "routing" is used, jobs from different customers can be delivered together in a shipment. This problem with a fixed number of customers k is at least ordinarily NP-hard because when $k = 1$, it is already ordinarily NP-hard, as discussed in Sect. 3.4.4. When the number of customers k is arbitrary, however, this problem becomes strongly NP-hard because it contains the strongly NP-hard traveling salesman problem as a special case. Whether this problem with a fixed k is strongly NP-hard or not is apparently an open question.

3.5 Problems with Batch Delivery to Multiple Customers 97

Chen and Vairaktarakis (2005) propose a heuristic for this problem with a running time that is exponential in k and worst-case performance ratio of $2 - 1/m$. The idea of the heuristic is similar to Heuristic H3.2 presented in Sect. 3.4.4 for the special case of the problem with one customer, i.e., $P_m||V(\infty, c), direct|1|\sum D_j + TC$. The heuristic starts with an auxiliary single-machine problem, solves it by a dynamic programming algorithm, and transforms the solution for this problem into a feasible solution for the parallel-machine problem under study. Below, we discuss how the auxiliary problem is defined and solved. The rest of the heuristic is exactly the same as H3.2 described in Sect. 3.4.4 and hence is not discussed.

We first consider the single-machine case of the problem, i.e., $1||V(\infty, c), routing|k|\sum D_j + TC$. It can be shown that there exists an optimal schedule for the problem where the jobs from each customer are processed in SPT order on the machine. However, on each machine, the jobs of different customers do not necessarily form an SPT order.

Algorithm A3.11

Initialization Reindex the jobs in N_i from each customer $i \in K$ as $(i, 1), \ldots, (i, n_i)$ such that $p_{i,1} \leq \cdots \leq p_{i,n_i}$. Define set $Q_{ih} = \{(i, 1), \ldots, (i, h)\}$, and $R_{iuv} = Q_{iv} \setminus Q_{i,v-u} = \{(i, v-u+1), (i, v-u+2), \ldots, (i, v)\}$, and parameter $P_{ih} = \sum_{l=1}^{h} p_{il}$ for $h = 1, \ldots, n_i, v = u, \ldots, n_i, u = 1, \ldots, c$, and $i \in K$.

Value Function $F(j_1, \ldots, j_k)$ is the minimum objective value of a schedule for the $j_1 + \cdots + j_k$ jobs from $\cup_{i=1}^{k} Q_{i,j_i}$. In addition, define
$t_i(\tau, X) =$ the time needed to reach customer i from the plant in a given route τ covering all the customers associated with the jobs in the set X.
$g(\tau, q_1, \ldots, q_k) =$ the total transportation cost of a given route τ, which delivers q_u jobs to customer u for $u = 1, \ldots, k$ [hence route τ visits all the customers u with $q_u \geq 1$].

Initial Condition $F(0, \ldots, 0) = 0$.

Recurrence Relation For $j_i = 0, 1, \ldots, n_i; i = 1, 2, \ldots, k$.

$$F(j_1, \ldots, j_k) = \min_{q_1,\ldots,q_k;\tau} \left\{ F(j_1 - q_1, \ldots, j_k - q_k) \right.$$

$$+ \sum_{i \in K} q_i \left(\sum_{l \in K} P_{l,j_l} + t_i(\tau, \cup_{l \in K} R_{l,q_l,j_l}) \right) + g(\tau, q_1, \ldots, q_k)$$

$$\left. \mid q_i \leq j_i \text{ for } i \in K \text{ and } 1 \leq \sum_{i \in K} q_i \leq c; \tau \in \mathscr{T}(\cup_{l \in K} R_{l,q_l,j_l}) \right\},$$

where $\mathscr{T}(\cup_{l \in K} R_{l,q_l,j_l})$ is the set of all possible routes covering all the customers associated with the jobs in $\cup_{l \in K} R_{l,q_l,j_l}$.

Optimal Solution Value $F(n_1, \ldots, v_k)$.

98　　3　Integrated Production and Outbound Distribution Scheduling: Offline Problems

Chen and Vairaktarakis (2005) show that Algorithm A3.11 finds an optimal schedule for problem $1||V(\infty, c), routing|k| \sum D_j + TC$ in $O(n^k c^k k^{k-1})$ time. When k is fixed, this algorithm has a polynomial time complexity.

The auxiliary problem used in the heuristic given in Chen and Vairaktarakis (2005) for problem $P_m||V(\infty, c), routing|k| \sum D_j + TC$ is defined in exactly the same way as the auxiliary problem used in Heuristic H3.2 described in Sect. 3.4.4: Find a way to partition the job set N into subsets $S_1, S_2, \ldots$ such that the number of jobs in each subset S_q is no more than c, and deliver each subset of jobs S_q in one shipment with departure time d_q equal to the maximum between (i) $\max\{p_j | j \in S_1 \cup \ldots \cup S_q\}$, and (ii) $\sum_{j \in S_1 \cup \ldots \cup S_q} p_j / m$, so as to minimize the objective function $\sum D_j + TC$.

Remark 3.3 It can be seen that this auxiliary problem is the same as the single-machine problem $1||V(\infty, c), direct|k| \sum D_j + TC$, except that the departure time of a shipment is calculated as the maximum of (i) and (ii) in the earlier problem, whereas it is the completion time of the job completed last in a shipment in the latter problem.

Chen and Vairaktarakis (2005) show that the auxiliary problem can be solved by a modified version of Algorithm A3.11, where the recurrence relation is replaced by the recurrence relation below:

$$
\begin{aligned}
F(j_1, \ldots, j_k) = \min_{q_1, \ldots, q_k; \tau} \Bigg\{ & F(j_1 - q_1, \ldots, j_k - q_k) \\
& + \sum_{i \in K} q_i \Bigg[\max \Big\{ \max\{p_{l, j_l} | l = 1, \ldots, k\}, \sum_{l \in K} P_{l, j_l} / m \Big\} \\
& + t_i(\tau, \cup_{l=1}^{k} R_{l, q_l, j_l}) \Bigg] \\
& + g(\tau, q_1, \ldots, q_k) \\
& \Big| \ q_i \le j_i \text{ for } i \in K \text{ and } 1 \le \textstyle\sum_{i \in K} q_i \le c; \tau \in \mathscr{T}(\cup_{l \in K} R_{l, q_l, j_l}) \Bigg\}.
\end{aligned}
$$

The computational tests conducted by Chen and Vairaktarakis (2005) show that their heuristic can generate near-optimal solutions. However, the computational time taken by the heuristic is quite sensitive to the number of customers k. When $k \le 3$, the heuristic can solve instances with up to 160 jobs quickly. When $k = 4$ or 5, the heuristic can generate solutions for instances with up to 80 jobs in a reasonable amount of time.

Chen and Vairaktarakis (2005) also study the value of production-distribution integration by comparing the integrated approach reflected in problem $P_m||V(\infty, c), direct|k| \sum D_j + TC$ where production and distribution scheduling are considered jointly, with a typical sequential approach that considers production and distribution scheduling sequentially. The *value of integration* is defined as the relative improvement of the objective value from the sequential approach to the inte-

3.5 Problems with Batch Delivery to Multiple Customers 99

grated approach. In a typical sequential approach (SA), the production part assumes that each job $j \in N_i$ once completed is delivered to its customer immediately, i.e., $D_j = C_j + t_i$, and minimizes the total delivery time $\sum D_j$ (equivalently, minimizing $\sum C_j$) without considering how jobs are actually delivered. The distribution part in this approach minimizes the total transportation cost TC given the production schedule generated from the production part. This is a vehicle routing problem which can be solved by a modified version of Algorithm A3.11 described above, where the value function $V(j_1, \cdots, j_k)$ is redefined as the total transportation cost of the jobs involved, and the recurrence relation is revised as

$$F(j_1, \ldots, j_k) = \min_{q_1, \ldots, q_k; \tau} \left\{ F(j_1 - q_1, \ldots, j_k - q_k) + g(\tau, q_1, \ldots, q_k) \right.$$

$$\left. | \; q_i \leq j_i \text{ for } i \in K \text{ and } 1 \leq \sum_{i \in K} q_i \leq c; \tau \in \mathscr{T}(\cup_{l \in K} R_{l, q_l, j_l}) \right\}.$$

The computational results in Chen and Vairaktarakis (2005) show that (i) the value of integration is more than 5% for most of the test instances and more than 10% for many test instances with $k \geq 4$, and (ii) the value of integration increases with the number of customers k and vehicle capacity c.

3.5.3 Problems with a Limited Number of Vehicles and Direct Shipping

In this section, we consider problems $1||V(v, c), direct|k|D_{max}$ and $1||V(v, c), direct|k|\sum D_j$. We first describe some optimality properties of these problems in the following lemma. Some of the properties are proved by Chen (2010) and the rest are straightforward. Hence, we do not give proofs.

Lemma 3.10

(i) *For problems $1||V(v, c), direct|k|D_{max}$ and $1||V(v, c), direct|k|\sum D_j$, there exists an optimal schedule where (1) the jobs from each customer are processed in nondecreasing sequence of their processing times (call such a sequence a customer-SPT sequence), (2) jobs delivered in the same shipment are processed consecutively, and (3) a shipment containing jobs completed earlier departs no later than a shipment containing jobs completed later.*

(ii) *For problem $1||V(v, c), direct|k|D_{max}$, the jobs from each customer $i \in K$ are delivered in $e_i = \lceil n_i/c \rceil$ shipments, where if n_i/c is not an integer, then the first shipment contains $u_i = n_i - (e_i - 1)c$ jobs and every other shipment contains c jobs, and otherwise, every shipment contains c jobs.*

We first focus on problem $1||V(v, c), direct|k|D_{max}$. Different cases of the problem $1||V(v, c), direct|k|D_{max}$ may have different tractability. As shown in Sect. 3.4.5, the problem with a single customer (i.e., $k = 1$) is solvable in $O(n \log n)$ time. Chen (2010) shows that (i) the problem with a single vehicle and an arbitrary number of customers, i.e., $1||V(1, c), direct|k|D_{\max}$ is solvable in polynomial time, and (ii) the problem with at least two vehicles $v \geq 2$ and an arbitrary number of customers is strongly NP-hard. Below, we show that this problem with an arbitrary number of vehicles and a fixed number of customers can be solved in polynomial time.

We briefly describe how the problem $1||V(v, c), direct|k|D_{\max}$ with a fixed k can be solved in polynomial time. By Lemma 3.10, we can batch the n jobs into e shipments, where $e = e_1 + \cdots + e_k$, and by treating each of the e batches as a single combined job, the problem can then be viewed as equivalent to $1||V(v, 1), direct|k|D_{\max}$. In this equivalent problem $1||V(v, 1), direct|k|D_{\max}$, there are e_i combined jobs from each customer $i \in K$, where the processing time of a combined job (i, j) is equal to the total processing time of the corresponding individual jobs, and is denoted as P_{ij}. Thus, in the following, we focus on solving problem $1||V(v, 1), direct|k|D_{\max}$, where there are e_i jobs from each customer $i \in K$, and the total number of jobs is $e = e_1 + \cdots + e_k$.

Applying Lemma 3.10 to problem $1||V(v, 1), direct|k|D_{\max}$, we can see that in an optimal solution the jobs are processed in customer-SPT sequence. Reindex the jobs of each customer in SPT order. We observe that there are at most e^k different schedules for processing the e jobs in the problem that are customer-SPT sequences. By Lemma 3.10, we observe that to find an optimal solution for problem $1||V(v, 1), direct|k|D_{\max}$, we can enumerate all possible customer-SPT sequences for processing jobs, and for the job processing schedule corresponding to each such sequence, use a delivery schedule that satisfies Property (i)(3) of the lemma. Furthermore, we observe that given any job processing sequence, the following delivery schedule is optimal among those that satisfy Property (i)(3) of the lemma: Whenever a job completes processing, if there is at least one vehicle waiting at the plant, assign it to any such vehicle; if there is no vehicle available at the plant, assign it to the next returning vehicle. For any given processing schedule, it takes $O(ev)$ time to create such a delivery schedule.

The overall procedure provided above for solving problem $1||V(v, c), direct|k|D_{\max}$ has a time complexity $O(e^k + ev) = O((n/c)^k + nv/c)$, which is polynomial in v, but exponential in k.

Next, we consider problem $1||V(v, c), direct|k|\sum D_j$. The complexity spectrum of the various cases of this problem is as follows. As shown in Sect. 3.4.5, when there is a single customer ($k = 1$), the problem with a fixed number of vehicles is solvable in polynomial time, and the problem with an arbitrary v is open. When there are multiple customers ($k \geq 2$), the problem with a single vehicle (i.e., $1||V(1, c), direct|k|\sum D_j$) is polynomially solvable if k is fixed (Li et al., 2005a), and strongly NP-hard if k is arbitrary (Chen, 2010). For problem $1||V(v, c), direct|k|\sum D_j$, we show below that when both k and v are fixed, a polynomial time algorithm can be constructed for the problem by applying the ideas of Li et al. (2005a) for their problem $1||V(1, c), direct|k|\sum D_j$, and Algorithm A3.8 given in Sect. 3.4.5 for problem $1||V(v, c), direct|1|\sum D_j$. However, to our knowledge, the complexity of this problem remains open when either k or v or both are arbitrary.

3.5 Problems with Batch Delivery to Multiple Customers

By Lemma 3.10, for problem $1||V(v, c), direct|k| \sum D_j$, we only consider processing schedules that are customer-SPT sequences. In any schedule that is a customer-SPT sequence, the completion time of any job can be expressed as $\sum_{i=1}^{k} \sum_{j=1}^{x_i} p_{ij}$, for some $(x_1, \ldots, x_k)$ with $0 \leq x_i \leq n_i$ for $i = 1, \ldots, k$. Thus, there are at most $\prod_{i=1}^{k} (n_i + 1) \leq n^k$ different values of job completion times. Let the set of these different values of job completion times be Γ. Following the discussion in Sect. 3.4.5 and the idea of Procedure DepTime given there, we observe that a vehicle can depart at any possible job completion time $C_{ij} \in \Gamma$ and any possible return time after it completes consecutive round-trips without any idle time, i.e., $C_{ij} + \sum_{l=1}^{k} 2y_l t_l$, for some $y_1, \ldots, y_k$ with $y_1 + \cdots + y_k \leq n$. Then, corresponding to each $C_{ij} \in \Gamma$, there are at most n^k possible departure times. Thus, the total number of possible departure times of a shipment is no more than n^{2k}. Let Ω be the set of all possible departure times of a shipment.

By a similar idea to Algorithm A3.8, which is given in Sect. 3.4.5 for problem $1||V(v, c), direct|1| \sum D_j$, problem $1||V(v, c), direct|k| \sum D_j$ can be solved by the following dynamic programming algorithm.

Algorithm A3.12

Initialization Reindex the jobs of each customer in SPT order. Calculate possible departure times as discussed above.

Value Function Define $F(j_1, \ldots, j_k; s_1, \ldots, s_v; r_1, \ldots, r_v)$ to be the minimum total delivery time of a partial schedule containing the first j_i jobs of each customer i, i.e., jobs $(i, 1), \ldots, (i, j_i)$ for $i = 1, \ldots, k$, provided that the v vehicles last depart from the plant at times $\tau_1, \ldots, \tau_v$, and going to customers $r_1, \ldots, r_v$, respectively, where $\tau_l \in \Omega$ and $r_l \in K$, for $l = 1, \ldots, v$.

Boundary Conditions
$F(0, \ldots, 0; 0, \ldots, 0; 0, \ldots, 0) = 0;$
$\quad F(j_1, \ldots, j_k; \tau_1, \ldots, \tau_v; r_1, \ldots, r_v) = \infty$ for any state satisfying one of the following:

(a) $\max_{1 \leq l \leq v} \{\tau_l\} < \sum_{i \in K} \sum_{x=1}^{j_i} p_{ix}$.
(b) for every $1 \leq l \leq v$ with $s_l = \max_{1 \leq u \leq v} \{s_u\}$, $j_{r_l} = 0$.

Recurrence Relation
For $j_i = 0, \ldots, n_i$ for $i = 1, \ldots, k$, and $\tau_l \in \Omega$ and $r_l \in K$ for $l = 1, \ldots, v$:

$$F(j_1, \ldots, j_k; \tau_1, \ldots, \tau_v; r_1, \ldots, r_v)$$

$$= \min_{i \in I; \ 1 \leq h_i \leq \min\{c, j_i\}} \left\{ F(j_1, \ldots, j_{i-1}, j_i - h_i, j_{i+1}, j_k; \right.$$

$$\tau_1', \ldots, \tau_v'; r_1', \ldots, r_v') + h_i(t_i + \tau_{\delta_i})$$

$$\left. | \ \tau_1', \ldots, \tau_v' \text{ and } r_1', \ldots, r_v' \text{ satisfy the conditions (i) and (ii) described below} \right\},$$

where I is the set consisting of every customer $i \in K$ that satisfies the following: There is a vehicle, denoted as $\delta_i \in \{1, \ldots, v\}$, such that $r_{\delta_i} = i$, $s_{\delta_i} = \max_{1 \le u \le v}\{s_u\}$, and $s_{\delta_i} \ge \sum_{i \in K} \sum_{x=1}^{j_i} p_{ix}$. [i.e., vehicle δ_i departs at the latest time currently, its departure time is no earlier than the completion time of the current last job, and is going to customer i]. The two conditions (i) and (ii) involved in the recurrence relation are

(i) $\tau'_l = \tau_l$ and $r'_l = r_l$ for $l = 1, \ldots, \delta_i - 1, \delta_i + 1, \ldots, v$,
(ii) $\tau'_{\delta_i} \in \Omega$ with $\tau'_{\delta_i} + 2t_{r'_{\delta_i}} \le \tau_{\delta_i}$, and $r'_{\delta_i} \in \{1, \ldots, k\}$.

Optimal Solution Value $\min\{F(n_1, \ldots, n_k; \tau_1, \ldots, \tau_v; r_1, \ldots, r_v)\}$ over all possible $\tau_1, \ldots, \tau_v$ and $r_1, \ldots, r_v$ with $\tau_l \in \Omega$ and $r_l \in K$.

Theorem 3.11 *Algorithm A3.12 solves problem $1||V(v,c), direct|k|\sum D_j$ to optimality in $O(ck^{v+2}n^{(2v+3)k})$ time.*

Proof We provide a sketch of the proof. The optimality of the above algorithm is quite straightforward. The recurrence relation considers every possible configuration of the last shipment in the current partial schedule. The last shipment can be for jobs from any customer $i \in I$ with a size varying from 1 to $\min\{c, j_i\}$. The two conditions (i) and (ii) ensure the feasibility of the vehicle departure times and their destinations when transitioning from state $(\tau'_1, \ldots, \tau'_v; r'_1, \ldots, r'_v)$ to state $(\tau_1, \ldots, \tau_v; r_1, \ldots, r_v)$.

In the algorithm, there are $O(n^k)$ combinations of $(j_1, \ldots, j_k)$, $O(n^{2kv})$ combinations of $(\tau_1, \ldots, \tau_v)$, and $O(k^v)$ combinations of $(r_1, \ldots, r_v)$. Thus, there are a total of $O(n^k n^{2kv} k^v) = O(n^{(2v+1)k} k^v)$ possible states. To calculate the value of each state, the recurrence relation is run over $O(kc)$ possible combinations of i and h_i, and for each such combination, $O(|\Omega|k)$ possibilities of $(\tau'_{\delta_i}, r'_{\delta_i})$ are considered. Thus, the computation time for each state is $O(kcn^{2k}k) = O(ck^2n^{2k})$. Therefore, the overall time complexity of the algorithm is $O(ck^{v+2}n^{(2v+3)k})$. $\square$

3.6 Problems with Fixed Delivery Departure Dates

Problems with fixed delivery departure dates arise in applications where delivery vehicles have fixed departure times such as trains, liner ships, and air flights, and in applications where delivery is carried out by logistics service providers that pick up orders at preannounced times, e.g., 10:00 a.m. and 3:00 p.m. every weekday (e.g., Hall et al., 2001; Leung & Chen, 2013; Stecke & Zhao, 2007). Problems with fixed delivery departure dates can be classified generally into two classes: (1) problems with *homogeneous vehicles* where to reach a given customer destination, all the vehicles have the same travel time and incur the same cost, and (2) problems with *heterogeneous vehicles* where to reach a given customer destination, different vehicles may have different travel times and travel costs. We discuss several representative problems in each class in Sects. 3.6.1 and 3.6.2, respectively.

3.6.1 Problems with Homogeneous Vehicles

We consider several problems with a single machine, a single customer, and a finite number of homogeneous vehicles. They can all be represented as $1||V(v, c), fdep|1|\gamma$, where $\gamma \in \{f(D), f(D)+TC\}$ and $f(D)$ is a nondecreasing function of $D = (D_1, \ldots, D_n)$.

Before we discuss any specific problem, we first define some additional notation unique to this class of problems. In these problems, we let h ($h \leq v$) denote the number of distinct fixed vehicle departure times, let $T_1, \ldots, T_h$ be these departure times with $T_1 < \cdots < T_h$, and let $v_1, \ldots, v_h$ be the number of vehicles that depart at these departure times, respectively, where $v = v_1 + \cdots + v_h$ is the total number of vehicles available. Each vehicle can deliver up to c jobs. All the vehicles are homogeneous in terms of their travel time and cost. We use t and f to denote the transportation time and cost of a delivery shipment between the plant and the customer, respectively. Without loss of generality, we assume that $T_h \geq P = \sum_{j \in N} p_j$. Without this assumption, not all jobs can be delivered and hence the problem is infeasible. However, the problem could still be infeasible even if $T_h \geq P$. The following simple two-step procedure can be used to check the feasibility of these problems:

Feasibility Check for Problems $1||V(v, c), fdep|1|\gamma$
Step 1: Process the jobs on the single machine in SPT sequence.
Step 2: For $i = 1, \ldots, h$, do the following: Let x_i be the number of jobs that have completed processing by time T_i but have not been delivered. Deliver $y_i = \min\{cv_i, x_i\}$ of the x_i jobs by the available vehicles that are to depart at time T_i. If $y_h = x_h$, then the problem is feasible; otherwise, the problem is infeasible.

It is easy to see that under the SPT processing sequence in Step 1, a maximum number of jobs is completed by any point in time. In Step 2, as many jobs as possible are delivered by each departure time. Therefore, this procedure maximizes the total number of jobs that are delivered.

Without loss of generality, we henceforth assume that all the problems considered in this section are feasible. We first present some optimality properties for the class of problems $1||V(v, c), fdep|1|\gamma$, which are given in Chen (2010).

Lemma 3.11 *For any problem $1||V(v, c), fdep|1|\gamma$ that is feasible, where $\gamma \in \{f(D), f(D) + TC\}$ and $f(D)$ is a nondecreasing function of $D = (D_1, \ldots, D_n)$, there exists an optimal schedule satisfying all of the following:*

(i) There is no idle time between the jobs on the machine;
(ii) For each delivery batch, all the jobs in the batch are processed consecutively on the machine;
(iii) Jobs that are processed earlier on the machine are delivered no later than those processed later on the machine;

104 3 Integrated Production and Outbound Distribution Scheduling: Offline Problems

(iv) *At each departure time T_i, for $i = 1, \ldots, h$, all the delivery batches, except possibly one batch, are full; and if a partial batch is delivered at time T_i, then all the jobs completed by T_i are delivered by T_i;*

(v) *For each $i = 1, \ldots, h$, if not all the v_i delivery vehicles with the departure time T_i are used, then there are less than c jobs that complete processing by T_i but are delivered at a later departure time.*

3.6.1.1 Problem $1||V(v, c), fdep|1| \sum D_j + TC$

We first consider problem $1||V(v, c), fdep|1| \sum D_j + TC$. By a pairwise interchange argument, we can show that processing jobs in SPT sequence is optimal. Based on this and the properties in Lemma 3.11, we use the SPT sequence for job processing, and given this sequence, optimally form batches of jobs and assign vehicles to these batches for delivery. Chen (2010) gives the following dynamic programming algorithm.

Algorithm A3.13

Initialization Reindex the jobs such that $p_1 \leq \cdots \leq p_n$. Process the jobs in the order $1, \ldots, n$. For $i = 1, \ldots, h$, let b_i be the number of jobs that have completed processing by time T_i under this processing sequence.

Value Function $F(i, u)$ = the minimum total contribution of the first u jobs $\{1, \ldots, u\}$ to the objective value in a solution satisfying the following two conditions: (1) All these jobs are delivered by vehicles with a departure time no later than T_i, and (2) all the other jobs $\{u + 1, \ldots, n\}$ are delivered by a vehicle with a departure time later than T_i.

Boundary Condition $F(0, 0) = 0$.

Recurrence Relation For $i = 1, \ldots, h$, and $u = 0, \ldots, b_i$:

$$F(i, u) = \min_{y} \left\{ F(i - 1, y) + (u - y)(T_i + t) + \lceil (u - y)/c \rceil f \right.$$

$$\left. | \max(0, u - cv_i) \leq y \leq u, \text{ and } C_y \leq T_{i-1} \right\}$$

Optimal Solution Value $F(h, n)$.

Chen (2010) proves the following theorem.

Theorem 3.12 *If problem $1||V(v, c), fdep|1| \sum D_j + TC$ is feasible, then Algorithm A3.13 solves it optimally in $O(n^2h)$ time.*

Proof For a given state (i, u), let x be the total number of jobs delivered at T_i. Clearly, $0 \leq x \leq \min\{u, cv_i\}$. Let $y = u - x$. Then by Lemma 3.11, the x jobs delivered at T_i are jobs $u, u - 1, \ldots, y + 1$, and the jobs $1, 2, \ldots, y$ are delivered no later than T_{i-1}. The recurrence relation of the algorithm considers all possible

3.6 Problems with Fixed Delivery Departure Dates 105

values of y (ranging from $\max(0, u - cv_i)$ to u), or equivalently all possible values of x ($= 0, \ldots, \min\{u, cv_i\}$). Therefore, all possible cases of x are considered by the recurrence relation. By Lemma 3.11, the number of batches delivered at T_i is $\lceil x/c \rceil = \lceil (u - y)/c \rceil$. The term $(u - y)(T_i + t)$ in the recurrence relation is the total contribution to $\sum D_j$ by the x jobs delivered at T_i, and the term $\lceil (u - y)/c \rceil f$ is the total transportation cost contributed by these jobs. This shows the correctness of the recurrence relation and hence the optimality of the algorithm. Since the number of states in the DP is bounded by hn, and for each state the computational time is bounded by $O(n)$, the overall complexity of the algorithm is $O(n^2 h)$. $\square$

3.6.1.2 Problem $1||V(v, c), fdep|1|L_{\max}$

Next, we consider problem $1||V(v, c), fdep|1|L_{\max}$. We describe the polynomial-time algorithm developed by Leung and Chen (2013) for this problem.

We first consider a related problem, which is to decide whether there is a feasible schedule such that the maximum lateness is less than or equal to a given value g. For a given g, each job $j \in N$ must be completed and delivered by time $d_j - t + g$. Thus, we can convert the due date of each job j to the *departure deadline $\bar{d}_j$*, where $\bar{d}_j$ is defined to be the latest departure time T_k that is less than or equal to $d_j - t + g$. For a given g, the following procedure decides whether there is a feasible schedule where all the jobs are delivered by their departure deadlines.

Procedure LF(g)

1. For each job $j \in N$, define its departure deadline $\bar{d}_i$ as the latest departure time T_k that is less than or equal to $d_j - t + g$.
2. For $i = 1$ to h, let $\mathcal{J}(i) = \{j \in N \mid \bar{d}_j = T_i\}$ be the subset of jobs with a deadline equal to T_i.
3. Let $T_0 = 0$; $\mathcal{J}(0) = \emptyset$; $A = \emptyset$; $T = \sum_{j \in N} p_j$.
4. For $i = h, h - 1, \ldots, 1$, do the following:

   (a) Let A be all the jobs in $\mathcal{J}(i)$, arranged in nondecreasing order of their processing times.
   (b) If $v_i c < |A|$, then take the first $|A| - v_i c$ jobs from A and merge them into $\mathcal{J}(i - 1)$. Update $\mathcal{J}(i - 1)$ and A accordingly. Update $\mathcal{J}(i) = A$.
   (c) Let $\tau = \sum_{j \in \mathcal{J}(i)} p_j$.
   (d) Schedule the jobs in $\mathcal{J}(i)$ from time $T - \tau$ to T, and deliver these jobs by the vehicles available at time T_i.
   (e) Let $T = T - \tau$.
   (f) If $T > T_{i-1}$, then stop; the problem is not feasible.

We briefly describe how the main steps of Procedure **LF**(g) work. In Step 4, we schedule the jobs backwards, starting at time $T = \sum_{j \in N} p_j$. We schedule the jobs in $\mathcal{J}(i), \mathcal{J}(i - 1), \ldots, \mathcal{J}(1)$ in this order. Suppose we are scheduling the jobs in $\mathcal{J}(i)$. We sort the jobs in $\mathcal{J}(i)$ in nondecreasing order of their processing times and assign them to the set A. If there are more than $v_i c$ jobs in A, then the

106   3 Integrated Production and Outbound Distribution Scheduling: Offline Problems

v_i vehicles with the departure time T_i cannot deliver all the jobs in A. In this case, we take the first $|A| - v_i c$ jobs out of A and merge them into $\mathscr{J}(i-1)$; these jobs will be delivered by the vehicles at T_{i-1} or earlier. The remaining jobs in A will be scheduled from time $T - \tau$ until T, and delivered by the vehicles at T_i. In Step 4(e), we decrease T by τ, and in Step 4(f), we check if T is larger that T_{i-1}. If T is larger than T_{i-1}, then there is a job in $\mathscr{J}(i-1)$ that must complete processing after T_{i-1}. This job cannot be delivered by any vehicles at T_{i-1}. Hence, there is no feasible schedule. On the other hand, if T is less than or equal to T_{i-1}, then we proceed to schedule the jobs in $\mathscr{J}(i-1)$.

We repeatedly call Procedure **LF**(g) with different values of g until we obtain the minimum $L_{\max}$. There are only a limited number of different values of g that we need to consider. Since there are only h possible delivery departure times, $T_1, \ldots, T_h$, the lateness of each job j has at most h possible values, $T_1 + t - d_i, \ldots, T_h + t - d_i$. Therefore, the n jobs together have at most hn possible values of $L_{\max}$.

The following algorithm solves problem $1||V(v,c), fdep|1|L_{\max}$.

Algorithm ML
1. Let $k \leq hn$ be the number of possible values of $L_{\max}$, and let these values be a_l, for $l = 1, \ldots, k$. Let the a_l's be sorted in increasing order; i.e., $a_1 < a_2 < \cdots < a_k$.
2. For $l = 1$ to k do the following:

    (a) Call Procedure **LF**(g) with $g = a_l$.
    (b) If the procedure returns a feasible solution, then stop and the optimal $L_{\max}$ is a_l.

Leung and Chen (2013) show that Algorithm **ML** finds an optimal solution for problem $1||V(v,c), fdep|1|L_{\max}$ in $O(h^2 n^2 \log n)$ time.

Leung and Chen (2013) further consider two related problems: (1) The problem of minimizing the total transportation cost (or equivalently the number of vehicles used) subject to the constraint that $L_{\max}$ is minimized, and (2) the problem of minimizing the weighted sum of $L_{\max}$ and the total transportation cost. They provide polynomial-time algorithms for both problems.

3.6.2   Problems with Heterogeneous Vehicles

In this section, we consider several problems with fixed delivery departure times and heterogeneous vehicles. The first problem, discussed in Sect. 3.6.2.1, is commonly faced by make-to-order companies with a so-called commit-to-deliver business model and has been studied by several authors (Stecke & Zhao, 2007; Zhong et al., 2010, and Melo & Wolsey, 2010). Several other problems, discussed in Sect. 3.6.2.2, are motivated by applications where each customer order has a delivery time window within which the order needs to be delivered to the customer and have been studied by Li et al. (2017).

3.6.2.1 Problem $1|\bar{d}_j|V_{het}(\infty, 1), fdep|1|TC$

We first briefly describe the business environment where such a scheduling problem arises. There are two business models that a make-to-order company uses, namely, *commit-to-ship* and *commit-to-deliver* (Stecke & Zhao, 2007). Under the commit-to-ship business model, the company commits to a *shipping date* for each order, which is the date by which the order has completed processing and shipped out. In this case, the company only needs to determine a production schedule based on the committed shipping dates, and the customer of each order needs to choose a shipping mode for order delivery and pay the shipping cost. Under the commit-to-deliver business mode, the company commits to a *delivery date* for each order, which is the date when the order is delivered to its customer. In this case, the company needs to determine both a production schedule and a shipping plan, and pay the shipping cost. In the commit-to-deliver case, if an order is completed early, a slow shipping mode should be chosen to deliver the order in order to minimize the shipping cost. On the other hand, if an order is completed late, a fast shipping mode may have to be used in order to meet the committed delivery due date. Therefore, in a commit-to-deliver situation, it is necessary to schedule production and delivery operations jointly.

In practice, companies often use third-party logistics (3PL) providers to deliver completed orders to customers. A 3PL provider typically offers multiple shipping modes with different shipping time guarantees (e.g., 1 day, 2 days, etc.) and charges a shipping cost for an order that is typically increasing with the order size and decreasing with the shipping time guaranteed. There are usually one or more fixed order pickup time points on each business day. The order pickup time points over a given planning horizon can be viewed as the fixed vehicle departure times, and each available shipping mode at an order pickup time can be viewed as a heterogeneous vehicle which has a distinct shipping time and a shipping cost. In many practical situations, production costs are independent of how orders are scheduled. Also, because completed orders are delivered shortly, inventory holding costs are negligible. Thus, transportation cost is the primary concern. Therefore, by the five-field notation given in Sect. 3.2, the joint production and delivery scheduling problem can be represented as $1|\bar{d}_j|V_{het}(\infty, 1), fdep|1|TC$.

We now define the problem in a way that is consistent with the application background described above. At the beginning of a planning horizon consisting of m days, a manufacturer has accepted n orders $N = \{1, 2, \ldots, n\}$ to be scheduled on a single production line. Each order $i \in N$ requires Q_i units of some products and has a delivery deadline d_i ($2 \le d_i \le m$) promised by the manufacturer. Without loss of generality, we assume that $m = \max\{d_i \mid i \in N\}$. All the products have the same unit weight and the same unit production capacity requirement. The production line can produce up to c units of products daily. We assume that $Q_i \le c$, for $i = 1, 2, \ldots, n$, and $\sum_{i=1}^{n} Q_i > c$.

A 3PL provider picks up the finished orders for shipping at the end of each day in the planning horizon. The manufacturer needs to choose a shipping time for each order to be shipped and pay a corresponding shipping cost to the 3PL. The shipping time that can be chosen varies from 1 day, 2 days, ..., to $m - 1$ days. The cost for shipping an order i with a shipping time of x days is calculated as the following function $G(x, Q_i) = Q_i g(x)$, where $g(x)$ is either a linear decreasing function of x, i.e., $g(x) = \alpha - \beta x$ with $\alpha, \beta > 0$ and $\alpha - \beta(m - 1) > 0$, or a convex decreasing function with $g(m - 1) > 0$. The conditions $\alpha - \beta(m - 1) > 0$ and $g(m - 1) > 0$ ensure that the unit shipping cost of each order is always positive even with the slowest shipping mode possible (i.e., $m - 1$ days of shipping time).

Define $S_j = \{i \in N \mid d_i \leq j + 1\}$, which is the subset of orders that must complete processing by the end of day j in order for them to be delivered no later than their deadlines. To ensure that a feasible schedule exists, we assume that there is enough production capacity, i.e.,

$$\sum_{i \in S_j} Q_i \leq c \cdot j, \quad \text{for } j = 1, 2, \ldots, m - 1. \tag{3.22}$$

Partial delivery may or may not be allowed. If partial delivery is not allowed, then all the units of any order i have to be delivered on the same day when the last unit of the order finishes processing. Otherwise, not all units of an order need to be delivered on the same day.

For ease of presentation, we use the term shipping mode and shipping time interchangeably. For example, we may say that the shipping mode for order i is r_i days, which is equivalent to saying that the shipping time for the order is r_i days.

Remark 3.4 Given that the shipping cost of an order decreases as the shipping time increases, it is optimal for the manufacturer to ship an order or a partial order as soon as possible using the slowest shipping mode possible without violating the promised delivery due date. Thus, if partial delivery is allowed, then if a fraction of order i completes processing on day t_i, this partial order should be shipped out at the end of that day using a shipping mode with the shipping time $r_i = d_i - t_i$ days. If partial delivery is not allowed, then an order should be shipped out at the end of the day when the last unit of the order completes processing, using the slowest possible shipping mode. This means that once a processing sequence of the orders is given, the shipping mode for each order or partial order and the total shipping cost are known, and hence a unique delivery schedule is known. Therefore, the only decision to make is to determine a processing sequence for the orders.

There are four cases of this problem, based on whether the cost function is linear or convex in shipping time and whether partial delivery is allowed. Stecke and Zhao (2007) are the first to study this problem. They show that the problem with partial delivery allowed and convex cost function in shipping time can be solved optimally by processing the orders in earliest due-date first (EDD) sequence and shipping the orders and partial orders that are finished in a day at the end of the day. However, for the problem with no partial delivery allowed, they show that the problem is strongly NP-hard even if the cost function is linear in shipping time. They also propose a heuristic for the problem with convex cost function in shipping time and no partial

3.6 Problems with Fixed Delivery Departure Dates

delivery allowed. Melo and Wolsey (2010) study the same problem by proposing an integer programming formulation that enables them to solve large size instances to optimality. Zhong et al. (2010) propose a heuristic for the problem with linear cost function in shipping time and no partial delivery allowed and show that their heuristic has a worst-case performance ratio of 2, and this bound is tight.

In the remainder of this section, we describe the heuristic by Stecke and Zhao (2007) for the problem with a convex cost function in shipping time and no partial delivery allowed, and the heuristic by Zhong et al. (2010) for the problem with a linear cost function in shipping time and no partial delivery allowed.

For ease of presentation, we introduce some additional definitions and notation:

- $k = \lceil \sum_{i \in N} Q_i / c \rceil$, the day when all the orders complete processing.
- $N_1 = \{i \in N | d_i = 2\}$, the set of orders with delivery due date 2.
- $N_2 = \{i \in N | d_i = 3\}$, the set of orders with delivery due date 3.
- $f(\sigma) = $ the total shipping cost of a given schedule σ.
- $f^* = $ the optimal total shipping cost.
- $\sigma[j] = $ the order that is started in day j but completed in day $j + 1$ in a given schedule σ, for $j = 1, \ldots, k - 1$.
- $P_{jl}^{\sigma} = $ the quantity of order $\sigma[j]$ that is completed in day j in a given schedule σ, for $j = 1, \ldots, k - 1$.
- $P_{jr}^{\sigma} = $ the quantity of order $\sigma[j]$ that is completed in day $j+1$ in a given schedule σ, for $j = 1, \ldots, k - 1$.

In a given schedule σ, order $\sigma[j]$ may not exist, and in this case, P_{jl}^{σ}, P_{jr}^{σ}, and $d_{\sigma[j]}$ are all defined to be 0. If order $\sigma[j]$ exists, we call it a *split order*. In this case, $Q_{\sigma[j]} = P_{jl}^{\sigma} + P_{jr}^{\sigma}$, and the part completed in day j (with quantity P_{jl}^{σ}) must be delivered in day $j + 1$ together with the rest of the order.

We call a sequence of orders an *EDD-LPT* sequence if they are sequenced according to the earliest delivery due date first rule, breaking ties by the longest processing time first rule. Let σ_1 denote the schedule where the orders are processed in EDD-LPT sequence and finished orders are delivered as soon as possible with no partial delivery allowed.

The idea of Stecke and Zhao's (2007) heuristic, denoted as Heuristic SZ, for the problem with a convex cost function is to start with schedule σ_1 and construct a new schedule by re-positioning some of the jobs in σ_1.

Heuristic SZ
Step 1: Generate schedule σ_1 as described above. Let $\sigma = \sigma_1$ and $j = k - 1$.
Step 2: Consider the following two cases:

- If in σ, order $\sigma[j]$ does not exist, then let $j = j - 1$. If $j = 0$, then stop. Otherwise, repeat Step 2.
- Otherwise, go to Step 3.

110   3   Integrated Production and Outbound Distribution Scheduling: Offline Problems

Step 3: Consider the following two cases.

- If in σ, every order started and finished in day $j + 1$ has a quantity larger than P^{σ}_{jl}, then let $j = j - 1$. If $j = 0$, then stop. Otherwise, go to Step 2.
- Otherwise, in σ, among all the orders started and finished in day $j + 1$ with a quantity less than or equal to P^{σ}_{jl}, find the order i with the largest quantity and move order i to the position right before order $\sigma[j]$, and update the value of P^{σ}_{jl} accordingly. Repeat this until every order started and finished in day $j + 1$ has a quantity larger than P^{σ}_{jl}. Let $j = j - 1$. If $j = 0$, then stop. Otherwise, go to Step 2.

Example 3.11 (Application of Heuristic SZ) Apply Heuristic SZ to the following instance of the problem with convex cost function in shipping time: planning horizon $m = 5$ days, daily production capacity $c = 100$, number of orders $n = 6$, number of days needed to complete all the orders $k = 3$. The order processing time and deadline information and the unit-weight cost function $g(x)$ in shipping time x are given in the following two tables, respectively. Observe that $g(x)$ is a convex decreasing function of shipping time x.

Step 1: Generate schedule $\sigma_1 = (1, 2, 3, 4, 5, 6)$. Let $\sigma = \sigma_1$. In σ, order 3 is started in day 1 but completed in day 2, i.e., $\sigma[1] = 3$ with 15 units of it completed in day 1, i.e., $P^{\sigma}_{11} = 15$. Similarly, order 5 is started in day 2 but completed in day 3, i.e., $\sigma[2] = 5$ with 50 units of it completed in day 2, i.e., $P^{\sigma}_{21} = 50$. Let $j = k - 1 = 2$.
Step 2: Since order $\sigma[2]$ exists, go to Step 3.
Step 3: Order 6 is found and moved to the position right before order $\sigma[2]$ (i.e., order 5). After this, P^{σ}_{21} becomes 45. Next consider $j = 1$. Go to Step 2.
Step 2: Since order $\sigma[1]$ exists, go to Step 3.
Step 3: Order 6 is found and moved to the position right before order $\sigma[1]$ (i.e., order 3). As a result, P^{σ}_{11} becomes 10. Every order started and finished in day 2 has a quantity larger than 10. Let $j = 0$. Stop.

Order j	1	2	3	4	5	6
Q_j	60	25	25	40	60	5
d_j	2	3	3	4	5	5

Shipping time x	1	2	3	4
Cost for shipping one unit, $g(x)$	2	1	0.25	0.2

The schedule generated by this heuristic is $(1, 2, 6, 3, 4, 5)$. The corresponding shipping time of each order is $(x_1, \ldots, x_6) = (1, 2, 1, 2, 2, 4)$ days. The total cost of this schedule is $\sum_{j=1}^{6} Q_j g(x_j) = 60(2) + 25(1) + 25(2) + 40(1) + 60(1) + 5(0.2) = 296$. We note that this is not an optimal schedule because the following schedule $(1, 4, 2, 6, 3, 5)$ with shipping time of each order $(x_1, \ldots, x_6) = (1, 1, 1, 3, 2, 3)$

3.6 Problems with Fixed Delivery Departure Dates

days has a lower total cost $60(2) + 25(2) + 25(2) + 40(0.25) + 60(1) + 5(0.25) = 291.25$.

Next, we discuss Zhong et al.'s (2010) heuristic for the problem with a linear cost function. Similar to Stecke and Zhao's (2007) heuristic, Zhong et al.'s heuristic uses σ_1 as the starting point and modifies σ_1 in different ways for many different cases involved. In some cases, schedule σ_1 is not modified at all, whereas in other cases, schedule σ_1 is modified multiple times, resulting in different schedules for the different subcases involved.

For ease of presentation, we introduce the following additional definitions that are all related to schedule σ_1:

- $N_3 = \{i \in N | d_i \le d_{\sigma_1[1]} - 1\}$.
- $N_4 = \{i \in N | d_i = d_{\sigma_1[1]}\} \setminus \{\sigma_1[1]\}$, defined for the case if $2c < \sum_{i \in N} Q_i < 3c$.
- N_5 = the set of the orders processed after order $\sigma_1[1]$ in σ_1, defined for the case if $c < \sum_{i \in N} Q_i \le 2c$ and $P_{1l}^{\sigma_1} > \sum_{i \in N} Q_i - c + \sum_{i \in N_3} Q_i$.

Note that if $\sigma_1[1]$ does not exist, then N_3 and N_4 are both empty. If $\sigma_1[1]$ exists, then $N_1 \subseteq N_3$, and in schedule σ_1 the orders in N_3 are all completed in day 1 before $\sigma_1[1]$. In addition, recall that by the notation introduced earlier, in a given schedule σ, if $\sigma[j]$ does not exist, then P_{jl}^{σ}, P_{jr}^{σ}, and $d_{\sigma[j]}$ are all defined to be 0.

We are ready to describe Zhong et al.'s (2010) heuristic, denoted as Heuristic ZCC, for the problem with a linear cost function.

Heuristic ZCC

Step 1: Generate schedule σ_1 as described above. If one of the following conditions is satisfied:

  (1) $\alpha - \beta d_{\sigma_1[1]} \ge 0$
  (2) $P_{1l}^{\sigma_1} \le \sum_{i \in N_3} Q_i$
  (3) $\sum_{i \in N} Q_i \ge 3c$
  (4) $2c < \sum_{i \in N} Q_i < 3c$ and $P_{1l}^{\sigma_1} \le \sum_{i \in N} Q_i - c - P_{2l}^{\sigma_1}$
  (5) $c < \sum_{i \in N} Q_i \le 2c$ and $P_{1l}^{\sigma_1} \le \sum_{i \in N} Q_i - c + \sum_{i \in N_3} Q_i$

  then output schedule σ_1, and stop.

Step 2: If $2c < \sum_{i \in N} Q_i < 3c$ and $P_{1l}^{\sigma_1} > \sum_{i \in N} Q_i - c - P_{2l}^{\sigma_1}$, then adjust schedule σ_1 by moving the orders between $\sigma_1[1]$ and $\sigma_1[2]$ and the orders after $\sigma_1[2]$ to the position right before $\sigma_1[1]$. Let the resulting schedule be σ_2. In σ_2, orders $\sigma_1[1]$ and $\sigma_1[2]$ are still split, and hence $\sigma_2[1] = \sigma_1[1]$ and $\sigma_2[2] = \sigma_1[2]$, respectively. Consider the following cases:

- Case 1: If $P_{1l}^{\sigma_2} \le \max\{\sum_{i \in N_3} Q_i, P_{1r}^{\sigma_2} + \sum_{i \in N} Q_i - 2c\}$, output schedule σ_2, and stop.
- Case 2: If $P_{1l}^{\sigma_2} > \max\{\sum_{i \in N_3} Q_i, P_{1r}^{\sigma_2} + \sum_{i \in N} Q_i - 2c\}$, consider two further cases:

  - (i) If $\sum_{i \in N_1} Q_i + Q_{\sigma_1[1]} + Q_{\sigma_1[2]} + \sum_{i \in N_2} Q_i \le 2c$, then consider the following two schedules:

$$\pi_1 = (N_1, \sigma_1[1], \sigma_1[2], N_2, N \setminus (N_1 \cup N_2 \cup \{\sigma_1[1], \sigma_1[2]\})),$$

$$\pi_2 = (N_1, \sigma_1[2], \sigma_1[1], N_2, N \setminus (N_1 \cup N_2 \cup \{\sigma_1[1], \sigma_1[2]\})).$$

Let σ_3 denote whichever of these two schedules has a lower total shipping cost incurred by orders $\sigma_1[1]$ and $\sigma_1[2]$.

- (ii) If $\sum_{i \in N_1} Q_i + Q_{\sigma_1[1]} + Q_{\sigma_1[2]} + \sum_{i \in N_2} Q_i > 2c$, then consider the following two schedules:

$$\pi_3 = (N_1, \sigma_1[1], N_2, N \setminus (N_1 \cup N_2 \cup \{\sigma_1[1], \sigma_1[2]\}), \sigma_1[2]),$$

$$\pi_4 = (N_1, \sigma_1[2], N_2, N \setminus (N_1 \cup N_2 \cup \{\sigma_1[1], \sigma_1[2]\}), \sigma_1[1]).$$

Let σ_3 denote whichever of these two schedules has a lower total shipping cost incurred by orders $\sigma_1[1]$ and $\sigma_1[2]$.

Output schedule σ_3, and stop.

Step 3: If $c < \sum_{i \in N} Q_i \le 2c$ and $P_{1l}^{\sigma_1} > \sum_{i \in N} Q_i - c + \sum_{i \in N_3} Q_i$, adjust σ_1 by moving all the orders in N_5 to the position right before $\sigma_1[1]$. Let the resulting schedule be σ_4. In σ_4, order $\sigma_1[1]$ is still split. Hence, $\sigma_4[1] = \sigma_1[1]$. Consider the following cases:

- Case 1: If one of the following two conditions is satisfied: (a) $P_{1l}^{\sigma_4} \le \sum_{i \in N} Q_i - c + \sum_{i \in N_3} Q_i$, (b) $P_{1l}^{\sigma_4} > \sum_{i \in N} Q_i - c + \sum_{i \in N_3} Q_i$ and $\sum_{i \in N_3 \setminus N_1} Q_i + \sum_{i \in N_5} Q_i < P_{1r}^{\sigma_4}$, then output schedule σ_4, and stop.
- Case 2: If $P_{1l}^{\sigma_4} > \sum_{i \in N} Q_i - c + \sum_{i \in N_3} Q_i$ and $\sum_{i \in N_3 \setminus N_1} Q_i + \sum_{i \in N_5} Q_i \ge P_{1r}^{\sigma_4}$, adjust schedule σ_4 by moving all the orders in $(N_3 \setminus N_1) \cup N_5$ to the end of the schedule. Let the resulting schedule be σ_5. Output schedule σ_5, and stop.

This heuristic generates one of the five possible schedules $\sigma_1, \sigma_2, \ldots, \sigma_5$ defined above, depending on particular cases, as the solution to our problem. Zhong et al. (2010) show that whichever schedule is output from this heuristic, its objective value is at most twice the optimal objective value, and hence the worst-case performance ratio of the heuristic is bounded by 2.

Example 3.12 (Application of Heuristic ZCC) If we apply Heuristic ZCC to the instance given in Example 3.11 with any linear cost function, then $N_3 = \{1\}$ and both conditions (2) and (4) in Step 1 are satisfied. This means that σ_1 is the output from this heuristic.

Example 3.13 (Application of Heuristic ZCC) Apply Heuristic ZCC to the following instance: planning horizon $m = 5$ days, daily production capacity $c = 100$, number of orders $n = 5$, number of days needed to complete all the orders $k = 3$. The unit-weight cost function in shipping time x is defined as $g(x) = 7 - 2x$. The order processing time and deadline information are given in the following table:

3.6 Problems with Fixed Delivery Departure Dates

Order j	1	2	3	4	5
Q_j	25	85	40	60	5
d_j	3	4	4	5	5

Step 1: Generate schedule $\sigma_1 = (1, 2, 3, 4, 5)$. We have $\sigma_1[1] = 2$ with $P_{1l}^{\sigma_1} = 75$, and $\sigma[2] = 4$ with $P_{2l}^{\sigma_1} = 50$. It can be seen that none of the 5 conditions in Step 1 is satisfied.

Step 2: The condition for Step 2 is satisfied. Adjust σ_1 by moving orders 3 and 5 to the position right before order 2. The resulting schedule $\sigma_2 = (1, 3, 5, 2, 4)$. In σ_2, $\sigma_2[1] = 2$ with $P_{1l}^{\sigma_2} = 30$ and $P_{1r}^{\sigma_2} = 55$. The condition for Case 1 is satisfied. Thus σ_2 is the output from this heuristic.

3.6.2.2 Problems $1|[a_j, b_j]|V_{het}(v, 1), fdep|k|IC + TC$

In this subsection, we consider problems with fixed delivery departure times with the following main characteristics: (1) There are a single machine, multiple customers, and a limited number of heterogeneous vehicles available at each given departure time, each with an unlimited delivery capacity, (2) each job has a delivery time window within which the job must be delivered to its customer (denoted as "$[a_j, b_j]$" in the five-field problem representation), (3) there is an inventory cost for keeping a job at the plant after it has completed processing but before it is delivered (denoted as "IC" in the five-field problem representation), and (4) the objective is to minimize the total inventory cost and total transportation cost.

Li et al. (2017) describe a business environment where such supply chain scheduling problems arise. Fierce competition in the steel industry worldwide is motivating many iron and steel enterprises to produce a significant portion of steel products in a make-to-order (MTO) fashion, under which steel coils are made according to specific customer orders. Compared to a traditional make-to-stock (MTS) production strategy, under which steel coils are made according to projected market demand, the MTO strategy has several advantages. These advantages include reducing warehousing and inventory costs, providing a larger variety of products, and achieving better customer service. Consider production and delivery decisions which a medium to small steel manufacturer has to make for the MTO steel coils ordered by large customers such as automobile manufacturers and shipbuilders. Since the customers often have more bargaining power than the steel supplier, the customers often negotiate with the steel supplier to specify when and how their orders should be delivered. In such situations, customers may set a delivery time window within which a finished order should be delivered for the following reasons. First, a steel coil is heavy and hence it incurs a large inventory handling and holding cost if the coil is not used soon after it is delivered and has to be put in temporary storage at the customer site. Second, temporary storage space at a customer site may be limited, particularly if the customer adopts a just-in-time

114 3 Integrated Production and Outbound Distribution Scheduling: Offline Problems

materials supply strategy. Therefore, an MTO order is associated with a delivery time window. Typically, a time window for an order varies from one to five days depending on the customer's bargaining power relative to the supplier.

Each order may consist of multiple coils. Usually different coils in an order can be delivered separately, as long as they are all delivered to the customer within the time window specified by the customer. This is referred to as *splittable delivery*. However, in some cases, to reduce handling cost, customers may require that all the coils within their order be delivered together in one shipment. This is referred as *non-splittable delivery*.

Delivery of finished steel coils to customer sites is often carried out by third-party logistics companies that use ships and freight trains to deliver heavy goods such as steel products. Ships and freight trains usually follow a fixed daily or weekly schedule with a fixed route and a fixed departure time at each stop on the route. To deliver a coil from the manufacturer's site to the destination of the order within its time window, an eligible set of ships and trains with specific departure times can be identified. When an order completes processing at the plant, if none of the ships and trains going to the destination of the order departs at the completion time of the order, the order must be kept in temporary storage first, which incurs an inventory cost, and delivered later when a ship or train becomes available. Given a set of orders to be processed and delivered, the manufacturer needs to find an integrated schedule for processing the orders, keeping finished orders in inventory if necessary, and delivering them to the customers within their time windows using available ships and trains, such that the total inventory and delivery cost is minimum. We note that during job processing, idle times between jobs may or may not be allowed. In steel production, due to the fact that it can be very expensive to resume production if it is stopped even temporarily, production runs continuously without any idle time until all the jobs are completed. However, in some other situations, idle times between jobs may be allowed if necessary.

As discussed in Li et al. (2017), similar decision problems exist in other industries where products are made-to-order and need to be delivered to customers in a timely manner. Automobile manufacturers such as Toyota, which use a just-in-time production model, often require their suppliers to deliver ordered parts within a narrow time window. Consequently, the suppliers have to carry inventory of the finished parts at their own sites if orders are produced some time prior to their delivery time window. Delivery of expensive parts in the automobile industries is often carried out by air flights which obviously have fixed schedules. The suppliers in these settings face the same issues as the steel manufacturer discussed earlier.

Motivated by these applications, Li et al. (2017) study a number of problems that can be represented as $1|[a_j, b_j]|V_{het}(v, 1), fdep|k|IC + TC$ using the five-field notation in Sect. 3.2. To be consistent with the application environment described above, we apply the notation and problem definitions used by Li et al. (2017) to describe these scheduling problems more precisely.

At the beginning of the planning horizon, a manufacturer has received a set of m orders $M = \{1, \ldots, m\}$, where each order consists of n_i jobs, and each job j from order i is denoted as (i, j). Let $N_i = \{(i, 1), \ldots, (i, n_i)\}$ denote the set of jobs that

3.6 Problems with Fixed Delivery Departure Dates

form order i, and let $n = n_1 + \cdots + n_m$ be the total number of jobs of all the orders together, and $N = \cup_{i=1}^{m} N_i$ be the set of all the jobs. Each job (i, j) has a weight of w_{ij} units and requires a processing time of p_{ij} time units. The processing time of a job is generally proportional to the weight of the job, i.e., $p_{ij} = r_{ij} w_{ij}$, where the r_{ij} are all equal to a constant r if all the jobs are homogeneous (e.g., all steel coils have the same grade and same thickness). The processing of the jobs is completed on a single production line from the beginning of the planning horizon (time 0) without interruption. Motivated by the application in steel coil production, we assume that no idle times between jobs are allowed during job processing. A completed job is kept in a temporary warehouse if it is not delivered to its customer immediately. If a job (i, j) is kept in the warehouse, it incurs an inventory cost of h_{ij} per unit weight unit per unit time.

Each order i has a delivery time window $[a_i, b_i]$ within which all of its jobs must be delivered. Order delivery is performed by a given number of transporters that are available within the planning horizon. Each transporter has a known departure time, arrival time at each stop of its route, and cost rate for each stop. For each order, we can identify all the transporters that can deliver the order to its customer within its time window. Without loss of generality, we can assume that no two transporters that are eligible to deliver a given order have the same departure time. This is because for any order, among all the eligible transporters with the same departure time, the one with the lowest cost rate is always chosen over the others. Therefore, we can associate each order i with a set of e_i distinct eligible departure times, denoted as $E_i = \{T_{i1}, \cdots, T_{ie_i}\}$, where each departure time T_{it} is associated with a unique transporter, which has a departure time T_{it} and can deliver order i to its destination within the order's time window at the cost rate c_{it} per unit weight.

The manufacturer needs to find a production schedule for the jobs, and decide how long each job is kept in the warehouse, and when the delivery departure time should be for each job, so that the total inventory and delivery cost is minimized. We consider problems with both splittable delivery (denoted as SD problems) and non-splittable delivery (denoted as NSD problems).

Remark 3.5 We note that, given a production schedule of the orders, the inventory and departure time decisions for each job can be made accordingly. For an SD problem, given a production schedule, it is optimal for each job (i, j) of an order i to use some departure time $T_{it} \in E_i$ such that $T_{it} \geq C_{ij}$, where C_{ij} is the processing completion time of job (i, j), and the total inventory and delivery cost is minimum possible, i.e.,

$$h_{ij} w_{ij} (T_{it} - C_{ij}) + c_{it} w_{ij} = \min_{T_{il} \in E_i; \ T_{il} \geq C_{ij}} \{h_{ij} w_{ij} (T_{il} - C_{ij}) + c_{il} w_{ij}\}.$$

Similarly, for an NSD problem, given a production schedule, it is optimal for all the jobs of an order i to use some departure time $T_{it} \in E_i$ such that $T_{it} \geq C_i$, where C_i is the processing completion time of order i (i.e., $C_i = \max\{C_{ij} \mid (i, j) \in N_i\}$), and the total inventory and delivery cost is minimum possible, i.e.,

$$\sum_{(i,j)\in N_i} h_{ij}w_{ij}(T_{it} - C_{ij}) + c_{it} \sum_{(i,j)\in N_i} w_{ij} = \min_{T_{il}\in E_i;\ T_{il}\geq C_i} \left\{ \sum_{(i,j)\in N_i} h_{ij}w_{ij}(T_{il} - C_{ij}) \right.$$

$$\left. + c_{il} \sum_{(i,j)\in N_i} w_{ij} \right\}.$$

As a result, we can focus on production scheduling decisions only.

Definition 3.1 We define an *Earliest Latest Eligible-Departure-Time first (ELEDT)* *schedule* of the orders as follows: The m orders are processed in nondecreasing order of their latest eligible departure times $d_i = \max\{T_{it} \mid T_{it} \in E_i\}$, and the jobs of each order are processed consecutively in any sequence.

It can be shown that both SD and NSD problems are feasible if and only if an ELEDT schedule is feasible.

In the following, we summarize some known results for various cases of the SD and NSD problems from the literature. We first consider these problems where each order consists of a single job, i.e., $n_i = 1$.

Problems with $n_i = 1$
We note that when there is only one job per order (i.e., $n_i = 1$ for $i \in M$) or each order is associated with a unique delivery vehicle that can deliver this order (i.e., $e_i = 1$ for $i \in M$), the SD problems and NSD problems are identical. Thus, every solvability result for a SD problem with $n_i = 1$ (or $e_i = 1$) applies to the same NSD problem with $n_i = 1$ (or $e_i = 1$) as well. When $n_i = 1$, for notational convenience, we use index i to represent the job of order i, and replace the symbols $p_{ij}, w_{ij}, r_{ij}, h_{ij}$ by p_i, w_i, r_i, h_i, respectively.

We first summarize known complexity results for some special cases of SD and NSD problems with $n_i = 1$ and $e_i = 1$. The classical single-machine scheduling problem (denoted as TWE) of minimizing the total weighted earliness $\sum_{i\in M} u_i G_i$ subject to no tardy jobs, where u_i is the penalty per unit of earliness for order i and G_i, defined as $\max\{0, d_i - C_i\}$, is the earliness of order i, can be viewed as a special case of SD and NSD problems with $n_i = 1$ and $e_i = 1$ and $h_i w_i = u_i$. Chand and Schneeberger (1988) show that several special cases of TWE are solvable by a simple rule in polynomial time. One of the special cases is when the p_i/u_i (i.e., h_i/r_i) values are identical, for which any EDD schedule is optimal. This means that any ELEDT schedule is optimal for SD and NSD problems with $n_i = 1$, $e_i = 1$, $h_i = h$, and $r_i = r$. Boysen et al. (2013) show that the unweighted version of TWE (i.e., all u_i's are identical) is strongly NP-hard. This means that SD and NSD problems with $n_i = 1$, $e_i = 1$, $h_i = h$, and identical w_i values and problems with $n_i = 1$, $e_i = 1$, $r_i = r$, and identical $h_i w_i$ values are also all strongly NP-hard.

Yang (2000) considers another unweighted version of the TWE problem where there are multiple departure dates for the jobs (i.e., $e_i \geq 1$). In Yang's problem, all the jobs have the same possible departure dates and no delivery costs are considered, whereas in our problems, each job may have a different set of possible departure dates and there are delivery costs. Yang's problem thus can be viewed as a special case of SD and NSD problems with $n_i = 1, e_i \geq 1, c_{it} = 0$, identical E_i, and identical $h_i w_i$. Yang shows that his problem is strongly NP-hard. Thus, SD and NSD problems with $n_i = 1, e_i \geq 1, h_i = h, c_{it} = 0$, identical w_i, and identical E_i are also strongly NP-hard. Li et al. (2017) show that SD and NSD problems with $n_i = 1, e_i \geq 1, h_i = h, r_i = r$ are also strongly NP-hard.

We now consider more general problems where each order may have more than one job, i.e., $n_i \geq 1$.

Problems with $n_i \geq 1$

Li et al. (2017) clarify the computational complexity of many different cases of SD and NSD problems with $n_i \geq 1$ and $e_i = 1$, or $n_i \geq 1$ and $e_i \geq 1$. We summarize below several main results from Li et al. (2017).

- When $n_1 \geq 1$ and $e_i = 1$,

  - Both SD and NSD problems with an arbitrary m, and $h_{ij} = h$ and $r_{ij} = r$, for all i, j, are polynomially solvable. Any ELEDT schedule is optimal.
  - Both SD and NSD problems with a fixed m are ordinarily NP-hard even if $c_{i1} = 0$, for all i.
  - Both SD and NSD problems with an arbitrary m are strongly NP-hard even if $h_{ij} = h$ or $r_{ij} = r$, for all i, j.

- When $n_1 \geq 1$ and $e_i \geq 1$,

  - SD problem is strongly NP-hard even with a fixed m, and $h_{ij} = 0$ and $r_{ij} = r$, for all i, j.
  - NSD problem with a fixed m is ordinarily NP-hard even if $c_{it} = 0$, for all i, t.
  - NSD problem with an arbitrary m is strongly NP-hard even if $p_{ij} = p, r_{ij} = r$ and $h_{ij} = 0$, for all i, j.
  - Both SD problem with an arbitrary m and $p_{ij} = p$, for all i, j, and NSD problem with a fixed m and $p_{ij} = p$, for all i, j, or a fixed m and $h_{ij} = 0$, for all i, j, or a fixed m and both $h_{ij} = h$ and $r_{ij} = r$, for all i, j, are polynomially solvable.

3.7 Problems with Multiple Plants

In this section, we discuss several IPODS problems studied by Chen and Pundoor (2006) where there are multiple production plants located at different locations that can process the jobs, and the jobs, after completion of processing, need to be delivered to a central distribution center (DC). Given a set of jobs, the decision maker needs to determine (1) which jobs to be assigned to which plants, (2) how to schedule the production of the assigned jobs at each plant, and (3) how to schedule the delivery of the completed jobs from each plant to the DC, so as to optimize a certain performance measure involving production and transportation costs and the total or maximum lead time of the jobs.

Such IPODS problems are often encountered by companies with an international supply chain. The following application is described in Chen and Pundoor (2006). A make-to-order manufacturer owns several plants located in foreign countries and a central DC in the USA located close to the retailers that this manufacturer serves. Shortly before a selling season, the manufacturer receives orders from the retailers and needs to assign the orders to the plants for processing and deliver them to the DC after they are processed for distribution to the retailers. In this supply chain, production costs and production rates may vary significantly from plant to plant, due to variations in labor costs and productivity in the different countries involved. Furthermore, since the DC is close to the retailers, the delivery time and cost between the DC and the retailers are negligible, compared to the delivery time and cost between the plants and the DC. Therefore, the manufacturer is faced with the job assignment and production and delivery scheduling decisions discussed above.

We now introduce necessary notation and precisely define the problems considered by Chen and Pundoor (2006). We are given n jobs, $N = \{1, \ldots, n\}$, at time 0, each of which is to be processed at one of the m given plants in a supply chain, $M = \{1, \ldots, m\}$. Each plant has a single machine (i.e., a single dedicated production line) and is capable of producing all the jobs. Each job needs to be processed by only one of the plants once without interruption. If job $j \in N$ is assigned to plant $i \in M$ for processing, it takes p_{ij} units of processing time and c_{ij} units of production cost. Completed jobs are delivered to a distribution center in the supply chain. The delivery time and delivery cost of a shipment from plant $i \in M$ to the DC are t_i and f_i, respectively. Each delivery shipment can carry up to b jobs. The problem is to assign each job to a plant, schedule the processing of the jobs assigned to each plant, and schedule the delivery of the completed jobs from each plant to the DC, so as to optimize a given objective function that takes into account delivery lead time of the jobs as well as the total cost of the jobs including total production cost and total shipping cost. For a given schedule of the problem, we define:

- TC = the total cost of the jobs including total production cost and total shipping cost.
- C_j = the completion time of job $j \in N$, which is the time when job j completes processing at the plant to which it is assigned.
- D_j = the delivery time of job $j \in N$, which is the time when job j is delivered to the DC.

Chen and Pundoor (2006) consider four problems, each with a different objective function as follows:

- **Problem 1:** Minimizing the sum of the total lead time of the jobs and the total cost, i.e., $\sum_{j \in N} D_j + TC$.

3.7 Problems with Multiple Plants 119

- **Problem 2:** Minimizing the total cost TC, subject to the constraint that the total lead time of the jobs is no more than a given threshold, i.e., $\sum_{j \in N} D_j \leq D$, where D is a given constant.
- **Problem 3:** Minimizing the sum of the maximum lead time of the jobs and the total cost, i.e., $D_{\max} + TC$, where $D_{\max} = \max\{D_j | j \in N\}$.
- **Problem 4:** Minimizing the total cost TC subject to the constraint that the maximum lead time $D_{\max}$ is no more than a given threshold, i.e., $D_{\max} \leq D$, where D is a given constant.

These problems differ from the other classes of problems discussed in this chapter in the following two aspects: (1) There are multiple plants in these problems such that job assignment is one of the decisions to make, whereas in all other problems there is a single plant and hence there is no job assignment decision, (2) production costs are part of the objective function in these problems, whereas production costs are fixed and hence not considered in other problems.

Chen and Pundoor (2006) show the following optimality properties for these four problems.

Lemma 3.12 *There exists an optimal solution for Problems 1–4 in which all of the following hold:*

(1) The jobs assigned to each plant are scheduled in the Shortest Processing Time (SPT) first order.

(2) There is no inserted idle time between jobs processed at each plant.

(3) The departure time of each shipment is the time when all the jobs in it complete processing.

(4) All the jobs that are delivered in the same shipment are processed consecutively at a plant.

(5) The number of jobs delivered in an earlier shipment from a plant is greater than or equal to the number of jobs delivered in a later shipment from the same plant.

In the following Sects. 3.7.1 and 3.7.2, we discuss how Problem 1 and Problem 3 can be solved, respectively. Most of the algorithms and results given below are from Chen and Pundoor (2006). We do not discuss how the other two problems can be solved since, as discussed in Chen and Pundoor (2006), these problems can be solved by algorithms similar to those for solving Problems 1 and 3.

3.7.1 Minimizing Total Delivery Time and Transportation Cost

Chen and Pundoor (2006) show that Problem 1 with an arbitrary number of plants is strongly NP-hard and mention that when the number of plants is fixed, the complexity of this problem is unknown. They propose a heuristic for solving Problem 1. The heuristic consists of an initialization step, where some parameters used in later steps are calculated, followed by a two-phase procedure, where the jobs are assigned to the plants in the first phase, and then the delivery schedule of the

120   3   Integrated Production and Outbound Distribution Scheduling: Offline Problems

jobs assigned to each plant is determined in the second phase. The job assignment problem in the first phase is solved as a standard assignment problem where the cost of assigning a job to a particular position of a plant is heuristically derived, based on relevant parameters of the job and the parameters calculated in the initialization step. The delivery scheduling problem in the second phase is solved by a dynamic programming algorithm.

One of the key parameters involved in the heuristic is the maximum possible size of a shipment containing job j at plant i in an optimal schedule, which is denoted as $b_{\max,i,j}$. If all the jobs are processed at plant i, denote the resulting SPT order of the jobs as $([i1], \ldots, [in])$. Suppose that the size of a shipment B containing order j at plant i is x, and B consists of orders $(< i1 >, \ldots, < ix >)$, where $(< i1 >, \ldots, < ix >)$ is in SPT order and a subset of $\{[i1], \ldots, [in]\}$. Clearly, $p_{i,<iu>} \geq p_{i,[iu]}$, for $u = 1, \ldots, x$. The following computational procedure finds an upper bound on x, and this upper bound is defined as $b_{\max,i,j}$.

Procedure MAXSIZE

Step 0: Initially, let $x = b$.

Step 1: Given x, check if the total cost of the jobs in any shipment B with x jobs, denoted as $B = \{< i1 >, \ldots, < ix >\}$, where $(< i1 >, \ldots, < ix >)$ is in SPT order, can be reduced by splitting it into two shipments. There are $x - 1$ different ways of splitting this shipment into two separate shipments, denoted as E_1 and E_2, with E_1 consisting of the first y jobs, i.e., $E_1 = \{< i1 >, \ldots, < iy >)\}$, and E_2 the last $x - y$ jobs, i.e., $E_2 = \{< i, y + 1 >, \ldots, < ix >\}$, for $y = 1, \ldots, x - 1$.

For each $y = 1, \ldots, x - 1$, compute a lower bound on the cost reduction due to the splitting, denoted as R_y, as follows:

$$R_y \geq y(p_{i,[i,y+1]} + p_{i,[i,y+2]} + \cdots + p_{i,[i,x-1]} + \max\{p_{i,[ix]}, p_{ij}\}) - f_i,$$

where $y(p_{i,[i,y+1]} + p_{i,[i,y+2]} + \cdots + p_{i,[i,x-1]} + \max\{p_{i,[ix]}, p_{ij}\})$ is a lower bound on the decrease in total lead time of the jobs in E_1 and f_i is the increase in delivery cost, after B splits into E_1 and E_2.

Step 2: Find $z \in \{1, \ldots, x - 1\}$ such that $R_z = \max\{R_y \mid y = 1, \ldots, x - 1\}$. If $R_z \geq 0$, then the shipment size x should be reduced; update $x = x - 1$ and go to Step 1. If $R_z < 0$, then stop, and the current x is the maximum size of a shipment containing job j at plant i.

We now describe the heuristic for Problem 1 given by Chen and Pundoor (2006).

Heuristic CP-H1

Initialization Run procedure MAXSIZE to derive the maximum shipment size $b_{\max,i,j}$ of any shipment that contains job j at plant i, for $i \in M$ and $j \in N$. Define parameters Δ_{ih} and e_{ui}, for $i \in M$, $h = 1, \ldots, n - 1$, and $u = 1, \ldots, b$, as follows:

3.7 Problems with Multiple Plants

$\Delta_{ih} = \min\{p_{i,[i,q+h]} - p_{i,[iq]} | q = 1, \ldots, n - h\}$, which is the minimum difference of the processing times of any two jobs $[iq]$ and $[i, q + h]$ in the SPT order of the jobs $[i1], \ldots, [in]$ at plant i [Δ_{ih} is always nonnegative],

$$e_{ui} = \begin{cases} \frac{1}{2u}[\Delta_{i1} + 3\Delta_{i3} + 5\Delta_{i5} + \cdots + (u - 1)\Delta_{i,u-1}], & \text{if } u \text{ is even,} \\ \frac{1}{2u}[2\Delta_{i2} + 4\Delta_{i4} + 6\Delta_{i6} + \cdots + (u - 1)\Delta_{i,u-1}], & \text{if } u \text{ is odd.} \end{cases}$$

Phase 1 For $k = 1, \ldots, n$, $i = 1, \ldots, m$, and $j = 1, \ldots, n$, define parameter $a_{(k,i)j}$ as the cost for scheduling job j as the kth last job at plant i, which is given as

$$a_{(k,i)j} = (kp_{ij} + t_i) + c_{ij} + \min_{1 \leq u \leq b_{\max,i,j}} \{p_{ij}(u - 1)/2 + f_i/u + e_{ui}\}. \tag{3.23}$$

Define a binary variable $x_{(k,i)j}$ to be 1 if job j is scheduled as the kth last job at plant i, and 0 otherwise. Solve the following assignment problem:

$$\text{Minimize} \quad G = \sum_{k \in N} \sum_{i \in M} \sum_{j \in N} a_{(k,i)j} x_{(k,i)j}$$

$$\text{subject to:} \quad \sum_{k \in N} \sum_{i \in M} x_{(k,i)j} = 1, \quad \text{for } j \in N,$$

$$\sum_{j \in N} x_{(k,i)j} \leq 1, \quad \text{for } k \in N, i \in M,$$

$$x_{(k,i)j} = 0 \text{ or } 1, \quad \text{for } k \in N, i \in M, j \in N.$$

Phase 2 In the solution generated in Phase 1 (which specifies how jobs are assigned and scheduled at each plant), suppose that there are n_i jobs processed by plant i, and they are reindexed in their SPT order as $[i1], \ldots, [in_i]$. Let $C_{[ij]}$ denote the time when job $[ij]$ completes processing at plant i. Given this solution, find an optimal delivery schedule for the jobs processed at each plant i with respect to the objective function of the problem using the following dynamic programming algorithm:

- *Value Function*: $V(j)$ = the minimum total cost of a schedule for the first j jobs $\{[i1], \ldots, [ij]\}$.
- *Initial Condition*: $V(0) = 0$.
- *Recurrence Relation*: For $j = 1, \ldots, n_i$,

$$V(j) = \min\{V(j - h) + h(C_{[ij]} + t_i) + f_i \mid h = 1, \ldots, \min\{b, j\}\}.$$

- *Optimal Solution*: $V(n_i)$.

In Phase 1 of the heuristic, the cost coefficient $a_{(k,i)j}$ defined in (3.23) and used in the assignment problem formulation is an approximation to the actual cost of job j if it is scheduled as the kth last job at plant i. The actual cost is $(k + r)p_{ij} + t_i + c_{ij} + f_i/q$ if we know that there are a total of q jobs in the shipment containing job j, and a total of r jobs scheduled before job j in this shipment. Since we do not know the values of q and r, the term $r p_{ij} + f_i/q$ is approximated by $\min_{1 \le u \le b_{\max,i,j}} \{p_{ij} (u - 1)/2 + f_i/u + e_{ui}\}$. In Phase 2, the optimality of the DP algorithm for finding an optimal delivery schedule for the n_i jobs processed at plant i follows from the fact that the recurrence relation compares the cost of every possible configuration of the last delivery shipment. This algorithm has a time complexity of $O(n_i b)$.

Chen and Pundoor (2006) show that the optimal objective value of the assignment problem solved in Phase 1 of Heuristic CP-H1 is a lower bound on the optimal objective value of Problem 1. Based on this result, they show that the worst-case performance ratio of the heuristic is bounded by $b_{\max}$, where $b_{\max} = \max\{b_{\max,i,j} \mid i \in M, j \in N\}$, and this bound is tight. Furthermore, they show that this heuristic is asymptotically optimal for Problem 1 when n goes to infinity but m and b are fixed. Finally, to improve the quality of the solutions generated by this heuristic, they modify the heuristic by lowering the maximum shipment size $b_{\max,i,j}$ for each $j \in N$ and $i \in M$ and re-running the heuristic with the revised $b_{\max,i,j}$. Their computational tests based on a large number of test instances with up to 200 orders, 8 plants, and shipment capacity of 12 show that this modified heuristic is capable of generating solutions with an average gap of 1.05% compared to the lower bound defined by the optimal objective value of the assignment problem in Phase 1.

3.7.2 Minimizing Maximum Delivery Time and Transportation Cost

Chen and Pundoor (2006) show that Problem 3 is at least ordinarily NP-hard, even with a fixed number of plants. They show that in addition to the properties stated in Lemma 3.12, Problem 3 also satisfies the following property.

Lemma 3.13 *There exists an optimal solution for Problem 3 in which all the delivery shipments from each plant to the DC, except possibly one shipment, are full. More specifically, if there are n_i jobs scheduled at plant $i \in M$, then ub jobs are delivered in u full shipments and v jobs are delivered in a partial shipment, where $u = \lfloor n_i/b \rfloor$ and $v = n_i - ub$.*

Chen and Pundoor (2006) propose a linear programming based heuristic for Problem 3. The idea of the heuristic is as follows. Since Problem 3 cannot be formulated precisely as an integer program because it is not known exactly how many jobs are in each shipment, a slightly different problem whose objective function is a lower bound on that of Problem 3 is instead considered and formulated as a binary integer program. We denote this slightly different problem as Problem $3'$. In this problem the subset of plants $Q \subseteq M$ that are used is specified explicitly. It is shown that there exists a subset of plants $U \subseteq M$ such that the optimal objective value of the LP relaxation of Problem $3'$ with U as the subset of the plants used

3.7 Problems with Multiple Plants

is a lower bound on the optimal objective value of Problem 3. Consequently, the solution of the LP relaxation of Problem 3′ with U as the subset of the plants used is applied to construct a feasible solution to Problem 3.

Now we describe Problem 3′ and the corresponding IP formulation in detail. Everything else in Problem 3′ is the same as in Problem 3 except that (i) the jobs are processed in a subset of plants $Q \subseteq M$, and (ii) each job is required to be delivered individually in a separate shipment and the transportation cost of a shipment from plant $i \in M$ to the DC is defined to be f_i/b. This problem can be formulated as the following binary integer program $IP(Q)$, where each binary variable x_{ij} is defined to be 1 if job j is assigned to plant $i \in Q$ and 0 otherwise, and the continuous variable $D_{\max}$ is the maximum delivery time of the jobs.

$$\textbf{IP(Q)}: \quad Z(Q) = \text{Minimize} \quad D_{\max} + \sum_{i \in Q} \sum_{j \in N} (c_{ij} + f_i/b) x_{ij} \tag{3.24}$$

$$\text{s.t.} \quad D_{\max} \geq \sum_{j \in N} p_{ij} x_{ij} + t_i, \quad \text{for } i \in Q, \tag{3.25}$$

$$\sum_{i \in Q} x_{ij} = 1, \quad \text{for } j \in N, \tag{3.26}$$

$$x_{ij} \in \{0, 1\}, \quad \text{for } i \in Q, j \in N. \tag{3.27}$$

In this formulation, constraint (3.25) defines $D_{\max}$ and constraint (3.26) ensures that each job is assigned to one of the plants in Q. It should be noted that constraint (3.25) implies that there is at least one job scheduled at each plant in Q, because otherwise $D_{\max}$ does not have to be greater than or equal to t_i. This means that Problem 3′ is not equivalent to formulation $IP(M)$. Instead, Problem 3′ is equivalent to the problem of finding a subset $Q \subseteq M$ with a minimum possible objective value $Z(Q)$.

Given any subset of plants $Q \subseteq M$, let the LP relaxation problem of $IP(Q)$ be denoted as $LP(Q)$, and let the optimal objective value of problem $LP(Q)$ be denoted as $Z_{LP}(Q)$. By the fact that for any given Q, the objective function of problem $LP(Q)$ is a lower bound on the optimal objective value of Problem 3 with the restriction that only the plants in Q can be used to process the jobs, we can see that $Z_{LP}(U) = \min\{Z_{LP}(Q)|Q \subseteq M\}$ is a lower bound of the optimal objective value of Problem 3. Chen and Pundoor (2006) show that there is no need to solve $LP(Q)$ for every possible subset Q of M in order to find the subset U that provides a lower bound $Z_{LP}(U)$ on the optimal objective value of Problem 3. They propose the following algorithm, which solves the LP relaxation problem $LP(Q)$ m times, each time with a different set Q, and show that the subset of plants U found by this algorithm satisfies $Z_{LP}(U) = \min\{Z_{LP}(Q)|Q \subseteq M\}$ and hence $Z_{LP}(U)$ is a valid lower bound on the optimal objective value of Problem 3.

Algorithm LB

Step 0: Reindex the plants in the nonincreasing order of the transportation times t_i between them and the DC. Let $Q_i = \{i, \ldots, m\}$ be the subset of the $m - i + 1$ plants with the shortest transportation times to the DC.

Step 1: For $i = 1, \ldots, m$, solve the LP relaxation problem $LP(Q_i)$ and obtain the optimal objective value $Z_{LP}(Q_i)$.

Step 2: Let $U = Q_l$ for some $l \in \{1, \ldots, m\}$ such that $Z_{LP}(Q_l) = \min\{Z_{LP}(Q_i) | 1 \leq i \leq m\}$, and let $u = |U|$.

Furthermore, Chen and Pundoor (2006) show that the solution of $LP(U)$ satisfies the following property.

Lemma 3.14 *If $n \geq u - 1$, then in an optimal basic solution of $LP(U)$, there are at least $(n - u + 1)$ x_{ij} variables that take the value 1, where U is the subset of the plants found by Algorithm LB and u is the number of plants in U.*

Now, we present the heuristic for Problem 3 proposed by Chen and Pundoor (2006).

Heuristic CP-H2

Step 1: Run Algorithm LB to obtain a subset of plants U and an optimal basic solution x^* of $LP(U)$. Define a subset of jobs $J = \{j \in N \mid x_{ij}^* = 1$ for some $i \in U\}$. [Lemma 3.14 implies that there are at least $n - u + 1$ jobs in J and hence at most $u - 1$ jobs in $N \setminus J$].

Step 2: (*Create a solution for the jobs in J*) Assign each job $j \in J$ to plant $i \in U$ with $x_{ij} = 1$. Schedule the jobs assigned to each plant in an arbitrary sequence. Schedule order delivery such that it satisfies Lemma 3.13. Denote the resulting partial solution (containing the jobs from J only) by σ_1.

Step 3: (*Create a separate solution for the jobs in $N \setminus J$*) Enumerate all possible assignments of the at most $u - 1$ jobs in $N \setminus J$ to the plants in U until the following termination condition is satisfied:

- For each such assignment, schedule the jobs at each plant in an arbitrary sequence. Schedule job delivery such that it satisfies Lemma 3.13. If in the resulting solution (containing the jobs from $N \setminus J$ only), the total contribution of the jobs to the objective value of Problem 3 is less than or equal to $Z_{LP}(U)$, then stop. Denote the resulting partial solution by σ_2.

If no solution satisfies the termination condition, then take the solution with the lowest total contribution to the objective value of Problem 3, and denote this partial solution by σ_2.

Step 4: Concatenate solutions σ_1 and σ_2 at each plant. Reschedule job delivery in the concatenated solution at each plant such that it satisfies Lemma 3.13. Denote the final solution by σ.

We note that the enumeration procedure in Step 3 may generate a maximum of u^{u-1} possible solutions for the jobs in $N \setminus J$. Thus the worst-case time complexity of this heuristic is polynomial in n but exponential in m. However, if m is fixed, this heuristic has polynomial running time. We also note that the termination condition in Step 3 may not always be satisfied. However, for a problem with a large number of jobs, $Z_{LP}(U)$ is sufficiently large such that the termination condition may be satisfied at an early stage, and hence only a small number of solutions may be generated in Step 3.

Chen and Pundoor (2006) show that for Problem 3, the worst-case performance ratio of Heuristic CP-H2 is bounded by $b + 1$, and this heuristic is asymptotically optimal when n goes to infinity with m and b fixed. Furthermore, their computational experiments based on a large number of randomly generated test instances show that the average gap of the solution generated by the heuristic compared to the lower bound $Z_{LP}(U)$ is 5.23%, 3.11%, and 1.96%, respectively, for test problems with 50, 100, and 200 jobs.

3.8 Problems with Two Stages of Delivery

All the problems discussed in the previous sections involve a single stage of job delivery. However, as discussed in Tang et al. (2019), there are practical settings where the delivery of completed jobs may involve two stages. One example is the delivery of make-to-order steel coils by Baosteel, the third largest steel company in the world. Baosteel delivers MTO steel coils first from its plant to a port by trailers, and then from the port to customer destinations by ships. Other examples involving two stages of delivery include some custom-made high-tech electronics (e.g., PCs) and picked-to-order organic vegetables. After PCs are assembled in a plant, they are first delivered to a consolidation center by vans, and from the consolidation center, PCs heading to different regions are shipped by trucks, trains, or air flights. Similarly, after being picked and collected from a farm, picked-to-order vegetables are first delivered from the farm by trucks or vans to a distribution center in a city, and then sent from the distribution center to customer homes by cars or bicycles. In all these examples, the underlying integrated production and distribution scheduling problem has a common structure as depicted in Fig. 3.3, where the pool point (e.g., port, consolidation center) represents the destination of the first-stage delivery and the origin of the second-stage delivery.

In this section, we focus on the two IPODS problems with two stages of delivery studied in Tang et al. (2019). These problems share the same production and delivery characteristics but with different objective functions. They are defined as follows. There are n jobs from k customers, $K = \{1, \ldots, k\}$, to be processed in a plant with a single machine or m ($m > 1$) identical parallel machine. Let n_i be the number of jobs from customer $i \in K$ such that $n = \sum_{i \in K} n_i$, and $N_i = \{(i, 1), \ldots, (i, n_i)\}$ be the set of jobs from customer $i \in K$, where (i, j) denotes the jth job of customer i. Let $N = \cup_{i \in K} N_i$ be the set of all the jobs together. Each job $(i, j) \in N$ has a required processing time of $p_{(i,j)}$. After jobs are processed in the plant, they are delivered to their respective customers through two stages of delivery: (1) First from the plant to a pool point (e.g., a port, a distribution, or a consolidation center) by

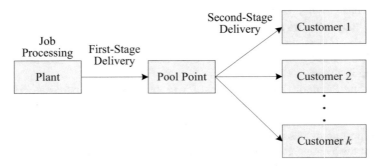

Fig. 3.3 A supply chain with two stages of delivery

homogeneous transporters (e.g., trailers, vans, or trucks), which we call *vehicles* to distinguish them from transporters used in the second stage of delivery, and (2) then from the pool point to the customers by transporters (e.g., ships, trucks, or vans) which we call *ships* to distinguish them from the transporters used in the first stage of delivery. In the first stage of delivery, there are sufficient homogeneous vehicles available whenever needed and each vehicle can deliver up to c_0 jobs in each shipment. Jobs from different customers can be delivered together in a vehicle shipment from the plant to the pool point. The transportation time and transportation cost of each vehicle shipment from the plant to the pool point are denoted as t_0 and f_0, respectively. In the second stage of delivery, jobs from different customers are not allowed to share a shipment because each ship only goes to one customer site. There are sufficient homogeneous ships available for each customer site whenever needed, but ships for different customer sites are generally heterogeneous. Each ship going to customer i can carry up to c_i jobs in each shipment. The transportation time and transportation cost from a shipment from the pool point to customer i are t_i and f_i, respectively.

For ease of presentation, the shipments by vehicles from the plant to the pool point and the shipments by ships from the pool point to the customers are denoted below as *v-shipments* and *s-shipments*, respectively. We need to determine (1) how to schedule jobs for processing in the plant; (2) how to batch jobs to form v-shipments and schedule the delivery of v-shipments from the plant to the pool point; and (3) how to batch jobs to form s-shipments and schedule the delivery of s-shipments from the pool point to the customers, so that a certain objective is optimized. In a given solution, we define:

- $D_{(i,j)}$ = the delivery time of job (i, j), which is the time when job (i, j) arrives at its customer.
- $C_{(i,j)}$ = the completion time of job (i, j) processed in the plant.
- TC = the total transportation cost.
- $D_{total} = \sum_{(i,j) \in N} D_{(i,j)}$, the total delivery time of all the jobs.
- $D_{\max} = \max_{(i,j) \in N} D_{(i,j)}$, the maximum delivery time of all the jobs.

3.8 Problems with Two Stages of Delivery

We consider the following two problems in this section.

- Problem P1: Minimizing the sum of the total delivery time and the total transportation cost, i.e., $D_{total} + TC$.
- Problem P2: Minimizing the sum of the maximum delivery time and the total transportation cost, i.e., $D_{max} + TC$.

Tang et al. (2019) show that problem P1 is strongly NP-hard even if there is a single machine or a single customer. Problem P2 with a single machine can be solved in polynomial time when the number of customers k is fixed, whereas problem P2 with parallel machines is NP-hard because it contains the NP-hard classical parallel-machine makespan problem $P_m||C_{max}$ as a special case.

In the remainder of this section, we first present some optimality properties in Sect. 3.8.1, and then present solution algorithms for these two problems in Sects. 3.8.2 and 3.8.3, respectively. All these results are from Tang et al. (2019).

3.8.1 Optimality Properties

There are five optimality properties derived by Tang et al. (2019). The first four apply to both problems, whereas the last one applies to problem 2 only. Since they are all straightforward, we do not show the proofs.

Property 3.1 For both problems, there exists an optimal solution that satisfies all of the following:

(i) There is no idle time between the jobs processed on any machine.
(ii) The jobs from the same customer and processed on the same machine are processed in the shortest processing time first (SPT) sequence. (In the remainder of the chapter, we call this property group-SPT property.)
(iii) The jobs in each v-shipment that are processed on the same machine are processed consecutively on the machine.
(iv) For each v-shipment, its departure time from the plant to the pool point is equal to the completion time of the last job in this shipment.
(v) For each s-shipment, its departure time from the pool point to its customer is equal to the arrival time of the last job in this shipment at the pool point.
(vi) Jobs from each customer that arrive earlier at the pool point are delivered by ships no later than jobs from the same customer that arrive later at the pool point.

Property 3.2 For both problems, there exists an optimal solution that satisfies the following: For each customer $i \in K$, at any time point t, if there are at least $x_i \geq c_i$ jobs from this customer waiting at the pool point, then there are $u_i = \lfloor x_i/c_i \rfloor$ full s-shipments carrying a total of $u_i c_i$ jobs, or u_i full s-shipments and 1 partial s-shipment carrying a total of x_i jobs that will depart immediately (i.e., at time t) from the pool point to the customer.

128   3 Integrated Production and Outbound Distribution Scheduling: Offline Problems

Based on Properties 3.1 and 3.2, Property 3.3 below characterizes all possible cases of the relationship between the number of jobs from each customer waiting at the pool point before a new v-shipment arrives at the pool point and the number of jobs from the same customer shipped away from the pool point after the v-shipment arrives at the pool point. For ease of presentation, we define the following three parameters for each $i \in K$:

- Let h_i denote the number of jobs from customer i waiting at the pool point immediately before a v-shipment arrives at the pool point.
- Let q_i denote the number of jobs from customer i in this v-shipment.
- Let e_i denote the number of jobs from customer i that are shipped away by s-shipments from the pool point to customer i immediately after this v-shipment arrives at the pool point.

Property 3.3 For both problems, there exists an optimal solution which satisfies one of the following cases, for each $i \in K$:

(i) Immediately after the arrival of the v-shipment, $e_i = \lfloor (h_i + q_i)/c_i \rfloor c_i$ of the $h_i + q_i$ jobs from customer i are shipped away from the pool point in $\lfloor (h_i + q_i)/c_i \rfloor$ s-shipments, and the remaining $l_i = h_i + q_i - e_i$ jobs from customer i are waiting at the pool point.

(ii) Immediately after the arrival of the v-shipment, all the $e_i = h_i + q_i$ jobs from customer i are shipped away from the pool point in $\lceil (h_i + q_i)/c_i \rceil$ s-shipments, and there is no job from customer i waiting at the pool point.

Property 3.4 For both problems, if there is only a single machine in the problems, then there exists an optimal solution in which jobs completed earlier in the plant are delivered by vehicles no later than those completed later in the plant.

Property 3.5 For problem P2, there exists an optimal solution in which the jobs from customer $i \in K$ are delivered by $\lceil n_i/c_i \rceil$ s-shipments and all the s-shipments except possibly the last one are full.

While Properties 3.1, 3.2, and 3.3 all hold for both problems under both the case with a single machine and the case with parallel machines, it can be shown that Property 3.5 does not hold for problem P1, and Property 3.4 does not hold for the case with parallel machines.

Based on these properties, we assume throughout the remainder of this section that the jobs from each customer $i \in K$ are indexed in SPT order such that $p_{(i,1)} \le p_{(i,2)} \le \cdots \le p_{(i,n_i)}$.

In the following sections, we apply these properties to solve problems P1 and P2, respectively.

3.8 Problems with Two Stages of Delivery   129

3.8.2 Solving the Total Delivery Time Problem

We first consider problem P1 with a single machine, denoted as P1-S, and solve it by a dynamic programming algorithm. This algorithm considers one v-shipment at each iteration and updates the state based on the time moment when the v-shipment arrives at the pool point. The formation and scheduling of each v-shipment follow from Properties 3.1 and 3.4. By Property 3.2, when a v-shipment arrives at the pool point, there are most $c_i - 1$ jobs waiting for delivery to each customer.

Algorithm TLC-DP1

Value Function $F(j_1, \ldots, j_k; l_1, \ldots, l_k)$ is the minimum objective value of a partial schedule where for each customer $i \in K$, the first j_i jobs, $(i, 1), \ldots, (i, j_i)$, have been processed on the machine and delivered from the plant to the pool point; the first $j_i - l_i$ jobs, $(i, 1), \ldots, (i, j_i - l_i)$, have been delivered from the pool point to customer i, and the remaining l_i jobs, $(i, j_i - l_i + 1), \ldots, (i, j_i)$, are kept at the pool point to be delivered to customer i later.

Initial Condition $F(0, \ldots, 0; 0, \ldots, 0) = 0$.

Recurrence Relation For $i = 1, \ldots, k$; $j_i = 0, \ldots, n_i$; $l_i = 0, \ldots, \min\{j_i, c_i - 1\}$:

$$
\begin{aligned}
&F(j_1, \ldots, j_k; l_1, \ldots, l_k) \\
&= \min_{(q_1, \ldots, q_k; h_1, \ldots, h_k)} \Bigg\{ F(j_1 - q_1, \ldots, j_k - q_k; h_1, \ldots, h_k) \\
&\quad + \sum_{i \in K} \left((h_i + q_i - l_i) \left(\sum_{u \in K} \sum_{r=1}^{j_u} p_{(u,r)} + t_0 + t_i \right) \right) \\
&\quad + f_0 + \sum_{i \in K} \lceil (h_i + q_i - l_i)/c_i \rceil f_i \\
&\quad \Big| \; 0 < \sum_{i \in K} q_i \leq c_0; \; 0 \leq q_i \leq \min\{j_i, c_0\}, \text{ for } i \in K; \\
&\quad\quad h_i \in H_i \cap \{0, \ldots, j_i - q_i\}, \text{ for } i \in K \Bigg\},
\end{aligned}
$$

where H_i is defined as follows:

$$
H_i = \begin{cases}
\{l_i - q_i\}, & \text{if } l_i \geq q_i; \\
\{0, \ldots, c_i - 1\}, & \text{if } l_i < q_i, l_i = 0; \\
\{l_i + c_i - q_i\}, & \text{if } l_i < q_i, l_i \neq 0, c_0 \leq c_i; \\
\{uc_i + l_i - q_i, \text{ for } u = 1, \ldots, \lfloor (q_i - l_i - 1)/c_i \rfloor + 1\}, & \text{if } l_i < q_i, l_i \neq 0, c_0 > c_i.
\end{cases}
$$

Optimal Solution Value $F(n_1, \ldots, n_k; 0, \ldots, 0)$.

130   3 Integrated Production and Outbound Distribution Scheduling: Offline Problems

Tang et al. (2019) show that this algorithm solves problem P1-S to optimality in $O(n^k (c_{max})^{2k})$ time, where $c_{max} = \max\{c_i | i \in K\}$.

Next, we consider the general version of problem P1 where there are m parallel machines. We describe below the heuristic algorithm developed by Tang et al. (2019) for this problem. The heuristic consists of two phases. In the first phase, a variant of problem P1-S is solved by a modified version of Algorithm TLC-DP1. In the second phase, the solution of this problem is converted to a feasible solution for problem P1.

Define a variant of problem P1-S, denoted as P1-S$'$, which is the same as problem P1-S except that the departure time of each v-shipment is calculated differently. In problem P1-S, the departure time of a v-shipment is equal to the completion time of the last job contained in it. However, in problem P1-S$'$, the departure time of a v-shipment is instead defined as follows. Suppose that jobs are delivered from the plant to the pool point by u v-shipments, denoted as $A_1, \ldots, A_u$, in increasing order of the completion times of their last jobs. For each v-shipment A_l, for $l = 1, \ldots, u$, its departure time δ_l from the plant is defined to be

$$\delta_l = \frac{1}{m} \sum_{r=1}^{l} \sum_{(i,j) \in A_r} p_{(i,j)} + \frac{m-1}{m} \max\{p_{(i,j)} | (i, j) \in A_1 \cup \cdots \cup A_l\}. \quad (3.28)$$

As will become clear in the following, the quantity defined in (3.28) is an upper bound on the completion time of the last job among the jobs in $A_1 \cup \cdots \cup A_l$ when these jobs are assigned to the m parallel machines in a certain way. This then ensures that the optimal objective value of problem P1-S$'$ is an upper bound on the objective value of the solution generated by the heuristic for problem P1 described below.

The following algorithm solves problem P1-S$'$ to optimality in $O(n^k (c_{max})^{2k})$ time.

Algorithm TLC-DP1$'$

Apply Algorithm TLC-DP1 except that the departure time of each v-shipment from the plant involved in the recursion of TLC-DP1, i.e., $\sum_{u \in K} \sum_{r=1}^{j_u} p_{(u,r)}$, is replaced by the redefined departure time for problem P1-S$'$ as in (3.28), i.e., $\frac{1}{m} \sum_{u \in K} \sum_{r=1}^{j_u} p_{(u,r)} + \frac{m-1}{m} \max\{p_{(u,r)} | u \in K, r = 1, \ldots, j_u\}$.

Now, we describe the heuristic algorithm developed by Tang et al. (2019) for problem P1. The heuristic first solves problem P1-S$'$ and then transforms the solution of this problem into a feasible solution for problem P1.

Heuristic TLC-H1

Step 1. Solve problem P1-S$'$ by Algorithm TLC-DP$'$. Denote the solution by σ. Suppose that in σ, there are a v-shipments, denoted as $A_1, \ldots, A_a$, in increasing order of the completion times of their last jobs at the plant, and b s-shipments, denoted as $B_1, \ldots, B_b$, in increasing order of the arrival times of their last jobs at the pool point.

Step 2. Convert solution σ to a solution π for problem P1 as follows. Solution π consists of the same v-shipments $A_1, \ldots, A_a$ and the same s-shipments,

3.8 Problems with Two Stages of Delivery

$B_1, \ldots, B_b$ as in solution σ, except that the jobs have a different processing schedule as described below in Step 2.1, which uniquely determines the departure time of each of these shipments as described below in Step 2.2.

Step 2.1. For $l = 1, \ldots, a$, sort the jobs of A_l in nondecreasing order of their processing times (i.e., SPT order), and then process them on the m parallel machines using the following earliest-available-machine (EAM) rule: Schedule the first unscheduled job to the earliest available machine until all the jobs in A_l are scheduled.

Step 2.2. For $l = 1, \ldots, a$, deliver the jobs of A_l in one v-shipment from the plant to the pool point when the last job in A_l completes processing at the plant. For $l = 1, \ldots, b$, deliver the jobs of B_l in one s-shipment from the pool point to the corresponding customer when the last job in B_l arrives at the pool point.

Tang et al. (2019) show that the worst-case performance ratio of Heuristic TLC-H1 for problem P1 is bounded by $2 - \frac{1}{m}$, and the heuristic is asymptotically optimal for the problem when the number of jobs n goes to infinity but the number of machines m is fixed.

They also consider a variant of problem P1 where jobs from different customers are not allowed to share v-shipments. They explain that there are practical settings where, for reasons such as possible contamination, insurance liability, and competition, jobs from different customers may have to be delivered separately in every stage of delivery. Consequently, both v-shipments and s-shipments can deliver jobs from a single customer only. They modify Heuristic TLC-H1 for this variant of problem P1 and show that the modified heuristic has a worst-case performance ratio of 2 or $\max\{2 - \frac{1}{m}, \max_{i \in K}\{c_i\}\}$, depending on certain conditions on some problem parameters.

3.8.3 Solving the Maximum Delivery Time Problem

By Property 5 in Sect. 3.8.1, in an optimal solution of problem P2, the jobs from each customer $i \in K$ are delivered by $\lceil n_i/c_i \rceil$ s-shipments and among these shipments at most one is not full. This means that the total transportation cost of the jobs from the pool point to the customer sites is fixed in an optimal solution. Furthermore, by Properties 1(v), 1(vi), and 5, the formation and schedule of each s-shipment to each customer is known once the arrival times of jobs to the pool point are known. Thus, to solve problem P2, we can focus on production scheduling, and formation and scheduling of the v-shipments from the plant to the pool point.

For problem P2 with a single machine, Tang et al. (2019) propose the following DP algorithm that can find an optimal solution in $O(n^{k+1}c_0^k/k^{k-1})$ time.

Algorithm TLC-DP2

Value Function $F(r; j_1, \ldots, j_k)$ as the minimum maximum delivery time of the jobs in a partial schedule where for each customer $i \in K$, the first j_i jobs

$(i, 1), \ldots, (i, j_i)$ have been processed and delivered to the pool point, and a total of r v-shipments are used to deliver all these $j_1 + \cdots + j_k$ jobs.

Initialization $F(0; 0, \ldots, 0) = 0$.

Recurrence Relation For $i \in K$; $j_i = 0, \ldots, n_i$; and $r = \lceil \sum_{i \in K} j_i / c_0 \rceil, \ldots, \sum_{i \in K} j_i$:

$$F(r; j_1, \ldots, j_k)$$

$$= \min_{(q_1, \ldots, q_k)} \left\{ \max \left\{ F(r - 1; j_1 - q_1, \ldots, j_k - q_k), \right. \right.$$

$$\left. G(r; j_1, \ldots, j_k; q_1, \ldots, q_k) \right\}$$

$$\left| (q_1, \ldots, q_k) \text{ satisfying: } 0 < \sum_{u \in K} q_i \leq c_0, \text{ and} \right.$$

$$\left. 0 \leq q_i \leq \min\{j_i, c_0\}, \text{ for } i \in K \right\},$$

where

$$G(r; j_1, \ldots, j_k; q_1, \ldots, q_k) = \max \left\{ \sum_{u \in K} \sum_{w=1}^{j_u} P_{(u,w)} + t_0 + t_l \right|$$

$$\left. \text{for } l \in K \text{ that satisfy } j_l = n_l \text{ or } j_l - \lfloor \frac{j_l - q_l}{c_l} \rfloor c_l \geq c_l \right\}$$

Optimal Solution The optimal solution value of the problem is determined as

$$\min \left\{ F(r; n_1, \ldots, n_k) + r f_0 | r = \lceil n/c_0 \rceil, \ldots, n \right\} + \sum_{i \in K} \lceil n_i / c_i \rceil f_i.$$

In the above algorithm, $G(r; j_1, \ldots, j_k; q_1, \ldots, q_k)$ is the maximum delivery time of the jobs in $\cup_{i=1}^{k} \{(i, j_i - q_1 + 1), \ldots, (i, j_i)\}$. The algorithm works as follows. At each iteration, for any feasible values of $(q_1, \ldots, q_k)$, the algorithm considers a v-shipment consisting of q_i jobs $\{(i, j_i - q_i + 1), \ldots, (i, j_i)\}$ from each customer $i \in K$. This v-shipment arrives at the pool point at time $\tau = \sum_{u \in K} \sum_{w=1}^{j_u} P_{(u,w)} + t_0$. Since the number of jobs from customer i waiting immediately before this v-shipment arrives at the pool point is $h_i = j_i - q_i - \lfloor \frac{j_i - q_i}{c_i} \rfloor c_i$, there is a total of $q_i + h_i$ jobs from customer i at the pool point when this v-shipment arrives at the pool point.

If $h_i + q_i \geq c_i$ (i.e., $j_i - \lfloor \frac{j_i - q_i}{c_i} \rfloor c_i \geq c_i$) and $j_i \neq n_i$, then, by Property 3.5, there are $\lfloor (h_i + q_i)/c_i \rfloor c_i$ jobs departing from the pool point to customer i at time τ and $h_i + q_i - \lfloor (h_i + q_i)/c_i \rfloor c_i$ jobs waiting to be delivered to customer i at a later time.

3.8 Problems with Two Stages of Delivery

If $j_i = n_i$, then all the $q_i + h_i$ jobs depart from the pool point to customer i at time τ. This implies that if $j_i - \lfloor \frac{j_i - q_i}{c_i} \rfloor c_i \geq c_i$ or $j_i = n_i$, then there are jobs departing to customer i at time τ, and their arrival time at customer i is $\tau + t_i$.

Otherwise, by Property 3.5, there is no job of customer i departing from the pool point at time τ. The first maximization in the recurrence relation of the DP calculates the maximum delivery time of the jobs by comparing the maximum delivery time of the earlier jobs, which is $F(r-1; j_1 - q_1, \ldots, j_k - q_k)$, and the maximum delivery time of the jobs departing at time τ, which is $G(r; j_1, \ldots, j_k; q_1, \ldots, q_k)$.

Tang et al. (2019) propose a heuristic for problem P2 with a general number of parallel machines. The idea of the heuristic can be described as follows. Customers are sequenced in nonincreasing order of the shipping times from the pool point to their sites, i.e., t_i. For each customer, jobs from this customer are first sorted in LPT order and then processed on the m machines in the plant using the EAM rule (defined in Step 2.1 of Heuristic TLC-H1). Given the production schedule, a delivery schedule is generated by forming v-shipments using a dynamic programming algorithm, and forming s-shipments following Property 3.5, as described below.

Heuristic TLC-H2

Step 1. Reindex the customers such that $t_1 \geq \cdots \geq t_k$. Reindex the jobs from customer $i \in K$ such that $p_{(i,1)} \geq \cdots \geq p_{(i,n_i)}$.

Step 2. Process the jobs from customer $1, \ldots, k$ in this order on the m machines by the EAM rule. Based on the completion times of the jobs $C_{(i,j)}$ in the resulting production schedule, reindex the jobs from customer $i \in K$ such that $C_{(i,1)} \leq \cdots \leq C_{(i,n_i)}$. Further reindex job (i, j) as $[\sum_{l=1}^{i-1} n_l + j]$ for $j = 1, \ldots, n_i$, and $i \in K$, so that the jobs are now reindexed as $[1], \ldots, [n]$. Their corresponding customers are denoted as, $e[1], \ldots, e[n]$, and their completion times as $C_{[1]}, \ldots, C_{[n]}$, respectively.

Step 3. Given the production schedule and new indices of the jobs as defined in the above steps, the formation and scheduling of v-shipments are obtained by the following dynamic programming algorithm.

- *Value Function*: $F(r, j)$ is the minimum maximum delivery time of the jobs $[1], \ldots, [j]$ in a partial schedule where these jobs have been processed and delivered to the pool point by r v-shipments. Define $\delta_i(x, y)$ as the number of jobs from customer i in the job set $\{[x], \ldots, [y]\}$.
- *Initialization*: $F(0, 0) = 0$.
- *Recurrence Relation*: For $r = \lceil j/c_0 \rceil, \ldots, j$, and $j = 1, \ldots, n$,

$$F(r, j_1) = \min_q \left\{ \max \left\{ F(r-1, j-q), G(r, j, q) \right\} \mid 0 < q \leq \min\{j, c_0\} \right\},$$

where

$$G(r, j, q) = \max_l \left\{ \max_w \left\{ C_{[w]} \mid w = j - q + 1, \ldots, j \right\} + t_0 + t_{e[l]} \right.$$

$$\left. \mid \text{for } l \in \{j - q + 1, \ldots, j\} \text{ and satisfy:} \right.$$

$$\delta_{e[l]}(1, j) = n_{e[l]} \text{ or}$$

$$\delta_{e[l]}(1, j) - \lfloor \frac{\delta_{e[l]}(1, j - q)}{c_{e[l]}} \rfloor c_{e[l]} \geq c_{e[l]} \Big\}.$$

- *Output*: The optimal value is determined as $\min\{F(r, n) + rf_0 | r = \lceil n/c_0 \rceil, \ldots, n\}$.

Suppose that the optimal solution generated by this DP algorithm contains a v-shipments, denoted as $A_1, \ldots, A_a$. Each of these v-shipments is delivered from the plant to the pool point at the time when the last job in it has completed processing in the plant.

Step 4. The formation and schedule of s-shipments follow Property 5. For each $i \in K$, whenever there are at least c_i customer-i jobs waiting at the pool point or the last job of customer i arrives at the pool point, deliver all the customer-i jobs at the pool point to customer i using a minimal number of s-shipments.

We note that in the DP algorithm in Step 3 for finding the optimal formation and schedule of v-shipments given the production schedule of the jobs, each iteration considers a v-shipment consisting of q jobs $[j - q + 1], \ldots, [j]$. The departure time of this v-shipment from the plant is $\max\{C_{[w]} \mid w = j - q + 1, \ldots, j\}$. This algorithm is similar to Algorithm TLC-DP2 for problem P2 with a single machine.

Tang et al. (2019) show that for problem P2, Heuristic TLC-H2 has a worst-case performance ratio of 2 or $3 - 1/m$, depending on whether a certain condition is satisfied in the solution obtained by the heuristic. They further show that this heuristic is asymptotically optimal for problem P2 when n goes to infinity but m is fixed.

Tang et al. (2019) also study online versions of some of the problems discussed here. In Chap. 4, we discuss these online problems, together with the online versions of some other problems covered in this chapter.

3.9 Future Research

Although a wide variety of IPODS problems have received a significant amount of research attention in the last two decades, there are still many gaps to be filled, including clarifying the complexity of many open problems, relaxing some commonly adopted assumptions to make the models studied more practical, and paying more attention to some problem classes that have been under-studied. We elaborate on each of these directions for future research.

- Within the problem class with the individual and immediate delivery method, problem $P_m|fd_j|V(v, 1), iid|n| \sum R_j$ is solved by Algorithm A3.2 in Sect. 3.3.3. This algorithm has a time complexity that is exponential in m and v. Whether this problem with arbitrary m and v can be solved in polynomial time

3.9 Future Research

remains open. Hence, this problem should be studied further. In addition, one can study problems within this class with an objective function other than $D_{\max}$ and $\sum R_j$. Such problems have received little attention.

- A large number of problems with a single customer and the batch delivery method have been investigated in the literature. The ones discussed in Sect. 3.4 are only a small representative subset of problems in this class. There are many interesting open problems left in the literature that can be studied further. Below we highlight several such problems.

  - Several problems with multiple delivery vehicles can be solved in polynomial time when the number of vehicles v is fixed, but their complexity remains open when v becomes arbitrary. They include problem $1||V(v, c), direct|1|\sum D_j$ discussed in Sect. 3.4.5, and problem $1||V(v, \infty), direct|1|L_{\max}+TC$ (Chen, 2010).
  - Several problems with an unlimited vehicle capacity (i.e., $c = \infty$), including $1||V(\infty, \infty), direct|1|\sum U_j + TC$ and $1||V(1, \infty), direct|1|\sum U_j + TC$ can be solved in polynomial time (Hall & Potts, 2003, 2005, and Section 7.2), but the complexity of these problems with a limited vehicle capacity remains unknown.
  - Several problems are known to be at least ordinarily NP-hard, including problem $P_m||V(\infty, c), direct|1|\sum D_j + TC$ with an arbitrary m, studied in Sect. 3.4.4, problem $P_2||V(1, \infty), direct|1|\sum D_j+TC$ (Hall & Potts, 2005), and problem $P_2||V(1, c), direct|1|\sum D_j$ (Lee & Chen, 2001). However, to our knowledge, it remains unknown whether these problems are strongly NP-hard.

- Problems discussed in Sect. 3.5 involve batch delivery to multiple customers. This class of problems has received much less attention than problems with batch delivery to a single customer. It would be useful to investigate several open problems left from the literature, as discussed below.

  - As shown in Sect. 3.5.1, problem $1||V(\infty, c), direct|k|L_{\max} + TC$ with an arbitrary number of customers k is at least ordinarily NP-hard. However, it is unknown whether this problem is strongly NP-hard. Also, it is open whether this problem is still at least ordinarily NP-hard when k is fixed.
  - As discussed in Sect. 3.5.2, problem $P_m||V(\infty, c), routing|k|\sum D_j +TC$ is strongly NP-hard when k is arbitrary, and at least ordinarily NP-hard when k is fixed. But whether the latter case is strongly NP-hard remains unknown.
  - As shown in Sect. 3.5.3, problem $1||V(v, c), direct|k|\sum D_j + TC$ with both k and v fixed is solvable in polynomial time. However, when one or both of k and v are arbitrary, the complexity of this problem remains unknown.

- Another valuable direction is to investigate problems that involve the routing delivery method for multiple customers. Only a handful of such problems have been studied in the literature (e.g., Chen & Vairaktarakis, 2005; Geismar et al., 2008; Li et al., 2005a). Such problems involve both production scheduling and vehicle routing and are generally more challenging than most other IPODS problems. It would be useful to develop algorithms that build on some existing methods from the vehicle routing literature.

- The problems with fixed delivery departure dates discussed in Sect. 3.6 and other problems within this class studied in the literature all involve a production environment where there is a single machine. It would also be valuable to consider this class of problems with a different production environment, e.g., parallel machines.

- Apparently, Chen and Pundoor (2006) is the only study on IPODS problems with multiple plants. As supply chains become more global, and more companies rely on overseas plants for production, an increasing number of applications give rise to scheduling and delivery problems that can be modeled as IPODS problems with multiple plants. Thus, more research in this area is needed.

- Problems with two or more stages of delivery have also received little attention. As most supply chains in practice involve multiple stages of distribution, it is clear that more research on IPODS problems with multiple delivery stages is also needed.

- Finally, in most existing IPODS problems, the capacity of a delivery vehicle is measured in terms of the number of jobs the vehicle can carry in a shipment by implicitly assuming that each job has an identical size such that they require an identical amount of vehicle capacity. Only a few papers (Chang & Lee, 2004; Chen & Pundoor, 2009; He et al., 2006; Zhong et al., 2007) have considered problems where each job may have a different size and the capacity of a vehicle is measured as the total size of jobs that it can carry. Clearly, modeling the job size and vehicle capacity in this way is more practical, but it also makes the underlying problems more challenging because the vehicle capacity constraint alone involves the strongly NP-hard bin packing problem. More research on such IPODS problems would be highly valuable.

Chapter 4
Integrated Production and Outbound Distribution Scheduling: Online Problems

Abstract In this chapter we discuss online integrated production and outbound distribution scheduling (O-IPODS) problems, which are extensions of the offline IPODS problems discussed in Chap. 3 to an online environment. In such problems, jobs arrive over time and the parameters associated with each job are not known until it arrives. Following the classification scheme described in Chap. 3 for offline IPODS problems, O-IPODS problems can also be classified into several different classes in a similar way, and most of them can also be represented by the five-field notation described in Chap. 3. For each class of O-IPODS problems, we discuss several representative problems, present the corresponding online algorithms for solving these problems, and describe the theoretical performance of these algorithms.

4.1 Introduction

One of the basic assumptions made in deterministic scheduling, including deterministic supply chain scheduling covered in other chapters of this book, is that all the jobs to be considered in a problem, along with their parameters, are known with certainty before scheduling decisions are made. However, this assumption is often not valid in practice. For example, manufacturers and retailers usually receive customer orders over time and do not have precise knowledge of future orders until they arrive (e.g., Chen & Chen, 2015; Fisher, 1997). One could use stochastic scheduling models to study scheduling problems that arise in such an environment. However, stochastic scheduling models assume that probability distributions of job parameters are known in advance. Such an assumption is not valid either in many practical settings, especially in settings where products are customized or have a short selling season; hence, there is little market information that can be used even to characterize future demand probabilistically (e.g., Daniels & Kouvelis, 1995; Perakis & Roels, 2008). In such cases, the underlying scheduling decisions may need to be made in an online fashion without assuming any knowledge of future orders or their parameters.

© Springer Nature Switzerland AG 2022

Z.-L. Chen, N. G. Hall, *Supply Chain Scheduling*, International Series in Operations Research & Management Science 323, https://doi.org/10.1007/978-3-030-90374-9_4

137

138   4 Integrated Production and Outbound Distribution Scheduling: Online Problems

In online scheduling problems, at any time instant, no information about a future job's arrival time, processing time, and other parameters is assumed to be known with certainty or even in a probabilistic sense until this job arrives. Therefore, compared to deterministic and stochastic scheduling problems, online scheduling problems involve the least information about problem parameters. Online scheduling algorithms, which are used to solve online scheduling problems, construct a schedule piece-by-piece in a serial fashion based on the known information about the jobs that have arrived. The performance of an online algorithm is often represented by its *competitive ratio*. Readers are referred to Sect. 2.3.4 for the definition of competitive ratio and a discussion of some related concepts.

There is an extensive literature on online scheduling (e.g., Pruhs et al., 2004; Tan & Zhang, 2013). However, most online scheduling problems studied in the literature are online classical scheduling problems, which involve only scheduling decisions for processing jobs on machines without involving other decisions such as job delivery that arise in supply chains. As e-commerce is becoming ever more popular around the world, we are witnessing an increasing number of applications where the underlying scheduling problems can be modeled as online integrated production and outbound distribution scheduling (O-IPODS) problems. Below we describe two such applications.

Direct-sell consumer electronics manufacturers such as Dell operate in make-to-order fashion where assembly operations for an order only begin after the order arrives. Once an order is processed, it needs to be delivered to the customer soon. To achieve a system-wide optimal solution, assembly and delivery operations must be considered together (Li et al., 2008; Stecke & Zhao, 2007). The underlying scheduling decisions about the assembly and delivery operations can be made in two ways: (1) on a rolling horizon basis where decisions are made periodically (e.g., once a day) such that all the orders that have arrived are considered together in the underlying decision problem, and (2) in an online fashion such that a decision is made whenever a new order arrives. The first approach involves an offline integrated production and delivery scheduling problem, which belongs to the class of problems studied in Chap. 3, whenever the problem is solved under a rolling horizon framework. However, the second approach involves an online integrated production and delivery scheduling problem. Either approach has advantages and disadvantages. Considering multiple orders together can potentially result in a solution that is less myopic, but waiting for more orders to arrive may lower capacity utilization and delay the delivery of orders, which can result in an inferior solution. Hence, in situations where processing or/and delivery capacity is/are tightly constrained, and customers expect short delivery lead time, online decision making may be preferable. Such situations occur during busy holiday shopping seasons, such as Thanksgiving, Christmas, and Labor Day, when a much higher than average demand occurs. In addition, during such time periods, there tends to be more competition among the companies selling similar products, and hence, fast delivery of orders becomes even more important.

Another example is the order fulfillment and delivery operations faced by online retailers such as Amazon and JD. In this case, order delivery lead time is often

4.2 Online Problems with Individual and Immediate Delivery 139

very short (e.g., 1 day or 2 days), and both fulfillment and delivery capacities are tightly constrained, particularly during busy shopping seasons. Similar to the above example, decision makers need to consider fulfillment and delivery operations jointly and should make scheduling decisions in an online fashion in order to utilize capacity fully and respond to online orders as quickly as possible (Zhang et al., 2018, 2019).

In this chapter, we focus on online integrated production and outbound distribution scheduling (O-IPODS) problems, which are the online versions of the IPODS problems discussed in Chap. 3. In Chap. 3, offline IPODS problems are classified into several different classes based on the number of plants, the number of delivery stages, and delivery method. Most IPODS problems involve a single plant and a single delivery stage. Such problems are represented in Chap. 3 by a five-field notation scheme. For ease of presentation, we extend the five-field representation scheme of Chap. 3 to represent online counterparts of IPODS problems with a single plant and a single delivery stage as follows. Given an offline problem $\alpha |r_j, \beta |\pi|\delta|\gamma$, we use $\alpha |online, r_j, \beta|\pi|\delta|\gamma$ to represent the corresponding O-IPODS problem with the same characteristics except that now jobs arrive over time (as represented by "r_j") and the parameters of a job, including its arrival time, are unknown until after its arrival.

There has been a growing research interest in O-IPODS problems in the last decade or so. However, the existing studies in this area have focused primarily on a small subset of problems where (i) certain delivery methods, such as individual and immediate delivery and direct delivery to a single customer, are used and (ii) specific objective functions, such as $D_{\max}$, $D_{\max} + TC$, $\sum D_j$, and $\sum D_j + TC$ are considered.

This chapter is organized as follows. We consider some representative O-IPODS problems with a single stage of delivery with the delivery method of individual and immediate delivery, direct shipping to a single customer, and direct shipping to multiple customers, in Sects. 4.2, 4.3, and 4.4, respectively. In Sect. 4.5, several problems with two stages of delivery are discussed. In Sect. 4.6, we illustrate the importance of choosing a suitable algorithm by comparing the computational performance of some online and offline algorithms. Finally, we discuss some possible future research directions in Sect. 4.7.

Figure 4.1 provides an overview of the topics covered in the remaining sections of this chapter.

4.2 Online Problems with Individual and Immediate Delivery

In this section, we focus on two online IPODS problems with the individual and immediate delivery methods: $1|online, r_j|V(\infty, 1), iid|n|D_{\max}$ and $P_2|online, r_j|V(\infty, 1), iid|n|D_{\max}$. They are discussed in Sects. 4.2.1 and 4.2.2, respectively.

140   4 Integrated Production and Outbound Distribution Scheduling: Online Problems

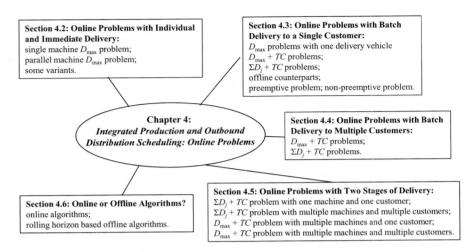

Fig. 4.1 Overview of the topics covered in Chap. 4

4.2.1 Single-Machine Maximum Delivery Time Problem and Some Variants

In this section, we consider problem $1|online, r_j|V(\infty, 1), iid|n|D_{\max}$ and some related problems. As shown in Sect. 3.3.1, problem $1|r_j|V(\infty, 1), iid|n|D_{\max}$, the offline counterpart of $1|online, r_j|V(\infty, 1), iid|n|D_{\max}$, is strongly NP-hard. For this offline problem, the heuristic Algorithm H3.1 given in Sect. 3.3.1 finds a solution with a worst-case performance ratio of 3/2 (see Theorem 3.2). However, by definition of online algorithms (see Sect. 2.3.4), this heuristic is not an online algorithm because it relies on the information about all the jobs when constructing a schedule.

There are several online algorithms for problem $1|online, r_j|V(\infty, 1), iid|n|D_{\max}$. The simplest online algorithm is Rule S described in Sect. 3.3.1. This algorithm has a competitive ratio of 2 (Hoogeveen & Vestjens, 2000; Kise et al., 1979). Hoogeveen and Vestjens (2000) show that for this problem any online algorithm has a competitive ratio of at least $(\sqrt{5} + 1)/2 \approx 1.61803$. Since their proof provides some useful insights about online scheduling, below we briefly summarize their proof, along with the insights that can be derived.

To show that for a given online problem, any online algorithm has a competitive ratio of at least α, a common approach is to construct a specific instance of the problem from an adversarial point of view such that for this instance, the competitive ratio of any online algorithm is at least α. Hoogeveen and Vestjens (2000) construct the following instance for any given online algorithm H:

- There are either one or two jobs that will arrive. Job 1 arrives at time 0 with $p_1 = 1$ and $t_1 = 0$. Depending on when the online algorithm H starts processing job 1, either no more jobs will arrive or a second job will arrive. If the starting

4.2 Online Problems with Individual and Immediate Delivery

time of job 1 is $S > (\sqrt{5} - 1)/2$, then no other jobs will arrive. Otherwise, job 2 with $p_2 = 0$ and $t_2 = 1$ will arrive at time $S + \epsilon$, where ϵ is positive but very close to 0.

- In the first case where $S > (\sqrt{5} - 1)/2$, the optimal schedule is to start job 1 at time 0, which gives optimal objective value $D^*_{max} = 1$, whereas the online algorithm H gives a solution with objective value $D_{max}(H) = S + 1$. Thus, for this case of the instance, the competitive ratio of H is $D_{max}(H)/D^*_{max} = S + 1 \geq (\sqrt{5} + 1)/2$.
- In the second case where $S \leq (\sqrt{5} - 1)/2$, the optimal schedule is to schedule job 2 before job 1 with both starting at time $S + \epsilon$, which gives $D^*_{max} = S + 1 + \epsilon$, whereas H schedules job 1 before job 2 with their starting time S and $S + 1$, respectively, which gives $D_{max}(H) = S + 2$. Thus, the competitive ratio of H for this case of the instance is $(S + 2)/(S + 1 + \epsilon)$, which is at least $(\sqrt{5} + 1)/2$ over the domain of $S \leq (\sqrt{5} - 1)/2$, when ϵ approaches 0.
- The two cases together show that the competitive ratio of H is at least $(\sqrt{5} + 1)/2$.

It can be seen from the above proof of Hoogeveen and Vestjens (2000) that for any online algorithm that does not wait intentionally, i.e., starts to process an available job as soon as the machine is available and there is at least one available job (that has arrived but has not been processed), the competitive ratio is at least 2. This is because under such an algorithm, the starting time of job 1 is $S = 0$, and hence, the second case in the above discussion applies. This means that Rule S given in Sect. 3.3.1 achieves the best possible competitive ratio (which is 2) among all online algorithms that do not wait intentionally. It also means that to have a competitive ratio strictly less than 2, an online algorithm needs a strategy for intentional waiting. The intuition is that while waiting, new jobs may arrive, which can then give additional information to the algorithm and enable it to generate better solutions. Clearly, there is a tradeoff: if the intentional waiting is too long, then the machine capacity is wasted, which can lead to inferior solutions. So, it is important to find a good waiting strategy that balances machine capacity waste and new information gained. Every online algorithm discussed in this chapter employs some waiting strategy for processing jobs and/or delivering jobs. The critical ratio of an online algorithm strongly depends on the specific waiting strategy used.

Hoogeveen and Vestjens (2000) give an online algorithm with the smallest possible competitive ratio, which is $(\sqrt{5} + 1)/2$, for problem $1|online, r_j|V(\infty, 1), iid\ |n|D_{max}$. Hence, their algorithm is an optimal (i.e., best possible) online algorithm for the problem. Their algorithm is a modified version of Rule S given in Sect. 3.3.1 with added intentional waiting whenever a certain condition is satisfied. The basic idea of the algorithm is the following: At any time when the machine is available and there is at least one available job (that has arrived but has not been processed), if none of the available jobs is *big* (i.e., has a long processing time, as defined below), then the job with the longest transportation time is scheduled, just as in Rule S; otherwise, various conditions are checked to determine whether to schedule the biggest job, schedule the job with the longest transportation time, or intentionally wait without scheduling any job.

142   4 Integrated Production and Outbound Distribution Scheduling: Online Problems

We now describe their algorithm. First, we define some necessary terms and notations used in the algorithm:

- $P(X)$ denotes the total processing time of all jobs in set X.
- A_τ is the set of the jobs that have arrived at or before time τ but have not been started by time τ.
- B_τ is the set of the jobs that have arrived at or before time τ but have not been completed before the last idle time period before time τ; if there is no idle time before time τ, then B_τ contains all the jobs that have arrived at or before time τ.
- g_τ is the job with the largest processing time in A_τ.
- q_τ is the job with the largest transportation time in A_τ.

The job sets A_τ and B_τ are determined by the algorithm, where B_τ is the set of jobs in A_τ plus the jobs continuously scheduled between the last idle time period before time τ and time τ. We call a job $j \in A_\tau$ *big* at time τ if $p_j > \frac{\sqrt{5}-1}{2}P(B_\tau)$. We note that since $\frac{\sqrt{5}-1}{2} > 1/2$, and $A_\tau \subset B_\tau$, there is at most one big job at any time.

The following is the online algorithm given by Hoogeveen and Vestjens (2000) for problem $1|online, r_j|V(\infty, 1), iid|n|D_{\max}$.

Algorithm A4.1

Whenever the machine is idle and a job is available, let this time be τ and do the following. Otherwise, wait until the machine is idle and a job is available:

Step 0: Determine job sets A_τ and B_τ, job g_τ, and job q_τ.

Step 1: If g_τ is not a big job, i.e., $p_{g_\tau} \leq \frac{\sqrt{5}-1}{2}P(B_\tau)$, then start processing job q_τ from time τ, let $\tau = \tau + p_{q_\tau}$, and go to Step 0. If g_τ is a big job, then check the condition of Step 2: if the condition of Step 2 is satisfied, go to Step 2; otherwise, go to Step 3.

Step 2: If $\tau + P(A_\tau) > r_{g_\tau} + \frac{\sqrt{5}+1}{2}p_{g_\tau}$, then consider two cases as follows:

- Case (i): If $t_{q_\tau} > \frac{\sqrt{5}-1}{2}p_{g_\tau}$, then start processing job q_τ from time τ, and let $\tau = \tau + p_{q_\tau}$. Go to Step 0.
- Case (ii): If $t_{q_\tau} \leq \frac{\sqrt{5}-1}{2}p_{g_\tau}$, then start processing job g_τ from time τ, and let $\tau = \tau + p_{g_\tau}$. Go to Step 0.

Step 3: If $\tau + P(A_\tau) \leq r_{g_\tau} + \frac{\sqrt{5}+1}{2}p_{g_\tau}$, then consider two cases as follows:

- Case (i): If $q_\tau \neq g_\tau$, then start processing job q_τ from time τ, and let $\tau = \tau + p_{q_\tau}$. Go to Step 0.
- Case (ii): If $q_\tau = g_\tau$, then consider two further cases: if job g_τ is not the only job in A_τ, then start processing any job j in A_τ but g_τ from time τ, let $\tau = \tau + p_j$, and go to Step 0; otherwise, do not start any job, let $\tau = \tau + 1$, and go to Step 0.

By this algorithm, at any time point τ, if none of the available jobs is big, then the job with the longest transportation time is scheduled. Otherwise, it is checked

4.2 Online Problems with Individual and Immediate Delivery 143

whether the available jobs can keep the machine busy until time $r_{g_\tau} + \frac{\sqrt{5}+1}{2} p_{g_\tau}$. If this is the case, then either the job with the longest transportation time or the big job is scheduled, depending on whether the job with the longest transportation time has a transportation time above some threshold or not. If the available jobs cannot keep the machine busy until time $r_{g_\tau} + \frac{\sqrt{5}+1}{2} p_{g_\tau}$, then the job with the longest transportation time is always scheduled unless this job is also the big job. In the case when the job with the longest transportation time is also the big job, then any other job is scheduled if there exists another job, or the machine waits if there are no other jobs. In the latter case, the machine waits intentionally until time $r_{g_\tau} + \frac{\sqrt{5}-1}{2} p_{g_\tau}$ or until a new job arrives if sooner.

Hoogeveen and Vestjens (2000) show that the competitive ratio of this algorithm is $(\sqrt{5} + 1)/2$ by contradiction where the concept of a *smallest counterexample* is used. A smallest counterexample is an instance of the problem with a minimum number of jobs, for which the algorithm generates a solution with the objective value more than $(\sqrt{5} + 1)/2$ times the optimal objective value of the corresponding offline instance. They show that if such a counterexample exists, then the solution generated by the algorithm for this instance satisfies some properties, which are then used to show that there is a contradiction and, hence, such a counterexample cannot exist.

To understand this algorithm better, we illustrate the steps of the algorithm when it is applied to the following numerical example.

Example 4.1 (Application of Algorithm 4.1) Consider a situation where four jobs arrive over time with the parameters given in the following table.

j	1	2	3	4
r_j	1	4	10	10
p_j	5	9	2	1
t_j	10	7	3	12

Applying the algorithm, the first time point to consider is $\tau = 1$ when job 1 arrives. *At $\tau = 1$, the algorithm runs the following steps:*

Step 0: $A_\tau = B_\tau = \{1\}$, $g_\tau = q_\tau = 1$.
Step 1: Job 1 is a big job; the condition of Step 2 is not satisfied, and go to Step 3.
Step 3: Case (ii); since job 1 is the only job in A_τ, do not start any job, let $\tau = 2$, and go to Step 0.

    At $\tau = 2$ and $\tau = 3$, the algorithm yields the same results as above and hence no job is started.

    At $\tau = 4$, the algorithm runs the following steps:
Step 0: $A_\tau = B_\tau = \{1, 2\}$, $g_\tau = 2$, $q_\tau = 1$.
Step 1: Job 2 is a big job; the condition of Step 2 is not satisfied, and go to Step 3.
Step 3: Case (i); start processing job 1 from time 4; let $\tau = 4 + p_1 = 9$, and go to Step 0.

144   4 Integrated Production and Outbound Distribution Scheduling: Online Problems

At $\tau = 9$, the algorithm runs the following steps:
Step 0: $A_\tau = \{2\}$, $B_\tau = \{1, 2\}$, $g_\tau = q_\tau = 2$.
Step 1: Job 2 is a big job; the condition of Step 2 is not satisfied, and go to Step 3.
Step 3: Case (ii); since job 2 is the only job in A_τ, do not start any job, let $\tau = 10$, and go to Step 0.
At $\tau = 10$, the algorithm runs the following steps:
Step 0: $A_\tau = \{2, 3, 4\}$, $B_\tau = \{2, 3, 4\}$, $g_\tau = q_\tau = 2$.
Step 1: Job 2 is a big job; the condition of Step 2 is satisfied, and go to Step 2.
Step 2: Case (i); start processing job 4 from time 10; let $\tau = 10 + p_4 = 11$, and go to Step 0.
At $\tau = 11$, the algorithm runs the following steps:
Step 0: $A_\tau = \{2, 3\}$, $B_\tau = \{2, 3, 4\}$, $g_\tau = 2$, $q_\tau = 4$.
Step 1: Job 2 is a big job; the condition of Step 2 is satisfied, and go to Step 2.
Step 2: Case (i); start processing job 2 from time 11; let $\tau = 10 + p_2 = 20$, and go to Step 0.
At $\tau = 20$, the algorithm runs the following steps:
Step 0: $A_\tau = \{3\}$, $B_\tau = \{2, 3, 4\}$, $g_\tau = q_\tau = 3$.
Step 1: Job 3 is not a big job; start processing job 3 from time 20; let $\tau = 20 + p_3 = 22$. Go to Step 0. No new jobs arrive. Stop.

The schedule generated by this algorithm in this example is $(1, 4, 2, 3)$ with starting times of the jobs 4, 10, 11, 20, respectively. This gives $D_1 = 19, D_2 = 27, D_3 = 25, D_4 = 23$. Thus, $D_{\max} = 27$. It can easily be checked that this solution happens to be an optimal solution for the offline problem of the given instance.

Several variants of problem $1|online, r_j|V(\infty, 1), iid|n|D_{\max}$ have been studied in the literature. Tian et al. (2008) and Liu et al. (2010) consider the same problem, except that each job's transportation time is bounded. When each job's transportation time t_j is assumed to be no more than its processing time p_j, Tian et al. (2008) give an online algorithm with a competitive ratio of $\sqrt{2}$ and show that this ratio is the best possible. When each job's transportation time t_j satisfies the condition: $\beta t_j \le p_j$, where $\beta \ge 1/2$ is a given constant, Liu et al. (2010) give an online algorithm with a competitive ratio of $\frac{1}{2}(\sqrt{5 + \beta^2 + 2\beta} + 1 - \beta)$ and show that this ratio is the best possible. It can be seen that when $\beta = 1$, the problem of Liu et al. (2010) reduces to that of Tian et al. (2008), and the competitive ratio of Liu et al.'s algorithm becomes the same as that of Tian et al.'s algorithm. Both their algorithms essentially follow the idea of Algorithm A4.1.

Some other variants of the problem where the machine is a so-called parallel batching machine have also been studied. A parallel batching machine is one that can process multiple jobs as a batch simultaneously, and the processing requirement of the batch is determined by the job with the longest processing time. A well-known application involving parallel batching machines is the scheduling of burn-in operations in semiconductor manufacturing (Lee & Uzsoy, 1999; Lee et al., 1992). Tian et al. (2012) study problem $1|online, r_j|V(\infty, 1), iid|n|D_{\max}$ with a parallel batching machine with an unbounded batch size and give an online algorithm with

4.2 Online Problems with Individual and Immediate Delivery 145

a competitive ratio of $2\sqrt{2} - 1$. Yuan et al. (2009) and Tian et al. (2011) consider similar problems where there are lower or upper bounds on the transportation times of the jobs.

4.2.2 Parallel-Machine Maximum Delivery Time Problem

We consider problem $P_2|online, r_j|V(\infty, 1), iid|n|D_{max}$ in this section. Some offline problems related to this online problem are discussed in Sect. 3.3.3. For this online problem, Vestjens (1997) shows that any online algorithm has a competitive ratio of at least 3/2. Liu and Lu (2015) give the following algorithm for this online problem and show that its competitive ratio is $(\sqrt{5} + 1)/2$ and this bound is tight.

Algorithm A4.2
Let $\alpha = (\sqrt{5} - 1)/2$. Set $\tau = 0$.

Step 0: If there is no available job at time τ, then wait until a new job arrives, and reset τ to be this time.

Step 1: If both machines are idle at time τ, then select an available job with the largest transportation time, and start to process the job at time τ on one of the machines. Go to Step 0.

Step 2: If only one machine is idle at time τ, let j be the job being processed by the other machines at time τ and C_j be the completion time of this job, and consider the following two cases:
Case (i): If $\tau \geq \alpha^2 C_j$, then select an available job with the largest transportation time and start to process the job at time τ on the idle machine. Go to Step 0.
Case (ii): If $\tau < \alpha^2 C_j$, then reset τ to be $\alpha^2 C_j$. Go to Step 0.

Step 3: If both machines are busy at time τ, reset τ to be the earliest time instant after τ at which at least one machine becomes idle. Go to Step 0.

We give a numerical example in the following to illustrate the steps of this algorithm.

Example 4.2 (Application of Algorithm A4.2) Consider an instance where five jobs arrive over time with the parameters given in the following table.

j	1	2	3	4	5
r_j	1	4	7	7	10
p_j	5	16	12	6	8
t_j	10	7	3	12	9

Applying Algorithm A4.2, *at $\tau = 0$, the algorithm runs the following steps:*

Step 0: Since there is no available job at τ, wait until job 1 arrives, and reset $\tau = 1$.

Step 1: Since both machines are idle at τ, the only available job, which is job 1, is processed on machine 1 from time 1 to 6.

At $\tau = 1$, the algorithm runs the following steps:

Step 0: Since there is no available job at τ, wait until job 2 arrives, and reset $\tau = 4$.

Step 2: Since only machine 2 is idle at τ, the job being processed by machine 1 at time τ is identified, which is job 1 with $C_1 = 6$. Case (i) holds and the only available job, which is job 2, is processed on machine 2 from time 4 to 20.

At $\tau = 4$, the algorithm runs the following steps:

Step 0: Since there is no available job at τ, wait until time 7 when jobs 3 and 4 arrive, and reset $\tau = 7$.

Step 2: Since only machine 1 is idle at τ, the job being processed by machine 2 at time τ is identified, which is job 2 with $C_2 = 20$. Case (ii) holds, and reset $\tau = 20\alpha^2$, which is greater than 7.

At $\tau = 20\alpha^2$, the algorithm runs the following steps:

Step 0: Jobs 3 and 4 are available at τ.

Step 2: Since only machine 1 is idle at τ, the job being processed by machine 2 at time τ is identified, which is job 2 with $C_2 = 20$. Case (i) holds, and job 4 is selected and processed on machine 1 from time $20\alpha^2$ to $6 + 20\alpha^2$.

At $\tau = 20\alpha^2$, the algorithm runs the following steps:

Step 0: Job 3 is available at τ.

Step 3: Since both machines are busy at time τ, reset $\tau = 6 + 20\alpha^2$ when machine 1 is available.

At $\tau = 6 + 20\alpha^2$, the algorithm runs the following steps:

Step 0: Jobs 3 and 5 are available at τ.

Step 2: Since only machine 1 is idle at τ, the job being processed by machine 2 at time τ is identified, which is job 2 with $C_2 = 20$. Case (i) holds, and job 5 is selected and processed on machine 1 from time $6 + 20\alpha^2$ to $14 + 20\alpha^2$.

At $\tau = 6 + 20\alpha^2$, the algorithm runs the following steps:

Step 0: Job 3 is available at τ.

Step 3: Since both machines are busy at τ, reset $\tau = 20$ when machine 2 is available.

At $\tau = 20$, the algorithm runs the following steps:

Step 0: Job 3 is available at τ.

Step 2: Since only machine 2 is idle at τ, the job being processed by machine 1 at time τ is identified, which is job 5 with $C_5 = 14 + 20\alpha^2$. Case (i) holds, and job 3 is processed on machine 2 from time 20 to 32. Stop.

The schedule generated for this example is the following: machine 1 processed jobs 1, 4, and 5 with starting time 1, $20\alpha^2$ and $6 + 20\alpha^2$, respectively, and machine 2 processed jobs 2 and 3 with the starting times 4 and 20, respectively. Thus, $D_1 = 16$, $D_2 = 27$, $D_3 = 35$, $D_4 = 18 + 20\alpha^2$, $D_5 = 23 + 20\alpha^2$, and $D_{\max} = 35$.

Although Algorithm A4.2 is quite straightforward, the competitive analysis given in Liu and Lu (2015) is not. We do not present their analysis here. They also conduct computational experiments, which show that the performance of this algorithm based on randomly generated instances is much better than the theoretical worst-case bound.

4.3 Online Problems with Batch Delivery to a Single Customer

It would be interesting to see whether the idea of this algorithm can be extended to the more general problem $P_m|online, r_j|V(\infty, 1), iid|n|D_{\max}$, where there are more than two machines. To our knowledge, there are no existing online algorithms for this problem.

4.3 Online Problems with Batch Delivery to a Single Customer

All the problems considered in this section involve a single customer with the direct shipping delivery method. We consider two representative problems each with the objective functions $D_{\max}$, $D_{\max} + TC$, and $\sum D_j + TC$ in Sects. 4.3.1, 4.3.2, and 4.3.3, respectively.

4.3.1 Maximum Delivery Time Problems

In this section, we consider two related problems $1|online, r_j, pmtn|V(1, c), direct|1|D_{\max}$ and $1|online, r_j|V(1, c), direct|1|D_{\max}$. They both involve a single machine and a single capacitated vehicle delivering all the jobs in batches with the objective of minimizing $D_{\max}$, the time when all the jobs are delivered to the customer. The first problem allows preemption when processing jobs on the machine, whereas the second problem does not. In these problems, the single delivery vehicle can deliver at most $c \geq 1$ jobs in each trip, and the travel time from the plant to the customer site and that from the customer site back to the plant are assumed to be identical and denoted as t.

We first discuss briefly the offline counterparts of these problems in Sect. 4.3.1.1 and then discuss each of the online problems in Sects. 4.3.1.2 and 4.3.1.3, respectively.

4.3.1.1 Offline Counterparts

We are not aware of any existing papers that study the offline problems $1|r_j, pmtn|V(1, c), direct|1|D_{\max}$ and $1|r_j|V(1, c), direct|1|D_{\max}$. However, Lu et al. (2008) consider the closely related problems $1|r_j, pmtn|V(1, c), direct|1|F_{\max}$ and $1|r_j|V(1, c), direct|1|F_{\max}$, where the objective function $F_{\max} = D_{\max} + t$ is the time when the vehicle returns to the plant after delivering the last batch of jobs. Since t is a given constant, the offline problems $1|r_j, pmtn|V(1, c), direct|1|D_{\max}$ and $1|r_j|V(1, c), direct|1|D_{\max}$ are equivalent to the offline problems studied by Lu et al. (2008), respectively, in the sense that optimal solutions to the former problems are also optimal for the latter problems and vice versa.

148   4 Integrated Production and Outbound Distribution Scheduling: Online Problems

However, the optimal objective value of $1|r_j, pmtn|V(1, c), direct|1|F_{max}$ (resp. $1|r_j|V(1, c), direct|1|F_{max}$) differs from that of $1|r_j, pmtn|V(1, c), direct|1|D_{max}$ (resp. $1|r_j|V(1, c), direct|1|D_{max}$) by a constant, t.

Several results derived by Lu et al. (2008) for $1|r_j, pmtn|V(1, c), direct|1|F_{max}$ are also valid for problem $1|r_j, pmtn|V(1, c), direct|1|D_{max}$ and are hence stated as properties for the latter problem in the following.

For problem $1|r_j, pmtn|V(1, c), direct|1|D_{max}$, it is optimal to process the jobs on the machine using the *shortest remaining processing time* (SRPT) rule, which, together with a simple tie-breaking rule, can be stated formally as follows:

SRPT Rule At each time instant τ, process the job with the smallest remaining processing time among all the jobs that have arrived but have not been completed, with ties broken by giving priority to the job with the smallest index.

Example 4.3 (Application of SRPT Rule) Apply the SRPT rule to the following instance where four jobs arrive over time with the following parameters.

j	1	2	3	4
r_j	1	4	10	11
p_j	9	5	3	1

Job 1 is started at time 1 but preempted at time 4 by job 2. Job 2 is processed from time 4 without interruption until it is completed at time 9. Job 1 is resumed at time 9 but preempted at time 10 by job 3. Job 3 is processed for one time unit before it is preempted at time 11 by job 4. Job 4 is processed from time 11 without interruption, until it is completed at time 12. At time 12, job 1 has 5 units of processing time remaining, and job 3 has 2 units of processing time remaining. Thus, at time 12, job 3 is selected for processing and is completed at time 14. Finally, job 1 is processed from time 14 to time 19. In this solution, the job completion times are, in increasing order, $C_2 = 9$, $C_4 = 12$, $C_3 = 14$, $C_1 = 19$.

Furthermore, for problem $1|r_j, pmtn|V(1, c), direct|1|D_{max}$, there is an optimal solution where (i) a job with an earlier completion time is delivered no later than any job with a later completion time, and (ii) each delivery batch, except possibly the first batch, contains exactly c jobs. Based on these properties, the following polynomial-time algorithm solves problem $1|r_j, pmtn|V(1, c), direct|1|D_{max}$ to optimality.

Algorithm A4.3

Step 1: Process the jobs following the SRPT rule. Reindex the jobs as $[1], \ldots, [n]$ in nondecreasing order of their completion times resulting from the application of SRPT rule.

Step 2: Form $\lceil n/c \rceil$ delivery batches such that the first batch consists of the first $n - (\lceil n/c \rceil - 1)c$ consecutively completed jobs, and the ith batch consists of the c consecutively completed jobs, $[x + 1], [x + 2], \ldots, [x + c]$, where $x = n - (\lceil n/c \rceil - 1)c + (i - 2)c$, for $i = 2, \ldots, \lceil n/c \rceil$. Deliver these batches

4.3 Online Problems with Batch Delivery to a Single Customer

one by one as soon as possible in the order of their completion times (which are the completion times of the last jobs in the batches).

Lu et al. (2008) show that problem $1|r_j|V(1,c), direct|1|F_{\max}$ is strongly NP-hard, and give an approximation algorithm with a tight worst-case performance bound of 5/3. Clearly, problem $1|r_j|V(1,c), direct|1|D_{\max}$ has exactly the same complexity as $1|r_j|V(1,c), direct|1|F_{\max}$ and hence is also strongly NP-hard. However, if Lu et al.'s approximation algorithm is applied to our problem, the worst-case performance bound is not 5/3 because of the difference in the objective function. Instead, we have the following result.

Remark 4.1 The worst-case performance bound of Lu et al.'s approximation algorithm, when applied to problem $1|r_j|V(1,c), direct|1|D_{\max}$, is no more than 7/3. This is because of the fact that $F_{\max}(H) \leq (5/3)F_{\max}^*$, and $F_{\max}(H) = D_{\max}(H)+t$ and $F_{\max}^* = D_{\max}^*+t$ implies that $D_{\max}(H) \leq 5D_{\max}^*/3+2t/3 \leq (7/3)D_{\max}^*$, where $D_{\max}(H)$ and $D_{\max}^*$ (which is clearly at least t) are the maximum delivery times in the solution generated by Lu et al.'s approximation algorithm and in the optimal solution, respectively.

4.3.1.2 Algorithm for the Preemptive Problem

For the online problem $1|online, r_j, pmtn|V(1,c), direct|1|D_{\max}$, since the SRPT rule described in Sect. 4.3.1.1 can be implemented online, applying this rule for processing the jobs on the machine is optimal. Therefore, the SRPT rule should be used for processing the jobs in any online algorithm for this problem. When $c = 1$, each job is delivered individually. Thus, for problem $1|online, r_j, pmtn|V(1,1), direct|1|D_{\max}$, it is optimal to process the jobs using the SRPT rule and deliver the jobs one by one as soon as possible in the order of their completion times.

However, when $c \geq 2$, apparently a simple optimal solution cannot be identified because when $c \geq 2$, a vehicle may deliver one or two jobs in a trip, and hence, a waiting strategy needs to be developed, which is not straightforward. In this case, Algorithm 4.3 given in Sect. 4.3.1.1 for the offline counterpart of this problem cannot be implemented online and hence cannot be used for the online problem.

Ng and Lu (2012) study a closely related online problem $1|online, r_j, pmtn|V(1,c), direct|1|F_{\max}$, where the objective function $F_{\max} = D_{\max} + t$. They show that any deterministic online algorithm H for this problem with $c \geq 2$ has a competitive ratio of at least $\frac{\sqrt{5}+1}{2}$, and develop an online algorithm with a competitive ratio of $\frac{\sqrt{5}+1}{2}$. Their online algorithm can be applied to our problem $1|online, r_j, pmtn|V(1,c), direct|1|D_{\max}$ and generate exactly the same solution. However, since our problem has a different objective function from their problem, their algorithm also has a different competitive ratio when applied to our problem.

150   4 Integrated Production and Outbound Distribution Scheduling: Online Problems

While writing this chapter, we contacted Dr. Chi To Ng of Hong Kong Polytechnic University, the lead author of the paper Ng and Lu (2012), about applying their online algorithm to our problem. In response to our inquiry, Ng and Lu (2020) show that for our problem $1|online, r_j, pmtn|V(1, c), direct|1|D_{max}$ with $c \geq 2$, any online algorithm H has a competitive ratio of at least 2 by constructing an instance of the problem. We modify their instance slightly to make it more straightforward as follows:

- There are one or two jobs that will arrive, depending on what the algorithm does. Job 1 arrives at time 0 with $p_1 = 0$.
- If the vehicle delivers job 1 with departure time $\tau > t$, then no other jobs arrive. In this case, $D_{max}(H) > 2t$. However, the optimal solution is to deliver job 1 at time 0, resulting in $D^*_{max} = t$. Thus, $D_{max}(H)/D^*_{max} > 2$.
- If the vehicle delivers job 1 with departure time $\tau \leq t$, then job 2 with $p_2 = 0$ arrives at time $\tau + \epsilon$. In this case, $D_{max}(H) \geq \tau + 3t$. However, the optimal solution is to deliver both jobs at time $\tau + \epsilon$, resulting in $D^*_{max} = \tau + \epsilon + t$. Thus, $D_{max}(H)/D^*_{max} \geq \frac{\tau+3t}{\tau+\epsilon+t} = 1 + \frac{2t-\epsilon}{\tau+\epsilon+t} \geq 2$ when ϵ goes to 0.

Ng and Lu (2020) propose the following online algorithm for solving problem $1|online, r_j, pmtn|V(1, c), direct|1|D_{max}$ with any $c \geq 2$. It is a modified version of the online algorithm given in Ng and Lu (2012) for problem $1|online, r_j, pmtn|V(1, c), direct|1|F_{max}$ with $c \geq 2$.

Algorithm A4.4

Step 1: At the production stage, process the jobs by the SRPT rule given in Sect. 4.3.1.1.

Step 2: At the delivery stage, keep the vehicle idle until time t.

Step 3: At any time point $\tau \geq t$, if there is at least one job that has completed processing but has not been delivered, then the vehicle carries as many completed jobs as possible and departs at time τ, set $\tau = \tau + 2t$, and go to Step 3. Otherwise, set τ to be the earliest time after the current τ when a job completes processing, let the vehicle wait until time τ, and go to Step 3.

Example 4.4 (Application of Algorithm A4.4) Apply Algorithm A4.4 to the instance given in Example 4.3 with vehicle capacity $c = 2$ and one-way transportation time $t = 2$. Given the SRPT schedule described in Example 4.3, we can see that the earliest time point to be considered is $\tau = 9$ when the first job in the SRPT schedule is completed. At $\tau = 9$, deliver job 2, and set $\tau = 9 + 2t = 13$. At time $\tau = 13$, job 4 is available for delivery and hence is delivered. Set $\tau = 13 + 2t = 17$. At $\tau = 17$, job 3 is available and is hence delivered. Set $\tau = 17 + 2t = 21$. At time $\tau = 21$, job 1 is available and hence delivered. This solution gives the delivery times of the jobs, in increasing order, $D_2 = 11, D_4 = 15, D_3 = 19, D_1 = 23$, and hence $D_{max} = 23$. An optimal offline solution for this instance is to deliver jobs 2 and 4 together at time 12, and deliver jobs 1 and 3 together at time 19, which yields $D_{max} = 21$.

4.3 Online Problems with Batch Delivery to a Single Customer

Ng and Lu (2020) show that for problem $1|online, r_j, \; pmtn|V(1,c)$, $direct|1|D_{\max}$, Algorithm A4.4 satisfies Lemma 3.2 given in Ng and Lu (2012). This lemma is stated and proved below.

Lemma 4.1 *For any given instance I of problem $1|online, \; r_j, pmtn|V(1,c)$, $direct|1|D_{\max}$, $D_{\max}^H(I) \leq D_{\max}^*(I) + 2t$, where $D_{\max}^H(I)$ is the maximum delivery time in the solution generated by Algorithm A4.4 for the instance, and $D_{\max}^*(I)$ is the maximum delivery time in the optimal offline solution for the instance.*

Proof For any given instance of the problem, let π and π^* be the solution generated by Algorithm A4.4, and the optimal offline solution, respectively. Since processing the jobs by the SRPT rule is optimal, we can assume that π and π^* have the same job processing schedule. Let $[j]$ denote the jth completed job in the job processing schedule of π and π^*, for $j = 1, \ldots, n$. Suppose that there are b delivery batches in π and they are denoted as $B_1, \ldots, B_b$, where a batch with a smaller index is delivered earlier than a batch with a larger index. Let $d(B_i)$ denote the departure time of batch B_i. By Algorithm A4.4, $d(B_1) = \max\{t, r_{[1]}\}$.

Let B_k be the earliest delivery batch such that $B_k, \ldots, B_b$ are delivered continuously without any vehicle idle time. Thus, $D_{\max}^H(I) = d(B_k) + 2t(b - k) + t$. If $k = b$, then the vehicle is idle between the time it returns to the plant after delivering batch B_{b-1} and the time it departs from the plant carrying batch B_b, which is time $d(B_b)$. By the algorithm, this means that $d(B_b)$ is equal to the processing completion time of the first job in it, denoted as time C_0. Thus, $D_{\max}^H(I) = C_0 + t$. Clearly, $D_{\max}^*(I) \geq C_0 + t$. This implies that $D_{\max}^H(I) \leq D_{\max}^*(I)$.

If $k < b$, then there are two cases to consider as follows. First, if all the batches $B_k, \ldots, B_{b-1}$ contain c jobs, there are two further cases. If $k = 1$, then $b = \lceil n/c \rceil \leq b^*$. Thus, $D_{\max}^H(I) = \max\{t, r_{[1]}\} + 2t(\lceil n/c \rceil) - t$. Since $D_{\max}^*(I) \geq r_{[1]} + 2t(\lceil n/c \rceil) - t$, we have $D_{\max}^H(I) \leq D_{\max}^*(I) + t$. If $k > 1$, then the vehicle is idle between the time it gets back to the plant after delivering batch B_{k-1}, which is denoted as time E, and the time it departs from the plant carrying batch B_k, which is time $d(B_k)$. From the algorithm, this means that $d(B_k)$ is equal to the processing completion time of the first job in it, which further implies that $c - 1$ jobs in B_k have a zero processing time. Let the completion time of the first job in B_k be denoted as C_0. Thus $D_{\max}^H(I) = C_0 + 2t(b - k) + t$. Furthermore, we can see that in π^*, there are at least $\lceil (c(b - k) + 1)/c \rceil = b - k + 1$ batches with a departure time greater than or equal to C_0. Thus $D_{\max}^*(I) \geq C_0 + 2t(b - k) + t = D_{\max}^H(I)$. Thus $D_{\max}^H(I) \leq D_{\max}^*(I)$.

Second, suppose some batches $B_k, \ldots, B_{b-1}$ contain less than c jobs. Let B_l be the last batch among these batches containing less than c jobs. There are two subcases. First, if $l = b - 1$, then all the jobs in B_b complete processing after time $d(B_{b-1})$. This means that $D_{\max}^*(I) \geq d(B_{b-1}) + t$, and $D_{\max}^H(I) = d(B_{b-1}) + 3t$. Thus, $D_{\max}^H(I) \leq D_{\max}^*(I) + 2t$. Second, if $l < b - 1$, then every batch $B_{l+1}, \ldots, B_{b-1}$ contains c jobs and all the jobs in these batches complete processing after $d(B_l)$. Thus, there are at least $(b - l - 1)c + 1$ jobs in the batches $B_{l+1}, \ldots, B_b$. This implies that in π^* there are at least $b - l$ delivery batches that depart after

$d(B_l)$. Thus, $D_{\max}^*(I) \geq d(B_l) + 2t(b - l - 1) + t$. On the other hand, we know $D_{\max}^H(I) = d(B_l) + 2t(b - l) + t$. Thus, $D_{\max}^H(I) \leq D_{\max}^*(I) + 2t$.

As shown above, in every possible case, we have $D_{\max}^H(I) \leq D_{\max}^*(I) + 2t$, hereby establishing the lemma. $\square$

Based on this lemma, Ng and Lu (2020) show the following result.

Theorem 4.1 *For problem* $1|online, r_j, pmtn|V(1, c), direct|1|D_{\max}$, *the competitive ratio of Algorithm A4.4 is 2.*

Proof If $D_{\max}^*(I) \geq 2t$, then by Lemma 4.1, $D_{\max}^H(I) \leq D_{\max}^*(I) + 2t$. Thus, we have $D_{\max}^H(I) \leq 2D_{\max}^*(I)$. If $D_{\max}^*(I) < 2t$, then in the optimal offline solution, all the jobs complete processing at or before time t and all the jobs are delivered in one batch, which implies that $c \geq n$. Since the SRPT schedule is optimal for processing the jobs even for the offline problem, the processing schedule in the solution generated by Algorithm A4.4 is the same as that in the optimal offline solution. This means that all the jobs complete processing at or before time t in the solution generated by Algorithm A4.4. Thus, from Step 3 of the algorithm, all the jobs are delivered together at time t, which implies that $D_{\max}^H(I) = 2t$. Since $D_{\max}^*(I) \geq t$, we have $D_{\max}^H(I) \leq 2D_{\max}^*(I)$. $\square$

4.3.1.3 Algorithms for the Nonpreemptive Problem

Next, we consider the nonpreemptive problem $1|online, r_j|V(1, c), direct|1|D_{\max}$. Ng and Lu (2012) consider a closely related problem, $1|online, r_j|V(1, c), direct|1|F_{\max}$. They show that any deterministic online algorithm H for this problem has a competitive ratio of at least $\frac{\sqrt{5}+1}{2}$, and develop an online algorithm with a competitive ratio of $\frac{\sqrt{5}+1}{2}$ when $c = 1$, and an asymptotic competitive ratio of the same value when $c \geq 2$. Their online algorithm can be applied to our problem $1|online, r_j|V(1, c), direct|1|D_{\max}$ and generate the same solution with a different objective value. However, since our problem has a different objective function, their algorithm has a different competitive ratio when applied to our problem.

In the following, we first apply Ng and Lu's (2012) algorithm directly to solve our problem $1|online, r_j|V(1, c), direct|1|D_{\max}$ and show that for our problem, this algorithm has a competitive ratio of $\sqrt{5}$ when $c = 1$ and an asymptotic competitive ratio of $\frac{\sqrt{5}+1}{2}$ when $c \geq 2$. We then present another algorithm that has a competitive ratio of 2.5 for our problem with any value of c.

We first describe the algorithm from Ng and Lu (2012). We introduce some additional notation as follows:

- $P(S)$ denotes the total processing time of all the jobs in set S.
- A_τ is the set of jobs that have arrived at or before time τ but have not started processing by time τ.
- e_τ is the earliest time such that the machine is always busy in time interval $[e_\tau, \tau]$.
- B_τ is the set of jobs that are processed on the machine in time interval $[e_\tau, \tau]$.

4.3 Online Problems with Batch Delivery to a Single Customer   153

- s_τ is the job with the shortest processing time in A_τ.
- l_τ is the job with the longest processing time in A_τ.

The algorithm consists of two phases: the first phase generates a production schedule, and the second phase generates a delivery schedule based on the production schedule from the first phase.

Algorithm A4.5

Phase 1: At the production stage, assign the jobs for processing on the machine as follows. Set $\alpha = \frac{\sqrt{5}-1}{2}$, and $\tau = 0$.

Step 1: If A_τ is empty, wait until the time a new job arrives and reset τ to be this time. If $|A_\tau| \geq 2$, go to Step 2. If $|A_\tau| = 1$, then we denote the only job in A_τ as job s_τ and consider two cases as follows.

Case (i): If $\tau < r_{s_\tau} + \alpha(p_{s_\tau} + 2t)$, then wait until either the time a new job arrives or the time becomes $r_{s_\tau} + \alpha(p_{s_\tau} + 2t)$, whichever is earlier. Reset τ to be this time. Go to Step 1.

Case (ii): If $\tau \geq r_{s_\tau} + \alpha(p_{s_\tau} + 2t)$, then start to process job s_τ from time τ. Reset $\tau = \tau + p_{s_\tau}$. Go to Step 1.

Step 2: If $|A_\tau| \geq 2$, consider two cases as follows:

Case (i): If at least one of the following three conditions holds: (1) $p_{s_\tau} \leq 2t/c$, (2) $\tau + p_{s_\tau} \leq \max\{r_{l_\tau} + \alpha(p_{l_\tau} + 2t), \alpha(P(A_\tau \cup B_\tau) + 2t)\}$, (3) $p_{l_\tau} \leq \alpha P(A_\tau \cup B_\tau)$, then start to process job s_τ from time τ. Reset $\tau = \tau + p_{s_\tau}$. Go to Step 1.

Case (ii): Otherwise, start to process job l_τ from time τ. Reset $\tau = \tau + p_{l_\tau}$. Go to Step 1.

Phase 2: At the delivery stage, assign the finished jobs in Phase 1 for delivery by the vehicle as follows. Set $\tau = 0$.

Step 1: If there is at least one job that has completed processing but has not been delivered by time τ, then the vehicle carries as many completed jobs as possible and departs at time τ, set $\tau = \tau + 2t$, and go to Step 1. Otherwise, reset τ to be the earliest future time when a job is completed processing, let the vehicle wait until time τ, and go to Step 1.

Example 4.5 (Application of Algorithm A4.5) Apply Algorithm A4.5 to the instance given in Example 4.3 with vehicle capacity $c = 2$ and one-way transportation time $t = 2$. Applying Phase 1 of the algorithm, the first time point to consider is $\tau = 1$ when job 1 arrives. *At $\tau = 1$, the algorithm runs the following steps of Phase 1:*

Step 1: $A_\tau = \{1\}$, B_τ is empty, $s_\tau = l_\tau = 1$; Case (i) is satisfied; wait until time $1 + \alpha(9 + 4) = 1 + 13\alpha$ or when the next job arrives, whichever is earlier. This means wait until time 4 when job 2 arrives. Set $\tau = 4$. *At $\tau = 4$, the algorithm runs the following steps of Phase 1:*

Step 1: $A_\tau = \{1, 2\}$, B_τ is empty, $s_\tau = 2$, $l_\tau = 1$; since $|A_\tau| \geq 2$, go to Step 2.

Step 2: Since Condition (2) is satisfied, start to process job 2 at time 4. Set $\tau = 4 + 5 = 9$. *At $\tau = 9$, the algorithm runs the following steps of Phase 1:*

Step 1: $A_\tau = \{1\}$, $B_\tau = \{2\}$, $s_\tau = l_\tau = 1$; Case (i) is satisfied; wait until time $1 + \alpha(9 + 4) = 1 + 13\alpha$ or time 10 when the next job arrives, whichever is earlier. Since $1 + 13\alpha < 10$, wait until time $1 + 13\alpha < 10$. Set $\tau = 1 + 13\alpha$. At $\tau = 1 + 13\alpha$, the algorithm runs the following steps of Phase 1:

Step 1: $A_\tau = \{1\}$, B_τ is empty, $s_\tau = l_\tau = 1$; Case (ii) is satisfied; start to process job 1 at time $1 + 13\alpha$. Set $\tau = 10 + 13\alpha$. At $\tau = 10 + 13\alpha$, the algorithm runs the following steps of Phase 1:

Step 1: $A_\tau = \{3, 4\}$, $B_\tau = \{1\}$, $s_\tau = 4$, $l_\tau = 3$; since $|A_\tau| \geq 2$, go to Step 2.

Step 2: Since Condition (1) is satisfied; start to process job 4 at time $10 + 13\alpha$. Set $\tau = 11 + 13\alpha$. At $\tau = 11 + 13\alpha$, the algorithm runs the following steps of Phase 1:

Step 1: $A_\tau = \{3\}$, $B_\tau = \{1, 4\}$, $s_\tau = l_\tau = 3$; Case (ii) is satisfied; start to process job 3 at time $11 + 13\alpha$. Set $\tau = 14 + 13\alpha$. No new jobs arrive after that. Stop. Applying Phase 2 of the algorithm, the first time point to consider is $\tau = 9$ when job 2 is completed. Deliver job 2 at time 9. Set $\tau = 9 + 2t = 13$. Wait until job 1 is completed processing at time $\tau = 10 + 13\alpha$. Deliver job 1 at this time. Set $\tau = 10 + 13\alpha + 2t = 14 + 13\alpha$. At this time, jobs 3 and 4 are both available. Deliver them together at this time. The solution generated has the objective value $D_{max} = 16 + 13\alpha \approx 24.03$.

An optimal offline solution is to schedule the jobs in the sequence $(1, 3, 2, 4)$ without inserted idle time such that their completion times are $C_1 = 10, C_3 = 13, C_2 = 18, C_4 = 19$, and deliver jobs 1 and 3 together at time 13, and jobs 2 and 4 together at time 19. The optimal objective value is 21.

Theorem 4.2 *For problem* $1|online, r_j|V(1, c), direct|1|D_{max}$, *Algorithm A4.5 has a competitive ratio of* $\sqrt{5}$ *when* $c = 1$ *and has an asymptotic competitive ratio of* $\frac{\sqrt{5}+1}{2}$ *when* $c \geq 2$.

Proof Ng and Lu (2012) show that for any instance I of problem $1|online, r_j|$ $V(1, c), direct|1|F_{max}$ with $c = 1$, the solution from this algorithm satisfies: $F_{max}^H(I) \leq \frac{\sqrt{5}+1}{2} F_{max}^*(I)$, i.e., the algorithm has a competitive ratio of $\frac{\sqrt{5}+1}{2}$. This means that $D_{max}^H(I) + t \leq \frac{\sqrt{5}+1}{2}(D_{max}^*(I) + t)$. Thus, $D_{max}^H(I) \leq \frac{\sqrt{5}+1}{2} D_{max}^*(I) + \frac{\sqrt{5}-1}{2}t$. Since $t \leq D_{max}^*(I)$, we have: $D_{max}^H(I) \leq (\sqrt{5})D_{max}^*(I)$. This establishes the first half of the theorem.

Ng and Lu (2012) also show that for any instance I of problem $1|online, r_j|$ $V(1, c), direct|1|F_{max}$ with $c \geq 2$, the solution from this algorithm satisfies: $F_{max}^H(I) \leq \frac{\sqrt{5}+1}{2} F_{max}^*(I) + (2t)(2c - 1)/c$, i.e., the algorithm has an asymptotic competitive ratio of $\frac{\sqrt{5}+1}{2}$. This means that $D_{max}^H(I) + t \leq \frac{\sqrt{5}+1}{2}(D_{max}^*(I) + t) + (2t)(2c - 1)/c$. Thus,

$$D_{max}^H(I) \leq \left(\frac{\sqrt{5}+1}{2}\right) D_{max}^*(I) + \beta,$$

4.3 Online Problems with Batch Delivery to a Single Customer   155

where $\beta = \frac{\sqrt{5}-1}{2}t + (2t)(2c-1)/c$ is a fixed constant. This establishes the second half of the theorem. $\qquad\square$

Theorem 4.2 does not show if Algorithm A4.5 has a constant competitive ratio for problem $1|online, r_j|V(1,c), direct|1|D_{max}$ with $c \geq 2$. It is not known whether this algorithm has a constant competitive ratio for our problem with $c \geq 2$.

However, as we show next, there is another algorithm that can be proven to have a constant competitive ratio for the same problem with any value of c. This algorithm and the competitive ratio analysis presented below are from Ng (2021).

Algorithm A4.6
Step 1: In the production stage, at any moment when the machine is available, process any job that has arrived.
Step 2: Same as in Algorithm A4.4.
Step 3: Same as in Algorithm A4.4.

Example 4.6 (Application of Algorithm A4.6) Apply Algorithm A4.6 to the instance given in Example 4.3 with vehicle capacity $c = 2$ and one-way transportation time $t = 2$.

Step 1: A production schedule $(1, 2, 3, 4)$ is generated with $C_1 = 10, C_2 = 15, C_3 = 18, C_4 = 19$.
Step 2: Keep the vehicle idle until time 2.
Step 3: At time $\tau = 10$, the first job, which is job 1, completes processing and is delivered. Reset $\tau = 10 + 2t = 14$. At this time, there is no job available for delivery. Reset τ to be 15, the time when the next job, job 2, completes processing. At $\tau = 15$, job 2 is delivered. Reset $\tau = 15 + 2t = 19$. At $\tau = 19$, both jobs 3 and 4 complete processing and hence are delivered together. This gives $D_{max} = 19 + 2 = 21$, which happens to be the same as the optimal offline objective value, as calculated in Example 4.5.

Theorem 4.3 *For problem $1|online, r_j|V(1,c), direct|1|D_{max}$ with any value of vehicle capacity c, Algorithm A4.6 has a competitive ratio of 2.5.*

Proof Given any instance of the problem, let π be the solution generated by this algorithm, and π^* be the optimal solution for the offline version of the instance. We denote the maximum completion time of the jobs and the maximum delivery time of the jobs in π as $C_{max}(\pi)$ and $D_{max}(\pi)$, respectively. Similarly, we denote these measures in π^* as $C_{max}(\pi^*)$ and $D_{max}(\pi^*)$, respectively.

We observe that Step 1 of the algorithm generates a production schedule with the minimum possible completion time of the last job, i.e., $C_{max}(\pi) \leq C_{max}(\pi^*)$. We can also observe that

$$D_{max}(\pi^*) \geq C_{max}(\pi^*) + t \geq C_{max}(\pi) + t, \tag{4.1}$$

$$D_{max}(\pi^*) \geq 2t(\lceil n/c \rceil - 1) + t. \tag{4.2}$$

156   4 Integrated Production and Outbound Distribution Scheduling: Online Problems

Suppose that in π there are h delivery batches with a departure time greater than or equal to $C_{\max}(\pi)$. Denote these batches as $B_1, \ldots, B_h$. Since all the jobs have completed processing by $C_{\max}(\pi)$, each of the batches $B_1, \ldots, B_{h-1}$ must contain c jobs, and batch B_h may contain c or fewer jobs. Thus, $h \leq \lceil n/c \rceil$.

We consider two cases about the relationship between $C_{\max}(\pi)$ and t as follows.

Case 1 If $C_{\max}(\pi) \leq t$, then all the delivery batches in π have a departure time greater than or equal to $C_{\max}(\pi)$, which means $h = \lceil n/c \rceil$, and

$$D_{\max}(\pi) = t + 2t(h-1) + t = 2t(\lceil n/c \rceil - 1) + 2t. \tag{4.3}$$

From (4.2) and (4.3), we have

$$D_{\max}(\pi) \leq 2D_{\max}(\pi^*). \tag{4.4}$$

Case 2 If $C_{\max}(\pi) > t$, then from (4.1), we have

$$D_{\max}(\pi^*) \geq C_{\max}(\pi^*) + t \geq 2t,$$

which implies that

$$t \leq D_{\max}(\pi^*)/2. \tag{4.5}$$

Since in solution π there is at most one delivery batch for which the vehicle departs before time $C_{\max}(\pi)$ and returns to the production facility after time $C_{\max}(\pi)$, we have

$$D_{\max}(\pi) \leq C_{\max}(\pi) + 2t + 2t(h-1) + t,$$

which, along with (4.1) and (4.2), implies

$$D_{\max}(\pi) \leq 2D_{\max}(\pi^*) + t,$$

which, along with (4.5), further implies

$$D_{\max}(\pi) \leq 2.5 D_{\max}(\pi^*). \tag{4.6}$$

The theorem then follows from (4.4) and (4.6). $\square$

4.3.2 Maximum Delivery Time and Transportation Cost Problems

In this section, we consider two related problems $1|online, r_j|V(\infty, c), direct|1|D_{\max} + TC$ and $P_m|online, r_j|V(\infty, c), direct|1|D_{\max} + TC$. They involve a single machine or multiple parallel machines and a sufficient number

4.3 Online Problems with Batch Delivery to a Single Customer

of capacitated delivery vehicles, with the objective of minimizing the sum of the maximum delivery time of the jobs and the total delivery cost.

We first briefly discuss their offline counterparts. The offline problem $1|r_j|V(\infty, c), direct|1|D_{\max} + TC$ can be solved easily as follows: Process the jobs in nondecreasing order of their release times, and deliver them at time $C_{\max}$ using $\lfloor n/c \rfloor$ full batches if n is an integer multiple of c, or using $\lfloor n/c \rfloor$ full batches and one partial batch if n is not an integer multiple of c. However, the offline parallel-machine problem $P_m|r_j|V(\infty, c), direct|1|D_{\max} + TC$ is much more difficult to solve; it is strongly NP-hard, since a special case of the problem, the classical machine scheduling problem without job delivery, $P_m|r_j|C_{\max}$, is itself strongly NP-hard (Garey & Johnson, 1979).

For the online problem $1|online, r_j|V(\infty, c), direct|1|D_{\max} + TC$, Han et al. (2015) show that no online algorithm can have a competitive ratio less than $\max\{\frac{\sqrt{5}+1}{2}, 2 - \frac{1}{c}\}$, and give an online algorithm with a competitive ratio of 2. We present a modified version of their algorithm below and give a simpler proof than theirs for the competitive ratio result.

Algorithm A4.7

Step 1: In the production stage, consider the jobs in the order of their arrival and start to process the next job as soon as the machine is available.

Step 2: In the delivery stage, at any time point $\tau = lf$ where $l = 1, 2, \ldots$, if there is no job being processed, then deliver all the jobs that have been completed but have not been delivered; otherwise, do not deliver any job.

Theorem 4.4 *For problem $1|online, r_j|V(\infty, c), direct|1|D_{\max} + TC$, Algorithm A4.7 has a competitive ratio of 2.*

Proof Given any instance, let π be the solution generated by this algorithm, and π^* be the optimal solution for the offline version of the instance. Clearly, the way the arriving jobs are processed in this algorithm yields the shortest possible completion time of all the jobs. Thus, $C_{\max}(\pi) = C_{\max}(\pi^*)$.

Let Lf be the departure time of the last delivery batch in π, for some positive integer L. Clearly, $Lf \leq C_{\max}(\pi) + f$. Thus $D_{\max}(\pi) = Lf + t \leq C_{\max}(\pi) + t + f$. Let x and y be the total number of full batches and the total number of partial batches delivered in π, respectively. Thus, $TC(\pi) = (x + y)f$. From the algorithm, it can be seen that there is at most one partial batch at each time point lf, for $l = 1, \ldots, L$. Thus, $y \leq L$, and hence $yf \leq C_{\max}(\pi) + f$.

Now, consider the optimal solution π^*. Clearly, $D_{\max}(\pi^*) \geq C_{\max}(\pi^*) + t$, and $TC(\pi^*) \geq (x + 1)f$ if $y > 0$ and $TC(\pi^*) \geq xf$ if $y = 0$.

If $y = 0$, then $x \geq 1$. We have

$$
\frac{Z(\pi)}{Z(\pi^*)} = \frac{D_{\max}(\pi) + TC(\pi)}{D_{\max}(\pi^*) + TC(\pi^*)}
$$

$$
\leq \frac{C_{\max}(\pi) + t + f + xf}{C_{\max}(\pi^*) + t + xf}
$$

158   4 Integrated Production and Outbound Distribution Scheduling: Online Problems

$$\leq 1 + \frac{f}{C_{\max}(\pi^*) + t + xf}$$

$$\leq 2.$$

If $y \geq 1$, we have

$$
\begin{aligned}
\frac{Z(\pi)}{Z(\pi^*)} &= \frac{D_{\max}(\pi) + TC(\pi)}{D_{\max}(\pi^*) + TC(\pi^*)} \\
&\leq \frac{C_{\max}(\pi) + t + f + (x + y)f}{C_{\max}(\pi^*) + t + (x + 1)f} \\
&\leq 1 + \frac{yf}{C_{\max}(\pi^*) + t + (x + 1)f} \\
&\leq 1 + \frac{C_{\max}(\pi) + f}{C_{\max}(\pi^*) + t + (x + 1)f} \\
&\leq 2.
\end{aligned}
$$

$\square$

For the online problem $P_m|online, r_j|V(\infty, c), direct|1|D_{\max} + TC$, Han et al. (2015) also show that no online algorithm can have a competitive ratio less than $\max\{\frac{\sqrt{5}+1}{2}, 2 - \frac{1}{c}\}$, and give an online algorithm with a competitive ratio of 2. We present their algorithm, along with their competitive analysis of the algorithm.

Algorithm A4.8

Step 1: In the production stage, process the arriving jobs following the online longest processing time (LPT) rule: whenever a machine becomes available, start to process the available job with the longest processing time.

Step 2: In the delivery stage, at any time point $\tau = lf$ where $l = 1, 2, \ldots,$ if there is no job being processed on any machine, then deliver all the jobs that have been completed but have not been delivered using a minimum number of vehicles; otherwise, do not deliver any job.

Example 4.7 (Application of Algorithm A4.8) Apply Algorithm A4.8 to the following instance where $m = 2$, $f = 5$, $c = 2$, $t = 2$, and there are five jobs that arrive over time with their parameters given in the following table.

j	1	2	3	4	5
r_j	2	4	4	5	10
p_j	8	3	5	20	4

Denote the two machines as M1 and M2. Step 1 schedules jobs 1, 5, 2 on M1 in the time intervals [2, 10], [10, 14], and [14, 17], respectively, and jobs 3, 4 on M2 in the time intervals [4, 9], and [9, 29], respectively. This gives $C_{\max} = 29$. Step

4.3 Online Problems with Batch Delivery to a Single Customer 159

2 checks time points $5l$ for $l = 1, 2, \ldots$. At time $\tau = 5l$ for $l = 1, \ldots, 5$, since there is always at least one job being processed, no job delivery takes place. At time $\tau = 30$, no job is being processed on any machine. Thus, at this time, all the jobs are delivered by a total of 3 vehicles. This means that $D_{\max} = 30 + 2 = 32$ and the total transportation cost is $TC = 3f = 15$. Thus, the objective value of the solution generated is $32 + 15 = 47$.

It can be easily verified that the following solution is optimal: Schedule jobs 1, 2, 3 and 5 on M1 in the time intervals [2, 10], [10, 13], [13, 18], and [18, 22], respectively, and job 4 on M2 in the time interval [5, 25]; deliver all the jobs at time 25 using 3 vehicles. The optimal objective value is $25 + 2 + 15 = 42$.

We note that for the classical online problem without the delivery part, i.e., problem $P_m|online, r_j|C_{\max}$, Chen and Vestjens (1997) show that the online LPT rule has a competitive ratio of 3/2. This result is used by Han et al. (2015) in their competitive analysis of Algorithm A4.8, which we now discuss.

Theorem 4.5 *For problem* $P_m|online, r_j|V(\infty, c), direct|1|D_{\max} + TC$, *Algorithm A4.8 has a competitive ratio of 2.*

Proof Given any instance, let π be the solution generated by this algorithm, and π^* be an optimal solution for the offline version of the instance. In π, let Lf be the departure time of the last delivery batch in π, for some positive integer L, and Hf be the latest departure time before Lf at which no job is being processed. If there is no such departure time, then let $H = 0$. From the algorithm, it can be seen that $Lf \leq C_{\max}(\pi) + f$, and all the jobs processed after time Hf arrive after this time and are all delivered at the departure time Lf. Thus, if we only consider the jobs that arrive after Hf, by the result from Chen and Vestjens (1997), we obtain the following result: $C_{\max}(\pi) - Hf \leq \frac{3}{2}(C_{\max}(\pi^*) - Hf)$. This means that $C_{\max}(\pi) \leq \frac{3}{2}C_{\max}(\pi^*) - \frac{Hf}{2}$. Thus,

$$D_{\max}(\pi) = Lf + t \leq C_{\max}(\pi) + t + f \leq \frac{3}{2}C_{\max}(\pi^*) - \frac{Hf}{2} + t + f. \quad (4.7)$$

In π, we further let x and y denote the total number of full batches and the total number of partial batches delivered at time Hf or earlier, and let u denote the total number of batches delivered at the departure time Lf. Clearly, $y \leq H$, and among the u batches that depart at Lf, at most one of them is a partial batch. Thus, $TC(\pi) = (x + y + u)f$.

Based on the above definitions, we can see that in π^*, $C_{\max}(\pi^*) \geq HF$ and $TC(\pi^*) \geq (x + u)f$. By (4.7), we have

$$\frac{Z(\pi)}{Z(\pi^*)} = \frac{D_{\max}(\pi) + TC(\pi)}{D_{\max}(\pi^*) + TC(\pi^*)}$$

$$\leq \frac{\frac{3}{2}C_{\max}(\pi^*) - \frac{Hf}{2} + f + t + (x + y + u)f}{C_{\max}(\pi^*) + t + (x + u)f}$$

$$\leq 1 + \frac{\frac{1}{2}C_{\max}(\pi^*) - \frac{Hf}{2} + f + yf}{C_{\max}(\pi^*) + t + (x+u)f}$$

$$\leq 1 + \frac{\frac{1}{2}C_{\max}(\pi^*) + \frac{Hf}{2} + f}{C_{\max}(\pi^*) + t + (x+u)f}$$

$$\leq 1 + \frac{C_{\max}(\pi^*) + f}{C_{\max}(\pi^*) + t + (x+u)f} \leq 2.$$

$\square$

In addition to the two problems discussed above, Han et al. (2015) also consider a number of other online problems with a closely related objective function $F_{\max} + TC$, where $F_{\max} = D_{\max} + t$, including problems $1|online, r_j|V(1, c), direct|1|F_{\max} + TC$ and $P_m|online, r_j|V(1, c), direct|1| F_{\max} + TC$ where there is a single delivery vehicle only. They propose online algorithms for these problems and conduct competitive analyses. As discussed in Sect. 4.3.1.1, $F_{\max}$ is the time when the vehicle returns to the plant after delivering the last batch of jobs. By a similar argument to the one in Sect. 4.3.1.3, the online algorithm given by Han et al. (2015) for $1|online, r_j|V(1, c), direct|1|F_{\max} + TC$ (resp., $P_m|online, r_j|V(1, c), direct|1| F_{\max} + TC$) can be applied to $1|online, r_j|V(1, c), direct|1|D_{\max} + TC$ (resp., $P_m|online, r_j|V(1, c), direct|1|D_{\max} + TC$) and generates exactly the same solution. However, the competitive ratio result for $1|online, r_j|V(1, c), direct|1|F_{\max} + TC$ (resp., $P_m|online, r_j|V(1, c), direct|1|F_{\max} + TC$) is not the same for $1|online, r_j|V(1, c), direct|1|D_{\max} + TC$ (resp., $P_m|online, r_j|V(1, c), direct|1| D_{\max} + TC$) because of the difference in the objective value.

4.3.3 Total Delivery Time and Transportation Cost Problems

In this section, we consider two related problems $1|online, r_j, pmtn|V(\infty, c), direct|1|\sum D_j + TC$ and $1|online, r_j|V(\infty, c), direct|1|\sum D_j + TC$. Both involve a single machine and the use of batch delivery to a single customer. There are a sufficient number of capacitated delivery vehicles with the objective of minimizing the sum of the total delivery time of the jobs and the total delivery cost. The first problem allows preemption when processing jobs on the machine, whereas the second problem does not. We first briefly discuss some closely related offline and online problems in Sect. 4.3.3.1 and then describe an algorithm for $1|online, r_j, pmtn|V(\infty, c), direct|1|\sum D_j + TC$ and $1|online, r_j|V(\infty, c), direct|1|\sum D_j + TC$, respectively, in Sects. 4.3.3.2 and 4.3.3.3.

4.3.3.1 Closely Related Problems

We first note that the offline problems without delivery corresponding to these online problems are the classical machine scheduling problems $1|r_j, pmtn| \sum C_j$ and $1|r_j| \sum C_j$, respectively. The latter problem is strongly NP-hard (Lenstra et al., 1977), whereas the earlier problem is solved by applying the SRPT rule defined in Sect. 4.3.1.1 (Schrage, 1968).

Clearly, the offline problem with delivery $1|r_j|V(\infty, c), direct|1| \sum D_j + TC$ is more general than that without delivery $1|r_j| \sum C_j$ and hence is also strongly NP-hard. However, the offline problem with delivery and preemption $1|r_j, pmtn|V(\infty, c), direct|1| \sum D_j + TC$ can be solved in polynomial time. It can be seen that for this problem, the SRPT rule is optimal for processing the jobs. Given the processing schedule, a dynamic programming algorithm can be designed to find a delivery schedule to minimize the objective function. Averbakh (2010) provides such an algorithm.

As can be seen, the SRPT rule can be implemented online and hence is optimal for the online problem $1|online, r_j, pmtn| \sum C_j$. For the nonpreemptive online problem, $1|online, r_j| \sum C_j$, Hoogeveen and Vestjens (1996) show that any deterministic online algorithm has a competitive ratio of at least 2. Lu et al. (2003) propose a so-called *shifted shortest processing time* (SSPT) rule for this problem and show that it achieves a competitive ratio of 2. The SSPT rule can be formally stated as follows:

SSPT Rule Whenever a job j arrives, shift its arrival time r_j to a later time r'_j, where r'_j is an arbitrary number in the interval $[\max\{r_j, p_j\}, r_j + p_j]$. At each time instant τ when the machine becomes available, process the job with the shortest processing time among all the jobs that are available (based on r'_j), with ties broken by giving priority to the job with the smallest index.

Example 4.8 (Application of the SSPT Rule) Apply the SSPT rule to the following instance where there are four jobs that arrive over time with their parameters given in the table below.

j	1	2	3	4
r_j	2	4	6	8
p_j	5	3	1	6

At time 2, job 1 arrives and its arrival time is shifted to 6 ($\in [5, 7]$). At time 4, job 2 arrives, but its arrival time remains as 4 ($\in [4, 7]$). Thus, job 2 is processed in time interval $[4, 7]$. At time 6, job 3 arrives and its arrival time remains as 6 ($\in [6, 7]$). At time 7 when the machine becomes available next, there are two available jobs $\{1, 3\}$. Job 3 is picked and processed in interval $[7, 8]$. At time 8, job 4 arrives and its arrival time is shifted to 14 ($\in [8, 14]$). At time 8, job 1 is picked and processed

162   4 Integrated Production and Outbound Distribution Scheduling: Online Problems

in interval [8, 13]. At time 13, no job is available. At time 14, job 4 is picked and processed in interval [14, 20].

To analyze the competitive ratio of the SSPT rule for problem $1|online, r_j|\sum C_j$, Lu et al. (2003) show some preliminary results. Since these results are also used later in Sect. 4.3.3.3, we describe them here, but without providing proofs.

For any given instance I of the problem $1|online, r_j|\sum C_j$, let σ be a solution produced by the SSPT rule. We define another instance of the problem $I(\sigma)$ as follows.

Definition 4.1 Given an instance I and a solution σ generated by the SSPT rule, an instance $I(\sigma)$ is defined as consisting of the same n jobs, where each job j has the same processing time p_j as in I, but its ready time is shifted to $\bar{r}_j = \min\{S_j, 2r_j + p_j\}$, where S_j is the starting time of job j in solution σ.

Lemma 4.2 *For any instance I of $1|online, r_j|\sum C_j$, the corresponding solution σ for instance I produced by the SSPT rule, and the corresponding instance $I(\sigma)$ that can be constructed based on I and σ, as described above, we have:*

(i) $Z^*(I(\sigma)) \le 2Z^*(I)$, where $Z^*(I(\sigma))$ and $Z^*(I)$ are the optimal objective values of the instance $I(\sigma)$ and I of the offline problem $1|r_j|\sum C_j$, respectively.
(ii) The solution that can be generated by applying the SRPT rule to the instance $I(\sigma)$ is the same as solution σ.

Based on the results in this lemma, Lu et al. (2003) prove the following result.

Lemma 4.3 *For problem $1|online, r_j|\sum C_j$, the SSPT rule has a competitive ratio of 2.*

Proof Since SSPT does not allow preemption, there is no job preemption in solution σ. Part (ii) of Lemma 4.2 means that although the SRPT rule allows preemption, when applying the SRPT rule to the instance $I(\sigma)$, no job is preempted. As discussed earlier, the SRPT rule is optimal for both the offline and online problems with preemption: $1|r_j, pmtn|\sum C_j$ and $1|online, r_j, pmtn|\sum C_j$. Thus, from part (ii) of Lemma 4.2, we can conclude that solution σ is optimal for instance $I(\sigma)$ of both the offline and online problems with preemption. Since there is no preemption in solution σ, this solution is also optimal for instance $I(\sigma)$ of both the offline and online problems without preemption. Thus, the objective value of σ is equal to $Z^*(I(\sigma))$. This, together with part (i) of Lemma 4.2, implies that for problem $1|online, r_j|\sum C_j$, the SSPT rule has a competitive ratio of 2.   □

4.3.3.2 Algorithm for the Preemptive Problem

We consider problem $1|online, r_j, pmtn|V(\infty, c), direct|1|\sum D_j + TC$ in this section. Averbakh (2010) gives an online algorithm for this same problem but with the objective of minimizing the sum of the total flow time of the jobs and the total transportation cost. The flow time of a job j is defined as $D_j - r_j$. Averbakh (2010)

4.3 Online Problems with Batch Delivery to a Single Customer

shows that his algorithm has a competitive ratio of 2 and that no online algorithm can achieve a better competitive ratio. His algorithm as well as the competitive ratio analysis given in his paper can be directly applied to the problem considered here. However, the instance he uses to show that no algorithm can have a competitive ratio lower than 2 cannot be applied to our problem.

The idea of Averbakh's algorithm is the following. First, it can be shown that the SRPT rule given in Sect. 4.3.1.1 is optimal for processing the jobs. Thus, the problem is reduced to making delivery batching decisions. If there are already c jobs that have completed processing but have not been delivered, then they need to be delivered immediately as a full batch. But if there are fewer than c jobs available for delivery, there are two options: (i) wait and do not deliver any job, and (ii) deliver all the jobs together in a batch immediately. The algorithm uses a concept called the *total delay time* of finished but undelivered jobs to determine which of the two options to use. At any given time point τ, the delay time of a finished but undelivered job j is equal to $\tau - C_j$. If the total delay time is equal to the delivery cost of a batch f, the algorithm chooses option (ii); otherwise, it chooses option (i).

We now describe Averbakh's algorithm below.

Algorithm A4.9

Step 1: At the production stage, process the jobs by the SRPT rule given in Sect. 4.3.1.1.

Step 2: At the delivery stage, at any time point, if at least one of the following conditions is satisfied (a) there are c finished but undelivered jobs, (b) the total delay time of the finished but undelivered jobs is equal to f, then deliver all the jobs together in a batch.

Before we analyze the performance of this algorithm, we define some terms and notations.

Definition 4.2 A delivery batch is called *saturated* if it is full, i.e., it contains c jobs; otherwise, it is called *unsaturated*.

Given the solution σ generated by Algorithm A4.8, the last delivery batch in σ is always considered unsaturated even if it contains c jobs. Let $k \geq 1$ be the total number of unsaturated batches in σ, and let $\tau_1 < \cdots < \tau_k$ be the times when the k unsaturated batches depart from the processing plant. Let $\tau_0 = 0$. Define k time intervals $\Omega_1 = [\tau_0, \tau_1]$, and $\Omega_i = (\tau_{i-1}, \tau_i]$, for $i = 2, \ldots, k$. Let $Z(\sigma)$ be the objective value of σ.

Theorem 4.6 *For problem* $1|online, r_j, pmtn|V(\infty, c), direct|1| \sum D_j + TC$, *the competitive ratio of Algorithm A4.9 is 2.*

Proof Let σ^* be an optimal solution and $Z(\sigma^*)$ the optimal objective value for the offline version of the problem, i.e., $1|r_j, pmtn|V(\infty, c), direct|1| \sum D_j + TC$. For this problem, as discussed in Sect. 4.3.1.1, the SRPT schedule is optimal for processing the jobs. Thus, we can assume that the job processing schedule in σ^* is the same as that in σ.

164   4 Integrated Production and Outbound Distribution Scheduling: Online Problems

We first focus on the solution σ generated by the algorithm. Consider any time interval Ω_i, for $i = 1, \ldots, k$. Let $q_i \geq 0$ be the number of saturated batches that depart during Ω_i in σ. Let $\tilde{\tau}_i$ denote the time when the last saturated batch departs, where $\tilde{\tau}_i = \tau_{i-1}$ if $q_i = 0$. Thus, there are a total of $q_i + 1$ batches that depart during Ω_i. Let $\phi(\sigma, \Omega_i)$ be the total contribution of the jobs that complete processing in interval Ω_i under solution σ, defined as the sum of the total delay time of the jobs that complete processing in interval Ω_i and the total delivery cost of the batches that depart during interval Ω_i. From Step 2 of the algorithm, the total delay time of the jobs in each batch that departs during Ω_i is no more than f. Thus, $\phi(\sigma, \Omega_i) \leq 2f(q_i + 1)$.

Now, consider the optimal solution σ^* for the offline problem. Consider the same time interval Ω_i. Since $q_i c$ jobs are completed during the interval $(\tau_{i-1}, \tilde{\tau}_i]$, in σ^*, there must be at least q_i delivery batches that depart during this interval. If in σ^* there is no batch that departs during the interval $(\tilde{\tau}_i, \tau_i]$, then the total delay time of the jobs completed in this interval is at least f. Therefore, the total contribution of the jobs completed in interval Ω_i in σ^*, denoted as $\phi(\sigma^*, \Omega_i)$, is at least $f(q_i + 1)$.

Let C_j be the completion time of job j in the SRPT schedule and t be the delivery time from the processing plant to the customer location. The delivery time D_j of job j is thus equal to the sum of C_j, its delay time, and t. Based on this, we have

$$Z(\sigma) = \sum_{j=1}^{n}(C_j + t) + \sum_{i=1}^{k}\phi(\sigma, \Omega_i) \leq \sum_{j=1}^{n}(C_j + t) + 2f\sum_{i=1}^{k}(q_i + 1) \quad (4.8)$$

$$Z(\sigma^*) = \sum_{j=1}^{n}(C_j + t) + \sum_{i=1}^{k}\phi(\sigma^*, \Omega_i) \geq \sum_{j=1}^{n}(C_j + t) + f\sum_{i=1}^{k}(q_i + 1). \quad (4.9)$$

From (4.8) and (4.9), we can see that $Z(\sigma) \leq 2Z(\sigma^*)$. This shows that the competitive ratio of the algorithm is bounded by 2. $\qquad \square$

It is apparently not known whether Algorithm A4.9 is optimal (i.e., best possible) for problem $1|online, r_j, pmtn|V(\infty, c), direct|1|\sum D_j + TC$.

4.3.3.3   Algorithm for the Nonpreemptive Problem

Now, we consider problem $1|online, r_j|V(\infty, c), direct|1|\sum D_j + TC$. Feng et al. (2016) give an online algorithm for this problem with a competitive ratio of 3. Their algorithm combines the idea of Lu et al. (2003) for scheduling job processing and the idea of Averbakh (2010) for scheduling job delivery. Their algorithm can be described as follows.

Algorithm A4.10
Step 1: At the production stage, process the jobs by the SSPT rule given in Sect. 4.3.3.1.

4.3 Online Problems with Batch Delivery to a Single Customer

Step 2: At the delivery stage, at any time point, if at least one of the following conditions is satisfied (a) there are c finished but undelivered jobs, (b) the total delay time of the finished but undelivered jobs is equal to $2f$, then deliver all the jobs together in a batch.

Example 4.9 (Application of Algorithm A4.10) Apply this algorithm to the instance given in Example 4.8 with the additional parameters: $t = 0, c = 2, f = 3$. Given the SSPT schedule shown in Example 4.8 for this instance, Step 2 of the algorithm generates the following delivery schedule: at time 8, condition (a) is satisfied, and hence, jobs 2 and 3 are delivered together at time 8; at time 19, the total delay time of job 1 becomes $2f = 6$ (i.e., condition (b) is satisfied), and hence, job 1 is delivered; at time 26, the total delay time of job 4 becomes $2f$, and hence, job 4 is delivered. In this solution, $D_2 = D_3 = 8$, $D_1 = 19$, and $D_4 = 26$, and there are 3 delivery batches. The objective value of this solution is $8 + 8 + 19 + 26 + 3f = 70$.

It can be verified that the following solution is optimal for the offline version of the instance: schedule the jobs on the machine in the order of 1, 3, 2, 4 without inserted idle time, which yields $D_1 = 7$, $D_3 = 8$, $D_2 = 11$, $D_4 = 17$, and deliver jobs 1 and 3 at time 8, deliver job 2 at time 11, and deliver job 4 at time 17. This solution has an objective value of $8 + 8 + 11 + 17 + 3f = 53$.

Before we analyze the performance of this algorithm, we introduce some new notation. For any given instance I of the problem, let σ denote the solution generated by Algorithm A4.10, and $F(I)$ be the objective value of this solution. Let σ_p and σ_d denote the production schedule and delivery schedule of solution σ, respectively. Let σ^* be the optimal offline solution for instance I, and σ_p^* and σ_d^* the production schedule and delivery schedule of σ^*, respectively. Let $F^*(I)$ be the objective value of σ^*, and TT_{σ^*} and TC_{σ^*} be the total delivery time of the jobs and the total delivery cost in this solution, respectively. Thus, $F^*(I) = TT_{\sigma^*} + TC_{\sigma^*}$.

Given instance I and solution σ, we construct a corresponding instance $I(\sigma)$ in exactly the same way as in Definition 4.1 given in Sect. 4.3.3.1. For the constructed instance $I(\sigma)$, we construct a solution $\bar{\sigma}$ that allows preemption during job processing, as follows: (1) apply the SRPT rule in the production stage, and let $\bar{\sigma}_p$ denote the production schedule generated; (2) follow the same configuration as in σ_d^* to schedule the delivery, and denote the delivery schedule generated as $\bar{\sigma}_d$. By Lemma 4.2(ii), production schedule $\bar{\sigma}_p$ is the same as σ_p and hence does not involve job preemption. Suppose that in σ_d^* for instance I there are s delivery batches and their departure times are at the completion times of the i_1st, ..., i_sth completed jobs, respectively. Then in $\bar{\sigma}_d$ for instance $I(\sigma)$, there are also s delivery batches with departure times at the completion times of the i_1st, ..., i_sth completed jobs, respectively. Let $\bar{F}$ be the objective value of solution $\bar{\sigma}$ for instance $I(\sigma)$, and $TT_{\bar{\sigma}}$ and $TC_{\bar{\sigma}}$ be the total delivery time of the jobs and the total delivery cost in this solution, respectively. Thus, $\bar{F} = TT_{\bar{\sigma}} + TC_{\bar{\sigma}}$.

Lemma 4.4 $\bar{F} + TC_{\bar{\sigma}} \leq 2F^*(I)$.

Proof It is clear that $TC_{\bar{\sigma}} = TC_{\sigma^*}$. Thus, we can prove this lemma by showing that $TT_{\bar{\sigma}} \leq 2TT_{\sigma^*}$. To this end, we construct another solution π for instance I based on

166 4 Integrated Production and Outbound Distribution Scheduling: Online Problems

σ^* as follows: (1) let the starting time of each job j be $S'_j = 2C^*_j - p_j$, where C^*_j is the completion time of job j in schedule σ^*_p; (2) use the same delivery batches as in σ^*_d (i.e., use the same number of batches and deliver exactly the same jobs in each batch), but with the departure time of each batch determined by the completion time of the last job in the batch. It can easily be shown that π is a feasible solution to instance $I(\sigma)$ and that the departure time of each batch in π is twice that of the same batch in σ^*. Thus, the total delivery time of the jobs in π, $TT_\pi = 2TT_{\sigma^*}$.

Since the production schedule in $\bar{\sigma}$ is generated by the SRPT rule, it contains the most jobs that have completed processing by any time t for the instance $I(\sigma)$, compared to any other schedule for the same instance (Pruhs et al., 2004). Furthermore, the delivery configuration in $\bar{\sigma}$ is the same as that in σ^* and π, which implies that for instance $I(\sigma)$, the departure time of the ith batch in $\bar{\sigma}$ is no later than that of the ith batch in π, for $i = 1, \ldots, s$. Hence, $TT_{\bar{\sigma}} \leq TT_\pi = 2TT_{\sigma^*}$. This, along with the result that $TC_{\bar{\sigma}} = TC_{\sigma^*}$, implies that $\bar{F} + TC_{\bar{\sigma}} \leq 2F^*(I)$. $\qquad \square$

We are now ready to evaluate the performance of Algorithm A4.10. The following result is proved by Feng et al. (2016).

Theorem 4.7 *For problem* $1|online, r_j|V(\infty, c), direct|1| \sum D_j + TC$, *Algorithm A4.9 is 3-competitive.*

Proof We apply some terms and notations used in Sect. 4.3.3.2. Given any instance I of problem $1|online, r_j|V(\infty, c), direct|1| \sum D_j + TC$, and the corresponding solution σ generated by Algorithm A4.10, we define the concept of saturated and unsaturated batches as in Definition 4.2 (see Sect. 4.3.3.2), as well as the following terms and notations, as before. Let $k \geq 1$ be the total number of unsaturated batches in σ. The last batch in σ is always treated as unsaturated even if it contains c jobs. Let the departure times of these batches in σ be $\tau_1, \ldots, \tau_k$, respectively. Let the number of jobs in these batches in σ be $v_1, \ldots, v_k$, respectively. Create k time intervals, $\Omega_1 = [\tau_0, \tau_1]$, where $\tau_0 = 0$, and $\Omega_i = (\tau_{i-1}, \tau_i]$, for $i = 2, \ldots, k$. We say a job j is in Ω_i if its completion time C_j is in this interval. Let $q_i \geq 0$ be the number of saturated batches that depart during interval Ω_i in solution σ. Define the delay time of a job as in Sect. 4.3.3.2. Let $g(\Omega_i)$ be the total delay time of the jobs that complete processing in interval Ω_i in solution σ.

In solution σ, for each $i = 1, \ldots, k$, there are a total of $q_i + 1$ delivery batches— q_i saturated and 1 unsaturated—that depart during each interval Ω_i. Thus, $TC_\sigma = \sum_{i=1}^{k}(q_i + 1)f$. By the algorithm, the total delay time of the jobs in each batch is no more than $2f$. Hence, $g(\Omega_i) \leq 2f(q_i + 1)$ for each interval Ω_i. Therefore, we have

$$F(I) = TT_\sigma + TC_\sigma \qquad (4.10)$$

$$= \sum_{i=1}^{k} \left(\sum_{j \in \Omega_i} C_j + g(\Omega_i) \right) + \sum_{i=1}^{k}(q_i + 1)f$$

4.3 Online Problems with Batch Delivery to a Single Customer 167

$$= \sum_{i=1}^{k} \sum_{j \in \Omega_i} C_j + \sum_{i=1}^{k} g(\Omega_i) + \sum_{i=1}^{k} (q_i + 1) f$$

$$\leq \sum_{i=1}^{k} \sum_{j \in \Omega_i} C_j + 3 \sum_{i=1}^{k} (q_i + 1) f. \tag{4.11}$$

Now, consider solution $\bar{\sigma}$, which is constructed for instance $I(\sigma)$ in the paragraph before Lemma 4.2. As discussed there, the production schedule in $\bar{\sigma}$ (i.e., $\bar{\sigma}_p$) is the same as the production schedule in σ (i.e., σ_p) and hence does not involve job preemption. Thus, $\bar{\sigma}$ is also a feasible solution to instance I of problem $1|online, r_j|V(\infty, c), direct|1| \sum D_j + TC$. For each job j, let $\bar{C}_j$ and $\bar{D}_j$ be the completion time and delivery time of j in $\bar{\sigma}$. Thus, $\bar{C}_j = C_j$. Let $TT_{\bar{\sigma}}^i$ and $TC_{\bar{\sigma}}^i$ denote the total delivery time and total delivery cost of the jobs in $\bar{\sigma}$ that complete processing in interval Ω_i and have a departure time also in this interval.

Consider interval Ω_i. Since $q_i c + v_i$ jobs complete processing in this interval, there are at least q_i delivery batches made in this interval in solution $\bar{\sigma}$. We consider two cases as follows.

Case 1: There are at least $q_i + 1$ delivery batches made in Ω_i in solution $\bar{\sigma}$. In this case, clearly, $TT_{\bar{\sigma}}^i \geq \sum_{j \in \Omega_i} \bar{C}_j = \sum_{j \in \Omega_i} C_j$, and $TC_{\bar{\sigma}}^i \geq (q_i + 1) f$.

Case 2: There are exactly q_i batches delivered in Ω_i in solution $\bar{\sigma}$. In this case, there must be less than $(q_i + 1)c$ jobs that complete processing in Ω_i in $\bar{\sigma}_p$. From the fact that $\bar{\sigma}_p = \sigma_p$, we conclude that in σ the last batch that departs in Ω_i, which has a departure time τ_i, contains less than c jobs. Thus, by Algorithm A4.9, in solution σ, at time τ_i, the total delay of the jobs in the batch that departs at time τ_i is equal to $2f$. Clearly, in solution $\bar{\sigma}$, the q_i delivery batches made in interval Ω_i contain a total of no more than $q_i c$ jobs. This means that all the jobs contained in the batch that departs at τ_i in solution σ are delivered in batches that depart after time τ_i in solution $\bar{\sigma}$. Thus, the total delay time of these jobs in solution $\bar{\sigma}$ is greater than or equal to that in solution σ (which is $2f$). This means that $TT_{\bar{\sigma}}^i \geq \sum_{j \in \Omega_i} \bar{C}_j + 2f = \sum_{j \in \Omega_i} C_j + 2f$, and $TC_{\bar{\sigma}}^i \geq q_i f$.

From the above two cases, we have, for $i = 1, \ldots, k$,

$$TT_{\bar{\sigma}}^i + 2TC_{\bar{\sigma}}^i \geq \sum_{j \in \Omega_i} C_j + 2(q_i + 1) f.$$

This, along with (4.11), gives

$$F(I) \leq \sum_{i=1}^{k} \sum_{j \in \Omega_i} C_j + 3 \sum_{i=1}^{k} (q_i + 1) f < \frac{3}{2} \sum_{i=1}^{k} \left(\sum_{j \in \Omega_i} C_j + 2(q_i + 1) f \right)$$

$$\leq \frac{3}{2} \sum_{i=1}^{k} (TT_{\bar{\sigma}}^i + 2TC_{\bar{\sigma}}^i) = \frac{3}{2} (\bar{F} + TC_{\bar{\sigma}}). \tag{4.12}$$

From (4.12) and Lemma 4.4, we have $F(I) \leq 3F^*(I)$. $\qquad\square$

168 4 Integrated Production and Outbound Distribution Scheduling: Online Problems

Apparently, it is not known whether there are online algorithms with a competitive ratio less than 3 for problem $1|online, r_j|V(\infty, c), direct|1| \sum D_j + TC$.

4.4 Online Problems with Batch Delivery to Multiple Customers

Online IPODS problems with multiple customers are considerably more challenging than those with a single customer. There are very few results in the existing literature on online IPODS problems with multiple customers. We have derived some new results for two problems with the objective function of $D_{\max} + TC$, which are given in Sect. 4.4.1. We also present results from the literature on another two problems with the objective function of $\sum D_j + TC$ in Sect. 4.4.2. Following the notation defined in Sect. 3.5.1, in all the problems considered in this section, the set of customers is denoted as $K = \{1, \ldots, k\}$, where $k \geq 1$ is the number of customers, the set of jobs from customer $i \in K$ is denoted as $N_i = \{(i, 1), \ldots, (i, n_i)\}$, where (i, j) is the jth job from customer i, and n_i is the number of jobs from customer i, which is not known in advance in an online setting. The processing time of job (i, j) is denoted as p_{ij}, and the transportation time and cost from the plant to customer $i \in K$ are denoted as t_i and f_i, respectively.

4.4.1 Maximum Delivery Time and Transportation Cost Problems

We consider two related problems in this section: $1|online, r_j, pmtn|V(\infty, c), direct|k|D_{\max} + TC$ and $1|online, r_j|V(\infty, c), direct|k|D_{\max} + TC$. The corresponding offline problem without preemption $1|r_j|V(\infty, c), direct|k|D_{\max} + TC$ is strongly NP-hard because a special case of this problem, where there are n customers each having one job and the transportation costs f_i are all 0, is equivalent to problem $1|r_j|V(\infty, 1), iid|n|D_{\max}$, which is shown to be strongly NP-hard in Sect. 3.3.1. However, the corresponding offline problem with preemption $1|r_j, pmtn|V(\infty, c), direct|k|D_{\max} + TC$ can be solved in polynomial time by the following simple procedures: (1) process the jobs using the *longest transportation time* (LTT) rule, as described below, and (2) deliver all the jobs from customer $i \in K$ at the completion time of the last job from customer i.

LTT Rule At each time instant τ whenever a new job arrives, process the job with the longest transportation time among all the jobs that have arrived but have not been completed, including the jobs that have been partially processed, with ties broken by giving priority to the job with the smallest customer index among the jobs from different customers, and to the job with the smallest job index among the jobs from the same customer.

4.4 Online Problems with Batch Delivery to Multiple Customers

The optimality of the LTT rule can be proved by a simple job exchange argument. Clearly, the LTT rule can be implemented in an online fashion.

We first propose an online algorithm for problem $1|r_j, pmtn|V(\infty, c), direct|k| D_{\max} + TC$. The algorithm uses the LTT rule to process the jobs and allows shipments of jobs to depart only at some pre-specified time points when a condition described below is satisfied.

Algorithm A4.11

Step 1: At the production stage, process the arriving jobs by the LTT rule, as described above.

Step 2: At the delivery stage, for each $i \in K$, at each time point $\tau_l^i = l(\sqrt{k} f_i)$, for $l = 1, 2, \ldots$, if all the jobs from customer i that arrived before this time have completed processing, then deliver them all to customer i using a minimum number of vehicles. Otherwise, do not deliver any jobs from customer i.

Example 4.10 (Application of Algorithm A4.11) We apply Algorithm A4.11 to the instance with five jobs that arrive over time with their parameters shown in the table below. The vehicle capacity is $c = 2$. It is also known in advance that there are 2 customers (i.e., $k = 2$) with $t_1 = f_1 = 5$ and $t_2 = f_2 = 10$.

Arrival index	1	2	3	4	5
From customer i	1	2	1	1	2
Job index (i, j)	$(1,1)$	$(2, 1)$	$(1, 2)$	$(1, 3)$	$(2, 2)$
r_{ij}	2	4	10	12	15
p_{ij}	4	2	6	2	3

Step 1 creates the following schedule for processing the jobs. Job $(1,1)$ is started at time 2 but preempted at time 4 when job $(2, 1)$ arrives because the latter has a longer transportation time. Job $(2, 1)$ is completed at time 6. Job 1 is then resumed at time 6 and completed at time 8. No job is processed from time 8 to 10. Job 3 is started at time 10 but is preempted at time 15 by job $(2, 2)$ because the latter has a longer transportation time. Job $(2, 2)$ is completed at time 18. Job 3 resumes at time 18 and is completed at time 19. Finally, job 4 is started at time 19 and completed at time 21. In this schedule, the job completion times, in increasing order, are $C_{21} = 6, C_{11} = 8, C_{22} = 18, C_{12} = 19, C_{13} = 21$.

Step 2 checks the jobs from customer 1 at time points $\tau_l^1 = 5l\sqrt{2}$, for $l = 1, 2, \ldots$, and checks the jobs from customer 2 at time points $\tau_l^2 = 10l\sqrt{2}$, for $l = 1, 2, \ldots$. At τ_1^1 and τ_2^1, not all jobs from customer 1 that have arrived have completed processing. Hence, there is no delivery to customer 1 at these time points. At time τ_3^1, all jobs from customer 1 that have arrived have been completed. Thus, all the jobs $(1, 1), (1, 2), (1, 3)$ are delivered at time $\tau_3^1 = 15\sqrt{2}$ using two delivery batches. For jobs from customer 2, at time τ_1^2, the only job from customer 2 that has arrived, i.e., job $(2,1)$, has been completed and hence is delivered. At time τ_2^2, the other job from customer 2, i.e., job $(2,2)$, has been completed and hence is delivered. This

170   4 Integrated Production and Outbound Distribution Scheduling: Online Problems

solution gives $D_{\max} = \tau_2^2 + 10 = 20\sqrt{2} + 10$ and the total transportation cost $TC = 2f_1 + 2f_2 = 30$. Thus, the objective value of this solution is $20\sqrt{2} + 40$.

For the offline version of this instance, as discussed above, the job processing schedule generated by the LTT rule is optimal. Given this schedule, an optimal delivery schedule is as follows: deliver all the jobs from customer 1 at time 21, when all of them have completed processing, and deliver all the jobs from customer 2 at time 18. This gives the optimal objective value $28 + 2f_1 + f_2 = 48$.

We now evaluate the performance of Algorithm A4.11.

Theorem 4.8 *For problem* $1|online, r_j, pmtn|V(\infty, c), direct|k|D_{\max} + TC$, *Algorithm A4.11 is* $(\sqrt{k} + 1)$-*competitive.*

Proof For any given instance of the problem, let π be the solution generated by this algorithm. Let $C_{\max}^i$, $D_{\max}(\pi)$, and $TC(\pi)$ be the completion time of the last job from customer i, the maximum delivery time, and the total transportation cost in solution π, respectively. Similarly, let $D_{\max}^*$ and TC^* be the maximum delivery time and the total transportation cost in an optimal solution, respectively. Since LTT gives an optimal production schedule for the problem, we can assume without loss of generality that in an optimal solution, the completion time of the last job from customer i is the same as that in π, i.e., $C_{\max}^i$.

Let $\tau_{h_i}^i$ be the departure time of the last shipment for customer i in solution π, for some integer $h_i \geq 1$. From the algorithm, $\tau_{h_i-1}^i \leq C_{\max}^i \leq \tau_{h_i}^i$. Thus, $C_{\max}^i \geq \tau_{h_i}^i - \sqrt{k} f_i$, and we have

$$D_{\max}(\pi) = \max_{i \in K}\{\tau_{h_i}^i + t_i\} \leq \max_{i \in K}\{C_{\max}^i + \sqrt{k} f_i + t_i\}, \tag{4.13}$$

$$D_{\max}^* = \max_{i \in K}\{C_{\max}^i + t_i\}. \tag{4.14}$$

Clearly, $TC^* \geq \max_{i \in K}\{f_i\}$. Thus, the above relations (4.13) and (4.14) imply that

$$D_{\max}(\pi) \leq D_{\max}^* + \sqrt{k} TC^*. \tag{4.15}$$

Now, let x_i and y_i be the number of full batches and the number of partial batches delivered to customer i in solution π, respectively. Thus,

$$TC(\pi) = \sum_{i \in K}(x_i + y_i) f_i. \tag{4.16}$$

Clearly, there is at most one partial batch at each departure time. Thus $y_i \leq h_i$. The total number of batches delivered to customer i in an optimal solution is at least $x_i + \delta_i$, where $\delta_i = 0$ if $y_i = 0$ and $\delta_i = 1$ if $y_i \geq 1$. Thus,

$$TC^* \geq \sum_{i \in K}(x_i + \delta_i) f_i. \tag{4.17}$$

4.4 Online Problems with Batch Delivery to Multiple Customers   171

Furthermore, we have $y_i - \delta_i \le h_i - 1$, which implies that

$$\sum_{i \in K}(y_i - \delta_i) f_i \le \sum_{i \in K}(h_i - 1) f_i = \frac{1}{\sqrt{k}}\sum_{i \in K}\tau^i_{h_i-1} \le \frac{1}{\sqrt{k}}\sum_{i \in K}C^i_{\max} \le \sqrt{k}D^*_{\max}.$$

(4.18)

From (4.15) - (4.18), we have

$$\frac{D_{\max}(\pi) + TC(\pi)}{D^*_{\max} + TC^*} \le \frac{D^*_{\max} + \sqrt{k}TC^* + \sum_{i \in K}(x_i + y_i) f_i}{D^*_{\max} + TC^*}$$

$$= 1 + \frac{\sqrt{k}TC^* + \sum_{i \in K}(x_i + y_i) f_i - TC^*}{D^*_{\max} + TC^*}$$

$$\le 1 + \frac{\sqrt{k}TC^* + \sum_{i \in K}(x_i + y_i) f_i - \sum_{i \in K}(x_i + \delta_i) f_i}{D^*_{\max} + TC^*}$$

$$= 1 + \frac{\sqrt{k}TC^* + \sum_{i \in K}(y_i - \delta_i) f_i}{D^*_{\max} + TC^*}$$

$$\le 1 + \frac{\sqrt{k}TC^* + \sqrt{k}D^*_{\max}}{D^*_{\max} + TC^*} \le 1 + \sqrt{k}.$$

$\square$

We next propose an online algorithm for the nonpreemptive problem $1|online, r_j|V(\infty, c), direct|k|D_{\max} + TC$. Since preemption is not allowed, the LTT rule can no longer be used for processing the jobs. Instead, the algorithm schedules any available job whenever the machine is available.

Algorithm A4.12
Let $\alpha = \frac{1+\sqrt{1+4k}}{2}$.

Step 1: At the production stage, process any available job whenever the machine becomes available.
Step 2: At the delivery stage, for each $i \in K$, at each time point $\tau^i_l = l(\alpha f_i)$, for $l = 1, 2, \ldots$, if all the jobs from customer i that arrived before this time have completed processing, then deliver them all to customer i using a minimum number of vehicles. Otherwise, do not deliver any jobs from customer i.

Example 4.11 (Application of Algorithm A4.12) Apply Algorithm A4.12 to the instance given in Example 4.10. First of all, given $k = 2$, we have $\alpha = 2$. We observe that Step 1 provides a lot of flexibility. Suppose that it schedules the jobs in the order of their arrival. This gives the following job completion times, in increasing order: $C_{11} = 6, C_{21} = 8, C_{12} = 16, C_{13} = 18, C_{22} = 21$. Step 2 checks the jobs from customer 1 at time points $\tau^1_l = 10l$, for $l = 1, 2, \ldots$, and checks the jobs from customer 2 at time points $\tau^2_l = 20l$, for $l = 1, 2, \ldots$. For the jobs from customer 1, at time 10, job (1,1) is delivered; and at time 20, jobs (1,2) and (1,3) are delivered

172   4 Integrated Production and Outbound Distribution Scheduling: Online Problems

together. Similarly, for the jobs from customer 2, at time 20, no job delivery takes place, but at time 40, jobs (2,1) and (2,2) are delivered together. This solution gives $D_{\max} = 40 + t_2 = 50$ and the total transportation cost $TC = 2f_1 + f_2 = 20$. Thus, the objective value of this solution is 70.

For the offline version of this instance, an optimal solution is to process the jobs in the following order (1, 1), (2, 1), (1, 2), (2, 2), (1, 3). This gives $C_{11} = 6, C_{21} = 8, C_{12} = 16, C_{22} = 19, C_{13} = 21$. Given this schedule, an optimal delivery schedule is as follows: deliver all the jobs from customer 1 at time 21, and deliver all the jobs from customer 2 at time 19. This gives $D_{\max} = 29$, and the optimal objective value $29 + 2f_1 + f_2 = 49$.

Theorem 4.9 *For problem $1|online, r_j|V(\infty, c), direct|k|D_{\max} + TC$, Algorithm A4.12 is $(1 + \alpha)$-competitive.*

Proof For any given instance of the problem, let π be the solution generated by this algorithm. Let $C_{\max}^i(\pi)$ and $C_{\max}^i$ be the completion time of the last job from customer i in solution π and in an optimal solution, respectively. In general, they are not the same. We follow the same notation defined in the proof of Theorem 4.8 for all other parameters. In addition, we define $C_{\max}$ to be the completion time of the last job in solution π. Clearly, $C_{\max} = \max_{i \in K}\{C_{\max}^i\}$, and the completion time of the last job in an optimal solution is also $C_{\max}$.

The relation between $D_{\max}(\pi)$ and $D_{\max}^*$ given in (4.15) in the proof of Theorem 4.8 no longer holds partly because the possible time points at which a delivery can occur in Algorithm A4.12 differ from those in Algorithm A4.11. To derive their relationship, first we observe that

$$D_{\max}(\pi) = \max_{i \in K}\{\tau_{h_i}^i + t_i\} \le \max_{i \in K}\{C_{\max}^i(\pi) + \alpha f_i + t_i\}$$

$$\le C_{\max} + \alpha \max_{i \in K}\{f_i\} + \max_{i \in K}\{t_i\},$$

$$D_{\max}^* \ge \max\{C_{\max}, \max_{i \in K}\{t_i\}\},$$

$$TC^* \ge \max_{i \in K}\{f_i\}.$$

The above relations imply that

$$D_{\max}(\pi) \le 2D_{\max}^* + \alpha TC^*. \tag{4.19}$$

We still have the same relationship between y_i and δ_i as in the proof of Theorem 4.8, i.e., $y_i - \delta_i \le h_i - 1$. Thus, we have the following result, which is similar to (4.18).

$$\sum_{i \in K}(y_i - \delta_i)f_i \le \sum_{i \in K}(h_i - 1)f_i = \frac{1}{\alpha}\sum_{i \in K}\tau_{h_i - 1}^i \le \frac{1}{\alpha}\sum_{i \in K}C_{\max}^i(\pi) \le \frac{k}{\alpha}D_{\max}^*.$$

$$\tag{4.20}$$

4.4 Online Problems with Batch Delivery to Multiple Customers 173

From (4.19), (4.20), and the two results (4.16) and (4.17) shown in the proof of Theorem 4.8, we have

$$
\begin{aligned}
\frac{D_{\max}(\pi) + TC(\pi)}{D^*_{\max} + TC^*} &\leq \frac{2D^*_{\max} + \alpha TC^* + \sum_{i \in K}(x_i + y_i)f_i}{D^*_{\max} + TC^*} \\
&= 1 + \frac{D^*_{\max} + \alpha TC^* + \sum_{i \in K}(x_i + y_i)f_i - TC^*}{D^*_{\max} + TC^*} \\
&\leq 1 + \frac{D^*_{\max} + \alpha TC^* + \sum_{i \in K}(y_i - \delta_i)f_i}{D^*_{\max} + TC^*} \\
&\leq 1 + \frac{D^*_{\max} + \frac{k}{\alpha}D^*_{\max} + \alpha TC^*}{D^*_{\max} + TC^*} \leq 1 + \alpha.
\end{aligned}
$$

The last inequality above is due to the fact that $\alpha = 1 + \frac{k}{\alpha}$, which is implied by the given value of α. $\qquad\square$

For problem $1|online, r_j|V(\infty, c), direct|k|D_{\max} + TC$, from Theorem 4.9, the competitive ratio of Algorithm A4.12 is 2.618 (respectively, 3) if $k = 1$ (resp., $k = 2$).

4.4.2 Total Delivery Time and Transportation Cost Problems

We consider two related problems in this section: $1|online, r_j, pmtn|V(\infty, c), direct|k|\sum D_j + TC$ and $1|online, r_j|V(\infty, c), direct|k|\sum D_j + TC$. The corresponding offline problem without preemption $1|r_j|V(\infty, c), direct|k|\sum D_j + TC$ is strongly NP-hard because it contains a strongly NP-hard classical problem without the delivery component, $1|r_j|\sum C_j$ (Lenstra et al., 1977), as a special case. However, the complexity of the corresponding offline problem with preemption $1|r_j, pmtn|V(\infty, c), direct|k|\sum D_j + TC$ remains open (Chen, 2010). The corresponding online problems with a single customer are discussed in Sects. 4.3.3.2 and 4.3.3.3, where an online algorithm with a competitive ratio of 2 for the problem with preemption and an online algorithm with a competitive ratio of 3 for the problem without preemption are given, respectively.

Below, we first present the online algorithm given by Averbakh (2010) for problem $1|online, r_j, pmtn|V(\infty, c), direct|k|\sum D_j + TC$. This algorithm extends directly from Algorithm A4.9 given in Sect. 4.3.3.2 for the corresponding problem with a single customer. At any given time point, we define the delay time of a finished but undelivered job exactly as in Sect. 4.3.3.2.

174   4 Integrated Production and Outbound Distribution Scheduling: Online Problems

Algorithm A4.13
Step 1: At the production stage, schedule the arriving jobs by the SRPT rule given in Sect. 4.3.1.1.
Step 2: At the delivery stage, for each customer $i \in K$, as soon as one of the following two conditions is satisfied: (i) there are c finished but undelivered jobs from customer i; (ii) the total delay time of the finished but undelivered jobs from customer i is equal to f_i, deliver all the finished but undelivered jobs from customer i together in one batch to customer i.

Theorem 4.10 *For problem* $1|online, r_j, pmtn|V(\infty, c), direct|k| \sum D_j + TC,$ *Algorithm A4.13 is* (2γ)-*competitive, where* $\gamma = \min\{c, 1 + (1 - \frac{1}{c})(\frac{\sum_{i \in K} f_i}{f_{\min}})\}$ *and* $f_{\min} = \min_{i \in K} f_i$.

Proof We provide a sketch of the proof given by Averbakh (2010). For any given instance of the problem, let π be the solution generated by this algorithm and π^* be an optimal offline solution. Let $\tau_1 < \tau_2 < \cdots < \tau_q$ be the consecutive departure times of delivery batches in π^*. Note that at each of these time points there may be multiple deliveries to the same or different customers.

Consider another solution π_1 obtained as follows: jobs are scheduled by the SRPT rule, as in Algorithm A4.12, and deliveries are scheduled at time points $\tau_1, \ldots, \tau_q$. At each time point τ_j, use a minimum number of delivery batches to deliver all the jobs that are finished in time interval $(\tau_{j-1}, \tau_j]$ such that there is no more than one partial delivery batch to any customer.

Let $TD(\sigma), TC(\sigma)$, and $Z(\sigma) = TD(\sigma) + TC(\sigma)$ be the total delivery time, the total transportation cost, and the objective value of a given solution σ, respectively.

Averbakh (2010) proves the theorem by showing the following three results: (i) $Z(\pi) \leq 2Z(\pi_1)$, (ii) $TD(\pi_1) \leq TD(\pi^*)$, and (iii) $TC(\pi_1) \leq \gamma TC(\pi^*)$. Result (i) can be proved by arguments similar to the proof of Theorem 4.6. Result (ii) can be proved by the following fact: for any time point τ, the production schedule generated by the SRPT rule yields at least as many completed jobs in the time interval $[0, \tau]$ as in any other production schedule including the production schedule in solution π^*.

To show result (iii), Averbakh (2010) first shows some results about the number of delivery batches in π^* and that in π_1. Let x_i be the number of delivery batches to customer i in solution π^*, and y_1^i, y_2^i be the number of full and partial delivery batches to customer i in solution π_1. Clearly, $cy_1^i + y_2^i \leq cx_i$, for $i \in K$. Also, since $\sum_{i \in K} x_i \geq q$ and in π_1 there is at most one partial delivery to customer i at each departure time $\tau_1, \ldots, \tau_q$, we have $y_2^i \leq \sum_{i \in K} x_i$, for $i \in K$. Based on these results, it can be shown that

$$y_1^i + y_2^i \leq \frac{1}{c}\left(cx_i + (c-1)\sum_{j \in K} x_j\right).$$

From this inequality, result (iii) can be proved. □

4.5 Online Problems with Two Stages of Delivery 175

Next, we present the online algorithm given by Feng et al. (2016) for problem $1|online, r_j|V(\infty, c), direct|k| \sum D_j + TC$. This algorithm extends directly from Algorithm A4.10 given in 4.3.3.3 for the corresponding problem with a single customer.

Algorithm A4.14

Step 1: At the production stage, process the jobs by the SSPT rule given in Sect. 4.3.3.1.

Step 2: At the delivery stage, for each customer $i \in K$, as soon as one of the following two conditions is satisfied:

(i) There are c finished but undelivered jobs from customer i.
(ii) The total delay time of the finished but undelivered jobs from customer i is equal to f_i, deliver all the finished but undelivered jobs from customer i together in one batch to customer i.

Theorem 4.11 *For problem* $1|online, r_j|V(\infty, c), direct|k| \sum D_j + TC$, *Algorithm A4.14 is* (2γ)-*competitive, where* γ *is defined in Theorem 4.10.*

Proof We provide a sketch of the proof given by Feng et al. (2016). For any given instance of the problem, let π be the solution generated by this algorithm and π^* be the optimal offline solution. Let $Z(\pi)$ and $Z(\pi^*)$ be the objective values of π and π^*, respectively. Let $\tau_1 < \tau_2 < \cdots < \tau_q$ be the consecutive departure times of delivery batches in π^*. Note that at each of these time points there may be multiple deliveries to the same or to different customers.

Consider a solution π_1 for the preemptive version of the problem as follows: jobs are scheduled by the SRPT rule, as in Algorithm A4.12, and deliveries are scheduled at time points $2\tau_1, \ldots, 2\tau_q$. At each time point $2\tau_j$, use a minimum number of delivery batches to deliver all the jobs that are finished in time interval $(2\tau_{j-1}, 2\tau_j]$ such that there is no more than one partial batch delivery to any customer. Let $\tilde{Z}(\pi_1)$ be the objective value of solution π_1 for the preemptive version of the problem instance.

Feng et al. (2016) prove this theorem by showing the following two results: (1) $\tilde{Z}(\pi_1) \leq \gamma Z(\pi^*)$ and (2) $Z(\pi) \leq 2\tilde{Z}(\pi_1)$. These results can be proved using similar arguments as in the proofs of Theorem 4.10, Lemma 4.3, and Theorem 4.7. $\square$

4.5 Online Problems with Two Stages of Delivery

In Sect. 3.8, we consider two offline integrated production and distribution scheduling problems involving two stages of delivery, namely, problem P1 with the objective of minimizing $\sum D_j + TC$, and problem P2 with the objective of minimizing $D_{\max} + TC$. In both problems, a given set of jobs is first processed on a single machine or m parallel machines in a plant, and then delivered from the

176 4 Integrated Production and Outbound Distribution Scheduling: Online Problems

plant to a pool point and from the pool point to the corresponding customer sites. It is shown in Sect. 3.8 that these problems are generally NP-hard, but they can be solved in polynomial time when there are only a single machine and a fixed number of customers.

In this section, we consider the online version of these two problems where jobs arrive over time and are not known until they arrive. However, all necessary information about the customers from whom the jobs originate, including the number of customers and their locations, is known in advance. Since the difficulty of a problem and the corresponding competitive analysis for the problem are mainly determined by the number of machines (i.e., m) and the number of customers (i.e., k) involved in the problem, we consider four different cases of the online problems as follows:

- Online problem P1 with a single machine and a single customer, which is denoted as OP1 with $m = 1$ and $k = 1$.
- Online problem P1 with a general number of parallel machines and a general number of customers, which is denoted as OP1 with $m \geq 1$ and $k \geq 1$.
- Online problem P2 with a general number of parallel machines and a single customer, which is denoted as OP2 with $m \geq 1$ and $k = 1$.
- Online problem P2 with a general number of parallel machines and a general number of customers, which is denoted as OP2 with $m \geq 1$ and $k \geq 1$.

Tang et al. (2019) propose an online algorithm and conduct a competitive analysis of the algorithm for each of these four problems. We present their algorithms and competitive analysis results in the following without giving the proofs. We refer the interested reader to Tang et al.'s paper for all the technical details.

We use the notation introduced in Sect. 3.8. Specifically, the following symbols defined in Sect. 3.8 are explicitly used in this section: (i, j) denotes the jth job from customer i, $r_{(i,j)}$ its arrival time, and $p_{(i,j)}$ its processing time. In a given schedule, we use $C_{(i,j)}$ to denote the completion time of job (i, j) at the plant. The shipment capacity, transportation time, and transportation cost from the plant to the pool point are denoted as c_0, t_0, and f_0, respectively, and those from the pool point to customer i are denoted as c_i, t_i, and f_i, respectively. Shipments from the plant to the pool point are called v-shipments, and shipments from the pool point to the customers are called s-shipments.

For problem OP1 with $m = 1$ and $k = 1$, Tang et al. (2019) propose the following online algorithm and show that its competitive ratio is 4.

Algorithm A4.15

Step 1. At the production stage, schedule the arriving jobs by the SSPT rule given in Sect. 4.3.3.1.

Step 2. At the first delivery stage, at any time point τ from 0 onward, do the following. Let h be the number of completed jobs waiting at the plant and q be the number of jobs waiting at the pool point.

- If the sum of the total delay time of the h jobs waiting at the plant, the total delay time of the q jobs waiting at the pool point, and qt_0 is equal to $f_0 + f_1$,

4.5 Online Problems with Two Stages of Delivery 177

then deliver all these h jobs to the pool point using $\lceil h/c_0 \rceil$ v-shipments, where the delay time of a job (i, j) waiting at the plant is defined as $\tau - C_{(i,j)}$, and that of a job (i, j) waiting at the pool point is defined as $\tau - C_{(i,j)} - t_0$.

- Otherwise, deliver only the first $\lfloor h/c_0 \rfloor c_0$ of these h jobs to the pool point using $\lfloor h/c_0 \rfloor$ v-shipments.

Step 3. At the second delivery stage, at any time point τ from 0 onward, let q be the number of jobs waiting at the pool point.

- If the total delay time of the q jobs is equal to $f_0 + f_1$, then deliver all these q jobs to the customer using $\lceil q/c_1 \rceil$ s-shipments.
- Otherwise, deliver only the first $\lfloor q/c_1 \rfloor c_1$ of the q jobs to the customer using $\lfloor q/c_1 \rfloor$ s-shipments.

Example 4.12 (Application of Algorithm A4.15) We apply Algorithm A4.15 to the instance given in the table below, which also shows the jobs' shifted arrival times $r'_j \in [\max\{r_j, p_j\}, r_j + p_j]$ following the SSPT rule in Step 1 of the algorithm. The other parameters of the instance include $m = 1, k = 1$ and $t_0 = 1, t_1 = 3, f_0 = 2, f_1 = 5, c_0 = 2, c_1 = 3$.

j	1	2	3	4	5
r_j	2	4	6	8	15
p_j	5	3	1	6	2
r'_j	6	4	6	14	15

In Step 1, the SSPT rule schedules the jobs in the order $(2, 3, 1, 4, 5)$ with the starting time S_j and completion time C_j of each job as follows: $S_2 = 4, C_2 = 7, S_3 = 7, C_3 = 8, S_1 = 8, C_1 = 13, S_4 = 14, C_4 = 20, S_5 = 20, C_5 = 22$.

Check any time τ from 0 onward. Steps 2 and 3 need to be considered simultaneously because Step 2 involves jobs waiting at the plant as well as the jobs waiting at the pool point. At time $\tau = 12$, Step 2 finds that there are $h = 2$ jobs (jobs 2 and 3) waiting at the plant and $q = 0$ jobs waiting at the pool point, and their total delay time is 7, which is equal to $f_0 + f_1$. Thus, a v-shipment carrying jobs 2 and 3 departs at time 11 from the plant and arrives at the pool point at time 12. At time $\tau = 12$, Step 3 finds that there are $q = 2$ jobs (job 2 and 3) waiting at the pool point and their total delay time is 7 $(= f_0 + f_1)$. Thus, an s-shipment carrying these jobs departs at time 12 and arrives at the customer site at time 15.

At time $\tau = 20$, Step 2 finds that the total delay time of the two jobs (jobs 1 and 4) waiting at the plant is 7. Thus, they are delivered by a v-shipment with departure time 20 and arrive at the pool point at time 21. At time $\tau = 21$, Step 3 finds that the total delay time of the two jobs (jobs 1 and 4) waiting at the pool point is 7. Thus, they are delivered by an s-shipment with departure time 21 and arrive at the customer site at time 24.

At time $\tau = 29$, Step 2 finds that the total delay time of the job (job 5) waiting at the plant is 7. Thus, it is delivered by a v-shipment with departure time 29 and

178   4   Integrated Production and Outbound Distribution Scheduling: Online Problems

arrives at the pool point at time 30. At time $\tau = 30$, Step 3 finds that the total delay time of the job (job 5) waiting at the pool point is 7. Thus, it is delivered by an s-shipment with departure time 30 and arrives at the customer site at time 33.

It can be seen that in the above described schedule $\sum D_j = 2(15) + 2(24) + 33 = 111$, and $TC = 3f_0 + 3f_1 = 21$. Thus, the total cost of this schedule is 132.

It can also be verified that the following solution is optimal for this instance: schedule the jobs on the machine in the order $(1, 3, 2, 4, 5)$ with the starting time S_j and completion time C_j of each job as follows: $S_1 = 2, C_1 = 7, S_3 = 7, C_3 = 8, S_2 = 8, C_2 = 11, S_4 = 11, C_4 = 17, S_5 = 17, C_5 = 19$. Jobs 1 and 3 are delivered in a v-shipment with departure time 8 from the plant; they arrive at the pool point at time 9, and then are delivered in an s-shipment immediately with arrival time 12 at the customer site, i.e., $D_1 = D_3 = 12$. Job 2 is delivered in a v-shipment with departure time 11 and arrival time 12 at the pool point and is delivered in an s-shipment immediately from the pool point with arrival time 15 at the customer site, i.e., $D_2 = 15$. Finally, jobs 4 and 5 are delivered in a v-shipment with departure time 19 from the plant and arrival time 20 at the pool point and then are delivered in an s-shipment immediately with arrival time 23 at the customer site (i.e., $D_4 = D_5 = 23$). In this solution, $\sum D_j = 2(12) + 15 + 2(23) = 85$, and $TC = 3f_0 + 3f_1 = 21$. Thus, the total cost of this solution is 106.

We observe that problem $1|online, r_j|V(\infty, c), direct|1|\sum D_j + TC$ considered in Sect. 4.3.3.3 is a special case of problem OP1 with $m = 1$ and $k = 1$ with a single delivery stage. It is shown there that Algorithm A4.10 given there for this problem has a competitive ratio of 3. We can see that the first two steps of Algorithm A4.15 here are somewhat similar to Algorithm A4.10, in that both employ a delay strategy.

For the more general problem OP1 with $m \geq 1$ and $k \geq 1$, Tang et al. (2019) propose the following online algorithm and show that its competitive ratio is $c_{max} + 1$, where $c_{max} = \max\{c_i|0 \leq i \leq k\}$.

Algorithm A4.16

Step 1. At the production stage, reset the arrival time $r_{(i,j)}$ of each arriving job (i, j) to be $\max\{r_{(i,j)}, p_{(i,j)}\}$. Whenever there is a machine available, schedule an available job (based on the reset arrival times) with the shortest processing time on this machine.

Step 2. At the first delivery stage, at any time point τ, do the following. For each customer $i \in K$, let h_i be the number of completed jobs from customer i waiting at the plant. Check if the following condition is satisfied: the total delay time of these h_i jobs is equal to $\max\{f_0/c_0, f_i/c_i\}$.

- If this condition is satisfied for customer i, then deliver all these h_i jobs to the pool point using $\lceil h_i/c_0 \rceil$ v-shipments.
- For the customers for which the above condition is not satisfied, let l be the total number of completed jobs waiting at the plant that belong to these customers. Deliver the first $\lfloor l/c_0 \rfloor c_0$ of these l jobs from the plant to the pool point using $\lfloor l/c_0 \rfloor$ v-shipments.

4.5 Online Problems with Two Stages of Delivery

Step 3. At the second delivery stage, at any time point τ, for each customer $i \in K$, let q_i be the number of jobs from customer i waiting at the pool point.

- If the total delay time of these q_i jobs is greater than or equal to $\max\{f_0/c_0, f_i/c_i\}$, then deliver all these q_i jobs to customer i using $\lceil q_i/c_i \rceil$ s-shipments.
- Otherwise, deliver only the first $\lfloor q_i/c_i \rfloor c_i$ of the q_i jobs to customer i using $\lfloor q_i/c_i \rfloor$ s-shipments.

We observe that problem $1/online, r_j|V(\infty, c), direct|k| \sum D_j + TC$ considered in Sect. 4.4.2 is a special case of problem OP2 with $m = 1, k \geq 1$ and identical c_i and with a single delivery stage. It is shown there that Algorithm A4.14 given there for $1/online, r_j|V(\infty, c), direct|k| \sum D_j + TC$ has a competitive ratio that depends on problem parameters.

For problem OP2 with $m \geq 1$ and $k = 1$, Tang et al. (2019) propose an online algorithm and show that the competitive ratio of their algorithm is 2 and that this is the best possible competitive ratio that any online algorithm can achieve for this problem. In the following, we provide a modified version of their algorithm, where the procedure for the first stage of delivery is made more similar to Algorithm A4.7 and Algorithm A4.18 given below.

Algorithm A4.17
Step 1. At the production stage, whenever there is a machine available, schedule an available job with the longest processing time on this machine.
Step 2. At the first delivery stage, at each time point $\tau = l(f_0 + f_1)$, for $l = 1, 2, \ldots$, let h be the number of completed jobs waiting at the plant. If both of the following two conditions are satisfied: (1) there are no new jobs arriving at the plant at this time point and (2) the jobs that arrived before this time point have all completed processing by this time point, then deliver all these h jobs to the pool point using $\lceil h/c_0 \rceil$ v-shipments.
Step 3. At the second delivery stage, at any time point τ, if there are any v-shipments that arrive at the pool point, then let q be the number of jobs at the pool point after the arrival of these v-shipments, and deliver all these q jobs to the customer using $\lfloor q/c_1 \rfloor$ s-shipments.

We note that problem $P_m|online, r_j|V(\infty, c), direct|1|D_{\max} + TC$ considered in Sect. 4.3.2 is a special case of problem OP2 with $m \geq 1, k = 1$ and a single stage of delivery. It is shown there that Algorithm A4.8 given there has a competitive ratio of 2 for this problem.

Finally, for problem OP2 with $m \geq 1$ and $k \geq 1$, Tang et al. (2019) propose the following online algorithm. They show that the competitive ratio of this algorithm is $k + 2$.

Algorithm A4.18
Step 1. At the production stage, whenever there is a machine available, schedule an available job with the longest processing time on this machine.

180   4   Integrated Production and Outbound Distribution Scheduling: Online Problems

Step 2. At the first delivery stage, at each time point $\tau = lf_0$, for $l = 1, 2, \ldots$, let h be the number of completed jobs waiting at the plant. If both of the following two conditions are satisfied: (1) there are no new jobs arriving at the plant at this time point and (2) the jobs that arrived before this time point have all completed processing, then deliver all these h jobs to the pool point using $\lceil h/c_0 \rceil$ v-shipments. Otherwise, deliver only the first $\lfloor h/c_0 \rfloor c_0$ of the h jobs to the pool point using $\lfloor h/c_0 \rfloor$ v-shipments.

Step 3. At the second delivery stage, at any time point τ, for each customer $i \in K$ at each time point $\tau_i = lf_i$ for $l = 1, 2, \ldots$, let q_i be the number of jobs from this customer waiting at the pool point. If both of the following two conditions are satisfied: (1) there are no new jobs from this customer arriving at the plant at this time point and (2) the jobs from this customer that arrived before this time point have all been completed processing and delivered to the pool point, then deliver all these q_i jobs to the customer using $\lceil q_i/c_i \rceil$ s-shipments.

Example 4.13 (Application of Algorithm A4.18) We apply Algorithm A4.18 to the instance given in the table below, where there are $m = 2$ parallel machines and $k = 2$ customers. The other parameters of the instance include $t_0 = 1, t_1 = 2, t_2 = 3, f_0 = 4, f_1 = 6, f_2 = 9, c_0 = 2, c_1 = c_2 = 3$.

j	1	2	3	4	5
Customer	2	1	1	2	2
r_j	4	5	6	13	15
p_j	3	5	1	5	2

Step 1 generates the following schedule for processing the jobs on the two machines: machine 1 processes jobs 1, 3, 4 in this order with their starting times and completion times as follows: $S_1 = 4, C_1 = 7, S_3 = 7, C_3 = 8, S_4 = 13, C_4 = 18$; machine 2 processes jobs 2 and 5 in this order with $S_2 = 5, C_2 = 10, S_5 = 15, C_5 = 17$.

Step 2 checks the jobs waiting at the plant at time points $\tau = 4l$, for $l = 1, 2, \ldots$, and at each time point determines whether to deliver some jobs from the plant to the pool point. At $\tau = 4$, it does nothing because none of the jobs have been completed (i.e., $h = 0$). At $\tau = 8, h = 2$ (jobs 1 and 3), but neither of the two conditions is satisfied. However, since $c_0 = h$, these two jobs are delivered together in a v-shipment with arrival time 9 at the pool point. At $\tau = 12, h = 1$ (job 2), and the two conditions are satisfied. Thus, job 2 is delivered to the pool point with arrival time 13. At $\tau = 16, h = 0$. At $\tau = 20, h = 2$ (jobs 4 and 5), and the two conditions are satisfied. Thus, jobs 4 and 5 are delivered to the pool point with arrival time 21.

Step 3 checks the jobs from customer 1 waiting at the pool point at time points $\tau = 6l$, for $l = 1, 2, \ldots$, and checks the jobs from customer 2 waiting at the pool point at time points $\tau = 9l$, for $l = 1, 2, \ldots$. First, consider customer 1. At time $\tau = 6, q_1 = 0$. At time $\tau = 12, q_1 = 1$ (job 3), but condition (2) is not satisfied for customer 1 because job 2 has not been delivered to the pool point. At time $\tau = 18$,

4.6 Online or Offline Algorithms? 181

$q_1 = 2$ (jobs 2 and 3), and both conditions are satisfied for customer 1. Thus, jobs 2 and 3 are delivered to customer 1 with arrival time 20. Now consider customer 2. At time $\tau = 9$, $q_2 = 1$ (job 1), and both conditions are satisfied for customer 2. Thus, job 1 is delivered to customer 2 with arrival time 12. At time $\tau = 18$, $q_2 = 0$. At time $\tau = 27$, $q_2 = 2$ (jobs 4 and 5), and both conditions are satisfied. Thus, jobs 4 and 5 are delivered to customer 2 with arrival time 30.

It can be seen that in the above described schedule, $D_{\max} = 30$ and $TC = 3f_0 + f_1 + 2f_2 = 36$. Thus, the total cost of this schedule is 66. It can also be verified that the following solution is optimal for this instance: schedule the jobs on the two machines the same way as in the solution described above. At the first stage of delivery, deliver jobs 1 and 3 at time 8 to the pool point with arrival time 9; deliver job 2 at time 10 to the pool point with arrival time 11; deliver jobs 4 and 5 at time 18 to the pool point with arrival time 19. At the second stage of delivery, deliver jobs 2 and 3 at time 11 to customer 1 with arrival time 13; deliver jobs 1, 4, and 5 at time 19 to customer 2 with arrival time 22. This solution has $D_{\max} = 22$ and $TC = 3f_0 + f_1 + f_2 = 27$ and hence a total cost of 49.

We note that problem $1|online, r_j|V(\infty, c), direct|k|D_{\max} + TC$ considered in Sect. 4.4.1 is a special case of problem OP2 with $m = 1$, $k \geq 1$, and a single stage of delivery. It is shown there that Algorithm A4.12 given there has a competitive ratio of $\frac{3+\sqrt{1+4k}}{2}$ for this problem.

Comparing the four algorithms, Algorithms A4.15–A4.18, we observe the following similarities and differences:

- The algorithms for the two cases of problem OP1, where the objective function is $\sum D_j + TC$, i.e., Algorithms A4.15 and A4.16 both use an SPT based strategy to schedule the jobs in the production stage and use a strategy based on the total delay time of the waiting jobs to schedule job delivery in both delivery stages. Similar strategies are also used in Algorithms A4.9, A4.10, A4.13, and A4.14 for similar problems but with a single stage of delivery.
- The algorithms for the two cases of problem OP2, where the objective function is $D_{\max} + TC$, i.e., Algorithms A4.17 and A4.18 both use an LPT based strategy to schedule the jobs in the production stage and use a strategy that periodically checks the status of the system to schedule job delivery in both delivery stages. Similar strategies are also used in Algorithms A4.8, A4.11, and A4.12 for similar problems but with a single stage of delivery.

4.6 Online or Offline Algorithms?

As discussed in Sect. 4.1, to solve an online problem, the decision maker can either follow a rolling horizon approach in which the underlying problem is treated and solved as an offline problem within each planning horizon using an offline algorithm, or treat and solve the problem in an online fashion using an online algorithm.

However, all the existing studies on online IPODS problems develop online algorithms to solve the underlying online problems, and only one study, discussed below, also uses rolling horizon based offline algorithms. Furthermore, the most existing studies on online IPODS problems evaluate the performance of online algorithms by performing competitive analysis, which compares the solutions generated by the online algorithms with the optimal offline solutions in the worst case. This is not necessarily the most reasonable way of evaluating online algorithms because optimal offline solutions for a problem are obtained under the assumption that one has the complete information of all the problem parameters in advance. A fairer, or at least more practical, way of evaluating online algorithms is to compare their solutions with the best possible solutions that can be generated by offline algorithms that use the same amount of information as the online algorithms.

Tang et al. (2019) is the only paper on online IPODS problems that uses both online and rolling horizon based offline algorithms to solve the underlying online problems. They evaluate the performance of their online algorithms by doing theoretical worst-case based competitive analysis, which is discussed in Sect. 4.5, as well as comparing with rolling horizon based offline algorithms. For the two online problems, OP1 with $m \geq 1$ and $k \geq 1$ and OP2 with $m \geq 1$ and $k \geq 1$, described in Sect. 4.5, in addition to the online algorithms described in Sect. 4.5, Tang et al. (2019) also propose two offline approaches, denoted as OFF4 and OFF1, as follows. Suppose that in the online problems, jobs arrive over time in a given planning horizon $[0, T]$:

- OFF4: The problem is solved four times at time point $T/4, T/2, 3T/4$, and T, respectively, and at each time it is treated as an offline problem with all the information available up to this time point. The heuristics for the offline problems, described in Sect. 3.8, are used to solve these offline problems.
- OFF1: The problem is solved only once after all the jobs have arrived, i.e., at time T, using the same heuristics of Sect. 3.8.

Clearly, online algorithms make real-time decisions and, hence, have the highest decision frequency, whereas OFF1 makes decisions only once for all the jobs together and has the lowest decision frequency. The decision frequency of OFF4 is somewhere in between. Their computational tests show that among the three approaches (online algorithms, OFF1 and OFF4), OFF4 performs the best for most test instances.

For the problems studied in Tang et al. (2019), because jobs do not have delivery deadlines, and there are infinitely many delivery vehicles that can be used at any time point, we can choose to solve the problem in any way we want. For example, we can choose any number of time points within the planning horizon in any way and solve the corresponding offline problem at each chosen time point with the information available up to this time. However, in various applications, there are constraints on delivery times (e.g., a job must be delivered to its customer site by a pre-specified time) and/or constraints on vehicle availability (e.g., there are only a limited number of vehicles available, and they are available only at certain time points). In these

4.7 Future Research

situations, we have to choose the time points in a way that guarantees problem feasibility if we want to solve the problem by solving the corresponding offline problem at the chosen time points.

4.7 Future Research

For future research directions, first there are several open questions from the previous sections of this chapter that need to be clarified. They include:

- As discussed in Sect. 4.2.2, there is no existing online algorithm for problem $P_m|online, r_j|V(\infty, 1), iid|n|D_{\max}$ with a general number of machines. One can try to extend Algorithm A4.2 to this problem and perform a competitive analysis.
- As discussed in Sect. 4.3.1.3, for problem $1|online, r_j|V(1, c), direct|1|D_{\max}$ with $c \geq 2$, Algorithm A4.5 is shown to have an asymptotic competitive ratio of $\frac{\sqrt{5}+1}{2}$, whereas Algorithm A4.6 is shown to have a competitive ratio of 2.5. These two ratios differ significantly. Thus, there are two questions that can be investigated. First, can we show tighter competitive ratios for these algorithms? Second, is there another algorithm with a competitive ratio between $\frac{\sqrt{5}+1}{2}$ and 2.5?
- As discussed in Sect. 4.3.2, Han et al. (2015) give an online algorithm (i.e., Algorithm A4.8) with a competitive ratio of 2 for problem $P_m|online, r_j|V(\infty, 1), direct|n|D_{\max}+TC$, but show that no online algorithm can have a competitive ratio less than $\max\{\frac{\sqrt{5}+1}{2}, 2 - \frac{1}{c}\}$. A question that remains is whether there is another algorithm for this problem that has a smaller competitive ratio than Algorithm A4.8.
- A similar question remains for problem $1|online, r_j|V(\infty, c), direct|1|\sum D_j + TC$. Is there an alternative algorithm for this problem that has a smaller competitive ratio than Algorithm A4.10? Similarly, for problem $1|online, r_j|V(\infty, c), direct|k|D_{\max} + TC$, is there another algorithm with a smaller competitive ratio than Algorithm A4.12?

While a wide variety of offline IPODS problems have received a significant amount of research attention in the last two decades, online IPODS problems have received much less attention. As discussed in the previous sections of this chapter, the existing research on O-IPODS problems has been mostly focused on a small subset of problems only. We believe that more research is needed on the following classes of O-IPODS problems:

- Problems with a limited number of delivery vehicles. Most O-IPODS problems that have been studied involve a sufficient number of vehicles such that vehicle availability is not a constraint. In such problems, each vehicle is used at most for one trip. However, in real-world situations, there is often limited vehicle availability such that a vehicle may need to be used for multiple trips.

- Problems with fixed delivery departure dates. We are not aware of any existing results on online problems where vehicle departure dates are fixed in advance. We can consider the online versions of several such offline problems discussed in Sect. 3.6.
- Problems with multiple customers. Section 4.4 has discussed several O-IPODS problems with multiple customers. However, all these problems involve the direct shipping method where each shipment goes to one customer only. Apparently, no existing studies have considered online problems with a "routing" delivery method where a shipment is allowed to cover multiple customers. Clearly, such online problems will be more difficult to solve. We suggest that research should start with the online version of the problem discussed in Sect. 3.5.2 with a single machine, i.e., problem $1|online, r_j|V(\infty, c), routing|k| \sum D_j + TC$.
- Problems with objective functions other than $D_{\max}$, $D_{\max} + TC$, $\sum D_j$, $\sum D_j + TC$. Almost all the existing O-IPODS problems involve one of these objective functions. In reality, jobs may have different importance weights, due dates that can be violated with a penalty, and deadlines that cannot be violated. This means that objective functions such as the total weighted delivery time, maximum lateness, the total tardiness, and a total number of tardy jobs may be relevant and should also be studied.
- Semi-online problems. Unlike in a purely online environment where nothing about the future (including the number of jobs to arrive in the future, and any parameters about a future job) is known, in a semi-online setting, some information about the future is known in advance. For example, in practice, although we may not know everything about the jobs that will arrive in the future, we may know some information about the jobs, e.g., specific time points when new jobs may arrive (Hall et al., 2009), bounds of the job processing times, bounds of the transportation times, etc. Another example is that we may know everything about the jobs that will arrive in the near future, although we may know nothing about the jobs that will arrive in the distant future. A handful of existing studies (Averbakh & Baysan, 2012, 2013; Liu et al., 2010; Tian et al., 2008) have considered some semi-online IPODS problems. More research is certainly needed on such problems, especially given that real-world situations are more likely to be semi-online than purely online.
- Alternative approaches for solving online problems. As discussed in Sect. 4.6, for online problems, online algorithms may not be the best approaches. Instead, rolling horizon based offline approaches could generate better solutions. It will be valuable to investigate whether similar approaches can beat online algorithms for the other online IPODS problems covered in this chapter.

Chapter 5
Coordinated Product Pricing and Scheduling Decisions

Abstract In this chapter, we discuss various coordinated product pricing and production scheduling problems that commonly arise in make-to-order environments. We first briefly discuss some practical situations where such problems arise, followed by an investigation of two classes of such problems, namely problems with a single time period and problems with multiple periods. For each class of problems, various exact and approximation algorithms and heuristics, their performance, and related managerial insights are discussed. For several problems, we also evaluate the benefit of pricing–scheduling coordination.

5.1 Introduction

It has long been recognized in practice that operations issues such as capacity management, production planning, and inventory policies often interplay closely with marketing decisions such as demand management, pricing, and sales promotion decisions. Therefore, marketing and production decisions should be made in a coordinated manner in order to maximize system-wide efficiency and profitability in the supply chain. Coordinated product pricing and production planning or/and inventory decisions have received significant research attention in the past three decades. Comprehensive literature surveys are provided by Eliashberg and Steinberg (1993), Yano and Gilbert (2004), Tang (2010), and Chen and Simchi-Levi (2012).

A majority of the existing joint pricing–production models consider production decisions from an *aggregate planning* point of view. That is, the *detailed scheduling* of each individual order is not considered. Furthermore, these models consider *aggregate planning costs*—setup, production, and finished product inventory holding costs. However, it is relevant to consider detailed order-by-order scheduling decisions and individual order based costs in many practical environments. We provide several examples, as follows:

- For perishable products and many make-to-order products, each order typically has a short due date by which the order must be delivered. As a result, the total cost and overall service level measures depend on how each individual order

© Springer Nature Switzerland AG 2022
Z.-L. Chen, N. G. Hall, *Supply Chain Scheduling*, International Series in Operations Research & Management Science 323, https://doi.org/10.1007/978-3-030-90374-9_5

185

is scheduled. Costs and service level measures from aggregate planning models are not accurate because they assume simultaneous delivery of all completed orders at the end of a planning time period and fail to consider individual order performance.

- In many make-to-order production systems for time-sensitive products, there is little or no finished product inventory, and hence finished product inventory cost is negligible when considering the total cost. However, in such systems, a significant amount of components is kept as work-in-process (WIP) inventory and the associated costs can be significant. Here, an aggregate planning approach is not sufficiently precise, since the WIP inventory cost depends on when each order is scheduled.
- In a production system involving multiple production lines or multiple stages, such as a flowshop (Pinedo, 2016), capacity usage cannot be estimated accurately without knowing a detailed order-by-order schedule. This is particularly problematic in a joint pricing–production model, since in such a model available capacity should be considered during the pricing decision. Therefore, an aggregate planning approach cannot efficiently plan capacity usage.
- In some make-to-order systems, each arriving customer is quoted a price with a certain delivery lead time guarantee, and based on the given quotation, the customer decides whether to place an order or not (So & Song, 1998; Celik & Maglaras, 2008). The lead time of an order is determined by the completion time of the order and hence can only be calculated accurately when detailed order-by-order scheduling is considered.

By considering scheduling costs and service performance at the individual order (or item) level, more complete and more accurate measurements of production costs and service levels are obtained. This in turn provides more accurate estimates of the benefit from coordinated pricing and production decisions relative to uncoordinated decision making.

Motivated by the practical relevance discussed above, a growing number of studies (Charnsirisakskul et al., 2006; Chen & Hall, 2010; Liu et al., 2012, 2020; Lu et al., 2013; Wang & Wang, 2019; Yue et al., 2019) have investigated *coordinated pricing and production scheduling* (CPPS) decisions. This chapter is dedicated to CPPS problems. Such problems extend traditional production scheduling problems, as well as traditional pricing and price quotation problems. Traditional production scheduling assumes that a set of available orders is given and needs to be processed at minimum cost subject to capacity constraints without considering the revenue from the orders, whereas coordinated product pricing and production scheduling considers the impact of pricing decisions on available orders, the associated revenue, and the required capacity. Traditional pricing and price quotation ignore production capacity constraints or treat production decisions in an aggregate way without considering detailed order-by-order scheduling, whereas coordinated product pricing and production scheduling considers the interdependence of pricing, capacity and detailed scheduling decisions, and their impact on revenue and cost.

5.2 Single-Period Product Based Problems

The objective functions of CPPS problems involve costs or/and service levels that can only be calculated by looking into the detailed schedule of the incoming orders. Thus, making detailed scheduling decisions is a necessary part of these problems.

Existing CPPS problems can be divided into two classes: (1) problems with a single period where the pricing decision is static (i.e., it is made once for the entire planning horizon), and (2) problems with multiple periods where the pricing decision is dynamic (i.e., it is made multiple times over the planning horizon). Most of the problems studied by Chen and Hall (2010), Liu et al. (2012, 2020), Lu et al. (2013), and Wang and Wang (2019) involve a single period, whereas the problems considered by Charnsirisakskul et al. (2006) and Yue et al. (2019) involve multiple periods.

Among the problems involving a single period, the problems of Chen and Hall (2010) and Wang and Wang (2019) differ from those of Liu et al. (2010, 2012) and Lu et al. (2013) mainly in their modeling of demand. Chen and Hall (2010) and Wang and Wang (2019) assume that there are a number of known products and the demand for a product is a deterministic function of the price set for the product. We call such problems *single-period product based problems*. However, in the problems considered by Liu et al. (2012, 2020) and Lu et al. (2013), it is assumed that there are a number of known order inquiries and there is a probability that an order is actually placed, where this probability of order placement is a function of the price set for the order. We call such problems *single-period order based problems*.

In Sects. 5.2–5.4, we discuss the three single-period product based problems studied by Chen and Hall (2010), some of the single-period order based problems considered by Liu et al. (2012) and Lu et al. (2013), and the three multi-period problems studied by Yue et al. (2019), respectively. Finally, in Sect. 5.5, we highlight some future research topics.

Figure 5.1 provides an overview of the topics discussed in this chapter.

5.2 Single-Period Product Based Problems

We discuss the three single-period problems considered in Chen and Hall (2010). All these problems share the same sequence of events as follows:

- The decision maker makes a pricing decision for each product at the beginning of the period.
- The demand realizes, given the prices.
- The decision maker schedules the incoming orders for processing.

We apply the notation and problem definitions given in Chen and Hall (2010). There are n available products, $N = \{1, \ldots, n\}$. For each product $j \in N$, the decision maker can set the price of the product using one of the m_j allowable prices for the product. Let $q_{1j} > \cdots > q_{m_j,j}$ denote these allowable prices. We assume knowledge of a deterministic, nonincreasing discrete demand for product $j \in N$ as a function $g_j(q_{ij})$ of the price q_{ij} set for this product, for $i =$

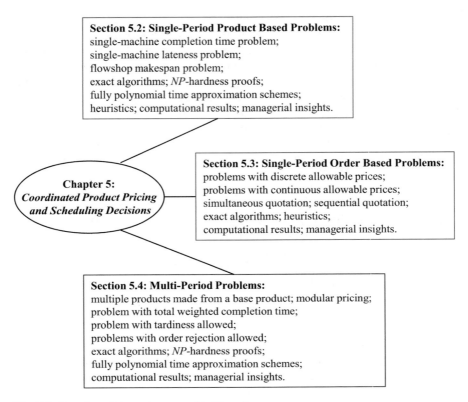

Fig. 5.1 Overview of the topics covered in Chap. 5

$1, \ldots, m_j$, where $g_j(q_{ij})$ denotes the number of orders (or items) of product j that are demanded at price q_{ij}. We assume that q_{1j} is a sufficiently high price that $g_j(q_{1j}) = 0$. This is a reasonable assumption since in many practical situations, setting the price high enough that there is no demand is an available option. We let $Q_j = \{q_{1j}, \ldots, q_{m_j,j}\}$, $m_{\max} = \max_{1 \le j \le n}\{m_j\}$, and $M = \sum_{j=1}^{n} m_j$. We also let $\bar{g}_j = g_j(q_{m_j,j})$ denote the maximum possible demand for product j, and $\bar{g}_{\max} = \max_{1 \le j \le n}\{\bar{g}_j\}$. It follows that the revenue for product j at price q_{ij} is $R_j(q_{ij}) = q_{ij} g_j(q_{ij})$.

The assumption that there are a finite number of allowable prices that can be used for a product is commonly adopted in the dynamic pricing literature (e.g., Chen & Chen, 2015) and can be easily justified from a practical point of view, as follows. Although in theory the price of a product can be any number within a certain interval, there are some price points at which customers are more willing to purchase, and hence companies often use a small set of popular prices for a product (see, e.g., Anderson & Simester, 2003).

After setting the prices for the products, orders arrive and need to be scheduled for processing in a given production environment. We consider a production envi-

5.2 Single-Period Product Based Problems

ronment with either a single-machine configuration, where all incoming orders are processed, or a two-machine flowshop configuration, where all incoming orders are first processed on the first machine M_1 and then processed on the second machine M_2. In a single-machine environment, we let $p_j > 0$ denote the processing time of an order of product j. Alternatively, in a two-machine flowshop environment, we let $p_{1j} > 0$ and $p_{2j} > 0$ denote the processing time of an order for product j on machines M_1 and M_2, respectively. Some problems that we consider also have a weight $w_j > 0$ or a due date $d_j > 0$, for each order of product j. We assume throughout that all p_j, d_j, and w_j are known integers. We further assume that all the orders are available for processing at the start of the planning horizon.

Since price is a decision variable in our work, and the demand function is deterministic, the decision maker effectively chooses the demand. Therefore, it is reasonable to assume that the demand which is implied by the pricing decision for each product must be satisfied in full. This assumption is particularly realistic where the demand function has many discrete points, which enables the decision maker to choose the demand precisely. The results in this section can be easily extended to the case where part or all of incoming demand can be rejected.

A solution σ to a problem consists of a price $x_j \in Q_j$ for each product $j \in N$ and a schedule π of all the incoming orders. Given a solution σ, we define the following parameters:

$$R(\sigma) = \sum_{j \in N} R_j(x_j), \text{ the total revenue of the incoming orders;}$$

$$C_{ij}(\sigma) = \text{the completion time of the } i\text{th order of product } j, \text{ for } i = 1, \ldots, g_j(x_j), j \in N;$$

$$U_{ij}(\sigma) = \begin{cases} 1, & \text{if } C_{ij}(\sigma) > d_j \\ 0, & \text{otherwise.} \end{cases}, \text{ for } i = 1, \ldots, g_j(x_j), \ j \in N.$$

where the solution being used is clear from the context, we simplify $R(\sigma)$, $C_{ij}(\sigma)$, and $U_{ij}(\sigma)$ to R, C_{ij}, and U_{ij}, respectively.

We consider three specific problems as follows:

- *Single-machine completion time problem*: single-machine production environment with the objective of maximizing the net profit, defined as the total revenue minus the total weighted completion time of the orders, i.e., $\sum_{j \in N} R_j(x_j) - \sum_{j \in N} \sum_{i=1}^{g_j(x_j)} w_j C_{ij}$, where $x_j \in Q_j$ is the price for product j.
- *Single-machine lateness problem*: single-machine production environment with the objective of maximizing the net profit, defined as the total revenue minus the total weight of late orders, i.e., $\sum_{j \in N} R_j(x_j) - \sum_{j \in N} \sum_{i=1}^{g_j(x_j)} w_j U_{ij}$, where $x_j \in Q_j$ is the price for product j.
- *Flowshop makespan problem*: two-machine flowshop production environment with the objective of maximizing the net profit, defined as the total revenue minus the makespan $C_{\max}$ (i.e., the completion time of the last order), i.e., $\sum_{j \in N} R_j(x_j) - C_{\max}$, where $x_j \in Q_j$ is the price for product j, and $C_{\max} = \max_{1 \le i \le g_j(x_j), \ 1 \le j \le n} \{C_{ij}\}$.

For ease of presentation, we may write the objective functions of these problems simply as $R - \sum\sum w_j C_{ij}$, $R - \sum\sum w_j U_{ij}$, and $R - C_{\max}$, respectively. We assume that the revenue function is normalized to match the time-based units of the scheduling cost incurred in these problems. The total weighted completion time represents the work-in-process inventory cost (Pinedo, 2016). Also, it is appropriate to use the total weight of late orders as the scheduling cost in situations where orders can be delivered late but with a reduction in the revenue, such as a late fee or a required discount. Finally, the makespan of a schedule represents overhead and capacity cost.

Although these problems do not consider production cost, a linear production cost can easily be incorporated into the objective functions by redefining the price q_{ij} to be $q_{ij} - c_j$, where c_j is the unit production cost for processing an order of product j. The assumption of linearity for production costs is very common in the operations management literature.

Chen and Hall (2010) show that all these problems can be solved by pseudo-polynomial time dynamic programming algorithms and further show that these problems are all ordinarily NP-hard, even when $p_j = 1$ and $w_j = 1$ for all $j \in N$ for the single-machine completion time problem and when both d_j's and w_j's are identical for all $j \in N$ for the single-machine lateness problem. They develop fast heuristics and estimate the value of coordinating pricing and scheduling decisions. Finally, they develop fully polynomial time approximation schemes (FPTASs) for the problems.

We organize this section as follows, based on the work of Chen and Hall (2010). Section 5.2.1 describes the pseudo-polynomial time algorithms for finding optimal solutions for all these problems. Section 5.2.2 shows the NP-hardness proofs for all these problems. Section 5.2.3 presents the FPTAS for two of the problems. Section 5.2.4 describes the heuristics for all the problems. Finally, Sect. 5.2.5 reports the computational results and related insights.

5.2.1 Exact Algorithms

The exact dynamic programming algorithms given by Chen and Hall (2010) are all based on an optimality property that, for the underlying scheduling problems without the pricing decisions, it is optimal to schedule the orders in a particular pre-specified sequence. More specifically, for the single-machine completion time problem, it is optimal to schedule the orders by the *shortest weighted processing time* (SWPT) rule, in which the orders are sequenced by nonincreasing ratio of weight to processing time (Smith, 1956). For the single-machine lateness problem, it is optimal to schedule the orders by the *earliest due date* (EDD) rule, in which orders are sequenced by nondecreasing due date (Jackson, 1955). For the flowshop makespan problem, it is optimal to schedule the orders by the sequencing rule of Johnson (1954), which is elaborated below.

5.2 Single-Period Product Based Problems

The following algorithms SMCT, SML, and FSM solve the single-machine completion time problem, single-machine lateness problem, and flowshop makespan problem, respectively. All these algorithms consider the products in the corresponding sequence (SWPT, EDD, or the sequence specified by Johnson's rule) and enumerate all possible prices for a product.

Algorithm SMCT

Input

Given $q_{ij}, g_j(q_{ij}), i = 1, \ldots, m_j, j = 1, \ldots, n; p_j, w_j, j = 1, \ldots, n$.

Initialization

Index the products in SWPT order.

Value Function

$f_j(t)$ = maximum net profit from the orders of products $1, \ldots, j$, given that after the orders of product j are scheduled, the makespan of the schedule is t.

Boundary Condition

$f_0(0) = 0; f_j(t) = -\infty$, for $t < 0, j = 1, \ldots, n$.

Optimal Solution Value

$$\max_{0 \le t \le \sum_{j=1}^n \bar{g}_j p_j} \{f_n(t)\}.$$

Recurrence Relation

$$f_j(t) = \max_{1 \le i \le m_j} \{q_{ij} g_j(q_{ij}) - w_j g_j(q_{ij})[t - p_j g_j(q_{ij})] - w_j p_j g_j(q_{ij})[g_j(q_{ij}) \\ + 1]/2 + f_{j-1}(t - p_j g_j(q_{ij}))\}.$$

Algorithm SMCT considers each product in turn in SWPT sequence and chooses the optimal number of orders of that product for the demand and the schedule. The second term in the recurrence relation is the increment to total cost that results from starting $g_j(q_{ij})$ orders of product j at time $[t - p_j g_j(q_{ij})]$. The third term is the additional cost of scheduling those orders individually.

Chen and Hall (2010) show that Algorithm SMCT finds an optimal schedule for the single-machine completion time problem in $O(M \sum_{j=1}^n \bar{g}_j p_j)$ time.

We now describe the algorithm for the single-machine lateness problem.

Algorithm SML

Input

Given $q_{ij}, g_j(q_{ij}), i = 1, \ldots, m_j, j = 1, \ldots, n; p_j, w_j, d_j, j = 1, \ldots, n$.

Initialization

Index the products in EDD order.

Value Function

$f_j(t)$ = maximum net profit from products $1, \ldots, j$, given that after product j is scheduled, the makespan of the schedule of on-time orders is t.

Boundary Condition

$f_0(0) = 0; f_j(t) = -\infty$, for $t > d_j$ or $t < 0, j = 1, \ldots, n$.

Optimal Solution Value

$$\max_{0 \le t \le \sum_{j=1}^n \bar{g}_j p_j} \{f_n(t)\}.$$

Recurrence Relations
$$f_j(t) = \max_{1 \leq i \leq m_j,\, 0 \leq X \leq g_j(q_{ij})} \{q_{ij} X + (q_{ij} - w_i)(g_j(q_{ij}) - X) + f_{j-1}(t - X p_j)\},$$
if $t \leq d_j$.

Algorithm SML considers each product in turn in EDD sequence and chooses the optimal price and the optimal number of orders, X, to schedule on time. In the recurrence relation, the first term is the revenue from scheduling orders on time, and the second term is the revenue from scheduling orders late.

Chen and Hall (2010) show that Algorithm SML finds an optimal schedule for the single-machine lateness problem in $O((\sum_{j=1}^{n} m_j \bar{g}_j)(\sum_{j=1}^{n} \bar{g}_j p_j))$ time.

Finally, we describe Chen and Hall's algorithm for the flowshop makespan problem. As discussed above, the products are scheduled in the sequence proposed by Johnson (1954). That is, the products are first partitioned into two sets, $S_1 = \{j | p_{1j} \leq p_{2j}\}$ and $S_2 = \{j | p_{1j} > p_{2j}\}$. The orders of the products in S_1 are scheduled first in nondecreasing p_{1j} sequence, followed by the orders of the products in S_2 in nonincreasing p_{2j} sequence. To illustrate how Johnson's sequencing rule works, we provide a numerical example as follows.

Example 5.1 (Application of Johnson's Rule) We apply Johnson's rule to the instance with 5 products shown in the table below:

j	1	2	3	4	5
p_{1j}	3	4	5	8	7
p_{2j}	6	4	3	5	2

The products are divided into two sets $S_1 = \{1, 2\}$ and $S_2 = \{3, 4, 5\}$. Since $p_{11} \leq p_{12}$, the products in S_1 are sequenced in the order $(1, 2)$. Similarly, since $p_{42} > p_{32} > p_{52}$, the products in S_2 are sequenced in the order $(4, 3, 5)$. The overall sequence of the products is $(1, 2, 4, 3, 5)$ on both machines. All the orders of a product are sequenced consecutively.

In the dynamic programming algorithm below, we also use the following concept.

Definition 5.1 The *profile* of a partial schedule is defined as the difference between the completion time of the last order on machine M_2 and that on machine M_1.

Algorithm FSM
Input
Given $q_{ij}, g_j(q_{ij}), i = 1, \ldots, m_j, j = 1, \ldots, n; p_{1j}, p_{2j}, j = 1, \ldots, n$.
Initialization
Index the products in the sequence proposed by Johnson (1954).
Value Function
$f_j(\delta)$ = maximum net profit from products $1, \ldots, j$, given that after product j is scheduled, the profile of the schedule is δ.

5.2 Single-Period Product Based Problems

Boundary Condition

$$f_0(0) = 0; \ f_j(\delta) = -\infty, \text{ for } \delta < p_{2j} \text{ or } \delta > \textstyle\sum_{i=1}^{j} p_{2i}, \ j = 1, \ldots, n.$$

Optimal Solution Value

$$\max_{0 \le \delta \le \sum_{j=1}^{n} \bar{g}_j p_{2j}} \{f_n(\delta)\}.$$

Recurrence Relations

(i) If $\delta > p_{2j}$

$$f_j(\delta)$$

$$= \begin{cases} \displaystyle\max_{1 \le i \le m_j} \left\{ q_{ij} g_j(q_{ij}) - p_{2j} g_j(q_{ij}) + f_{j-1}(\delta + (p_{1j} - p_{2j})g_j(q_{ij})) \right\}, & \text{if } p_{1j} \le p_{2j} \\[2em] \displaystyle\max_{1 \le i \le m_j \ | \ g_j(q_{ij}) \le \lfloor[\delta + g_j(q_{ij})(p_{1j} - p_{2j}) - p_{2j}]/(p_{1j} - p_{2j})\rfloor} \left\{ q_{ij} g_j(q_{ij}) - p_{2j} g_j(q_{ij}) \right. \\[0.5em] \hspace{4cm} \left. + f_{j-1}(\delta + (p_{1j} - p_{2j})g_j(q_{ij})) \right\}, & \text{if } p_{1j} > p_{2j}. \end{cases}$$

(ii) If $\delta = p_{2j}$

$$f_j(p_{2j})$$

$$= \begin{cases} \displaystyle\max_{1 \le i \le m_j} \left\{ q_{ij} g_j(q_{ij}) - p_{2j} g_j(q_{ij}) + f_{j-1}(\delta + (p_{1j} - p_{2j})g_j(q_{ij})) \right\}, & \text{if } p_{1j} \le p_{2j} \\[2em] \displaystyle\max_{0 \le \delta' \le \sum_{k=1}^{j-1} \bar{g}_k p_{2k}, \ 1 \le i \le m_j \ | \ g_j(q_{ij}) > \lfloor(\delta' - p_{2j})/(p_{1j} - p_{2j})\rfloor} \left\{ q_{ij} g_j(q_{ij}) - p_{1j} g_j(q_{ij}) - p_{2j} \right. \\[0.5em] \hspace{4cm} \left. + \delta' + f_{j-1}(\delta') \right\}, & \text{if } p_{1j} > p_{2j}. \end{cases}$$

Algorithm FSM considers each product in the sequence proposed by Johnson (1954) and chooses the optimal price for that product. There are two cases for the profile δ. Consider the first case, where $\delta > p_{2j}$. If $p_{1j} \le p_{2j}$, then no additional idle time is created on machine M_2 by the scheduling of $g_j(q_{ij})$ orders of product j. Alternatively, if $p_{1j} > p_{2j}$, then the profile is reduced by scheduling $g_j(q_{ij})$ orders of product j; however, this case only occurs if $g_j(q_{ij})$ is small enough that no additional idle time is created on machine M_2. Now, consider the second case, where $\delta = p_{2j}$. If $p_{1j} \le p_{2j}$, then the above argument for the same condition still applies. Alternatively, if $p_{1j} > p_{2j}$, then the new profile of p_{2j} can only be achieved if $g_j(q_{ij})$ is large enough that the completion time of the last order on machine M_1 is no earlier than the completion time of the second last order on machine M_2.

Chen and Hall (2010) show that Algorithm FSM finds an optimal schedule for the flowshop makespan problem in $O(M \sum_{j=1}^{n} \bar{g}_j p_{2j})$ time.

5.2.2 *N P-Hardness Proofs*

Chen and Hall (2010) prove that all the three problems discussed above are ordinarily NP-hard. We present their proofs below.

Theorem 5.1 *The single-machine completion time problem is ordinarily* NP-*hard, even when* $p_1 = \cdots = p_n$ *and* $w_1 = \cdots = w_n$.

Proof We show below that this problem is at least ordinarily NP-hard, by a reduction from the Partition problem, which is known to be binary *NP*-complete. This, together with the pseudo-polynomial time algorithm SMCT given in Sect. 5.2.1, implies that this problem is exactly ordinarily NP-hard. The Partition problem can be described as follows:

Partition (Garey & Johnson, 1979): given t elements with integer sizes $a_1, \ldots, a_t$, where $\sum_{i=1}^{t} a_i = 2A$, does there exist a partition S_1, S_2 of the index set $\{1, \ldots, t\}$ such that $\sum_{i \in S_1} a_i = \sum_{i \in S_2} a_i = A$?

Consider the following instance of the recognition version of the single-machine completion time problem:

$$
\begin{aligned}
n &= t, \\
p_j &= 1, & j &= 1, \ldots, n \\
w_j &= 1, & j &= 1, \ldots, n \\
m_j &= 2, & j &= 1, \ldots, n \\
q_{1j} &= 2A, & j &= 1, \ldots, n \\
q_{2j} &= A + 1/2, & j &= 1, \ldots, n \\
g_j(q_{1j}) &= 0, & j &= 1, \ldots, n \\
g_j(q_{2j}) &= a_j, & j &= 1, \ldots, n \\
Z &= A^2/2,
\end{aligned}
$$

where Z denotes the threshold net profit.

We prove that there exists a feasible schedule for this instance of the single-machine completion time problem with $R - \sum \sum w_j C_{ij} \geq Z$ if and only if there exists a solution to Partition.

($\Rightarrow$) Assume that there exists a solution S_1, S_2 to Partition. For each product $j \in S_1$, set the price equal to q_{2j}, and schedule a_j incoming orders consecutively. For the other products, set the price equal to q_{1j}, and hence there are no orders to schedule. Therefore, the net profit is

$$
R - \sum \sum w_j C_{ij} = (A + 1/2) \sum_{j \in S_1} a_j - \sum_{j \in S_1} \left[a_j(a_j + 1)/2 + a_j \sum_{i \in S_1, i < j} a_i \right]
$$

$$
= A^2 + A/2 - \sum_{j \in S_1} a_j/2 - \left[\sum_{j \in S_1} a_j \right]^2 / 2
$$

$$
= Z.
$$

5.2 Single-Period Product Based Problems

($\Leftarrow$) Let S denote the set of products that are priced at $A + 1/2$. Thus, there are a_j incoming orders of each product $j \in S$. Then, $R = (A + 1/2) \sum_{j \in S} a_j$. Since $p_j = 1$ and $w_j = 1$ for $j \in S$, any sequence of the incoming orders yields the same total weighted completion time. Therefore, we assume that the orders are scheduled in the order of their product indices. This implies that $\sum \sum w_j C_{ij} = \sum_{j \in S} [a_j (a_j + 1)/2 + a_j \sum_{i \in S, i < j} a_i]$. Therefore, the net profit is

$$R - \sum \sum w_j C_{ij} = (A + 1/2) \sum_{j \in S} a_j - \sum_{j \in S} \left[a_j (a_j + 1)/2 + a_j \sum_{i \in S, i < j} a_i \right]$$

$$= (A + 1/2) \sum_{j \in S} a_j - \sum_{j \in S} a_j/2 - \left[\sum_{j \in S} a_j \right]^2 /2$$

$$= \left(\sum_{j \in S} a_j \right) \left(2A - \sum_{j \in S} a_j \right) /2. \tag{5.1}$$

Now, (5.1) achieves its maximum over all possible sets S when $\sum_{j \in S} a_j = 2A - \sum_{j \in S} a_j$, where $R - \sum \sum w_j C_{ij} = A^2/2 = Z$. Therefore, if $R - \sum \sum w_j C_{ij} \geq Z$, then $(S, N \setminus S)$ is a solution to Partition. $\qquad \square$

Theorem 5.2 *The single-machine lateness problem is ordinarily NP-hard, even when $w_1 = \cdots = w_n$ and $d_1 = \cdots = d_n$.*

Proof We show below that this problem is at least ordinarily NP-hard, which, together with the pseudo-polynomial time algorithm SML given in Sect. 5.2.1, implies that this problem is exactly ordinarily NP-hard.

We use a reduction from Partition, as described in the proof of Theorem 5.1. Consider the following instance of the recognition version of the single-machine lateness problem, where $w_1 = \cdots = w_n$ and $d_1 = \cdots = d_n$:

$$
\begin{aligned}
n &= t, \\
p_j &= a_j, & j &= 1, \ldots, n \\
w_j &= 2A, & j &= 1, \ldots, n \\
d_j &= A, & j &= 1, \ldots, n \\
m_j &= 2, & j &= 1, \ldots, n \\
q_{1j} &= 2A, & j &= 1, \ldots, n \\
q_{2j} &= a_j, & j &= 1, \ldots, n \\
g_j(q_{1j}) &= 0, & j &= 1, \ldots, n \\
g_j(q_{2j}) &= 1, & j &= 1, \ldots, n \\
Z &= A,
\end{aligned}
$$

where Z denotes the threshold net profit.

196   5 Coordinated Product Pricing and Scheduling Decisions

We prove that there exists a feasible schedule for this instance of the single-machine lateness problem with $R - \sum\sum w_j U_{ij} \geq Z$ if and only if there exists a solution to Partition.

($\Rightarrow$) Assume that there exists a solution S_1, S_2 to Partition. For each product $j \in S_1$, set the price equal to q_{2j}, which generates one order. For the other products, set the price equal to q_{1j}, which generates no orders. Schedule all the orders in arbitrary order. Since the total processing time of the orders is equal to $\sum_{j \in S_1} a_j = A = d_k$, for $k = 1, \ldots, n$, no order is late, and hence $\sum\sum w_j U_{ij} = 0$. Therefore, the net profit is $\sum_{j \in S_1} q_{2j} = \sum_{j \in S_1} a_j = A = Z$.

($\Leftarrow$) Let S denote the set of products with price q_{2j}. Thus, there is one order of each product $j \in S$, and there are no orders of any other product. Then, $R = \sum_{j \in S} a_j$. Since $w_j - q_{2j} > Z$, for $j = 1, \ldots, n$, no order is scheduled late. It follows that (i) $\sum_{j \in S} p_j \leq d_k$ for $k \in S$, which implies $\sum_{j \in S} a_j \leq A$ and (ii) $R \geq Z$, which implies $\sum_{j \in S} a_j \geq A$. Therefore, $\sum_{j \in S} a_j = A$ and $(S, N \setminus S)$ is a solution to Partition. $\qquad\square$

Theorem 5.3 *The flowshop makespan problem is ordinarily* NP-*hard.*

Proof We show below that this problem is at least ordinarily NP-hard, which, together with the pseudo-polynomial time algorithm FSM given in Sect. 5.2.1, implies that this problem is exactly ordinarily NP-hard.

We use a reduction from Partition, as described in the proof of Theorem 5.1. We consider the following instance of the flowshop makespan problem:

$$
\begin{aligned}
n &= t + 1 \\
p_{1j} &= 0, & j &= 1, \ldots, n-1 \\
p_{1n} &= A \\
p_{2j} &= a_j, & j &= 1, \ldots, n-1 \\
p_{2n} &= 1 \\
m_j &= 2, & j &= 1, \ldots, n \\
q_{1j} &= A, & j &= 1, \ldots, n-1 \\
g_j(q_{1j}) &= 0, & j &= 1, \ldots, n-1 \\
q_{1n} &= 2A^2 \\
g_n(q_{1n}) &= 0 \\
q_{2j} &= a_j/2, & j &= 1, \ldots, n-1 \\
g_j(q_{2j}) &= 1, & j &= 1, \ldots, n-1 \\
q_{2n} &= A^2 \\
g_n(q_{2n}) &= 1 \\
Z &= A^2 - A/2 - 1,
\end{aligned}
$$

where Z denotes the threshold net profit.

We prove that there exists a feasible schedule for this instance of the flowshop makespan problem with the net profit greater than or equal to Z if and only if there exists a solution to Partition.

5.2 Single-Period Product Based Problems 197

($\Rightarrow$) Suppose that there exists a solution S_1, S_2 to Partition. Price each product $j \in S_1 \cup \{n\}$ at q_{2j}, thereby creating a demand of one unit for that product. Price each product $j \in S_2$ at q_{1j}, thereby creating no demand. Schedule the order of product n in the interval $[0, A]$ on machine M_1 and the interval $[A, A + 1]$ on machine M_2. Schedule one order of each product in S_1 in the interval $[0, A]$ on machine M_2. The revenue R from scheduling the order of product n and the orders of S_1 is $A^2 + A/2$. Also, by construction, $C_{\max} = A + 1$. Therefore, the net profit is $R - C_{\max} = (A^2 + A/2) - (A + 1) = A^2 - A/2 - 1 = Z$.

($\Leftarrow$) Since $\sum_{j=1}^{n-1} q_{2j} < Z$, any solution to the pricing and scheduling problem with $R - C_{\max} \geq Z$ must schedule an order of product n. Since $C_n \geq A + 1$ in any schedule that includes an order of product n, the net profit from all other orders must be at least $Z - [A^2 - (A + 1)] = A/2$. Let S denote the set of other orders which are scheduled and thus priced at q_{2j}. Since $p_{2j} = 2q_{2j}$, for $j \in S$, such orders can only be scheduled if they do not increase $C_{\max}$, i.e., they must be scheduled in the available idle time in $[0, A]$ on machine M_2. It follows that $\sum_{j \in S} a_j \leq A$. However, if $\sum_{j \in S} p_{2j} < A$, then the additional net revenue earned from the orders of S is $\sum_{j \in S} q_{2j} = \sum_{j \in S} p_{2j}/2 < A/2$, hence $R - C_{\max} < Z$. Therefore, we must have $\sum_{j \in S} p_{2j} = A$, which implies that $(S, \{1, \ldots, n\} \setminus S)$ is a solution to Partition. $\qquad \square$

5.2.3 Fully Polynomial Time Approximation Schemes

Chen and Hall (2010) develop a fully polynomial time approximation scheme (FPTAS) for each problem. As defined in Sect. 2.3.4, an FPTAS is a family of algorithms $\{A_\epsilon\}$ such that, for any given $\epsilon > 0$, A_ϵ delivers a solution that is within a relative error ϵ from optimality and has a running time that is polynomial in both the size of the input data and $1/\epsilon$.

Chen and Hall's approximation schemes for the three problems are based on dynamic programming algorithms that are similar to Algorithms SMCT, SML, and FSM given in Sect. 5.2.1, respectively, with a key difference: the value function is treated as a state variable. Their approximation schemes start with a state space trimming approach that is often used to design approximation schemes for classical scheduling problems without pricing decisions (Schuurman & Woeginger, 2011). However, in a classical scheduling problem, the number of orders is given, whereas in our problems the number of orders is controlled by pricing decisions. Consequently, the techniques developed by Chen and Hall (2010) extend the existing approach.

For the single-machine total completion time problem, their approximation scheme requires partitioning the range of possible net profit values into intervals of equal width Δ. However, for the single-machine lateness problem and the flowshop makespan problem, it is necessary to use intervals of geometrically increasing width $\Delta, \Delta^2, \ldots$. Within each interval, only one partial schedule is retained, and the others

198   5 Coordinated Product Pricing and Scheduling Decisions

are discarded. This enables the dynamic program to run in a polynomial number of steps, while controlling the loss of accuracy by adjusting the value of Δ.

In Sects. 5.2.3.1 and 5.2.3.2, we describe Chen and Hall's approximation schemes for two of the three problems: the single-machine completion time problem and the flowshop makespan problem, respectively. We refer the interested readers to Chen and Hall (2010) for their approximation scheme for the single-machine lateness problem.

5.2.3.1 FPTAS for the Single-Machine Completion Time Problem

We begin our analysis of the single-machine completion time problem with a preliminary result from Chen and Hall (2010).

Lemma 5.1 *The optimal objective value of the single-machine completion time problem, denoted as* $R(\sigma^*) - \sum\sum w_j C_{ij}(\sigma^*)$, *satisfies* $F_0 \leq R(\sigma^*) - \sum\sum w_j C_{ij}(\sigma^*) \leq n F_0$, *where* $F_0 = \max_{1 \leq j \leq n, 1 \leq i \leq m_j} \{q_{ij} g_j(q_{ij}) - w_j p_j g_j(q_{ij})[g_j(q_{ij}) + 1]/2\}$.

Proof F_0 is a lower bound on optimal net profit which is found by considering only one product. Since this value is calculated as the maximum over all products, an upper bound on optimal net profit is found by taking n times this value and ignoring the interactive cost terms between products.   □

We now describe the FPTAS developed by Chen and Hall (2010) for the single-machine completion time problem. This scheme is based on a dynamic programming algorithm with states (j, t, v), indicating that products $1, \ldots, j$ have been considered, and the schedule has makespan t and net profit v. Given two partial schedules (j, t', v') and (j, t'', v''), where the values of v' and v'' are similar, we eliminate the second partial schedule if $t' \leq t''$, and the first partial schedule otherwise. For a value of x such that $i\Delta \leq x < (i + 1)\Delta$, we define the label $\Delta(x) = \Delta i$.

Algorithm CAS$_\epsilon$

Initialization:

Index the products in SWPT order.

Define $F_0 = \max_{1 \leq j \leq n, 1 \leq i \leq m_j} \{q_{ij} g_j(q_{ij}) - w_j p_j g_j(q_{ij})[g_j(q_{ij}) + 1]/2\}$. Set $\Delta = \epsilon F_0/n$.

State Variables:

(j, t, v) corresponds to a partial schedule that has considered products $1, \ldots, j$, where the schedule has makespan t and net profit v.

Initial State:

$(0, 0, 0)$.

Trial State Generation:

For each state (j, t, v), generate m_{j+1} trial states $(j + 1, t', v')$ by pricing product

5.2 Single-Period Product Based Problems

$j + 1$ at $q_{i,j+1}$ and then scheduling the resulting demand of $g_{j+1}(q_{i,j+1})$ orders, for $i = 1, \ldots, m_{j+1}$.

Trial State Labeling:
For each trial state $(j + 1, t', v')$, attach the label $(j + 1, \Delta(v'))$.

Trial State Elimination:
For each pair of trial states $(j + 1, t', v')$ and $(j + 1, t'', v'')$ with identical labels, eliminate the second state if $t' \leq t''$, and eliminate the first state otherwise.

Termination Test:
If $j + 1 < n$, then set $j = j + 1$ and return to the Trial State Generation step. Otherwise, select a state $(n, \tilde{t}, \tilde{v})$ for which $\tilde{v}$ is largest, and backtrack to find the corresponding schedule $\tilde{\sigma}_\epsilon$.

At the Initialization step, the value of Δ is set such that $n\Delta/\epsilon = F_0$, where from Lemma 5.1, F_0 is a lower bound on optimal net profit. The Trial State Generation step chooses the price $q_{i,j+1}$, where $1 \leq i \leq m_{j+1}$, for product $j + 1$ that generates a demand $g_{j+1}(q_{i,j+1})$ for that product and then schedules those orders. The Trial State Labeling step labels each trial state, based on the number of orders considered and the net profit value. The Trial State Elimination step compares the profile of all trial states with the same label, keeps only one with the smallest makespan, and discards the others.

Theorem 5.4 *The family of algorithms $\{CAS_\epsilon\}$, for $\epsilon > 0$, is an FPTAS for the single-machine completion time problem, with $O(n^3 m_{\max}/\epsilon)$ running time.*

Proof We start by analyzing the net profit of the solution delivered by Algorithm CAS_ϵ. The proof is by induction on the number of products that have been considered for scheduling. The induction hypothesis is as follows:

- Given any state (j, t, v) that is obtained under the exact dynamic program, Algorithm CAS_ϵ generates a state $(j, \tilde{t}, \tilde{v})$, where $\tilde{t} \leq t$ and $\tilde{v} \geq v - j\Delta$.

The hypothesis clearly holds for $j = 0$. Suppose that the hypothesis holds for $j = 0, 1, \ldots, k$. Let (k, t, v) define a state in the exact dynamic program.

We assume that the exact dynamic program prices product $k + 1$ at $q_{i,k+1}$, for some $1 \leq i \leq m_{k+1}$, and therefore that $g_{k+1}(q_{i,k+1})$ orders of product $k + 1$ are scheduled. We further assume that, in the exact dynamic program, this yields a state $(k + 1, t', v')$. From the induction hypothesis, we have a state $(k, \tilde{t}, \tilde{v})$ in the approximate dynamic program where $\tilde{t} \leq t$ and $\tilde{v} \geq v - k\Delta$. The trial state, S, that is generated from $(k, \tilde{t}, \tilde{v})$ by pricing product $k + 1$ at $q_{i,k+1}$ and scheduling $g_{k+1}(q_{i,k+1})$ orders of product $k+1$ in Algorithm CAS_ϵ is denoted by $(k+1, \tilde{t}', \tilde{v}')$. We prove the following two claims about this state:

(i) $\tilde{t}' \leq t'$. From the induction hypothesis, $\tilde{t} \leq t$. Moreover, the same orders are added in the approximate and exact dynamic programs, and therefore the increase in makespan is the same, i.e., $\tilde{t}' - \tilde{t} = t' - t$. Combining these inequalities establishes the claim.

(ii) $\tilde{v}' \geq v' - (k+1)\Delta$. From the induction hypothesis, $\tilde{v} \geq v - k\Delta$. Now, $R_{k+1} = q_{i,k+1}g_{k+1}(q_{i,k+1})$ in both the exact and approximate dynamic programs. Since state $(k+1, t', v')$ is generated from state (k, t, v), we have

$$v' = v + R_{k+1} - tg_{k+1}(q_{i,k+1})w_{k+1} - g_{k+1}(q_{i,k+1})[g_{k+1}(q_{i,k+1}) + 1]p_{k+1}w_{k+1}/2. \tag{5.2}$$

Similarly, since state $(k+1, \tilde{t}', \tilde{v}')$ is generated from state $(k, \tilde{t}, \tilde{v})$, we have

$$\tilde{v}' = \tilde{v} + R_{k+1} - \tilde{t}g_{k+1}(q_{i,k+1})w_{k+1} - g_{k+1}(q_{i,k+1})[g_{k+1}(q_{i,k+1}) + 1]p_{k+1}w_{k+1}/2. \tag{5.3}$$

Equations (5.2) and (5.3), together with the induction hypothesis, imply that $\tilde{v}' \geq v' - k\delta > v' - (k+1)\delta$.

It follows from claims (i) and (ii) that if trial state S exists in Algorithm CAS_ϵ, then the induction argument is complete.

However, trial state S may be eliminated by another trial state $S' = (k+1, \tau_1, \tau_2)$, where $\tau_1 \leq \tilde{t}'$ and $\tau_2 \geq \tilde{v}' - \Delta$, where the last bound holds because S and S' have the same label. If this happens, then we have: (i) $\tau_1 \leq \tilde{t}' \leq t'$ and (ii) $\tau_2 \geq \tilde{v}' - \Delta \geq v' - (k+1)\Delta$ for S'. Thus, the induction hypothesis holds.

We now show that Algorithm CAS_ϵ delivers a solution with the required performance guarantee. Let the state (n, t, v^*) correspond to an optimal solution with value v^*. Then, the above induction argument shows that Algorithm CAS_ϵ generates a solution $\tilde{\sigma}$ and a corresponding final state $(n, \tilde{t}, \tilde{v})$ with value $\tilde{v}$, where $\tilde{v} \geq v^* - n\Delta$. Therefore,

$$\frac{(R(\sigma^*) - \sum\sum w_j C_{ij}(\sigma^*)) - (R(\tilde{\sigma}) - \sum\sum w_j C_{ij}(\tilde{\sigma}))}{R(\sigma^*) - \sum\sum w_j C_{ij}(\sigma^*)} \leq \frac{n\Delta}{R(\sigma^*) - \sum\sum w_j C_{ij}(\sigma^*)}$$

$$\leq \epsilon,$$

where the last inequality follows from the specification of Δ in the Initialization step and from Lemma 5.1.

Finally, we analyze the time complexity of Algorithm CAS_ϵ. We first evaluate the number of different labels that are used in the Trial State Labeling step. There are $O(n)$ values of $j + 1$. From the specification of Δ in the Initialization step and from Lemma 5.1, there are $O(n^2/\epsilon)$ possible labels for $\Delta(v')$. Thus, the total number of labels is $O(n^3/\epsilon)$. Each state generates at most $O(m_{\max})$ trial states. It follows that the overall time complexity of Algorithm CAS_ϵ is $O(n^3 m_{\max}/\epsilon)$. $\qquad\square$

5.2.3.2 FPTAS for the Flowshop Makespan Problem

Chen and Hall's (2010) FPTAS for the flowshop makespan problem is based on a dynamic programming algorithm with states (j, h, v), indicating that products

5.2 Single-Period Product Based Problems

$1, \ldots, j$ have been considered, and the schedule has profile h and net profit v. Given two partial schedules for the orders of products $1, \ldots, j$, with similar net profit values, the partial schedule with a smaller profile is eliminated.

This FPTAS requires partitioning the range of possible net profit values into intervals of geometrically increasing width $\Delta, \Delta^2, \ldots$, where

$$\Delta = 1 + \epsilon/2n, \tag{5.4}$$

which implies the inequality

$$\Delta^n \leq 1 + \epsilon, \qquad \text{for } 0 \leq \epsilon \leq 2. \tag{5.5}$$

Within each interval, only one partial schedule is retained and the others are discarded. This enables the dynamic program to run in a polynomial number of steps, while controlling the loss of accuracy by adjusting the value of Δ.

For a value of x such that $\Delta^i \leq x < \Delta^{i+1}$, we define the label $\Delta(x) = \Delta^i$.

Algorithm MAS$_\epsilon$

Initialization:
Index the products in the sequence according to Johnson's rule (Johnson, 1954). Set $\Delta = 1 + \epsilon/2n$.
State Variables:
(j, h, v) corresponds to a partial schedule that has considered products $1, \ldots, j$, where the schedule has profile h and net profit v.
Initial State:
$(0, 0, 0)$.
Trial State Generation:
For each state (j, h, v), generate m_{j+1} trial states $(j + 1, h', v')$ by pricing product $j + 1$ at $q_{i,j+1}$ and then scheduling the resulting demand of $g_{j+1}(q_{i,j+1})$ orders, for $i = 1, \ldots, m_{j+1}$.
Trial State Labeling:
For each trial state $(j + 1, h', v')$, attach the label $(j + 1, \Delta(v'))$.
Trial State Elimination:
For each pair of trial states $(j + 1, h', v')$ and $(j + 1, h'', v'')$ with identical labels, eliminate the second state if $h' \geq h''$, and eliminate the first state otherwise.
Termination Test:
If $j + 1 < n$, then set $j = j + 1$ and return to the Trial State Generation step. Otherwise, select a state $(n, \tilde{h}, \tilde{v})$ for which $\tilde{v}$ is largest, and backtrack to find the corresponding schedule $\tilde{\sigma}_\epsilon$.

Theorem 5.5 *The family of algorithms* $\{MAS_\epsilon\}$, *for* $\epsilon > 0$, *is an FPTAS for the flowshop makespan problem, with* $O(n^2 m_{\max} \log(n \max_{1 \leq j \leq n, 1 \leq i \leq m_j} \{q_{ij} g_j(q_{ij})\})/\epsilon)$ *running time.*

Proof We start by analyzing the cost of the solution delivered by Algorithm MAS$_\epsilon$. Our proof uses induction on j. The induction hypothesis is that, given any state

202   5 Coordinated Product Pricing and Scheduling Decisions

(j, h, v) that is obtained under the exact dynamic program, Algorithm MAS$_\epsilon$ generates a state $(j, \tilde{h}, \tilde{v})$, where $\tilde{h} \geq h$ and $\tilde{v} \geq v/\Delta^j$. The hypothesis clearly holds for $j = 0$. Suppose that the hypothesis holds for $j = 0, 1, \ldots, k$. Let (k, h, v) define a state in the exact dynamic program.

We assume that the exact dynamic program prices product $k + 1$ at $q_{i,k+1}$, for some $1 \leq i \leq m_{k+1}$, and therefore that $g_{k+1}(q_{i,k+1})$ orders of product $k + 1$ are scheduled. We further assume that, in the exact dynamic program, this yields a state $(k + 1, h', v')$. From the induction hypothesis, we have a state $(k, \tilde{h}, \tilde{v})$ in the approximate dynamic program, where $\tilde{h} \geq h$ and $\tilde{v} \geq v/\Delta^k$. The trial state, S, that is generated from $(k, \tilde{h}, \tilde{v})$ by pricing product $k + 1$ at $q_{i,k+1}$ and scheduling $g_{k+1}(q_{i,k+1})$ orders of product $k+1$ in Algorithm MAS$_\epsilon$ is denoted by $(k+1, \tilde{h}', \tilde{v}')$. We prove the following two claims about this state.

(i) $\tilde{h}' \geq h'$. From the induction hypothesis, $\tilde{h} \geq h$. The state $(k + 1, \tilde{h}', \tilde{v}')$ in the approximate dynamic program is generated from $(k, \tilde{h}, \tilde{v})$ by adding the same set of orders as those that are added when $(k + 1, h', v')$ is generated from (k, h, v) in the exact dynamic program. The fact that $\tilde{h} \geq h$ then implies that $\tilde{h}' \geq h'$.

(ii) $\tilde{v}' \geq v'/\Delta^{k+1}$. From the induction hypothesis, $\tilde{v} \geq v/\Delta^k$. Now, $R_{k+1} = q_{i,k+1}g_{k+1}(q_{i,k+1})$ in both the exact and approximate dynamic programs. By the same argument as in the proof of claim (i), it follows that the increase in makespan that results from the scheduling of product $k + 1$ is no larger in the approximate dynamic program than in the exact dynamic program. Combining these facts, we have $\tilde{v}' - \tilde{v} \geq v' - v \geq v'/\Delta^k - v/\Delta^k$. This implies that $\tilde{v}' \geq \tilde{v} + v'/\Delta^k - v/\Delta^k \geq v'/\Delta^k \geq v'/\Delta^{k+1}$, where the second inequality follows from the induction hypothesis.

It follows from claims (i) and (ii) that if trial state S exists in Algorithm MAS$_\epsilon$, then the induction argument is complete.

However, trial state S may be eliminated by another trial state $S' = (k+1, \tau_1, \tau_2)$, where $\tau_1 \geq \tilde{h}'$, and $\tau_2 \geq \tilde{v}'/\Delta$, and where the second bound holds because S and S' have the same label. Then, we have: (i) $\tau_1 \geq \tilde{h}' \geq h'$ and (ii) $\tau_2 \geq \tilde{v}'/\Delta \geq v'/\Delta^{k+1}$ for S'. Thus, the presence of trial state S' in Algorithm MAS$_\epsilon$ establishes that the induction hypothesis holds.

We now show that Algorithm MAS$_\epsilon$ delivers a solution with the required performance guarantee. Let the state (n, h, v) correspond to an optimal solution with value v^*. Then, the above induction argument shows that Algorithm MAS$_\epsilon$ generates a solution $\tilde{\sigma}$ and a corresponding final state $(n, \tilde{h}, \tilde{v})$ with value $\tilde{v}$, where $\tilde{v} \geq v^*/\Delta^n$. Therefore,

$$[(R(\sigma^*) - C_{\max}(\sigma^*)) - (R(\tilde{\sigma} - C_{\max}(\tilde{\sigma}))]/[R(\sigma^*) - C_{\max}(\sigma^*)] \leq 1 - 1/\Delta^n \leq 1 - 1/(1+\epsilon) \leq \epsilon,$$

where the second last inequality follows from (5.5).

Finally, we analyze the time complexity of Algorithm MAS$_\epsilon$. We first evaluate the number of different labels that are used in the Trial State Labeling step. There are $O(n)$ values of $j + 1$. Since an upper bound on optimal net profit is given by

5.2 Single-Period Product Based Problems

$n \max_{1 \leq j \leq n, 1 \leq i \leq m_j} \{q_{ij} g_j(q_{ij})\}$, the number of possible values for the label $\Delta(v')$ is no more than

$$\lceil \log_\Delta (n \max_{1 \leq j \leq n, 1 \leq i \leq m_j} \{q_{ij} g_j(q_{ij})\}) \rceil = \lceil \log(n \max_{1 \leq j \leq n, 1 \leq i \leq m_j} \{q_{ij} g_j(q_{ij})\}) / \log \Delta \rceil$$

$$\leq \lceil (1 + 2n/\epsilon) \log(n \max_{1 \leq j \leq n, 1 \leq i \leq m_j} \{q_{ij} g_j(q_{ij})\}) \rceil,$$

where the last inequality follows from (5.4) and the inequality $\log x \geq (x-1)/x$ for all $x > 1$. Thus, the total number of labels is $O(n^2 \log(n \max_{1 \leq j \leq n, 1 \leq i \leq m_j} \{q_{ij} g_j (q_{ij})\})/\epsilon)$. Each state generates at most $O(m_{max})$ trial states. Thus, the overall time complexity of Algorithm MAS$_\epsilon$ is $O(n^2 m_{max} \log(n \max_{1 \leq j \leq n, 1 \leq i \leq m_j} \{q_{ij} g_j(q_{ij})\}) /\epsilon)$. $\qquad\square$

5.2.4 Heuristics

Chen and Hall (2010) develop three heuristics with an increasing level of coordination between pricing and scheduling decisions and use them to evaluate the value of pricing–scheduling coordination through a computational experiment. The three heuristics are:

- An uncoordinated Heuristic H1 where pricing and scheduling decisions are made independently,
- A partially coordinated Heuristic H2 that uses only basic information about scheduling that a marketing department typically knows,
- A simple Heuristic H3 for solving the coordinated problem.

They are described in this section. In Sect. 5.2.5, we describe the computational experiments performed by Chen and Hall (2010) that compare the solutions generated by these heuristics and the optimal solutions generated by the exact algorithms given earlier and report the related managerial insights.

In the first Heuristic, H1, there is no coordination between pricing and scheduling decisions. The pricing decision is made first by maximizing the total revenue without considering its impact on scheduling costs. Since scheduling is not considered, the pricing decision can be made separately for each product. Given the demand, which is determined by the pricing decision, the scheduling decision is then made by minimizing the total scheduling cost. A formal description follows.

Heuristic H1

Step 1: For $j = 1, \ldots, n$, choose price $q_{k_j, j}$ for product j, where $k_j = \arg \max_{1 \leq i \leq m_j} \{q_{ij} g_j(q_{ij})\}$.

Step 2: Given $g_j(q_{k_j, j})$ orders of product j, for $j = 1, \ldots, n$, schedule these orders optimally to minimize the total scheduling cost. More specifically, for the single-machine completion time problem, it is optimal to schedule the given orders in

SWPT order (Smith, 1956). Similarly for the flowshop makespan problem, it is optimal to schedule the orders by Johnson's rule (Johnson, 1954). However, the single-machine lateness problem in Step 2 is NP-hard (Karp, 1972). Therefore, we use the pseudo-polynomial time dynamic program of (Lawler & Moore, 1969) to solve this problem.

In the second Heuristic, H2, there is partial coordination between pricing and scheduling decisions. The pricing decision is again made separately for each product, but the cost of scheduling the demand for that product alone is considered when the pricing decision is made. However, the contribution of that product to the scheduling cost of the other products and the contribution of the other products to the scheduling cost of that product are both ignored.

Heuristic H2

Step 1: For $j = 1, \ldots, n$, choose price $q_{k_j,j}$ for product j, where $k_j = \arg\max_{1 \leq i \leq m_j} \{q_{ij} g_j(q_{ij}) - z_j(g_j(q_{ij}))\}$, where $z_j(g_j(q_{ij}))$ is the cost of scheduling $g_j(q_{ij})$ orders of product j, starting from time 0. The scheduling cost $z_j(g_j(q_{ij}))$ is calculated assuming that there are no other products on the machine(s). For the single-machine completion time problem and the flowshop makespan problem, the scheduling cost $z_j(g_j(q_{ij}))$ can easily be calculated because all the orders of a product are identical. However, for the single-machine lateness problem, we first schedule as many orders as possible on time subject to the due date constraint and then compute the cost of scheduling the remaining orders after the due date.

Step 2: The same as Step 2 of Heuristic H1.

In contrast to Heuristics H1 and H2 where there is either no coordination or only partial coordination, the exact algorithms SMCT, SML, and FSM described in Sect. 5.2.1 jointly optimize the pricing and scheduling decisions. However, it may be difficult to implement these complex and relatively time-consuming algorithms in practice. Therefore, Chen and Hall (2010) propose a third heuristic, H3, that considers the pricing and scheduling decisions jointly but is much easier to implement and runs much faster than the exact dynamic programming algorithms. If the marketing and manufacturing departments fully coordinate their operations, knowledge of the production sequence is available to the marketing department and hence may be used in its pricing decisions. Thus in H3, the products are considered in a sequence that is optimal with respect to the scheduling cost, and the heuristic pricing decision for each product is made based on both revenue and scheduling cost information.

Heuristic H3

Step 0: Index the products in SWPT order, EDD order, or the order prescribed by Johnson's rule (Johnson, 1954), for the single-machine completion time problem, the single-machine lateness problem, and the flowshop makespan problem, respectively.

Step 1: For $j = 1, \ldots, n$, choose price $q_{k_j,j}$ for product j, where $k_j = \arg\max_{1 \leq i \leq m_j} \{q_{ij} g_j(q_{ij}) - y_j(g_j(q_{ij}))\}$, where $y_j(g_j(q_{ij}))$ is the cost of scheduling $g_j(q_{ij})$ orders of product j, after the $g_1(q_{k_1 1})$ orders of product 1, $\ldots$,

5.2 Single-Period Product Based Problems

$g_{j-1}(q_{k_{j-1},j-1})$ orders of product $j - 1$, that have been scheduled earlier. The cost function $y_j(g_j(q_{ij}))$ is computed similarly to $z_j(g_j(q_{ij}))$ in Heuristic H2. However, whereas $z_j(g_j(q_{ij}))$ in H2 assumes that the orders start at time 0, $y_j(g_j(q_{ij}))$ in H3 considers the processing time of orders that have already been scheduled. Note that the decisions about q_{ij} made in this way are locally optimal, in that the net profit of the current product j, but not of the whole schedule, is being maximized.
Step 2: The same as Step 2 of Heuristic H1.

To illustrate how these heuristics work, we apply them to a simple instance of the single-machine completion time problem below.

Example 5.2 (Application of Heuristics H1, H2, and H3) We apply Heuristics H1, H2, and H3 to the following instance of the single-machine completion time problem with 3 products.

Product j	1	2	3
p_j	1	2	4
w_j	2	1	1
Allowable prices Q_j	{5, 10, 20}	{15, 25}	{20, 35}
Corresponding demand g_j	{5, 2, 1}	{3, 2}	{3, 1}

First, we apply H1 to this instance. Step 1 chooses an allowable price for each product that maximizes the revenue of this product. This means that for products 1, 2, and 3, allowable prices 5, 25, and 20 are chosen, respectively. This results in 5, 2, and 3 orders of products 1, 2, and 3, respectively. Step 2 schedules these orders in the SWPT sequence of the products, which is $(1, 2, 3)$. In this solution, the total revenue is $5(5) + 25(2) + 20(3) = 135$, and the total weighted completion time of the orders is $2(1 + 2 + 3 + 4 + 5) + 1(7 + 9) + 1(13 + 17 + 21) = 97$. Thus, the net profit is $135 - 97 = 38$.

Next, we apply H2. Step 1 chooses an allowable price for each product that maximizes the revenue of this product minus the total weighted completion time of the orders of this product, without considering the orders of other products. For product 1, if allowable price 5 is chosen, then the net profit of this product is $5(5) - 2(1 + 2 + 3 + 4 + 5) = -5$; if allowable price 10 is chosen, then the net profit is $10(2) - 2(1 + 2) = 14$; and if allowable price 20 is chosen, then the net profit is $20(1) - 2(1) = 18$. Thus, allowable price 20 is used for product 1 with a demand of 1 order. Similarly, we can find that for product 2 allowable price 25 is chosen with a demand of 2 orders, and for product 3 allowable price 20 is chosen with a demand of 3 orders. Step 2 schedules these orders in the SWPT sequence. In this solution, the total revenue is $20(1) + 25(2) + 20(3) = 130$, and the total weighted completion time of the orders is $2(1) + 1(3 + 5) + 1(9 + 13 + 17) = 49$. Thus, the net profit is $130 - 49 = 81$.

Finally, we apply H3. Step 1 chooses an allowable price for each product that maximizes the revenue of this product minus the total weighted completion time of the orders of this product, taking into account the orders of the other products that have already been scheduled. For product 1, since no other products have been considered, the same allowable price as in H2 is chosen, i.e., allowable price 20 is used for product 1 with a demand of 1 order. For products 2 and 3, however, when choosing the best allowable price, the cost contribution of the product is calculated based on a starting time equal to the total processing time of the orders that have already been scheduled. Thus, for product 2, the starting time for any order is 1, not 0, because 1 order of product 1 has been scheduled. If allowable price 15 is chosen, then the net profit of this product is $15(3) - 1(3 + 5 + 7) = 30$, and if allowable price 25 is chosen, then the net profit is $25(2) - 1(3 + 5) = 42$. Thus for product 2, allowable price 25 is chosen with a demand of 2. Now for product 3, the starting time is 5. It can be easily verified that for product 3, allowable price 35 is chosen with a demand of 1. This solution has a total revenue $20(1) + 25(2) + 35(1) = 105$ and a total weighted completion time of the orders $2(1)+1(3+5)+1(9) = 19$. Thus the net profit of this solution is $105 - 19 = 86$. This heuristically derived solution happens to be an optimal one.

The computational results from Chen and Hall (2010) are reported in the next subsection. These results show that for all the three problems, on average, H3 performs better than H2 which performs better than H1. In fact, Chen and Hall (2010) prove more strongly that for the single-machine completion time problem, the performance of H3 dominates that of H2 which dominates that of H1 for every instance. This is shown in the theorem below. However, for the other two problems, their computational results show that there exist problem instances for which H1 performs better than H2, and there exist problem instances for which H2 performs better than H3.

Theorem 5.6 *For any instance of the single-machine completion time problem, the profit generated by Heuristic H3 is at least as large as the profit generated by Heuristic H2, which is at least as large as the profit generated by Heuristic H1.*

Proof Let $k_{j1}, k_{j2}, k_{j3} \in \{1, \ldots, m_j\}$ denote the price level chosen for product $j \in N$ by Heuristics H1, H2, and H3, respectively. By comparing the ways in which these heuristics choose prices for the products, it is evident that $g_j(q_{k_{j1},j}) \geq g_j(q_{k_{j2},j}) \geq g_j(q_{k_{j3},j})$, and hence $k_{j1} \leq k_{j2} \leq k_{j3}$, for $j \in N$. Let z_{ji} denote the cost of scheduling $g_j(q_{k_{ji},j})$ orders of product j, starting from time 0, for $i = 1, 2, 3$ and $j \in N$. Let $R_{ji} = q_{k_{ji},j} g_j(q_{k_{ji},j})$, for $i = 1, 2, 3$. Let F_1, F_2, and F_3 denote the net profit of the solution generated by H1, H2, and H3, respectively. We have

$$F_i = \sum_{j \in N} R_{ji} - \sum_{j \in N} z_{ji} - \sum_{j \in N} \left[w_j g_j(q_{k_{ji},j}) \sum_{v=1}^{j-1} p_v g_v(q_{k_{vi},v}) \right], \quad \text{for } i = 1, 2, 3.$$

$$(5.6)$$

From Step 1 of Heuristic H2,

$$R_{j2} - z_{j2} \geq R_{j1} - z_{j1}, \quad \text{for } j \in N. \tag{5.7}$$

5.2 Single-Period Product Based Problems

The fact that $g_j(q_{k_{j1},j}) \geq g_j(q_{k_{j2},j})$, for $j \in N$, implies that

$$w_j g_j(q_{k_{j1},j}) \sum_{v=1}^{j-1} p_v g_v(q_{k_{v1},v})$$

$$\geq w_j g_j(q_{k_{j2},j}) \sum_{v=1}^{j-1} p_v g_v(q_{k_{v2},v}), \quad \text{for } j \in N. \tag{5.8}$$

Then, from (5.6), (5.7), and (5.8), we have $F_2 \geq F_1$.

Furthermore, from Step 1 of Heuristic H3,

$$R_{j3} - z_{j3} - w_j g_j(q_{k_{j3},j}) \sum_{v=1}^{j-1} p_v g_v(q_{k_{v3},v})$$

$$\geq R_{j2} - z_{j2} - w_j g_j(q_{k_{j2},j}) \sum_{v=1}^{j-1} p_v g_v(q_{k_{v3},v}), \quad \text{for } j \in N. \tag{5.9}$$

The fact that $g_j(q_{k_{j2},j}) \geq g_j(q_{k_{j3},j})$, for $j \in N$, implies that

$$w_j g_j(q_{k_{j2},j}) \sum_{v=1}^{j-1} p_v g_v(q_{k_{v2},v}) \geq w_j g_j(q_{k_{j2},j}) \sum_{v=1}^{j-1} p_v g_v(q_{k_{v3},v}), \quad \text{for } j \in N. \tag{5.10}$$

Then, from (5.6), (5.9), and (5.10), we have $F_3 \geq F_2$. $\qquad\square$

5.2.5 Computational Results and Managerial Insights

We summarize the computational experiments performed by Chen and Hall (2010) and the associated results and insights. Their computational experiments are conducted to address the following questions: (i) how much improvement in net profit can be achieved between the uncoordinated Heuristic H1, the partially coordinated Heuristic H2, the fully coordinated Heuristic H3, and the optimally coordinated algorithm? (ii) how do these improvements vary with problem parameters? and (iii) what other solution characteristics change as the level of coordination increases?

Following guidelines about the design of computational experiments from Hall and Posner (2001), Chen and Hall (2010) generate a large set of test instances to cover a wide variety of practical situations. The number of products varies from 10 to 50, the number of allowable prices for each product ranges from 2 to 12, a linear demand function $g_j(q_{ij}) = \max\{0, \lfloor \alpha_j - \beta_j q_{ij} \rfloor\}$ is used with varying ranges for α_j and β_j, and all other parameters such as order processing times, weights, and due dates are generated from varying intervals. We show in Table 5.1 the overall average

Table 5.1 Comparison of heuristics and optimal solutions

	Profit gap %						Demand gap %		
	H1		H2		H3		H1	H2	H3
Problem	Mean	Stdev	Mean	Stdev	Mean	Stdev	Mean	Mean	Mean
Single-machine completion time problem	32.32	15.66	25.94	12.30	4.44	2.38	32.29	28.89	11.45
Single-machine lateness problem	7.35	3.75	5.38	3.07	2.02	1.66	16.53	13.53	0.03
Flowshop makespan problem	15.96	7.81	4.09	3.37	2.84	3.33	21.77	−7.84	−2.05

of each performance measure for each problem, as reported in Chen and Hall (2010). Each row in Table 5.1 is based on thousands of instances tested. In this table, the columns under "Profit gap" show the relative gap (expressed as a percentage) in net profit between the solutions generated by Heuristics H1, H2, and H3 described in Sect. 5.2.4 and the optimal coordinated solution generated by the corresponding dynamic programming algorithm described in Sect. 5.2.1, respectively. The columns under "Demand gap" show the relative gap (expressed as a percentage) in total realized demand of all the products (i.e., the total number of orders) between the solution of H1, H2, and H3 and the optimal coordinated solution. The columns "Mean" and "Stdev" represent the mean and standard deviation of the results over a large number of random instances, respectively. Chen and Hall (2010) find that each heuristic takes less than 10 CPU seconds and each dynamic programming algorithm takes less than 100 CPU seconds to solve any test problem on a 1 GHz personal computer.

We first discuss the overall performance of the three heuristics. The value of partial coordination in Heuristic H2 compared to no coordination in Heuristic H1 can be seen in reduced mean profit gaps in all the three problems. Further significant improvements are offered by full coordination in Heuristic H3 for the three problems, respectively. Moreover, for all the three problems, the standard deviations of the profit gaps associated with H3 are significantly smaller than those associated with H2, which are smaller than those associated with H1. This implies that the performance of H3 is more robust than that of H2, which is more robust than that of H1. Since Heuristic H3 routinely delivers solutions that are close to optimal, we recommend it as a faster and simpler alternative to the implementation of the optimal dynamic programming algorithms described in Sect. 5.2.1.

Chen and Hall (2010) also report the following sensitivity analysis results regarding total net profit:

1. For all the three problems, when demand is more sensitive to price, all three heuristics show much larger profit gaps under every configuration of the other parameters. This is because high sensitivity of demand to price magnifies heuristic errors in price choices.

5.2 Single-Period Product Based Problems

2. For the single-machine completion time and lateness problems, when the order weights (w_j) are larger, all three heuristics show much larger profit gaps under every configuration of the other parameters. Similarly, for the flowshop makespan problem, when processing times (p_{1j}, p_{2j}) are larger, all three heuristics show much larger profit gaps under every configuration of the other parameters. This is because Heuristics H1 and H2 fail to fully consider the scheduling costs that are more significant when w_j in the first two problems and p_{1j} and p_{2j} in the last problem are larger.

3. For the single-machine lateness problem, when due dates are tighter, Heuristics H1 and H2 show much larger profit gaps under every configuration of the other parameters. This is because difficulty in meeting the due dates magnifies the cost of heuristic errors in scheduling choices. On the contrary, the performance of Heuristic H3 does not vary much with the tightness of due dates and hence is more robust than H1 and H2.

Chen and Hall (2010) also make the following observations about the total demand scheduled by the three heuristics and the optimal algorithm. Since it does not consider cost, Heuristic H1 receives substantially more orders than the optimal algorithm. Since Heuristic H2 partially considers cost, the excess demand it receives compared to the optimal algorithm is less than that in the case of H1 for the first two problems, respectively. However, for the flowshop makespan problem, H2 results in a demand shortfall compared to the optimal algorithm, due to overestimation of the increase in flowshop makespan when an order is added. Since Heuristic H3 evaluates cost more accurately, it produces a much lower excess demand than the other heuristics for the single-machine completion time problem and gets very close to the same total demand as the optimal algorithm for the other two problems.

Based on the above discussions, Chen and Hall (2010) offer the following insights that can be useful for practitioners:

1. In situations where demand is sensitive to price or where profit margins are relatively small, the coordination of pricing and scheduling decisions is particularly important. For managers who require a solution that is easier to implement, we recommend using Heuristic H3, which routinely provides near-optimal coordinated solutions for all the three problems studied here.

2. In situations where communication between marketing and production is poor and full coordination is therefore impossible, it is still valuable to use the partially coordinated Heuristic H2, since it provides a significant improvement in average profit over the uncoordinated Heuristic H1.

3. While profit is in many cases the primary objective, an important secondary objective is market share, as measured by the percentage of realized demand enjoyed by the company. Here, the heuristics generally perform well; however, Heuristic H2 does not typically achieve a good market share for the flowshop makespan problem.

4. For consistent success, it is best to align the incentives of the marketing and production departments. Therefore, performance incentives within the marketing department should be based on net profit rather than revenue. Implementing such

5.3 Single-Period Order Based Problems

Liu et al. (2012) and Lu et al. (2013) study single-period coordinated price quotation and scheduling problems involving the following sequence of events:

- a known set of order inquiries arrive simultaneously at the beginning of the time period;
- the decision maker (DM) quotes a price to every order either simultaneously or sequentially;
- each order is placed with a certain probability as a function of the quoted price;
- the decision maker schedules the placed orders for processing on a single machine.

Two schemes for price quotation are studied. Under a simultaneous quotation scheme, the DM quotes a price for every order inquiry simultaneously and waits for a confirmation from the customer of each inquiry that the order is either placed or not. Liu et al. (2012) explain that in practice, order inquiries arrive dynamically over time, but the manufacturer often postpones the quotation decisions until a sufficient number of order inquiries have arrived or the deadline for quotation is reached. This enables the manufacturer to use a simultaneous quotation scheme for a set of order inquiries that have arrived over a given period of time.

Under a sequential quotation scheme, the DM handles order inquiries that have arrived one by one and quotes a price for an inquiry after knowing the customers' decisions on all the inquiries that have been quoted before that. Clearly, sequential quotation benefits the DM because more information is available when a price quotation is made.

In the problem studied in Lu et al. (2013), there is a discrete set of allowable prices that can be quoted for each order, whereas in the problem studied in Liu et al. (2012) any price from a given interval can be quoted. There are two major differences between these problems and those studied in Chen and Hall (2010) and discussed in Sect. 5.2: (i) in the former problems, the size of an order is known beforehand and independent of the price quoted for the order, whereas in the latter problems the order size for a product is a function of the price set for this product and (ii) in the former problems, whether an order is placed or not is uncertain, with its probability as a function of the price quoted, whereas in the latter problems each order is placed with certainty. As a result, the latter problems are stochastic and their objective functions involve the *expected* total profit, whereas the former problems are deterministic and their objective functions involve the total profit.

In Sects. 5.3.1 and 5.3.2 below, we discuss the problems considered in Lu et al. (2013) and Liu et al. (2012), respectively.

5.3 Single-Period Order Based Problems

5.3.1 Discrete Allowable Prices

We use the notation given in Lu et al. (2013) to describe the problem they study. A manufacturer receives a set of n order inquiries $N = \{1, \ldots, n\}$ at the beginning of the planning horizon and needs to quote a price to every order simultaneously. There are m_j allowable prices that can be quoted for inquiry $j \in N$. Let $q_{1j} > \cdots > q_{m_j,j}$ denote these allowable prices. The probability that inquiry j materializes as a firm order (i.e., the order is actually placed), which we call the *placement probability*, is a known decreasing function of the price quoted. Let π_{ij} be the placement probability if the price quoted is q_{ij}. If inquiry j becomes a firm order after it is quoted a price $R_j \in \{q_{1j}, \ldots, q_{m_j,j}\}$, then the manufacturer needs to process it, which takes the manufacturer p_j time units to complete and earns a revenue of R_j. Each order inquiry j is associated with a weight w_j. If inquiry j materializes and its order completes processing at time C_j, then the cost contribution of this inquiry is its weighted completion time, i.e., $w_j C_j$. The manufacturer's decision problem is to make price quotations as discussed above to maximize its expected net profit, which is the expected total revenue minus the expected total weighted completion time of the given n order inquiries. We note that in this problem the order size, as represented by its processing time p_j, is not a function of the quoted price, unlike in the problems of Chen and Hall (2010).

To solve this problem, we first make two observations. First, for each order inquiry $j \in N$, given the one-to-one relationship between each allowable price q_{ij} that can be quoted and the corresponding placement probability π_{ij}, for $i = 1, \ldots, m_j$, finding optimal price quotations for the given inquiries is equivalent to finding the placement probabilities for these inquiries. Second, since the cost contribution of each order inquiry is its weighted completion time, it is thus optimal to schedule the placed orders in the shortest weighted processing time (SWPT) order (Smith, 1956). Thus, without loss of generality, we assume that the order inquiries are indexed such that $p_1/w_1 \leq p_2/w_2 \leq \cdots \leq p_n/w_n$.

Lu et al. (2013) provide the following results. Since these results are fairly straightforward, we do not show their proofs.

Theorem 5.7 *For any given placement probabilities for the n inquiries, $\pi_1, \ldots, \pi_n$, where $\pi_j \in \{\pi_{1j}, \ldots, \pi_{m_j,j}\}$, for $j \in N$, the expected total weighted completion is equal to*

$$\sum_{j=1}^{n} \pi_j w_j \left(\sum_{i=1}^{j-1} \pi_i p_i + p_j \right) \tag{5.11}$$

and is also equal to

$$\sum_{j=1}^{n} \pi_j p_j \left(\sum_{i=j+1}^{n} \pi_i w_i + w_j \right). \tag{5.12}$$

Lu et al. (2013) point out that this problem contains a known NP-hard scheduling problem with rejection (Engels et al., 2003) as a special case and hence is at least ordinarily NP-hard. They give a pseudo-polynomial time dynamic programming algorithm for solving the problem. The pseudo-polynomial time complexity of the algorithm relies on the following practical assumption:

Assumption: The placement probabilities of orders, π_{ij}, for $i = 1, \ldots, m_j$ and $j \in N$, can all be expressed as integer multiples of a small positive fractional number δ.

This assumption holds automatically if all π_{ij} values are rational numbers. Under this assumption, if the placement probabilities of the first j inquiries are $\pi_1, \ldots, \pi_j$, respectively, then the total expected processing time incurred by these inquiries, $\sum_{i=1}^{j} \pi_i p_i$, is an integer multiple of δ, which as shown below guarantees that the computational time of the algorithm is pseudo-polynomial.

Now we describe the algorithm of Lu et al. (2013).

Algorithm TWCP

Input

Given $m_j, p_j, w_j, q_{ij}, \pi_{ij}$ for $i = 1, \ldots, m_j$ and $j = 1, \ldots, n$.

Initialization

Index the order inquiries in the SWPT order.

Value Function

$f(j, r)$ = maximum expected profit from order inquiries $1, \ldots, j$, given that the expected total processing time of the orders corresponding to these inquiries is r (i.e., $\sum_{i=1}^{j} \pi_i p_i = r$ if the placement probabilities of these inquiries are $\pi_1, \ldots, \pi_n$).

Boundary Condition

$f(0, r) = 0$, if $r = 0$; and $-\infty$, if $r \neq 0$.

Optimal Solution Value

$$\max_{r \in \{0, \delta, 2\delta, \ldots, P-\delta, P\}} f(n, r), \text{ where } P = \sum_{j \in N} p_j.$$

Recurrence Relation

For $j = 1, \ldots, n$ and $r = 0, \delta, 2\delta, \ldots, P - \delta, P$:

$$f(j, r) = \max_{i=1,\ldots,m_j} \left\{ f(j - 1, r - \pi_{ij} p_j) + \pi_{ij} q_{ij} - \pi_{ij} w_j (r - \pi_{ij} p_j + p_j) \right\}.$$

In the recurrence equation of the algorithm, every allowable price for inquiry j is compared to maximize the expected profit from the first j inquiries, given that the expected total processing time resulting from these inquiries is r. The term $\pi_{ij} q_{ij}$ is the expected revenue from inquiry j, $r - \pi_{ij} p_j$ is the expected total processing time from the first $j - 1$ inquiries, and $\pi_{ij} w_j (r - \pi_{ij} p_j + p_j)$ is the expected weighted completion time contributed by inquiry j. Lu et al. (2013) show that the time complexity of this algorithm is $O(n m_{\max} P / \delta)$, where $m_{\max} = max\{m_j | j \in N\}$.

5.3 Single-Period Order Based Problems

By Theorem 5.7, the expected total cost can also be written as (5.12). Based on this, Lu et al. (2013) provide a second dynamic programming algorithm for solving their problem. It is presented below. It uses the same input and initialization step as Algorithm TWCP.

Algorithm TWCW

Value Function

$f(j, r)$ = maximum expected profit from order inquiries $1, \ldots, j$, given that the expected total weight of the orders corresponding to these inquiries is r (i.e., $\sum_{i=1}^{j} \pi_i w_i = r$ if the placement probabilities of these inquiries are $\pi_1, \ldots, \pi_n$).

Boundary Condition

$f(n + 1, r) = 0$, if $r = 0$; and $-\infty$, if $r \neq 0$.

Optimal Solution Value

$$\max_{r \in \{0, \delta, 2\delta, \ldots, W - \delta, W\}} f(1, r), \text{ where } W = \sum_{j \in N} w_j.$$

Recurrence Relations

For $j = n - 1, \ldots, 1$ and $r = 0, \delta, 2\delta, \ldots, W - \delta, W$:

$$f(j, r) = \max_{i=1, \ldots, m_j} \left\{ f(j + 1, r - \pi_{ij} w_j) + \pi_{ij} q_{ij} - \pi_{ij} p_j (r - \pi_{ij} w_j + w_j) \right\}.$$

Lu et al. (2013) show that the time complexity of this algorithm is $O(n m_{\max} W / \delta)$. Furthermore, for the special case of the problem where the weights of the order inquiries w_j are identical (i.e., the cost function in the problem becomes the expected total completion time of the order inquiries), this algorithm has a polynomial time complexity $O(n^2 m_{\max} / \delta)$. This is because in this case, $W = nw$, where w is the identical weight for all the order inquiries, and for any $j = 1, \ldots, n$, only the states (j, r) with $r = 0, w\delta, 2w\delta, \ldots, W - w\delta, W$ need to be considered in the dynamic program.

We highlight some of the computational results and insights derived by Lu et al. (2013).

- They show that both algorithms TWCP and TWCW are very efficient and can solve large instances of the problem quickly.
- In their problem, it is assumed that there is a finite number of allowable prices that can be quoted for each order inquiry. They investigate the potential profit loss caused by a limit on the number of allowable prices (m_j), by varying m_j from 2 to 50. In practice, a company may limit the number of allowable prices it uses in order to simplify its decision process. They find that the expected profit loss relative to the maximum possible expected profit that can be achieved when $m_j = 50$ decreases rapidly from more than 10% to less than 1% as m_j increases from 2 to 10. However, it approaches a constant level near 0 when $m_j \geq 15$. This suggests that the benefit of considering more possible prices to quote diminishes once $m_j \geq 15$.
- In their problem, the manufacturer can quote a distinct price for each order. Although price discrimination may not be illegal, quoting different prices to different customers could be perceived as unfair. They therefore investigate the expected profit loss if an identical unit price scheme is used across different

orders. With an identical unit pricing scheme, the manufacturer can choose a unit price R and quote price $R_j = Rp_j$ for each order inquiry $j \in N$. In addition, the manufacturer also has the option to reject an order inquiry. In other words, an inquiry j is either rejected or quoted a price $R_j = Rp_j$, where the unit price R is a decision to be made and can be chosen from a discrete set of allowable prices. Their computational results show that the expected profit loss from identical unit pricing increases as customers (or orders) become more heterogeneous. Moreover, even when customers are quite similar, the profit loss is quite significant, especially when the price probability function is nonlinear.

5.3.2 Continuous Allowable Prices

Liu et al. (2012) study two problems with continuous allowable prices, one with simultaneous price quotation and the other with sequential quotation. For ease of presentation, we denote these problems as SIMQ and SEQ, respectively. We discuss these two problems in Sects. 5.3.2.1 and 5.3.2.2, respectively.

5.3.2.1 Simultaneous Quotation

Problem SIMQ is similar to the problem described in Sect. 5.3.1 with the following two differences: (i) the price that can be quoted for inquiry j can be any value from an interval, and (ii) the placement probability is a linear function of the quoted price for every inquiry. For convenience of analysis, Liu et al. (2012) treat the placement probability for each inquiry j, π_j, as a decision to be made by the manufacturer, and given this decision, the corresponding unit price that is quoted to inquiry j is a function of π_j, denoted as $R_j(\pi_j)$. This function is assumed to be linear, with the inquiry independent coefficients:

$$R_j(\pi_j) = a\pi_j + b, \tag{5.13}$$

where a and b are given coefficients with $a < 0$ and $b \geq |a|$ and $0 \leq \pi_j \leq u$ for a positive constant $u \leq 1$. Liu et al. (2012) make the following assumption about some of the problem parameters:

Assumption $w_{\max} < \min\{-2a, b\}$, where $w_{\max} = \max\{w_j | j \in N\}$.

This is a reasonable assumption for the following reasons. By (5.13), the price p_j can vary from $au + b$ to b, and hence the price range is $-au \leq -a$. Thus, the assumption that $w_{\max} < -2a$ means that the unit scheduling cost w_j cannot be too large relative to the price range. Similarly, the assumption that $w_{\max} < b$ ensures that the unit scheduling cost is not too large relative to the order revenue.

The problem is to find placement probabilities $\pi_1, \ldots, \pi_n$ such that the expected total profit, defined as the expected total revenue minus the expected total weighted

5.3 Single-Period Order Based Problems

completion time, is maximized subject to the constraint that $0 \le \pi_j \le u$ for $j \in N$, where $u \le 1$ is the maximum placement probability possible and corresponds to the minimum possible price that can be quoted.

Without loss of generality, the inquiries are indexed in SWPT order. We can derive the total expected profit as a function of the placement probabilities $\pi_1, \ldots, \pi_n$ as follows. Given $\pi_1, \ldots, \pi_n$, the total expected revenue of the n inquiries is

$$\sum_{j=1}^{n} \pi_j p_j R_j(\pi_j),$$

and the total expected weighted completion time of the inquiries is

$$\sum_{j=1}^{n} \left[w_j \pi_j \left(\sum_{i=1}^{j-1} \pi_i p_i + p_j \right) \right].$$

With each quoted unit price $R_j(\pi_j)$ defined in (5.13), we have the expected total profit, denoted as $G(\pi_1, \ldots, \pi_n)$, as follows:

$$G(\pi_1, \ldots, \pi_n) = \sum_{j=1}^{n} \left[ap_j \pi_j^2 + bp_j \pi_j - w_j \pi_j \left(\sum_{i=1}^{j-1} \pi_i p_i + p_j \right) \right].$$

Let $H(\pi_1, \ldots, \pi_n) = -G(\pi_1, \ldots, \pi_n)$, then the problem is equivalent to

$$\max\{H(\pi_1, \ldots, \pi_n) \mid 0 \le \pi_j \le u, j \in N\}. \tag{5.14}$$

Liu et al. (2012) show the results stated in the following theorem.

Theorem 5.8 *Function $H(\pi_1, \ldots, \pi_n)$ is strictly convex and the formulation (5.14) can be solved as a convex quadratic program in polynomial time.*

Proof We first prove that the Hessian matrix of function H is positive definite. The first-order partial derivatives of H are as follows:

$$\frac{\partial H}{\partial \pi_j} = -(2ap_j \pi_j + bp_j) + w_j \left(\sum_{i=1}^{j-1} \pi_i p_i + p_j \right) + p_j \sum_{i=j+1}^{n} w_i \pi_i,$$

and the second-order partial derivatives are

$$\frac{\partial^2 H}{\partial \pi_j \partial \pi_k} = \begin{cases} w_k p_j & \text{if } j < k, \\ -2ap_j & \text{if } j = k, \\ w_j p_k & \text{if } j > k. \end{cases}$$

Let the Π denote the vector $(\pi_1, \ldots, \pi_n)^T$. The function H can be rewritten as $H(\Pi) = \frac{1}{2}\Pi^T A \Pi + s\Pi$, where matrix $A = (a_{jk})_{n \times n}$ and vector $s = (s_1, \ldots, s_n)$ are given as follows: $a_{jk} = \frac{\partial^2 H}{\partial \pi_j \partial \pi_k}$, and $s_j = (w_j - b)p_j$, for $j, k = 1, \ldots, n$.

Given the assumption $w_{\max} < -2a$, we can see that matrix A is positive definite, and hence function H is strictly convex. Consequently, the formulation (5.14) is a convex quadratic program, which can be solved in polynomial time (Bazaraa et al., 2013). $\qquad\square$

We use the following numerical instance to illustrate the formulation (5.14) and Theorem 5.8.

Example 5.3 (Illustration of Function H) Consider an example with $n = 2$ order inquiries with $p_1 = 5, p_2 = 4, w_1 = 2, w_2 = 1, R_j(\pi_j) = -2\pi_j + 3$, for $0 \leq \pi_j \leq 1$, for $j = 1, 2$. For this example, the total expected profit as a function of placement probabilities, π_1, π_2, is

$$G(\pi_1, \pi_2) = p_1 \pi_1 R_1(\pi_1) + p_2 \pi_2 R_2(\pi_2) - [w_1 \pi_1 p_1 + w_2 \pi_2(p_1 \pi_1 + p_2)]$$
$$= 5\pi_1(3 - 2\pi_1) + 4\pi_2(3 - 2\pi_2) - (10\pi_1 + \pi_2(5\pi_1 + 4))$$
$$= -10\pi_1^2 + 5\pi_1 - 8\pi_2^2 + 8\pi_2 - 5\pi_1\pi_2.$$

Thus, $H(\pi_1, \pi_2) = -G(\pi_1, \pi_2) = 10\pi_1^2 + 8\pi_2^2 + 5\pi_1\pi_2 - 5\pi_1 - 8\pi_2$. It can easily be verified that the Hessian matrix of H is A and $H(\pi_1, \pi) = \frac{1}{2}\Pi^T A \Pi + s\Pi$, where $\Pi = (\pi_1, \pi_2)^T$, and A and s are as follows:

$$A = \begin{pmatrix} 20 & 5 \\ 5 & 16 \end{pmatrix}, \qquad s = (-5, -8).$$

Clearly, A is a positive definite matrix, and hence H is a strictly convex function.

For the special case where all the order inquiries have an identical weight, i.e., $w_j = w$ for $j \in N$, Liu et al. (2012) show that the optimal unit prices to quote satisfy $R_1^* \geq \cdots \geq R_n^*$, where the inquiries are indexed by the shortest processing time (SPT) rule, i.e., $p_1 \leq \cdots \leq p_n$. This means that when all of the customers are equally important, as reflected by the identical weight, the manufacturer should quote a lower price to an inquiry with a larger order, which is equivalent to giving a discount that increases with the order size.

For the special case where the order weight is proportional to the order size, i.e., $w_j = wp_j$ for some constant w, for $j \in N$, Liu et al. (2012) show that the optimal unit prices to quote satisfy $R_1^* \leq \cdots \leq R_n^*$, where the inquiries are indexed by the SPT rule. This means that when larger orders have larger cost weights, larger orders are less attractive and should be priced higher.

5.3.2.2 Sequential Quotation

With sequential quotation, order inquiries are handled one by one such that when making the quotation decision for an order, the manufacturer knows the responses from all the inquiries that have been quoted for earlier. Two sequences need to be determined in a sequential quotation scheme: (i) what sequence to use for price quotation of inquiries? and (ii) what sequence to use for processing confirmed orders? Liu et al. (2012) consider two types of sequential quotation, namely, consistent quotation and general quotation, defined as follows.

Definition 5.2 *Consistent quotation* requires that price quotation and order processing follow the same sequence, whereas *general quotation* does not require these two actions to follow the same sequence.

Consistent quotation has the following positive feature: during quotation it can provide the customer the start and completion times of the order if the order materializes. General quotation, however, provides the manufacturer the most flexibility and hence the highest expected profit. For ease of presentation, we use SEQC and SEQG to denote the sequential quotation problem with consistent quotation and that with general quotation, respectively.

We observe that although inquiries are handled sequentially in both problems SEQC and SEQG, all the order inquiries arrive simultaneously at the beginning of the planning horizon, and no new inquiries arrive over time. Even though in these problems the underlying decisions are made in a sequential multi-stage fashion, these problems are still essentially single-period problems and hence differ from the multi-period problems discussed in Sect. 5.4 where orders come in over time and pricing decisions for the same products are made repeatedly over time.

Next, we discuss how the problem SEQC can be solved. Suppose that N_1 is the set of remaining order inquiries to be handled, and t is the total processing time of the firm orders that have resulted from the inquiries that have already been handled, i.e., the inquiries in $N \setminus N_1$. By Definition 5.2 about consistent quotation, the orders that result from the order inquiries of N_1 can only be processed starting from time t. Thus, the optimal quotation and scheduling decisions for the inquiries in N_1 depend on t and N_1 only and do not depend on any other specific characteristics of the inquiries in $N \setminus N_1$ or the confirmed orders from these inquiries. Based on this observation, Liu et al. (2012) develop the following dynamic programming algorithm for solving the problem SEQC with general revenue functions $R_j(\pi_j)$ and general cost functions $f_j(C_j)$. Since linear revenue functions and/or special cost functions such as weighted completion time do not reduce the complexity of the problem, this same algorithm is needed to solve the problem with a linear revenue function and the total weighted completion time as the cost function.

Algorithm DP-SEQC

Input:
Given p_j, $f_j()$, $R_j()$, for $j \in N$.
Value Function:
$F(t, N_1)$ = maximum expected total profit from the inquiries in N_1, given a start time t.
Boundary Condition:
$F(t, \phi) = 0$.
Maximum Expected Profit:
$F(0, N)$.
Recurrence Relation:

$$F(t, N_1) = \max_{j \in N_1} \left\{ \max_{0 \le \pi_j \le u} \left\{ \pi_j \left[p_j R_j(\pi_j) - f_j(t + p_j) + F(t + p_j, N_1 \setminus \{j\}) \right] \right. \right.$$

$$\left. \left. + \left[(1 - \pi_j) F(t, N_1 \setminus \{j\}) \right] \right\} \right\}.$$

In the recurrence relation, any inquiry j from N_1 and any possible placement probability of this inquiry π_j are considered. Given inquiry j, the recurrence relation considers two possibilities: the order materializes with probability π_J, or the order does not materialize with probability $1 - \pi_j$. Liu et al. (2012) show that this algorithm solves problem SEQC to optimality in $O(n^2 2^n)$ time, if an optimal π_j can be found via a constant number of computations for given j in the recurrence equation. This algorithm is therefore computationally efficient for small values of n.

Finally, we discuss how the more general problem SEQG can be solved. Suppose that N_1 is the set of remaining order inquiries to be handled, and among the inquiries $N \setminus N_1$ that have been handled, J is the subset of inquiries that have resulted in firm orders. By Definition 5.2 about general quotation, the order processing sequence can be different from the price quotation sequence. This means that the orders in J can be processed later than the orders arising from price quotation decisions for the inquiries in N_1. Thus, we cannot make scheduling decisions for the inquiries in N_1 alone without considering the orders in J. Therefore, the optimal quotation decisions for the inquiries in N_1 depend on which specific orders are in J. However, which specific prices are quoted for the orders in J does not have an impact on quotation decisions for the inquiries in N_1. Based on these observations, Liu et al. (2012) develop the following algorithm for solving the problem SEQG with general revenue functions $R_j(\pi_j)$ and general cost functions $f_j(C_j)$.

Algorithm DP-SEQG

Input:
Given p_j, $f_j()$, $R_j()$, for $j \in N$.
Initialization:
For any subset of orders $J \in N$, find the minimum cost, denoted as $g(J)$, of processing the orders in J with a start time 0.

5.3 Single-Period Order Based Problems

Value Function:
$F(J, N_1)$ = maximum expected total profit of the problem, given that price quotation decisions have already been made for the order inquiries in $N \setminus N_1$, the orders in $J \subseteq N \setminus N_1$ have materialized, and the remaining order inquiries in N_1 have not been quoted for.

Boundary Condition:
$F(J, \phi) = g(J)$ for any $J \subseteq N$.

Maximum Expected Profit:
$F(\phi, N)$.

Recurrence Relation:
For any subset of firm orders $J \subseteq N$ and any subset of inquiries $N_1 \subseteq N$ such that $J \cap N_1 = \phi$, considered in the following sequence: $|J| = n, \ldots, 1, 0$, and $|N_1| = 0, 1, \ldots, n$,

$$F(J, N_1) = \max_{j \in N_1} \left\{ \max_{0 \leq \pi_j \leq u} \left\{ \pi_j \left[p_j R_j(\pi_j) + F(J \cup \{j\}, N_1 \setminus \{j\}) \right] \right. \right.$$

$$\left. \left. + \left[(1 - \pi_j) F(J, N_1 \setminus \{j\}) \right] \right\} \right\}.$$

In the recurrence equation, every inquiry $j \in N_1$ and every possible order placement probability π_j are considered for price quotation decisions. The two possible events, an order placed with probability π_j and no order placed with probability $1 - \pi_j$, are considered in the expected revenue calculation. The recurrence equation considers the expected revenue explicitly, whereas the scheduling cost is included in the boundary condition.

Liu et al. (2012) show that algorithm DP-SEQG optimally solves the general sequential quotation problem in $O(n3^n)$ time, if an optimal π_j can be found via a constant number of computations for given j in the recurrence equation.

Given the exponential time complexity of the algorithms DP-SEQC and DP-SEQG, it is unlikely that they can solve large instances of problems SEQC and SEQG, respectively. Liu et al. (2012) therefore propose a heuristic algorithm. The heuristic first fixes a sequence for price quotation and order processing, and given this sequence finds an optimal price quotation solution.

Heuristic SEQ-FIX

Input:
Given $p_j, f_j(), R_j()$, for $j = 1, \ldots, n$, where inquiries are indexed according to a pre-specified sequence.

Value Function:
$F(t, j)$ = maximum expected total profit from the inquiries $j, \ldots, n$ with a start time t.

Boundary Condition:
$F(t, n + 1) = 0$.

Maximum Expected Profit:
$F(0, 1)$.

Recurrence Relation:
For $t = P, \ldots, 0$, and $j = n, \ldots, 1$:

$$F(t, j) = \max_{j \in N_1} \left\{ \max_{0 \leq \pi_j \leq u} \left\{ \pi_j \left[p_j R_j(\pi_j) - f_j(t + p_j) + F(t + p_j, j + 1) \right] \right. \right.$$

$$\left. \left. + \left[(1 - \pi_j) F(t, j + 1) \right] \right\} \right\}.$$

It can be seen that the time complexity of this algorithm is $O(n^2 P)$ if an optimal π_j can be found via a constant number of computations for given j in the recurrence equation.

Liu et al. (2012) conduct computational experiments of the above discussed algorithms for the corresponding problems where all the orders have the same weights, i.e., $w_1 = \cdots = w_n = w$. Their computational results show that the expected profit of an optimal solution of problem SEQC is quite close to that of the problem SEQG, based on a variety of test instances. This means that the advantage of the general quotation scheme over the consistent quotation scheme is small. However, the optimal expected profit of problem SIMQ often deviates a lot from those of problems SEQC and SEQG. This means that there is a big advantage to using sequential quotation over simultaneous quotation.

Liu et al. (2012) also test the performance of heuristic SEQ-FIX with shortest processing time (SPT) or longest processing time (LPT) sequence of the orders as the pre-specified sequence. The performance of the heuristic is mixed. Specifically, when w is small, the heuristic with SPT as the pre-specified sequence performs very well and can generate expected profit close to that of the optimal expected profit of problem SEQC. However, when w gets larger, the performance of the heuristic with SPT as the pre-specified sequence deteriorates. The performance of the heuristic with LPT as the pre-specified sequence is the opposite: it performs very well when w is large, but it performs poorly when w is small.

5.4 Multi-Period Problems

In this section, we discuss several CPPS problems with multiple periods studied by Yue et al. (2019). We first discuss the practical setting where their problems arise. Many manufacturers using a make-to-order strategy do not make customized products from scratch. Instead, they make customized products after receiving customer orders by customizing the last few steps of production based on a base product that is already made beforehand (Simchi-Levi et al., 2008). Motivated by this, Yue et al. (2019) assume that in their problems, a manufacturer makes multiple customized products from a common base product. They further assume that the price for each customized product is the price for the base product plus a given

5.4 Multi-Period Problems

differential for the specific customization involved, such that once the price for the base product is set, the price for each customized product is also set accordingly. The manufacturer uses dynamic pricing to match capacity with demand over a planning horizon consisting of multiple time periods. It needs to determine simultaneously a price for the base product and a production schedule for incoming orders at the beginning of each period over a given planning horizon, with the goal of maximizing its revenue while considering customer service.

Yue et al. (2019) give an example of the operations of a real company to justify their model assumptions. This company makes and sells a variety of customized canvas bags, mugs, T-shirts, and other consumer products and customizes its products by adding features to what it calls basic products, e.g., basic canvas bags and mugs without images printed on them. Customers can customize their orders at the company's website by choosing a basic product and specifying whether or not to have an image printed on the product and whether the image should be printed on one side or both sides of the product in case an image is needed. In order to achieve timely delivery, the company keeps a sufficient inventory of basic products, based on which customized products can be made quickly by adding customized features. The company uses a modular pricing scheme for most of its products such that the price for a customized product is equal to the price for the basic product plus the price for the added customized feature(s). Each available customized feature has a price that is often fixed and does not vary over time. For example, the price for having an image printed on one side of a bag is 17 RMB, whereas the price for having an image printed on both sides of a bag is 27 RMB. These prices remain unchanged regardless of how the basic product is priced. Thus, if the company prices a basic canvas bag at X, then it prices the same bag with an image printed on one side of the bag and the same bag with an image printed on both sides of the bag at $X + 17$, and $X + 27$, respectively. The company adjusts the prices for its products two to three times in each season, based on their demand forecasts and available capacity. To manage each product category, the company needs to adjust the price of the basic product involved (based on which all products in the category are made) periodically and create a production schedule so as to maximize its revenue subject to on-time delivery of orders.

The modular pricing scheme used by this company is also common practice in several other industries. For example, although automobile dealers may adjust the prices of the cars that they sell from time to time, they often fix prices for additional features that they sell, e.g., $750 for a sun roof and $2500 for a technology add-on. This means that if a basic car model without any add-ons is priced at $\$X$, then the same car with a sun roof and technology add-on is priced at $\$X + 3250$. Modular pricing schemes are easy to implement and simple for customers to understand. However, we are not aware of any existing models in the dynamic pricing literature (e.g., Elmaghraby & Keskinocak, 2003, Talluri & van Ryzin, 2004, and Chen & Chen, 2015) that study such pricing schemes.

To define the problems considered by Yue et al. (2019) precisely, we adopt the notation used in their paper. A manufacturer produces n customized products, $1, \ldots, n$, based on a common base product over a planning horizon with T time periods, $1, \ldots, T$, where the starting time of the horizon is zero and the length of each period is L time units (e.g., days), for some positive integer L. At the beginning of each period t, the manufacturer sets a price for the base product, which in turn determines the price for each customized product. Given the prices of the customized products, customers place orders at the beginning of the period. Let $p_1 > \cdots > p_m$ denote the m allowable prices that can be set for the base product in each period t. Suppose that $P_t \in \{p_1, \ldots, p_m\}$ is the price chosen by the manufacturer for the base product in period t. For product j ($j = 1, \ldots, n$), an additional price v_j is charged for the customization, where v_j is fixed and is not a decision variable. As a result, the actual price of product j in period t is $P_t + v_j$. Given the prices of the n products in period t, the demand for each product j in this period is a function of these prices. Since $P_t + v_j$ is determined by P_t for all products $j = 1, \ldots, n$, the demand for each product j in period t is then simply a function of the price of the base product P_t, denoted as $d_{tj}(P_t)$, which is assumed to be a nonnegative integer. All the incoming orders in a period arrive at the beginning of the period.

Each product j may be associated with an importance weight w_j. Each incoming order that arrives at time Z may be assigned a due date $Z + kL$, where kL (i.e., k time periods) can be viewed as the delivery lead time promised for the order. This represents a typical practice used by companies operating in a make-to-order business mode, which often promise a common delivery lead time for all incoming orders. The manufacturer may or may not accept all the incoming orders. If an incoming order of product j is accepted, then each unit of the order must be processed nonpreemptively for q_j time units on a single machine. Following common business practice, it is assumed that orders that arrive in an earlier period are always processed before orders that arrive in a later period. Note that the manufacturer makes the last pricing decision at the beginning of period T (i.e., at time $(T-1)L$), whereas the production process continues until all accepted orders in the last period are completed. The parameters defined here w_j, k, q_j are all positive integers.

Yue et al. (2019) consider the following three specific coordinated production pricing and scheduling problems with different order acceptance rules and objective functions:

- *Problem with total weighted completion time*: the manufacturer accepts and processes all incoming orders with the objective of maximizing the total revenue minus the total weighted completion time of the orders.
- *Problem with tardiness allowed*: the manufacturer accepts all incoming orders, but some incoming orders are allowed to be completed after their due dates with tardiness penalties. If an order is completed after its due date, there is a penalty of β units per unit of tardiness. The objective is to maximize the total profit, defined as the total revenue less the total tardiness penalty.
- *Problem with order rejection allowed*: the manufacturer is allowed to reject some incoming orders of each product, but all accepted orders must be completed no

5.4 Multi-Period Problems

later than their due dates. The objective is to maximize the total revenue from accepted orders.

Example 5.4 (An Instance and a Feasible Solution for Each Problem) We provide a numerical instance and a corresponding solution to illustrate each of the above defined problems. Consider an instance with $T = 3$ periods, each with $L = 24$ time units, $n = 2$ products, $m = 3$ allowable prices, which are $p_1 = 100$, $p_2 = 80$, and $p_3 = 60$. The demand for each product j is time-invariant and hence is written as $d_j(P_t)$, where P_t is the price of the base product set for period t. The parameters w_j, v_j, q_j, and $d_j(p_i)$ are given in the following table. Let $k = 1$, i.e., the common delivery lead time is L time units, which means that orders arriving at the beginning of period t ($t = 1, 2, 3$) have a due date equal to the end of the period. Let the unit tardiness penalty be $\beta = 10$.

Product j	v_j	w_j	q_j	$d_j(p_1)$	$d_j(p_2)$	$d_j(p_3)$
1	5	2	1	5	8	10
2	10	3	2	3	6	10

Given this instance, we construct a feasible solution to each of the three problems as follows. For all the problems, we set the price for each period $t = 1, 2, 3$ as $P_1 = p_3 = 60$, $P_2 = p_2 = 80$, and $P_3 = p_1 = 100$, respectively. Given these prices, in each period $t = 1, 2, 3$, the demand realizations for the two products over each period are as follows:

Product j	$d_j(P_1)$	$d_j(P_2)$	$d_j(P_3)$
1	10	8	5
2	10	6	3

For the first two problems, for which all the incoming orders must be processed, we use the following production schedule: in each period, after the remaining orders from previous periods are completed, we process the incoming orders of product 1 first, followed by the incoming order of product 2.

In this solution, the total revenue is $\sum_{j=1}^{2} \sum_{t=1}^{3} (P_t + v_j) d_j(P_t) = [(60 + 5)(10) + (80+5)(8) + (100+5)(5)] + [(60+10)(10) + (80+10)(6) + (100+10)(3)] = 1855 + 1570 = 3425$.

For the first problem, the total weighted completion time of the orders can be calculated as follows:

- In period 1, 10 incoming orders of product 1 are processed from time 0 to 10, and 10 incoming orders of product 2 are processed from time 10 to 30. Thus, the total completion time of the 10 orders of product 1 is $1+2+\cdots+10 = 55$. Similarly, the total completion time of the 10 orders of product 2 is $12+14+\cdots+30 = 210$.

Thus, the total weighted completion time of the orders that arrive in the first period is $55w_1 + 210w_2 = 55(2) + 210(3) = 740$.

- In period 2, eight incoming orders of product 1 are processed from time 30 to 38, and six incoming orders of product 2 are processed from time 38 to 50. Thus, the total completion time of the eight orders of product 1 is $31 + 32 + \cdots + 38 = 276$ and that of the six orders of product 2 is $40 + 42 + \cdots + 50 = 270$. Thus, the total weighted completion time of the orders that arrive in the second period is $276w_1 + 270w_2 = 276(2) + 270(3) = 1362$.

- In period 3, five incoming orders of product 1 are processed from time 50 to 55, and three incoming orders of product 2 are processed from time 55 to 61. Thus, the total completion time of the five orders of product 1 is $51 + 52 + \cdots + 55 = 265$ and that of the three orders of product 2 is $57 + 59 + 61 = 177$. Thus, the total weighted completion time of the orders that arrive in the third period is $265w_1 + 177w_2 = 265(2) + 177(3) = 1061$.

Thus, the total weighted completion time of all the orders is $740 + 1362 + 1061 = 3163$. Therefore, for the first problem, the total profit of this solution is $3425 - 3163 = 262$.

For the second problem, the total tardiness penalty can be calculated as follows. As calculated above, the completion time of the last order that arrives at the beginning of period 1 is 30, which implies that the last three orders of product 2 that arrive in the first period are tardy, each with a tardiness of 2, 4, and 6 units, respectively. Similarly, we can observe that the last order of product 2 that arrives in the second period is tardy with a tardiness of 2. None of the orders that arrive in the third period is tardy. Thus, the total tardiness penalty is $\beta(2 + 4 + 6 + 2) = 140$. Thus, for the second problem, the total profit of this solution is $3425 - 140 = 3285$.

For the third problem, we may have to reject some incoming orders so that all accepted orders complete processing by their due dates. Given the prices and the demand realizations as discussed above, some orders would be tardy if all the orders were accepted, as shown above. We construct a feasible solution as follows. Reject the last three orders of product 2 that arrive in the first period and accept all other incoming orders and use the same scheduling policy as above, i.e., in each period, accepted orders of product 1 are processed before those of product 2. This results in a completion time of 24 for the last order that arrives in the first period and a completion time of 44 for the last order that arrives in the second period. The orders that arrive in the third period must be processed from time 48 to 59. We can observe that this is a feasible solution. Thus, the total revenue of this solution for the third problem is $[(60 + 5)(10) + (80 + 5)(8) + (100 + 5)(5)] + [(60 + 10)(7) + (80 + 10)(6) + (100 + 10)(3)] = 1855 + 1360 = 3215$.

Yue et al. (2019) provide pseudo-polynomial time algorithms for solving all these problems and show that they are all NP-hard in the ordinary sense even with a single product, i.e., $n = 1$. They further provide an FPTAS for each of these problems. In Sects. 5.4.1, 5.4.2, and 5.4.3, we present the exact pseudo-polynomial time algorithms for all the problems, the NP-hardness proofs for two of the problems, and the FPTAS for one of the problems, respectively. In Sect. 5.4.4, we show some computational results and related managerial insights derived by Yue et al. (2019).

5.4.1 Exact Algorithms

In this section, we describe some optimality properties derived by Yue et al. (2019) for the three problems and the optimal pseudo-polynomial time dynamic programming algorithms developed by them for these problems based on these properties.

The following optimality properties for these problems are fairly straightforward and hence are stated without proofs.

Lemma 5.2

(i) *For the problem with total weighted completion time, the shortest weighted processing time (SWPT) rule is optimal for processing all incoming orders in each time period.*

(ii) *For the problem with tardiness allowed, it is optimal to process incoming orders in each period by the shortest processing time (SPT) rule.*

(iii) *For the problem with order rejection allowed, accepted orders in each period can be processed in an arbitrary sequence.*

The problem with total weighted completion time can be solved by the following dynamic programming algorithm.

Algorithm MP-DP1

Input: Given q_j, v_j, w_j, for $j = 1, \ldots, n$; and p_i, for $i = 1, \ldots, m$. Define S_t as the latest possible starting time for processing incoming orders in period t for $t = 1, \ldots, T$. The value of S_t can be calculated recursively as follows:
$S_1 = 0$, and
$S_t = \max\{(t-1)L, S_{t-1} + \sum_{j=1}^{n} d_{tj}(p_m)q_j\}$, for $t = 2, \ldots, T$.
Initialization: Reindex the products in SWPT order.
Value Function: $f_t(h)$ as the maximum total profit (i.e., the total revenue minus the total weighted completion time) from period t through period T, given that h is the starting time for processing incoming orders in period t.
Boundary Condition:
$f_{T+1}(h) = 0$, for $h > 0$;
$f_t(h) = -\infty$, if $h < (t-1)L$ or $h > S_t$, for $t = 1, \ldots, T$.
Optimal Solution Value: $f_1(0)$.
Recurrence Relation:
For $t = 1, \ldots, T$, and $(t-1)L \le h \le S_t$,

$$
f_t(h) = \max_{1 \le i \le m} \left\{ \sum_{j=1}^{n} d_{tj}(p_i)(p_i + v_j) - W_{hit} + f_{t+1}\left(\max\left\{ h + \sum_{j=1}^{n} d_{tj}(p_i)q_j, tL \right\} \right) \right\},
$$

where W_{hit} is the total weighted completion time of the orders that arrive in period t if the price is set at p_i in period t and the starting time for processing these orders is h. The value of W_{hit} is calculated as follows:

$$W_{hit} = \sum_{j=1}^{n} w_j \left(\sum_{r=1}^{d_{tj}(p_i)} C_{hijrt} \right),$$

where C_{hijrt} denotes the completion time of the rth incoming order for product j in period t if the price is set at p_i and the starting time is h, for $i = 1, \ldots, m$, $j = 1, \ldots, n, r = 1, \ldots, d_{tj}(p_i)$, and $t = 1, \ldots, T$, and is calculated as $C_{hijrt} = h + \sum_{l=1}^{j-1} d_{tl}(p_i)q_l + rq_j$.

The recurrence relation in Algorithm MP-DP1 compares all the m allowable prices for period t based on the total profit. Given price p_i, the term $\sum_{j=1}^{n} d_{tj}(p_i)(p_i + v_j)$ is the total revenue from the incoming orders in period t, and the term $\max\{h + \sum_{j=1}^{n} d_{tj}(p_i)q_j, tL\}$ is the starting time for processing the incoming orders in period $t + 1$.

Yue et al. (2019) show that Algorithm MP-DP1 finds an optimal solution for the problem with total weighted completion time in $O(mTS_T^2)$ time. This is therefore a pseudo-polynomial time algorithm. In Sect. 5.4.2 below, we show that the problem with the weighted completion time is NP-hard. This implies that Algorithm MP-DP1 is the best type of result achievable for this problem, unless $P = NP$.

Next, we describe the dynamic programming algorithm for the problem with tardiness allowed given in Yue et al. (2019).

Algorithm MP-DP2

Input: Given q_j, v_j, for $j = 1, \ldots, n$; and p_i, for $i = 1, \ldots, m$. Define S_t as the latest possible starting time for processing incoming orders in period t, for $t = 1, \ldots, T$. The value of S_t can be calculated in exactly the same way as in Algorithm MP-DP1.

Initialization: Reindex the products in SPT order.

Value Function: Define $f_t(h)$ as the maximum total revenue minus the total tardiness penalty from period t through period T, given that the starting time for processing the incoming orders in period t is h.

Boundary Condition:

$f_{T+1}(h) = 0$, for $h > 0$;

$f_t(h) = -\infty$, if $h < (t - 1)L$ or $h > S_t$, for $t = 1, \ldots, T$.

Optimal Solution Value: $f_1(0)$.

Recurrence Relation:

For $t = 1, \ldots, T$, and $(t - 1)L \leq h \leq S_t$,

$$f_t(h) = \max_{1 \leq i \leq m} \left\{ \sum_{j=1}^{n} d_{tj}(p_i)(p_i + v_j) - \beta g_{hit} + f_{t+1} \left(\max \left\{ (h + \sum_{j=1}^{n} d_{tj}(p_i)q_j, tL \right\} \right) \right\},$$

5.4 Multi-Period Problems

where g_{hit} is the total tardiness of the orders that arrive in period t when the price is set at p_i and the starting time for processing the incoming orders is h. As in Algorithm MP-DP1, define $C_{hijrt} = h + \sum_{l=1}^{j-1} d_{tl}(p_i)q_l + rq_j$ as the completion time of the rth incoming order for product j in period t when the price is set at p_i and the starting time is h, for $r = 1, \ldots, d_{tj}(p_i)$, $j = 1, \ldots, n$, $t = 1, \ldots, T$, and $i = 1, \ldots, m$. Thus, based on the fact that the due date of incoming orders in period t is $(t - 1 + k)L$, we have $g_{hit} = \sum_{j=1}^{n} \sum_{r=1}^{d_{tj}(p_i)} \max\{0, C_{hijrt} - (t - 1 + k)L\}$.

The recurrence relation of Algorithm MP-DP2 compares the net profits of all the m allowable prices for period t based on the total profit. Given price p_i, the term $\sum_{j=1}^{n} d_{tj}(p_i)(p_i + v_j)$ is the total revenue from the incoming orders in period t, and the term $\max\{h + \sum_{j=1}^{n} d_{tj}(p_i)q_j, tL\}$ is the starting time for processing the incoming orders in period $t + 1$.

Yue et al. (2019) show that Algorithm MP-DP2 finds an optimal solution for the problem with tardiness allowed in $O(mTS_T^2)$ time. Below in Sect. 5.4.2, we show that the problem with tardiness allowed is NP-hard. This implies that Algorithm MP-DP2 is the best type of result achievable for this problem, unless $P = NP$.

In the following, we describe the dynamic programming algorithm given in Yue et al. (2019) for finding an optimal solution to the problem with order rejection allowed.

Algorithm MP-DP3

Input: Given q_j, v_j, for $j = 1, \ldots, n$; and p_i, for $i = 1, \ldots, m$.
Initialization: Index the products in an arbitrary order.
Value Function: Define $f_t(h)$ = maximum total revenue from period t through period T, given that the starting time for processing the accepted orders in period t is h.
Boundary Condition:
   $f_{T+1}(h) = 0$, for $h > 0$;
   $f_t(h) = -\infty$, if $h < (t - 1)L$ or $h > (t - 2 + k)L$, for $t = 1, \ldots, T$.
Optimal Solution Value: $f_1(0)$.
Recurrence Relation:
For $t = 1, \ldots, T$, and $(t - 1)L \le h \le (t - 2 + k)L$,

$$f_t(h) = \max_{1 \le i \le m} \left\{ \max_{0 \le \tau_{hit} \le \bar{\tau}_{hit}} \{g(\tau_{hit}) + f_{t+1}(\max\{h + \tau'_{hit}, tL\})\} \right\},$$

where the parameters $\tau_{hit}, \bar{\tau}_{hit}, g(\tau_{hit})$, and τ'_{hit} are defined as follows: τ_{hit} is the maximum possible total processing time of accepted orders when the price set in period t is p_i and the processing starting time is h, $\bar{\tau}_{hit}$ is an upper bound of τ_{hit}, defined as $\bar{\tau}_{hit} = \min\{\sum_{j=1}^{n} d_{tj}(p_i)q_j, (t-1+k)L - h\}$, $g(\tau_{hit})$ is the total revenue from accepted orders in period t when the total processing time of accepted orders is no greater than τ_{hit}, and τ'_{hit} is the resulting total processing time of accepted orders. Given τ_{hit}, the value of $g(\tau_{hit})$ is the optimal objective value of the following bounded knapsack problem, where decision variable x_{jt} is the number of accepted orders for product j in period t.

$$\max \quad \sum_{j=1}^{n} (p_i + v_j) x_{jt}$$

$$\text{s.t.} \quad \sum_{j=1}^{n} q_j x_{jt} \leq \tau_{hit}$$

$$0 \leq x_{jt} \leq \min\{d_{tj}(p_i), \lfloor kL/q_j \rfloor\}, x_{jt} \text{ integer, for } j = 1, \ldots, n.$$

This knapsack problem can be solved using the dynamic programming algorithm given in (Kellerer et al., 2004, p. 190). Given the optimal solution of this knapsack problem x_{jt}^*, $\tau_{hit}' = \sum_{j=1}^{n} q_j x_{jt}$.

The recurrence relation of Algorithm MP-DP3 compares all the m allowable prices for period t based on the total revenue of accepted orders. Given price p_i, the algorithm selects an optimal maximum total processing time τ_{hit} for accepted orders and determines the optimal number of accepted orders x_{jt} for each product by solving the above defined bounded knapsack problem. Finally, all accepted orders are scheduled in arbitrary order. In the recurrence relation, the term $\max\{h + \tau_{hit}', tL\}$ is the starting time for processing the accepted orders in period $t + 1$, where $h + \tau_{hit}'$ is the completion time of the accepted orders in period t.

Define $V = \min\left\{\max_{1 \leq t \leq T}\left\{\sum_{j=1}^{n} d_{tj}(p_m)q_j\right\}, kL\right\}$. It can be seen that V is an upper bound on $\bar{\tau}_{hit}$. To solve the bounded knapsack problem, the dynamic programming algorithm given in Kellerer et al. (2004) has a running time of $O(nV \log V)$.

Yue et al. (2019) show that Algorithm MP-DP3 finds an optimal solution for the problem with order rejection allowed in $O(mnkLTV^2 \log V)$ time. As in the case for Algorithms MP-DP1 and MP-DP2, this algorithm is the best type of result achievable for this problem unless $P = NP$.

5.4.2 *NP-Hardness Proofs*

We show below the NP-hardness proofs given by Yue et al. (2019) for the first two problems. The NP-hardness of the third problem can be proved similarly to the second problem and hence is not provided.

Theorem 5.9 *The problem with total weighted completion time is ordinarily NP-hard, even if the manufacturer produces only a single product, i.e., $n = 1$.*

5.4 Multi-Period Problems

Proof We show below that this problem is at least ordinarily NP-hard, which, together with the pseudo-polynomial time algorithm MP-DP1 given in Sect. 5.4.1, implies that this problem is exactly ordinarily NP-hard. We use a reduction from the partition problem, a well-known NP-hard problem (Garey & Johnson, 1979). Partition Problem: Given a set of u elements $U = \{1, \dots, u\}$, a positive integer a_j associated with each element $j \in U$, and $\sum_{j=1}^{u} a_j = A$, do there exist two disjoint subsets U_1 and U_2 of U such that $\sum_{j \in U_1} a_j = \sum_{j \in U_2} a_j = \frac{1}{2}A$?

Construct an instance of the problem with a single product as follows:

- The number of time periods is $T = u$, with the length of each period $L = A$ time units.
- The number of allowable prices in each period is $m = 2$, with prices $p_1 = A^2 + 2A + 2$ and $p_2 = A^2 + 2A$.
- Demand corresponding to each price p_i in period t is denoted as D_{ti}, for $i = 1, 2$ and $t = 1, \dots, u$. Let $D_{t1} = Aa_t$ and $D_{t2} = (A + 2)a_t$, for $t = 1, \dots, u$.
- Each order of the product has a processing time $q = 1$.
- For the product, the additional charge is $v = \frac{1}{2}$, and the unit weight of completion time is $w = 1$.
- Threshold value for the total profit is $Z = \frac{1}{2}A^4 + 2A^3 + \frac{5}{2}A^2$.

We first formulate the objective function. Since there is only one product, all incoming orders in each period can be processed in an arbitrary sequence. Also, since the demand in each period under any price is greater than the length of the period, all orders over the planning horizon are processed consecutively without any idle time. Let P_t and $d_t(P_t)$ be the price and the demand in period t, respectively, and let C_{jt} denote the completion time of the jth order in period t, for $j = 1, \dots, d_t(P_t)$ and $t = 1, \dots, u$. The total weighted completion time over u time periods can be written as

$$\sum_{t=1}^{u} \sum_{j=1}^{d_t(P_t)} C_{jt} = \sum_{t=1}^{u} \left[d_t(P_t) \sum_{j=1}^{t-1} d_j(P_j) + \frac{1}{2} d_t(P_t)(d_t(P_t) + 1) \right]$$

$$= \frac{1}{2} \left[\sum_{t=1}^{u} d_t(P_t) \right]^2 + \frac{1}{2} \sum_{t=1}^{u} d_t(P_t).$$

Thus, the objective function is

$$\sum_{t=1}^{u} (P_t + v) d_t(P_t) - \sum_{t=1}^{u} \sum_{j=1}^{d_t(P_t)} C_{jt} = \sum_{t=1}^{u} P_t d_t(P_t) - \frac{1}{2} \left[\sum_{t=1}^{u} d_t(P_t) \right]^2. \tag{5.15}$$

In the following, we prove that there is a solution to the above instance of our problem with the objective value greater than or equal to Z if and only if there is a solution to the instance of the Partition Problem.

$(\Rightarrow)$ If there exist two disjoint subsets U_1 and U_2 of U such that $\sum_{j\in U_1} a_j = \sum_{j\in U_2} a_j = \frac{1}{2}A$, we construct a solution to the instance of our problem as follows. Set the price P_t for period t as $P_t = p_1$ if $t \in U_1$ and $P_t = p_2$ if $t \in U_2$, for $t = 1, \ldots, u$. Thus, by (5.15), the objective value of this solution is

$$
\sum_{t\in U_1} p_1 D_{t1} + \sum_{t\in U_2} p_2 D_{t2} - \frac{1}{2}\left[\sum_{t\in U_1} D_{t1} + \sum_{t\in U_2} D_{t2}\right]^2
$$

$$
= \sum_{t\in U_1} Aa_t(A^2 + 2A + 2) + \sum_{t\in U_2} (A+2)a_t(A^2 + 2A) - \frac{1}{2}\left[\sum_{t\in U_1} Aa_t + \sum_{t\in U_2} (A+2)a_t\right]^2
$$

$$
= \frac{1}{2}A^4 + 2A^3 + \frac{5}{2}A^2 = Z.
$$

$(\Leftarrow)$ In a solution to the instance of our problem with the total profit greater than or equal to Z, let U_1 denote the set of periods that are priced at p_1 and U_2 denote the set of periods that are priced at p_2. Thus, there are Aa_t incoming orders in each period $t \in U_1$ and $(A+2)a_t$ incoming orders in each period $t \in U_2$. Let $E = \sum_{j\in U_2} a_j$. Then, by (5.15), the total profit in this solution is

$$
\sum_{t\in U_1} Aa_t(A^2 + 2A + 2) + \sum_{t\in U_2} (A+2)a_t(A^2 + 2A) - \frac{1}{2}\left[\sum_{t\in U_1} Aa_t + \sum_{t\in U_2} (A+2)a_t\right]^2
$$

$$
= A^4 + 2A^3 + 2A^2 + 2(A^2 + A)E - \frac{1}{2}(A^2 + 2E)^2
$$

$$
= Z - 2\left(\frac{A}{2} - E\right)^2.
$$

Since the total profit has to be greater than or equal to Z, we have $-2(\frac{A}{2} - E)^2 \geq 0$, which implies that $E = \frac{1}{2}A$ and $\sum_{j\in U_1} a_j = \sum_{j\in U_2} a_j = \frac{1}{2}A$. This completes the proof. $\square$

Next, we provide a similar result for the problem with tardiness allowed, but with a quite different proof technique.

Theorem 5.10 *The problem with tardiness allowed is ordinarily NP-hard, even if there is only a single customized product, i.e., $n = 1$.*

Proof We show below that this problem is at least ordinarily NP-hard, which, together with the pseudo-polynomial time algorithm MP-DP2 given in Sect. 5.4.1, implies that this problem is exactly ordinarily NP-hard. We use a reduction from the Subset Sum (SS) problem, another well-known NP-hard problem (Garey & Johnson, 1979).

5.4 Multi-Period Problems

SS: Given a set of u elements, $U = \{1, \ldots, u\}$, a positive integer a_j associated with each element $j \in U$, and a positive integer B, does there exist a subset S of U such that $\sum_{j \in S} a_j = B$?

Let $A = \sum_{j \in U} a_j$ and $H = M^1 + M^2 + \cdots + M^u + B$, where M is a sufficiently large positive integer (e.g., $M = A^u$) such that $M > uA$ and $M^i > M^1 + 2M^2 + \cdots + (i - 1)M^{i-1} + B$, for any $i = 2, \ldots, u$. We construct an instance of our problem with a single product based on the above instance of SS as follows:

- The number of time periods is $T = u$ with the length of each period $L = H$ time units.
- The number of allowable prices in each period is $m = 2u$, with prices $p_{2i-1} = \frac{1}{H+M^i} + \frac{1}{2}$ and $p_{2i} = \frac{1}{H+M^i+a_i} + \frac{1}{2}$, for $i = 1, \ldots, u$.
- Demand corresponding to each allowable price is time-invariant and denoted as D_j for price p_j, $j = 1, \ldots, 2u$, where $D_{2i-1} = H + M^i$ and $D_{2i} = H + M^i + a_i$, for $i = 1, \ldots, u$.
- Each order has a processing time of $q = 1$ time unit. The due date of an order that arrives at the beginning of time period t is $(t + 1)L$, for $t = 1, \ldots, T$, i.e., $k = 2$.
- The additional charge for the product is $v = \frac{1}{2}$.
- The penalty per time unit of tardiness is $\beta = (u + 1)H + u$.
- Threshold value for the total revenue minus the total tardiness penalty is $Z = (u + 1)H + u$.

Clearly, the above instance can be constructed in polynomial time. In this instance, by construction, the following hold: $p_1 > \cdots > p_{2u}$, $D_1 < \cdots < D_{2u}$, and $(p_1 + v)D_1 < \cdots < (p_{2u} + v)D_{2u}$.

In the following, we prove that there is a solution to the above instance of our problem with the total profit greater than or equal to Z if and only if there is a solution to the instance of SS.

($\Rightarrow$) If there is a subset S of U such that $\sum_{j \in S} a_j = B$, we construct a solution to the instance of our problem as follows. Set the price in period i as $P_i = p_{2i-1}$ if $i \notin S$ and $P_i = p_{2i}$ if $i \in S$, for $i = 1, \ldots, T$. Process all the incoming orders in an arbitrary sequence. It can be seen that in the constructed solution, none of the orders that arrive in the first $T - 1$ periods are tardy. The total demand over T time periods is

$$\sum_{i \in S} D_{2i} + \sum_{i \in U \setminus S} D_{2i-1} = \sum_{i \in S} (H + M^i + a_i) + \sum_{i \in U \setminus S} (H + M^i)$$

$$= uH + (M^1 + M^2 + \cdots + M^u) + B = (u + 1)H.$$

Thus, the completion time of the last order is equal to $(T + 1)L$, which is the due date of the orders that arrive in the last period. Hence, none of these orders are tardy.

232   5   Coordinated Product Pricing and Scheduling Decisions

The total revenue of the orders processed is thus

$$\sum_{i \in S} (p_{2i} + v) D_{2i} + \sum_{i \in U \setminus S} (p_{2i-1} + v) D_{2i-1}$$

$$= \sum_{i \in S} (H + M^i + a_i + 1) + \sum_{i \in U \setminus S} (H + M^i + 1)$$

$$= (u + 1)H + u = Z.$$

Since there is no tardiness penalty, the total profit of the constructed solution for the instance of our problem is equal to the threshold value Z.

($\Leftarrow$) If there is a solution to the instance of our problem with a total profit greater than or equal to Z, we prove by induction that for each $i = 1, \ldots, u$, there is exactly one period where one of the two prices p_{2i-1} and p_{2i} is used. We first prove the result for $i = u$ by contradiction. Suppose that none of the two prices p_{2u-1} and p_{2u} are used. In each period, the maximum revenue earned is at most $(p_{2u-2} + v) D_{2u-2} = H + M^{u-1} + a_{u-1} + 1$. Thus, the total revenue is at most $uH + uM^{u-1} + uA + u < Z$. This shows that at least one of these two prices is used for some period. Now, suppose that there are at least two periods where one of these prices is used. This results in a total demand of at least $uH + 2M^u > (u + 1)H$. Since the due date of the last batch of orders (that arrive at the beginning of the last period) is $(u + 1)H$, this implies that some orders are tardy. Given the large unit tardiness penalty β, this means that the total profit is less than Z. By contradiction, this shows that there is exactly one period where one of the two prices p_{2u-1} and p_{2u} is used.

Now, suppose that, for some $1 \leq j \leq u - 1$, there is exactly one period where one of the two prices p_{2i-1} and p_{2i} is used, for each $i = u, \ldots, j + 1$. We prove that the same result holds for $i = j$. The total demand over the $u - j$ time periods where one of the $2(u - j)$ prices $p_{2u}, p_{2u-1}, \ldots, p_{2j+2}, p_{2j+1}$ is used is at least $e_1 = H(u-j) + \sum_{i=j+1}^{u} M^i$, and the total revenue over these periods is at most $e_2 = H(u - j) + \sum_{i=j+1}^{u} M^i + (u - j)(A + 1)$. Suppose that there is no period where one of the two prices p_{2j-1} and p_{2j} is used. The revenue earned in any of the j time periods where a price p_i with $i < 2j-1$ is used is less than $H + M^{j-1} + A + 1$. Thus, the total revenue across all time periods is at most $e_2 + Hj + jM^{j-1} + j(A+1) < Z$. Now suppose that there are at least two periods where one of the two prices p_{2j-1} and p_{2j} is used. The total demand over the j time periods where a price other than $p_{2u}, p_{2u-1}, \ldots, p_{2j+2}, p_{2j+1}$ is used is at least $jH + 2M^j$. Thus, the total demand across all the time periods is at least $e_1 + jH + 2M^j > (u + 1)H$. This implies that some orders are tardy. Given the value of unit tardiness penalty β, this means that the total profit is less than Z. This shows that there is exactly one period where one of the two prices p_{2j-1} and p_{2j} is used. Therefore, by induction, we have proved that there is exactly one period where one of the two prices p_{2i-1} and p_{2i} is used for each $i = 1, \ldots, u$.

5.4 Multi-Period Problems

Define a subset $S \subseteq U$ such that for each $i \in S$, price p_{2i} is used in some period in the given solution for the instance of our problem. The subset $U \setminus S$ includes the indices i such that price p_{2i-1} is used in some period. The total revenue of the solution is

$$\sum_{i \in S}(H + M^i + a_i + 1) + \sum_{i \in U \setminus S}(H + M^i + 1) = uH + (M^1 + \ldots + M^u) + u + \sum_{i \in S} a_i.$$

Since this total revenue is at least Z, we can conclude that $\sum_{i \in S} a_i \geq B$, and there are no tardy orders in the solution. The total demand in this solution is

$$\sum_{i \in S}(H + M^i + a_i) + \sum_{i \in U \setminus S}(H + M^i) = uH + (M^1 + \ldots + M^u) + \sum_{i \in S} a_i.$$

Since there are no tardy orders, the total demand must be no more than the largest due date $(u+1)H$. This means that $\sum_{i \in S} a_i \leq B$, and hence we have $\sum_{i \in S} a_i = B$.

$\square$

5.4.3 Approximation Algorithm

In this section, we describe the FPTAS developed by Yue et al. (2019) for the problem with total weighted completion time. The FPTASs they develop for the other two problems use similar techniques and hence are not presented here.

We first describe a preliminary result without showing the proof. Let F^* be the optimal profit for the problem with total weighted completion time.

Lemma 5.3 *In the problem with total weighted completion time, the optimal profit F^* satisfies $F_0 \leq F^* \leq T F_0$, where*

$$F_0 = \max_{1 \leq i \leq m, 1 \leq t \leq T} \left\{ \sum_{j=1}^{n} d_{tj}(p_i)(p_i + v_j) - W_{it} \right\},$$

and

$$W_{it} = \sum_{j=1}^{n} w_j \left[\sum_{r=1}^{d_{tj}(p_i)} \left((t-1)L + \sum_{l=1}^{j-1} d_{tl}(p_i)q_l + rq_j \right) \right]$$

is the total weighted completion time of the orders that arrive in a single period t if price p_i is used in this period and the starting time for processing the orders is the beginning time of period t (i.e., time $(t-1)L$).

The idea of the FPTAS provided by Yue et al. (2019) for the problem with total weighted completion time is similar to that of the FPTAS given in Sect. 5.2.3.1 for the problem with a single period studied there. The FPTAS is based on a redesigned dynamic programming algorithm for the problem and applies a state space trimming technique to ensure that the DP can run in polynomial time. The new dynamic programming algorithm differs from Algorithm MP-DP1 by defining states differently and using a labeling scheme to handle the states. The new DP algorithm uses state (t, C, R) to indicate a partial schedule where periods $1, \ldots, t$ have been considered, the completion time of the last order is C, and the profit is R. For states (t, C, R), we label them based on the value of profit R. Given multiple states $(t, C_1, R), (t, C_2, R), \ldots$ with the same t and same label (i.e., the same profit value R), we only keep the state with the smallest completion time of the last order and eliminate all the other such states.

Algorithm MP-APP

Input: all parameters of the problem with total weighted completion time and the approximation precision parameter $\epsilon > 0$.

State Variables: (t, C, R) corresponds to a partial schedule that has considered periods $1, \ldots, t$ and has the total completion time (or makespan) C and profit R.

Initialization: Reindex the products in SWPT order. Define F_0 as in Lemma 5.3, and partition the profit dimension R in the state space into intervals with equal length $\Delta = \epsilon F_0 / T$.

Initial State: $(0, 0, 0)$.

Forward Recursion:

For $t = 0, \ldots, T - 1$, run the following steps:

(1) *State Generation*. For each state (t, C, R), generate m trial states $(t + 1, C', R')$ by pricing the base product in period $t+1$ at p_i and then scheduling all the incoming orders in SWPT order, for $i = 1, \ldots, m$.

(2) *State Labeling*. For each state $(t + 1, C', R')$, attach the label $(t + 1, \Delta i)$ if the value of the profit R' satisfies $i \Delta \leq R' < (i + 1)\Delta$, where $i = 0, 1, \ldots$.

(3) *State Elimination*. For any two partial schedules $(t + 1, C'_1, R'_1)$ and $(t + 1, C'_2, R'_2)$ with identical labels, i.e., $R'_1 = R'_2$, eliminate the second schedule if $C'_1 \leq C'_2$ and the first schedule otherwise.

Optimal Solution: Select a state (T, C, R) for which R is the largest, and backtrack the forward recursion process to find the corresponding solution σ_ϵ.

In Algorithm MP-APP, the initialization step sets the value of Δ such that $T F_0 = \Delta T^2 / \epsilon$, where from Lemma 5.3, F_0 is a lower bound on the optimal profit. For each period $t = 1, \ldots, T$, the forward recursion step first generates trial states by choosing the price and scheduling all incoming orders, then labels each trial state based on the profit value, and finally eliminates trial states by comparing the makespan of all trial states with the same label, keeping one with the smallest value, and discards all the others. The final step obtains the optimal solution by selecting a state with the largest total profit over all time periods and backtracking the forward recursion process.

5.4 Multi-Period Problems

Theorem 5.11 *For any $\epsilon > 0$, Algorithm MP-APP is an FPTAS for the problem with total weighted completion time with $O(n \log n + mT^3/\epsilon)$ running time.*

Proof We prove the theorem by induction on the number of time periods t. The induction hypothesis is that, given any state (t, C, R) that is obtained under the exact dynamic program Algorithm MP-DP1, Algorithm MP-APP generates a state $(t, \tilde{C}, \tilde{R})$, where $\tilde{C} \leq C$ and $\tilde{R} \geq R - t\Delta$. The hypothesis clearly holds for $t = 0$. Suppose that the hypothesis holds for $t = 0, 1, \ldots, l$. Now, we prove that for any state $(l + 1, C', R')$ generated in Algorithm MP-DP1, there is a state $(l + 1, \tilde{C}', \tilde{R}')$ generated by Algorithm MP-APP such that $\tilde{C}' \leq C'$ and $\tilde{R}' \geq R' - (l + 1)\Delta$.

Let (l, C, R) be the state in Algorithm MP-DP1 from which $(l + 1, C', R')$ is generated by applying price p_i, for some $1 \leq i \leq m$, and scheduling all the $d_{l+1}(p_i)$ orders in period $l + 1$. From the induction hypothesis, we have a state $(l, \tilde{C}, \tilde{R})$ generated in the approximate program where $\tilde{C} \leq C$ and $\tilde{R} \geq R - l\Delta$. In Algorithm MP-APP, for a trial state $(l + 1, \tilde{C}', \tilde{R}')$ that is generated from $(l, \tilde{C}, \tilde{R})$ by pricing in period $l + 1$ at p_i and scheduling $d_{l+1}(p_i)$ orders, we prove the following two claims.

Claim (i): $\tilde{C}' \leq C'$. Since $\tilde{C} \leq C$ and the same orders are added in Algorithm MP-DP1 and Algorithm MP-APP, the increase in the makespan in Algorithm MP-APP is no more than that in Algorithm MP-DP1, i.e., $\tilde{C}' \leq C'$. This proves Claim (i).

Claim (ii): $\tilde{R}' \geq R' - (l + 1)\Delta$. In both Algorithm MP-DP1 and Algorithm MP-APP, the total revenue of incoming orders in period $l + 1$ is $\delta = \sum_{j=1}^{n} d_{l+1,j}(p_i)(p_i + v_j)$. Let W' and $\tilde{W}'$ be the total weighted completion time in period $l + 1$ under Algorithm MP-DP1 and Algorithm MP-APP, respectively. Then, according to the trial state generation process, for state $(l + 1, C', R')$, we have $R' = R + \delta - W'$. For state $(l + 1, \tilde{C}', \tilde{R}')$, we have $\tilde{R}' = \tilde{R} + \delta - \tilde{W}'$.

Due to the fact that $\tilde{C}' \leq C'$ and the same orders are added in Algorithm MP-DP1 and Algorithm MP-APP, we have $\tilde{W}' \leq W'$. These relations, together with the induction hypothesis $\tilde{R} \geq R - l\Delta$, imply that $\tilde{R}' \geq R' - (l + 1)\Delta$. This proves Claim (ii).

If the trial state $(l + 1, \tilde{C}', \tilde{R}')$ is not eliminated, then this state is what we need in our induction proof and satisfies $\tilde{C}' \leq C'$ and $\tilde{R}' \geq R' - (l + 1)\Delta$. If this state is eliminated, then there is another state $(l + 1, \bar{C}, \bar{R})$ such that $\bar{C} \leq \tilde{C}'$ and $\bar{R} \geq \tilde{R}' - \Delta$. Thus, $\bar{C} \leq C'$ and $\bar{R} \geq R' - (l + 1)\Delta$, and state $(l + 1, \bar{C}, \bar{R})$ is what we need in our induction proof.

We now show that Algorithm MP-APP delivers a solution with the required performance guarantee. Let the state (T, C^*, R^*) correspond to an optimal solution σ^* with total profit R^* in Algorithm MP-DP1. Then, the above induction argument shows that Algorithm MP-APP generates a solution σ_ϵ and a corresponding state $(T, \tilde{C}, \tilde{R})$ with total profit $\tilde{R}$, where $\tilde{R} \geq R^* - T\Delta$. From Lemma 5.3 and the definition of Δ, we have $(R^* - \tilde{R})/R^* \leq T\Delta/R^* \leq \epsilon$. Therefore, according to the Optimal Solution step of Algorithm MP-APP, the optimal profit $\tilde{R}^*$ in the optimal solution σ_ϵ^* generated by Algorithm MP-APP satisfies $(R^* - \tilde{R}^*)/R^* \leq \epsilon$.

Finally, we analyze the time complexity of Algorithm MP-APP. First, Algorithm MP-APP sequences all products in SWPT order, which requires $O(n \log n)$ time.

Next, we evaluate the number of states (i.e., labels) in the forward recursion step. In this step, for each period, from the definition of Δ and Lemma 5.3, the number of labels to generate trial states is no more than T^2/ϵ and each label generates at most m trial states. Since there are T periods, the total number of labels is bounded by $O(mT^3/\epsilon)$. Hence, the overall time complexity of the approximation algorithm is $O(n \log n + mT^3/\epsilon)$, which is a polynomial function of n, m, T, and $1/\epsilon$. $\qquad\square$

5.4.4 Computational Results and Managerial Insights

In this section, we summarize the computational results obtained by Yue et al. (2019) on the performance of the exact dynamic programming algorithms and FPTAS for the three problems studied. We also present managerial insights from these results. For ease of presentation, we denote the three problems—the problem with total weighted completion time, the problem with tardiness allowed, and the problem with order rejection allowed—as TWC, TA, and ORA, respectively.

Yue et al. (2019) conduct an extensive set of computational experiments on randomly generated test instances of all the three problems with a number of time periods T varying from 4 to 8, a number of products n from 5 to 20, and a number of price levels m from 2 to 6. Half of the instances have a small demand, which involves, on average, 11 to 3 incoming orders for each product in each period when n goes from 5 to 20. The other half of the instances have a large demand, which involves, on average, 18 to 5 incoming orders for each product in each period when n goes from 5 to 20.

Their computational results show that for any test instance of the first two problems TWC and TA, their exact algorithms given in Sect. 5.4.2 find optimal solutions quickly. This means that we can rely on these algorithms to solve the first two problems and do not need to use approximation algorithms when the problem instance has a similar size or even slightly larger size than those tested by Yue et al. (2019).

For problem ORA, however, their test results show that the exact algorithm MP-DP3 given in Sect. 5.4.2 can be very time-consuming, especially for instances with a large demand and a large number of time periods. They therefore conduct further computational experiments to evaluate the performance of their FPTAS for problem ORA. Their test results show that (1) the FPTAS takes significantly less time than the optimal DP algorithm for all test instances, (2) the FPTAS with the allowed error $\epsilon = 20\%$ generates solutions within 10% optimality gap for all test instances with a small demand and most test instances with a large demand, and (3) the FPTAS with the allowed error $\epsilon = 40\%$ generates solutions within 15% optimality gap for all test instances with a small demand and most test instances with a large demand. Consequently, it can be concluded that the FPTAS developed for the problem ORA generates near-optimal solutions in much shorter times than the exact algorithm MP-DP3.

5.4 Multi-Period Problems

For managerial insights, we first discuss the relationship between the number of price levels (i.e., m) and the total profit over the planning horizon. In their experiments, the number of price levels tested varies from 1 to 7. The average percentage gap of the total profit under a smaller value of m relative to the total profit under a larger value of m is calculated. The average gaps based on test instances with $T = 8$, $n = 20$ and large demand are shown in Table 5.2, where each percentage gap value shown for row $m = x$ and column $m = y$ is the relative percentage deviation of the optimal total profit of the problem with $m = x$, compared to that of the same problem with $m = y$. Similar experimental results are observed across other values of the parameters T and n and other sizes of demand.

From Table 5.2, we can make the following observations. For problems TWC and TA, when the number of price levels m increases from 1 to 2 or higher or from 2 to 3 or higher, there is a significant increase in the total profit, more than 45% for problem TWC in most cases and more than 15% for problem TA in many cases. However, when m increases from 3 or 4 to a higher value, there is only a small increase in the total profit, less than 5% in most cases of TWC and TA. For problem ORA, when m increases from 1 to a higher value, the total profit shows a big increase, but when m increases from 2 or more to a higher value, there is little change in total profit.

For all the three problems, when there are three price levels, the total profit that can be generated is already very close to the profit that can be generated when there are more price levels. Therefore, in practice, using three price levels (e.g.,

Table 5.2 Percentage gap of total profits under different values of m

	Problem	$m = 2$	$m = 3$	$m = 4$	$m = 5$	$m = 6$	$m = 7$
$m = 1$	TWC	0.9%	45.7%	46.3%	47.8%	48.4%	49.0%
	TA	5.0%	15.2%	16.8%	17.6%	18.5%	18.7%
	ORA	7.6%	8.5%	10.2%	11.2%	12.3%	12.4%
$m = 2$	TWC		45.1%	45.8%	47.3%	47.8%	48.4%
	TA		10.2%	11.9%	12.7%	13.7%	14.0%
	ORA		1.0%	2.8%	3.9%	5.0%	5.1%
$m = 3$	TWC			1.1%	3.5%	4.5%	6.0%
	TA			1.7%	2.5%	3.5%	3.8%
	ORA			1.9%	2.9%	4.1%	4.2%
$m = 4$	TWC				2.5%	3.4%	5.0%
	TA				0.9%	1.9%	2.2%
	ORA				1.1%	2.2%	2.4%
$m = 5$	TWC					1.0%	2.5%
	TA					1.1%	1.3%
	ORA					1.2%	1.4%
$m = 6$	TWC						1.6%
	TA						0.3%
	ORA						0.2%

Table 5.3 Benefits of dynamic pricing compared with constant pricing

Problem	Demand	$T = 4$			$T = 6$			$T = 8$		
		$n = 5$	$n = 10$	$n = 20$	$n = 5$	$n = 10$	$n = 20$	$n = 5$	$n = 10$	$n = 20$
TWC	Small	10.4%	31.3%	27%	40.2%	11%	14.8%	19%	35.3%	29.7%
	Large	14.1%	13.7%	17.1%	10.1%	20%	27.8%	19%	20.1%	18.5%
TA	Small	5.9%	6.3%	4.5%	7.8%	9.2%	10.4%	8.1%	6.2%	5.3%
	Large	5.4%	3.9%	5.3%	13.5%	7.8%	4.4%	13.5%	10.6%	23.1%
ORA	Small	4.3%	13.1%	16.2%	12.5%	10.8%	14.2%	5.8%	5.1%	7.5%
	Large	3.9%	9.1%	8.9%	10.3%	5.3%	11.5%	12.2%	7.7%	6.7%

a low price, a medium price, and a high price) should be sufficient to generate a near-optimal total profit. In fact, in practice, practitioners may prefer to use a small number of price levels for several reasons. With a small number of price levels, it is generally not as time-consuming to solve the problem as with a large number of price levels. Also, the solution obtained with a small number of price levels generally involves less frequent price changes over time and hence is easier to implement and less annoying to customers, as compared to the solution for the case with a large number of price levels.

Finally, we discuss the benefits of dynamic pricing policy by comparing the total profit that can be generated in the current problems where dynamic pricing is used and the total profit that can be generated in the same problems using a constant pricing policy. Under a constant pricing policy, a single price is used for all the time periods, and the allowable price that yields the maximum total profit is adopted. Table 5.3 shows the average percentage gap between the total profit generated from the constant pricing policy and the total profit generated from the current problems, as reported in Yue et al. (2019). We observe that for all the three problems, compared to the constant pricing policy, the dynamic pricing policy generates more profit for firms under any parameter combination of T, n, and demand size. Dynamic pricing yields an average of 20% more profit for problem TWC and an average of 10% more profit for both problems TA and ORA.

Table 5.4 shows the average number of price changes over the planning horizon in the optimal solution of the current problems. It can be seen that in the optimal solution of these problems, the price is indeed dynamically adjusted over time. Specifically, on average, one or two price changes occur over the planning horizon for the problem TWC, and two or three price changes occur for the problems TA and ORA.

These results indicate that when a is faced with a production capacity limit and changing demand over time, dynamic pricing is a useful tool to match supply with demand and achieve satisfactory performance.

Table 5.4 Average number of price changes

Problem	Demand	T = 4			T = 6			T = 8		
		$n = 5$	$n = 10$	$n = 20$	$n = 5$	$n = 10$	$n = 20$	$n = 5$	$n = 10$	$n = 20$
TWC	Small	1.8	1.8	1.3	1.9	2	1.9	1.9	2.2	3.3
	Large	1.6	1	0.7	0.9	0.8	1.5	1.1	0.2	1.4
TA	Small	2.2	1.6	1.9	3	3.2	3.1	3.9	2.3	4
	Large	1.6	1.9	1.8	2.9	2.4	2.3	2.4	4	3.3
ORA	Small	1.6	1.9	1.8	2.9	2.4	2.3	2.4	4	3.3
	Large	2.1	1.2	2.5	2.2	2.5	2.9	3.7	4.6	5.7

5.5 Future Research

Most existing models on coordinated pricing and scheduling involve independent products or orders with simple demand functions, special scheduling cost functions such as total weighted completion time, and a single-machine production environment.

In the following, we highlight some possible new problem classes as future research topics.

- Problems with a parallel-machine or a job-shop production environment have not been studied. For problems with a parallel-machine environment, when the number of parallel machines is fixed, it is likely that the algorithms presented in Sects. 5.2 and 5.4 can be extended and may still be computationally efficient. However, when the number of machines is arbitrary, most of the ordinarily NP-hard problems shown earlier may become strongly NP-hard.
- In make-to-order environments, where customers are waiting to receive their completed orders, tardiness is an important customer service measure, and hence tardiness related cost functions deserve more research. For example, one can consider the total weighted tardiness of orders as the cost function in the single-period problem setting studied in Sect. 5.2. Another example is that one can use the weighted number of late orders as the cost function in the multi-period problem setting considered in Sect. 5.4.
- Problems with stochastic or unknown demand functions have received little attention. One can borrow some existing demand models for multiple products from the dynamic pricing literature (e.g., Chen & Chen, 2015). Demand for a product can be stochastic with a known probability distribution as a function of the prices of the products or can be uncertain with limited information (e.g., only the support of the demand distribution is known). In the latter case, robust optimization may be used to address the underlying problem (e.g., Chen & Chen, 2018). It would be valuable to see how some of the existing multi-product dynamic pricing models can be extended to include job scheduling decisions.
- Problems where different products or orders are correlated, e.g., substitutable or complementary, have not been studied. In reality, however, it is common that

demand for one product is often correlated with the demand for another product. In such cases, the demand functions are much more complex. One can use some existing models from the dynamic pricing literature (e.g., Chen & Chen, 2015) for multiple products that are inter-dependent.

- Problems involving multiple stages of price quotation decisions have not been considered. Such problems extend from the single-stage price quotation problems discussed in Sect. 5.3.
- In addition to price quotation, one could also consider due date quotation in combination with scheduling decisions. Such models, which integrate price and due date quotation with scheduling, would be more difficult to solve. There are existing models on joint due date quotation and scheduling (e.g., Panwalkar et al., 1982, Kaminsky & Kaya, 2008). One could investigate how existing solution methods from this literature can be used to solve the more complex problems discussed here.
- From a supply chain perspective, it would also be valuable to coordinate decisions such as distribution in combination with pricing and scheduling. One could incorporate pricing decisions into the integrated production and distribution scheduling problems studied in Chap. 3.
- Finally, it would be interesting to investigate the online version of many of the problems studied in the previous sections and those discussed here.

In addition, from a solution methodology point of view, most existing solution methods in the literature have been dynamic programming algorithms. The design and worst-case analysis of simple heuristics for intractable coordinated pricing and scheduling problems remains an open area. Another possible area of research is the design of branch-and-bound algorithms for such problems.

Chapter 6
Joint Subcontracting and Scheduling Decisions

Abstract In this chapter, we discuss centralized supply chain scheduling problems that involve an in-house processing facility and one or more subcontractors by which jobs can also be processed. The decision maker needs to determine jointly a subset of jobs to be subcontracted and a schedule for the jobs processed in-house, and in some situations may also need to construct a schedule for the subcontracted jobs. We discuss several representative problems, and for each problem considered, we study its complexity and describe exact or heuristic solution algorithms, analyze the performance of these algorithms, and present relevant practical insights.

6.1 Introduction

The problems considered in the previous three chapters involve two different stages of a supply chain (i.e., production and distribution) or two different functional areas of a firm (i.e., production and marketing), where the centralized decision maker needs to take into consideration the inter-dependency of the multiple supply chain stages or functional areas when making decisions.

There is another class of centralized supply chain scheduling problems that involve multiple production facilities where jobs can be processed. Scheduling problems involving multiple facilities are commonly encountered in practice. We describe two practical situations where such problems arise.

- First, a large number of manufacturing firms have multiple in-house production facilities. Due to the time urgency of received orders, the company many need to utilize more than one of its facilities to process incoming orders. Section 3.7 discusses integrated production and distribution scheduling problems involving multiple processing plants owned by a single firm. In such problems, the firm is responsible for both assigning the jobs to the plants and creating a schedule for processing the assigned jobs at each plant.
- Second, it is a common practice in many industries for a manufacturer to subcontract some operations or outsource an entire line of production because of the many advantages this practice can bring to the firm. The global market for

© Springer Nature Switzerland AG 2022
Z.-L. Chen, N. G. Hall, *Supply Chain Scheduling*, International Series
in Operations Research & Management Science 323,
https://doi.org/10.1007/978-3-030-90374-9_6

outsourced services in 2019 was more than \$92 billion (Statista, 2021). When a firm subcontracts out some of its tasks or outsources an entire set of operations, it allows the firm to concentrate on its core competencies. Subcontracting lowers investment requirements, and hence the financial risk of the firm. It also helps the firm improve its response to customer demand and lower the risk associated with fluctuating demand. Clearly, scheduling problems that arise in such a setting involve multiple facilities, including an in-house plant and the plants of the subcontractors involved.

Since Sect. 3.7 covers several problems with multiple in-house plants, in this chapter, we focus on problems with an in-house plant and one or more subcontractors. The subcontractors may process jobs at a faster rate but with a higher production cost. In some cases, the jobs processed by the subcontractors may need to be delivered back to the in-house facility, which incurs an additional transportation cost and time. The firm needs to determine (1) a subset of jobs to be outsourced to each subcontractor, (2) a processing schedule for the in-house facility, and (3) possibly also a delivery schedule to send the completed jobs from each subcontractor to the in-house facility. In most such problems, it is assumed that the decision maker is not responsible for creating schedules for subcontractors because they do not belong to the same entity. However, there are also some situations where the decision maker needs to create schedules for subcontractors.

We consider several subclasses of joint subcontracting and scheduling (JSS) problems and related issues in the following subsections.

- In Sect. 6.2, we consider a JSS problem where the decision maker can subcontract some jobs to multiple available subcontractors with the objective of minimizing the total subcontracting cost, subject to a lead time performance guarantee on the jobs. Some variants of the problem are also considered.
- In Sect. 6.3, we investigate the value of subcontracting based on the problems discussed in Sect. 6.2 by comparing the objective value of a problem with and without the subcontracting option.
- In Sect. 6.4, we study JSS problems where there is a budget constraint on the total subcontracting cost.
- All the problems considered in the other sections involve a production environment where a job only has one processing stage. In Sect. 6.5, we consider JSS problems involving a flowshop production environment where each job consists of multiple operations.
- In Sect. 6.6, we consider JSS problems where the decision maker needs to schedule both the in-house jobs as well as the subcontracted jobs and the subcontracted jobs must be delivered to the in-house facility after completion. The problems considered in all the other sections do not involve such complications.
- Finally, in Sect. 6.7 we consider JSS problems where the subcontractor employs a quantity discount scheme for the subcontracting cost. The subcontracting cost structure in the problems considered here is more general than those studied in Sects. 6.2 through 6.6.

6.2 Problem with a Lead Time Performance Guarantee

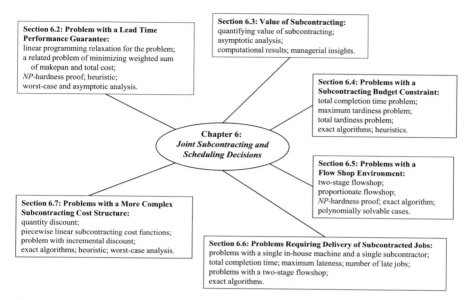

Fig. 6.1 Overview of the topics covered in Chap. 6

Figure 6.1 provides an overview of the topics discussed in this chapter.

Several decentralized supply chain scheduling problems involving subcontracting decisions are studied in Sects. 8.7, 9.2, and 9.3. These problems are modeled as cooperative or noncooperative games, unlike the problems studied in this chapter, which are modeled as centralized optimization problems.

6.2 Problem with a Lead Time Performance Guarantee

We first consider a problem studied by Chen and Li (2008). At the beginning of a planning horizon, a manufacturer has received a set of jobs, and can either process each of them on one of the multiple identical machines available in-house, or subcontract it to one of the multiple subcontractors available. The objective of the model is to minimize the total cost of production and subcontracting, subject to a constraint on the delivery lead time of the orders. Below, we define the model following the notation introduced in Chen and Li (2008), and discuss the results developed there, including the computational complexity of the model, a heuristic algorithm, and worst-case and asymptotic performance of the heuristic. We also discuss a related problem.

6.2.1 Problem Definition

A manufacturer receives a set of n jobs $N = \{1, \ldots, n\}$ at the beginning of a planning horizon. For each job, the manufacturer has two options: It can either process the job at its own plant or subcontract it to a subcontractor for processing. There are m identical parallel machines $M = \{1, \ldots, m\}$ available at the manufacturer's plant, such that if a job is processed at the manufacturer's plant, it only needs to be processed by one of the machines. There are k subcontractors $K = \{1, \ldots, k\}$ available. Each job is assumed to be indivisible; that is, it has to be processed entirely by an in-house machine or subcontracted to one of the subcontractors entirely. This assumption is justified by convenience of accounting, packaging, and delivery purposes. If job $j \in N$ is processed at the manufacturer's own plant, a processing time p_{0j} is required and the cost to the manufacturer is q_{0j}. If job $j \in N$ is subcontracted to subcontractor $h \in K$, then the delivery lead time is p_{hj} (i.e., it takes subcontractor p_{hj} units of time to complete the job and deliver the job to the in-house plant) and the cost incurred is q_{hj} dollars. We do not explicitly define the workload or size of each job. However, if necessary, the workload of a job $j \in N$ can be easily incorporated into the time and cost parameters defined here. We can set these parameters such that they are proportional to the workload of job j. For example, if the workload of job j is w_j, a possible instance of these parameters can be $p_{ij} = \alpha_i w_j$, and $q_{hj} = \beta_i w_j$ for $i \in 0, 1, \ldots, k$ and $j \in N$, where $\alpha_i, \beta_i > 0$ are facility-dependent parameters.

We further assume that for each subcontractor $h \in K$, the delivery lead time p_{hj} and subcontracting cost q_{hj} for a job $j \in N$ are independent of the total workload of the subcontractor. This assumption is made and justified in the literature. For example, Bertrand and Sridharan (2001) and Bukchin and Hanany (2007) make the same assumption on the subcontracting lead time of a job. Bukchin and Hanany (2007) assume that the subcontractor has an unlimited capacity and that the subcontracting lead time of a job is a constant factor multiplied by the in-house processing time of the job. They point out that the assumption that the subcontractor has unlimited capacity is reasonable when the subcontractor's available capacity is significantly higher than the manufacturer's required capacity, and in this case, a contract can be signed that clearly defines a due date commitment on the subcontractor's side. In the models of Chung et al. (2005), Bukchin and Hanany (2007), and Qi (2008), it is also assumed that the subcontracting cost of a job is independent of the other jobs processed by the same subcontractor. This assumption is appropriate if each subcontractor makes independent offers to the individual jobs from the manufacturer with a promise to deliver a finished job within a certain deadline at a certain cost.

The manufacturer needs to determine (1) a subset of jobs to be subcontracted to each of the k subcontractors, and (2) a production schedule for the jobs processed on the m machines at its own plant, such that the total production cost is minimized, subject to the constraint that the makespan (i.e., the maximum completion time of the jobs) is no more than a given threshold. Each subcontractor determines its own production schedule for the jobs subcontracted from the manufacturer and

6.2 Problem with a Lead Time Performance Guarantee

delivers completed jobs to the manufacturer by the pre-specified lead times. The delivery time and cost are not explicitly considered, but can be viewed as already incorporated into p_{hj} and q_{hj}, respectively.

In a solution to this problem, let C_j denote the completion time of job $j \in N$. If job $j \in N$ is subcontracted to a subcontractor $h \in K$, then $C_j = p_{hj}$. If job $j \in N$ is processed in-house, then C_j is determined by the schedule for the jobs processed in-house. Define the makespan of all the jobs to be the maximum completion time of the jobs, and denote it as $C_{\max} = \max\{C_j | j \in N\}$. Here, $C_{\max}$ represents the time when all the customer orders are completed. By imposing a constraint on $C_{\max}$, we guarantee that all jobs are completed within a given time limit. Let G denote the total cost of a given solution, including the production costs at the manufacturer's plant and the subcontracting costs. The problem is to minimize the total cost G subject to the constraint $C_{\max} \leq C$, where C is a pre-specified threshold value. We denote this problem as $\min\{G \mid C_{\max} \leq C\}$. This problem can be used to determine all Pareto-optimal solutions with respect to G and $C_{\max}$ if we solve this problem repeatedly for different values of C.

Remark 6.1 The problem described above can be viewed as a generalized version of the classical parallel-machine scheduling problems, for example, $P_m||C_{\max}$. In classical parallel-machine scheduling problems, no production costs are involved, while some performance measure of job completion times is optimized. In our problem, the objective is to minimize the total operating cost, and each subcontractor $h \in K$ can be viewed as having a sufficient number (e.g., n) of identical parallel machines, such that each of these machines only needs to handle at most one job.

6.2.2 Complexity and Heuristic Analysis

We first show that problem $\min\{G \mid C_{\max} \leq C\}$ is at least ordinarily NP-hard even with a special structure. Then, we propose a heuristic and analyze its performance. All the results are from Chen and Li (2008).

Theorem 6.1 *Problem $\min\{G \mid C_{\max} \leq C\}$ is at least ordinarily NP-hard even if there is only a single machine at the manufacturer, there is a single subcontractor, and the in-house production costs are proportional to the production times.*

Proof Clearly, this problem contains the classical parallel-machine makespan problem $P_m||C_{\max}$ as a special case. Thus, when there is an arbitrary number of machines, the problem is strongly NP-hard because $P_m||C_{\max}$ with an arbitrary m is known to be strongly NP-hard (Garey & Johnson, 1978).

In the remainder of the proof, we show that the special case of the problem with a single machine at the manufacturer, and a single subcontractor, where in-house production costs are proportional to the production times, is ordinarily NP-hard. To this end, we first show that this special case of the problem is at least ordinarily NP-hard by a reduction from the Subset Sum problem, a known NP-complete problem

(Garey & Johnson, 1979). After this, we show that there is a pseudo-polynomial time algorithm to solve the problem to optimality.

The Subset Sum (SS) problem can be defined as follows: Given a set of items $V = \{1, 2, \ldots, v\}$, a size $a_j \in Z^+$ for each item $j \in V$, and a positive integer A, the problem asks if there is a subset $U \in V$ such that $\sum_{j \in U} a_j = A$. We define $B = \sum_{j \in V} a_j$. We can assume $B \geq A + 1$ because otherwise $A = B$ and the problem is trivial.

Given an instance of SS, we construct the following instance for our problem $\min\{G \mid C_{\max} \leq C\}$:

- Number of machines at the manufacturer, $m = 1$.
- Number of subcontractors, $k = 1$.
- Number of jobs, $n = v + 1$, and job set: $N = V \cup \{v + 1\}$.
- Processing time at the manufacturer: $p_{0j} = La_j$ for $j \in N$, and $p_{0,v+1} = LB$, where L is any positive integer.
- Delivery lead time if subcontracted: $p_{1j} = La_j$ for $j \in N$, and $p_{1,v+1} = LA$.
- Production cost if processed in-house: $q_{0j} = a_j$ for $j \in N$, and $q_{0,v+1} = B$.
- Production cost if subcontracted: $q_{1j} = 2a_j$ for $j \in N$, and $q_{1,v+1} = 2A$.
- Constraint for the makespan: $C = LA$.
- Threshold for the objective value: $Z_0 = A + 2B$.

Since in the above instance $q_{0j} = p_{0j}/L$ for all $j \in N$, in-house production costs are proportional to the processing times. We prove that there is a feasible solution to the constructed instance of our problem with objective value no more than Z_0 if and only if there is a solution to SS.

($\Rightarrow$) Given a solution to SS, we construct a solution to our problem as follows: Subcontract all the jobs in $N \setminus U$ to the only subcontractor available, and process the jobs in U in-house in any sequence. Clearly, in this solution $C_{\max} = LA = C$ and $G = A + 2B = Z_0$.

($\Leftarrow$) Given a solution to our problem with an objective value G no more than Z_0, let H denote the subset of the jobs processed in-house. Clearly, $v + 1 \notin H$, because otherwise $C_{\max} \geq LB \geq L(A + 1)$, implying that the objective value exceeds Z_0. Thus, $C_{\max} = p_{1,v+1} = LA = C$. Also, $\sum_{j \in H} a_j \leq A$, because otherwise $C_{\max} \geq L(A + 1) > C$. If $\sum_{j \in H} a_j < A$, then the total cost is

$$G = \sum_{j \in H} q_{0j} + \sum_{j \in N \setminus H} q_{1j} = \sum_{j \in H} a_j + 2A + \sum_{j \in V \setminus H} 2a_j$$

$$= 2A + 2B - \sum_{j \in H} a_j > A + 2B = Z_0,$$

which is a contradiction. This implies that $\sum_{j \in H} a_j = A$.

Finally, we briefly show that a pseudo-polynomial time dynamic programming algorithm can be constructed to solve the special case of the problem to optimality. We design a DP algorithm that considers jobs $1, \ldots, n$ in the sequence of their indices one by one, and for each job j, tries to process it in-house, or subcontract it. Define value function $F(j, E_1, E_2)$ as the minimum total cost of a solution for jobs

6.2 Problem with a Lead Time Performance Guarantee

$1, \ldots, j$, where the makespan of the in-house jobs is E_1 and the longest lead time of a subcontracted job is E_2. Then, the recurrence relation of the dynamic program is the following:

$$F(j, E_1, E_2) = \min\{F(j-1, E_1 - p_{0j}, E_2) + q_{0j}, \ Z + q_{1j}\},$$

where

$$Z = \begin{cases} F(j-1, E_1, E_2), & \text{if } E_2 \geq p_{1j} \\ \min\{F(j-1, E_1, x) \mid x \leq p_{1j}\}, & \text{if } E_2 = p_{1j} \\ \infty, & \text{if } E_2 < p_{1j} \end{cases}$$

The optimal solution is found by solving the problem: $\min\{F(n, E_1, E_2) \mid E_1 \leq C, E_2 \leq C\}$. Clearly this algorithm has a pseudo-polynomial running time. $\square$

We now discuss the heuristic proposed by Chen and Li (2008). This heuristic is based on an integer programming formulation of the problem and exploits a special property of the LP-relaxation of the IP formulation. For each job $j \in N$, we find all the subcontractors that can process job j with a delivery time no later than the required threshold of the makespan, C. Denote the subset of such subcontractors as S_j. Thus, $S_j = \{h \in K \mid p_{hj} \leq C\}$. Define $V = \{j \in N \mid S_j \neq \emptyset\}$ to be the set of jobs that can be subcontracted. For each $j \in V$, define a subcontractor $s_j = \arg\min_{v \in S_j}\{q_{vj}\}$, which is the subcontractor that can process job j at a minimum cost with a delivery time no later than C. With this additional notation defined, the problem can then be formulated as the following mixed integer program, where each binary variable x_{ij} is defined to be 1 if job j is assigned to machine $i \in M$ at the manufacturer's own plant, and 0 otherwise; variable y_j is defined to be 1 if job j is assigned to subcontractor s_j, and 0 otherwise; and variable $C_{\max}$ is the makespan.

$$IP(C): \quad \text{Minimize} \quad \sum_{i=1}^{m}\sum_{j=1}^{n} q_{0j}x_{ij} + \sum_{j \in V} q_{s_j,j}y_j \tag{6.1}$$

subject to

$$\sum_{i=1}^{m} x_{ij} + y_j = 1, \quad \text{for } j \in V, \tag{6.2}$$

$$\sum_{i=1}^{m} x_{ij} = 1, \quad \text{for } j \in N \setminus V \tag{6.3}$$

$$C_{\max} \geq \sum_{j=1}^{n} p_{0j}x_{ij}, \quad \text{for } i \in M, \tag{6.4}$$

$$C_{\max} \leq C, \tag{6.5}$$

$$x_{ij} \in \{0, 1\}, \quad \text{for } i \in M \text{ and } j \in N \tag{6.6}$$

$$y_j \in \{0, 1\}, \quad \text{for } j \in V. \tag{6.7}$$

248   6 Joint Subcontracting and Scheduling Decisions

In the above formulation, objective function (6.1) is the total production and subcontracting cost. Constraints (6.2) and (6.3) ensure that each job $j \in V$ is either assigned to an in-house machine or subcontracted to s_j, and that each job $j \in N \setminus V$ is assigned to an in-house machine. Constraints (6.4) and (6.5) define the makespan and ensure that the threshold on the makespan is met.

We focus on the LP-relaxation problem of $IP(C)$, denoted as $LP(C)$, which is the same formulation as $IP(C)$ except that variables x_{ij} and y_j are allowed to take any nonnegative values. Constraints (6.2) and (6.3) enforce these variables to take values between 0 and 1. We have the following result about problem $LP(C)$.

Lemma 6.1 *If $n \geq m$, then in an optimal basic solution of $LP(C)$, at least $n - m$ of the variables x_{ij} and y_j take the value 1.*

Proof There are $n + m + 1$ constraints in $LP(C)$ in addition to the nonnegativity constraints. Hence, in an optimal basic solution, no more than $n + m + 1$ variables take positive values. Given that variable $C_{\max}$ must take a positive value, at most $n + m$ of the x_{ij} and y_j variables take positive values in an optimal basic solution.

Given an optimal basic solution of $LP(C)$, let Ω_j denote the subset of variables among $x_{1j}, x_{2j}, \ldots, x_{mj}, y_j$ that take a nonzero value when $j \in V$, or the subset of variables among $x_{1j}, x_{2j}, \ldots, x_{mj}$ that take a nonzero value when $j \in N \setminus V$. Define $N_1 = \{j \in N \mid |\Omega_j| = 1\}$ and $N_2 = \{(j \in N \mid |\Omega_j| \geq 2\}$. If $j \in N_1$, then there is only one nonzero variable among the variables $x_{1j}, x_{2j}, \ldots, x_{mj}, y_j$. Constraints (6.2) and (6.3) imply that this nonzero variable must have a value 1. Clearly, each Ω_j contains a distinct set of variables, i.e., $\Omega_j \cap \Omega_{j'} = \emptyset$ if $j \neq j'$. Thus,

$$n + m \geq |N_1| + 2|N_2| = |N_1| + 2(n - |N_1|) = 2n - |N_1|,$$

which implies that $|N_1| \geq n - m$. □

From Lemma 6.1, we can conclude that in an optimal basic solution of $LP(C)$, there are at most m jobs with fractional values assigned to the corresponding x_{ij} or y_j variables. We show in the following that we do not have to use a linear programming algorithm to obtain an optimal basic solution of $LP(C)$. Instead, there is a simple strongly polynomial-time algorithm that can find an optimal basic solution of $LP(C)$ with at most m jobs having fractional values of the corresponding x_{ij} or y_j variables.

We first consider the following auxiliary problem, denoted as P_{AUX}, which is a subproblem in the procedure to solve problem $LP(C)$ given below. We are given a set of h jobs $H = \{1, \ldots, h\}$ to be scheduled on the m parallel identical machines in-house, where each job $j \in H$ has a processing time a_j. Each job j can be split into subjobs, where each subjob has a processing time less than a_j such that the total processing time of all subjobs of job j is equal to a_j. The subjobs of a job are mutually independent and can be processed on different machines simultaneously if needed. Problem P_{AUX} is to split at most m jobs into subjobs and find a schedule for all the resulting subjobs and unsplit jobs on the m identical parallel machines, such that the makespan of the schedule is equal to $A_H = \frac{1}{m} \sum_{j \in H} a_j$.

6.2 Problem with a Lead Time Performance Guarantee

Problem P_{AUX} can be solved by the following procedure. The idea is to assign the jobs sequentially to the machines and divide a job into subjobs whenever necessary in order to make the total processing time of each machine equal to A_H.

Procedure PRO1 for Problem P_{AUX}

Step 1: Assign jobs $1, 2, \ldots$ one by one to machine 1. Suppose job u_1 is the first job such that after it is assigned to machine 1, the total processing time on machine 1, i.e., $\sum_{j=1}^{u_1} a_j$ becomes greater than or equal to A_H. Job u_1 is divided into two subjobs $u_1[1]$ and $u_1[2]$ such that the total processing time of jobs $1, \ldots, u_1 - 1$ and $u_1[1]$ is exactly A_H. Let the processing time of subjob $u_1[2]$ be denoted as $a_{u_1[2]}$. Call $u_1[2]$ the leftover subjob from machine 1.

Step 2: For $i = 2, \ldots, m$, assign the leftover subjob $u_{i-1}[2]$ from machine $i - 1$, and the remaining jobs $u_{i-1} + 1, u_{i-1} + 2, \ldots$ one by one to machine i. There are two cases:

Case (i): If $a_{u_{i-1}[2]} < A_H$, then let job u_i be the first job such that $a_{u_{i-1}[2]} + \sum_{j=u_{i-1}+1}^{u_i} a_j \geq A_H$. Divide job u_i into two subjobs $u_i[1]$ and $u_i[2]$ such that the total processing time of jobs $u_{i-1}[1], u_{i-1}+1, \ldots, u_i - 1$ and $u_i[1]$ is exactly A_H. Denote the processing time of subjob $u_i[2]$ by $a_{u_i[2]}$. Call $u_i[2]$ the leftover subjob from machine i.

Case (ii): If $a_{u_{i-1}[2]} \geq A_H$, then subjob $u_{i-1}[2]$ is divided further into two subjobs, denoted as $u_i[1]$ and $u_i[2]$, such that the processing time of $u_i[1]$ is equal to A_H and that of $u_i[2]$, denoted as $a_{u_i[2]}$, is equal to $a_{u_{i-1}[2]} - A_H$. Call subjob $u_i[2]$ the leftover job from machine i.

In the above procedure, in Step 1, the processing time of subjob $u_1[2]$ is $a_{u_1}[2] = \sum_{j=1}^{u_1} a_j - A_H$, and in Case (i) of Step 2, the processing time of subjob $u_i[2]$ is $a_{u_i[2]} = a_{u_{i-1}[2]} + \sum_{j=u_{i-1}+1}^{u_i} a_j - A_H$. Furthermore, there is at most one new job that is split going from machine i to machine $i + 1$. Thus, it results in a total of at most $m - 1$ split jobs. It is not difficult to check that this procedure takes $O(h + m)$ time.

Example 6.1 (Application of Procedure PRO1) We apply Procedure PRO1 to the following instance of problem P_{AUX}: Assign 8 jobs $H = \{1, \ldots, 8\}$ with the processing times $a_1 = a_2 = a_3 = 4, a_4 = a_5 = 5, a_6 = 8, a_7 = a_8 = 6$ to $m = 3$ identical parallel machines such that the makespan of the schedule is equal to $A_H = (\sum_{j=1}^{8} a_j)/3 = 42/3 = 14$.

For this example, in Step 1, we assign jobs 1, 2, 3, 4 to machine 1 with u_1 being job 4. Split job 4 into two parts $u_1[1]$ with processing time 2 and $u_1[2]$ with processing time 3 such that the total processing time of jobs 1, 2, 3, and $u_1[1]$ is 14. In Step 2, for machine 2, we assign subjob $u_1[2]$ and jobs 5 and 6 to machine 2 with u_2 being job 6. Split job 5 into two parts $u_2[1]$ with processing time 6 and $u_2[2]$ with processing time 2. As a result, the total processing time of jobs $u_1[2], 5, u_2[1]$ is equal to 14. The remaining jobs, $u_2[2], 7, 8$ are assigned to machine 3 with total processing time 14.

Next, we present a procedure that either concludes that the linear relaxation problem $LP(C)$ is infeasible or finds an optimal solution of the problem if it is feasible. We first define some of the notation used in this procedure:

- U denotes the set of in-house jobs and subjobs.
- N_1 and N_2 denote the set of unsplit and split jobs, respectively, as defined in the proof of Lemma 6.1.
- W denotes the set of jobs that have not been subcontracted but can be subcontracted if needed.

Procedure PRO2 for $LP(C)$

Step 1: Initialize $U = N$, $N_1 = \emptyset$, and $N_2 = \emptyset$. For each job $j \in V$, if $q_{s_j,j} \le q_{0j}$, then assign job j to subcontractor s_j, i.e., set $y_j = 1$ and $x_{ij} = 0$ for $i \in M$, and set $U = U \setminus \{j\}$, and $N_1 = N_1 \cup \{j\}$. Set $W = U \cap V$.

Step 2: If $\frac{1}{m}\sum_{j \in U} p_{0j} \le C$, then all the jobs in U are assigned to the manufacturer's in-house plant. Define auxiliary problem P_{AUX} involving the jobs in U and the m in-house machines. Call Procedure PRO1 to schedule these jobs on the m machines. This results in at most $m - 1$ jobs being split into subjobs. These jobs are added to set N_2. The other jobs are added to set N_1. For each job $j \in U \cap N_1$, let $x_{ij} = 1$, where i is the machine to which job j is assigned. For each job $j \in U \cap N_2$ and each machine $i \in M$, let $x_{ij} = \tau_{ij}/p_{0j}$, where τ_{ij} is the total processing time of the subjobs of job j assigned to machine i. Stop.

Step 3: If $\frac{1}{m}\sum_{j \in U} p_{0j} > C$ and W is empty, then $LP(C)$ is infeasible, and stop.

Step 4: If $\frac{1}{m}\sum_{j \in U} p_{0j} > C$ and W is not empty, then some jobs in W must be subcontracted. Let $\Delta = \sum_{j \in U} p_{0j} - mC$, which is the total processing time of jobs in W that need to be subcontracted in an optimal solution of $LP(C)$. Suppose that there are w jobs in W. Reindex the jobs in W as $[1], [2], \ldots, [w]$ such that

$$\frac{q_{s_{[1]},[1]} - q_{0,[1]}}{p_{0,[1]}} \le \frac{q_{s_{[2]},[2]} - q_{0,[2]}}{p_{0,[2]}} \le \cdots \le \frac{q_{s_{[w]},[w]} - q_{0,[w]}}{p_{0,[w]}}.$$

Set $v = 1$, and consider the following two cases:

(a) If $\Delta = 0$, then define auxiliary problem P_{AUX} involving the jobs in U and the m in-house machines and call Procedure PRO1 to schedule the jobs in U on the m in-house machines. This results in at most $m - 1$ split jobs. These jobs are added to set N_2. The other jobs are added to set N_1. For each job $j \in U \cap N_1$, set $x_{ij} = 1$, where i is the machine to which job j is assigned. For each job $j \in U \cap N_2$ and each machine $i \in M$, let $x_{ij} = \tau_{ij}/p_{0j}$, where τ_{ij} is the total processing time of the subjobs of job j assigned to machine i. Stop.

(b) If $\Delta > 0$, then consider the following two subcases:

(i) If $\Delta < p_{0,[v]}$, then split job $[v]$ into two subjobs $g_1([v])$ and $g_2([v])$ with a processing time $p_{0,[v]} - \Delta$ and Δ, respectively. Assign subjob $g_2([v])$ to subcontractor $s_{[v]}$ (and let $y_{[v]} = \Delta/p_{0,[v]}$). Set $U = (U \setminus \{[v]\}) \cup g_1([v])$. Define auxiliary problem P_{AUX} involving the jobs in U (including subjob $g_1([v])$) and the m in-house machines and call Procedure PRO1 to schedule the jobs in U on the m in-house machines. This results in at most m split

6.2 Problem with a Lead Time Performance Guarantee 251

jobs, including job $[v]$. These jobs are added to set N_2. All the other jobs are added to set N_1. For each job $j \in U \cap N_1$, set $x_{ij} = 1$, where i is the machine to which job j is assigned. For each job $j \in U \cap N_2$ and each machine $i \in M$, let $x_{ij} = \tau_{ij}/p_{0j}$, where τ_{ij} is the total processing time of the subjobs of job j assigned to machine i. Stop.

(ii) If $\Delta \geq p_{0,[v]}$, then assign job $[v]$ to subcontractor $s_{[v]}$. Let $y_{[v]} = 1$, and add job $[v]$ to N_1. Update $\Delta = \Delta - p_{0,[v]}$ and $U = U \setminus \{[v]\}$. If $v < w$, then set $v = v + 1$ and repeat Steps 4(a) and 4(b). If $v = w$ and $\Delta = 0$, then repeat Step 4(a) and stop. If $v = w$ and $\Delta > 0$, then $LP(C)$ is infeasible, and stop.

We briefly explain the validity of the above procedure. Clearly, for each job $j \in V$, if $q_{s_j,j} \leq q_{0j}$, then job j should be subcontracted to subcontractor s_j in an optimal solution. This is part of what Step 1 does. Steps 2, 3, and 4 consider three possible cases. Step 4 subcontracts the jobs in W one by one following the sequence $[1], \ldots, [w]$. Here the following rule is used for subcontracting jobs: The remaining job in W with the smallest ratio $(q_{s[j],[j]} - q_{0,[j]})/p_{0,[j]}$ is subcontracted first. This rule minimizes the total subcontracting cost.

We state the following result without a detailed proof. Interested readers are referred to Chen and Li (2008).

Lemma 6.2 *If $LP(C)$ is infeasible, then Procedure PRO2 validates that this problem is infeasible. If $LP(C)$ is feasible, then Procedure PRO2 finds an optimal solution to $LP(C)$ with no more than m split jobs in $O(n \log n + m)$ time.*

Now, we describe the heuristic of Chen and Li (2008) for solving problem $\min\{G \mid C_{\max} \leq C\}$. The heuristic assigns each job either to an in-house machine or to a subcontractor based on the solution of $LP(C)$ obtained by Procedure PRO2, which generates a set of unsplit jobs N_1 and a set of split jobs N_2. The heuristic assigns each job $j \in N_1$ with $x_{ij} = 1$ for some $i \in M$ to in-house machine i, and each job $j \in N_1 \cap V$ with $y_j = 1$ to subcontractor s_j. This creates a schedule σ_1 for jobs in N_1. Next, each job in N_2 is either assigned to a subcontractor or an in-house machine based on its cost parameters and the workload of each in-house machine in schedule σ_1.

Heuristic $H1$ for Problem $\min\{G \mid C_{\max} \leq C\}$

Step 1: Solve $LP(C)$ by Procedure PRO2. If $LP(C)$ is infeasible, then problem $\min\{G \mid C_{\max} \leq C\}$ is infeasible and stop. Otherwise, based on the solution of $LP(C)$, define $J_i = \{j \in N_1 \mid x_{ij} = 1\}$ for $i \in M$.

Step 2: For each $i \in M$, assign each job $j \in J_i$ to machine i at the manufacturer. Schedule the jobs on each machine in an arbitrary sequence. For each job $j \in N_1 \cap V$ with $y_j = 1$ assign job j to subcontractor s_j. Denote the resulting schedule (containing the jobs from N_1 only) by σ_1. Define the workload of each in-house machine under solution σ_1 as the total processing time of the jobs assigned to this machine in σ_1.

Step 3: For each $j \in N_2$, do the following. If $S_j \neq \emptyset$ and $q_{s_j,j} \leq q_{0j}$, then assign job j to subcontractor s_j. If $S_j \neq \emptyset$ and $q_{s_j,j} > q_{0j}$, or if $S_j = \emptyset$, then assign job j to an in-house machine with the minimum workload under solution σ_1 and update the workload of this machine accordingly. Denote the final schedule as σ.

252   6 Joint Subcontracting and Scheduling Decisions

In the above heuristic $H1$, determining $S_1, S_2, \ldots, S_n$ and $s_1, s_2, \ldots, s_n$ takes $O(nk)$ time, where k is the number of subcontractors in the problem. Once these values are known, Steps 2 and 3 of the heuristic require $O(n)$ time. Since $LP(C)$ involved in Step 1 of the heuristic is solved by Procedure PRO1 in $O(n \log n + m)$ time, the overall time complexity of the heuristic is $O(nk + n \log n)$.

Example 6.2 (Application of Heuristic H1) We apply Heuristic H1 to the following instance of problem $\min\{G \mid C_{\max} \leq C\}$: $m = 2, k = 2, n = 6$, where p_{ij} and q_{ij} are given in the following table. Consider two cases of the threshold value of $C_{\max}$: $C = 10$ or $C = 15$.

j	1	2	3	4	5	6
p_{0j}	5	5	8	6	5	3
p_{1j}	10	6	9	6	7	4
p_{2j}	6	4	8	7	8	5
q_{0j}	2	4	2	5	5	3
q_{1j}	5	3	4	6	6	2
q_{2j}	4	3	3	7	6	4
$q_{s_j,j}$	4	3	3	6	6	2

In the table, the $q_{s_j,j}$ values are added as the last row. It can be seen that in both cases of C, every job can be subcontracted if needed, i.e., $V = N$. We first apply Heuristic H1 to the case with $C = 10$.

Step 1. Use Procedure PRO2 to solve problem $LP(C)$.

- Step 2 of this procedure subcontracts jobs 2 and 6 because $q_{s_2,2} \leq q_{02}$ and $q_{s_6,2} \leq q_{06}$. Thus, $U = \{1, 3, 4, 5\}$, $N_1 = \{2, 6\}$, and $W = U$.
- Since $\frac{1}{m} \sum_{j \in U} p_{0j} = 12 > C$, Step 4 of Procedure PRO2 is run next. Compute $\Delta = \sum_{j \in U} p_{0j} - mC = 4$. For each $j \in W$, calculate the ratio $(q_{s_j,j} - q_{0j})/p_{0j}$. Job 3 has the smallest ratio $1/8$.

  - Since $\Delta < p_{03}$, Case (i) of Step 4(b) applies. Job 3, denoted as [1], is thus split into two subjobs, $g_1([1]), g_2([1])$, each with a length of 4 units. Job $g_2([1])$ is subcontracted, while job $g_1([1])$ is kept for in-house processing. Update $U = \{1, g_1([1]), 4, 5\}$. Call Procedure PRO1 to schedule the jobs in U on the two in-house machines. Applying Procedure PRO1, $E_T = (\sum_{j \in U} p_{0j})/2 = 10$.

The solution generated is as follows: Split job 4 into two parts such that part 1 is 1 unit long, while part 2 is 5 units long; assign job 1, $g_1([1])$ and part 1 of job 4 to machine 1 (which gives the total processing time of 10), and assign part 2 of job 4 and job 5 to machine 2 (which also gives the total processing time 10). Now return to Step 1 of the heuristic. Based on the solution of $LP(C)$ generated by Procedure PRO2, $J_1 = \{1\}$, $J_2 = \{5\}$, and $N_2 = \{3, 4\}$.

6.2 Problem with a Lead Time Performance Guarantee

Step 2. Assign job 1 to machine 1 and job 5 to machine 2. Subcontract jobs 2 and 6. This gives a partial solution σ_1. The workload of each machine in this solution is 5.

Step 3. Assign job 3 to machine 1 and job 4 to machine 2. This gives the final solution. The C_{max} value of this solution is 13, and hence no feasible solution is found.

Next we apply Heuristic H1 to the case with $C = 15$.

Step 1. Use Procedure PRO2 to solve problem $LP(C)$.

- Step 2 of this procedure is the same as that in the case with $C = 10$. Thus, $U = \{1, 3, 4, 5\}$, $N_1 = \{2, 6\}$, and $W = U$.
- Since $\frac{1}{m} \sum_{j \in U} p_{0j} = 12 < C$, Step 3 of Procedure PRO2 is run next. Call Procedure PRO1 to schedule the jobs in U on the two in-house machines with $E_T = 1/2 \sum_{j \in U} p_{0j} = 12$. The solution generated is as follows: Split job 3 into two parts such that part 1 is 7 units long, while part 2 is 1 unit long; assign job 1 and part 1 of job 3 to machine 1 (which gives the total processing time of 12), and assign part 2 of job 3 and job 4 and 5 to machine 2 (which also gives the total processing time 12).
- Now return to Step 1 of the heuristic. Based on the solution of $LP(C)$ generated by Procedure PRO2, $J_1 = \{1\}$, $J_2 = \{4, 5\}$, and $N_2 = \{3\}$.

Step 2. Assign job 1 to machine 1 and job 4 and 5 to machine 2. Subcontract job 2 and 6. This gives a partial solution σ_1. In this solution, the workload of machine 1 is 5, while that of machine 2 is 11.

Step 3. Assign job 3 to machine 1. This gives the final solution. The C_{max} of this solution is 13 and hence this solution is feasible. In fact, this solution is optimal.

If problem $LP(C)$ is infeasible (which can be detected by Step 1 of heuristic $H1$), then problem $\min\{G \mid C_{max} \le C\}$ is infeasible as well. If problem $\min\{G \mid C_{max} \le C\}$ is feasible, then problem $LP(C)$ is feasible and heuristic $H1$ generates schedule σ. However, schedule σ generated by $H1$ may not always be feasible for problem $\min\{G \mid C_{max} \le C\}$ even if this problem is feasible, as stated in the following lemma.

Lemma 6.3 *There does not exist a polynomial-time heuristic which can always generate a feasible schedule for every feasible instance of* $\min\{G \mid C_{max} \le C\}$, *unless* $P = NP$.

Proof We prove the lemma by contradiction. If there is such a heuristic H, then this heuristic can always find a feasible schedule for every feasible instance of the following special case of the problem: All in-house production costs are zero (i.e., $q_{0j} = 0$ for all $j \in N$), all subcontracting costs are strictly positive (i.e., $q_{ij} > 0$ for all $i \in M$ and $j \in N$), and the threshold C is the minimum makespan of the jobs if all the jobs are processed in-house. It can be seen that finding a feasible schedule for this problem is equivalent to finding an optimal schedule for the classical parallel-machine makespan minimization problem $P_m||C_{max}$, which is known to be NP-hard (Garey & Johnson, 1978). Thus, heuristic H can be used to solve this NP-hard problem optimally, hence $P = NP$. □

We show below that when the given threshold of the makespan C satisfies a certain condition, then schedule σ generated by Heuristic $H1$ is guaranteed to be feasible for problem $\min\{G \mid C_{max} \leq C\}$.

Theorem 6.2 *If* $C \geq \frac{1}{m} \sum_{j \in N} p_{0j} + p_{0,max}$, *where* $p_{0,max} = \max\{p_{0j} | j \in N\}$, *then the solution generated by Heuristic $H1$ is a feasible solution to problem* $\min\{G \mid C_{max} \leq C\}$.

Proof We first show that if $C \geq \frac{1}{m} \sum_{j \in N} p_{0j} + p_{0,max}$, then problem $\min\{G \mid C_{max} \leq C\}$ is feasible. We construct a feasible solution to the problem as follows: Process all the jobs by the m in-house machines using the following scheduling rule: For $j = 1, 2, \ldots, n$, schedule job j to a machine with the minimum workload and update the workload of that machine accordingly. In the resulting schedule π, let C_{max} denote the makespan and C^i denote the total processing time of the jobs assigned to machine i, for $i \in M$. By this scheduling rule, it is clear that the start time of the last job on each machine must be no more than $\frac{1}{m} \sum_{j \in N} p_{0j}$. Thus, $C^i \leq \frac{1}{m} \sum_{j \in N} p_{0j} + p_{0,max}$ for every $i \in M$, which implies that

$$C_{max} = \max\{C^i | i \in M\} \leq \frac{1}{m} \sum_{j \in N} p_{0j} + p_{0,max} \leq C.$$

Thus, schedule π is feasible. This means that problem $\min\{G \mid C_{max} \leq C\}$ has a feasible solution and, hence, $LP(C)$ is feasible. It is evident that schedule σ_1 generated in Step 2 for the jobs in N_1 is feasible. Let $C^i(\sigma_1)$ denote the total processing time of the jobs assigned to machine i, i.e., the total workload of machine i, in schedule σ_1. Define $\Delta^i(\sigma_1) = C - C^i(\sigma_1)$ to be the slack of machine i, for $i \in M$. We can see that a schedule is feasible if the slack of every machine is nonnegative. The fact that σ_1 is feasible means that $\Delta^i(\sigma_1) \geq 0$, for all $i \in M$. Since some jobs of N_1 may be subcontracted in schedule σ_1, we have

$$\sum_{i=1}^{m} C^i(\sigma_1) \leq \sum_{j \in N_1} p_{0j} = \sum_{j \in N} p_{0j} - \sum_{j \in N_2} p_{0j}. \tag{6.8}$$

The fact that $C \geq \frac{1}{m} \sum_{j \in N} p_{0j} + p_{0,max}$, along with (6.8), implies that

$$\sum_{i=1}^{m} \Delta^i(\sigma_1) = mC - \sum_{i=1}^{m} C^i(\sigma_1) \geq mp_{0,max} + \sum_{j \in N_2} p_{0j}. \tag{6.9}$$

6.2 Problem with a Lead Time Performance Guarantee

Let N_3 denote the subset of the jobs in N_2 that are assigned to an in-house machine by Step 3 of the heuristic. Define $w = |N_3|$ as the number of jobs in N_3. Clearly, $w \leq m$. Let $[h]$ denote the index of the hth job of N_3 added to an in-house machine in Step 3 of $H3$, for $h = 1, 2, \ldots, w$. By the scheduling rule used in Step 3, whenever a job in N_3 is added to an in-house machine, it is added to a machine with the minimum workload, i.e., a machine with the maximum slack. Let i_h denote the in-house machine where job $[h]$ of N_3 is added, for $h = 1, 2, \ldots, w$. Thus, immediately before job $[1]$ is added, machine i_1 has the minimum total workload under schedule σ_1. From (6.9), this means that $\Delta^{i_1}(\sigma_1) \geq p_{0,\max}$. This implies that after job $[1]$ is added, the updated total workload of machine i_1 is no more than C, and hence the resulting schedule remains feasible. From (6.9), we can see that after job $[1]$ is added, the total updated slack of the m machines is

$$\sum_{i=1}^{m} \Delta^i(\sigma_1) \geq m p_{0,\max} + \sum_{j \in N_2 \setminus \{[1]\}} p_{0j}. \tag{6.10}$$

Next, we consider job $[2]$. By a similar argument and using (6.10), we can prove that immediately after job $[2]$ is added to an in-house machine, the resulting schedule remains feasible, and the total updated slack of the m machines is

$$\sum_{i=1}^{m} \Delta^i(\sigma_1) \geq m p_{0,\max} + \sum_{j \in N_2 \setminus \{[1],[2]\}} p_{0j}.$$

Repeatedly applying this argument, we can conclude that the schedule remains feasible after all the jobs of N_3 are added to the schedule. □

Remark 6.2 The usefulness of the result in Theorem 6.2 is that whether the condition $C \geq \frac{1}{m} \sum_{j \in N} p_{0j} + p_{0,\max}$ holds or not can be checked from the data, without running the heuristic. If the condition is satisfied, then we know that running the heuristic will deliver a feasible solution.

Clearly, it is not meaningful to discuss worst-case or asymptotic performance of a heuristic if the solution generated by the heuristic may not even be feasible. However, by Theorem 6.2, when the condition that $C \geq \frac{1}{m} \sum_{j \in N} p_{0j} + p_{0,\max}$ is satisfied, Heuristic $H1$ is guaranteed to generate a feasible solution. Hence, we study the worst-case and asymptotic performance of our heuristic under this condition.

Let Z^{H1} denote the total cost of the schedule σ generated by $H1$, and Z^* denote the optimal total cost of problem $\min\{G \mid C_{\max} \leq C\}$. We have the following results for the worst-case and asymptotic performance of our heuristic.

Theorem 6.3 $Z^{H1} \leq 2Z^*$ *for any instance of problem* $\min\{G \mid C_{\max} \leq C\}$ *with* $C \geq \frac{1}{m} \sum_{j \in N} p_{0j} + p_{0,\max}$.

Proof Heuristic $H1$ generates a partial schedule σ_1 before generating the final schedule σ. Let $Z(\sigma_1)$ denote the total cost of schedule σ_1, and $Z(N_2)$ the total cost of the jobs in N_2 in schedule σ. Let $Z_{LP(C)}$ denote the optimal total cost of problem $LP(C)$. Clearly, $Z_{LP(C)}$ is a lower bound of Z^*. Since σ_1 generated in Step 2 of the heuristic only includes the jobs in N_1, we have $Z(\sigma_1) \leq Z_{LP(C)}$. In Step 3 of Heuristic $H1$, each job in N_2 is assigned to a subcontractor or an in-house machine in a way that it incurs the minimum cost. Thus, $Z(N_2) \leq Z^*$. Therefore,

$$Z^{H1} = Z(\sigma_1) + Z(N_2) \leq Z_{LP(C)} + Z^* \leq 2Z^*.$$

This completes the proof. □

Theorem 6.4 *For problem* $\min\{G \mid C_{\max} \leq C\}$ *with* $C \geq \frac{1}{m}\sum_{j \in N} p_{0j} + p_{0,\max}$, *if the processing times and production costs of the jobs are distributed over the intervals* $[X_1, X_2]$ *and* $[Y_1, Y_2]$, *respectively, where* $0 < X_1 < X_2 < \infty$ *and* $0 < Y_1 < Y_2 < \infty$, *and if* m *and* k *are fixed, then, as* n *approaches infinity, the solution* σ *generated by Heuristic* $H1$ *is asymptotically optimal.*

Proof Since m is fixed, the contribution of the jobs in N_2 to the total cost of a schedule is always bounded from above. On the other hand, the optimal total cost of any schedule approaches infinity as n goes to infinity. Therefore,

$$\lim_{n \to \infty} \frac{Z(N_2)}{Z^*} = 0. \tag{6.11}$$

As we have shown in the proof of Theorem 6.3, $Z(\sigma_1) \leq Z^*$. This, along with (6.11), implies that

$$\lim_{n \to \infty} \frac{Z(\sigma) - Z^*}{Z^*} \leq \lim_{n \to \infty} \frac{Z(\sigma_1) + Z(N_2) - Z^*}{Z^*}$$
$$= \lim_{n \to \infty} \frac{Z(\sigma_1) - Z^*}{Z^*} \leq 0.$$

This completes the proof. □

The result in Theorem 6.4 shows the asymptotic performance of the heuristic and provides motivation for studying its computational performance in the following section.

6.2.3 Computational Results

Chen and Li (2008) conduct computational experiments to evaluate the performance of Heuristic $H1$. We summarize their experiments and corresponding results below.
  A large number of test problems are generated randomly as follows:

- Number of jobs $n \in \{50, 100, 200, 400\}$, number of in-house parallel machines $m \in \{2, 4, 8\}$, and number of subcontractors $k \in \{1, 3, 9\}$. We note that a small (large) m relative to k means a relative small (large) in-house capacity compared

6.2 Problem with a Lead Time Performance Guarantee

to available subcontracting options. The nine possible combinations of m and k here represent a wide range of this relative relationship.

- Job processing times p_{0j} are drawn from the discrete uniform distribution over the interval $[1, 100]$, and $p_{1j}, p_{2j}, \ldots, p_{kj}$ are drawn from the discrete uniform distribution over the interval $[1, 100\mu]$, where $\mu \in \{1, 2, 4\}$. These values of μ represent situations where the delivery lead time of a subcontracted job is about the same as, twice, or four times the processing time of the job if it is processed in-house.
- Production costs of jobs q_{0j} are drawn from the discrete uniform distribution over the interval $[1, 100]$, and $q_{1j}, q_{2j}, \ldots, q_{kj}$ follow the discrete uniform distribution over the interval $[1, 100\nu]$, where $\nu \in \{0.5, 1, 4\}$. These values of ν represent situations in which the production cost of a job charged by a subcontractor is about half, the same as, or four times the in-house production cost of the job.
- The makespan threshold value C is set as $\lceil \alpha(\sum_{j \in N} p_{0j})/m \rceil + p_{0,\max}$, where $\alpha \in \{0.3, 0.6, 1.0\}$. With C generated this way, typically at least $(1 - \alpha) \times 100\%$ of the jobs have to be subcontracted in order to satisfy the given constraint on the makespan.

For each possible combination of the values of parameters n, m, k, μ, ν, and α, 10 random test instances are generated. It is found that Heuristic $H1$ can solve every test instance in less than 1 CPU second on a 2-GHz processor. Therefore, we do not report CPU times for the test instances.

The LP-relaxation problem $LP(C)$ is infeasible for some of the test problems. Even if $LP(C)$ is feasible for a test problem, the test problem itself may not be feasible; and even if the test problem is feasible, the solution generated by the heuristic may not be feasible. We report in Table 6.1 the percentage of test instances

Table 6.1 Percentage of test instances of $\min\{G \mid C_{\max} \leq C\}$ for which Heuristic $H1$ generates feasible/optimal solutions

n	m	$k = 1$		$k = 3$		$k = 9$	
		$\alpha = 0.3$	$\alpha = 0.6$	$\alpha = 0.3$	$\alpha = 0.6$	$\alpha = 0.3$	$\alpha = 0.6$
50	2	90.0%	100%	100%	96.0%	95.7%	100%
	4	88.9%	95.0%	96.7%	100%	96.1%	100%
	8	67.4%	73.8%	83.6%	92.8%	87.3%	100%
100	2	100%	100%	100%	91.7%	100%	100%
	4	90.0%	100%	90.0%	92.3%	91.7%	100%
	8	73.3%	100%	95.0%	93.1%	82.9%	100%
200	2	83.3%	95.2%	85.7%	100%	100%	100%
	4	100%	100%	100%	87.5%	95.2%	100%
	8	100%	90.9%	100%	91.7%	95.0%	100%
400	2	90.9%	100%	100%	100%	100%	100%
	4	90.9%	100%	100%	100%	100%	100%
	8	90.9%	100%	95.2%	90.9%	100%	100%

for which $H1$ generates a feasible solution among all the test problems where $LP(C)$ is feasible. Since a problem may still be infeasible even if the corresponding $LP(C)$ is feasible, the percentage reported in Table 6.1 is a lower bound on the percentage of feasible problems for which the heuristic generates a feasible solution. Each entry in the table corresponds to a given combination of n, m, k, and α based on 90 test problems, i.e., 9 combinations of μ and v, and 10 test problems for each combination. By Theorem 6.2, when $\alpha = 1.0$, the solution generated by the heuristic is always feasible. Hence, only the problems with = 0.3 or 0.6 are reported in Table 6.1. From this table, we conclude that the heuristic often (with an overall probability of more than 90%) generates a feasible solution when the given problem instance is feasible. We also observe that Heuristic $H1$ tends to be more successful in generating feasible solutions when $\alpha = 0.6$ than when $\alpha = 0.3$. This is because, when α is larger, the test instances generated are more likely to be feasible.

More importantly, among those test instances where Heuristic $H1$ generates feasible solutions, the heuristic solution values are always equal to the optimal objective values of the corresponding $LP(C)$ solutions. In other words, for all of our test problems, if the solution generated by the heuristic is feasible, then it is optimal. This means that Heuristic $H1$ is highly effective at solving problem $\min\{G \mid C_{\max} \leq C\}$.

6.2.4 A Related Problem

In the problem considered in Sects. 6.2.1–6.2.3, there is a pre-specified threshold value C on the makespan of the schedule. This problem represents applications where there is an explicit overall service level constraint. However, for some other applications, a different problem variant may be more appropriate. In this section we discuss such a problem that is studied by Chen and Li (2008).

The problem has the same setting as in problem $\min\{G \mid C_{\max} \leq C\}$, but with a different objective, which is to minimize a weighted sum of makespan and the total cost, i.e., $\lambda C_{\max} + (1 - \lambda)G$, where $0 \leq \lambda \leq 1$, without a constraint on service level. Denote this problem as $\min\{\lambda C_{\max} + (1 - \lambda)G\}$. This problem is motivated by a situation where the manufacturer wants to achieve a balance between the lead time performance $C_{\max}$ and the total production and subcontracting cost G. The manufacturer can choose a weighting parameter $\lambda \in [0, 1]$ and consider the weighted sum of the two measures $C_{\max}$ and G.

By a reduction from the Subset Sum problem with a similar construction to that in the proof of Theorem 6.1, it is not difficult to show that when $0 < \lambda < 1$, this problem is at least ordinarily NP-hard even if there is only a single machine at the manufacturer, there is a single subcontractor, and the in-house production costs are proportional to the production times. To solve this problem, Chen and Li (2008) propose a heuristic algorithm. The heuristic divides the problem into a number of subproblems and then uses a similar idea to the heuristic developed in Sect. 6.2.2 to solve each subproblem.

6.2 Problem with a Lead Time Performance Guarantee

Suppose that there are L, $L \leq nk$, distinct values among all delivery lead times $\{p_{hj} | j \in N, h \in K\}$ specified by the subcontractors. Let $\pi_1, \pi_2, \ldots, \pi_L$ denote these L values, where $\pi_1 > \pi_2 > \cdots > \pi_L$. Define $\pi_{L+1} = 0$. We consider $L + 1$ subproblems. For $l = 1, 2, \ldots, L + 1$, subproblem l is defined to be the original problem with two additional requirements:

- Requirement (i): The maximum delivery lead time among all of the subcontracted jobs is no more than π_l.
- Requirement (ii): The makespan $C_{\max}$ is calculated as the maximum of π_l and the completion time of the last job completed at the manufacturer's own plant.

Clearly, any feasible solution to the original problem is also a feasible solution to at least one of the subproblems with the same objective value. Thus, the minimum of the optimal objective values of the subproblems is the optimal objective value of the original problem. This means that we can solve the original problem by solving these $L + 1$ subproblems.

For each job $j \in N$ and each $l = 1, 2, \ldots, L + 1$, define a subset of subcontractors $S_{lj} = \{h \in K | p_{hj} \leq \pi_l\}$, which are the subcontractors that can process job j with a delivery time no later than π_l. Define $V_l = \{j \in N \mid S_{lj} \neq \emptyset\}$, which is the set of jobs that can be subcontracted in subproblem l. For each $j \in V_l$, define a subcontractor $s_{lj} = \arg\min_{v \in S_{lj}} \{q_{vj}\}$, which is the subcontractor that can process job j at a minimum cost with a delivery lead time no later than π_l. Requirements (i) and (ii) of subproblem l imply that if a job $j \in V_l$ is to be subcontracted, it is optimal to subcontract it to subcontractor s_{lj}. In subproblem $L + 1$, since $\pi_{L+1} = 0$, no job can be subcontracted and, hence, $V_{L+1} = \emptyset$.

For $l = 1, \ldots, L + 1$, subproblem l can be formulated as the following mixed integer program which is similar to the formulation $IP(C)$ given in Sect. 6.2.2:

$$IP_l: \quad \text{Minimize} \quad \lambda C_{\max} + (1 - \lambda) \sum_{i=1}^{m} \sum_{j=1}^{n} q_{0j} x_{ij} + (1 - \lambda) \sum_{j \in V_l} q_{s_{lj}, j} y_j$$

subject to

$$\sum_{i=1}^{m} x_{ij} + y_j = 1, \quad \text{for } j \in V_l,$$

$$\sum_{i=1}^{m} x_{ij} = 1, \quad \text{for } j \in N \setminus V_l$$

$$C_{\max} \geq \sum_{j=1}^{n} p_{0j} x_{ij}, \quad \text{for } i \in M,$$

$$C_{\max} \geq \pi_l,$$

$$x_{ij} \in \{0, 1\}, \quad \text{for } i \in M \text{ and } j \in N$$

$$y_j \in \{0, 1\}, \quad \text{for } j \in V_l.$$

We study the LP-relaxation problem of $I P_l$, denoted as $L P_l$. By a similar proof to that of Lemma 6.1, we can show that in an optimal basic solution of $L P_l$, if $n \geq m$, then at least $n - m$ of the x_{ij} and y_j variables take the value of 1. Therefore, in an optimal basic solution of $L P_l$, there are at most m jobs with some fractional values assigned to the x_{ij} or y_j variables. An efficient procedure similar to Procedure PRO2 given in Sect. 6.2.2 can be designed to find an optimal solution to problem $L P_l$ with at most m split jobs. Based on this optimal solution, a heuristic similar to Heuristic $H1$ given in Sect. 6.2.2 can be designed to solve subproblem l. The heuristic for the overall problem $\min\{\lambda C_{\max} + (1 - \lambda)G\}$ can then be summarized as follows.

Heuristic $H2$ for Problem $\min\{\lambda C_{\max} + (1 - \lambda)G\}$
Step 1: For $l = 1, 2, \ldots, L + 1$, solve subproblem l by a heuristic similar to $H1$ (as discussed above) and obtain the solution σ_l.
Step 2: Choose the solution with the minimum objective value among the $L + 1$ solutions $\sigma_1, \sigma_2, \ldots, \sigma_{L+1}$ generated in Step 1.

Chen and Li (2008) show that (i) the worst-case performance ratio of Heuristic $H2$ is 2 and this bound is tight, and (ii) under similar conditions to those in Theorem 6.4, the solution generated by Heuristic $H2$ is asymptotically optimal as n approaches infinity.

Remark 6.3 Note that Heuristic $H2$ always generates a feasible solution to problem $\min\{\lambda C_{\max} + (1 - \lambda)G\}$. Thus, although both problems $\min\{\lambda C_{\max} + (1 - \lambda)G\}$ and $\min\{G \mid C_{\max} \leq C\}$ are NP-hard, it is easier to obtain a feasible solution with a worst-case performance guarantee for the former problem than obtaining a feasible solution for the latter problem.

Chen and Li (2008) test the performance of Heuristic $H2$ using various test problems similar to those described in Sect. 6.2.3. They report that the average relative error among all test instances equals 0.62%, indicating that Heuristic $H2$ is highly effective overall. Their computational results also show that the relative error of the heuristic decreases as n increases, and it approaches 0 as n tends to infinity. This is consistent with the fact that the heuristic is asymptotically optimal.

6.3 Value of Subcontracting

The value of subcontracting is well understood in a qualitative sense (e.g., Bazinet et al., 1998, Craumer, 2002, Kolawa, 2004). In contrast, few works have quantitatively evaluated the value of subcontracting. Chen and Li (2005, 2008) are apparently the first such studies in the context of detailed operations scheduling. They build on the problems $\min\{G \mid C_{\max} \leq C\}$ and $\min\{\lambda C_{\max} + (1 - \lambda)G\}$ discussed in Sect. 6.2 to evaluate the possible benefits that can be obtained by using the subcontracting option. In the following, we describe the analysis and results from Chen and Li (2005, 2008). Their analysis provides a tool for deriving various

6.3 Value of Subcontracting

managerial insights and performing sensitivity analysis in practice, for example, how the solution with or without the subcontracting option changes with various parameters of the problem.

Let ω and $Z(\omega)$ denote the optimal solution and optimal objective value of a problem without the subcontracting option, respectively. Similarly, let σ and $Z(\sigma)$ denote the optimal solution and optimal objective value to the same problem but with the subcontracting option, respectively. We investigate the relative reduction in the objective value that can be achieved when subcontracting is an available option. The relative reduction in the objective value is given as

$$\frac{Z(\omega) - Z(\sigma)}{Z(\omega)} = 1 - \frac{Z(\sigma)}{Z(\omega)}. \tag{6.12}$$

With the subcontracting option, we can apply a Heuristic H to obtain a solution σ^H whose objective value $Z(\sigma^H)$ is an upper bound on the optimal objective value $Z(\sigma)$. Then (6.12) implies that

$$\frac{Z(\omega) - Z(\sigma)}{Z(\omega)} \geq 1 - \frac{Z(\sigma^H)}{Z(\omega)}. \tag{6.13}$$

Thus, given a problem instance, the right-hand side of (6.12) provides a lower bound on the relative cost reduction that can be achieved. In the following Sects. 6.3.1 and 6.3.2, respectively, we describe the results from Chen and Li (2008) based on problem $\min\{G \mid C_{\max} \leq C\}$ and the results from Chen and Li (2005) based on problem $\min\{\lambda C_{\max} + (1 - \lambda)G\}$.

6.3.1 Value of Subcontracting in the Total Cost Problem

Without the subcontracting option, all of the jobs are processed on the m in-house machines. Hence, the total production cost is fixed and independent of how the jobs are scheduled. Therefore, for problem $\min\{G \mid C_{\max} \leq C\}$, $Z(\omega)$ in (6.13) is $\sum_{j \in N} q_{0j}$. We use Heuristic $H1$ given in Sect. 6.2.2 to solve problem $\min\{G \mid C_{\max} \leq C\}$, which means that $Z(\sigma^H)$ in (6.13) is equal to the total cost of the solution obtained by Heuristic $H1$.

We use the same set of test instances with $\alpha = 1.0$ generated in the experiments reported in Sect. 6.2.3. The instances with $\alpha = 0.3$ or 0.6 are not used here because the problem without the subcontracting option is likely to be infeasible with those values of α. With $\alpha = 1.0$, the problem without the subcontracting option is always feasible, and Heuristic $H1$ is also guaranteed to generate a feasible solution. We report in Tables 6.2 and 6.3 both the average relative cost reduction and the minimum relative cost reduction, in terms of n and k, and in terms of v, respectively. Since the relative cost reduction due to subcontracting does not change much with the number of machines m or the average subcontractors' processing

Table 6.2 Relative cost reduction due to the subcontracting option based on problem $\min\{G \mid C_{\max} \leq C\}$: results in terms of n and k

n	k	Avg reduction (%)	Min reduction (%)
50	1	34.7%	4.6%
	3	53.8%	12.4%
	9	71.8%	37.8%
100	1	34.1%	4.4%
	3	53.0%	16.0%
	9	72.2%	43.2%
200	1	33.1%	7.1%
	3	53.0%	17.1%
	9	72.0%	43.6%
400	1	32.8%	7.3%
	3	52.6%	18.1%
	9	72.6%	44.9%

Table 6.3 Relative cost reduction due to the subcontracting option based on problem $\min\{G \mid C_{\max} \leq C\}$: results in terms of v

v	Avg reduction (%)	Min reduction (%)
0.5	74.5%	52.1%
1	57.9%	28.0%
4	25.8%	4.4%

time (represented by μ), we do not report the results in terms of m or μ. The results in Table 6.2 are based on 90 test problems with $m = 4$ (10 for each of the 9 combinations of the values of μ and v). The results in Table 6.3 are based on 360 test problems with $\mu = 2$, i.e., 10 for each of the 36 combinations of the values of n, m, and k.

The results in these tables demonstrate that there is a significant cost reduction from using the subcontracting option for almost every problem tested. The relative cost reduction increases quickly with the number of subcontractors k and decreases quickly with the average subcontracting cost (represented by v).

6.3.2 Value of Subcontracting in the Weighted Sum of Makespan and Total Cost Problem

For problem $\min\{\lambda C_{\max} + (1 - \lambda)G\}$ without the subcontracting option, since all of the jobs are processed on the m in-house machines, in the optimal objective value $Z(\omega) = \lambda C_{\max}(\omega) + (1 - \lambda)G(\omega)$, the total production cost $G(\omega)$ is equal to $\sum_{j \in N} q_{0j}$, and the makespan of the jobs $C_{\max}(\omega)$ is the minimum makespan of the jobs when they are all processed on the m in-house machines.

6.3 Value of Subcontracting

Since the parallel-machine makespan minimization problem is NP-hard, it is impractical to find the exact value of $C_{\max}(\omega)$. We use the following lower bound on $C_{\max}(\omega)$ to replace $C_{\max}(\omega)$ in $Z(\omega)$: $LB(\omega) = \frac{1}{m}\sum_{j \in N} p_{0j}$.

If the subcontracting option is available, we can apply Heuristic $H2$ given in Sect. 6.2.4 to obtain a solution σ^{H2}. Clearly, the objective value of σ^{H2}, i.e., $\lambda C_{\max}(\sigma^{H2}) + (1 - \lambda)G(\sigma^{H2})$, is an upper bound on the optimal objective value $\lambda C_{\max}(\sigma) + (1 - \lambda)G(\sigma)$. This implies that (6.13) can be rewritten as

$$\frac{Z(\omega) - Z(\sigma)}{Z(\omega)} \geq 1 - \frac{\lambda C_{\max}(\sigma^{H2}) + (1 - \lambda)G(\sigma^{H2})}{\lambda LB(\omega) + (1 - \lambda)G(\omega)}. \tag{6.14}$$

Hence, given any problem instance, the right-hand side of (6.14) provides a lower bound for the relative cost reduction that can be computed efficiently.

Next, we provide an asymptotic analysis on the relative cost reduction that can be achieved by subcontracting as the number of jobs in the problem approaches infinity. We make the following assumption about the problem parameters:

Assumption A All parameters in a problem instance are integers, and independent and uniformly distributed as follows:

(i) $p_{0j} \sim U[P_{0l}, P_{0u}]$ and $q_{0j} \sim U[Q_{0l}, Q_{0u}]$, for all $j \in N$, and
(ii) $p_{hj} \sim U[P_{1l}, P_{1u}]$ and $q_{hj} \sim U[Q_{1l}, Q_{1u}]$, for all $h \in K$ and $j \in N$,

where $P_{0l}, P_{0u}, Q_{0l}, Q_{0u}, P_{1l}, P_{1u}, Q_{1l}, Q_{1u}$ are integers and satisfy $0 < P_{0l} < P_{0u} < \infty, 0 < Q_{0l} < Q_{0u} < \infty, 0 < P_{1l} < P_{1u} < \infty$, and $0 < Q_{1l} < Q_{1u} < \infty$.

We note that it is a common assumption in the literature that job processing times follow uniform distributions (e.g., Tsai, 1992; Cheng & Liu, 2004).

For ease of presentation, we define the following notation:

- $q_{\min, j} = \min\{q_{hj}|h \in K\}$, for $j \in N$.
- $Prob(x, y, z)$ = probability that a job $j \in N$ satisfies $p_{0j} = x$, $q_{\min, j} = y$, and $q_{0j} = z$.
- $\delta_S(x, y, z) = 1$ if $\lambda x > (1 - \lambda)(y - z)m$, and 0 otherwise.
- $\delta_M(x, y, z) = 1$ if $\lambda x \leq (1 - \lambda)(y - z)m$, and 0 otherwise.
- $R_S(x, y) = \sum_{z=Q_{0l}}^{Q_{0u}} Prob(x, y, z) \cdot \delta_S(x, y, z)$.
- $R_M(x, z) = \sum_{y=Q_{1l}}^{Q_{1u}} Prob(x, y, z) \cdot \delta_M(x, y, z)$.

The exact formula for $Prob(x, y, z)$, for all integers x, y, and z satisfying $P_{0l} \leq x \leq P_{0u}$, $Q_{1l} \leq y \leq Q_{1u}$ and $Q_{0l} \leq z \leq Q_{0u}$, can be derived as follows:

$$Prob(x, y, z) = Pr(p_{0j} = x) \cdot Pr(q_{\min, j} = y) \cdot Pr(q_{0j} = z)$$

$$= Pr(p_{0j} = x) \cdot [Pr(q_{\min, j} \geq y) - Pr(q_{\min, j} \geq y + 1)] \cdot Pr(q_{0j} = z)$$

$$= \frac{1}{P_{0u} - P_{0l} + 1} \cdot \left[\left(\frac{Q_{1u} - y + 1}{Q_{1u} - Q_{1l} + 1}\right)^k - \left(\frac{Q_{1u} - y}{Q_{1u} - Q_{1l} + 1}\right)^k\right]$$

$$\cdot \frac{1}{Q_{0u} - Q_{0l} + 1}.$$

Note that as k goes to infinity, $Prob(x, y, z)$ approaches $\frac{1}{[(P_{0u}-P_{0l}+1)(Q_{0u}-Q_{0l}+1)]}$ if $y = Q_{1l}$, $P_{0l} \leq x \leq P_{0u}$, and $Q_{0l} \leq z \leq Q_{0u}$, and it approaches 0, otherwise. Chen and Li (2005) show the following result.

Theorem 6.5 *For problem* $\min\{\lambda C_{\max} + (1 - \lambda)G\}$, *under Assumption A, if m is fixed, then as the number of jobs n approaches infinity, the relative cost reduction achieved by subcontracting satisfies the following:*

$$\lim_{n\to\infty} \frac{Z(\omega) - Z(\sigma)}{Z(\omega)}$$

$$= 1 - \frac{\frac{\lambda}{m} \sum_{x=P_{0l}}^{P_{0u}} \sum_{z=Q_{0l}}^{Q_{0u}} x R_M(x, z) + (1 - \lambda) \sum_{x=P_{0l}}^{P_{0u}} \left(\sum_{y=Q_{1l}}^{Q_{1u}} y R_S(x, y) + \sum_{z=Q_{0l}}^{Q_{0u}} z R_M(x, z) \right)}{\frac{\lambda}{2m}(P_{0l} + P_{0u}) + \frac{1-\lambda}{2}(Q_{0l} + Q_{0u})},$$

$$(6.15)$$

almost surely (a.s.).

Proof Without the subcontracting option, the optimal solution ω satisfies the following two properties:

(i) $\frac{1}{m} \sum_{j\in N} p_{0j} \leq C_{\max}(\omega) \leq \frac{1}{m} \sum_{j\in N} p_{0j} + P_{0u}$, and (ii) $G(\omega) = \sum_{j\in N} q_{0j}$.

Since $p_{0j} \sim U[P_{0l}, P_{0u}]$ and $q_{0j} \sim U[Q_{0l}, Q_{0u}]$ for all $j \in N$ and they are all independent, by the Law of Large Numbers, we have

$$\lim_{n\to\infty} \frac{C_{\max}(\omega)}{n} = \frac{1}{m} \lim_{n\to\infty} \frac{1}{n} \sum_{j\in N} p_{0j} = \frac{P_{0l} + P_{0u}}{2m}, \quad a.s. \quad (6.16)$$

$$\lim_{n\to\infty} \frac{G(\omega)}{n} = \lim_{n\to\infty} \frac{1}{n} \sum_{j\in N} q_{0j} = \frac{Q_{0l} + Q_{0u}}{2}, \quad a.s. \quad (6.17)$$

We now focus on the case with the subcontracting option. We propose the following simple rule to derive a solution:

Heuristic Rule For each $j \in N$, if $\lambda p_{0j} > (1-\lambda)(q_{\min,j} - q_{0j})m$, then subcontract job j to subcontractor $s'_j = \arg\min_{h\in K}\{q_{hj}\}$, otherwise assign job j to the earliest available machine at the in-house facility. We denote the solution generated as σ'.

In the following, we show that σ' is asymptotically optimal and characterize the objective value of σ' and thus also the optimal objective value of the problem in the asymptotic sense.

Consider any solution ρ for the case with the subcontracting option. Let N_M and N_S denote the subset of the jobs processed in-house and the subset of the jobs subcontracted, respectively, in ρ. Let $T(\rho) = \sum_{j\in N_M} p_{0j}$ be the total

6.3 Value of Subcontracting

processing time of the jobs processed in-house in ρ. Clearly, $G(\rho) = \sum_{j \in N_M} q_{0j} + \sum_{j \in N_S} q_{\min, j}$ and

$$\frac{1}{m} T(\rho) \leq C_{\max}(\rho) \leq \max \left\{ \frac{1}{m} T(\rho) + P_{0u}, P_{1u} \right\}. \tag{6.18}$$

This, along with the fact that $\lim_{n \to \infty}(P_{0u}/n) = \lim_{n \to \infty}(P_{1u}/n) = 0$, implies that

$$\lim_{n \to \infty} \frac{Z(\rho)}{n} = \lim_{n \to \infty} \frac{\lambda C_{\max}(\rho) + (1 - \lambda)G(\rho)}{n} = \lim_{n \to \infty} \frac{\frac{\lambda}{m} T(\rho) + (1 - \lambda)G(\rho)}{n},$$

or equivalently,

$$\lim_{n \to \infty} \frac{Z(\rho)}{n} = \lim_{n \to \infty} \frac{1}{n} \left[\sum_{j \in N_M} \left(\frac{\lambda p_{0j}}{m} + (1 - \lambda)q_{0j} \right) + \sum_{j \in N_S} (1 - \lambda)q_{\min, j} \right].$$

It is evident that the proposed heuristic rule minimizes the right-hand side of the above equation. Therefore, solution σ' is asymptotically optimal.

Next, we characterize the objective value of σ'. By the proposed heuristic rule and the definition of $R_S(x, y)$, it is easy to see that $R_S(x, y)$ is the probability that a given job j is assigned to a subcontractor and satisfies $p_{0j} = x$ and $q_{\min, j} = y$. Similarly, $R_M(x, z)$ is the probability that a given job j is assigned to a machine at the manufacturer and satisfies $p_{0j} = x$ and $q_{0j} = z$. Define:

$n_S(x, y)$ = number of jobs j with $p_{0j} = x$ and $q_{\min, j} = y$ that are subcontracted;
$n_M(x, z)$ = number of jobs j with $p_{0j} = x$ and $q_{0j} = z$ that are processed in-house.

Clearly, by the Law of Large Numbers,

$$\lim_{n \to \infty} \frac{n_S(x, y)}{n} = R_S(x, y), \quad a.s. \tag{6.19}$$

$$\lim_{n \to \infty} \frac{n_M(x, z)}{n} = R_M(x, z), \quad a.s. \tag{6.20}$$

The total production cost of solution σ' is given as

$$G(\sigma') = \sum_{x=P_{0l}}^{P_{0u}} \sum_{y=Q_{1l}}^{Q_{1u}} y \cdot n_S(x, y) + \sum_{x=P_{0l}}^{P_{0u}} \sum_{z=Q_{0l}}^{Q_{0u}} z \cdot n_M(x, z), \tag{6.21}$$

where the first term is the contribution of the subcontracted jobs, and the second term is the contribution of the jobs processed in-house. From (6.19), (6.20), and (6.21), we have

$$\lim_{n\to\infty} \frac{G(\sigma')}{n} = \lim_{n\to\infty} \sum_{x=P_{0l}}^{P_{0u}} \sum_{y=Q_{1l}}^{Q_{1u}} y \cdot \frac{n_S(x,y)}{n} + \lim_{n\to\infty} \sum_{x=P_{0l}}^{P_{0u}} \sum_{z=Q_{0l}}^{Q_{0u}} z \cdot \frac{n_M(x,z)}{n}$$

$$= \sum_{x=P_{0l}}^{P_{0u}} \sum_{y=Q_{1l}}^{Q_{1u}} y R_S(x,y) + \sum_{x=P_{0l}}^{P_{0u}} \sum_{z=Q_{0l}}^{Q_{0u}} z R_M(x,z), \quad a.s. \quad (6.22)$$

In solution σ', the total processing time of the jobs processed at the manufacturer is given by

$$T(\sigma') = \sum_{x=P_{0l}}^{P_{0u}} \sum_{z=Q_{0l}}^{Q_{0u}} x \cdot n_M(x,z).$$

Applying (6.18) to σ', we have,

$$\lim_{n\to\infty} \frac{C_{\max}(\sigma')}{n} = \frac{1}{m} \lim_{n\to\infty} \frac{T(\sigma')}{n}$$

$$= \frac{1}{m} \lim_{n\to\infty} \sum_{x=P_{0l}}^{P_{0u}} \sum_{z=Q_{0l}}^{Q_{0u}} x \cdot \frac{n_M(x,z)}{n} = \frac{1}{m} \sum_{x=P_{0l}}^{P_{0u}} \sum_{z=Q_{0l}}^{Q_{0u}} x R_M(x,z), \quad a.s. \quad (6.23)$$

From (6.22) and (6.23), we have

$$\lim_{n\to\infty} \frac{Z(\sigma')}{n} = \lim_{n\to\infty} \frac{\lambda C_{\max}(\sigma') + (1-\lambda)G(\sigma')}{n}$$

$$= \frac{\lambda}{m} \sum_{x=P_{0l}}^{P_{0u}} \sum_{z=Q_{0l}}^{Q_{0u}} x R_M(x,z)$$

$$+ (1-\lambda) \sum_{x=P_{0l}}^{P_{0u}} \left(\sum_{y=Q_{1l}}^{Q_{1u}} y R_S(x,y) + \sum_{z=Q_{0l}}^{Q_{0u}} z R_M(x,z) \right), \quad a.s.$$

This, along with (6.16) and (6.17) and the fact that σ' is asymptotically optimal, completes the proof of the theorem. $\square$

Remark 6.4 Note that in Theorem 6.5, we do not assume that the number of subcontractors, k, is fixed. Thus, the asymptotic result (6.15) holds for both the case with a fixed k and the case with k approaching infinity. From the proof of Theorem 6.5, we can see that the terms in Eq. (6.15) represent the average

6.3 Value of Subcontracting

contributions to $C_{\max}$ and the total production cost as follows. The terms $(P_{0l} + P_{0u})/2m$ (denoted as $\bar{C}_{\max}^1$) and $(Q_{0l} + Q_{0u})/2$ (denoted as $\bar{G}^1$) are the average contribution per job to $C_{\max}$ and the average contribution per job to the total production cost (as n approaches infinity) in the case with no subcontracting option. Similarly, the terms $\frac{1}{m} \sum_{x=P_{0l}}^{P_{0u}} \sum_{z=Q_{0l}}^{Q_{0u}} x R_M(x, z)$ (denoted as $\bar{C}_{\max}^2$) and $\sum_{x=P_{0l}}^{P_{0u}} (\sum_{y=Q_{1l}}^{Q_{1u}} y R_S(x, y) + \sum_{z=Q_{0l}}^{Q_{0u}} z R_M(x, z))$ (denoted as $\bar{G}^2$) are the corresponding average contributions per job in the case with the subcontracting option.

Theorem 6.5 and the associated average contribution terms observed in the above remark (i.e., $\bar{C}_{\max}^1$, $\bar{C}_{\max}^2$, $\bar{G}^1$, and $\bar{G}^2$) enable us to estimate the following performance measures for problems with a large number of jobs (e.g., $n \geq 500$):

(i) The makespan in the optimal solution with or without the subcontracting option, which is $n\bar{C}_{\max}^1$ or $n\bar{C}_{\max}^2$.
(ii) The total production cost in the optimal solution with or without the subcontracting option, which is $n\bar{G}^1$ or $n\bar{G}^2$.
(iii) The benefit of subcontracting, which is given by (6.15).

Given the number of machines (i.e., m), the number of subcontractors (i.e., k), the ranges of processing times (i.e., P_{0l}, P_{0u}, P_{1l}, and P_{1u}), the ranges of production costs (i.e., Q_{0l}, Q_{0u}, Q_{1l}, and Q_{1u}), and the weighting parameter λ, measurements (i), (ii), and (iii) can be calculated easily using the functions $Prob(x, y, z)$, $R_M(x, z)$, and $R_S(x, y)$.

Furthermore, the result of Theorem 6.5, along with the above observations, can be used to perform sensitivity analysis in practice. For example, in situations where the manufacturer is faced with a large number of jobs, the manufacturer can use the results derived here to answer a number of important managerial questions, such as:

1. How will the makespan and total production cost change if some additional subcontractors are used and/or some additional machines are added for in-house processing?
2. How will the benefit of subcontracting change if some problem parameters change?

Some general insights can also be obtained from the result of Theorem 6.5. It can be easily proved that the relative cost reduction given in Theorem 6.5 increases with the number of subcontractors k and the weighting parameter λ, but decreases with the number of machines m. These insights are intuitively correct (as explained below where some computational results are reported), but we can use the result of Theorem 6.5 to verify those insights analytically.

Finally, we describe the computational results about the value of subcontracting reported in Chen and Li (2005) based on problem $\min \lambda C_{\max} + (1 - \lambda)G$. For problem instances with a finite n, the lower bound on the relative cost reduction given in (6.14) is used. For problem instances with an infinite n, the asymptotic relative cost reduction derived in Theorem 6.5 is used. For the case with a finite n, test instances are randomly generated in the same way as those used in the

Table 6.4 Relative cost reduction due to the subcontracting option based on problem $\min\{\lambda C_{\max} + (1 - \lambda)G\}$

n	m	$k = 1$		$k = 3$		$k = 9$	
		Avg red	Min red	Avg red	Min red	Avg red	Min red
50	2	42.97%	5.14%	59.82%	13.63%	75.38%	40.15%
	4	37.24%	4.73%	54.19%	12.91%	70.54%	38.34%
	8	32.61%	4.23%	47.15%	8.67%	58.45%	26.54%
100	2	44.06%	4.73%	61.37%	16.92%	77.89%	45.68%
	4	38.96%	4.55%	56.52%	16.26%	74.04%	44.32%
	8	35.32%	4.46%	53.00%	16.03%	69.17%	41.25%
200	2	44.20%	7.70%	62.27%	18.42%	78.73%	45.72%
	4	39.18%	7.33%	57.80%	17.68%	75.32%	44.54%
	8	35.87%	7.17%	54.79%	17.38%	71.66%	43.96%
400	2	44.22%	8.08%	62.45%	19.00%	79.75%	47.18%
	4	39.22%	7.57%	58.12%	18.49%	76.63%	45.94%
	8	35.96%	7.41%	55.26%	18.27%	74.35%	45.41%
∞	2	44.46%	11.06%	62.80%	23.17%	80.20%	49.44%
	4	39.51%	8.53%	58.54%	22.46%	77.26%	48.37%
	8	36.31%	8.39%	55.76%	22.13%	75.16%	47.86%

computational experiment reported in Sect. 6.2.3, except that slightly different values of λ, ν are used here: $\lambda \in \{0.2, 0.5, 0.8\}$, $\nu \in \{1, 2, 4\}$. For the case with $n = \infty$, the only relevant parameters are $m, k, P_{0l}, P_{0u}, Q_{0l}, Q_{0u}, Q_{1l}, Q_{1u}$, and λ. We generate these parameters as in the case with a finite n.

We report in Table 6.4 both average and minimum relative cost reductions due to the subcontracting option. For each combination of (n, m, k) with a finite n reported in the table, the results are based on 270 test problems (10 for each of the 27 combinations of the values of μ, ν, and λ). Each entry in the columns Avg red (Min red) is the average (minimum) relative cost reduction over the 270 test problems for the corresponding (n, m, k) combination. In the case with $n = \infty$, the lower bounds derived in Theorem 6.5 are reported for each row based on the 27 lower bounds, one for each combination of μ, ν, and λ.

The results in Table 6.4 demonstrate that there is a significant reduction in cost by using the subcontracting option for almost every problem tested. The relative cost reduction increases quickly with the number of subcontractors k, increases slightly with the number of jobs n, and decreases slightly with the number of machines m at the manufacturer. This can be explained intuitively. As k increases, there is more flexibility in using the subcontracting option; hence, the overall cost should go down. On the other hand, as m decreases or n increases, the capacity of the manufacturer becomes tighter, and the relative value of subcontracting becomes larger. Note that the cost reduction does not change much when n increases from 50 to ∞ for fixed m and k. This means that the subcontracting option is beneficial even if the manufacturer is faced with a small number of jobs. Although no results are explicitly reported as a function of λ in the table, Chen and Li (2005) discuss how their results show that the value of subcontracting increases with λ. This can be explained as follows. The impact of $C_{\max}$ on the overall objective function increases with λ, and this measure decreases if more jobs are subcontracted. As a result, one can typically expect that as λ increases, more jobs should be subcontracted. In summary, we conclude that the value of subcontracting mainly depends on the availability of subcontractors (k), the in-house capacity (m), and the weighting parameter in the objective function (λ).

6.4 Problems with a Subcontracting Budget Constraint

Lee and Sung (2008a,b) consider several scheduling problems with subcontracting options where there is a budget constraint on the total subcontracting cost. In all their problems, a single in-house machine and a single subcontractor are available.

We first define the problems of Lee and Sung (2008a,b), following most of the notation introduced in their work. A manufacturer needs to process a set of n given jobs $N = \{1, \ldots, n\}$ using either a single machine in-house or a subcontractor. If a job $j \in N$ is processed on the in-house machine, the processing time required is p_j; but if it is subcontracted to the subcontractor, the lead time (i.e., the completion time) of the job is l_j regardless of how many jobs are handled by the subcontractor. Furthermore, if a job $j \in N$ is subcontracted, there is a subcontracting cost s_j, which can be viewed as the additional cost incurred due to subcontracting relative to the in-house processing cost (which is not explicitly considered). Each job $j \in N$ has a due date d_j. In a given schedule, let S denote the set of subcontracted jobs, and $SC = \sum_{j \in S} s_j$ the total subcontracting cost. There is a given budget B such that the total subcontracting cost cannot exceed this budget, i.e., it is required that $SC \leq B$ in a feasible schedule.

Given a schedule, let C_j denote the completion time of job j, which is l_j if job j is subcontracted, and the total processing time of all the jobs scheduled before it on the in-house machine plus p_j if it is processed in-house. Let $T_j = \max\{0, C_j - d_j\}$ be the tardiness of job j. Three scheduling measures are considered, namely,

- Total completion time of the jobs, denoted as $\sum C_j$, which is equal to $\sum_{j \in N} C_j$.
- Maximum tardiness of the jobs, denoted as $T_{\max}$, which is equal to $\max_{j \in N} \{T_j\}$.
- Total tardiness of the jobs, denoted as $\sum T_j$, which is equal to $\sum_{j \in N} T_j$.

Lee and Sung (2008a,b) consider three specific objective functions:

1. Weighted sum of the total completion time of the jobs and the total subcontracting cost, denoted as $\alpha \sum C_j + (1 - \alpha)SC$, where the weighting parameter $\alpha \in [0, 1]$ represents the relative importance between the two measures involved from the manufacturer's point of view.
2. Weighted sum of the maximum tardiness the jobs and the total subcontracting cost, denoted as $\alpha T_{\max} + (1 - \alpha)SC$.
3. Weighted sum of the total tardiness of the jobs and the total subcontracting cost, denoted as $\alpha \sum T_j + (1 - \alpha)SC$.

270   6 Joint Subcontracting and Scheduling Decisions

For ease of presentation, we simply call the corresponding problems with these objective functions *the total completion time problem, the maximum tardiness problem*, and *the total tardiness problem*, respectively.

Lee and Sung (2008a,b) show that all these problems are ordinarily NP-hard. We do not present their NP-hardness proofs. Instead, we focus on how these problems can be solved either exactly or heuristically. In the following Sects. 6.4.1, 6.4.2, and 6.4.3, we discuss exact and heuristic algorithms for each of these problems, respectively. All the results are from Lee and Sung (2008a,b).

6.4.1 The Total Completion Time Problem

For this problem, since the total completion time of the jobs is a part of the objective function to be minimized, it is optimal to schedule the jobs that are processed on the in-house machine in the shortest processing time first (SPT) order.

Lee and Sung (2008b) propose a pseudo-polynomial time dynamic programming algorithm to solve this problem with time complexity $O(n^2 B)$. We describe this algorithm below.

Algorithm DP-TCT

Initialization Reindex the jobs in SPT order, i.e., $p_1 \leq \cdots \leq p_n$.

Value Function $f(j, m, b)$ = the minimum total completion time of a partial schedule for jobs $j, \ldots, n$ where m ($m \leq n - j + 1$) of these jobs are subcontracted and the total subcontracting cost of these jobs is b.

Boundary Conditions $f(n + 1, 0, 0) = 0$.

Recurrence Relation For $j = n, \ldots, 1, m = 1, \ldots, n - j + 1$, and $b = 0, 1, \ldots, B$:

$$f(j, m, b) = \begin{cases} (n - j + 1)p_j + f(j + 1, m, b) & \text{if } m = 0, \\ \infty & \text{if } n - j + 1 = m \text{ and } s_j > b, \\ l_j + f(j + 1, m - 1, b - s_j) & \text{if } n - j + 1 = m \text{ and } s_j \leq b, \\ (n - j - m + 1)p_j + f(j + 1, m, b) & \text{if } n - j + 1 > m > 0 \text{ and } s_j > b, \\ \min\{(n - j - m + 1)p_j + f(j + 1, m, b), \\ \qquad l_j + f(j + 1, m - 1, b - s_j)\} & \text{if } n - j + 1 > m > 0 \text{ and } s_j \leq b. \end{cases}$$

Optimal Solution Value The optimal solution value is found by solving the following problem:

$$\min_{0 \leq m \leq n, 0 \leq b \leq B} \{\alpha f(1, m, b) + (1 - \alpha)b)\}.$$

The recurrence relation compares all five possible cases of (j, m, b): (1) $m = 0$, where all the jobs $j, \ldots, n$ are processed in-house; (2) $m = n - j + 1$, where all the

6.4 Problems with a Subcontracting Budget Constraint

jobs $j, \ldots, n$ are subcontracted out, and $s_j > b$; (3) $m = n - j + 1$ and $s_j \le b$; (4) $n - j + 1 > m > 0$, where some of the jobs $j, \ldots, n$ are processed in-house and some are subcontracted out, and $s_j > b$; (5) $n - j + 1 > m > 0$, and $s_j \le b$. Case (2) is not possible and hence the value function is ∞. In Cases (1) and (4), job j must be processed in-house, whereas in Case (3), job j must be subcontracted out. In Case (5), job j can either be processed in-house or subcontracted out.

In addition, Lee and Sung (2008b) give two heuristics and a branch-and-bound exact algorithm for the total completion time problem. We describe one of their heuristics. The idea is first to solve the problem without considering the budget constraint, which may result in a solution with too many jobs subcontracted out, and then gradually remove some of the jobs from the set of the subcontracted jobs until the budget constraint is satisfied. Before presenting this heuristic, we first discuss how the total completion time problem without the budget constraint can be solved. Lee and Sung (2008b) give a polynomial-time exact dynamic programming algorithm with time complexity $O(n^2)$ to solve this problem. This algorithm is described in the following.

Algorithm DP-TCT-NB

Initialization Reindex jobs in SPT order, i.e., $p_1 \le \cdots \le p_n$.

Value Function $f(j, m)$ = the minimum objective value of a partial schedule for jobs $j, \ldots, n$ where m ($m \le n - j + 1$) of these jobs are subcontracted out.

Boundary Conditions $f(n + 1, 0) = 0$.

Recurrence Relation For $j = n, \ldots, 1$, and $m = 1, \ldots, n - j + 1$:

$$
f(j, m) = \begin{cases}
\alpha(n - j + 1)p_j + f(j + 1, 0) & \text{if } m = 0, \\
\alpha l_j + (1 - \alpha)s_j + f(j + 1, m - 1) & \text{if } n - j + 1 = m, \\
\min\{\alpha(n - j - m + 1)p_j + f(j + 1, m), \\
\quad \alpha l_j + (1 - \alpha)s_j + f(j + 1, m - 1)\} & \text{if } n - j + 1 > m > 0.
\end{cases}
$$

Optimal Solution Value The optimal solution value is found by solving the following problem:
$\min_{0 \le m \le n}\{f(1, m)\}$.

Now we describe the heuristic. It generates three feasible schedules and chooses the one with the lowest objective value as the solution.

Heuristic TCT

Step 1: Solve the total completion time problem without the budget constraint by Algorithm DP-TCT-NB. Let the solution be denoted as π, and let the set of the subcontracted jobs be denoted as $S(\pi)$. If $\sum_{j \in S(\pi)} s_j \le B$, then π is also an optimal solution to the original problem with the budget constraint, and stop.

Step 2: Let $S_1 = S2 = S3 = S(\pi)$. Generate three solutions based on π as follows.

272   6 Joint Subcontracting and Scheduling Decisions

1. Remove the jobs with the shortest processing times from S_1, one by one, until $\sum_{j \in S_1} s_j \leq B$. Construct a feasible solution as follows: The jobs in the final set S_1 are subcontracted out, and the rest are processed in-house in SPT order. Let π_1 denote this solution, and $f(\pi_1)$ denote its objective value.
2. Remove the jobs with the largest subcontracting costs from S_2, one by one, until $\sum_{j \in S_2} s_j \leq B$. Construct a feasible solution as follows: The jobs in the final set S_2 are subcontracted out, and the rest are processed in-house in SPT order. Let π_2 denote this solution, and $f(\pi_2)$ denote its objective value.
3. Remove the jobs with the longest lead times provided by the subcontractor (i.e., l_j) from S_3, one by one, until $\sum_{j \in S_3} s_j \leq B$. Construct a feasible solution as follows: The jobs in the final set S_3 are subcontracted out, and the rest are processed in-house in SPT order. Let π_3 denote this solution, and $f(\pi_3)$ denote its objective value.

Step 3: Select the solution with the lowest objective value among π_1, π_2, π_3 as the heuristic solution.

The computational results reported in Lee and Sung (2008b) show that this heuristic performs well, particularly when the budget B is relatively large.

Example 6.3 (Application of Heuristic TCT) We apply Heuristic TCT to the following instance of the total completion time problem: $\alpha = 0.5$, $B = 9$, and p_j, l_j, s_j are given in the following table.

j	1	2	3	4
p_j	2	4	6	8
l_j	4	3	2	2
s_j	8	4	4	6

Step 1. Solve the problem without the budget constraint by Algorithm DP-TCT-NB. The optimal solution π is as follows: process jobs 1 and 2 in-house, but subcontract jobs 3 and 4 (i.e., $S(\pi) = \{3, 4\}$). This solution has an objective value of 11. The total subcontracting cost of this solution is 10, which violates the budget constraint.

Step 2. $S_1 = \{3, 4\}$. Since job 3 has a shorter processing time than job 4, job 3 is removed from S_1. After this, $\sum_{j \in S_1} s_j = s_4 = 6 < B$, and a feasible solution π_1 is generated in which job 4 is subcontracted, but jobs 1, 2 and 3 are processed in-house. The objective value of this solution is 14 with the total subcontracting cost of 6.

Step 3. $S_2 = \{3, 4\}$. Since job 4 has a larger subcontracting cost than job 3, job 4 is removed from S_2. After this, $\sum_{j \in S_2} s_j = s_3 = 4 < B$, and a feasible solution π_2 is generated in which job 3 is subcontracted, but jobs 1, 2 and 4 are processed in-house. The objective value of this solution is 16 with the total subcontracting cost of 4.

6.4 Problems with a Subcontracting Budget Constraint   273

Step 4. This step generates the same solution as in Step 3.
Step 5. π_1 is selected as the solution for this example.

An optimal solution for this example is to subcontract jobs 2 and 3, and process jobs 1 and 4 in-house. This solution has an objective value of 12.5 with total subcontracting cost of 8.

6.4.2 The Maximum Tardiness Problem

Since in this problem the maximum tardiness of the jobs is a part of the objective function to be minimized, it is optimal to schedule the jobs that are processed on the in-house machine in earliest due date first (EDD) order. Thus, we only need to consider the EDD order for the jobs processed in-house in any solution.

Lee and Sung (2008a) propose a pseudo-polynomial time dynamic programming algorithm to solve this problem with time complexity $O(nBP)$, where $P = \sum_{j \in N} p_j$. We describe this algorithm below.

Algorithm DP-MT

Initialization Reindex the jobs in EDD order, i.e., $d_1 \leq \ldots \leq d_n$.

Value Function $f(j, t, b)$ = the minimum maximum tardiness of a partial schedule for jobs $1, \ldots, j$ where the total processing time of the jobs processed in-house is t and the total subcontracting cost of these jobs is b.

Boundary Conditions $f(0, 0, 0) = 0$

Recurrence Relation For $j = 1, \ldots, n$, $t = 1, \ldots, P$, and $b = 0, 1, \ldots, B$:

$$
f(j, t, b) = \begin{cases}
\infty & \text{if } p_j > t \text{ and } s_j > b, \\
\max\{\max\{0, l_j - d_j\}, f(j-1, t, b-s_j)\} & \text{if } p_j > t \text{ and } s_j \leq b, \\
\max\{\max\{0, t - d_j\}, f(j-1, t - p_j, b)\} & \text{if } p_j \leq t \text{ and } s_j > b, \\
\min\{\max\{\max\{0, t - d_j\}, f(j-1, t - p_j, b)\}, & \\
\qquad \max\{\max\{0, l_j - d_j\}, f(j-1, t, b-s_j)\}\} & \text{if } p_j \leq t \text{ and } s_j \leq b.
\end{cases}
$$

Optimal Solution Value The optimal solution value is found by solving the following problem:

$$
\min_{0 \leq t \leq P, 0 \leq b \leq B} \{\alpha f(n, t, b) + (1 - \alpha)b)\}.
$$

The logic of this algorithm is very similar to that of Algorithm DP-TCT given in Sect. 6.4.1.

274   6   Joint Subcontracting and Scheduling Decisions

Lee and Sung (2008a) give two heuristics, one of which is similar to Heuristic TCT given in the previous subsection for the total completion time problem. We do not describe these heuristics here.

6.4.3   The Total Tardiness Problem

Lee and Sung (2008a) propose a pseudo-polynomial time dynamic programming algorithm to solve this problem with time complexity $O(n^3 BP)$, where $P = \sum_{j \in N} p_j$. The idea of their algorithm is based on the well-known pseudo-polynomial dynamic programming algorithm given by Lawler (1977) for the classical single-machine total tardiness problem without subcontracting options, i.e., problem $1 || \sum T_j$, which can be viewed as a special case of the total tardiness problem studied here.

Lawler's algorithm for problem $1 || \sum T_j$ is based on the following important property. Consider a problem of scheduling any given subset of l jobs $i_1, \ldots, i_l$. Find an optimal schedule starting at a given time t that minimizes the total tardiness of the jobs. Suppose the jobs are indexed in EDD order, i.e., $d_{i_1} \leq \ldots \leq d_{i_l}$. Let i_k be the job with the longest processing time, i.e., $p_{i_k} = \max\{p_{i_1}, \ldots, p_{i_l}\}$. Lawler (1977) proves the following property.

Lemma 6.4 *There exists some job $i_q \in \{i_{k+1}, \ldots, i_l\}$ such that there is an optimal schedule for the problem that starts at time t and is a concatenation of the following three segments:*

(i)   *Some sequence of jobs $i_1, \ldots, i_{k-1}, i_{k+1}, \ldots, i_q$.*
(ii) *Followed by job i_k.*
(iii) *Followed by some sequence of jobs $i_{q+1}, \ldots, i_l$.*

Clearly, to have an overall optimal schedule, both the sequence of the first segment (i.e., the sequence for the jobs $i_1, \ldots, i_{k-1}, i_{k+1}, \ldots, i_q$) and the sequence of the third segment (i.e., the sequence for the jobs $i_{q+1}, \ldots, i_l$) must be optimal. This provides the foundation for a dynamic programming based algorithm. Below, we briefly summarize the main idea of Lawler's DP algorithm, since essentially the same idea is used by Lee and Sung (2008a) to design their algorithm for the problem with subcontracting options.

Lawler's DP algorithm uses a job set as a part of a DP state. Suppose that all the jobs $1, \ldots, n$ are reindexed in EDD order, i.e., $d_1 \leq \cdots \leq d_n$. For any j, l, k with $j \leq l$, define a job set $J(j, l, k)$ to be the subset of jobs in $\{j, j+1, \ldots, l-1, l\} \setminus \{k\}$ with processing times less than or equal to p_k, i.e.,

$$J(j, l, k) = \{i \in \{j, j+1, \ldots, l-1, l\} \setminus \{k\} | p_i \leq p_k\}$$

We note that although $J(j, l, k)$ is a set, the members in $J(j, l, k)$ are uniquely determined by three numbers, j, l, k. Thus, keeping track of this set in a DP algo-

6.4 Problems with a Subcontracting Budget Constraint

rithm is equivalent to keeping tracking of j, l, k, which requires only polynomial time.

With $J(j, l, k)$ defined as above, Lawler's DP algorithm uses value function $V(J(j, l, k), t)$ to denote the minimum total tardiness of the jobs in the set $J(j, l, k)$, given that the processing of the first job starts at time t. Let $k^* = \arg\max_{i \in J(j,l,k)}\{p_i\}$. Then by Lemma 6.4 described earlier, $V(J(j, l, k), t)$ can be computed recursively as follows:

$$V(J(j, l, k), t) = \min_{k^* \leq q \leq l} \{V(J(j, q, k^*), t) + \max(0, C_{k^*}(q) - d_{k^*})$$

$$+ V(J(q + 1, l, k^*), C_{k^*}(q)))\},$$

where $C_{k^*}(q) = \sum_{i \in J(j,q,k^*)} p_i + p_{k^*}$ is the completion time of job k^*. This algorithm has a time complexity $O(n^4 P)$, and hence is pseudo-polynomial. This, together with the NP-hardness proof given by Du and Leung (1990), implies that problem $1||\sum T_j$ is ordinarily NP-hard.

Now we consider the problem with subcontracting options. Clearly, for the jobs processed in-house, the property stated in Lemma 6.4 holds. Based on this fact, Lee and Sung (2008a) propose the following DP algorithm for solving this problem. The algorithm can be viewed as an extension of Lawler's (1977) algorithm.

Algorithm DP-TT

Initialization Reindex jobs in EDD order, i.e., $d_1 \leq \cdots \leq d_n$.

Value Function $f(J(j, l, k), a, b, c)$ = the minimum objective value of a schedule for jobs in the set $J(j, l, k)$ where the jobs processed in-house are processed in the interval $[a, b]$ and the total subcontracting cost of the jobs subcontracted out is c.

Boundary Conditions $f(\emptyset, 0, 0, 0) = 0$.

Recurrence Relation For $j = 1, \ldots, n, l = j, \ldots, n, k = 1, \ldots, n, a = 0, \ldots, P, b = a, \ldots, P$, and $c = 0, \ldots, B$:

$$f(V(j, l, k), a, b, c) = \begin{cases} \infty & \text{if } p_{k^*} > b - a \text{ and } s_{k^*} > c, \\ f_1(V(j, l, k), a, b, c) & \text{if } p_{k^*} > b - a \text{ and } s_{k^*} \leq c, \\ f_2(V(j, l, k), a, b, c) & \text{if } p_{k^*} \leq b - a \text{ and } s_{k^*} > c, \\ f_3(V(j, l, k), a, b, c) & \text{if } p_{k^*} \leq b - a \text{ and } s_{k^*} \leq c, \end{cases}$$

where $k^* = \arg\max_{i \in J(j,l,k)}\{p_i\}$, and

$$f_1(V(j, l, k), a, b, c) = f(V(j, l, k^*), a, b, c - s_{k^*})$$

$$+ \alpha \max(0, l_{k^*} - d_{k^*}) + (1 - \alpha)s_{k^*}$$

$$f_2(V(j, l, k), a, b, c)$$

$$= \min_{k^* \le q \le l, 0 \le u \le b - a - p_{k^*}, 0 \le v \le c} \left\{ \begin{array}{l} f(J(j, q, k^*), a, a + u, v) \\ + \alpha \max(0, a + u + p_{k^*} - d_{k^*}) \\ + f(J(q + 1, l, k^*), a + u + p_{k^*}, b, c - v) \end{array} \right\}$$

$$f_3(V(j, l, k), a, b, c)$$

$$= \min \left\{ \begin{array}{l} f(J(j, l, k^*), a, b, c - s_{k^*}) + \alpha \max(0, l_{k^*} - d_{k^*}) + (1 - \alpha)s_{k^*}, \\ \min_{k^* \le q \le l, 0 \le u \le b - a - p_{k^*}, 0 \le v \le c} \left\{ \begin{array}{l} f(J(j, q, k^*), a, a + u, v) \\ + \alpha \max(0, a + u + p_{k^*} - d_{k^*}) \\ + f(J(q + 1, l, k^*), a + u + p_{k^*}, b, c - v) \end{array} \right\} \end{array} \right\}.$$

Optimal Solution Value The optimal solution value is found by solving the following problem: $\min_{0 \le b \le P, 0 \le c \le B}\{f(N, 0, b, c)\}$.

The recurrence relation of the above DP algorithm considers four possible cases: (i) $p_{k^*} > b - a$ and $s_{k^*} > c$, (ii) $p_{k^*} > b - a$ and $s_{k^*} \le c$, (iii) $p_{k^*} \le b - a$ and $s_{k^*} > c$, and (iv) $p_{k^*} \le b - a$ and $s_{k^*} \le c$. Case (i) is infeasible because job k^* cannot be processed in-house or subcontracted. Case (ii) means that job k^* must be subcontracted. Case (iii) means that job k^* must be processed in-house during the interval $[a + u, a + u + p_{k^*}]$. Case (iv) means that job k^* can be processed in-house or subcontracted, depending on whichever option gives a lower cost.

Lee and Sung (2008a) also give heuristics and a branch-and-bound algorithm. We do not elaborate on these procedures here.

6.5 Problems with a Flowshop Environment

In this section, we discuss a joint subcontracting and scheduling problem studied by Lee and Choi (2011) that arises in a two-stage flowshop production environment. In a two-stage flowshop, each given job needs to undergo two processing operations— it is processed first on a machine in the first stage, and then on a machine in the second stage. In Lee and Choi's problem, the in-house plant has two machines which can process the stage-one and stage-two operations of any given job, respectively. One or both operations of a job can be subcontracted at a cost that is proportional to the processing time of the operation(s) involved. The objective is to minimize the sum of the makespan of the jobs processed in-house and the total subcontracting cost. It is implicitly assumed that the subcontracted job operations are completed instantaneously so that they do not delay the remaining operations of the jobs involved. This essentially means that we can treat a subcontracted operation of a job as if it is processed in-house but with zero processing time.

6.5 Problems with a Flowshop Environment

We now define the problem. There is a given set of n jobs $N = \{1, \ldots, n\}$ to be processed. Each job j consists of two operations, denoted as $(1, j)$ as its stage-one operation and $(2, j)$ as its stage-two operation, respectively. There are two in-house machines, M_1 and M_2, which can process stage-one operations and stage-two operations, respectively. Either or both operations of a job can be processed in-house or subcontracted. For $i = 1, 2$ and $j \in N$, if operation (i, j) is processed in-house, it requires a processing time of p_{ij} on machine M_i; if this operation is subcontracted, it costs $\alpha_i p_{ij}$, where α_i is the subcontracting cost per unit of in-house processing time.

Let C_{ij} denote the completion time of operation (i, j) if it is processed in-house, for $i = 1, 2, j \in N$. Let C_j denote the completion time of job j if at least one of its two operations is processed in-house, for $j \in N$. If only the second-stage operation $(2, j)$ or both operations of job j are processed in-house, then $C_j = C_{2j}$. If only the first-stage operation $(1, j)$ of job j is processed in-house, then $C_j = C_{1j}$. The problem is to find a set of jobs S_1 whose stage-one operations are subcontracted, a set of jobs S_2 whose stage-two operations are subcontracted, and a schedule σ for the operations processed in-house such that the following objective function is minimized:

$$F(S_1, S_2, \sigma) = C_{\max}(\sigma) + \alpha_1 \sum_{j \in S_1} p_{1j} + \alpha_2 \sum_{j \in S_2} p_{2j},$$

where $C_{\max}(\sigma) = \max\{C_j | j \in \sigma\}$ is the makespan of schedule σ (i.e., the completion time of the last operation in-house).

Given S_1 and S_2, the problem is reduced to finding a schedule σ for the two in-house machines to process the operations kept in-house with a minimum makespan $C_{\max}(\sigma)$. Since this problem is the classical two-machine flowshop makespan minimization problem, a schedule given by Johnson's rule (Johnson, 1954, also see Sect. 5.2.1) is optimal. For ease of presentation, in the remainder of this section, we use (S_1, S_2, σ) to denote a solution of the problem, where S_1, S_2, σ are defined as above.

Lee and Choi (2011) provide the following results:

- If $\alpha_1 + \alpha_2 > 1$, and $\alpha_1 < 1$, $\alpha_2 < 1$, then the problem is at least ordinarily NP-hard.
- If $\alpha_1 + \alpha_2 > 1$, and $\max\{\alpha_1, \alpha_2\} \geq 1$, $\min\{\alpha_1, \alpha_2\} < 1$, then the problem is at least ordinarily NP-hard.
- If $\alpha_1 + \alpha_2 > 1$, and $\alpha_1 \geq 1$, $\alpha_2 \geq 1$, then the problem can be solved in polynomial time.
- If $\alpha_1 + \alpha_2 \leq 1$, then the problem can be solved in polynomial time.

We show that there is a pseudo-polynomial time algorithm for solving the general case of the problem. Thus, the problem under the first two cases above is ordinarily NP-hard. In addition, Lee and Choi (2011) provide a polynomial-time heuristic for the problem with $\alpha_1 + \alpha_2 > 1$, and $\alpha_1 < 1$, $\alpha_2 < 1$ and show that its worst-case performance ratio is bounded by a constant. They also consider the problem where the two operations of each job have the same processing time (i.e., $p_{1j} = p_{2j}$, for all $j \in N$). The corresponding flowshop environment is called a proportionate flowshop (see e.g., Pinedo, 2016, Section 8.3.7). In the following, we present an NP-hardness proof for the problem with $\max\{\alpha_1, \alpha_2\} \geq 1$, $\min\{\alpha_1, \alpha_2\} < 1$ in Sect. 6.4.1, discuss the two cases that can be solved in polynomial time in Sect. 6.4.2, and finally discuss the problem with the proportionate flowshop in Sect. 6.4.3. We refer the reader to Lee and Choi (2011) for an NP-hardness proof for the problem with $\alpha_1 + \alpha_2 > 1$, and $\alpha_1 < 1$, $\alpha_2 < 1$, and for their heuristic and related analysis for the problem with $\alpha_1 + \alpha_2 > 1$, and $\alpha_1 < 1$, $\alpha_2 < 1$.

6.5.1 NP-Hardness Proof

We first consider the problem with $\max\{\alpha_1, \alpha_2\} \geq 1$ and $\min\{\alpha_1, \alpha_2\} < 1$. Lee and Choi (2011) prove the following result.

Theorem 6.6 *The problem with* $\max\{\alpha_1, \alpha_2\} \geq 1$ *and* $\min\{\alpha_1, \alpha_2\} < 1$ *is at least ordinarily NP-hard.*

Proof We show that the problem with any given values of α_1, α_2 satisfying $\alpha_1 < 1$ and $\alpha_2 \geq 1$ is NP-hard by a reduction from Partition Problem (PP), a known NP-hard problem (Garey & Johnson, 1979). In PP, we are given h integers, $a_1, \ldots, a_h$ such that $\sum_{j=1}^{h} a_j = A$. The question asks whether there is a subset $Q \subseteq \{1, \ldots, h\}$ such that $\sum_{j \in Q} = A/2$. Given an instance of PP, construct an instance of our problem as follows: $n = h + 2$ jobs, with the processing times p_{ij} given below, and a threshold $Z = 2A + \frac{4}{3}\alpha_1$ on the objective value.

$$p_{1j} = \begin{cases} a_j, & \text{if } j = 1, \ldots, h \\ \frac{3A}{2}, & \text{if } j = h + 1 \\ 0, & \text{if } j = h + 2 \end{cases} \qquad p_{2j} = \begin{cases} 0, & \text{if } j = 1, \ldots, h \\ 0, & \text{if } j = h + 1 \\ 2A, & \text{if } j = h + 2 \end{cases}$$

Below, we show that there exists a solution (S_1, S_2, σ) to the above constructed instance of our problem with objective value $T(S_1, S_2, \sigma) \leq Z$ if and only if there is a solution to PP.

($\Rightarrow$) If there exists a subset $Q \subseteq \{1, \ldots, h\}$ such that $\sum_{j \in Q} = A/2$, we construct the following solution (S_1, S_2, σ) for the instance of our problem: Let $S_1 = Q$, $S_2 = \emptyset$, and schedule the operations kept in-house following Johnson's rule (see Sect. 5.2.1). Since $p_{2j} = 0$ for $j = 1, \ldots, h + 1$ and $p_{1,h+2} = 0$, the completion times of the operations on M_1 do not have any impact on those on M_2. Let $\bar{S}_1 = \{1, \ldots, h + 2\} \setminus Q$. We have

$$C_{\max}(\sigma) = \max\{\sum_{j \in \bar{S}_1} p_{1j}, p_{2,h+2}\} = \max\{2A, 2A\} = 2A.$$

6.5 Problems with a Flowshop Environment

Thus, the objective value of the solution is

$$F(S_1, S_2, \sigma) = C_{\max}(\sigma) + \alpha_1 \sum_{j \in S_1} p_{1j} = 2A + \alpha_1(A/2) = Z.$$

($\Leftarrow$) If there is a solution (S_1, S_2, σ) for the instance of our problem with $F(S_1, S_2, \sigma) \leq Z$, we first show that both operations $(1, h + 1)$ and $(2, h + 2)$ must be processed in-house, i.e., $h + 1 \notin S_1$ and $h + 2 \notin S_2$. We prove this by contradiction. There are two cases. First, if $(2, h + 2)$ is subcontracted, then its contribution to the objective value is $2A\alpha_2 \geq 2A$, and the contribution from any stage-one operation $(1, j)$, for $j = 1, \dots, h + 2$, is at least $\alpha_1 p_{1j}$, regardless of whether it is subcontracted or processed in-house. This means that if $(2, h + 2)$ is subcontracted, then the objective value of the solution is at least $2A + \alpha_1 \sum_{j=1}^{h+2} p_{1j} = 2A + (5A/2)\alpha_1 > Z$, a contradiction.

Alternatively, if $(1, h + 1)$ is subcontracted, then its contribution to the objective value is $(3A/2)\alpha_1$. The contribution of operation $(2, h+2)$ is at least $2A$, regardless of whether it is subcontracted or processed in-house. This means that if $(1, h + 1)$ is subcontracted, then the objective value of the solution is at least $2A + (3A/2)\alpha_1 > Z$, a contradiction.

Therefore, both operations $(1, h + 1)$ and $(2, h + 2)$ are processed in-house in the solution (S_1, S_2, σ). Thus, the objective value of this solution is

$$F(S_1, S_2, \sigma) = \max\{5A/2 - \sum_{j \in S_1} p_{1j}, 2A\} + \alpha_1 \sum_{j \in S_1} p_{1j}. \tag{6.24}$$

We show that the fact that $F(S_1, S_2, \sigma) \leq Z$ means that $\sum_{j \in S_1} p_{1j} = A/2$. First, if $\sum_{j \in S_1} p_{1j} > A/2$, then (6.24) implies that $F(S_1, S_2, \sigma) = 2A + \alpha_1 \sum_{j \in S_1} p_{1j} > 2A + (A/2)\alpha_1 = Z$, leading to a contradiction. Alternatively, if $\sum_{j \in S_1} p_{1j} < A/2$, then (6.24) implies that

$$F(S_1, S_2, \sigma) = 2A + (A/2 - \sum_{j \in S_1} p_{1j}) + \alpha_1 \sum_{j \in S_1} p_{1j}$$

$$= Z + (1 - \alpha_1)(A/2 - \sum_{j \in S_1} p_{1j}) > Z,$$

leading to a contradiction. Thus, $\sum_{j \in S_1} p_{1j} = A/2$, and hence there is a solution to PP. $\qquad \square$

Next, we give a pseudo-polynomial time dynamic programming algorithm for the general case of the problem. The algorithm is based on the following observation. From Johnson's rule, there is an optimal solution where on the two in-house machines, the jobs with the first-stage operations subcontracted are scheduled first, the jobs with both operations processed in-house are scheduled next, and the jobs with the second-stage operations subcontracted are scheduled last.

Algorithm FS

Initialization Reindex the jobs following Johnson's rule (see Sect. 5.2.1). Define $P_{1j} = \sum_{k=1}^{j} p_{1j}$ and $P_{2j} = \sum_{k=1}^{j} p_{2j}$ for $j = 1, \ldots, n$, and let $P_1 = P_{1n}$ and $P2 = P_{2n}$.

Value Function $F(j, x, y, z_1, z_2, w)$ = the minimum completion time of the second operation of the last job processed in-house in a schedule for jobs $1, \ldots, j$ where (1) among the jobs $1, \ldots, j$ with both operations processed in-house, the total processing time of stage-one operations of these jobs is x, and the total processing time of stage-two operations of these jobs is y, (2) among the jobs $1, \ldots, j$ with stage-two operations subcontracted, the total processing time of stage-one operations of these jobs is z_1, (3) among the jobs $1, \ldots, j$ with stage-one operations subcontracted, the total processing time of stage-two operations of these jobs is z_2, and (4) in the final schedule after all the n jobs are considered, among the jobs with stage-one operations subcontracted, the total processing time of stage-two operations of these jobs is w.

Boundary Conditions

$F(0, 0, 0, 0, 0, w) = w$, for $0 \geq w \geq P_2$,
$F(0, x, y, z_1, z_2, w) = \infty$ for $x > 0$ or $y > 0$,
$F(j, x, y, z_1, z_2, w) = \infty$ if any one of the following conditions holds: $x + z_1 > P_1$, $y + z_2 > P_2, z_2 > w$.

Recurrence Relation For $j = 1, \ldots, n, x = 0, 1, \ldots, P_{1j}, y = 0, 1, \ldots, P_{2j}$, $z_1 = 0, 1, \ldots, P_{1j} - x, z_2 = 0, 1, \ldots, w, w = 0, 1, \ldots, P_2$:

$$F(j, x, y, z_1, z_2, w) = \min\{F_1, F_2, F_3, F_4\},$$

where

$$F_1 = F(j - 1, x, y, z_1, z_2, w),$$

$$F_2 = F(j - 1, x, y, z_1, z_2 - p_{2j}, w),$$

$$F_3 = F(j - 1, x, y, z_1 - p_{1j}, z_2, w),$$

$$F_4 = \max\left\{x + p_{1j}, \ F(j - 1, x - p_{1j}, y - p_{2j}, z_1, z_2, w)\right\} + p_{2j}.$$

Optimal Solution Value The optimal solution value is found by solving the following problem:

$$\min\left\{\alpha_1(P_1 - x - z_1) + \alpha_2(P_2 - y - w) + \max\{x + z_1, F(n, x, y, z_1, w, w)\}\right.$$
$$\left| \ x = 0, 1, \ldots, P_1; y = 0, 1, \ldots, P_2; z_1 = 0, 1, \ldots, P_1 - x; \right.$$
$$\left. w = 0, 1, \ldots, P_2 - y\right\}.$$

6.5 Problems with a Flowshop Environment

Theorem 6.7 *Algorithm FS finds an optimal solution for the general case of the problem with a flowshop environment in $O(n P_1^2 P_2^3)$ time.*

Proof The validity of the algorithm can be shown by the following observations. The recurrence relation of the above algorithm compares all the four options for job j: (i) Both operations are subcontracted, which corresponds to F_1, (ii) stage-one operation is subcontracted but stage-two operation is processed in-house, which corresponds to F_2, (iii) stage-two operation is subcontracted but stage-one operation is processed in-house, which corresponds to F_3, and (iv) both operations are processed in-house, which corresponds to F_4. The makespan of the final schedule is $\max\{x + z_1, F(n, x, y, z_1, w, w)\}$ since it is the maximum between the completion time of the last first-stage operation (which is $x + z_1$) and the completion time of the last second-stage operation (which is $F(n, x, y, z_1, w, w)$).

It can be shown that this algorithm has a time complexity $O(n P_1^2 P_2^3)$. Thus, it is a pseudo-polynomial time algorithm. $\qquad\square$

This theorem, together with Theorem 6.6, implies that the problem with $\max\{\alpha_1, \alpha_2\} \geq 1$ and $\min\{\alpha_1, \alpha_2\} < 1$ is ordinarily NP-hard.

6.5.2 Polynomially Solvable Cases

We now consider the two polynomially solvable cases of the problem: (i) $\alpha_1 + \alpha_2 \leq 1$, and (ii) $\alpha_1 \geq 1$ and $\alpha_2 \geq 1$. Lee and Choi (2011) prove the following results.

Theorem 6.8 *For the problem with $\alpha_1 + \alpha_2 \leq 1$, there is an optimal solution where all the operations are subcontracted out (i.e., $S_1 = S_2 = N$).*

Proof Consider any solution (S_1, S_2, σ). Its objective value satisfies

$$F(S_1, S_2, \sigma) \geq \max\left\{\sum_{j\in N\setminus S_1} p_{1j}, \sum_{j\in N\setminus S_2} p_{2j}\right\} + \alpha_1 \sum_{j\in S_1} p_{1j} + \alpha_2 \sum_{j\in S_2} p_{2j}.$$
(6.25)

Since $\alpha_1 + \alpha_2 \leq 1$, we have

$$\max\left\{\sum_{j\in N\setminus S_1} p_{1j}, \sum_{j\in N\setminus S_2} p_{2j}\right\} \geq \alpha_1 \sum_{j\in N\setminus S_1} p_{1j} + \alpha_2 \sum_{j\in N\setminus S_2} p_{2j}.$$

This, along with (6.25), means that

$$F(S_1, S_2, \sigma) \geq \alpha_1 \sum_{j\in N} p_{1j} + \alpha_2 \sum_{j\in N} p_{2j}.$$
(6.26)

However, if all the jobs are subcontracted out, the objective value is in fact $\alpha_1 \sum_{j\in N} p_{1j} + \alpha_2 \sum_{j\in N} p_{2j}$. This, along with (6.26), implies that subcontracting all the jobs out is an optimal solution. $\qquad\square$

Theorem 6.9 *For the problem with $\alpha_1 \geq 1$ and $\alpha_2 \geq 1$, there is an optimal solution where all the operations are processed in-house (i.e., $S_1 = S_2 = \emptyset$) following Johnson's rule.*

Proof Given any solution (S_1, S_2, σ) where $S_1 \neq \emptyset$. For any $j \in S_1$, in this solution, operation $(1, j)$ is subcontracted. If this operation is instead processed in-house, then the makespan of σ increases by at most p_{1j}, but the subcontracting cost decreases by $\alpha_1 p_{1j} \geq p_{1j}$. This means that it may improve the current solution to process operation $(1, j)$ in-house instead. Thus, we revise the given solution by keeping operation $(1, j)$ in-house. We repeat this process until all the stage-one operations are kept in-house. The resulting solution has an objective value no more than that of the original solution. If $S_2 \neq \emptyset$, we can apply the same logic to any $j \in S_2$ by keeping operation $(2, j)$ in-house. Eventually, we arrive at a solution with an objective value no more than that of the original solution by keeping all the stage-two operations in-house. $\qquad\square$

6.5.3 Proportionate Flowshop

As defined above, in a two-stage proportionate flowshop, $p_{1j} = p_{2j}$ for $j \in N$. For notational convenience, we replace both p_{1j} and p_{2j} by p_j. The joint subcontracting and scheduling problem with a two-stage proportionate flowshop is a special case of the problem with a general two-stage flowshop. Thus, the polynomially solvable cases discussed in Sect. 6.5.2 are still solvable in polynomial time under a proportionate flowshop. When $\alpha_1 + \alpha_2 > 1$ and $\alpha_1 < 1, \alpha_2 < 1$, the NP-hardness proof given by Lee and Choi (2011) for the problem with a general flowshop also works for the problem with a proportionate flowshop. Similarly, the pseudo-polynomial time algorithm given in Sect. 6.5.2 for the problem with a general flowshop also works for the problem with a proportionate flowshop. Thus, when $\alpha_1 + \alpha_2 > 1$ and $\alpha_1 < 1, \alpha_2 < 1$, the problem with a proportionate flowshop is still ordinarily NP-hard.

However, for the case with $\max\{\alpha_1, \alpha_2\} \geq 1$ and $\min\{\alpha_1, \alpha_2\} < 1$, the problem complexity changes when the production environment changes from a general flowshop to a proportionate flowshop. It is NP-hard with a general flowshop, as shown in Sect. 6.5.1. The problem with a proportionate flowshop is polynomially solvable, as shown below.

Theorem 6.10 *For the problem with a two-machine proportionate flowshop,*

(i) *If $\alpha_1 < 1 \leq \alpha_2$, there is an optimal solution where only the first-stage operation of the largest job is subcontracted out and all other operations are processed in-house.*

(ii) *If $\alpha_2 < 1 \leq \alpha_1$, there is an optimal solution where only the second-stage operation of the largest job is subcontracted out and all other operations are processed in-house.*

6.5 Problems with a Flowshop Environment

Proof We prove (i) below. Suppose that the jobs are reindexed such that $p_1 \leq p_2 \leq \cdots \leq p_n$. First, consider the solution where only the first-stage operation of the largest job is subcontracted out, denoted as $(\{n\}, \emptyset, \sigma^*)$, where σ^* follows Johnson's rule. In σ^*, M_1 processes the jobs in the order $(1, 2, \ldots, n - 1)$, and M_2 processes the jobs in the order $(n, 1, \ldots, n - 1)$. Thus, the objective value of this solution is

$$F(\{n\}, \emptyset, \sigma^*) = \sum_{j=1}^{n} p_j + \alpha_1 p_n. \tag{6.27}$$

Now, consider any given solution (S_1, S_2, σ) with $S_2 \neq \emptyset$. If operation $(2, j)$ for any $j \in S_2$ is processed in-house instead of being subcontracted in the current solution, the subcontracting cost decreases by $\alpha_2 p_{2j}$ whereas the makespan of σ increases by at most p_{2j}. Since $\alpha_2 \geq 1$, processing operation $(2, j)$ in-house does not increase the overall objective value. We repeat this until the stage-two operations of all the jobs in S_2 are processed in-house without increasing the objective value. This means that there exists an optimal solution where all the stage-two operations are kept in-house. We consider such solutions below.

Given any solution $(S_1, \emptyset, \sigma)$ where operation $(1, n)$ is not subcontracted, i.e., $n \notin S_1$, we compare the objective value of this solution, $F(S_1, \emptyset, \sigma)$ with $F(\{n\}, \emptyset, \sigma^*)$ given in (6.27). Clearly,

$$F(S_1, \emptyset, \sigma) \geq \max \left\{ \sum_{j \in N \setminus S_1} p_j + p_n, \sum_{j=1}^{n} p_j \right\} + \alpha_1 \sum_{j \in S_1} p_j. \tag{6.28}$$

There are two possible cases. If $\sum_{j \in S_1} p_j \geq p_n$, then from (6.28) and (6.27), we have

$$F(S_1, \emptyset, \sigma) \geq \sum_{j=1}^{n} p_j + \alpha_1 p_n = F(\{n\}, \emptyset, \sigma^*). \tag{6.29}$$

If $\sum_{j \in S_1} p_j < p_n$, then from (6.28) and (6.27) and the fact that $\alpha_1 < 1$ (which is assumed in part (i) statement of the theorem), we have

$$F(S_1, \emptyset, \sigma) \geq \sum_{j \in N \setminus S_1} p_j + p_n + \alpha_1 \sum_{j \in S_1} p_j$$

$$= \sum_{j \in N} p_j + \left(p_n - \sum_{j \in S_1} p_j \right) + \alpha_1 \sum_{j \in S_1} p_j$$

$$> \sum_{j \in N} p_j + \alpha_1 p_n = F(\{n\}, \emptyset, \sigma^*). \tag{6.30}$$

Inequalities (6.29) and (6.30) mean that solution $(\{n\}, \emptyset, \sigma^*)$ is optimal. This shows result (i).

Result (ii) can be shown similarly. $\qquad\square$

6.6 Problems Requiring Delivery of Subcontracted Jobs

In this section, we discuss several problems studied by Qi (2008, 2011) where subcontracted jobs, once completed, need to be delivered to the in-house plant in batches, which incurs a transportation delay and transportation cost. The problems discussed in the other sections of this chapter do not explicitly involve delivery of subcontracted jobs. This is one major difference. Another major difference is that in the problems considered by Qi (2008, 2011), a schedule for processing subcontracted jobs needs to be determined for the subcontractor, in addition to a schedule for the jobs kept for in-house processing. In all the problems considered in the other sections of this chapter, no scheduling decision needs to be made for subcontracted jobs.

We first consider in Sect. 6.6.1 three problems where there is a single in-house machine, and there is a single subcontractor with a single machine that can be used to process subcontracted jobs, and then consider in Sect. 6.6.2 several problems with a two-stage flowshop.

6.6.1 Single In-House Machine and Single Subcontractor's Machine

We first describe three of the problems considered in Qi (2008), using their notation, which are distinguished by their objective functions. There are n jobs, each of which can be either processed on a single machine in-house or subcontracted and processed on a single machine owned by the subcontractor. If a job j is processed in-house, the processing time is p_j, and it becomes αp_j if the job is processed on the subcontractor's machine, where α represents that the subcontractor's machine operates at a different speed from the in-house machine. If a job j is subcontracted, it incurs an extra processing cost βp_j, which is assumed to be proportional to the processing time requirement of the job. Subcontracted jobs, after completing processing, must be delivered in batches to the in-house facility. The delivery of a batch incurs a fixed transportation cost K and a transportation time τ. There is no capacity constraint on a delivery batch. Each job j may have a due date d_j. The decision maker needs to decide which jobs to be subcontracted out, how to schedule the in-house jobs on the single in-house machine, how to schedule the subcontracted jobs on the single subcontractor's machine, and how to batch the subcontracted jobs for delivery to the in-house facility so that the sum of the total subcontracting and

6.6 Problems Requiring Delivery of Subcontracted Jobs

transportation cost and a performance measure based on the job completion times is minimized.

In a given schedule, let C_j denote the completion time of job j. If a job j is processed in-house, then C_j is the time it completes processing, but if it is subcontracted, then C_j is the time when it is delivered to the in-house facility after being processing by the subcontractor. We consider three performance measures based on $C_1, \ldots, C_n$ as follows:

- Total completion time of the jobs, $\sum_{j=1}^{n} C_j$
- Maximum lateness of the jobs, $L_{\max} = \max\{C_j - d_j | j = 1, \ldots, n\}$
- Number of late jobs, $\sum_{j=1}^{n} U_j$, where $U_j = 1$ if $C_j > d_j$ and 0 otherwise

For ease of presentation, we call the problem of minimizing the sum of the total subcontracting and transportation cost and each of the above completion time based performance measures the total completion time problem, the maximum lateness problem, and the number of late jobs problem, respectively.

Qi (2008) shows that for the total completion time problem, there exists an optimal solution where both the jobs kept in-house and the jobs subcontracted out are processed in their SPT order on the respective machine. Based on this, he gives an $O(n^4)$ dynamic programming algorithm to solve the total completion time problem. This algorithm is described below.

Algorithm DP-CT

Initialization Reindex jobs in SPT order, i.e., $p_1 \leq \cdots \leq p_n$.

Value Function $F(j, m, h, h') =$ the minimum objective value of a schedule for jobs $j, \ldots, n$ where (a) there are m jobs kept for in-house processing (and hence $n - j + 1 - m$ jobs subcontracted), (b) among these jobs, the earliest one subcontracted is in a batch where there will be a total of h jobs in the end, but there are currently h' ($h' \leq h$) jobs.

Boundary Conditions

$F(n, 0, h, 1) = K + hp_n + \tau$, for $h = 1, \ldots, n$.
$F(n, 0, h, h') = \infty$, for $h' \neq 1$.
$F(j, m, 0, 0) = \infty$ if $m \neq n - j + 1$, and $\sum_{i=j}^{n} (n - i + 1)p_i$ if $m = n - j + 1$.

Recurrence Relation For $j = n, \ldots, 1, m = 0, \ldots, n - j + 1, h = 1, \ldots, n - j + 1 - m$, and $h' = 1, \ldots, h$:
If $h' = 1$, then

$$F(j, m, h, 1) = \min \begin{cases} F(j + 1, m - 1, h, 1) + mp_j, \\ (n - j - m + h)\alpha p_j + \tau + \beta p_j + K + \min_{v \leq n - j - m}\{F(j + 1, m, v, v)\}. \end{cases}$$

If $h' > 1$, then

$$F(j, m, h, h') = \min \begin{cases} F(j + 1, m - 1, h, h') + mp_j, \\ (n - j + 1 - m + h - h')\alpha p_j + \tau + \beta p_j + F(j + 1, m, h, h' - 1)\}. \end{cases}$$

Optimal Solution Value The optimal solution value is found by solving the following problem:

$$\min\{F(1, m, h, h)|m = 0, 1, \ldots, n; h = 0, 1, \ldots, n - m\}.$$

The optimality of the above algorithm can be validated by checking the recurrence relation. There are two options for job j: Either it is subcontracted out, or it is processed in-house. First, consider the case when $h' = 1$. If job j is processed in-house, then the value of the state $(j, m, h, 1)$ is equal to $F(j+1, m-1, h, 1) + mp_j$. If job j is subcontracted out, then job j is the first one in the batch containing it. In this case, the value of the state $(j, m, h, 1)$ is equal to $(n - j - m + h)\alpha p_j + \tau + \beta p_j + K + \min_{v \leq n-j-m}\{F(j+1, m, v, v)\}$, where the last part (the min operator) considers all possible sizes (v) for the delivery batch that follows the batch containing job j. The recurrence relation chooses the lower cost one of these two options. This shows the validity of the recurrence relation when $h' = 1$. When $h' > 1$, the recurrence relation again considers the two options for job j and can similarly be shown to be valid.

Both the maximum lateness problem and the number of late jobs problem are at least ordinarily NP-hard because under the special case with no subcontracting cost (i.e., $\beta = 0$) and no delivery requirement for the subcontracted jobs (i.e., $\tau = 0$, $K = 0$), these problems reduce to the classical parallel-machine scheduling problem of minimizing the maximum lateness $P_m||L_{\max}$, and that of minimizing the number of late jobs $P_m||\sum U_j$, respectively, which are both known to be ordinarily NP-hard (Pinedo, 2016). Qi (2008) provides pseudo-polynomial time algorithms for solving these problems. Therefore, these problems are ordinarily NP-hard.

Below we present the pseudo-polynomial time algorithms of Qi (2008) for these problems. Their algorithms are based on the following straightforward properties: (i) For the maximum lateness problem, there exists an optimal solution in which both the jobs kept in-house and the jobs subcontracted are processed in their EDD order on the respective machine; (ii) for the number of late jobs problem, there exists an optimal solution where the jobs subcontracted are all on time and scheduled in their EDD order, and among the jobs that are kept in-house, the ones that are on time are processed in their EDD order before the ones that are tardy.

For the maximum lateness problem, the algorithm is as follows.

Algorithm DP-ML

Initialization Reindex the jobs in EDD order, i.e., $d_1 \leq \ldots \leq d_n$. Define $P_j = \sum_{k=1}^{j} p_j$ for $j = 1, \ldots, n$, and let $P = P_n$.

Value Function $F(j, x, h, t) = $ the minimum maximum lateness of the jobs in a schedule for jobs $1, \ldots, j$ where (a) the total processing time of the subcontracted jobs is αx, (b) among the jobs $1, \ldots, j$, the last one subcontracted is in the hth batch when it is delivered from the subcontractor to the in-house plant, and (c) the hth batch is completed on the subcontractor's machine at time αt.

6.6 Problems Requiring Delivery of Subcontracted Jobs

Boundary Conditions

$$F(1, x, h, t) = \begin{cases} p_1 - d_1, & \text{if } x = 0, h = 0, t = 0, \\ \alpha t + \tau - d_1, & \text{if } x = p_1, h = 1, t \geq p_1, \\ \infty, & \text{otherwise.} \end{cases}$$

Recurrence Relation For $j = 1, \ldots, n$, $x = 0, 1, \ldots, P_j$, $h = 0, 1, \ldots, j$, and $t = x, x + 1, \ldots, P$:

$$F(j, x, h, t) = \min\{F_1(j, x, h, t), F_2(j, x, h, t)\},$$

where

$$F_1(j, x, h, t) = \max\{F(j - 1, x, h, t), P_j - x - d_j\}$$

$$F_2(j, x, h, t) = \max \begin{cases} \alpha t + \tau - d_j, \\ \min\{F(j - 1, x - p_j, h - 1, x - p_j), F(j - 1, x - p_j, h, t)\} \end{cases}$$

Optimal Solution Value The optimal solution value is found by solving the following problem:

$$\min\{F(n, x, h, x) + \beta x + hK \,|\, x = 0, 1, \ldots, P; h = 0, 1, \ldots, n\}.$$

In the recurrence relation of the above algorithm, $F_1(j, x, y, t)$ is the value of the state (j, x, y, t) if job j is subcontracted out, and $F_2(j, x, y, t)$ is that if job j is processed in-house. The recurrence relation for F_1 is quite clear. For F_2, the second term (i.e., the term with the min operator) considers the two possibilities for the job j: It is either the first job in the hth batch of the subcontracted jobs, or not. The optimality of the algorithm is based on comparing the values of all feasible state transitions.

For the number of late jobs problem, the algorithm is as follows.

Algorithm DP-LJ

Initialization Reindex the jobs in EDD order, i.e., $d_1 \leq \ldots \leq d_n$. Define $P_j = \sum_{k=1}^{j} p_j$ for $j = 1, \ldots, n$, and let $P = P_n$.

Value Function $F(j, x, y, t)$ = the minimum objective value of a schedule for jobs $1, \ldots, j$ where (a) the total processing time of the subcontracted jobs is αx, (b) the total processing time of the jobs processed in-house that are on time is y, and (c) the last batch that contains at least one of the jobs $1, \ldots, j$ is completed on the subcontractor's machine at time αt.

Boundary Conditions

$$F(1, x, y, t) = \begin{cases} 0, & \text{if } x = 0, y = p_1, p_1 \leq d_1, \\ K, & \text{if } x = p_1, y = 0, t + \tau \leq d_1, \\ 1, & \text{if } x = 0, y = 0, \\ \infty, & \text{otherwise.} \end{cases}$$

Recurrence Relation For $j = 1, \ldots, n, x = 0, 1, \ldots, P_j, y = 0, 1, \ldots, P_j - x$, and $t = x, x + 1, \ldots, P$:

$$F(j, x, y, t) = \min\{F_1(j, x, y, t), F_2(j, x, y, t), F_3(j, x, y, t)\},$$

where

$$F_1(j, x, y, t) = \begin{cases} \infty, & \text{if } t + \tau > d_j, \\ \min\{F(j - 1, x - p_j, y, t), F(j - 1, x - p_j, y, x - p_j) + K\}, & \text{if } t + \tau \leq d_j. \end{cases}$$

$$F_2(j, x, y, t) = \begin{cases} \infty, & \text{if } y > d_j, \\ F(j - 1, x, y - p_j, t), & \text{if } y \leq d_j. \end{cases}$$

$$F_3(j, x, y, t) = F(j - 1, x, y, t) + 1.$$

Optimal Solution Value The optimal solution value is found by solving the following problem:

$$\min\{F(n, x, y, x) | x = 0, 1, \ldots, P; y = 0, 1, \ldots, P - x\}.$$

In the recurrence relation of the above algorithm, $F_1(j, x, y, t)$ is the value of the state (j, x, y, t) if job j is subcontracted out, $F_2(j, x, y, t)$ is that if job j is processed in-house and on time, and $F_3(j, x, y, t)$ is that if job j is processed in-house and tardy. The optimality of the algorithm follows from comparing the values of all feasible state transitions.

We note that a Stackelberg game, which consists of a subcontractor as the leader and a manufacturer as the follower and is built on a problem similar to the ones discussed above, is studied in Qi (2012) and discussed in Sect. 9.3.2. In this game, first the subcontractor sets the unit price β for processing the manufacturer's jobs. Then, the manufacturer decides which jobs to subcontract, as well as a schedule for processing the jobs kept in-house, and a schedule for processing the subcontracted jobs on the subcontractor's machine.

6.6 Problems Requiring Delivery of Subcontracted Jobs

6.6.2 Two-Stage Flowshop

In this section, we discuss two problems studied by Qi (2011). Both problems involve scheduling with subcontracting options in a two-stage flowshop environment. The subcontracting mechanism is different from that in the flowshop problem discussed in Sect. 6.5. To subcontract a job, both stage-one and stage-two operations of the job must be subcontracted out together. In the first problem of Qi (2011), there is a single subcontractor that handles both operations of every subcontracted job, whereas in the second problem of Qi (2011) there are two independent subcontractors, each dealing with one operation of each subcontracted job. We define each of these problems and show how it can be solved below, respectively.

We consider the first problem. There are n jobs, each of which consists of two operations. For each job j, the processing time of its stage-one operation is p_j, and that of its stage-two operation is q_j. There are two in-house machines, one for stage-one operations, and the other for stage-two operations. There is a single subcontractor available that also has two machines, one for stage-one operations, and the other for stage-two operations. If a job is subcontracted out, both of its operations must be processed by the subcontractor. The processing time of an operation remains the same whether it is processed in-house or by the subcontractor. Subcontracted jobs, once completed, need to be delivered to the in-house facility in batches. Each batch can deliver any number of jobs and incurs a fixed delivery cost μ, and a fixed transportation time τ.

The in-house production cost of an operation may differ from the subcontracting cost of the same operation. It is assumed that for each job j, the difference between the subcontracting cost of the job's stage-one operation and the in-house production cost of the same operation is proportional to its processing time, i.e., $\alpha_1 p_j$, where α_1 is identical for all the jobs. Similarly, it is assumed that, for each job j, the difference between the subcontracting cost of the job's stage-two operation and the in-house production cost of the same operation is $\alpha_2 p_j$, where α_2 is identical for all the jobs. Here α_1, α_2 can be negative if the subcontracting cost is lower.

The problem is to find a subset of jobs to subcontract out, a schedule for the jobs kept for in-house processing, a schedule for the jobs subcontracted out, and a delivery schedule for the subcontracted jobs from the subcontractor to the in-house facility, so as to minimize the sum of the makespan of the jobs and the total subcontracting and delivery cost.

This problem is ordinarily NP-hard because it contains the NP-hard classical parallel-machine scheduling problem $P_2||C_{\max}$ as a special case when the second-stage operations all have a zero processing time, and the transportation time from the subcontractor to the in-house facility τ is 0.

To solve this problem, we first observe that all the subcontracted jobs are delivered together in one batch at the time when all these jobs are completed by the subcontractor. Thus, the delivery cost is fixed as μ and independent of how other decisions are made. In the discussion below for this problem, we do not consider delivery cost. Qi (2011) proposes a pseudo-polynomial time dynamic programming algorithm for solving this problem. We describe that algorithm below.

Algorithm DP-FS1

Initialization Reindex the jobs following Johnson's rule (see Sect. 5.2.1). Define $P_j = \sum_{k=1}^{j} p_j$ and $Q_j = \sum_{k=1}^{j} q_j$ for $j = 1, \ldots, n$, and let $P = P_n$ and $Q = Q_n$.

Value Function $F(j, x, y, z)$ = the minimum makespan of the jobs processed in-house in a schedule for jobs $1, \ldots, j$ where (a) the total processing time of the stage-one operations of the subcontracted jobs is x (hence that of the jobs processed in-house is $P_j - x$), (b) the total processing time of the stage-two operations of the subcontracted jobs is y, and (c) the makespan of the jobs processed by the subcontractor is no more than z.

Boundary Conditions

$F(0, 0, 0, z) = 0$, for $z = 0, 1, \ldots, P + Q$,
$F(0, x, y, z) = \infty$ for $x > 0$ or $y > 0$.

Recurrence Relation For $j = 1, \ldots, n$, $x = 0, 1, \ldots, P_j$, $y = 0, 1, \ldots, Q_j$, and $z = \max(x, y), \max(x, y) + 1, \ldots, x + y$:

$$F(j, x, y, z) = \min\{F_1(j, x, y, z), F_2(j, x, y, z)\},$$

where

$$F_1(j, x, y, z) = \max\{F(j - 1, x, y, z), P_j - x\} + q_j,$$

$$F_2(j, x, y, t) = \begin{cases} \infty, & \text{if } x + q_j > z, \\ F(j - 1, x - p_j, y - q_j, z - q_j), & \text{if } x + q_j \leq z. \end{cases}$$

Optimal Solution Value

$$\min\{\alpha_1 x + \alpha_2 y + \max\{F(n, x, y, z), z + \tau\} \mid x = 0, 1, \ldots, P;$$

$$y = 0, 1, \ldots, Q; z = \max(x, y), \ldots, x + y\}.$$

In the recurrence relation of the above algorithm, $F_1(j, x, y, z)$ and $F_2(j, x, y, z)$ are the value of the state (j, x, y, z) if job j is processed in-house and if job j is subcontracted out, respectively. The recurrence relation for $F_1(j, x, y, z)$ is quite straightforward. For $F_2(j, x, y, z)$, if $x + q_j > z$, then the completion time of the second-stage operation of job j, which defines the makespan of the subcontracted jobs among the first j jobs (denoted as $C_{\max}^j$) would be more than z, a contradiction. Since $C_{\max}^j = \max\{x, C_{\max}^{j-1}\} + q_j$, where $C_{\max}^{j-1}$ is the makespan of the subcontracted jobs among the first $j - 1$ jobs, if $x + q_j \leq z$ and $C_{\max}^{j-1} + q_j \leq z$, then $C_{\max}^j \leq z$. This shows the validity of the recurrence relation for $F_2(j, x, y, z)$.

6.6 Problems Requiring Delivery of Subcontracted Jobs

Qi (2011) also considers a special case of this problem where no subcontracting cost is considered. A simplified version of Algorithm DP-FS1 can be used to solve this problem. Since the subcontracting cost is not considered, we do not need to keep track of the total processing time of the second-stage operations of the subcontracted jobs, i.e., we can drop the y variable from each state in the algorithm. The same recurrence relations apply.

We now consider the second problem studied by Qi (2011). It is the same as the first problem discussed above, except that now there are two subcontractors, denoted as $S1$ and $S2$, respectively, that handle subcontracted jobs sequentially such that $S1$ processes the stage-one operations and $S2$ processes the stage-two operations of subcontracted jobs, and all the jobs completed at $S1$ are delivered together in one batch to $S2$. The transportation time from $S1$ to $S2$ is τ_1. Completed jobs at $S2$ are shipped to the in-house facility in batches, where each delivery batch incurs a transportation time τ_2.

This problem is at least ordinarily NP-hard because it is more general than the first problem. Also, as in the first problem, we observe that there exists an optimal solution where all the completed jobs at $S2$ are delivered together in one batch. Hence, the total delivery cost is fixed and independent of how other decisions are made. In the discussion below for this problem, we do not consider delivery cost. Finally, by the requirement in the problem that all the jobs completed at $S1$ are delivered together to $S2$ in one batch, we can see that (i) an arbitrary schedule can be used for the jobs processed at $S1$ and those processed at $S2$, and (ii) the makespan of the subcontracted jobs is simply the sum of the total processing time of the two operations together of the subcontracted jobs, and the total transportation delay, i.e., $\tau_1 + \tau_2$.

Qi (2011) proposes a pseudo-polynomial time dynamic programming algorithm for solving this problem. We describe that algorithm below.

Algorithm DP-FS2

Initialization Reindex jobs following Johnson's rule (see Sect. 5.2.1). Define $P_j = \sum_{k=1}^{j} p_j$ and $Q_j = \sum_{k=1}^{j} q_j$ for $j = 1, \ldots, n$, and let $P = P_n$ and $Q = Q_n$.

Value Function $F(j, x, y)$ = the minimum makespan of the jobs processed in-house in a schedule for jobs $1, \ldots, j$ where (i) the total processing time of the stage-one operations of the subcontracted jobs is x (and hence that of the in-house jobs is $P_j - x$), and (ii) the total processing time of the stage-two operations of the subcontracted jobs is y.

Boundary Conditions

$F(0, 0, 0) = 0$; $F(0, x, y) = \infty$ for $x, y > 0$;
$F(j, x, y) = \infty$ for $j = 1, \ldots, n$, and $x, y < 0$.

Recurrence Relation For $j = 1, \ldots, n$, $x = 0, 1, \ldots, P_j$, and $y = 0, 1, \ldots, Q_j$:

$$F(j, x, y) = \min \begin{cases} F(j - 1, x - p_j, y - q_j), \\ \max\{F(j - 1, x, y), P_j - x\} + q_j. \end{cases}$$

Optimal Solution Value

$$\min \left\{ \alpha_1 x + \alpha_2 y + \max\{F(n, x, y), x+y+\tau_1+\tau_2\} | x = 0, 1, \ldots, P; \ y = 0, 1, \ldots, Q \right\}.$$

The recurrence relation in the above algorithm considers two cases of job j: (1) it is subcontracted out, and in this case, $F(j, x, y) = F(j-1, x-p_j, y-q_j)$, (2) it is processed in-house, and in this case the completion time of job j (which is defined as $F(j, x, y)$) is $\max\{F(j-1, x, y), P_j - x\} + q_j$. This shows the validity of the recurrence relation.

6.7 Problems with a More Complex Subcontracting Cost Structure

In all the problems discussed in the previous sections, it is assumed that the subcontracting cost of a job is independent of the total subcontracted workload. However, in practice, due to fixed overhead and necessary setups, production costs often exhibit economies of scale. This means that the higher the volume a subcontractor handles, the lower the unit production cost is for the subcontractor. Hence, a subcontractor may be willing to lower the subcontracting cost of a job if the partnering manufacturer can subcontract a larger amount of work to the subcontractor. Discount schemes like this are called *quantity discounts*, and studied extensively in the inventory management and lot-sizing literature (e.g., Pereira & Costa, 2015 and Munson & Jackson, 2015).

In this section, we consider several JSS problems with a quantity discount scheme applied to the subcontracting cost. These problems are studied by Lu et al. (2021). Below, we first describe these problems and summarize the results derived by Lu et al. (2021) in Sect. 6.7.1, followed by an in-depth analysis of two problems in Sect. 6.7.2.

6.7.1 Problem Description

A manufacturer receives a set of n jobs $N = \{1, \ldots, n\}$. Each job is processed either on a single machine available in-house at the manufacturer or subcontracted to a subcontractor. Each job $j \in N$ is associated with a release time r_j, a processing time p_j if it is processed in-house, and an original subcontracting cost e_j if it is processed by the subcontractor. Let $S \subseteq N$ be the set of subcontracted jobs, and $Q(S) = \sum_{j \in S} e_j$ be the total original subcontracting cost. Based on the value of $Q(S)$, the subcontractor applies a quantity discount scheme to determine the actual total subcontracting cost for the manufacturer. Consequently, the actual total subcontracting cost is a function of $Q(S)$, denoted as $f(Q(S))$. The manufacturer

6.7 Problems with a More Complex Subcontracting Cost Structure

needs to determine a subset of jobs S to be subcontracted such that the sum of the makespan of the in-house jobs, denoted as $C_{\max}(N \setminus S)$, and the total subcontracting cost $f(Q(S))$ is minimized.

Lu et al. (2021) consider four quantity discount schemes, all representable by a piece-wise linear subcontracting cost function $f(Q(S))$. The basic idea of all these discount schemes is the same: The domain for the total original subcontracting cost is divided into m ($m \le n$) disjoint intervals $[W_0, W_1), [W_1, W_2), \ldots, [W_{m-1}, W_m)$, where $W_0 = 0$ and $W_m = \infty$, such that the discount applied increases over these intervals, i.e., the larger the total original subcontracting cost $Q(S)$, the larger the discount the manufacturer receives. These discount schemes differ in the functional form of the discount applied. Below we describe the discount function as well as the actual subcontracting cost $f(Q(S))$ under each discount scheme.

- Under every discount scheme, if $Q(S) \in [W_0, W_1)$, there is no discount, i.e., $f(Q(S)) = Q(S)$.
- Discount scheme (i): If $Q(S) \in [W_k, W_{k-1})$ for some $k \in \{1, \ldots, m-1\}$, the discount offered is a constant α_k such that $f(Q(S)) = Q(S) - \alpha_k$, where $\alpha_1 < \alpha_2 < \cdots < \alpha_{m-1}$.
- Discount scheme (ii): If $Q(S) \in [W_k, W_{k-1})$ for some $k \in \{1, \ldots, m-1\}$, the discount offered is a linear function $Q(S) - \beta_k$ such that $f(Q(S)) = Q(S) - (Q(S) - \beta_k) = \beta_k$, where $\beta_1 < \beta_2 < \cdots < \beta_{m-1}$ are constants.
- Discount scheme (iii): If $Q(S) \in [W_k, W_{k-1})$ for some $k \in \{1, \ldots, m-1\}$, the discount offered is a linear function $(1 - \gamma_k)Q(S)$ such that $f(Q(S)) = Q(S) - (1 - \gamma_k)Q(S) = \gamma_k Q(S)$, where $1 > \gamma_1 > \gamma_2 > \cdots > \gamma_{m-1} > 0$ are constants.
- Discount scheme (iv): If $Q(S) \in [W_k, W_{k-1})$ for some $k \in \{1, \ldots, m-1\}$, the discount offered is a complex linear function such that $f(Q(S)) = W_1 + \theta_1(W_2 - W_1) + \cdots + \theta_{k-1}(W_k - W_{k-1}) + \theta_k(Q(S) - W_k)$, where $1 > \theta_1 > \theta_2 > \cdots > \theta_{m-1} > 0$ are constants.

It can be seen that under the discount schemes (ii), (iii), and (iv), $f(Q(S))$ is a step-wise function, all-unit discount function, and an incremental discount function, over the domain $[W_1, W_m)$, respectively.

To illustrate, we give a numerical example of each discount scheme as follows.

Example 6.4 (Discount Schemes) Suppose that the domain of $Q(S)$ is divided into 3 intervals, $[0, 100), [100, 200), [200, \infty)$, i.e., $W_1 = 100, W_2 = 200$, and $W_3 = \infty$. Let $\alpha_1 = 10, \alpha_2 = 30$. Then under discount scheme (i), we have

$$f(Q(S)) = \begin{cases} Q(S), & \text{if } Q(S) \in [0, 100), \\ Q(S) - 10, & \text{if } Q(S) \in [100, 200), \\ Q(S) - 30, & \text{if } Q(S) \in [200, \infty). \end{cases}$$

Let $\beta_1 = 100$, $\beta_2 = 200$. Then, under discount scheme (ii), we have

$$f(Q(S)) = \begin{cases} Q(S), & \text{if } Q(S) \in [0, 100), \\ 100, & \text{if } Q(S) \in [100, 200), \\ 200, & \text{if } Q(S) \in [200, \infty). \end{cases}$$

Let $\gamma_1 = 0.8$, $\gamma_2 = 0.6$. Then, under discount scheme (iii), we have

$$f(Q(S)) = \begin{cases} Q(S), & \text{if } Q(S) \in [0, 100), \\ 0.8Q(S), & \text{if } Q(S) \in [100, 200), \\ 0.6Q(S), & \text{if } Q(S) \in [200, \infty). \end{cases}$$

Let $\theta_1 = 0.8$, $\theta_2 = 0.6$. Then, under discount scheme (iv), we have

$$f(Q(S)) = \begin{cases} Q(S), & \text{if } Q(S) \in [0, 100), \\ 100 + 0.8(Q(S) - 100), & \text{if } Q(S) \in [100, 200), \\ 100 + 0.8(100) + 0.6(Q(S) - 200), & \text{if } Q(S) \in [200, \infty). \end{cases}$$

Lu et al. (2021) consider both the general problem where the jobs have different release times r_j, denoted as $1|r_j|C_{\max}(N \setminus S) + f(Q(S))$, and the special case where all the jobs have the same release time (or equivalently, $r_j = 0$ for $j \in N$), denoted as $1||C_{\max}(N \setminus S) + f(Q(S))$, under each of the four discount schemes. They show that (1) both problems $1||C_{\max}(N \setminus S) + f(Q(S))$ and $1|r_j|C_{\max}(N \setminus S) + f(Q(S))$ under the discount scheme (i), (ii), or (iii) are ordinarily NP-hard; (2) problem $1||C_{\max}(N \setminus S) + f(Q(S))$ under the discount scheme (iv) is polynomially solvable, whereas problem $1|r_j|C_{\max}(N \setminus S) + f(Q(S))$ under the discount scheme (iv) is ordinarily NP-hard. In addition, they provide a polynomial time heuristic for problem $1|r_j|C_{\max}(N \setminus S) + f(Q(S))$ under the discount scheme (iv) with a tight worst-case performance ratio of 2. In the following subsection, we provide an in-depth analysis of the two problems under the discount scheme (iv).

6.7.2 Analysis of Problems with Incremental Discount

In this section we analyze problems $1||C_{\max}(N \setminus S) + f(Q(S))$ and $1|r_j|C_{\max}(N \setminus S) + f(Q(S))$ under the incremental discount scheme, i.e., discount scheme (iv).

Lemma 6.5 *There is an optimal solution for problem* $1||C_{\max}(N \setminus S) + f(Q(S))$ *with the incremental discount scheme in which any subcontracted job* $u \in S$ *and any job processed in-house* $v \in N \setminus S$ *must satisfy* $p_u/e_u \geq p_v/e_v$.

Proof We prove the lemma by contradiction. Given an optimal solution π^*, suppose that there are two jobs in this solution, $u \in S$ and $v \in N \setminus S$ satisfy $p_u/e_u < p_v/e_v$.

6.7 Problems with a More Complex Subcontracting Cost Structure

Suppose that $Q(S) = \sum_{j \in S} e_j \in [W_k, W_{k+1})$ for some $k \in \{0, \ldots, m-1\}$. Let $\theta_0 = 1$.

First, consider another solution π_1 where job u is processed in-house whereas the status of every other job is the same as in π^*. Compared to π^*, in π_1 the makespan of the in-house jobs is p_u units longer, but the subcontracting cost is at least $\theta_k e_u$ units lower because of the incremental discount scheme. Thus, the objective function of π_1 is higher than that of π^* by at most $p_u - \theta_k e_u$. Since π^* is optimal, $p_u - \theta_k e_u \geq 0$, which implies that $\theta_k \leq p_u/e_u$. Since $p_u/e_u < p_v/e_v$, we have

$$\theta_k < p_v/e_v. \tag{6.31}$$

Next, consider another solution π_2 where job v is subcontracted whereas the status of every other job is the same as in π^*. Compared to π^*, in π_2 the makespan of the in-house jobs is p_v units shorter, but the subcontracting cost is at most $\theta_k e_v$ units higher because of the incremental discount scheme. Thus, the objective function of π_2 is higher than that of π^* by at most $\theta_k e_v - p_v$. Since π^* is optimal, $\theta_k e_v - p_v \geq 0$, which implies that $\theta_k \geq p_v/e_v$, which is a contradiction with (6.31). Thus, the condition that $p_u/e_u < p_v/e_v$ does not hold. $\qquad\square$

Reindex the jobs such that $p_1/e_1 \geq \cdots \geq p_n/e_n$. Lemma 6.5 implies that there exists an optimal solution to problem $1||C_{\max}(N \setminus S) + f(Q(S))$ with the incremental discount scheme, in which, for some $h \in \{0, 1, \ldots, n\}$, the first h jobs $1, \ldots, h$ are subcontracted and the remaining jobs are processed in-house. Based on this observation, we can solve this problem by the following algorithm, which has a time complexity of $O(n \log n)$.

Algorithm A6.7.1

Step 1: Reindex the jobs such that $p_1/e_1 \geq \cdots \geq p_n/e_n$. Let $P_0 = \sum_{j=1}^{n} p_j$, $E_0 = 0$, and $Z_0 = P_0$.

Step 2: For $j = 1, \ldots, n$, compute $P_j = P_{j-1} - p_j$, and $E_j = E_{j-1} + e_j$, and $Z_j = P_j + f(E_j)$.

Step 3: Find $h = \arg \min\{Z_j \mid j = 0, 1, \ldots, n\}$. Let $S = \emptyset$ if $h = 0$, and $S = \{1, \ldots, h\}$ otherwise. [An optimal solution is found where the jobs in S are subcontracted and the rest are processed in-house. The optimal objective value is Z_h.]

Next, we consider problem $1|r_j|C_{\max}(N \setminus S) + f(Q(S))$ with the incremental discount scheme. Consider a special case of this problem with $m = 1$, i.e., $f(Q(S)) = Q(S)$ over the entire domain of $Q(S)$. There is no discount on the subcontracting cost. If a job j is subcontracted, its contribution to the total subcontracting cost is e_j. This special case of the problem is equivalent to the scheduling problem with rejection, denoted as $1|r_j|C_{\max} + \sum_{j \in R} w_j$, where jobs have generally different release times and can be rejected with a penalty $w_j = e_j$ and the objective is to minimize the makespan of the accepted jobs and the total penalty of the rejected jobs (whose job set is denoted as R). This problem is known to be NP-hard (Zhang et al., 2009). Thus, our problem $1|r_j|C_{\max}(N \setminus S) + f(Q(S))$ with the incremental discount scheme is NP-hard. Below we give a pseudo-

296   6 Joint Subcontracting and Scheduling Decisions

polynomial time dynamic programming algorithm for solving this problem, which implies that this problem is ordinarily NP-hard.

The algorithm is based on the straightforward property that the jobs processed in-house are scheduled by earliest release times first (ERT) rule in an optimal solution. By this property, the algorithm considers the jobs in ERT order, and for each job, decides whether to subcontract it or process it in-house.

Algorithm A6.7.2

Initialization Reindex the jobs following the ERT rule, i.e, $r_1 \leq \cdots \leq r_n$.

Value Function $F(j, Q)$ = the minimum makespan of the jobs processed in-house in a solution for jobs $1, \ldots, j$, where the total original subcontracting cost, without discount, of the subcontracted jobs is Q.

Boundary Conditions
$$F(0, 0) = 0; F(0, Q) = \infty \text{ for } Q > 0.$$

Recurrence Relation For $j = 1, \ldots, n$, $Q = 0, 1, \ldots, \sum_{j=1}^{n} e_j$:

$$F(j, Q) = \min\left\{\max\{F(j-1, Q), r_j\} + p_j, F(j-1, Q - e_j)\right\}.$$

Optimal Solution Value

$$\min\{F(n, Q) + f(Q) \mid 0 \leq Q \leq \sum_{j=1}^{n} e_j\}.$$

The recurrence relation of the above algorithm considers both the case with job j processed in-house, under which the makespan of the schedule is $\max\{F(j-1, Q), r_j\} + p_j$, and the case with job j subcontracted, under which the makespan of the schedule is $F(j-1, Q - e_j)$. The time complexity of this algorithm is $O(n \sum_{j \in N} e_j)$.

Finally, we give a polynomial time heuristic for problem $1|r_j|C_{\max}(N \setminus S) + f(Q(S))$ with the incremental discount scheme and analyze its worst-case performance. For ease of presentation, we refer to this problem as the original problem. The idea of the heuristic is to solve n auxiliary problems of the original problem and choose one of the resulting solutions with the lowest objective value as the solution to the original problem. We first define these auxiliary problems, denoted as $AP_1, \ldots, AP_n$. Reindex the jobs such that $r_1 \leq \cdots \leq r_n$ and $e_j \geq e_{j+1}$ in case $r_j = r_{j+1}$ for every such j. For $l = 1, \ldots, n$, auxiliary problem AP_l is the original problem with the following two additional constraints:

- Job l is the job with the largest index that is processed in-house, which means that all the jobs in $V_l = \{l + 1, \ldots, n\}$ are subcontracted.
- The jobs processed in-house (which consist of a subset of the first $l - 1$ jobs and job l) must start at time r_l consecutively without any idle time.

6.7 Problems with a More Complex Subcontracting Cost Structure

Problem AP_l is to find a subset of jobs $U_l \subseteq \{1, \ldots, l-1\}$ such that the jobs in $S_l = U_l \cup V_l$ are subcontracted and the jobs in $N \setminus S_l$ are processed in-house.

It is not difficult to see that Lemma 6.5 holds for every auxiliary problem AP_l, for $l = 1, \ldots, n$. This means that if we reindex the jobs in $\{1, \ldots, l-1\}$ as $[1], \ldots, [l-1]$ such that $p_{[1]}/e_{[1]} \geq \cdots \geq p_{[l-1]}/e_{[l-1]}$, then there exists an optimal solution to problem AP_l where jobs $[1], \ldots, [h]$, for some $0 \leq h \leq l-1$, are subcontracted and the remaining jobs are processed in-house.

We can thus solve every problem AP_l with fixed l, for $l = 1, \ldots, n$, by a slightly modified version of Algorithm A6.7.1. It is described below. This is used as a subroutine for Heuristic H6.7.4 below.

Algorithm A6.7.3

Step 1: Let $V_l = \{l+1, \ldots, n\}$. Let $P_0 = r_l + \sum_{j=1}^{l} p_j$, $E_0 = \sum_{j \in V_l} e_j$, and $Z_0 = P_0 + f(E_0)$. Reindex the jobs in $\{1, \ldots, l-1\}$ as $[1], \ldots, [l-1]$ such that $p_{[1]}/e_{[1]} \geq \cdots \geq p_{[l-1]}/e_{[l-1]}$.

Step 2: For $j = 1, \ldots, l-1$, compute $P_j = P_{j-1} - p_{[j]}$, $E_j = E_{j-1} + e_{[j]}$, and $Z_j = P_j + f(E_j)$.

Step 3: Find $h = \arg\min\{Z_j \mid j = 0, 1, \ldots, l-1\}$. Let $U_l = \emptyset$ if $h = 0$, and $U_l = \{[1], \ldots, [h]\}$ otherwise. [An optimal solution is found for problem AP_l where the jobs in $U_l \cup V_l$ are subcontracted and the rest are processed in-house. The optimal objective value is Z_h.]

The time complexity of the above algorithm is $O((l-1) \log(l-1))$.

We now describe the heuristic for the original problem, $1|r_j|C_{\max}(N \setminus S) + f(Q(S))$ with the incremental discount scheme.

Heuristic H6.7.4

Step 1: Reindex the jobs such that $r_1 \leq \cdots \leq r_n$, and $e_j \geq e_{j+1}$ in case $r_j = r_{j+1}$ for every such j.

Step 2: Create solution σ_0 in which all the n jobs are subcontracted.

Step 3: For $l = 1, \ldots, n$, solve auxiliary problem AP_l using Algorithm A6.7.3. Let σ_l be the solution.

Step 4: Among the solutions generated, $\sigma_0, \ldots, \sigma_n$, choose one with the lowest objective value as the final solution.

Theorem 6.11 *Heuristic H6.7.4 generates a solution for problem $1|r_j|C_{\max}(N \setminus S) + f(Q(S))$ with the incremental discount scheme with a tight worst-case ratio of 2 in $O(n^2 \log n)$ time.*

Proof First, since the heuristic applies Algorithm A6.7.3 n times, and the lth time when this algorithm is applied, its running time is $O((l-1) \log(l-1))$, the total time taken by Step 3 of the heuristic is thus $O(n^2 \log n)$. The other steps of the heuristic together take less than this time. Thus, the overall time complexity of the heuristic is $O(n^2 \log n)$.

Next, we analyze the worst-case performance of the heuristic. Reindex the jobs such that $r_1 \leq \cdots \leq r_n$, and $e_j \geq e_{j+1}$ in case $r_j = r_{j+1}$ for every such j. Let π^* be an optimal solution of the problem, and σ^* be the solution generated by the heuristic. We denote the objective value of any feasible solution η as $Z(\eta)$. If no job is processed in-house in π^*, then σ_0 has the same objective value as π^*, which implies that the solution generated by the heuristic, σ^*, is optimal, i.e., $Z(\sigma^*) = Z(\pi^*)$. Suppose that in π^*, job u is the largest indexed job processed in-house. This means that all the jobs $u+1, \ldots, n$ and possibly a subset of the jobs in $\{1, \ldots, u-1\}$ are subcontracted. We create a new solution π' based on π^* as follows: π' has the same set of jobs subcontracted and the same set of jobs processed in-house with the same sequence as in π^*, but shifts the schedule of the jobs processed in-house later such that the first job starts exactly at time r_u.

Clearly, solution π' is feasible for auxiliary problem P_u. Thus, $Z(\pi') \geq Z(\sigma^*)$. Furthermore, the way π' is constructed implies that $Z(\pi') \leq r_u + Z(\pi^*) \leq 2Z(\pi^*)$. Therefore, $Z(\sigma^*) \leq 2Z(\pi^*)$, meaning that the worst-case ratio of the heuristic is bounded above by 2.

Next, we show that the worst-case bound of 2 is tight. Consider an instance where there are two jobs, with $r_1 = 0$, $p_1 = 1$, $e_1 = 3$ and $r_2 = 1$, $p_2 = 0$, $e_2 = 3$. The subcontracting cost function $f(Q) = Q$ for any $Q \geq 0$. For this instance, the following solution is optimal: Process all jobs in-house with job 1 processed in interval $[0, 1]$ and job 2 at time point 1. This solution has an objective value 1. Using the heuristic, three solutions are generated: (1) σ_0 which subcontracts all the jobs, and hence has an objective value 6, (2) σ_1 which subcontracts job 2 and processes job 1 in-house with starting time 0, and hence has an objective value 4, and (3) σ_2 which processes both jobs in-house with starting time 1, and hence has an objective value 2. Thus, solution σ_2 is chosen as the final solution to this instance with an objective value 2. This implies that the performance bound of the heuristic for this instance is exactly 2. $\square$

In addition to the results presented here, Lu et al. (2021) also provide an FPTAS for problem $1|r_j|C_{\max}(N \setminus S) + f(Q(S))$ with the incremental discount scheme.

6.8 Future Research

Most existing research on joint subcontracting and scheduling problems that we are aware of has made quite restrictive assumptions, including,

(i) Any job can be subcontracted if necessary.
(ii) A subcontractor has an unlimited capacity such that it can process as many jobs as assigned to it and still guarantee a promised lead time for each job, or there is only a single machine available at a subcontractor.
(iii) The subcontracting cost rate per unit processing time is a constant, independent of the total subcontracted amount, or the subcontracting cost for a subcontracted job is fixed, independent of the other subcontracted jobs.
(iv) There is a fixed number of machines in-house and all these machines can be used to process jobs without incurring any fixed cost for using a machine or treating the fixed cost as a sunk cost.

6.8 Future Research

However, these assumptions may not be valid in some practical settings. Below, we discuss several situations where these assumptions may not hold, and possible new problems that can be studied when these assumptions are relaxed.

- In practice, some jobs may have precedence constraints because of inherent characteristics of the jobs (Pinedo, 2016). For example, suppose jobs 1 and 2 are two sequential production steps (or service procedures) applied to a given component (or customer). Clearly, job 1 needs to be processed first before job 2, and because they deal with the same component, either both jobs are subcontracted or both jobs are processed in-house. In such a case, assumption (i) above is not valid. To reflect the example given here, we can replace this assumption by the following: There are subsets of jobs such that if one of the jobs in a subset is subcontracted, then all the jobs in this subset must be subcontracted together to the same subcontractor. It would be useful to study various problems with this new assumption.
- In reality, every subcontractor has a capacity limit, and hence assumption (ii) above may not hold. A subcontractor may set lower and upper bounds on how much work it can take in from a manufacturer. For example, on one hand, a subcontractor may not want to process only one job for a manufacturer because it is not worth the fixed cost involved (such as paperwork, machine setup, and overhead). On the other hand, its limited capacity may allow it to accept at most 10 jobs or 10 h of work from a manufacturer. Furthermore, the lead time that a subcontractor can guarantee may depend on how much work it processes. Clearly, the corresponding problems with such practical capacity and lead time complications will be more complex to solve.
- Because of economies of scale and fixed costs that are present, the unit production cost usually decreases with the production volume. Thus, a subcontractor may charge less per unit if a larger amount of work is subcontracted to it. In such a case, assumption (iii) above may not hold. A more practical problem then involves a subcontracting cost as a nonlinear function (e.g., nondecreasing concave function) of the total amount processed by a subcontractor. As discussed in Sect. 6.7, Lu et al. (2021) study some problems with such a subcontracting cost function. More research on such problems is needed.
- The main reason why companies subcontract or outsource jobs is to lower investment cost for in-house production capacity. For example, a company can use fewer in-house machines by subcontracting more jobs, which can lower the cost for using the machines but increase the subcontracting cost. Hence, there is a tradeoff between the fixed cost for using a certain number of in-house machines and the subcontracting cost if some jobs are subcontracted out. Thus, assumption (iv) above may not hold. To examine such issues, we would need to consider problems where a fixed cost is incurred whenever an in-house machine is used, and part of the decision is the number of in-house machines to use.

In addition to these possible directions for future research, there are several issues related to the specific problems studied in the previous sections of this chapter that need to be addressed.

- The majority of the problems studied in this chapter are NP-hard. Although pseudo-polynomial time algorithms are provided for many of these problems, there are few existing fast heuristics for these problems with a constant worst-case performance ratio. Thus, designing efficient heuristics with a theoretical performance guarantee for many of these problems is a future research direction.
- We are not aware of any online joint subcontracting and scheduling problems studied in the existing literature. Hence, another future research direction is to investigate online versions of the problems studied in this chapter.

Part II
Decentralized Supply Chain Scheduling

Part II of the book consists of Chaps. 7 through 9 on decentralized supply chain scheduling problems. Chapter 7 presents some early foundational works on supply chain scheduling that use optimization techniques from classical scheduling. Typical results here include describing efficient algorithms, identifying the solvability boundary of various problems, evaluation of the cost of conflict when decision makers fail to coordinate their decisions, and evaluation of the benefit of cooperation when they do. Chapter 8 applies cooperative solution concepts to decentralized scheduling problems and addresses issues such as the stability of cooperation and how to divide the benefit of cooperation to ensure stability. Chapter 9 applies noncooperative solution concepts to study the existence of equilibria and their effect on the performance of an overall system. In scheduling systems where decision makers have private information, we investigate mechanisms that ensure truthful reporting of that information to a central planner, in some cases with the help of a payment or cost allocation scheme. In addition to covering a variety of supply chain scheduling applications, Chaps. 8 and 9 also include sufficient background to serve as an introduction to cooperative and noncooperative games, respectively.

Chapter 7
Optimization and Conflict

Abstract This chapter discusses decentralized supply chain scheduling applications and related models that use optimization methodology. We study four problems that have both a scheduling component and a second component that arises from the structure of the supply chain and the self-interest of the different parties. We discuss mathematical models to evaluate the cost of conflict experienced by one party when another party dominates the decision making process and also to evaluate the benefit of cooperation between the parties. Methods by which one party can compensate others, in order to achieve such cooperation, are also discussed.

7.1 Introduction

This chapter presents four foundational works on optimization approaches to decentralized supply chain scheduling problems. They focus, respectively, on the following issues that fall within the scope of scheduling and related decisions in supply chains:

1. The coordination of schedule formation with the quantity and timing of batch deliveries
2. The coordination of the delivery schedules of parts suppliers with a manufacturer's final assembly schedule
3. The coordination of a manufacturer's production schedule and a downstream distributor's delivery schedule
4. The coordination of sequences involving setup costs between consecutive stages of a supply chain

Together, these issues and the related works we discuss illustrate the extensive variety of problems, issues, solution methods, and insights that arise within the optimization of supply chain scheduling problems. Chapter 8 studies similar issues using cooperative game theory. In Chap. 9, we examine how noncooperative game theory can be applied to these issues.

© Springer Nature Switzerland AG 2022
Z.-L. Chen, N. G. Hall, *Supply Chain Scheduling*, International Series
in Operations Research & Management Science 323,
https://doi.org/10.1007/978-3-030-90374-9_7

In decentralized supply chain scheduling, the overall performance of the supply chain is affected by the decisions of several self-interested parties. As a result, the performance achieved by those parties and by the overall supply chain depends not only on their own decisions but also on those of others. Two challenges that arise both naturally and frequently here are discussed within the context of the above four issues.

The first challenge is *avoiding conflict*. Consider two decision making parties, A and B, in a supply chain. It may happen that A imposes on B a decision that restricts B's options. This typically occurs for one of the two reasons. First, party A has greater decision making power in the supply chain than party B does. Second, the position of party A in the supply chain enables it to make decisions that arise earlier in the supply chain than those of party B. This restriction may reduce the best possible outcome achievable by B. This reduction is party B's *cost of conflict*. We typically assume that the decision chosen by party A is optimal for its own problem, and those decisions are presented to party B as already given. This conflict arises frequently in the literature of supply chain management. However, we study it here within the context of scheduling problems. We discuss ways in which the cost of this conflict can be estimated, in various scheduling environments. These include a supplier that batches jobs for multiple manufacturers, an assembly supply chain, and supply chains consisting of either a manufacturer and a distributor or a supplier and a manufacturer.

The second challenge is *encouraging cooperation* between the various parties, for the purpose of achieving an improved outcome for the entire supply chain. The base case for defining the benefit of cooperation is that each party in the supply chain makes its own self-interested decisions, either optimally or heuristically. Given these decisions, the resulting performance of the overall supply chain can be estimated. However, it is also possible that the various players cooperate to find a commonly agreed solution, and this solution may provide improved, perhaps even globally optimal, performance of the supply chain. The relative improvement in overall supply chain performance is the *benefit of cooperation*. A mechanism is needed to initiate this cooperation, and this mechanism naturally varies with the supply chain environment. For the supply chain scheduling environments described above, we assess the potential benefit of cooperation and identify practical incentives and methods within the scope of optimization for establishing cooperation.

As we demonstrate in this chapter, both the cost of conflict and the benefit of cooperation are substantial in various supply chain scheduling environments. This chapter therefore studies the challenges of avoiding conflict and encouraging cooperation as they arise in supply chain scheduling problems. Differences among the four environments studied originate from varying characteristics of resources, jobs, costs, constraints, decisions that need to be made, and other specifications. As a result, there exists a rich literature that recommends a wide variety of algorithms and heuristic solution procedures for these problems, and the works presented here are central to this literature. For each supply chain environment studied, we discuss these solution procedures, which enables us to study the resulting conflict and cooperation issues that arise when self-interested but potentially cooperative parties use those solution procedures. An overview of this chapter now follows.

Section 7.2 is based on the work of Hall and Potts (2003) on scheduling and batching problems. Several works motivate the study of supply chain scheduling and batching problems. Thomas and Griffin (1996) provide an extensive review and discussion of the literature of supply chain management. They emphasize that for many products, logistics expenditures can constitute over 30% of the cost of goods sold. Sarmiento and Nagi (1999) survey the literature of integrated production and distribution models. They motivate the importance of such models by pointing out that the modern trend toward reduced inventory levels creates the need for closer coordination between consecutive stages of a supply chain. This work is specifically motivated by their discussion of possible topics for future research. Hall et al. (2001) analyze a variety of problems with different machine environments where a set of available times, at which batches may be delivered, is fixed before the schedule is determined.

The work of Hall and Potts (2003) considers a variety of scheduling, batching, and delivery problems that arise in an arborescent supply chain where a supplier makes deliveries to several manufacturers, who also make deliveries to customers. The objective is to minimize the overall scheduling and delivery cost, using several classical scheduling objectives to represent scheduling cost. This is achieved by scheduling jobs and forming them into batches, each of which is delivered to the next downstream stage as a single shipment. Optimal algorithms and limits to computational tractability are identified. It is shown that cooperation between a supplier and a manufacturer may reduce the total system cost substantially, but to an extent that depends on the scheduling objective. Incentives and practical mechanisms for achieving cooperation are also discussed.

Section 7.3 is based on the work of Chen and Hall (2007) on scheduling in assembly systems. Reductions in inventory levels (Rajagopalan & Malhotra, 2001; Walts, 2020) motivate the need for closer coordination within supply chains. It is well known (Cachon, 2003; Chen, 2003) that cooperation between companies can improve efficiency. However, most supply chain cooperation models in the literature consider inventory control decisions. Within traditional supply chain management research, the literature that is most closely related to this work is on production and distribution systems with multiple stages. There are at least two previous studies of scheduling problems in assembly systems. Lee et al. (1993) consider the minimization of makespan in an assembly system with two suppliers and one manufacturer. They prove that this problem is intractable, provide an enumerative algorithm, and analyze special cases and heuristics. Potts et al. (1995) consider a more general problem with several suppliers and one manufacturer and describe heuristics with small worst-case error bounds. However, these works do not discuss conflict and cooperation between decision makers, which are the main focus of Sect. 7.3. Many electronics manufacturers, including Dell Computer, have adopted assemble-to-order production approaches (The Economist, 2001), where the coordination of suppliers' production schedules with that of the manufacturer is critical. This is the environment we discuss.

The work of Chen and Hall (2007) considers an assembly system with several suppliers and one manufacturer. Each supplier provides parts to the manufacturer. The manufacturer waits until all the parts for a job have arrived and then initiates a final stage of manufacturing. As is customary in assembly systems, different parts of the same job can be processed simultaneously by different suppliers. The objective is to minimize the overall scheduling cost. The best schedule for the suppliers' scheduling problem can be far from optimal for the corresponding manufacturer's problem, and vice versa. Moreover, it may be the case that neither's best schedule is close to optimal for the overall supply chain. Evaluating the cost of conflict and the benefit of cooperation under various definitions of cost requires the solution of various scheduling problems by the suppliers, the manufacturer, and the overall system. Efficient optimal algorithms or heuristics with guaranteed performance are provided. The cost saving realized by cooperation between the decision makers is significant in many cases.

Section 7.4 is based on the work of Dawande et al. (2006), which considers tradeoffs between production cost and downstream costs in a supply chain consisting of a manufacturer and a distributor. The need for coordination between a manufacturer and a distributor arises in many practical situations. Chen and Vairaktarakis (2005) study an integrated scheduling model involving production and distribution operations, using an objective that considers both customer service level and distribution costs. This paper provides efficient algorithms, proofs of intractability, and heuristic analysis but does not explicitly model conflict and coordination issues in a manufacturing and distribution system. Specific practical situations that motivate the need for such coordination include perishable products where inventory immediately loses value and applications with significant setup costs when changing between the manufacture of different products.

The work of Dawande et al. (2006) considers a supply chain where a manufacturer makes products that are shipped to customers by a distributor. Both the manufacturer and the distributor have an ideal schedule, determined by cost and capacity considerations. However, these two schedules are in general not well coordinated, which leads to poor overall performance. Two practical problems are studied. In both problems, the manufacturer focuses on production costs, i.e., minimizing unproductive time. However, the distributor minimizes downstream costs, which include customer cost measures in the first problem and inventory holding cost in the second problem. The work discussed in Sect. 7.4 first evaluates each party's conflict, which is the relative increase in cost that results from using the other party's optimal schedule. Since this conflict is often significant, we consider several practical scenarios about the level of cooperation between the manufacturer and the distributor. These scenarios define various scheduling problems for the manufacturer, the distributor, and the overall system. For each of these scheduling problems, we provide an algorithm. We demonstrate that the cost saving provided by cooperation between the decision makers is usually significant. Finally, we discuss the implications of our work for how manufacturers and distributors negotiate, coordinate, and implement their supply chain schedules in practice.

Section 7.5, based on the work of Agnetis et al. (2006), considers the problem of resequencing when successive stages of a manufacturing process prefer different production sequences. This most typically occurs due to different production setup or changeover times at different stages. The work discussed considers operational issues that are important to the scheduling of supply chains organized to achieve just-in-time (JIT) goals (Hernandez, 1989; Ohno, 1988). At the operational level, decision makers at different stages of the chain need to consider various factors such as their immediate customers' due dates, production deadlines, changeover costs and times. For example, an assembly facility that has to ship jobs to different customers may wish to process the materials in the chronological sequence of the customers' due dates. On the other hand, according to JIT concepts, scheduling decisions at an upstream stage must also comply with the actual time at which the supplier will dispatch the raw materials and with technological requirements that may make certain schedules infeasible. Nellemann and Smith (1982) identify the punctual delivery of materials at different stages to be among the most important elements of a successful JIT system. Hence, the schedule that is used at each stage depends on the requirements at the other stages. Agnetis et al. (2001) consider the problem of finding a common sequence that minimizes the number of setups between the two departments. They provide intractability results and design and test a heuristic.

The work of Agnetis et al. (2006) considers two consecutive stages of a supply chain, consisting of one supplier and several manufacturers, respectively. The costs and requirements specific to each stage (for example, changeover times, resource availability, and deadlines) define an ideal schedule in which the jobs should be processed. This ideal schedule minimizes overall costs subject to resource constraints at that stage. Resequencing between a supplier and a manufacturer requires the use of a buffer, which may incur additional cost. An interchange cost, which models buffer storage cost, is incurred by the supplier or a manufacturer whenever the relative order of two jobs in its actual schedule is different from that in its ideal schedule. The problems of finding an optimal supplier's schedule, an optimal manufacturer's schedule, and an optimal schedule for the overall system are considered. The objective functions considered are the minimization of total interchange cost and of total interchange plus buffer storage cost. Algorithms for all the supplier's and manufacturers' problems, as well as for a special case of the overall system scheduling problem, are provided. The running time of these algorithms is polynomial in both the number of jobs and the number of manufacturers. Finally, conditions are identified under which cooperation between the supplier and a manufacturer reduces their total cost.

Section 7.6 uses the current literature of supply chain scheduling to identify several suggestions for future research. Figure 7.1 provides an overview of the topics within the optimization of supply chain scheduling problems that are discussed in this chapter.

7.2 Scheduling and Batching in a Supply Chain

This section, based on the work of Hall and Potts (2003), considers the objective of minimizing the total batch delivery cost plus a scheduling cost that models the inconvenience of the downstream party based on the delivery time of the batch. This objective is a natural extension of the classical scheduling literature

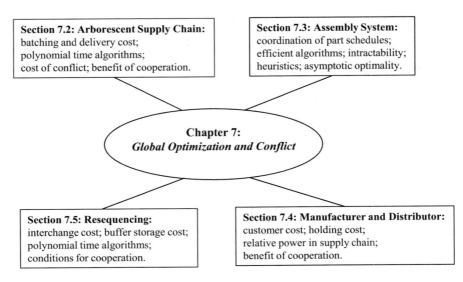

Fig. 7.1 Overview of the topics covered in Chap. 7

to allow for batch delivery cost. An important example of decision making that affects both a supplier and a manufacturer is the delivery process between the two. The supplier processes jobs and delivers them to the manufacturer. The manufacturer may prefer to receive frequent deliveries of small batches from the supplier, because this enables the manufacturer to achieve better resource utilization. However, the supplier may be reluctant to deliver very frequently because of the resulting high delivery cost. Furthermore, the manufacturer may prefer to receive parts earlier rather than later, because this enlarges the manufacturer's scheduling options and improves utilization. Also, because of production capacity constraints at the supplier, scheduling decisions may prioritize the processing of certain parts, perhaps for specific high value or long-standing customers, over others. Importantly, scheduling decisions must be coordinated with the related batching and delivery decisions. This problem is studied from the viewpoint of the supplier.

The manufacturer also has downstream customers. The decision problem faced by the manufacturer is therefore similar to that faced by the supplier, with the difference that the scheduling, batching, and delivery decisions made by the supplier define *batch release dates*, before which the manufacturer cannot begin work on any job in that batch. Analysis of this problem shows that these batch release dates can be incorporated into scheduling, batching, and delivery models. The batch release dates defined for the manufacturer by the supplier's decisions may be less than ideal from the viewpoint of the manufacturer. This suggests that it may be mutually advantageous for the supplier and manufacturer to cooperate in developing combined models that incorporate the total costs of both parties. Therefore, models for cooperative decision making between the supplier and the manufacturer are also developed.

7.2 Scheduling and Batching in a Supply Chain

This section is organized as follows. In Sect. 7.2.1, we describe our notation and classification scheme. We also provide some general results for all our scheduling objectives, and we present an overview of our algorithmic and computational complexity results. Section 7.2.2 considers the minimization of the total scheduling and delivery cost, using a variety of classical scheduling objectives, from the viewpoint of the supplier. In Sect. 7.2.3, we consider the same problems from the viewpoint of the manufacturer. The problem of minimizing the total system cost of a supplier and a manufacturer who cooperate is studied in Sect. 7.2.4. The potential benefits from such cooperation, and practical mechanisms for achieving it, are discussed in Sect. 7.2.5.

7.2.1 Preliminaries

This section describes the notation and assumptions used, provides some general results that simplify the subsequent analysis, and summarizes results for algorithms and intractability issues.

7.2.1.1 Notation and Classification

Consider three categories of problems that arise in an arborescent supply chain. In the *supplier's problem*, n^S jobs are to be scheduled on a single machine, M_S, by the supplier $\mathscr{S}$. Each job is produced for one of G manufacturers $\mathscr{M}_1, \ldots, \mathscr{M}_G$, and the jobs for each manufacturer are delivered in batches. The supplier's problem is illustrated in Fig. 7.2, where the asterisk indicates that scheduling, batching, and delivery decisions by the supplier are required.

Similarly, in the *manufacturer's problem*, one of the manufacturers (without loss of generality, $\mathscr{M}_1$, as indicated by an asterisk) uses jobs from the supplier to

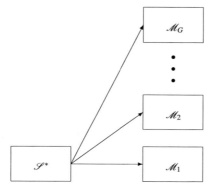

Fig. 7.2 Structure of the supplier's problems

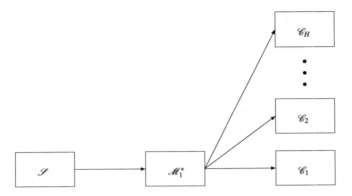

Fig. 7.3 Structure of the manufacturer's problems

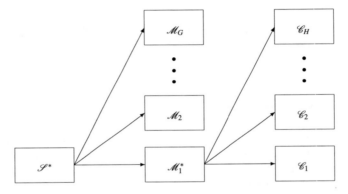

Fig. 7.4 Structure of the combined problems

produce n^m jobs on a single machine, M_M, for customers $\mathscr{C}_1, \ldots, \mathscr{C}_H$. These jobs are scheduled and delivered in batches to the customers, as shown in Fig. 7.3.

Finally, in the *combined problem*, it is necessary to find an overall schedule for the supplier $\mathscr{S}$ and manufacturer $\mathscr{M}_1$ that creates batches to be delivered from the supplier to each of the manufacturers and from manufacturer $\mathscr{M}_1$ to the customers. Figure 7.4 shows the structure of the combined problem, where again the asterisks shown at the supplier $\mathscr{S}$ and manufacturer $\mathscr{M}_1$ indicate by which parties scheduling, batching, and delivery decisions are required.

A description of the notation used starts with the supplier's problem. Let $N^S = \{1, \ldots, n^S\}$ denote the set of jobs. We refer to the jobs processed for manufacturer $\mathscr{M}_g$, as $(1, g), \ldots, (n_g, g)$, for $g = 1, \ldots, G$. Job (j, g) has a processing time p_{jg}^S on machine M_s, for $j = 1, \ldots, n_g$. Where relevant, job (j, g) has a weight (or value) w_{jg}^S and a due date d_{jg}^S. For the manufacturer's problem, the set of jobs is $N^M = \{1, \ldots, n^M\}$, and the jobs for customer $\mathscr{C}_h$ are $(1, h), \ldots, (n_h, h)$, for $h = 1, \ldots, H$. Job (j, h) has a processing time p_{jh}^M and, where relevant, has a weight w_{jh}^M and a due date d_{jh}^M, for $j = 1, \ldots, n_h$. The time when job (j, h) is

7.2 Scheduling and Batching in a Supply Chain

delivered from the supplier to the manufacturer defines a release date r_{jh}^M, which is the earliest time when the manufacturer can start to process this job. For the combined problem, the set of jobs is $N^C = \{1, \ldots, n^C\}$. The jobs processed for customer $\mathscr{C}_h$ are $(1, h), \ldots, (n_h, h)$, for $h = 1, \ldots, H$, and these two-stage jobs require first machine M_S and then machine M_M. Furthermore, the jobs processed for manufacturer $\mathscr{M}_g$ are $(1, H + g - 1), \ldots, (n_{H+g-1}, H + g - 1)$, for $g = 2, \ldots, G$, and these single-stage jobs require machine M_S only. Job (j, h) has a processing time p_{jh}^S on machine M_S and a processing time p_{jh}^M on machine M_M and where relevant has a weight w_{jh}^M and a due date d_{jh}^M, for $h = 1, \ldots, H$ and $j = 1, \ldots, n_h$. Also, job (j, g) has a processing time p_{jg}^S on machine M_S and where relevant has a weight w_{jg}^S and a due date d_{jg}^S, for $g = H + 1, \ldots, H + G - 1$ and $j = 1, \ldots, n_g$. Consistent with the classical scheduling literature, it is assumed that all processing times, weights, and release dates are positive integers and that G and H are fixed so that they do not form part of the input data for a particular instance. Also, let P denote the sum of all the processing times in the specified problem, $W^S = \sum_{g=1}^{G} \sum_{j=1}^{n_g} w_{jg}^S$ and $W^M = \sum_{h=1}^{H} \sum_{j=1}^{n_h} w_{jh}^M$. Where there is no ambiguity, we write n instead of n^S or n^M or n^C and W instead of W^S or W^M.

The due dates are set as follows. Customers specify due dates by which the corresponding jobs should ideally be delivered from the manufacturer. To specify a due date for the supplier, the manufacturer assumes a specific (but not necessarily optimal) schedule for the processing of its jobs, i.e., one in which all jobs can be delivered to the customers on time. Then, the due date of each job at the supplier is equal to the start time of that job in the manufacturer's given schedule.

A group of jobs forms a batch for the supplier if all of these jobs are delivered from the supplier to a single manufacturer at the same time. A batch for the manufacturer is defined analogously. Let D_g^S and D_h^M denote the cost of delivering each batch from the supplier to manufacturer $\mathscr{M}_g$ for $g = 1, \ldots, G$ and from manufacturer $\mathscr{M}_1$ to customer $\mathscr{C}_h$ for $h = 1, \ldots, H$, respectively, independent of the contents of the batch.

The following definitions are functions of the *variable* σ, which denotes the supplier's schedule:

$$C_j^S(\sigma) = \text{the time at which job } j \text{ is delivered to the relevant manufacturer;}$$
$$F_j^S(\sigma) = C_j^S(\sigma), \text{ the flow time of job } j;$$
$$U_j^S(\sigma) = \begin{cases} 0 & \text{if job } j \text{ is delivered to the relevant manufacturer by its due date,} \\ 1 & \text{if job } j \text{ is late;} \end{cases}$$
$$y_g^S(\sigma) = \text{the number of deliveries to manufacturer } \mathscr{M}_g \text{ in } \sigma.$$

The quantities $C_j^M(\sigma)$, $U_j^M(\sigma)$, and $y_h^M(\sigma)$ are defined analogously for a manufacturer's schedule σ, and $F_j^M(\sigma) = C_j^M(\sigma) - r_j^M$. For the combined problem, define $C_j^C(\sigma)$ to be $C_j^S(\sigma)$ for the single-stage jobs j that are produced for manufacturers $\mathscr{M}_2, \ldots, \mathscr{M}_G$, and $C_j^M(\sigma)$ for the two-stage jobs that are produced for customers

$\mathscr{C}_1, \ldots, \mathscr{C}_H$, from which the analogous variables $F_j^C(\sigma) = C_j^C(\sigma)$ and $U_j^C(\sigma)$ are computed. When there is no ambiguity, we simplify $C_j^S(\sigma)$, $F_j^S(\sigma)$, $U_j^S(\sigma)$, and $y_g^S(\sigma)$ to C_j^S, F_j^S, U_j^S, and y_g^S, respectively, and similarly for the manufacturer's problem and the combined problem. We also refer to C_j^S and C_j^M as the completion times of job j (as perceived by the manufacturer and customer, respectively). Observe that, for any two-stage job j, $F_j^C = F_j^S + F_j^M$ when $r_j^M = C_j^S = F_j^S$.

The scheduling objectives that we consider are classical ones motivated either by internal costs or by external costs or target dates. First, in the absence of due dates, we consider total (weighted or unweighted) completion or flow time objectives that model internal holding costs. Since we are considering a supply chain which ultimately delivers jobs to a customer, it is natural to use the definitions of C_j^S, C_j^M, and C_j^C in the previous paragraph. In models, that minimize the (weighted or unweighted) number of late jobs, we assume that a job that would be late is neither produced nor delivered. This assumption is relevant where late deliveries are not accepted. When the aim is to meet due dates, the number of late jobs is a standard measure of performance in the scheduling literature (Pinedo, 2016).

The standard classification scheme for scheduling problems (Graham et al., 1979) is $\alpha|\beta|\gamma$, as defined in Chap. 2. Under β, we may have "r_j," which denotes that each of the manufacturer's jobs has a release date r_{jh}^M that defines the earliest time at which job (j, h) becomes available for processing. The objective functions studied under γ comprise a delivery cost and a scheduling cost. The delivery cost for the supplier is $\sum D_g^S y_g^S$ and for the manufacturer is $\sum D_h^M y_h^M$. The scheduling cost is

$$\sum (w_j) F_j^X = \text{the total (weighted) flow time of the jobs;}$$
$$\sum (w_j) U_j^X = \text{the total (weighted) number of late jobs,}$$

where $X = S$ for the supplier, $X = M$ for the manufacturer, and $X = C$ for the combined problem. For the combined problem, we consider the total delivery cost $\sum D_g^S y_g^S + \sum D_h^M y_h^M$, the supplier's scheduling cost for those jobs of N^S that are produced for manufacturers $\mathscr{M}_2, \ldots, \mathscr{M}_G$, and the scheduling cost incurred by manufacturer $\mathscr{M}_1$ for all jobs of N^M. Since the combined problem considers the complete system as illustrated in Fig. 7.4, the supplier's scheduling cost for the jobs of N^S that are produced for manufacturer $\mathscr{M}_1$ is assumed to represent a performance measure for work in process and hence does not affect the total system cost.

7.2.1.2 General Assumptions and Properties

For problems where the scheduling objective is to minimize the number of late jobs, we assume that it is sufficient to construct a delivery schedule for the on-time jobs only, and the delivery cost of the late jobs is ignored.

7.2 Scheduling and Batching in a Supply Chain

We present some results that apply to various problems, irrespective of the scheduling objective. The first result eliminates inserted idle time from the schedules we construct and follows directly from the assumption of costs that are nondecreasing in time.

Lemma 7.1 *There exists an optimal schedule where:*

(a) *In any of the supplier's and combined problems which we consider, there is no idle time between the jobs on machine M_S.*
(b) *In any of the manufacturer's problems which we consider, each job starts processing on machine M_M either at its release date or immediately after another job.*

The next result restricts the choice of times at which batch deliveries are scheduled.

Lemma 7.2 *There exists an optimal schedule with the following properties:*

(a) *In any problem, each delivery from the supplier $\mathcal{S}$ to any manufacturer (respectively, each delivery from manufacturer $\mathcal{M}_1$ to any customer) occurs when some job destined for the relevant manufacturer (respectively, customer) completes processing.*
(b) *In any of the supplier's or combined problems, a delivery from the supplier $\mathcal{S}$ to some manufacturer $\mathcal{M}_g$ that occurs when some job (j, g) completes processing comprises a group of jobs destined for manufacturer $\mathcal{M}_g$, including (j, g), that are processed consecutively on machine M_S.*

Proof

(a) Consider an optimal schedule with a delivery from the supplier $\mathcal{S}$ to a manufacturer $\mathcal{M}_g$ at some time t, where no job for $\mathcal{M}_g$ completes processing at t. Let job (j, g) be the last job for manufacturer $\mathcal{M}_g$ that completes processing before time t. Move the delivery at t earlier so that it occurs at the time when job (j, g) completes processing. Since no job is delivered later, and the number of deliveries is unchanged, the new schedule is also optimal. A similar argument establishes that each delivery from manufacturer $\mathcal{M}_1$ to a customer can also be scheduled when a job for that customer completes processing.

(b) Now consider the delivery from the supplier $\mathcal{S}$ to manufacturer $\mathcal{M}_g$ that is scheduled when job (j, g) completes processing. If there is another job (i, g) that is delivered in the same batch as job (j, g) but is processed immediately before another job (k, l) that is not delivered in this batch, then interchange jobs (i, g) and (k, l). Also, if there is a delivery when job (k, l) completes processing in the original schedule, then schedule that delivery p_{ig}^S units earlier, at the time when job (k, l) completes processing in the new schedule. Repeat this adjacent job interchange process a finite number of times until all the jobs that are delivered in the batch containing job (j, g) are processed consecutively, finishing at the completion time of job (j, g). Since no job is delivered later, and the number of deliveries is unchanged, the new schedule is also optimal. □

The third result restricts the processing orders on machines M_S and M_M in combined problems.

Lemma 7.3 *In any of the combined problems, there exists an optimal schedule in which the jobs on machine M_M are processed in the same order as the corresponding jobs are processed on machine M_S.*

We refer the reader to Hall & Potts (2003) for a proof.

Schedules that satisfy Lemma 7.3 are called *permutation schedules*.

The final result in this section provides a complexity hierarchy between a classical scheduling problem $\alpha|\beta|\gamma$, a supplier's problem $\alpha|\beta|\gamma^S$, a manufacturer's problem $\alpha|\beta, r_j|\gamma^M$, and a combined problem $\alpha|\beta|\gamma^C$. Given two problems P_1 and P_2, let the notation $P_1 \propto P_2$ denote that P_2 is a generalization of P_1.

Theorem 7.1 $\alpha|\beta|\gamma \propto \alpha|\beta|\gamma^S \propto \alpha|\beta, r_j|\gamma^M$ and $\alpha|\beta|\gamma^S \propto \alpha|\beta|\gamma^C$.

Proof If $D_g^S = 0$ for $g = 1, \ldots, G$, then without loss of generality all batches in problem $\alpha|\beta|\gamma^S$ contain a single job, and consequently problems $\alpha|\beta|\gamma$ and $\alpha|\beta|\gamma^S$ are equivalent. Also, when $r_j^M = 0$ for $j \in N^M$, problems $\alpha|\beta|\gamma^S$ and $\alpha|\beta, r_j|\gamma^M$ are equivalent. Finally, if $D_h^M = 0$ for $h = 1, \ldots, H$ and all the manufacturer's processing times are zero, then problems $\alpha|\beta|\gamma^S$ and $\alpha|\beta|\gamma^C$ are equivalent. □

7.2.1.3 Overview of the Results

We provide an overview of the algorithm and intractability results in this work. Because the cost and the feasibility of a schedule can be evaluated in $O(n)$ time, the recognition versions of all the problems considered in this work belong to the class *NP*. Table 7.1 presents a summary of our results for the supplier's, manufacturer's, and combined problems. For the manufacturer's problems, our polynomial-time algorithms are derived under the assumption of batch consistency, which means that, if some job i is delivered to the manufacturer before another job j, then i cannot be scheduled for delivery by the manufacturer strictly later than j. For various manufacturer's problems within Table 7.1, we also assume SPT-batch consistency, EDD-batch consistency, or EDD-batch consistency for the on-time jobs, which means that jobs with the same release date that are destined for the same customer are sequenced in SPT order, i.e., nondecreasing order of processing times (Smith, 1956), in EDD order, i.e., nondecreasing order of due dates (Jackson, 1955), or in EDD order for the on-time jobs, respectively. For the combined problems, we assume a given ordering of the jobs for each of the manufacturers $\mathcal{M}_2, \ldots, \mathcal{M}_G$ and for each of the customers $\mathcal{C}_1, \ldots, \mathcal{C}_H$. All these assumptions are motivated and discussed below. The first column of Table 7.1 specifies the scheduling objective. The second, third, and fourth columns show the running time of the fastest known

Table 7.1 Algorithm and complexity results for supply chain scheduling problems

Scheduling objective	Supplier's problem		Manufacturer's problem		Combined problem	
$\sum C_j$ or $\sum F_j$	$O(n^{G+1})$	Theorem 7.2	$UNPC$	Theorem 7.1	$UNPC$	Theorem 7.1
			$O(n^{3H})$ [a]	Theorem 7.6	$O(n^{2G+7H-2})$ [b]	Theorem 7.9
$\sum w_j C_j$ or $\sum w_j F_j$	$UNPC$	Theorem 7.3	$UNPC$	Theorem 7.1	$UNPC$	Theorem 7.1
$\sum U_j$	$O(n^{2G+2})$	Theorem 7.4	$UNPC$	Theorem 7.1	$UNPC$	Theorem 7.1
					$BNPC$ [c]	Theorem 7.10
			$O(n^{3H+1})$ [d]	Theorem 7.7	$O(n^{G+2H-1}P^3)$ [c]	Theorem 7.11
$\sum w_j U_j$	$BNPC$	Theorem 7.5	$UNPC$	Theorem 7.1	$UNPC$	Theorem 7.1
			$BNPC$ [d]	Theorem 7.8	$BNPC$ [c]	Theorem 7.10
	$O(n^{2G+1}W)$	Theorem 7.5	$O(n^{3H}W)$ [d]	Theorem 7.8	$O(n^{G+2H-1}P^3)$ [c]	Theorem 7.11

[a] Result applies for SPT-batch consistency
[b] Result applies for total SPT within groups sequencing
[c] Result applies for EDD within groups sequencing for the on-time jobs
[d] Result applies for EDD-batch consistency for the on-time jobs

polynomial or pseudo-polynomial time algorithm for the supplier's, manufacturer's, and combined problem, respectively, if such an algorithm exists. Otherwise, we use *UNPC* (respectively, *BNPC*) to indicate that the equivalent recognition version of a problem is *NP*-complete with respect to a unary (respectively, binary) encoding of the data, respectively. Related definitions can be found in Garey and Johnson (1979). Included in the appropriate cell is a reference to where a proof of that result can be found.

7.2.2 The Supplier's Problem

In this section, we describe models for minimizing the sum of scheduling and delivery cost in various environments, from the viewpoint of the supplier. For some of the models, we establish the processing order of jobs for the same manufacturer in an optimal schedule and then use dynamic programming to form batches for delivery. Our dynamic programs are forward algorithms that append either a single job or a batch to a previously constructed partial schedule of jobs.

7.2.2.1 Sum of Flow Times

Lemma 7.4 *For problem $1 || \sum F_j^S + \sum D_g^S y_g^S$, the cost is minimized by sequencing the jobs for each manufacturer $\mathcal{M}_g$ according to a shortest processing time (SPT) rule.*

Proof The result is established by a standard job interchange argument. □

From Lemma 7.4, we assume throughout this subsection that the jobs for each manufacturer $\mathcal{M}_g$ are indexed in SPT order, so that $p_{1g}^S \leq \cdots \leq p_{n_g,g}^S$, for $g = 1, \ldots, G$. Generalizing ideas from Albers and Brucker (1993) for a similar problem with $G = 1$, we propose the following dynamic programming algorithm to solve problem $1 || \sum C_j^S + \sum D_g^S y_g^S$.

Algorithm SF
Value Function
$f(q) = f(q_1, \ldots, q_G) = $ the minimum total cost of scheduling and delivering jobs $(1, g), \ldots, (q_g, g)$ for $g = 1, \ldots, G$, where the last delivery is at time $\sum_{g=1}^{G} \sum_{j=1}^{q_g} p_{jg}^S$, and where $0 \leq q_g \leq n_g$.
Boundary Condition
$f(0, \ldots, 0) = 0$.
Optimal Solution Value
$f(n_1, \ldots, n_G)$.
Recurrence Relation
$$f(q) = \min_{(q_g', g) \in J} \{ (q_g - q_g')T + D_g^S + f(q') \},$$

7.2 Scheduling and Batching in a Supply Chain

where

$$J = \{(q'_g, g) \mid 1 \le g \le G, \; q_g > 0, \; 0 \le q'_g < q_g\},$$
$$T = \sum_{g=1}^{G} \sum_{j=1}^{q_g} p_{jg}^{S} \text{ and}$$
$$q' = (q_1, \ldots, q_{g-1}, q'_g, q_{g+1}, \ldots, q_G).$$

The recurrence relation selects a batch $\{(q'_g + 1, g), \ldots, (q_g, g)\}$ of jobs to be delivered to manufacturer $\mathcal{M}_g$ at time T. Each of these jobs contributes a flow time of T to the total scheduling cost, and a delivery cost of D_g^S is also incurred.

Theorem 7.2 *Algorithm SF finds an optimal schedule for problem* $1 || \sum C_j^S + \sum D_g^S y_g^S$ *in* $O(n^{G+1})$ *time.*

Proof The dynamic program exploits structural properties of an optimal schedule that are established in part (a) of Lemmas 7.1, 7.2, and 7.4. There are $O(n^G)$ states $(q_1, \ldots, q_G)$, and for each state the recurrence relation requires $O(n)$ time. Therefore, the overall time complexity of Algorithm SF is $O(n^{G+1})$. $\qquad\square$

However, we now show that the weighted version of this problem is intractable, even when there is only one manufacturer.

Theorem 7.3 *The recognition version of problem* $1 || \sum w_j F_j^S + \sum D_g^S y_g^S$ *is unary NP-complete, even for* $G = 1$.

Proof Hall and Potts (2003) provide a reduction from 3-Partition. $\qquad\square$

7.2.2.2 Number of Late Jobs

First, we state the following result for weighted and unweighted number of late jobs problems.

Lemma 7.5 *For problem* $1 || \sum w_j U_j^S + \sum D_g^S y_g^S$, *the cost is minimized by sequencing the on-time jobs for each manufacturer according to an earliest due date (EDD) rule.*

Proof The result is established by a standard job interchange argument. $\qquad\square$

As a result of Lemma 7.5, we assume throughout this subsection that the jobs for each manufacturer $\mathcal{M}_g$ are indexed in EDD order. For problem $1 || \sum U_j^S + \sum D_g^S y_g^S$, we describe a dynamic programming algorithm that either appends a job to some previous schedule of on-time jobs or specifies that this job is late and therefore not scheduled. A subsequent decision is made about whether a batch delivery is scheduled on completion of an appended on-time job. To enable checking that all the jobs of the current batch are on time when the batch is delivered, we store the index $(j, \bar{g})$ of the lowest indexed job in this batch as a state variable. Since the jobs are indexed in EDD order, all the jobs in the batch are on time if and only if the lowest indexed job is. Since the number of values for the makespan of the current

318   7 Optimization and Conflict

partial schedule of on-time jobs is pseudo-polynomial, the makespan is used as the function value, while the number of late jobs u is treated as a state variable.

Algorithm SU

Value Function

$f(q, y, u, j, \bar{g}) = f(q_1, \ldots, q_G, y_1, \ldots, y_G, u, j, \bar{g}) =$ the minimum makespan for the on-time jobs from $(1, g), \ldots, (q_g, g)$ for $g = 1, \ldots, G$, given that (i) for manufacturer $\mathcal{M}_g$, all on-time jobs are delivered using y_g deliveries for $g = 1, \ldots, \bar{g} - 1, \bar{g} + 1, \ldots, G$, (ii) if $y_{\bar{g}} > 0$, then all processed jobs from $(1, \bar{g}), \ldots, (j - 1, \bar{g})$ for manufacturer $\mathcal{M}_{\bar{g}}$ are delivered using $y_{\bar{g}} - 1$ deliveries, (iii) if $j > 0$, then $(j, \bar{g})$ is the first (i.e., earliest due date) job in the last batch of the current partial schedule that is not yet scheduled for delivery, and (iv) the total number of late jobs is u, where $0 \le y_g \le q_g \le n_g$, $0 \le u \le n$, $0 \le j \le q_{\bar{g}}$, and $1 \le \bar{g} \le G$. If $j > 0$ and $f(q, y, u, j, \bar{g}) > d^S_{j\bar{g}}$, then we define $f(q, y, u, j, \bar{g}) = \infty$.

Boundary Condition

$f(0, \ldots, 0, 0, \ldots, 0, 0, 0, 0) = 0.$

Optimal Solution Value

$$\min \left\{ u + \sum_{g=1}^{G} D^S_g y_g \mid \min_{(j,\bar{g}) \in N^S} \{ f(n_1, \ldots, n_G, y_1, \ldots, y_G, u, j, \bar{g}) \} < \infty, \ 0 \le u \le \right.$$

$$\left. n, \ 0 \le y_g \le n_g \text{ for } g = 1, \ldots, G \right\}.$$

Recurrence Relation

$$f(q, y, u, j, \bar{g}) =$$

$$\min \begin{cases} f(q', y, u - 1, j, \bar{g}) \\ p^S_{q_{\bar{g}}, \bar{g}} + f(q', y, u, j, \bar{g}), & \text{if } 0 < j < q_{\bar{g}} \text{ and } f(q', y, u, j, \bar{g}) \\ & \quad + p^S_{q_{\bar{g}}, \bar{g}} \le d^S_{j\bar{g}} \\ \min_{(j', \bar{g}') \in J} \{ p^S_{q_{\bar{g}}, \bar{g}} + f(q', y', u, j', \bar{g}') \}, & \text{if } j = q_{\bar{g}}, \end{cases}$$

where

$q' = (q_1, \ldots, q_{\bar{g}-1}, q_{\bar{g}} - 1, q_{\bar{g}+1}, \ldots, q_G),$

$y' = (y_1, \ldots, y_{\bar{g}-1}, y_{\bar{g}} - 1, y_{\bar{g}+1}, \ldots, y_G),$ and

$J = \{ (j', \bar{g}') \mid 0 \le \bar{g}' \le G,$

$j' = 0$ if $\bar{g}' = 0;$

$1 \le j' \le q_{\bar{g}} - 1$ if $\bar{g}' = \bar{g} \neq 0;$

$1 \le j' \le q_{\bar{g}'}$ if $\bar{g}' \neq \bar{g}$ and $\bar{g}' \neq 0;$

$f(q', y', u, j', \bar{g}') \} + p^S_{q_{\bar{g}}, \bar{g}} \le d^S_{q_{\bar{g}}, \bar{g}} \}.$

The first term in the minimization in the recurrence relation schedules job $(q_{\bar{g}}, \bar{g})$ to be late. The second term schedules job $(q_{\bar{g}}, \bar{g})$ to be on time and belonging to the current batch of jobs for customer $\mathcal{M}_{\bar{g}}$, provided that job $(q_{\bar{g}}, \bar{g})$ can be completed no later than time $d^S_{j\bar{g}}$, so that job $(j, \bar{g})$ can be dispatched by its due date. No decision has yet been made about when to deliver the batch containing jobs $(j, \bar{g})$ and $(q_{\bar{g}}, \bar{g})$. The third term schedules a delivery for a batch containing $(j', \bar{g}')$ as

7.2 Scheduling and Batching in a Supply Chain

its first job if $j' > 0$, starts a new batch with job (q_g, g) which is scheduled to be on time, and accounts for a delivery that will eventually need to be made to manufacturer $\mathcal{M}_{\bar{g}}$, since a new batch destined for that manufacturer has been started. In the definition of J, we distinguish the case where customers $\bar{g}'$ and $\bar{g}$ are the same and therefore the first job $(j', \bar{g}')$ in the delivered batch satisfies $j' \leq q_{\bar{g}} - 1$, from the case where those customers are different and therefore the first job can also be $(q_{\bar{g}'}, \bar{g}')$.

Theorem 7.4 *Algorithm SU finds an optimal schedule for problem* $1|| \sum U_j^S + \sum D_g^S y_g^S$ *in* $O(n^{2G+2})$ *time.*

Proof The dynamic program exploits structural properties of an optimal schedule that are established in part (a) of Lemmas 7.1, 7.2, and 7.5. There are $O(n^{2G+2})$ states $(q_1, \ldots, q_G, y_1, \ldots, y_G, u, j, \bar{g})$. The first and second terms in the recurrence relation require constant time for each state. The third term requires $O(n)$ time for each of the $O(n^{2G+1})$ states for which $j = q_{\bar{g}}$. Therefore, the overall time complexity of Algorithm SU is $O(n^{2G+2})$. □

We now consider the corresponding problem with the weighted number of late jobs as a scheduling objective.

Theorem 7.5 *An optimal solution for problem* $1|| \sum w_j U_j^S + \sum D_g^S y_g^S$ *can be found in* $O(n^{2G+1} W^S)$ *time. The recognition version of this problem is binary* NP-*complete.*

Proof We modify Algorithm SU by replacing the state variable u that represents the number of late jobs by one that specifies the total weight of late jobs. The original time complexity of $O(n^{2G+2})$ in Algorithm SU becomes $O(n^{2G+1} W^S)$ with this modification. The second result follows from the binary *NP*-completeness of the recognition version of the classical problem $1|| \sum w_j U_j$ (Karp, 1972) and from Theorem 7.1. □

7.2.3 The Manufacturer's Problem

We first describe models for minimizing the sum of scheduling cost plus delivery cost from the viewpoint of one particular manufacturer, $\mathcal{M}_1$. In these models, the time at which each job j is delivered from the supplier to the manufacturer defines a release date r_j^M from the perspective of the manufacturer.

Remark 7.1 Unfortunately, neither the SPT ordering of Lemma 7.4 nor the EDD ordering of Lemma 7.5 can be generalized to give a sequence of jobs for each customer in this case because the jobs have different release dates. However, by making some natural assumptions about the processing order of jobs for each customer, we are still able to provide dynamic programming algorithms that generate an optimal schedule in polynomial or pseudo-polynomial time. The algorithms here are more complicated than those in Sect. 7.2.2. This is because part (b) of Lemma 7.2 does not generalize to batches that are delivered from a manufacturer to a customer, due to the presence of release dates.

Definition 7.2 A supplier's batch schedule and a manufacturer's batch schedule are *batch consistent* if for each pair of jobs (i, h) and (j, h) that are processed by the supplier $\mathscr{S}$ and manufacturer $\mathscr{M}_1$, where $1 \le h \le H$, $1 \le i, j \le n_h$, and $i \ne j$, whenever job (i, h) is in a strictly earlier batch than job (j, h) in the supplier's batch schedule, then job (i, h) is in an earlier batch or in the same batch as job (j, h) in the manufacturer's batch schedule.

The algorithms developed by Ahmadi et al. (1992) for serial production processes with both discrete and batch processors provide schedules that meet this assumption. Moreover, this assumption is a natural and practical simplification of the production planning process, since it permits some scheduling decisions to be made without waiting for the next incoming batch. Another practical justification for making this assumption is that it reduces the need for resequencing and for storage buffers.

7.2.3.1 Sum of Flow Times

From the unary *NP*-completeness of the recognition version of the classical problem $1|r_j|\sum F_j$ (Lenstra et al., 1977) and Theorem 7.1, the recognition version of problem $1|r_j|\sum F_j^M + \sum D_h^M y_h^M$ is also unary *NP*-complete.

We derive a dynamic programming algorithm for problem $1|r_j|\sum F_j^M + \sum D_h^M y_h^M$ under the assumption of batch consistency. We make the further assumption of *SPT-batch consistency*, in which jobs with the same release date (that is, jobs delivered in one batch by the supplier) and for the same customer are processed by the manufacturer in SPT order. Thus, for customer $\mathscr{C}_h$, we index the jobs such that $r_{1h}^M \le \cdots \le r_{n_h,h}^M$, for $h = 1, \ldots, H$, where $r_{jh}^M = r_{j+1,h}^M$ implies that $p_{jh}^M \le p_{j+1,h}^M$ for $j = 1, \ldots, n_h - 1$. This assumption is motivated by a local optimization rule that minimizes the $\sum F_j^M$ objective within a batch.

We now provide a dynamic programming algorithm for problem $1|r_j|\sum F_j^M + \sum D_h^M y_h^M$ under the assumption of SPT-batch consistency.

Remark 7.2 We need additional state variables besides those in Algorithm SF, first because we consider the jobs one at a time here and therefore some jobs may have been processed and not yet delivered, and second because the presence of release dates may cause machine idle time which affects the makespan of the current partial schedule. To control the machine idle time, we partition the partial schedule into *blocks*, where a block is a maximal set of jobs that are processed with no idle time in between. Thus, the first job in a block is either the first job in the schedule or it is preceded by idle time. In either case, the first job in a block starts processing at its release date.

7.2 Scheduling and Batching in a Supply Chain

Algorithm MF

Value Function

$f(q, s, b, \bar{h}) = f(q_1, \ldots, q_H, s_1, \ldots, s_H, b_1, \ldots, b_H, \bar{h}) =$ the minimum total cost (where flow time is evaluated on the basis of zero release dates) for processing jobs $(1, h), \ldots, (q_h, h)$ and delivering jobs $(1, h), \ldots, (s_h, h)$ for $h = 1, \ldots, H$, given that (i) the last block contains jobs $(b_h + 1, h), \ldots, (q_h, h)$ for $h = 1, \ldots, H$, (ii) if $\bar{h} > 0$, then the last block starts with job $(b_{\bar{h}} + 1, \bar{h})$, (iii) $0 \leq s_h \leq q_h \leq n_h$, and $0 \leq b_h \leq q_h$, (iv) if $\bar{h} > 0$, then $b_{\bar{h}} < q_{\bar{h}}$, and (v) $0 \leq \bar{h} \leq H$.

Boundary Condition

$f(0, \ldots, 0, 0, \ldots, 0, 0, \ldots, 0, 0) = 0.$

Optimal Solution Value

$$\min_{(b_1, \ldots, b_H, \bar{h}) \in B} \{f(n_1, \ldots, n_H, n_1, \ldots, n_H, b_1, \ldots, b_H, \bar{h})\} - \sum_{h=1}^{H} \sum_{j=1}^{n_h} r_{jh}^M,$$

where $B = \{(b_1, \ldots, b_H, \bar{h}) \mid 0 \leq b_h \leq n_h \text{ for } 1 \leq h \leq H, \; b_{\bar{h}} < n_{\bar{h}}, \; 1 \leq \bar{h} \leq H\}$.

Recurrence Relation

$f(q, s, b, \bar{h}) =$

$$\min \begin{cases} \min_{h \in G_1} \{f(q', s, b, \bar{h})\} \\ \min_{h \in G_2} \left\{ \min_{0 \leq s_h' < s_h} \{(q_h - s_h')T + D_h^M + f(q', s', b, \bar{h})\} \right\} \\ \min_{(b', \bar{h}') \in B_1} \{f(q'', s, b', \bar{h}')\}, & \text{if } b = q'', s_{\bar{h}} < q_{\bar{h}} \\ \min_{(b', \bar{h}') \in B_1} \left\{ \min_{0 \leq s_{\bar{h}}'' < s_{\bar{h}}} \{(q_{\bar{h}} - s_{\bar{h}}'')T + D_{\bar{h}}^M + f(q'', s'', b', \bar{h}')\} \right\}, & \text{if } b = q'', \; s_{\bar{h}} = q_{\bar{h}}, \end{cases}$$

where

$q' = (q_1, \ldots, q_{h-1}, q_h - 1, q_{h+1} \ldots, q_H),$

$s' = (s_1, \ldots, s_{h-1}, s_h', s_{h+1} \ldots, s_H),$

$q'' = (q_1, \ldots, q_{\bar{h}-1}, q_{\bar{h}} - 1, q_{\bar{h}+1} \ldots, q_H),$

$s'' = (s_1, \ldots, s_{\bar{h}-1}, s_{\bar{h}}'', s_{\bar{h}+1} \ldots, s_H),$

$G_1 = \{h \mid 1 \leq h \leq H, \; s_h < q_h, \; b_h < q_h, \; b_{\bar{h}} + 1 < q_h \text{ if } h = \bar{h}, \; r_{q_h, h}^M \leq T'\},$

$G_2 = \{h \mid 1 \leq h \leq H, \; s_h = q_h, \; b_h < q_h, \; b_{\bar{h}} + 1 < q_h \text{ if } h = \bar{h}, \; r_{q_h, h}^M \leq T'\},$

$B_1 = \{(b_1', \ldots, b_H', \bar{h}') \mid 0 \leq \bar{h}' \leq H, \; 0 \leq b_h' \leq b_h \text{ for } h = 1, \ldots, H, \; b_{\bar{h}'}' < b_{\bar{h}'}, \; r_{q_{\bar{h}}, \bar{h}}^M > T'' \text{ if } \bar{h} > 0\},$

$T = r_{b_{\bar{h}}+1, \bar{h}}^M + \sum_{h=1}^{H} \sum_{j=b_h+1}^{q_h} p_{jh}^M,$

$T' = r_{b_{\bar{h}}+1, \bar{h}}^M + \sum_{l=1}^{H} \sum_{j=b_l+1}^{q_l'} p_{jl}^M, \text{ and}$

$T'' = r_{b_{\bar{h}'}+1, \bar{h}'}^M + \sum_{l=1}^{H} \sum_{j=b_l'+1}^{q_l''} p_{jl}^M.$

In the recurrence relation, the first term in the minimization schedules job (q_h, h) to be processed at the end of the current block and does not schedule a delivery upon completion of this job. The set G_1 ensures that $s_h < q_h$ so that job (q_h, h) is not delivered, that $b_h < q_h$ so that job (q_h, h) is in the last block, and that there is no idle time immediately before job (q_h, h) is processed. The second term is similar, except that a batch $\{(s'_h + 1, h), \ldots, (q_h, h)\}$ is scheduled for delivery to customer $\mathscr{C}_h$ when job (q_h, h) completes processing. In this case, the set G_2 ensures that $q_h = s_h$, so that the current state is consistent with such a delivery. The third and fourth terms in the recurrence relation correspond to the case where job $(q_{\bar{h}}, \bar{h})$ is the last job in the current schedule and starts a new block. Specifically, the third term considers the case where $s_{\bar{h}} < q_{\bar{h}}$, so that no delivery is scheduled on completion of job $(q_{\bar{h}}, \bar{h})$, whereas $s_{\bar{h}} = q_{\bar{h}}$ in the fourth term so that a batch delivery for jobs $\{(s''_{\bar{h}} + 1, \bar{h}), \ldots, (q_{\bar{h}}, \bar{h})\}$ is scheduled. The set B_1 defines b' and $\bar{h}'$ for a previous state that allows the processing of job $(q_{\bar{h}}, \bar{h})$ to start at its release date and be preceded by machine idle time.

Theorem 7.6 *Algorithm MF finds an optimal SPT-batch consistent schedule for problem* $1|r_j| \sum_j F_j^M + \sum_h D_h^M y_h^M$ *in* $O(n^{3H})$ *time.*

Proof The dynamic program exploits structural properties of an optimal schedule that are established in part (b) of Lemma 7.1, part (a) of Lemma 7.2, and the assumption of SPT-batch consistency. There are $O(n^{3H})$ states $(q, s, b, \bar{h})$. In the recurrence relation, the first term in the minimization requires constant time. The second term requires $O(n)$ time but is only applied for the $O(n^{3H-1})$ states for which $s_h = q_h$. The third term requires $O(n^H)$ time but is only applied for the $O(n^{2H})$ states for which $b_l = q_l$ for $l \neq \bar{h}$ and $b_{\bar{h}} = q_{\bar{h}} - 1$. Similarly, the fourth term requires $O(n^{H+1})$ time but is only applied for the $O(n^{2H-1})$ states for which $b_l = q_l$ for $l \neq \bar{h}$, $b_{\bar{h}} = q_{\bar{h}} - 1$, and $s_{\bar{h}} = q_{\bar{h}}$. Therefore, the overall time complexity of Algorithm MF is $O(n^{3H})$. $\qquad\square$

7.2.3.2 Number of Late Jobs

From the unary *NP*-completeness of the recognition version of the classical problem $1|r_j| \sum U_j$ (Lenstra et al., 1977) and Theorem 7.1, the recognition version of problem $1|r_j| \sum U_j^M + \sum D_h^M y_h^M$ is also unary *NP*-complete. Thus, we again restrict the class of schedules that we consider.

We assume *EDD-batch consistency for the on-time jobs*. Accordingly, we index the jobs such that $r_{1h}^M \leq \cdots \leq r_{n_h,h}^M$ for $h = 1, \ldots, H$, where $r_{jh}^M = r_{j+1,h}^M$ implies that $d_{jh}^M \leq d_{j+1,h}^M$ for $j = 1, \ldots, n_h - 1$. This assumption is motivated by a local rule that satisfies due dates for on-time jobs within a batch.

We now provide a dynamic programming algorithm for problem $1|r_j| \sum U_j^M + \sum D_h^M y_h^M$, under the assumption of EDD-batch consistency for the on-time jobs.

Following the approach in Algorithm SU, we define the value function to be the makespan of the current partial schedule of on-time jobs. This avoids the need to use state variables of the type defined in Algorithm MF for storing information about blocks. However, we introduce state variables to store the undelivered on-time job with the smallest due date for each customer, in order to check that all jobs of a batch are on time when a delivery is scheduled.

7.2 Scheduling and Batching in a Supply Chain

Algorithm MU

Value Function

$f(q, v, y, u) = f(q_1, \ldots, q_H, v_1, \ldots, v_H, y_1, \ldots, y_H, u) =$ the minimum makespan for the on-time jobs from $(1, h), \ldots, (q_h, h)$ for $h = 1, \ldots, H$, given that (i) y_h deliveries are used for completed batches for customer $\mathscr{C}_h$, (ii) job (v_h, h) is the job with the smallest due date among the undelivered on-time jobs for customer $\mathscr{C}_h$, for $h = 1, \ldots, H$, (iii) the total number of late jobs is u, and (iv) $0 \leq y_h \leq q_h \leq n_h$, $0 \leq v_h \leq q_h$, and $0 \leq u \leq n$. If $v_h > 0$ and $f(q, v, y, u) > d^M_{v_h, h}$ for any h, where $1 \leq h \leq H$, then we define $f(q, v, y, u) = \infty$ and this replaces any assigned value. We define $v_h = 0$ if there are no undelivered on-time jobs for customer $\mathscr{C}_h$, and $d_{0h} = \infty$.

Boundary Condition

$f(0, \ldots, 0, 0, \ldots, 0, 0, \ldots, 0, 0) = 0.$

Optimal Solution Value

$$\min\left\{ u + \sum_{h=1}^{H} D^M_h y_h \mid f(n_1, \ldots, n_H, 0, \ldots, 0, y_1, \ldots, y_H, u) < \infty, \ 0 \leq u \leq \right.$$

$$\left. n, \ 0 \leq y_h \leq n_h \text{ for } h = 1, \ldots, H \right\}.$$

Recurrence Relation

$$f(q, v, y, u) = \min \begin{cases} \min_{h \in G_1} \{ f(q', v, y, u - 1) \} \\ \min_{h \in G_2} \left\{ p^M_{q_h, h} + \max\{ f(q', v, y, u), r^M_{q_h, h} \} \right\} \\ \min_{h \in G_3} \left\{ \min_{v'_h \in V_1} \left\{ p^M_{q_h, h} + \max\{ f(q', v', y, u), r^M_{q_h, h} \} \right\} \right\} \\ \min_{h \in G_4} \left\{ \min_{v'_h \in V_2} \left\{ p^M_{q_h, h} + \max\{ f(q', v', y', u), r^M_{q_h, h} \} \right\} \right\}, \end{cases}$$

where

$q' = (q_1, \ldots, q_{h-1}, q_h - 1, q_{h+1} \ldots, q_H),$

$v' = (v_1, \ldots, v_{h-1}, v'_h, v_{h+1} \ldots, v_H),$

$y' = (y_1, \ldots, y_{h-1}, y_h - 1, y_{h+1} \ldots, y_H),$

$G_1 = \{ h \mid 1 \leq h \leq H, \ 0 \leq v_h < q_h \},$

$G_2 = \{ h \mid 1 \leq h \leq H, \ 0 < v_h < q_h, \ d^M_{v_h, h} \leq d^M_{q_h, h} \},$

$G_3 = \{ h \mid 1 \leq h \leq H, \ v_h = q_h > 0 \},$

$G_4 = \{ h \mid 1 \leq h \leq H, \ v_h = 0, \ q_h > 0 \},$

$V_1 = \{ v'_h \mid v'_h = 0, \ \text{or } 0 < v'_h < q_h \text{ and } d^M_{v'_h, h} > d^M_{q_h, h} \}$ and

$V_2 = \{ v'_h \mid 0 \leq v'_h < q_h, \ \max\{ f(q', v', y', u), r^M_{q_h, h} \} + p^M_{q_h, h} \leq \min\{ d^M_{v'_h, h}, d^M_{q_h, h} \} \}.$

In the recurrence relation, the first term in the minimization schedules job (q_h, h) to be late, whereas job (q_h, h) is on time in the schedule corresponding to the other three terms. In the second term, no delivery is scheduled when job (q_h, h) completes processing, and job (v_h, h) remains the undelivered job with the smallest due date for customer $\mathscr{C}_h$. The third term similarly does not schedule a delivery when job (q_h, h) completes processing, but as specified by V_1, (q_h, h) is either the only undelivered on-time job for customer $\mathscr{C}_h$ or it has a smaller due date than the job (v'_h, h) which has the smallest due date among undelivered on-time jobs for customer $\mathscr{C}_h$ in the previous schedule. Thus, the third term is used only when $v_h = q_h$. The fourth term schedules a delivery when job (q_h, h) completes processing and therefore is applied only when $v_h = 0$. The condition specified in V_2 ensures that all jobs of the batch that is scheduled for delivery are on time.

Theorem 7.7 *Algorithm MU finds an optimal EDD-batch consistent schedule of on-time jobs for problem $1|r_j| \sum U_j^M + \sum D_h^M y_h^M$ in $O(n^{3H+1})$ time.*

Proof The dynamic program exploits structural properties of an optimal schedule that are established in part (b) of Lemma 7.1, part (a) of Lemma 7.2, and the assumption of EDD-batch consistency for the on-time jobs. There are $O(n^{3H+1})$ states (q, v, y, u). The first two terms in the recurrence relation require constant time. The third term requires $O(n)$ time but is only applied for the $O(n^{3H})$ states where $v_h = q_h$ for some h. Similarly, the fourth term requires $O(n)$ time but is only applied for the $O(n^{3H})$ states where $v_h = 0$ for some h. Therefore, the overall time complexity of Algorithm MU is $O(n^{3H+1})$. $\qquad\square$

We now consider the corresponding weighted problem $1|r_j| \sum w_j U_j^M + \sum D_h^M y_h^M$.

Theorem 7.8 *An optimal EDD-batch consistent schedule of on-time jobs for problem $1|r_j| \sum w_j U_j^M + \sum D_h^M y_h^M$ can be found in $O(n^{3H} W^M)$ time. The recognition version of this problem, under the assumption of EDD-batch consistency for the on-time jobs, is binary NP-complete.*

Proof We modify Algorithm MU by replacing the number of late jobs state variable u by one that specifies the total weight of late jobs. The original time complexity of $O(n^{3H+1})$ in MU becomes $O(n^{3H} W)$ with this modification. The second result follows from the binary NP-completeness of the recognition version of the classical problem $1|| \sum w_j U_j$ (Karp, 1972) and Theorem 7.1, where the latter is valid under the assumption of EDD-batch consistency for the on-time jobs. $\qquad\square$

7.2.4 The Combined Problem

Here we assume that the supplier $\mathscr{S}$ and manufacturer $\mathscr{M}_1$ cooperate to solve a combined problem of minimizing the total system cost. There are single-stage jobs which the supplier $\mathscr{S}$ produces for manufacturers $\mathscr{M}_2, \ldots, \mathscr{M}_G$ with indexes (j, g), for $g = H + 1, \ldots, H + G - 1$ and $j = 1, \ldots, n_g$. There are also two-stage jobs for which parts are produced by the supplier and the final product is produced by manufacturer $\mathscr{M}_1$ for customers $\mathscr{C}_1, \ldots, \mathscr{C}_H$ with indexes (j, h), for $h = 1, \ldots, H$ and $j = 1, \ldots, n_h$. We refer to jobs $(1, k), \ldots, (n_k, k)$ for $k = 1, \ldots, H + G - 1$ as *group* k. Thus, all the jobs in group k are destined for customer $\mathscr{C}_k$ if $1 \le k \le H$

7.2 Scheduling and Batching in a Supply Chain   325

and for manufacturer $\mathcal{M}_{k-H+1}$ if $H + 1 \leq k \leq H + G - 1$. We need to determine schedules for machines M_S and M_M and to specify a batch delivery schedule from the supplier $\mathcal{S}$ to all manufacturers and from manufacturer $\mathcal{M}_1$ to all customers. The scheduling cost of the two-stage jobs is based on delivery times from $\mathcal{M}_1$ to the customers. This combined problem is a two-machine flowshop with batch deliveries and with some missing operations at the second stage.

Since the recognition versions of the classical problems $F_2||\sum F_j$ and $F_2||\sum U_j$ are unary NP-complete (Garey et al., 1976; Lenstra et al., 1977) and from Theorem 7.1, the recognition versions of the combined problems $1||\sum F_j^C + \sum D_g^S y_g^S + \sum D_h^M y_h^M$ and $1||\sum U_j^C + \sum D_g^S y_g^S + \sum D_h^M y_h^M$, respectively, are also unary NP-complete. Therefore, we first describe and then motivate a simplifying assumption for both these problems. For the sum of flow times problem, we make the natural and practical assumption that the single-stage jobs for each of the manufacturers $\mathcal{M}_2, \ldots, \mathcal{M}_G$ are sequenced in SPT order by the supplier according to the processing time on machine M_S and that the two-stage jobs for each customer are sequenced by both the supplier and the manufacturer $\mathcal{M}_1$ in SPT order according to the total processing time on machines M_S and M_M. We refer to this assumption as *total SPT within groups*. This assumption enables us to develop a polynomial-time dynamic programming algorithm for that problem. Similarly, by making an *EDD within groups for the on-time jobs* assumption for the number of late jobs problem, we provide a pseudo-polynomial time dynamic programming algorithm. Both assumptions are motivated by a heuristic scheduling rule for the particular objective being considered. These assumptions produce a permutation schedule, as defined in Lemma 7.3.

Let τ denote the set of all possible completion times on machine M_M. The following result shows that τ contains only a polynomial number of values.

Lemma 7.6 *For problem* $1||\sum F_j^C + \sum D_g^S y_s + \sum D_g^M y_M$, *assuming a given ordering of the jobs within each group, we have* $|\tau| = O(n^{G+3H-1})$.

We refer the reader to Hall and Potts (2003) for a proof.

7.2.4.1 Sum of Flow Times

In this subsection, we adopt the total SPT within groups assumption for problem $1||\sum F_j^C + \sum D_g^S y_g^S + \sum D_h^M y_h^M$. Thus, we index the jobs such that $p_{1h}^S + p_{1h}^M \leq \cdots \leq p_{n_h,h}^S + p_{n_h,h}^M$ for $h = 1, \ldots, H$ and $p_{1g}^S \leq \cdots \leq p_{n_g,g}^S$ for $g = H + 1, \ldots, H + G - 1$.

Our dynamic programming algorithm combines the enumeration schemes used in Algorithms SF and MF. Thus, we schedule batches of jobs on machine M_S and individual jobs on machine M_M. We define a state variable t which denotes the completion time of the current partial schedule on machine M_M. When scheduling a job on machine M_M, we ensure that it does not start before time T, the completion time of the current partial schedule on M_S.

Algorithm CF

Value Function

$f(q, \bar{q}, s, t) = f(q_1, \ldots, q_{H+G-1}, \bar{q}_1, \ldots, \bar{q}_H, s_1, \ldots, s_H, t)$ = the minimum total cost for (i) the supplier processing jobs $(1, h), \ldots, (q_h, h)$ and delivering them to manufacturer $\mathcal{M}_1$ for $h = 1, \ldots, H$, (ii) the supplier processing jobs $(1, H + g - 1), \ldots, (q_{H+g-1}, H + g - 1)$ and delivering them to manufacturer $\mathcal{M}_g$ for $g = 2, \ldots, G$, and (iii) for manufacturer $\mathcal{M}_1$ processing jobs $(1, h), \ldots, (\bar{q}_h, h)$ and delivering jobs $(1, h), \ldots, (s_h, h)$ to customer $\mathcal{C}_h$ for $h = 1, \ldots, H$, where the last job processed by manufacturer $\mathcal{M}_1$ completes at time t, and where $0 \le s_h \le \bar{q}_h \le q_h \le n_h, 0 \le q_{H+g-1} \le n_{H+g-1}$, and $t \in \tau$.

Boundary Condition

$f(0, \ldots, 0, 0, \ldots, 0, 0, \ldots, 0, 0) = 0.$

Optimal Solution Value

$$\min_{t \in \tau} \left\{ f(n_1, \ldots, n_{H+G-1}, n_1, \ldots, n_H, n_1, \ldots, n_H, t) \right\}.$$

Recurrence Relation

$$f(q, \bar{q}, s, t) = \min \begin{cases} \min_{q' \in Q'} \{f(q', \bar{q}, s, t)\} + D_1^S \\ \min_{g \in G_1} \left\{ \min_{0 \le q_g'' < q_g} \{(q_g - q_g'')T + D_{g-H+1}^S + f(q'', \bar{q}, s, t)\} \right\} \\ \min_{h \in I_1} \{f^*(q, \bar{q}', s, t - p_{\bar{q}_h, h}^M)\} \\ \min_{h \in I_2} \{f(q, \bar{q}', s, t - p_{\bar{q}_h, h}^M)\} \\ \min_{h \in I_3} \left\{ \min_{0 \le s_h' < s_h} \{(\bar{q}_h - s_h')t + D_h^M + f^*(q, \bar{q}', s', t - p_{\bar{q}_h, h}^M)\} \right\} \\ \min_{h \in I_4} \left\{ \min_{0 \le s_h' < s_h} \{(\bar{q}_h - s_h')t + D_h^M + f(q, \bar{q}', s', t - p_{\bar{q}_h, h}^M)\} \right\}, \end{cases}$$

where

$f^*(q, \bar{q}, s, t) = \min_{0 \le t' \le t} \{f(q, \bar{q}, s, t')\},$

$q'' = (q_1, \ldots, q_{g-1}, q_g'', q_{g+1}, \ldots, q_{H+G-1}),$

$\bar{q}' = (\bar{q}_1, \ldots, \bar{q}_{h-1}, \bar{q}_h - 1, \bar{q}_{h+1}, \ldots, \bar{q}_H),$

$s' = (s_1, \ldots, s_{h-1}, s_h', s_{h+1}, \ldots, s_H),$

$Q' = \{(q_1', \ldots, q_H', q_{H+1}, \ldots, q_{H+G-1}) \mid \bar{q}_h \le q_h' \le q_h \text{ for } 1 \le h \le H, q_h' < q_h \text{ for some } h\},$

7.2 Scheduling and Batching in a Supply Chain

$$G_1 = \{g \mid H+1 \le g \le H+G-1, \ q_g > 0\},$$
$$I_1 = \{h \mid 1 \le h \le H, \ s_h < \bar{q}_h, \ p^M_{\bar{q}_h,h} = t - T\},$$
$$I_2 = \{h \mid 1 \le h \le H, \ s_h < \bar{q}_h, \ p^M_{\bar{q}_h,h} < t - T\},$$
$$I_3 = \{h \mid 1 \le h \le H, \ s_h = \bar{q}_h > 0, \ p^M_{\bar{q}_h,h} = t - T\},$$
$$I_4 = \{h \mid 1 \le h \le H, \ s_h = \bar{q}_h > 0, \ p^M_{\bar{q}_h,h} < t - T\}, \text{ and}$$
$$T = \sum_{h=1}^{H+G-1} \sum_{j=1}^{q_h} p^S_{jh}.$$

In the recurrence relation, the first term schedules a batch containing the two-stage jobs $(q'_h + 1, h), \ldots, (q_h, h)$ for $h = 1, \ldots, H$ to be processed on machine M_S, and this batch is delivered to manufacturer $\mathcal{M}_1$ on completion of its processing at time T. The condition $\bar{q}_h \le q'_h$ in the definition of Q' ensures that jobs of this batch are not currently scheduled on machine M_M. At this stage, no scheduling cost is incurred for this batch of jobs. The second term schedules a batch $\{(q''_g + 1, g), \ldots, (q_g, g)\}$ of single-stage jobs, where $H + 1 \le g \le H + G - 1$, for processing on machine M_S and subsequent delivery to manufacturer $\mathcal{M}_{g-H+1}$ at time T, and evaluates the completion time and delivery cost of this batch accordingly. The third through sixth terms schedule the two-stage job $(\bar{q}_h, h)$ to be processed on machine M_M in the interval $[t - p^M_{\bar{q}_h,h}, t]$, so that it completes at time t. The time t' at which machine M_M completes processing the previous job in the partial schedule is such that $t' \le T$ in the third and fifth terms and such that $t' = t - p^M_{\bar{q}_h,h} > T$ in the fourth and sixth terms. In the third and fourth terms, $s_h < \bar{q}_h$, and thus no delivery of a batch containing job $(\bar{q}_h, h)$ to customer $\mathcal{C}_h$ occurs at time t. However, in the fifth and sixth terms, $s_h = \bar{q}_h$, and thus a delivery of batch $\{(s'_h + 1, h), \ldots, (\bar{q}_h, h)\}$ to customer $\mathcal{C}_h$ is scheduled at time t.

Theorem 7.9 *Algorithm CF finds an optimal total SPT within groups schedule for problem* $1 \mid\mid \sum F^C_j + \sum D^S_g y^S_g + \sum D^M_h y^M_h$ *in* $O(n^{2G+7H-2})$ *time.*

Proof The dynamic program exploits structural properties of an optimal schedule that are established in part (a) of Lemmas 7.1, 7.2, 7.3, and the assumption of total SPT within groups. For any $(q, \bar{q}, s, t)$, where $t \ge 1$, $f^*(q, \bar{q}, s, t) = \min\{f^*(q, \bar{q}, s, t-1), f(q, \bar{q}, s, t)\}$ can be computed recursively in constant time. From Lemma 7.6, there are $O(n^{2G+6H-2})$ states $(q, \bar{q}, s, t)$. In the recurrence relation, the first term in the minimization requires $O(n^H)$ time, while the other terms require no more than $O(n)$ time. Therefore, the overall time complexity of Algorithm CF is $O(n^{2G+7H-2})$. $\qquad \square$

7.2.4.2 Number of Late Jobs

The first result shows that, assuming an EDD within groups sequence for the on-time jobs, problem $1 \mid\mid \sum U^C_j + \sum D^S_g y^S_g + \sum D^M_h y^M_h$ is intractable, even when there is only one manufacturer and one customer.

Theorem 7.10 *The recognition version of problem* $1 || \sum U_j^C + \sum D_g^S y_g^S + \sum D_h^M y_h^M$, *assuming an EDD within groups schedule for the on-time jobs, is binary* NP-*complete.*

Proof Hall and Potts (2003) provide a reduction from Partition. □

Although Theorem 7.10 provides a negative result, we still describe a computationally practical algorithm for the more general problem $1 || \sum w_j U_j^C + \sum D_g^S y_g^S + \sum D_h^M y_h^M$, assuming an EDD within groups schedule for the on-time jobs. We index the jobs such that $d_{1h}^M \leq \cdots \leq d_{n_h,h}^M$ for $h = 1, \ldots, H$, and $d_{1g}^S \leq \cdots \leq d_{n_g,g}^S$ for $g = H + 1, \ldots, H + G - 1$.

Our dynamic programming algorithm schedules one job at a time. To prevent a job being processed on M_M before it is delivered from the supplier, we assign a state variable to represent the time at which the current supplier's batch is to be delivered, and only schedule any further processing on machine M_M after this time.

Algorithm CU

Value Function

$f(q, v, t, z, \bar{t}, k) = f(q_1, \ldots, q_{H+G-1}, v_1, \ldots, v_H, t, z, \bar{t}, k)$ = the total cost of (a) scheduling the on-time jobs from $(1, l), \ldots, (q_l, l)$ on machine M_S and delivering them to the relevant manufacturer for $l = 1, \ldots, H + G - 1$ and (b) scheduling the on-time jobs from $(1, h), \ldots, (q_h, h)$ on machine M_M and delivering those jobs except $(v_h, h), \ldots, (q_h, h)$ if $v_h > 0$ to customer $\mathscr{C}_h$ for $h = 1, \ldots, H$, given that (i) machine M_S completes processing the on-time jobs at time t, (ii) the delivery of the current batch from M_S to M_M is scheduled at time z, (iii) machine M_M completes processing the on-time jobs at time $\bar{t}$, and (iv) k is the group of the last on-time job on machine M_S if $k > 0$, where $0 \leq v_h \leq q_h \leq n_h$ for $h = 1, \ldots, H$; $0 \leq q_g \leq n_g$ for $g = H + 1, \ldots, H + G - 1$; $0 \leq t \leq z \leq \bar{t} \leq \sum_{h=1}^{H+G-1} \sum_{j=1}^{n_h} p_{jh}^S + \sum_{h=1}^{H} \sum_{j=1}^{n_h} p_{jh}^M$; $z \leq \sum_{h=1}^{H+G-1} \sum_{j=1}^{n_h} p_{jh}^S$; and $0 \leq k \leq H + G - 1$. If there are no undelivered on-time jobs for customer $\mathscr{C}_h$, then we set $v_h = 0$; otherwise, (v_h, h) is the undelivered job with the smallest due date.

Boundary Condition

$f(0, \ldots, 0, 0, \ldots, 0, 0, 0, 0, 0) = 0.$

Optimal Solution Value

$$\min_{(t,z,\bar{t},k) \in Y} \{f(n_1, \ldots, n_{H+G-1}, 0, \ldots, 0, t, z, \bar{t}, k)\},$$

where $Y = \{(t, z, \bar{t}, k) \mid 0 \leq t \leq z \leq P^S, \ 0 \leq z \leq \bar{t} \leq P^S + P^M, \ 0 \leq k \leq H + G - 1\}$, $P^S = \sum_{h=1}^{H+G-1} \sum_{j=1}^{n_h} p_{jh}^S$ and $P^M = \sum_{h=1}^{H} \sum_{j=1}^{n_h} p_{jh}^M$.

7.2 Scheduling and Batching in a Supply Chain

Recurrence Relation

$$
f(q, v, t, z, \bar{t}, k) =
$$

$$
\min \begin{cases}
\min_{1 \le k' \le H} \{ w^M_{q_{k'}, k'} + f(q', v, t, z, \bar{t}, k) \}, & \text{if } k = 0 \\[2mm]
\min_{H < k' \le H+G-1} \{ w^S_{q_{k'}, k'} + f(q', v, t, z, \bar{t}, k) \}, & \text{if } k = 0 \\[2mm]
w^M_{q_k, k} + f(q'', v, t, z, \bar{t}, k), & \text{if } 1 \le k \le H, \ q_k > v_k \\[2mm]
w^S_{q_k, k} + f(q'', v, t, z, \bar{t}, k), & \text{if } H < k \le H+G-1 \\[2mm]
f^*_1(q'', v, t - p^S_{q_k, k}, z, \bar{t} - p^M_{q_k, k}), & \text{if } k \in K_1, \ q_k > v_k > 0 \\[2mm]
f^*_1(q'', v', t - p^S_{q_k, k}, z, \bar{t} - p^M_{q_k, k}), & \text{if } k \in K_1, \ q_k = v_k > 0 \\[2mm]
\min_{v''_k \in V_1} \{ f^*_1(q'', v'', t - p^S_{q_k, k}, z, \bar{t} - p^M_{q_k, k}) \} + D^M_k, & \text{if } k \in K_1, \ v_k = 0 \\[2mm]
f^*_1(q'', v, t - p^S_{q_k, k}, t - p^S_{q_k, k}, \bar{t} - p^M_{q_k, k}) + D^S_1, & \text{if } k \in K_1, \ q_k > v_k > 0, \\
& \quad \bar{t} - p^M_{q_k, k} > z \\[2mm]
\min_{0 \le \bar{t}' \le z} \{ f^*_1(q'', v, t - p^S_{q_k, k}, t - p^S_{q_k, k}, \bar{t}') \} + D^S_1, & \text{if } k \in K_1, \ q_k > v_k > 0, \\
& \quad \bar{t} - p^M_{q_k, k} = z \\[2mm]
f^*_1(q'', v', t - p^S_{q_k, k}, t - p^S_{q_k, k}, \bar{t} - p^M_{q_k, k}) + D^S_1, & \text{if } k \in K_1, \ q_k = v_k > 0, \\
& \quad \bar{t} - p^M_{q_k, k} > z \\[2mm]
\min_{0 \le \bar{t}' \le z} \{ f^*_2(q'', v', t - p^S_{q_k, k}, t - p^S_{q_k, k}, \bar{t}') \} + D^S_1, & \text{if } k \in K_1, \ q_k = v_k > 0, \\
& \quad \bar{t} - p^M_{q_k, k} = z \\[2mm]
\min_{v''_k \in V_1} \{ f^*_1(q'', v'', t - p^S_{q_k, k}, t - p^S_{q_k, k}, \bar{t} - p^M_{q_k, k}) \} + D^S_1 + D^M_k, & \text{if } k \in K_1, \ v_k = 0, \\
& \quad \bar{t} - p^M_{q_k, k} > z \\[2mm]
\min_{v''_k \in V_1} \left\{ \min_{0 \le \bar{t}' \le z} \{ f^*_2(q'', v'', t - p^S_{q_k, k}, t - p^S_{q_k, k}, \bar{t}') \} \right\} + D^S_1 + D^M_k, & \text{if } k \in K_1, \ v_k = 0, \\
& \quad \bar{t} - p^M_{q_k, k} = z \\[2mm]
f(q'', v, t - p^S_{q_k, k}, z, \bar{t}, k), & \text{if } k \in K_2 \\[2mm]
\min_{0 \le k' \le H+G-1} \{ f(q'', v, t - p^S_{q_k, k}, t - p^S_{q_k, k}, \bar{t}, k') \} + D^S_{k-H+1}, & \text{if } k \in K_2,
\end{cases}
$$

where

$$f^*_1(q, v, t, z, \bar{t}) = \min_{1 \le k \le H} \{ f(q, v, t, z, \bar{t}, k) \},$$
$$f^*_2(q, v, t, z, \bar{t}) = \min_{0 \le k \le H} \{ f(q, v, t, z, \bar{t}, k) \},$$
$$q' = (q_1, \ldots, q_{k'-1}, q_{k'} - 1, q_{k'+1}, \ldots, q_{H+G-1}),$$
$$q'' = (q_1, \ldots, q_{k-1}, q_k - 1, q_{k+1}, \ldots, q_{H+G-1}),$$
$$v' = (v_1, \ldots, v_{k-1}, 0, v_{k+1}, \ldots, v_H),$$
$$v'' = (v_1, \ldots, v_{k-1}, v''_k, v_{k+1}, \ldots, v_H),$$
$$V_1 = \{ v''_k \mid 0 \le v''_k < q_k, \ v''_k = 0 \text{ or } d^M_{k, v''_k} \ge \bar{t} \},$$
$$K_1 = \{ k \mid 1 \le k \le H, \ d^M_{q_k, k} \ge \bar{t} \}, \text{ and}$$
$$K_2 = \{ k \mid H < k \le H+G-1, \ d^S_{q_k, k} \ge z \}.$$

In the recurrence relation, there are 15 terms. The first two terms in the minimization schedule a job $(q_{k'}, k')$ to be late when no jobs are currently scheduled to be on time. In the first term, $(q_{k'}, k')$ is a two-stage job, whereas in the second term it is a single-stage job. The third and fourth terms schedule job (q_k, k) to be late when the schedule contains at least one on-time job. In the third term, the condition $q_k > v_k$ allows the two-stage job k to be late, whereas the fourth term schedules a single-stage job to be late. The fifth through thirteenth terms schedule the two-stage job (q_k, k) in the interval $[t - p^S_{q_k,k}, t]$ on machine M_S and in the interval $[\bar{t} - p^M_{q_k,k}, \bar{t}]$ on machine M_M, so that it is on time. In the fifth, sixth, and seventh terms, job (q_k, k) does not start a new batch on machine M_S, and the previous job in the batch is in some group k', where $1 \leq k' \leq H$. In the fifth term, $v_k > 0$, thereby preventing a delivery to customer $\mathscr{C}_k$ when job (q_k, k) completes processing. The sixth term applies for $q_k = v_k > 0$, so that no delivery is scheduled on completion of job (q_k, k); however, (q_k, k) is the first undelivered job in group k and the previous schedule has no undelivered job in group k. The seventh term has $v_k = 0$ so that a delivery to customer $\mathscr{C}_k$ is scheduled upon completion of job (q_k, k) on machine M_M at time $\bar{t}$. The condition on v''_k in the definition of V_1 in the seventh term ensures that all jobs in this batch are delivered to the customer by their due dates. The eighth through thirteenth terms correspond to the situation in which job (q_k, k) starts a new batch on machine M_S. The first two of these terms are analogous to the fifth term, the next two are analogous to the sixth term, and the last two are analogous to the seventh term. There are two terms in each case, depending upon whether job (q_k, k) starts processing on machine M_M at time z and is preceded by idle time in some interval $[\bar{t}', z]$, or job (q_k, k) is processed on machine M_M immediately after the previous job. The eleventh and thirteenth terms allow scheduling of the first on-time job. The fourteenth and fifteenth terms schedule the single-stage job (q_k, k), where $k > H$, in the interval $[t - p^S_{q_k,k}, t]$ on machine M_S so that it is on time. In the fourteenth term, this job is scheduled in the same batch as the previous job, whereas in the last term job (q_k, k) starts a new batch at time $t - p^S_{q_k,k}$ when the previous batch completes.

Theorem 7.11 *Algorithm CU finds an optimal EDD within groups schedule for problem* $1 || \sum w_j U^C_j + \sum D^S_g y^S_g + \sum D^M_h y^M_h$, *in* $O(n^{G+2H-1} P^3)$ *time.*

Proof The dynamic program exploits structural properties of an optimal schedule that are established in part (a) of Lemmas 7.1, 7.2, 7.3, and the assumption of EDD within groups for on-time jobs. There are $O(n^{G+2H-1} P^3)$ states $(q, v, t, z, \bar{t}, k)$. An analysis of the recurrence relation similar to that in the proof of Theorem 7.9 shows that the overall time complexity of Algorithm CU is $O(n^{G+2H-1} P^3)$. □

7.2 Scheduling and Batching in a Supply Chain

7.2.5 *Cooperation*

We first show through three examples that substantial benefits can result from cooperation between the supplier $\mathscr{S}$ and the manufacturer $\mathscr{M}_1$. Then, using two further examples, we discuss the stability of such cooperations and mechanisms for achieving them.

7.2.5.1 Benefits of Cooperation

We present an example for both of the scheduling objectives analyzed above. Each example shows that the solution that results from the supplier and manufacturer acting independently is considerably more costly than the solution of the combined problem.

Example 7.1 (Benefit of Cooperation in a Flowtime Problem) Consider the following instance of the combined problem $1|| \sum F_j^C + \sum D_g^S y_g^S + \sum D_h^M y_h^M$. There are two jobs ($n = 2$), both produced by a single manufacturer ($G = 1$) for a single customer ($H = 1$), where the processing times and delivery costs are given in Table 7.2, and where K is an integer such that $K > 3$.

A straightforward cost comparison shows that there is an optimal schedule in which both the supplier and the manufacturer process the jobs in the order $(1, 2)$ on machines M_S and M_M, respectively. For the supplier, processing of the two jobs is completed at times 1 and $K + 1$, respectively. Therefore, if the jobs are delivered in two separate batches, the scheduling cost is $\sum F_j^S = 1 + (K + 1) = K + 2$. On the other hand, if the jobs are delivered in a single batch, then $\sum F_j^S = 2(K + 1)$. Thus, the overall costs $\sum F_j^S + \sum D_g^S y_g^S$ for two deliveries and one delivery are $(K + 2) + 2(K - 1) = 3K$ and $2(K + 1) + (K - 1) = 3K + 1$, respectively. Consequently, the supplier's decision is to deliver the two jobs in separate batches to arrive at the manufacturer at times 1 and $K + 1$, respectively.

For the manufacturer's problem, using release dates $r_1^M = 1$ and $r_2^M = K + 1$, processing of the two jobs is completed at times 2 and $K + 2$, respectively. Using two separate batches, the overall cost is $\sum F_j^M + \sum D_h^M y_h^M = 2K + 2$. Alternatively, using a single-batch delivery, $\sum F_j^M + \sum D_h^M y_h^M = (K + 2) + K = 2K + 2$. Thus, the minimum total cost for the manufacturer's problem is $2K + 2$. In order to evaluate this schedule with respect to the combined problem, we add the supplier's optimal cost of $3K$, giving a total cost of $5K + 2$.

Table 7.2 Data for Example 7.1

	Supplier		Manufacturer	
Job	1	2	1	2
Processing time	1	K	1	1
Delivery cost	$K - 1$		K	

Table 7.3 Data for Example 7.2

	Supplier				Manufacturer			
Job	1	...	$n-1$	n	1	...	$n-1$	n
Processing time	K	...	K	$K-1$	1	...	1	$(n-1)K+1$
Due date	$K-n+1$	...	$K-1$	K	$(n-1)K+1$	...	$(n-1)K+1$	$nK+1$
Delivery cost	0				0			

However, an optimal schedule for the combined problem is to deliver both jobs from the supplier to the manufacturer in a single batch at time $K+1$. At time $K+3$, after the manufacturer has processed both jobs, they are delivered to the customer in a single batch. The overall cost of this schedule is $\sum F_j^C + \sum D_g^S y_g^S + \sum D_h^M y_h^M = 2(K+3) + (K-1) + K = 4K + 5$. Therefore, the ratio of the cost incurred in the combined problem when the supplier and the manufacturer make separate decisions to the optimal cost is $(5K+2)/(4K+5)$, which can be arbitrarily close to 5/4 if K is large. Thus, cooperation provides a 20% reduction in the total system cost.

Example 7.2 (Benefit of Cooperation in a Late Jobs Problem) Consider the following instance of the combined problem $1 || \sum U_j^C + \sum D_g^S y_g^S + \sum D_h^M y_h^M$, where $G = H = 1$. The processing times, due dates, and delivery costs are given in Table 7.3, where K is an integer and $K \geq n \geq 2$. The supplier's due dates are based on a schedule for the manufacturer in which jobs $1, \ldots, n-1$ are scheduled consecutively in the interval $[K-n+1, K]$ and job n is scheduled in the interval $[K, nK+1]$.

A unique optimal solution of the supplier's problem schedules job n to be on time and all other jobs to be late and not delivered to the manufacturer. The manufacturer consequently schedules job n to be on time. Thus, the total cost is equal to $n-1$.

However, an optimal schedule for the combined problem schedules jobs $1, \ldots, n-1$ on time, where each job is delivered separately, and job n late, giving an optimal cost of 1. Thus, cooperation provides a reduction in the total system cost that can be arbitrarily close to 100%.

The potential benefits of cooperation identified in Examples 7.1 and 7.2 can be viewed in the context of similar results from the supply chain management literature. For example, Parlar and Weng (1997) consider a problem of coordination between a firm's supply and manufacturing departments and estimate the benefit of cooperation to total profit to be at least 26%.

7.2.5.2 Mechanisms for Cooperation

We now present two further examples for problem $1 || \sum F_j^C + \sum D_g^S y_g^S + \sum D_h^M y_h^M$. If the supplier's and manufacturer's schedules are used to form a

7.2 Scheduling and Batching in a Supply Chain

Table 7.4 Data for Example 7.3

	Supplier		Manufacturer	
Job	1	2	1	2
Processing time	1	K	1	1
Delivery cost		$K/2$	K	

Table 7.5 Cost matrix for Example 7.3

		Manufacturer	
		1 batch	2 batches
Supplier	1 batch	$(5K/2 + 2, K + 4) : 7K/2 + 6$	$(5K/2 + 2, 2K + 3) : 9K/2 + 5$
	2 batches	$(2K + 2, 2K + 2) : 4K + 4$	$(2K + 2, 2K + 2) : 4K + 4$

combined schedule, then $F_j^C = F_j^S + F_j^M$. Thus, the overall cost in the combined problem is equal to the supplier's total cost plus the manufacturer's total cost.

Example 7.3 (Benefit of Cooperation in a Flowtime Problem) Consider the following instance of problem $1 || \sum F_j^C + \sum D_g^S y_g^S + \sum D_h^M y_h^M$, where $n = 2$, $G = 1$, and $H = 1$. The processing times and delivery costs are given in Table 7.4, where $K > 8$ is an integer.

Some insights about cooperation can be gained from summarizing the results for Example 7.3 in the form of a cost matrix, as in Table 7.5, where the notation $(c_1, c_2) : c_1 + c_2$ denotes that the supplier's cost is c_1, the manufacturer's cost is c_2, and the total cost is $c_1 + c_2$. As in Example 7.1, the jobs are processed in the order $(1, 2)$ on machines M_S and M_M.

It is easy to see that the solution that minimizes total cost in Table 7.5 requires both the supplier and the manufacturer to use a single batch. However, this solution is not a Nash equilibrium (Myerson, 1981; Nash, 1951), since the supplier can benefit by unilaterally deviating from it and using two batches. Mechanisms by which the manufacturer can encourage the supplier's cooperation include:

1. Offering an incentive if all the jobs in the order are delivered together, to an extent sufficient to compensate the supplier for the increased cost
2. Offering to share holding costs for completed jobs at the supplier

A situation analogous to that in the first mechanism above arises in the personal computer industry, as discussed by Lee et al. (2000). Because of rapid innovation and new product development, leading to frequent declines in retail prices, retailers of personal computers tend to delay purchases, so as to avoid being caught with expensive inventory that can only be sold cheaply. In this situation, computer manufacturers may offer price protection packages to encourage earlier purchases. Regarding the second mechanism above, our recommendations are similar to Propositions 1 and 2 of Moses and Seshadri (2000), where a necessary and sufficient condition for decision makers at two stages to agree on a stocking level is an agreement to share holding costs at the second stage. Also, Agrawal and Seshadri (2000) consider a model that determines the timing of replenishments from a

334 7 Optimization and Conflict

Table 7.6 Data for Example 7.4

		Supplier		Manufacturer	
Job		1	2	1	2
Processing time		1	K	K	K
Delivery cost		$3K/2$		K	

Table 7.7 Cost matrix for Example 7.4

		Manufacturer	
		1 batch	2 batches
Supplier	1 batch	$(7K/2 + 2, 5K) : 17K/2 + 2$	$(7K/2 + 2, 5K) : 17K/2 + 2$
	2 batches	$(4K + 2, 4K) : 8K + 2$	$(4K + 2, 4K) : 8K + 2$

supplier to multiple retail stores. Their discussion of the tradeoff between immediate and delayed replenishment is analogous to our batching decision.

In the event that attempts at cooperation fail, the manufacturer can still attempt to force the supplier to deliver only one batch. Mechanisms for doing so include refusing to accept delivery before a certain date or refusing to accept delivery of partial orders.

Example 7.4 (Benefit of Cooperation in a Flowtime Problem) Consider the following instance of problem $1|| \sum F_j^C + \sum D_g^S y_g^S + \sum D_h^M y_h^M$ with $n = 2$, $G = 1$, and $H = 1$. The processing times and delivery costs are given in Table 7.6, where K is an integer such that $K \geq 2$.

The costs for Example 7.4 are summarized in Table 7.7, using the same format as Table 7.5, where the optimal processing order on machines M_S and M_M is $(1, 2)$.

Mechanisms by which the manufacturer can encourage the supplier to deliver the first batch earlier include:

1. Offering an incentive for earlier delivery of part of the order, to an extent sufficient to compensate the supplier for the increased delivery cost
2. Offering to pick up part of the order, perhaps as part of an existing logistics operation
3. Offering to share the extra delivery costs

The linkages to the supply chain management literature discussed following Example 7.3 are again relevant here. Agrawal and Seshadri (2000) address related timing issues in the balancing of inventory between a supplier and several manufacturers. If attempts at cooperation fail, then the manufacturer can still attempt to force the supplier to deliver a batch earlier, for example, by refusing to accept delivery of job 1 after a certain date.

In both Examples 7.3 and 7.4, the supplier and manufacturer can bargain over the savings in the total system cost that are achieved by an optimal cooperative strategy, relative to a solution found by independent decision making. These savings are $(4K+4)-(7K/2+6) = K/2-2$ in Table 7.5 and $(17K/2+2)-(8K+2) = K/2$ in Table 7.7. The bargaining solution theory of Nash (1950, 1953) suggests that neither player will bargain at a cost greater than they can achieve independently. Thus, a solution with $c_1 \leq 2K + 2$ and $c_2 \leq 2K + 2$ is found for Example 7.3, and a solution with $c_1 \leq 7K/2 + 2$ and $c_2 \leq 5K$ is found for Example 7.4. The supply chain management literature offers some guidance about how the profits from cooperation should be divided. For example, Weng (1995) develops models that share the increased profit from cooperation. A similar methodology can be used here, subject to the above constraints.

It is clear from Tables 7.5 and 7.7 that the supplier's cost is independent of the manufacturer's decisions, and therefore the supplier has no incentive to persuade the manufacturer to change behavior. For this reason, if cooperation is to lead to a solution that is optimal for the system as a whole, then that cooperation must be initiated by the manufacturer. Although our analysis focuses on supply chains with three stages, namely a supplier, manufacturers, and customers, more generally there may be s stages, where stage s corresponds to the customers. In this case, cooperation should be initiated at stage $s - 1$ by discussion with stage $s - 2$. If this cooperation is successfully achieved, then stages $s - 2$ and $s - 1$ can jointly approach stage $s - 3$ about cooperation. Continuing in this way, the negotiations work their way upstream until all parts of the supply chain are cooperating for maximum benefit.

The study of scheduling and batching presented in this section is important for applications that involve significant transportation cost. Another relevant factor is the availability of sufficient transportation resources—either internally or through third party logistics—to make frequent deliveries in order to satisfy customer deadlines.

7.3 Sequencing in an Assembly System

This section focuses on the important issues of conflict and cooperation between decision makers in an *assembly system*. The issues of conflict and cooperation between the suppliers and the manufacturer arise from the requirement that all parts required for a job must be received before the final stage of manufacturing for that job can begin. Therefore, the performance of the manufacturer depends on the last supplier to deliver a part for each job and thus on decisions made by all the suppliers. However, the suppliers are concerned about their own costs which are not, in general, optimized by the same scheduling decisions that optimize the manufacturer's cost. How these conflicts are resolved depends on the *relative bargaining power* of the suppliers and the manufacturer, and cooperation mechanisms that achieve this resolution need to be developed. In order to focus on conflict and coordination issues instead of the constraints faced by the manufacturer, we assume that this final stage is nonbottleneck; however, none of the cooperation mechanisms discussed in this section rely on this assumption. In nonbottleneck manufacturing, as many products as needed can be processed through the final stage simultaneously.

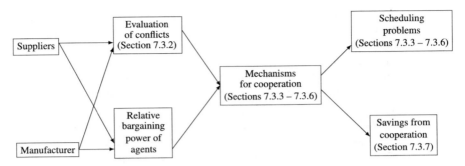

Fig. 7.5 Logical flow of the assembly system study

Practical examples of nonbottleneck final manufacturing stages include outsourced assembly, packaging, and delivery.

We assume that all the suppliers act as a single agent when negotiating with the manufacturer. This is motivated by the common practice that sellers (or buyers) act together to negotiate collectively with buyers (or sellers) in order to increase their bargaining power (Moore & Gray, 2011). It is necessary to evaluate the cost saving from cooperation between the decision makers, in order to understand when cooperation is worthwhile. This in turn requires the solution of the various scheduling problems that these mechanisms define for solution by the suppliers, the manufacturer, and the overall system. Figure 7.5 provides an overview of the logical flow of this section.

7.3.1 Notation and Assumptions

The assembly system studied in this section consists of s suppliers $S_1, \ldots, S_s$, which supply parts to a manufacturer M. Each supplier operates a dedicated production line for the manufacturer. This situation occurs commonly in practice, for example, when (i) the jobs from the manufacturer are customized and require special tools and (ii) the supplier and manufacturer have a long-term relationship. Each supplier may produce one or more parts for each job. Because the cost functions considered are nondecreasing in job completion time, there exists an optimal schedule in which the parts produced for a single job by the same supplier are scheduled consecutively.

The manufacturer receives a set of jobs $N = \{1, \ldots, n\}$ from its customer(s) at the beginning of the planning horizon. Each job consists of several parts to be processed nonpreemptively at suppliers $S_1, \ldots, S_s$. The parts of a particular job can be processed concurrently by different suppliers. Since it has been shown in practice (Stein & Sweat, 1998) and in the academic literature that sharing information vertically among the supply chain members helps the system operate more efficiently, we assume that the manufacturer passes the known information about all the jobs to the suppliers simultaneously. Therefore, all parts become

7.3 Sequencing in an Assembly System

simultaneously available for processing by the suppliers. Let p_{ij} denote the total processing time of the parts processed by supplier S_i for job j, for $i = 1, \ldots, s$, $j = 1, \ldots, n$. Each job j may have a due date d_j, for $j = 1, \ldots, n$. We assume that all parameters p_{ij} and d_j are nonnegative integers.

We define a *schedule* in any problem in this section to consist of $s + 1$ subschedules, one for each of the suppliers $S_1, \ldots, S_s$ and the manufacturer M. We define the following decision variables in a given schedule σ:

$$C_{ij}(\sigma) = \text{the time at which the parts for job } j \text{ are delivered from supplier } S_i$$
$$\text{to the manufacturer;}$$
$$C_j(\sigma) = \max_{1 \le i \le s}\{C_{ij}(\sigma)\}, \text{ the time at which the last part for job } j \text{ is delivered}$$
$$\text{to the manufacturer;}$$
$$L_j(\sigma) = C_j(\sigma) - d_j, \text{ the lateness of job } j.$$

We assume that the delivery time from a supplier to the manufacturer is negligible, relative to the processing times of the jobs at the supplier. The insights about conflict and cooperation issues which we discuss still hold without this assumption. However, the solvability of the implied scheduling problems may change in the more general case. Since we consider the manufacturer's operations as nonbottleneck, we assume without loss of generality that the processing time of each job at the manufacturer is zero. Therefore, $C_j(\sigma)$ is not only the delivery time of the last part for job j to the manufacturer but also the completion time of job j at the manufacturer. We use a shortest processing time (SPT) ordering of the parts or jobs, where they are scheduled in nondecreasing order of their processing times. We also use an earliest due date (EDD) ordering, where the jobs are scheduled in nondecreasing order of their due dates.

We consider various scheduling problems denoted by the classification scheme $\psi_1|\psi_2|\psi_3$ (Graham et al., 1979). Except where stated, we let $\psi_1 = As$, which denotes an assembly system with s suppliers and one manufacturer. We also refer to problems with $\psi_1 = 1$, which denotes a single-machine problem, or $\psi_1 = F_2$, which denotes a two machine flowshop problem. Under ψ_2, we may have *coseq* which specifies that the suppliers use a common job sequence, t_{ij} which denotes a transportation time for the parts of job j from supplier S_i to the manufacturer, or a constraint on cost.

In order to model conflict and cooperation issues in our assembly system, we consider four problems.

1. *Supplier S_i's problem.* An individual supplier S_i acts alone to minimize a performance measure F_i.
2. *The suppliers' problem.* The suppliers act jointly to minimize a total performance measure $\sum_{i=1}^{s} F_i$.
3. *The manufacturer's problem.* The manufacturer acts alone to minimize a performance measure G.
4. *The system problem.* All the suppliers and the manufacturer act jointly to minimize their total cost $\alpha \sum_{i=1}^{s} F_i + (1 - \alpha)G$.

Remark 7.3 We consider the suppliers as a single agent; however, the first definition helps in understanding the cost function of an individual supplier. In the system problem, α is used to convert the performance measures of the suppliers and the manufacturer into common cost units. For example, if one unit of $\sum_{i=1}^{s} F_i$ costs \$2 and one unit of G costs \$3, then $\alpha = 0.4$. Here, αF_i represents the cost of supplier S_i, for $i = 1, \ldots, s$, and $(1 - \alpha)G$ represents the cost of the manufacturer.

The models discussed here are applicable to an assembly system with any F_i and G cost functions. We now describe and motivate our specific choice of cost functions under ψ_3. Since the suppliers do not deal directly with customers, their objective is internally focused; therefore, we use the minimization of work-in-process cost. We note that the total completion time of a set of jobs is often used in the scheduling literature (Lane & Sidney, 1993; Ng et al., 2003) as a surrogate for the work-in-process inventory cost of the jobs. Furthermore, minimizing the total completion time of the jobs in a plant is equivalent to minimizing the average number of jobs in the plant and hence minimizing the congestion of the plant (Hopp & Spearman, 2000; Pinedo & Chao, 1999). For the manufacturer, however, customer service is important; therefore, we use total lead time and maximum lateness as cost measures. Total lead time measures average customer service, whereas maximum lateness measures worst-case customer service. These scheduling cost functions are among the most commonly used in manufacturing practice (Pinedo, 2016). Other objective functions, such as the total tardiness or the total number of tardy jobs, could also be considered. Therefore, our discussion focuses on the following cost function F_i for supplier S_i, for $i = 1, \ldots, s$,

$$\sum_{j \in N} C_{ij}(\sigma) = \text{total completion time of the parts at supplier } S_i \text{ in schedule } \sigma$$
$$\text{representing the work-in-process cost of the supplier,}$$

and the following two cost functions G for the manufacturer

$$\sum_{j \in N} C_j(\sigma) = \text{total completion time of the jobs at the manufacturer}$$
$$\text{in schedule } \sigma;$$
$$L_{\max}(\sigma) = \max\{L_j(\sigma) \mid j \in N\}, \text{maximum lateness of the jobs at the}$$
$$\text{manufacturer in schedule } \sigma.$$

When the schedule being used is clear from the context, we write $C_{ij}(\sigma)$, $C_j(\sigma)$, and $L_{\max}(\sigma)$ as C_{ij}, C_j, and $L_{\max}$, respectively.

7.3.2 Conflicts Between Suppliers and Manufacturer

We study the extent to which an optimal schedule for the manufacturer's problem can be suboptimal for the suppliers' problem, and *vice versa*. Let ν and γ

7.3 Sequencing in an Assembly System

denote an optimal schedule for the suppliers' problem $As||\sum_{i=1}^{s} F_i$ and for the manufacturer's problem $As||G$, respectively. Also, let π denote an optimal schedule for the system problem, $As||\alpha \sum_{i=1}^{s} F_i + (1-\alpha)G$. The levels of conflict between the suppliers and the manufacturer are measured by the following relative errors between v and γ:

(i) $\left[\sum_{i=1}^{s} F_i(\gamma) - \sum_{i=1}^{s} F_i(v)\right] / \sum_{i=1}^{s} F_i(v)$ and (ii) $[G(v) - G(\gamma)]/G(\gamma)$,

where (i) represents the relative error of the optimal schedule for the manufacturer's problem when used for the suppliers' problem, and (ii) represents the relative error of the optimal schedule for the suppliers' problem when used for the manufacturer's problem.

For the analysis in this section, we use the following notations:

$p_j = \max\{p_{ij} \mid i = 1, \ldots, s\};$
$N_g = \{j \in N \mid p_j = g\};$
$M_g = \{j \in N \mid \sum_{i=1}^{s} p_{ij} = g\};$
$N_{ig} = \{j \in N \mid p_{ij} = g\};$
$n_g = |N_g| = $ number of jobs with $p_j = g;$
$m_g = |M_g| = $ number of jobs with $\sum_{i=1}^{s} p_{ij} = g;$
$n_{ig} = |N_{ig}| = $ number of jobs with $p_{ij} = g;$
$r_g = \min\{n_{ig} \mid i = 1, \ldots, s\};$
$m_{igh} = $ number of jobs with $p_{ij} = h$ and $p_j \le g;$
$q_{gh} = \max\{m_{igh} \mid i = 1, \ldots, s\}.$

7.3.2.1 Completion Time and Completion Time

We firstevaluate the relative error of the optimal schedule v for the supplier's problem $As||\sum\sum C_{ij}$ when it is used for the manufacturer's problem $As||\sum C_j$, i.e.,

$$\frac{\sum_{j\in N} C_j(v) - \sum_{j\in N} C_j(\gamma)}{\sum_{j\in N} C_j(\gamma)}.$$

As a preliminary step, we analyze the solvability of these two problems. We define an individual shortest processing time (ISPT) schedule to be one obtained when supplier S_i schedules its parts in SPT order, i.e., such that $p_{i1} \le \cdots \le p_{in}$, for $i = 1, \ldots, s$.

Theorem 7.12 *Problem $As||\sum\sum C_{ij}$ is solved optimally by an ISPT order of the jobs, which can be found in $O(n \log n)$ time.*

Proof The result follows from Smith (1956). □

Theorem 7.13 *The recognition version of problem $As||\sum C_j$ is unary NP-complete.*

Proof By reduction from the following problem, which is known to be unary *NP*-complete. □

3-Partition (Garey & Johnson, 1979, p. 224): given $3m$ elements with integer sizes $a_1, \ldots, a_{3m}$, where $\sum_{i=1}^{3m} a_i = mB$ and $B/4 < a_i < B/2$, for $i = 1, \ldots, 3m$, does there exist a partition $H_1, \ldots, H_m$ of the index set $H = \{1, \ldots, 3m\}$ such that $|H_j| = 3$ and $\sum_{i \in H_j} a_i = B$, for $j = 1, \ldots, m$? As part of this definition, we assume that, if there exists a solution to 3-Partition, then the elements are numbered such that $a_{3i-2} + a_{3i-1} + a_{3i} = B$, for $i = 1, \ldots, m$.

Consider an instance of the recognition version of problem $As || \sum C_j$ defined by

$$
\begin{aligned}
n &= 4m, \\
s &= 4, \\
p_{1j} &= 4B, && \text{for } j = 1, \ldots, 3m, \\
p_{2j} &= 4B - a_j, && \text{for } j = 1, \ldots, 3m, \\
p_{3j} &= 3B + a_j, && \text{for } j = 1, \ldots, 3m, \\
p_{4j} &= 0, && \text{for } j = 1, \ldots, 3m, \\
p_{1j} &= 0, && \text{for } j = 3m + 1, \ldots, 4m, \\
p_{2j} &= B, && \text{for } j = 3m + 1, \ldots, 4m, \\
p_{3j} &= 2B, && \text{for } j = 3m + 1, \ldots, 4m, \\
p_{4j} &= 12B, && \text{for } j = 3m + 1, \ldots, 4m, \text{ and} \\
C &= 24m^2 B + 12mB,
\end{aligned}
$$

where C is a threshold cost. We prove that there exists a schedule for this instance of $As || \sum C_j$ with cost less than or equal to C if and only if there exists a solution to 3-Partition.

($\Rightarrow$) Consider the sequence $(1, 2, 3, 3m + 1, \ldots, 3m - 2, 3m - 1, 3m, 4m)$. The bottleneck supplier for the first three jobs is S_1, and those jobs are completed at times $4B$, $8B$, and $12B$, respectively. Each of the four suppliers completes job $3m + 1$ at time $12B$. Each subsequent subset of four jobs is scheduled similarly, requiring a total processing time of $12B$ at each supplier. It can be shown that the total cost of the schedule is equal to C.

($\Leftarrow$) Assume the existence of a schedule σ for problem $As || \sum C_j$ for which $\sum C_j \leq C$. Without loss of generality, suppose that the jobs $\{1, \ldots, 3m\}$ are sequenced in this order at supplier S_1 and that the jobs $\{3m + 1, \ldots, 4m\}$ are sequenced in this order at supplier S_4. Then, it can be shown that $C_j \geq C_{1j} = 4jB$ for $j \in \{1, \ldots, 3m\}$ and $C_j \geq C_{4j} = 12(j - 3m)B$ for $j \in \{3m + 1, \ldots, 4m\}$. Hence, $\sum C_j \geq C$, and $\sum C_j \leq C$ if and only if $C_j = 4jB$ for $j \in \{1, \ldots, 3m\}$ and $C_j = 12(j - 3m)B$ for $j \in \{3m + 1, \ldots, 4m\}$. This means that, in σ, $C_{2j} \leq 4jB$ and $C_{3j} \leq 4jB$ for $j \in \{1, \ldots, 3m\}$, and $C_{2j} \leq 12(j - 3m)B$ and $C_{3j} \leq 12(j - 3m)B$ for $j \in \{3m + 1, \ldots, 4m\}$.

Now consider the following four jobs: 1, 2, 3, and $3m+1$. They are all completed no later than time $12B$ at both suppliers S_2 and S_3. Thus, $p_{21}+p_{22}+p_{23}+p_{2,3m+1} = 13B-(a_1+a_2+a_3) \leq 12B$, and $p_{31}+p_{32}+p_{33}+p_{3,3m+1} = 11B+(a_1+a_2+a_3) \leq 12B$. This implies that $a_1 + a_2 + a_3 = B$. Therefore, the four jobs are completed exactly at $12B$ at each supplier. This argument can be repeated for each group of

7.3 Sequencing in an Assembly System

four jobs $\{3j-2, 3j-1, 3j, 3m+j\}$ to show that $a_{3j-2} + a_{3j-1} + a_{3j} = B$, for $j = 2, \ldots, m$. This implies the existence of a solution to 3-Partition. $\square$

In view of Theorem 7.13, we use schedule ρ generated by the following heuristic, instead of γ, to evaluate the performance of ν.

Heuristic SMPT Schedule the jobs in nondecreasing order of p_j at all the suppliers, where $p_j = \max\{p_{ij} \mid i = 1, \ldots, s\}$.

Clearly, $\sum_{j \in N} C_j(\gamma) \leq \sum_{j \in N} C_j(\rho)$. Therefore,

$$\frac{\sum_{j \in N} C_j(\nu) - \sum_{j \in N} C_j(\gamma)}{\sum_{j \in N} C_j(\gamma)} \geq \frac{\sum_{j \in N} C_j(\nu) - \sum_{j \in N} C_j(\rho)}{\sum_{j \in N} C_j(\rho)}. \tag{7.1}$$

The following result provides an asymptotic analysis for the relative error as $n \to \infty$.

Theorem 7.14 *Assume that the job processing times p_{ij} are integer valued and follow an independent and identical discrete uniform distribution over a finite interval $[l, u]$, where l and u are nonnegative integers. If the optimal schedule ν for the suppliers' problem is used for the manufacturer's problem $As\|\sum C_j$, then the relative error between the cost of ν and the optimal manufacturer's cost satisfies*

$$\lim_{n \to \infty} \frac{\sum_{j \in N} C_j(\nu) - \sum_{j \in N} C_j(\gamma)}{\sum_{j \in N} C_j(\gamma)}$$

$$\overset{a.s.}{\geq} \frac{\sum_{g=l}^{u} (g^2 - l^2 - g + l) \left[(g-l+1)^s - (g-l)^s \right]}{\sum_{g=l}^{u} \left[(g^2 - l^2 + g + l) \left(\frac{g-l+1}{u-l+1} \right)^{s-1} \right] \left[(g-l+1)^s - (g-l)^s \right]} - 1. \tag{7.2}$$

Proof From the Laws of Large Numbers (see Remark 2.2 in Sect. 2.3.4.1) and the stated assumption on the probability distribution of the p_{ij} values, we have, for $i = 1, \ldots, s, g = l, \ldots, u$, and $h = l, \ldots, g$,

$$\lim_{n \to \infty} \frac{n_{ig}}{n} \overset{a.s.}{=} \Pr[p_{ij} = g] = \frac{1}{u-l+1}, \tag{7.3}$$

$$\lim_{n \to \infty} \frac{n_g}{n} \overset{a.s.}{=} \Pr[p_j = g] = \Pr[p_j \leq g] - \Pr[p_j \leq g-1]$$

$$= \left(\frac{g-l+1}{u-l+1} \right)^s - \left(\frac{g-l}{u-l+1} \right)^s, \quad \text{and} \tag{7.4}$$

$$\lim_{n \to \infty} \frac{m_{igh}}{n} \overset{a.s.}{=} \Pr[p_{ij} = h, p_j \leq g] = \Pr[p_j \leq g] \times \Pr[p_{ij} = h \mid p_j \leq g]$$

$$= \left(\frac{g-l+1}{u-l+1} \right)^s \times \frac{1}{g-l+1} = \frac{(g-l+1)^{s-1}}{(u-l+1)^s}. \tag{7.5}$$

342   7 Optimization and Conflict

It follows from (7.3) and (7.5) that

$$\lim_{n \to \infty} \frac{r_g}{n} \overset{a.s.}{=} \frac{1}{u - l + 1}, \quad \text{and} \tag{7.6}$$

$$\lim_{n \to \infty} \frac{q_{gh}}{n} \overset{a.s.}{=} \frac{(g - l + 1)^{s-1}}{(u - l + 1)^s}. \tag{7.7}$$

We provide a lower bound on the cost of v in the manufacturer's problem. From Theorem 7.12, in schedule v, the parts are processed at each supplier S_i in SPT order of their processing times p_{ij}. Thus, each supplier S_i processes the jobs from the same subset N_{ig} consecutively, for $g = l, \ldots, u$, and the jobs from different subsets in the order $(N_{il}, N_{i,l+1}, \ldots, N_{iu})$. Let E_{ig} denote the starting time of the first job from N_{ig} at supplier S_i. We have, for each $j \in N_g$,

$$C_j(v) \geq \min\{E_{ig} \mid i = 1, \ldots, s\} = \min\left\{\sum_{k=l}^{g-1} kn_{ik} \mid i = 1, \ldots, s\right\}$$

$$\geq \sum_{k=l}^{g-1} k \min\{n_{ik} \mid i = 1, \ldots, s\} = \sum_{k=l}^{g-1} kr_k.$$

This implies that

$$\sum_{j \in N} C_j(v) = \sum_{g=l}^{u} \sum_{j \in N_g} C_j(v) \geq \sum_{g=l}^{u} \left[n_g \sum_{k=l}^{g-1} kr_k\right]. \tag{7.8}$$

Then, from (7.4), (7.6), and (7.8), we have

$$\lim_{n \to \infty} \frac{\sum_{j \in N} C_j(v)}{n^2} \geq \lim_{n \to \infty} \sum_{g=l}^{u} \frac{n_g}{n} \left[\sum_{k=l}^{g-1} \frac{r_k}{n} k\right] = \sum_{g=l}^{u} \left(\lim_{n \to \infty} \frac{n_g}{n}\right) \left[\sum_{k=l}^{g-1} \left(\lim_{n \to \infty} \frac{r_k}{n}\right) k\right]$$

$$\overset{a.s.}{=} \sum_{g=l}^{u} \left[\left(\frac{g - l + 1}{u - l + 1}\right)^s - \left(\frac{g - l}{u - l + 1}\right)^s\right] \left[\sum_{k=l}^{g-1} \frac{k}{u - l + 1}\right]$$

$$= \frac{1}{2(u - l + 1)^{s+1}} \sum_{g=l}^{u} \left[(g - l + 1)^s - (g - l)^s\right] \left[g^2 - l^2 - g + l\right]. \tag{7.9}$$

Next, we derive an upper bound on the optimal manufacturer's cost, $\sum_{j \in N} C_j(\gamma)$, using schedule ρ from Heuristic SMPT and (7.1). In schedule ρ, the jobs from the same subset N_g, for $g = 1, \ldots, s$, are scheduled consecutively, and the jobs from different subsets are scheduled in the order $(N_l, N_{l+1}, \ldots, N_u)$. Let D_g be the completion time of the last job from the subset N_g and H_{ig} be the total processing time of the jobs from $\bigcup_{k=l}^{g} N_k$ at supplier S_i. Thus, for $g = l, \ldots, u$,

7.3 Sequencing in an Assembly System

$$D_g = \max\{H_{ig} \mid i = 1, \ldots, s\} = \max\left\{\sum_{k=l}^{g} km_{igk} \mid i = 1, \ldots, s\right\}$$

$$\leq \sum_{k=l}^{g} k \max\{m_{igh} \mid i = 1, \ldots, s\} = \sum_{k=l}^{g} kq_{gk}. \tag{7.10}$$

Since $C_j(\rho) \leq D_g$ for $j \in N_g$, from (7.10), we have

$$\sum_{j \in N} C_j(\rho) = \sum_{g=1}^{u} \sum_{j \in N_g} C_j(\rho) \leq \sum_{g=l}^{u} n_g D_g \leq \sum_{g=l}^{u} n_g \left[\sum_{k=l}^{g} kq_{gk}\right]. \tag{7.11}$$

Then, we have

$$\lim_{n \to \infty} \frac{\sum_{j \in N} C_j(\gamma)}{n^2} \leq \lim_{n \to \infty} \frac{\sum_{j \in N} C_j(\rho)}{n^2} \leq \lim_{n \to \infty} \sum_{g=l}^{u} \left[\frac{n_g}{n} \sum_{k=l}^{g} \frac{q_{gk}}{n} k\right], \quad \text{from (7.11)}$$

$$= \sum_{g=l}^{u} \left[\left(\lim_{n \to \infty} \frac{n_g}{n}\right) \sum_{k=l}^{g} \left(\lim_{n \to \infty} \frac{q_{gk}}{n}\right) k\right]$$

$$\overset{a.s.}{=} \sum_{g=l}^{u} \left[\frac{(g-l+1)^s - (g-l)^s}{(u-l+1)^s}\right] \sum_{k=l}^{g} \left[\frac{(g-l+1)^{s-1}}{(u-l+1)^s} k\right], \quad \text{from (7.4) and (7.7)}$$

$$= \frac{1}{2(u-l+1)^{s+1}} \sum_{g=l}^{u} \left[(g-l+1)^s - (g-l)^s\right]\left[g^2 - l^2 + g + l\right]\left[\frac{(g-l+1)^{s-1}}{(u-l+1)^{s-1}}\right]. \tag{7.12}$$

The main result, (7.2), then follows from (7.9) and (7.12). $\qquad\square$

Theorem 7.14 provides an asymptotic lower bound on the relative error between schedules v and γ for the manufacturer's problem, as $n \to \infty$. For finite values of n, we compute the lower bound in (7.1), using random test problems that are generated as follows: (i) the number of suppliers $s \in \{2, 4, 8, 16\}$, (ii) the number of jobs $n \in \{50, 100, 200, 400\}$, and (iii) job processing times p_{ij} are independently drawn from a uniform integer distribution over the interval $[l, u]$, where $l \in \{10, 50\}$, and $u \in \{100, 500, 1000\}$. For a small number of randomly generated test problems, we have $\sum_{j \in N} C_j(v) < \sum_{j \in N} C_j(\rho)$. For these problems, we record the relative error as 0 because the actual relative error between v and γ is always nonnegative. For each (s, l, u, n) combination, the mean lower bound over 10 random instances is reported in Table 7.8. We also compute the lower bound in (7.2) for each (s, l, u) combination and report the results in the columns with $n = \infty$ in Table 7.8. Since

Table 7.8 Lower bounds on relative error in the manufacturer's problem $\left(\sum C_j\right)$

s	l	u	Lower bound on relative error					s	l	u	Lower bound on relative error				
			$n=50$	$n=100$	$n=200$	$n=400$	$n=\infty$				$n=50$	$n=100$	$n=200$	$n=400$	$n=\infty$
2	10	100	21.94%	23.29%	24.42%	25.13%	22.66%	2	50	100	28.55%	29.58%	29.98%	30.28%	24.89%
		500	19.91%	21.29%	22.68%	23.52%	24.58%			500	21.93%	23.31%	24.48%	25.22%	25.97%
		1000	19.63%	20.99%	22.42%	23.30%	24.79%			1000	20.74%	22.08%	23.40%	24.21%	25.55%
4	10	100	39.34%	43.98%	45.70%	47.32%	45.73%	4	50	100	50.03%	52.59%	53.85%	54.53%	47.29%
		500	36.45%	41.62%	43.38%	45.09%	49.21%			500	39.49%	44.12%	45.83%	47.33%	50.71%
		1000	35.99%	41.21%	43.04%	44.80%	49.61%			1000	37.65%	42.60%	44.36%	45.99%	50.43%
8	10	100	54.34%	57.11%	61.53%	65.08%	61.18%	8	50	100	66.33%	68.22%	70.56%	72.38%	58.84%
		500	50.94%	53.89%	58.80%	62.99%	68.30%			500	54.20%	57.03%	61.39%	65.15%	69.33%
		1000	50.48%	53.46%	58.47%	62.70%	69.15%			1000	52.23%	55.12%	59.87%	63.85%	69.74%
16	10	100	62.63%	67.95%	72.80%	75.24%	66.35%	16	50	100	75.54%	78.42%	81.56%	82.44%	57.97%
		500	59.42%	64.71%	70.49%	73.24%	79.93%			500	62.70%	67.66%	72.95%	75.28%	80.38%
		1000	59.00%	64.43%	70.25%	72.96%	81.63%			1000	60.79%	65.87%	71.49%	74.04%	81.95%

7.3 Sequencing in an Assembly System

the relative error is at least 19.6% for all the (s, l, u, n) combinations considered, we conclude that there is substantial conflict between the two schedules. The results in Table 7.8 indicate that the relative errors increase significantly with the number of suppliers, s. This can be explained as follows. As s increases, C_j increases, since it is the maximum of C_{ij} over $i = 1, \ldots, s$. Also, the increase of C_j under schedule ν is likely to be larger than that under schedule ρ, because schedule ρ uses the same job sequence at all the suppliers, whereas schedule ν does not. The relative errors also increase slightly with n, for $50 \leq n \leq 400$.

We next evaluate the relative error of the optimal schedule γ for the manufacturer's problem $As|| \sum C_j$ when it is used for the suppliers' problem $As|| \sum \sum C_{ij}$, i.e.,

$$\frac{\sum_{i=1}^{s} \sum_{j \in N} C_{ij}(\gamma) - \sum_{i=1}^{s} \sum_{j \in N} C_{ij}(\nu)}{\sum_{i=1}^{s} \sum_{j \in N} C_{ij}(\nu)}.$$

We first analyze the solvability of these two problems. In view of Theorems 7.12 and 7.13, we use schedule ξ generated by the following shortest total processing time rule to evaluate the performance of γ.

Heuristic STPT Schedule the jobs in nondecreasing order of $\sum_{i=1}^{s} p_{ij}$ at each supplier.

We need the following two preliminary results to provide some insight.

Theorem 7.15 *Heuristic STPT finds an optimal schedule for problem $As|coseq| \sum \sum C_{ij}$ in $O(n \log n)$ time.*

Proof Consider a hypothetical schedule in which job k immediately precedes job j in some common sequence σ, where $\sum_{i=1}^{s} p_{ik} > \sum_{i=1}^{s} p_{ij}$. Let t_i denote the total processing time of the jobs that are scheduled before j and k at supplier S_i, for $i = 1, \ldots, s$. Then, the total completion time of jobs k and j is

$$\sum_{i=1}^{s} (C_{ik} + C_{ij}) = \sum_{i=1}^{s} 2t_i + \sum_{i=1}^{s} 2p_{ik} + \sum_{i=1}^{s} p_{ij}.$$

If we interchange jobs j and k to obtain a sequence σ', then the total completion time of jobs k and j becomes

$$\sum_{i=1}^{s} (C'_{ik} + C'_{ij}) = \sum_{i=1}^{s} 2t_i + \sum_{i=1}^{s} 2p_{ij} + \sum_{i=1}^{s} p_{ik}.$$

Since $\sum_{i=1}^{s} p_{ik} > \sum_{i=1}^{s} p_{ij}$, we have

$$\sum_{i=1}^{s} (C'_{ik} + C'_{ij}) - \sum_{i=1}^{s} (C_{ik} + C_{ij}) = \sum_{i=1}^{s} (p_{ij} - p_{ik}) < 0.$$

346   7   Optimization and Conflict

Thus, the total completion time of sequence σ' is lower than that of σ. Repeating this argument proves the theorem. $\qquad\square$

Lemma 7.7 *For any manufacturer's problem with a regular objective function of* $(C_1, \ldots, C_n)$ *denoted by* $As| \cdot |\max_{1 \leq j \leq n} \{f_j(C_j)\}$ *or* $As| \cdot |\sum f_j(C_j)$, *where* $f_j(\cdot)$ *is a nondecreasing function, and without processing times at the manufacturer or transportation times, there exists an optimal schedule that uses identical job sequences at all suppliers.*

Proof Consider a schedule with two jobs i and j such that job i is scheduled before job j at supplier S_1 and job j is scheduled before job i at supplier S_2. If $C_{1j} \leq C_{2k}$, then interchange jobs k and j at supplier S_1. Alternatively, if $C_{1j} > C_{2k}$, then interchange jobs k and j at supplier S_2. In both cases, the completion time of each job is either unchanged or decreased in the new schedule. $\qquad\square$

From Theorem 7.15, schedule ξ minimizes $\sum \sum C_{ij}$ over all schedules that require identical job sequences at the suppliers. From Lemma 7.7, we may assume without loss of generality that schedule γ has identical job sequences at the suppliers. Therefore, we have

$$\sum_{i=1}^{s} \sum_{j \in N} C_{ij}(\gamma) \geq \sum_{i=1}^{s} \sum_{j \in N} C_{ij}(\xi) \qquad (7.13)$$

$$\Rightarrow \quad \frac{\sum_{i=1}^{s} \sum_{j \in N} C_{ij}(\gamma) - \sum_{i=1}^{s} \sum_{j \in N} C_{ij}(v)}{\sum_{i=1}^{s} \sum_{j \in N} C_{ij}(v)}$$

$$\geq \frac{\sum_{i=1}^{s} \sum_{j \in N} C_{ij}(\xi) - \sum_{i=1}^{s} \sum_{j \in N} C_{ij}(v)}{\sum_{i=1}^{s} \sum_{j \in N} C_{ij}(v)}. \qquad (7.14)$$

The following result provides an asymptotic analysis for the relative error as $n \to \infty$.

Theorem 7.16 *Assume that the job processing times* p_{ij} *are integer valued and follow an independent and identical discrete uniform distribution over a finite interval* $[l, u]$, *where* l *and* u *are nonnegative integers. If the optimal schedule* γ *for the manufacturer's problem is used for the suppliers' problem* $As||\sum \sum C_{ij}$, *then the relative gap between the cost of* γ *and the optimal manufacturer's cost satisfies*

$$\lim_{n \to \infty} \frac{\sum_{i=1}^{s} \sum_{j \in N} C_{ij}(\gamma) - \sum_{i=1}^{s} \sum_{j \in N} C_{ij}(v)}{\sum_{i=1}^{s} \sum_{j \in N} C_{ij}(v)} \overset{a.s.}{\geq} \frac{\sum_{g=sl}^{su} \left[r_{sg} \sum_{h=sl}^{g-1} h r_{sh} \right]}{s \left[\sum_{g=l}^{u} (g^2 - l^2 + g + l) \right] / [2(u - l + 1)^2]} - 1,$$

$$(7.15)$$

7.3 Sequencing in an Assembly System   347

where r_{sk} is the probability that the total processing time $\sum_{i=1}^{s} p_{ij}$ of any job is equal to k, for $sl \leq k \leq su$.

Proof From the Laws of Large Numbers and the given assumption on the probability distribution of the p_{ij} values, we have, for $i = 1, \ldots, s$, $g = l, \ldots, u$, and $h = sl, \ldots, su$,

$$\lim_{n \to \infty} \frac{m_h}{n} \stackrel{a.s.}{=} \Pr\left[\sum_{i=1}^{s} p_{ij} = h\right] = r_{sh}. \tag{7.16}$$

We first derive an upper bound on $\sum_{i=1}^{s} \sum_{j \in N} C_{ij}(v)$. From Theorem 7.12, jobs are in SPT order at each supplier in schedule v. Thus, each supplier S_i processes the jobs from the same subset N_{ig} consecutively, for $g = l, \ldots, u$, and the jobs from different subsets in the order $(N_{il}, N_{i,l+1}, \ldots, N_{iu})$. At supplier S_i, the completion time of each job $j \in N_{ig}$ satisfies $C_{ij}(v) \leq \sum_{k=l}^{g} k n_{ik}$. This implies that

$$\sum_{j \in N} C_{ij}(v) = \sum_{g=l}^{u} \sum_{j \in N_{ig}} C_{ij}(v) \leq \sum_{g=l}^{u} \left(n_{ig} \sum_{k=l}^{g} k n_{ik}\right). \tag{7.17}$$

Then, from (7.3) and (7.17), we have

$$\lim_{n \to \infty} \frac{\sum_{i=1}^{s} \sum_{j \in N} C_{ij}(v)}{n^2} \leq \lim_{n \to \infty} \frac{\sum_{i=1}^{s} \sum_{g=l}^{u} \left(n_{ig} \sum_{k=l}^{g} k n_{ik}\right)}{n^2}$$

$$= \lim_{n \to \infty} \sum_{i=1}^{s} \sum_{g=l}^{u} \left(\frac{n_{ig}}{n} \sum_{k=l}^{g} \frac{n_{ik}}{n} k\right)$$

$$\stackrel{a.s.}{=} \frac{1}{(u-l+1)^2} \sum_{i=1}^{s} \sum_{g=l}^{u} \sum_{k=l}^{g} k$$

$$= \frac{s}{2(u-l+1)^2} \sum_{g=l}^{u} (g^2 - l^2 + g + l). \tag{7.18}$$

Next, we derive a lower bound on $\sum_{i=1}^{s} \sum_{j \in N} C_{ij}(\gamma)$, using schedule ξ from Heuristic STPT and (7.13). In schedule ξ, the jobs from the same subset M_g, for $g = sl, \ldots, su$, are scheduled consecutively, and the jobs from different subsets are scheduled in the order $(M_{sl}, M_{sl+1}, \ldots, M_{su})$. Thus, for each job $j \in M_g$ for $g \in \{sl, \ldots, su\}$, we have $C_{ij}(\xi) \geq \sum_{h=sl}^{g-1} \sum_{j \in M_h} p_{ij}$, and hence

$$\sum_{i=1}^{s} C_{ij}(\xi) \geq \sum_{h=sl}^{g-1} \sum_{j \in M_h} \sum_{i=1}^{s} p_{ij} = \sum_{h=sl}^{g-1} \sum_{j \in M_h} h = \sum_{h=sl}^{g-1} h m_h.$$

348   7   Optimization and Conflict

This implies that

$$\sum_{i=1}^{s}\sum_{j\in N}C_{ij}(\gamma) \geq \sum_{i=1}^{s}\sum_{j\in N}C_{ij}(\xi) = \sum_{g=sl}^{su}\sum_{j\in M_g}\left[\sum_{i=1}^{s}C_{ij}(\xi)\right]$$

$$\geq \sum_{g=sl}^{su}\sum_{j\in M_g}\sum_{h=sl}^{g-1}hm_h = \sum_{g=sl}^{su}\left[m_g\sum_{h=sl}^{g-1}hm_h\right]. \tag{7.19}$$

Then, from (7.16) and (7.19), we have

$$\lim_{n\to\infty}\frac{\sum_{i=1}^{s}\sum_{j\in N}C_{ij}(\gamma)}{n^2} \geq \lim_{n\to\infty}\frac{\sum_{g=sl}^{su}\left[m_g\sum_{h=sl}^{g-1}hm_h\right]}{n^2}$$

$$= \lim_{n\to\infty}\sum_{g=sl}^{su}\left[\frac{m_g}{n}\sum_{h=sl}^{g-1}h\frac{m_h}{n}\right] \overset{a.s.}{=} \sum_{g=sl}^{su}\left[r_{sg}\sum_{h=sl}^{g-1}hr_{sh}\right]. \tag{7.20}$$

The main result, (7.15), then follows from (7.18) and (7.20).   □

Theorem 7.16 provides an asymptotic lower bound on the relative gap between schedules γ and ν for the suppliers' problem, as $n \to \infty$. The probability parameters r_{sk} can be calculated recursively for given l and u, as follows. First, when $s = 1$, we have $r_{1k} = 1/(u - l + 1)$ for $l \leq k \leq u$. Suppose that we have already calculated r_{sk} for $s = 1,\ldots,i$ for some i. Then, the values of $r_{i+1,k}$ can be found from the following formula: $r_{i+1,k} = \sum_{j=l}^{\min\{u,k\}} r_{i,k-j}/(u - l + 1)$, for $(i+1)l \leq k \leq (i+1)u$. For finite values of n, we compute the lower bound in (7.14), using random test problems that are generated similarly to those in Table 7.8. The results are reported in Table 7.9. We also compute the lower bound in (7.15) for each (s, l, u) combination and report the results in the columns with $n = \infty$ in Table 7.9. Since the relative error is at least 10% for most (s, l, u, n) combinations considered, we conclude that there is substantial conflict between the two schedules. Since in (7.14) schedules γ and ξ use a common sequence for all the suppliers, whereas schedule ν does not, the relative errors increase with s.

7.3.2.2   Completion Time and Maximum Lateness

We first evaluate the performance of the optimal schedule ν for the supplier's problem $As||\sum\sum C_{ij}$ when it is used for the manufacturer's problem $As||L_{\max}$, i.e.,

$$\frac{L_{\max}(\nu) - L_{\max}(\gamma)}{L_{\max}(\gamma)}.$$

Table 7.9 Lower bounds on relative error in the suppliers' problem ($\sum \sum C_{ij}$)

s	l	u	Lower bound on relative error					s	l	u	Lower bound on relative error				
			$n=50$	$n=100$	$n=200$	$n=400$	$n=\infty$				$n=50$	$n=100$	$n=200$	$n=400$	$n=\infty$
		100	10.60%	11.13%	11.26%	11.23%	8.73%			100	3.56%	3.72%	3.74%	3.72%	0.06%
2	10	500	13.16%	13.80%	13.99%	13.97%	13.64%	2	50	500	10.50%	11.00%	11.14%	11.11%	10.74%
		1000	13.53%	14.19%	14.39%	14.37%	14.31%			1000	12.05%	12.64%	12.81%	12.78%	12.70%
		100	17.29%	17.94%	18.74%	18.78%	16.82%			100	5.82%	5.98%	6.22%	6.24%	3.07%
4	10	500	21.42%	22.28%	23.31%	23.35%	23.50%	4	50	500	17.12%	17.76%	18.55%	18.59%	18.61%
		1000	22.02%	22.91%	23.97%	24.01%	24.44%			1000	19.64%	20.41%	21.33%	21.37%	21.73%
		100	23.56%	24.48%	24.47%	24.60%	22.46%			100	7.90%	8.16%	8.15%	8.18%	5.18%
8	10	500	29.19%	30.41%	30.41%	30.59%	30.38%	8	50	500	23.32%	24.24%	24.23%	24.36%	24.09%
		1000	30.01%	31.27%	31.27%	31.46%	31.51%			1000	26.76%	27.85%	27.85%	28.00%	28.01%
		100	27.27%	27.95%	28.47%	28.46%	26.43%			100	9.13%	9.33%	9.48%	9.46%	6.67%
16	10	500	33.81%	34.70%	35.38%	35.38%	35.21%	16	50	500	27.00%	27.68%	28.19%	28.18%	27.94%
		1000	34.76%	35.68%	36.38%	36.39%	36.47%			1000	30.99%	31.79%	32.40%	32.39%	32.43%

As a preliminary step, we briefly discuss the solvability of these two problems. Problem $As||\sum\sum C_{ij}$ is studied in Theorem 7.12. For problem $As||L_{\max}$, the following result generalizes that of Jackson (1955) for the single-machine scheduling problem $1||L_{\max}$.

Theorem 7.17 *An optimal schedule for problem $As||L_{\max}$ is provided by an earliest due date (EDD) ordering of the jobs, which can be found in $O(n\log n)$ time.*

Proof From Lemma 7.7, we assume that the suppliers use a common sequence. Consider a hypothetical schedule in which job k immediately precedes job j in sequence σ, where $d_j < d_k$. Let t_i denote the total processing time of the jobs before j and k at supplier S_i, for $i = 1, \ldots, s$. Then the maximum lateness among jobs j and k is given by

$$L_{\max} = \max\Big\{ \max_{1 \le i \le s}\{t_i + p_{ik}\} - d_k, \ \max_{1 \le i \le s}\{t_i + p_{ik} + p_{ij}\} - d_j \Big\}.$$

If we interchange jobs j and k to obtain a sequence σ', then the maximum lateness among jobs j and k is given by

$$L'_{\max} = \max\Big\{ \max_{1 \le i \le s}\{t_i + p_{ij}\} - d_j, \ \max_{1 \le i \le s}\{t_i + p_{ij} + p_{ik}\} - d_k \Big\},$$

where since $d_j < d_k$, the second term in $L_{\max}$ is larger than the second term in $L'_{\max}$. Thus, $L'_{\max} \le L_{\max}$. The jobs can be sorted in EDD order in $O(n\log n)$ time. $\square$

The following result provides an asymptotic analysis for the relative error as $n \to \infty$.

Theorem 7.18 *Assume that*

(i) *The job processing times p_{ij} are integer valued and follow an independent and identical discrete uniform distribution over a finite interval $[l, u]$, where l and u are nonnegative integers.*

(ii) *The job due dates d_j follow an independent and identical uniform distribution over the interval $[0, n\bar{p}]$, where $\bar{p} = (l + u)/2$ is the average processing time of a job at a supplier.*

(iii) *The p_{ij} and d_j values are independent.*

If the optimal schedule v for the suppliers' problem is used for the manufacturer's problem $As||L_{\max}$, then the relative error between the maximum lateness of v and the optimal manufacturer's maximum lateness satisfies

$$\lim_{n\to\infty} \frac{L_{\max}(v) - L_{\max}(\gamma)}{L_{\max}(\gamma)} \stackrel{a.s.}{=} \infty. \tag{7.21}$$

Proof Classify the jobs into m classes, $D_1, \ldots, D_m$, where m is an arbitrary positive integer, and $D_k = \{j \in N \mid n\bar{p}(k - 1)/m \le d_j < n\bar{p}k/m\}$, for

7.3 Sequencing in an Assembly System

$k = 1, \ldots, m$. Define $N_{igk} = N_{ig} \cap D_k$, and let n_{igk} be the number of jobs in N_{igk}, for $i = 1, \ldots, s$, $g = l, \ldots, u$, and $k = 1, \ldots, m$. From the Laws of Large Numbers and the given assumption on the probability distributions of the p_{ij} and d_j values, we have

$$\lim_{n \to \infty} \frac{n_{igk}}{n} \overset{a.s.}{=} \Pr[p_{ij} = g, n\bar{p}(k-1)/m \leq d_j < n\bar{p}k/m] = \frac{1}{m(u-l+1)}.$$
(7.22)

Equation (7.22) means that, almost surely, N_{igk} contains an infinite number of jobs. Consider a job $j \in N_{iu1}$ in schedule ν. Since in ν, jobs are processed in SPT order at each supplier, all the jobs from $N_{il} \cup \ldots \cup N_{i,u-1}$ are scheduled before j. Thus,

$$C_{ij}(\nu) \geq \sum_{h=l}^{u-1} hn_{ih}.$$
(7.23)

Now, (7.23) implies that

$$L_{\max}(\nu) \geq L_{ij}(\nu) = C_{ij}(\nu) - d_j \geq \sum_{h=l}^{u-1} hn_{ih} - d_j$$

$$\geq \sum_{h=l}^{u-1} hn_{ih} - n\bar{p}/m.$$
(7.24)

From (7.3), (7.24) implies that

$$\lim_{n \to \infty} \frac{L_{\max}(\nu)}{n} \geq \lim_{n \to \infty} \sum_{h=l}^{u-1} hn_{ih}/n - \bar{p}/m$$

$$\overset{a.s.}{\geq} \sum_{h=l}^{u-1} h/(u-l+1) - \bar{p}/m = \frac{(u-l)(u+l-1)}{2(u-l+1)} - \bar{p}/m.$$
(7.25)

Next, we consider schedule γ. Since, from Theorem 7.17, jobs are processed in EDD order at each supplier in schedule γ, we have, for $i = 1, \ldots, s$, $j \in D_k$, and $k = 1, \ldots, m$,

$$C_{ij}(\gamma) \leq \sum_{h=1}^{k} \sum_{g=l}^{u} gn_{igh}.$$
(7.26)

Then, from (7.26), we have

$$\lim_{n\to\infty} \frac{L_{ij}(\gamma)}{n} = \lim_{n\to\infty} \frac{C_{ij}(\gamma) - d_j}{n} \le \lim_{n\to\infty} \frac{\sum_{h=1}^{k} \sum_{g=l}^{u} g n_{igh} - n\bar{p}(k-1)/m}{n}$$

$$= \lim_{n\to\infty} \left(\sum_{h=1}^{k} \sum_{g=l}^{u} g n_{igh}/n - \bar{p}(k-1)/m \right)$$

$$\stackrel{a.s.}{=} \sum_{h=1}^{k} \sum_{g=l}^{u} g/[m(u-l+1)] - \bar{p}(k-1)/m, \qquad \text{from (7.22)}$$

$$= \bar{p}k/m - \bar{p}(k-1)/m = \bar{p}/m. \tag{7.27}$$

Since (7.27) holds for $i = 1, \ldots, s$ and $j \in N$, we have

$$\lim_{n\to\infty} \frac{L_{\max}(\gamma)}{n} \stackrel{a.s.}{\le} \bar{p}/m. \tag{7.28}$$

Now, (7.25) and (7.28) hold for any given m. Therefore, as $m \to \infty$, (7.25) and (7.28) imply the main result, (7.21). □

Theorem 7.18 implies that, as $n \to \infty$, the relative error between schedules v and γ for the manufacturer's problem becomes, almost surely, arbitrarily large. For finite values of n, we compute the relative error using random test problems where the parameters s, n, l, u, and p_{ij} are generated similarly to those in Tables 7.8 and 7.9 and where the parameter d_j is independently drawn from a discrete uniform distribution over the interval $[0, n(l + u)/2]$. For each (s, l, u, n) combination, the mean relative error over 10 random instances is reported in Table 7.10. As can be seen there, large relative errors occur over all (s, l, u, n) combinations considered, indicating huge conflict between the two schedules. These errors are much larger than those observed in Tables 7.8 and 7.9 because lower bounds on the value of $L_{\max}$ may be small. The relative errors increase strongly with n, since as the number of jobs increases, the error caused by a single job with large processing times but a small due date being at the end of schedule v increases.

We next evaluate the relative error of the optimal schedule γ for the manufacturer's problem $As||L_{\max}$ when it is used for the suppliers' problem $As|| \sum \sum C_{ij}$, i.e.,

$$\frac{\sum_{i=1}^{s} \sum_{j\in N} C_{ij}(\gamma) - \sum_{i=1}^{s} \sum_{j\in N} C_{ij}(v)}{\sum_{i=1}^{s} \sum_{j\in N} C_{ij}(v)}.$$

The following result provides an asymptotic analysis of the relative error as $n \to \infty$.

7.3 Sequencing in an Assembly System

Table 7.10 Relative errors in the manufacturer's problem (L_{max})

s	l	u	Relative error				
			$n = 50$	$n = 100$	$n = 200$	$n = 400$	$n = \infty$
2	10	100	764%	1006%	1465%	2059%	∞
		500	636%	875%	1288%	1765%	∞
		1000	621%	864%	1270%	1730%	∞
4	10	100	627%	1084%	1258%	2227%	∞
		500	552%	936%	1062%	1769%	∞
		1000	543%	917%	1042%	1722%	∞
8	10	100	603%	873%	1337%	2286%	∞
		500	511%	739%	1078%	1814%	∞
		1000	504%	724%	1050%	1771%	∞
16	10	100	436%	786%	1185%	1992%	∞
		500	372%	677%	952%	1565%	∞
		1000	366%	660%	930%	1515%	∞
2	50	100	1305%	1419%	2066%	2962%	∞
		500	722%	956%	1397%	1730%	∞
		1000	662%	905%	1322%	1803%	∞
4	50	100	991%	1542%	2035%	3633%	∞
		500	611%	999%	1189%	1978%	∞
		1000	572%	958%	1103%	1825%	∞
8	50	100	1013%	1398%	2148%	3964%	∞
		500	582%	830%	1223%	2035%	∞
		1000	538%	770%	1118%	1875%	∞
16	50	100	669%	1317%	2361%	3739%	∞
		500	421%	763%	1087%	1789%	∞
		1000	391%	703%	992%	1621%	∞

Theorem 7.19 *Assume that*

(i) *The job processing times p_{ij} are integer valued and follow an independent and identical discrete uniform distribution over a finite interval $[l, u]$, where l and u are nonnegative integers.*

(ii) *The job due dates d_j follow an arbitrary independent and identical distribution.*

(iii) *The p_{ij} and d_j values are independent.*

If the optimal schedule γ for the manufacturer's problem is used for the suppliers' problem $As||\sum\sum C_{ij}$, then the relative error between the cost of γ and that of ν satisfies

$$\lim_{n\to\infty} \frac{\sum\limits_{i=1}^{s}\sum\limits_{j\in N} C_{ij}(\gamma) - \sum\limits_{i=1}^{s}\sum\limits_{j\in N} C_{ij}(\nu)}{\sum\limits_{i=1}^{s}\sum\limits_{j\in N} C_{ij}(\nu)} \overset{a.s.}{\geq} \frac{(u+l)(u-l+1)^2}{2\sum\limits_{g=l}^{u}(g^2 - l^2 + g + l)} - 1. \qquad (7.29)$$

We refer the reader to (Chen & Hall, 2007) for a proof.

Theorem 7.19 provides an asymptotic lower bound on the relative error between schedules γ and ν for the suppliers' problem. For finite values of n, we compute the relative error using random test problems which are generated similarly to those in Table 7.10. For each (s, l, u, n) combination, the mean relative error over 10 random instances is reported in Table 7.11. We also compute the lower bound in (7.29) for each (s, l, u) combination and report the results in the columns with $n = \infty$ in Table 7.11. Since the relative error is at least 10.3% for all (s, l, u, n) combinations considered, we conclude that there is substantial conflict between the schedules. The explanation of the results is similar to that for Table 7.9.

7.3.3 Suppliers Dominate and Manufacturer Negotiates

Motivated by the evidence of significant cost of conflict found in Sect. 7.3.2, we investigate in Sects. 7.3.3–7.3.6 how different bargaining power scenarios lead to various resolutions of this conflict. Figure 7.5 provides an overview of this work. We first consider a situation where the suppliers have dominant bargaining power in the supply chain and choose their optimal schedule, ν. Here, the manufacturer may wish to compensate the suppliers for using some alternative schedule σ which is cheaper for the manufacturer than ν. The bargaining theory of Nash (1950, 1953) suggests that this incentive has to be sufficient to persuade the suppliers to select schedule σ (to be determined) instead of ν, while the resulting cost to the manufacturer has to be no more than that of ν. Recall that αF_i denotes the cost of supplier S_i, and

Table 7.11 Relative errors in the suppliers' problem ($\sum\sum c_{ij}$)

s	l	u	Relative error					s	l	u	Relative error				
			n = 50	n = 100	n = 200	n = 400	n = ∞				n = 50	n = 100	n = 200	n = 400	n = ∞
2	10	100	34.78%	36.19%	36.82%	37.17%	36.01%	2	50	100	11.64%	12.02%	12.19%	12.35%	10.34%
		500	43.11%	44.96%	45.83%	46.20%	46.82%			500	34.40%	35.80%	36.44%	36.79%	37.20%
		1000	44.31%	46.25%	47.15%	47.52%	48.38%			1000	39.50%	41.16%	41.93%	42.30%	43.03%
4	10	100	36.50%	37.23%	37.44%	37.64%	36.01%	4	50	100	12.20%	12.37%	12.47%	12.53%	10.34%
		500	45.26%	46.28%	46.50%	46.77%	46.82%			500	36.11%	36.84%	37.06%	37.26%	37.20%
		1000	46.53%	47.60%	47.82%	48.10%	48.38%			1000	41.47%	42.36%	42.59%	42.83%	43.03%
8	10	100	35.99%	37.03%	37.66%	37.65%	36.01%	8	50	100	12.02%	12.36%	12.55%	12.52%	10.34%
		500	44.65%	45.96%	46.78%	46.79%	46.82%			500	35.62%	36.66%	37.28%	37.27%	37.20%
		1000	45.90%	47.26%	48.10%	48.12%	48.38%			1000	40.91%	42.11%	42.84%	42.84%	43.03%
16	10	100	36.06%	37.19%	37.59%	37.80%	36.01%	16	50	100	12.09%	12.42%	12.52%	12.55%	10.34%
		500	44.68%	46.15%	46.70%	47.01%	46.82%			500	35.70%	36.82%	37.22%	37.42%	37.20%
		1000	45.93%	47.45%	48.03%	48.35%	48.38%			1000	40.96%	42.28%	42.77%	43.03%	43.03%

$(1 - \alpha)G$ denotes the cost of the manufacturer. Therefore, the incentive u_i provided to each supplier S_i must satisfy

$$\alpha F_i(\sigma) - u_i \leq \alpha F_i(v), \text{ for } i = 1, \ldots, s, \quad \text{and} \quad (7.30)$$

$$(1 - \alpha)G(\sigma) + \sum_{i=1}^{s} u_i \leq (1 - \alpha)G(v). \quad (7.31)$$

Also, the manufacturer chooses σ to minimize its total cost $(1 - \alpha)G(\sigma) + \sum_{i=1}^{s} u_i$. Thus, the manufacturer is faced with the following optimization problem in determining σ and $u_1, \ldots, u_s$:

$$\min_{\sigma, u_1, \ldots, u_s} (1 - \alpha)G(\sigma) + \sum_{i=1}^{s} u_i, \text{ s.t. } (7.30), (7.31), \text{ and } u_i \geq 0, \quad i = 1, \ldots, s.$$

$$(7.32)$$

Theorem 7.20 *The solution* $(\sigma, u_1, \ldots, u_s)$ *defined by* $\sigma = \pi$ *and* $u_i = \alpha[F_i(\pi) - F_i(v)]$, *for* $i = 1, \ldots, s$, *where* π *is a schedule that minimizes* $\alpha \sum_{i=1}^{s} F_i(\sigma) + (1 - \alpha)G(\sigma)$, *is optimal for problem (7.32).*

Proof By definition of π, we have $\alpha \sum_{i=1}^{s} F_i(\pi) + (1-\alpha)G(\pi) \leq \alpha \sum_{i=1}^{s} F_i(v) + (1 - \alpha)G(v)$. Thus, the solution $(\sigma, u_1, \ldots, u_s)$ satisfies (7.31). Since by construction it also satisfies (7.30), it follows that this solution is feasible for problem (7.32). From (7.30), given any feasible solution $(\sigma, u_1, \ldots, u_s)$ to problem (7.32), its cost to the manufacturer, denoted by $Z(\sigma, u_1, \ldots, u_s)$, satisfies

$$Z(\sigma, u_1, \ldots, u_s) \geq \alpha \sum_{i=1}^{s} F_i(\sigma) + (1 - \alpha)G(\sigma) - \alpha \sum_{i=1}^{s} F_i(v). \quad (7.33)$$

Since $\alpha \sum_{i=1}^{s} F_i(\sigma) + (1 - \alpha)G(\sigma)$ is minimized when $\sigma = \pi$, the right-hand side of (7.33) is minimized when $\sigma = \pi$. Therefore, $\alpha \sum_{i=1}^{s} F_i(\pi) + (1 - \alpha)G(\pi) - \alpha \sum_{i=1}^{s} F_i(v)$ is a lower bound on optimal cost in problem (7.32). However, the cost of the solution given in the theorem equals this lower bound. Therefore, this solution is optimal for problem (7.32). $\square$

Theorem 7.20 implies that (i) problem (7.32) is feasible and hence the proposed cooperation mechanism can always be used, and (ii) the optimal strategy of the manufacturer is to provide an incentive of $u_i = \alpha[F_i(\pi) - F_i(v)]$ to each supplier S_i, for $i = 1, \ldots, s$. Consequently, the suppliers agree to use schedule π. It follows that the manufacturer's cost is equal to the optimal cost in problem (7.32), i.e., $\alpha \sum_{i=1}^{s}[F_i(\pi) - F_i(v)] + (1 - \alpha)G(\pi)$. In the absence of cooperation, schedule v is used and the manufacturer's cost is $(1 - \alpha)G(v)$. Thus, the net saving to the manufacturer from obtaining the suppliers' cooperation is

7.3 Sequencing in an Assembly System

$$(1 - \alpha)G(v) - \alpha \sum_{i=1}^{s} [F_i(\pi) - F_i(v)] - (1 - \alpha)G(\pi)$$

$$= \left[\alpha \sum_{i=1}^{s} F_i(v) + (1 - \alpha)G(v) \right] - \left[\alpha \sum_{i=1}^{s} F_i(\pi) + (1 - \alpha)G(\pi) \right], \quad (7.34)$$

which is also the difference between the total system cost under schedule v and under schedule π.

Remark 7.4 If v is not optimal for the system problem, then the net saving to the manufacturer in (7.34) is positive, hence the manufacturer should encourage the suppliers to use schedule π by providing the incentive u_i given in Theorem 7.20 to each supplier S_i, for $i = 1, \ldots, s$. However, if v is optimal for the system problem, then no incentive provided to the suppliers creates a net saving to the manufacturer. In this case, the suppliers use schedule v. In either case, the suppliers' total cost is no greater than the optimal cost given by schedule v. Since the suppliers use a schedule which is optimal for the system problem (i.e., either π or v if v is optimal for the system problem), the proposed cooperation mechanism is equivalent to centralized decision making for the system as a whole.

Theorem 7.20 shows that, whether $\pi = v$ or not, the optimal system schedule π is always achieved. Therefore, we need to operationalize this result by studying the solvability of the two system problems defined by our cooperation mechanism. In doing so, we note that α is fixed, and therefore the system problem does not directly generalize the related suppliers' or manufacturer's problem.

First, we consider problem $As||\alpha \sum\sum C_{ij} + (1 - \alpha) \sum C_j$.

Theorem 7.21 *The recognition version of problem $As||\alpha \sum\sum C_{ij} + (1-\alpha) \sum C_j$, where $0 < \alpha < 1$ is a fixed parameter, is unary NP-complete.*

Proof We first prove a similar result for problem $As|coseq|\alpha \sum\sum C_{ij} + (1 - \alpha) \sum C_j$. The proof is by reduction from 3-Partition, as described in the proof of Theorem 7.13. Construct an instance of problem $As|coseq|\alpha \sum\sum C_{ij} + (1 - \alpha) \sum C_j$ with $n = 4m$ and $s = 5$, where the job processing times at the first four suppliers are exactly the same as in the instance in the proof of Theorem 7.13, and the job processing times at supplier S_5 are identical to those at supplier S_1. Let the threshold cost be $C = \alpha[15Bn(n + 1)/2] + (1 - \alpha)(24m^2 B + 12mB)$. We prove that there exists a schedule for this instance of problem $As|coseq|\alpha \sum\sum C_{ij} + (1 - \alpha) \sum C_j$ with cost less than or equal to C if and only if there exists a solution to 3-Partition.

($\Rightarrow$) Consider the sequence $(1, 2, 3, 3m+1, \ldots, 3m-2, 3m-1, 3m, 4m)$. From the ($\Rightarrow$) part of the proof of Theorem 7.13, $(1 - \alpha) \sum C_j = (1 - \alpha)(24m^2 B + 12mB)$. Also, since $\sum_{i=1}^{s} p_{i1} = \cdots = \sum_{i=1}^{s} p_{in} = 15B$, we have $\alpha \sum\sum C_{ij} = \alpha[15B(1 + \cdots + n)] = \alpha[15Bn(n+1)/2]$. Thus, the total cost is $\alpha \sum\sum C_{ij} + (1-\alpha) \sum C_j = \alpha[15Bn(n + 1)/2)] + (1 - \alpha)(24m^2 B + 12mB) = C$.

$(\Leftarrow)$ Since $\sum_{i=1}^{s} p_{i1} = \cdots = \sum_{i=1}^{s} p_{in} = 15B$, and from Theorem 7.15, we have $\alpha \sum \sum C_{ij} = \alpha[15Bn(n+1)/2]$ for any sequence. The remainder of the proof follows from the $(\Leftarrow)$ part of the proof of Theorem 7.13.

We can now proceed to our main result for problem $As||\alpha \sum \sum C_{ij} + (1 - \alpha) \sum C_j$. The proof is by reduction from problem $As|coseq|\alpha \sum \sum C_{ij} + (1 - \alpha) \sum C_j$. Given an arbitrary instance of problem $As|coseq|\alpha \sum \sum C_{ij} + (1 - \alpha) \sum C_j$ defined by α, processing times p'_{ij}, and threshold cost C', we construct an instance of problem $As||\alpha \sum \sum C_{ij} + (1 - \alpha) \sum C_j$ with $p_{ij} = p'_{ij} + (C'+1)/(1-\alpha)$ and a threshold cost $C = C' + \alpha sn(n+1)(C'+1)/[2(1-\alpha)] + n(n+1)(C'+1)/2$. We prove that there exists a schedule for this instance of problem $As||\alpha \sum \sum C_{ij} + (1 - \alpha) \sum C_j$ with $\alpha \sum \sum C_{ij} + (1 - \alpha) \sum C_j \leq C$ if and only if there exists a schedule for problem $As|coseq|\alpha \sum \sum C_{ij} + (1 - \alpha) \sum C_j$ with $\alpha \sum \sum C_{ij} + (1 - \alpha) \sum C_j \leq C'$.

$(\Rightarrow)$ Let σ' denote a schedule for problem $As|coseq|\alpha \sum \sum C_{ij} + (1 - \alpha) \sum C_j$ that has $\alpha \sum \sum C_{ij} + (1 - \alpha) \sum C_j \leq C$. From the construction of the p_{ij} values, we have $\alpha \sum \sum C_{ij} + (1 - \alpha) \sum C_j \leq C' + \alpha sn(n+1)(C'+1)/[2(1-\alpha)] + n(n+1)(C'+1)/2 = C$ for σ' in the constructed instance of $As||\alpha \sum \sum C_{ij} + (1 - \alpha) \sum C_j$.

$(\Leftarrow)$ Let σ denote a schedule for the constructed instance of problem $As||\alpha \sum \sum C_{ij} + (1 - \alpha) \sum C_j$ that has $\alpha \sum \sum C_{ij} + (1 - \alpha) \sum C_j \leq C$. From the construction of the p_{ij} values, we have $\sum C'_j \leq C - \alpha sn(n+1)(C'+1)/[2(1-\alpha)] - n(n+1)(C'+1)/2 = C'$. It remains to prove that σ satisfies the common sequence requirement. First, in the constructed instance of problem $As||\alpha \sum \sum C_{ij} + (1 - \alpha) \sum C_j$, we must have

$$\sum \sum C_{ij} \geq \frac{sn(n+1)(C'+1)}{2(1-\alpha)}, \tag{7.35}$$

where this lower bound is obtained by assuming that $p_{ij} = 0$ for $i = 1, \ldots, s$, $j = 1, \ldots, n$. Second, if σ does not satisfy the common sequence requirement, then using the same assumption,

$$\sum C_j \geq \frac{(C'+1)[(1+\cdots+n)+1]}{(1-\alpha)} = \frac{n(n+1)(C'+1)}{2(1-\alpha)} + \frac{(C'+1)}{(1-\alpha)}. \tag{7.36}$$

Finally, from (7.35) and (7.36), we obtain

$$\alpha \sum \sum C_{ij} + (1-\alpha) \sum C_j \geq \frac{\alpha sn(n+1)(C'+1)}{2(1-\alpha)} + \frac{n(n+1)(C'+1)}{2} + (C'+1) > C.$$

This contradiction completes the proof. $\qquad\square$

Theorem 7.21 motivates the use of ISPT as a heuristic for problem $As||\alpha \sum \sum C_{ij} + (1 - \alpha) \sum C_j$.

7.3 Sequencing in an Assembly System 359

Theorem 7.22 *For problem $As||\alpha \sum \sum C_{ij} + (1 - \alpha) \sum C_j$, let the value of the solution delivered by ISPT be F^H and the optimal objective value be F^*. Then, $F^H \leq [s/(\alpha s - \alpha + 1)]F^*$.*

Proof Let C_{ij}^H and C_j^H denote the completion time of job j at supplier S_i and that at the manufacturer, respectively, in the schedule obtained by Heuristic ISPT and C_{ij}^* and C_j^* the job completion time of job j at supplier S_i and that at the manufacturer, respectively, in the optimal schedule. Since $\sum_{j \in N} C_j^* = \sum_{j \in N} \max_{1 \leq i \leq s}\{C_{ij}^*\} \geq \sum_{i=1}^s \sum_{j \in N} C_{ij}^*/s$, we have

$$F^* = \alpha \sum_{i=1}^s \sum_{j \in N} C_{ij}^* + (1 - \alpha) \sum_{j \in N} C_j^* \geq [\alpha + (1 - \alpha)/s] \sum_{i=1}^s \sum_{j \in N} C_{ij}^*$$

$$\geq [\alpha + (1 - \alpha)/s] \sum_{i=1}^s \sum_{j \in N} C_{ij}^H, \tag{7.37}$$

where the last inequality follows from Smith (1956). Also, since $\sum_{j \in N} C_j^H \leq \sum_{i=1}^s \sum_{j \in N} C_{ij}^H$, we have

$$F^H = \alpha \sum_{i=1}^s \sum_{j \in N} C_{ij}^H + (1 - \alpha) \sum_{j \in N} C_j^H \leq \sum_{i=1}^s \sum_{j \in N} C_{ij}^H. \tag{7.38}$$

Finally, from (7.37) and (7.38), we have

$$F^H \leq 1/[\alpha + (1 - \alpha)/s]F^* = [s/(\alpha s - \alpha + 1)]F^*. \qquad \square$$

Remark 7.5 It follows from Theorem 7.22 that Heuristic ISPT is optimal for problem $As|| \sum \sum C_{ij}$ and also performs well for problem $As||\alpha \sum \sum C_{ij} + (1 - \alpha) \sum C_j$ when α is close to 1. Alternatively, when α is close to zero, the problem is similar to $As|| \sum C_j$, for which we discuss a heuristic in Sect. 7.3.5.

Second, we consider problem $As||\alpha \sum \sum C_{ij} + (1-\alpha)L_{\max}$. Hoogeveen and van de Velde (1995) describe an $O(n^3 \log n)$ time algorithm for finding all the Pareto-optimal solutions for problem $1||F(\sum C_j, L_{\max})$, where F denotes an arbitrary linear additive objective function, and C_j denotes the completion time of job j on the single machine. We propose the following algorithm.

Algorithm SCL

1. For each supplier, apply the algorithm of Hoogeveen and van de Velde (1995) to find all the Pareto-optimal ($\sum C_j, L_{\max}$) pairs.

2. Sort the Pareto-optimal solutions for each supplier $i = 1, \ldots, s$ by nondecreasing order of $L_{\max}$ values. Let $(l_{i1}, \ldots, l_{ik_i})$ and $(\pi_{i1}, \ldots, \pi_{ik_i})$ denote the resulting list of $L_{\max}$ values and the associated schedules of supplier S_i, respectively, where k_i is the number of Pareto-optimal solutions for supplier S_i. Merge the lists $(l_{i1}, \ldots, l_{ik_i})$, for $i = 1, \ldots, s$, to create a single list $(l_{[1]}, \ldots, l_{[q]})$, where $l_{[1]} \leq \cdots \leq l_{[q]}$, and q is the number of different values of l_{ih}, for $i = 1, \ldots, s$, and $h = 1, \ldots, k_i$.
3. For each $l_{[h]}$, for $h = 1, \ldots, q$, do the following:
4. For each $i = 1, \ldots, s$, find index u_i from the list $(l_{i1}, \ldots, l_{ik_i})$ such that $l_{u_i} \leq l_{[h]}$ and l_{u_i} is closest to $l_{[h]}$ in this list.
5. Compute the total cost $\alpha \sum_{i=1}^{s} \sum_{j \in N} C_{ij}(\pi_{iu_i}) + (1 - \alpha)l_{[h]}$.
6. Select a solution with the minimum total cost.

Theorem 7.23 *Algorithm SCL solves problem* $As||\alpha \sum \sum C_{ij} + (1 - \alpha)L_{\max}$ *in* $O(sn^3 \log n)$ *time.*

Proof We first prove the optimality of Algorithm SCL. The total cost, $\alpha \sum \sum C_{ij} + (1 - \alpha)L_{\max}$, changes only at values of $L_{\max}$ that identify a Pareto-optimal solution. Therefore, it is only necessary to identify $L_{\max}$ values at which at least one supplier has such a solution. This is achieved for individual suppliers in Step 1 and by merging the suppliers' lists in Step 2. The comparison of all candidate solutions' costs in Step 3 thus identifies an optimal solution.

We now consider the time required by Algorithm SCL. From Hoogeveen and van de Velde (1995), Step 1 requires $O(sn^3 \log n)$ time. They also show that the list of Pareto-optimal points for a single supplier has $O(n^2)$ entries. Therefore, the lists can be sorted and merged in Step 2 in $O(sn^2 \log n + sn^2)$ time. Since each Pareto-optimal solution needs to be considered only once when $L_{\max}$ is monotonically increasing, Step 3 requires constant time for each of the entries in the merged list, i.e. $O(sn^2)$ time. Therefore, the overall time requirement of Algorithm SCL is $O(sn^3 \log n)$. □

7.3.4 Manufacturer Dominates and Suppliers Negotiate

Referring to Fig. 7.5, we consider a situation where the manufacturer has dominant bargaining power and chooses its optimal schedule γ. Here, the suppliers may prefer the manufacturer to choose some other schedule which is cheaper than γ for the suppliers. To resolve this conflict, we propose the following cooperation mechanism.

The suppliers collectively offer an incentive to the manufacturer to use a schedule that is cheaper for them than γ. Let v and σ denote the incentive provided by the suppliers and the schedule which the suppliers want the manufacturer to use,

7.3 Sequencing in an Assembly System

respectively. Similar to the derivation of (7.32), the suppliers are faced with the following optimization problem:

$$\min_{\sigma, v} \ \alpha \sum_{i=1}^{s} F_i(\sigma) + v \tag{7.39}$$

$$\text{s.t.} \ (1 - \alpha)G(\sigma) - v \le (1 - \alpha)G(\gamma) \tag{7.40}$$

$$\alpha \sum_{i=1}^{s} F_i(\sigma) + v \le \alpha \sum_{i=1}^{s} F_i(\gamma) \tag{7.41}$$

$$v \ge 0. \tag{7.42}$$

Theorem 7.24 *The solution (σ, v) defined by $\sigma = \pi$ and $v = (1 - \alpha)[G(\pi) - G(\gamma)]$ is optimal for problem (7.39)–(7.42), where π is the schedule that minimizes $\alpha \sum_{i=1}^{s} F_i(\sigma) + (1 - \alpha)G(\sigma)$.*

Proof The proof is similar to that of Theorem 7.20. □

Theorem 7.24 implies that (i) problem (7.39)–(7.42) is feasible, and therefore the proposed cooperation mechanism can always be used if the suppliers are willing to negotiate collectively with the manufacturer, and (ii) the optimal strategy of the suppliers is to provide collectively an incentive of $v = (1 - \alpha)[G(\pi) - G(\gamma)]$ to the manufacturer. Consequently, the manufacturer agrees to use schedule π, and the net saving to the suppliers from the manufacturer's cooperation is given by

$$\Delta = \alpha \sum_{i=1}^{s} F_i(\gamma) - \left\{ \alpha \sum_{i=1}^{s} F_i(\pi) + (1 - \alpha)[G(\pi) - G(\gamma)] \right\} \tag{7.43}$$

$$= \left[\alpha \sum_{i=1}^{s} F_i(\gamma) + (1 - \alpha)G(\gamma) \right] - \left[\alpha \sum_{i=1}^{s} F_i(\pi) + (1 - \alpha)G(\pi) \right] \ge 0.$$

The first and second terms in (7.43) are the suppliers' total cost without and with the manufacturer's cooperation, respectively.

Remark 7.6 If γ is not optimal for the system problem, then the net saving to the suppliers in (7.43) is positive, and hence the suppliers as a whole benefit from the manufacturer's cooperation. Here, the suppliers work together to provide the incentive v in Theorem 7.24 to the manufacturer, so that the manufacturer chooses schedule π. Theorem 7.24 shows that the suppliers prefer schedule π to v. If γ is optimal for the system problem, then the suppliers do not bargain with the manufacturer because they as a whole do not benefit from the manufacturer's cooperation.

7.3.5 Manufacturer Dominates and Suppliers Adjust

Again referring to Fig. 7.5, we recognize the reality that, in some practical supply chains, the manufacturer may not allow its suppliers to bargain. This occurs when a manufacturer is much larger and/or financially stronger than all of its suppliers. Here, since the suppliers have no bargaining power, they need to meet any requirements imposed by the manufacturer without compensation. We consider situations where the manufacturer's dominance allows it to impose two self-interested but natural requirements on the suppliers.

The first requirement arises from the manufacturer's choice of production sequence, γ. This requirement can be interpreted in two alternative ways: either that the suppliers face due dates implied by γ for all parts or that some delays in the manufacturer's schedule are permitted, subject to a predetermined limit on the resulting cost increase to the manufacturer. In either case, this requirement can be implemented by the suppliers individually, without cooperation between them.

The second requirement is that the suppliers all send the jobs to the manufacturer in some common sequence, so that the manufacturer's average lead time is minimized (see Lemma 7.7). One possible cooperation strategy for the suppliers is as follows. They find a schedule with the same sequence at each supplier that minimizes the total cost of the suppliers over all such sequences. We denote the problem of finding such a schedule by $As|coseq|\sum_{i=1}^{s} F_i$. We consider problem $As|coseq|\sum_{i=1}^{s} F_i$ with various objective functions. Let μ denote an optimal schedule to problem $As|coseq|\sum_{i=1}^{s} F_i$, which is chosen by the suppliers. Since μ is by definition no better than ν for supplier S_i, the cost of each supplier S_i increases by $\alpha[F_i(\mu) - F_i(\nu)] \geq 0$ when using μ instead of ν. Suppliers with a lower than average cost increase may need to compensate other suppliers.

In order to understand the scheduling problems faced by the suppliers as a result of the above requirements imposed by the manufacturer, we now discuss the solvability of the two manufacturer's problems, $As||\sum C_j$ and $As||L_{\max}$. Recall that Theorem 7.13 establishes the intractability of problem $As||\sum C_j$. Therefore, we now describe a heuristic, Batch, for this problem. We demonstrate that, under the following mild Assumption A about the job processing times, Batch provides solutions that are asymptotically optimal in the number of jobs.

Assumption A: The processing times p_{ij} take only integer values and follow an independent and identical discrete distribution $\Phi(\cdot)$ over a finite interval $[L_p, U_p]$, where L_p and U_p are nonnegative integers.

The intuition behind Heuristic Batch is to schedule most of the jobs in nondecreasing order of $\sum_{i=1}^{s} p_{ij}$ and use special sequences within jobs that have identical value of $\sum_{i=1}^{s} p_{ij}$. The heuristic first divides the jobs into different subsets based on their processing times. We refer to the vector of data $(p_{1j}, \ldots, p_{sj})$ associated with a job j as the *parameter vector* of this job. We divide the jobs in N into different *classes* such that all the jobs in a class have the same parameter vector, i.e., they are identical. Let $N_1, \ldots, N_K$ denote those classes of jobs, where $N = \cup_{k=1}^{K} N_k$. Note that K is finite even as $n \to \infty$.

7.3 Sequencing in an Assembly System

The following $O(sK^2)$ time subroutine partitions the set N into classes $N_1, \ldots, N_K$.

Subroutine Class

1. Define the first class by $N_1 = \{1\}$. Let $K = 1$.
2. For $j = 2, \ldots, n$, compare the parameter vector of job j with that of each of the K classes already created, $N_1, \ldots, N_K$. If job j is identical to the jobs in N_k for some k, $1 \le k \le K$, then let $N_k = N_k \cup \{j\}$. Otherwise, create a new class, $N_{K+1} = \{j\}$, and let $K = K + 1$.

Given a parameter vector $(x_1, x_2, \ldots, x_s)$, we define $s - 1$ *shifted vectors* (Kaminsky & Simchi-Levi, 1998) as follows:

$$(x_2, x_3, \ldots, x_s, x_1), (x_3, x_4, \ldots, x_s, x_1, x_2), \ldots, (x_s, x_1, \ldots, x_{s-1}).$$

We use the following $O(sK^2)$ time subroutine to combine the job classes $N_1, \ldots, N_K$ into $H \le K$ groups, $G_1, \ldots, G_H$, such that the parameter vector of each class in a group is a shifted vector of each of the other classes in this group. It follows that there are at most s classes in a group. We denote $G_h = \{Q_{1h}, \ldots, Q_{sh}\}$, where, for each $i = 1, \ldots, s$, Q_{ih} is either empty or $Q_{ih} = N_k$ for some k with $1 \le k \le K$. Note that H is finite even when $n \to \infty$.

Subroutine Group

1. Define the first group by $G_1 = \{N_1\}$. Let $H = 1$.
2. For $k = 2, \ldots, K$, compare the parameter vector of class N_k with that of each class in each group already created, $G_1, \ldots, G_H$. If the parameter vector of class N_k is a shifted vector of that of a class in some group G_h, for $1 \le h \le H$, then let $G_h = G_h \cup \{N_k\}$. Otherwise, create a new group, $G_{H+1} = \{N_k\}$, and let $H = H + 1$.

By construction, each job j in each group G_h (i.e., $j \in \cup_{i=1}^{s} Q_{ih}$) has identical total processing time $P_h = \sum_{i=1}^{s} p_{ij}$. We assume for the remainder of this section that groups $G_1, \ldots, G_H$ are indexed such that $P_1 \le \cdots \le P_H$. Let n_{ih} denote the number of jobs in class Q_{ih}, and define $n_h = \min\{n_{ih} \mid 1 \le i \le s\}$. Also, let $g_h = \sum_{i=1}^{s} n_{ih}$ denote the total number of jobs in group G_h, and define $\delta_h = \sum_{i=1}^{s} (n_{ih} - n_h)$.

Heuristic Batch

1. Divide the jobs of N into the H groups $G_1, \ldots, G_H$ as described above, by calling Subroutines Class and Group.
2. For each group $h = 1, \ldots, H$, do the following:
3. Form n_h batches of jobs, denoted as $B_{1h}, \ldots, B_{n_h,h}$, such that each batch consists of exactly s jobs, one from each job class Q_{ih} in G_h, for $i = 1, \ldots, s$.
4. For $k = 1, \ldots, n_h$, schedule the s jobs of batch B_{kh} consecutively in arbitrary order.
5. Schedule the jobs in $N \setminus (\cup_{h=1}^{H} \cup_{k=1}^{n_h} B_{kh})$ in arbitrary order at the end.

Steps 1 and 2 each requires $O(n)$ time. Thus, the overall time requirement of Heuristic Batch is $O(\max\{sK^2, n\})$. The job sequence generated by Heuristic Batch is

$$B_{11}, \ldots, B_{n_1,1}, B_{12}, \ldots, B_{n_2,2}, \ldots, B_{1H}, \ldots, B_{n_H,H}, N \setminus (\cup_{h=1}^{H} \cup_{k=1}^{n_h} B_{kh}).$$

For each batch B_{kh}, since the parameter vector of each of the s jobs in B_{kh} is a shifted vector of that of each other job, the total processing time of the s jobs of B_{kh} at each supplier S_i is the same and equal to P_h, i.e., $\sum_{j \in B_{kh}} p_{ij} = P_h$, for $i = 1, \ldots, s$. We begin our analysis of the performance of Heuristic Batch with two preliminary results.

Lemma 7.8 *The total completion time, Z^{Batch}, of the schedule generated by Heuristic Batch satisfies*

$$Z^{Batch} \leq \sum_{h=2}^{H} sn_h \left(\sum_{j=1}^{h-1} n_j P_j \right) + \sum_{h=1}^{H} P_h sn_h (n_h + 1) / 2 + \left(\sum_{h=1}^{H} \delta_h \right) \left(\sum_{h=1}^{H} (n_h + \delta_h) P_h \right).$$

Proof First, consider the jobs of B_{kh} for given k and h. It can be seen that the completion time of the last job of B_{kh} is $(\sum_{j=1}^{h-1} n_j P_j) + kP_h$. Thus, the total completion time of the s jobs in B_{kh} is no more than $s[(\sum_{j=1}^{h-1} n_j P_j) + kP_h]$. This implies that the total completion time of the jobs in $\cup_{h=1}^{H} \cup_{k=1}^{n_h} B_{kh}$ is no more than

$$\sum_{h=1}^{H} \sum_{k=1}^{n_h} s \left[\left(\sum_{j=1}^{h-1} n_j P_j \right) + kP_h \right] = \sum_{h=2}^{H} sn_h \left(\sum_{j=1}^{h-1} n_j P_j \right) + \sum_{h=1}^{H} P_h sn_h (n_h + 1) / 2. \tag{7.44}$$

Now, consider the jobs in the subset $N \setminus (\cup_{h=1}^{H} \cup_{k=1}^{n_h} B_{kh})$. The completion time of the last job in this subset is no more than $\sum_{h=1}^{H} (n_h + \delta_h) P_h$. Since in this subset there are exactly $\sum_{h=1}^{H} \delta_h$ jobs, the total completion time of the jobs in this subset is at most

$$\left(\sum_{h=1}^{H} \delta_h \right) \left(\sum_{h=1}^{H} (n_h + \delta_h) P_h \right). \tag{7.45}$$

The lemma then follows immediately from (7.44) and (7.45). $\square$

7.3 Sequencing in an Assembly System

Lemma 7.9 *The total completion time, Z^{OPT}, of an optimal schedule for problem $As||\sum C_j$ satisfies*

$$Z^{OPT} \geq \frac{1}{s}\left[\sum_{h=2}^{H} g_h \left(\sum_{j=1}^{h-1} g_j P_j\right) + \sum_{h=1}^{H} P_h \left(g_h^2 + g_h\right)/2\right].$$

We refer the reader to Chen and Hall (2007) for a proof.

Theorem 7.25 *If the processing times are generated according to Assumption A, then Heuristic Batch provides solutions that are asymptotically optimal in the number of jobs for problem $As||\sum C_j$. The time complexity of Batch is $O(\max\{sK^2, n\})$.*

Proof First, under Assumption A, for each $h = 1, \ldots, H$, there exists a constant θ_h with $0 < \theta_h < 1$ and $\sum_{h=1}^{H} \theta_h = 1$ such that $\lim_{n\to\infty} \frac{n_{ih}}{n} \overset{a.s.}{=} \theta_h$ for each $i = 1, \ldots, s$ and that $\lim_{n\to\infty} \frac{n_h}{n} \overset{a.s.}{=} \theta_h$, $\lim_{n\to\infty} \frac{g_h}{n} \overset{a.s.}{=} s\theta_h$, and $\lim_{n\to\infty} \frac{\delta_h}{n} \overset{a.s.}{=} 0$.

It is easy to see that the total completion time of the last batch of jobs in the schedule constructed by Heuristic Batch satisfies

$$\lim_{n\to\infty} \left(\sum_{h=1}^{H} \delta_h\right)\left(\sum_{h=1}^{H} (n_h + \delta_h) P_h\right)/n^2 = 0.$$

Thus, from Lemmas 7.8 and 7.9, respectively, we have

$$\lim_{n\to\infty} \frac{Z^{Batch}}{n^2} \leq \sum_{h=2}^{H} s\theta_h \left(\sum_{j=1}^{h-1} \theta_j P_j\right) + \sum_{h=1}^{H} s P_h \theta_h^2/2, \quad \text{and}$$

$$\lim_{n\to\infty} \frac{Z^{OPT}}{n^2} \geq \sum_{h=2}^{H} s\theta_h \left(\sum_{j=1}^{h-1} \theta_j P_j\right) + \sum_{h=1}^{H} s P_h \theta_h^2/2.$$

Since the right-hand sides of the above two inequalities are finite, these inequalities imply that

$$\lim_{n\to\infty} \frac{Z^{Batch} - Z^{OPT}}{n^2} \overset{a.s.}{=} 0, \quad \text{and}$$

$$\lim_{n\to\infty} \frac{Z^{Batch} - Z^{OPT}}{Z^{OPT}} \overset{a.s.}{=} 0.$$

The time requirement of Step 0 is determined by the running time of Subroutines Class and Group, as discussed above. Steps 1 and 2 each requires $O(n)$ time. Therefore, the overall computation time of Heuristic Batch is $O(\max\{sK^2, n\})$. $\quad\square$

Remark 7.7 Theorem 7.25 shows that, although problem $As||\sum C_j$ is formally intractable, close to optimal schedules can be found efficiently for large instances.

The other manufacturer's problem we consider is $As||L_{\max}$. Recall that Theorem 7.17 shows that this problem can be solved in $O(n \log n)$ time by sequencing the jobs in nondecreasing due date order.

Having studied the schedules which the manufacturer may choose, we now consider the solvability of the resulting suppliers' problems. Here, we first consider problems where the suppliers face due dates implied by the manufacturer's choice of schedule γ. In this case, it is natural for the suppliers to minimize their total cost, subject to a constraint "$L_{\max} \leq L$" on the maximum lateness with respect to those due dates. We show that this suppliers' problem is efficiently solvable.

Theorem 7.26 *Problem $As|L_{\max} \leq L|\sum\sum C_{ij}$ is solvable in $O(sn \log n)$ time.*

Proof In problem $As|L_{\max} \leq L|\sum\sum C_{ij}$, the constraint $L_{\max} \leq L$ can be enforced by requiring job j and therefore each part ij, where $i = 1, \ldots, s$, to satisfy $C_{ij} \leq \bar{d}_j = d_j + L$. This decomposes the problem into s instances of problem $1|\bar{d}_j|\sum C_j$, where $\bar{d}_j$ denotes a deadline on the maximum completion time of job j. From Smith (1956), these instances can be solved in a total of $O(sn \log n)$ time. $\quad\square$

As discussed above, an alternative interpretation of the requirement implied by the manufacturer's choice of schedule γ is that an upper bound constraint "$\sum C_j \leq C$" is imposed on the manufacturer's cost.

Theorem 7.27 *The recognition version of problem $As|\sum C_j \leq C|\sum\sum C_{ij}$ is unary NP-complete.*

We refer the reader to Chen and Hall (2007) for a proof that uses the result in Theorem 7.13.

Next, we consider the suppliers' scheduling problem implied by the second requirement to process all jobs in a common sequence or problem $As|coseq|\sum\sum C_{ij}$. Recall that Theorem 7.15 shows that this problem can be solved in $O(n \log n)$ time.

Finally, we consider problems where *both* requirements are imposed by the manufacturer on the suppliers. That is, they need to take schedule γ into account and also process the jobs in a common sequence.

Theorem 7.28 *The recognition version of problem $As|coseq, L_{\max} \leq L|\sum\sum C_{ij}$ is unary NP-complete.*

Proof Chen and Hall (2007) provide a reduction from 3-Partition. $\quad\square$

Theorem 7.29 *The recognition version of problem $As|coseq, \sum C_j \leq C|\sum\sum C_{ij}$ is unary NP-complete.*

7.3 Sequencing in an Assembly System

We refer the reader to Chen and Hall (2007) for a proof that uses the result in Theorem 7.13.

7.3.6 Suppliers and Manufacturer Cooperate

Once again referring to Fig. 7.5, we discuss conflict and cooperation where the suppliers and the manufacturer are all subsidized or fully owned by a single company. The company would like the suppliers and the manufacturer to use the system optimal schedule π because it minimizes the company's total cost. However, since π is in general not optimal for either the suppliers' or the manufacturer's problem, the company may have to provide an incentive for them to use π. We propose one possible incentive scheme that the company can use. Without cooperation between the suppliers and the manufacturer, either schedule v or schedule γ will be implemented, depending on whether the suppliers or the manufacturer selects the schedule. Thus, the potential reduction in total cost due to cooperation is at least

$$R_c = \min \left\{ \alpha \sum_{i=1}^{s} [F_i(v) - F_i(\pi)] + (1-\alpha)[G(v) - G(\pi)], \right.$$

$$\left. \alpha \sum_{i=1}^{s} [F_i(\gamma) - F_i(\pi)] + (1-\alpha)[G(\gamma) - G(\pi)] \right\}. \quad (7.46)$$

The suppliers and the manufacturer can be compensated using the cost saving R_c given in (7.46). Let u_i and v denote the amount of compensation provided to the supplier S_i, for $i = 1, \ldots, s$, and the manufacturer, respectively. Since the compensation is funded by the total cost saving, we require

$$\sum_{i=1}^{s} u_i + v \le R_c. \quad (7.47)$$

From Nash (1950, 1953), in order for the suppliers and the manufacturer to adopt schedule π, the compensation they receive, $(u_1, \ldots, u_s, v)$, must make them better off compared to their own optimal schedules. Thus, $(u_1, \ldots, u_s, v)$ must satisfy

$$\alpha F_i(\pi) - u_i \le \alpha F_i(v), \quad \text{for } i = 1, \ldots, s, \quad \text{and} \quad (7.48)$$

$$(1-\alpha)G(\pi) - v \le (1-\alpha)G(\gamma). \quad (7.49)$$

In general, if there exists a solution $(u_1, \ldots, u_s, v)$ satisfying (7.47), (7.48), and (7.49), then this mechanism can be used to achieve cooperation. This discussion leads to the following result.

Theorem 7.30 *There exists a solution* $(u_1, \ldots, u_s, v)$ *satisfying (7.47), (7.48), and (7.49), if and only if schedules* v, γ, *and* π *satisfy the following conditions:*

$$(1 - \alpha)[G(v) - G(\pi)] \geq 2\alpha \sum_{i=1}^{s} [F_i(\pi) - F_i(v)] + (1 - \alpha)[G(\pi) - G(\gamma)]$$

$$(7.50)$$

$$\alpha \sum_{i=1}^{s} [F_i(\gamma) - F_i(\pi)] \geq 2(1 - \alpha)[G(\pi) - G(\gamma)] + \alpha \sum_{i=1}^{s} [F_i(\pi) - F_i(v)].$$

$$(7.51)$$

Proof Let

$$u_i = \alpha[F_i(\pi) - F_i(v)], \quad \text{for } i = 1, \ldots, s, \quad \text{and} \tag{7.52}$$

$$v = (1 - \alpha)[G(\pi) - G(\gamma)]. \tag{7.53}$$

Clearly, the solution $(u_1, \ldots, u_s, v)$ satisfies (7.48) and (7.49). Since $\sum_{i=1}^{s} u_i + v = \alpha \sum_{i=1}^{s} [F_i(\pi) - F_i(v)] + (1 - \alpha)[G(\pi) - G(\gamma)]$, Eqs. (7.50) and (7.51) imply, respectively,

$$\sum_{i=1}^{s} u_i + v \leq \alpha \sum_{i=1}^{s} [F_i(v) - F_i(\pi)] + (1 - \alpha)[G(v) - G(\pi)], \quad \text{and} \tag{7.54}$$

$$\sum_{i=1}^{s} u_i + v \leq \alpha \sum_{i=1}^{s} [F_i(\gamma) - F_i(\pi)] + (1 - \alpha)[G(\gamma) - G(\pi)]. \tag{7.55}$$

It follows from (7.54) and (7.55) that the solution $(u_1, \ldots, u_s, v)$ satisfies (7.47). ($\Leftarrow$) Given a solution $(u_1, \ldots, u_s, v)$ satisfying (7.47), (7.48), and (7.49), we have

$$\alpha \sum_{i=1}^{s} [F_i(\pi) - F_i(v)] + (1 - \alpha)[G(\pi) - G(\gamma)] \leq \sum_{i=1}^{s} u_i + v \leq R_c,$$

which, using (7.46), implies

$$\alpha \sum_{i=1}^{s} [F_i(\pi) - F_i(v)] + (1 - \alpha)[G(\pi) - G(\gamma)]$$

$$\leq \alpha \sum_{i=1}^{s} [F_i(v) - F_i(\pi)] + (1 - \alpha)[G(v) - G(\pi)], \quad \text{and}$$

7.3 Sequencing in an Assembly System

$$\alpha \sum_{i=1}^{s} [F_i(\pi) - F_i(\nu)] + (1 - \alpha)[G(\pi) - G(\gamma)]$$

$$\leq \alpha \sum_{i=1}^{s} [F_i(\gamma) - F_i(\pi)] + (1 - \alpha)[G(\gamma) - G(\pi)],$$

which further imply (7.50) and (7.51), respectively. □

Theorem 7.30 shows that if schedules ν, γ, and π satisfy (7.50) and (7.51), then the proposed cooperation mechanism can be implemented. Checking these conditions requires finding schedules ν, γ, and π. Results for the suppliers' problems, to obtain ν, can be found in Theorems 7.12, 7.15, 7.26, 7.27, 7.28, and 7.29. Results for the manufacturer's problems, to obtain γ, can be found in Theorems 7.13, 7.17, and 7.25. Results for the system problems, to obtain π, can be found in Theorems 7.21, 7.22, and 7.23.

Remark 7.8 Some interpretation of (7.50) and (7.51) is useful here. Note that $F_i(\pi) \geq F_i(\nu)$, for $i = 1, \ldots, s$, and $G(\pi) \geq G(\gamma)$. Condition (7.50) means that, in order for the proposed cooperation mechanism to work, the maximum possible cost increase to the manufacturer as a result of no cooperation must be at least twice the total cost increase to all the suppliers plus the cost increase to the manufacturer as a result of cooperation. Similarly, condition (7.51) means that the maximum possible total cost increase to the suppliers as a result of no cooperation must be at least twice the cost increase to the manufacturer plus the total cost increase to the suppliers as a result of cooperation.

We now show how the solutions to the suppliers' and manufacturer's problems can be used to check whether the conditions of Theorem 7.30 can be satisfied, even if π is unknown. In general, the suppliers' problem $As||\sum_{i=1}^{s} F_i$ and the manufacturer's problem $As||G$ are easier to solve than the system problem $As||\alpha \sum_{i=1}^{s} F_i + (1 - \alpha)G$. Assuming that we already know ν and γ but not π, we find an upper bound on the cost of schedule π for the system problem as follows. Condition (7.50) implies that

$$\alpha \sum_{i=1}^{s} F_i(\pi) + (1 - \alpha)G(\pi) \leq \alpha \sum_{i=1}^{s} F_i(\nu) + (1 - \alpha)[G(\nu) + G(\gamma)]/2. \qquad (7.56)$$

Similarly, condition (7.51) implies that

$$\alpha \sum_{i=1}^{s} F_i(\pi) + (1 - \alpha)G(\pi) \leq \alpha \sum_{i=1}^{s} [F_i(\nu) + F_i(\gamma)]/2 + (1 - \alpha)G(\gamma). \qquad (7.57)$$

Combining (7.56) and (7.57), we obtain an upper bound on $\alpha \sum_{i=1}^{s} F_i(\pi) + (1 - \alpha)G(\pi)$ given by

$$
UB(\pi) = \alpha \sum_{i=1}^{s} F_i(\nu)/2 + (1 - \alpha)G(\gamma)/2
$$

$$
+ \frac{1}{2} \min \left\{ \alpha \sum_{i=1}^{s} F_i(\nu) + (1 - \alpha)G(\nu), \alpha \sum_{i=1}^{s} F_i(\gamma) + (1 - \alpha)G(\gamma) \right\}.
$$

$$(7.58)$$

Suppose that we have also found a lower bound, denoted by $LB(\pi)$, on $\alpha \sum_{i=1}^{s} F_i(\pi) + (1 - \alpha)G(\pi)$, by using mathematical programming techniques. Then, using (7.58), if $LB(\pi) > UB(\pi)$, we do not need to know π exactly in order to establish that the proposed cooperation mechanism is not implementable.

7.3.7 Cost Saving from Cooperation

We now computationally evaluate the cost saving from the various mechanisms for cooperation between the suppliers and the manufacturer proposed in Sects. 7.3.3, 7.3.4, and 7.3.6.

First, where the suppliers have dominant power in the supply chain, the mechanism for cooperation proposed in Sect. 7.3.3 provides a net saving given by (7.34) to the manufacturer. Without cooperation, the suppliers impose schedule ν, and therefore the relative cost saving to the manufacturer is

$$
z_{man} = \frac{\left[\alpha \sum_{i=1}^{s} F_i(\nu) + (1 - \alpha)G(\nu)\right] - \left[\alpha \sum_{i=1}^{s} F_i(\pi) + (1 - \alpha)G(\pi)\right]}{(1 - \alpha)G(\nu)}.
$$

$$(7.59)$$

Second, where the manufacturer has dominant power in the supply chain, the mechanism for cooperation proposed in Sect. 7.3.4 provides a total net saving given by (7.43) to the suppliers. Without cooperation, the manufacturer imposes schedule γ, and therefore the relative cost saving to the suppliers is

$$
z_{sup} = \frac{\left[\alpha \sum_{i=1}^{s} F_i(\gamma) + (1 - \alpha)G(\gamma)\right] - \left[\alpha \sum_{i=1}^{s} F_i(\pi) + (1 - \alpha)G(\pi)\right]}{\alpha \sum_{i=1}^{s} F_i(\gamma)}.
$$

$$(7.60)$$

Finally, where there is a decision maker in the supply chain who makes centralized decisions for the system, the mechanism for cooperation proposed in Sect. 7.3.6

7.3 Sequencing in an Assembly System

provides a net saving given by (7.46) to the system. There are two cases to be considered.

Case 1: If schedule ν is used without cooperation, then the relative cost saving to the system is

$$z_{sys(\nu)} = \frac{\left[\alpha \sum_{i=1}^{s} F_i(\nu) + (1-\alpha)G(\nu)\right] - \left[\alpha \sum_{i=1}^{s} F_i(\pi) + (1-\alpha)G(\pi)\right]}{\alpha \sum_{i=1}^{s} F_i(\nu) + (1-\alpha)G(\nu)}. \tag{7.61}$$

Case 2: If schedule γ is used without cooperation, then the relative cost saving to the system is

$$z_{sys(\gamma)} = \frac{\left[\alpha \sum_{i=1}^{s} F_i(\gamma) + (1-\alpha)G(\gamma)\right] - \left[\alpha \sum_{i=1}^{s} F_i(\pi) + (1-\alpha)G(\pi)\right]}{\alpha \sum_{i=1}^{s} F_i(\gamma) + (1-\alpha)G(\gamma)}. \tag{7.62}$$

As throughout this section, we consider two combinations of cost functions: (1) the suppliers' cost function $F_i = \sum_{j \in N} C_{ij}$, for $i = 1, \ldots, s$, and the manufacturer's cost function $G = \sum_{j \in N} C_j$ and (2) the suppliers' cost function $F_i = \sum_{j \in N} C_{ij}$, for $i = 1, \ldots, s$, and the manufacturer's cost function $G = L_{\max}$. In the following subsections, we estimate the four relative cost savings defined by (7.59)–(7.62).

7.3.7.1 Completion Time and Completion Time

From Theorem 7.12, schedule ν consists of an SPT order of the jobs at each supplier. However, from Theorems 7.13 and 7.21, finding schedules γ and π, respectively, is intractable. Therefore, instead of finding γ and π exactly, we compute an upper or a lower bound on the cost of an optimal schedule. We derive an upper bound $UB_{sys}(\pi)$ on the system cost $\alpha \sum\sum C_{ij}(\pi) + (1-\alpha)\sum C_j(\pi)$, a lower bound $LB_{sup}(\gamma)$ on the suppliers' total cost $\alpha \sum\sum C_{ij}(\gamma)$, and a lower bound $LB_{man}(\gamma)$ on the manufacturer's cost $(1-\alpha)\sum C_j(\gamma)$.

The upper bound $UB_{sys}(\pi)$ is found using a simulated annealing (Koulamas et al., 1994) heuristic for problem $As \| \alpha \sum\sum C_{ij} + (1-\alpha)\sum C_j$. An initial schedule is given by an SPT order of the jobs at each supplier. The neighborhood used is pairwise exchange of job positions at a supplier. Any schedule σ that is found becomes the new seed schedule with probability $e^{-a\Delta(\sigma)}$, where $\Delta(\sigma)$ is the relative difference in the costs of σ and the incumbent schedule, and a is a positive parameter. The value of a increases from 10 to 50 during the procedure. If no new incumbent schedule is found during 10,000 consecutive iterations, then the heuristic terminates.

We let $LB_{sup}(\gamma) = \alpha \sum \sum C_{ij}(\rho)$, where schedule ρ is generated by Heuristic STPT described in Sect. 7.3.2.1. From (7.13), $LB_{sup}(\gamma)$ provides a lower bound on $\alpha \sum \sum C_{ij}(\gamma)$.

The lower bound $LB_{man}(\gamma)$ is derived from the following observations. It is easy to show that for any given parameters $(v_1, \ldots, v_s)$ with $v_i \geq 0$ and $\sum_{i=1}^{s} v_i = 1$, we have

$$\sum_{j \in N} C_j(\gamma) = \sum_{j \in N} \max_{i=1,\ldots,s} \{C_{ij}(\gamma)\} \geq \sum_{j \in N} \sum_{i=1}^{s} v_i C_{ij}(\gamma). \tag{7.63}$$

It can be shown that the term $\sum_{j \in N} \sum_{i=1}^{s} v_i C_{ij}$ is minimized over schedules with identical sequences at all suppliers if the jobs are scheduled in nondecreasing order of $\sum_{i=1}^{s} v_i p_{ij}$ at all suppliers. Let the schedule corresponding to nondecreasing order of $\sum_{i=1}^{s} v_i p_{ij}$ be denoted by $\theta(v_1, \ldots, v_s)$. From Lemma 7.7, we may assume that schedule γ uses identical sequences at all suppliers. Therefore,

$$\sum_{j \in N} \sum_{i=1}^{s} v_i C_{ij}(\gamma) \geq \sum_{j \in N} \sum_{i=1}^{s} v_i C_{ij}(\theta(v_1, \ldots, v_s)). \tag{7.64}$$

Then, for any nonnegative numbers $v_1, \ldots, v_s$ with $\sum_{i=1}^{s} v_i = 1$, (7.63) and (7.64) imply that

$$\sum_{j \in N} C_j(\gamma) \geq \sum_{j \in N} \sum_{i=1}^{s} v_i C_{ij}(\theta(v_1, \ldots, v_s)). \tag{7.65}$$

We use a simulated annealing heuristic to search for values of $v_1, \ldots, v_s$ such that the right-hand side of (7.65) is as large as possible. This heuristic is similar to that used to find $UB_{sys}(\pi)$. Let the values of $v_1, \ldots, v_s$ found by this heuristic be denoted by $\bar{v}_1, \ldots, \bar{v}_s$, respectively. Let $LB_{man}(\gamma) = (1 - \alpha) \sum_{j \in N} \sum_{i=1}^{s} \bar{v}_i C_{ij}(\theta(\bar{v}_1, \ldots, \bar{v}_s))$. It follows from (7.65) that $LB_{man}(\gamma)$ is a lower bound on $(1 - \alpha) \sum_{j \in N} C_j(\gamma)$.

Using the bounds $UB_{sys}(\pi)$, $LB_{sup}(\gamma)$, and $LB_{man}(\gamma)$ to replace, respectively, $\alpha \sum \sum C_{ij}(\pi) + (1 - \alpha) \sum C_j(\pi)$, $\alpha \sum \sum C_{ij}(\gamma)$, and $(1 - \alpha) \sum C_j(\gamma)$ in (7.59)–(7.62), we obtain

$$z_{man} \geq \max \left\{ 0, \frac{\alpha \sum_{i=1}^{s} \sum_{j \in N} C_{ij}(v) + (1 - \alpha) \sum_{j \in N} C_j(v) - UB_{sys}(\pi)}{(1 - \alpha) \sum_{j \in N} C_j(v)} \right\}, \tag{7.66}$$

$$z_{sup} \geq \max \left\{ 0, 1 - \frac{UB_{sys}(\pi) - LB_{man}(\gamma)}{LB_{sup}(\gamma)} \right\}, \tag{7.67}$$

7.3 Sequencing in an Assembly System

$$z_{sys(v)} \geq \max\left\{0, 1 - \frac{UB_{sys}(\pi)}{\alpha \sum_{i=1}^{s}\sum_{j\in N} C_{ij}(v) + (1-\alpha)\sum_{j\in N} C_j(v)}\right\}, \quad \text{and}$$

(7.68)

$$z_{sys(\gamma)} \geq \max\left\{0, 1 - \frac{UB_{sys}(\pi)}{LB_{sup}(\gamma) + LB_{man}(\gamma)}\right\}.$$

(7.69)

We compute the lower bounds in (7.66)–(7.69) using random test problems generated as follows: (i) the number of suppliers $s \in \{2, 4, 8\}$, (ii) the number of jobs $n \in \{25, 50, 100\}$, (iii) the job processing times p_{ij} are independently drawn from a uniform integer distribution over the interval [10, 100], and (iv) the relative cost parameter $\alpha \in \{0.2, 0.5, 0.8\}$. For each (s, n, α) combination, 10 random instances are generated and the lower bounds on z_{man}, z_{sup}, $z_{sys(v)}$, and $z_{sys(\gamma)}$ are computed. The mean lower bounds over the 10 random instances are reported in Table 7.12(a). The cost saving depends on the relative cost parameter (α) and the problem size (s, n). The relative cost saving to the manufacturer (z_{man}) and to the system ($z_{sys(v)}$) when the suppliers' optimal schedule v is used without cooperation is larger when α is small. For example, z_{man} and $z_{sys(v)}$ are always at least 12.5% when $\alpha \leq 0.2$. By contrast, the relative cost saving to the suppliers as a whole (z_{sup}) and to the system ($z_{sys(\gamma)}$) when the manufacturer's optimal schedule γ is used without cooperation is larger when α is large. In particular, z_{sup} and $z_{sys(\gamma)}$ are always at least 10.1% when $\alpha \geq 0.5$ and $s \geq 8$. The relative cost savings on z_{man} (respectively, z_{sup}) are consistently larger than those on $z_{sys(v)}$ (respectively, $z_{sys(\gamma)}$). The reason is that a schedule typically has more impact on an individual party in the system (i.e., the suppliers or the manufacturer) than on the entire system. This is because positive and negative effects may cancel each other out within the system objective, and hence the overall system performance may not be as good (or as bad).

7.3.7.2 Completion Time and Maximum Lateness

From Theorem 7.12, schedule v is an SPT order of the jobs at each supplier. From Theorem 7.17, schedule γ is an EDD order of the jobs. Schedule π, which is optimal for problem $As||\alpha \sum\sum C_{ij} + (1-\alpha)L_{max}$, can be found by Algorithm SCL which from Theorem 7.23 runs in polynomial time (see Sect. 7.3.3).

We compute the relative cost savings z_{man}, z_{sup}, $z_{sys(v)}$, and $z_{sys(\gamma)}$ defined, respectively, in (7.59), (7.60), (7.61), and (7.62), using random test problems generated as follows: (i) s, n, and p_{ij} are generated as in Sect. 7.3.7.1, (ii) the job due dates d_j are independently drawn from a uniform integer distribution over the interval $[10, 55n]$, and (iii) the relative cost parameter $\alpha = \beta/n$, where $\beta \in \{0.5, 2, 8\}$. The values of α are selected such that both cost components play a significant role and that a wide range of values for the relative cost saving is considered. Since the completion time of the last job is approximately $55n$ and the due dates are generated from the interval $[10, 55n]$, it can be expected that L_{max}

Table 7.12 Relative cost saving from cooperation

s	n	α	(a) Lower bound on relative cost saving				s	n	α	(b) Relative cost saving			
			z_{man}	z_{sup}	$z_{sys(v)}$	$z_{sys(\gamma)}$				z_{man}	z_{sup}	$z_{sys(v)}$	$z_{sys(\gamma)}$
2	25	0.2	16.76%	0.00%	12.50%	0.00%	2	25	0.5/25	69.85%	12.68%	47.00%	9.29%
		0.5	10.93%	1.66%	4.63%	1.10%			2/25	56.12%	16.50%	18.35%	15.22%
		0.8	4.30%	6.45%	0.67%	5.72%			8/25	34.67%	21.34%	2.87%	21.02%
2	50	0.2	18.58%	0.00%	13.76%	0.00%	2	50	0.5/50	78.35%	13.46%	54.74%	10.71%
		0.5	12.15%	1.53%	5.08%	1.02%			2/50	66.35%	17.58%	23.90%	16.53%
		0.8	4.62%	5.82%	0.70%	5.17%			8/50	46.07%	21.94%	5.06%	21.64%
2	100	0.2	18.51%	0.00%	13.79%	0.00%	2	100	0.5/100	82.37%	12.70%	58.38%	10.74%
		0.5	11.54%	1.99%	4.87%	1.33%			2/100	69.26%	17.14%	25.97%	16.40%
		0.8	3.75%	6.71%	0.58%	5.96%			8/100	50.01%	22.13%	6.18%	21.90%
4	25	0.2	23.95%	0.00%	15.57%	0.00%	4	25	0.5/25	64.00%	16.76%	33.89%	13.63%
		0.5	14.99%	6.17%	4.75%	4.90%			2/25	49.63%	19.70%	10.83%	18.69%
		0.8	6.07%	11.33%	0.63%	10.64%			8/25	28.18%	22.71%	1.32%	22.48%
4	50	0.2	25.89%	0.03%	16.88%	0.01%	4	50	0.5/50	74.85%	16.86%	41.24%	14.73%
		0.5	16.06%	6.88%	5.12%	5.49%			2/50	60.18%	20.23%	13.81%	19.55%
		0.8	5.95%	11.92%	0.62%	11.21%			8/50	39.81%	23.45%	2.44%	23.27%
4	100	0.2	26.31%	0.00%	17.17%	0.00%	4	100	0.5/100	77.63%	15.76%	43.37%	14.19%
		0.5	15.93%	7.01%	5.09%	5.60%			2/100	62.38%	19.88%	14.86%	19.36%
		0.8	4.28%	12.04%	0.45%	11.32%			8/100	43.73%	23.45%	3.00%	23.31%
		0.2	24.94%	2.66%	13.07%	1.73%			0.5/25	60.68%	19.17%	22.54%	17.08%

8	25	0.5	15.08%	11.47%	3.25%	10.12%	8	25	2/25	44.25%	21.52%	5.40%	20.91%
		0.8	6.04%	15.41%	0.39%	14.91%			8/25	24.01%	23.55%	0.60%	23.42%
8	50	0.2	26.76%	3.71%	14.05%	2.45%			0.5/50	68.37%	19.00%	26.59%	17.50%
		0.5	16.07%	12.31%	3.48%	10.91%	8	50	2/50	51.56%	21.93%	6.91%	21.49%
		0.8	4.59%	16.23%	0.3%	15.72%			8/50	32.76%	24.18%	1.08%	24.07%
8	100	0.2	27.02%	3.49%	14.24%	2.32%			0.5/100	71.17%	18.51%	28.14%	17.43%
		0.5	14.28%	12.16%	3.11%	10.80%	8	100	2/100	54.05%	22.31%	7.51%	21.98%
		0.8	0.13%	16.41%	0.01%	15.91%			8/100	36.69%	24.84%	1.34%	24.75%

(a) Completion time and completion time

(b) Completion time and maximum lateness

should be $O(n)$, almost surely. Since $\sum\sum C_{ij}$ is $O(n^2)$, by using $\alpha = O(1/n)$ in our experiment, the magnitude of $\alpha \sum\sum C_{ij}$ matches that of $(1 - \alpha)L_{\max}$ at $O(n)$, which makes our test problems representative. For each (s, n, α) combination, 10 random instances are generated and the values of z_{man}, z_{sup}, $z_{sys(v)}$, and $z_{sys(\gamma)}$ are computed. The mean values of these measures over the 10 random instances are reported in Table 7.12b. From these results, we conclude that, in most cases, the proposed cooperation mechanism results in significant cost reductions for the decision makers. In fact, all results for z_{man}, z_{sup}, and $z_{sys(\gamma)}$ show a relative cost saving of at least 9.2%. The explanation of the results is similar to that for Table 7.12a.

7.3.8 Extensions

Chen and Hall (2007) study two practical extensions of the assembly system model, for nonzero transportation times between the suppliers and the manufacturer and for bottleneck processing operations at the manufacturer. Let t_{ij} denote the transportation time for part i of job j. We briefly summarize the results.

Theorem 7.31 *Problem $As|t_{ij}|L_{\max}$ is solvable in $O(ns \log n)$ time.*

Proof For $i = 1, \ldots, s$, define $d_{ij} = d_j - t_{ij}$ and $L_{ij} = C_{ij} - d_{ij}$, for $j = 1, \ldots, n$, and $L_{\max}^i = \max_{1 \le j \le n}\{L_{ij}\}$. Here, d_{ij} represents the due date by which all parts for job j must be completed at supplier S_i if job j is on time. Since $L_{\max} = \max_{1 \le i \le s}\{L_{\max}^i\}$, it follows from Jackson (1955) that an optimal schedule is found when each supplier S_i sequences its parts in nondecreasing d_{ij} order. $\square$

Theorem 7.32 *Problem $As|t_{ij}|\alpha \sum\sum C_{ij} + (1 - \alpha)L_{\max}$ is solvable in $O(sn^3 \log n)$ time.*

Proof Define d_{ij}, L_{ij}, and $L_{\max}^i$ as in the proof of Theorem 7.31. Apply Algorithm SCL, replacing $L_{\max}$ by $L_{\max}^i$ throughout. The proof follows that of Theorem 7.23. $\square$

Theorem 7.33 *Problem $As|t_{ij}, L_{\max} \le L|\sum\sum C_{ij}$ is solvable in $O(ns \log n)$ time.*

Proof Define d_{ij} as in the proof of Theorem 7.31. The constraint $L_{\max} \le L$ can be enforced by requiring each part ij to satisfy $C_{ij} \le d_{ij} + L$. The remainder of the proof follows that of Theorem 7.26. $\square$

In the presence of bottleneck operations at the manufacturer, the recognition versions of manufacturer's or system problems with $\sum C_j$ objective are unary NP-complete, since they are generalizations of problem $As||\sum C_j$, as discussed in Theorem 7.13. Also, the recognition versions of the manufacturer's and system problems with $L_{\max}$ objective are unary NP-complete, since they are generalizations of the two-machine flowshop problem $F_2||L_{\max}$ (Lenstra et al., 1977).

The study of assembly systems presented in this section highlights the need for coordination between suppliers in delivering their parts in a horizontal supply chain. This issue assumes increasing importance as a result of the more frequent use of platform-based supply networks which often unite suppliers who have not worked together previously.

7.4 Manufacturer and Distributor

This section studies coordinated decision making between a manufacturer and a distributor in two practical distribution systems. Problem 1 is motivated by Hurter and van Buer (1996), who study coordination between the printing (i.e., manufacturing) and distribution departments of a newspaper company. Here, the printing department prefers to produce jobs according to an ideal schedule that minimizes overall production time, whereas the distribution department prefers that products which will be shipped over longer distances are produced first. Hurter and van Buer's objective is to reduce the number of vans required to deliver the newspapers to drop-off points while satisfying the vehicle capacity and time constraints. Their methodology is to solve several instances of the capacitated vehicle routing problem with time windows and then to design a production schedule that supports the resulting routes. They assume that the printing and distribution departments cooperate on this schedule. They compare their results with the prevailing practice at a medium-sized newspaper company and demonstrate a significant reduction in the number of vans required and the total distribution time.

In a more general context, Problem 1 is a scheduling problem in which a manufacturer produces variations of a single perishable product and a distributor must deliver the appropriate variation to each of several customers by specified times within a single day. A setup time occurs when the manufacturer changes from the production of one variation of the product to another. Conflict arises because the manufacturer prefers a schedule with a minimum number of setups, whereas the distributor prefers a schedule in which all products are delivered by a certain time.

Problem 2 is motivated by Blumenfeld et al. (1991), who consider a coordination problem in which one producer makes several products and has several customers, each cyclically receiving its specific product type. The production sequence is based on setup and in-process inventory costs; however, the distribution schedule depends on freight and in-transit inventory costs. Their objective is the minimization of overall inventory costs, and they analyze the tradeoff between the benefits of coordination and increased management complexity.

More generally, Problem 2 is a scheduling problem in which a manufacturer produces two products on a single production line, and a distributor has to manage inventory and deliver specified combinations of the different products to several retailers within a planning horizon. There is a setup cost when the manufacturer changes from the production of one product to another. This problem arises, among other situations, in the manufacture and distribution of household cleaners (Lee

& Tse, 1992) and in food processing (Claassen et al., 2016). The manufacturer prefers a schedule that produces individual products in large batch sizes, in order to minimize total setup costs. However, in order to minimize its inventory holding cost, the distributor prefers a schedule that batches products which are shipped together to retailers.

Both of these problems create a need for the manufacturer and the distributor to coordinate their decisions within the supply chain. In each, the manufacturer and the distributor may or may not be part of the same company. For example, in some cities with two newspapers, one newspaper is printed on presses owned by the other but distributed separately; in this case, schedules and fees must be negotiated. Ideally, the manufacturer and the distributor can agree on a common schedule that minimizes the overall system cost. In each problem, we computationally evaluate the benefits of cooperation using performance measures from classical scheduling.

This section is organized as follows. In Sect. 7.4.1, we formally define the two problems considered and describe our notation and assumptions. Section 7.4.2 presents an evaluation of the conflict that results when one decision maker imposes its optimal schedule on the other. Section 7.4.3 considers the effect of different assumptions about the relative bargaining power of the manufacturer and the distributor. This requires solving the scheduling problem of the nondominant decision maker under a constraint imposed by the dominant decision maker. In Sect. 7.4.4, we solve the overall system problems and evaluate the cost savings that result from coordination between the manufacturer and the distributor. We also discuss how manufacturers and distributors can negotiate, coordinate, and implement their supply chain schedules in practice.

7.4.1 Problem Descriptions

7.4.1.1 Problem 1

Besides the newspaper application mentioned above, Problem 1 is also applicable to various process industries, such as industrial chemicals (Lei et al., 2006). Consider a newspaper publisher, for example, the *Dallas Morning News*, which serves a large metropolitan area. Each day, it produces an issue that contains five standard sections: *News*, *Metropolitan*, *Sports*, *Business*, and *Living*. There are also supplements, such as community news, event listings, and advertisements, that are specific to downtown or suburban zones within the metropolitan area. Each zone receives its own specific version of each day's issue. To formulate this problem for a general newspaper, let n be the number of different editions printed, one for each of n delivery zones. Zone Z_i, for $i = 1, \ldots, n$, is divided into ℓ_i subzones, each with a single local distribution center. The jth distribution center in zone Z_i is denoted by Z_{ij}.

We describe the manufacturing process. The printer generally does not begin processing until midnight, so that it can include information (including zone-specific

7.4 Manufacturer and Distributor

379

news) that is as up to date as possible. Let job J_{ij} denote the printing of enough copies of all sections and supplements required to serve distribution center Z_{ij}. Let schedule σ denote the order in which all jobs J_{ij}, for $i = 1, \ldots, n$, $j = 1, \ldots, \ell_i$, are processed nonpreemptively in the production system. In Corollary 7.1 below, we show that there is no advantage for either the printer or the distributor to consider preemptive schedules. If the printer uses schedule σ, then the time at which the printing of job J_{ij} completes is denoted by $C_{ij}^M(\sigma)$. Before printing a job for a subzone within Z_i, the printing presses must be set up for that zone, which requires time s_i. If jobs for two different subzones within the same zone are performed, then no additional setup is required between them.

Now consider the distribution process. Newspapers are delivered by truck from the plant to the distribution centers. In large metropolitan areas, adult carriers using automobiles then pick up the newspapers from the distribution centers and deliver them to subscribers' homes (Hurter & van Buer, 1999). Subscribers are allocated to carriers, and carriers are assigned to distribution centers so that each distribution center receives and distributes one truckload of newspapers. The travel time from the plant to distribution center Z_{ij} is denoted by t_{ij}. The delivery of newspapers to center Z_{ij} has due date d_{ij}, which is based on the time required by the carriers for delivery; for most distribution centers, this time is between 4:00 AM and 4:30 AM. If the printer uses schedule σ and the distributor uses schedule ν, then the time at which the delivery to center Z_{ij} is completed is denoted by $C_{ij}^D(\sigma, \nu)$.

Our assumption that each distribution center receives and distributes one truckload of newspapers is not restrictive. If multiple truckloads are demanded by a distribution center, then this assumption can be made without loss of generality, since we can treat that center's location as though it has multiple distribution centers, each of which demands one truckload. Hence, the time required for the printer to produce enough newspapers for any distribution center within zone Z_i is a constant, which we denote by p_i.

Since the printer does not deal directly with the customers, its goal is to minimize its overhead costs. Hence, its objective is to find a schedule σ^m that minimizes $C_{\max}^M(\sigma) = \max_{1 \leq i \leq n} \max_{1 \leq j \leq \ell_i} \{C_{ij}^M(\sigma)\}$ over all production schedules σ. The distributor aims to deliver each truckload of newspapers before its due date. This objective can be operationalized by using maximum lateness, a number of tardy jobs, or total tardiness objectives. We choose the maximum lateness objective over the number of tardy jobs because it is preferred to have several subzones' newspapers delivered to customers slightly late (for example, at 6:10 AM instead of at 6:00 AM) rather than one or two subzones' newspapers delivered very late (for example, at 7:30 AM or 8:00 AM). The total tardiness objective does not capture precisely the late deliveries to individual customers and is, therefore, not an attractive choice; moreover, the total tardiness problem is known to be *NP*-hard (Du & Leung, 1990).

Therefore, we consider the distributor's objective to minimize

$$L_{\max}^D(\sigma, v) = \max_{1 \le i \le n} \max_{1 \le j \le \ell_i} \{L_{ij}^D(\sigma, v)\}$$

for a given σ, over all v, where $L_{ij}^D(\sigma, v) = C_{ij}^D(\sigma, v) - d_{ij}$.

The system problem is to minimize

$$\alpha C_{\max}^M(\sigma) + (1 - \alpha) L_{\max}^D(\sigma, v),$$

where α is a parameter satisfying $0 \le \alpha \le 1$, over all schedules σ and v.

7.4.1.2 Problem 2

In Problem 2, two closely related products P_1 and P_2 are manufactured on the same production line. The products are to be distributed to n retailers $R_i, i = 1, \dots, n$, by trucks, each with a fixed capacity C. Define a *period* as the time required to produce one truckload of items. This time is Ct, where t is the fixed length of the interval between the completion of two consecutive items and t is the same for each product. After the production line starts producing a product, it restricts production to that product for a duration of time which is an integer multiple of Ct. This process is used because a setup is required for changing the production from one product to the other. The cost of each setup is μ.

At the end of each period, the manufacturer transfers one truckload containing a single product to the distributor. Let the ratio of the demands for the two products for retailer R_i be $r_{1i} : r_{2i}$, where $r_{1i} + r_{2i} = 1, i = 1, \dots, n$. For some retailer R_i of the distributor's choosing, the distributor sends a shipment containing $b_{1i} = r_{1i}C$ units of product P_1 and $b_{2i} = r_{2i}C$ units of product P_2. Thus, within time nCt, which represents a complete *distribution cycle*, each retailer receives exactly one truckload of the products. That is, the plant is operating at full capacity and the total demand from each retailer during each distribution cycle is at least C, so the total demand is not necessarily satisfied.

Remark 7.9 If multiple truckloads are demanded by a retailer R_i, we assume that each delivered truckload is required to have a mix of the two products in the ratio $r_{1i} : r_{2i}$. This assumption is natural in that it matches supply with demand at the retailers as well as defining a simple truck loading policy for the distributor. Under this assumption, it can be further assumed without any loss of generality that each retailer demands one truckload of products. If multiple truckloads are demanded by a retailer, then we treat that retailer as multiple retailers, each of which demands one truckload.

Assuming that the inventory for each product at the beginning of the distribution cycle must equal the inventory at the end of the distribution cycle, the total number of periods devoted to producing product P_j during the distribution cycle is $k_j =$

7.4 Manufacturer and Distributor

$\frac{\sum_{i=1}^{n} b_{ji}}{C}$. Hence, $k_1 + k_2 = n$. We assume k_1 and k_2 to be integers. The distribution cycle's schedule is defined by a *production sequence* σ that specifies which product is produced during each of the n periods, and a *distribution sequence* v that specifies which retailer is served at the end of each of the n periods. This cyclic schedule is then repeated until the end of the planning horizon. This model is suitable for products that have a stable demand over the planning horizon. For example, the demand for laundry products is typically stable during the winter period in North America (Lee & Tse, 1992).

Let I_{js} denote the inventory level of product P_j, $j = 1, 2$, at the end of period s. At the beginning of each distribution cycle, some initial inventory I_{j0} of product P_j is kept in order to satisfy demand in the early periods, if needed; this amount depends on the production sequence and the delivery sequence. The inventory holding cost per production period for product P_j is h_j per unit. The holding cost for product P_j in a period s is computed using the period's average inventory: $h_j(I_{js-1} + I_{js})/2$, $j = 1, 2$.

We assume a make-to-order manufacturer. Since the manufacturer knows the exact demands of the two products during a distribution cycle, it does not need to hold any inventory. The manufacturer's problem is to minimize the total manufacturing cost (i.e., production cost + setup cost) per distribution cycle. Since the production cost during a distribution cycle is constant, minimizing the total manufacturing cost is equivalent to minimizing the total setup cost. Let $S(\sigma)$ denote the total setup cost in one distribution cycle for schedule σ. For the distributor, it is necessary to hold inventory. This is because the production lots for both the products are in multiples of C, the fixed truck capacity. At the end of each period, one truckload of C units consisting entirely of one product is delivered to the distributor. However, in each period, the distributor has to supply a retailer, say R_i, with a mix of the two products with quantities $b_{1i} = r_{1i}C$ and $b_{2i} = r_{2i}C$, respectively, where $r_{1i} + r_{2i} = 1$. Thus, the distributor must incur inventory holding cost.

Given σ, the distributor's problem is to find a distribution sequence $v(\sigma)$ that minimizes its total inventory cost, $T(\sigma, v(\sigma))$.

The system problem is to minimize $\alpha S(\sigma) + (1 - \alpha)T(\sigma, v(\sigma))$, where α is a parameter, $0 \le \alpha \le 1$, over all production sequences σ and distribution sequences v.

7.4.2 Cost of Conflict

We consider the extent to which one decision maker's cost is larger than optimal when the other decision maker imposes its optimal schedule. This is the *cost of conflict*. Calculating the cost of conflict requires first solving the manufacturer's and the distributor's individual problems optimally. We then perform computational experiments to measure the average cost of conflict for both the manufacturer and the distributor in each problem. We show that this cost is significant in all cases, which motivates the subsequent study of different power relationships and the benefit of cooperation.

7.4.2.1 Conflict in Problem 1

The manufacturer (i.e., the printer), motivated by the objective of minimizing overhead cost, solves a makespan minimization problem. This problem can be written as

$$\min_{y_i \geq 1} C_{\max} = \sum_{i=1}^{n} \ell_i p_i + \sum_{i=1}^{n} s_i y_i, \qquad (7.70)$$

where the first term is a constant and $y_i \geq 1$ is a decision variable specifying the number of setups for the jobs in zone Z_i. This problem is easily solved, and hence the result is stated without proof.

Proposition 7.1 *The printer's Problem 1 is solved by any schedule with $y_1 = \cdots = y_n = 1$.*

We refer to schedules that are characterized by Proposition 7.1 as *block family* schedules, since all jobs for the same zone are produced consecutively. In the newspaper context, this means that the jobs for all subzones of a particular zone are printed consecutively. Furthermore, the manufacturer's cost is unaffected by the order in which it processes the blocks.

To understand how the distributor can determine its optimal schedules for production and distribution, we first discuss how jobs are released to the distributor. After a job is printed, which requires time p_i for a job for zone Z_i, it is transferred to the packaging center. This transfer requires time δ. At the packaging center, the newspapers are collated, compiled with their inserts, and loaded into a truck. This process is performed in time q_i for each job for zone Z_i. Based on typical industry data (Hurter & van Buer, 1996), we assume that $q_i \leq p_i$ for all i, and $\max_{1 \leq i \leq n}\{q_i\} \leq \min_{1 \leq i \leq n}\{s_i + p_i\}$; hence, no bottlenecks occur at the packaging center. We also assume that a sufficient number of trucks is available so that a compiled job can be dispatched immediately. This process is illustrated in Fig. 7.6.

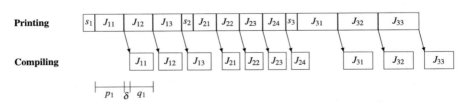

Fig. 7.6 Operations of the printer and the packaging center

7.4 Manufacturer and Distributor

Job J_{ij} is released to the distributor at time $C_{ij}^M(\sigma) + \delta + q_i$, it arrives at distribution center Z_{ij} at time $C_{ij}^D(\sigma, \nu(\sigma)) = C_{ij}^M(\sigma) + \delta + q_i + t_{ij}$, and its lateness is $L_{ij}^D(\sigma, \nu(\sigma)) = C_{ij}^D(\sigma, \nu(\sigma)) - d_{ij}$. Conversely, since by assumption a truck is always available to make a delivery, the distributor's due dates d_{ij} can be translated into implied due dates d_{ij}^M for the printer, as follows:

$$d_{ij}^M = d_{ij} - \delta - q_i - t_{ij}, \quad i = 1, \ldots, n; \ j = 1, \ldots, \ell_i. \tag{7.71}$$

This discussion leads to the following result, which simplifies the search for the distributor's optimal production and distribution schedules.

Lemma 7.10 *For a given printer's schedule σ^m, the distributor's cost $L_{\max}$ is minimized if it uses a schedule that is the same as the printer's schedule, i.e., $\nu(\sigma^m) = \sigma^m$.*

Proof Since the printer uses a single production line to process the jobs, it releases the jobs to the distributor in the same sequence, σ^m, in which it begins them. Under the assumption that a truck is always available for delivery when a job is ready to be loaded, the distributor minimizes its maximum lateness by delivering each job as soon as possible, which is achieved by setting $\nu(\sigma^m) = \sigma^m$. □

Lemma 7.10 allows us to simplify our notation from $L_{ij}(\sigma, \nu(\sigma))$ to $L_{ij}(\sigma)$.

Corollary 7.1 *In either the printer's or distributor's Problem 1, there exists an optimal schedule in which no job is preempted during processing at the printer.*

We refer the reader to Dawande et al. (2006) for a proof. □

The implied due dates d_{ij}^M defined in (7.71) are used in the lemma and algorithm which follow. The algorithm finds a schedule that minimizes the distributor's maximum lateness over all schedules. It requires the following structural result.

Lemma 7.11 *In the distributor's Problem 1, there exists an optimal schedule in which the jobs for zone Z_i are processed in earliest due date (EDD) order based on the implied due dates d_{ij}^M from (7.71).*

Proof For a given nonpreemptive schedule σ, the jobs for zone Z_i are released to the distributor at times $r_{ij} = C_{ij}^M + \delta + q_i$, $j = 1, \ldots, \ell_i$. This holds for any permutation of these jobs for zone Z_i. However, the distributor's objective function ($L_{\max}$) depends only on the values r_{ij}, $j = 1, \ldots, \ell_i$. Since each job for zone Z_i requires the same processing time p_i, the result follows from Jackson (1955). □

Lemma 7.11 motivates the following optimal algorithm for the distributor's problem of minimizing the maximum lateness in Problem 1.

Algorithm P1D

Input

Given d_{ij}, t_{ij} for $i = 1, \ldots, n, j = 1, \ldots, \ell_i$; p_i, q_i, s_i for $i = 1, \ldots, n$, and δ.

Indexing
Index the jobs for each zone Z_i such that $d_{i1}^M \leq \cdots \leq d_{i\ell_i}^M$, for $i = 1, \ldots, n$.
Value Function
$f(v_1, \ldots, v_n; u_1, \ldots, u_n; j) = $ minimum value of the maximum lateness for scheduling jobs $1, \ldots, v_i$ using $u_i \leq v_i$ setups for zone Z_i, for $i = 1, \ldots, n$, where the last job scheduled is for zone Z_j if $j \geq 0$. [Zone Z_0 is assumed to be a dummy zone that requires a zero setup time and consists of a single dummy job that is scheduled at time zero. The dummy job has zero processing time and its due date is infinity.]
Boundary Condition
$f(0, \ldots, 0; 0, \ldots, 0; 0) = -\infty$.
Optimal Solution Value
$\min_{1 \leq j \leq n, 1 \leq u_1 \leq \ell_1, \ldots, 1 \leq u_n \leq \ell_n} \{f(\ell_1, \ldots, \ell_n; u_1, \ldots, u_n; j)\}$.
Recurrence Relation

$$f(v_1, \ldots, v_n; u_1, \ldots, u_n; j) =$$
$$\min \begin{cases} \max\{\sum_{i=1}^n (v_i p_i + u_i s_i) - d_{jv_j}^M, f(v_1, \ldots, v_{j-1}, v_j - 1, v_{j+1}, \ldots, \\ \qquad v_n; u_1, \ldots, u_n; j)\} \\ \min_{1 \leq i \leq n, i \neq j}\{\max\{\sum_{i=1}^n (v_i p_i + u_i s_i) - d_{jv_j}^M, \\ \qquad\qquad f(v_1, \ldots, v_{j-1}, v_j - 1, v_{j+1}, \ldots, v_n; u_1, \ldots, \\ \qquad\qquad u_{j-1}, u_j - 1, u_{j+1}, \ldots, u_n; i)\}\}. \end{cases}$$

In the first term in the recurrence relation, no setup is needed because the zone served, Z_j, is the same as that for the previous job. In the second term, the choice of a job for a different zone necessitates a setup at the printer.

Theorem 7.34 *Algorithm P1D finds an optimal schedule for the distributor's problem of minimizing the maximum lateness in Problem 1 in $O(n^2 \prod_{i=1}^n \ell_i^2)$ time.*

Proof It follows from Lemma 7.11 that Algorithm P1D compares the cost of all possible optimal state transitions and therefore finds an optimal schedule. We consider the time complexity of Algorithm P1D. Since $u_i, v_i \leq \ell_i$ for $i = 1, \ldots, n$, and $j \leq n$, the number of possible values for the state variables is $O(n \prod_{i=1}^n \ell_i^2)$. The second term in the recurrence relation requires the most computation, which is $O(n)$. Thus, the overall time complexity of Algorithm P1D is $O(n^2 \prod_{i=1}^n \ell_i^2)$, which is polynomial for fixed n. $\qquad\square$

The distributor's conflict arises when it must follow the printer's schedule. From Theorem 7.1, the printer is content to select a block family schedule randomly. From Lemma 7.11, we assume that within each block the jobs are ordered by EDD.

We define the relative increase in cost resulting from the distributor's conflict as

$$[L_{\max}^D(\sigma^m) - L_{\max}^D(\sigma^d)] / L_{\max}^D(\sigma^d), \tag{7.72}$$

7.4 Manufacturer and Distributor

where σ^d is a printer's schedule that allows the distributor to achieve minimum customer cost over all printer's schedules, and σ^m is a *randomly chosen* block family schedule for the printer. The use of a randomly chosen block family schedule models the case in which there is no cooperation between the parties. In Sect. 7.4.3.1 below, we find a manufacturer's block family schedule that minimizes the distributor's maximum lateness.

We evaluate (7.72) computationally by examining 100 random instances for each of three different configurations, as follows. Each configuration has three zones and a total of 10 subzones. Different configurations are created by varying the number of subzones per zone. In the first configuration, there are four subzones in zone 1, three subzones in zone 2, and three subzones in zone 3. In the second configuration, there are five, four, and one subzones in the three zones, respectively. Finally, in the third configuration, there are seven, two, and one subzones in the three zones, respectively. For the setup time, processing time, and due date, each is generated from one of two distributions. Specifically, the setup times are randomly generated integers from a $U[1, 50]$ distribution or a $U[1, 100]$ distribution, the processing times are integers from a $U[1, 50]$ or a $U[1, 100]$ distribution, and the due dates are integers from a $U[400, 600]$ or a $U[200, 800]$ distribution. This variety creates $2 \times 2 \times 2 = 8$ different data sets for each configuration. These ranges are designed to be representative of those arising in a wide variety of manufacturing problems.

Table 7.13 presents our results. The first two columns show the lower and upper bounds on setup times and processing times, respectively. Column 3 (respectively, Column 4) shows the relative percentage increase in distributor's cost (computed as the mean over 300 randomly generated instances, including 100 for each configuration) resulting from conflict for due dates generated from a $U[400, 600]$ (respectively, $U[200, 800]$) distribution. These results indicate that if the printer randomly chooses a block family schedule, then the overall average relative increase in maximum lateness from the distributor's conflict is 15.81%. We note that the relative lateness cost almost doubles when the due dates are more dispersed.

Table 7.13 Distributor's cost of conflict in Problem 1

Setup times		Processing times		Due dates $l = 400, \ u = 600$	Due dates $l = 200, \ u = 800$
l	u	l	u	Conflict	Conflict
1	50	1	50	16.47%	20.16%
1	50	1	100	8.73%	22.83%
1	100	1	50	10.55%	18.87%
1	100	1	100	7.30%	21.59%
Overall averages				10.76%	20.86%

386 7 Optimization and Conflict

Table 7.14 Manufacturer's cost of conflict in Problem 1

Setup times		Processing times		Due dates	
				$l = 400, \ u = 600$	$l = 200, \ u = 800$
l	u	l	u	Conflict	Conflict
1	50	1	50	6.07%	3.18%
1	50	1	100	1.57%	5.46%
1	100	1	50	2.85%	14.61%
1	100	1	100	1.24%	8.65%
Overall averages				2.93%	7.97%

The printer incurs a cost of conflict when it must produce according to a distributor's optimal schedule σ^d. If σ^m is a block family schedule, then we define the relative increase in cost that results from the printer's conflict as

$$[C_{\max}(\sigma^d) - C_{\max}(\sigma^m)]/C_{\max}(\sigma^m). \tag{7.73}$$

We evaluate expression (7.73) computationally using the same test data as for (7.72). The results are shown in Table 7.14.

The mean relative increase in cost resulting from the printer's conflict is 5.45%. A 5.45% increase in the length of an eight-hour shift is almost 30 minutes. Hence, the resulting overtime pay for the production staff represents a significant cost to the printer. Therefore, each party in this production–distribution system faces a significant cost of conflict if forced to use the other's optimal schedule. This motivates our investigations of supply chain dominance in Sect. 7.4.3 and of the benefit of cooperation in Sect. 7.4.4.

7.4.2.2 Conflict in Problem 2

As in Problem 1, the manufacturer's problem is solved by minimizing the number of setups. The result here is similarly stated without proof.

Proposition 7.2 *The manufacturer's Problem 2 is solved by any schedule that has one setup for each product.*

To determine a production sequence and a delivery schedule that jointly minimize the distributor's overall inventory cost, we formulate the problem as the following assignment problem with side constraints. Recall that k_1 is the total number of periods during which product P_1 is produced. Let $y_s = 1$ if P_1 is produced during period s, and $y_s = 0$ otherwise. Let $x_{si} = 1$ if the distributor delivers to retailer i at the end of period s, and $x_{si} = 0$ otherwise. The objective is to minimize the total inventory holding cost. Since the average inventory level in period s for product j is $h_j(I_{j,s-1} + I_{j,s})/2$, the total inventory holding cost for a distribution cycle is

7.4 Manufacturer and Distributor

$h_1[I_{1,0}+2\sum_{s=1}^{n-1} I_{1,s}+I_{1,n}]/2+h_2[I_{2,0}+2\sum_{s=1}^{n-1} I_{2,s}+I_{2,n}]/2$. Since $I_{j,0}=I_{j,n}$, this reduces to $\sum_{s=1}^{n}(h_1 I_{1,s}+h_2 I_{2,s})$, which enables the following model.

Minimize $\sum_{s=1}^{n}(h_1 I_{1,s}+h_2 I_{2,s})$

$$\text{s.t.} \quad \sum_{i=1}^{n} x_{si}=1, \qquad s=1,\ldots,n \tag{7.74}$$

$$\sum_{s=1}^{n} x_{si}=1, \qquad i=1,\ldots,n \tag{7.75}$$

$$I_{1,s}=I_{1,s-1}+Cy_s-\sum_{i=1}^{n} b_{1i}x_{si}, \qquad s=1,\ldots,n \tag{7.76}$$

$$I_{2,s}=I_{2,s-1}+C(1-y_s)-\sum_{i=1}^{n} b_{2i}x_{si}, \qquad s=1,\ldots,n \tag{7.77}$$

$$I_{1,0}=I_{1,n} \tag{7.78}$$

$$I_{2,0}=I_{2,n} \tag{7.79}$$

$$\sum_{s=1}^{n} y_s=k_1 \tag{7.80}$$

$$I_{1,s}\geq 0, \qquad s=1,\ldots,n \tag{7.81}$$

$$I_{2,s}\geq 0, \qquad s=1,\ldots,n \tag{7.82}$$

$$y_s \in \{0,1\}, \qquad s=1,\ldots,n \tag{7.83}$$

$$x_{si} \in \{0,1\}, \qquad i=1,\ldots,n, \quad s=1,\ldots,n. \tag{7.84}$$

Constraints (7.74) and (7.75) ensure that exactly one retailer is served at the end of each period. Constraints (7.76) and (7.77) define each period's ending inventory level for each product. Constraints (7.78) and (7.79) ensure that the distribution cycle's ending inventory level equals its starting inventory level for each product. Constraint (7.80) ensures that the required amount of each product is manufactured.

As in Problem 1, the distributor's conflict arises when the manufacturer solves its problem independently from the distributor. We perform a computational study to determine the cost of the distributor's conflict. We compare its costs under the following two alternative scenarios:

1. The manufacturer uses its optimal schedule σ^m, and the distributor then determines its best schedule $v(\sigma^m)$, given the manufacturer's schedule. The distributor's inventory holding cost in this scenario is denoted as $T(\sigma^m, v(\sigma^m))$.
2. The manufacturer produces according to a schedule σ^d preferred by the distributor, which then uses an optimal delivery schedule $v(\sigma^d)$. That is, the distributor chooses σ^d for the manufacturer such that $v(\sigma^d)$ is optimal for the

388   7 Optimization and Conflict

distributor. The distributor's inventory holding cost in this scenario is denoted as $T(\sigma^d, v(\sigma^d))$.

The data set includes two products delivered to six retailers; the truck capacity is 100 units. The manufacturer, therefore, produces 100 units of one product during each of the six periods, and each retailer receives a total of 100 units, mixed according to its demand ratio. The demand ratios across all retailers sum to 50:50. To simulate this, the demand for product P_1 is a randomly generated integer from $U[1, 99]$ for each of the first five retailers, and $b_{16} = 300 - \sum_{i=1}^{5} b_{1i}$. Infeasible instances where $b_{16} \leq 0$ or $b_{16} \geq 100$ are discarded. Also, $b_{2i} = 100 - b_{1i}$, for $i = 1, \ldots, 6$. One set of these six pairs of demands defines an instance. Each of 100 instances is tested for several combinations of holding costs for product P_1 ($h_1 \in \{5, 10, 20, 40\}$) and product P_2 ($h_2 \in \{1, 5, 10, 20, 40\}$).

The distributor's cost of conflict for an instance is computed as $[T(\sigma^m, v(\sigma^m)) - T(\sigma^d, v(\sigma^d))]/T(\sigma^d, v(\sigma^d))$, i.e., the percentage increase in the distributor's inventory cost if the manufacturer uses its optimal schedule. For each combination of holding costs, the mean cost of conflict over 100 instances is computed. The distributor's problem (i.e., the assignment problem with side constraints) is solved as a linear mixed integer program using CPLEX (version 8.1). The results are shown in Table 7.15. The distributor's cost in Table 7.15 is symmetric with respect to holding costs, as discussed below in Corollary 7.2 in Sect. 7.4.3.3.

The manufacturer incurs a cost of conflict when it produces according to a schedule chosen by the distributor. This can increase the number of setups from the manufacturer's optimal number (which is the number of products, in this case two) to as many as the number of periods, n. This increases the manufacturer's cost from 2μ to $n\mu$. Since the number of setups required by the distributor's optimal schedule is $S(\sigma^d)/\mu$, the manufacturer's cost of conflict is computed as $[S(\sigma^d)/\mu - 2]/2$, the relative increase in the number of setups. Our computational study includes two products and six retailers, with 1000 random instances of demand ratios generated as described above. In none of the instances tested does the distributor's optimal schedule allow the manufacturer to have only two setups, i.e., the schedule $(P_1 P_1 P_1 P_2 P_2 P_2)$. In 24.6% of these instances, the manufacturer performs four setups, i.e., $(P_1 P_1 P_2 P_1 P_2 P_2)$ or $(P_1 P_1 P_2 P_2 P_1 P_2)$. In the other 75.4% of the instances, the manufacturer performs six setups, i.e., $(P_1 P_2 P_1 P_2 P_1 P_2)$. These data show that the mean number of setups increases from 2.00 to 5.51; therefore, the manufacturer's mean cost of conflict is 175.5%.

Table 7.15 Distributor's cost of conflict in Problem 2

	$h_2 = 1$	$h_2 = 5$	$h_2 = 10$	$h_2 = 20$	$h_2 = 40$
$h_1 = 5$	87.96%	89.28%	88.26%	87.94%	88.10%
$h_1 = 10$	88.19%	88.26%	89.28%	88.26%	87.94%
$h_1 = 20$	88.46%	87.94%	88.26%	89.28%	88.26%
$h_1 = 40$	88.66%	88.10%	87.94%	88.26%	89.28%

7.4.3 Supply Chain Dominance

In this section, we consider two alternative scenarios for each problem with respect to supply chain dominance. In the first scenario, the manufacturer is dominant and insists on a schedule that serves as a constraint for the distributor. In the second scenario, the roles are reversed. In each scenario, we discuss how the decision maker which is not dominant can minimize its cost under the constraint imposed by the dominant decision maker.

7.4.3.1 Dominance in Problem 1: Printer Dominates

Since there is no difference in the printer's cost between all block family schedules, a rational printer is willing to use any block family schedule the distributor requests. Thus, we now determine which block family schedule is best for the distributor. Recall that the distributor's due dates can be translated into printer's due dates d_{ij}^M using (7.71). Consequently, the distributor's minimum maximum lateness can be found by solving a maximum lateness scheduling problem at the printer.

To study this problem, we need a measure to compare the lateness of jobs within a block. Index the jobs such that $d_{i1}^M \leq \cdots \leq d_{i\ell_i}^M$, for $i = 1, \ldots, n$. Thus, $C_{i\ell_i}^M(\sigma)$ denotes the time at which the last job for zone Z_i is completed by the printer. Since jobs are ordered by EDD within each block, for each $j \in \{1, \ldots, \ell_i\}$, $C_{ij}^M(\sigma) - C_{i\ell_i}^M(\sigma)$ is constant for all block family schedules. For each zone Z_i, we define the constant

$$X_i = \max_{1 \leq j \leq \ell_i} \{C_{ij}^M(\sigma) - C_{i\ell_i}^M(\sigma) - d_{ij}^M\}.$$

We are now ready to solve the maximum lateness block scheduling problem.

Theorem 7.35 *Among all of the printer's block family schedules, one which minimizes the maximum lateness is given by sequencing the blocks $i = 1, \ldots, n$, in nonincreasing order of X_i.*

Proof By adjacent pairwise interchange. Consider scheduling the blocks in reverse order, i.e., starting at $C_{\max}$ and moving backward. Suppose we have just scheduled a block whose starting time is B. Assume that block i is selected at this point, and then block k is selected to precede block i, where $X_k \leq X_i$, as shown in Fig. 7.7. Here, the maximum lateness within blocks i and k is

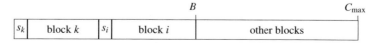

Fig. 7.7 Schedule where Block k precedes Block i

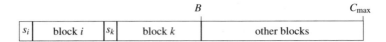

Fig. 7.8 Schedule where Block i precedes Block k

Table 7.16 Distributor's cost of conflict and its improvement from Theorem 7.35

Setup times		Processing times		Due dates $l = 400$, $u = 600$		$l = 200$, $u = 800$	
l	u	l	u	Conflict	Improvement	Conflict	Improvement
1	10	1	50	3.54%	10.06%	6.73%	10.25%
1	10	1	100	0.58%	6.82%	7.39%	11.45%
1	50	1	50	1.68%	7.33%	6.39%	9.68%
1	50	1	100	0.64%	5.71%	6.38%	11.38%
Overall averages				1.61 %	7.48%	6.72%	10.69%

$\max\{X_i + B, X_k + B - \ell_i p_i - s_i\} = X_i + B$. However, if we interchange blocks i and k (Fig. 7.8), then the maximum lateness within those blocks is $\max\{X_i + B - \ell_k p_k - s_k, X_k + B\} \leq X_i + B$. □

We perform a computational study similar to the one in Sect. 7.4.2.1. That study evaluates the distributor's conflict for a randomly chosen block family schedule. In this case, however, we evaluate the distributor's conflict from using a block family schedule $\sigma_{7.35}^m$ that satisfies Theorem 7.35, which is $[L_{\max}(\sigma_{7.35}^m) - L_{\max}(\sigma^d)]/L_{\max}(\sigma^d)$. We also evaluate the *improvement* in the distributor's maximum lateness from the use of such a block family schedule rather than a randomly chosen one, denoted by σ_r^m, which is $[L_{\max}(\sigma_r^m) - L_{\max}(\sigma_2^m)]/L_{\max}(\sigma_r^m)$. The results are shown in Table 7.16. The mean reduction in the distributor's maximum lateness that results from the printer using the most favorable block family schedule is 9.08%, which still leaves an average distributor's conflict of 4.17%. As in Table 7.13, the distributor's cost of conflict is significantly larger for the case of more dispersed due dates.

Remark 7.10 The results in Table 7.16 suggest that approximately one-third of the distributor's conflict computed in Sect. 7.4.2.1 arises from the printer's use of a block family schedule, and the remainder comes from the choice of which block family schedule the printer uses.

7.4.3.2 Dominance in Problem 1: Distributor Dominates

If the distributor has dominant power in the supply chain, then it may impose a limit, Δ, on the maximum lateness that results from the printer's decisions. The printer then minimizes its cost, subject to this constraint. We now show how this can be modeled.

7.4 Manufacturer and Distributor

Lemma 7.12 *In the printer's problem of minimizing* $C_{\max}$ *subject to the constraint* $L_{\max} \leq \Delta$, *there exists an optimal schedule in which the jobs for zone* Z_i *are processed in EDD order based on* d_{ij}^M.

Proof Similar to Lemma 7.11. □

Algorithm P1MC finds a schedule that minimizes the printer's makespan, while satisfying the distributor's requirement that $L_{\max} \leq \Delta$. It is the same as Algorithm P1D, except for the Optimal Solution Value step shown below.

Algorithm P1MC
Optimal Solution Value
$\min_{1 \leq j \leq n, 1 \leq u_1 \leq \ell_1, \ldots, 1 \leq u_n \leq \ell_n} \{\sum_{i=1}^{n} u_i s_i \mid f(\ell_1, \ldots, \ell_n; u_1, \ldots, u_n; j) \leq \Delta\}$.

Theorem 7.36 *Algorithm P1MC finds an optimal schedule for the printer's version of Problem 1 with the* $L_{\max} \leq \Delta$ *constraint in* $O(n^2 \prod_{i=1}^{n} \ell_i^2)$ *time.*

Proof Similar to Theorem 7.34. □

In order to evaluate the cost incurred by the printer if it must satisfy a maximum lateness constraint imposed by the distributor, we compute the relative cost increase resulting from the printer's conflict. If σ^m denotes any block family schedule, and $\sigma^d(\Delta)$ denotes the printer's schedule derived from Algorithm P1MC, then we define the relative increase in cost resulting from the printer's conflict as

$$[C_{\max}(\sigma^d(\Delta)) - C_{\max}(\sigma^m)]/C_{\max}(\sigma^m). \tag{7.85}$$

We evaluate this expression computationally, as for (7.73) in Sect. 7.4.2.1. The results appear in Table 7.17. For each combination of setup times, processing times, and due dates, we evaluate (7.85) for three values of Δ. Let $L_{\max}^*$ be the optimum $L_{\max}$ value from Algorithm P1D and $Z = L_{\max}(\sigma^m) - L_{\max}^*$. The three values of Δ for which each instance is tested are $\Delta = L_{\max}^* + 0.25Z$, $\Delta = L_{\max}^* + 0.5Z$, and $\Delta = L_{\max}^* + 0.75Z$. Recall that values for $\Delta = L_{\max}^*$ can be found in Table 7.14, whereas for $\Delta = L_{\max}(\sigma^m)$ the cost of conflict is zero.

The results in Table 7.17 show that most of the printer's conflict is incurred when the weakest constraint, $L_{\max} \leq \Delta = L_{\max}^* + 0.75Z$, is imposed by the distributor. By comparing Table 7.17 with Table 7.14, we observe that on average 68.0% of the printer's total conflict is incurred as a result of this first marginal reduction in allowable $L_{\max}$ value from $L_{\max}(\sigma^m)$ to $L_{\max}^* + 0.75Z$. It follows that the largest marginal reduction in conflict occurs when the printer first uses a schedule that is not a block family schedule.

7.4.3.3 Dominance in Problem 2: Manufacturer Dominates

The manufacturer produces so that it has only two setups per distribution cycle, one for each product. Given this production sequence, the distributor seeks a distribution

Table 7.17 Printer's cost of conflict in Problem 1 as Δ varies

Setup times		Processing times		Due dates					
				$l = 400,\ u = 600$			$l = 200,\ u = 800$		
				Maximum allowable lateness (Δ)			Maximum allowable lateness (Δ)		
l	u	l	u	$L_{max}^* + 0.25Z$	$L_{max}^* + 0.5Z$	$L_{max}^* + 0.75Z$	$L_{max}^* + 0.25Z$	$L_{max}^* + 0.5Z$	$L_{max}^* + 0.75Z$
1	50	1	50	5.31%	4.42%	3.99%	2.64%	1.94%	1.79%
1	50	1	100	1.46%	1.28%	1.24%	4.46%	3.49%	3.11%
1	100	1	50	2.77%	2.70%	2.63%	12.15%	9.59%	8.69%
1	100	1	100	1.24%	1.20%	1.18%	6.97%	5.79%	5.22%
Overall averages				2.70%	2.40%	2.26%	6.56%	5.20%	4.70%

7.4 Manufacturer and Distributor

sequence that minimizes its cost over all possible distribution sequences. This distribution sequence is then repeated throughout the planning horizon.

The manufacturer produces product P_1 for k_1 consecutive periods and then produces product P_2 for k_2 consecutive periods. Let $v = (v(1), \ldots, v(n))$ denote the delivery sequence. We first explain how the inventory level of product P_j, for $j = 1, 2$, can be computed over the distribution cycle time nCt and then specify the distributor's best distribution sequence, given this production sequence. Let the total inventory holding cost from period 1 through period k_1 for product P_1 be denoted by T_{1,k_1}^1 and the total inventory holding cost for both products from period 1 through period n be denoted by $T_{1,n}$.

Lemma 7.13 *For production sequence $(P_1 \cdots P_1 P_2 \cdots P_2)$, the distributor's inventory cost in Problem 2 is*

$$T_{1,n} = n I_{1,0} h_1 + n I_{2,k_1} h_2 + \left(\frac{k_1^2}{2} + k_1 k_2 + \frac{k_1}{2} \right) h_1 C + \left(\frac{k_2^2}{2} + k_1 k_2 + \frac{k_2}{2} \right) h_2 C$$

$$- \sum_{s=1}^{n} (n - s + 1) \left(h_1 b_{1v(s)} + h_2 b_{2v(k_1+s)} \right),$$

where $b_{2v(s)} = b_{2v(n+s)}$, $s = 0, 1, \ldots, n$.

We refer the reader to Dawande et al. (2006) for a proof.

We now find the distributor's best delivery sequence if the manufacturer uses its optimal schedule.

Theorem 7.37 *Suppose that $h_1 \geq h_2$ and that the retailers are indexed such that $b_{11} \geq \cdots \geq b_{1n}$. For production sequence $(P_1 \ldots P_1 P_2 \ldots P_2)$, the distributor's inventory cost in Problem 2 can be minimized by using the delivery sequence $v = (1, \ldots, n)$.*

Proof Because $I_{1,0} = I_{2,k_1} = 0$ for this production sequence, we can prove the result by showing that the non-constant term $\sum_{s=1}^{n} (n-s+1)(h_1 b_{1v(s)} + h_2 b_{2v(k_1+s)})$ in Lemma 7.13 is maximized by the proposed sequence v. First, observe that since the distribution sequence is cyclic,

$$\sum_{s=1}^{n} (n - s + 1) h_2 b_{2v(k_1+s)} = \sum_{s=1}^{k_1} (k_1 - s + 1) h_2 b_{2v(s)} + \sum_{s=k_1+1}^{n} (n + k_1 - s + 1) h_2 b_{2v(s)}.$$

Suppose that v_o is a distribution schedule in which the retailers' demands are not served in nonincreasing order. Then, there must be two adjacent periods i and $j = i + 1$ in v_o such that $b_{1v_o(i)} < b_{1v_o(j)}$. We perform a pairwise interchange on the demands served in those periods and thus obtain a new schedule v'. We show that $T_{1,n}(v') - T_{1,n}(v_o) \leq 0$. If $2 \leq j \leq k_1$, then

$$T_{1,n}(v') - T_{1,n}(v_o) = -h_1[(n - i + 1)(b_{1v_o(j)} - b_{1v_o(i)}) + (n - j + 1)(b_{1v_o(i)} - b_{1v_o(j)})]$$
$$- h_2[(k_1 - i + 1)(b_{2v_o(j)} - b_{2v_o(i)}) + (k_1 - j + 1)(b_{2v_o(i)} - b_{2v_o(j)})]$$
$$= -h_1(j - i)(b_{1v_o(j)} - b_{1v_o(i)}) - h_2(j - i)(b_{2v_o(j)} - b_{2v_o(i)})$$
$$= (h_2 - h_1)(b_{1v_o(j)} - b_{1v_o(i)}) \le 0.$$

Thus, any distribution schedule can be rearranged into nonincreasing order of the b_{1i} values without increasing the total inventory cost. The proof is similar for $k_1 + 1 \le j \le n$. $\square$

Remark 7.11 The result in Theorem 7.37 leads to the symmetry with respect to holding costs observed in Table 7.15: the distributor's optimal inventory cost remains the same if the holding costs of the two products are interchanged.

Corollary 7.2 *For the production sequence $(P_1 \ldots P_1 P_2 \ldots P_2)$, the distributor's optimal inventory cost in Problem 2 is symmetric with respect to the holding costs h_1 and h_2.*

Proof Theorem 7.37 implies that if $h_2 \ge h_1$, then for production sequence $(P_1 \ldots P_1 P_2 \ldots P_2)$, the distributor's inventory cost in Problem 2 is minimized by using delivery order $v' = (k_1, k_1 - 1, \ldots, 1, n, n - 1, \ldots, k_1 + 1)$.

We consider two different problems. In each, the production sequence is $(P_1 \ldots P_1 P_2 \ldots P_2)$. In the first, $h_1 \ge h_2$ and the distributor uses delivery order $v = (1, 2, \ldots, n - 1, n)$. Inventory levels are represented by $I_{j,s}$. In the second, $h_2 \ge h_1$ and the distributor uses delivery order $v' = (k_1, k_1 - 1, \ldots, 1, n, n - 1, \ldots, k_1 + 1)$. Inventory levels are represented by $I'_{j,s}$. We prove Corollary 7.2 by showing that $I_{1,s} = I'_{2,k_1-s}$ for $s = 0, \ldots, k_1$, and $I_{1,s} = I'_{2,n+k_1-s}$ for $s = k_1, \ldots, n - 1$. We have

$$I_{1,0} = I'_{2,k_1} = 0$$

$$I_{1,1} = I_{1,0} + C - b_{1,v(1)} = I'_{2,k_1} + C - b_{1,v'(k_1)} = I'_{2,k_1} + b_{2,v'(k_1)} = I'_{2,k_1-1}$$

$$\vdots$$

$$I_{1,k_1} = I_{1,0} + k_1 C - \sum_{i=1}^{k_1} b_{1,v(i)} = I'_{2,k_1} + \sum_{i=1}^{k_1}(C - b_{1,v'(i)}) = I'_{2,k_1} + \sum_{i=1}^{k_1} b_{2,v'(i)} = I'_{2,0}$$

$$I_{1,k_1+1} = I_{1,k_1} - b_{1,v(k_1+1)} = I'_{2,0} - C + b_{2,v'(n)} = I'_{2,n-1}$$

$$\vdots$$

$$I_{1,n-1} = I_{1,k_1} - \sum_{i=k_1+1}^{n-1} b_{1,v(i)} = I'_{2,0} - \sum_{i=k_1+2}^{n} b_{1,v'(i)} = I'_{2,0} - \sum_{i=k_1+2}^{n}(C - b_{2,v'(i)}) = I'_{2,k_1+1}.$$

$\square$

7.4 Manufacturer and Distributor

Recall that for Problem 1 in Sect. 7.4.3.1, we show how the distributor can benefit by finding a production sequence that improves $L_{\max}$ and does not degrade $C_{\max}$. However, since the manufacturer's optimal schedule in Problem 2 is simply $(P_1 \ldots P_1 P_2 \ldots P_2)$, no such improved schedule exists in this case. Hence, no computational study is needed here. Therefore, the contribution of this section is to show that the problem of finding the best distribution schedule, given a manufacturer's schedule $(P_1 \ldots P_1 P_2 \ldots P_2)$, is polynomially solvable via a sorting algorithm.

7.4.3.4 Dominance in Problem 2: Distributor Dominates

If the distributor has dominant power in the supply chain, then it may impose a limit, I^*, on the total inventory holding cost that results from the decisions of the manufacturer. The manufacturer then minimizes its cost, subject to this constraint, by solving a variant of the assignment problem with side constraints in Sect. 7.4.2.2. We let $g_s = 1$ if a setup is required in period s; otherwise, $g_s = 0$.

$$\text{Minimize} \quad g_2 + g_3 + \cdots + g_{n+1} \tag{7.86}$$

$$\text{s.t.} \quad \sum_{s=1}^{n} (h_1 I_{1,s} + h_2 I_{2,s}) \leq I^* \tag{7.87}$$

$$y_s - y_{s-1} \leq g_s, \qquad s = 2, \ldots, n+1 \tag{7.88}$$

$$y_{s-1} - y_s \leq g_s, \qquad s = 2, \ldots, n+1 \tag{7.89}$$

$$g_s \in \{0, 1\}, \qquad s = 2, \ldots, n+1$$

$$\text{and} \quad (7.74)\text{–}(7.84).$$

Constraint (7.87) enforces the inventory holding cost limitation. Constraints (7.88) and (7.89) determine whether a setup is required in period s.

We perform a computational study to evaluate how different values of I^* affect the manufacturer's cost. The same data set generated for the study of the manufacturer's conflict in Sect. 7.4.2.2 is used to compute the mean number of setups, $S(\sigma(I^*))/\mu$, required for the manufacturer to meet the given inventory cost constraint and to compute the mean relative cost increase, $[S(\sigma(I^*))/\mu - 2]/2$. This is performed for five values of I^*. Let $T(\sigma^m, v(\sigma^m))$ be the distributor's total inventory holding cost for the manufacturer's optimal production sequence, $T((\sigma^d, v(\sigma^d))$ be the distributor's optimal total inventory holding cost, and $Y = T(\sigma^m, v(\sigma^m)) - T((\sigma^d, v(\sigma^d))$. The five values of I^* for which 100 instances are tested are $I^* = T((\sigma^d, v(\sigma^d))$, $I^* = T((\sigma^d, v(\sigma^d)) + 0.25Y$, $I^* = T((\sigma^d, v(\sigma^d)) + 0.5Y$, $I^* = T((\sigma^d, v(\sigma^d)) + 0.75Y$, and $I^* = T(\sigma^m, v(\sigma^m))$. Holding cost values $h_1 = 5$ and $h_2 \in \{5, 10, 20, 40\}$ are used. Mean results over the 100 instances are shown in Table 7.18.

Table 7.18 Manufacturer's cost of conflict in Problem 2 as I^* varies

	$T((\sigma^d, \nu(\sigma^d)))$		$T((\sigma^d, \nu(\sigma^d))) + 0.25Y$		$T((\sigma^d, \nu(\sigma^d))) + 0.5Y$		$T((\sigma^d, \nu(\sigma^d))) + 0.75Y$		$T(\sigma^m, \nu(\sigma^m))$	
	Setups	Cost	Setups	Cost	Setups	Cost	Setups	Cost	Setups	Cost
$h_2 = 5$	5.26	163%	4.32	116%	4.00	100%	4.00	100%	2.00	0%
$h_2 = 10$	5.62	181%	4.36	118%	4.00	100%	4.00	100%	2.00	0%
$h_2 = 20$	5.50	175%	4.38	119%	4.00	100%	4.00	100%	2.00	0%
$h_2 = 40$	5.45	172%	4.43	121%	4.00	100%	4.00	100%	2.00	0%
Averages	5.46	173%	4.37	119%	4.00	100%	4.00	100%	2.00	0%

7.4 Manufacturer and Distributor 397

The results in Table 7.18 show that 57.8% of the manufacturer's cost of conflict is incurred when the weakest constraint, $I^* = T((\sigma^d, \nu(\sigma^d)) + 0.75Y$, is imposed by the distributor.

7.4.4 Benefit of Cooperation

In this section, we compare the total system cost in a situation where the manufacturer and the distributor cooperate fully, to the total system cost that results if either party makes an independent decision. For each problem, the combined objective function is a convex combination of the individual objectives. This model is chosen for generality; we evaluate the objective for different values of the combination parameter α. In any practical system consisting of a manufacturer and a distributor, the value of α is defined either by an executive decision if they are in the same company or by the two parties' relative negotiating power otherwise. We conclude this section with a discussion of methods for encouraging and implementing supply chain cooperation.

7.4.4.1 Problem 1

For the newspaper example, various reasonable objectives for the combined problem can be formulated. In practice, the distributor's goal may not be to minimize $L_{\max}$, but rather to ensure that $L_{\max} = 0$. In this case, the discussion in Sect. 7.4.3.2 and the results in Table 7.17 are applicable. Similarly, the printer may not want to minimize $C_{\max}$ as much as requiring that $C_{\max} \leq C^*$, where C^* is a value which ensures that production can be completed without the use of overtime labor. Here, the printer can offer the distributor the opportunity to design and request a production sequence with a fixed number of extra setups allowed. Each of these scenarios is more likely if the printer and the distributor are in the same company, which is typical but not ubiquitous in the newspaper industry.

If the printer and distributor cooperate, then they select a schedule σ^c that minimizes the convex combination $\alpha C_{\max}^M(\sigma) + (1 - \alpha)L_{\max}^D(\sigma)$, for some fixed α. Given α, Algorithm P1C below, which differs from Algorithm P1D only in the Input and Optimal Solution Value steps, finds such a schedule.

In order for the distributor to agree to a certain value of $L_{\max}$, it is important for the distributor to assess the cost implication of choosing this value. We now describe an approach to assess this cost in practice. The demand of each distribution center Z_{ij} typically consists of demand from individual subscribers and from newsstands. Late deliveries may affect these demands; the demand at newsstands is particularly time sensitive. Using historical data, each distribution center Z_{ij} can express the dollar value of lost sales, $G_{ij}(L_{ij})$, as a function of the lateness L_{ij}. Typically, $G_{ij}(L_{ij})$ is an increasing function of L_{ij}. Thus, by agreeing to a specific value of

L_{max}, the distributor may incur a maximum total cost of $\sum_{i=1}^{n} \sum_{j=1}^{\ell_i} G_{ij}(L_{\max})$. We note that this is a worst-case scenario in which the lateness of each distribution center is $L_{\max}$. In practice, when a solution with given $L_{\max}$ value is implemented, the distributor's cost will typically be much less than the maximum committed, i.e., $\sum_{i=1}^{n} \sum_{j=1}^{\ell_i} G_{ij}(L_{\max})$. In Algorithm P1C, the boundary condition and recurrence relation are the same as in Algorithm P1D. The other details appear below.

Algorithm P1C

Input

Given d_{ij}, t_{ij} for $i = 1, \ldots, n, j = 1, \ldots, \ell_i$; p_i, q_i, s_i for $i = 1, \ldots, n$; δ and α.

Optimal Solution Value

$\min_{1 \le j \le n, 1 \le u_1 \le \ell_1, \ldots, 1 \le u_n \le \ell_n} \{\alpha \sum_{i=1}^{n} (\ell_i p_i + u_i s_i) + (1 - \alpha) f(\ell_1, \ldots, \ell_n; u_1, \ldots, u_n; j)\}$.

Theorem 7.38 *Algorithm P1C finds an optimal schedule for the combined version of Problem 1 in $O(n^2 \prod_{i=1}^{n} \ell_i^2)$ time.*

Proof Similar to Theorem 7.34. $\qquad\qquad\qquad\qquad\qquad\qquad\qquad\qquad\qquad\square$

In order to evaluate the benefit of cooperation, we compare the schedule derived by Algorithm P1C to the printer's optimal schedule and to the distributor's optimal schedule. As in Sect. 7.4.2.1, we use eight combinations of ranges for the setup times, processing times, and due dates. For each combination, we generate 100 random instances for each of the three configurations defined in Sect. 7.4.2.1 and for $\alpha \in \{0.2, 0.4, 0.6, 0.8\}$. Then we compute:

1. A random block family schedule σ^m and its cost $\Gamma^m = \alpha C_{\max}(\sigma^m) + (1 - \alpha) L_{\max}(\sigma^m)$
2. The schedule σ^d found by Algorithm P1MC, where the printer is required to satisfy $L_{\max} \le \Delta = L_{\max}^*$, and its cost $\Gamma^d = \alpha C_{\max}(\sigma^d) + (1 - \alpha) L_{\max}(\sigma^d)$
3. The optimal system schedule σ^c found by Algorithm P1C and its cost $\Gamma^c = \alpha C_{\max}(\sigma^c) + (1 - \alpha) L_{\max}(\sigma^c)$

The benefit of cooperation relative to the cost of the printer's optimal schedule, $(\Gamma^m - \Gamma^c)/\Gamma^m$, is shown in Table 7.19. The corresponding information, $(\Gamma^d - \Gamma^c)/\Gamma^d$, for the distributor's optimal schedule is shown in Table 7.20.

Our results show that the mean benefit of cooperation relative to using the printer's optimal schedule is 6.50% and relative to using the distributor's optimal schedule is 1.28%. The parameter that has the greatest effect on the benefit of cooperation is due dates. For more dispersed due dates (200–800 *vs.* 400–600), the benefit of cooperation is relatively 81.35% greater (8.37% *vs.* 4.62%) when compared to the printer's optimal schedule, and it is relatively 206.43% greater (1.92% *vs.* 0.63%) when compared to the distributor's optimal schedule. These results imply that cooperation is more valuable when due dates are more dispersed. This observation is consistent with the results in Tables 7.13 and 7.16.

7.4 Manufacturer and Distributor

Table 7.19 Benefit of cooperation *vs.* printer's optimal schedule in Problem 1

Setup times		Processing times		Due dates		Savings over manufacturer's optimal schedule			
l	u	l	u	l	u	$\alpha = 0.2$	$\alpha = 0.4$	$\alpha = 0.6$	$\alpha = 0.8$
1	50	1	50	400	600	9.69%	7.49%	5.22%	2.56%
1	50	1	100	400	600	6.81%	5.06%	3.31%	1.77%
1	100	1	50	400	600	7.86%	5.48%	3.78%	2.09%
1	100	1	100	400	600	4.94%	3.93%	2.54%	1.36%
1	50	1	50	200	800	13.64%	10.07%	7.36%	3.59%
1	50	1	100	200	800	14.04%	10.25%	6.77%	3.63%
1	100	1	50	200	800	12.30%	9.79%	6.81%	3.96%
1	100	1	100	200	800	12.63%	9.72%	6.09%	3.34%
Averages						10.24%	7.72%	5.24%	2.79%

Table 7.20 Benefit of cooperation *vs.* distributor's optimal schedule in Problem 1

Setup times		Processing times		Due dates		Savings over Distributor's optimal schedule			
l	u	l	u	l	u	$\alpha = 0.2$	$\alpha = 0.4$	$\alpha = 0.6$	$\alpha = 0.8$
1	50	1	50	400	600	0.08%	0.45%	1.30%	2.54%
1	50	1	100	400	600	0.03%	0.17%	0.40%	0.79%
1	100	1	50	400	600	0.12%	0.50%	1.03%	1.72%
1	100	1	100	400	600	0.02%	0.11%	0.28%	0.51%
1	50	1	50	200	800	0.14%	0.66%	1.92%	4.55%
1	50	1	100	200	800	0.05%	0.38%	1.23%	2.95%
1	100	1	50	200	800	0.30%	1.37%	3.55%	6.86%
1	100	1	100	200	800	0.15%	0.77%	1.99%	3.92%
Averages						0.11%	0.55%	1.46%	2.98%

7.4.4.2 Problem 2

Whereas in Problem 1 the decision makers minimize time, in Problem 2 they minimize cost. Therefore, there is no obvious scenario in which one party will freely relinquish its optimal schedule without compensation, even if the parties are within the same company. We again use a convex combination of the individual objectives to define a combined objective function.

If the manufacturer and the distributor cooperate, then they can find a manufacturer's schedule σ^c and a distributor's schedule $\nu(\sigma^c)$ that jointly minimize $\alpha S(\sigma) + (1 - \alpha) T(\sigma, \nu(\sigma))$ by solving an assignment problem with side constraints that is similar to that in Sect. 7.4.3.4. The only changes are to remove the first constraint and to change the objective function to

$$\text{Minimize } \alpha(g_2 + g_3 + \cdots + g_{n+1})\mu + (1 - \alpha) \sum_{s=1}^{n} (h_1 I_{1,s} + h_2 I_{2,s}).$$

We perform a computational study to determine the relative cost saving to the supply chain that results from cooperation between the two parties. The same data generated for the study of the manufacturer's conflict in Sect. 7.4.2.2 are used, under three different scenarios:

1. The manufacturer uses its optimal schedule σ^m, and then the distributor uses Theorem 7.37 to determine its best schedule $v(\sigma^m)$. We denote the total cost of this scenario by $\Gamma^m = \alpha S(\sigma^m) + (1 - \alpha)T(\sigma^m, v(\sigma^m))$.
2. The manufacturer uses a schedule σ^d, derived from the assignment problem with side constraints in Sect. 7.4.3.4, that enables the distributor to achieve its overall minimum total inventory holding cost. We denote the total cost of this scenario by $\Gamma^d = \alpha S(\sigma^d) + (1 - \alpha)T(\sigma^d, v(\sigma^d))$.
3. A production schedule σ^c that minimizes the overall system cost is used. We denote the total cost of this scenario by $\Gamma^c = \alpha S(\sigma^c) + (1 - \alpha)T(\sigma^c, v(\sigma^c))$.

The setup cost is $\mu = 200$ throughout. The relative gain from using the cooperative schedule over the manufacturer's optimal schedule is computed as $(\Gamma^m - \Gamma^c)/\Gamma^m$. The mean benefit of cooperation for various combinations of holding costs and different values of α is shown in Table 7.21.

The relative gain from using the cooperative schedule over the distributor's optimal schedule is computed as $(\Gamma^d - \Gamma^c)/\Gamma^d$. The mean benefit of cooperation for various combinations of holding costs and different values of α is shown in Table 7.22.

As in Table 7.15, the results in Tables 7.21 and 7.22 are approximately symmetric with respect to holding costs. Here, the manufacturer does not use production sequence $(P_1 \ldots P_1 P_2 \ldots P_2)$ in all instances, however analogs to Corollary 7.2 can be similarly proven for the different production sequences.

From Tables 7.21 and 7.22, the average benefit of cooperation over the manufacturer's optimal schedule is 25.26%, whereas the average benefit of cooperation over the distributor's optimal schedule is 6.02%.

Additional computational results show that the improvement over the manufacturer's optimal schedule decreases and the improvement over the distributor's optimal schedule grows as μ increases. This is to be expected because a larger setup cost gives more weight to the manufacturer's cost in the combined objective. Similar reasoning applies to two other observations from the results: (i) as holding costs increase, the benefit of cooperation relative to the manufacturer's optimal schedule increases, and the benefit relative to the distributor's optimal schedule decreases and (ii) as α increases, the benefit of cooperation relative to the manufacturer's optimal schedule decreases, and the benefit relative to the distributor's optimal schedule increases.

7.4.4.3 Implementing Cooperation

In both the problems considered, a benefit of cooperation arises when the dominant player agrees not to use its individually optimal schedule. Unless the distributor

Table 7.21 Benefit of cooperation vs. manufacturer's optimal schedule in Problem 2

$\alpha = 0.2$					
h_1	$h_2 = 1$	$h_2 = 5$	$h_2 = 10$	$h_2 = 20$	$h_2 = 40$
5	30.10%	36.44%	37.83%	39.73%	41.32%
10	35.35%	37.83%	39.93%	40.49%	41.50%
20	39.05%	39.73%	40.49%	41.79%	41.92%
40	41.29%	41.32%	41.50%	41.92%	42.74%

$\alpha = 0.4$					
h_1	$h_2 = 1$	$h_2 = 5$	$h_2 = 10$	$h_2 = 20$	$h_2 = 40$
5	15.64%	26.72%	30.31%	34.32%	37.96%
10	25.15%	30.31%	34.33%	36.16%	38.58%
20	32.60%	34.32%	36.16%	38.72%	39.58%
40	37.56%	37.96%	38.58%	39.58%	41.17%

$\alpha = 0.6$					
h_1	$h_2 = 1$	$h_2 = 5$	$h_2 = 10$	$h_2 = 20$	$h_2 = 40$
5	1.86%	13.13%	18.94%	25.78%	32.17%
10	11.33%	18.94%	25.04%	28.98%	33.34%
20	22.54%	25.78%	28.98%	33.30%	35.36%
40	31.22%	32.17%	33.34%	35.36%	38.13%

$\alpha = 0.8$					
h_1	$h_2 = 1$	$h_2 = 5$	$h_2 = 10$	$h_2 = 20$	$h_2 = 40$
5	0.07%	0.00%	1.72%	9.21%	19.19%
10	0.10%	1.72%	7.49%	13.73%	21.49%
20	5.31%	9.21%	13.73%	20.50%	25.28%
40	17.11%	19.19%	21.49%	25.28%	30.34%

Table 7.22 Benefit of cooperation *vs.* distributor's optimal schedule in Problem 2

$\alpha = 0.2$						$\alpha = 0.4$					
h_1	$h_2 = 1$	$h_2 = 5$	$h_2 = 10$	$h_2 = 20$	$h_2 = 40$	h_1	$h_2 = 1$	$h_2 = 5$	$h_2 = 10$	$h_2 = 20$	$h_2 = 40$
5	1.92%	0.23%	0.46%	0.18%	0.03%	5	7.21%	2.03%	2.38%	0.87%	0.26%
10	0.70%	0.46%	0.01%	0.12%	0.05%	10	3.57%	2.38%	0.57%	0.74%	0.28%
20	0.24%	0.18%	0.12%	0.00%	0.04%	20	1.41%	0.87%	0.74%	0.04%	0.22%
40	0.08%	0.03%	0.05%	0.04%	0.00%	40	0.47%	0.26%	0.28%	0.22%	0.00%

$\alpha = 0.6$						$\alpha = 0.8$					
h_1	$h_2 = 1$	$h_2 = 5$	$h_2 = 10$	$h_2 = 20$	$h_2 = 40$	h_1	$h_2 = 1$	$h_2 = 5$	$h_2 = 10$	$h_2 = 20$	$h_2 = 40$
5	17.83%	6.81%	6.71%	3.43%	1.32%	5	40.24%	23.44%	18.71%	11.16%	5.60%
10	9.42%	6.71%	2.46%	2.80%	1.06%	10	27.53%	18.71%	9.66%	9.19%	4.96%
20	4.53%	3.43%	2.80%	0.73%	0.91%	20	13.99%	11.16%	9.19%	3.86%	4.12%
40	1.86%	1.32%	1.06%	0.91%	0.07%	40	6.48%	5.60%	4.96%	4.12%	1.25%

7.4 Manufacturer and Distributor

can assert itself as dominant, the manufacturer is dominant because it chooses its schedule first, i.e., it is a Stackelberg leader (Frank & Parker, 2004). When the supply chain switches from the dominant party's schedule to the overall optimal schedule, the dominant player's cost increases, but the nondominant party's cost decreases by a larger amount. We note in Sect. 7.4.4.1 that there are situations in which the dominant party may accept a suboptimal schedule. However, in general the nondominant party must use some of its cost saving to compensate the dominant party for changing its schedule. Classical game theory Nash (1953) states that for the dominant party to agree to cooperate, this compensation should exceed the amount by which its cost increases in the overall optimal schedule.

More formally, suppose $S(\pi)$ is the manufacturer's cost and $T(\pi)$ is the distributor's cost if schedule π is used. Suppose the manufacturer is dominant, and σ is its preferred schedule. The total cost of the non-coordinated schedule is thus $S(\sigma) + T(\sigma)$. Let σ^c denote an optimal coordinated system schedule. The total cost savings from implementing the coordinated schedule are thus $p^* = [S(\sigma) + T(\sigma)] - [S(\sigma^c) + T(\sigma^c)]$. The dominant party's increase in cost from agreeing to use the coordinated schedule is $p = S(\sigma^c) - S(\sigma)$. Since the nondominant party's cost decreases by more than p in an optimal coordinated schedule, the system has a surplus of $p^* - p > 0$. A possible mechanism for cooperation is for the dominant party to receive a lump sum side payment of $p + \beta(p^* - p)$, where $0 < \beta < 1$; the value of β typically depends on the difference in negotiating power between the two parties. Under this mechanism, both parties have an incentive to cooperate, since the dominant party's net cost is $S(\sigma^c) - p - \beta(p^* - p) < S(\sigma)$ and the nondominant party's net cost is $T(\sigma^c) - (1 - \beta)(p^* - p) < T(\sigma)$. A similar argument applies to the case in which the distributor is dominant.

The distribution of the surplus between the two parties is determined by the value of β. Marketing research (Corfman & Lehman, 1993; Lehman, 2001) and management research (Ouchi, 1980; Williamson, 1975) suggest that the surplus should be divided equitably to ensure continued cooperation. A perfectly equitable split of the surplus, however, would require that the parties accurately and continuously share their cost data in a verifiable way. The related topic of strategic misreporting of private data is discussed in Sects. 9.4 and 9.5.

An alternative approach is one that is more market-oriented. For either problem, if the manufacturer dominates, then it can negotiate a price to be paid by the distributor for each additional setup that the manufacturer performs. This price should be at least the manufacturer's cost for the additional setup and at most the distributor's benefit from the resulting increase in scheduling flexibility. Because the result of this negotiation is an easily verified job release schedule to which compensation is tied, the manufacturer is unable to cheat without being detected. If the distributor dominates, then a similar negotiation determines the price paid by the manufacturer for the right to impose on the distributor a larger maximum lateness in Problem 1 or a larger inventory cost in Problem 2. Again, the results are easily verified. In both situations, the burden of initiating cooperation and of determining an alternative schedule is borne by the nondominant party.

7.5 Resequencing in a Supply Chain

Consider two consecutive stages of a production system that prefer different sequences. A single supplier fills orders for several manufacturers. A typical situation is that the two stages determine their job sequences independently, without regard for the resulting cost to the other. In some other situations, one of the two stages imposes its own ideal schedule on the other. Then, the other stage has to optimize its own schedule, subject to this given schedule and a limited resequencing capability in a storage buffer. Neither of these situations is typically optimal for the overall system performance.

More generally, in a situation where it is costly to resequence work, we are interested in minimizing the distance between the actual schedules at the various stages of the chain and their respective ideal schedules. For this purpose, the distance between the actual and ideal schedules at any stage of the supply chain is measured by the minimum number of adjacent pairwise interchanges that are necessary to transform one schedule into the other. The pairwise interchange cost is a standard measure of the distance between sequences. It is used, for example, in genome sequencing (Mahajan et al., 2003).

In the context of classical scheduling problems, consider an ideal sequence as being defined by changeover times, such as might occur in various process industries including paint, chemicals, and fertilizer. Suppose that, in these applications, the ideal and least costly sequence (1,2,3) is from light to dark or from mild to toxic. In this case, the sequence $\sigma = (3, 1, 2)$ which has two interchanges is worse than the sequence $\sigma' = (1, 3, 2)$ which has only one interchange. This is because the "increasing job index" changeovers $(1, 2)$ in σ and $(1, 3)$ in σ' have zero or minimal cost, whereas the cost of the "decreasing job index" changeover $(3, 1)$ in σ is likely to be greater than that for $(3,2)$ in σ', due to greater dissimilarity between the products.

Such situations are studied from the point of view of a manufacturer and also from that of an immediately upstream supplier. Both these problems are considered under two different objectives. In the first objective, there is an interchange cost but no storage cost. In the second objective, the addition of storage cost discourages the use of the buffer. A second situation we consider occurs when both stages compromise in order to reach an overall schedule that is satisfactory to both parties. That is, they both schedule the jobs in a less than ideally self-interested way, in order to achieve a fair redistribution of the overall costs. We study this problem under the objective of minimizing the interchange cost and show by example that some intuitive results do not hold in the presence of buffer costs.

This section is organized as follows. In Sect. 7.5.1, we describe our notation and scheme for classifying changeover cost supply chain scheduling problems, and we provide a brief overview of our results. In Sect. 7.5.2, we analyze several problems where one of the manufacturers has to follow the supplier's ideal schedule. In Sect. 7.5.3, the roles are reversed and the supplier has to follow several manufacturers' ideal schedules. Section 7.5.4 considers the joint supplier–

7.5 Resequencing in a Supply Chain

manufacturer decision problem that minimizes the overall system cost and identifies conditions for profitable cooperation between the supplier and the manufacturer. Some incentives and practical mechanisms for cooperation are also discussed.

7.5.1 Notation and Classification

We begin with a description of our notation and assumptions and then provide a brief overview of our results. Let $N = \{1, \ldots, n\}$ denote a set of jobs to be processed. In a two-stage supply chain, each job is processed first by the supplier and then by the manufacturer who ordered it, as in a typical flowshop. A single supplier supplies G manufacturers. The time horizon is divided into T time slots. Processing of a job takes one time slot, for both the supplier and a manufacturer. We consider a balanced flow situation where each manufacturer can process at most one job in each time slot, whereas the supplier can process at most G jobs in each time slot. It is possible that two or more jobs processed by the supplier in a given time slot may have been ordered by the same manufacturer. We assume zero transportation time between the supplier and the manufacturer. Hence, a job that is processed by the supplier in time slot t can be processed by a manufacturer either in time slot $t + 1$ or later. If it is not processed immediately, the job must wait in an intermediate buffer of given capacity $b < n$. We assume that the buffer is controlled by the specified decision maker(s) in each problem considered. The set of available jobs in the buffer during time slot t is denoted by $\beta(t)$, where $|\beta(t)| \leq b$. Figure 7.9 illustrates the arborescence structure of the two-stage supply chain.

As discussed above, both the supplier and each manufacturer have an ideal schedule in which they would like to process the jobs. We denote by S, S^I, and S^* a feasible schedule of jobs for the supplier, an ideal schedule for the supplier, and an optimal schedule that minimizes the supplier's cost while meeting the manufacturer's requirements defined below, respectively. A feasible schedule is one

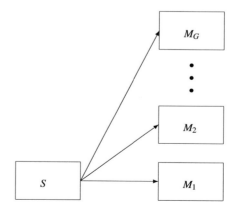

Fig. 7.9 Structure of the two-stage supply chain

that does not exceed the available buffer capacity, b, at any time. Also, we denote by $S(t)$ (respectively, $S^I(t)$, $S^*(t)$) the set of jobs processed by the supplier in time slot t in schedule S (respectively, S^I, S^*). We let $\sigma(j)$ (respectively, $\sigma^I(j)$, $\sigma^*(j)$) denote the time slot in which job j is processed by the supplier in schedule S (respectively, S^I, S^*). Analogously for the manufacturers, we let M_r, M_r^I, and M_r^* denote a feasible schedule for the rth manufacturer, an ideal schedule for the rth manufacturer, and an optimal schedule for the rth manufacturer, respectively. We use the notation M, M^I, and M^* when referring to all the G manufacturers as a whole. Hence, $M(t)$ (respectively, $M^I(t)$, $M^*(t)$) denotes the set of jobs processed by the G manufacturers during time slot t in schedule M (respectively, M^I, M^*), while $M_r(t)$ (respectively, $M_r^I(t)$, $M_r^*(t)$) has the same meaning for the rth manufacturer. We also denote by $\mu(j)$ (respectively, $\mu^I(j)$, $\mu^*(j)$) the time slot in which job j is processed by some manufacturer in schedule M (respectively, M^I, M^*).

If a decision maker processes one or more jobs during a time slot, then that time slot is said to be *active*; otherwise, it is said to be *idle*. Consider the supplier's ideal schedule, S^I. We use $i \prec^S j$ to denote that job i precedes job j in S^I. For the ideal sequence of the rth manufacturer, we use the notation $i \prec^{M_r} j$, omitting the subscript where the identity of the manufacturer is clear from the context. We say that an interchange occurs whenever job i is processed strictly before j, whereas in the ideal schedule j strictly precedes i. We define the cost of an interchange relative to an ideal schedule to be 1. The cost of storing one job in a buffer for one time slot is denoted by w. Depending upon which model is being studied, the decisions to be made include finding:

  (i) An optimal supplier's schedule S^*
 (ii) An optimal schedule M_r^* for the rth manufacturer where $1 \le r \le G$
(iii) An optimal combined schedule S^*, M_r^*

Here, the decision maker(s) are either the supplier, the rth manufacturer, or both jointly, respectively.

Using the standard classification scheme of Graham et al. (1979), we let $\psi_1 = S$ where the decision maker is a supplier and $\psi_1 = M_r$ where the decision maker is manufacturer M_r. Where both these parties are joint decision makers, we let $\psi_1 = S, M_r$. Under ψ_2, we use b to describe the buffer capacity. The objective functions that we consider under ψ_3 are

$$C \qquad = \text{the total cost of interchanges, relative to the decision maker's ideal schedule;}$$
$$C + W = \text{the total cost of interchanges plus storage.}$$

We first show that the number of time slots that need to be considered to construct an optimal schedule is small. For simplicity, we consider the case $G = 1$, but the extension to $G \ge 2$ is straightforward.

Lemma 7.14 *The number of time slots in which processing may occur in an optimal schedule is $O(nb)$.*

7.5 Resequencing in a Supply Chain

Proof Consider a feasible schedule for the supplier and a manufacturer, and suppose that the supplier releases one job at time t. There are $|\beta(t)|$ jobs in the buffer at time t. Suppose that the supplier releases the next job at time t', where $t' > t + |\beta(t)| + 1$. Furthermore, suppose that the manufacturer processes a job in a time slot between $t + |\beta(t)| + 2$ and t'. Here, at least one time slot between $t + 1$ and $t + |\beta(t)| + 1$ is idle for both the supplier and the manufacturer. Removing this time slot clearly does not affect schedule feasibility, nor does it alter interchange costs. Storage costs, if present, can decrease but not increase as a result. Thus, for each of the $O(n)$ jobs released by the supplier, we consider at most $b + 1$ time slots in the schedule. $\square$

In view of Lemma 7.14, we discard irrelevant time slots and hence number the remaining time slots $1, \ldots, T$, where $T = O(nb)$, in all the following discussion.

7.5.2 Manufacturer's Problems

We consider problems where the decision maker is the rth of the G manufacturers. We let S^I denote the ideal supplier's schedule *relative* to this manufacturer, i.e., the ideal schedule of the jobs which are ordered by this manufacturer. Hence, job sets $S^I(t)$ may be empty for some time slots t. In the manufacturer's problem, the jobs are released by the supplier according to schedule S^I. The rth manufacturer also has its own ideal schedule, M_r^I. The manufacturer can resequence the jobs by storing them in a buffer when they arrive from the supplier and then retrieving them in a sequence that is different from that in which they were received. However, the given capacity $b < n$ of the buffer limits this resequencing option. Let z be the last time slot t during which jobs are released by the supplier, i.e., $z = \max\{t : |S^I(t)| > 0\}$.

7.5.2.1 Interchange Costs

We first consider problem $M_r|b|C$, i.e., the minimization of interchange cost for the manufacturer. At each time slot, based on the current jobs in the buffer, the manufacturer decides whether or not to produce a job. We let $u_t = 1$ if time slot t is idle and $u_t = 0$ if a job is scheduled at time t. Note that $u_1 = 1$, since the supplier releases no jobs before time slot 1.

Definition 7.3 We define the vector $U = [u_1, \ldots, u_T]$ to be the *profile* of a schedule M_r. The profile of a schedule identifies which time slots are active and which are idle in the manufacturer's schedule but does not specify the order in which the jobs are processed.

We let $q_t = \sum_{i=1}^{t-1} |S^I(i)| - t$, and $Q_t = \max_{t \le v \le T}\{q_v\} - q_t = \max_{t \le v \le T}\{\sum_{i=t}^{v-1} |S^I(i)| - (v - t)\}$. Observe that Q_t represents the minimum amount of buffer space that needs to be set aside for jobs arriving in the future, in order to ensure feasibility. In fact,

$$Q_t = \max_{v=t,\dots,T}\{q_v\} - q_t. \tag{7.90}$$

Hence, $Q_t \geq 0$.

We now establish a series of structural results about a solution to problem $M_r|b|C$.

Lemma 7.15 *A schedule for problem $M_r|b|C$ satisfies the buffer capacity constraint if and only if $q_t + \sum_{i=1}^{t} u_i \leq b$, for $t = 1, \dots, T$.*

Proof Observe that from time slot 1 through time slot t, the supplier supplies $\sum_{i=1}^{t-1} |S^I(i)|$ jobs, and only $t - \sum_{i=1}^{t} u_i$ of them have so far been processed by the manufacturer. Hence, the number of jobs in the buffer during time slot t is exactly $q_t + \sum_{i=1}^{t} u_i$. □

Given a partial schedule from time slot 1 to time slot t, we let $\psi(t) = Q_t + q_t + \sum_{i=1}^{t} u_i$. Note that $\psi(t)$ is the total buffer requirement at time t, including both the space required to store the jobs currently in the buffer and also the space that needs to be set aside for jobs arriving in the future.

Lemma 7.16 *Given a partial schedule from 1 to t, if $\psi(t) > b$, then no feasible schedule exists from time $t + 1$ on.*

Proof Given t, let $v^* \geq t$ be such that $Q_t = \sum_{i=t}^{v^*-1} |S^I(i)| - (v^* - t)$. Then, $Q_t + q_t = \sum_{i=1}^{v^*-1} |S^I(i)| - t - (v^* - t) = q_{v^*}$ by definition. Hence, if $\psi(t) > b$, and since $t \leq v^*$, we have $q_{v^*} + \sum_{i=1}^{v^*} u_i \geq q_{v^*} + \sum_{i=1}^{t} u_i = \psi(t) > b$. Then, from Lemma 7.15, it follows that no feasible schedule exists. □

Lemma 7.17 $Q_{t-1} = \max\{0, Q_t + q_t - q_{t-1}\}$, *for $t = 2, \dots, T$.*

Proof From (7.90) and $Q_{t-1} = \max_{t-1 \leq v \leq T}\{q_v\} - q_{t-1}$, we obtain $Q_{t-1} = \max\{q_{t-1}, Q_t + q_t\} - q_{t-1} = \max\{0, Q_t + q_t - q_{t-1}\}$. □

Lemma 7.18 *In any feasible schedule, given a time slot t such that $u_t = 0$, we have $\psi(t) \leq \psi(t - 1)$.*

Proof By definition, and since $u_t = 0$, we have $\psi(t) - \psi(t - 1) = (Q_t + q_t + \sum_{i=1}^{t} u_i) - (Q_{t-1} + q_{t-1} + \sum_{i=1}^{t-1} u_i) = (Q_t + q_t - q_{t-1}) - Q_{t-1} \leq 0$ from Lemma 7.17. □

Remark 7.12 The result in Lemma 7.18 provides a condition that is satisfied by an optimal solution to Problem $M_r|b|C$. Consider a profile U such that $u_t = 0$ if and only if $q_t + Q_t + \sum_{i=1}^{t-1} u_i = b$ for $t = 1, \dots, z$. Intuitively, this means that the manufacturer delays the processing of the next job until the widest possible choice of jobs is available; this occurs when the buffer is full. A manufacturer's profile that satisfies this property is said to be *packed*. If a profile is packed, then the position

7.5 Resequencing in a Supply Chain

of the idle time slots from 1 to z is uniquely determined by the supplier's ideal schedule S^I.

Lemma 7.19 *There exists an optimal schedule for problem $M_r|b|C$ that has a packed profile.*

Proof First, observe that in a feasible schedule, $u_t = 1$ implies $q_t + Q_t + \sum_{i=1}^{t-1} u_i = \psi(t) - u_t < b$. In fact, if $\psi(t) - u_t = b$ and $u_t = 1$, then from Lemma 7.16, a buffer overflow occurs at some time slot after t. Hence, to prove the lemma, it is sufficient to show that, given any feasible schedule for problem $M_r|b|C$, there exists another feasible schedule with the same or smaller interchange cost and a packed profile. Consider any feasible manufacturer's schedule without a packed profile.

Suppose there is a time slot t such that $u_t = 0$, $u_{t+1} = 1$ and $\psi(t) - u_t < b$. We can move the idle time earlier from $t + 1$ to t, which delays the processing of the job from time slot t to $t + 1$. This solution is still feasible, since in the new schedule $\psi(t)$ increases by 1 (and cannot therefore exceed b), and all the other $\psi(i)$ values, for $i = 1, \ldots, T, i \neq t$, remain the same. Clearly, no new job interchange occurs when moving idle time slots earlier. Repeating this argument, we obtain a feasible schedule in which all the active time slots t preceding an idle time slot $t + 1$ satisfy the property $\psi(t) - u_t = b$.

Alternatively, suppose that $u_t = 0$, $u_{t+1} = 0$ and $\psi(t + 1) - u_{t+1} = b$. Since $u_{t+1} = 0$, from Lemma 7.18, we have $\psi(t) \geq \psi(t + 1) = b$. Also, from Lemma 7.16, $\psi(t) \leq b$, and hence $\psi(t) = b$. Repeating this argument backward in the schedule, we obtain $\psi(i) - u_i = b$ for all consecutive active time slots i between any two idle time slots. Thus, the resulting profile is packed. □

Definition 7.4 In a manufacturer's problem, given a set of jobs X, we say that $j \in X$ is the *leftmost* job in M_r^I if $j \prec^M k$ for all $k \in X$. Further, $j \in X$ is the *rightmost* job in M_I^r if $k \preceq^M j$ for all $k \in X$.

Lemma 7.20 *A schedule $\tilde{M}_r$ for problem $M_r|b|C$ has the minimum number of interchanges among all schedules with a given profile if and only if, whenever a job is scheduled in time slot $t + 1$, it is the leftmost job in M_r^I among those in $\beta(t) \cup S(t)$.*

We refer the reader to Agnetis et al. (2006) for a proof.

Lemmas 7.15 through 7.20 suggest the following algorithm.

Algorithm M-C

1. Given S^I, M_r^I, b. Let z be the last slot in which some job is released by the supplier.
2. For $t = 1, \ldots, z$, compute $q_t = \sum_{i=1}^{t-1} |S^I(i)| - t$, and
$$Q_t = \max_{t \leq v \leq T} \{\sum_{i=t}^{v-1} |S^I(i)| - (v - t)\}.$$
3. For $t = 1, \ldots, T$:
   If $Q_t + q_t + \sum_{i=1}^{t-1} u_i \geq b$ and there are no jobs available to the manufacturer, then no feasible schedule exists. Terminate.
   If $Q_t + q_t + \sum_{i=1}^{t-1} u_i < b$, then schedule idle time and set $u_t = 1$.

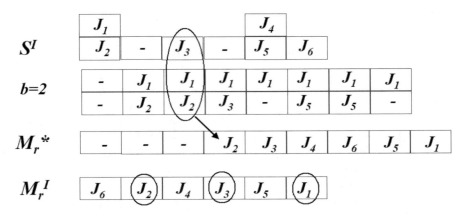

Fig. 7.10 Illustration of Algorithm M-C

Otherwise, schedule the available job which is leftmost in M_r^I, and set $u_t = 0$.

4. For $t = z + 1, \ldots, T$:
    Schedule the job in the buffer which is leftmost in M_r^I. Terminate.

Example 7.5 (Application of Algorithm M-C) Consider the example in Fig. 7.10. There are $n = 6$ jobs and the buffer has capacity $b = 2$. The ideal supplier's and manufacturer's schedules are also shown in Fig. 7.10. The time slot in which the last job is released by the supplier is $z = 6$. At time 1, $u_1 = 1$. At time 2, $q_2 = |S^I(1)| - 2 = 2 - 2 = 0$ and $Q_2 = \max\{0, 0 - 1, 1 - 2, 1 - 3, 3 - 4, 4 - 5\} = 0$. Hence, $q_2 + Q_2 + u_1 = 1 < b = 2$, so again an idle time slot is scheduled ($u_2 = 1$). Similarly, $q_3 = -1$ and $Q_3 = 0$, $q_3 + Q_3 + u_1 + u_2 = -1 + 2 = 1 < 2$, and $u_3 = 1$. For $t = 4$, $q_4 = \sum_{i=1}^{3} |S^I(i)| - 4 = -1$, $Q_4 = 0$, and hence $q_4 + Q_4 + u_1 + u_2 + u_3 = 2 = b$. Since there are available jobs (1, 2, and 3), the leftmost in M_r^I among them (i.e., job 2) is scheduled at $t = 4$, so that $u_4 = 0$. Continuing thus, $q_5 = -2$, $Q_5 = 1$ (obtained for $v = 6$), and therefore $q_5 + Q_5 + u_1 + u_2 + u_3 + u_4 = 2 = b$. Again there are available jobs, so job 3 is scheduled and $u_5 = 0$. At time $t = 6$, $q_6 = -1$, $Q_6 = 0$, and $q_6 + Q_6 + u_1 + u_2 + u_3 + u_4 + u_5 = 2 = b$, so job 4 is scheduled and $u_6 = 0$. After slot z, the buffer is emptied by repeatedly scheduling the leftmost job in M_r^I, which yields the remaining sequence (6, 5, 1). □

Theorem 7.39 *Algorithm M-C finds an optimal schedule for Problem $M_r|b|C$ in $O(nb \log b)$ time.*

Proof Algorithm M-C schedules idle time whenever $\psi(t) - u_t < b$. Hence, from Lemmas 7.15 through 7.18, the profile of the resulting schedule is packed, and therefore Algorithm M-C finds a feasible solution if one exists. Finally, it follows from Lemmas 7.19 and 7.20 that the schedule found by Algorithm M-C has minimum cost.

7.5 Resequencing in a Supply Chain

We consider the time complexity of Algorithm M-C. From the definitions of q_t and Q_t and from Lemma 7.17, it follows that Step 2 requires $O(T)$ time. Step 3 requires $O(T)$ repetitions of the choice of next job to schedule. The jobs in the buffer are stored in a list ordered by the M_r^I schedule. Each arriving job is inserted in this list, using binary search, in $O(\log b)$ time. The next (i.e., leftmost) job is taken from the front of the list. Step 3 requires $O(T)$ insertions in the list, each requiring $O(\log b)$ time. Therefore, the overall time complexity of Algorithm M-C is $O(T \log b)$, which from Lemma 7.14 equals $O(nb \log b)$. $\qquad\square$

7.5.2.2 Interchange and Storage Costs

Consider the problem of the rth manufacturer where the objective function also includes storage costs, $M_r|b|C + W$. Recall that the cost of holding one job in the buffer for one time slot is w. We describe two dynamic programming algorithms for problem $M_r|b|C + W$. The first, M-CW1, has running time that is polynomial in n, but exponential in the buffer capacity, b. The second, M-CW2, has running time that is polynomial in both n and b. However, neither algorithm is more efficient than the other for all problem instances. For both algorithms, the following preliminary result simplifies the choice of which job to schedule next. The proof is similar to the "only if" part of Lemma 7.20 and is omitted.

Lemma 7.21 *There exists an optimal schedule M_r^* for problem $M_r|b|C + W$, in which whenever a job is scheduled in time slot $t + 1$, it is the leftmost job in M_r^I among those in $\beta(t) \cup S(t)$.*

In the description of Algorithm M-CW1 that follows, given a set B of jobs, we let v denote the leftmost job in the manufacturer's ideal schedule M_r^I among the jobs in $B \cup S(t)$. We also let $F(t, j)$ denote the number of jobs that are released by the supplier at or after time slot t and which precede job j in M_r^I.

Algorithm M-CW1
Preprocessing
$F(t, j) = |\{i : i \in \cup_{h=t}^{T} S(h), i \prec^M j\}|$, for $t = 1, \ldots, T, j = 1, \ldots, n$.
Value Function
$f_t(B) = $ the minimum total (interchange plus storage) cost to solve the problem over the time slots from $t + 1$ through T, if $\beta(t) = B$.
Boundary Conditions
$f_T(\emptyset) = 0$.
$f_{t+1}(B \cup S(t) \setminus \{j\}) = +\infty$, if $B \cup S(t) = \emptyset$, for $t = 0, \ldots, T, j = 1, \ldots, n$.
$f_t(B) = +\infty$ if $|B| > b$, for $t = 0, \ldots, T + 1$.
Optimal Solution Value
$f_0(\emptyset)$.

412   7 Optimization and Conflict

Recurrence Relation

$$f_t(B) = \min \begin{cases} w|B \cup S(t)| + f_{t+1}(B \cup S(t)) \\ w(|B \cup S(t)| - 1) + F(t+1, v) + f_{t+1}(B \cup S(t) \setminus \{v\}). \end{cases}$$

The main result for Algorithm M-CW1 now follows.

Theorem 7.40 *Algorithm M-CW1 finds an optimal schedule for problem $M_r|b|C + W$ in $O(n^{b+2}b)$ time.*

Proof The first alternative in the recurrence relation computes the cost of scheduling one unit of idle time and thus incurring the storage cost of delaying the $|B \cup S(t)|$ jobs in the buffer by one time unit. The second alternative computes the interchange cost of processing job v in M_r before any jobs which precede v in M_r^I. Since, by definition, at time $t + 1$ job v is the leftmost job in M_r^I among those in $B \cup S(t)$, no job in $B \cup S(t)$ causes an interchange cost when v is scheduled. Hence, the interchange cost created when processing v at time t equals the number of jobs that are not available before time $t + 1$ and that precede v in M_r^I, i.e., $F(t + 1, v)$. In the second alternative, exactly the jobs in $B \cup S(t) \setminus \{v\}$ remain in the buffer at time $t+1$. Consequently, Algorithm M-CW1 compares the cost of all nondominated state transitions and thus finds an optimal schedule.

We now consider the time complexity of Algorithm M-CW1. Observe that, for any given j, each job i appears in only one set $S(h)$, thus requiring $O(\max\{n, T\})$ time in the preprocessing step. Therefore, the overall time requirement for preprocessing is $O(nT)$. Also, the recurrence relation is computed for $f_t(B)$, where $0 \le t \le T$, and for all possible subsets B where $|B| \le b$. This requires a total of $O(n^b T)$ applications of the recurrence relation. Since $B \cup S(t)$ can be computed in $O(n)$ time, the overall time complexity of Algorithm M-CW1 is $O(n^{b+1}T)$, which from Lemma 7.14 equals $O(n^{b+2}b)$ time. $\qquad\square$

Below, we present a second algorithm, M-CW2, for problem $M_r|b|C + W$. In order to describe Algorithm M-CW2, we need some additional notation. Let $J(i, j, k)$ be the set of jobs that are processed by the supplier in the time slots from i through j and that precede job k in M_r^I, i.e., $J(i, j, k) = \{q | q \prec^M k, i \le \sigma^I(q) \le j\}$. We let $J(i, j, k, l)$ denote the set $J(i, j, k)$ with the addition of $l \ge 0$ idle time slots. Also, we let $|J(i, j, k)|$ denote the number of jobs in $J(i, j, k)$, and we note that $|J(i, j, k, l)| = |J(i, j, k)| + l$.

Before describing the algorithm, several definitions and preliminary results are needed.

Lemma 7.22 *If $i \preceq^S j$ and $i \prec^M j$, then in every optimal schedule M_r^*, i precedes j.*

Proof Since $i \preceq^S j$, whenever j is available for processing in M_r^*, either i has already been processed or it is also available. In the first case, the proof is complete. In the second case, it follows immediately from Lemma 7.21 that, without loss of generality, job i can be scheduled before job j in M_r^*. $\qquad\square$

7.5 Resequencing in a Supply Chain

Definition 7.5 Given a feasible manufacturer's schedule M_r, a set $J(i, j, k, l)$ is *compact* in M_r if all the elements of $J(i, j, k, l)$ (including the idle time slots) are sequenced consecutively in M_r, i.e., they are scheduled in time slots $i + 1, \ldots, i + |J(i, j, k, l)|$. That is, if $J(i, j, k, l)$ is compact, then no job or idle time slot that is not in $J(i, j, k, l)$ can be scheduled in the time interval $[i + 1, i + |J(i, j, k, l)|]$.

Definition 7.6 A set $J(i, j, k, l)$ is *compact-feasible* if there exists a feasible schedule M_r such that $J(i, j, k, l)$ is compact in M_r. For a set to be compact-feasible, l can only assume certain values. There must be a sufficient number of idle time slots in M_r to account for the time slots in which no job from $J(i, j, k)$ can be scheduled. More precisely, if $J(i, j, k, l)$ is compact in M_r, in the $t - i + 1$ time slots from $i + 1$ through $t + 1$ (where $i \le t \le j$), only jobs in $J(i, t, k)$ can be scheduled, and the other time slots must be idle.

Using Definitions 7.5 and 7.6, a lower bound on l is given by

$$l_{\min}(i, j, k) = \max\{0, \max_{t=i,\ldots,j} \{t - i + 1 - |J(i, t, k)|\}\}. \tag{7.91}$$

Let h be the rightmost job of $J(i, j, k)$ in M_r^I, and let

$$P(i, j, k) = \{t | \sigma^I(h) \le t \le j, S^I(t) \cap (J(i, j, k) \setminus \{h\}) = \emptyset\}.$$

Note that $P(i, j, k)$ contains all the time slots, from $\sigma^I(h)$ through j, in which no job in $J(i, j, k) \setminus \{h\}$ is processed by the supplier. In particular, $P(i, j, k)$ contains time slot $\sigma^I(h)$ if and only if no other job in $J(i, j, k)$, other than h, becomes available from the supplier in time slot $\sigma^I(h)$. Moreover, from the definition of $l_{\min}(i, j, k)$ in Eq. (7.91), it follows that $l_{\min}(i, j, k) = 0$ if $j < i$ and, for all $j \ge i$,

$$l_{\min}(i, j, k) = \max\{l_{\min}(i, j - 1, k), j - i + 1 - |J(i, j, k)|\}. \tag{7.92}$$

The following lemma identifies the time slots that are candidates to process job h.

Lemma 7.23 *Given an optimal schedule M_r^* and a set $J(i, j, k, l)$, let h be the last job of $J(i, j, k, l)$ in M_r^I. Then,*

(i). All jobs $u \in J(i, j, k) \setminus \{h\}$ such that $\sigma^I(u) \le \sigma^I(h)$ precede h in M_r^*.

(ii). Either h is scheduled in time slot $p + 1$, for some $p \in P(i, j, k)$, or h is the last job from $J(i, j, k)$ in M_r^*.

Proof We consider each part in turn.

(i) The result follows immediately from Lemma 7.22.

(ii) Suppose that h is not the job scheduled last among those of $J(i, j, k)$ in M_r^*, and further suppose for contradiction that h is scheduled in time slot $q + 1$ in M_r^*, where $q \notin P(i, j, k)$. Then, by definition of h and $P(i, j, k)$, $S^I(q) \cup \beta(q)$ contains a job $v \in J(i, j, k)$ such that $v \prec^M h$. Since jobs v and h are both

414   7 Optimization and Conflict

available for processing by the manufacturer at time $q + 1$, processing job h violates Lemma 7.21, a contradiction. □

The following two preliminary results consider the two cases in part (ii) of Lemma 7.23, respectively. Each result describes a decomposition of the schedule of the jobs and idle time slots of $J(i, j, k, l)$, thereby specifying which jobs precede and which jobs follow job h.

Lemma 7.24 *Given an optimal schedule M_r^* and a set $J(i, j, k, l)$ that is compact in M_r^*, let h be the last job in the M_r^l schedule in that set. If h is scheduled in a time slot $p + 1$, where $p \in P(i, j, k)$, then, letting $l' = l_{\min}(i, p - 1, h)$:*

(i) *The jobs and the idle time slots of set $J(i, j, k, l)$ that precede h in M_r^* are $A(p) = J(i, p - 1, h, l')$, where $l' \leq l$.*

(ii) *The jobs and the idle time slots of set $J(i, j, k, l)$ that follow h in M_r^* are $B(p) = J(p + 1, j, h, l - l')$, where $l - l' \geq l_{\min}(p + 1, j, h)$.*

(iii) *Sets $A(p)$ and $B(p)$ are compact in M_r^*.*

Proof We consider each part in turn.

(i) It follows from Lemma 7.21 that any job $q \in J(i, p - 1, h, l')$ precedes h in M_r^*. Since $J(i, j, k, l)$ is compact in M_r^*, from time slot $i + 1$ through time slot p exactly $p - i$ jobs and idle time slots are scheduled in M_r^*. Since M_r^* is feasible, $l' \leq l$.

(ii) After h in M_r^*, the remaining jobs from $J(i, j, k, l)$ must be scheduled with $l - l'$ idle time slots, thus yielding the set $B(p) = J(p + 1, j, h, l - l')$. Since M_r^* is feasible, $l - l' \geq l_{\min}(p + 1, j, h)$.

(iii) Note that $A(p) \cup B(p) \cup \{h\} = J(i, j, k, l)$. Then, the compactness of $A(p)$ and $B(p)$ follows from that of $J(i, j, k, l)$. □

From Lemma 7.24, the schedule of $J(i, j, k, l)$ consists of the jobs and idle time slots of $A(p)$, followed by job h, followed by the jobs and idle time slots of $B(p)$. In the following discussion, we refer to the case considered in Lemma 7.24 as *h-intermediate*.

Lemma 7.25 *Given an optimal schedule M_r^* and a set $J(i, j, k, l)$ that is compact in M_r^*, let h be the last job in the M_r^l schedule in that set. If h is the last job from $J(i, j, k, l)$ in M_r^*, then the jobs and idle time slots of set $J(i, j, k, l)$ that precede h in M_r^* are the set $J(i, j, h, l')$, for some $l_{\min}(i, j, h) \leq l' \leq l$, where $J(i, j, h, l')$ is compact in M_r^*.*

Proof From the lemma conditions, the set of jobs of $J(i, j, k)$ preceding h in M_r^* is $J(i, j, k) \setminus \{h\} = J(i, j, h)$. Since $J(i, j, k, l)$ is compact in M_r^*, there is a minimum number of idle time slots $l_{\min}(i, j, h)$ that must precede h in M_r^*. The remaining $l - l_{\min}(i, j, h)$ idle time slots can be scheduled either before h, thus contributing to l', or after h. Finally, the compactness of $J(i, j, h, l')$ follows from that of $J(i, j, k, l)$. □

7.5 Resequencing in a Supply Chain

Remark 7.13 From Lemma 7.25, the schedule of $J(i, j, k, l)$ consists of the jobs of $J(i, j, k) \setminus \{h\}$ and l' idle time slots, followed by job h, followed by $l - l'$ idle time slots. In the following discussion, we refer to the case considered in Lemma 7.25 as *h-last*. Note that, if $l_{\min}(i, j, h) > l$, then h cannot be scheduled last among jobs in $J(i, j, k)$ in M_r^*. Moreover in that case, from the definition of $l_{\min}(i, j, h)$, $J(i, j, h, l)$ is not compact-feasible.

Lemmas 7.23, 7.24, and 7.25 identify all the possible candidate time slots for processing job h in M_r^* and suggest a dynamic programming algorithm to solve problem $M_r|b|C + W$. In order to construct such an algorithm, we need to identify the contribution of $J(i, j, k, l)$ to the objective function in the cases considered in Lemmas 7.24 and 7.25. Let $V(J(i, j, k, l))$ be the minimum total interchange plus storage cost to schedule the set $J(i, j, k, l)$. If we add a dummy job 0 at the end of the M_r^I schedule, then $J(1, T, 0)$ is the entire set of jobs to be scheduled. Then, $l_{\min}(1, T, 0)$ is the minimum number of idle time slots that must be inserted in any feasible schedule M_r of the rth manufacturer. Adding more than b idle time slots to $l_{\min}(1, T, 0)$, within the interval $[1, z]$, would necessarily result in buffer overflow. Therefore, the value of the optimal solution can be computed as $V(J(1, T, 0, b + l_{\min}(1, T, 0)))$.

We now describe our dynamic programming algorithm for problem $M_r|b|C + W$. By convention, the value obtained by minimization over an empty set is $+\infty$.

Algorithm M-CW2

Preprocessing
$l_{\min}(i, j, k) = \max\{0, \max_{t=i,\ldots,j}\{t - i + 1 - |J(i, t, k)|\}\}$, for $i, k = 1, \ldots, n, j > i$.
$P(i, j, k) = \{t | \sigma^I(h) \leq t \leq j, S^I(t) \cap (J(i, j, k) \setminus \{h\}) = \emptyset\}$, for $i, k = 1, \ldots, n, j > i$.

Value Function
$V(J(i, j, k, l)) = $ minimum total interchange plus storage cost to schedule the set $J(i, j, k, l)$.

Boundary Condition
$V(J(i, j, k, l)) = 0$ if $|J(i, j, k)| \leq 1, l \geq 0$.

Optimal Cost
$V(J(1, T, 0, b + l_{\min}(1, T, 0)))$.

Recurrence Relation

$$
V(J(i, j, k, l)) = \min \left\{
\begin{array}{l}
\min_{p \in P(i,j,k)} \left\{
\begin{array}{l}
V(A(p)) + V(B(p)) + w(p - \sigma^I(h)) \\
+ |\{f, g | f \in A(p), g \in B(p), g \prec^M f\}| \\
+ |J(p + 1, j, h)|
\end{array}
\right\}, \\
\min_{l_{\min}(i,j,h) \leq l' \leq l} \left\{ V(J(i, j, h, l')) + w(i + |J(i, j, h, l')| - \sigma^I(h)) \right\},
\end{array}
\right.
$$

where $A(p) = J(i, p - 1, h, l_{\min}(i, p - 1, h))$,
$B(p) = J(p + 1, j, h, l - l_{\min}(i, p - 1, h))$, and
h is the last job of $J(i, j, k, l)$ in M_r^I.

416   7 Optimization and Conflict

We provide an explanation of Algorithm M-CW2, followed by a numerical example. The two alternatives in the recurrence relation represent the h-intermediate and h-last cases, respectively. Consider first the h-intermediate case. From Lemma 7.24, if h is scheduled in time slot $p + 1$, then the schedule decomposes into three parts, namely $A(p)$, h, and $B(p)$. Besides $V(A(p))$ and $V(B(p))$, we need to account for the contributions of h to the storage and interchange costs, plus the interchange costs between $A(p)$ and $B(p)$. Since job h is first available for processing by the manufacturer in time slot $\sigma^I(h) + 1$ and is scheduled in time slot $p + 1$, the storage cost of job h is $w(p - \sigma^I(h))$. By definition of h, there are no interchanges between h and any job in $A(p)$, whereas there is one interchange between h and every job in $B(p)$. This provides $|J(p + 1, j, h)|$ interchanges. Finally, there is one interchange for each pair (f, g) such that $f \in A(p)$, $g \in B(p)$, and $g \prec^M f$.

Consider now the h-last case. From Lemma 7.25, and since $f \prec^M h$ for all $f \in J(i, j, h)$, we need only add to $V(J(i, j, h, l'))$ the contribution of job h to the storage costs. All jobs and idle time slots in $J(i, j, h, l')$ are scheduled before h, starting from time slot $i + 1$. Hence, job h is scheduled in time slot $i + 1 + |J(i, j, h, l')|$, and its contribution to storage costs is $w(i + |J(i, j, h, l')| - \sigma^I(h))$.

Regarding the boundary condition, when $J(i, j, k)$ is either empty or a singleton, there are no interchanges within that set. Moreover, if $|J(i, j, k)| = 1$, then there is no reason not to schedule the single job h immediately, i.e., in time slot $\sigma^I(h) + 1$. We note that this is always possible, due to the fact that $J(i, j, k, l)$ is compact. We now provide an example of Algorithm M-CW2.

Example 7.6 (Application of Algorithm M-CW2) Consider the following instance of problem $M_r|b|C + W$. There are $n = 5$ jobs. The ideal supplier's schedule releases exactly one job in each time slot, i.e., $S^I = 1, 2, 3, 4, 5, 0$. From (7.91), $l_{\min}(1, 5, 0) = 0$. There is a buffer of capacity $b = 1$. The manufacturer's ideal schedule is $M_r^I = 2, 3, 5, 1, 4, 0$. Finally, the storage cost is $w = 1/3$.
Let $*$ denote an idle time slot. Our objective is to compute $V(J(1, n, 0, b + l_{\min}(1, 5, 0))) = V(J(1, 5, 0, 1))$.

$\boxed{V(J(1, 5, 0, 1))}$

The set $J(1, 5, 0, 1)$ includes all the jobs, so the rightmost element in M_r^I within the set is $h = 4$. We first consider the h-intermediate case. Let us consider $P(i, j, k) = P(1, 5, 0)$. Since $\sigma^I(h) = \sigma^I(4) = \{4\}$, we have $J(i, j, k) \setminus \{h\} = J(1, 5, 0) \setminus \{4\} = \{1, 2, 3, 5\}$ and $P(1, 5, 0) = \{t | 4 \le t \le 5, S^I(t) \cap (J(1, 5, 0) \setminus \{4\}) = \emptyset\}$. The only value of t for which $S^I(t) \cap (J(i, j, k) \setminus \{h\}) = \emptyset$ is thus $t = 4$. Therefore, we evaluate the recurrence relation for $p = 4$ only. To consider the h-intermediate case, we need to compute $l_{\min}$. For $t = 1$, $J(1, 1, 4)$ includes the jobs released from 1 to 1 which precede 4 in M_r^I, i.e., job 1 only. Thus, $|J(1, 1, 4)| = 1$ and $t - i + 1 - |J(i, t, k)| = 1 - 1 + 1 - 1 = 0$. For $t = 2$, $J(1, 2, 4) = \{1, 2\}$ and hence $t - i + 1 - |J(i, t, k)| = 2 - 1 + 1 - 2 = 0$. Similarly, for $t = 3$, $J(1, 3, 4) = \{1, 2, 3\}$, so $t - i + 1 - |J(i, t, k)| = 3 - 1 + 1 - 3 = 0$, and therefore $l_{\min}(1, 3, 4) = 0$. Thus, we have $A(p) = A(4) = J(i, p - 1, h, l_{\min}(i, p - 1, h)) = J(1, 3, 4, 0) = \{1, 2, 3\}$ and $B(p) = B(4) = J(p + 1, j, h, l - l_{\min}(i, p - 1, h)) = J(5, 5, 4, 1) = \{5, *\}$.

7.5 Resequencing in a Supply Chain

We now consider the h-last case. We first compute $l_{\min}(1, 5, 4)$. Besides the previously considered sets $J(1, 1, 4)$, $J(1, 2, 4)$, and $J(1, 3, 4)$, we must consider $J(1, 4, 4) = \{1, 2, 3\}$ and $J(1, 5, 4) = \{1, 2, 3, 5\}$. For $t = 4$, we have $t - i + 1 - |J(i, t, k)| = 4 - 1 + 1 - 3 = 1$, and for $t = 5$, we have $t - i + 1 - |J(i, t, k)| = 5 - 1 + 1 - 4 = 1$. Therefore, $l_{\min}(1, 5, 4) = 1$. Since $l = 1$, we have $l' = 1$. In this case, $|J(i, j, h, l')| = |J(1, 5, 4, 1)| = 5$ and $\sigma^I(h) = 4$, and hence the second term in the recurrence relation is $V(J(1, 5, 4, 1)) + (1 + 5 - 4)w$. Thus,

$$V(J(1, 5, 0, 1)) = \min \begin{cases} V(J(1, 3, 4, 0)) + V(J(5, 5, 4, 1)) + w(4 - 4) + 1 + 1 \\ V(J(1, 5, 4, 1)) + 2w. \end{cases}$$

In computing $V(J(1, 3, 4, 0))$, since $l = 0$, we are forced to schedule the jobs in $J(1, 3, 4) = \{1, 2, 3\}$ in the same order as in S^I, which results in two interchanges with respect to M_r^I and no storage costs. Hence, $V(J(1, 3, 4, 0)) = 2$. From the boundary condition, $V(J(5, 5, 4, 1)) = 0$. Therefore, it only remains to compute $V(J(1, 5, 4, 1))$.

$\boxed{V(J(1, 5, 4, 1))}$

As above, we compute $h = 1$. For the h-intermediate case, we obtain $P(1, 5, 4) = \{1, 4\}$. Therefore, we evaluate the recurrence relation for $p = 1$ and $p = 4$.

$p = 1$:
$l_{\min}(1, 0, 1) = 0$.
$A(1) = J(1, 0, 1, 0) = \emptyset$.
$B(1) = J(2, 5, 1, 1) = \{2, 3, 5, *\}$.

$p = 4$:
$l_{\min}(1, 3, 1) = 1$.
$A(4) = J(1, 3, 1, 1) = \{2, 3, *\}$.
$B(4) = J(5, 5, 1, 0) = \{5\}$.

We now consider the h-last case. Since $l_{\min}(1, 5, 1) = 2 > 1 = l$, there are no feasible values for l', i.e., job 1 cannot be scheduled last in $J(1, 5, 4, 1)$. Thus,

$$V(J(1, 5, 4, 1)) = \min \begin{cases} \min \begin{cases} V(J(1, 0, 1, 0)) + V(J(2, 5, 1, 1)) + w(1 - 1) + 0 + 3 \\ V(J(1, 3, 1, 1)) + V(J(5, 5, 1, 0)) + w(4 - 1) + 0 + 1 \end{cases} \\ +\infty. \end{cases}$$

Observe that $V(J(1, 0, 1, 0)) = 0$ and $V(J(5, 5, 1, 0)) = 0$ from the boundary condition. Therefore, to evaluate $V(J(1, 5, 4, 1))$, we need to only compute $V(J(2, 5, 1, 1))$ and $V(J(1, 3, 1, 1))$.

$\boxed{V(J(2, 5, 1, 1))}$

As above, we compute $h = 5$ and $P(2, 5, 1) = \{5\}$. Therefore, we evaluate the recurrence relation for $p = 5$ only.

$p = 5$:
$l_{\min}(2, 4, 5) = 1$.
$A(5) = J(2, 4, 5, 1) = \{2, 3, *\}$.
$B(5) = J(6, 5, 5, 0) = \emptyset$.

Since $l_{\min}(2, 5, 5) = 2 > 1 = l$, there are no feasible values for l' in the h-last case. Thus,

$$V(J(2, 5, 1, 1)) = \min \begin{cases} V(J(2, 4, 5, 1)) + V(J(6, 5, 5, 0)) + w(5 - 5) + 0 + 0 \\ +\infty. \end{cases}$$

Observe that $V(J(6, 5, 5, 0)) = 0$ from the boundary condition. Therefore, to evaluate $V(J(2, 5, 1, 1))$, we need to only compute $V(J(2, 4, 5, 1))$.

$\boxed{V(J(1, 3, 1, 1))}$

As above, we compute $h = 3$ and $P(1, 3, 1) = \{3\}$. Therefore, we evaluate the recurrence relation for $p = 3$ only.

$p = 3$:
$l_{\min}(1, 2, 3) = 1$.
$A(3) = J(1, 2, 3, 1) = \{2, *\}$.
$B(3) = J(4, 3, 3, 0) = \emptyset$.
Since $l_{\min}(1, 3, 3) = 2 > 1 = l$, there are no feasible values for l' in the h-last case. Thus,

$$V(J(1, 3, 1, 1)) = \min \begin{cases} V(J(1, 2, 3, 1)) + V(J(4, 3, 3, 0)) + w(3 - 3) + 0 + 0 \\ +\infty. \end{cases}$$

Observe that $V(J(1, 2, 3, 1)) = 0$ and $V(J(4, 3, 3, 0)) = 0$ from the boundary condition.

$\boxed{V(J(2, 4, 5, 1))}$

In this case, $h = 3$ and $P(2, 4, 5) = \{3, 4\}$. We evaluate the recurrence relation for $p = 3$ and $p = 4$.

$p = 3$:
$l_{\min}(2, 2, 3) = 0$.
$A(3) = J(2, 2, 3, 0) = \{2\}$.
$B(3) = J(4, 4, 3, 1) = \{*\}$.
$p = 4$:
$l_{\min}(2, 3, 3) = 1$.
$A(4) = J(2, 3, 3, 1) = \{2, *\}$.
$B(4) = J(5, 4, 3, 0) = \emptyset$.
Since $l_{\min}(2, 4, 3) = 2 > 1 = l$, there are no feasible values for l' in the h-last case. Thus,

$$V(J(2, 4, 5, 1)) = \min \begin{cases} \min \begin{cases} V(J(2, 2, 3, 0)) + V(J(4, 4, 3, 1)) + w(3 - 3) + 0 + 0 \\ V(J(2, 3, 3, 1)) + V(J(5, 4, 3, 0)) + w(4 - 3) + 0 + 0 \end{cases} \\ +\infty. \end{cases}$$

Observe that $V(J(2, 3, 3, 0))$, $V(J(4, 4, 3, 1))$, $V(J(2, 3, 3, 1))$, and $V(J(5, 4, 3, 0))$ are all equal to 0 from the boundary condition.

7.5 Resequencing in a Supply Chain 419

Optimal Schedule Construction

First, we evaluate all the above value functions.

$$V(J(2, 4, 5, 1)) = \min\{0 + 0 + w(0) + 0 + 0, 0 + 0 + w(1) + 0 + 0, +\infty\} = 0 \text{ for } p = 3$$
$$V(J(1, 3, 1, 1)) = \min\{0 + 0 + w(0) + 0 + 0, +\infty\} = 0 \text{ for } p = 3$$
$$V(J(2, 5, 1, 1)) = \min\{0 + 0 + w(0) + 0 + 0, +\infty\} = 0 \text{ for } p = 5$$
$$V(J(1, 5, 4, 1)) = \min\{0 + 0 + w(0) + 0 + 3, 0 + 0 + w(3) + 0 + 1, +\infty\} = 2$$
$$\text{for } p = 4, \text{ since } w = 1/3$$
$$V(J(1, 5, 0, 1)) = \min\{2 + 0 + w(0) + 1 + 1, 2 + w(2)\} = 8/3 \text{ for } l' = 1.$$

We now backtrack to find the optimal schedule. In the summary table of the backtracking process which follows, $\{\ldots\}$ is used to denote an unordered subset of the jobs and idle times.

$V(J(i, j, k, l))$	h	p	l'	Schedule
$V(J(1, 5, 0, 1))$	4		1	$\{1,2,3,5,*\}4$
$V(J(1, 5, 4, 1))$	1	4		$\{2,3,*\}1\ 5\ 4$
$V(J(1, 3, 1, 1))$	3	3		$\{2,*\}3\ 1\ 5\ 4$
$V(J(1, 2, 3, 1))$	2	2		$\{*\}2\ 3\ 1\ 5\ 4$

The optimal schedule is $* \ 2\ 3\ 1\ 5\ 4$. The buffer contains job 1 for three time slots and job 4 for two time slots, yielding a buffer cost of $5/3$. There is one interchange between M_r^* and M_r^I, for jobs 1 and 5. Therefore, the total cost is $V(J(1, 5, 0, 1)) = 8/3$.

The main result for Algorithm M-CW2 now follows.

Theorem 7.41 *Algorithm M-CW2 finds an optimal schedule for problem $M_r|b|C + W$ in $O(n^5 b^4)$ time.*

Proof First, we prove the optimality of Algorithm M-CW2. Since any optimal schedule contains only jobs and idle times, the set $J(1, T, 0, b + l_{\min}(1, T, 0))$ is compact. Lemma 7.23 shows that, for a compact set of jobs and idle times, there exists an optimal schedule M_r^* where the job that is last in M_r^I is scheduled in one of the two alternative ways. Lemma 7.24 (respectively, Lemma 7.25) provides a decomposition of the schedule in the first (respectively, second) case. Algorithm M-CW2 compares the costs of all possible decompositions in both cases. Since, from Lemmas 7.24 and 7.25, each subset resulting from the decomposition of a compact set is also compact, this procedure can be applied recursively. It then follows that Algorithm M-CW2 finds an optimal schedule for problem $M_r|b|C + W$.

We consider the time complexity of Algorithm M-CW2. First, consider the sets $J(i, j, k)$. For each pair i, j, we can identify all jobs preceding k in M^I which are released by the supplier between time slots i and j, in $O(n)$ time. It follows that, since i, j, and k may assume T, T, and n different values, respectively, all sets $J(i, j, k)$ can be generated in $O(T^2 n)$ time. From Eq. (7.92), each value of $l_{\min}(i, j, h)$ can be computed in constant time. Each set $P(i, j, k)$ can be computed in $O(T)$ time by checking whether each job released by the supplier from i to j belongs to $J(i, j, k)$ or not. Hence, the entire preprocessing step requires $O(T^3 n)$ time. The recurrence relation requires the computation of $O(T^2 nb)$ values of $V(J(i, j, k, l))$. For each $p \in P(i, j, k)$, the total number of interchanges between $A(p)$ and $B(p)$ can be computed in $O(n)$ time, as follows. We scan M^I from left to right, labeling each job $g \in B(p)$ with the number of jobs from $A(p)$ following g (i.e., still to be encountered). Adding up all the labels gives the total number of interchanges for that value of p. For the computation of $V(J(i, j, k, l))$, p and l' may assume $O(T)$ and $O(b)$ values, respectively, where $O(b) < O(T)$ from Lemma 7.14. Thus, each value of $V(J(i, j, k, l))$ requires $O(nT)$ computation time. Therefore, the overall time complexity of the recurrence step is $O(T^3 n^2 b)$, which dominates that of the preprocessing step. Recalling from Lemma 7.14 that $T = O(nb)$, the result follows. $\qquad\square$

Since Algorithm M-CW1 has time complexity $O(n^{b+2} b)$ and Algorithm M-CW2 has time complexity $O(n^5 b^4)$, neither algorithm is more efficient than the other in general.

7.5.3 Supplier's Problems

We consider problems where the decision maker is the supplier. We assume that the jobs must be delivered by the supplier according to the G ideal manufacturers' schedules. The supplier needs to find a schedule that enables it to achieve this at minimum cost.

Remark 7.14 The supplier's problem and the manufacturer's problem are not symmetric, due to the different processing capacities of the supplier and of each manufacturer. A symmetric scenario would involve G suppliers and one manufacturer who can process G jobs during a time slot, similar to the assembly system discussed in Sect. 7.3. Here, it would be possible to derive results that are symmetric to those illustrated in this section. However, the case of one supplier and G manufacturers is common in practice, since for a given item, a specialized supplier serves multiple manufacturers. This case is therefore considered here.

Recall from Sect. 7.5.1 that M_r^I and S^I denote the ideal rth manufacturer's schedule and the ideal supplier's schedule, respectively, and $M^I(t)$ denotes the set of jobs requested by all manufacturers in time slot t. Let $d_t = |M^I(t)|$, and, given a supplier's schedule S, let I_t and x_t denote the number of jobs in the buffer and the number of jobs produced by the supplier during time slot t, respectively. The vector $X = [x_1, \ldots, x_T]$ is referred to as the *profile* of a supplier's schedule. The following inventory balance equations hold in any feasible schedule:

$$I_t + x_t = d_{t+1} + I_{t+1}, \quad \text{for } t = 1, \ldots, T - 1. \tag{7.93}$$

7.5.3.1 Interchange Costs

We first consider problem $S|b|C$, where there are no storage costs, and thus the objective is the minimization of interchange costs relative to S^I. The demand pattern of each manufacturer requires the production of at most one unit at every time slot. By assumption, the supplier can supply up to G jobs in each time slot. Jobs that have been produced by the supplier, but not yet delivered to the manufacturers, enter the buffer of capacity b.

We propose an algorithm based on the following two preliminary results. The first result is the supplier's counterpart of Lemma 7.20.

Definition 7.7 In a supplier's problem, given a set of jobs $\mathscr{J}$, we say that $A \subseteq \mathscr{J}$ is the *rightmost* (respectively, *leftmost*) job set in S^I if no job in $\mathscr{J} \setminus A$ strictly follows (resp., precedes) a job of A in the supplier's ideal schedule S^I.

Lemma 7.26 *In problem $S|b|C$, given a profile, a schedule $\tilde{S}$ has the minimum number of interchanges among all the schedules having that profile, if and only if, whenever a set of jobs is scheduled in time slot $t - 1$, those jobs are the rightmost jobs in S^I among the jobs in $\beta(t) \cup M(t)$.*

We refer the reader to Agnetis et al. (2006) for a proof.

We assume that the first request for a job by the manufacturers occurs in time slot 2. Also, we allow $I_1 > 0$, which is equivalent to assuming that the supplier can start producing before time slot 1.

Definition 7.8 We define a supplier's profile to be *packed* if there exists a time slot $\bar{t}$ such that:

(i) $I_t = b$, for all $t = 1, \ldots, \bar{t} - 1$.
(ii) $I_{\bar{t}} < b$.
(iii) $x_t = 0$, for all $t = \bar{t}, \ldots, T$.

We observe that, if $\bar{t}$ exists, then (i)–(iii) uniquely define it.

The following result is the supplier's counterpart of Lemma 7.19.

Lemma 7.27 *There exists an optimal schedule for problem $S|b|C$ that has a packed profile.*

Proof Let S^* be any optimal schedule, and let $\bar{\tau}$ be such that, for all $1 \leq t \leq \bar{\tau} - 1$, $I_t = b$, and $I_{\bar{\tau}} < b$. Since it follows that $I_{\bar{\tau}} + d_{\bar{\tau}} < G + b$, Eq. (7.93) implies $x_{\bar{\tau}-1} < G$. If $x_t = 0$ from time $\bar{\tau}$ on, then the proof is complete. Else, let $\hat{t} \geq \bar{\tau}$ be the first time slot in S^* after $\bar{\tau}$ in which some job is produced by the supplier. Since no job is produced from $\bar{\tau}$ through $\hat{t} - 1$, the buffer is never full in that time interval. Let j be the leftmost in S^I among the jobs produced in $\hat{t}$. Consider the schedule $\hat{S}$ obtained from S^* by scheduling job j earlier, in time slot $\bar{\tau} - 1$. Since, in S^*, $x_{\bar{\tau}-1} < G$, and the buffer is not full from $\bar{\tau}$ through $\hat{t} - 1$, $\hat{S}$ is also feasible. Since j is the leftmost in S^I among the jobs produced in $\hat{t}$, the number of interchanges in $\hat{S}$ is not greater than in S^*, and thus $\hat{S}$ is also optimal. Repeating the above argument, we can move other jobs earlier until we obtain an optimal schedule that has a packed profile. □

Lemmas 7.26 and 7.27 suggest an algorithm for finding an optimal schedule. The algorithm constructs the supplier's schedule in reverse order. In each time slot, Lemma 7.27 determines how many jobs must be produced by the supplier in the current time slot, while Lemma 7.26 indicates which jobs those are.

Algorithm S-C

1. Given S^I, M_r^I for all $r = 1, \ldots, G$, and b. Set $\beta(T) = \emptyset$, $I_{T+1} = 0$, and $d_{T+1} = 0$.
2. For $t = T, \ldots, 1$, do:

   - Compute $x_t = \max\left\{0, I_{t+1} + d_{t+1} - b\right\}$.
   - Schedule in time slot t the set $S(t)$ formed by the x_t rightmost jobs in S^I from the set $\beta(t+1) \cup M^I(t+1)$.
   - Set $\beta(t) = (\beta(t+1) \cup M^I(t+1)) \setminus S(t)$, and $I_t = |\beta(t)|$.

3. Schedule the job set $\beta(1)$ before time slot 1, and terminate.

Theorem 7.42 *Algorithm S-C finds an optimal schedule for Problem $S|b|C$ in $O(nb \log(G + b))$ time.*

Proof Lemma 7.27 guarantees that there exists an optimal schedule which has a packed profile. Scheduling $\max\left\{0, I_{t+1} + d_{t+1} - b\right\}$ jobs at each time slot t guarantees that the profile of the schedule built by Algorithm S-C is packed. Since at each time slot t the scheduled jobs are selected according to Lemma 7.26, the schedule produced by Algorithm S-C has lowest cost among the schedules that have a packed profile and therefore is optimal.

We consider the time complexity of Algorithm S-C. Step 2 is repeated $O(T)$ times. During the execution of the algorithm, each job is inserted into and deleted from an ordered list containing at most $G + b$ elements exactly once. The time required for each such insertion or deletion is $O(\log(G+b))$. Therefore, the overall time complexity of Algorithm S-C is $O(T \log(G + b))$, which from Lemma 7.14 equals $O(nb \log(G + b))$. □

7.5.3.2 Interchange and Storage Costs

We now consider the more general supplier's problem with both interchange and storage costs, $S|b|C + W$. We propose an algorithm, S-CW, which is the supplier's counterpart of Algorithm M-CW1. The main difference from M-CW1 is that, in S-CW, we must decide how many jobs up to G to process in each time slot. Algorithm S-CW proceeds forward in time. The set of jobs to be processed in time slot t is determined by the jobs which are in the buffer during time slot $t + 1$ and by schedule M^I.

7.5 Resequencing in a Supply Chain

Let $f_t(B)$ denote the minimum cost for the problem restricted to time slots from 0 through t, given that the set of jobs in the buffer during time slot $t + 1$ is $\beta(t + 1) = B$. We observe that Lemma 7.26, which is proved for problem $S|b|C$, also holds for problem $S|b|C + W$. This is because the storage cost is determined only by the profile and not by which jobs are scheduled. Thus, from Lemma 7.26, if the supplier decides to produce x_t jobs in time slot t, these are the x_t rightmost jobs in S^I from the set $B \cup M^I(t + 1)$. We denote this set by $V(x_t)$. We also denote by $F(t, h)$ the number of interchanges due to the supplier processing job h in time slot t. This equals the number of jobs that have already been processed by the supplier, but which follow h in S^I. Since $h \in V(x_t)$, all the jobs in $\beta(t)$ precede h in S^I and therefore do not contribute to $F(t, h)$, thus $F(t, h) = \left| \{i \mid i \in \cup_{j=1}^{t} M^I(j), h \prec^S i\} \right|$.

There are three cost components in $f_t(B)$. The first is the storage cost due to the jobs in the buffer during time slot $t + 1$, i.e., $w|B|$. The second is the total interchange cost associated with the jobs in $V(x_t)$, which equals $\sum_{h \in V(x_t)} F(t, h)$. The last component is the optimal cost up to time slot $t - 1$, with $\beta(t)$ including all the jobs of $B \cup M^I(t + 1)$ which are not in $V(x_t)$. This discussion motivates the following algorithm.

Algorithm S-CW

Preprocessing
$F(t, h) = \left| \{i \mid i \in \cup_{j=1}^{t} M^I(j), h \prec^S i\} \right|$, for $t = 1, \ldots, T, h = 1, \ldots, n$.
Value Function
$f_t(B) = $ minimum cost for the problem from 0 to t, given that $\beta(t + 1) = B$.
Boundary Conditions
$f_0(B) = w|B|$, for all $B \subseteq N, |B| \leq b$.
$f_t((B \cup M^I(t + 1)) \setminus V(x_t)) = +\infty$, if $x_t > d_{t+1} + |B|$.
$f_t((B \cup M^I(t + 1)) \setminus V(x_t)) = +\infty$, if $x_t < d_{t+1} + |B| - b$.
Optimal Solution Value
$f_T(\emptyset)$.
Recurrence Relation

$$f_t(B) = \min_{x_t = 0, \ldots, G} \left\{ w|B| + \sum_{h \in V(x_t)} F(t, h) + f_{t-1}\left((B \cup M^I(t+1)) \setminus V(x_t)\right) \right\}.$$

Since $0 \leq I_t \leq b$ and $I_{t+1} = |B|$, from Eq. (7.93), x_t must be at least $d_{t+1} + |B| - b$ and must not exceed $d_{t+1} + |B|$. The boundary conditions enforce these requirements.

Theorem 7.43 *Algorithm S-CW finds an optimal schedule for problem $S|b|C + W$ in $O(n^{b+1} b(G + b) \log(G + b))$ time.*

Proof From Lemmas 7.26 and 7.27, Algorithm S-CW compares the cost of all nondominated feasible partial schedules and thus finds an optimal schedule. In the preprocessing step, the computation of $F(t, h)$ can be performed in $O(Tn)$

424   7 Optimization and Conflict

time, using a labeling procedure similar to that in the proof of Theorem 7.41. There are $O(n^b)$ possible sets B for each time slot t, for $t = 0, \ldots, T - 1$. For each pair (t, B), the recurrence relation requires computing a minimum over $O(G)$ values. All sets $V(x_t)$ can be found by ordering the set $B \cup M^I(t + 1)$, which requires $O((G + b) \log(G + b))$ time. Therefore, the overall time complexity of Algorithm S-CW is $O(Tn^b(G + b) \log(G + b))$, which from Lemma 7.14 equals $O(n^{b+1}b(G + b) \log(G + b))$. $\qquad\qquad\qquad\qquad\qquad\qquad\qquad\qquad\qquad\qquad\square$

7.5.4 Combined Problems

We analyze the combined problem $S, M|b|C$, for the special case where $G = 1$. Hence, we omit the subscript on M_r. Here, the supplier and the only manufacturer have their own ideal schedules, which may process the jobs in different orders. The first objective we consider is the minimization of overall interchange costs. The analysis of this problem requires the following definition.

Definition 7.9 Given two schedules S and M, we say that they are *b-compatible* if the manufacturer can feasibly schedule the jobs according to M after the supplier releases them according to S, when the buffer has capacity b. Also, given two schedules S and M, we say that a job k is a *no-wait job* if it is processed by the supplier and by the manufacturer in consecutive time slots, i.e., if $\mu(k) = \sigma(k) + 1$; otherwise, it is a *wait job*.

Our main result now follows.

Theorem 7.44 *Given the ideal schedules M^I and S^I, let M^* and S^* be optimal schedules for problems $M|b|C$ and $S|b|C$, respectively. Let k_m (respectively, k_s) denote the minimum number of interchanges between M^I and M^* (respectively, S^I and S^*).*

(i) *There exist two schedules $\mathscr{S}_i^I$ and $\mathscr{M}_i^*$ which are b-compatible, such that $\mathscr{S}_i^I$ differs from S^I by i interchanges and $\mathscr{M}_i^*$ differs from M^I by $k_m - i$ interchanges, for $1 \le i \le k_m$.*

(ii) *There exist two schedules $\mathscr{M}_j^I$ and $\mathscr{S}_j^*$ which are b-compatible, such that $\mathscr{M}_j^I$ differs from M^I by j interchanges and $\mathscr{S}_j^*$ differs from S^I by $k_s - j$ interchanges, for $1 \le j \le k_s$.*

(iii) *Let S' differ from S^I by q_s interchanges, and M' differ from M^I by q_m interchanges. Then, if $q_s + q_m < k_m$, schedules M' and S' are not b-compatible.*

Proof If $k_m = 0$ or $k_s = 0$, then the theorem is trivially true. We consider each part in turn.

(i). We first consider $i = 1$. Since $k_m > 0$, there is at least one pair of consecutively processed jobs g, h in M^* such that $h \prec^M g$. Note that g is released by the supplier before h. From the "only if" part of Lemma 7.20, when g is scheduled

7.5 Resequencing in a Supply Chain

in M^*, h is not available yet, and therefore since h immediately follows g in M^*, h is no-wait. We consider two subcases, depending on whether g is a no-wait or a wait job.

Assume first that g is a no-wait job. Then, g and h are consecutive in both S^I and M^*. By interchanging jobs g and h in both S^I and M^*, we obtain two new schedules, $\mathscr{S}_1^I$ and $\mathscr{M}_1^*$, respectively, such that there are exactly one interchange between $\mathscr{S}_1^I$ and S^I and exactly $k_m - 1$ interchanges between $\mathscr{M}_1^*$ and M^I. Moreover, these two schedules are b-compatible, by construction.

Alternatively, assume that job g is a wait job, and consider the job k processed by the supplier in time slot $\sigma^I(h) - 1$. Observe that, since jobs g and h are consecutive in M^*, job k is scheduled after them in M^* (see Fig. 7.11). From the "only if" part of Lemma 7.20, $h \prec^M k$ and $g \prec^M k$. Hence, by interchanging jobs g and h in M^* and jobs k and h in S^I, we again obtain two schedules, $\mathscr{S}_1^I$ and $\mathscr{M}_1^*$, respectively. The only difference in buffer usage resulting from these interchanges is that the pair of schedules S^I, M^* has job k in the buffer during time slot $\sigma^I(h)$, whereas the pair $\mathscr{S}_1^I$, $\mathscr{M}_1^*$ has job g in the buffer during that time slot. Thus, $\mathscr{S}_1^I$ and $\mathscr{M}_1^*$ are b-compatible. Moreover, $\mathscr{S}_1^I$ differs from S^I by exactly one interchange, and $\mathscr{M}_1^*$ differs from M^I by exactly $k_m - 1$ interchanges. For $i > 1$, we set $S^I = \mathscr{S}_1^I$ and $M^* = \mathscr{M}_1^*$ and repeat the above argument.

(ii). The proof is similar to that of part (i), by symmetry.

(iii). For contradiction, assume that two b-compatible schedules S' and M' exist, such that $q_s + q_m < k_m$. From part (ii), we can find two b-compatible schedules S'' and M'' requiring $q_s - 1$ and $q_m + 1$ interchanges, where the total number of interchanges required is still $(q_s - 1) + (q_m + 1) < k_m$. By applying this argument another $q_s - 1$ times, we can find two b-compatible schedules $\mathscr{S}_{q_s}^* = S^I$ and $\mathscr{M}_{q_s}^I$, such that $\mathscr{M}_{q_s}^I$ differs from M^I by exactly $q_s + q_m < k_m$

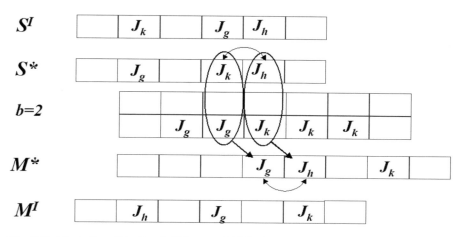

Fig. 7.11 Illustration of the Proof of Theorem 7.44 if g is a wait job

426   7 Optimization and Conflict

interchanges. This implies that the schedule found by Algorithm M-C which contained k_m interchanges was not optimal, a contradiction. □

Theorem 7.44 has an important implication for the solvability of problem $S, M|b|C$, as shown in the following result.

Theorem 7.45 *An optimal schedule for problem $S, M|b|C$ where $G = 1$ can be found in $O(nb \log b)$ time.*

Proof It follows from Theorem 7.44 that an optimal schedule for problem $M|b|C$ and an optimal schedule for problem $S|b|C$ are both optimal for problem $S, M|b|C$ where $G = 1$. Therefore, we can apply either Algorithm M-C which runs in $O(nb \log b)$ time (see Theorem 7.39), or Algorithm S-C which runs in $O(nb \log(G + b))$ time in general (see Theorem 7.42) and therefore in $O(nb \log b)$ time when $G = 1$. □

The complexity status of problem $S, M|b|C$, where $G \geq 2$, remains open.

Remark 7.15 It follows from Theorem 7.44 is that, when there are no storage costs, the interchange cost incurred by the two parties can be divided between them in various ways. However, the supplier and the manufacturer cannot decrease the total interchange cost by cooperation.

On the other hand, if storage costs are also considered as in problem $S, M|b|C + W$, cooperation between the supplier and the manufacturer *can* provide an improvement in total cost, as shown by the following example.

Example 7.7 (Benefit of Cooperation with Storage Costs Considered) Consider the following instance of problem $S, M|b|C + W$: $b = 2$; $S^I = 1, 2, 3, 4, 5, 6, 7, 8, 9, 10$; $M^I = 4, 5, 2, 1, 3, 9, 10, 6, 8, 7$; $w = 0.1$.
Let "$*$" denote an idle time period.
The optimal solution, M^*, to problem $M|2|C + W$ (which can be found by Algorithm M-CW1 or Algorithm M-CW2) is the following, with the total cost of $C + W = 4 + 19(0.1) = 5.9$.

$$
\begin{array}{llllllllllll}
S^I & 1 & 2 & 3 & 4 & 5 & 6 & 7 & 8 & 9 & 10 \\
M^* & * & 2 & * & 4 & 5 & 1 & 3 & 6 & 9 & 10 & 8 & 7 \\
M^I & 4 & 5 & 2 & 1 & 3 & 9 & 10 & 6 & 8 & 7
\end{array}
$$

The optimal solution, S^*, to problem $S|2|C + W$ can be found by Algorithm S-CW. Note that, for the manufacturer to process job 4 in time slot 2, the supplier must process jobs 1 and 2 before time slot 1. The algorithm yields the following solution, also with the total cost of $C + W = 4 + 19(0.1) = 5.9$.

$$
\begin{array}{llllllllllll}
S^I & & 1 & 2 & 3 & 4 & 5 & 6 & 7 & 8 & 9 & 10 \\
S^* & 1 & 2 & 4 & 5 & 3 & 6 & 7 & 9 & 10 & * & 8 & * \\
M^I & & 4 & 5 & 2 & 1 & 3 & 9 & 10 & 6 & 8 & 7
\end{array}
$$

However, the following solution for the combined problem $S, M|2|C + W$ has a smaller total cost of $C + W = 4 + 16(0.1) = 5.6$:

$$
\begin{array}{lllllllllllll}
S^I & & 1 & 2 & 3 & 4 & 5 & 6 & 7 & 8 & 9 & 10 \\
S^* & 1 & 2 & 4 & 5 & * & * & 3 & 6 & 7 & 8 & 9 & 10 \\
M^* & & 4 & 5 & 2 & 1 & 3 & 6 & * & * & 9 & 10 & 8 & 7 \\
M^I & & 4 & 5 & 2 & 1 & 3 & 9 & 10 & 6 & 8 & 7
\end{array}
$$

Example 7.7 shows that cooperation can provide a reduction in the total system cost when that cost includes storage. Finally, we note that the complexity class of problem $S, M|b|C + W$ remains open.

The work discussed in this section demonstrates the importance of supply chain scheduling in practical situations where setup costs between products are significant and preferred production sequences vary between production stages. The significant benefits of coordination which are demonstrated here are sufficient to motivate companies to document these costs and schedule preferences in detail.

7.6 Future Research

In this section, we describe several important directions for future research on supply chain scheduling, organized according to the four issues discussed in this chapter. For each issue, we first mention some future research suggestions from the foundational work and then provide a discussion of more recent works and their own forward-looking perspectives.

- As discussed in Sect. 7.2, Hall and Potts (2003) discuss a variety of models that evaluate tradeoffs between scheduling and batching costs. They motivate the enhancement of their results by the development of dominance rules and lower bounds and also the design and analysis of heuristics. Generalizations to multistage supply chains are recommended. Their other recommendations relate to game theory models that are discussed in detail in Chaps. 8 and 9. Finally, their recommendation to quantify the potential benefits of cooperation is now greatly supported by the availability of large and current data sets in many planning situations.
- Hall and Potts (2005) study the coordination of scheduling and batching in single and parallel machine environments where the objective is to minimize the total cost, which is determined by batch delivery time. They provide efficient algorithms for some problems and intractability results for others.
- We refer the reader to Chaps. 3 and 4 for an extensive discussion of scheduling and batch delivery within the context of centralized decision making.
- Agnetis et al. (2014a) consider a variation of the scheduling and batch delivery model of Hall and Potts (2003). A third-party logistics provider delivers semifinished products in batches from one production location to another owned

by the same manufacturer. They consider scheduling and batching problems under the two alternative assumptions that the manufacturer or the logistics provider dominates the decision making process. Algorithms and intractability results are described. Several problems remain open for future research. When the manufacturer dominates, there are several open complexity issues. When the logistics provider dominates, there is a need for heuristic design and analysis. Finally, a model with balanced negotiation power motivates the study of integrated decision making and the benefit of cooperation, along with the design of mechanisms to motivate supply chain cooperation.

- As discussed in Sect. 7.3, Chen and Hall (2007) study the coordination of the schedules of parts suppliers in an assembly system. They recommend extension of their work to multi-stage assembly systems. Another possible research topic is the modeling of cooperation between the suppliers. Also of importance is the development of models of the bargaining process between suppliers and a manufacturer that take into account practical issues such as imperfect or asymmetric information. Another significant issue is how, if necessary, to enforce cooperation between the parties. Finally, it is important to examine how the benefits of cooperation in supply chains may influence organizational integration, since vertical integration makes cooperation easier to establish and maintain.

- In related work, Sawik (2009) proposes a mixed integer programming model for a three-stage assembly system. The objective is to minimize the total inventory holding, production startup, and shipping costs. Results are presented for a comparison of an integrated approach that simultaneously determines manufacturing, supply, and assembly schedules, with a disaggregated approach.

- Ren et al. (2013) consider the suppliers' problem of minimizing the weighted number of tardy jobs, which Chen and Hall (2007) show is binary NP-hard in Theorem 7.8. They strengthen this result by proving unary NP-hardness. They also prove a similar result for the suppliers' problem of minimizing the total late work of parts.

- İnkaya and Akansel (2017) consider coordinated scheduling of transfer lots in an assembly-type supply chain. Lot streaming is used to enhance product flow and reduce work-in-process inventory. They develop a mathematical model to find optimal transfer lot sizes in the supply chain. Their objective is the minimization of the sum of weighted flow and inventory costs. A genetic algorithm is developed and tested. Experimental results show that the proposed GA-based approaches provide acceptable results in a reasonable amount of time and that coordination with lot streaming provides improvements in supply chain performance.

- As discussed in Sect. 7.4, Dawande et al. (2006) study conflict and cooperation issues arising in a supply chain where a manufacturer makes products that are shipped to customers by a distributor. They recommend the consideration of other customer-related objectives that are relevant, including minimization of the number of late jobs and the total tardiness of the jobs. A second important research topic is to extend the cooperation mechanisms described to multiple-stage supply chains. Also valuable is the development of models of the bargaining

7.6 Future Research

process between a manufacturer and a distributor that generalize the models presented here to consider imperfect or asymmetric information. Finally, as in the work of Chen and Hall (2007), cooperation between a manufacturer and a distributor should be evaluated within a study of the benefits and costs of vertical supply chain integration.

- In related work, Manoj et al. (2008) study coordinated decision making in a supply chain consisting of a manufacturer, a distributor, and several retailers. Finished goods industry is managed by the distributor. An ideal schedule of either the manufacturer or the distributor, if imposed on the other party, results in a substantial cost of conflict. They show that integrated decision making can generate savings that are sufficient to compensate both parties. They present computational results for up to 30 retailers in the distributor's problem and up to nine retailers in the combined problem. They recommend the solution of larger instances of the problem and suggest that this will require the design and application of efficient heuristic solution methods.
- Geismar and Murthy (2015) study a paper manufacturing plant that minimizes its production cost by using long production runs that combine the demands from its various customers. Distribution is achieved using one railcar for each customer. However, the tradeoff involved in this policy is that it requires holding completed jobs within the distribution facility, which is costly. The problem of minimizing the distribution cost, given a production schedule, is solved. A coordination mechanism is proposed and shown to reduce distribution cost by 25% on average. Also, the total system cost is reduced by a further 4% on average. A possible extension is to use a rolling horizon model. Another extension is to consider uncertainty in the arrival dates and condition of railcars. Also, the railcar distribution system can be augmented by the use of trucks.
- As discussed in Sect. 7.5, a critical issue in supply chain scheduling is coordinating the decisions made by decision makers at different stages, for example, a supplier and one or several manufacturers. Agnetis et al. (2006) model this issue by assuming that the supplier and each manufacturer have an ideal schedule, determined by their own costs and constraints. It would be valuable to extend their models to multiple-stage supply chains. Second, it is important to develop mechanisms by which decision makers at different stages of a supply chain can cooperate and to design incentives for this cooperation. Third, it would be valuable to extend their analysis to account for additional practical complications, such as due dates for the jobs. Finally, there is a need to develop models that allow for imperfect or asymmetric information in the negotiations between suppliers and manufacturers.
- In work that is related to Agnetis et al. (2006), Manoj et al. (2012) study a production system with two consecutive stages and an intermediate buffer. The first stage minimizes inventory cost measured by the sum of completion times, and the second stage minimizes the tardiness cost of late delivery plus the cost of resequencing in the buffer. This work provides intractability results and describes a heuristic solution procedure. Computational results show that the cost

of conflict for the second stage increases more rapidly than that for the first stage as the number of jobs increases.

- The resequencing problem studied in Sect. 7.5 is mathematically similar to the one found in manufacturing settings which mass-produce highly customized products, as in the automobile industry. In this context, the sequencing problem, which decides on the succession of workpieces launched down the line, has major effects on efficiency. Boysen et al. (2012) review research on resequencing in a mixed-model assembly line context. Relevant problem settings, alternative buffer configurations, and resulting decision problems are described. While the problems described there are centralized, there is the potential to extend the results to the decentralized setting considered in this chapter.

In several other manufacturing environments, besides those considered here, potentially significant cost savings motivate research into supply chain scheduling issues. For example, Ullrich and Herrmann (2013) study a supplier and a manufacturer, both of which face a machine scheduling and delivery problem. They conclude that, on average, supply chain scheduling reduces costs by up to 35%. As the substantial supply chain management literature attests, there are also several other types of decisions where cooperation can be valuable. However, the benefits there are often not as easy to identify and evaluate as they are for scheduling decisions. This observation emphasizes the central importance of supply chain scheduling in achieving improved system performance.

Chapter 8
Cooperative Supply Chain Scheduling

Abstract This chapter discusses the application of cooperative solution methods, especially cooperative game theory, to decentralized supply chain scheduling problems. We consider many scheduling situations that model diverse applications, and that have classically been analyzed from the perspective of a centralized decision maker. By viewing the jobs or resources within those situations as individual self-interested players, cooperative supply chain scheduling games are defined over those situations. The analysis of these games applies all the main concepts of cooperative games, from the perspective of achieving and sustaining cooperation among the players. Mechanisms for achieving cooperation, and many examples of supply chain scheduling applications, are discussed.

8.1 Introduction

This chapter discusses five supply chain scheduling application areas that are modeled and solved using methodology from cooperative game theory and optimization. In each case, a group of players may benefit from cooperating among themselves in order to find improved solutions to supply chain scheduling problems.

The first application area is *sequencing games*. Consider a group of customers, or equivalently in a scheduling context a group of jobs where each is owned by a different customer, that are initially arranged in an arbitrarily ordered queue in front of a single server or machine. It may be the case that the last customer in the queue has an urgent appointment elsewhere, whereas the first customer in the queue has no pressing appointments and would not object to waiting longer. In this situation, a resequencing of the queue would potentially benefit the customers as a whole. But, if the first customer surrenders his place, he should be compensated for doing so. This raises the question of how the total benefit of the resequencing should be allocated among the customers. In order to ensure the participation of the customers, this allocation must meet the stability conditions of a cooperative game. Ideally, the compensation system should also satisfy some axiomatic properties. Finally, customers who are not part of a swapping agreement should not be

© Springer Nature Switzerland AG 2022
Z.-L. Chen, N. G. Hall, *Supply Chain Scheduling*, International Series
in Operations Research & Management Science 323,
https://doi.org/10.1007/978-3-030-90374-9_8

431

adversely affected by such an agreement, which raises the issue of which revised sequences are admissible. While this summary describes the simplest sequencing game environment, several variations regarding the scheduling environment, the admissible behavior of the customers, or details about groupings of the customers, are also motivated by applications.

The second application area considers *scheduling games*. Scheduling games are similar to sequencing games in that a set of customers with various levels of urgency and different length tasks arrive seeking service from a common server. However, a fundamental difference is that, in a scheduling game, all the customers arrive simultaneously. Thus, there is no initial arrangement of the customers. As a result, the admissibility restrictions found in sequencing games, which typically exclude jobs that are outside a given coalition in the initial sequence from participating in a resequencing arrangement, do not apply. Nonetheless, customers with higher levels of urgency may be willing to compensate others in order to obtain earlier service. Also, the value of a coalition is not measured by cost savings relative to an initial sequence; instead, it can be measured by the total scheduling cost of the coalition. Alternatively, it is possible to design an artificial initial sequence to use as a benchmark, which we demonstrate in various ways. The issues that arise in scheduling games are similar to those that arise in sequencing games. Within scheduling games, we also discuss methods for encouraging cooperation where it does not occur spontaneously, for example, by invoking a penalty on players who leave the coalition, providing a subsidy to those who remain, or some combination of these measures.

The third application area considers *project management games*. There are two perspectives under which project management can be modeled as a cooperative game. The first perspective applies at the planning stage, when project performance has not yet been realized. Here, subcontractors who can provide resources to the project compete for the opportunity to do so, with a view to sharing rewards from the project client when the project is completed sooner due to the use of those resources. The second perspective focuses on issues that arise after the project is finished. Then, if the project is delayed, as happens frequently in practice, an issue is how the penalty cost of the delay, as typically defined in a contract with the project owner, should be shared among the players who represent the tasks of the project. Symmetrically, if the project is delivered early and thus earns a reward from the project owner, it is necessary to determine how this reward should be shared. Under both these perspectives, the stability of the coalition is of importance. This issue is addressed by studying the emptiness of the core of the game, and also the design of single-point cost or reward allocations where the entire vector of payments for the players is uniquely specified.

While the three applications mentioned above focus exclusively on cooperative game solutions, the last two applications we consider demonstrate the integration of cooperative game and optimization methodologies in the solution of supply chain scheduling problems. The fourth application area studies the *allocation of scarce capacity* within a fixed capacity supply chain. For example, suppose a manufacturer receives orders from several distributors, but has insufficient capacity to meet all

8.1 Introduction

those orders. Then, the manufacturer has to make a decision about how to allocate its available capacity to the different distributors. The manufacturer can benefit by making this decision in consideration of its scheduling cost and its capacity restrictions. This allocation provides new information to the distributors, which will cause them to reprioritize their orders and resubmit them. If they choose to do so, then they may resubmit their revised orders individually. Important issues that are studied here using cooperative games include whether they can achieve a better outcome by sharing their allocated capacity as a coalition, and also the stability of such a coalition. A further issue is whether it is worthwhile for the manufacturer to cooperate with all the distributors, leading to vertical cooperation in the supply chain. Finally, the manufacturer needs to schedule the revised and resubmitted orders efficiently, for example, to minimize its cost, which can be defined in several practically relevant ways.

The fifth application area considers the *acquisition of outsourced capacity* by several manufacturers, either individually or in a coalition. The motivation for using this option is the technical capability of a third-party supplier, which enables the manufacturer to outsource specialized components for its products in order to focus on their main operations. Many examples arise in semiconductor manufacturing, pharmaceutical research, and biotechnology. In such situations, the third-party facility announces time slots, amounts of available capacity at those times, and their prices. Then, the manufacturers have the option to reserve those time slots as needed for their manufacturing processes. While the manufacturers may make their reservation decisions individually, they may alternatively benefit from making them as a coalition, and this problem forms a cooperative game. It is important to study the stability of this coalition. A second problem that is studied within this application area involves the purchase of outsourced capacity that is used concurrently with capacity that is owned by each manufacturer, in order to achieve faster completion of work. In this case, the outsourced capacity must be purchased in competition with other manufacturers.

This chapter is organized as follows. Section 8.2 provides a review of solution concepts within cooperative game theory. Section 8.3 introduces sequencing games, establishes connections with other topics within cooperative games, and then identifies approaches to establishing balancedness and to allocating the gains achieved by resequencing. Section 8.4 analyzes scheduling games and discusses issues that are similar to those for sequencing games. Section 8.5 studies the modeling of projects as cooperative games. Section 8.6 discusses the issue of capacity allocation in a fixed capacity supply chain that includes a manufacturer and several distributors. Section 8.7 considers the possibility of introducing concurrent external capacity, in the form of specialized manufacturing capability provided by a third party, into a supply chain. Section 8.8 identifies future research topics of value within the study of cooperative games for supply chain scheduling. We refer the reader to Sect. 2.3.5 for a brief introduction to, and definitions of standard concepts within, cooperative games.

Figure 8.1 provides an overview of the topics within cooperative solutions to decentralized supply chain scheduling problems that are discussed in this chapter.

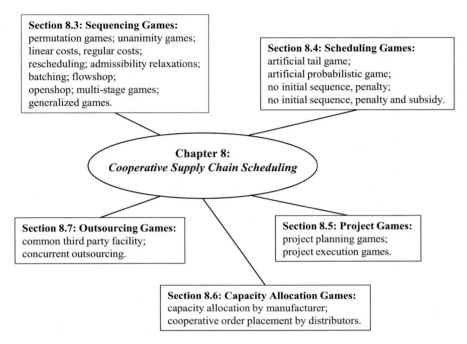

Fig. 8.1 Overview of the topics covered in Chap. 8

8.2 Cooperative Game Solutions

This section provides an overview of important definitions and solution concepts within the theory of cooperative games. A comprehensive introduction to cooperative game theory is provided by Peleg and Sudhölter (2007). Some key concepts of cooperative games are described in Sect. 2.3.5. We use the following simple optimization problem and associated cooperative game introduced by Dragan (2013) to illustrate these definitions and concepts. In general, the participants in a supply chain scheduling cooperative game are described as *agents* or *players* and typically represent jobs or resources. In this work, because of our focus on supply chain scheduling applications rather than theoretical development, we use the more natural term for a participant in a game, i.e., player.

Consider a single machine that processes a set of jobs $N = \{1, \ldots, n\}$ nonpreemptively around a common due date d. Without loss of generality, we assume that the jobs have processing times $p_1 \geq \cdots \geq p_n > 0$. While several variations of this problem are discussed in the literature, we make the simplifying assumption that $d \geq \sum_{j \in N} p_j$. The objective of the problem is to minimize the total deviation of completion times around d. It should be immediately clear that there exists an optimal schedule without idle time between the jobs. Moreover, an optimal schedule can be fully characterized by a sequence for the jobs and a starting time for the schedule.

8.2 Cooperative Game Solutions

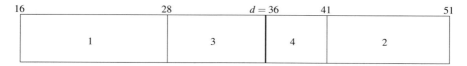

Fig. 8.2 Optimal Schedule σ^* in Example 8.1

If the completion time of job j in a given schedule σ is denoted by $C_j(\sigma)$, then this objective can be written as the minimization of $\sum_{j \in N} |C_j(\sigma) - d|$, where $|\cdot|$ denotes absolute value. Given a schedule σ, we say that a job j is *early* if $C_j(\sigma) \leq d$ and *tardy* if $C_j(\sigma) > d$.

This scheduling problem and its variations have been studied extensively in the operations research literature. Kanet (1981) provides an optimal algorithm that requires $O(n \log n)$ time. This algorithm takes the jobs in index order, i.e., nonincreasing processing time order, and schedules the odd numbered jobs to complete at time d (where necessary, moving previously scheduled early jobs earlier), and the even numbered jobs to start at time d (where necessary, moving previously scheduled late jobs later). Hall (1986) develops optimality conditions that establish the existence of many optimal solutions for this problem, and extends the results of Kanet (1981) to multiple parallel machines. Hall and Posner (1991) study a generalization of this problem with weighted deviations for the jobs. Hall et al. (1991) study a generalization with a restrictive common due date, i.e., $d < \sum_{j \in N} p_j$. We consider an example of this scheduling problem. Let $z(\sigma)$ denote the cost of any schedule σ in this problem.

Example 8.1 (Instance of an Earliness–Tardiness Problem) Let $N = \{1, 2, 3, 4\}$, where $p_1 = 12$, $p_2 = 10$, $p_3 = 8$, and $p_4 = 5$. Also, let $d = 36 > \sum_{j=1}^{4} p_j = 35$. The algorithm of Kanet (1981) finds an optimal schedule σ^* where job 1 is scheduled from time 16 to time 28, job 2 is scheduled from 41 to 51, job 3 is scheduled from 28 to 36, and job 4 is scheduled from 36 to 41. Then, $z(\sigma^*) = (36 - 28) + (51 - 36) + (36 - 36) + (41 - 36) = 8 + 15 + 0 + 5 = 28$. Figure 8.2 shows schedule σ^*, where the common due date $d = 36$ is indicated with a bold vertical line.

We consider a cooperative game defined over the above scheduling problem, where the players represent jobs in the game. We use Example 8.1 to illustrate various concepts within cooperative games for supply chain scheduling applications.

Let (N, v) denote a cooperative game described over the above scheduling problem, where N is the set of players and $v : 2^N \to \mathbb{R}$ defines the *coalition value* of any possible coalition formed from N. If all the players of N cooperate, then they form the *grand coalition*. All cooperative games considered in this book are *transferable utility* (TU) games, which means that members of a coalition can costlessly share the utility of the coalition between them, for example, through the use of a common currency. For any subset $S \subseteq N$, we let $v(S)$ represent the value achieved by coalition S if it acts alone, which is a benchmark against which the

Fig. 8.3 Initial Schedule σ_0 in Example 8.1

value that coalition S can achieve within the grand coalition can be compared. For the purposes of this example, we assume that the jobs have the initial schedule σ_0 shown in Fig. 8.3, where $z(\sigma_0) = (48 - 36) + (58 - 36) + (36 - 36) + (36 - 28) = 12 + 22 + 0 + 8 = 42$. The value of a coalition in this game represents nonnegative cost savings which it can achieve relative to schedule σ_0, without the assistance of other players.

Next, we discuss the issue of *admissibility*, i.e., which coalitions should be allowed to reschedule their jobs, and how this should be implemented. Here, we apply two rules. First, a coalition $S \subseteq N$ must consist of consecutive jobs in σ_0. The coalitions that meet this rule, from Figure 8.3, are as follows: $v(\{i\}), i = 1, \ldots, 4$; $v(\{1, 2\}), v(\{1, 3\}), v(\{3, 4\}; v(\{1, 2, 3\}), v(\{1, 3, 4\})$, and $v(\{1, 2, 3, 4\})$. Second, the schedule of jobs in $N \setminus S$ cannot be changed by rescheduling the jobs of S. The second rule implies that the full interval in which the jobs of S are scheduled remains unchanged by the rescheduling.

Based on this identification of the admissible coalitions, we provide an example of the calculation of coalition values in this game.

Example 8.2 (Coalition Values in an Earliness–Tardiness Game) Using the instance from Example 8.1, the value of each coalition is the maximum cost savings which it can achieve, relative to σ_0 and following the given admissibility rules. Observe that a single job cannot achieve any rescheduling by itself without changing the schedule of other jobs; hence, $v(\{i\}) = 0, i = 1, \ldots, 4$. The values of the other admissible coalitions are as follows:

$v(\{1, 2\}) = 2$, from schedule (4, 3, 2, 1);
$v(\{1, 3\}) = 0$, since interchanging jobs 1 and 3 increases the cost of the schedule from 42 to 46, and coalition value cannot be negative;
$v(\{3, 4\}) = 3$, from schedule (3, 4, 1, 2);
$v(\{1, 2, 3\}) = 2$, from schedule (4, 3, 2, 1);
$v(\{1, 3, 4\}) = 3$, from either schedule (1, 4, 3, 2) or schedule (3, 4, 1, 2); and
$v(\{1, 2, 3, 4\}) = 14$, from schedule (1, 3, 4, 2), as shown in Fig. 8.2.

Other coalitions that are not admissible as defined above may also have value that is inherited from their subset coalitions. For example, (1, 2, 4) is not admissible, but $v(\{1, 2, 4\}) = v(\{1, 2\}) = 2$, and similarly (2, 3, 4) is not admissible, but $v(\{2, 3, 4\}) = v(\{3, 4\}) = 3$.

In general, cooperative game theory studies ways in which the players can be compensated so that they participate in the game. For example, suppose the players

8.2 Cooperative Game Solutions

represent jobs that require resources for processing. Then, the costs that are allocated to the players for this processing, which form a *cost allocation scheme*, need to be sufficiently small that the players are willing to pay them. Alternatively, if the players represent resources, then they need to receive sufficiently large payments, in the form of a *payment scheme*, in order to accept the work. Example 8.2 is similar to the latter case, where gains, i.e., cost savings, are available for sharing among the players through a payment scheme.

Before studying several concepts for cooperative games, we identify various properties that such schemes should possess. In the following description of these properties, a player's *outcome* is his cost allocation or payment that results from application of the scheme. Individual supply chain scheduling games discussed in this book may also use additional properties specific to those games.

1. *Existence*: The scheme is well defined for any cooperative game.
2. *Efficiency*: The scheme exactly divides the value of the complete game among the players.
3. *Individual Rationality*: No player receives a worse outcome than if he refuses to participate.
4. *Coalitional Rationality*: No coalition of players can improve their outcome by splitting off from the grand coalition.
5. *Monotonicity*: The player's outcome is a weakly monotonic function of his marginal value or marginal cost to the game.
6. *Zero Outcome for Null Players*: A player who adds nothing to the value of any coalition should receive zero outcome.
7. *Symmetry*: If we can swap two players who are in different coalitions with equal value and the coalition values remain equal, then those players should have the same outcome.
8. *Computational Tractability*: The scheme should be computable in time that increases only polynomially with the number of players.

Let y_i, $i \in N$, denote a payment scheme for the game described in Example 8.2. This scheme compensates the players for staying within the grand coalition, by making payments to them that are at least as much as they could obtain by forming a coalition to leave and enjoy the coalition value cost savings by themselves. The payment scheme is said to be in the *core of the game* if:

(i) $\sum_{i \in N} y_i = v(N)$, and
(ii) $\sum_{i \in S} y_i \geq v(S)$, for $\emptyset \subset S \subset N$.

These conditions require some interpretation. Condition (i), the Efficiency property, requires that the total cost of the payment scheme used is exactly the value of the grand coalition. Condition (ii), the Coalitional Rationality property ensures that no coalition of players can do better by leaving the grand coalition. This condition includes as a special case:

(ii′) $y_i \geq v(\{i\})$, $i \in N$.

Condition (ii′), the Individual Rationality property, ensures participation by individual players.

438   8 Cooperative Supply Chain Scheduling

A major focus in studying various cooperative games is the identification of a core solution. The core is the set of Efficient payment or cost allocation vectors that satisfy the Coalitional and Individual Rationality properties, i.e., Conditions (ii) and (ii′) above. In a typical game, it can be conceptualized as a region within an n-dimensional payment or cost allocation space, which allows for some flexibility that may be useful for negotiation between the players in practical situations. A cooperative game that has a nonempty core for all instances is said to be *balanced*. Nonetheless, an unbalanced game may, for some instances, have a core solution. We provide an example of a core solution for the above Earliness–Tardiness game.

Example 8.3 (Example of a Core Solution) Using the instance from Example 8.2, consider the payment scheme $y = (1, 3, 4, 6)$. We examine whether this payment scheme is in the core of the game. Since $\sum_{i \in N} y_i = 1 + 3 + 4 + 6 = 14 = v(N)$, condition (i) is satisfied. For condition (ii′), observe that $y_i \geq 0 = v(\{i\}), i \in N$. More generally for condition (ii), $y_1 + y_2 = 4 \geq 2 = v(\{1, 2\})$, $y_1 + y_3 = 5 \geq 0 = v(\{1, 3\})$, $y_3 + y_4 = 10 \geq 3 = v(\{3, 4\})$; $y_1 + y_2 + y_3 = 8 \geq 2 = v(\{1, 2, 3\})$, $y_1 + y_3 + y_4 = 11 \geq 3 = v(\{1, 3, 4\})$.
Further, consider any admissible coalition S above. Then, any coalition S', where $S \subset S' \subseteq N$, satisfies $\sum_{i \in S'} y_i \geq \sum_{i \in S} y_i \geq v(S) = v(S')$, and therefore condition (ii) is also satisfied for coalition S'.

Therefore, by consideration of all admissible coalitions, we conclude that $y = (1, 3, 4, 6)$ is a core solution of the game. One insight this example provides is that the process used here for checking conditions (i) and (ii) for all coalitions is not in general computationally efficient. Within this book, we discuss several methods to address this issue for specific supply chain scheduling games.

For cooperative games that have an empty core, a useful concept is the *least core* of a game (N, w) with agents $N = \{1, \ldots, n\}$, which is the set of payoff allocations $x \in \mathbb{R}$ that solves the linear program

$$z^* = \min\{z \mid \sum_{i \in N} x_i = v(N), \sum_{i \in S} x_i \geq v(S) - z, \text{ for } S \subset N, S \neq \emptyset\}. \tag{8.1}$$

In (8.1), z^* is the *least core value*. The least core value can be interpreted as the minimum penalty required to prevent any coalition from leaving the grand coalition. We refer the reader to Sects. 8.4.3 and 8.4.4 for applications of the least core value concept.

As mentioned above, core solutions typically represent a range of possible payments. However, cooperative game theory also defines various single-point solutions where the entire vector of payments is uniquely specified. Among the best known of these is the Shapley value (Shapley, 1953), denoted as $\phi_i(v), i \in N$. Let $S \subseteq N$ denote a coalition of players that does not contain a particular player $i \in N$. The Shapley value of player i is given by:

$$\phi_i(v) = \sum_{S \subset N \setminus \{i\}} \frac{|S|! \, (n - |S| - 1)!}{n!} [v(S \cup \{i\}) - v(S))], \quad i \in N, \tag{8.2}$$

8.2 Cooperative Game Solutions

where the sum includes all subsets S of N that do not contain player i. An intuitive explanation is that the bracketed term in (8.2) is the marginal value from adding player i to any coalition S that did not previously contain it. However, this value depends on the coalition S to which player i is added. Hence, the Shapley value takes the average over all possible such coalitions S. The Shapley value is the unique scheme that satisfies the Efficiency, Symmetry, and Monotonicity properties.

Example 8.4 (Example of Shapley Value Calculations) Using the instance from Example 8.2, we have the following calculations. For each job i, we consider all admissible coalitions that include i, and compute the value lost if i is removed from the coalition.
For job 1:

   (i) $v(\{1, 2\}) - v(\{2\}) = 2 - 0 = 2$;
  (ii) $v(\{1, 3\}) - v(\{3\}) = 0 - 0 = 0$;
 (iii) $v(\{1, 2, 3\}) - v(\{2, 3\}) = 2 - 0 = 2$;
 (iv) $v(\{1, 2, 4\}) - v(\{2, 4\}) = 2 - 0 = 2$;
  (v) $v(\{1, 3, 4\}) - v(\{3, 4\}) = 3 - 3 = 0$;
 (vi) $v(\{1, 2, 3, 4\}) - v(\{2, 3, 4\}) = 14 - 3 = 11$.

Then, from (8.2), the Shapley value for job 1, $\phi_1(v)$, is the total found by multiplying terms (i)–(ii) for $|S| = 1$ by $1/12$, terms (iii)–(v) for $|S| = 2$ by $(1)(2)/(24) = 1/12$, and term (vi) for $|S| = 3$ by $(6)(1)/24 = 1/4$. Thus, $\phi_1(v) = (2 + 2 + 2)/12 + 11/4 = 39/12 = 3.25$.
Similar calculations provide $\phi_2(v) = (2 + 2 + 2)/12 + 11/4 = 39/12 = 3.25$, $\phi_3(v) = (3 + 3 + 3)/12 + 12/4 = 45/12 = 3.75$, and $\phi_4(v) = (3 + 3 + 3)/12 + 12/4 = 45/12 = 3.75$. Then, $\sum_{i=1}^{4} \phi_i(v) = 3.25 + 3.25 + 3.75 + 3.75 = 14 = v(N)$, which establishes Efficiency as required.

As the Shapley value formula in (8.2) suggests, in a general game, finding the Shapley value requires an exponential time computation. However, we discuss several games where the Shapley value is efficiently computable. A further useful characteristic of the Shapley value is that, in some classes of games, including convex games (Bondareva, 1963; Shapley, 1967), it is in the core.

Another important single-point concept in cooperative game theory is the *nucleolus*, introduced by Schmeidler (1969). Given a payment scheme $f \in \mathbb{R}^n$ and a coalition $S \subseteq N$, $S \neq \emptyset$, define the *excess*

$$e(f, S) = \sum_{i \in S} f_i - v(S).$$

Intuitively, the larger the excess, the greater the safety margin provided by the payment scheme to coalition S with respect to keeping S from leaving the grand coalition. Further, define the *excess vector* $e(f) = (e(f, S_1), \ldots, e(f, S_m))$, where $S_i \subset N$, $S_i \neq \emptyset$, and $m = 2^n - 2$ since $S = N$ and $S = \emptyset$ are excluded. In this definition, the elements of $e(f)$ are arranged in nondecreasing order. Then, the nucleolus, $v_i(v)$, $i \in N$, is a payment scheme with lexicographically greatest excess vector. The nucleolus satisfies the Existence, Efficiency, Individual Rationality and Symmetry properties. It is a unique element of the game. In a game with a nonempty core, the nucleolus is in the core.

Iñarra et al. (2019) give the following example of nucleolus calculations that provides helpful intuition.

Example 8.5 (Example of Nucleolus Calculations) Consider a cooperative game with a set $N = \{1, 2, 3\}$ of players and the following coalition values: $v(\{1\}) = v(\{2\}) = v(\{3\}) = 0$, $v(\{1, 2\}) = 20$, $v(\{1, 3\}) = 30$, $v(\{2, 3\}) = 40$, $v(N) = 42$. We study three payment schemes.

First, consider a payment scheme x where $v_1(v) = v_2(v) = v_3(v) = 14$, which divides the value of the game equally among the players. Then, the ordered excess vector is:

$$e(x) = (14 + 14 - 40, 14 + 14 - 30, 14 + 14 - 20, 14 - 0, 14 - 0, 14 - 0)$$
$$= (-12, -2, 8, 14, 14, 14, 14),$$

where the sequence of coalitions is $(\{2, 3\}, \{1, 3\}, \{1, 2\}, \{1\}, \{2\}, \{3\})$.

Intuitively, since the worst treated coalition is $\{2, 3\}$, we should transfer some utility from player 1 to players 2 and 3. For example, consider a payment scheme y where $v_1(v) = 4$, $v_2(v) = 24$, $v_3(v) = 14$. In this case, the ordered excess vector is:

$$e(y) = (4 + 14 - 30, 24 + 14 - 40, 4 - 0, 4 + 24 - 20, 14 - 0, 24 - 0)$$
$$= (-12, -2, 4, 8, 14, 24),$$

where the sequence of coalitions is $(\{1, 3\}, \{2, 3\}, \{1\}, \{1, 2\}, \{3\}, \{2\})$.

Recall that we are trying to find the lexicographically largest excess vector. Disappointingly then, the solution y is not as good as the original solution x. Now, consider a solution z where $v_1(v) = 4$, $v_2(v) = 14$, $v_3(v) = 24$. In this case, the ordered excess vector is:

$$e(z) = (4 + 14 - 20, 4 + 24 - 30, 14 + 24 - 40, 4 - 0, 14 - 0, 24 - 0)$$
$$= (-2, -2, -2, 4, 14, 24),$$

where the sequence of coalitions is $(\{1, 2\}, \{1, 3\}, \{2, 3\}, \{1\}, \{2\}, \{3\})$. The vector z happens to be the nucleolus, where $v_1(v) = 4$, $v_2(v) = 14$ and $v_3(v) = 24$.

The nucleolus is not computationally tractable. In a general cooperative game, finding the nucleolus involves solving a sequence of linear programs which may have size that is exponential in the number of players. Leng and Parlar (2010) provide a review of algorithms for this problem, as well as an easily computable closed form expression for games with three players. See Sect. 8.5.1 for an example of a game where the nucleolus can be found more efficiently for games of any size.

8.2 Cooperative Game Solutions

A final single-point solution discussed here is the τ-value, introduced by Tijs (1981). In that work and also Driessen and Tijs (1985), it is shown that the τ-value satisfies several useful properties, including Individual Rationality, Efficiency and Symmetry.

An explanation of the τ-value for a cost savings allocation game requires several definitions. Given a game (N, v), we first define the *marginal value vector* $b^v = (b_1^v, \ldots, b_n^v)$ as the reduction in the value of the game when each job individually is removed from the grand coalition. Thus, $b^v(i) \in \mathbb{R}$ is defined as

$$b_i^v = v(N) - v(N \setminus \{i\}). \tag{8.3}$$

Next, for any coalition $S \subseteq N$, the *gap function* $g^v(S)$ is defined as

$$g^v(S) = \sum_{i \in S} b_i^v - v(S). \tag{8.4}$$

The gap function of a coalition is the difference between the total marginal value of its members, and its value as a coalition; observe that this difference is always nonnegative. Next, the *concession vector* $\lambda^v \in \mathbb{R}^n$ of the game is defined as

$$\lambda_i^v = \min\{g^v(S) \mid S \subseteq N, i \in S\}, \quad i \in N. \tag{8.5}$$

Thus, λ_i^v is the minimum gap for a coalition containing player i, or more intuitively the potential concession of player i from his marginal value. Each player surrenders some part of this concession as a reduction from his marginal value in (8.3), in proportion to his concession value in (8.5). However, there is a unique fraction of how much total concession needs to be surrendered if the Efficiency property is to be satisfied. Finding this limit requires first calculating $\lambda^v(N) = \sum_{i \in N} \lambda_i^v$. Then, for a balanced game, the τ-value is given by

$$\tau_i(v) = b_i^v - \left[\frac{g^v(N)}{\lambda^v(N)}\right]\lambda_i^v, \quad i \in N. \tag{8.6}$$

The normalization term $g^v(N)/\lambda^v(N)$ in (8.6) computes the unique fraction of the concessions of all the players from their marginal values, such that $\sum_{i \in N} \tau_i(v) = v(N)$. This normalization ensures that the payment allocation by the τ-vector satisfies the Efficiency property.

Example 8.6 (Example of τ-Value Calculations) Using the instance from Example 8.2, we have the following calculations.

From (8.3), $b_1^v = 14 - 3 = 11, b_2^v = 14 - 3 = 11, b_3^v = 14 - 2 = 12$, and $b_4^v = 14 - 2 = 12$.
From (8.4), $g^v(\{1\}) = 11, g^v(\{2\}) = 11, g^v(\{3\}) = 12$, and $g^v(\{4\}) = 12$;

$g^v(\{1, 2\}) = 22 - 2 = 20, g^v(\{1, 3\}) = 23 - 0 = 23, g^v(\{3, 4\}) = 24 - 3 = 21;$
$g^v(\{1, 2, 3\}) = 34 - 2 = 32, g^v(\{1, 3, 4\}) = 35 - 3 = 32, g^v(\{2, 3, 4\}) = 35 - 3 = 32;$

and $g^v(\{1, 2, 3, 4\}) = 46 - 14 = 32$.

From (8.5), $\lambda_1^v = 11, \lambda_2^v = 11, \lambda_3^v = 12$, and $\lambda_4^v = 12$, hence $\lambda^v(N) = \sum_{i=1}^4 \lambda_i^v = 11 + 11 + 12 + 12 = 46$.

We use the above calculations $g^v(N) = 32$ and $\lambda^v(N) = 46$ to calculate the normalization factor 32/46 to apply to the maximal concessions of the players, starting from their marginal values.

Thus, from (8.6), we have $\tau_1(v) = 11 - 11(32)/46 = 77/23, \tau_2(v) = 11 - 11(32)/46 = 77/23, \tau_3(v) = 12 - (12)(32)/46 = 84/23$, and $\tau_4(v) = 12 - (12)(32)/46 = 84/23$. Then, $\sum_{i=1}^4 \tau_i(v) = (77 + 77 + 84 + 84)/23 = 14 = v(N)$, as required.

Due to (a) its positioning as a compromise between the total of the marginal values within a coalition and the value of that coalition, and (b) its satisfaction of several key properties, the τ-value is an appealing solution concept for balanced cooperative games. As with the Shapley value and nucleolus, the discussion of sequencing games below identifies games where the τ-value can be found efficiently.

The following sections provide many examples of how the cooperative game concepts discussed above can be applied to supply chain scheduling problems.

8.3 Sequencing Games

In this section, we consider the substantial class of sequencing games within the field of cooperative games. The classic cooperative game issues of determining balancedness, identifying core members, and efficiently calculating single-point solutions such as the Shapley value (Shapley, 1953), run throughout this class of games. Section 8.3.1 discusses two games that are taken from outside the class of sequencing games, but which nevertheless provide useful results for games within this class. The remaining sections are ordered from simple games where the main results are relatively easy to prove using what are now considered as standard techniques, to more complex generalizations of those games that require different, and in some cases more game-specific, proof techniques. Section 8.3.2 discusses games with costs that are linear functions of job completion times. A more general environment with regular costs is discussed in Sect. 8.3.3. Section 8.3.4 discusses games where the arrival of new work results in rescheduling. Section 8.3.5 studies the effect of relaxing the classical assumptions about the admissibility of sequences with respect to coalition membership. Sequencing games where multiple jobs can be processed simultaneously in batches are considered in Sect. 8.3.6. We provide examples of sequencing games for multiple machine scheduling environments, using a proportionate flowshop game in Sect. 8.3.7, and an openshop game in Sect. 8.3.8.

8.3 Sequencing Games 443

An extension to multi-stage sequencing games is studied in Sect. 8.3.9. Finally, Sect. 8.3.10 provides some perspectives on methods for establishing balancedness in generalized games.

8.3.1 General Related Games

Two classes of cooperative games are closely related to sequencing games, and provide results that assist in the analysis of some sequencing games. Therefore, we discuss them first. They are *permutation games* and *unanimity games*.

8.3.1.1 Permutation Games

Tijs et al. (1984) introduce the class of permutation games. A permutation game contains a set $N = \{1, \ldots, n\}$ of players, each with a single job in a service system, who are waiting in a queue for service at a counter. The order σ_0 in which they expect to receive service is assigned randomly; therefore, without loss of generality, we assume that player i is in position i, i.e., $\sigma_0(i) = i$, for $i = 1, \ldots, n$. The service time for each player is the same, hence also without loss of generality we define it as one time unit. There is no benefit to the server being idle, hence we assume that the jobs are processed consecutively. Therefore, if no rearrangement of the players occurs, player j receives their service in the time interval $[j - 1, j]$. However, the players have different costs of waiting, which in practice are motivated by the value of alternative activities foregone while waiting or receiving service in the system described. Thus, the cost to player i of being the jth player to receive service is denoted as a known constant k_{ij}.

The players can form coalitions to rearrange their positions, thereby reducing their total cost, and share the resulting cost savings among them. A coalition can consist of non-consecutive players in the initial sequence, for example, the players in the first and third positions could form a coalition and swap positions without the involvement of the player in second position. However, any coalition S only has available its own set of initial positions and cannot access positions that are not occupied by members of S in σ_0. For any coalition, the problem of minimizing the total cost of the coalition is a linear assignment problem. Let $\pi \in \Pi_S$ denote an assignment of the players in coalition S to the available positions in the queue, where Π_S denotes all possible assignments, i.e., permutations, of S. A permutation game (N, c) has player set N and characteristic function $c : 2^N \to \mathbb{R}$, where $c(\emptyset) = 0$, and for $S \in 2^N \setminus \emptyset$,

$$c(S) = \min_{\pi \in \Pi_S} \sum_{i \in S} k_{i\pi(i)}. \tag{8.7}$$

8 Cooperative Supply Chain Scheduling

Example 8.7 (Example of a Permutation Game) Consider a game with four players. The game has the following cost matrix, where the entry in row i and column j is k_{ij} as defined above, and where negative values denote profit:

$$
\begin{pmatrix}
0 & -1 & -2 & -1 \\
-4 & 0 & -1 & 1 \\
-3 & -2 & 0 & -1 \\
2 & -3 & -2 & 0
\end{pmatrix}.
$$

The value of the various possible coalitions is as follows:
$c(\{1\}) = c(\{2\}) = c(\{3\}) = c(\{4\}) = 0;\ c(\{1, 2\}) = -5, c(\{1, 3\}) = -5, c(\{1, 4\}) = 0, c(\{2, 3\}) = -3, c(\{2, 4\}) = -2, c(\{3, 4\}) = -3; c(\{1, 2, 3\}) = -8, c(\{1, 2, 4\}) = -8, c(\{1, 3, 4\} = -6, c(\{2, 3, 4\}) = -5;$ and $c(\{1, 2, 3, 4\}) = -10$. It is easy to check that an optimal assignment solution $\pi(1) = 3, \pi(2) = 1, \pi(3) = 4, \pi(4) = 2$ also has a cost of -10.

Tijs et al. (1984) prove that permutation games are balanced. More strongly, they prove that permutation games are totally balanced, i.e., each subgame of a permutation game is balanced. The assumption of a permutation game that the service time of each player is the same is somewhat restrictive for the purposes of classical scheduling and sequencing. Essentially, it implies that all jobs in a scheduling situation have the same processing time. Nonetheless, there are some sequencing games where the balancedness results of Tijs et al. (1984) prove useful. We provide an application to a relaxed sequencing game in Sect. 8.3.5.

8.3.1.2 Unanimity Games

Also of relevance to the analysis of sequencing games are *unanimity games*, introduced by Harsanyi (1981). An unanimity game is a cooperative game (N, u) on any given subset $T, \emptyset \neq T \subseteq N$,

$$
u_T(S) = \begin{cases} 1, & \text{if } S \supseteq T \\ 0, & \text{otherwise.} \end{cases} \tag{8.8}
$$

Observe that, from (8.8), a coalition S has value 1 if it contains all the players of T, and 0 otherwise. Shapley (1953) shows that any cooperative game (N, v) can be written as a unique linear combination of unanimity games, as follows:

$$
v = \sum_{\emptyset \neq T \subseteq N} \mu_T u_T, \tag{8.9}
$$

8.3 Sequencing Games

where $\mu_\emptyset = 0$, and the coefficients μ_S are recursively defined as $\mu_{\{i\}} = v(\{i\})$, $i \in N$, and for $S \subseteq N$, $|S| \geq 2$,

$$\mu_S = v(S) - \sum_{T \subset S} \mu_T. \tag{8.10}$$

The following example illustrates the decomposition of an arbitrary cooperative game into unanimity games.

Example 8.8 (Decomposition into Unanimity Games) Consider a cooperative game (N, v) with three players and the following coalition values: $v(\{1\}) = 2$, $v(\{2\}) = 3$, $v(\{3\}) = 5$, $v(\{1, 2\}) = 7$, $v(\{1, 3\}) = 11$, $v(\{2, 3\}) = 14$, $v(\{1, 2, 3\}) = 35$. Then, the corresponding decomposition of this game into a unanimity game, using (8.9) and (8.10), is

$$
\begin{aligned}
v &= \mu_1 u_1 + \mu_2 u_2 + \mu_3 u_3 + \mu_{12} u_{12} + \mu_{13} u_{13} + \mu_{23} u_{23} + \mu_{123} u_{123} \\
&= 2u_1 + 3u_2 + 5u_3 + (7-2-3)u_{12} + (11-2-5)u_{13} \\
&\quad + (14-3-5)u_{23} + (35-2-3-5-2-4-6)u_{123} \\
&= 2u_1 + 3u_2 + 5u_3 + 2u_{12} + 4u_{13} + 6u_{23} + 13u_{123}.
\end{aligned}
$$

We also show that the values of $v(S)$, $S \subseteq N$, given above, can be reconstructed from the coefficients μ of the vector v in (8.9). Thus, $v(\{1\}) = \mu_1 = 2$, $v(\{2\}) = \mu_2 = 3$, $v(\{3\}) = \mu_3 = 5$; $v(\{1, 2\}) = \mu_1 + \mu_2 + \mu_{12} = 2+3+2 = 7$, $v(\{1, 3\}) = \mu_1 + \mu_3 + \mu_{13} = 2+5+4 = 11$, $v(\{2, 3\}) = \mu_2 + \mu_3 + \mu_{23} = 3+5+6 = 14$; and $v(\{1, 2, 3\}) = \mu_1 + \mu_2 + \mu_3 + \mu_{12} + \mu_{13} + \mu_{23} + \mu_{123} = 2+3+5+2+4+6+13 = 35$.

Intuition about unanimity games is provided by considering how a coalition S should allocate gains or costs in such a game. A gain, or cost saving, of 1 is achieved if and only if all players of T are involved in cooperation. Therefore, any allocation of gain or cost that divides the total gain or cost among the members of $S \cap T$ is a core solution, but members of $S \setminus T$ receive or pay nothing.

For a sequencing game where a decomposition into unanimity games can be accomplished efficiently, this makes two contributions toward the analysis of that sequencing game. First, it provides an efficient calculation for the Shapley value Shapley (1953) of the game, which in general requires averaging over an exponential number of possible coalitions, as in (8.2). The second contribution makes use of the following result.

Theorem 8.1 *A cooperative game (N, v) is convex if and only if, for all $i, j \in N$, $i \neq j$, and each $S \subseteq N \setminus \{i, j\}$,*

$$\sum_{U \subseteq S} \mu_{U \cup \{i, j\}} \geq 0.$$

Proof Let $i, j \in N, i \neq j$, and $S \subseteq N \setminus \{i, j\}$. Given these definitions, a cooperative game (N, v) is convex, as defined in Sect. 2.3.5, if and only if

$$[v(S \cup \{i, j\}) - v(S \cup \{j\})] - [v(S \cup \{i\}) - v(S)] \geq 0$$

$$\Leftrightarrow [\sum_{T \subseteq S \cup \{i, j\}} \mu_T - \sum_{T \subseteq S \cup \{j\}} \mu_T] - [\sum_{T \subseteq S \cup \{i\}} \mu_T - \sum_{T \subseteq S} \mu_T] \geq 0$$

$$\Leftrightarrow \sum_{U \subseteq S \cup \{j\}} \mu_{U \cup \{i\}} - \sum_{U \subseteq S} \mu_{U \cup \{i\}} \geq 0$$

$$\Leftrightarrow \sum_{U \subseteq S} \mu_{U \cup \{i, j\}} \geq 0.$$

$\square$

Observe that if, for a sequencing game, $\mu_S \geq 0$, for $\emptyset \neq S \subseteq N$, as in Example 8.8, then from Theorem 8.1, this is sufficient to establish convexity of that game. This is described as decomposition into a nonnegative linear combination of unanimity games. We describe applications of this procedure to a rescheduling game in Sect. 8.3.4, a batch sequencing game in Sect. 8.3.6, and a proportionate flowshop game in Sect. 8.3.7.

8.3.2 Linear Costs

A *sequencing problem* is one where a solution is completely characterized by a sequence of customers or jobs. Within the more general class of scheduling problems, sequencing problems arise where the sequence completely specifies the time and resource allocations of all activities being processed. A common reason why this occurs is the use of a *regular* cost function, i.e., one that is nondecreasing in job completion times. When a regular cost function is used, there typically exists an optimal schedule that includes no inserted, i.e., unnecessary, idle time. Sequencing problems with costs that are *linear* in job completion times provide a regular measure of overall service time performance across a set of orders for multiple customers. Much of the classical scheduling literature (Pinedo, 2016) uses linear costs to model a variety of different environments and objectives, as defined by internal costs or external contracts with customers.

Let $N = \{1, \ldots, n\}$ denote a queue of jobs that are waiting for service from a single machine. We assume that the queue follows an arbitrary given permutation σ_0 of the jobs. That is, $\sigma_0(i) = j$ means that job i is in the jth position in the queue. Let $p_i > 0$ denote the processing time of job i, and w_i a measure of its urgency

8.3 Sequencing Games

that in classical scheduling is known as a *weight*. We make the natural assumptions that:

(a) Each job experiences a cost that is determined only by its own completion time and not that of other jobs.
(b) The overall cost of a solution is equal to the total of all the individual job costs.

Let $h_i(C_i)$ denote the cost of job i if it completes processing at time C_i. While the regular cost function $h_i(\cdot)$ can be more general, as discussed, for example, in Sect. 8.3.3, here we consider a simple case with linear costs, where $h_i(C_i) = w_i C_i$ and the total cost to be minimized is $\sum_{i=1}^{n} w_i C_i$. In a situation of centralized planning, i.e., where all the jobs have the same customer, an optimal sequence is found by sequencing the jobs in order of nonincreasing w_i/p_i ratio (Smith, 1956), which is known as *shortest weighted processing time* (SWPT) order.

We observe that if $\sigma_0(i) = k$ and $\sigma_0(j) = k+1$, then interchanging the positions of jobs i and j results in a change in total cost of $w_i p_j - w_j p_i$, irrespective of the positions of the adjacent jobs i and j in σ_0 and also of their start times. It may be possible for the players to cooperate and resequence their positions to reduce their total cost, however, players who move earlier may need to compensate those who move later in order to obtain the agreement of the latter to the move. Since we are interested in cost reductions from interchanging jobs, we define the *gain* from interchanging jobs i and j, where $\sigma_0(i) = \sigma_0(j) - 1$, as

$$g_{ij} = \max\{w_j p_i - w_i p_j, 0\}. \tag{8.11}$$

The *sequencing situation* thus defined can be described concisely as (σ_0, w, p), where $w = \{w_1, \ldots, w_n\}$ and $p = \{p_1, \ldots, p_n\}$. Let $P_j(\sigma_0) = \{i \in N \mid \sigma_0(i) < \sigma_0(j)\}$ denote the set of jobs that precede j in σ_0.

From the above sequencing situation, we now define a sequencing game which falls within the class of cooperative games described in Sect. 2.3.5. Each player represents a job in N. The following definition is needed.

Definition 8.1 A coalition S is *connected* if its jobs form a *connected component* of σ_0, i.e., if it contains consecutive jobs in σ_0. That is, for all $i, k \in S$ with $\sigma_0(i) < \sigma_0(k)$, any $j \in N$ with $\sigma_0(i) < \sigma_0(j) < \sigma_0(k)$ is also in S.

For $S \subseteq N$, we define the characteristic function $v(S)$ as the maximal cost savings that a connected coalition can achieve by rearranging the positions of its members in the queue. Observe that, when we interchange the positions of jobs i and j with $\sigma_0(i) < \sigma_0(j)$ and $w_i/p_i < w_j/p_j$, the total cost decreases by g_{ij}. Hence, for a connected coalition $S \subseteq N$, we have

$$v(S) = \sum_{j \in S} \sum_{i \in S \mid \sigma_0(i) < \sigma_0(j)} g_{ij}. \tag{8.12}$$

More generally, a coalition T may not be completely connected but may have one or more connected components, as defined by σ_0. Each component consists of one or more consecutive jobs in σ_0. This requires another definition.

Definition 8.2 Given a coalition T, a connected component S of T is *maximally connected* with respect to σ_0 if no strict superset of any component of T under σ_0 is connected. For example, if $\sigma_0 = \{1, 2, 3, 4, 5, 6\}$, and $T = \{1, 4, 5\}$, then the maximally connected components of T are $\{1\}$ and $\{4, 5\}$, since in the first case $\{2\} \notin T$ and in the second case $\{3\}, \{6\} \notin T$. The given coalition T is equal to the union of its connected components.

Let $T|\sigma_0$ denote the set of components of T that are maximally connected with respect to σ_0. Then, the characteristic function of T is

$$v(T) = \sum_{S \subseteq T|\sigma_0} v(S). \tag{8.13}$$

The above definitions are sufficient to form a sequencing game.

Theorem 8.2 *Consider the sequencing situation (σ_0, w, p) and the corresponding sequencing game (N, v) described above. Then, the game (N, v) is balanced.*

Proof Recall the definition of a convex game in Sect. 2.3.5. Then, for components $T_1, U_1 \in S_1|\sigma_0 \cup \{\emptyset\}$ and $T_2, U_2 \in S_2|\sigma_0 \cup \{\emptyset\}$ where $T_1 \subset T_2$ and $U_1 \subset U_2$, we have

$$v(S_1 \cup \{i\}) - v(S_1) = \sum_{k \in T_1} g_{ki} + \sum_{j \in U_1} g_{ij} + \sum_{k \in T_1, j \in U_1} g_{kj},$$

from (8.12) and (8.13)

$$\leq \sum_{k \in T_2} g_{ki} + \sum_{j \in U_2} g_{ij} + \sum_{k \in T_2, j \in U_2} g_{kj},$$

since $T_1 \subset T_2$ and $U_1 \subset U_2$

$$= v(S_2 \cup \{i\}) - v(S_2).$$

Thus, the sequencing game (N, v) is convex. Then from Bondareva (1963) and Shapley (1967), the game is balanced. $\square$

The result in Theorem 8.2 is intuitive. It specifies that adding player i is more valuable to a larger existing coalition than a smaller one. This encourages cooperation and working together within the grand coalition.

As discussed in Sect. 8.1, when the customers are resequenced to achieve a lower total cost, it is necessary to share the resulting gains equitably. For this purpose, the following definition is useful.

8.3 Sequencing Games

Definition 8.3 An *allocation rule* is a payment scheme $f(\sigma_0, w, p) = (f_1(\sigma_0, w, p), \ldots, f_n(\sigma_0, w, p))$ that assigns to every job i a share of the gain, such that:

(i) $f_i(\sigma_0, w, p) \geq 0$, $i = 1, \ldots, n$, and
(ii) $\sum_{i \in N} f_i(\sigma_0, w, p) = C(\sigma_0) - C(\sigma^*)$,

where $C(\gamma)$ is the total cost of sequence γ, and σ^* is a sequence that minimizes the total cost. Condition (i) implements Individual Rationality, and Condition (ii) implements the Efficiency Property. However, Conditions (i) and (ii) are by themselves insufficient to define a core solution, since the Coalitional Rationality property is not considered.

Curiel et al. (1989) describe a rule for dividing the gains from interchanging positions which they name Equal Gain Splitting (EGS). Recall that (8.11) defines g_{ij} as the gain from interchanging adjacent jobs i and j. Then, EGS gives $g_{ij}/2$ to both i and j, i.e.,

$$f_i^{EGS}(\sigma_0, w, p) = \sum_{k \mid \sigma_0(k) < \sigma_0(i)} g_{ki}/2 + \sum_{j \mid \sigma_0(i) < \sigma_0(j)} g_{ij}/2, \qquad i \in N. \qquad (8.14)$$

The idea of splitting the gain equally between the interchanging players turns out to be powerful in a variety of supply chain scheduling applications.

The analysis of EGS begins with the following result. Observe that, by repeatedly interchanging jobs in adjacent positions whenever a gain can be achieved by doing so, an optimal sequence σ^* can be found.

Theorem 8.3 *EGS is a payment scheme.*

Proof We need only show that the scheme satisfies properties (i) and (ii) of Definition 8.3 above. First, from (8.11), $g_{ij} \geq 0$, hence $f_i^{EGS}(\cdot, \cdot, \cdot) \geq 0$. Second, each time a pair of jobs is interchanged to reduce total cost, the exact cost saving is added to $\sum_{i \in N} f_i^{EGS}(\sigma_0, w, p)$. Thus, by construction, the total cost saving between the initial cost $C(\sigma_0)$ and the optimal cost $C(\sigma^*)$ appears in $\sum_{i \in N} f_i^{EGS}(\sigma_0, w, p)$, and the Efficiency property is finally satisfied. $\qquad \square$

The following three axiomatic properties are relevant to an analysis of the *EGS* payment scheme.

(i) An allocation rule satisfies the *dummy property* if it allocates no gain to a job that does not contribute to cost savings since it is already optimally sequenced in σ_0. A job j is optimally sequenced in σ_0 if there exists an optimal sequence where the set of jobs preceding j is exactly the set of jobs preceding j in σ_0, in which case j is a *dummy job*.

(ii) Given two sequencing situations, we say that one is the *ij inverse* of the other if it is obtained from the first one by switching the positions of jobs i and j in the initial sequence. Then, an allocation rule $f(\cdot)$ possesses the *switch property* if for any pair of sequencing situations (σ_1, w, p) and its ij-inverse (σ_2, w, p), we have

$$f_i(\sigma_2, w, p) - f_i(\sigma_1, w, p) = f_j(\sigma_2, w, p) - f_j(\sigma_1, w, p), \qquad i, j \in N.$$

(iii) Two sequencing situations (σ_1, w, p) and (σ_2, w, p) are i-*equivalent* if job i has exactly the same predecessors in the two original sequences of these situations, i.e., $P_i(\sigma_1) = P_i(\sigma_2)$. Then, an allocation rule $f(\cdot)$ possesses the *equivalence property* if for each job $i \in N$ and each pair of i-equivalent situations, the allocation to job i is equal.

The validity and axiomatic uniqueness of the EGS rule for sequencing games with linear scheduling costs are demonstrated by the next result of Curiel et al. (1989) that makes use of the above three properties.

Theorem 8.4

(a) The EGS rule possesses the dummy, switch, and equivalence properties.
(b) The EGS rule is the only rule that possesses all three properties.

Proof

(a) First, if i is a dummy job, then by definition $g_{ki} = 0$ for $k \in P_i(\sigma_0)$, and $g_{ij} = 0$ for j such that $i \in P_j(\sigma_0)$, which satisfies the dummy property. Second, if (σ, w, p) and (σ', w, p) are two sequencing situations that are identical except that adjacent jobs i and j are interchanged where $\sigma(i) < \sigma(j)$, then $f_i^{EGS}(\sigma', w, p) - f_i^{EGS}(\sigma, w, p) = g_{ji}/2 - g_{ij}/2 = f_j^{EGS}(\sigma', w, p) - f_j^{EGS}(\sigma, w, p)$, which establishes the switch property. Third, if $P_i(\sigma) = P_i(\sigma')$, then $N \setminus P_i(\sigma) = N \setminus P_i(\sigma')$, and then from (8.14), $f_i^{EGS}(\sigma, w, p) = f_i^{EGS}(\sigma', w, p)$, which establishes the equivalence property.
(b) Let $f(\sigma, w, p)$ denote an allocation rule that satisfies the dummy, switch, and equivalence properties. Consider a sequencing situation (σ, w, p). Let the adjacent pairs of jobs that are out of optimal SWPT sequence in σ be denoted as: $S_\sigma = \{(i, j) \mid \sigma(i) = \sigma(j) + 1, w_i/p_i > w_j/p_j\}$. If $S_\sigma = \emptyset$, then each job is a dummy and $f(\sigma, w, p) = (0, \ldots, 0) = f^{EGS}(\sigma, w, p)$. Suppose $f(\sigma, w, p) = f^{EGS}(\sigma, w, p)$ holds for $|S_\sigma| = g$, $g = 1, \ldots, h$. The proof uses induction on the number of pairs of adjacent jobs that are out of sequence to show that this result holds for $h + 1$. Let the sequencing situation (ϕ, w, p) have $|S_\phi| = h + 1$. Hence, there is a sequencing situation (σ, w, p) and a pair of jobs $(k, l) \in S_\phi$ such that $\sigma(i) = \phi(i)$ for $i \neq k, l$, $\sigma(k) = \phi(l)$, and $\sigma(l) = \phi(k)$. Therefore, $S_\sigma = S_\phi \setminus \{(k, l)\}$. Then, from the induction hypothesis, $f_i(\phi, w, p) = f_i(\sigma, w, p) = f_i^{EGS}(\phi, w, p) = f_i^{EGS}(\sigma, w, p)$, for $i \neq k, l$. Further, $C(\phi) - C(\sigma) = g_{lk}$. Then, from part (a) of the theorem,

$$\begin{aligned} f_k(\phi, w, p) &= f_k(\sigma, w, p) + g_{lk}/2 \\ &= f_k^{EGS}(\sigma, w, p) + g_{lk}/2 \\ &= f_k^{EGS}(\phi, w, p), \end{aligned}$$

8.3 Sequencing Games

and similarly for job l. We now have $f_j(\phi, w, p) = f_j^{EGS}(\phi, w, p)$, for all $j \in N$, which completes the proof.

$\square$

We provide an example of cost savings allocations by the EGS rule.

Example 8.9 (Application of the EGS Rule) Let $N = \{1, 2, 3\}$; $\sigma_0(i) = 1, i = 1, 2, 3$; $w = (2, 10, 30)$, and $p = (1, 3, 5)$. Sequence σ_0 has a total cost $C(\sigma_0) = 2 + 40 + 270 = 312$. Now, since $w_1/p_1 = 2$, $w_2/p_2 = 4$ and $w_3/p_3 = 6$, an optimal sequence $(3, 2, 1)$ has total cost $C(\sigma^*) = 150 + 80 + 18 = 248$, a saving of 64 relative to $C(\sigma_0)$. Now, $g_{12} = 4$, $g_{21} = 0$, $g_{13} = 20$, $g_{31} = 0$, $g_{23} = 40$ and $g_{32} = 0$. Hence,

$$f_1^{EGS}(\sigma, w, p) = (g_{12} + g_{13})/2 = (4 + 20)/2 = 12$$

$$f_2^{EGS}(\sigma, w, p) = (g_{12} + g_{23})/2 = (4 + 40)/2 = 22$$

$$f_3^{EGS}(\sigma, w, p) = (g_{13} + g_{23})/2 = (20 + 40)/2 = 30.$$

Observe that the EGS rule allocates the total cost saving of $12 + 22 + 30 = 64 = 312 - 248 = C(\sigma_0) - C(\sigma^*)$ among the three jobs, as required.

Let Π_N denote the set of all possible sequences of jobs. The next result establishes that the EGS rule finds a core solution.

Theorem 8.5 *Let (σ, w, p) be a sequencing situation and let (N, v) be the corresponding sequencing game. Then, $f^{EGS}(\sigma, w, p)$ is in the core of the sequencing game.*

Proof From the Efficiency property, let $\pi_1, \ldots, \pi_r \in \Pi(N)$ be the sequence of permutations produced by adjacent pairwise interchanges when changing an initial sequence σ_0 into an optimal sequence σ^*. Let $C(\sigma_0)$ denote the cost of the initial sequence σ_0, $C(\pi_k)$ denote the cost of the schedule after k interchanges, and $C(\sigma^*) = C(\pi_r)$ denote the cost of an optimal sequence. Then, we have $C(\sigma_0) - C(\sigma^*) = \sum_{k=0}^{r-1}[C(\pi_k) - C(\pi_{k+1})]$, where we define $C(\pi_0) = C(\sigma_0)$, and $C(\pi_r) = C(\sigma^*)$, and $C(\pi_q) - C(\pi_{q+1}) = g_{ij}, 0 \leq q \leq r - 1$. Therefore, $\sum_{i \in N} f_i^{EGS}(\sigma_o, w, p) = C(\sigma_0) - C(\sigma^*)$, which confirms that EGS satisfies the Efficiency Property.

Now, consider any coalition $S \subset N$. We have

$$\sum_{i \in S} f_i^{EGS}(\sigma_0, w, p) = \sum_{i \in S} \Big(\sum_{k \in P_i(\sigma_0)} g_{ki} + \sum_{j | i \in P_j(\sigma_0)} g_{ij} \Big)/2$$

$$\geq \sum_{i \in S} \Big(\sum_{k \in P_i(\sigma_0) \cap S} g_{ki} + \sum_{j \in S | i \in P_j(\sigma_0)} g_{ij} \Big)/2$$

$$= \sum_{i \in S} \sum_{k \in P_i(\sigma_0) \cap S} g_{ki}$$

$$\geq v(S).$$

Thus, no coalition has an incentive to leave the grand coalition. $\qquad\square$

It is also useful to consider single-point solutions, specifically the Shapley value and the τ-value, for the linear sequencing game. Curiel et al. (1989) prove the following result.

Theorem 8.6 *For the sequencing situation (σ, w, p) and corresponding sequencing game (N, v), the Shapley values $\phi_1, \ldots, \phi_n$ are given by*

$$\phi_i(v) = \sum_{\sigma_0(k) \leq \sigma_0(i) \leq \sigma_0(j)} \frac{g_{kj}}{\sigma_0(j) - \sigma_0(k) + 1}, \quad i \in N.$$

Also, Driessen and Tijs (1985) prove the following result.

Theorem 8.7 *For the sequencing situation (σ, w, p) and corresponding sequencing game (N, v), the τ-values $(\tau_1, \ldots, \tau_n)$ are given by*

$$\tau_i(v) = \frac{v(N) \cdot M_i(v)}{\sum_{i \in N} M_i(v)}, \quad where$$

$$M_i(v) = v(N) - v(N \setminus \{i\}) = \sum_{\sigma(k) \leq \sigma(i) \leq \sigma(j)} g_{kj}.$$

Since, from the proof of Theorem 8.2, the sequencing game is convex, we can apply a result of Shapley (1971) about the set of core solutions.

Theorem 8.8 *For a given sequence $\pi \in \Pi_N$, let $\psi_\pi(v) = (\psi_{1,\pi}(v), \ldots, \psi_{n,\pi}(v))$, where*

$$\psi_{i,\pi}(v) = v(P_i(\pi) \cup \{i\}) - v(P_i(\pi)), \quad i \in N. \tag{8.15}$$

Intuitively, $\psi_{i,\pi}(v)$ is the marginal value added when job i joins a coalition that is formed in sequence π. Now, Shapley (1971) proves that the core of a convex game is the convex hull of the vectors $\psi_\pi(v)$, $\pi \in \Pi_N$. Thus, every core solution $x \in \mathbb{R}^n$ can be written as a convex combination of the marginal vectors defined in (8.15), i.e.,

$$x = \lambda_{\pi \in \Pi_N} \psi_\pi(v), \tag{8.16}$$

where $\lambda \in \mathbb{R}_+^{\Pi_N}$, $\sum_{\pi \in \Pi_N} \lambda_\pi = 1$, and $\pi \in \Pi_N$.

The following example demonstrates the application of the results in Theorems 8.6–8.8.

8.3 Sequencing Games

Example 8.10 (Example of Shapley, τ-Value, and Convex Hull Calculations) Consider the sequencing situation in Example 8.9. The corresponding sequencing game (N, v) is defined by $v(\{1\}) = v(\{2\}) = v(\{3\}) = 0$, $v(\{1, 2\}) = 4$, $v(\{1, 3\}) = 0$, $v(\{2, 3\}) = 40$, and $v(\{1, 2, 3\}) = 64$.

Then, from Theorem 8.6, we compute the Shapley values as follows: $\phi_1(v) = 4/2 + 20/3 = 26/3$, $\phi_2(v) = 4/2 + 20/3 + 0 + 40/2 = 86/3$ and $\phi_3(v) = 20/3 + 40/2 + 0 = 80/3$, and $\sum_{i=1}^{3} \phi_i(v) = 26/3 + 86/3 + 80/3 = 64 = v(N)$, as required.

Also, from Theorem 8.7, we compute the τ values as follows: $M_1^v = 24$, $M_2^v = 64$ and $M_3^v = 60$, therefore $\sum_{i=1}^{3} M_i^v = 24 + 64 + 60 = 148$. Then, we have $\tau_1(v) = 64(64 - 40)/148 = 384/37$, $\tau_2(v) = 64(64 - 0)/148 = 1024/37$, $\tau_3(v) = 64(64 - 4)/148 = 960/37$, and $\sum_{i=1}^{3} \tau_i(v) = (384 + 1024 + 960)/37 = 64 = v(N)$, as required.

Finally, for any sequence of jobs $\pi \in \Pi_N$, we use (8.15) to compute the vector $\psi_\pi(v) = v(P_i(\pi) \cup \{i\}) - v(P_i(\pi))$, for $\pi \in \Pi_N, i \in N$, as follows: $\psi_{1,2,3} = (0, 4, 60)$, $\psi_{1,3,2} = (0, 64, 0)$, $\psi_{2,1,3} = (4, 0, 60)$, $\psi_{2,3,1} = (24, 0, 40)$, $\psi_{3,1,2} = (0, 64, 0)$ and $\psi_{3,2,1} = (24, 40, 0)$. Removing duplication and applying Theorem 8.8, the core of the game (N, v) is the convex hull of the vectors $(0, 4, 60)$, $(0, 64, 0)$, $(4, 0, 60)$, $(24, 0, 40)$ and $(24, 40, 0)$. Then, from Shapley (1971), every core solution can be written as a convex combination of these vectors.

The seminal work of Curiel et al. (1989) on the simple sequencing game described above has inspired a variety of generalizations based on the introduction of problems and practical issues from classical scheduling as well as related to assumptions of the games defined. Several of these generalizations are discussed in the following sections.

8.3.3 Regular Costs

We now consider the use of a more general than linear, but still regular, cost function for the jobs. A regular cost function for a job is one that is nondecreasing in its completion time. Regular costs are typically defined by contract penalties for the delivery of make-to-order work. Within classical scheduling, regular but nonlinear costs are commonly used to model problems with due dates. They define problems with objectives that include, for example, the minimization of the number of late jobs (Moore, 1968), and the minimization of total tardiness (Lawler, 1977). Such costs also arise frequently in project management due to contract penalties for late delivery (Klastorin, 2012). By contrast with the game considered in Sect. 8.3.2, the resulting sequencing game is not in general convex, as demonstrated by the following example.

Example 8.11 (Counterexample to Convexity with General Regular Costs) $N = \{1, 2, 3\}$, where $\sigma_0(i) = i$, $p_i = 4$, for $i = 1, 2, 3$. We define the following cost functions: $h_1(C) = C$, $h_2(C) = \min\{40, 10\max\{0, C - 4\}\}$, and $h_3(C) = 5(\max\{0, C - 6\})^2$. The cost of sequence σ_0 is $4 + 40 + 180 = 224$. However, the cost of an optimal sequence $\sigma^* = (2, 3, 1)$ is $0 + 20 + 12 = 32$. Therefore, $v(\{1, 2, 3\}) = 224 - 32 = 192$. In this game, $v(\{j\}) = 0, j \in N$. Also, $v(\{1, 2\}) = 44 - (0 + 8) = 36$ and $v(\{2, 3\}) = 220 - (20 + 40) = 160$. Then, $v(\{1, 2\}) + v(\{2, 3\}) = 36 + 160 = 196 > 192 = v(\{1, 2, 3\}) + v(\{2\})$, which shows that the cost saving game is not superadditive, and therefore not convex.

Curiel et al. (1994) propose a rule for sharing cost savings in sequencing games with nonlinear but regular costs. They name it the β-rule. This rule calculates the marginal increase in savings achieved by adding job i to an earlier sequence of jobs in σ_0, and similarly to a later sequence of jobs in σ_0, and allocates the average of these two quantities to job i. This is an intuitive generalization of the EGS-rule discussed in Sect. 8.3.2, to allow for the possibility that costs are not linear in this case. A formal description now follows.

Let $G(i) = \{j \in N \mid \sigma_0(j) \le \sigma_0(i)\}$, $G'(i) = \{j \in N \mid \sigma_0(j) < \sigma_0(i)\}$, $H(i) = \{j \in N \mid \sigma_0(j) \ge \sigma_0(i)\}$, and $H'(i) = \{j \in N \mid \sigma_0(j) > \sigma_0(i)\}$. Given these definitions, let $f_i^\beta(v)$ denote the allocation of the resequencing gain to player i under the β-rule, for $i \in N$, as defined by:

$$f_i^\beta(v) = [v(G(i)) - v((G'(i))]/2 + [v(H(i)) - v(H'(i))]/2, \qquad i \in N. \qquad (8.17)$$

To interpret (8.17), observe that $[v(G(i)) - v(G'(i))]$ (respectively, $[v(H(i)) - v(H'(i))]$) is the marginal increase in cost savings from adding job i to the sequence of jobs before (resp., after) i in σ.

Example 8.12 (Application of the β-Rule) Using the same instance as in Example 8.11, we calculate the allocations from the β-rule, as follows:

$f_1^\beta(v) = [v(\{1, 2, 3\}) - v(\{2, 3\}) + v(\{1\}) - 0]/2 = (192 - 160)/2 = 16.$
$f_2^\beta(v) = [v(\{1, 2\}) - v(\{1\}) + v(\{2, 3\}) - v(\{3\})]/2 = (36 + 160)/2 = 98.$
$f_3^\beta(v) = [v\{(1, 2, 3\}) - v(\{1, 2\}) + v(\{3\}) - 0]/2 = (192 - 36)/2 = 78.$

We observe that $f_1^\beta(v) + f_2^\beta(v) + f_3^\beta(v) = 16 + 98 + 78 = 192 = 224 - 32 = v(\sigma_0) - v(\sigma^*)$, which shows that the β-rule satisfies the Efficiency property.

Recall Definition 8.1 for connected coalitions. Finally, we check that the connected coalitions $\{1, 2\}$ and $\{2, 3\}$ receive sufficient allocation of the gains from resequencing that they do not leave the grand coalition:

$f_1^\beta(v) + f_2^\beta(v) = 16 + 98 = 114 > 36 = v(\{1, 2\})$
$f_2^\beta(v) + f_3^\beta(v) = 98 + 78 = 176 > 160 = v(\{2, 3\}).$

A useful definition within the context of sequencing games is σ_0-*component additivity*.

Definition 8.4 A cooperative game (N, v) is σ_0-component additive if:

(i) $v(i) \geq 0, i \in N$
(ii) the game is superadditive, i.e., $v(S) + v(T) \leq v(S \cup T)$ for $S, T \subset N$, when $S \cap T = \emptyset$, and
(iii) $v(S) = \sum_{T \in S|\sigma_0} v(T)$, where $S|\sigma_0$ is a partition of the maximally connected components of S with respect to sequence σ_0.

To interpret Condition (iii) in Definition 8.4, T is a subset of jobs that form a connected component of S with respect to σ_0. The cooperative game value of the jobs in T as an independent coalition is defined as $v(T)$. Then, the value of the coalitions of jobs S, denoted by $v(S)$, is additive over all the connected components T of S.

Curiel et al. (1994) prove the following result.

Lemma 8.1 *Every one-machine scheduling problem with an additive and regular cost function defines a cost savings game that is σ_0-component additive.*

Proof If S_1 and S_2 are disjoint coalitions, any resequencing of S_1 and S_2 can be combined into a feasible resequencing of $S_1 \cup S_2$, where the total cost saving equals the sum of the cost savings from the individual resequencing of S_1 and S_2. This establishes superadditivity. Then, σ_0-component additivity follows from the definition of $v(\cdot)$. $\qquad \square$

Corollary 8.1 *It follows from Lemma 8.1 and Le Breton et al. (1992) that a one-machine scheduling problem with an additive and regular cost function is balanced.*

Let $\lambda(i) = \sigma^{-1}(i), i \in N$, i.e., $\lambda(i)$ is the job in position i in σ. The main result of Curiel et al. (1994) which now follows shows the usefulness of the β-rule in supporting cooperation.

Theorem 8.9 *Let (N, v) denote a cooperative game defined by a one-machine scheduling problem with an additive and regular cost function. Then, the β-rule finds a core allocation of the game (N, v).*

Proof From Lemma 8.1, the game described in the theorem statement is superadditive.

Now, consider the σ_0-connected coalition $T = \{i \in N \mid a \leq \sigma_0(i) \leq b\}$, for integers a and b. For this coalition, the β-rule gives

$$2 \sum_{i \in T} f_i^\beta(v) = \sum_{i \in T} [v(G(i)) - v((G'(i)) + v(H(i)) - v(H'(i))]$$

$$= v(G(\lambda(b))) - v(G'(\lambda(a))) + v(H(\lambda(a))) - v(H'(\lambda(b)))$$

$$\geq 2v(T),$$

where $G'(\lambda(b)) = G(\lambda(a)) \cup T$, $H'(\lambda(a)) = H(\lambda(b)) \cup T$, and the inequality follows from superadditivity. $\qquad \square$

456 8 Cooperative Supply Chain Scheduling

Remark 8.1 It is important to note that the result in Theorem 8.9 depends on (a) each job having a cost that is a regular function of its completion time, and (b) the admissibility only of coalitions of jobs that are consecutive in σ_0, or composed of smaller coalitions of jobs that are consecutive in σ_0.

8.3.4 Rescheduling Games

This section studies two situations where a planned schedule is disrupted, due to either a change in work requirements or a change in resource availability. As a result, rescheduling is needed to avoid significant costs. We study how the gains achieved by rescheduling should be divided among the jobs. Models for rescheduling in the event of disruptions are provided by Bean et al. (1991) and Wu et al. (1993).

In the first rescheduling situation we consider, jobs arrive in batches, as occurs frequently in manufacturing. Here, a job that arrives in an earlier batch has certain privileges over a job that arrives in a later batch. Hall and Potts (2004) model this problem from an optimization perspective, by defining this privilege as the maximum number of positions by which an earlier job can be moved later by a later arriving job, which is known as its *disruption level*. The motivation for modeling the disruption level is that the disruption causes resources, possibly including outsourced ones, to be rescheduled. This may result in stress on other activities and increased costs. Hence, the imposition of a constraint on maximum disruption is designed to limit such costs.

We consider a rescheduling problem with two batches. Let $N_1 = \{1, \ldots, n_1\}$ and $N_2 = \{n_1 + 1, \ldots, n_1 + n_2\}$ denote the sets of jobs in the first and second batch, respectively, and let $N = N_1 \cup N_2$. Using classical scheduling notation, the problem of minimizing the total completion time of the jobs is denoted as $1|D_{\max}(\sigma_0) \leq k|\sum C_j$. Here, σ_0 represents an initial, not necessarily optimal, sequence. Also, $D_{\max}(\sigma_0)$ denotes the maximum disruption in the position in sequence of any job in N_1, and the constraint $D_{\max}(\sigma_0) \leq k$ requires that no job in N_1 be more than k positions later in a feasible solution to the rescheduling game than it was in the sequence σ_0 before the second batch arrived. For problem $1|D_{\max}(\sigma_0) \leq k|\sum C_j$, Hall and Potts (2004) describe the following algorithm.

Algorithm MultiBatch
1. Input the jobs of N_1 in SPT order as $1, \ldots, n_1$.
2. Sequence the jobs of N_2 separately in SPT order as $n_1 + 1, \ldots, n_1 + n_2$.
3. Schedule the jobs $1, \ldots, n_1 + k$ in SPT order at the front of the schedule.
4. Schedule the jobs $n_1 + k + 1, \ldots, n_1 + n_2$ in SPT order at the back of the schedule.
   They prove that Algorithm MultiBatch finds an optimal schedule for problem $1|D_{\max}(\sigma_0) \leq k|\sum C_j$ in $O(n_1 + n_2 + n_2 \log n_2)$ time.

Gerichhausen and Hamers (2009) define a *partition sequencing situation* $(N_1, N_2, \sigma^0, p, k)$ that is closely related to the above problem, but with two differences. The first difference is that the jobs of the first batch arrive in an arbitrary

8.3 Sequencing Games

order that defines the initial sequence for the purposes of computing cost savings, or gains, achieved by resequencing. The second difference is that the authors define the maximum disruption constraint differently from that defined by Hall and Potts (2004) described above. Instead, it is defined as a weaker requirement that each job $i \in N_1$ is sequenced in one of the first $n_1 + k$ positions after the second batch is added. Additionally, since this is a cooperative game, the initial sequence is defined to include all the players, i.e., all the jobs in $N_1 \cup N_2$, in order to provide a benchmark for the calculation of overall cost savings. A numerical example follows.

Example 8.13 (Instance of a Partition Sequencing Situation) $N_1 = \{1, 2, 3, 4\}$, $N_2 = \{5, 6, 7\}$, $k = 1$, $p = (3, 10, 2, 5, 8, 1, 6)$.
The original schedule, $\sigma_0 = (1, 2, 3, 4, 5, 6, 7)$, has cost $\sum_{j=1}^{7} C_j(\sigma_0) = 3 + 13 + 15 + 20 + 28 + 29 + 35 = 143$. An optimal schedule $\sigma^* = (6, 3, 1, 4, 2, 7, 5)$, has cost $\sum_{j=1}^{7} C_j(\sigma^*) = 1 + 3 + 6 + 11 + 21 + 27 + 35 = 104$, for a cost saving of 39. This schedule is feasible since the jobs of $N_1 = \{1, 2, 3, 4\}$ are all in the first $n_1 + k = 5$ positions in σ^*.

Over a partition sequencing situation, a *partition sequencing game* is defined. Recall Definition 8.1 for a connected component. The partition sequencing game requires the following admissibility rule: a feasible schedule is *admissible* with respect to σ_0 if and only if the jobs in a connected component S in σ_0 do not jump over other jobs outside S. However, a coalition may contain multiple connected components. Gerichhausen and Hamers (2009) describe a Partition Equal Gain Sharing rule, or PEGS-rule, for allocating cost savings from resequencing the jobs. This rule operates by disaggregation of cost savings. A disaggregated solution allocation is defined by a matrix $F^{PEGS} \in \mathbb{R}^{n \times n}$, where each element f_{ij}^{PEGS} of F denotes the nonnegative allocation of costs savings to job i for cooperating with job j, and $f_{ij}^{PEGS} = f_{ji}^{PEGS}$. Then, the total allocation to job i is $\sum_{j=1}^{n} f_{ij}^{PEGS}$.

Let $g_{ij} = \max\{p_i - p_j, 0\}$ denote the potential cost savings from interchanging adjacent jobs i and job j, where i precedes j in the same connected component in σ^0.

Let S_j, $j = n_1 + k, \ldots, n_1 + n_2$, be defined as:

$$S_j = \begin{cases} \{n_1 + 1, \ldots, n_1 + k\}, & \text{if } j = n_1 + k \\ S_{j-1} \cup \{j\} \setminus \{v_j\}, & \text{if } j \in \{n_1 + k + 1, \ldots, n_1 + n_2\}, \end{cases} \tag{8.18}$$

where v_j is the lowest indexed job that has the largest processing time in the set $S_{j-1} \cup \{j\}$. Observe that S_j is defined recursively from S_{j-1} by (a) the addition of job j, and (b) the removal of a single job with largest processing time, which could also be job j. Intuitively, S_j is an iteratively updated set of the k smallest jobs i, such that $n_1 + 1 \le i \le j$.

The PEGS-rule is defined by:

$$f_{ij}^{PEGS} = \begin{cases} g_{ij}/2, & \text{if } i, j \in N_1, \text{ or if } i, j \in N_2, \text{ or if } i \in N_1, j \in S_{n_1+k} \\ (g_{ij} - g_{iv_j})/2, & \text{if } i \in N_1, j \in N_2 \setminus S_{n_1+k}. \end{cases}$$

The first definition of f_{ij}^{PEGS} divides the cost savings from an interchange of jobs i

and j between those two jobs. The second term in the second definition compensates for the fact that job v_j cannot interchange with jobs of N_1 due to the maximum disruption constraint.

Example 8.14 (Application of the PEGS-Rule) Using the same instance as in Example 8.13, $N_1 = \{1, 2, 3, 4\}$, $N_2 = \{5, 6, 7\}$, $p = (3, 10, 2, 5, 8, 1, 6)$, $\sigma_0 = (1, \ldots, 7)$, and $k = 1$. Then,

$$
F^{PEGS} = \begin{pmatrix}
0 & 0 & 0.5 & 0 & 0 & 1.0 & 0 \\
0 & 0 & 4.0 & 2.5 & 1.0 & 3.5 & 0 \\
0.5 & 4.0 & 0 & 0 & 0 & 0.5 & 0 \\
0 & 2.5 & 0 & 0 & 0 & 2.0 & 0 \\
0 & 1.0 & 0 & 0 & 0 & 3.5 & 1.0 \\
1.0 & 3.5 & 0.5 & 2.0 & 3.5 & 0 & 0 \\
0 & 0 & 0 & 0 & 1.0 & 0 & 0
\end{pmatrix}.
$$

As examples of the calculations in F^{PEGS}, $f_{13}^{PEGS} = g_{13}/2 = \max\{3 - 2, 0\}/2 = 0.5$, and $f_{26}^{PEGS} = (g_{26} - g_{25})/2 = (\max\{10 - 1, 0\})/2 - (\max\{10 - 8, 0\})/2 = 3.5$. From the disaggregated allocation F^{PEGS} of cost savings, the row or column sums provide the aggregated allocation $(1.5, 11.0, 5.0, 4.5, 5.5, 10.5, 1.0)$. The total allocation is thus $39 = \sum_{j \in N_1 \cup N_2}[C_j(\sigma^0) - C_j(\sigma^*)] = 143 - 104$, as in Example 8.13. This shows that all cost savings are allocated, i.e., the Efficiency property is satisfied, as required.

Recall Definition 8.2 for a maximally connected component. A coalition of jobs may consist of multiple maximally connected components. Given σ_0, we define a new sequence as admissible for S with respect to σ_0 if the jobs in $N \setminus S$ that precede job i are the same in σ_0 and the new sequence, for $i \in N$. Let $\mathscr{A}(S)$ denote the set of admissible sequences for coalition S. Now, consider the maximal cost savings of such a coalition $S \subset N$. Then, the characteristic function of a partition sequencing game (N, v) is defined by:

$$
v(S) = \max_{\sigma \in \mathscr{A}(S)} \left\{ \sum_{i \in S}[C_i(\sigma_0) - C_i(\sigma)] \right\}, \tag{8.19}
$$

where the value of a disconnected coalition is the sum of the values of its maximally connected components, as defined in (8.13).

We introduce the following preliminary result. We refer the reader to Gerichhausen and Hamers (2009) for a proof.

Lemma 8.2 $\sum_{i,j \in S} f_{ij}^{PEGS} = \sum_{i \in S}[C_i(\sigma^0) - C_i(\sigma^*)]$, *for all* $S \subseteq N$.

The unanimity game (N, u) on any given subset $T \subset N$ is defined by $u_T(S) = 1$ if $T \subseteq S$, and $= 0$ otherwise, as introduced in Sect. 8.3.1.2. As discussed below, Gerichhausen and Hamers (2009) show that a partition sequencing game

8.3 Sequencing Games

can be written as a nonnegative linear combination of unanimity games. A further preliminary result is needed.

Lemma 8.3 *Let* $(N_1, N_2, \sigma^0, p, k)$ *be a partition sequencing situation, and let* (N, v) *be the corresponding partition sequencing game. Then,*

$$v(S) = \sum_{i,j \in N_1 \cup N_2} g_{ij} u_{[i,j]} + \sum_{j \in N_1, j \in S_{n_1+k}} g_{ij} u_{[i,j]} + \sum_{i \in N_1, j \in N_2 \setminus S_{n_1+k}} (g_{ij} - g_{iv_j}) u_{[i,j]},$$

where $[i, j] = \{i, i+1, \ldots, j\}$ *and* S_{n_1+k} *and* v_j *are defined in (8.18).*

Proof From the admissibility rule, the value of a coalition can be written as the sum of values of its maximally connected components. Therefore, the proof need only consider connected components S. Let σ^* denote an optimal order of S. Define $u_{[i,j]}(S) = u[i, j]$ if $\{i, i+1, \ldots, j\} \in S$, and $= 0$ otherwise. Then, we have

$$v(S) = \sum_{i \in S} [C_i(\sigma_0) - C_i(\sigma^*)], \quad \text{from (8.19)}$$

$$= \sum_{i \in S} \sum_{j=1}^{n} f_{ij}^{PEGS}, \quad \text{from Lemma 8.2}$$

$$= \sum_{i,j \in (N_1 \cup N_2) \cap S} g_{ij} + \sum_{i \in N_1 \cap S, j \in S_{n_1+k} \cap S} g_{ij}$$

$$\quad + \sum_{i \in N_1 \cap S, j \in (N_2 \setminus S_{n_1+k}) \cap S} (g_{ij} - g_{iv_j})$$

$$= \sum_{i,j \in N_1 \cup N_2} g_{ij} u_{[i,j]}(S) + \sum_{j \in N_1, j \in S_{n_1+k}} g_{ij} u_{[i,j]}(S)$$

$$\quad + \sum_{i \in N_1, j \in N_2 \setminus S_{n_1+k}} (g_{ij} - g_{iv_j}) u_{[i,j]}(S),$$

where the third equality follows from (8.19), and the last equality follows from the definition of unanimity games. $\square$

This leads immediately to the following result.

Theorem 8.10 *Partition sequencing games are convex.*

Proof Recall that unanimity games, as defined in Sect. 8.3.1.2, are convex. Lemma 8.3 shows that partition sequencing games are a linear combination of unanimity games. Moreover, since $g_{ij} - g_{iv_j} \geq 0$ by definition of v_j, this is a nonnegative linear combination. The result then follows from Theorem 8.1. $\square$

We now turn our attention to the Shapley value of a partition sequencing game. For many cooperative games, the calculation of the Shapley value is computationally challenging, since it depends on averaging over an exponential number of possible

460   8 Cooperative Supply Chain Scheduling

coalitions. However, a useful result for partition sequencing games is that the Shapley value for job i, denoted by $\phi_i(v)$, can be computed efficiently.

Theorem 8.11 *Let $(N_1, N_2, \sigma_0, p, k)$ be a partition sequencing situation, and let (N, v) be the corresponding partition sequencing game. Then, for $i \in N$,*

$$\phi_i(v) = \frac{\sum_{h,j\in N_1, h\leq i\leq j} g_{hj}}{j-h+1} + \frac{\sum_{h,j\in N_2, h\leq i\leq j} g_{hj}}{j-h+1} + \frac{\sum_{h\in N_1, j\in S_{n_1}+k, h\leq i\leq j} g_{hj}}{j-h+1} +$$

$$\frac{\sum_{h\in N_1, j\in N_2\setminus S_{n_1}+k, h\leq i\leq j}(g_{hj}-g_{hv_j})}{j-h+1}, \textit{ where } S_{n_1+k} \textit{ is defined in } (8.18).$$

Proof Define $h_{ij} = \begin{cases} g_{ij}, & \text{if } i, j \in N_1 \cup N_2, \text{ or if } i \in N_1, j \in S_{n_1+k} \\ (g_{ij} - g_{iv_j}), & \text{if } i \in N_1, j \in N_2 \setminus S_{n_1+k}. \end{cases}$

Now, from Lemma 8.3, $v(S) = \sum_{i<j} h_{ij} u_{[i,j]}(S)$, $S \subseteq N$. Then, from Curiel et al. (1993), $\phi_l(v) = \sum_{i\leq l\leq j, i\neq j} h_{ij}/(j-i+1)$. □

Example 8.15 (Shapley Value Calculations in a Partition Sequencing Game) Consider job $i = 4$ in Example 8.13. From Theorem 8.11, noting that $v(\{6\}) = 5$, we have

$$\phi_4(v) = (g_{16} - g_{15})/6 + g_{24}/3 + g_{25}/4 + (g_{26} - g_{25})/5$$
$$+(g_{36} - g_{35})/4 + (g_{46} - g_{45})/3$$
$$= 2/6 + 5/3 + 2/4 + 7/5 + 1/4 + 4/3$$
$$= 329/60.$$

Also, noting that $v(\{7\}) = 7$, similar calculations for the other jobs provide the vector of Shapley values: $(2/3, 494/60, 509/60, 329/60, 479/60, 449/60, 2/3)$, where $\sum_{i=1}^{7} \phi_i(v) = 39 = 143 - 104 = \sum_{j\in N_1\cup N_2}[C_j(\sigma^0) - C_j(\sigma^*)]$, as required.

Remark 8.2 Gerichhausen and Hamers (2009) generalize their above results to partition sequencing situations with more than two sets, which corresponds to a situation where multiple batches of jobs arrive sequentially, before any processing occurs. The corresponding optimization problem is studied by Hall et al. (2007). As a first step, they extend Algorithm MultiBatch of Hall and Potts (2004) for this problem. The main results are similar to those for the case with two batches, including a proof of convexity and an efficiently computable solution for the Shapley value. They also show that their generalized allocation rule is the unique non-aggregated rule that satisfies the Efficiency, Symmetry, and Consistency properties. Consistency means that connected subcoalitions obtain the same division between them if they renegotiate the current solution after some players leave. They also show that, if the partition sequencing game is generalized to consider the weighted objective function $\sum_{j\in N_1\cup N_2} w_j C_j$, the game is no longer convex; however, it remains balanced.

In the second rescheduling situation we consider, after an optimal schedule π^* has been found but not yet implemented, production resources become unavailable for a single interval of time $[T_1, T_2]$. Some processing has typically been scheduled

8.3 Sequencing Games

within this interval. Hence, due to the period of unavailability, rescheduling is needed. Let $N = \{1, \ldots, n\}$ denote the set of jobs. Each job j has a processing time p_j and a weight or urgency value w_j.

The jobs are required to be processed nonpreemptively, i.e., without interruption. As in Hall and Potts (2004) and Gerichhausen and Hamers (2009), a constraint is imposed on the maximum disruption to any job as a result of the necessary rescheduling. This constraint is of the form $\Delta_{\max} \leq k$, which requires that each job is scheduled no more than k time units either earlier or later in a feasible solution than it was in π^*. Using classical scheduling notation, this problem is denoted as $1 | \Delta_{\max} \leq k | \sum w_j C_j$. Liu et al. (2018b) study this problem, for which they provide a pseudo-polynomial time optimal algorithm, which they name Algorithm 1. After sequencing the jobs according to the SWPT rule of Smith (1956), i.e., by nonincreasing w_j / p_j value, Algorithm 1 applies dynamic programming to schedule each job either before time T_1 or after time T_2. Observe that Algorithm 1 may need to insert idle time, in order to satisfy the maximum disruption time constraint. Let z^* denote the cost of the optimal schedule thus obtained. The computational requirement of the optimal algorithm is $O(n^2 T_1)$ time. The authors also provide a fully polynomial-time approximation scheme. These results show that, while the problem is known to be binary NP-hard as a generalization of a problem studied by Adiri et al. (1989), it is only ordinarily NP-hard.

Consider a cooperative game defined over the above problem. Let the jobs be indexed in SWPT order, which we define as sequence π^*. It is necessary to define a baseline schedule against which any cost savings from cooperative rescheduling can be compared. This baseline schedule is found as follows. Algorithm H schedules each job as early as possible, given the sequence π^*.

Algorithm H
1. Let $\pi^* = (1, 2, \ldots, n)$, where $w_1/p_1 \geq \cdots \geq w_n/p_n$.
2. Find $j' = \min\{j \mid C_j(\pi^*) > T_1\}$.
3. Schedule jobs $1, \ldots, j' - 1$ sequentially without idle time in the interval $[0, \sum_{i=1}^{j'-1} p_i]$, and jobs $j', \ldots, n$ sequentially without idle time in the interval $[T_2, T_2 + \sum_{i=j'}^{n} p_i]$.

Let σ^H denote the schedule found by Algorithm H, and z^H its cost. In the supply chain scheduling game discussed below, a coalition can only be formed from jobs processed consecutively in σ^H, which is a standard admissibility requirement for coalitions in sequencing games. The discussion of these issues requires the following definition.

Definition 8.5 A *usable time period* for a coalition begins at the start time of the first job in the coalition and ends at the completion time of the last job in the coalition in σ_0, excluding the interval $[T_1, T_2]$.

Then, the *rescheduling game* (N, v) is defined by a characteristic function $v(S), S \subseteq N$, where $v(S)$ is the cost saving achieved by coalition S from rescheduling its jobs within its usable time period, relative to its total cost in schedule σ^H. The total cost saving is $z^H - z^*$.

462   8 Cooperative Supply Chain Scheduling

Observe that the time interval $[0, T_1]$ is fixed. It follows that, as a coalition increases in size, there is less space for a new job to add value. Hence, the game is not convex. However, Liu et al. (2018b) show that the game is σ_0-component additive, hence a core solution is found by the β-rule of Curiel et al. (1994) as discussed in Sect. 8.3.3. More directly, however, a core solution is identified by the following result.

Theorem 8.12 *The vector x, where*

$$x_j = 0, \text{ for } j = 1, \ldots, j' - 2, j' + 1, \ldots, n,$$
$$x_{j'-1} = \delta(z^H - z^*), \text{ and}$$
$$x_{j'} = (1 - \delta)(z^H - z^*),$$

for any $0 \le \delta \le 1$, is a core solution of the rescheduling game.

Proof It is easy to check that $\sum_{i=1}^n x_i = z^H - z^*$, as required by the Efficiency property. Observe that any coalition not containing either job $j' - 1$ or job j' cannot be better off acting by itself, from the definition of a usable time period. Also, a coalition that contains both jobs $j' - 1$ and j' has a maximum cost saving of $z^H - z^*$, which is achieved by the values $x_1, \ldots, x_n$ in the theorem statement. $\square$

For this game, Liu et al. (2018b) also show that an efficient computation of the Shapley value is available. Consider a coalition $S(j, l)$ that contains jobs $j, \ldots, l$ processed consecutively in that sequence in σ^H, where $1 < j' \le j_1 - 1$ and $j' \le l < n$. The marginal contribution of job i, $j \le i \le l$ to coalition $S(j, l)$ is defined as $\bar{v}_i(j, l) = v(S(j, l)) - v(S(j, l) \setminus \{i\})$.

Theorem 8.13 *The Shapley value of the rescheduling game is given, for $i \in N$, by $\phi_i(v) = \sum_{1 < j \le j'-1, \, j' \le l < n, \, j \le i \le l} \frac{2\bar{v}(j,l)}{(l-j+1)(l-j+2)(l-j+3)} + \sum_{j' \le l < n, \, i \le l} \frac{\bar{v}(1,l)}{l(l+1)} + \sum_{1 < j \le j'-1, \, j \le i} \frac{\bar{v}(j,n)}{(n-j+1)(n-j+2)} + \frac{\bar{v}(1,n)}{n}$, which can be computed in $O(n^3 T_1)$ time.*

Proof We consider how a player i can contribute to a coalition. There are four cases.

Case 1. Consider $j > 1$ and $l < n$. Any set of jobs not containing job j' or $j' - 1$ cannot achieve cost saving through rescheduling. Therefore, the marginal contribution of job i to any coalition that contains jobs $j, \ldots, l$ but excludes $j - 1$ and $l + 1$ is $\bar{v}(j, l) = v(S(j, l)) - v(S(j, l) \setminus \{i\})$. The total number of permutations that yield this marginal contribution is $2(l - j)!(l - j + 4)(l - j + 5) \cdots (n - 1)n$, which is a fraction

$$\frac{2}{(l - j + 1)(l - j + 2)(l - j + 3)}$$

of the total possible number of permutations $n!$.

Case 2. Now consider $j = 1$ and $l < n$. The analysis is similar to Case 1, and the number of possible permutations in this case is $(l - 1)!(l + 2)(l + 3) \cdots (n - 1)n$, which is a fraction $1/l(l + 1)$ of the total number of permutations.

Case 3. Similarly, for $j > 1$ and $l = n$, the number of possible permutations is a fraction $1/(n - j + 1)(n - j + 2)$ of the total number of partitions.

8.3 Sequencing Games

Case 4. Similarly, for $j = 1$ and $l = n$, the number of possible permutations is a fraction $1/n$ of the total number of partitions.

Finally, the time requirement is determined by the need to enumerate all possible coalitions within their admissible time periods. The characteristic function values required can be computed using $O(n)$ applications of Algorithm 1 in Liu et al. (2018b), each of which requires $O(n^2 T_1)$ time. $\square$

Example 8.16 (Shapley Value Calculations in a Rescheduling Game) $N = \{1, 2, 3, 4\}$; $p = (2, 2, 5, 1)$; $w = (2, 2, 6, 3)$; $[T_1, T_2] = [5, 6]$; $k = 7$; $\pi^* = (1, 2, 3, 4)$. Schedule σ^H processes job 1 from time 0 to 2, job 2 from 2 to 4, job 3 from 6 to 11, and job 4 from 11 to 12. The cost of schedule σ^H, allowing for the unavailable processing time, is $2(2) + 2(4) + 6(11) + 3(12) = 114$. Observe that, since $C_4(\sigma^H) = 12$ and $k = 7$, we have $C_4(\sigma^*) \geq 12 - 7 = 5$. Therefore, an optimal reschedule processes job 3 from 0 to 5, job 4 from 6 to 7, job 1 from 7 to 9, and job 2 from 9 to 11, for a total cost of $6(5) + 3(7) + 2(9) + 2(11) = 91$, giving a total cost saving of 23. The coalition values are $v(\{1, 2\}) = v(\{2, 3\}) = 0$, $v(\{3, 4\}) = 9$, $v(\{1, 2, 3\}) = 12$, $v(\{2, 3, 4\}) = 21$, and $v(\{1, 2, 3, 4\}) = 23$. The vector of Shapley values, showing the four terms in Theorem 8.13 separately, is $\phi_1(v) = 0 + 1.0 + 0 + 0.5 = 1.5$, $\phi_2(v) = 0 + 1.0 + 1.0 + 3.5 = 5.5$, $\phi_3(v) = 0 + 1.0 + 1.75 + 5.75 = 8.5$, and $\phi_4(v) = 0 + 0 + 1.75 + 5.75 = 7.5$. Hence, $\sum_{i=1}^{4} \phi_i(v) = 1.5 + 5.5 + 8.5 + 7.5 = 23.0$, as required.

Remark 8.3 The availability of an efficiently computable solution for the Shapley value of this game is very useful in establishing cooperation for this game. Liu et al. (2018b) conduct a computational study involving 18,600 instances, and observe that the Shapley value is in the core in about 93% of those cases.

8.3.5 Relaxed Sequencing Games

As discussed in the previous sections, the standard admissibility assumption in a sequencing game is that members of a coalition cannot jump over other players, in this case jobs, outside the coalition. Hence, the only admissible interchanges of position are within connected components of a coalition; there can be several such components within a coalition. Curiel et al. (1993) consider more general situations where admissible moves include (a) a change of position in the sequence for an outside job, either earlier or later, and (b) a change of starting time for an outside job, earlier but not later, and both (a) and (b). Our focus is on both relaxations (a) and (b), since it is the most general case, and hence establishing the main result immediately implies the same result for the other cases. The relaxation of the traditional admissibility assumption under (b) is reasonable in the sense that players outside the coalition are not necessarily harmed by the additional flexibility given to the coalition. Moreover, the relaxation provides the potential for additional cost savings for the coalition.

We consider a sequencing situation with $N = \{1, \ldots, n\}$ jobs that need to be processed nonpreemptively on a single machine. Each job j has a processing time p_j, and a weight or urgency value w_j. The jobs are initially queued in a given sequence σ_0. Let $C_j(\sigma)$ denote the completion time of job j in a sequence σ. The sequencing objective is to minimize the total weighted completion time of the jobs, i.e., $\sum_{j \in N} w_j C_j$. Over this sequencing situation, we define a sequencing game (N, v) under both the above admissibility relaxations (a) and (b).

Example 8.17 (Instance of a Sequencing Game under Admissibility Relaxations) Consider a sequencing situation (N, σ_0, p, w) where $N = \{1, 2, 3, 4\}$, $\sigma_0 = (1, 2, 3, 4)$, $p = (6, 7, 2, 1)$, and the weight vector w is arbitrary. Observe that the job starting times in σ_0 are $(0, 6, 13, 15)$. Now, consider the coalition $S = \{1, 3, 4\}$. The corresponding sequencing game (N, v) under relaxations (a) and (b) above has an admissible schedule $\sigma = (3, 4, 2, 1)$, where job $2 \notin S$ has moved from position 2 to position 3 in the sequence, and has a starting time of $3 < 6$.

Slikker (2006) proves the balancedness of the game illustrated in Example 8.17. This result holds for real-valued processing times. However, consistent with the usual convention in classical scheduling problems, we present the analysis for the more intuitive and more practical special case of integer processing times. The balancedness of this game is established by first considering a sequencing situation and corresponding game where each job is broken into pieces with unit processing times. The following definitions are needed for analysis of the unit processing time game.

Definition 8.6 Given a sequencing situation (N, σ_0, p, w), we define a corresponding relaxed *unit sequencing situation* $(\bar{N}, \bar{\sigma}_0, \bar{p}, \bar{w})$ where each job $i \in N$ is replaced by p_i unit processing time jobs and the weight of the job, w_i, is shared equally between the p_i unit size jobs, such that each has weight w_i / p_i. Thus, $\bar{N} = \cup_{i=1}^{n} N_i$, where $N_i = \{j_{i1}, \ldots, j_{ip_i}\}, i \in N$; $\bar{\sigma}_0 = (j_{11}, \ldots, j_{1p_1}, \ldots, j_{n1}, \ldots, j_{np_n})$; $p_{ik} = 1, i \in N, k \in \{1, \ldots, p_i\}$; and $w_{ik} = w_i / p_i, i \in N, k \in \{1, \ldots, p_i\}$.

Example 8.18 (Instance of a Relaxed Unit Sequencing Situation) Given a sequencing situation $N = \{1, 2, 3\}$, $\sigma_0 = (1, 2, 3)$, $p = (3, 2, 1)$, and $w = (3, 4, 5)$, the associated unit sequencing situation is:

$\bar{N} = \{j_{11}, j_{12}, j_{13}, j_{21}, j_{22}, j_{31}\}$; $\bar{\sigma}_0 = (j_{11}, j_{12}, j_{13}, j_{21}, j_{22}, j_{31})$; $p_{ik} = 1$, for all (i, k) such that $j_{ik} \in \bar{N}$; and $\bar{w}_{11} = \bar{w}_{12} = \bar{w}_{13} = 1, \bar{w}_{21} = \bar{w}_{22} = 2, \bar{w}_{31} = 5$.

Associated with the relaxed unit sequencing situation $(\bar{N}, \bar{\sigma}_0, \bar{p}, \bar{w})$ is a *relaxed unit sequencing game*, $(\bar{N}, u)$. The following result in Slikker (2006) characterizes this game.

Lemma 8.4 *If* (N, σ_0, p, w) *is a sequencing situation, then the relaxed unit sequencing game* $(\bar{N}, u)$ *is balanced.*

Proof Since the relaxed unit sequencing game is a permutation game (see Sect. 8.3.1.1), the result follows from Tijs et al. (1984). □

We know from Lemma 8.4 that there exists a core element of $(\bar{N}, u)$ that defines a fair allocation of the cost savings from resequencing. Let this core element be denoted by $y_{ik}, i \in N, 1 \le k \le p_i$. We now show that the aggregated solution $x_i = \sum_{k=1}^{p_i} y_{ik}, i \in N$, is a core element of the relaxed sequencing game $(\bar{N}, v)$. In any schedule σ, let $C_{j_{ik}}(\sigma)$ denote the completion time of job j_{ik}, and for any $\bar{S} \subseteq \bar{N}$ let $C_{\bar{S}}(\sigma) = \sum_{j_{ik} \in \bar{S}} C_{j_{ik}}$.

Slikker (2006) proves the following result.

Lemma 8.5 *If (N, σ_0, p, w) is a sequencing situation, and $(\bar{N}, u)$ is the corresponding relaxed unit sequencing game, then $v(S) \le u(\bar{S})$ for all $S \subseteq N$ and $v(N) = u(\bar{N})$.*

Proof Consider a coalition $S \subseteq N$, where σ is an admissible sequence for S. Correspondingly, $\bar{S}$ is a coalition of unit size jobs, where $\bar{S} \subseteq \bar{N}$ in the relaxed unit sequencing game. Then, $\bar{\sigma}$ is also admissible for $\bar{S}$, since jobs outside S do not start later than they did in σ_0, which satisfies rule (b) of the relaxation. Further, additional cost savings that are not available to S may be available to $\bar{S}$ by moving jobs in $\bar{N} \setminus \bar{S}$ later into their original positions and moving the jobs in $\bar{S}$ earlier without changing their internal sequence.

Let Δ_i denote the cost difference of job $i \in N$ between the relaxed sequencing game and the unit sequencing game with the same sequence. Then, $\Delta_i = w_i p_i - \sum_{k=1}^{p_i} k w_i / p_i = w_i(p_i - 1)/2$. It follows that, for any sequence π,

$$
\begin{aligned}
C_i(\pi) &= w_i \sum_{k \mid \pi(k) \le \pi(i)} p_k \\
&= w_i p_i + w_i \sum_{k \mid \pi(k) < \pi(i)} p_k \\
&= \Delta_i + \sum_{k=1}^{p_i} k \frac{w_i}{p_i} + \sum_{k=1}^{p_i} \left(\frac{w_i}{p_i} \sum_{k \mid \pi(k) < \pi(i)} p_k \right) \\
&= \Delta_i + \sum_{k=1}^{p_i} C_{j_{ik}}(\bar{\pi}).
\end{aligned}
$$

Then, for any coalition $S \subseteq N$, we have

$$
C_S(\pi) = C_{\bar{S}}(\bar{\pi}) + \sum_{i \in S} \Delta_i. \tag{8.20}
$$

Let σ_S denote an optimal sequence for S, and $\bar{\sigma}_S$ its associated schedule, which we know from the above discussion is admissible for $\bar{S}$. Let $\sigma_{\bar{S}}$ denote an optimal schedule for $\bar{S}$. Then, we have

$$u(\bar{S}) = C_{\bar{S}}(\bar{\sigma}_0) - C_{\bar{S}}(\sigma_{\bar{S}})$$

$$\geq C_{\bar{S}}(\bar{\sigma}_0) - C_{\bar{S}}(\overline{\sigma_S}), \qquad \text{from the optimality of } \sigma_{\bar{S}} \text{ for } \bar{S}$$

$$= C_{\bar{S}}(\bar{\sigma}_0) + \sum_{i \in S} \Delta_i - [C_{\bar{S}}(\overline{\sigma_S}) + \sum_{i \in S} \Delta_i]$$

$$= C_S(\sigma_0) - C_S(\sigma_S), \qquad \text{from (8.20)}$$

$$= v(S).$$

Finally, we consider N. Let σ_N denote an optimal sequence for N, and $\overline{\sigma_N}$ the associated order for $\bar{N}$. Then, from Smith (1956), the associated order $\bar{\sigma}_N$ is optimal for $\bar{N}$. Hence,

$$u(\bar{N}) = C_{\bar{N}}(\bar{\sigma}_0) - C_{\bar{N}}(\overline{\sigma_N})$$

$$= C_{\bar{N}}(\bar{\sigma}_0) + \sum_{i \in N} \Delta_i - [C_{\bar{N}}(\overline{\sigma_N}) + \sum_{i \in N} \Delta_i]$$

$$= C_N(\sigma_0) - C_N(\sigma_N), \qquad \text{from (8.20)}$$

$$= v(N).$$

$\square$

We are now ready to prove the main result for relaxed sequencing games.

Theorem 8.14 *If (N, σ_0, p, w) is a sequencing situation, then the associated relaxed sequencing game (N, v) is balanced.*

Proof Let $y_{ik}, i \in N, 1 \leq k \leq p_i$, be a core element of $(\bar{N}, u)$ which, from Lemma 8.4, exists. Let $x_i = \sum_{k=1}^{p_i} y_{ik}, i \in N$. Then,

$$\sum_{i \in S} x_i \geq u(\bar{S}) \geq v(S), \qquad \text{and}$$

$$\sum_{i \in N} x_i \geq u(\bar{N}) = v(N),$$

from the definition of y_{ik} and Lemma 8.5. $\square$

From a practical perspective, the relaxations considered here may be useful in negotiating agreements between coalitions, since they provide additional flexibility to one coalition that is not necessarily harmful to another. As mentioned above, Slikker (2006) extends the above results to games with any real-valued processing times.

8.3 Sequencing Games

Musegaas et al. (2015) study a class of games using a different relaxation, where any player is allowed to step out of his position in the processing sequence and step in at a later position. They show that sequencing games, as defined in Curiel et al. (1989), have a nonempty core under this relaxation. This relaxation can also be used to study the more general games discussed below in this chapter.

8.3.6 Batch Sequencing Games

In batch manufacturing problems, several jobs can be processed simultaneously. Such problems occur, for example, where several processing resources can be used concurrently on the same job(s). A well-known application of batch processing is "burn-in" processing of computer chips (Hochbaum & Landy, 1997; Lee & Tse, 1992). Çiftçi et al. (2013) study scheduling games that are motivated by such applications. In the batch sequencing problem studied here, the processing time of a batch, denoted by t, is independent both of the number of jobs in the batch and of their individual characteristics; hence, this time is simply a known constant. However, the maximum number of jobs in the batch, defined by processing capacity, is L. Each job j has a priority weight, w_j. The objective is to minimize the total weighted completion time of the jobs, where the completion time of a job is the completion time of the batch that contains it. Intuitively, (a) it would never be advantageous to use less than a full batch of jobs while some jobs remain unassigned to a batch, and (b) each batch should contain the L jobs with largest weights until fewer than L jobs remain. This intuition is formalized below. This is a *batch sequencing situation*, for which Çiftçi et al. (2013) define and analyze a corresponding cooperative *batch sequencing game*.

Let $N = \{1, \ldots, n\}$ be a set of jobs. Let $\sigma_0 = (1, \ldots, n)$ denote an initial sequence of the jobs. This implies that, initially, jobs $1, \ldots, L$ are in batch 1 with completion time t, jobs $L + 1, \ldots, 2L$ are in batch 2 with completion time $2t$, and so on. Let B_k denote the subset of jobs in the kth batch. For simplicity, we assume that $t = 1$. The resulting batch cost is $\sum_{i \in B_k} w_i k$, the weighted completion time of that batch. Given a schedule σ, let $C(\sigma)$ denote its total cost. Formally, a batch sequencing situation is defined as (N, σ_0, w, L), where $w \in \mathbb{R}_+^n$, and $L \in \mathbb{Z}_+$.

Lemma 8.6 *An optimal schedule is defined by processing the jobs in maximum capacity batches and in nonincreasing job weight order, which implies nonincreasing total weight of batches.*

Proof This result, based on adjacent pairwise interchanges of jobs, follows from Smith (1956). $\square$

For a given schedule σ, let $b_\sigma(i) = \lceil \sigma(i)/L \rceil$ denote the index of the batch in which job i is scheduled. Let $\mathscr{A}(S)$ denote the set of all admissible sequences. Recall from Definition 8.1 that a connected coalition occupies consecutive positions in σ. Using Definition 8.2, a σ_0-component of S is a maximally connected component of S with respect to σ_0, and $S|\sigma_0$ is the set of all such components in S. We let $con(\sigma_0)$ denote the set of coalitions that are connected with respect to σ_0. Formally, a batch sequencing game is defined by (N, v), where for all $S \subseteq N$,

$$v(S) = \max_{\sigma \in \mathscr{A}(S)} \left\{ \sum_{i \in S} w_i [b_{\sigma_0}(i) - b_\sigma(i)] \right\}. \tag{8.21}$$

The next result establishes the existence of a core solution.

Lemma 8.7 *Batch sequencing games are balanced.*

Proof It is clear that batch sequencing games are superadditive. In a batch sequencing game, a resequencing σ of the jobs by coalition S is admissible if and only if the set of jobs that precede any job $j \in N \setminus S$ is the same in the original sequence σ_0 and in σ. This requirement ensures that batch sequencing games are σ_0-component additive. Then, from Le Breton et al. (1992), such games are balanced. $\square$

As a result of Lemma 8.7, we turn our focus to obtaining an understanding of the convexity of the game, and also obtaining an efficiently computable expression for the Shapley value. These are achieved through the use of unanimity games, as defined in Sect. 8.3.1.2. The value of coalition $S \subseteq N$ is the maximum cost savings that the coalition can achieve by an admissible resequencing from σ_0, and we now provide an example. Let $b_\sigma(i)$ denote the number of the batch in which job i is included in a given schedule σ.

Example 8.19 (Instance of a Batch Sequencing Game) Let $N = \{1, \ldots, 5\}$, $w = (1, 2, 4, 5, 8)$ and $L = 2$. Let $\sigma_0 = (1, 2; 3, 4; 5)$, where we use ";" to indicate the start of a new batch, i.e., $b_{\sigma_0}(1) = b_{\sigma_0}(2) = 1, b_{\sigma_0}(3) = b_{\sigma_0}(4) = 2$, and $b_{\sigma_0}(5) = 3$. The cost of σ_0, denoted by $C(\sigma_0)$ is $1(1 + 2) + 2(4 + 5) + 3(8) = 45$. Consider a coalition $S = \{2, 3, 4, 5\}$. The optimal rearrangement σ^* that is admissible for S is $(1, 5; 4, 3; 2)$, where $b_{\sigma^*}(1) = b_{\sigma^*}(5) = 1, b_{\sigma^*}(4) = b_{\sigma^*}(3) = 2$, and $b_{\sigma^*}(2) = 3$, with a cost of $1(1 + 8) + 2(5 + 4) + 3(2) = 33$, a saving of $C(\sigma_0) - C(\sigma^*) = v(S) = 45 - 33 = 12$. Using (8.21), we also obtain $v(S) = 2(1 - 3) + 4(2 - 2) + 5(2 - 2) + 8(3 - 1) = 12 = 45 - 33$, as required.

For any coalition $S \subseteq N$, it is useful to characterize the first and last member of S, as scheduled in σ_0, i.e.,

$$f(S) = \arg \min_{i \in S} \{\sigma_0(i)\}, \quad \text{and}$$

$$l(S) = \arg \max_{i \in S} \{\sigma_0(i)\},$$

respectively. Note that $\sigma_S^{-1}(y)$ is the job in position y in schedule σ_S. Using these definitions, Çiftçi et al. (2013) prove the following result.

8.3 Sequencing Games

Theorem 8.15 *Let (N, σ_0, w, L) be a batch sequencing situation, and (N, v) be the corresponding batch sequencing game. Further, let $\sum_{S \subseteq N} \lambda_S u_S$ be a linear decomposition of (N, v) into unanimity games. Then, for $S \in con(\sigma_0)$,*

$$\lambda_S = \begin{cases} \sum_{k|b_{\sigma_S}(l(S)) \leq k < b_{\sigma_S}(f(S))} [w_{\sigma_S^{-1}(kL)} - w_{\sigma_S^{-1}(kL+1)}], & \text{if } b_{\sigma_S}(l(S)) < b_{\sigma_S}(f(S)) \\ 0, & \text{otherwise.} \end{cases} \tag{8.22}$$

Observe that the summation in (8.22) is over all batches that contain any jobs of the coalition S (which is connected with respect to σ_0), excluding the last such batch. The result in Theorem 8.15 is useful in that it enables efficient computation of the values of all coalitions and also for the Shapley value. We now summarize these results.

Theorem 8.16 *Let (N, σ_0, w, L) be a batch sequencing situation, and (N, v) be the corresponding batch sequencing game. Then,*

(i) (N, v) is convex.
(ii) For all $S \subset N$, $v(S) = \sum_{k | b_{\sigma_S}(l(S)) \leq k < b_{\sigma_S}(f(S))} [w_{\sigma_S^{-1}(kL)} - w_{\sigma_S^{-1}(kL+1)}]$.
(iii) For all $i \in N$, the Shapley value of job i, $\phi_i(v)$, is given by

$$\phi_i(v) = \sum_{S \in con(\sigma_0), i \in S} \quad \sum_{k | b_{\sigma_S}(l(S)) \leq k < b_{\sigma_S}(f(S))} \frac{w_{\sigma_S^{-1}(kL)} - w_{\sigma_S^{-1}(kL+1)}}{|S|}.$$

$$\tag{8.23}$$

(iv) For all $i \in V$, $\phi_i(v)$ is in the core of the game.

Proof

(i) Follows from the fact that Theorem 8.15 shows that batch sequencing games are nonnegative combinations of unanimity games, and therefore convex (see Sect. 8.3.1.2).
(ii) Follows from (8.22).
(iii) Follows from (i) and Theorem 8.15.
(iv) Follows from (i) and Shapley (1971).

$\square$

The following example applies the results in Theorem 8.16 to compute the values of all coalitions, and the Shapley values of all jobs, efficiently in batch sequencing games.

Example 8.20 (Coalition and Shapley Values in a Batch Sequencing Game) Consider the batch sequencing game in Example 8.19. We discuss the calculations for the values of the coalitions and the Shapley value in Table 8.1. First, recall from Example 8.19 that $C(\sigma_0) = 45$. Also, from Lemma 8.6, an optimal schedule is $\sigma^* = (5, 4; 3, 2; 1)$, with $C(\sigma^*) = 1(8 + 5) + 2(4 + 2) + 3(1) = 28$. Hence, $C(\sigma_0) - C(\sigma^*) = 45 - 28 = 17$, which is the total value of all coalitions in the fourth column of Table 8.1. More generally, from Theorem 8.16, part (ii), the value

8 Cooperative Supply Chain Scheduling

Table 8.1 Coalition and Shapley values in Example 8.20

Row	S	σ_S	$v(S)$	Shapley
1	$\{1, 2\}$	$(2, 1; 3, 4; 5)$	0	0
2	$\{2, 3\}$	$(1, 3; 2, 4; 5)$	$w_3 - w_2 = 2$	$2/2 = 1$
3	$\{3, 4\}$	$(2, 1; 4, 3; 5)$	0	0
4	$\{4, 5\}$	$(2, 1; 3, 5; 4)$	$w_5 - w_4 = 3$	$3/2 = 1.500$
5	$\{1, 2, 3\}$	$(3, 2; 1, 4; 5)$	$w_2 - w_1 = 1$	$1/3 = 0.333$
6	$\{2, 3, 4\}$	$(1, 4; 3, 2; 5)$	$w_4 - w_3 = 1$	$1/3 = 0.333$
7	$\{3, 4, 5\}$	$(1, 2; 5, 4; 3)$	$w_4 - w_3 = 1$	$1/3 = 0.333$
8	$\{1, 2, 3, 4\}$	$(4, 3; 2, 1; 5)$	$w_3 - w_2 = 2$	$2/4 = 0.500$
9	$\{2, 3, 4, 5\}$	$(1, 5; 4, 3; 2)$	$(w_3 - w_2) + (w_5 - w_4) = 2 + 3 = 5$	$5/4 = 1.250$
10	$\{1, 2, 3, 4, 5\}$	$(5, 4; 3, 2; 1)$	$(w_4 - w_3) + (w_2 - w_1) = 1 + 1 = 2$	$2/5 = 0.400$
Total			17	

of any coalition can be found from adding the number in the fourth column of the table over all its subcoalitions, including itself. For example, consider the coalition $S = \{2, 3, 4, 5\}$. Recall from Example 8.19, that $v(\{2, 3, 4, 5\}) = 12$. This result can be found by adding the values in the fourth column of all rows except 1,5,8, and 10 for coalitions which contain $\{1\}$, giving $2 + 0 + 3 + 1 + 1 + 5 = 12$.

We also calculate the Shapley value of each job from Table 8.1, using the result in Theorem 8.16, part (iii). For each task i, we add the entry in the last column of the table, for each row where $i \in S$. Thus, we obtain:
$\phi_1(v) = 0 + 0.333 + 0.5 + 0.4 = 1.233$; $\phi_2(v) = 0 + 1 + 0.333 + 0.333 + 0.5 + 1.25 + 0.4 = 3.817$; $\phi_3(v) = 1 + 0 + 0.333 + 0.333 + 0.333 + 0.5 + 1.25 + 0.4 = 4.15$; $\phi_4(v) = 0 + 1.5 + 0.333 + 0.333 + 0.5 + 1.25 + 0.4 = 4.317$; and $\phi_5(v) = 1.5 + 0.333 + 1.25 + 0.4 = 3.483$. Then, $\sum_{i=1}^{5} \phi_i(v) = 1.233 + 3.817 + 4.15 + 4.317 + 3.483 = 17 = C(\sigma_0) - C(\sigma^*)$, as required.

Çiftçi et al. (2013) extend their work in two different directions. First, they relax the standard condition on admissibility to allow the players in coalition S to take any position, provided that the players outside S remain in the same position as in the original schedule. Batch sequencing games under this relaxation are not convex. However, a useful connection with assignment games (Shapley & Shubik, 1972) is established. Every relaxed batch sequencing game can be written as the sum of specific assignment games. Then, since assignment games are balanced, this establishes the balancedness of relaxed batch sequencing games. Second, they study batch sequencing games defined on flowshops. In general, such games are neither convex nor σ_0-component additive. However, some special cases of such games reduce to batch sequencing games defined on an easily identified bottleneck machine in the flowshop.

8.3 Sequencing Games

8.3.7 *Proportionate Flowshops*

Estévez-Fernández et al. (2008) consider cooperative games defined over proportionate flowshops (PFS). In a flowshop problem, a group of jobs has to be processed through a fixed number of machines, and the order of the machines in which the jobs have to be processed is the same for all jobs. A proportionate flowshop problem is a special case of the flowshop problem where processing times vary between jobs, but for any job they are the same on all machines. A typical application of this occurs where the processes at the different machines are simple and similar operations, an example being the addition of various layers of paint to products, i.e., jobs, of different sizes.

We describe a PFS application where the objective is to minimize the total weighted completion time of the jobs on the last machine. A PFS situation can be described by a 4-tuple (M, N, p, w), where $M = \{M_1, \ldots, M_m\}$ is the set of machines, $N = \{1, \ldots, n\}$ denotes the set of jobs, $p \in \mathbb{R}_+^n$ is the vector of processing times of the jobs, and $w_i \in \mathbb{R}_+^n$ denotes the cost of job i per unit of waiting time. Let $\Pi(N, M)$ denote the set of all possible schedules. A schedule $\sigma \in \Pi(N, M)$ is defined by $\sigma = (\sigma^1, \ldots, \sigma^m)$, where σ^j is the sequence of jobs on machine M_j. Given a schedule σ^j for machine M_j, let $P_i(\sigma^j) = \{h \in N \mid \sigma^j(h) < \sigma^j(i)\}$ denote the set of jobs that precede job i on machine M_j.

Definition 8.7 If $\sigma_1 = \cdots = \sigma_m$, then the schedule is called a *permutation schedule*, or an *order*.

Shakhlevich et al. (1998) show that there exists an optimal schedule for a PFS problem that is a permutation schedule. The completion time of job i on machine j in schedule σ is denoted as $C_i^j(\sigma)$, $i \in N$, $j \in M$. The overall completion time of job i in schedule σ is its completion time on the last machine on which processing occurs for all jobs, i.e., machine M_m, and is thus denoted by $C_i^m(\sigma)$. The objective is to minimize the total cost $c_N(\sigma) = \sum_{i \in N} c_i(\sigma)$, where $c_i(\sigma) = w_i C_i^m(\sigma)$, $i \in N$.

Definition 8.8 Given a schedule σ, job i is defined to be a *new-max job under σ* if $p_i > \max_{j \in P_i(\sigma)}\{p_j\}$. That is, job i is the largest job in σ up to this point. This definition enables a partitioning of the jobs into *segments* where each segment starts with the next new-max job.

We assume an initial schedule σ_0. Given a coalition $S \subset N$, we define $S|\sigma_0^j$ as the set of all maximally connected components of S according to σ_0^j. Also, given $S \subset N$, the set of admissible schedules of S with respect to σ_0, denoted by $A(S, \sigma_0)$, consists of all schedules σ such that

(i) $S|\sigma^j = S|\sigma_0^j$, $j \in M$, and
(ii) $C_i^j(\sigma) = C_i^j(\sigma_0)$, $i \in N \setminus S$, $j \in M$.

Condition (i) specifies that a schedule is admissible for a coalition S with respect to the initial schedule σ_0 if changes on any machine j with respect to its local initial schedule σ_0^j occur within connected components. Condition (ii) requires that the completion time of no job in $N \setminus S$ is changed from schedule σ_0 to schedule σ.

Consider a PFS cooperative game defined as follows. Let (M, N, p, w, σ_0) denote an instance of a PFS scheduling problem. Then, the associated PFS game (N, v) is defined by

$$v(S) = \max_{\sigma \in A(S, \sigma_0)} \{c_S(\sigma_0) - c_S(\sigma)\},$$

for $S \subset N$, where $c_S(\sigma) = \sum_{i \in S} c_i(\sigma)$. Estévez-Fernández et al. (2008) prove the following result.

Theorem 8.17 *PFS games are balanced.*

Proof There are two cases.

Case 1. Suppose σ_0 is a permutation schedule. Then,

    (i) $v(i) \geq 0, i \in N$,
    (ii) (N, v) is superadditive, and
    (iii) $v(S) = \sum_{T \in S | \sigma_0} v(T)$.

Hence (N, v) is σ_0-component additive, and from Le Breton et al. (1992) it is balanced.

Case 2. Let the initial schedule σ_0 be an arbitrary schedule. Define $\tilde{\sigma}_0$ by $\sigma_0^j = \sigma_0^m$, for $j \in M$. That is, the job sequence of σ_0 on the last machine M_m is applied to all machines, in order to create a permutation schedule. Let (N, w) be the PFS game associated with the PFS situation $(N, M, p, w, \tilde{\sigma}_0)$. Let $a_i = c_i(\sigma_0) - c_i(\tilde{\sigma}_0), i \in N$. Then, since the optimal schedule for N belongs to both $A(N, \sigma_0)$ and $A(N, \tilde{\sigma}_0)$, we have

$$v(N) = w(N) + \sum_{i \in N} a_i. \tag{8.24}$$

Further, since for every $\sigma \in A(S, \sigma_0)$, we can define $\tilde{\sigma}$ by $\tilde{\sigma}^j = \sigma^m, j \in M$, we have

$$v(S) \leq w(S) + \sum_{i \in S} a_i. \tag{8.25}$$

Then, since $\tilde{\sigma}$ is a permutation schedule, $\tilde{\sigma} \in A(S, \tilde{\sigma}_0)$, hence

$$v(S) = \max_{\sigma \in A(S, \sigma_0)} \{c_S(\sigma_0) - c_S(\sigma)\}$$

$$= c_S(\sigma_0) - \min_{\sigma \in A(S, \sigma_0)} \{c_S(\sigma)\}$$

$$= c_S(\sigma_0) - c_S(\tilde{\sigma}_0) + c_S(\tilde{\sigma}_0) - \min_{\sigma \in A(S, \sigma_0)} \{c_S(\sigma)\}$$

8.3 Sequencing Games

$$\leq c_S(\sigma_0) - c_S(\tilde{\sigma}_0) + c_S(\tilde{\sigma}_0) - \min_{\sigma \in A(S,\sigma_0)} \{c_S(\tilde{\sigma})\}$$

$$\leq c_S(\sigma_0) - c_S(\tilde{\sigma}_0) + c_S(\tilde{\sigma}_0) - \min_{\sigma \in A(S,\tilde{\sigma}_0)} \{c_S(\sigma)\}$$

$$= c_S(\sigma_0) - c_S(\tilde{\sigma}_0) + \max_{\sigma \in A(S,\tilde{\sigma}_0)} \{c_S(\tilde{\sigma}_0) - c_S(\sigma)\}$$

$$= \sum_{i \in S} a_i + w(S).$$

Here, the first inequality follows from $C_S(\sigma) \geq C_S(\tilde{\sigma})$, for $\sigma \in A(S,\sigma_0)$ (Shakhlevich et al., 1998). The second inequality follows because $A(S,\tilde{\sigma}_0) \supseteq A(S,\sigma_0)$. The last equality follows by definition of a_i, since $c_S(\sigma_0) - c_S(\tilde{\sigma}_0) = \sum_{i \in S} c_i(\sigma_0) - \sum_{i \in S} c_i(\tilde{\sigma}_0) = \sum_{i \in S} a_i$.

Finally, by Case 1, (N, w) is balanced. Let $y \in \mathbb{R}^n$ be in the core of that game, and define $x \in \mathbb{R}^n$ such that $x = y + a$. It follows from (8.24) and (8.25) that x is in the core of (N, v), and (N, v) is balanced. □

The remainder of our discussion of PFS games considers a natural and practical special case. We make the assumption that σ_0 is an *urgency permutation* of the jobs, i.e., each machine schedules the jobs in the sequence $1, \ldots, n$, where $w_1/p_1 \geq \cdots \geq w_n/p_n$, the SWPT order of Smith (1956). We write this assumption as $\sigma_0 = \sigma_u$.

Estévez-Fernández et al. (2008) describe a procedure to generate an optimal order which we denote as $\hat{\sigma}^S_{i_S}, \ldots, \hat{\sigma}^S_{j_S}$ for a connected coalition $S = \{i_S, \ldots, j_S\}$. In this procedure, $\hat{\sigma}^S_{i_S} = \sigma_u$. Then, the procedure recursively computes $\hat{\sigma}^S_i$ from $\hat{\sigma}^S_{i-1}$, by adding a new job at the end of the current sequence of jobs, and then resequencing the jobs. We refer the reader to their work for details of this procedure.

Let $G^S_i \geq 0$ be defined as the cost savings obtained by adding job $i \in S$ to the sequence, and then resequencing the jobs to find an optimal sequence from resequencing job $i \in S$. Thus, Estévez-Fernández et al. (2008) define

$$G^S_i = c_N(\hat{\sigma}^S_{i-1}) - c_N(\hat{\sigma}^S_i), \quad i \in S,$$

from which it follows that

$$v(S) = \sum_{i=i_s}^{j_s} [c_N(\hat{\sigma}^S_{i-1}) - c_N(\hat{\sigma}^S_i)]$$

$$= \sum_{i \in S} G^S_i.$$

Given an urgency permutation σ_u of the jobs, let $\{a_1, \ldots, a_s\}$ denote the corresponding set of new-max jobs, where $a_1 < \cdots < a_s$. Recall that these jobs are successively the largest job so far in σ_u, and since σ_u is a permutation, they are well defined.

Definition 8.9

(i) If i is a new-max job in σ_u, then let $r(i)$ be the index of job i, that is, $a_{r(i)} = i$.

(ii) If i is not a new-max job in σ_u, then let $r(i)$ be the index of the new-max job that precedes job i.

We now show how to derive an efficiently computable closed form expression for the value of any coalition, and also for the Shapley value of the game (N, v). This result uses a decomposition into unanimity games, as defined in Sect. 8.3.1.2.

Theorem 8.18

(i) *In a PFS game (N, v) with initial urgency permutation σ_0,*

$$v(T) = \sum_{k \in N} \sum_{r=1}^{r(k)} [G_k^{\{a_r,...,n\}} - G_k^{\{a_{r+1},...,n\}}] u_{\{a_r,...,k\}}(T),$$

for $T \subset N$, and where $G_k^{\{a_{r(k)}+1,...,n\}}$ is defined to be 0.

(ii) *The Shapley value of the game (N, v) is*

$$\phi_i(v) = \sum_{k=i}^{n} \sum_{r=1}^{r(i)} \frac{G_k^{\{a_r,...,n\}} - G_k^{\{a_{r+1},...,n\}}}{|\{a_r, ..., k\}|}, \quad i \in N.$$

Proof

(i) Let $T \subset N$ be a connected coalition, where we let $T = \{i_T, ..., j_T\}$. There are two cases.

Case 1. $T \cap \{a_1, ..., a_s\} = \emptyset$. Then, since Shakhlevich et al. (1998) show that there exists an optimal schedule that follows urgency order within segments, $\hat{\sigma}_k^T = k, k \in T$, and therefore $G_k^T = 0, k \in T$. Hence, $v(T) = 0$. Further, $\{a_r, ..., k\} \not\subset T$ for every new-max job a_r and every $k \geq a_r$. Hence, $u_{\{a_r,...,k\}}(T) = 0$, and

$$\sum_{k \in N} \sum_{r=1}^{r(k)} [G_k^{\{a_r,...,n\}} - G_k^{\{a_{r+1},...,n\}}] u_{\{a_r,...,k\}}(T) = 0 = v(T).$$

Case 2. $T \cap \{a_1, ..., a_s\} = \{a_u, ..., a_w\}$ with $a_u \leq \cdots \leq a_w$. Then, from Shakhlevich et al. (1998), $\hat{\sigma}_k^T(k) = k$, for $i_T \leq k < a$ and $\hat{\sigma}_k^T = \hat{\sigma}_k^{\{a_u,...,n\}}$, for $k \geq a_u$. Hence, $G_k^T = 0$ for $i_T \leq k < a_u$ and $G_k^T = G_k^{\{a_u,...,n\}}$ for $j_T \geq k \geq a_u$. Therefore, $v(T) = \sum_{k=a_u}^{j_T} G_k^{\{a_u,...,n\}}$. Further,

$$\sum_{k \in N} \sum_{r=1}^{r(k)} \left[G_k^{\{a_r,...,n\}} - G_k^{\{a_{r+1},...,n\}} \right] u_{\{a_r,...,k\}}(T)$$

$$= \sum_{k=a_u}^{j_T} \sum_{r=u}^{r(k)} \left[G_k^{\{a_r,...,k\}} - G_k^{\{a_{r+1},...,n\}} \right] u_{\{a_r,...,k\}}(T)$$

8.3 Sequencing Games

Table 8.2 Cost savings achieved by job j in various coalitions

	1	2	3	4	5	6	7	8	9
G_i^N	0	0	2500	0	1480	800	0	130	0
$G_i^{\{2,\dots,9\}}$		0	1300	0	720	800	0	0	0
$G_i^{\{9\}}$									0

$$= \sum_{k=a_u}^{j_T} \left[\left(G_k^{\{a_u,\dots,n\}} - G_k^{\{a_u+1,\dots,n\}} \right) + \left(G_k^{\{a_u+1,\dots,n\}} - G_k^{\{a_u+2,\dots,n\}} \right) \right.$$
$$\left. + \cdots + \left(G_k^{\{a_{r(k)}-1,\dots,n\}} - G_k^{\{a_{r(k)},\dots,n\}} \right) + G_k^{\{a_{r(k)},\dots,n\}} \right]$$

$$= \sum_{k=a_u}^{j_T} G_k^{\{a_u,\dots,n\}}$$

$$= v(T),$$

where the first equality follows from the fact that if either $a_r < a_u \le k$, or $k > j_T$ and $a_r \le k$, then $\{a_r, \dots, k\} \not\subset T$ and hence $u_{\{a_r,\dots,k\}}(T) = 0$. Also, the second equality follows because if $a_u \le a_r \le a_{r(k)}$ and $a_r \le k \le j_T$, then $\{a_r, \dots, k\} \subset T$ and hence $u_{\{a_r,\dots,k\}}(T) = 1$.

Let $T \subset N$. If T is unconnected, then $v(T) = \sum_{U \in T|\sigma_0} v(U)$, and

$$\sum_{k \in N} \sum_{r=1}^{r(k)} (G_k^{\{a_r,\dots,n\}} - G_k^{\{a_r+1,\dots,n\}}) u_{\{a_r,\dots,k\}}(T)$$

$$= \sum_{U \in T|\sigma_0} \sum_{k \in N} \sum_{r=1}^{r(k)} (G_k^{\{a_r,\dots,n\}} - G_k^{\{a_r+1,\dots,n\}}) u_{\{a_r,\dots,k\}}(U),$$

since unanimity games are defined for connected coalitions.

(ii) The proof follows immediately from part (i) of the theorem, and the definition of Shapley value.

$\square$

Example 8.21 (Cost Savings and Shapley Value Calculations in a PFS Game) Consider a PFS problem with $M = \{M_1, M_2, M_3\}$, $N = \{1, \dots, 9\}$, $p = (20, 30, 10, 30, 10, 20, 30, 10, 40)$, and $w = (200, 270, 80, 210, 69, 130, 180, 59, 200)$. The urgency index order is $\sigma_0 = (1, \dots, 9)$. The cost $\sum_{i \in M} w_i C_i$ of a schedule in urgency order is 224,020. An optimal schedule is $(3, 5, 8, 1, 6, 2, 4, 7, 9)$, with a cost of 219,110. Hence, $v(N) = 224{,}020 - 219{,}110 = 4{,}910$.

Observe that the new-max jobs are 1,2, and 9. In order to calculate the Shapley value of this game, we first need to compute (a) $G_i^N, i \in N$, (b) $G_i^{\{2,\dots,9\}}, i \in \{2, \dots, 9\}$, and (c) $G_9^{\{9\}}$. These values are shown in Table 8.2.

Table 8.3 Calculation of Shapley values

Players	1	2	3	4	5	6	7	8	9
$G_3^N - G_3^{\{2,\dots,9\}} = 1200$	400.00	400.00	400.00						
$G_5^N - G_5^{\{2,\dots,9\}} = 760$	152.00	152.00	152.00	152.00	152.00				
$G_8^N - G_8^{\{2,\dots,9\}} = 130$	16.25	16.25	16.25	16.25	16.25	16.25	16.25	16.25	
$G_3^{\{2,\dots,9\}} - G_3^{\{9\}} = 1300$		650.00	650.00						
$G_5^{\{2,\dots,9\}} - G_5^{\{9\}} = 720$		180.00	180.00	180.00	180.00				
$G_6^{\{2,\dots,9\}} - G_6^{\{9\}} = 800$		160.00	160.00	160.00	160.00	160.00			
Shapley value	568.25	1558.25	1558.25	508.25	508.25	176.25	16.25	16.25	0

Table 8.3 shows the calculation of the Shapley values, based on the result in Theorem 8.18, part (ii). Each row in the table corresponds to a segment defined by the new-max jobs.

Observe that $\sum_{i=1}^{9} \phi_i(v) = 568.25 + 1558.25 + 1558.25 + 508.25 + 508.25 + 176.25 + 16.25 + 16.25 + 0 = 4{,}910 = v(N)$, as required.

Remark 8.4 The Shapley value of a PFS game can be interpreted as follows. Player i needs players $a_{r(i)}, \dots, i - 1$ to obtain some cost savings, which are divided equally among those players and i. If a new segment is added to the left of this group of jobs, then the extra cost savings are divided among the now larger group $a_{r(i)-1}, \dots, a_{r(i)}, \dots, i - 1$ of participating jobs, and this process repeats.

8.3.8 Openshops

Atay et al. (2019) study games defined over openshop scheduling problems with unit processing times. In openshop scheduling problems, each job has to complete a number of operations on designated machines; however, the sequence of those operations is left to scheduling decisions. Let $N = \{1, \dots, n\}$ denote the set of jobs, and $M = \{1, \dots, m\}$ the set of machines. Each operation of every job has a unit processing time. Each job i has unit waiting cost. Given a schedule s, the completion time of job i is $C_i(s) = \max_{j \in M}\{C_i^j(s)\}$, where $C_i^j(s)$ is the completion time of the operation of job i on machine j in schedule s. For any schedule s and set of jobs $S \subseteq N$, let $c_S = \sum_{i \in S} C_i(s)$. This work considers the problem of minimizing the total completion time of jobs with unit processing times in an openshop environment with m machines, or problem $Om|p_{ij} = 1|\sum C_i$.

In studying this problem, it is important to distinguish an *openshop scheme* σ from an *openshop schedule* s. A scheme specifies the sequence of operations on every machine, i.e., $\sigma^j(i) = k$ specifies that the operation of job i is in position k on machine j. A scheme does not specify the order of operations of any job. However, a schedule specifies the start time of all operations on every machine. Consequently, a schedule defines a unique scheme, but a scheme can be associated with various schedules associated with different priority choices between sequences of operations for the jobs.

8.3 Sequencing Games

Assume an arbitrary initial schedule s_0, and let $\sigma_0 \in \Sigma$ denote the unique scheme associated with it, where Σ is the set of all possible schemes. With each job, we associate a player of a cooperative game (N, v). In this game, N is the set of players, and the characteristic function v assigns a real number $v(T)$ to each coalition $T \subseteq N$, where $v(\emptyset) = 0$. For any coalition $\emptyset \neq T \subseteq N$, we denote by $c_T(s) = \sum_{i \in T} C_i(s)$ the cost of the coalition T in schedule s. Then, $v(\cdot)$ assigns to every coalition the maximal cost savings it can achieve by means of admissible schedules starting from s_0. Thus,

$$v(T) = c_T(s_0) - c_T(s^*),$$

where s^* minimizes $c_T(s)$ over all admissible schedules and their associated schemes.

The definition of which schedules are admissible by a coalition T requires particular specification for this game. The reason for this is that a standard sequencing game definition, for example, as used by Curiel et al. (1989) in Sect. 8.3.2, which requires that rearrangement is possible within connected components of T, is insufficient. The reasons for this are (a) a job outside T may be delayed, and (b) resequencing may require active participation by players outside T. Atay et al. (2019) give an example of both situations. Therefore, a stronger definition of admissibility is needed. We specify that a schedule s with unique associated scheme σ is admissible if, for a given coalition $T \subseteq N$,

$$\{k \in N \mid \sigma^j(k) < \sigma^j(i)\}$$
$$= \{k \in N \mid \sigma_0^j(k) < \sigma_0^j(i)\}, \ i \in N \setminus T, \ j \in M, \quad \text{and} \quad (8.26)$$

$$C_i(s) \leq C_i(s_0), \quad i \in N \setminus T. \tag{8.27}$$

Condition (8.26) requires that switches are only possible between players within connected coalitions, and condition (8.27) ensures that the completion times of players outside T are not increased. Examples show that this game is not superadditive and hence not convex, nor is it σ-component additive. However, in order to establish that a game is balanced, it is possible to consider a specific allocation of cost savings. If such an allocation can be shown to be a core solution, then the game is balanced.

Atay et al. (2019) prove the following structural result.

Lemma 8.8 *Given a unit time openshop scheduling problem with initial schedule* (N, M, s_0), *for any given machine* $j \in M$, *there exists an optimal schedule for N which we denote by* s_N^{*j}, *such that:*

(a) the unique scheme $\sigma^* \in \Sigma$ *associated with* s_N^{*j} *satisfies* $\sigma^{*j} = \sigma_0^j$, *and*
(b) machine j does not incur any idle time, i.e., the operations on machine j are processed continuously.

Part (a) of Lemma 8.8 specifies that, for any single machine (but not for all machines simultaneously), it is possible to find an optimal schedule where the associated scheme on that machine is the same as the initial scheme on that machine. Let $C_i(s_N^{*j})$ denote the completion time of the operation of job i on machine j in an optimal schedule.

Now, define the *machine j-based allocation* $\mu^j(N, M, s_0) \in \mathbb{R}^N$ by:

$$\mu_i^j(N, M, s_0) = C_i(s_0) - C_i(s_N^{*j}), \quad i \in N. \tag{8.28}$$

The allocation in (8.28) is efficient, since

$$\sum_{i \in N} \mu_i^j(N, M, s_0) = \sum_{i \in N}[w_i C_i(s_0) - w_i C_i(s_N^{*j})] = v(N),$$

from the optimality of s_N^{*j}. This allocation does not in general provide a core allocation. However, it provides a path to one, which is found by averaging the machine-based allocations, i.e.,

$$\bar{\mu}(N, M, s_0) \equiv \frac{1}{m} \sum_{j \in M} \mu^j(N, M, s_0), \qquad i \in N. \tag{8.29}$$

In order to analyze this possibility, Atay et al. (2019) prove the following preliminary result.

Lemma 8.9 *For all $\emptyset \neq T \subset N$,*

$$\frac{1}{m} \sum_{j \in M}[C_i(s_0) - \lceil \frac{C_i^j(s_T^*)}{m} \rceil m] \geq C_i(s_o) - C_i(s_T^*), \tag{8.30}$$

where s_T^* is an optimal admissible schedule for coalition T.

The main result can now be stated.

Theorem 8.19 *Let (N, M, s_0) be a unit time openshop scheduling game with initial schedule s_0. Then, $\bar{\mu}(N, M, s_0)$ is a core allocation of the game.*

Proof To show that $\bar{\mu}(N, M, s_0)$ is efficient, we have

$$\bar{\mu}(N, M, s_0) = \sum_{i \in N} \bar{\mu}_i$$

$$= \sum_{i \in N} \frac{1}{m} \sum_{j \in M} \left[C_i(s_0) - C_i(s_N^{*j}) \right]$$

$$= \frac{1}{m} \sum_{j \in M} \sum_{i \in N} \left[C_i(s_0) - C_i(s_N^{*j}) \right]$$

8.3 Sequencing Games

$$= \frac{1}{m} \sum_{j \in M} \left[c_N(s_0) - c_N(s_N^{*j}) \right]$$

$$= \frac{1}{m} m \left[c_N(s_0) - c_N(s_N^*) \right]$$

$$= v(N),$$

where the last equality follows from $c_N(s_N^{*j}) = c_N(s_N^{*j'}) = c_N(s_N^*)$, for $j, j' \in M$, $j \neq j'$.

It remains to prove that $\bar{\mu}(T) \geq v(T)$, for $T \subset N$. Let $T|\sigma$ denote the set of all maximally connected components of T under σ. We have

$$\bar{\mu}(T) = \sum_{i \in T} \bar{\mu}_i$$

$$= \sum_{i \in T} \frac{1}{m} \sum_{j \in M} \mu_i^j$$

$$= \sum_{i \in T} \frac{1}{m} \sum_{j \in M} \left[C_i(s_0) - C_i(s_N^{*j}) \right]$$

$$= \sum_{i \in T} \frac{1}{m} \sum_{j \in M} \left[C_i(s_0) - \left\lceil \frac{\sigma_0^j(i)}{m} \right\rceil m \right]$$

$$= \frac{1}{m} \sum_{j \in M} \left[\sum_{i \in T} C_i(s_0) - \sum_{i \in T} \left\lceil \frac{\sigma_0^j(i)}{m} \right\rceil m \right]$$

$$= \frac{1}{m} \sum_{j \in M} \left[\sum_{i \in T} C_i(s_0) - \sum_{T' \in T|\sigma_0^j} \sum_{i \in T'} \left\lceil \frac{\sigma_0^j(i)}{m} \right\rceil m \right]$$

$$\geq \frac{1}{m} \sum_{j \in M} \left[\sum_{i \in T} C_i(s_0) - \sum_{T' \in T|\sigma_0^j} \sum_{i \in T'} \left\lceil \frac{C_i^j(s_T^*)}{m} \right\rceil m \right]$$

$$= \frac{1}{m} \sum_{j \in M} \left[\sum_{i \in T} C_i(s_0) - \sum_{i \in T} \left\lceil \frac{C_i^j(s_T^*)}{m} \right\rceil m \right]$$

$$= \sum_{i \in T} \frac{1}{m} \sum_{j \in M} \left[C_i(s_0) - \left\lceil \frac{C_i^j(s_T^*)}{m} \right\rceil m \right]$$

$$\geq \sum_{i \in T} \left[C_i(s_0) - C_i(s_T^*) \right]$$

$$= v(T).$$

The fourth equality follows from Lemma 8.8 and from Adiri and Amit (1984), which together imply $C_i(s_N^{*j}) = \lceil \frac{\sigma_0^j(i)}{m} \rceil m$. The first inequality follows from the definition of admissibility, under which players in $T'|\sigma_0^j$ can only switch positions with other players in T'. Then, if $T' = \{i_1, \ldots, i_q\}$ and σ_T^* is the unique optimal scheme associated with s^*, we have $\{\sigma_0^j(i_1), \ldots, \sigma_0^j(i_q)\} = \{\sigma_0^{*j}(i_1), \ldots, \sigma_0^{*j}(i_q)\}$. Moreover, for $i_k \in T'$, $C_{i_k}^j(s_T^*) \geq \sigma_T^j(i_k)$, and hence $\sum_{i \in T'} \lceil \frac{\sigma_0^j(i)}{m} \rceil m \leq \sum_{i \in T'} \lceil \frac{C_i^j(s_T^*)}{m} \rceil m$. The last inequality follows from Lemma 8.9.
$\square$

Remark 8.5 The balancedness result in Theorem 8.19 still holds if the admissibility condition is relaxed by continuing to require (8.27), but replacing (8.26) with the following weaker condition

$$\sigma_0^j(i) = \sigma^j(i), \quad i \in N \setminus T, \ j \in M, \tag{8.31}$$

where σ is the unique scheme associated with s. This relaxation allows the players in coalition T to jump over players outside T, provided that such a move does not hurt those outside players.

8.3.9 Multi-Stage Sequencing Games

Consider a service process where multiple retailers place orders with a manufacturer repeatedly over a number of periods. For example, each retailer places a weekly order for a single job, where a job could represent a production run that needs to be performed nonpreemptively, i.e., without interruption. Examples of this requirement occur commonly in the chemical and fertilizer industries, where mixing of products is potentially dangerous. The manufacturer allocates its capacity to the incoming orders and completes their processing each week. However, the orders received from a given retailer vary from week to week. Typically, based on their current inventory level and anticipated sales to their customers, retailers may order more or less in a particular week, and may also place a different priority on the urgency of their orders. The possibility exists that the retailers may form coalitions to submit combined orders which can then be processed more efficiently by the manufacturer, thereby adding value to all participants. In this case, maintaining the stability of such coalitions presents an interesting problem. Viewing the retailers from the perspective of the manufacturer as customers, Curiel (2010) models this problem as a multi-stage sequencing game.

In multi-stage sequencing games, as discussed further below, cost allocations that are stable at each stage separately do not, in general, provide stable solutions for the overall problem. This provides independent motivation for studying multi-stage games. Curiel (2015) extends her earlier work to consider m-stage sequencing situations with $m \geq 2$, and games defined over them, with a focus on the design of stable cost allocation rules.

8.3 Sequencing Games

Consider an m-stage sequencing situation with a set of customers $N = \{1, \ldots, n\}$. This sequencing situation is defined by $(\sigma_0, w^1, p^1, \ldots, w^m, p^m)$, where $w^q \in \mathbb{R}^n$ is a measure of cost or urgency for the jobs in period q, and $p^q \in \mathbb{R}^n$ is the processing time of the jobs in that period. Also, $\sigma_0 \in \Pi_N$ is an initial sequence from the set of all possible permutations of N.

Let $P_i(\sigma_0) = \{j \mid \sigma_0(j) < \sigma_0(i)\}$ and $F_i(\sigma_0) = \{j \mid \sigma_0(j) > \sigma_0(i)\}$ denote the set of predecessors and successors of i with respect to σ_0, respectively. If job i immediately precedes job j in stage q, then the change in cost (of unrestricted sign) from interchanging them is

$$h_{ij}^q \equiv w_j^q p_i^q - w_i^q p_j^q, \tag{8.32}$$

and we also define

$$g_{ij}^q = \max\{h_{ij}^q, 0\},$$

which is the potential cost saving from the interchange. The following discussion recalls the use of g_{ij} in the EGS-rule in Sect. 8.3.2.

At each stage, the initial order of the jobs is the sequence inherited from the previous stage. This raises the issue of how cost savings should be defined. If they are defined relative to the sequence from the previous stage, this game is called a *short history m-stage sequencing game*. Alternatively, if they are defined relative to the initial sequence σ_0, this game is called a *long history m-stage sequencing game*. While Curiel (2015) studies both games, the analysis is similar, hence we focus on the long history game. In the long history game, the value of a connected coalition of customers $T \subseteq N$ is given by

$$v(T) = \sum_{i \in T} \sum_{k \in P_i(\sigma_0)} (g_{ki}^1 + g_{ki}^2 + \cdots + g_{ki}^m).$$

Remark 8.6 For purposes of tiebreaking, we assume that, in the event of there being multiple optimal sequences, the sequence that requires fewer job interchanges is chosen.

Counterexamples show that aggregation of the EGS-rule and the one-stage Shapley value do not yield stable solutions for the multi-stage game. The reason is that, when player i evaluates the allocation that he receives in the long history m-stage sequencing game when a rule f is used to allocate the cost savings in each stage, he takes into account the implicit gain or loss he starts with at the beginning of stage q compared to his starting position at the beginning of stage 1. It is shown in Curiel (2010) that, even adjusting for implicit gains and losses, there does not exist a single-stage allocation rule that, when aggregated, provides stable solutions for the m-stage game. This provides a strong motivation for studying the m-stage game. To achieve stable solutions in this game requires the design of a *compensation rule*, as now defined.

Definition 8.10 Consider the sequencing situation $(\sigma_0, w^{q-1}, p^{q-1}, w^q, p^q)$. A *compensation rule* is a function that assigns to the jobs a division of the implicit gains and losses of the jobs created by the change from the starting sequence σ_0 of the first stage to the optimal order of stage $(q-1)$.

We consider a class of compensation rules that divide the implicit losses and gains that occur when two jobs switch, between them. More specifically, the challenge is to design a compensation rule that distributes the implicit losses and gains that occur between two stages, along with a rule that distributes the cost savings in the sequencing game at each stage, which together identify a core element of the m-stage sequencing game.

Let $0 \leq \lambda \leq 1$. We give λh_{ij}^q to i and $(1-\lambda)h_{ij}^q$ to j. Thus, we define a compensation rule $CR\lambda$, for $0 \leq \lambda \leq 1$, by

$$CR\lambda_i(\sigma_0, w^{q-1}, p^{q-1}, w^q, p^q) = \sum_{j \in F_i(\sigma_0) \cap P_i(\sigma_*^{q-1})} \lambda h_{ij}^q + \sum_{k \in F_i(\sigma_0) \cap P_i(\sigma_*^{q-1})} (1-\lambda)h_{ki}^q,$$

where σ_*^{q-1} is an optimal sequence at stage $q-1$, if necessary using the tiebreaking rule described in Remark 8.6.

Consider a $CR\lambda$-compensation rule that is used together with the EGS-rule from Sect. 8.3.2 to allocate the cost savings in an m-stage sequencing game. We denote such a cost allocation rule by λEGS. Let σ_*^q denote an optimal sequence for the sequencing situation at stage $q > 0$, and $\sigma_*^0 = \sigma_0$. We define, for $i \in N$,

$$\lambda EGS_i(\sigma_0, w^1, p^1, \ldots, w^m, p^m) = \sum_{q=1}^m EGS_i(\sigma_*^{q-1}, w^q, p^q)$$

$$+ \sum_{q=2}^m CR\lambda_i(\sigma_0, w^{q-1}, p^{q-1}, w^q, p^q).$$

$$(8.33)$$

The main result now follows.

Theorem 8.20 *Let* $(\sigma_0, w^1, p^1, \ldots, w^m, p^m)$ *be an m-stage sequencing situation and let* (N, v) *be the corresponding long history m-stage sequencing game. Then,* $\lambda EGS(\sigma_0, w^1, p^1, \ldots, w^m, p^m)$ *is in the core of this game if* $\lambda = 1/2$.

Proof Let $\lambda = 1/2$ and $T \subset N$. Then,

$$\sum_{i \in T} \lambda EGS_i(\sigma_0, w^1, p^1, \ldots, w^m, p^m) = \sum_{i \in T} \Big[\sum_{q=1}^m EGS_i(\sigma_*^{q-1}, w^q, p^q)$$

$$+ \sum_{q=2}^m CR\lambda_i(\sigma_0, w^{q-1}, p^{q-1}, w^q, p^q) \Big]$$

8.3 Sequencing Games

$$= \sum_{i \in T} \Big[\Big(\sum_{q=1}^{m} \sum_{j \in F_i(\sigma_*^{q-1})} g_{ij}^q + \sum_{k \in P_i(\sigma_*^{q-1})} g_{ki}^q \Big)$$

$$+ \sum_{q=2}^{m} \Big(\sum_{j \in F_i(\sigma_0) \cap P_i(\sigma_*^{q-1})} h_{ij}^q$$

$$+ \sum_{k \in P(\sigma_0) \cap F_i(\sigma_*^{q-1})} h_{ki}^q \Big) \Big] / 2. \qquad (8.34)$$

Further,

$$v(T) = \sum_{i \in T} \sum_{k \in P_i(\sigma_0) \cap T} (g_{ki}^1 + g_{ki}^2 + \cdots + g_{ki}^m). \qquad (8.35)$$

The result is established by showing that the contribution of any job to (8.34) is at least as large as that job's contribution to (8.35). Let $i \in T$. Consider the contribution of a player $k \in N \setminus \{i\}$ to (8.34) and (8.35). There are two cases. For Case 1, suppose $k \notin T$. Then k does not contribute to (8.35), and it only remains to show that the contribution of k to (8.34) is nonnegative. We consider four subcases.

Case 1a. $k \in P_i(\sigma_0) \cap P_i(\sigma_*^{q-1})$: the contribution of k is $g_{ki}^q/2 \geq 0$ for $1 \leq q \leq m$.
Case 1b. $k \in P_i(\sigma_0) \cap F_i(\sigma_*^{q-1})$: the contribution of k is $(g_{ik}^q + h_{ki}^q)/2 \geq 0$ for $2 \leq q \leq m$, and $g_{ik}^1/2 \geq 0$ for $q = 1$.
Case 1c. $k \in F_i(\sigma_0) \cap P_i(\sigma_*^{q-1})$: the contribution of k is $(g_{ki}^q + h_{ik}^q)/2 \geq 0$ for $2 \leq q \leq m$, and $g_{ki}^1/2 \geq 0$ for $q = 1$.
Case 1d. $k \in F_i(\sigma_0) \cap F_i(\sigma_*^{q-1})$: the contribution of k is $g_{ik}^q/2 \geq 0$ for $1 \leq q \leq m$.
Summarizing Cases 1a through 1d, when $k \notin T$, its contribution to (8.34) is greater than or equal to its contribution to (8.35).

For Case 2, suppose $k \in T$, and consider the same four subcases.

Case 2a. The contribution of k to (8.35) is g_{ki}^q, for $1 \leq q \leq m$. The contribution of k to (8.34) is also g_{ki}^q, where half comes from $\lambda EGS_i(v)$ and half comes from $\lambda EGS_k(v)$.
Case 2b. The contribution of k to the sum in (8.35) equals g_{ki}^q, for $1 \leq q \leq m$. The contribution of k to (8.34) is $g_{ik}^q + h_{ki}^q = g_{ki}^q$.
Case 2c. The contribution of k to (8.35) is g_{ik}^q, for $1 \leq q \leq m$. The contribution of k to (8.34) is $g_{ki}^q + h_{ik}^q = g_{ik}^q$.
Case 2d. The contribution of k to (8.35) is g_{ik}^q. The contribution of k to (8.34) is also g_{ik}^q.
Summarizing Cases 2a through 2d, when $k \in T$, its contribution to (8.34) equals its contribution to (8.35).

484   8 Cooperative Supply Chain Scheduling

Combining these results, we have

$$\sum_{i \in T} \lambda EGS_i(\sigma_0, w^1, p^1, \ldots, w^m, p^m) \geq v(T),$$

for $T \subset N$, and therefore $\lambda EGS_i(\sigma_0, w^1, p^1, \ldots, w^m, p^m)$ is in the core of the m-stage sequencing game. $\qquad\qquad\square$

We provide an example of how the result in Theorem 8.20 can be used to find a core solution for the m-stage game.

Example 8.22 (Coalition and Compensation Values and Core Allocations in a Multi-Stage Game) Consider a game with $m = 3$ stages, where $N = \{1, 2, 3, 4\}$. Let σ^q denote the sequence of the jobs in stage q, where $\sigma^0 = (1, 2, 3, 4)$, which is the starting sequence of stage 1. The processing time of job i in stage q is 1, for $i \in N, 1 \leq q \leq m$. The weights of the jobs are given by the vectors $w^1 = (1, 2, 3, 4)$, $w^2 = (10, 5, 3, 12)$ and $w^3 = (7, 2, 4, 5)$. Now, $\sigma^1 = (4, 3, 2, 1)$, which is the ending sequence of stage 1 and the starting sequence of stage 2. Also, $\sigma^2 = (4, 1, 2, 3)$ is the ending sequence of stage 2 and the starting sequence of stage 3. Finally, $\sigma^3 = (1, 4, 3, 2)$ is the ending sequence of stage 3.

Table 8.4 shows the coalition values for all possible coalitions that have nonzero value over the three stages.

We first compute the values $EGS_i(\sigma_*^{q-1}, w^q, p^q), i \in N, q = 1, \ldots, m$ from (8.33). Note that, since we are considering the long history game, the positions of the jobs in the sequence are evaluated relative to σ^0.

$i = 1$: In stage 1, job 1 swaps with jobs 2, 3, and 4, for a total gain of $1 + 2 + 3 = 6$, of which job 1 receives $6/2 = 3$. In stage 2, job 1 swaps with jobs 2 and 3, for a total gain of $5 + 7 = 12$, of which job 1 receives $12/2 = 6$. In stage 3, job 1 swaps with job 4, for a total gain of 2, of which job 1 receives $2/2 = 1$. The total gain of job 1 is therefore $3 + 6 + 1 = 10.0$.

$i = 2$: Similarly, job 2 has a gain of 2 in stage 1, 3.5 in stage 2, and 1 in stage 3, for a total gain of 6.5.

$i = 3$: Similarly, job 3 has a gain of 2 in stage 1, 4.5 in stage 2, and 1 in stage 3, for a total gain of 7.5.

$i = 4$: Similarly, job 4 has a gain of 3 in stage 1, 0 in stage 2, and 1 in stage 3, for a total gain of 4.0.

Table 8.4 Coalition values in Example 8.22

Coalition S	$\{1, 2\}$	$\{1, 4\}$	$\{2, 3\}$	$\{3, 4\}$	$\{1, 2, 3\}$	$\{1, 2, 4\}$	$\{1, 3, 4\}$	$\{2, 3, 4\}$	$\{1, 2, 3, 4\}$
$v^1(S)$	1	0	1	1	4	1	1	4	10
$v^2(S)$	5	0	2	0	14	5	0	2	14
$v^3(S)$	0	2	2	0	2	2	2	2	4
$v(S)$	1	0	3	11	6	1	11	26	34

8.3 Sequencing Games

Table 8.5 Interstage compensation values in Example 8.22

Jobs i, j	1,2	1,3	1,4	2,3	2,4	3,4
h_{ij}^2	−5	−7	2	−2	−7	9
h_{ij}^3	−5	−3	−2	2	3	1

Observe that the total gain allocated is $10.0 + 6.5 + 7.5 + 4.0 = 28 < 34 = v(N)$. Also, since $v(\{2, 3, 4\}) = 26$ and $v(N) = 34$, the current allocation of $10.0 > 34 − 26$ to job 1 is excessive. Hence, the current allocations need to be adjusted. This is accomplished using the compensation rule $CR\lambda_i(\sigma_0, w^{q-1}, p^{q-1}, w^q, p^q), i \in N, q = 2, 3$.

Table 8.5 shows the pairwise swap compensation terms h_{ij}^q from (8.33) for all pairs of jobs over stages 2 and 3.

We repeat the above process for each job in turn, using the data in Table 8.5, and once again comparing the new sequence with σ^0.

$i = 1$: In stage 1, job 1 swaps with jobs 2, 3, and 4, for a total compensation in stage 2 of $−5 − 7 + 2 = −10$, of which job 1 receives $−10/2 = −5$. In stage 2, job 1 swaps with job 4, for a compensation of $−2$, of which job 1 receives $−2/2 = −1$. The total compensation of job 1 is therefore $−5 − 1 = −6.0$.

$i = 2$: Similarly, job 2 has a compensation of 0 in stage 2, and 1.5 in stage 3, for a total compensation of 1.5.

$i = 3$: Similarly, job 3 has compensation of 0 in stage 2, and 0.5 in stage 3, for a total compensation of 0.5.

$i = 4$: Similarly, job 4 has a compensation of 9 in stage 2, and 1 in stage 3, for a total compensation of 10.0.

It remains to compute the core allocations by combining, for each job, its gains from swapping with other jobs and its interstage compensation values: job 1 : $10.0 − 6.0 = 4.0$; job 2: $6.5 + 1.5 = 8.0$; job 3: $7.5 + 0.5 = 8.0$; job 4: $4.0 + 10.0 = 14.0$. Then, the total allocation is $4.0 + 8.0 + 8.0 + 14.0 = 34.0 = v(N)$, as required (see Table 8.4). It is easy to check that the value $v(S)$ for each coalition $S \subset N$ is covered by this allocation, which is therefore a core solution.

Remark 8.7 Curiel (2015) shows that the condition $\lambda = 1/2$ in Theorem 8.20 is not only sufficient but also necessary. Further, if $m = 2$, the λEGS allocation rule possesses the stage-1 dummy property, the equivalence property, and the switch property, and moreover is the unique rule that does so. See Sect. 8.3.2 for the definitions of these properties.

8.3.10 Balancedness in Generalized Games

Several generalizations that are developed in classical scheduling theory have also been studied in the context of sequencing games. These generalizations include ready times (Hamers et al., 1995), due dates (Borm et al., 2002), and precedence constraints between the jobs (Hamers et al., 2002). Sequencing games that correspond to multiple machine scheduling situations are studied by Van den Nouweland et al. (1992), Hamers et al. (1999) and Calleja et al. (2002).

In the studies of sequencing games discussed in the preceding sections, the important concept of balancedness is typically established either:

(a) By proving that the game is convex and then invoking the theorem of Bondareva (1963) and Shapley (1967) (see Sects. 8.3.2 and 8.3.4)
(b) By reduction to a game that is known to be balanced, for example, a permutation game (see Sect. 8.3.1.1) or a unanimity game that satisfies convexity conditions (see Sect. 8.3.1.2)
(c) By showing that the game is σ_0-component additive and then invoking the result of Le Breton et al. (1992) (see Sects. 8.3.3, 8.3.6, and 8.3.7)
(d) By using the balancedness of a closely related game as a path to proving balancedness (see Sect. 8.3.5)

We now discuss two practically important sequencing games where none of these approaches can be applied. In these games, a particular solution is specified and shown to be a core solution. This approach is also used in Sects. 8.3.8 and 8.3.9. Both the games studied below use the concept of a *marginal vector*, defined below, although it is applied in different ways in the two games.

8.3.10.1 Controllable Processing Times

Sequencing problems with controllable processing times for jobs are studied by, for example, Vickson (1980), Alidaee and Ahmadian (1993), Wan et al. (2010), and Oron (2014). Shabtay and Steiner (2007) provide a review of the literature on this topic. These situations are motivated by the availability of various resources that, in many environments, can be applied to expedite processing times. Using additional resources in this way involves a tradeoff between time and cost.

van Velzen (2006) studies sequencing games that are derived from sequencing situations of the type now described. A sequencing situation with controllable processing times, or *cp-situation*, has a job set $N = \{1, \ldots, n\}$ waiting in front of a server, in the initial sequence $\sigma_0 = (1, \ldots, n)$. For $i \in N$, job i has a standard processing time p_i but it is possible to crash, i.e., expedite, this time by an amount y_i, where $y_i \leq p_i - \bar{p}_i$ and $\bar{p}_i$ is a lower limit on processing time. Such limits are in practice imposed by physical or logistical limitations on processing. Job i also has a weight or urgency cost w_i, and a crashing cost per unit of time β_i. In schedule σ_0, all jobs are at their standard processing times, i.e., there is no crashing and $y_i = 0, i \in N$.

Let $C_i(\sigma, y)$ denote the completion time of job i in a schedule σ that uses a vector of crash times y. Then, the scheduling problem is

$$\min_{i \in N, y \in \mathbb{R}^+} \sum \left[\beta_i y_i + w_i \sum_{j \in N \mid \sigma(j) \leq \sigma(i)} (p_j - y_j) \right].$$

A cp-situation is defined by the 6-tuple $(N, \sigma_0, w, \beta, p, \bar{p})$.

8.3 Sequencing Games

In order to define a *cp-game* corresponding to a cp-situation, we need to specify rules for the admissibility of rescheduling by a coalition $S \subseteq N$. First, the chosen crashing time of job i, y_i, cannot change for $i \in N \setminus S$. Second, $0 \le y_i \le p_i - \bar{p}_i$, $i \in S$. Third, jumps over jobs in $N \setminus S$ are not allowed. Let $\mathscr{A}(S)$ denote the set of admissible schedules (σ, y) for S thus defined.

Corresponding to the cp-situation is the cp-game (N, v) defined by these rules, where

$$v(S) = \sum_{i \in S} C_i(\sigma_0, 0) - \min_{(\sigma, y) \in \mathscr{A}(S)} \sum_{i \in S} C_i(\sigma, y).$$

Hence, the value of any coalition is the maximum cost savings which it can obtain by means of an admissible processing schedule, relative to the initial sequence without crashing. van Velzen (2006) shows that general techniques for proving balancedness cannot be applied to this game. By examples, it is shown that this game is not convex, nor is it σ_0-component additive. However, it is superadditive.

The following result simplifies the search for an optimal solution to the scheduling problem.

Lemma 8.10 *For any coalition $S \subseteq N$, there exists an optimal schedule where the processing time of every job is either equal to its initial processing time p_i, or to its fully crashed processing time $\bar{p}_i$.*

The analysis of this game requires the following definition.

Definition 8.11 The *marginal vector $m^\sigma(v) \in \mathbb{R}^N$* with respect to $\sigma \in \Pi(N)$, which is the set of all possible sequences, is defined as

$$m_i^\sigma(v) = v(P_i(\sigma) \cup \{i\}) - v(P_i(\sigma)),$$

where $P_i(\sigma) = \{j \in N \mid \sigma(j) < \sigma(i)\}$ is the set of predecessors of job $i \in N$ in sequence σ.

A related concept that is also useful here is *permutational convexity*.

Definition 8.12 A cooperative game (N, v) is *permutationally convex* if there exists a sequence σ that satisfies

$$v(P_i(\sigma) \cup \{i\} \cup T) - v(P_i(\sigma) \cup \{i\}) \le v(P_j(\sigma) \cup \{j\} \cup T) - v(P_j(\sigma) \cup \{j\}),$$

for $i, j \in N, \sigma(i) < \sigma(j)$, where $T \subset \{h \in N \mid \sigma(h) > \sigma(j)\}$ is the set of successors of job j with respect to σ. In this case, σ is a *permutationally convex sequence*.

Observe that permutational convexity is the analog of convexity (as defined in Sect. 2.3.5) with respect to a given sequence σ. Hence, a game that is convex is also permutationally convex with respect to any schedule σ, but the reverse is not true. Permutational convexity of a sequence σ is a sufficient condition for

488   8   Cooperative Supply Chain Scheduling

the corresponding marginal vector $m^\sigma(v) \in \mathbb{R}^n$ to be a core element (Granot & Huberman, 1982). This enables the following result by van Velzen (2006).

Theorem 8.21 *Let $(N, \sigma_0, w, \beta, p, \bar{p})$ be a cp-situation and let (N, v) be the corresponding game. Let $j \in \{1, \ldots, n\}$. Let $\sigma : \{1, \ldots, n\} \to N$ be defined such that*

(i) $\sigma(i) = n + 1 - i, 1 \leq i < j$,
(ii) $\sigma(i) = n + 2 - i, j < i \leq n$, and
(iii) $\sigma(j) = 1$.

Then, σ is a permutationally convex sequence, and $m^\sigma(v)$ is an element of the core of the game.

This result shows that sequences where the jobs are in reverse order with respect to σ_0, but job 1 is scheduled in an arbitrary position, are permutationally convex. Since the choice of $j \in \{1, \ldots, n\}$ is arbitrary in Theorem 8.21, this result identifies potentially many marginal vectors that are elements of the core of the game. Moreover, they are all close to each other and easy to compute, offering the players access to multiple potentially agreeable solutions, which improves the chance that they can find one which is acceptable to all of them.

8.3.10.2   Family Sequencing

Another important and practical generalization of sequencing games is family sequencing games. In a family sequencing situation, a job does not need a setup time when it follows another member of the same family, but it does require a family setup time when it follows a member of another family. Numerous examples exist in manufacturing processes where a change of engineering specification, product size, or color, requires resetting of equipment when changing between the scheduling of different job families on the same production line. There is a substantial literature of scheduling with setup times. Bruno and Downey (1978) study the solvability of scheduling problems with deadlines, setup times and changeover costs. Monma and Potts (1989) analyze the performance of heuristics for scheduling problems where jobs have sequence-dependent setup times. Potts and Kovalyov (2000) review the literature of family scheduling problems. Allahverdi et al. (2008) review the literature of scheduling problems with both sequence-dependent and sequence-independent setups.

Consider a set of jobs $N = \{1, \ldots, n\}$. Let F be the set of families, indicating membership of the jobs within the families. The number of jobs in family k is denoted by n_k. A job in family k requires a setup time s_k if it follows a job of another family. All jobs of family k have the same processing time p_k and the same linear cost $w_k t$, where t is the job completion time. A family sequencing situation is denoted by $(N, F, \sigma_0, s, p, w)$. For this problem, Santos and Magazine (1985) define an optimal sequencing rule that sequences the jobs of each family contiguously, by nonincreasing order of $n_k w_k / (s_k + n_k p_k)$. Let $\Pi(N)$ denote the set of all possible sequences.

8.4 Scheduling Games 489

With respect to proving balancedness, family sequencing games turn out to be even more challenging than sequencing games with controllable processing times. Grundel et al. (2013) show by examples that family sequencing games are not convex, nor are they σ_0-component additive, nor are they even permutationally convex. This leaves a proof of balancedness to a directly constructive approach, i.e., finding an allocation and showing that it belongs to the core of the family sequencing game.

The main result now follows. We refer the reader to Grundel et al. (2013) for the proof.

Theorem 8.22 *Let $(N, F, \sigma_0, s, p, w)$ be a family sequencing situation, and (N, v) be the corresponding family sequencing game. Then, the marginal vector $m^{\sigma_0}(v)$ is an element of the core of the game.*

Interestingly, Theorem 8.22 shows that the initial order σ_0 provides a marginal vector that is an element of the core of the game. While this establishes that the core of a family sequencing game is nonempty, it may not be practical in some situations, since the first job in σ^0 receives no allocation. Indeed, it is easy to imagine situations where this would lead to obstructive behavior by the first player.

Based on naturally occurring shop floor practice, it may be that the initial sequence σ_0 is *family ordered*, i.e., all jobs that belong to the same family are processed consecutively. This assumption defines a special case of the family sequencing situation and the corresponding family sequencing game. In this case, the subgame defined by the exclusion of the last job in σ_0 is convex. Moreover, a simple characterization of a core solution from Shapley values is also possible, as shown in the following result. Let job n be the job scheduled last in the initial schedule σ_0.

Theorem 8.23 *The marginal vector for an arbitrary sequence $\sigma \in \Pi(N)$ such that $\sigma(n) = n$ is in the core of the family ordered sequencing game.*

This completes our discussion of sequencing games. The above discussion shows that this literature has evolved strongly from the consideration of games defined over simple classical scheduling problems, to include a variety of practical generalizations. Besides the theoretical and practical value of these games themselves, the variety of techniques and results that are now available within this topic provide a useful and accessible introduction both to the literature of cooperative games and also to the many supply chain scheduling applications we discuss in this book.

8.4 Scheduling Games

Sequencing games have an initial schedule, as discussed in Sect. 8.3. Our definition of scheduling games, however, models situations where all players arrive simultaneously at a resource, and hence no initial schedule exists. This implies that an alternative benchmark is needed to estimate the savings achieved by a coalition in order to define the characteristic function of the game. Further, in sequencing games, the resequencing problem faced by a coalition typically includes an admissibility requirement that only jobs which are contiguous in the initial sequence and within the coalition can be resequenced. Without the presence of an initial sequence, this restriction does not apply, and the coalition's resequencing problem may therefore be less constrained. Since costs tend to accumulate superlinearly in scheduling problems as the number of jobs increases, the absence of an initial schedule in scheduling games to provide a benchmark may result in there being no core solution. This is one of the issues addressed in this section.

For situations where there is no initial order, a cooperative game can be modeled using three different approaches. The first approach is to define an *artificial initial sequence* to serve as a reference point for cost savings, under various possible assumptions. Thus, Sect. 8.4.1 uses the assumption that a coalition's jobs are arranged at the end of the overall job set, but in an optimal sequence within the coalition. Section 8.4.2 uses an alternative assumption of a *probabilistic initial sequence*, where a coalition's jobs are either all at the front or all at the back of the overall job set, with known probability. A third approach is to ignore the need for a reference point, and simply *base the value of a coalition on its cost*. This tends to make games unbalanced. The game discussed in Sect. 8.4.3 illustrates this point, and suggests how this issue can be resolved for a supply chain scheduling game with supermodular costs. Finally, a methodology for combining the use of penalties and subsidization in games without a core solution, in order to sustain cooperation within the grand coalition, is studied in Sect. 8.4.4 for a scheduling game.

8.4.1 Artificial Initial Sequence: Tail Game

In a variety of practical situations, arriving jobs do not have an initial sequence. For example, a set of orders that is downloaded daily from a website will typically be treated as a single batch without an initial order. Similarly, arriving mail has no initial order. Klijn and Sánchez (2006) discuss a business process where cars owned by different customers are delivered overnight to a repair shop, and the time at which they arrived is unknown for the purposes of scheduling them. More generally, various administrative processes would not recognize an initial order over work requests. For such applications, there may be a significant cost difference between sequences, but due to the lack of an initial sequence to serve as a benchmark, it is not clear how cost savings from the development of an efficient sequence should be allocated. In order to do so, one possible approach is to define an artificial initial sequence.

Let $N = \{1, \ldots, n\}$ denote a set of jobs. Each job j has a processing time p_j and a weight or urgency factor w_j. The jobs need to be processed nonpreemptively on a single machine. This *uncertainty sequencing situation* is denoted by a triple (N, p, w). Klijn and Sánchez (2006) define two alternative artificial initial orders. The first is a "tail" game, where each coalition assumes that its jobs are initially

8.4 Scheduling Games

consecutively sequenced, in the coalition's optimal order, at the end of the jobs of N. Thus, all jobs in $N \setminus S$ initially appear at the front of σ_0. The second is a "pessimistic" game, where each coalition assumes that its jobs are initially sequenced by an adversary who maximizes the coalition's costs. The following discussion focuses on the tail game, since it is simpler to analyze and the two games provide similar intuition. Let $\Pi(S)$ denote all possible admissible orders for the jobs of coalition $S \subseteq N$. Let $P_k(\sigma_S) = \{j \in S \mid \sigma_S(j) < \sigma_S(k)\}$ and $F_k(\sigma_S) = \{j \in S \mid \sigma_S(j) > \sigma_S(k)\}$, i.e., the predecessors and successors of job k in schedule σ_S, respectively.

Formally, the uncertainty tail scheduling game (N, c_{tail}) is defined by the characteristic function

$$c_{tail}(S) = \min_{\sigma_S \in \Pi(S)} \sum_{k \in S} w_k C_k, \quad S \subseteq N,$$

where the completion time of job k is $C_k = \sum_{i \in (N \setminus S) \cup P_k(\sigma_S) \cup \{k\}} p_i$, i.e., the processing time includes: first, the jobs of $N \setminus S$; second, the predecessors of job k within S; and finally, job k itself.

Example 8.23 (Calculation of Coalition Values in a Tail Scheduling Game) Consider an instance of the game with $N = \{1, 2, 3\}$, $p = (1, 2, 3)$ and $w = (5, 4, 3)$. Then, $c_{tail}(\{1\}) = 5(1 + 2 + 3) = 30$, $c_{tail}(\{2\}) = 4(1 + 2 + 3) = 24$, $c_{tail}(\{3\}) = 3(1 + 2 + 3) = 18$; $c_{tail}(\{1, 2\}) = 5(1 + 3) + 4(1 + 2 + 3) = 44$, $c_{tail}(\{1, 3\}) = 5(1+2)+3(1+2+3) = 33$, $c_{tail}(\{2, 3\}) = 4(1+2)+3(1+2+3) = 30$; $c_{tail}(\{1, 2, 3\}) = 5(1) + 4(1 + 2) + 3(1 + 2 + 3) = 35$.

The analysis of the tail game requires the following definition.

Definition 8.13 A cost game (N, c) is *concave* if, for all $S \subset T \subseteq N \setminus \{i\}$,

$$c(T \cup \{i\}) - c(T) \leq c(S \cup \{i\}) - c(S).$$

To interpret Definition 8.13, in a concave cost game, the marginal cost contribution to a given coalition is smaller than its marginal cost contribution to a smaller coalition. Intuitively then, it is always beneficial to group the players, in this case represented by jobs, together. We study the concavity and balancedness of the uncertainty tail cost game using the following result.

Theorem 8.24 *The game (N, c_{tail}) is balanced.*

Proof From Smith (1956), there exists an optimal sequence in which the jobs are ordered by nonincreasing value of w_i/p_i. Hence, there exist optimal sequences $\sigma^*_{S \setminus \{i\}} \in \Pi(S \setminus \{i\})$ and $\sigma^*_S \in \Pi(S)$ such that, for $k \in S \setminus \{i\}$,

$$P_k(\sigma^*_S) = \begin{cases} P_k(\sigma^*_{S \setminus \{i\}}) \cup \{i\}, & \text{if } w_i/p_i > w_k/p_k \\ P_k(\sigma^*_{S \setminus \{i\}}), & \text{otherwise.} \end{cases}$$

492 8 Cooperative Supply Chain Scheduling

Then, for any $S \subseteq N$ where $i \in S$,

$$c_{tail}(S) - c_{tail}(S \setminus \{i\}) = w_i(p_i + \sum_{h \in N \setminus S} p_h) + \sum_{k \in S \,|\, w_k/p_k > w_i/p_i} (w_i p_k - w_k p_i).$$

(8.36)

Observe that the first term in this expression is the cost of sequencing job i immediately after all the jobs of $N \setminus S$, and the negative part of the second term is the cost reduction from any adjacent pairwise interchanges with some job k that move job i later. Now, let $S \subset T \subseteq N$. Then, for $U = S, T$, from (8.36),

$$c_{tail}(U) - c_{tail}(U \setminus \{i\}) = w_i(p_i + \sum_{h \in N \setminus U} p_h) + \sum_{k \in U \,|\, w_k/p_k > w_i/p_i} (w_i p_k - w_k p_i).$$

Further, since $S \subset T$, we have $\sum_{h \in N \setminus S} p_h \geq \sum_{h \in N \setminus T} p_h$ and $\{k \in T \mid w_k/p_k > w_i/p_i\} \supseteq \{k \in S \mid w_k/p_k > w_i/p_i\}$. Hence, for all $S \subset T \subseteq N$,

$$c_{tail}(S) - c_{tail}(S \setminus \{i\}) \geq c_{tail}(T) - c_{tail}(T \setminus \{i\}),$$

which from Definition 8.13 establishes that the cost game (N, c_{tail}) is concave. Therefore, from Bondareva (1963) and Shapley (1967), it is balanced. □

Remark 8.8 Klijn and Sánchez (2006) prove that the core of the tail game is a subset of the core of the pessimistic game, and therefore from Theorem 8.24 the pessimistic game is also balanced. Also, for games with equal processing times, they describe two efficiently computable allocation rules that are both core solutions of both games.

The above analysis can be extended to provide an efficiently computable closed form expression for the Shapley value in the tail scheduling game. Mishra and Rangarajan (2007) provide a concise analysis for this problem, as follows. Let σ^* denote an optimal SWPT sequence of the jobs, i.e., $w_1/p_1 \geq \cdots \geq w_n/p_n$. Let $P_i(\sigma^*) = \{j \mid w_j/p_j \geq w_i/p_i\}$ and $F_i(\sigma^*) = \{j \mid w_j/p_j < w_i/p_i\}, i \in N$. Then, they prove the following result for the Shapley value, $\phi_i(ctail), i \in N$.

Theorem 8.25 $\phi_i(c_{tail}) = w_i p_i + (w_i \sum_{j \in P_i(\sigma^*)} p_j + p_i \sum_{j \in F_i(\sigma^*)} w_j)/2, \quad i \in N.$

We provide an example of the result in Theorem 8.25.

Example 8.24 (Shapley Value Calculations in a Tail Scheduling Game) Consider the tail scheduling game in Example 8.23. First, observe that, from Smith (1956), an optimal schedule is $\sigma^* = (1, 2, 3)$, with an optimal cost of $5(1)+4(1+2)+3(1+2+3) = 35.0$. The predecessors and successors of each job in σ^* are as follows: $P_1(\sigma^*) = \emptyset, P_2(\sigma^*) = \{1\}, P_3(\sigma^*) = \{1, 2\}, F_1(\sigma^*) = \{2, 3\}, F_2(\sigma^*) = \{3\}$ and $F_3(\sigma^*) = \emptyset$. Then, $\phi_1(c_{tail}) = 5(1) + [5(0) + 1(4 + 3)]/2 = 8.5, \phi_2(c_{tail}) = 4(2) + [4(1) + 2(3)]/2 = 13.0, \phi_3(c_{tail}) = 3(3) + [3(1 + 2) + 3(0)]/2 = 13.5$, and $\sum_{i=1}^{3} \phi_i(c_{tail}) = 8.5 + 13.0 + 13.5 = 35.0$, as required. It is easy to verify, from the coalition values shown in Example 8.23, that these cost allocations are sufficiently small that no coalition has an incentive to leave the grand coalition.

Remark 8.9 Mishra and Rangarajan (2007) define various axioms for the tail scheduling game, and show that their Shapley value solution satisfies them. Moreover, they show that any fair and reasonable cost sharing mechanism, under their definitions, is equivalent to the Shapley value solution identified.

8.4.2 Artificial Initial Sequence: Probabilistic Game

The cooperative game described here combines features of both the capacity allocation game of Hall and Liu (2010) which is discussed in Sect. 8.6, and the scheduling game of Klijn and Sánchez (2006) discussed in Sect. 8.4.1. A set of manufacturers orders capacity from a common supplier. Manufacturers may coordinate their ordering decisions prior to scheduling decisions being made, in which case there is no predetermined allocation of capacity to orders. Maniquet (2003) studies a similar capacity allocation problem, but assumes unit processing time of each order. He finds the Shapley value (Shapley, 1953) of the cooperative game thus defined. Schulz and Uhan (2010), as discussed in Sect. 8.4.3, consider the least core of a cooperate game defined over a similar capacity allocation problem where each set of manufacturers expects its orders to be processed *before* all the other orders.

Essentially, Klijn and Sánchez (2006) assume highly pessimistic manufacturers, whereas Schulz and Uhan (2010) assume highly optimistic manufacturers. The balancedness of the two resulting games is different: the game is balanced with pessimistic manufacturers and unbalanced with optimistic manufacturers. Interestingly, the Shapley values of the two games are the same (Maniquet, 2003; Mishra & Rangarajan, 2007). The model discussed here is therefore proposed as a more practical and reasonable alternative between these two extreme assumptions, where each set of manufacturers has a probability that its orders are processed first and last. Exact conditions for this cooperative game to be balanced are identified.

Hall and Liu (2016) consider a capacity allocation problem where a set of manufacturers orders capacity from a common supplier. The capacity is time sensitive and each capacity unit corresponds to a single time slot. The supplier has available time slots over a limited time horizon. These time slots can be either sufficient or insufficient to process all the manufacturers' orders. Each processed order generates a value and incurs a scheduling cost for its owner. An unprocessed order has no value or cost for its owner. Order processing cannot be preempted. The manufacturers place their orders for capacity simultaneously and no initial sequence of their orders is known. We investigate how manufacturers can cooperate in making their ordering decisions to receive higher profit. An important question is how manufacturers can share the increased profit from cooperation.

Let $N = \{1, \ldots, n\}$ denote a set of manufacturers. The supplier has a unit available capacity per time slot over a time horizon $1, \ldots, T$. Each manufacturer i has an order to place, with capacity requirement, i.e., order size p_i, value v_i if processed, and scheduling cost $w_i C_i$ if completed at time C_i, where w_i is a nonnegative weight or urgency measure. We assume that each order is profitable even if it completes at time T, i.e., $v_i \geq w_i T$, $i \in N$. Preemption of order processing is not allowed. Let P denote the total capacity requirement of the n manufacturers, i.e., $P = \sum_{i=1}^{n} p_i$. Since a customer has no incentive to order any capacity at a time slot later than P, the case with sufficient capacity can be modeled as $T = P$. However, as in the classical scheduling literature, it is useful also to consider the case of insufficient capacity, here defined by $T < P$.

Since we assume that an incomplete order has no value, it follows that every order is either processed completely or not at all. Consider a manufacturer, or equivalently an order, as a player. From the perspective of whether a core allocation exists, assuming that each manufacturer has a single order is not restrictive, because a manufacturer having multiple orders can be viewed as a coalition of multiple manufacturers each having a single order. Let $p_S = \sum_{i \in S} p_i$ denote the total capacity required by coalition S.

We define a *head-tail allocation (HTA)* characteristic function $v(S)$ for a capacity allocation game (N, v), as follows:

$$v(S) = q \mathscr{A}(S, R_{S,h}) + (1 - q)\mathscr{A}(S, R_{S,t}), \tag{8.37}$$

where $R_{S,h}$ is the set of time slots $1, \ldots, \min\{p_S, T\}$ in a *head allocation* allocated with a *head probability* q, $R_{S,t}$ is the set of time slots $P - p_S + 1, \ldots, T$ in a *tail allocation* allocated with a *tail probability* $1 - q$, and for $k \in \{h, t\}$, $\mathscr{A}(S, R_{S,k})$ is the value of the jobs processed minus their scheduling cost, in a solution found by an Algorithm $\mathscr{A}$ for coalition S using time slots in $R_{S,k}$. For the purposes of the definition in (8.37), Algorithm $\mathscr{A}$ need not be an optimal algorithm.

The head probability q is a measure of the degree of optimism of each coalition: a more optimistic coalition would assume a higher value of the head probability. The consideration of head and tail allocations, with total probability of 1, has a useful economic interpretation: each firm incorporates best case (head allocation) and worst-case (tail allocation) scenarios into its decision making. This approach provides a convenient way for firms competing for time sensitive capacity to rationalize their expectations when cooperating over their decisions. The head-tail allocation generalizes the consideration of head-only and tail-only allocations in the literature (Klijn & Sánchez, 2006; Maniquet, 2003; Mishra & Rangarajan, 2007; Schulz & Uhan, 2010).

We first consider the capacity allocation game with sufficient capacity to process all orders, i.e., $T = P$. Smith (1956) shows that the *shortest weighted processing time* (SWPT) rule, where orders are sequenced by nondecreasing ratio of size to weight, minimizes the total weighted completion time in single-machine processing. Therefore, we assume that Algorithm $\mathscr{A}$ in the characteristic function (8.37) uses

8.4 Scheduling Games

the SWPT rule and thus is optimal. We show that under a reasonable condition on q, the HTA value defines a convex game for the capacity allocation problem.

Theorem 8.26 *For the capacity allocation game where the capacity is sufficient and a job's scheduling cost is a linear function of its completion time, the HTA defines a convex and thus also balanced game if $q \leq 0.5$. Moreover, the condition $q \leq 0.5$ is also necessary.*

Proof Consider a player i and two coalitions S_1 and S_2, where $S_1 \subset S_2 \subseteq N \setminus \{i\}$. Assume that orders are indexed by the SWPT rule, i.e., $w_1/p_1 \geq \cdots \geq w_n/p_n$. Let $S_1^A = \{j \in S_1 \mid j > i\}$, and $S_2^A = \{j \in S_2 \mid j > i\}$. Let $S_1^B = S_1 \setminus S_1^A$ and $S_2^B = S_2 \setminus S_2^A$. Let $w_S = \sum_{i \in S} w_i$ be the total weight of orders in $S \subseteq N$. We have

$$[v(S_2 \cup \{i\}) - v(S_2)] - [v(S_1 \cup \{i\}) - v(S_1)]$$

$$= q(v_i - w_i(p_{S_2^B} + p_i) - w_{S_2^A} p_i) + (1-q)(v_i - w_i(P - p_{S_2^A}) + w_{S_2^B} p_i)$$

$$\quad -q(v_i - w_i(p_{S_1^B} + p_i) - w_{S_1^A} p_i) - (1-q)(v_i - w_i(P - p_{S_1^A}) + w_{S_1^B} p_i)$$

$$= (1-q)p_i(w_{S_2^B} - w_{S_1^B}) - q w_i(p_{S_2^B} - p_{S_1^B}) + (1-q)w_i(p_{S_2^A} - p_{S_1^A})$$

$$\quad -q p_i(w_{S_2^A} - w_{S_1^A})$$

$$\geq [p_i(w_{S_2^B} - w_{S_1^B}) - w_i(p_{S_2^B} - p_{S_1^B}) + w_i(p_{S_2^A} - p_{S_1^A}) - p_i(w_{S_2^A} - w_{S_1^A})]/2$$

$$= [(p_i w_{S_2^B \setminus S_1^B} - w_i p_{S_2^B \setminus S_1^B}) + (w_i p_{S_2^A \setminus S_1^A} - p_i w_{S_2^A \setminus S_1^A})]/2$$

$$\geq 0,$$

where the first inequality follows from the assumptions that $q \leq 0.5$ and $S_1 \subset S_2$. The second inequality follows from (a) $p_i/w_i \geq p_j/w_j$ for any $j \in S_2^B \setminus S_1^B$ if j exists, which implies $p_i/w_i \geq p_{S_2^B \setminus S_1^B}/w_{S_2^B \setminus S_1^B}$, and (b) $p_i/w_i \leq p_j/w_j$ for any $j \in S_2^A \setminus S_1^A$ if j exists, which implies $p_i/w_i \leq p_{S_2^A \setminus S_1^A}/w_{S_2^A \setminus S_1^A}$. Therefore, the game is convex, and thus also balanced from Bondareva (1963) and Shapley (1967).

The condition $q \leq 0.5$ is also necessary for balancedness. Consider an instance with $n = 3$, $p_1 = p_2 = p_3 = 1$, $v_1 = v_2 = v_3 = 3$, and $w_1 = w_2 = w_3 = 1$. Let $q = 0.5 + \delta$, where $0 < \delta \leq 0.5$. Now, $v(N) = 3$, and a coalition of any two orders has value $2 + 2\delta$. If we let (x_1, x_2, x_3) denote a payoff vector in the core, we must have $x_1 + x_2 \geq 2 + 2\delta$, $x_1 + x_3 \geq 2 + 2\delta$ and $x_2 + x_3 \geq 2 + 2\delta$, i.e., $x_1 + x_2 + x_3 \geq 3(2 + 2\delta)/2 = 3 + 3\delta > 3 = v(N)$, a contradiction. It follows that, for any $q > 0.5$, there exists a game instance with an empty core, and thus the game is unbalanced. $\qquad \square$

When capacity is insufficient, i.e., $T < P$, the condition $q \leq 0.5$ does not guarantee balancedness of the game. This is shown by the instance constructed in the proof of Theorem 8.27 below, which shows the intractability of deciding whether a given game instance has a nonempty core. We note that when $T < P$, even computing the value of the grand coalition is binary *NP*-hard. However, this result does not immediately imply intractability of the core emptiness test.

The following result is analogous to that in Theorem 8.46 discussed in Sect. 8.6.

Theorem 8.27 *The problem of deciding whether an instance of the capacity allocation game with $T \leq P$ has an empty core is binary NP-hard for any $0 < q \leq 0.5$, even when the weight of each job is 0.*

Proof By reduction from the following problem.

Partition (Garey & Johnson, 1979): Given $2t$ elements with positive integer sizes $a_1, \ldots, a_{2t}$, where $a_i < A$ for $i \in \{1, \ldots, 2t\}$, and $\sum_{i=1}^{2t} a_i = 2A$, does there exist a partition S_1, S_2 of the index set $\{1, \ldots, 2t\}$ such that $\sum_{i \in S_1} a_i = \sum_{i \in S_2} a_i = A$?

Given an instance of Partition, we construct an instance of the capacity allocation game. Consider the following four cases.

Case 1: $0 < q < 1/3$. Let K be the largest integer no greater than $1/q - 2$. If $1/q - 2 = K$, then let $n = 2t + K$, $T = A$, $v_i = p_i = a_i$ for $i = 1, \ldots, 2t - 1$, $v_{2t} = p_{2t} = a_{2t} + K\varepsilon$, $v_i = p_i = A - \varepsilon$ for $i = 2t + 1, \ldots, 2t + K$, and $w_i = 0$ for $i = 1, \ldots, 2t + K$, where $0 < \varepsilon < 1/K$ is a constant. If $1/q - 2 > K$, then let $n = 2t + K + 2$, $T = A$, $v_i = p_i = a_i$ for $i = 1, \ldots, 2t - 1$, $v_{2t} = p_{2t} = a_{2t} + K\varepsilon$, $v_{2t+1} = 0$, $p_{2t+1} = \varepsilon$, $v_{2t+2} = p_{2t+2} = ((1/q - 2) - K)A - \varepsilon$, $v_i = p_i = A - \varepsilon$ for $i = 2t + 3, \ldots, 2t + K + 2$, and $w_i = 0$ for $i = 1, \ldots, 2t + K + 2$, where $0 < \varepsilon < \min\{1/K, ((1/q - 2) - K)A\}$ is a constant.

Case 2: $q = 1/3$. Let $n = 2t + 1$, $T = A$, $v_i = p_i = a_i$ for $i = 1, \ldots, 2t - 1$, $v_{2t} = p_{2t} = a_{2t} + \varepsilon$, $v_{2t+1} = p_{2t+1} = A - \varepsilon$, and $w_i = 0$ for $i = 1, \ldots, 2t + 1$, where $0 < \varepsilon < 1$ is a constant.

Case 3: $1/3 < q < 1/2$. Let $n = 2t + 2$, $T = A$, $v_i = p_i = a_i$ for $i = 1, \ldots, 2t$, $v_{2t+1} = 0$, $p_{2t+1} = \varepsilon$, $v_{2t+2} = p_{2t+2} = (1/q - 2)A - \varepsilon$, and $w_i = 0$ for $i = 1, \ldots, 2t + 2$, where $0 < \varepsilon < 1$ is a constant.

Case 4: $q = 1/2$. Let $n = 2t$, $T = A$, and for each order i, $v_i = p_i = a_i$ and $w_i = 0$.

For example, consider Case 4. We show that the capacity allocation game instance has a nonempty core if and only if the instance of Partition has a solution.

($\Rightarrow$) If the instance of Partition has a solution, then consider the payoff vector $(p_1/2, \ldots, p_n/2)$. It is easy to check that the value of the grand coalition value is $\sum_{i=1}^n a_i = A$, which is equal to the total payoff. Also, no coalition S can generate a value greater than the payoff $p_S/2$ it receives from the payoff vector. Therefore, the proposed payoff vector is a core allocation.

($\Leftarrow$) If the instance of Partition has no solution, then the grand coalition generates a value that is strictly less than $A = P/2$. However, each individual order can generate a value $p_i/2$ by itself, and thus the core is empty.

In each of the other three cases above, it is similarly straightforward to verify that the instance of the capacity allocation game has a nonempty core if and only if the instance of Partition has a solution. $\square$

8.4 Scheduling Games

The study of this cooperative game adds to the literature that addresses how, in the absence of an initial solution, a benchmark solution for the evaluation of cost savings in a sequencing game can reasonably be specified.

8.4.3 No Initial Sequence: Penalty

Supply chain scheduling games without an initial sequence against which gains can be defined tend to be unbalanced, because cost accumulates more quickly as more jobs are added to a coalition. It is intuitive that, in such a case, cooperation between players may be difficult to sustain. This section considers the use of a penalty to resolve this problem. Section 8.4.4 applies a combination of both a penalty and a subsidy to the same issue.

We consider the problem of finding the minimum amount of penalty necessary to penalize each coalition in order to achieve their cooperation. For this purpose, the *least core* of a cooperate game (N, v) with players $N = \{1, \ldots, n\}$, as also defined in Sect. 8.2, is the set of cost allocations $x \in \mathbb{R}^n$ that solves the linear program

$$z^* = \min\{z \mid \sum_{i \in N} x_i = v(N), \sum_{i \in S} x_i \leq v(S) + z, \text{ for } S \subset N, S \neq \emptyset\}. \quad (8.38)$$

In (8.38), z^* is known as the *least core value*. In a scheduling problem, the least core value can be interpreted as the minimum penalty required to prevent any coalition from leaving the grand coalition and opening its own machine. As defined in Sect. 2.3.5, a cooperative game with *supermodular costs* is one that satisfies

$$v(S \cup \{j\}) - v(S) \leq v(S \cup \{j, k\}) - v(S \cup \{k\}),$$

for all $j, k \in N$, $j \neq k$, $S \subseteq N \setminus \{j, k\}$.

For general cooperative games with supermodular costs, Schulz and Uhan (2010) show that computing the least core value is a strongly *NP*-hard problem that cannot even be approximated within a ratio of 17/16, unless $P = NP$ (see Garey & Johnson, 1979).

However, they consider a particular scheduling game that has supermodular costs. Let N denote a set of customers. Each customer $i \in N$ has a single job i with processing time $p_i > 0$ and a weight or value w_i that, in this context, describes the urgency of the task. The jobs need to be scheduled nonpreemptively on a single machine. The scheduling cost is defined as the weighted completion time of the jobs, or $\sum_{j=1}^{n} w_j C_j$. No initial order is defined for the jobs, hence each job has the same access to any position in the schedule. We assume that the jobs are indexed in their globally optimal sequence defined by Smith (1956), i.e., $w_1/p_1 \geq \cdots \geq w_n/p_n$. This implies that $v(S) = \sum_{i \in S} w_i \sum_{j=1 \mid j \in S}^{i} p_j$, for $S \subseteq N$. The following result shows that, for this game, it is easy to compute a cost allocation $x_1, \ldots, x_n$ that is in the least core.

498   8 Cooperative Supply Chain Scheduling

Theorem 8.28 *The cost allocation*

$$x_i = (w_i \sum_{j=1}^{i} p_j + p_i \sum_{j=i}^{n} w_j)/2, \quad i = 1, \ldots, n, \tag{8.39}$$

is an element of the least core of the scheduling game (N, v).

Proof For any $S \subseteq N$, let $\bar{x}(S) = \sum_{i \in S} x_i$. Then, for any $S \subseteq N$, the cost allocation $(x_1, \ldots, x_n)$ defined in (8.39) satisfies

$$2[\bar{x}(S) - v(S)] = \sum_{i \in S} \sum_{j=1}^{i} w_i p_j + \sum_{i \in S} \sum_{j=i}^{n} w_j p_i - 2 \sum_{i \in S} \sum_{j=1|j \in S}^{i} w_i p_j$$

$$= \sum_{i \in S} \sum_{j=1}^{i} w_i p_j + \sum_{i \in S} \sum_{j=i}^{n} w_j p_i - \sum_{i \in S} \sum_{j=1|j \in S}^{i} w_i p_j$$

$$- \sum_{i \in S} \sum_{j=i|j \in S}^{n} w_j p_i$$

$$= \sum_{i \in S} \sum_{j=1|j \in N \setminus S}^{i} w_i p_j + \sum_{i \in S} \sum_{j=i|j \in N \setminus S}^{n} w_j p_i$$

$$= \sum_{i \in S} \sum_{j=1|j \in N \setminus S}^{i} w_i p_j + \sum_{i \in N \setminus S} \sum_{j=1|j \in S}^{i} w_i p_j$$

$$= \sum_{i \in N} \sum_{j=1}^{i} w_i p_j - \sum_{i \in S} \sum_{j=1}^{i} w_i p_j - \sum_{i \in N \setminus S} \sum_{j=1}^{i} w_i p_j$$

$$+ \sum_{i \in S} \sum_{j=1|j \in N \setminus S}^{i} w_i p_j + \sum_{i \in N \setminus S} \sum_{j=1|j \in S}^{i} w_i p_j$$

$$= \sum_{i \in N} \sum_{j=1}^{i} w_i p_j - \sum_{i \in S} \sum_{j=1|j \in S}^{i} w_i p_j - \sum_{i \in N \setminus S} \sum_{j=1|j \in N \setminus S}^{i} w_i p_j$$

$$= v(N) - v(S) - v(N \setminus S). \tag{8.40}$$

Define $\bar{z} = \max_{S \subset N, S \neq \emptyset} \{v(N) - v(S) - v(N \setminus S)\}/2$. From (8.40), the solution $(\bar{x}, \bar{z})$ is a feasible solution to the linear program (8.38). Let (x^*, z^*) be an optimal solution to (8.38). Adding the inequalities $x^*(S) \leq v(S) + z^*$ and $x^*(N \setminus S) \leq v(N \setminus S) + z^*$ for $S \subset N$, $S \neq \emptyset$ and from $x^*(N) = v(N)$, we have

$$z^* \geq [v(N) - v(S) - v(N \setminus S)]/2, \quad S \subset N, S \neq \emptyset. \tag{8.41}$$

8.4 Scheduling Games

It follows that $z^* \geq \bar{z}$. Thus, the cost allocation $\bar{x}$ is an element of the least core of the scheduling game (N, v). $\square$

We provide the following example of the least core element defined in (8.39).

Example 8.25 (Least Core Calculations in a Supermodular Cost Scheduling Game)
$N = \{1, 2, 3, 4\}$, $p = (5, 6, 7, 8)$, $w = (4, 3, 2, 1)$. From Smith (1956), an optimal sequence is $(1, 2, 3, 4)$ with $\sum_{j=1}^{4} w_j C_j = 4(5) + 3(5+6) + 2(5+6+7) + 1(5+6+7+8) = 115$.
The coalition values are: $v(\{1\}) = 20$, $v(\{2\}) = 18$, $v(\{3\}) = 14$, $v(\{4\}) = 8$; $v(\{1, 2\}) = 53$, $v(\{1, 3\}) = 44$, $v(\{1, 4\}) = 33$, $v(\{2, 3\}) = 44$, $v(\{2, 4\}) = 32$, $v(\{3, 4\}) = 29$; and $v(\{1, 2, 3\}) = 89$, $v(\{1, 2, 4\}) = 72$, $v(\{1, 3, 4\}) = 64$, $v(\{2, 3, 4\}) = 65$.
From (8.39), the cost allocations are: job 1: $(20 + 50)/2 = 35.0$; job 2: $(33 + 36)/2 = 34.5$; job 3: $(36 + 21)/2 = 28.5$; and job 4: $(26 + 8)/2 = 17.0$, where $35.0 + 34.5 + 28.5 + 17.0 = 115.0$, as required.
The least core value is: $(x_1 + x_3) - v(\{1, 3\}) = 63.5 - 44 = 19.5 = 51.5 - 32 = (x_2 + x_4) - v(\{2, 4\})$. Intuitively, the coalitions $\{1, 3\}$ and $\{2, 4\}$ can be viewed as those which are equally most likely to leave the grand coalition.

The cost allocations $x_1, \ldots, x_n$ also specify the Shapley values for the scheduling game (Mishra and Rangarajan, as discussed in Sect. 8.4.1). However, the problem of computing the least core value requires solution of the problem

$$z^* = \max_{S \subset N, S \neq \emptyset} \{v(N) - v(S) - v(N \setminus S)\}/2, \tag{8.42}$$

which is equivalent to the classical scheduling problem $P_2 || \sum w_j C_j$, and hence is at least binary NP-hard (Bruno et al., 1974).

8.4.4 No Initial Sequence: Penalty and Subsidy

This section, like the previous one, considers supply chain scheduling games without an initial sequence, and as a result, without a core solution. For cooperative game instances where there is no core solution, mechanisms can be developed to sustain players' cooperation within the grand coalition, and implemented by a central planner. Two general methods are imposition of a penalty on players who may leave the grand coalition (see Sect. 8.4.3), and provision of a subsidy to those who remain. However, potentially problematic issues arise in the use of either mechanism. In the case of penalties, players may believe that they are being unfairly targeted and become dissatisfied. On the other hand, providing a subsidy typically requires the use of resources from outside the game, which involves an opportunity cost for the unavailability of those resources elsewhere. To investigate the complex tradeoff between the use of these two mechanisms, Liu et al. (2018a) develop a "carrot-and-stick" approach to ensuring cooperation. This approach uses a *combination* of a penalty and a subsidy. We introduce each mechanism in turn.

The problem of finding the *minimum penalty* $z^* \in \mathbb{R}$ for leaving the grand coalition, along with a cost allocation $\beta^* \in \mathbb{R}^n$, such that, for any coalition $S \subset N$, its assigned cost $\beta^*(S)$ is not larger than its own cost as a separate coalition $c(S)$ plus the penalty z, can be written as the following linear program:

$$z^* = \min_{\beta, z}\{z \mid \beta(N) = c(N), \beta(S) \le c(S) + z, \ S \subset N, z \in \mathbb{R}, \beta \in \mathbb{R}^n\}. \tag{8.43}$$

The minimum penalty z^* is the *least core value*, and the optimal solution β^* is the *least core cost allocation*.

In the discussion below, we use the following notation for cost allocations: $\beta \in \mathbb{R}^n$, where $\beta = (\beta_1, \ldots, \beta_n)$, and $\beta(s) = \sum_{i \in s} \beta_i$, for $s \subseteq N$. Also, $\beta(i, z)$ is defined as the value of β_i given a penalty $z \in \mathbb{R}$.

The other alternative for sustaining cooperation is subsidization. The problem of finding the *minimum subsidy* ω^* along with a cost allocation $\alpha^* \in \mathbb{R}^n$ that satisfies the coalitional stability constraints can be formulated as the following linear program:

$$\omega^* = \min_{\alpha \in \mathbb{R}^n}\{c(N) - \alpha(N) \mid \alpha(s) \le c(s), \text{ for } s \subseteq N\}. \tag{8.44}$$

The optimal solution α^* is the *optimal cost allocation*. Here, ω^* is nonnegative, and it is strictly positive only if the scheduling game (N, c) is unbalanced.

The following definition helps to unify the above two mechanisms.

Definition 8.14 In a cooperative game (N, c), for any given penalty $z \in \mathbb{R}$, consider the following linear program with cost allocations $\beta(s), s \subset N$, as decision variables:

$$\omega(z) = \min_{\beta}\{c(N) - \beta(N) \mid \beta(s) \le c(s) + z, \text{ for } s \subset N, \beta \in \mathbb{R}^n\}. \tag{8.45}$$

The optimal solution to this linear program, denoted by $\beta(\cdot, z)$, is a *z-penalized optimal cost allocation*, and its optimal objective value $\omega(z)$ is the *z-penalized minimum subsidy*. Also, $\omega(z)$ is the *penalty-subsidy function*.

This definition of the penalty-subsidy function allows exploration of various combinations of penalty and subsidy. The requirement is that, under the combined effect of a suitable combination of penalty z and subsidy $\omega(z)$, the Coalitional Rationality constraints can be satisfied and cooperation of all members within the grand coalition can be achieved. We present an example of how this can be achieved.

Example 8.26 (Penalty, Subsidy, and Cost Allocations in a Scheduling Game) Consider a scheduling game defined over the classical scheduling problem $1 \| \sum w_j C_j$. There are four players, $N = \{1, 2, 3, 4\}$. Each player $k \in N$ has a job with processing time p_k and weight w_k, where $p_1 = 5, p_2 = 6, p_3 = 7, p_4 = 8;$

8.4 Scheduling Games

Table 8.6 Penalty, subsidy, and cost allocations in Example 8.26

Penalty z	0.00	5.00	10.00	15.00	19.50
Subsidy $\omega(z)$	55.00	35.00	20.00	9.00	0.00
$\beta(1, z)$	20.00	25.00	29.29	31.62	35.00
$\beta(2, z)$	18.00	23.00	28.00	31.45	34.50
$\beta(3, z)$	14.00	19.00	24.00	27.38	28.50
$\beta(4, z)$	8.00	13.00	13.71	15.55	17.00
$\sum_{i=1}^{4} \beta(i, z) + \omega(z)$	115.00	115.00	115.00	115.00	115.00

and $w_1 = 4$, $w_2 = 3$, $w_3 = 2$, $w_4 = 1$. Each coalition $S \subseteq N$ minimizes its total weighted completion time by processing its jobs on a single machine. From Smith (1956), the optimal solution is $\sigma^* = (1, 2, 3, 4)$ with cost $4(5) + 3(5 + 6) + 2(5 + 6 + 7) + 1(5 + 6 + 7 + 8) = 20 + 33 + 36 + 26 = 115$.

The range of tradeoffs between penalty and subsidy is illustrated in Table 8.6. For any given value of the penalty z, the corresponding column in the table represents a vector of cost allocations $\beta(1, z), \ldots, \beta(4, z)$ to players 1 through 4, respectively.

The last row of Table 8.6 shows the total penalty plus subsidization, which in each case equals the optimal total cost of 115. Observe that the last column of Table 8.6 allows for no subsidy, hence the solution shown is found entirely from the application of penalties.

The problem of computing, for a given penalty z, the z-penalized minimum subsidy that ensures cooperation, is strongly *NP*-hard for general scheduling games (Liu et al., 2018a). This result remains true even for some special case games where the computation of the cost $c(s)$ of a coalition s is polynomially solvable. For scheduling games in general, Liu et al. (2018a) develop a cutting plane algorithm. This algorithm starts with a restricted coalition set and finds a solution to a relaxed problem with only a subset of constraints included. It then solves the *separation problem*

$$\delta = \min_{s \subset N} \{c(s) + z - \sum_{k \in s} \beta(k, z)\}. \tag{8.46}$$

If $\delta < 0$, then the violated constraint is added to the coalition set. Otherwise, information is obtained to update the search process for optimal z and $\beta(\cdot, z)$.

The computational bottleneck in this process is solving the separation problem (8.46), which in general cannot be performed efficiently. However, for some scheduling games, efficient solution of the separation problem, and thus also of the penalty-subsidy function, is possible.

One such game is now described. Consider a scheduling problem with a set of jobs $N = \{1, \ldots, n\}$, where each job has a processing time p_i and needs to be processed using one of m identical parallel machines, to minimize the total completion time. From the perspective of a single player who controls all the jobs, this is the classical scheduling problem $P_m || \sum C_i$. Over this problem, we define a scheduling game (N, c), where each player $i \in N$ is represented by a job. Each coalition $s \subseteq N$ chooses machines for processing its jobs to minimize the total completion time of its jobs on the m machines.

It is well-known (Smith, 1956) that an optimal schedule for problem $P_m || \sum C_i$ can be found by sorting the jobs such that $p_1 \leq \cdots \leq p_n$, i.e., SPT order, and scheduling them sequentially, in index order, on the first machine that becomes available. If job i is scheduled on a machine as the jth to last job on a machine that processes it, it contributes the amount $j p_i$ to the total completion time. This is the "positional penalty" approach that is familiar from classical scheduling problems, which describes the number of jobs that are delayed by the processing of job i.

Since positional penalties are being used to define costs, it is necessary to work from the back of the schedule to the front. Therefore, we reindex the jobs such that $p_1 \geq \cdots \geq p_n$, i.e., LPT order, and schedule the lower indexed, i.e., longer, jobs first. For each (i, u) with $i \in \{1, \ldots, n\}$ and $u \in \{0, 1, \ldots, n\}$, we let $f(i, u)$ denote the minimum objective value of the separation problem for coalition s, given that coalition $s \subseteq \{1, \ldots, i\}$ and $|s| = u$. These definitions enable the solution of the separation problem using the following dynamic program.

Algorithm Separation

Preprocessing
  Index the jobs such that $p_1 \geq \cdots \geq p_n$.

Value Function
  $f(i, u) =$ the minimum objective value of a solution to the separation problem, where $s \subseteq \{1, \ldots, i\}$ and $|s| = u$.

Boundary Conditions
  $f(1, 0) = z$, $f(1, 1) = p_1 - \beta_1 + z$;
  $f(i, u) = +\infty$, if $u > i$, for $i \in N$.

Recurrence Relation For $i \in \{1, \ldots, n\}$, $u \in \{0, \ldots, n\}$:
$$f(i, u) = \begin{cases} f(i - 1, u), \\ f(i - 1, u - 1) + \lceil u/m \rceil p_i - \beta_i. \end{cases}$$

Optimal Solution
  $\delta = \min_{1 \leq u \leq v - 1}\{f(n, u)\}$.

In the recurrence relation, the first term applies when s^* does not contain job i, whereas in the second term it does so. If an optimal s^* for $f(i, u)$ contains player i, it is optimal to process job i on machine $[1 + (u - 1) \bmod m]$ as the $\lceil u/m \rceil$th to last job, thus contributing $\lceil u/m \rceil p_i$ to the total completion time. The sign of δ in the Optimal Solution step reveals the solution to the separation problem (8.46). Algorithm Separation enables the following result.

Theorem 8.29 *For the scheduling game (N, c), the separation problem can be solved in $O(n^2)$ time.*

Proof Algorithm Separation enumerates all relevant coalitions and hence finds an optimal one, s^*. Since $i \leq n$ and $u \leq n$, and the recurrence relation uses $O(1)$ comparisons, the running time is $O(n^2)$. □

Further, Liu et al. (2018a) show that the penalty-subsidy function has $O(n^4)$ breakpoints. This result, and Theorem 8.29 enable the main result that follows.

Theorem 8.30 *For the scheduling game (N, c), the penalty-subsidy function can be computed in polynomial time.*

Liu et al. (2018a) extend their methodology to find computationally efficient solution methods for three more general cooperative scheduling games. These games are based on the corresponding classical scheduling problems:

(i) The minimization of total completion time on unrelated parallel processors, i.e., $R_m || \sum C_i$;
(ii) The minimization of total weighted completion time on identical parallel processors, i.e., $P_m || \sum w_i C_i$; and
(iii) The minimization of total weighted completion time on unrelated parallel processors, i.e., $R_m || \sum w_i C_i$.

It is an interesting research challenge to understand the full range of problems for which the methodology of Liu et al. (2018a) can be applied efficiently. See Sect. 8.8 for additional comments.

8.5 Project Games

In this section, we discuss two examples of supply chain scheduling games defined on projects. We describe these games as *project planning games* and *project execution games*, respectively. A formal definition of a project is a "temporary business endeavor undertaken to create a unique product or service" (Project Management Institute, 2021). More operationally, a project is defined as a business activity composed of several discrete *tasks* or *activities* that can be scheduled independently, but may have some precedence relations between them. It is difficult to overestimate the importance of project management as a business process. The global economic value of projects is approximately $27 trillion, representing about 30% of the world's economic activity (Hu et al., 2015). Background about project management is provided by Klastorin (2012) and Kerzner (2013). Hall (2016) provides an overview of research and teaching opportunities in project management. A major component of successful project management in practice, and also a major focus of research on project management, is the scheduling of the individual tasks, i.e., *project scheduling*. Efficient project scheduling is needed to ensure timely delivery of the product or service being created, although in practice many projects are delivered late (The Standish Group, 2020).

504   8 Cooperative Supply Chain Scheduling

In practice, projects are rarely centralized operations. Even within a single organization, various resources and departments contribute to the project at different times and under constraints related to their other operations. More generally, external resources are needed to complete the project. In both cases, cooperation is needed to ensure complete and timely contributions to support the project, which motivates the topics discussed in this section. We study two different perspectives on cooperative game theory for project scheduling.

One cooperative game perspective, discussed in Sect. 8.5.1, studies projects at the planning stage and associates players not with tasks but with external resource-holding companies. Either individually or within coalitions, those companies can provide resources to the project, but require sufficient compensation for doing so. In this context, within the class of balanced games are two classes of games with useful properties, 1-convex games and big boss games. In these games, the realized details of project execution are not used to evaluate the various solutions obtained. We describe such games as project planning games.

A second cooperative game perspective, discussed in Sect. 8.5.2, studies projects that are already executed. This approach views the tasks of a completed project as players who need to share the rewards of early project completion or the costs of project delay. Those rewards or costs are typically defined in contracts with a project client. Then, they should be shared with the players whose performance was responsible for the successful or unsuccessful outcome of the project. We describe such games as project execution games. In the event that a project is early, or *expedited*, a reward from the project owner is used to define a *project execution reward game*. When a project is late, which incurs a penalty cost from a contract with the project owner, that cost is used to define a *project execution cost game*. The work discussed below focuses mainly on the stability of coalitions as defined by the core of the game, although alternative approaches that are more axiomatic are also discussed.

8.5.1 Project Planning Games

Curiel (2011) studies situations where a central project company relies on work that is outsourced from external subcontractors to complete a project for a client efficiently. The external companies can cooperate in order to decrease the makespan, or *earliest completion time* (ECT), of a project that consists of several tasks. However, they require sufficient compensation to do so. For this purpose, the earliest completion times of individual tasks are equivalent to the *early finish times* computed under the critical path method (Kelley Jr and Walker, 1959), and are the actual completion times if no task delays or expeditions occur. Since the stochastic performance of the project under actual execution is not modeled here, this analysis can be considered as ex-ante, or occurring at the planning stage of the project. The external companies own resources that can expedite the performance of tasks, and thereby expedite the project.

8.5 Project Games

There is a project owner who wants the project to be completed as soon as possible. Indeed, the project owner is willing to pay more for an earlier completion time. The total payment must be allocated among the companies that cooperate to provide their resources. From a cooperative game perspective, the players are the external companies which can provide resources to the project and hence expedite it. Each company must be sure that its own payment, or reward allocation, is sufficient to induce it to cooperate. Since the core of a cooperative game can contain many, even infinitely many, solutions, it is also valuable to study single-point solution concepts in this game, including the τ-value, nucleolus and Shapley value.

The earliest completion time of the whole project is the length of the longest path, or makespan. The client compares all the earliest completion times and assigns the project to the company, or coalition of companies, that offers the best one. Companies may decide to work together in coalitions. Companies that decide to work together can combine their resources to create greater reductions and therefore reach a more favorable earliest completion time with a resulting greater payoff from the client that can be shared agreeably among them.

Consider a typical project that is defined using the activity-on-arcs format (Kerzner, 2013; Klastorin, 2012). Let V denote the vertices of a network G that represents the project. An arc set $\mathscr{A} = \{A_1, \ldots, A_m\}$ represents the activities of the project. Let $N = \{1, \ldots, n\}$ denote a set of external resource-owning companies that compete to support the project, but need to be compensated for doing so. The nominal duration of activity A_j, where none of the external companies support it and reduce its duration, is denoted as $D(A_j)$. If no external companies participate, the project makespan is calculated from the activity durations $D(A_1), \ldots, D(A_m)$.

However, each external company $i \in N$ can provide a vector of potential activity time reductions $r^i_{A_1}, \ldots, r^i_{A_m}$. The choice to do so is binary; either the external company participates and provides its available resources in full, or it does not participate. The reduction vector of a coalition $S \subseteq N$ of external companies is denoted as $r^S = (r^S_{A_1}, \ldots, r^S_{A_m})$, where $r^S_{A_k} = \sum_{i \in S} r^i_{A_k}$. As in every practical project, however, each activity A_j has a minimum achievable duration, denoted as $L(A_j)$. This minimum value is typically defined by physical or logistical limitations of the activity. Thus, the duration function $d(A_j)$ of activity A_j, if a set $S \subseteq N$ of external companies participates, is given by

$$d(A_j) = \max\{D(A_j) - \sum_{i \in S} r^i_{A_j}, \ L(A_j)\}.$$

Let M denote the maximum amount that the project owner would be willing to pay for a project completed at time 0. The cost of participation for company i is $c_i, i \in N$, which needs to be compensated by the client's payoff function $P(t) = M - pt$, where t is the project duration achieved by using the external companies' resources, and p is an incentive per unit time. The total cost of participation by a coalition $S \subseteq N$ is $c_S \equiv \sum_{i \in S} c_i$.

A *project management situation* is defined by A, N, the network structure, the duration functions, and the value of p. The corresponding cooperative *project planning game* (N, v) is defined by N and the value of each coalition. Let ECT_i denote the earliest completion time that an individual external company can offer to the project company by sharing its resources. Observe that a coalition S only has value if the earliest completion time which it bids to the project company, denoted by ECT_S, is at least as good as what the remaining external companies could bid. Thus, for all coalitions $S \subset N$, the value of coalition S is given by

$$v(S) = \begin{cases} M - p \cdot ECT_S - c_S, & \text{if } ECT_S \leq ECT_{N \setminus S} \\ 0, & \text{otherwise.} \end{cases} \tag{8.47}$$

In (8.47), the first two terms represent the amount which the project owner is willing to pay for a project with delivery date ECT_S and the last term is the cost of coalition S for participating in the project.

Assume that the resources of every external company, if hired alone, would generate the same critical path in the project, although with various durations. This assumption is typical of a situation where the external resources being provided are fairly standard and therefore induce similar, although not in general identical, reductions in duration regardless of which company provides them. Given this assumption, Curiel (2011) provides conditions under which this implies that the combined effect of using the resources provided by every possible coalition results in the same critical path, once again with various durations. We denote this critical path by CP.

In the following result, Curiel (2011) proves necessary and sufficient conditions for balancedness.

Theorem 8.31 *Consider a project management situation given by the sets A, N, the precedence graph G, the reduction vectors $\{r^i, i \in N\}$, the duration functions $d_A(r) = \max\{D(A_i) - r, m_A\}$ for all $A \in \mathscr{A}$, and the payoff function $P(t) = M - pt$, where every coalition $S \subset N$ has the same unique critical path denoted by CP. Further, assume:*

(i) $D(A_i) - r_{A_i}^N \geq L_{A_i}$, $i = 1, \ldots, A_{|\mathscr{A}|}$, *and*
(ii) $ECT_{N \setminus \{i\}} \leq ECT_{\{i\}}$, $i \in N$.

Then, the core of the game is nonempty if and only if

$$\frac{M}{\sum_{A \in CP} D_A} \leq p.$$

In Theorem 8.31, Condition (i) means that the combined reduction in duration of all the companies working together could not achieve a duration that is smaller than the minimum duration m_A of any activity A. Condition (ii) means that no single company dominates, i.e., provides a makespan reduction that is smaller than that provided by all the other companies combined. The result in the theorem can be explained intuitively, as follows. If the penalty for later completion, or equivalently the saving for earlier completion, is sufficiently large, then this provides sufficient

8.5 Project Games

incentives for the players to cooperate and maintain stability of the grand coalition. Condition (ii) is modified below in order to study a relevant class of games.

The remainder of the discussion of project planning games studies two special cases of such games that have useful properties. First, Driessen and Tijs (1985) introduce the class of *1-convex* cooperative games, for which the following definition provides some background.

Definition 8.15 An n-person game is called *1-convex* if its core (when the core is non-singular) is a regular simplex with n vertices which is obtained from the marginal value vector (as discussed below) by decreasing *only one coordinate* to obtain an efficient vector.

A useful property of this class of games is that reduction to a 1-convex game enables the application of several known properties, as shown below. These games require the following definitions. First, recall the definition of a marginal value vector from (8.3), which we write here as $M_i^v = v(N) - v(N \setminus \{i\}), i \in N$. For a coalition $S \subseteq N$, let $M^v(S) = \sum_{i \in S} M_i^v$.

Definition 8.16 Recall from (8.4) that the *gap function* of the game (N, v) is

$$g^v(S) = \sum_{i \in S} M_i^v - v(S), \quad S \in 2^N.$$

Then, the game is called *1-convex* if

$$0 \le g^v(N) \le g^v(S), \quad \emptyset \neq S \subset N.$$

Theorem 8.32 *Let (N, v) be a project planning game that satisfies the conditions of Theorem 8.31. Then (N, v) is a 1-convex game.*

Proof The marginal value vector M^v of (N, v) is given by

$$M_i^v = v(N) - v(N \setminus \{i\}) = p \sum_{A \in CP} r_A^i - c_i, \quad i \in N.$$

For the gap function g^v,

$$g^v(S) = M^v(S) - v(S) = \begin{cases} -M + p \sum_{A \in CP} D_A, & \text{if } v(S) > 0 \\ p \sum_{A \in CP} r_A^S - c_S, & \text{otherwise.} \end{cases} \quad (8.48)$$

In the first row of (8.48), we have $M^v(S) - v(S) = p \sum_{A \in CP} r_A^S - c_S - (M - p \cdot ECT_S - c_S)$, which yields the expression shown. In the second row of (8.48), the result follows immediately by setting $v(S) = 0$.

Since the game (N, v) is balanced, we have $g^v(N) \ge 0$. Let $S \subset N$. If $v(S) > 0$, then $g^v(N) = g^v(S)$. Alternatively, if $v(S) = 0$, then

508   8 Cooperative Supply Chain Scheduling

$$0 \leq M - p \cdot ECT_S - c_S = M - p \sum_{A \in CP} (D_A - r_A^S) - c_S$$

$$\Rightarrow -M + p \sum_{A \in CP} D_A \leq p \sum_{A \in CP} r_A^S - c_S$$

$$\Rightarrow g^v(N) \leq g^v(S).$$

Therefore, $0 \leq g^v(N) \leq g^v(S)$ for all $S \subset N$, and hence the game (N, v) is 1-convex. $\qquad\square$

Theorem 8.32 enables the use of a previously known result to establish the τ-value of this game. Driessen and Tijs (1985) show that, for all 1-convex games, the τ-value and nucleolus coincide, and are given by

$$\tau_i(v) = v_i(v) = M_i^v - g^v(N)/n, \quad i \in N. \tag{8.49}$$

This result can be applied to find closed form solutions for the τ-value and nucleolus of the game (N, v), as shown by the following result.

Theorem 8.33 *For a project planning game (N, v) that satisfies the conditions of Theorem 8.31,*

$$\tau_i(v) = v_i(v) = \frac{1}{n}[M - p \cdot ECT_N + (n-1)p \sum_{A \in CP} r_A^i - p \sum_{A \in CP} r_A^{N \setminus \{i\}}] - c_i.$$

Proof From (8.49), we have, for $i \in N$,

$$\tau_i(v) = v_i(v) = p \sum_{A \in CP} r_A^i - c_i - (-M + p \sum_{A \in CP} D_A)/n$$

$$= \frac{1}{n}[M - p \sum_{A \in CP} (D_A - r_A^N) - p \sum_{A \in CP} r_A^N + np \sum_{A \in CP} r_A^i] - c_i$$

$$= \frac{1}{n}[M - p \cdot ECT_N + (n-1)p \sum_{A \in CP} r_A^i - p \sum_{A \in CP} r_A^{N \setminus \{i\}}] - c_i.$$

$\qquad\square$

Remark 8.10 In the 1-convex game (N, v), the τ-value and nucleolus can be found by dividing the payoff to the grand coalition equally, and then making adjustments that depend on the company's contribution to the value of the grand coalition. This can be accomplished without computing the coalition values. The contribution of company i to the value of the grand coalition from the reduction in project completion time if it participates is $p \sum_{A \in CP} r_A^i$, and company i receives a fraction $(n-1)/n$ of it. The total contribution of the other companies to the payoff is

8.5 Project Games

$p \sum_{A \in CP} r_A^{N\setminus\{i\}}$, and company i has to pay a fraction $1/n$ of it. Also, each company is responsible for its own costs.

We provide an example of the result in Theorem 8.33.

Example 8.27 (τ-Value and Nucleolus Calculations in a 1-Convex Project Planning Game) Let $N = \{1, 2, 3\}$, $\mathscr{A} = \{A, B, C, D, E\}$, $M = 1200$, and $p = 10$. The costs are $c_i = 20$, $i \in N$. The precedence constraints, reduction vectors $r_{A_k}^i$ of the companies, and the duration functions of the activities are shown in Table 8.7.

For this example, Table 8.8 shows the earliest completion times, the values of the coalitions, the values of the upper vector $m^v(S)$, and the values of the gap function $g^v(S)$. If all three companies participate in crashing the project, we have $d_A(8 + 6 + 12) = 50 - 26 = 24 > m_A = 5$, $d_B(12 + 9 + 20) = 45 - 41 = 4 = m_B$, $d_C(3+3+5) = 30-11 = 19 > m_C = 2$, $d_D(2+5+18) = 30-25 = 5 > m_D = 2$, and $d_E(5 + 6 + 10) = 50 - 21 = 29 > m_E = 10$. Then, the critical path length is $\max\{d_A+d_C+d_E, d_B+d_D+d_E\} = \max\{24+19+29, 4+5+29\} = \max\{72, 38\} = 72$, and the critical path is (A, C, E).

Finally, Table 8.9 shows the calculations for the equal distribution of the payoff to the members of the grand coalition, followed by the adjustments described in Remark 8.10. Observe that the τ and nucleolus values in the last row are found by adding all the entries in the column.

Observe that the total allocation is $(320 + 290 + 650)/3 = 420 = M - p \cdot ECT_N - \sum_{i \in N} c_i$, as required.

Table 8.7 Data of Example 8.27

Activity	A	B	C	D	E
Predecessors			A	B	C, D
Company 1	8	12	3	2	5
Company 2	6	9	3	5	6
Company 3	12	20	5	18	10
$d_{A_k}(r)$	$\max\{50 - r, 5\}$	$\max\{45 - r, 4\}$	$\max\{30 - r, 2\}$	$\max\{30 - r, 2\}$	$\max\{50 - r, 10\}$

Table 8.8 Preliminary calculations in Example 8.27

S	$\{1\}$	$\{2\}$	$\{3\}$	$\{1, 2\}$	$\{1, 3\}$	$\{2, 3\}$	$\{1, 2, 3\}$
ECT_S	114	115	103	99	87	88	72
$v(S)$	0	0	0	170	290	280	420
$M^v(S)$	140	130	250	270	390	380	520
$g^v(S)$	140	130	250	100	100	100	100

Table 8.9 Solutions in Example 8.27

i	1	2	3
$(M - pECT_N)/3$	160	160	160
$2p \sum_{A \in CP} r_A^i/3$	320/3	100	180
$-p \sum_{A \in CP} r_A^{N\setminus\{i\}}/3$	-140	$-430/3$	$-310/3$
$-c_i$	-20	-20	-20
$\tau_i(v) = v_i(v)$	320/3	290/3	650/3

510   8 Cooperative Supply Chain Scheduling

Besides 1-convex games, the class of balanced project planning games includes another interesting subclass. Muto et al. [1988] introduce *big boss* games, as follows.

Definition 8.17 A game (N, v) is a *big boss game* if there exists a single player $i^* \in N$ such that

(i) $v(S) = 0$, if $i^* \notin S$.
(ii) $v(N) - v(S) \geq \sum_{i \in N \setminus S} [v(N) - v(N \setminus \{i\})]$, if $i^* \in S$.

In this case, player i^* is the big boss.

Intuitively in a big boss game one player, who is here denoted by i^*, dominates. A coalition that does not include i^* has no value, as in Condition (i). Moreover, the loss of value from the grand coalition if i^* leaves is greater than the total loss if all the other players leave, as in Condition (ii). However, by working together, the other players can benefit from working with the big boss. Clearly, there cannot exist more than one big boss in a game.

Theorem 8.34 *Consider a project planning game (N, v) that satisfies the conditions of Theorem 8.31 except $ECT_{N \setminus \{i\}} \leq ECT_i, i \in N$. Then, (N, v) is a big boss game, where player i^* is the big boss.*

Proof Let i^* be such that $ECT_{i^*} < ECT_{N \setminus \{i\}}$. There are two cases.

Case 1. Let $S \subset N \setminus \{i^*\}$. Then,

$$
\begin{aligned}
ECT_S &= \sum_{A \in CP} (D_A - r_A^S) \\
&\geq \sum_{A \in CP} (D_A - r_A^{N \setminus \{i^*\}}) \\
&> \sum_{A \in CP} (D_A - r_A^{i^*}) \\
&\geq \sum_{A \in CP} (D_A - r_A^{N \setminus S}) \\
&= ECT_{N \setminus S}.
\end{aligned}
$$

The first inequality follows from $S \subset N \setminus \{i^*\}$, and $r_{A_j}^i \geq 0, i \in N, j = 1, \ldots, m$. The second inequality follows from the excepted condition in the theorem statement. The third inequality follows from $i^* \in N \setminus S$, and $r_{A_j}^i \geq 0, i \in N, j = 1, \ldots, m$. Since coalition $N \setminus S$ provides a smaller completion time than coalition S, we have $v(S) = 0$, i.e., Condition (i).

8.5 Project Games

Case 2. Consider a coalition S with $i^* \in S$. Then,

$$
\begin{aligned}
v(N) - v(S) &= p(ECT_S - ECT_N) - c_{N \setminus S} \\
&= p \sum_{A \in CP} r_A^{N \setminus S} - c_{N \setminus S} \\
&= \sum_{i \in N \setminus S} [v(N) - v(N \setminus \{i\})].
\end{aligned}
$$

$\square$

Theorem 8.35 *Let (N, v) be a project planning game that satisfies the conditions of Theorem 8.34, and is therefore a big boss game, where player i^* is the big boss. Then,*

$$
\tau_{i^*}(v) = v_{i^*}(v) = \phi_{i^*}(v) = M - p \sum_{A \in CP} D_A
$$

$$
+ p \sum_{A \in CP} (r_A^N + r_A^{i^*})/2 - (c_N + c_{i^*})/2, \quad and
$$

$$
\tau_i(v) = v_i(v) = \phi_i(v) = (p \sum_{A \in CP} r_A^i - c_i)/2, \quad i \in N \setminus \{i^*\}.
$$

Proof From Muto et al. (1988) and Theorem 8.34 the game is convex, and $\tau(v) = v(v) = \phi(v)$. Hence, it is sufficient to show the result for $\tau(v)$. From Driessen and Tijs (1985), the τ-value for a convex game (N, v) is given by

$$
\lambda(v(1), \ldots, v(n)) + (1 - \lambda)(M_1^v, \ldots, M_n^v),
$$

where the value of λ is uniquely determined by the Efficiency property $\sum_{i \in N} \tau_i(v) = v(N)$, and $(M_1^v, \ldots, M_n^v)$ is the marginal value vector. Now, since (N, v) is a convex big boss game, $v(i) = 0$ for $i \in N \setminus i^*$, and $M_{i^*}^v = v(N)$. Hence,

$$
\sum_{i \in N} \tau_i(v) = \lambda v(\{i^*\}) + (1 - \lambda)[\sum_{i \in N \setminus \{i^*\}} M_i^v + v(N)] = v(N)
$$

$$
\Leftrightarrow \lambda v(\{i^*\}) + (1 - \lambda) \sum_{i \in N \setminus \{i^*\}} M_i^v - \lambda v(N) = 0
$$

$$
\Leftrightarrow \lambda = \frac{\sum_{i \in N \setminus \{i^*\}} M_i^v}{v(N) - v(\{i^*\}) + \sum_{i \in N \setminus \{i^*\}} M_i^v} = 1/2,
$$

where the last equality follows from

$$
v(N) - v(\{i^*\}) = p \sum_{A \in CP} r_A^{N \setminus \{i^*\}} - c_{N \setminus \{i^*\}} = \sum_{i \in N \setminus \{i^*\}} M_i^v.
$$

512   8 Cooperative Supply Chain Scheduling

It follows that

$$\tau_{i*}(v) = [v(\{i^*\}) + v(N)]/2$$

$$= \Big[M - p \sum_{A \in CP} (D_A - r_A^{i*}) - c_{i*} + M - p \sum_{A \in CP} (D_A - r_A^N) - c_N\Big]/2$$

$$= M - p \sum_{A \in CP} D_A + p \sum_{A \in CP} (r_A^N + r_A^{i*})/2 - (c_N + c_{i*})/2.$$

Finally, for $i \in N \setminus \{i^*\}$, we have

$$\tau_i(v) = M_i^v/2 = p(\sum_{A \in CP} r_A^i - c_i)/2.$$

$\square$

We present an example of the payment calculations in a big boss project planning game.

Example 8.28 (τ-Value, Nucleolus, and Shapley Value Calculations in a Big Boss Project Planning Game) Let $N = \{1, 2, 3\}$, $\mathscr{A} = \{A, B, C, D, E\}$, $M = 1200$, and $p = 10$. The precedence constraints, reduction vectors of the companies, and the duration functions of the activities are shown in Table 8.10. The costs are $c_i = 20$, $i \in N$.

For this example, Table 8.11 shows the earliest completion times, the values of the coalitions, the values of the upper vector, and the values of the gap function. Observe that this is a big boss game, where player 3 is the big boss. If all three companies participate in crashing the project, we have $d_A(8+6+22) = 50-36 = 14 > m_A = 5$, $d_B(12 + 9 + 20) = 45 - 41 = 4 = m_B$, $d_C(3 + 3 + 18) = 30 - 24 = 6 > m_C = 2$, $d_D(2 + 5 + 18) = 30 - 25 = 5 > m_D = 2$, and $d_E(5 + 6 + 24) = 50 - 35 = 15 > m_E = 10$. Then, the critical path length is $\max\{d_A + d_C + d_E, d_B + d_D + d_E\} = \max\{14 + 6 + 15, 4 + 5 + 15\} = \max\{35, 24\} = 35$, and the critical path is (A, C, E).

Since this is a big boss game, the Shapley value, τ-value and nucleolus all assign to the big boss, company 3, the amount $[v(N) + v(\{3\})]/2 = (790 + 520)/2 = 655$.

Table 8.10 Data of Example 8.28

Activity	A	B	C	D	E
Predecessors			A	B	C, D
Company 1	8	12	3	2	5
Company 2	6	9	3	5	6
Company 3	22	20	18	18	24
$d_{A_k}(r)$	$\max\{50 - r, 5\}$	$\max\{45 - r, 4\}$	$\max\{30 - r, 2\}$	$\max\{30 - r, 2\}$	$\max\{50 - r, 10\}$

8.5 Project Games

Table 8.11 Preliminary calculations in Example 8.28

S	{1}	{2}	{3}	{1, 2}	{1, 3}	{2, 3}	{1, 2, 3}
ECT_S	114	115	66	99	50	51	35
$v(S)$	0	0	520	0	660	650	790
$M^v(S)$	140	130	790	270	930	920	1060
$g^v(S)$	140	130	270	270	270	270	270

Also, Company 1 receives $M_1^v/2 = 140/2 = 70$, and Company 2 receives $M_2^v/2 = 130/2 = 65$, hence the total payoff is $655 + 70 + 65 = 790$, as required.

There are several reasons why many projects require the use of external resources to reduce project completion time. This becomes necessary, for example, to address market competition, or to compensate for previous delays or unexpected project complications. The use of external resources to expedite a project is a standard procedure for crashing a project. The work of Curiel (2011) on cooperative project planning games provides decision support for this procedure. Besides the impressive statistics on the influence of project management described at the beginning of Sect. 8.5, the importance of this topic is further emphasized by the fact that the global market for outsourced services in 2019 was more than \$92 billion (Statista, 2021).

8.5.2 Project Execution Games

The concept of decentralized scheduling for supply chain scheduling problems naturally includes project scheduling problems where different players are responsible for various parts of a project. An important difference from the discussion in Sect. 8.5.1 is that here we consider a project that has already completed. We discuss the fair compensation of players within a project company. Each player has completed his task(s) and the resulting execution times may result in an increase or a reduction in the overall delivery time of the project, or makespan. If the realized project makespan is less than planned, then the project owner provides a reward. Alternatively, if the project takes longer than expected, penalties defined by a project contract may be required. Project execution games model how such rewards or penalties should be shared among the players. However, from the interconnectedness of many tasks in a project through the project network, a reduction or increase in makespan is not uniquely attributable to a single player, but rather to a subset of players. This subset of players may be viewed as a coalition for the purposes of cooperative games. An important issue is how to compensate each coalition and individual player for their performance during project execution.

Projects rarely complete exactly on time. Occasionally, they compete early, but as the long series of CHAOS reports (The Standish Group, 2020) documents, frequently they complete late. A consistent stream of literature studies project execution games. In such games, there are many players, and each player controls one or more tasks of the project, for example, by deciding how long it takes, within some limits. If the project is delayed and therefore incurs penalties specified in a contract with a project client, an issue arises as to how to allocate costs to the players to recover those penalties. Symmetrically, if a project is completed early and therefore receives an incentive reward from the project client, that reward needs to be shared equitably among the players. While the main focus of our discussion is on the identification of single-player reward or cost allocations, following that analysis we also provide a discussion of set-valued allocations.

Brânzei et al. (2002) analyze the problem of sharing the total delay of a project within the framework of taxation. They propose a two-step allocation rule: first, the total delay of the project is allocated among the paths based on the aggregated delays observed; second, the delay assigned to a path is shared among the activities in that path proportionately to their delay. Castro et al. (2007), also in the same delayed project setting, propose a parameterized family of rules stemming from the cost sharing literature. However, these works do not directly make use of game theory concepts. Estévez-Fernández et al. (2007) is apparently the first study to approach the related allocation problem directly from a game theoretical point of view and to analyze both delayed and expedited project problems. Still, that study is restricted to project problems where the penalty or reward function is proportional with respect to the total delay or expedition of the project.

Estévez-Fernández (2012) extends the above work by analyzing project problems with arbitrary but nondecreasing penalty and reward functions, and also by taking into account whether an activity can be started before its planned starting time. A first step is to allocate the reward associated with the delay or expedition of each path (i.e., the total delay or total expedition created by its activities) among its activities, using a reward or cost sharing mechanism. However, the total amount allocated from studying the performance of the paths may exceed the total reward or penalty of the project. Then, in a second step, a cooperative game is used to share the reward of the project among all its activities, using the initial allocations as reference points.

We define a project as $(A, \{P_i\}_{i \in A})$, where A is the set of activities and P_i is the set of predecessors of i, i.e., the tasks that must complete before task i starts. Symmetrically, let $F_i = \{j \in A \mid i \in P_j\}$ denote the set of activities that cannot start until task i has completed. We identify a project with the set of all its paths $\{N_1, \ldots, N_m\}$. Thus, we consider a project problem $(\{N_1, \ldots, N_m\}, p, r, R)$, where $\{N_1, \ldots, N_m\}$ is the set of paths through the project network, p denotes planned activity times, r denotes realized activity times after execution, and R is a nondecreasing reward function of the difference between the planned and real times of the overall project. In practice, p is determined by a project manager before the start of project execution. However, r represents data that is collected during project execution, for example, as part of standard project monitoring processes such as Earned Value Management (Klastorin, 2012). Since our perspective is that the project has already completed, all the above information is assumed to be known.

We define the *delay* of activity i as

$$d(i) = \max\{r(i) - p(i), 0\}, \quad i \in A,$$

8.5 Project Games

and the *expedition* of activity i as

$$e(i) = \max\{p(i) - r(i), 0\}, \quad i \in A.$$

Associated with this project problem, we define a project execution game where the set of players is the set of activities, and the value of a coalition is determined by taking into account the performance of both delayed and expedited activities. A project execution game can be a project execution reward game in the case of expedition, or a project execution cost game in the case of delay. The duration of a path N_α, denoted as $D(N_\alpha)$, is the sum of activity durations on the path. The project length D is the maximum length of any path. Let $D(p)$ denote the planned makespan of the project, which is known. Finally, let $\mathcal{D} = \{i \in A \mid r(i) > p(i)\}$ denote the set of delayed activities, and $\mathcal{E} = \{i \in A \mid r(i) < p(i)\}$ the set of expedited activities,

Definition 8.18 For any path N_α in the project network, the *slack* of N_α, denoted by $slack(N_\alpha, p)$, is given by $slack(N_\alpha, p) = D(p) - D(N_\alpha)$, and represents the maximum delay that can occur on the path without delaying the overall project.

In computing the value of a coalition $S \subseteq A$ we assume that:

(a) The durations of all delayed activities in A are as realized during project execution.
(b) The durations of all expedited activities outside the coalition are at their planned values.

Intuitively, for any coalition $S \subseteq A$, this computation involves taking the observed durations of all the tasks, and recomputing the performance of the project by adjusting the observed durations of the expedited activities outside S to their planned values. These assumptions can be viewed as pessimistic, since all responsibility for the delay is incurred by the coalition. See Klijn and Sánchez (2006) in Sect. 8.4.1 for another example of pessimistically determined value of a coalition. Such definitions make it easier to achieve cooperation.

Recall that $D(p)$ denotes the planned duration of the project. Then, following the above discussion, we let $D(p_{|\mathcal{E}\setminus S}, r_{|A\setminus(\mathcal{E}\setminus S)})$ denote the realized duration of the project, as adjusted for the performance of the tasks of coalition S. In this expression, the condition on p implements assumption (b) above by replacing the realized values of the expedited activities in $A \setminus S$ with their planned values, and the condition on r implements assumption (a) above by using the realized values of all delayed activities in A in calculating the adjusted project duration.

If the adjusted duration of the project is larger than $D(p)$, then we have a project execution cost game for coalition S. Otherwise, the value of the coalition is positive and is determined through a project execution reward game for coalition S. Formally, given the project problem described above, a cost sharing mechanism

y, and a surplus sharing mechanism z, we denote by (A, u_{yz}) the associated project execution game, where the characteristic function of the project game is given by

$$u_{yz}(S) = \begin{cases} -c_y(S), & \text{if } D(p_{|\mathscr{E} \setminus S}, r_{|A \setminus (\mathscr{E} \setminus S)}) \geq D(p), \\ v_z(S), & \text{if } D(p_{|\mathscr{E} \setminus S}, r_{|A \setminus (\mathscr{E} \setminus S)}) < D(p), \end{cases} \qquad (8.50)$$

where $c_y(S)$ and $v_z(S)$ are defined below for the cost game and the reward game, respectively.

We first consider the cost game, where there is a delay in project execution. In order to define the characteristic function of this game, the pessimistic assumption is made that the activities in a path N_α cannot make use of either (a) any slack that existed in the original plan defined by the project network and p, or (b) any expedition in the execution of other tasks in the path. Therefore, activities have to pay the cost associated with their total delay. We let y_i^α represent the share of the total delay on path N_α for which task i is accountable under assumptions (a) and (b). Based on this reference point, the activities of coalition S that are in path N_α are not held responsible for more than the total cost assigned to them by the cost sharing mechanism.

Thus, we define

$$c_y(S) = \max_{\alpha \in \mathscr{P}(S)} \left\{ \min \left\{ \sum_{i \in N_\alpha \cap S} y_i^\alpha, K\big(D(N_\alpha, p_{|\mathscr{E} \setminus S}, r_{|A \setminus (\mathscr{E} \setminus S)})\big) - D(p) \right\} \right\}, \qquad (8.51)$$

where $\mathscr{P}(S)$ represents the set of paths in which one or more tasks of S appear, and $K(t) = -R(-t)$ if $t > 0$ and $K(t) = 0$ otherwise. Observe that $c_y(A) = K(D(r) - D(p))$.

The cost game (A, c_y) defined in this way is not concave. Nonetheless, Estévez-Fernández (2012) proves the following result.

Theorem 8.36 *Let $(\{N_1, \ldots, N_m\}, p, r, a, R)$ be a project problem, and let y be a cost sharing mechanism as defined above. Then, the project execution cost game (A, c_y) has a nonempty core.*

We provide a brief outline of the proof of Theorem 8.36, which considers a related taxation game that is known to be concave. It is shown that the values of the grand coalition A are equal in the two games. Now, consider a coalition $S \subset A$. It is shown that the value of S in the project execution game is greater than or equal to that in the taxation game. Hence, coalition S will not defect in the project execution game whenever it does not do so in the taxation game. The result then follows from the balancedness of the taxation game. We refer the reader to Estévez-Fernández (2012) for additional details.

Next, we consider the reward game for a situation where project execution is expedited. First, consider an optimistic allocation of the part of the expedition that each path could contribute to among the activities of that path. Then, using these initial allocations for reference, we define the characteristic function of the game.

8.5 Project Games

We now provide an intuitive explanation of the process and refer the interested reader to Estévez-Fernández (2012) for full details of the sharing mechanism z. The following definition is needed for this explanation.

Definition 8.19 For any path N_α in the project network, the *remaining slack* of N_α, denoted by $rslack(N_\alpha, p, r)$, is the slack of N_α if its delayed activities had acted according to plan, i.e., $rslack(N_\alpha, p, r) = slack(N_\alpha, p) - \sum_{i \in N_\alpha \cap \mathscr{D}} d(i)$, where $slack(N_\alpha, p)$ is specified in Definition 8.18.

Let J_1 denote the set of paths with remaining slack equal to zero, and then for $k \geq 2$ let J_k contain all paths that would have remaining smallest slack if the paths in $J_1, \ldots, J_{k-1}$ were not present. Then clearly, $rslack(J_i) \leq \cdots \leq rslack(J_{i+1})$, for $i \geq 1$. Then, we define g such that $rslack(J_g) < D(p) - D(r) \leq rslack(J_{g+1})$ if $D(p) > D(r)$, and $g = 0$ otherwise. For $k = 1, \ldots, g$, let F^k represent the marginal contribution of the paths in $J_1, \ldots, J_k$ to the total expedition or reward. Thus,

$$
F^k = \begin{cases} R(rslack(J_{k+1})) - R(rslack(J_k)), & \text{if } 1 \leq k < g \\ R(D(p) - D(r)) - R(rslack(J_g)), & \text{if } k = g. \end{cases} \tag{8.52}
$$

Observe that $\sum_{k=1}^{g} F^k = R(D(p) - D(r))$.

Two further definitions are necessary. We define z_i^α as the maximum amount that activity i can claim according to the reward sharing mechanism if its path N_α is rewarded with the total expedition that it can bring to the project. Then, we define the *vector of maximal rewards*, f^z, by $f_i^z = \max_{\alpha | N_\alpha \ni i} \{z_i^\alpha\}, i \in A$, as the maximum reward that activity i can claim from the expedition of the project when the sharing mechanism z is used. Intuitively, this definition is optimistic, since each activity receives the full reward that is attributable to it. The characteristic function of the game (A, v_z) is then defined as

$$
v_z(S) = \sum_{k=1}^{g} \left(F^k - w_z^k(S) \right), \tag{8.53}
$$

where $w_z^k(S) \geq 0$ represents the part of the contribution to the total reward F^k that players in S maximally would have to give to players in the paths corresponding to $\cup_{l=1}^{k} J_l$ outside S, taking into account rewards previously given, and $v_z(A)$ equals the total expedition of the project. More formally,

$$
w_z^k(S) = \min \left\{ \sum_{i \in (\cup_{l=1}^{k} N_{j_l}) \setminus S} f_i^z - \sum_{l=1}^{k-1} w_z^l(S), \ F^k \right\}, \tag{8.54}
$$

for $k \in \{1, \ldots, g\}$, where $N_{j_l} = \cup_{\alpha \in J_l} N_\alpha$.

518   8 Cooperative Supply Chain Scheduling

For the reward game, Estévez-Fernández et al. (2007) and Estévez-Fernández (2012) prove the following result.

Theorem 8.37 *Let* $(\{N_1, \ldots, N_m\}, p, r, a, R)$ *be a project problem, and let z be a surplus sharing mechanism. Then, the project execution reward game (A, v_z) is convex.*

We refer the reader to Estévez-Fernández (2012) for a proof.

As a result of Theorem 8.37, the reward game is balanced from Bondareva (1963) and Shapley (1967).

Theorems 8.36 and 8.37 are now used to establish the following unifying result. Recall that $\mathscr{D}$ denotes the set of delayed activities, and $\mathscr{E}$ the set of expedited activities.

Theorem 8.38 *Project execution games have a nonempty core.*

Proof Let $(\{N_1, \ldots, N_m\}, p, r, a, R)$ be a project problem. Let y be a cost sharing mechanism and z be a reward sharing mechanism, and let (N, u_{yz}) as defined in (8.50) be the associated project execution game. We consider these two games separately.

For project execution cost games where $D(p) \leq D(r)$, then $D(p) \leq D(r) \leq D(p_{|\mathscr{E}\backslash S}, r_{|N\backslash(\mathscr{E}\backslash S)})$ for $S \subset N$, and $u_{yz}(S) = -c_y(S)$ for $S \subset N$. Then, from Theorem 8.36, (N, u_{yz}) has a nonempty core.

For project execution reward games where $D(p) > D(r)$, then $u_{yz}(N) = v_z(N)$ and $u_{yz}(S) \leq v_z(S)$ for $S \subset N$. From Theorem 8.37, the game (N, v_z) is convex and therefore has a nonempty core. Let x be in the core of (N, v_z), then $\sum_{i \in N} x_i = v_z(N) = u_{yz}(N)$ and $\sum_{i \in S} x_i \geq v_z(S) \geq u_{yz}(S)$ for $S \subset N$. Therefore, x is in the core of the game (N, u_{yz}). $\square$

We provide an example of the cost and reward allocation rules developed above.

Example 8.29 (Allocation of Costs and Rewards in a Project Execution Game) Consider a project problem with three activities $N = \{A, B, C\}$, where both activities A and B are predecessors of C. There are two paths, which we designate as $N_1 = (A, C)$ and $N_2 = (B, C)$. The planned activity times are $p(A) = 15, p(B) = 10$ and $p(C) = 8$. The realized activity times are $r(A) = 7, r(B) = 8$ and $r(C) = 12$. The available times of the activities, i.e., the times at which their predecessors have all completed processing, are 0 for activities A and B, and 7 for activity C. The project cost and reward function is

$$R(t) = \begin{cases} t^3 - 100, & \text{if } t < 0 \\ 0, & \text{if } t = 0 \\ t^3 + 200, & \text{if } t > 0. \end{cases}$$

Now, activity A achieves an expedition of $15 - 7 = 8$ units, but since activity B finishes at time 8, one unit of this expedition is wasted from the perspective of minimizing project completion time. Thus, activity C starts at time 8 and finishes at

8.5 Project Games

Table 8.12 Project execution game in Example 8.29

S	$\{A\}$	$\{B\}$	$\{C\}$	$\{A, B\}$	$\{A, C\}$	$\{B, C\}$	$\{A, B, C\}$
Makespan	$10 + 12 = 22$	$15 + 12 = 27$	$15 + 12 = 27$	$8 + 12 = 20$	$10 + 12 = 22$	$15 + 12 = 27$	$8 + 12 = 20$
$-c_y(S)$	0	0	-164	0	0	-164	0
$v_z(S)$	201	0	0	227	201	0	227
$u_{yz}(S)$	201	0	-164	227	201	-164	227

time 20. Then $D(p) - D(r) = 23 - 20 = 3 = t$, and a reward of $R(3) = 227$ is available for allocation.

Now, from (8.52), we have $F^1 = R(1) - R(0) = 201$ and $F^2 = R(3) - R(1) = 227 - 201 = 26$. The coalition values of the game are shown in Table 8.12.

In Table 8.12, the makespan for a coalition S is computed using the planned times for activities in $\mathscr{E} \setminus S$ and realized activity times for all other activities, i.e., $D(p_{|\mathscr{E} \setminus S}, r_{|N \setminus (\mathscr{E} \setminus S)})$. The core of this game is the convex hull of the vectors $(391, 0, -164)$, $(365, 26, -164)$, $(201, 26, 0)$ and $(227, 0, 0)$.

The above discussion focuses on the identification of single-player reward and cost allocations. However, in some practical situations, the project manager cannot reasonably expect delayed activities to compensate other activities. In such situations, a set-valued allocation that we now propose may be easier to implement. It uses the analysis of single-player solutions above, and the following principles:

(i) If the project is exactly on time, then no payments are made or received.
(ii) If the project is delayed, then there should be a solution in which the delayed activities pay exactly the total cost associated with the total delay, i.e., the expedited activities are not compensated.
(iii) If the project is expedited, then there should be a solution in which expedited activities get exactly the total reward associated with their total expedition, i.e., the delayed activities do not need to compensate the expedited activities.

This discussion leads to the following result.

Theorem 8.39 *Let* $(\{N_1, \ldots, N_m\}, p, r, R)$ *denote a project problem. Let* (N, u_{yz}), *as defined in (8.50), be the associated project execution game.*

(i) *If the project is delayed, then there exists a core solution* x *to the game* (N, u_{yz}) *such that* $x_i = 0$ *for* $i \in N \setminus \mathscr{D}$.
(ii) *If the project is exactly on time, then* $x = 0$ *is a core solution to the game* (N, u_{yz}).
(iii) *If the project is expedited, then there exists a core solution* x *to the game* (N, u_{yz}) *such that* $x_i = 0$ *for* $i \in N \setminus \mathscr{E}$.

Proof

(i) If $D(p) < D(r)$, then $D(p) < D(r) \leq D(p_{|\mathscr{E} \setminus S}, r_{|N \setminus (\mathscr{E} \setminus S)})$ for $S \subset N$, and $u_{yz}(S) = -c_y(S)$ for $S \subset N$. Let $\hat{\alpha} \in \{1, \ldots, m\}$ be such that $D(r) =$

$D(N_{\hat{a}}, r)$, i.e., the path $N_{\hat{a}}$ is responsible for the total delay of the project. Consider a taxation game $(N, E^{\hat{a}}, C^{\hat{a}})$ where $E^{\hat{a}} = K(\sum_{i \in N_{\hat{a}}} (d(i) - e(i)) - slack(N_{\hat{a}}, p))$ is the amount of tax that must be collected, $K(\cdot)$ is a penalty function for late project completion, and the ability of the players to pay is given by $c_i^{\hat{a}} = y_i^{\hat{a}}$ if $i \in N_{\hat{a}}$ and $c_i^{\hat{a}} = 0$ if $i \in N \setminus N_{\hat{a}}$. From the proof of Theorem 8.38, the core of the taxation game is a subset of the core of the project execution cost game. Since any x in the core of the taxation problem satisfies $0 \le x \le c^{\hat{a}}$, we have $x_i = 0$ for $i \in N \setminus \mathcal{D}$.

(ii) If $D(p) = D(r)$, then $D(p) = D(r) \le D(p_{|\mathcal{E}\setminus S}, r_{|N\setminus(\mathcal{E}\setminus S)})$ for $S \subset N$, and therefore $u_{yz}(S) = -c_y(S) \le 0$, for $S \subset N$. Also, $u_{yz}(N) = 0$ and hence $x = 0$ is a core solution.

(iii) If $D(p) > D(r)$, then $u_{yz}(N) = v_z(N)$ and $u_{yz}(S) \le v_z(S)$, for $S \subset N$. Then, the core of the game (N, v_z) is a subset of the core of the game (N, u_{yz}). Since $f_i^z = 0$ for $i \in N \setminus \mathcal{E}$, it follows that $v_z(S \cup \{i\}) = v_z(S)$ for $i \in N \setminus \mathcal{E}$, and therefore $x_i = 0$ for every x in the core of the game (N, v_z) and $i \in N \setminus \mathcal{E}$.

$\square$

The results in Theorem 8.39 improve the implementability of the allocation rules described in the above analysis.

Remark 8.11 An alternative approach to the analysis of project performance is provided by Castro et al. (2007). That work proposes desirable properties of separability, non-manipulability by splitting, and independent slack. Since there are some features of the allocations achieved by this analysis that are not consistent with the model of Estévez-Fernández (2012), but which nonetheless provide a valuable alternative perspective, we refer the reader to that work.

8.6 Capacity Allocation Games

This section demonstrates the synergistic use of optimization and cooperative game methodologies within a supply chain scheduling context. Hall and Liu (2010) consider a supply chain that includes a manufacturer, several distributors, and customers. The optimization problems faced by the manufacturer and the distributors are described in Sect. 8.6.1. Initially, the supply chain is considered as uncoordinated, and discussed in Sect. 8.6.2. Following the placement of orders by the distributors, the manufacturer may determine that its capacity is insufficient to meet all those orders. In this case, the manufacturer's *capacity allocation problem* determines how much capacity to allocate to each distributor. Following this distribution, the distributors can resubmit their orders under this new constraint. However, there is the possibility to improve their overall profitability by submitting their orders together; this problem forms a cooperative *distributors' game*. Finally, it is also possible for the manufacturer and the distributors to coordinate their

8.6.1 Supply Chain Scheduling Problems

Let $M = \{1, \ldots, m\}$ denote the m products produced by the manufacturer, and $N = \{1, \ldots, n\}$ denote the n distributors. Let $q = mn$. We assume that only a single order can be processed at any time by the manufacturer, hence capacity and production time are equivalent measures. Let $T > 0$ denote the manufacturer's available production capacity. An order from distributor j for one or more units of product i is denoted by v_{ij}. Let p_{ij} denote the capacity required by order v_{ij}. We allow the allocation of fractional units of capacity. Let $P_j = \sum_{i \in M} p_{ij}$, and $P_{\max} = \max_{j \in N}\{P_j\}$.

We allow orders to be filled either fractionally, or only entirely, by the manufacturer. The manufacturer allocates capacity y_{ij} to order v_{ij}. If partial orders are allowed, then $0 \leq y_{ij} \leq p_{ij}$; otherwise, $y_{ij} \in \{0, p_{ij}\}$. Each order consists of a single product, and we assume that the entire order quantity is delivered at the same time, which reduces transportation and stocking costs. Therefore, we only consider schedules where no preemption is allowed in the processing of the orders. However, different orders from the same distributor may be delivered by the manufacturer at different times. Suppose each order v_{ij} generates a revenue u_{ij} for the manufacturer and a profit v_{ij} for distributor j. Then, the revenue per unit of capacity from order v_{ij} is $\bar{u}_{ij} = u_{ij}/p_{ij}$ for the manufacturer, and the profit per unit of capacity is $\bar{v}_{ij} = v_{ij}/p_{ij}$ for distributor j. This model allows *lot splitting* (Trietsch & Baker, 1993). In practice, combined orders are often split for delivery purposes in order to improve customer service, especially for time-sensitive products (Chen, 2010).

Given a schedule σ of orders, let $C_{ij}(\sigma)$ denote the completion time of each order v_{ij}. Let S denote the set of orders scheduled. The manufacturer maximizes its total profit, which is its revenue from the orders processed less its scheduling cost. The scheduling cost is the total weighted completion time, $\sum_{v_{ij} \in S} w_{ij} C_{ij}(\sigma)$, where w_{ij} represents either a holding cost per unit time or the value already added to order v_{ij}. This is a widely used measure of work-in-process inventory cost in manufacturing systems (Pinedo, 2016). We assume that the cost of a partially filled order is proportional to its capacity requirement. Thus, for a partially filled order with processing time $y_{ij} < p_{ij}$, the weight of the order is $w_{ij} y_{ij}/p_{ij}$.

Each distributor $j \in N$ is allocated capacity $X_j \leq P_j$ by the manufacturer. Let $\overline{X} = \sum_{j \in N} X_j \leq T$. Each order v_{ij} is given a maximum resubmittable size $\hat{p}_{ij} \leq p_{ij}$ by the manufacturer. Let $\hat{P}_j = \sum_{i \in M} \hat{p}_{ij}$, and $\hat{P}_{\max} = \max_j\{\hat{P}_j\}$. Let $\hat{v}_{ij} = \hat{p}_{ij} v_{ij}/p_{ij}$ be the profit of order v_{ij} with size $\hat{p}_{ij}$. Let V denote the maximum profit of the grand coalition.

8.6.2 Uncoordinated Supply Chain

In this section, we consider a manufacturer which has received orders that it cannot meet in full. In Sect. 8.6.2.1, we study the manufacturer's initial capacity allocation problem. In Sect. 8.6.2.2, we study the manufacturer's problem of scheduling the distributors' revised orders. The distributors' problem of resubmitting orders is then studied, with partial orders allowed in Sect. 8.6.2.3, and with only full orders allowed in Sect. 8.6.2.4.

8.6.2.1 Manufacturer: Capacity Allocation

We consider the manufacturer's problems of scheduling initial orders and also of scheduling revised orders submitted by the distributors. We first introduce two simple and widely used rules for capacity allocation, *Proportional Allocation* (PA) and *Linear Allocation* (LA), respectively (Cachon & Lariviere, 1999; Laffont, 1988; Lee et al., 1997). The PA rule allocates capacity to each distributor proportionately to its capacity requirement:

$$X_j = \min\{P_j, P_j T / \sum_{k \in N} P_k\}.$$

The LA rule awards each distributor j its capacity requirement minus the common deduction that satisfies the capacity constraint, or 0 if this difference is negative. If we index the distributors by nonincreasing capacity requirements, i.e., $P_1 \geq \cdots \geq P_n$, then:

$$X_j = \begin{cases} P_j - \frac{1}{\tilde{n}} \max\{0, \sum_{k=1}^{\tilde{n}} P_k - T\}, & \text{if } j \leq \tilde{n}, \\ 0, & \text{otherwise,} \end{cases}$$

where $\tilde{n}$ is the largest integer no greater than n such that $P_{\tilde{n}} - \max\{0, \sum_{j=1}^{\tilde{n}} P_j - T\}/\tilde{n} \geq 0$.

These allocation rules are *equitable* between the distributors, in that the capacity allocation is nondecreasing in the capacity requirement. However, both the PA and LA rules are based solely on order requirements. Since they do not consider revenue or scheduling cost, the resulting capacity allocations may generate small revenues and large costs for the manufacturer. To resolve this problem, we propose the following algorithm, which integrates both equity considerations and scheduling information into the capacity allocation decisions. Let $r > 0$ denote a measure of the bargaining power of the distributors, relative to that of the manufacturer. Following presentation of the algorithm, further details of the steps are discussed below.

8.6 Capacity Allocation Games

Proportional Allocation Algorithm (PAAr)

1. Given u_{ij}, p_{ij}, w_{ij}, T and r.
2. The manufacturer finds a schedule that maximizes its total net profit, subject to the capacity constraint. Suppose in this schedule each order v_{ij} is processed at size p'_{ij}.
3. The manufacturer allocates capacity $X_j = \min\{P_j, P_j T / \sum_{k \in N} P_k\}$ to distributor j, for $j = 1, \ldots, n$.
4. The manufacturer allocates a set of resubmittable orders with total capacity requirement $\hat{P}_j \geq r X_j$ to distributor j, for $j = 1, \ldots, n$. Allocate all the orders that appear in the manufacturer's optimal schedule in Step 2, each with a maximum resubmittable size $\hat{p}_{ij} = p'_{ij}$. If the total resubmittable size of those orders is less than $r X_j$, then allocate other orders in nonincreasing order of revenue per unit of capacity, until $\hat{P}_j \geq r X_j$, where the maximum resubmittable size $\hat{p}_{ij}$ is equal to p_{ij} for each of those allocated orders except for the last one, and is equal to the minimum feasible value satisfying $\hat{P}_j \geq r X_j$ for the last allocated order.

It is important to note that, although the capacity of the resubmittable orders can exceed the allocated capacity X_j by a ratio r, the total capacity requirement of the resubmitted orders cannot exceed X_j. Hence, all the revised orders can be feasibly scheduled.

The set of resubmittable orders is selected without knowing the distributors' profits. A larger r value provides the distributors greater flexibility in revising their orders, hence the manufacturer has less assurance of achieving a high profit level from the resubmitted orders. If r is not large, then the manufacturer, in Step 4 of PAAr, excludes from the set of resubmittable orders those which are less profitable. In practice, either the distributors (Bish et al., 2005) or the manufacturer (Engels et al., 2003) may have dominant bargaining power. Carr and Duenyas (2000) provide an example of the latter case, where a major glass manufacturer allocates capacity on the basis of each individual order. Our definition of r parametrizes the situations in between these two extreme cases.

We now study the manufacturer's scheduling problem with partial orders in Step 2 of PAAr. The first result characterizes the sequence of orders in an optimal schedule for the manufacturer.

Lemma 8.11 *For the manufacturer's scheduling problem with partial orders, an optimal schedule processes complete or partial orders in SWPT sequence.*

Proof Given a set of complete and partial orders to be processed, the total revenue of those orders is independent of their processing sequence. Thus, the maximum total profit from those orders is found by a schedule that minimizes the total weighted completion time. The result then follows from Smith (1956). □

In view of Lemma 8.11, we assume for the remainder of this section that the orders are reindexed in SWPT sequence, i.e., $p_1/w_1 \leq \cdots \leq p_q/w_q$.

524   8 Cooperative Supply Chain Scheduling

The manufacturer's scheduling problem, which we denote by QP, can be formulated as:

$$\max \quad \sum_{j=1}^{q} \overline{u}_j y_j - \sum_{j=1}^{q} [w_j y_j (\sum_{k=1}^{j} y_k)/p_j] \qquad (8.55)$$

$$\text{s.t.} \quad \sum_{j=1}^{q} y_j \leq T \qquad (8.56)$$

$$0 \leq y_j \quad \leq \quad p_j, \qquad j = 1, \ldots, q. \qquad (8.57)$$

The objective function (8.55) maximizes the net profit of the manufacturer. Constraint (8.56) ensures that the total capacity requirement of the scheduled orders does not exceed the total available capacity. Constraints (8.57) ensure that each scheduled order is no larger than the corresponding order placed by the distributor. Let L denote the length of a binary encoding of the data for problem QP.

Theorem 8.40 *Problem QP can be solved optimally in $O(m^3 n^3 L)$ time.*

Proof The optimality of the SWPT indexing of the variables in problem QP follows from Lemma 8.11. Observe that the objective function of problem QP is a quadratic function of the form $uy - y^T Q y$, where the matrix Q is positive semidefinite and y^T denotes the transpose of the vector y. It follows that the objective function is concave. The result then follows from Goldfarb and Liu (1993). $\qquad \square$

When partial orders are not allowed, we propose the following procedure to solve the manufacturer's scheduling problem in Step 1 of PAAr.

Procedure Man

Input
    $p_j, \overline{u}_j, w_j$, for $j = 1, \ldots, q$, where $p_1/w_1 \leq \cdots \leq p_q/w_q$; T.

Value Function
    $F(j, t)$ = the maximum profit from orders $1, \ldots, j$ achieved by a partial schedule that completes at time t.

Boundary Condition
$$F(0, t) = \begin{cases} 0, & \text{if } t = 0 \\ -\infty, & \text{otherwise.} \end{cases}$$

Recurrence Relation
$$F(j, t) = \max_{y_j \in \{0, p_j\}} \{\overline{u}_j y_j - w_j t y_j / p_j + F(j - 1, t - y_j)\}.$$

Optimal Solution Value
$$\max_{t \in \{0, \ldots, T\}} \{F(q, t)\}.$$

8.6 Capacity Allocation Games

In the recurrence relation, y_j can only take on a value of p_j if order j is processed, or 0 if not. In the former case, a profit of $\bar{u}_j y_j$ is earned, a scheduling cost of $w_j t y_j / p_j$ is incurred, and state variables $j - 1$ and $t - y_j$ are updated to j and t, respectively.

Theorem 8.41 *For the manufacturer's scheduling problem without partial orders, Procedure Man finds a schedule with maximum total profit in $O(mnT)$ time.*

Proof The optimality of Procedure Man follows from Lemma 8.11. In the value function, there are $O(mn)$ possible values of j, and $O(T)$ possible values of t. In the recurrence relation, the maximum profit values resulting from the two possible choices for y_j are compared. Therefore, the overall time complexity of Procedure Man is $O(mnT)$. □

Remark 8.12 When partial orders are not allowed, the manufacturer's scheduling problem is binary *NP*-hard, even without the capacity constraint (Engels et al., 2003).

8.6.2.2 Manufacturer: Scheduling Revised Orders

We now consider the manufacturer's problem of scheduling the distributors' revised orders. Observe from Step 3 of Algorithm PAA*r* that the total capacity requirement of the revised orders of distributor j must not exceed its allocated capacity, X_j. Hence, a feasible schedule is guaranteed and all the revised orders are fully processed. The total revenue is fixed by the manufacturer's requirement to schedule revised orders within the allocated capacity and the set of resubmittable orders. Therefore, maximizing profit is equivalent to minimizing total weighted completion time. We have the following result.

Corollary 8.2 *The manufacturer's problem of scheduling the revised orders to maximize the total profit can be solved in $O(mn \log mn)$ time.*

Proof Since all the revised orders are scheduled, revenue is fixed. Therefore, the SWPT sequence minimizes the scheduling cost and maximizes the total profit (Smith, 1956). □

8.6.2.3 Distributors: Resubmitting Partial Orders

We describe the distributors' problem of resubmitting orders in response to resource allocations from manufacturers, using cooperative game theory. We consider two versions of this problem, depending on whether partial orders are allowed.

First, we consider the situation where the distributors can resubmit partial orders. The capacity sharing and order revision problem of each distributor or coalition of distributors can be modeled as a linear program (LP). If a coalition contains a set N' of distributors each having allocated capacity X_j, then this problem is:

$$\max \quad \sum_{i \in M} \sum_{j \in N'} \overline{v}_{ij} x_{ij} \tag{8.58}$$

$$\text{s.t.} \quad \sum_{i \in M} \sum_{j \in N'} x_{ij} \leq \sum_{j \in N'} X_j \tag{8.59}$$

$$0 \leq x_{ij} \leq \hat{p}_{ij}, \quad i \in M, \ j \in N'. \tag{8.60}$$

The objective function (8.58) maximizes the total profit of the coalition, where $\overline{v}_{ij}$ is the profit per unit of manufacturing capacity from order v_{ij} for distributor j. Constraint (8.59) ensures that the total capacity requirement of the revised orders does not exceed the total allocated capacity. Constraints (8.60) ensure that each revised order is no larger than the corresponding resubmittable size, $\hat{p}_{ij}$. The constraints in problem (8.58)–(8.60) include only a single constraint (8.59) with integer coefficients all equal to 1, and simple integer upper bound constraints (8.60). Therefore, the LP has an optimal integer solution.

The distributors' capacity allocation problem is a *linear programming game* (Owen, 1975). In any LP game, some core members (the *Owen set*) can be found by solving the dual problem of the grand coalition's LP. In the distributors' game, there are $mn + 1$ constraints in the LP model of the grand coalition. Letting γ_{ij}, for $i \in M, \ j \in N$, and γ be the $mn + 1$ dual variables, the dual problem is:

$$\min \quad \sum_{i \in M, j \in N} \hat{p}_{ij} \gamma_{ij} + \gamma \sum_{j \in N} X_j \tag{8.61}$$

$$\text{s.t.} \quad \gamma_{ij} + \gamma \geq \overline{v}_{ij}, \quad i \in M, \ j \in N \tag{8.62}$$

$$\gamma_{ij}, \gamma \geq 0, \quad i \in M, \ j \in N. \tag{8.63}$$

The following algorithm finds a core member of the distributors' LP game efficiently.

Algorithm LPCore

Input
$\hat{p}_{ij}, \overline{v}_{ij}$, for $i \in M, \ j \in N$; X_j for $j \in N$.

Step 1. Find $\overline{v} = \min\{\overline{v}_{ij} : i \in M, j \in N, \sum_{k \in M, \ l \in N, \ \overline{v}_{kl} > \overline{v}_{ij}} \hat{p}_{kl} \leq \sum_{j \in N} X_j\}$.
Step 2. Let $\gamma = \overline{v}$, and $\gamma_{ij} = \max\{\overline{v}_{ij} - \overline{v}, 0\}$, for $i \in M, \ j \in N$. Let the payoff division $(\chi_1, \ldots, \chi_n)$ be:

$$\chi_j = \sum_{i \in M} \hat{p}_{ij} \gamma_{ij} + X_j \gamma, \quad j \in N. \tag{8.64}$$

Theorem 8.42 *Algorithm LPCore finds a core member of the distributors' LP game in $O(mn)$ time.*

8.6 Capacity Allocation Games

Proof From constraints (8.62) and (8.63), the objective function (8.61) is minimized by setting $\gamma_{ij} = \max\{\bar{v}_{ij} - \gamma, 0\}$. Therefore, in (8.61), if γ increases by 1, then $\sum_{i \in M, j \in N} \hat{p}_{ij} \gamma_{ij}$ decreases by $\sum_{i \in M, j \in N, \bar{v}_{ij} > \gamma} \hat{p}_{ij}$, and $\gamma \sum_{j \in N} X_j$ increases by $\sum_{j \in N} X_j$. Consequently, from the definition of $\bar{v}$, Step 2 of Algorithm LPCore finds an optimal solution. The core membership of the payoff vector defined by (8.64) follows from Owen (1975). The time complexity follows from the median finding algorithm of Schönhage et al. (1976). $\qquad\square$

The following example shows that the Owen set does not fully cover the core of the distributors' LP game.

Example 8.30 (Core of the Distributor's Game and Owen Set) Two distributors 1 and 2 order a single product, with profits 2 and 3 per unit of capacity used, and capacity requirements of their orders 20 and 10, respectively. Previously, the manufacturer has allocated capacity 18 and 9 to distributors 1 and 2, respectively, without restricting the resubmittable orders. Without coordination, distributors 1 and 2 obtain a profit of $2(18) = 36$ and $3(9) = 27$, respectively. If the two distributors form a coalition, then their LP game is:

$$\max 2x_1 + 3x_2$$

$$\text{s.t.} \quad \begin{aligned} x_1 &\leq 20 \\ x_2 &\leq 10 \\ x_1 + x_2 &\leq 18 + 9 = 27, \end{aligned}$$

where an optimal solution is $x_1 = 17$ and $x_2 = 10$, with solution value 64. Letting γ_1, γ_2 and γ denote the three dual variables, the dual of this game is:

$$\min 20\gamma_1 + 10\gamma_2 + 27\gamma$$

$$\text{s.t.} \quad \begin{aligned} \gamma_1 + \gamma &\geq 2 \\ \gamma_2 + \gamma &\geq 3 \\ \gamma_1, \gamma_2, \gamma &\geq 0, \end{aligned}$$

where the unique optimal solution is $\gamma_1 = 0$, $\gamma_2 = 1$ and $\gamma = 2$. Thus, the unique fair payoff division in the Owen set is $(36, 28)$. However, any payoff division $(36 + a, 28 - a)$, where $0 \leq a \leq 1$, is in the core.

Core solutions that are not in the Owen set may be more reasonable than those that are. In Example 8.30, the payoff division $(36, 28)$ derived from the unique Owen set solution seems to favor distributor 2, which receives all the extra payoff from cooperation. Hence, it is likely that distributor 1 will propose a different payoff division. In order to evaluate whether this payoff division is in the core, we need to answer the *core membership test*: given an instance of the distributors' game and a payoff vector, is that vector in the core of the instance? In a general LP game, the core membership test is unary co-*NP*-complete (Fang et al., 2002).

However, in our distributors' game, the Owen set is a proper subset of the core, while the core membership test, although binary co-*NP*-complete, is solvable in pseudo-polynomial time.

We propose a dynamic programming algorithm for the core membership test in the distributors' LP game. For any given payoff vector $(\chi_1, \ldots, \chi_n)$ and coalition $N' \subset N$, let the *surplus profit* of N' be defined as the difference between the maximum profit generated by N' and the total payoff paid to N'. We use $F(j, t)$ to denote the maximum surplus profit of a potentially defecting coalition from distributors $\{1, \ldots, j\}$, given that those distributors have a total allocated capacity t. We assume without loss of generality that the payoff vector $(\chi_1, \ldots, \chi_n)$ is efficient, i.e., $\sum_{j \in N} \chi_j$ equals the total profit of the grand coalition; otherwise, the payoff vector is not in the core.

Algorithm LPCoreTest

Input
    $\hat{p}_{ij}, \overline{v}_{ij}$, for $i \in M$, $j \in N$; X_j, for $j \in N$; $\overline{X}$; and an efficient payoff vector $(\chi_1, \ldots, \chi_n)$.

Initialization
    For each distributor j, find the maximum profit $\phi(j, t)$ that can be generated using capacity t, for $t = 0, \ldots, \min\{\hat{P}_j, \overline{X}\}$, where $\hat{P}_j = \sum_{i \in M} \hat{p}_{ij}$.

Value Function
    $F(j, t) =$ the maximum surplus profit of any coalition formed by distributors from $1, \ldots, j$, for the given payoff vector $(\chi_1, \ldots, \chi_j)$, where distributors $1, \ldots, j$ have a total allocated capacity t.

Boundary Condition
    $F(0, t) = 0$, where $t \geq 0$.

Recurrence Relation
$$F(j, t) = \max \begin{cases} F(j-1, t - X_j) \\ \displaystyle\max_{x_j \in \{0, \ldots, \min\{t, \hat{P}_j\}\}} \{\phi(j, x_j) - \chi_j + F(j-1, t - x_j)\}. \end{cases}$$

Optimal Solution Value
    $F(n, \overline{X})$.

Core Membership Test
    The payoff vector $(\chi_1, \ldots, \chi_n)$ is a core member if and only if $F(n, \overline{X}) = 0$.

In the recurrence relation, the first equation excludes distributor j from the coalition being built. The second equation includes distributor j in the coalition and allocates capacity x_j to it, where the value of x_j is chosen to maximize the surplus profit. Recall that $\hat{P}_{\max} = \max_{j \in N} \{\hat{P}_j\}$.

8.6 Capacity Allocation Games   529

Theorem 8.43 *For a given instance of the distributors' LP game, Algorithm LPCoreTest determines whether a given payoff vector is in the core in $O(n \max\{m, \overline{X}\} \min\{\overline{X}, \hat{P}_{\max}\})$ time.*

Proof Observe that the surplus profit of any coalition of the distributors is defined as the difference between the optimal solution of the coalition's optimization problem (8.58)–(8.60) and the total payoff to the coalition given by the payoff vector χ. Since this difference is independent of the sequence of the distributors, it is sufficient to consider a single arbitrary sequence. It follows that the surplus profits of all possible state transitions are compared, and hence Algorithm LPCoreTest generates the maximum surplus profit. Therefore, a finding that $F(n, \overline{X}) > 0$ implies the identification of a subset of distributors that will leave the coalition. Alternatively, a finding that $F(n, \overline{X}) = 0$ implies that no such coalition exists, and therefore the payoff vector $(\chi_1, \ldots, \chi_n)$ is a core member. In the recurrence relation, there are $O(n)$ possible values of j, and $O(\overline{X})$ possible values of t. For each j and t, there are $O(\min\{\overline{X}, \hat{P}_{\max}\})$ values of x_j to enumerate. Therefore, the overall time complexity of Algorithm LPCoreTest is $O(n \max\{m, \overline{X}\} \min\{\overline{X}, \hat{P}_{\max}\})$. $\square$

Theorem 8.43 shows Algorithm LPCoreTest is a pseudo-polynomial time algorithm. However, the next result shows that this problem cannot be solved efficiently.

Theorem 8.44 *The core membership problem in the distributors' LP game is binary co-NP-complete, even for a single product.*

Proof Given a payoff vector and a coalition, it can be verified in polynomial time that the payoff vector is not in the core. Therefore, the core membership test belongs to the class co-NP. The co-NP-completeness proof is by reduction from the following problem.

Partition (Garey & Johnson, 1979, p. 223) Given $2t$ elements with integer sizes $a_1, \ldots, a_{2t}$, where $\sum_{j=1}^{2t} a_j = 2A$, does there exist a partition S_1 and S_2 of the index set $\{1, \ldots, 2t\}$ such that $\sum_{j \in S_1} a_j = \sum_{j \in S_2} a_j = A$? Without loss of generality, we assume that $A \geq 3$.

Given an instance of Partition, we construct an instance of the distributors' LP game, where $m = 1$ and $n = 2t + 2$. This instance is shown in Table 8.13, where for each distributor j, $\overline{v}_j$ is the profit of its order per unit of capacity requirement, $\hat{p}_j$ is the capacity requirement of its resubmittable order, X_j is the capacity allocated by the manufacturer, and χ_j is the payoff received. Let $\varepsilon > 0$ be defined sufficiently small that $\varepsilon(2A^2 - A - 2) < 1$.

First, note that $\sum_{j=1}^{2t+2} X_j = (2A - 1) \sum_{j=1}^{2t} a_j - 2 = (2A - 1)2A - 2 < (2A-1)2A = \hat{p}_{2t+1} + \hat{p}_{2t+2}$. Also, $\overline{v}_{2t+1} = \overline{v}_{2t+2} = 2A + 1$ is the maximum profit per unit of production capacity. Therefore, the grand coalition generates a profit of $(2A+1) \sum_{j=1}^{2t+2} X_j = (2A+1)[(2A-1)2A-2] = 8A^3 - 6A - 2$. Let Y denote this value of total profit. Also, the total payoff is $\sum_{j=1}^{2t+2} \chi_j = (4A - 2)a_1 - 4 + (4A - 2)a_2 + \cdots + (4A-2)a_{2t} + 2(4A^2 - 1)(A-1) = (4A-2)2A - 4 + 2(4A^2 - 1)(A-1) = 8A^3 - 6A - 2 = Y$. Hence, the payoff vector is feasible.

Table 8.13 Instance of the distributors' LP game in Theorem 8.44

j	1	2	$\ldots$	$2t$	$2t+1$	$2t+2$
$\overline{v}_j$	ε	ε	$\ldots$	ε	$2A+1$	$2A+1$
X_j	$(2A-1)a_1-2$	$(2A-1)a_2$	$\ldots$	$(2A-1)a_{2t}$	0	0
$\hat{p}_j$	$(2A-1)a_1$	$(2A-1)a_2$	$\ldots$	$(2A-1)a_{2t}$	$(2A-1)A$	$(2A-1)A$
χ_j	$(4A-2)a_1-4$	$(4A-2)a_2$	$\ldots$	$(4A-2)a_{2t}$	$(4A^2-1)(A-1)$	$(4A^2-1)(A-1)$

We now show that the given payoff vector $(\chi_1, \ldots, \chi_n)$ is not in the core if and only if the instance of Partition has a solution.

($\Rightarrow$) If the instance of Partition has a solution, then there exists at least one coalition N' with $\sum_{j \in N'} X_j = (2A-1)A$. Coalition N' includes exactly one of the two distributors $2t+1$ and $2t+2$, but does not include distributor 1. The total payoff received by coalition N' is $\sum_{j \in N'} \chi_j = (4A^2-1)(A-1) + 2\sum_{j \in N'} X_j = (4A^2-1)(A-1)+(2A-1)2A = (4A^2-1)A-(2A-1) < (4A^2-1)A = (2A+1)(2A-1)A$, which is the total profit generated by this coalition. Hence, the given payoff vector $(\chi_1, \ldots, \chi_n)$ is not in the core.

($\Leftarrow$) If the instance of Partition has no solution, we consider the only possible three types of coalition.

1. Coalitions not containing distributor $2t+1$ or $2t+2$. In this case, every coalition with total allocated capacity $\overline{X}$ has a profit of $\varepsilon \overline{X}$, which is less than the payoff $2\overline{X}$ received from the payoff vector.
2. Coalitions containing both distributors $2t+1$ and $2t+2$. In this case, for every coalition N', the profit generated is $Y - (2A+1)\sum_{j \notin N'} X_j \le Y - 2\sum_{j \notin N'} X_j = Y - \sum_{j \notin N'} \chi_j$, where the last term is the total payoff received from the payoff vector.
3. Coalitions containing exactly one of distributors $2t+1$ and $2t+2$. In this case, the profit generated by a coalition is no greater than that of a coalition containing all orders except for order $2t+2$: $\overline{v}_{2t+1}\hat{p}_{2t+1} + \varepsilon(\sum_{j=1}^{2t} X_j - \hat{p}_{2t+2}) = (2A+1)(2A-1)A + \varepsilon[(2A-1)A-2] = 4A^3 - A + \varepsilon(2A^2 - A - 2)$. Since the instance of Partition has no solution, the total capacity allocated to such a coalition cannot fall in the interval $((2A-1)(A-1), (2A-1)[(A+1)-2))$. If the total capacity is no greater than $(2A-1)(A-1)$, then the total profit generated is no greater than $(2A+1)(2A-1)(A-1) = (4A^2-1)(A-1)$, which is the payoff received by distributor $2t+1$ or $2t+2$ alone. Alternatively, if the total capacity is no less than $(2A-1)(A+1) - 2$, then the total payoff received is at least $(4A^2-1)(A-1) + 2[(2A-1)(A+1)-2] = 4A^3 + A - 5$. Since $A \ge 3$ and $\varepsilon(2A^2 - A - 2) < 1$, the difference between the total payoff received by the distributors and their total profit is $(4A^3+A-5)-[4A^3-A+\varepsilon(2A^2-A-2)] > (4A^3 + A - 5) - (4A^3 - A + 1) = 2A - 6 \ge 0$.

Therefore, in all cases, the total payoff received by any coalition is no less than the profit generated by the coalition. Hence, the given payoff vector is a core member. $\qquad\square$

8.6 Capacity Allocation Games

From Garey and Johnson (1979), the result in Theorem 8.44 implies that there does not exist a polynomial-time algorithm to find a core member of the distributor's LP game, unless $P = NP$.

8.6.2.4 Distributors: Resubmitting Full Orders

We now consider the situation where partial orders are not allowed. This problem is modeled as a knapsack game, defined by Eqs. (8.58)–(8.60) except that Eq. (8.60) is changed to $x_{ij} \in \{0, \hat{p}_{ij}\}$, for $i \in M$, $j \in N'$. Each coalition $N' \subseteq N$ faces a zero-one knapsack problem with knapsack size $\sum_{j \in N'} X_j$, where each item has a size $\hat{p}_{ij}$ and a value $\hat{v}_{ij}$.

We develop a dynamic programming algorithm that finds an integer core member if one exists. The algorithm uses the same definition of surplus profit as Algorithm LPCoreTest in Sect. 8.6.2.3.

Algorithm KPCore

Input
$\quad \hat{p}_{ij}, \hat{v}_{ij}$, for $i \in M$, $j \in N$; X_j, for $j \in N$; and $\overline{X}$.

Initialization
$\quad$ For each distributor j, find the maximum profit $\phi(j, t)$ which it can achieve using capacity t, for $t \in \{0, \ldots, \min\{\hat{P}_j, \overline{X}\}\}$. Find V, the maximum profit of the grand coalition, by solving the grand coalition's zero-one knapsack problem.

Value Function
$\quad F(j, t, \overline{\chi}) = $ the minimum value of the maximum surplus profit of any coalition formed by distributors $1, \ldots, j$, if those distributors have a total allocated capacity t and receive a total payoff $\overline{\chi}$.

Boundary Condition
$$F(1, t, \overline{\chi}) = \begin{cases} \phi(1, t) - \overline{\chi}, & \text{if } t < X_1, \text{ or } t \geq X_1 \text{ and } \phi(1, t) \geq \overline{\chi}, \text{ where } t, \overline{\chi} \geq 0 \\ 0, & \text{if } t \geq X_1 \text{ and } \phi(1, t) < \overline{\chi}, \text{ where } t, \overline{\chi} \geq 0. \end{cases}$$

Recurrence Relation
$$F(j, t, \overline{\chi}) = $$
$$\min_{\chi_j \in \{\phi(j, X_j), \ldots, \overline{\chi}\}} \max \begin{cases} F(j - 1, t - X_j, \overline{\chi} - \chi_j) \\ \max_{x_j \in \{0, \ldots, \min\{t, \hat{P}_j\}\}} \{\phi(j, x_j) - \chi_j + F(j - 1, t - x_j, \overline{\chi} - \chi_j)\}. \end{cases}$$

Optimal Solution Value
$\quad F(n, \overline{X}, V)$.

Core Emptiness Test
$\quad$ If $F(n, \overline{X}, V) > 0$, then the integer core is empty;
If $F(n, \overline{X}, V) = 0$, then the Optimal Solution Value identifies an integer core member.

In the boundary condition, when $t < X_1$, distributor 1's capacity is being used by other distributors. Hence, it must belong to a coalition containing other distributors. Otherwise, the value function takes the larger value achieved by whether or not distributor j joins a coalition. The recurrence relation first enumerates all possible values of the payoff χ_j to distributor j. Note that in any fair payoff division, each distributor j receives a payoff no less than its own profit $\phi(j, X_j)$. Then, for each fixed χ_j, the first equation excludes distributor j from the coalition. The second equation includes distributor j in the coalition and allocates capacity x_j to distributor j, where all possible values of x_j are considered.

Theorem 8.45 *Algorithm KPCore finds an integer core member of an instance of the knapsack game if it has a nonempty integer core, in $O(n\overline{X}\min\{\overline{X}, \hat{P}_{\max}\}V^2)$ time.*

Proof For fixed χ_j, in order for a coalition to achieve the maximum surplus profit, each distributor in the coalition must use capacity x_j to generate as much profit as possible. Since the surplus profit of the grand coalition is 0, $F(n, \overline{X}, V) \geq 0$. If $F(n, \overline{X}, V) > 0$, then Algorithm KPCore determines that the core of the instance is empty; otherwise $F(n, \overline{X}, V) = 0$, and retracing from the Optimal Solution Value identifies a core member.

In the Initialization step, V and the $\phi(j, t)$ values are found in $O(mn\overline{X})$ time. In the recurrence relation, there are $O(n)$ values of j, $O(\overline{X})$ values of t, and $O(V)$ values of $\overline{\chi}$. To find $F(j, t, \overline{\chi})$ for fixed j, t and $\overline{\chi}$ requires $O(V\min\{\overline{X}, \hat{P}_{\max}\})$ time. Therefore, the recurrence relation requires $O(n\overline{X}\min\{\overline{X}, \hat{P}_{\max}\}V^2)$ computation time, which is also the overall time complexity of Algorithm KPCore. $\quad\square$

Theorem 8.45 shows that finding a core member of the knapsack game, if one exists, can be performed in pseudo-polynomial time. The following result shows that the existence of a polynomial-time algorithm for this problem is unlikely. It also shows, by example, that the knapsack game is not balanced.

Theorem 8.46 *The problem of deciding whether an instance of the knapsack game has an integer core member in binary NP-hard, even for a single product.*

Proof By reduction from Partition, which is defined in the proof of Theorem 8.44. Given an arbitrary instance of Partition, we construct an instance of the knapsack game, where $m = 1$ and $n = 2t+1$. The detailed information is shown in Table 8.14, using the same notation as in Table 8.13. The last row of Table 8.14 contains an example payoff vector.

Table 8.14 Knapsack game of Theorem 8.46

j	1	2	$\ldots$	$2t$	$2t + 1$
$\bar{v}_j$	A	A	$\ldots$	A	$A - 1$
$\hat{p}_j$	$2A$	$2A$	$\ldots$	$2A$	A
X_j	a_1	a_2	$\ldots$	a_{2t}	A
χ_j	$a_1 A$	$a_2 A$	$\ldots$	$a_{2t} A$	$A(A - 1)$

8.6 Capacity Allocation Games

Next, we show that the knapsack game instance has an empty core if and only if the instance of Partition has a solution.

($\Rightarrow$) If the instance of Partition has a solution, then consider three coalitions 1, 2, and 3, where coalitions 1 and 2 are disjoint and each contains distributors from $\{1, \ldots, 2t\}$ with total capacity allocation A, and coalition 3 contains only distributor $2t + 1$. Any two of these three coalitions can jointly achieve a profit of $2A^2$. Let χ_1, χ_2, and χ_3 be the payoffs of coalitions 1, 2, and 3, respectively. Then any fair payoff division (χ_1, χ_2, χ_3) satisfies

$$\chi_1 + \chi_2 \geq 2A^2$$
$$\chi_1 + \chi_3 \geq 2A^2$$
$$\chi_2 + \chi_3 \geq 2A^2.$$

Hence, $\chi_1 + \chi_2 + \chi_3 \geq 3A^2$. However, the grand coalition can generate profit of at most $2A^2 + A(A - 1)$, which implies that $\chi_1 + \chi_2 + \chi_3 = 3A^2 - A$. Therefore, no fair payoff division exists and the instance of the knapsack game has an empty core.

($\Leftarrow$) If the instance of Partition has no solution, we show that the payoff vector in the last row of Table 8.14 is a core member. We consider the only possible two types of coalition.

1. Coalitions not containing distributor $2t + 1$. Here, if a coalition has allocated capacity $2A$, then it can generate a profit of at most $2A^2$. This profit is equal to the total payoff received. Otherwise, since any single order requires capacity $2A$ which exceeds the allocated capacity, the maximum profit is 0.

2. Coalitions containing distributor $2t + 1$. Here, no coalition has allocated capacity of exactly $2A$, otherwise a solution exists for the instance of Partition. First, the grand coalition has capacity $3A$, and a profit of $2A^2 + A(A - 1) = 3A^2 - A$. Since $A \sum_{j=1}^{2t} a_j + A(A - 1) = 3A^2 - A$, this profit is equal to the total payoff received. Second, for coalitions having capacity less than $2A$, since only distributor $2t + 1$'s order is feasible, the maximum profit is $A(A - 1)$. However, since this payoff is received by distributor $2t + 1$ alone, the total payoff received is at least $A(A - 1)$. Finally, for coalitions having capacity less than $3A$ but greater than $2A$, only one order requiring capacity $2A$ can be selected. This order generates a profit of $2A^2$. However, the total allocated capacity is at least $A + 1$, and the payoff received by distributor $2t + 1$ is $A(A - 1)$. Therefore, the total payoff received by the distributors from $1, \ldots, 2t$ is at least $(A + 1)A$, and the total payoff received is at least $(A + 1)A + (A - 1)A = 2A^2$.

Therefore in all cases, no coalition can generate more profit than the payoff received from the given payoff vector. It follows that the given payoff vector is in the core.

$\square$

For the knapsack game with integer inputs, the maximum profit generated by each coalition is also integer. However, there may exist a core member with fractional payoffs. Moreover, an instance may have only fractional core members.

534   8 Cooperative Supply Chain Scheduling

Table 8.15 Instance of the knapsack game with only fractional core members

j	1	2	3	4
$\hat{v}_j$	3	3	3	3
$\hat{p}_j$	2	2	2	2
X_j	1	1	1	1
χ_j	3/2	3/2	3/2	3/2
χ'_j	2	2	2	1

An example appears in Table 8.15, where each of the four distributors has a single order. Observe that $(\chi_1, \ldots, \chi_4)$ is a fair payoff division. In order to pay each coalition an integer payoff no less than its own profit, a payoff of at least 7 is required, as with $(\chi'_1, \ldots, \chi'_4)$ in the last row of Table 8.15. However, the grand coalition has a profit of 6. Therefore, no integer core member exists.

Our knapsack game results fundamentally affect the order revision decisions of the distributors in the uncoordinated supply chain. If an instance of the game has a core member, then the grand coalition of the distributors solves its knapsack problem. Otherwise, the grand coalition cannot generate enough payoff to cover every coalition's profit. In this case, it is not possible for subsets of the distributors to form coalitions that are stable (Grieco, 1988), as we now show. Suppose there are several mutually exclusive and exhaustive coalitions of distributors that are stable. This implies that each player in the coalitions receives a sufficient payoff that no players can form a new coalition, including players in other coalitions, that improves their total payoff. However, in this case, combining all the stable coalitions creates a grand coalition that is stable. This contradicts the assumption that there is no core member. It follows that, in an instance with an empty core, each distributor revises its orders individually.

8.6.3 Coordinated Supply Chain

In this section, we consider the capacity allocation and scheduling problem when the manufacturer and distributors coordinate their decisions to maximize the profit of the overall supply chain. In the coordinated supply chain, the manufacturer and distributors simultaneously agree on how much should be produced in order to maximize the profit of the supply chain. This coordination does not require information sharing among the distributors. Hall and Liu (2010) prove the following result.

Theorem 8.47 *An optimal algorithm for problem QP and Procedure Man find a schedule that maximizes the overall supply chain profit, with or without partial orders, respectively.*

Proof We replace $\overline{u}_{ij}$ in both QP and Man by $\overline{u}_{ij} + \overline{v}_{ij}$. The remainder of the proof follows that of Theorems 8.40 and 8.41.   □

8.6 Capacity Allocation Games

Now, consider a supply chain game consisting of one manufacturer and n distributors, where each distributor j has allocated capacity X_j and a set of resubmittable orders. We consider coalitions formed by the manufacturer and the grand coalition of distributors. In the supply chain game, each coalition and its maximum profit are defined as follows. Let R denote the maximum profit of the grand coalition of the supply chain game, i.e., the maximum profit achieved by the coordinated supply chain. Let U_M denote the profit of the manufacturer outside of any coalition. Consequently, if the corresponding instance of the distributors' game has a nonempty (respectively, an empty) core, then U_M is the profit achieved by the manufacturer assuming that the distributors jointly (resp., individually) revise their orders. The reason to define U_M in this way is that under supply chain coordination, the manufacturer can access the distributors' information and predict each distributor's behavior if it leaves the grand coalition. Since all other coalitions contain only distributors, their maximum profits are the same as in the corresponding instance of the distributors' game.

We now describe our balancedness, core emptiness test, and core membership test results for the supply chain game. First, we consider the supply chain game with partial orders allowed. Hall and Liu (2010) prove the following result.

Theorem 8.48 *For the supply chain game with partial orders:*

(a) The game is balanced;
(b) Algorithm LPCore finds a core member of the game in $O(mn)$ time;
(c) Algorithm LPCoreTest determines whether a given payoff vector is in the core of a given instance in $O(n \max\{m, \overline{X}\} \min\{\overline{X}, P_{\max}\})$ time;
(d) The core membership test of the supply chain game is binary co-NP-complete, even for a single product.

Proof

(a) The maximum profit R of the grand coalition is no less than that of the uncoordinated supply chain where the distributors coordinate. Since the corresponding distributors' LP game is balanced, (a) holds.
(b) To find a core member, we first apply Algorithm LPCore to find a core member of the corresponding distributors' LP game, and then pay the manufacturer the remaining payoff, U_M, from R. Thus, the payoff division is fair, and hence (b) follows from Theorem 8.42.
(c) For the core membership test, compared with the corresponding distributors' LP game, the only additional work requires testing whether the payoff to the manufacturer is no less than U_M. Thus, (c) follows from Theorem 8.43.
(d) For each order, we can define both the revenue and the work-in-process cost for the manufacturer as 0, which makes the supply chain game equivalent to the distributors' LP game, hence (d) follows from Theorem 8.46.

$\square$

Next, we consider the supply chain game without partial orders allowed. Hall and Liu (2010) prove the following result.

536 8 Cooperative Supply Chain Scheduling

Theorem 8.49 *For the supply chain game without partial orders:*

(a) The game is unbalanced;

(b) Algorithm KPCore finds an integer core member, if one exists, in $O(n\overline{X}\min\{\overline{X}, P_{\max}\}(R - U_M)^2)$ time;

(c) It is binary NP-hard to decide whether an instance of the knapsack game has an integer core member, even for a single product.

Proof

(a) If we define the revenue of each order and the work-in-process cost for the manufacturer as 0, then the supply chain game is equivalent to the distributors' knapsack game and the result follows from Theorem 7 of Hall and Liu (2010).

(b) For the core emptiness test, we apply Algorithm KPCore. From Theorem 8.45, if $F(n, \overline{X}, R - U_M) > 0$, then the integer core is empty; otherwise, retracing from the Optimal Solution Value identifies a core member.

(c) The result follows from Theorem 8.46.

□

It is straightforward to observe that the supply chain game and the distributors' game have the following relationship.

Corollary 8.3 *For a given instance of the supply chain game, if a payoff vector is in the core, then the part of the payoff vector that applies to the distributors is also in the core of the corresponding instance of the distributors' game. If an instance of the distributors' game has a nonempty core, then the corresponding instance of the supply chain game also has a nonempty core.*

The work of Hall and Liu (2010) is among the first that simultaneously considers three significant operational coordination issues that arise in two-stage supply chains with a manufacturer and several distributors. First, the cost savings from integrating scheduling information into capacity allocation decisions are evaluated. Second, the additional profit that the distributors can earn by sharing their capacity allocations and coordinating their revised orders is studied. Third, the additional profit that becomes available to the overall supply chain when the manufacturer and the distributors coordinate their decisions is analyzed. Insights, based on sensitivity analysis, are provided about when coordinating decisions is likely to be more valuable. The three types of coordination are all valuable, and the benefit is typically between 1% and 15%. In general, the three types of coordination are especially valuable when the manufacturer and the distributors have conflicting priorities between orders. Coordination is also more valuable when the manufacturer's profit margins are small, in which case the scheduling cost savings delivered by the methodology we present become relatively more significant.

8.7 Outsourcing Games

In semiconductor manufacturing, biotechnology, and pharmaceutical development, it is common for manufacturers to use outsourced capacity. In such situations, different issues arise from those in the supply chains discussed in Sect. 8.6. We consider two different models of this situation. In Sect. 8.7.1, we consider a third party that provides outsourcing services to several manufacturers who may reserve its capacity individually or jointly. In Sect. 8.7.2, we consider a problem where manufacturers compete for outsourced capacity that can be used concurrently with their own dedicated resources. We refer the reader to Chap. 6 for extensive discussions of similar problems within a centralized supply chain scheduling environment.

8.7.1 Common Third-Party Facility

Cai and Vairaktarakis (2012) consider a group of manufacturers which outsources some work to a third-party (3P) facility that possesses specialized capabilities which the manufacturers do not. First, the 3P announces available times and prices for its capacity, which can include both regular time and overtime. Then, each manufacturer reserves blocks of time, and within that available time, schedules its jobs to minimize a cost function consisting of reservation, overtime, and tardiness costs for late delivery to customers.

Having received all the manufacturers' reservations, the 3P may see the potential to reduce the total costs of the manufacturers by combining their orders. However, in the process, some manufacturers may incur extra cost. The 3P then needs to design a scheme to share the resulting savings and compensate those manufacturers. This problem can be modeled as a cooperative game. Additionally, it may be necessary to design a mechanism that encourages truth-telling by the manufacturers about the data of their jobs.

Let M denote a set of manufacturers and 3P a single third party facility. Each manufacturer $m \in M$ has a set N_m of jobs that require scheduling, where $N = \cup_{m \in M} N_m$ and $|N| = n$. The process begins when the 3P announces a set of K available time intervals of equal length and corresponding prices, which each manufacturer $m \in M$ can reserve on a first-come first-served basis. Let $W_i = [a_i, b_i]$ denote the ith time interval, where each interval has an equal length $L = b_i - a_i$, with announced price h_i. Observe that, by assumption, these intervals have the same available capacity. Within an interval, overtime can also be reserved at a rate of α_i per unit, up to a limit of c_i time units, for $i = 1, \ldots, K$. Further, let $\mathscr{W}_m$ denote the subset of time intervals reserved by manufacturer m. In this reservation process, manufacturers do not share a time interval. Each job j is available at time 0, and has a processing time p_j, where $P = \sum_{j \in N} p_j$. It also has a due date d_j that is assumed to be the end of a manufacturing window. Job j needs to be completed by time d_j, otherwise a tardiness penalty β_j is incurred.

Each manufacturer m then schedules its jobs over the time intervals $\mathcal{W}_m$ which it has reserved. The objective of each manufacturer is to minimize its total cost, which consists of its reservation cost $\sum_{i \in \mathcal{W}_m} h_i$, plus any overtime cost, plus the tardiness penalty β_j for each job j that is completed after its due date d_j. Let the overall initial schedule of the 3P's capacity, which is defined by concatenation of the schedules of the individual manufacturers, be denoted by σ_0. Relevant assumptions include feasibility, i.e., the 3P has enough capacity to process all the jobs, and also that there are no sequence-dependent setup times between the jobs. Jobs can be processed preemptively, i.e., stopped at the end of a manufacturing window and resumed in a later one. As a result, the number of time intervals needed to process all the jobs is $\omega \geq \lceil P/L \rceil$.

Consider a situation in which all reservations have already been made. The objective of the 3P is to maximize the value of work that is delivered on time. Then, based on structural properties of the problem described, the overall rescheduling problem of the 3P can be solved by first sequencing the jobs in earliest due date order, and then applying a dynamic programming algorithm similar to that of Lawler and Moore (1969) for the classical scheduling problem $1 || \sum w_j U_j$. Further, by enumerating this problem over all possible reservations that the manufacturers could be persuaded to adopt, the 3P's overall cost minimization problem, i.e., finding an optimal schedule σ^*, can be solved in $O(\omega^2 n P)$ time for the problem without overtime, and $O(\omega^2 n \bar{O} P)$ for the problem with overtime, where $\bar{O}$ is the maximum available amount of overtime in a time period.

A cooperative game (M, v) among the manufacturers is defined as follows. Let $S \subset M$ be an arbitrary coalition of manufacturers and $N(S) = \cup_{m \in S} N_m$ be the set of jobs owned collectively by the members of S. The coalition S must respect an admissibility rule that, for all $j \in N \setminus S$, the predecessors of j must be the same after resequencing as they are in σ_0. This rule is justified by the need for fairness on the part of the 3P, and also to maintain good relations between the manufacturers in order to encourage cooperation. Subject to this constraint, the coalition of manufacturers looks for a resequencing of its orders that minimizes its total cost, i.e., maximizes its cost savings v.

Let $v(S)$ be the maximum cost savings obtained by optimally rescheduling the jobs in $N(S)$, for a coalition S of manufacturers, $S \subseteq M$. Here, $v(S)$ consists of three parts: (i) the total refund $(1 - \rho) \sum_{k \in \mathcal{W}_0(S) \setminus \mathcal{W}^*(S)} h_k$ that coalition S receives from the 3P for those windows that are released after the rescheduling, where $\mathcal{W}_0(S)$ is the set of time windows that are initially reserved by coalition S, $\mathcal{W}^*(S)$ is the set of time windows that are utilized after the rescheduling, and ρ is the share of the reservation fee retained by the 3P in the event of cancellation; (ii) the total refund for the reduced overtime; and (iii) the reduction in the tardiness costs of the jobs of S as a result of rescheduling. Then, the pair (M, v) defines the manufacturers' savings game.

A cooperative game among the jobs is also defined. This game treats each individual job as a player. Let $v_J(S)$ be the maximum cost savings achieved

8.7 Outsourcing Games

by an admissible reschedule σ for a coalition of jobs $N(S)$. The job game is denoted by (N, v_J). Analysis of the job game provides a pathway to analysis of the manufacturers' game.

Let $G\{a, b\} = \{\sigma_0(a), \sigma_0(a + 1), \ldots, \sigma_0(b)\}$, for $1 \leq a \leq b \leq n$, denote a contiguous coalition of jobs that occupy all positions from a to b in σ_0. For conciseness, we use $v_J\{a, b\}$ in place of $v_J(G\{a, b\})$ to denote the maximum savings from rescheduling the jobs in $G\{a, b\}$.

Consider the following savings allocation for the ith job:

$$x_i = [v_J\{1, i\} - v_J\{1, i - 1\} + v_J\{i, n\} - v_J\{i + 1, n\}]/2, \quad i \in N, \tag{8.65}$$

where we define $v_J\{1, 0\} = v_J\{n + 1, n\} = 0$. This rule allocates to job i the average of its marginal contributions when joining the coalitions of preceding and succeeding jobs. Further, this allocation can be used to define a savings distribution for manufacturer m, as

$$y_m = \sum_{i \in N_m} x_i, \quad m \in M, \tag{8.66}$$

which exploits the connection between the two games.

In order to discuss the balancedness of the two games defined above, the following result is needed.

Lemma 8.12 *The game (N, v_J) is superadditive.*

Proof Consider two contiguous coalitions $G\{a, b\}$ and $H\{c, d\}$, where $a \leq b < c \leq d$. There are two cases.

First, if $c = b + 1$, then let $I\{a, d\} = G\{a, b\} \cup H\{c, d\}$, which is a contiguous coalition. Let $\sigma^*(S)$ denote an optimally resequenced schedule for the jobs of S, respectively. Concatenate $\sigma^*(G)$ and $\sigma^*(H)$ to form a (not necessarily optimal) sequence $\sigma(I)$. Then, the cost saving achieved by an optimal sequence $\sigma^*(I)$ is at least that of $\sigma(I)$. It follows that $v_J(G \cup H) \geq v_J(G) + v_J(H)$.

Second, if $c > b + 1$, the two components $G\{a, b\}$ and $H\{c, d\}$ are disjoint. Then, $v_J(G \cup H) \geq v_J(G) + v_J(H)$ if $G \cup H$ contains a larger contiguous set than in G or H, else $v_J(G \cup H) = v_J(G) + v_J(H)$, which is sufficient for superadditivity. $\square$

We can now prove the following result.

Theorem 8.50 *The cost savings allocation $\{x_i \mid i \in N\}$ defined in (8.65) is in the core of the game (N, v_J).*

Proof By definition, $x_i \geq 0$, for $i \in N$. To establish Coalitional Rationality, we consider two cases.

Case 1. Consider contiguous coalitions $G\{a, b\} = \{\sigma_0(a), \sigma_0(a + 1), \ldots, \sigma_0(b)\}$. Then, we have

$$\sum_{i \in G\{a,b\}} x_i = \sum_{i \in G\{a,b\}} [v_J\{1,i\} - v_J\{1,i-1\} + v_J\{i,n\} - v_J\{i+1,n\}]/2,$$

$$= [v_J\{1,b\} - v_J\{1,a-1\} + v_J\{a,n\} - v_J\{b+1,n\}]/2$$

$$\geq v_J(G\{a,b\}), \quad \text{from Lemma 8.12.}$$

Case 2. Let $G_k\{a_k, b_k\}$ denote a contiguous coalition, as discussed in Case 1. Now, consider non-contiguous coalitions $G = \cup_k G_k\{a_k, b_k\}$. Then, since $\sum_{i \in G_k} x_i \geq v_J(G_k\{a_k, b_k\})$ for all k, the same result holds for $G = \cup_k G_k\{a_k, b_k\}$.

Finally, we establish Efficiency. If $a = 1$ and $b = n$, we have $\sum_{i \in N} x_i = [(v_J\{1,n\} - v_J\{1,0\}) + (v_J\{1,n\} - v_J\{n+1,n\})]/2 = v_J(N)$. $\square$

This result in Theorem 8.50 can now be applied to the manufacturer's game.

Theorem 8.51 *The cost savings allocation* $\{y_m \mid m \in M\}$ *defined in (8.66) is in the core of the game* (M, v).

Proof First, $x_i \geq 0, i \in N \Rightarrow y_j \geq 0, j \in M$. Now, consider an arbitrary coalition S of manufacturers, consisting of k_S contiguous job subsets, i.e., $N(S) = \cup_{i=1}^{k_S} G_i\{a_i, b_i\}$. Then,

$$\sum_{m \in S} y_m = \sum_{m \in S} \sum_{i \in N_m} x_i$$

$$= \sum_{i \in N(S)} x_i$$

$$= \sum_{k=1}^{k_S} \sum_{i \in G_k\{a_k,b_k\}} x_i$$

$$\geq \sum_{k=1}^{k_S} v_J(G_k\{a_k, b_k\})$$

$$= v(S),$$

where the inequality follows from Theorem 8.50 and the last equality follows from the fact that the total savings of coalition S are generated from the maximum savings of its k_S subsets.

Finally, to establish Efficiency, we have $\sum_{m \in M} y_m = \sum_{i \in N} x_i = v_J(N) = v(M)$. $\square$

Remark 8.13 Cai and Vairaktarakis (2012) further study the issue of false reporting of data by the manufacturers, and develop a mechanism to ensure truthful reporting. They assume that the due date d_j and tardiness penalty β_j of manufacturer $j \in M$ are private information. They describe a mechanism under which the revelation

8.7 Outsourcing Games 541

of true information is a strategy that enables all manufacturers to minimize their true cost. We refer the reader to their work for details, and also to Chap. 9 for a more extensive discussion of issues and solutions related to the truthful reporting of private information.

8.7.2 Concurrent Outsourcing

Aydinliyim and Vairaktarakis (2013) study a scheduling environment with both in-house and outsourced third-party (3P) resources. Each player, i.e., manufacturer, can schedule its work either on its own dedicated facility or through competitive outsourcing to the 3P. In order to complete its work as soon as possible, a player may divide it between the two resources and process it concurrently on them.

More formally, consider a set $M = \{1, \ldots, m\}$ of manufacturers, which need to satisfy demand using their own dedicated resources and a 3P's flexible resource which they must share competitively with other manufacturers. Each manufacturer i has a workload P_i. The decision process is as follows. First, the 3P announces a priority rule that it will use for sequencing work that it receives from the various players. For example, it may announce a first-come, first-served (FCFS) rule, or a shortest processing time (SPT) rule. Next, the players use this information to decide the amount of their work to subcontract. If a player chooses to subcontract t_i work, $0 \le t_i \le P_i$, then the remaining workload $P_i - t_i$ is processed on its dedicated machine. The subcontracting decisions of the manufacturers and the 3P's priority rule jointly determine an initial schedule σ_0. However, the initial schedule σ_0 may be changed, by cooperation between the manufacturers, into another schedule σ which may have a lower total cost $\sum_{i \in M} C_i(\sigma)$.

Observe that due to concurrent processing on the dedicated machine and the 3P's facility, in any schedule σ, the completion time C_i of player i's work is the later of its completion time on those two resources, i.e.,

$$C_i(\sigma) = \max\{P_i - t_i, \sum_{k \mid \sigma(k) \le \sigma(i)} t_k\}. \tag{8.67}$$

Consider the cooperative game (M, v), where

$$v(S) = \sum_{i \in S} [C_i(\sigma_0) - C_i(\sigma^*)], \tag{8.68}$$

and where for any coalition of players $S \subseteq M$, $C_i(\sigma_0)$ and $C_i(\sigma^*)$ represent the completion time values attained by player i in an initial schedule σ_0 and an optimal schedule σ^*, respectively. After the initial schedule σ_0 is formed, the players have an option to form a coalition $S \subseteq M$ and coordinate their subcontracting decisions, for the purpose of minimizing $\sum_{i \in S} C_i(\sigma)$. However, this schedule must be admissible. For the purposes of this game, a reschedule of the work of coalition S is admissible if (a) it does not require the active cooperation of players outside S, and (b) it does not adversely affect players outside S. From (a), a coalition must consist of work that is processed consecutively in σ_0. From (b) and (8.67), a coalition that does not end with the work of the last player has zero value. This is necessary because, from (8.68), the value of a coalition derives from increasing its subcontracting to the 3P, which will adversely affect any later players in the schedule. Hence, an admissible coalition with positive value must end with the last player. This result is formalized in part (i) of Lemma 8.13 below.

Let $S[a, b]$ denote a coalition of players whose work is processed consecutively in positions a through b in σ_0. This definition enables an efficient computation of the characteristic function $v(S)$ of any coalition $S \subseteq M$ in the game (M, v), without evaluating an exponential number of coalitions. As shown below, it also facilitates finding a closed form expression for a core allocation of the savings from the rescheduling of the jobs.

Aydinliyim and Vairaktarakis (2013) establish the following preliminary result. We refer the reader to their work for details of their proof.

Lemma 8.13

(i) $v(S[a, b]) = 0$, if $b \neq m$.
(ii) If T is a maximally connected coalition, i.e., $T = S[a_1, b_1] \cup \ldots \cup S[a_r, b_r]$, then

$$v(T) = \sum_{k=1}^{r} v(S[a_k, b_k]) = \begin{cases} v(S[a_r, b_r]), & \text{if } b_r = m \\ 0, & \text{otherwise.} \end{cases} \tag{8.69}$$

Lemma 8.13 is used to prove the following result.

Theorem 8.52 *The cooperative savings game (M, v) is convex.*

Proof First, consider connected coalitions. There are four cases.

(i) $S[a, b]$ and $S[a', b']$ with $a, a' \geq 1$ and $b, b' < m$. In this case, $v(S[a, b]) = v(S[a', b']) = 0$.
(ii) $S[a, m]$ and $S[a', b']$ with $a, a' \geq 1$ and $b, b' < m$. In this case, $v(S[a, m] \cup S[a', b']) + v(S[a, m] \cap S[a', b']) = v(S[\min\{a, a'\}, b']) + v(S[\max\{a, a'\}, b']) \geq v(S[a, m]) = v(S[a, m]) + v(S[a', b'])$. In this case, the inequality follows from the superadditivity of v, i.e., from $v(S[\min\{a, a'\}, m]) \geq v(S[a, m])$, and the last equality follows from $b' < m$ which implies $v(S[a', b']) = 0$.
(iii) $S[a, b]$ and $S[a', m]$ with $a, a' \geq 1$ and $b < m$. The proof is similar to (ii).
(iv) $S[a, m]$ and $S[a', m]$ with $a, a' \geq 1$. In this case, $v(S[a, m] \cup S[a', m]) + v(S[a, m] \cap S[a', m]) = v(S[\min\{a, a'\}, m]) + v(S[\max\{a, a'\}, m]) = v(S[a, m]) + v(S[a', m])$.

Finally, for disconnected coalitions, the result follows from Lemma 8.13, part (ii). □

From Theorem 8.52 and the work of Bondareva (1963) and Shapley (1967), we know that the cooperative game (M, v) is balanced and the Shapley value is a core solution.

8.7 Outsourcing Games

Again from Lemma 8.13, it suffices to consider only coalitions $S[a, m]$, for $1 \leq a < m$. Now, define arbitrary constants $0 \leq \lambda_1, \ldots, \lambda_{m-1} \leq 1$. Then, the characteristic function v can be written, for coalitions $S[a, m]$ where $1 \leq a < m$, as:

$$
v(S[a, m]) = \sum_{k=a}^{m-1} \lambda_k [v(S[k, m]) - v(S[k+1, m])]
$$

$$
+ \sum_{i=a+1}^{m} \sum_{k=a}^{i-1} \frac{(1 - \lambda_k)[v(S[k, m]) - v(S[k+1, m])]}{[\,|S[a, m]| - k + a - 1]}. \tag{8.70}
$$

We now provide an example of the expression in (8.70).

Example 8.31 (Coalition Value Calculations in a Concurrent Outsourcing Game) Consider $S[3, 6]$ for a game where $m = 6$. Then, from (8.70), we have

$$
v(S[3, 6]) = \lambda_3 [v(S[3, 6]) - v(S[4, 6])] + \frac{1 - \lambda_3}{3} [v(S[3, 6]) - v(S[4, 6])]
$$

$$
+ \lambda_4 [v(S[4, 6]) - v(S[5, 6])]
$$

$$
+ \frac{1 - \lambda_3}{3} [v(S[3, 6]) - v(S[4, 6])] + \frac{1 - \lambda_4}{2} [v(S[4, 6]) - v(S[5, 6])]
$$

$$
+ \lambda_5 v(S[5, 6])
$$

$$
+ \frac{1 - \lambda_3}{3} [v(S[3, 6]) - v(S[4, 6])] + \frac{1 - \lambda_4}{2} [v(S[4, 6]) - v(S[5, 6])]
$$

$$
+ (1 - \lambda_5) v(S[5, 6]).
$$

We now use (8.70) to define a cost savings allocation rule based on the Shapley value and show that it is a core solution. This rule distributes a fraction λ_i of the marginal savings achieved by adding the player processed in ith position on the outsourced resource to a coalition of his followers in σ_0, and distributes a fraction $(1 - \lambda_i)$ among those followers as compensation for facilitating rescheduling. The main result for this allocation rule now follows.

Theorem 8.53 *The cost savings allocation rule:*

$$
x_i = \lambda_i \big[v(S[i, m]) - v(S[i+1, m]) \big]
$$

$$
+ \sum_{k=1}^{i-1} \frac{(1 - \lambda_k)\big[v(S[k, m]) - v(S[k+1, m]) \big]}{(m - k)}, \quad i \in M, \tag{8.71}
$$

defines a core allocation for the cooperative game (M, v) defined in (8.68).

Proof Observe that $x_i \geq v(\{i\})$, for $i \in M$. Next,

$$
\sum_{i \in S[a,m]} x_i = \sum_{i=a}^{m-1} \lambda_i \big[v(S[i,m]) - v(S[i+1,m]) \big]
$$

$$
+ \sum_{j=2}^{m} \sum_{i=1}^{j-1} (1 - \lambda_i) \frac{[v(S[i,m]) - v(S[i+1,m])]}{(m-i)}
$$

$$
\geq \sum_{i=a}^{m-1} \lambda_i \big[v(S[i,m]) - v(S[i+1,m]) \big]
$$

$$
+ \sum_{j=a+1}^{m} \sum_{i=a}^{j-1} \frac{(1 - \lambda_i)[v(S[i,m]) - v(S[i+1,m])]}{[|S[a,m]| - i + a - 1]}
$$

$$
= v(S[a,m]),
$$

where the inequality follows from $a \geq 1$, and $|S[a,m]| - i + a - 1 = m - i$ if $i \geq a$. Finally, we have

$$
\sum_{i \in M} x_i = \sum_{i=1}^{m-1} \lambda_i \big[v(S[i,m]) - v(S[i+1,m]) \big]
$$

$$
+ \sum_{h=2}^{m} \sum_{i=1}^{h-1} \frac{(1 - \lambda_i) \big[v(S[i,m]) - v(S[i+1,m]) \big]}{(m-i)}
$$

$$
= \sum_{i=1}^{m-1} \lambda_i \big[v(S[i,m]) - v(S[i+1,m]) \big]
$$

$$
+ \sum_{i=1}^{m-1} \sum_{h=i+1}^{m} \frac{(1 - \lambda_i) \big[v(S[i,m]) - v(S[i+1,m]) \big]}{(m-i)}
$$

$$
= \sum_{i=1}^{m-1} \lambda_i \big[v(S[i,m]) - v(S[i+1,m]) \big]
$$

$$
+ \sum_{i=1}^{m-1} (1 - \lambda_i)[v(S[i,m]) - v(S[i+1,m])]
$$

$$
= \sum_{i=1}^{m-1} [v(S[i,m]) - v(S[i+1,m])]
$$

8.8 Future Research 545

$$= v(S[1, m])$$
$$= v(M).$$

$\square$

Remark 8.14 Aydinliyim and Vairaktarakis (2013) conduct a computational study that yields valuable insights about effective management of the flexible third-party resource. First, they demonstrate the benefit of processing the shortest subcontracted load first, rather than using the first-come, first-served rule that is commonly used in practice. Second, they observe that the subcontractor's sequencing priority scheme and the savings allocation scheme decisions should be coordinated, in order to achieve fair coordination of the manufacturers' subcontracting decisions.

The results presented in this section show that various subcontracting problems within supply chain scheduling can be effectively coordinated using cooperative games.

8.8 Future Research

We describe several topics of future research interest. These are organized around the sections of this chapter, i.e., sequencing games, scheduling games, project management games, capacity allocation games in supply chains, and outsourcing games.

- For the topic of sequencing games discussed in Sect. 8.3, Aydinliyim and Vairaktarakis (2011) provide a review of the related literature and several suggestions for future research. Related to the implementability of sequencing game solutions, they note that recent advances in information technology are substantially enhancing the information sharing capabilities of supply chain members. Hence, many coordination problems that have been studied in the supply chain management literature can be revisited to investigate the benefit of coordinating decisions at the detailed scheduling level. Several open research questions arise in this context, based on the assumptions of such games. The first is more detailed investigation of reasonable assumptions about initial schedules. For example, a common assumption is that jobs are sequenced as first-come, first-served (FCFS). However, since the players know that resequencing will be possible, the use of strategic behavior may modify this assumption. Also, typical models assume that one dollar lost in booking costs can be compensated by one dollar worth of improvements in the delivery time, which is a strong, although mathematically useful, assumption that can be relaxed. The use of Pareto-optimal schedules may generate new insights. Full information sharing is another common assumption. Alternative treatments of information include Bayesian models with asymmetric information, which motivates studying the benefits of sharing information and mechanisms that induce truth-telling by the players, as discussed in Chap. 9. Most manufacturing systems are more complex than those considered in the sequencing game works in the literature, which motivates the study of more general systems. These systems include the machine environments of classical scheduling: parallel machines, flowshops, jobshops, and openshops. Finally, resource sharing is of importance in large and complex projects where many different contractors are responsible for different groups of tasks. In such models, players who finish their tasks earlier can move their resources to other tasks in return for side payments, and this process of resource sharing can create additional value for the grand coalition.

- Within the class of sequencing games, Gerichhausen and Hamers (2009) consider a game defined over a partition sequencing situation. The underlying scheduling problem has strong similarities to that of Hall and Potts (2004). That work suggests several related problems. Other definitions of scheduling cost are also relevant, as are more general machine configurations. In related work, Hall and Potts (2010) consider rescheduling problems where, after a schedule has been formed, the release date of some jobs is delayed; it would be useful to study sequencing games defined over such problems.
- Curiel (2015) studies multi-stage sequencing games. For future research, she recommends the study of multi-stage permutation games (see Sect. 8.3.1.1) where compensation is needed for the loss of an advantageous position. Also of value is the study of multi-stage sequencing games that incorporate uncertainty, which can be modeled in various ways, or games that include dynamic compensation rules.
- For scheduling games, Liu et al. (2018a) develop a valuable new mechanism for maintaining cooperation by combining subsidization and penalties. This work suggests both technical and economic questions of interest. First, on the technical side, even the subproblem of finding the optimal subsidy for a given level of penalty is computationally challenging. Second, there are significant computational challenges that require better approximation and faster convergence when the penalty-subsidy function has a large number of breakpoints. Third, besides the scheduling game which we discuss in detail, the authors also provide results for three closely related scheduling games. This motivates the characterization of a new "complexity boundary", to identify which scheduling games admit an efficiently found penalty-subsidy function. On the economic side, it is intriguing to model the opportunity cost of subsidy decisions within various models. For example, the decision to implement a subsidy may create a cost that removes, or reduces the efficiency of, production capacity. With this perspective, the level and efficiency of production resources should be viewed endogenously, thereby enriching the analysis of the tradeoff between penalties and subsidies.
- Regarding the project planning game for subcontractors studied by Curiel (2011) and discussed in Sect. 8.5, further research should be directed toward relaxing the condition that all coalitions should have the same unique critical path. Generalization of the model by considering allocation schemes that are not linear and duration functions that are not piecewise linear provide other opportunities for further research. It is also relevant to consider a situation where, as long as the project is completed before a certain due date, no penalty is incurred.

8.8 Future Research

- The project execution game that is also discussed in Sect. 8.5 raises several significant research issues. A fundamental issue that is not fully resolved is what solution concepts are appropriate. Castro et al. (2007) model a project game based on what they argue are desirable properties: separability, non-manipulability by splitting, and independent slack. However, Estévez-Fernández (2012) questions the relevance of these concepts and provides counterexamples. Her own work concentrates on traditional solution concepts within cooperative games, especially the core. Nonetheless, Bergantiños et al. (2018) argue that, within projects, strategic stability has no clear definition, since no group of activities can do without the others. This means that concepts such as the core are not necessarily applicable. They therefore consider several fairness properties: cost monotonicity (i.e., no activity should pay more if it finishes ahead of schedule), dummy (i.e., an activity finishing on schedule pays nothing), anonymity (i.e., the allocation does not depend on the name of the activity), and symmetry (i.e., symmetric activities pay the same). Both approaches can provide valuable insights about appropriate rewards in project execution games.
- As a more general comment about project games, because of the precedence requirements of the project and also the resource sharing between activities that often occurs, it is problematic to define reasonable criteria for admissibility of rearrangements. Therefore, relaxations of admissibility requirements should be studied.
- Section 8.6 discusses capacity allocation games. Hall and Liu (2010) discuss several directions for further research. First, the problem of testing whether instances of the knapsack game have fractional core members remains open. Second, since several of the algorithms presented require pseudo-polynomial time, it would be useful to develop effective heuristics to solve instances with large data values. Third, other measures of scheduling cost besides the total weighted completion time can be considered. Also, other operational decisions such as distribution can be incorporated into the supply chain considered. Furthermore, the supply chain studied in that work, which consists of one manufacturer and multiple distributors, can be generalized to consider multiple competing manufacturers. Finally, the impact of strategic behavior, such as deliberate overordering, on the manufacturer's and distributors' coordination decisions, should be considered.
- Section 8.7 studies outsourcing games. In this context, Cai and Vairaktarakis (2012) suggest several opportunities for further investigation. One practical research direction is to consider multiple external resources, rather than only a single third party. More general cost functions of relevance could include cost of earliness (as a proxy for inventory holding cost) as well as lateness. Also of importance is the consideration of various other capacity reservation protocols, for example, based on an auction model. It would also be valuable to consider, in situations with private information, the effect of strategic behavior. Such models should yield many practical and challenging topics for future research.
- Also for outsourcing games, Aydinliyim and Vairaktarakis (2013) mention several interesting future research directions that address other practical subcontracting issues. Such research opportunities include considering pricing issues,

incorporating due dates, and varying the sensitivity to delay of the players. Asymmetric information issues and the resulting moral hazard problem can also be studied. Another topic worthy of investigation is sequential decision making settings where some of the players have more power and act as Stackelberg leaders. We refer the reader to Sect. 9.3.1 for related discussions.

To summarize this chapter, we observe that there are numerous practically important and mathematically challenging research problems within the area of cooperative supply chain scheduling.

Chapter 9
Noncooperative Supply Chain Scheduling

Abstract This chapter discusses the application of noncooperative solution methods, especially noncooperative game theory, to decentralized supply chain scheduling problems. We consider a wide variety of scheduling problems that have classically been modeled and analyzed from the perspective of a centralized decision maker. By viewing the jobs or resources within these applications as individual self-interested players, noncooperative supply chain scheduling games are defined over those problems. We consider games with complete information, first without and second with structural enhancements, as well as games where the players have private information which they may report untruthfully. Within private information games, we study mechanism design both without and with payments and illustrate various concepts of truthfulness that are established by deterministic or randomized mechanisms. Our analysis of these games applies all the main concepts of noncooperative games, from the perspective of finding equilibrium solutions and analyzing their quality.

9.1 Introduction

The literature of cooperative solutions to decentralized supply chain scheduling problems is impressive, as discussed in Chap. 8. However, there are various general situations where cooperation between agents (referred to as players in our work) is difficult, or even impossible, to achieve. One typical situation occurs where the players are fundamentally hostile toward each other and each seeks to drive the other players out of the market. Another frequently occurring situation occurs where the players do not trust each other sufficiently to share their information in a way that would enable cooperation. Another problem is that cooperative games require large amounts of information to be collected from many players, and this may be administratively difficult. Yet another problem is that the optimization problem of the grand coalition under cooperation is in many cases large and computationally intractable. Besides these general situations, there are other issues that are specific either to particular sets of players or to particular applications that

© Springer Nature Switzerland AG 2022
Z.-L. Chen, N. G. Hall, *Supply Chain Scheduling*, International Series
in Operations Research & Management Science 323,
https://doi.org/10.1007/978-3-030-90374-9_9

549

make it problematic to obtain cooperative solutions. To address these situations, an alternative and substantial body of work has developed that uses noncooperative solutions to provide insights about supply chain scheduling applications. Within this context, the information requirements and computational challenges are typically easier to meet in the case of noncooperative solutions than cooperative ones. Moreover, finding solutions may be possible through the use of local information and decisions involving local improvement, based on simple equilibrium concepts. This section discusses four different environments for the study of noncooperative solutions to supply chain scheduling problems.

The first environment studied is *complete information settings*. In such settings, all information is publicly known to all players and a central planner if there is one. More specifically, the players make public all the information about the data they use to determine a strategy, although without revealing the strategy itself. Even so, the outcome of an equilibrium solution is typically not optimal for the overall system. The identification of equilibrium solutions for a supply chain scheduling problem makes it important to measure its solution quality, relative to that of an optimal solution for the system. As measures of the resulting loss, the ratio between the cost of the worst equilibrium and the optimal system cost is known as the *price of anarchy*, and the difference between them is known as the *absolute price of anarchy*. However, the price or absolute price of anarchy is in many cases high, suggesting that some equilibrium solutions are very inefficient. A related issue of importance under complete information is specifying the rules under which the players may interact and how this affects the quality of the solutions obtained.

The second environment is *complete information settings with enhancement*. Because the quality of system equilibria can be poor relative to system optimal solutions, even when complete information is available, there is motivation to enhance the system. There are various approaches by which a noncooperative supply chain scheduling game can be enhanced, such that equilibrium outcomes are closer to an optimal system outcome. One approach is to allow the players to make their decisions sequentially, rather than simultaneously. We discuss some supply chain scheduling applications where this procedure leads to improved solutions. An alternative enhancement is to allow central control of some of the players. These players, or *leaders*, make their decisions first, motivated by optimizing system performance, with complete information about how the independent players, or *followers*, will respond. This leads to the study of *Stackelberg games*. Such games also model other supply chain scheduling applications where the leaders are selfish but anticipate the reactive decisions of other players. A third possible enhancement is the incentivization of decisions that are less selfish, i.e., at least partly altruistic, and therefore more supportive of the overall social welfare. Finally, we consider methods by which a central authority can manipulate players to move from a poor quality equilibrium to a better quality one, for example by public service announcements.

Both the third and fourth environments involve some private information that is known only to its owner. In this situation, players may not necessarily report their information truthfully, which makes it harder to achieve a good outcome of the game. For example, a player may believe that, by underreporting the processing

9.1 Introduction 551

time of his job, that job will be given an earlier position in the schedule. In the third environment, the study of *private information settings without payments*, the truthful reporting of this information is incentivized through algorithm design without the use of additional payments to players. There is also other information that is public and therefore known to all players, including a central planner. The central planner, with the objective of optimizing overall system performance, creates an outcome, i.e., a schedule, based on information reported by the players. We formally introduce the concept of a mechanism and provide a generic example. We identify three levels of truthfulness, the first of which is deterministic, while the second and third require randomization. The examples we provide demonstrate a deterministically truthful mechanism that also finds a socially optimal solution, and the use of randomization to obtain good approximation bounds under truthful reporting.

The fourth environment is the study of *private information settings with payments*. Again, the players know some private information about their data that is not known to other players or to the central scheduler. The main difference from the third environment is that we consider the use of payments to support a truthful algorithm. This is the topic of *algorithmic mechanism design*, for which supply chain scheduling models are a widely used application. In this environment, a mechanism has two components: an algorithm that takes the information reported by the players and uses it to develop an outcome, which in the supply chain scheduling context is typically a schedule, and a payment scheme that ensures truthful reporting by the players. We provide an overview of the main design concepts for this environment. We provide examples of how to design mechanisms at three different levels of truthfulness. Finally, we study an environment where players have probabilistic beliefs about the private information of other players, which requires the use of different design concepts.

In several of these environments, the term *mechanism* plays an important but varying role, and we now provide a clarification about its different uses. When we discuss supply chain scheduling games where all information is public, the role of a mechanism is to coordinate the decisions of selfish players around a solution that is socially optimal. For example, it may be possible to identify an optimal solution that is stable. We describe such a mechanism as a *coordination mechanism*. Alternatively, when we discuss a game that includes private information, a *truthful mechanism* is one that incentivizes all the players to report their information truthfully to a central authority. For game solutions that include not only an algorithm but also payments between the central authority and the players, we use the term *algorithmic mechanism*. Thus, within this book, an algorithmic mechanism is a truthful mechanism that includes a payment scheme.

This chapter is organized as follows. Section 9.2 introduces complete information settings, illustrates the use of equilibrium concepts to study scheduling problems, and defines the price of anarchy with several examples. We also provide examples of algorithms for finding a Nash equilibrium and results which show that, in some situations, doing so is an intractable problem. Section 9.3 discusses enhanced complete information settings. Section 9.4 demonstrates the design and application of truthful algorithms where some information is private but payments are not used. Section 9.5 studies settings with private information and focuses on algorithmic

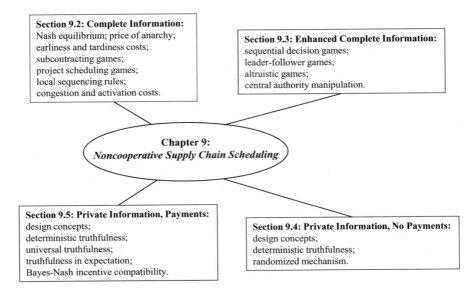

Fig. 9.1 Overview of the topics covered in Chap. 9

mechanism design, including the design of payment schemes, for supply chain scheduling problems. Section 9.6 identifies future research topics within the study of noncooperative games for supply chain scheduling.

Figure 9.1 provides an overview of the topics within noncooperative solutions to decentralized supply chain scheduling problems that are discussed in this chapter.

9.2 Complete Information Games

Complete information games provide a simple starting point for the study of noncooperative games. In Sect. 9.2.1, we describe the general environment of noncooperative games and define important noncooperative game concepts, including a Nash equilibrium, the price of anarchy, and the absolute price of anarchy. Section 9.2.2 provides several examples of how to find a Nash equilibrium for a supply chain scheduling problem. For some applications, doing so is shown to be intractable. For other applications, a Nash equilibrium can be found efficiently, but the imposition of a constraint on solution quality makes the problem intractable.

9.2.1 Noncooperative Game Concepts

Heydenreich et al. (2007) provide an inviting overview of noncooperative games that are defined for supply chain scheduling problems. Within the literature of

9.2 Complete Information Games

noncooperative games, it is common to refer to an instance of a scheduling problem as a *scheduling situation* and to refer to the corresponding instance of a related game as being *defined over a scheduling situation*. We briefly review the essential definitions for scheduling problems within the supply chain scheduling environment. These definitions arise within the study of classical scheduling problems and are independent of the assumptions of noncooperative games that are defined over them.

In the scheduling applications we consider, there is a set $N = \{1, \ldots, n\}$ of jobs. The jobs require processing, in most but not all cases nonpreemptively, i.e., without interruption, on a set $M = \{1, \ldots, m\}$ of machines. The data for the jobs is similar to that within classical scheduling: a processing time p_j and a weight or urgency measure w_j. In some problems, each job also has a due date d_j or a release date r_j. If $m \geq 2$, the m machines are configured in parallel. In this case, the processing time of a job j on machine i is p_j for $i \in M$ when the machines are *identical*; or p_j/s_i on machine i that has speed s_i when processing times are *proportional* or *uniform*; or p_{ij} when processing times are *unrelated* across the machines. For specific supply chain scheduling games discussed below, additional notation is defined as needed.

We now discuss some definitions for noncooperative supply chain scheduling games that involve a number of self-interested players. In many supply chain scheduling applications, we may think of the self-interested players as customers, each of whom owns one or more jobs; or equivalently, the jobs themselves can represent the players. Alternatively, we may view the machines as players. A player is defined by his *type*, which is his information about the scheduling problem, whether that information is public or private. Thus, player k has *type* t_k. Available to the players are several possible *actions*. For example, in some applications, a player may select any of several machines to schedule his job. An *allocation algorithm* computes an outcome, i.e., a schedule, from the known public or reported information and the actions of all the players. Let C_j, for $j \in N$, denote the set of job completion times in a schedule found by the allocation algorithm. To ensure that this schedule is well defined, it may be necessary to specify a local rule for the machines. For example, if the players each choose a machine for their jobs, then a local rule for each machine may specify that the jobs are sequenced in index order or shortest processing time (SPT) order. Once the jobs are assigned to the machines, the use of this rule is sufficient to define a schedule. More generally, the sequencing rule may vary between the machines.

While a focus is on the incentivization and decision making of the self-interested players, it is important to evaluate the overall system performance, typically measured by cost, that results from those decisions. Both the construction of the overall schedule and the evaluation of its utility, cost, or profit are performed by a *central authority*, or *central planner*, or *central scheduler*. The central authority optimizes a social objective for the overall system. In some applications, the central authority owns no resources, whereas in other applications the players own no resources and access resources owned by the central authority. Meanwhile, various players may value any given schedule differently. For example, since a player is self-interested, he is typically concerned only with the costs(s) of his own job(s). This is where the use of payments to enhance the game may be helpful, in that they

554   9 Noncooperative Supply Chain Scheduling

can be used to encourage the players to make decisions that improve the quality of the overall solution. To every action of a player, we associate a strategy. A game is a mapping from the set of strategies into the set of schedules. Let $u_k(x)$ denote the utility gained by player k from a vector of strategies for the n players, $x = (x_1, \ldots, x_n)$. The following three sections review and illustrate fundamental concepts within noncooperative games: a Nash equilibrium, the price of anarchy, and the absolute price of anarchy, respectively.

9.2.1.1 Nash equilibrium

An important concept for analyzing noncooperative games is a Nash equilibrium (Nash, 1951), as now defined. Consider a game of maximizing utility. The following definitions are needed. See Sect. 2.3.6 for a brief introduction to several related concepts. Let $N = \{1, \ldots, n\}$ denote a set of players. Let X_i denote the set of strategies available to player $i, i \in N$.

Definition 9.1 A *pure strategy* solution is one where each player makes his decisions and receives his outcome, deterministically. A vector of strategies for the n players, $x = (x_1, \ldots, x_n) \in X_1 \times \cdots \times X_n$, is a *pure strategy Nash equilibrium* if

$$u_k(x) \geq u_k(x_1, \ldots, x_{k-1}, x'_k, x_{k+1}, \ldots, x_n), \quad x'_k \in X_k, \ k = 1, \ldots, n. \quad (9.1)$$

Equation (9.1) states that, given the strategies of all other players, the utility of any individual player k cannot be improved by any other feasible strategy $x'_k \neq x_k$. Hence, no player has any incentive to change strategy unilaterally, and the system is in equilibrium. However, this equilibrium solution does not in general achieve an optimal outcome for the overall game, i.e., it may not be a *socially optimal solution*. In a supply chain scheduling game, a socially optimal solution maximizes the total profit or minimizes the total cost of the system. In a centralized supply chain scheduling context, as studied in Chaps 3 through 6, this is viewed more simply as an optimal solution for a single decision maker.

Importantly, not every game admits a pure strategy Nash equilibrium. We provide an example from supply chain scheduling, by considering the classical scheduling problem $P_2 || \sum C_j$, which requires minimization of the total completion time of all the jobs when they are scheduled on two identical parallel machines. There are two players, each of whom owns a subset of the jobs and minimizes his total completion time only over his own jobs. However, those costs may be influenced by the scheduling decisions of the other players. The strategy of each player consists of deciding on which of the two machines to schedule each of his jobs. A socially optimal solution in this game minimizes the total completion time of all the players.

Example 9.1 (A Game Without a Pure Strategy Nash equilibrium) Consider an example with two players, each of whom owns two jobs, and two machines. Player 1 owns jobs a and b, and player 2 owns jobs c and d. The processing times of the jobs are $p_a = 1$, $p_b = 4$, $p_c = 3$, and $p_d = 5$. Each machine sequences the jobs assigned to it in SPT order, as is known to be optimal for the classical scheduling problem

9.2 Complete Information Games

555

Table 9.1 Cost table for Example 9.1

$P1\backslash P2$	$\emptyset$	$\{c\}$	$\{d\}$	$\{c, d\}$
$\emptyset$	9, 17	6, 13	$9, 9^{\dagger}$	6, 11
$\{a\}$	8, 15	$5^{*}, 13$	$8, 9^{\dagger}$	$5^{*}, 13$
$\{b\}$	$5^{*}, 13$	$8, 9^{\dagger}$	$5^{*}, 13$	8, 15
$\{a, b\}$	6, 11	$9, 9^{\dagger}$	6, 13	9, 17

$P_2 || \sum C_j$ (Smith, 1956). Table 9.1 shows the cost table for both players, given their strategy of which job(s) to schedule on machine 1 shown in the row for player 1 and in the column for player 2. The other jobs are scheduled on machine 2. For example, suppose both players choose the strategy $\emptyset$, i.e., they schedule both of their jobs on machine 2. Implementing the SPT rule, the sequence of those jobs on machine 2 is shortest processing time (SPT), i.e., a, c, b, d. Hence, player 1 incurs costs of $C_a = 1$ and $C_b = 1 + 3 + 4 = 8$, for a total cost of 9, and player 2 incurs costs of $C_c = 1 + 3 = 4$ and $C_d = 1 + 3 + 4 + 5 = 13$, for a total cost of 17. Thus, the entry in Table 9.1 corresponding to the strategy of $\emptyset$ for both players shows their costs as 9, 17. The notation $*$ against the relevant cost for player 1 indicates that it is the best strategy for player 1 who chooses between the rows of the table, given player 2's strategy shown in the column. Similarly, the notation $\dagger$ against the relevant cost for player 2 indicates that it is the best strategy for player 2 who chooses between the columns of the table, given player 1's strategy shown in the row. For example, if player 2 chooses $\emptyset$, the best response of player 1 is $\{b\}$, with a cost of 5. Observe that there is no solution in Table 9.1 where both players have a best response, given the other player's strategy. This shows that there is no Nash equilibrium in pure strategy for this game.

A useful alternative for a game without a pure strategy equilibrium is a Nash equilibrium in *mixed strategy*, as now defined. Nash (1951) shows that for any game with a finite number of strategies, there exists an equilibrium in mixed strategies.

Definition 9.2 A *mixed strategy* is one where the decisions of each player are defined by a probability distribution over the possible strategies that are available. Under a mixed strategy, a player maximizes his *expected utility*. Formally, let $\Delta(X_k)$ denote the set of probability distributions over the set of available pure strategies X_k for player k, and let $\mathbb{E}[\cdot]$ denote expectation. Since this is a utility maximization problem, a vector of strategies for the n players, $x = (x_1, \ldots, x_n) \in \Delta(X_1) \times \cdots \times \Delta(X_n)$, is a mixed strategy Nash equilibrium if

$$\mathbb{E}[u_k(x)] \geq \mathbb{E}[u_k(x_1, \ldots, x_{k-1}, x'_k, x_{k+1}, \ldots, x_n)], \quad x'_k \in \Delta(X_k), \ k = 1, \ldots, n. \tag{9.2}$$

We now illustrate a mixed strategy equilibrium.

Example 9.2 (Mixed Strategy Nash equilibrium for the Game in Example 9.1) Consider Table 9.1 in Example 9.1. Observe that, irrespective of the strategy of player 2, it is always better for player 1 to use strategy $\{a\}$ over strategy $\emptyset$ and always better to use strategy $\{b\}$ over strategy $\{a, b\}$. Similarly, it is always better

556   9 Noncooperative Supply Chain Scheduling

for player 2 to use strategy $\{c\}$ over strategy $\emptyset$ and always better to use strategy $\{d\}$ over strategy $\{c, d\}$. Hence, the only pairs of strategies that are nondominated, and thus receive nonzero probability, are $(\{a\}, \{c\})$, $(\{a\}, \{d\})$, $(\{b\}, \{c\})$, and $(\{b\}, \{d\})$. A mixed strategy equilibrium is defined by $Pr(\{a\}) = Pr(\{b\}) = Pr(\{c\}) = Pr(\{d\}) = 0.5$, which results in an expected cost of 6.5 for player 1 and 11.0 for player 2, for a total of 17.5. The definition of this is that it does not increase the expected utility of either player unilaterally to change his probability distribution over his decisions.

Finally, observe that this solution does not minimize the total system cost, which is $8 + 9 = 17$, as achieved by the strategies $\{a\}$ for player 1 and $\{d\}$ for player 2, or symmetrically $\{b\}$ for player 1 and $\{c\}$ for player 2.

9.2.1.2 Price of Anarchy

In a typical game, there may be many Nash equilibrium solutions with varying levels of profit or cost for the overall system. From the perspective of a central authority, it is valuable to know the worst-case outcome for the overall system among those solutions. This information has practical importance, because the system may naturally evolve to it and, since it is in equilibrium, remain there.

Definition 9.3 Consider a cost minimization game, where z^* denotes the minimum total system cost, and $z^N(\sigma)$ denotes the cost of a pure Nash equilibrium solution σ. Then, the *price of anarchy* (PoA) is defined by Koutsoupias and Papadimitriou (1999) as

$$PoA = \max_{\sigma \in NE} \{z^N(\sigma)\}/z^*, \tag{9.3}$$

where NE is the set of strategies that are at a Nash equilibrium. Analogously, in a profit maximization game, we let $z^N(\sigma)$ denote the profit of a Nash equilibrium solution σ, and $PoA = z^*/\min_{\sigma \in NE}\{z^N(\sigma)\}$.

Exact analysis of the price of anarchy is possible for some supply chain scheduling games. Koutsoupias and Papadimitriou (1999) provide the following example.

Example 9.3 (PoA of a Mixed Strategy Nash equilibrium) Consider the classical scheduling problem $P_2||C_{\max}$, where jobs must be allocated to either of two machines to minimize the makespan of the schedule. Define a related game where the social objective is also to minimize the makespan. Each player minimizes the completion time of his own single job by choosing a machine on which to process it.

Consider an instance of this game where there are two players, each with one job, i.e., $n = 2$, and let $p_1 = p_2 = 1$. Let x_i^* denote the probability with which player i chooses to allocate his job to machine 1. A mixed strategy Nash equilibrium is given by $x_1^* = x_2^* = 0.5$, i.e., each player chooses to schedule his job on machine 1 and on machine 2 with equal probability. With probability 0.5, both jobs are scheduled on the same machine, which results in a makespan of 2, and with probability 0.5, the

9.2 Complete Information Games

jobs are scheduled on different machines, which results in a makespan of 1. Hence, the expected makespan is $0.5(1) + 0.5(2) = 1.5$. The optimal centralized solution schedules the jobs on different machines, resulting in a makespan of 1. Hence, the price of anarchy is *at least* 1.5. Moreover, Koutsoupias and Papadimitriou (1999) provide a matching upper bound that establishes that the PoA is *exactly* 1.5.

Remark 9.1 Since the set of mixed strategies contains the set of pure strategies as a subset, and from (9.3), the PoA over pure strategies is less than or equal to that over mixed strategies in a cost minimization or profit maximization game. That is, the PoA is no worse under pure strategies than under mixed strategies.

It is therefore interesting, for comparison, to consider the problem discussed in Example 9.3 over pure strategies. Heydenreich et al. (2007) prove the following result.

Theorem 9.1 *For problem $P_2||C_{max}$, the PoA of pure strategy Nash equilibria is 4/3.*

Proof There are n jobs in this game. To prove the upper bound, consider an arbitrary schedule in pure strategy Nash equilibria. Let T_1, T_2 denote the total processing time on machines 1 and 2, respectively; hence, $C_{max} = \max\{T_1, T_2\}$, where without loss of generality we let $T_2 = T_1 + \delta$, and $\delta \geq 0$. If machine 2 has only one job, then the schedule is optimal, i.e., $C_{max} = T^*$. Otherwise, any job on machine 2 must have a processing time of at least δ; else it would move to machine 1. Therefore, $T_1 + \delta \geq 2\delta \Rightarrow T_1 \geq \delta$. An optimal schedule cannot do better than divide δ equally between the two machines, hence $T^* \geq T_1 + \delta/2$. Therefore,

$$PoA = \frac{\max\{T_1, T_2\}}{T^*} = \frac{T_2}{T^*} \leq \frac{T_1 + \delta}{T_1 + \delta/2} \leq \frac{2\delta}{3\delta/2} = 4/3, \tag{9.4}$$

where the second inequality is obtained by setting T_1 as small as possible, i.e., $T_1 = \delta$.

The following example shows that the upper bound established in (9.4) is attainable in this game.

Example 9.4 (Lower Bound on PoA for a Two Machine Makespan Game) Consider an instance of a game defined over problem $P_2||C_{max}$, where $n = 4$, $p_1 = p_2 = 1$, and $p_3 = p_4 = 2$. An optimal solution schedules one job with processing time 1 and one job with processing time 2 on each machine, giving $C_{max} = 3$. However, consider a schedule with jobs 1 and 2 on machine 1, and jobs 3 and 4 on machine 2, giving $C_{max} = 4$. Since no job can move to a different machine and reduce its cost, this schedule is a pure strategy Nash equilibrium. Hence, $PoA \geq 4/3$. □

Lee et al. (2012) consider the price of anarchy in settings with two parallel uniform, i.e., proportional speed, machines. In a game they describe in this environment, the social objective is the minimization of the total completion time of all the jobs. Each player owns a single job. The objective of each player is to minimize the completion time of his job. The classical scheduling problem underlying this game is denoted as $Q_2|| \sum C_j$. To give some context for this analysis, we provide two related results for the identical parallel-machine case $P_2|| \sum C_j$ and the unrelated parallel-machine case $R_2|| \sum C_j$.

Theorem 9.2 *If each machine adopts a local SPT policy in problem $P_2|| \sum C_j$, then the PoA is 1.*

Proof The assumption in the theorem implies that, on each machine, jobs are scheduled in SPT order. Index the entire set of jobs in SPT order. Assume, without loss of generality, that the shortest job is scheduled on machine 1. Within all possible schedules that satisfy these conditions, we call a schedule in which all the odd numbered jobs are scheduled on machine 1 and all the even numbered jobs are scheduled on machine 2, an *alternating schedule*. We now show that any schedule with SPT ordering on both machines that is at a Nash equilibrium is an alternating schedule.

Observe that in an alternating schedule the total processing time on machine 1 is not smaller (respectively, not larger) than that on machine 2 after the scheduling of each odd (resp., even) numbered job. Let k denote the lowest indexed job that does not follow the alternating schedule. There are two cases. If k is odd but job k is scheduled on machine 2, then from the above observation, job k can move to machine 1 where its completion time will be smaller or the same. Alternatively, if k is even but job k is scheduled on machine 1, then the number of jobs on machine 1 is greater by two than the number on machine 2, and again from the above observation, job k can move to machine 2 where its completion time will be smaller or the same. It follows that any schedule with SPT ordering on both machines that is at a Nash equilibrium is an alternating schedule.

Next, observe that the total completion time cost $\sum C_j$ of any job sequence can be expressed as the sum of job processing times multiplied by a positional penalty that represents the number of jobs scheduled after job j and job j itself. Given this definition, it can be shown by adjacent pairwise interchange of jobs that the total cost is minimized if the jobs $p_n, p_{n-1}, \ldots, p_1$ are associated with the respective positional penalties $1, 1, 2, 2, \ldots, (n-1)/2, (n-1)/2, \lceil n/2 \rceil$ if n is odd, or $1, 1, 2, 2, \ldots, n/2, n/2$ if n is even. Finally, observe that an alternating schedule also associates the jobs and positional penalties in exactly this way. Therefore, an alternating schedule is a minimum cost schedule. Hence, any Nash equilibrium schedule is optimal, and the PoA is 1. $\square$

In the unrelated parallel-machines case, $R_2|| \sum C_j$, under the same local policy, Cole et al. (2011) show that the PoA in pure strategy Nash equilibria is at most 4. Intuitively, we expect that the result for two uniform machines, i.e., the Q_2 environment, interpolates between 1 and 4. This is indeed the case, as shown by Lee et al. (2012) in the following result.

Theorem 9.3 *Given two uniform parallel machines that adopt a local SPT policy and a central objective of minimizing the total completion time $\sum C_j$, then the PoA in pure strategy Nash equilibria satisfies $\frac{3+\sqrt{3}}{4} \leq PoA \leq \frac{1+\sqrt{5}}{2}$.*

9.2 Complete Information Games

Proof The upper bound is proved as follows. Without loss of generality, define the machine speeds as $s_2 = 1$ and $s_1 = s > 1$. Index the jobs in SPT order, i.e., $p_1 \leq \cdots \leq p_n$. Let $[j]$ denote the job with the jth smallest completion time in an optimal schedule σ^*. Then, for a schedule σ that is a Nash equilibrium,

$$\sum_{j=1}^{n} C_j(\sigma) = C_1(\sigma) + C_2(\sigma) + \cdots + C_n(\sigma)$$

$$\leq p_1/s + (p_1 + p_2)/s + \cdots + (p_1 + p_2 + \cdots + p_n)/s \quad (9.5)$$

$$= \sum_{j=1}^{n} \sum_{i=1}^{j} p_i/s.$$

Inequality (9.5) uses the scheduling of all jobs in SPT order on the faster machine as a reference point. For large values of s, this solution may be a Nash equilibrium. However, in all cases, its cost is an upper bound on any Nash equilibrium solution. Meanwhile, in an optimal schedule σ^*,

$$\sum_{j=1}^{n} C_j(\sigma^*) = C_{[1]}(\sigma^*) + C_{[2]}(\sigma^*) + \cdots + C_{[n]}(\sigma^*)$$

$$\geq p_{[1]}/(s+1) + (p_{[1]} + p_{[2]})/(s+1)$$

$$+ \cdots + (p_{[1]} + p_{[2]} + \cdots + p_{[n]})/(s+1) \quad (9.6)$$

$$= [np_{[1]} + (n-1)p_{[2]} + \cdots + 1p_{[n]}]/(s+1)$$

$$\geq [np_1 + (n-1)p_2 + \cdots + 1p_n]/(s+1) \quad (9.7)$$

$$= \sum_{j=1}^{n} \sum_{i=1}^{j} p_i/(s+1),$$

where the inequality (9.6) is obtained by allowing both machines to process the same job concurrently, and the inequality (9.7) follows from the SPT indexing of the jobs. Hence,

$$\frac{\sum_{j=1}^{n} C_j(\sigma)}{\sum_{j=1}^{n} C_j(\sigma^*)} \leq 1 + 1/s. \quad (9.8)$$

Recall that $s_2 = 1$ and $s_1 = s > 1$. Now, consider two machine environments that provide upper and lower bounds on cost in the environment that we are considering here: $s_1 = s_2 = 1$ and $s_1 = s_2 = s$. Let z_1 (respectively, z_2) denote the schedule from an SPT local policy in the first (resp., second) environment, given the same set of jobs. Then, $\sum_{j=1}^{n} C_j(\sigma) \leq z_1$ and $\sum_{j=1}^{n} C_j(\sigma^*) \geq z_2$. Therefore,

$$\frac{\sum_{j=1}^{n} C_j(\sigma)}{\sum_{j=1}^{n} C_j(\sigma^*)} \leq s. \quad (9.9)$$

Then, from (9.8) and (9.9),

$$\frac{\sum_{j=1}^{n} C_j(\sigma)}{\sum_{j=1}^{n} C_j(\sigma^*)} \leq \min\{1 + 1/s, s\}$$

$$\leq \frac{1 + \sqrt{5}}{2}.$$

An example instance is now used to establish the lower bound.

Example 9.5 (Lower Bound on PoA for a Two Machine Completion Time Game)
Let $n = 3$, $p_1 = s$, $p_2 = s/(s - 1)$, $p_3 = [s/(s - 1)]^2$, $s_1 = s = 1 + 1/\sqrt{3}$, and
$s_2 = 1$. Observe that $p_1 < p_2 < p_3$ here. Consider the schedule σ where jobs 1 and
2 are scheduled on machine 1 in that sequence in SPT order and job 3 is scheduled
on machine 2. Then, $C_1(\sigma) = 1$, $C_2(\sigma) = [1 + 1/(s - 1)]$, and $C_3(\sigma) = [s/(s - 1)]^2$;
hence,

$$\sum_{j=1}^{3} C_j(\sigma) = 1 + \left[1 + \frac{1}{(s - 1)}\right] + \left[\frac{s}{s - 1}\right]^2.$$

Observe that no job can reduce its cost by moving to another machine. Hence, this
solution is a Nash equilibrium in pure strategy. However, in an optimal schedule
σ^*, jobs 1 and 3 are scheduled on machine 1 in that sequence by SPT, and job 2 is
scheduled on machine 2. Then,

$$\sum_{j=1}^{3} C_j(\sigma^*) = 1 + \frac{s}{s - 1} + \left[1 + \frac{s}{(s - 1)^2}\right].$$

Therefore, the PoA in pure Nash equilibria satisfies

$$PoA \geq \frac{\sum_{j=1}^{3} C_j(\sigma)}{\sum_{j=1}^{3} C_j(\sigma^*)}$$

$$= \frac{2 + 1/(s - 1) + [s/(s - 1)]^2}{2 + s/(s - 1) + [s/(s - 1)^2]}$$

$$= 1 + \frac{s - 1}{3s^2 - 4s + 2}$$

$$= 1 + \frac{1}{2\sqrt{3} + 2}, \qquad \text{by definition of } s$$

$$= \frac{3 + \sqrt{3}}{4}.$$

□

9.2 Complete Information Games

From Theorem 9.3, the PoA for problem $Q_2 || \sum C_j$ is between $(3 + \sqrt{3})/4 \approx 1.183$ and $(1 + \sqrt{5})/2 \approx 1.618$, and clearly between 1 and 4, as expected from Theorem 9.2 and Cole et al. (2011).

Lee et al. (2012) also study the absolute price of anarchy for three classical scheduling objectives defined by due dates: maximum tardiness, total tardiness, and the number of tardy jobs.

Besides the performance of the worst Nash equilibrium, it is also of interest to evaluate the best Nash equilibrium. In general, the best Nash equilibrium solution need not be socially optimal. The following definition is useful for characterizing it.

Definition 9.4 Consider a cost minimization game, where z^* denotes the minimum total system cost and $z^N(\sigma)$ denotes the cost of a solution σ. Then, the *price of stability* (PoS) is defined by

$$PoS = \min_{\sigma \in NE} \{z^N(\sigma)\}/z^*, \tag{9.10}$$

where NE is the set of strategies that are at a Nash equilibrium in pure strategy. Analogously, in a profit maximization game, we let z^* denote the maximum total system profit and $z^N(\sigma)$ denote the profit of a Nash equilibrium solution σ. Then, $PoS = z^*/\max_{\sigma \in NE}\{z^N(\sigma)\}$.

9.2.1.3 Absolute Price of Anarchy

For scheduling problems with due dates, the value of an optimal solution may be zero or even negative. Hence, the conventional definition of the price of anarchy in (9.3) cannot be applied. As an alternative, Lee et al. (2012) define the *absolute price of anarchy* for a cost minimization game as

$$APoA = \max_{\sigma \in NE} \left[z^N(\sigma) - z^* \right]. \tag{9.11}$$

We illustrate the use of this performance measure for a supply chain scheduling game on m identical parallel machines. The central objective considered is minimization of the total tardiness, i.e., problem $P_m || \sum T_j$, where $T_j = \max\{C_j - p_j, 0\}$. There are n players. Each player owns a single job and minimizes the tardiness of that job, which is a nondecreasing function of its completion time. Since if $n \leq m$, all jobs can start processing at time 0, every schedule that starts at most one job on each machine is optimal. Hence, we assume that $n > m$. Let $P = \sum_{j=1}^{n} p_j$. Recall that an EDD policy (Jackson, 1955) schedules the jobs by nondecreasing order of due dates.

Theorem 9.4 *Given m identical parallel machines that adopt an EDD local policy, and a central objective of minimizing the total tardiness, then the APoA is $(n/m - 1)P$.*

562   9 Noncooperative Supply Chain Scheduling

Proof To prove the upper bound, observe that, in any feasible schedule, the completion time of job j is at least p_j. Thus, $T_j(\sigma^*) \geq \max\{0, p_j - d_j\}$. In a pure Nash equilibrium schedule, let $N^0 \subseteq N$ denote the set of jobs that start processing at time 0, and let $|N^0| = m$.

Now, for $j \in N^0$, we have

$$
\begin{aligned}
T_j(\sigma) &= \max\{0, C_j - d_j\} \\
&= \max\{0, p_j - d_j\} \\
&\leq T_j(\sigma^*).
\end{aligned}
\tag{9.12}
$$

On the other hand, for $j \in N \setminus N^0$, we have

$$
\begin{aligned}
T_j(\sigma) &= \max\{0, C_j - d_j\} \\
&\leq \max\{0, (P - p_j)/m + p_j - d_j\}, \quad \text{from property of a Nash equilibrium} \\
&\leq \max\{0, p_j - d_j\} + (P - p_j) \\
&\leq T_j(\sigma^*) + P/m.
\end{aligned}
\tag{9.13}
$$

Therefore, combining the last two results, we have

$$
\begin{aligned}
\sum_{j=1}^{n} T_j(\sigma) &= \sum_{j \in N^0} T_j(\sigma) + \sum_{j \in N \setminus N^0} T_j(\sigma) \\
&\leq \sum_{j \in N^0} T_j(\sigma^*) + \sum_{j \in N \setminus N^0} T_j(\sigma^*) + (n - m)P/m, \\
&\qquad \text{from (9.12) and (9.13)} \\
&\leq \sum_{j \in N} T_j(\sigma^*) + (n/m - 1)P.
\end{aligned}
$$

Thus, $APoA \leq (n/m - 1)P$ for this problem. The following example establishes the matching lower bound in this game.

Example 9.6 (Lower Bound on APoA in a Total Tardiness Game) Consider the following instance of the above game. For $l \in \mathbb{R}_+$, let there be $n = l \times m$ jobs to be scheduled on m machines. There are only two types of jobs. There are $(l - 1)m$ jobs of the first type and m jobs of the second type. Let $p_j = \epsilon > 0$ and small, and $d_j = \lceil j/m \rceil \epsilon$, for $j = 1, \ldots, (l - 1)m$. Let $p_j = x$, $d_j = 0$, for $j = (l - 1)m + 1, \ldots, lm$. Observe that $P = \sum_{j=1}^{n} p_j = (l - 1)m\epsilon + mx$ and also that $l = n/m$.

In an optimal schedule σ^*, jobs $1, \ldots, (l - 1)m$ are scheduled on machines 1 through m in EDD order, and jobs $(l - 1)m + 1, \ldots, lm$ are scheduled last on the m

9.2 Complete Information Games

machines. Thus, $T_j(\sigma^*) = 0$ for $j = 1, \ldots, (l-1)m$, and $T_j(\sigma^*) = (l-1)\epsilon + x$ for $j = (l-1)m + 1, \ldots, lm$. Therefore,

$$\sum_{j=1}^{n} T_j(\sigma^*) = [(l-1)\epsilon + x]m.$$

Consider a schedule σ where all jobs are scheduled in EDD order. Then, each machine processes one job with processing time x, followed by $(l-1)$ jobs with processing times ϵ, all of which are tardy by at least time x. Hence,

$$\sum_{j=1}^{n} T_j(\sigma) \geq xlm.$$

Moreover, since all machines complete processing at time $x + (l-1)\epsilon$, no job can move to another machine without increasing its completion time. Hence, schedule σ is a Nash equilibrium schedule.

Now, as $\epsilon \to 0$, it follows that $P \to xm$; hence, we have

$$APoA \geq xlm - [(l-1)\epsilon + x]m$$
$$= (l-1)xm - (l-1)\epsilon m$$
$$\to (n/m - 1)P \text{ as } \epsilon \to 0.$$

$\square$

The above definitions and examples provide a framework for studying the performance of Nash equilibrium solutions in various supply chain scheduling games in the following sections.

9.2.2 Finding and Evaluating an Equilibrium

This section contains six examples of supply chain scheduling problems for which we discuss the development of an algorithm to find a Nash equilibrium. Section 9.2.2.1 discusses a simple scheduling problem with unit processing times and both earliness and tardiness costs. Section 9.2.2.2 discusses two problems involving subcontracting. In the first problem, a set of manufacturers is supported by a third-party provider of capacity. In the second problem, various departments within an organization can use either a common resource shared with other departments or an external subcontractor. Section 9.2.2.3 describes a project scheduling game where the players own tasks which they can expedite at cost, if doing so generates a sufficient share of additional reward for improved project completion time provided by the project customer. Section 9.2.2.4 illustrates issues that arise in finding an

564   9   Noncooperative Supply Chain Scheduling

equilibrium when different machines use a variety of local prioritization rules for the jobs assigned to them. Section 9.2.2.5 discusses a scheduling game with both congestion and activation costs for machines, which generates interesting tradeoffs. In several of the problems studied in this section, finding a Nash equilibrium, and particularly finding one with a pre-specified bound on system cost, is shown to be an intractable problem.

9.2.2.1   Earliness and Tardiness Costs

The first supply chain scheduling game discussed in this section is chosen for its simplicity and the conciseness of its results. In a centralized decision making environment, a single machine problem with earliness and tardiness costs around a common due date is studied by Hall (1986) and Kanet (1981). The motivation for this problem is that earliness costs model the cost of holding inventory, whereas tardiness costs model penalties in delivery contracts with customers. A generalization of this problem with weighted earliness and tardiness penalties is studied by Hall and Posner (1991), who provide a pseudo-polynomial time algorithm and a proof of binary NP-completeness, as well as analysis of some special cases. Hall et al. (1991) provide similar results for an alternative version of the problem without weights where the common due date may be restrictively early. In a decentralized decision making environment, Glazer et al. (2018) study the problem of job arrivals to a single machine, where jobs incur both earliness and tardiness costs. We describe a noncooperative game defined over this supply chain scheduling problem.

Consider n customers or players, each of whom owns one or more jobs. Each job has a processing requirement of one time unit. The strategy of customer i is defined by s_i, the time at which he sends his jobs into the system for processing. Those jobs start processing immediately if and only if no other jobs are being processed or waiting for service. All jobs share a single server with a common due date, $d = 0$, which is not restrictive since negative start times are permitted. The earliness or tardiness cost of each job is measured by the absolute value of the time difference between its start time and the common due date d. There is a linear penalty c_e for each unit of earliness and a linear penalty c_l for each unit of tardiness. For example, the cost of starting job i at time $t > 0$ is $c_l t$. The dynamics of this noncooperative game are as follows:

1. Customers simultaneously decide, at time $-n$, when to send their jobs.
2. The server starts working when the first job arrives.
3. Jobs arriving at a busy server form a first-come, first-served queue if the server is busy, with simultaneous arrivals being sequenced according to a uniform random distribution over all possible sequences.
4. Once it completes processing a job, the server immediately processes a job at the head of the queue if there is one.
5. Customers pay a penalty for deviation of their service start time from the common due date.

9.2 Complete Information Games

We consider the scheduling environment defined above from the viewpoint of minimizing total cost, i.e., the total earliness and tardiness cost of the jobs. We first characterize an optimal solution (Glazer et al., 2018). Define $\tilde{s} = nc_l/(c_e + c_l)$.

Lemma 9.1 *A sequence of service start times is optimal if and only if there exists an indexing of the jobs such that $s_i = s_{i-1} + 1$, $i = 2, \ldots, n$, and:*

(i) If $\tilde{s}$ is integer, then $s_1 \in [-\tilde{s}, -\tilde{s} + 1]$.
(ii) If $\tilde{s}$ is not integer, then $s_1 = -\lfloor \tilde{s} \rfloor$.

Proof Without loss of generality, let $s_1 \leq \cdots \leq s_n$. Suppose the server is idle after job i where $s_i < 0$. Then, the earliness cost of all jobs up to i can be reduced by shifting them forward until there is no idle time, without affecting the timing of other jobs. A similar argument applies to the case where $s_i > 0$. Hence, processing of the unit size jobs is consecutive, i.e., $s_i = s_{i-1} + 1$, $i = 2, \ldots, n$, and the optimization problem reduces to a single decision variable, s_1. Letting $i_0 = \max\{i \mid s_i \leq 0\}$, the total cost function is

$$z(s_1) = \sum_{i=i_0+1}^{n} c_l(s_1 + i - 1) - \sum_{i=1}^{i_0} c_e(s_1 + i - 1)$$

$$= (c_l n - c_l i_0 - c_e i_0)s_1 + \sum_{i=i_0+1}^{n} c_l(i - 1) - \sum_{i=1}^{i_0} c_e(i - 1).$$

The slope of $z(s_1)$ is negative if $i_0 > \tilde{s}$, positive if $i_0 < \tilde{s}$, and 0 otherwise. The solution has two cases.

If $\tilde{s}$ is integer, then any s_1 that satisfies

$$-\tilde{s} \leq s_1 \leq -\tilde{s} + 1$$

is optimal.

Alternatively, if $\tilde{s}$ is not integer, then an optimal solution satisfies

$$-\tilde{s} < i_0 = \max\{i \mid s_1 + i - 1 \leq 0\} < -\tilde{s} + 1$$

and $s_1 + i_0 - 1 = 0$. Hence, $s_1 = -\lfloor \tilde{s} \rfloor$. $\qquad\square$

Recall that each job is owned by a player who decides when to release his job into the system. However, the job does not necessarily start immediately if other jobs are also waiting to start. We consider each player as the owner of a single job, with the objective of minimizing the cost of that job. The social objective is minimization of the total cost of all the players.

The following analysis provides necessary and sufficient conditions under which a socially optimal set of arrival times is an equilibrium. We define a strategy where all players make the same choice about when to release their jobs to the system to be

566   9 Noncooperative Supply Chain Scheduling

symmetric. Glazer et al. (2018) prove the following preliminary result for the game defined above:

Lemma 9.2

  (i) *There is no asymmetric equilibrium of the game in pure strategy.*
 (ii) *There is no asymmetric equilibrium of the game in mixed strategy.*
(iii) *There is no symmetric equilibrium of the game in mixed strategy.*

From Lemma 9.2, we restrict our discussion of equilibrium solutions to symmetric solutions in pure strategy. Now, let $c(s : t)$ denote the cost of a single player who chooses strategy s to minimize his individual cost when all the other players choose strategy t. As a special case of this definition, $c(t : t)$ is the cost of single player choosing strategy t when all other players choose t. The next result characterizes all possible equilibria.

Lemma 9.3 *Let $t = t_1$ be a solution of $c(t : t) = c_l(t + n - 1)$, and let $t = t_2$ be a solution of $c(t : t) = -c_e t$. Then, t_1 and t_2 are unique, and the set of all equilibria is given by the pure and symmetric strategies of all customers arriving together at time t, such that $t \in [t_1, t_2] \subset (-(n-1), 0)$, within which $t = -(n-1)[c_l/(c_e+c_l)]$ is an equilibrium.*

Proof Suppose all other customers arrive at some common time $t < 0$. Then, the expected cost for each of them, as determined by the uniformly generated random distribution of start times $t, \ldots, t + n - 1$, is

$$\sum_{i=0}^{n-1} \frac{t+i}{n} [c_l(|\{i \mid t + i \geq 0\}|) - c_e(|\{i \mid t + i < 0\}|)].$$

Besides the option of joining the other customers to arrive at time t, a single customer has only two reasonable alternatives: arriving before everyone else and incurring a cost of at least $-c_e t$, and waiting for everyone else to finish service and incurring a cost of at least $c_l(t + n - 1)$. Therefore,

$$c(s : t) = \begin{cases} -c_e s, & \text{if } s < t \\ [c_l \sum_{i=i_t+1}^{n-1}(t + i) - c_e \sum_{i=0}^{i_t}(t + i)]/n, & \text{if } s = t \\ c_l \max\{t + n - 1, s\}, & \text{if } s > t. \end{cases} \tag{9.14}$$

Let $i_t = \max\{i \mid t + i < 0\} > 0$. Then, the cost function $c(s : t)$ is piecewise linear with respect to t with a slope of

$$f(t) = \frac{c_l(n - 1 - i_t) - c_e i_t}{n}.$$

Now, if $t \in (-(n-1), 0)$, then $i_t \in (0, (n-1))$; hence, $f(t) < c_l$, and the solution t of $c(t : t) = c_l(t+n-1)$ is unique. Similarly, $c(t : t) = -c_e t$ has a unique solution.

9.2 Complete Information Games

Finally, $c(t : t) \leq c_l(t + n - 1)$ is satisfied for any $t \geq t_1$, and $c(t : t) \leq -c_e t$ is satisfied for any $t \leq t_2$. Summarizing, the interval $[t_1, t_2]$ is the set of all equilibria with pure symmetric strategies.

Finally, consider the symmetric solution $t = -(n - 1)[c_l/(c_e + c_l)]$. Using the expression under the condition $s = t$ from (9.14), we can write

$$
\begin{aligned}
c(t : t) &= -\frac{c_e t}{n} + \frac{[c_l \sum_{i=i_t+1}^{n-1}(t + i) - c_e \sum_{i=0}^{i_t}(t + i)]}{n} \\
&\leq c_l(t + n - 1) \\
&= -c_e t,
\end{aligned}
$$

and therefore, neither arriving before or after all other customers reduces the expected cost of a single customer. Hence, $t = -(n - 1)[c_l/(c_e + c_l)]$ is an equilibrium. $\square$

Next, we provide necessary and sufficient conditions for a socially optimal solution to be an equilibrium. The availability of such simple conditions is unusual within noncooperative supply chain scheduling games.

Theorem 9.5 *For the earliness–tardiness game, there exists a socially optimal symmetric arrival time that is also an equilibrium if and only if:*

(a) $n = 2$ *and* $c_e = c_l$.
(b) $n > 2$ *and*

$$
\frac{c_l}{c_e + c_l} \in [\frac{1}{n}, 1 - \frac{1}{n}].
$$

Proof From Lemma 9.1, it is socially optimal if all players arrive together at $t^* = -\lfloor nc_l/(c_e + c_l) \rfloor$. We consider conditions under which this solution is, or is not, an equilibrium, and where it is not, whether any equilibrium solutions exist. There are several cases:

Case 1. If $c_l/(c_e + c_l) < 1/n$, then $t^* = 0$, and any customer can reduce his cost by arriving momentarily before the others. Symmetrically, if

$$
\frac{c_l}{c_e + c_l} > 1 - \frac{n - 1}{n}, \tag{9.15}
$$

then $t^* = -(n - 1)$, and a player who arrives during $(-(n - 1), 0]$ incurs no cost. In either case, $nc_l/(c_e + c_l)$ is not an integer, and t^* is the unique equilibrium. Since t^* is not socially optimal, then it follows that no equilibrium is socially optimal.

Case 2. If $n = 2$, (9.15) is only satisfied if $c_e = c_l$. In this case, the unique equilibrium $t_1 = t_2 = -1/2$ is socially optimal.

Case 3. If $n > 2$ and

$$\frac{c_l}{c_e + c_l} \in \left[\frac{1}{n}, 1 - \frac{1}{n}\right],$$

then the social optimum is given by an integer t^* satisfying $-(n-2) \le t^* \le -1$. Since the total cost is $nc(t:t)$, minimizing the social cost is equivalent to minimizing the average customer cost. Let $k = -t^*$ and $m = n - 1 - k$. Then, $k/n = -t^*/n \ge 1/n$ is the proportion of early arrivals and $(m+1)/n = (n-k)/n \ge 1/n$ is the proportion of late arrivals including the costless job that arrives at time $d = 0$. The average cost of the early jobs is

$$c_e \sum_{i=1}^{k} i/k = c_e(k+1)/2. \tag{9.16}$$

The average cost of the late jobs and the one on-time job is

$$c_l \sum_{i=0}^{m} i/(m+1) = c_l m/2. \tag{9.17}$$

Collecting the costs from (9.16) and (9.17), the average customer cost is

$$c(t^* : t^*) = \frac{k}{n} \frac{c_e(k+1)}{2} + \frac{m+1}{n} \frac{c_l m}{2}. \tag{9.18}$$

Observe that the solution is in equilibrium unless a job can reduce its cost by moving from its expected cost position to an extreme schedule, i.e., the start of the schedule with cost kc_e or the end of the schedule with cost mc_l. Hence, a sufficient condition for t^* to be an equilibrium is that the average customer cost does not exceed $\min\{c_e k, c_l m\}$, the smaller of the two extreme schedule costs. There are again three cases (3a, 3b, 3c) that follow:

Case 3a. If $c_e k = c_l m$, then since $c_e(k+1)/2 < c_e k$ and $c_l m/2 < c_l m$, the average cost is smaller than the costs kc_e and mc_l of the two extreme schedules.

Case 3b. If $c_e k > c_l m$, then the early extreme schedule cost exceeds the average cost. Suppose $c_l m < kc_e/2$, then $kc_e > 2c_l m \ge c_l(m+1)$, in which case setting $t = -t^* + 1$ reduces the average cost, which is a contradiction. Then, the alternative case $c_l m \ge kc_e/2$ implies that the average cost does not exceed the late extreme schedule cost.

Case 3c. If $c_e k < c_l m$, then the late extreme cost immediately exceeds the average cost. Suppose $c_e k < c_l m/2$. Then, consider the special case $k = 1$ and $m = n - 1$ where $2c_e < c_l(n-1)$, in which case setting $t^* = -2$ reduces the average cost, which is a contradiction. Alternatively, $c_e k \ge c_l m/2$ implies that $c_e k \ge c(t^* : t^*)$, i.e., the early extreme cost exceeds the average cost.

$\square$

9.2 Complete Information Games

Theorem 9.5 provides the intuition that when n is not very small, there is a socially optimal equilibrium for reasonably symmetric values of c_e and c_l. However, if $c_e/(c_e + c_l)$ is too small (respectively, large), then the equilibrium arrivals are too early (resp., late) to coincide with an optimal solution.

Remark 9.2 Glazer et al. (2018) extend the results discussed above to consider several generalizations: a restricted interval during which service is offered, stochastic service times, a random number of customer arrivals, and heterogeneous customers with random cost functions. A general perspective is that their work develops interesting insights about whether, in equilibrium, customers arrive simultaneously.

The simple structure of the earliness–tardiness problem studied by Glazer et al. (2018) enables the characterization of necessary and sufficient conditions for a socially optimal solution to be an equilibrium and thereby provides clear insights about when the two types of solutions coincide.

9.2.2.2 Subcontracting

We discuss two noncooperative supply chain scheduling games that arise from a manufacturer's option to use subcontracting. This option has become widely used due to the need for increasingly specialized, often highly technical, work. The global market for subcontracted services in 2019 was more than \$92 billion (Statista, 2021). We refer the reader to Chapter 6 for extensive discussions of similar problems within a centralized supply chain scheduling environment.

Vairaktarakis (2013) considers a third-party (3P) supplier that provides outsourced capacity to a set of manufacturers, $M = \{1, \ldots, m\}$. Each manufacturer i has a set N_i of jobs that require the total processing time P_i. We number the manufacturers such that $P_1 \leq \cdots \leq P_m$. Each manufacturer i also has access to its own manufacturing resource that is denoted as M_i and the resource of the 3P that is denoted as F. This model can be used to illustrate a variety of Nash equilibrium solutions. The manufacturers compete or the 3P's capacity to optimize their own objective, which is the minimization of the completion time of their work, whether that occurs on their own facility or the 3P's. The 3P meanwhile has its own objective, which is to maximize the utilization of its capacity.

We discuss two alternative practical scheduling protocols: preemption with overlapping and nonpreemption. An overlapping preemptive protocol allows the processing of a job of manufacturer i to be divided between M_i and F and further allows concurrent processing of a job on M_i and F. By contrast, a nonpreemptive protocol requires that each *individual job* is processed either entirely on M_i or entirely on F, and processed from start to finish without interruption. However, even under the nonpreemptive protocol, manufacturer i may process some of its jobs on M_i and others on F. Let the decision variable $x_i, 0 \leq x_i \leq P_i$ denote the amount of processing subcontracted by manufacturer i to the 3P. The objective of each manufacturer i is to minimize its makespan, denoted by C_i, which is the later of its completion time on M_i and that on F in the event that its processing is

570   9 Noncooperative Supply Chain Scheduling

split between the two resources. The objective of the 3P is to maximize its revenue, which is modeled as $\sum_{i \in M} x_i$, i.e., the total work processed. All information, which consists of (a) $P_i, i \in M$, announced by the manufacturers, and (b) a priority rule to be used to schedule the jobs received as announced by the 3P, is public. As described below, the priority rule varies among different scheduling protocols.

We first consider the overlapping preemptive protocol. The subcontractor announces a priority rule under which the orders submitted by the manufacturers will be processed.

Priority Rule *Manufacturers' workloads x_i will be processed in SPT order, i.e., in nondecreasing order of x_i, with ties broken by index order.*

For this problem, we present the following result of Vairaktarakis (2013).

Theorem 9.6 *For the overlapping preemptive protocol, with the SPT priority rule used by the 3P, there exists a pure strategy Nash equilibrium where we define $x_0^* = 0$, and*

$$x_k^* = \min_{i \geq k} \left\{ \frac{P_i - \sum_{j=1}^{k-1} x_j^*}{i + 2 - k} \right\}, \quad k = 1, \ldots, m. \tag{9.19}$$

Proof If the manufacturers choose strategies $x_1^*, \ldots, x_m^*$, then the makespan C_i of manufacturer i is

$$C_i = \max \left\{ P_i - x_i^*, \sum_{k=1}^{i} x_k^* \right\} = P_i - x_i^*, \tag{9.20}$$

where the first term in the maximization is the completion time on M_i and the second term is the completion time on F. The second term represents the completion time of the work of manufacturer i on F since $x_1^* \leq \cdots \leq x_i^*$. Also, the equality in (9.20) holds because otherwise manufacturer i could decrease its outsourced workload, thereby reduce its makespan, and possibly even have its outsourced work processed earlier. Hence, for each manufacturer, its makespan is achieved on its own resource. As a result, $x_1^* + \cdots + x_{i-1}^* + 2x_i^* \leq P_i$, and from the SPT order, $(i + 1)x_1^* \leq P_i$ which implies $x_1^* \leq P_i/(i + 1)$, for $i \geq 1$.

Now, consider the outsourcing choice of manufacturer 1. If this manufacturer were the only player, then it would clearly outsource $P_1/2$ work. However, it needs to protect against competitive outsourcing of work P_2 by manufacturer 2, against competitive outsourcing of work P_3 by manufacturer M_3, and so on. Thus,

$$x_1^* = \min_{i \geq 1} \left\{ \frac{P_i}{i + 1} \right\}. \tag{9.21}$$

The outsourcing decisions of the other manufacturers are similar, except that the capacity used by the choices of the previous manufacturers has removed some

9.2 Complete Information Games

capacity from F. For example, $x_2^* = \min_{i \geq 2}\{\frac{P_i - x_1^*}{i}\}$. Proceeding similarly for the other manufacturers establishes the result. □

The following example provides intuition about the development of the players' strategies.

Example 9.7 (Nash Equilibrium Strategies in a Preemptive Outsourcing Game) Consider an instance of the game where $m = 4$ and $P_1 = 9$, $P_2 = 12$, $P_3 = 14$, and $P_4 = 19$. Then, $x_1^* = \min\{9/2, 12/3, 14/4, 19/5\} = 3.50$. The justification for this decision is that while manufacturer 1 would wish to outsource $9/2 = 4.50$ units of work, if it does so manufacturer 3 could set $x_3^* = 3.50$ and hence have its work scheduled before manufacturer 1's work on F under the 3P's SPT priority rule. As a result, manufacturer 1 outsources 3.50 units of work. Next, manufacturer 2 calculates $x_2^* = \min\{(12 - 3.50)/2, (14 - 3.50)/3, (19 - 3.50)/4\} = 3.50$ and also outsources 3.50 units of work. Then, manufacturer 3 calculates $x_3^* = \min\{(14 - 7)/2, (19 - 7)/3\} = 3.50$, with the same outsourcing decision. Finally, manufacturer 4 outsources $x_4^* = (19 - 10.50)/2 = 4.25$ units of work. The makespans of the manufacturers are: $C_1 = 9 - 3.50 = 5.50$, $C_2 = 12 - 3.50 = 8.50$, $C_3 = 14 - 3.50 = 10.50$, and $C_4 = 19 - 4.25 = 14.75$. Also, the 3P processes the total work of $\sum_{i=1}^{4} x_i^* = 3.50 + 3.50 + 3.50 + 4.25 = 14.75$. Finally, note that $\sum_{i=1}^{4} C_i = 5.50 + 8.50 + 10.50 + 14.75 = 39.25 = (9 + 12 + 14 + 19) - (3.50 + 3.50 + 3.50 + 4.25) = \sum_{i=1}^{4} P_i - \sum_{i=1}^{4} x_i^*$, due to the result in the proof of Theorem 9.6 that each manufacturer achieves its makespan on its own resource.

We next consider the nonpreemptive protocol. Recall that a manufacturer i can use only one of its two available resources, M_i and F, for any single job but can divide its jobs between them. The following definition is needed.

Definition 9.5 Let $f_i(w)$ denote the *maximum feasible workload* of any subset of jobs owned by a manufacturer i with a *total workload* that does not exceed w.

We provide an example of the relationship between the total workload and the maximum feasible workload in Definition 9.5.

Example 9.8 (Feasible Workloads in a Nonpreemptive Outsourcing Game) Suppose $P_i = 7$, where manufacturer i has two jobs with sizes 3 and 4 units. Then, $f_i(0) = f_i(1) = f_1(2) = 0$, $f_i(3) = 3$, $f_i(4) = f_i(5) = f_i(6) = 4$, $f_i(7) = 7$. For example, if the total workload is fixed at 6, the maximum feasible workload is 4.

The maximum feasible workload is typically a nondecreasing step function of the total workload. The variable w is similar to a knapsack capacity in this usage. The 3P forces the manufacturers to declare a value of the total workload w in order to have their jobs scheduled, and this value of w controls the amount of outsourcing by that manufacturer. Hence, in the following discussion, w_i is a total size from which manufacturer i chooses a feasible amount of outsourcing x_i^*, where $x_i^* = f_i(w_i)$.

The 3P has the objective of maximizing the utilization of its resource by the manufacturers. However, the 3P cannot control the outsourcing decisions of the manufacturers; thus the only way to achieve this is to guide the manufacturers into a Nash equilibrium solution that achieves this objective. For this purpose, the 3P announces to the manufacturers the following rule about the order in which it will process jobs that it receives.

Priority Rule *Manufacturers' workloads x_i will be processed in nondecreasing order of w_i, where x_i is the maximum feasible workload from a total workload w_i of manufacturer i's jobs, and with ties broken by smaller P_i values first.*

In Example 9.8, one solution that satisfies the priority rule is $w_i = 6$ and $x_i = 4$. This priority rule is designed to incentivize the manufacturers to make better utilization of F, by requiring them to maximize the utilization of a knapsack of size w. Each manufacturer i chooses its own value of w_i, taking into consideration the tradeoff that a larger value of w_i provides more options for subcontracting, but possibly a later processing time by the 3P.

Vairaktarakis (2013) proves the following preliminary result.

Lemma 9.4 *If there exists a pure strategy Nash equilibrium, then there exists one in which the jobs of the manufacturers are scheduled on F in nondecreasing order of their P_i values.*

We observe that Lemma 9.4 is not in conflict with the priority rule, since there exist total workload values $w_1, \ldots, w_m$ that satisfy both. From Lemma 9.4, we assume that the manufacturers are indexed such that $P_1 \leq \cdots \leq P_m$.

Theorem 9.7 *Let $i = 1, \ldots, m$ denote an SPT order of P_i values. We first define*

$$g_{ki}(w) = \max \left\{ P_i - f_i(w), \sum_{j=1}^{k-1} x_j^* + \sum_{j=k}^{i} f_j(w) \right\}, \quad and$$

$$h_{ki}(w) = \max \left\{ P_i - f_i(w), \sum_{j=1}^{k-1} x_j^* + f_i(w) \right\}, \quad 1 \leq k \leq i \leq m,$$

for use in the optimization model (9.22)–(9.23) below.

Then, the strategies defined by solving the following sequence of mathematical programs, for $k = 1, \ldots, m$:

$$x_k^* = \min_{w_k \geq w_{k-1}} g_{kk}(w_k) \tag{9.22}$$

$$s.t. \quad g_{ki}(w_k) \leq h_{ki}(w_i), \quad i > k \tag{9.23}$$

provide a pure strategy Nash equilibrium.

Proof We first interpret the mathematical model in the theorem statement. Manufacturer k chooses a value of w that implies an amount of outsourcing x_k^*. More specifically, the decision variables for manufacturer k are w_k and $x_k^* =$

9.2 Complete Information Games

$g_{kk}(w_k)$, where the choice of w_k is restricted by previous nondecreasing choices $w_1, \ldots, w_{k-1}$. It is clear that for the purpose of minimizing its makespan, manufacturer k may set $w_k > w_{k-1}$, provided that doing so does not provide an incentive for a later manufacturer $r > k$ to minimize its own makespan by setting $w_r < w_k$ and thereby having its jobs scheduled ahead of manufacturer k's according to the 3P's priority rule. The w_i values are determined in the sequence $w_1, \ldots, w_m$ and similarly for the x_i^* values $x_1, \ldots, x_m$.

Consider the problem faced by manufacturer 1:

$$x_1^* = \min_{w_1 \geq 0} g_{11}(w_1) \tag{9.24}$$

$$\text{s.t.} \quad g_{1i}(w) \leq h_{1i}(w_i), \quad 1 \leq i \leq m. \tag{9.25}$$

The objective (9.24) minimizes the makespan of manufacturer 1. Constraints (9.25) ensure that the subcontracting decision of manufacturer 1 does not encourage a later manufacturer to make a choice that moves the work of manufacturer 1 later.

Given $x_1^*, \ldots, x_i^*$, where $1 \leq i \leq m$, the equilibrium strategies $x_{i+1}^*, \ldots, x_m^*$ of the other manufacturers can be found recursively, using the mathematical program in the theorem statement. $\qquad \square$

The computational requirement of the procedure in Theorem 9.7 is $O(m^2 \max_{i \in M}\{N_i\} \max_{i \in M}\{P_i\})$ time. Although this running time is not formally efficient, it is computationally tractable to a reasonable size of problem instance. We provide an example of this procedure.

Example 9.9 (Nash equilibrium Strategies in a Nonpreemptive Outsourcing Game) Consider an instance of the game where $m = 4$, $\{p_{1j}\} = \{5, 4, 2, 1\}$, $\{p_{2j}\} = \{11, 2, 1\}$, $\{p_{3j}\} = \{7, 6, 5\}$ and $\{p_{4j}\} = \{8, 8, 7\}$. Because $P_1 = 12 < P_2 = 14 < P_3 = 18 < P_4 = 23$, and from Lemma 9.4, we assume for the purposes of finding a Nash equilibrium that the manufacturers will have their jobs processed on F in the sequence $1, 2, 3, 4$ if $w_1 \leq w_2 \leq w_3 \leq w_4$. Nonetheless, the total workload w_i of each player i on F must be set such that each subsequent player does not benefit from using a smaller total workload on F.

Consider the outsourcing decision of manufacturer 1. Since $P_1 = 12$, it is optimal for manufacturer 1 to set $w_1 = 6$ and subcontract $12/2 = 6 = 4 + 2$ units, i.e., set $x_1 = 6$. Under the priority rule, this requires each subsequent manufacturer $i \geq 2$ to use at least $w_i \geq 6$ as the total workload of a feasible subset of jobs from which it chooses its subcontracted jobs. This in turn creates a problem that occurs after manufacturer 2, for which $w_2 = 6$ and $f_2(6) = 3$, and subcontracts 3 units. Then, F has already processed 9 units for manufacturers 1 and 2. Then, $w_3 \geq w_2 = 6$, and since manufacturer 3 has jobs of sizes 5, 6, and 7, $f_3(6) = 6$, and subcontracting at least 6 units creates a makespan of at least $\max\{9 + 6, 5 + 7\} = 15$. However, if manufacturer 3 subcontracts 5 units, the makespan is $\max\{9 + 5, 6 + 7\} = 14 < 15$. This implies that manufacturer 1's choice of $w_1 = 6$ and subcontracting 6 units does not lead to an equilibrium solution.

Alternatively, if manufacturer 1 sets $w_1 = 5$, then we have $f_1(5) = 5 \Rightarrow x_1^* = 5$; next, manufacturer 2 sets $w_2 = 5$ and $f_2(5) = 3 \Rightarrow x_2^* = 3$; then, manufacturer 3 sets $w_3 = 5$ and $f_3(5) = 5 \Rightarrow x_3^* = 5$; and finally, manufacturer 4 sets $w_4 = 7$ and $f_4(7) = 7 \Rightarrow x_4^* = 7$, which is an equilibrium solution. This gives $\sum_{i=1}^4 x_i^* = 5 + 3 + 5 + 7 = 20$. Further, $\sum_{i=1}^4 C_i = \max\{7, 5\} + \max\{11, 8\} + \max\{13, 13\} + \max\{16, 20\} = 51$. By contrast with Example 9.7, we have $\sum_{i=1}^4 P_i - \sum_{i=1}^4 x_i^* = 67 - 20 = 47 < 51 = \sum_{i=1}^4 C_i$. This is because, in this nonpreemptive environment, a manufacturer i may attain its makespan C_i on F, in which case $C_i > P_i - x_i^*$.

A review of the above sequence of decisions provides some additional intuition. Manufacturer 1 has 12 units of work that can feasibly be divided into 6 units on its own resource and 6 units at the 3P, hence minimizing its makespan at a value of 6. Without any incentives by the 3P, manufacturer 1 will clearly do this because 6 is a lower bound on its makespan. However, the choice of priority rule by the 3P disincentivizes this decision, because it leads to a situation where another manufacturer's jobs are prioritized ahead of manufacturer 1's jobs by the 3P.

The two alternative models discussed above provide useful insights about Nash equilibrium solutions in subcontracting problems. We refer the reader to Vairaktarakis (2013) for analysis of an interesting and practical intermediate processing protocol that allows preemption but not overlapping.

We discuss a second example of a supply chain scheduling problem that includes an option for subcontracting. Bukchin and Hanany (2007) consider a problem with two alternative resources. There are several players, each of whom represents a department within the same organization. Each player owns one or more jobs. Jobs are scheduled either *in-house* on a machine shared by the other players or are subcontracted by the department that owns them.

If the jobs are subcontracted, then they do not need to compete with the jobs of the same department or those of other departments for processing time. Therefore, the completion time of a job is simply its processing time on the subcontracted resource, which is larger than on the in-house resource. The essentially unlimited concurrent capacity of the subcontractor is motivated by capacity reservation arrangements made in advance, as is common practice (Özer & Wei, 2006).

Let $C = \{1, \ldots, c\}$ denote the set of all jobs. The organization has departments $N = \{1, \ldots, n\}$, department i owns job set $C_i \subset C$, and each job is owned by a single department. Let p_j denote the in-house processing time of job j and αp_j denote its processing time that, as explained above, is also its completion time at the subcontractor, where $\alpha \geq 1$. For any set of jobs $V \subseteq C$, let $j_S(V)$ (respectively, $j_L(V)$) denotes the shortest (resp., longest) job in V.

The following notation applies to a given schedule. Let $M_i \subseteq C_i$ denote the set of department i's jobs that are scheduled on the shared in-house facility. Let S_i denote the set of jobs subcontracted by player i, where $S = \cup_{i=1}^n S_i$. Then clearly, $C_i = M_i \cup S_i, i = 1, \ldots, n$. Let M_{-i} denote the in-house processing decisions of all the players except i. Let $p_{M_i}(k)$ denote the length of the kth shortest job in M_i.

9.2 Complete Information Games

Player i, representing department i, minimizes his individual total completion time. The social objective is the minimization of the total cost of the players. Then, since both the centralized planner and the individual players use the minimization of the total completion time as their objective, we assume from Smith (1956) that the jobs are indexed in shortest processing time (SPT) order.

The cost of player i is composed of three parts and can be written as

$$F_i(M_i, M_{-i}) = \sum_{m=1}^{|M_i|} (|M_i| + 1 - m) p_{M_i}(m) + \sum_{j \in \cup M_{-i}} |\{j' \in M_i : j' > j\}| p_j$$

$$+ \alpha \sum_{j \in C_i \setminus M_i} p_i. \tag{9.26}$$

In (9.26), the first term is the total completion time of player i's jobs on the shared in-house machine, where they will be processed in SPT order (Smith, 1956), not yet considering delays caused by the processing of the other players' jobs. This expression applies a "positional penalty" ($|M_i| + 1 - m$) to the mth smallest processing time in M_i. The second term is the delays caused by the jobs of other players, when they precede the jobs of player j on the shared in-house facility. The third term is the completion time of player i's jobs that are sent to the subcontractor. Using Eq. (9.26), we can write the centralized objective as $\min \sum_{i \in N} F_i(M_i, M_{-i})$.

Bukchin and Hanany (2007) characterize a socially optimal solution, as follows. We refer the reader to that work for a proof. Observe that this problem is equivalent to the noncooperative game where $n = 1$, i.e., there is only one department.

Theorem 9.8 *There exists a socially optimal solution in which the organization keeps the $\lfloor \alpha \rfloor$ longest jobs on the shared in-house facility and sends the remaining $c - \lfloor \alpha \rfloor$ jobs to the subcontractor.*

However, a decentralized solution chosen by the players, i.e., a Nash equilibrium, may not be socially optimal. Therefore, Bukchin and Hanany (2007) establish bounds on the PoA. Furthermore, when the centralized solution is not a Nash equilibrium, it is important to develop a mechanism that coordinates the decentralized scheduling decisions of the players. We refer the reader to Sect. 9.1 for a definition of a coordination mechanism. The cost of implementing such a mechanism is assumed to be not more than the benefit from coordination and is therefore not considered further. The coordination mechanism needs to modify the incentive schemes of the departments so that all prefer to act according to the centralized objective. In achieving this, it needs to satisfy two conditions:

(i) It needs to be based on information that is available to the centralized authority.
(ii) Money transfers between the players should be zero-sum.

The proposed coordination mechanism modifies the SPT rule used for the in-house jobs, so that players representing the departments prefer not to deviate from the centralized solution. The mechanism requires that all in-house jobs other than the shortest are processed according to the SPT rule. The shortest in-house job is processed last if either (a) more than $\lfloor \alpha \rfloor$ jobs are processed in-house or (b) the longest job sent to the subcontractor is longer than the shortest in-house job. Otherwise, the shortest in-house job is processed first. No money transfers are required by the mechanism.

We now formally define the coordination mechanism, C-SPT, which finds an optimal centralized solution that is a pure Nash equilibrium. For any set of jobs $C' \subseteq C$, let $j_S(C')$ (respectively, $j_L(C')$) denote the shortest (resp., longest) job in C'.

Mechanism C-SPT

1. For any set M_i of department i's jobs that are manufactured in-house, all jobs $j \in (\cup_{i=1}^{n} M_i \setminus j_S(\cup_{i=1}^{n} M_i))$ are scheduled according to the SPT rule.
2. If either $| \cup_{i=1}^{n} M_i | > \lfloor \alpha \rfloor$ or $p_{j_L(C \setminus \cup_{i=1}^{n} M_i)} > p_{j_S(\cup_{i=1}^{n} M_i)}$, then job $j_S(\cup_{i=1}^{n} M_i)$ is scheduled in the last position on the shared in-house facility; otherwise, it is scheduled in the first position on the in-house facility.

Observe that mechanism C-SPT satisfies both the criteria (i) and (ii) above. First, the coordinator has enough information about the job in its processing time and does not need to know which department owns each job in order to complete the schedule. Second, there are no money transfers involved in the algorithm, and instead coordination is achieved merely by modifying the coordinator's scheduling policy. We now provide an example of mechanism C-SPT.

Example 9.10 (Application of Mechanism C-SPT) Consider an instance of the game defined above where $n = 2, c = 3, C_1 = \{1, 3\}, C_2 = \{2\}, p_1 = 2, p_2 = 4, p_3 = 6$, and $\alpha = 1.5$. Table 9.2 shows the cost table for both players, given their strategy of which job(s) to schedule on the shared in-house facility for player 1 in the row and for player 2 in the column. For example, if player 1 chooses strategy $\{1, 3\}$ and player 2 chooses strategy $\{2\}$, all three jobs are scheduled on the shared resource. From Step 2 of mechanism C-SPT, $|M_1 \cup M_2| = 3 > \lfloor 1.5 \rfloor = 1$; hence, the jobs are scheduled in the order 2,3,1, as a result of which $F_1 = (4 + 6) + (4 + 6 + 2) = 22$ and $F_2 = 4$, as shown in Table 9.2. The optimum centralized cost has $M_1 = \{3\}$, $M_2 = \emptyset$, where $F_1 = 6 + 1.5(2) = 9$ and $F_2 = (1.5)4 = 6$, and a total system cost of 15. The notation * against the relevant payoff for player 1 indicates that it is the best strategy for player 1 among the rows, given player 2's strategy in the column. Similarly, the notation † against the relevant payoff for player 2 indicates that it is the best strategy for player 2 among the columns, given player 1's strategy in the row. For example, if player 2 chooses $\{2\}$, the best response of player 1 is $\{3\}$, with

Table 9.2 Cost matrix for Example 9.10

$P_1 \backslash P_2$	$\emptyset$	$\{2\}$
$\emptyset$	$15, 6^\dagger$	$15, 4^\dagger$
$\{1\}$	$11, 6^\dagger$	$15, 4^\dagger$
$\{3\}$	$9^*, 6^\dagger$	$9^*, 10$
$\{1, 3\}$	$14, 6^\dagger$	$22, 4^\dagger$

9.2 Complete Information Games

a cost of 9. Observe that there is a solution in Table 9.1 where both players have a best response, given the other player's strategy, i.e., $M_1 = \{3\}$, $M_2 = \emptyset$, where $C_1 = 6 + 1.5(2) = 9$ and $C_2 = (1.5)4 = 6$, and a total system cost of 15. This is the unique Nash equilibrium in pure strategy, and also the optimum centralized solution, of the game.

We now provide the main result for coordination of the system.

Theorem 9.9 *Mechanism C-SPT finds a Nash equilibrium solution denoted by $\{M_i^*\}$ in pure strategy that is socially optimal, where $M_i^* = C_i \cap \{n + 1 - \lfloor \alpha \rfloor, \ldots, n\}$, $i = 1, \ldots, n$, and the jobs are indexed in SPT order.*

Proof It suffices to show that, for any $i = 1, \ldots, n$, M_i^* is a best response to M_{-i}^*. For a given i, let $M_i \subseteq C_i$ and $C' = (\cup_{j=1, j \neq i}^n M_j^*) \cup M_i$. There are two cases.

First, suppose $|C'| < \lfloor \alpha \rfloor$. In this case, there exists some job $h \in C_i \setminus M_i$, since $\lfloor \alpha \rfloor < c$ and player i fails to process its share of the $\lfloor \alpha \rfloor < c$ jobs in-house. Now, consider a new solution where a previously subcontracted job h is processed in-house. The resulting change in system cost is not more than $(|C'| - \alpha)p_h < (\lfloor \alpha \rfloor - \alpha)p_h \leq 0$; hence, M_i is not a best response to M_{-i}^* in this case.

Alternatively, suppose either $|C'| > \alpha$ or $|C'| = \alpha$, and $p_{j_L(C \setminus C')} > p_{j_S(C')}$. In this case, $j_S(C') \in C_i$, since player i fails to process its share of the $\lfloor \alpha \rfloor$ longest jobs in-house. Thus, under mechanism C-SPT, $j_S(C')$ is scheduled last. Now, consider a new solution where job $j_S(C')$ is removed from the in-house facility and subcontracted. The resulting change in system cost is

$$\alpha p_{j_S(C')} - \sum_{j \in C'} p_j < (\alpha - |C'|)p_{j_S(C')} \leq 0,$$

and hence, M_i is also not a best response to M_{-i}^* in this case.

Observing that since there must exist a best response to M_{-i}^*, and all alternatives to M_i^* have been exhausted, it follows that M_i^* is a best response to M_{-i}^*. In conclusion, finding a pure best response is equivalent to finding a socially optimal strategy. □

We remark that the intuition which underlies moving the shortest job to the end of the in-house schedule comes from comparing the positional penalty, i.e., the number of jobs with increased completion time due to the presence of the shortest job, with the increased processing time required by subcontracting.

9.2.2.3 Project Scheduling

As discussed in Sect. 8.5, project management is a globally important business process with a huge economic impact. Central to the success of project execution is efficient scheduling of the tasks of a project. Agnetis et al. (2015) study a project scheduling problem with multiple players and controllable processing times. The project customer provides a per unit time reward for shortening the makespan of

578   9 Noncooperative Supply Chain Scheduling

the project. This reward is shared by the players in fixed proportions that are known by the players in advance of their decision making. Each player has a choice about how long to take for his task, within a known interval. However, completing the task more quickly, i.e., *crashing* it, incurs a cost to the player. Hence, the player faces a situation where it is only worthwhile to crash his tasks if other players are doing likewise to the extent that a makespan reduction that generates a sufficient reward can be achieved. Each player maximizes his share of the project reward, less his crashing cost. The social objective is the minimization of the project makespan. We consider this problem as a noncooperative supply chain scheduling game and describe an algorithm to find a Nash equilibrium solution.

We describe some notation for this problem. Let $G = (N, U)$ denote an activity-on-arc graph that defines the activities of the project and their precedence relationships, where N is a set of nodes that represent project events, U is a set of arcs that represent tasks, and $|U| = n$. Let $A = \{1, \ldots, m\}$ denote the set of m players. Player i controls a set of tasks T_i. For each task (i, j), the normal and crashed durations are p_{ij}^U and p_{ij}^L, respectively, and task durations are assumed to be integer values in $[p_{ij}^L, p_{ij}^L + 1, \ldots, p_{ij}^U]$. The cost incurred for crashing activity (i, j) from p_{ij}^U to p_{ij} is $c_{ij}(p_{ij}^U - p_{ij})$. A reward for earlier project completion is defined by π per day of makespan reduction, and this reward can be shared among the tasks. Let $\bar{D}$ denote the makespan of the project if no crashing occurs. Then, the total reward given by the project owner for shortening the project makespan from any time $\bar{D}$ to any time $D < \bar{D}$ is $\pi(\bar{D} - D)$. Finally, $w = \{w_i \geq 0, 1 \leq i \leq m \mid \sum_{i=1}^m w_i = 1\}$ is a vector specifying the fraction of the total reward given to player i, which is the public information. Player i's strategy P_i is a vector of durations for the activities which it controls. An overall strategy profile $S = (P_1, \ldots, P_m)$ describes the strategies of all the individual players. An initial strategy in which no crashing of activities has occurred is denoted by $\bar{S} = (\bar{P}_1, \ldots, \bar{P}_m)$, which results in a project makespan of $\bar{D}$. In a profile S, let $z_i(S)$ denote the net profit, i.e., reward less crashing cost, of player $i, i \in M$. Observe that, given a strategy profile, the project makespan is well defined.

The following definition is used to reduce the set of strategies under consideration. It states that if an individual player can improve his net profit without changing the makespan, then the current strategy is not in equilibrium.

Definition 9.6 A strategy $S = (P_1, \ldots, P_m)$ with project makespan $D(S)$ is *dominated* if there exists a player u and an alternative strategy P_u' for that player such that $D(S') = D(S)$ and $z_u(S') > z_u(S)$, where $S' = (P_1, \ldots, P_{u-1}, P_u', P_{u+1}, \ldots, P_m)$.

Let $W_i(S)$ denote the crashing cost of player i in a strategy profile S. Further, let $W_i^+(S)$ (respectively, $W_i^-(S)$) denote the decrease (resp., increase) in player i's crashing cost if he acts unilaterally to increase (resp., decrease) the project makespan by one time unit, starting from strategy S. These definitions enable the following result, which establishes necessary and sufficient conditions for a Nash equilibrium in this game.

9.2 Complete Information Games

Lemma 9.5 *A nondominated strategy S is a Nash equilibrium if and only if, for each player i, $i = 1, \ldots, m$:*

$$W_i^-(S) \geq w_i \pi, \quad and \tag{9.27}$$

$$W_i^+(S) < w_i \pi. \tag{9.28}$$

Proof Consider a strategy S and an arbitrary player i. From Definition 9.6, player i can improve his situation only by decreasing or increasing the project makespan. Regarding a possible unit reduction of the makespan that increases player i's crashing cost, the player receives an increase in reward of $w_i \pi$, which however is insufficient to motivate a move to a new strategy if $w_i \pi \leq W_i^-(S)$, as in (9.27), since the increased reward does not exceed the increased cost incurred. In the other case, player i gives up an amount of reward $w_i \pi$; therefore, if $w_i \pi > W_i^+(S)$, as in (9.28), it is not worthwhile for the player to increase the makespan since the reduction in task cost does not fully cover the loss of reward. Therefore, strategy S is a Nash equilibrium if and only if conditions (9.27) and (9.28) hold. □

Agnetis et al. (2015) describe a procedure, Algorithm FindNash, that finds a Nash equilibrium solution of this noncooperative game. The idea of the algorithm is that the players sequentially crash their activities to a locally optimal solution. As a result of this decision, crashing decisions of earlier activities may need to be revisited and possibly reversed in whole or in part. We now provide a formal description of this algorithm. The net profit of player i consists of his reward based on the project makespan minus his crashing cost.

Algorithm FindNash
1. Input a starting set of players' strategies $(\bar{P}_1, \ldots, \bar{P}_m)$ where all activities are at their upper bound values, i.e., no crashing has been implemented.
2. For players $i = 1, \ldots, m$ do:
    Solve a linear program that finds a strategy P_i^* for player i. This program maximizes the net return to player i, subject to the current strategies of all the other players, i.e., $\max\{z_i \mid P_1, \ldots, P_{i-1}, P_{i+1}, \ldots, P_m\}$.
    Set $(P_1, \ldots, P_m)$ to $(P_1, \ldots, P_{i-1}, P_i^*, P_{i+1}, \ldots, P_m)$.
    For players $k = 1, \ldots, i - 1$ do:
        Increase their previously crashed, noncritical activities to the point where they become critical, or reach their upper bound value, while the project length remains unchanged.

The main result can now be stated. We provide a short version of the proof and refer the reader to Agnetis et al. (2015) for more details.

Theorem 9.10 *Algorithm FindNash finds a Nash equilibrium in polynomial time.*

Proof Since, by construction, Algorithm FindNash finds a strategy that satisfies the conditions of Lemma 9.5, it finds a Nash equilibrium solution. The computation time of the algorithm requires the solution of $O(m^2)$ linear programs, each of size no larger than the project graph G. □

580   9 Noncooperative Supply Chain Scheduling

However, as now shown by example, a Nash equilibrium solution may deliver an arbitrarily large makespan and PoA.

Example 9.11 (Arbitrarily Large PoA in a Project Crashing Game) Consider a problem with two players and one activity per player with durations in $\{p_{ij}^L = 1, p_{ij}^U = M\}$, where M is an arbitrarily large number. The two activities can be processed concurrently. Each activity has a crashing cost of 1, and a reward of 2 is obtained by each player if the makespan decreases by 1 time unit. Since unilateral crashing by one player does not reduce the makespan and hence results in no reward, the strategy profile $S = (M, M)$ is a Nash equilibrium, with a resulting makespan of M. It is clear that the socially optimal schedule profile sets the duration of each job to 1 time unit, with a resulting makespan of 1; therefore, the PoA is M.

Example 9.11 shows that it is important that the project is delivered with reasonable makespan, subject to ensuring stability. This motivates the issue of how to find a Nash equilibrium solution that meets a given upper bound on makespan. However, as we now show, this problem is intractable.

Theorem 9.11 *Given an upper bound $\Lambda \in \mathbb{R}^+$ on the project makespan $D(S)$, the recognition version of the problem of finding a Nash equilibrium solution S with $D(S) \leq \Lambda$ is unary NP-complete.*

Proof Given a strategy S, checking whether the solution is a Nash equilibrium and also whether $D(S) \leq \Lambda$ can be performed in polynomial time; hence, the problem is in *NP*. The remainder of the proof uses a reduction from the following problem, which is known (Garey & Johnson, 1979, p.224) to be unary *NP*-complete.

3-Partition Given a set $\Gamma = \{a_1, \ldots, a_{3k}\}$ of positive integers, such that $\sum_{j=1}^{3k} = kB$, and $B/4 < a_j < B/2$ for $j = 1, \ldots, 3k$, can Γ be partitioned into k subsets $\Gamma_1, \ldots, \Gamma_k$ such that $|\Gamma_i| = 3, 1 \leq i \leq k$, and $\sum_{j \in \Gamma_i} a_j = k, i = 1, \ldots, k$?

Given an arbitrary instance of 3-Partition, we construct an instance of the multiple player project scheduling problem as follows. The activity-on-arc graph G has $3k$ parallel paths, each consisting of k activities, plus two dummy nodes that are numbered 0 and $3k(k + 1) + 1$. The activities on the first path are $(1, 2), (2, 3), \ldots, (k, k+1)$, those on the second path are $(k + 2, k+3), (k + 3, k + 4), \ldots, (2k+1, 2k+2), \ldots$, and so on, until the $3k$th and last path contains activities $(3k(k+1)-k, 3k(k+1)-k+1), (3k(k+1)-k+1, 3k(k+1)-k+2), \ldots, (3k(k+1) - 1, 3k(k + 1))$. Nodes 0 and $3k(k + 1) + 1$ represent the start time and the finish time of the project, respectively. From node 0, there are dummy activities $(0, 1), (0, k+2), \ldots, (0, 3k(k+1)-k)$. Also, to node $3k(k+1)+1$, there are dummy activities $(k+1, 3k(k+1)+1), (2k+2, 3k(k+1)+1), \ldots, (3k(k+1), 3k(k+1)+1)$. There are k players. Player A_i owns the ith activity of each path, for $i = 1, \ldots, m$. All real, i.e., non-dummy, activities have $p_{ij}^L = 0$ and $p_{ij}^U = 1$. Also, the crashing cost of every activity on the jth path is $a_j, j = 1, \ldots, 3k$, where $B/4 < a_j < B/2$. Each player's unit reward is $w_u \pi = B + \epsilon$, where $\epsilon > 0$ and small.

9.2 Complete Information Games

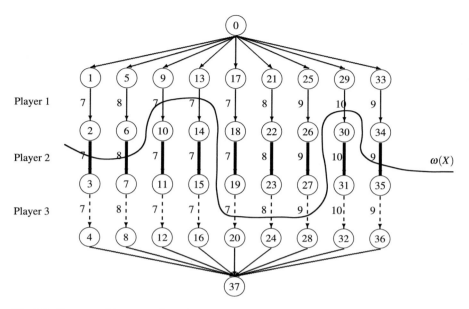

Fig. 9.2 Constructed instance of a project network in Theorem 9.11

Figure 9.2, which is reproduced from Agnetis et al. (2015), shows an example of the project network constructed as described above for an instance with $k = 3$, $(a_1, \ldots, a_{3k}) = (7, 8, 7, 7, 7, 8, 9, 10, 9)$, and $B = 24$. We show that there exists a Nash equilibrium strategy for which $D(S) < k$ in this project network if and only if there exists a solution to 3-Partition. Observe that if the activities on the cut $\omega(X)$ are crashed by one time unit, the result is a Nash equilibrium, with cost $D(s) < k$.
($\Rightarrow$) Consider the strategy S where all activities have normal duration, $p_{ij} = 1$. Then, the project makespan for S satisfies $D(S) = k$. If there exists a solution to 3-Partition, then for each player there exists a subset of three activities with total unit crashing cost of B. These $3k$ activities can be crashed, which from the topology of the project network, enables a decrease of the makespan to $D(S) < k$. Moreover, the crashing cost of each player is B, whereas his share of the reward for a reduction in the project makespan is $B + \epsilon$. Hence, the crashed solution is a Nash equilibrium.
($\Leftarrow$) In order to obtain a Nash equilibrium, for each player the total unit crashing cost of the crashed activities must not exceed B. Hence, not more than three crashed activities per player can be crashed. From the topology of the project network, in order to decrease the makespan, exactly $3k$ activities must be crashed. Therefore, for a Nash equilibrium with makespan smaller than k to exist, and from the definition of a_j, there must exist a subset of exactly three crashed activities per player, where the current task durations on all arcs are strictly greater than their lower bounds. The total crashing cost of such a set of activities is $\sum_{j=1}^{3k} a_j = kB$. Hence, in order for a Nash equilibrium to exist, the total crashing cost of the three activities selected

582 9 Noncooperative Supply Chain Scheduling

for each player must be exactly B. This implies the existence of a solution to 3-Partition. □

The work of Agnetis et al. (2015) is among the first to model the globally important application of project management as a noncooperative game. Their results highlight the difference in computational difficulty between on the one hand finding a Nash equilibrium solution and on the other hand finding one with a pre-specified bound on cost in a general case where a player may control more than one activity. We refer the reader to that work for consideration of a special case where each player controls only one activity, where finding a Nash equilibrium with minimum makespan can be performed efficiently.

9.2.2.4 Local Sequencing Rules

Vijayalakshmi et al. (2021) study the computational complexity of determining the existence of a Nash equilibrium for games defined over a class of scheduling problems. They consider a scheduling game on uniform parallel machines, where the players own jobs and minimize their completion time by choosing a machine on which their jobs are to be processed. The assumption is made that each player owns one job. An interesting feature of this problem is that each machine uses an individual priority list to decide the processing sequence for the jobs that are assigned to it. This is a *local sequencing rule*. The study of local sequencing rules is motivated by the use of different shop floor scheduling traditions within a distributed scheduling environment, for example, among local manufacturing plants.

An instance of a *scheduling game with local sequencing rules* is given by a tuple $G = (N; M; p_i, i \in N; s_j, \pi_j, j \in M)$, where N is a set of $n \geq 1$ jobs, M is a set of $m \geq 1$ machines, $p_i \in \mathbb{R}_+$ is the nominal processing time of job $i \in N$, $s_j \in \mathbb{R}_+$ denotes the speed of machine $j \in M$, and π_j is the job priority list of machine $j \in M$. A strategy profile σ assigns every job to a machine. Given a strategy profile, the jobs are processed according to their order in the machines' priority lists. Hence, the completion time of job i on machine j is the total of the nominal processing times of all the jobs that precede i on that machine and job i itself, divided by the machine speed s_j. Let $C_i(\sigma)$ denote this time. Vijayalakshmi et al. (2021) consider the alternative social objectives of minimizing makespan $\max_{i \in N}\{C_i(\sigma)\}$ and the total completion time of the jobs $\sum_{i \in N} C_i(\sigma)$. The results described here apply to both objectives. Each player i, representing job i, chooses a strategy $\sigma_i \in \Sigma_i$, where Σ_i is the set of strategies available to it, to minimize his cost C_i. A strategy profile $\sigma = (\sigma_1, \ldots, \sigma_n)$ is a pure Nash equilibrium if, for all $i \in N$ and all possible alternative choices $\sigma_i' \in \Sigma_i, \sigma_i' \neq \sigma_i$, we have $C_i(\sigma_1, \ldots, \sigma_n) \leq C_i(\sigma_1, \ldots, \sigma_{i-1}, \sigma_i', \sigma_{i+1}, \ldots, \sigma_n)$.

The following example shows that an instance G^* of the game G does not necessarily have a Nash equilibrium in pure strategy.

Example 9.12 (Nonexistence of a Pure NE in a Game with Local Sequencing Rules) Consider an instance G^* of the game G with $|N| = 5$, $N = \{a, b, c, d, e\}$, and

9.2 Complete Information Games

$M = \{M_1, M_2, M_3\}$. The nominal job processing times are $p_a = 5$, $p_b = 4$, $p_c = 4.5$, $p_d = 9.25$, and $p_e = 2$. The machine speeds are $s_1 = 1$, $s_2 = s_3 = 1/2$. The local sequencing rules on the machines are $\pi_1 = (a, b, c, d, e)$, $\pi_2 = \pi_3 = (e, d, b, c, a)$.

Because job a is ordered last on M_2 and M_3, it is clearly on M_1 in every Nash equilibrium. Similarly, job e is not on M_1 in an NE, since job e is first on M_2 or M_3. Since these two machines have the same local sequencing rule and speed, then without loss of generality, if an NE exists, then there exists an NE in which job e is on M_3. Thus, job a is first on M_1 and job e is first on M_3. Since job e is on M_3, job d prefers M_2 over M_3. Therefore, job d is on M_1 or M_2. We consider both cases:

1. Job d is on M_1. Then, since job b has the highest remaining priority between b and c on all machines, job b picks the machine that offers the lowest completion time that is M_2, and hence, job c is on M_1. As a result, job d prefers a completion time of $p_d/s_2 = 9.25/(1/2) = 18.5$ on M_2 over a completion time of $(p_a + p_c + p_d)/s_1 = (5 + 4.5 + 9.25)/1 = 18.75$ on M_1, and the solution is not in equilibrium.
2. Job d is on M_2. Then, since job b has the highest remaining priority between b and c on all machines, job b picks the machine with the lowest completion time that is M_1, and hence, job c is on M_3. As a result, job d prefers a completion time of $(p_a + p_b + p_d)/s_1 = (5 + 4 + 9.25)/1 = 18.25$ on M_1 over a completion time of $p_d/s_2 = 9.25/(1/2) = 18.5$ on M_2, and again the solution is not in equilibrium.

Thus, by examination of all nondominated schedules, G^* has no pure Nash equilibrium.

Example 9.12 raises the question of how difficult it is to determine whether a given instance of game G has a pure Nash equilibrium. The next result of Vijayalakshmi et al. (2021) answers this question.

Theorem 9.12 *Given an instance of the game G, it is unary NP-complete to decide whether the game has a Nash equilibrium in pure strategy.*

Proof Given a game and a schedule profile σ, verifying whether σ is a Nash equilibrium can be performed by checking for every job whether its current assignment is also its best response; hence, the problem is in *NP*. The reminder of the proof is by reduction from the following problem that is known to be unary *NP*-complete (Kann, 1991).

3-Bounded 3-Dimensional Matching (3DM-3) Given a set of triplets $T \subseteq X \times Y \times Z$, where $|T| \geq n$ and $|X| = |Y| = |Z| = n$, and where the number of occurrences of every element of $X \cup Y \cup Z$ in T is at most 3, does T have a 3-dimensional matching of size n, i.e., a subset $T' \subseteq T$, where $|T'| = n$ and every element in $X \cup Y \cup Z$ appears exactly once in T'?

Given an instance T of 3DM-3, we construct the following scheduling game, G_T. The set of jobs consists of:

584   9 Noncooperative Supply Chain Scheduling

1. The 5 jobs $\{a, b, c, d, e\}$ from the game G^* in Example 9.12
2. A single dummy job, f, with processing time 2
3. A set D of $|T| - n$ dummy jobs with processing time 3
4. A set U of $|T| + 1$ long dummy jobs with processing time 20
5. $3n$ jobs with processing time 1, one for each element in $X \cup Y \cup Z$

There are $m = |T| + 4$ machines, $M_1, M_2, \ldots, M_{|T|+4}$. All the machines except M_2 and M_3 have speed $s_j = 1$, whereas $s_2 = s_3 = 1/2$. The construction of G_T makes use of instance G^* from Example 9.12 through the local sequencing rules defined below.

The local sequencing rules are as follows. Where the list includes a set, it means that the set elements can appear in arbitrary order. For the first machine, $\pi_1 = (a, b, c, d, e, f, U, X, Y, Z, D)$. For the second and third machines, $\pi_2 = \pi_3 = (e, d, b, c, a, f, U, X, Y, Z, D)$. For the fourth machine, the local sequencing rule is $\pi_4 = (f, X, Y, Z, e, U, D, a, b, c, d)$. The remaining $|T|$ machines are defined as *triplet-machines*. For every triplet $t = (x_i, y_j, z_k) \in T$, the priority list of the triplet-machine corresponding to t is $(D, x_i, y_j, z_k, U, f, X \backslash x_j, Y \backslash y_j, Z \backslash z_j, a, b, c, d, e)$. Observe that in any Nash equilibrium, the dummy job f with processing time 2 is assigned as the first job on M_4. Also, the dummy jobs in D have the highest priority on the triplet-machines. Hence, in every Nash equilibrium, there are $|D| = |T| - n$ triplet-machines on which the first job is from D. Finally, in every Nash equilibrium, there is exactly one dummy job from U on each of the last $|T| + 1$ machines, due to the length of those jobs.

We provide some intuition about the proof that follows. First, the dummy jobs in U are long enough to guarantee that each of the jobs $\{a, b, c, d\}$ prefers the first three machines over the last $|T| + 1$ machines. Next, observe that, in Example 9.12, if job e is not on M_1, M_2, or M_3, then a Nash equilibrium exists. Since job e has last priority on the triplet-machines, it will always choose one of $M_1, \ldots, M_4$. Thus, it only remains to show that (a) if a 3DM-3 matching exists, then job e prefers M_4, thus leaving the first three machines for $\{a, b, c, d\}$ that results in a Nash equilibrium, and (b) if there is no 3DM-3 matching, then some job that originates from the elements in $X \cup Y \cup Z$ precedes job e on M_4, and e's best response is on M_2 or M_3, as in G^* in Example 9.12.

We now show that the constructed instance of the game has a pure NE if and only if the 3DM-3 instance has a matching of size n.

($\Rightarrow$) Let $T' \subseteq T$ be a matching of size n. Assign the jobs of $X \cup Y \cup Z$ on the triplet-machines corresponding to T' and the jobs of D on the remaining triplet-machines. Assign jobs f and e on M_4. Also, assign a single job from U on all but the first three machines. This leaves the jobs a, b, c, d that are assigned on the first three machines: a and d on M_1, b on M_2, and c on M_3. Observe that all the jobs originating from $X \cup Y \cup Z$ complete at time 3 or earlier and thus have no incentive to select M_4. Thus, job e completes at time $p_c/s_4 = 2/(1/2) = 4$ on M_4 and has no incentive to join the first three machines. Hence, the resulting assignment is a Nash equilibrium.

9.2 Complete Information Games

($\Leftarrow$) Assume that a matching of size n does not exist. Then, at least one job from $X \cup Y \cup Z$ is not assigned on its triplet-machine and thus prefers M_4, where it follows job f and its completion time is $(2 + 1)/1 = 3$. Thus, job e prefers to be first on M_2 or M_3, where its completion time is $p_2/(1/2) = 4$. The presence of the long dummy jobs guarantees that machines M_1, M_2, and M_3 process the five jobs $\{a, b, c, d, e\}$ and no others. Then, the game G^* of Example 9.12 is played on the first three machines, and as shown there, a Nash equilibrium does not exist. $\square$

Remark 9.3 Recall Definitions 9.3 and 9.4 for the PoA and PoS, respectively. Vijayalakshmi et al. (2021) study four special cases of the general problem discussed above, corresponding to (a) unit size jobs, (b) two machines, (c) identical machines, and (d) a global priority list, and evaluate the PoA and PoS in each case. They also study the problem of approximating the best Nash equilibrium solution within a given factor in case (c) and identify limits to approximability unless $P = NP$.

The work of Vijayalakshmi et al. (2021) described here provides an elegant illustration of the analysis of the computational complexity of determining the existence of a Nash equilibrium. It therefore provides a useful complement to the algorithms for finding a Nash equilibrium discussed elsewhere within Sect. 9.2.2.

9.2.2.5 Congestion and Activation Costs

Feldman and Tamir (2012) study a supply chain scheduling game that includes strategic resource allocation decisions. Let $N = \{1, \ldots, n\}$ denote a set of jobs to be processed, and $M = \{M_1, \ldots\}$ a set of identical parallel machines for processing them. These definitions specifically allow for the use of n machines, each with one job assigned to it. Jobs correspond to self-interested players who choose resources, i.e., machines, with the objective of minimizing their individual cost, which has two components. The first component is its *congestion cost*, which is the total processing time of the jobs assigned to the same machine; this cost increases with congestion, i.e., with the number of jobs sharing the same machine. The second component is the job's share of the machine's *activation cost*; this cost decreases with congestion. This creates an interesting tradeoff. More formally, given a schedule $s = (s_1, \ldots, s_n)$ where job j selects machine M_i, which is denoted as $s_j = M_i$, the cost of job j is given by $c_j(s) = L_i(s) + b_j(s)$, where $L_i(s)$ is the total load on machine M_i and $b_j(s)$ is the share of the activation cost of M_i paid by job j. Let B denote the activation cost of any machine. The activation cost of a machine is shared by the jobs assigned to that machine, according to two alternative rules that are discussed below. There is no cost consequence of the order of the jobs, since it is assumed they use a shared resource simultaneously. The social objective is the minimization of the total cost of all the jobs.

The activation cost component in the cost function of a job depends on a sharing rule. Under the *uniform sharing rule*, all the jobs assigned to a particular resource share its cost equally; hence, the share of activation cost incurred by job j with

$s_j = M_i$ is $b_j(s) = B/|\{k \in N \mid s_k = M_i\}|$. Alternatively, under the *proportional sharing rule*, the jobs assigned to a particular machine share its cost in proportion to their lengths; hence, the share of activation cost incurred by job j with $s_j = M_i$ is $b_j(s) = p_j B/L_i(s)$ since $L_i(s) = \sum_{k \in N \mid s_k = M_i} p_k$.

Example 9.13 (Alternative Cost Sharing Rules in a Congestion Game) Consider an instance with two jobs, lengths $p_1 = 2$, $p_2 = 3$, and activation cost $B = 10$. If schedule s assigns both jobs to the same machine, its workload is 5. Under the uniform sharing rule, $c_1(s) = c_2(s) = (2+3) + 10/2 = 10$. Under the proportional sharing rule, $c_1(s) = (2+3) + 2(10)/(2+3) = 9$ and $c_2(s) = (2+3) + 3(10)/(2+3) = 11$.

The choice of rule for sharing the activation cost of the jobs that are scheduled on the same machine has significant implications. Under the uniform sharing rule, a pure strategy Nash equilibrium does not in general exist, as shown by the following example.

Example 9.14 (Nonexistence of a Nash equilibrium in a Congestion Game) Consider an instance with two jobs, lengths $p_1 = 1$, $p_2 = 13$ and activation cost $B = 8$. If schedule s assigns both jobs to the same machine, $c_1(s) = c_2(s) = (1 + 13) + 8/2 = 18$. If schedule s assigns them to separate machines, $c_1(s) = 1 + 8 = 9$ and $c_2(s) = 13+8 = 21$. Hence, if the jobs are assigned to the same machine, job 1 will leave to join a dedicated machine, thereby reducing its cost from 18 to 9. But, if it does so, the increased cost to job 2 will incentivize it to join job 1, thereby reducing its cost from 21 to 18.

However, Feldman and Tamir (2012) show that, under the proportional sharing rule, a Nash equilibrium always exists, and moreover they provide a polynomial-time algorithm to find one. The remaining discussion in this section therefore focuses on the proportional sharing rule.

The longest processing time (LPT) rule, developed by Graham (1969), finds a Nash equilibrium in a load balancing problem without activation costs and with a fixed number of machines (Fotakis et al., 2002). For the present problem, this result does not hold, since there is the possibility to open a dedicated machine for each job. However, Feldman and Tamir (2012) show that a generalization of this rule, Algorithm LPT that is described below, computes a pure Nash equilibrium in polynomial time. A number of machines are set aside for the processing of one long job each. Any other machines that are used are designated as *LPT machines* in the algorithm and related discussion.

Algorithm LPT
1. Assign each "long job" j, i.e., job j where $p_j \geq B$, to a separate dedicated machine.
2. Assign the remaining "short jobs," i.e., those where $p_j < B$, one at a time in nonincreasing length order, to m *LPT machines*, where the assignment is to the machine that minimizes the job's total congestion and activation cost, and m is the minimal number of machines such that the schedule over the LPT machines

9.2 Complete Information Games 587

has makespan at most B. If that makespan would be exceeded by assigning the next job to any LPT machine, then that job is the first to be assigned to a newly opened LPT machine.

Observe that the assignment of jobs to machines in Step 2 is the application of Graham's (1969) LPT rule to identical parallel machines, except where the limit on makespan invokes the opening up of a new machine. Since all the jobs considered in Step 2 are short, and new machines can be opened as needed, a schedule with all machine loads not larger than B over the LPT machines is found by construction, if necessary using a separate machine for each short job. The running time of Algorithm LPT is $O(n \log^2 n)$. It is shown below that Algorithm LPT finds a Nash equilibrium.

Before presenting the main result, several preliminary results are needed. We refer the reader to Feldman and Tamir (2012) for the proofs. The first result defines necessary and sufficient conditions under which a job will move to another machine under the proportional sharing rule.

Lemma 9.6 *Consider the congestion game under the proportional sharing rule. Further, consider a given schedule where $s_j = M_i$. Then, job j will move from machine M_i to machine M_h if and only if either:*

(a) $L_h(s) + p_j > L_i(s)$ *and* $B > L_i(s)[L_h(s) + p_j]/p_j$, *in which case the maximum load on the two machines increases*

(b) $L_h(s) + p_j < L_i(s)$ *and* $B < L_i(s)[L_h(s) + p_j]/p_j$, *in which case the maximum load on the two machines decreases*

Also, Feldman and Tamir (2012) prove the following property of the LPT algorithm. Let $L_{\max}(s) = \max_{i \in M}\{L_i(s)\}$ denote the makespan of a schedule s.

Lemma 9.7 *Let N' be a set of n' jobs with sizes $p_1, \ldots, p_{n'}$. Let $C \in \mathbb{R}^+$ be such that $p_j < C$ for $j \in N'$, and $C \le \sum_{j \in N'} p_j$. Let s_k denote a schedule of the jobs of N' that uses k machines. Finally, let m denote the minimal number of machines such that $L_{\max}(s_m) \le C < L_{\max}(s_{m-1})$. Then, $L_i(s_m) + L_k(s_m) > C$, for $1 \le i \ne k \le m$.*

In order to establish that Algorithm LPT finds a Nash equilibrium, Feldman and Tamir (2012) also prove the following preliminary result.

Lemma 9.8 *Consider a schedule s found by Algorithm LPT. Then:*

(i) *No long job can benefit from migration to another machine.*

(ii) *No short job can benefit from migrating to a machine that has a long job, or from activating a new machine.*

The main result is now presented.

Theorem 9.13 *For an instance of the congestion game under the proportional sharing rule, every schedule found by Algorithm LPT is a Nash equilibrium.*

Proof Let s be any schedule that is found by Algorithm LPT. It is sufficient to show that no job unilaterally migrates from s. From Lemma 9.8, it remains to show that no short job can benefit from migrating to another LPT machine. If the total load of short jobs is not more than B, then LPT assigns them to a single machine, and no such migration is possible. It then remains to show that if the total load of short jobs is greater than B and LPT assigns them to multiple machines, no migration among those machines is beneficial.

Let j be a short job assigned to LPT machine M_i. We show that job j on machine M_i cannot reduce its cost by moving to some other LPT machine M_h. From a well-known property of LPT schedules, the load of M_h after the move is at least the load of M_i in s, i.e., $L_h(s) + p_j \geq L_i(s)$. Consequently, only load-increasing moves need to be considered. From Lemma 9.6, if $s_j = M_i$, a cost reduction is available to job j for moving from M_i to M_h if and only if either (a) $L_h(s) + p_j > L_i(s)$ and $Bp_j > L_i(s)[L_h(s) + p_j]$ or (b) $L_h(s) + p_j < L_i(s)$ and $Bp_j < L_i(s)[L_h(s) + p_j]$. Only (a) is load-increasing and (b) is not. Hence, it suffices to show that $B \leq L_i(s)[L_h(s) + p_j)]/p_j = L_i(s)L_h(s)/p_j + L_i(s)$. Now, since $p_j \leq L_i(s)$, we have $L_i(s)L_h(s)/p_j + L_i(s) \geq L_h(s) + L_i(s) \geq B$, where the last inequality follows from Lemma 9.7. $\qquad\square$

The following result is analogous with that of Theorem 9.11 of Agnetis et al. (2015), as discussed in Sect. 9.2.2.3. Although a Nash equilibrium can be found in polynomial time, finding a Nash equilibrium with social cost no larger than a given amount is an *NP*-hard problem, as shown by Feldman and Tamir (2012). However, the proof in this case is only of binary *NP*-hardness.

Theorem 9.14 *Given an instance of the congestion game under the proportional sharing rule, and a constant $c \in \mathbb{R}^+$, it is binary* NP-*hard to determine whether there exists a Nash equilibrium solution that achieves social cost less than or equal to c.*

Proof By reduction from Partition (Garey & Johnson, 1979, p.223): given a set of positive integers $A = \{a_1, \ldots, a_n\}$, with $\sum_{j=1}^{n} a_j = 2S$, does there exist a subset $A' \subset A$ such that $\sum_{j \in A'} a_j = S$?

Given A, consider an instance of the game containing n jobs with lengths $a_1, \ldots, a_n$ and machines with activation cost $B = S^2/a_{\max}$, where $a_{\max} = \max_{1 \leq j \leq n}\{a_j\}$, and where $c = 2S$. We show that this instance of the game admits a Nash equilibrium with a social cost of at most c if and only if A admits a partition. ($\Rightarrow$) Assume that A admits a partition, and consider a schedule s on two machines, each with a load of S. Because all the jobs incur the same load, the maximal cost is incurred by the longest job and is given by $S + a_{\max}B/S = 2S$. It remains to show that s is a Nash equilibrium. Consider a largest job j with length a_j.

From condition (a) in the proof of Theorem 9.13, moving to a nonempty machine reduces the cost of job j only if $B = S^2/a_{\max} > S(S+a_j)/a_j$, i.e., only if $S/a_{\max} > (S+a_j)/a_j = S/a_j + 1$, which is clearly impossible. From condition (b) in the proof of Theorem 9.13, moving to an empty machine reduces the cost of job j only if

9.3 Enhanced Complete Information Games 589

$B < S$, i.e., only if $S < a_{max}$, which is impossible from the existence of a partition. It follows that s is a Nash equilibrium.

($\Leftarrow$) Assume that A does not admit a partition. Hence, in any Nash equilibrium, the longest job is assigned to a machine with load $l \neq S$. The cost of the longest job is $l + a_{max}B/l$, which achieves its minimum value at $l = \sqrt{a_{max}B} = S$, where the cost is $\sqrt{a_{max}B} + a_{max}B/\sqrt{a_{max}B} = 2S = c$. It follows that, for any $l \neq S$, the cost of the longest job is strictly greater than c. $\square$

To summarize, the inclusion of both congestion effects and activation costs within supply chain scheduling games generates new and interesting results about the existence of Nash equilibria and the computational difficulty of finding them.

9.3 Enhanced Complete Information Games

The high price of anarchy in many noncooperative games and several practical concerns about the implementation of such games both provide motivation for the enhancement of noncooperative games to improve the performance of their equilibrium outcomes. This enhancement is possible in various ways. In Sect. 9.3.1, we consider games where the players make their strategic decisions sequentially, rather than simultaneously, and evaluate the resulting improvement in the price of anarchy. In Sect. 9.3.2, we consider games with a central planner who acts as a leader to improve the outcome of the game, as well as another game where a leader and follower are both selfish. In Sect. 9.3.3, we study the consequences of altruistic behavior, i.e., where some players' objectives are at least partly supportive of the social optimum. Finally, in Sect. 9.3.4, we discuss the use of manipulation by a central authority to guide players from a high cost equilibrium to a lower cost one.

9.3.1 Sequential Games

In this section, we discuss supply chain scheduling games where the players make their decisions sequentially rather than simultaneously. These games consist of homogeneous players making the same decisions with the same self-interested perspective, which distinguishes them from the leader–follower games studied in Sect. 9.3.2. As discussed below, sequential decision making enables improved performance for the worst-case outcomes of the games. Moreover, from a practical viewpoint, simultaneous playing of some games seems unnatural. It is not necessarily the case administratively that each player is ready to reach a decision at the same time, especially where the players are involved in various other revenue-generating activities. A common practical example arises in scheduling, where each player controls a job. The previous processing or preparation of the jobs may not complete at the same time for all players. For this reason, if the strategic decision of each player is to choose a machine on which to process his job, it is natural to allow players to select machines sequentially. Allowing sequential decision making may eliminate some bad quality equilibria and thereby reduce the price of anarchy. We provide two examples.

Leme et al. (2012) demonstrate improvements to the price of anarchy in two simple scheduling games that are played sequentially. Given n players, we assume that the game has n rounds, where player i only acts in round i, for $i = 1, \ldots, n$. The order of the players is arbitrary and is public information. All players are selfish utility maximizers. Since this is a complete information game, each player can predict with certainty how later players will react to his decision, and make his decision accordingly. The players have action sets $A_1, \ldots, A_n$, and functions $u_1, \ldots, u_n$ that map actions into costs. At each round i, player i observes the actions chosen by players $1, \ldots, i - 1$ and chooses an action $a_i \in A_i$. Hence, the strategy of player i is a mapping $s_i : A_1 \times \cdots \times A_{i-1} \to A_i$. Then, the outcome $a = (a_1, \ldots, a_n)$ is defined by: $a_1 = s_1(\emptyset), a_2 = s_2(a_1), a_3 = s_3(a_1, a_2), \ldots, a_i = s_i(a_1, \ldots, a_{i-1})$. Thus, the cost of player i is determined by his action, as well as by all previous and subsequent actions by other players. As a result, player i gains utility $u_i(a_i, \ldots, a_n)$.

Given pre-specified actions $\alpha_1, \ldots, \alpha_{i-1}$, an induced subgame of the original game is defined for players $i, i + 1, \ldots, n$. As defined in Section 2.3.6, a set of strategies $(s_1, \ldots, s_n)$ is a *subgame perfect equilibrium* if it is simultaneously an equilibrium of all subgames defined by the pre-specified actions which it observes (Osborne, 2004). It is also a Nash equilibrium of the original sequential game in the case where there are no pre-specified actions. Let SPE denote the set of all possible subgame perfect equilibrium solutions. The following definition is needed.

Definition 9.7 Given a social cost function $W(a)$ that maps actions into a positive real number, the *sequential price of anarchy (SPoA)* of a sequential game is the ratio between the cost of the worst subgame perfect equilibrium and the cost of the socially optimal solution $W^* = \min_{a \in A_1 \times \cdots \times A_n} \{W(a)\}$. Thus,

$$SPoA = \frac{\max_{a \in SPE} \{W(a)\}}{W^*}. \tag{9.29}$$

Consider a simple cost sharing game with a set N of n jobs and a set R of m identical parallel machines. Each player $i \in N$ can choose to place his job on any eligible machine in a given set $R_i \subseteq R$. Each machine j has a running cost c_j, independent of the number of jobs assigned to it, that is divided equally among the players choosing that machine. This is similar to the uniform sharing rule for activation cost of Feldman and Tamir (2012) discussed in Sect. 9.2.2.5 and is here described as a *fair cost allocation*. Then, if x players choose machine j, each incurs a cost c_j/x. We assume for simplicity that no combination of machine j and a number of players x choosing that machine produces the same cost allocation as another pair, i.e., $c_i/y \neq c_j/x$, for $1 \leq i \neq j \leq n, 0 < x, y \leq n$. If necessary, this assumption can be realized by a small perturbation of the data and hence is made

9.3 Enhanced Complete Information Games

without loss of generality. Each player minimizes the cost of his job. The social objective is minimization of the total cost of all the players. Leme et al. (2012) prove the following result.

Theorem 9.15 *For any machine cost sharing game with fair cost allocation and arbitrary costs, the sequential price of anarchy satisfies*

$$SPoA \leq O(\log n).$$

Proof Consider the following greedy algorithm: while there are jobs that are not yet assigned to machines, choose the machine that has the smallest ratio of its cost to the number of as yet unassigned jobs for which that machine is an available choice. This algorithm, originally developed for the classical set covering problem (Chvátal, 1979), has a worst-case bound, i.e., the ratio of the cost of a solution delivered by the greedy algorithm to an optimal cost, of $O(\log n)$.

We show that the outcome of this greedy algorithm is the unique subgame perfect equilibrium of this game. To solve the game, we calculate for $t = n, n - 1, \ldots, 1$ the best move player t has available at each round, which is unique due to the absence of ties. We show by backward induction that all players play according to the greedy algorithm. Let $r_1, \ldots, r_k$ be the machines in the order picked by the greedy algorithm, and let N_j denote the subset of jobs that are first allocated to machine r_j.

Consider the players in N_1, who incur cost $c_{r_1}/|N_1|$. From the definition of r_1 and the greedy choice rule, this is the smallest possible cost available. Hence, the last player in N_1 cannot do better and, since there are no ties, will choose r_1. Further, the second last player in N_1 also chooses r_1, since he knows that by doing so, the last player will choose r_1 too, thereby reducing his cost to $c_{r_1}/|N_1|$. Continuing similarly, all players in N_1 choose machine r_1, whatever other players do. From the definition of the greedy algorithm, the best possible cost for players in N_2 is $c_{r_2}/|N_2|$. The same argument again applies and can be repeated for the other machines. $\square$

In this problem, the price of anarchy of a simultaneous game is n (Anshlevich et al., 2004), whereas Theorem 9.15 shows that a subgame perfect equilibrium solution described above for the sequential game has a price of anarchy of $O(\log n)$. This improvement illustrates the benefit of sequential decision making in noncooperative supply chain scheduling games.

Corollary 9.1 *The subgame perfect equilibrium solution is independent of the order in which the players move. Moreover, the players do not need to know the order in which the rest of the players act to find their optimal move. Consequently, the subgame perfect equilibrium is also a Nash equilibrium of the sequential game described.*

As a second example of sequential games, consider a set M of m unrelated parallel machines and n players, each of whom owns a single job j. Let p_{ij} denote the processing time of job j on machine i. Recall the classical problem $R_m||C_{\max}$, which requires allocating the jobs nonpreemptively to the machines to minimize the makespan, i.e., the processing time of the most loaded machine. Our focus is on a noncooperative game defined over this scheduling problem. The objective of each player is the minimization of the load of the machine to which his job is assigned. The social objective is the minimization of the makespan. The classical simultaneous version of this game has an unbounded PoA, even for $n = m = 2$, as Leme et al. (2012) show by example. The purpose of this analysis is to establish a better price of anarchy through sequential decision making. They prove the following result.

Theorem 9.16 *The SPoA of the sequential game for unrelated parallel machine scheduling described above satisfies*

$$SPoA \leq O(m2^n).$$

Proof Let $M(\bar{L})$ denote the makespan resulting from a vector $\bar{L} = (L_1, \ldots, L_m)$ of machine loads. Let $\bar{L}_0$ denote a given vector of initial machine loads. Also, let $SPE(\bar{L}_0, k)$ denote the makespan of the subgame perfect equilibrium obtained when players $k, k + 1, \ldots, n$ make decisions starting from $\bar{L}_0$. Let $p_j^* = \min_{i \in M}\{p_{ij}\}$, i.e., the shortest processing time of job j on any machine. The result is proved using the induction hypothesis:

$$SPE(\bar{L}_0, k) \leq M(\bar{L}_0) + 2^{n-k} \sum_{j=k}^{n} p_j^*, \quad \bar{L}_0 \in \mathbb{R}_+^m.$$

Consider the last player, n. Since his cost is determined by the makespan of the machine which he chooses, he chooses the machine that provides the minimum makespan. Hence, the resulting makespan is at most $M(\bar{L}_0) + p_n^*$. Suppose the hypothesis holds for players $j = n, n - 1, \ldots, k + 1$. There are two cases:

Case 1. Player k allocates his job to the machine where he has processing time p_k^*, resulting in a new vector of machine loads denoted by $\bar{L}_1$. Then,

$$M(\bar{L}_1) \leq \sum_{j=k}^{n} p_j^* + M(\bar{L}_0). \tag{9.30}$$

Therefore, from the induction hypothesis,

$$SPE(\bar{L}_0, k) \leq M(\bar{L}_1) + 2^{n-k-1} \sum_{j=k+1}^{n} p_j^*$$

$$\leq M(\bar{L}_0) + 2^{n-k} \sum_{j=k}^{n} p_j^*, \quad \text{from (9.30)}.$$

9.3 Enhanced Complete Information Games 593

Case 2. Player k allocates his job to another machine i where his cost is lower because the machine is less loaded, resulting in a load vector $\bar{L}' = (L'_1, \ldots, L'_m)$. Hence,

$$L'_i \leq p^*_k + M(\bar{L}_0) + 2^{n-k-1} \sum_{j=k+1}^{n} p^*_j.$$

Then, since the load is unchanged for any machine $h \neq i$, we have

$$M(\bar{L}') \leq M(\bar{L}_0) + 2^{n-k-1} \sum_{j=k}^{n} p^*_j. \tag{9.31}$$

Therefore,

$$SPE(\bar{L}_0, k) = SPE(\bar{L}', k+1)$$

$$\leq M(\bar{L}') + 2^{n-k-1} \sum_{j=k+1}^{n} p^*_j, \quad \text{from the induction hypothesis}$$

$$\leq M(\bar{L}_0) + 2^{n-k} \sum_{j=k}^{n} p^*_j, \quad \text{from (9.31).}$$

Finally, the result is established by setting $\bar{L}_0 = 0$, $k = 1$, and noting that $\sum_{j=1}^{n} p^*_j$ is not larger than m times the optimal makespan. $\square$

Theorem 9.16 shows that a subgame perfect equilibrium solution described above for the sequential game has a price of anarchy of $O(m2^n)$, whereas in the equivalent simultaneous game the price of anarchy is unbounded. This result further illustrates how sequential decision making can improve the quality of a worst-case equilibrium.

Chen and Xu (2020) consider a scheduling situation where N is the set of n players, each of whom represents a job, and M the set of unrelated parallel machines, where $m = |M|$. Let p_{ij} denote the processing time of job j on machine i and $p^*_j = \min_{i \in M}\{p_{ij}\}$ denote the minimum processing time of job j on any machine. The players in publicly known sequence $1, \ldots, n$ choose one of the machines to process their job. A schedule $\sigma = (\sigma_1, \sigma_2, \ldots, \sigma_n)$ represents the sequence of machines chosen by jobs $1, \ldots, n$, respectively. The load $L_i(N) = \sum_{j|\sigma(j)=i} p_{ij}$ is the total processing on machine i.

Over this situation, they define a supply chain scheduling game where player i's objective is to minimize the load of the machine which he chooses, taking into account the choices of all predecessors and k successors. This objective is motivated by a situation where a machine delivers all its jobs together when all have completed processing. The social objective is the minimization of the makespan. In this environment, the players have *bounded rationality*, i.e., they are only able to look ahead to the next k decisions before making their own decision. Here, $0 \leq k \leq n - 1$, where $k = 0$ corresponds to an online greedy solution and $k = n - 1$ corresponds to perfect rationality as assumed in the work of Leme et al. (2012) discussed above. Bounded rationality is defined by Simon (1955) as "rational choice that takes account the cognitive limitations of the decision maker—limitations of both knowledge and computational capacity." A player has a *k-lookahead ability* in a sequential game if he computes his best decision using the decisions of his predecessors and his first $k - 1$ successors. This decision process can be conceptualized as follows: when a player makes a decision, he draws a $(k + 1)$-depth decision tree that includes his own node, assigns the corresponding costs to the leaves, and then performs backward induction to determine what decision to make. If $k = 0$, he assumes that his successors will choose machines with minimum processing times, which defines his best choice. This game always has a subgame perfect equilibrium (see Definition 2.13). However, finding one that minimizes the central objective of the makespan is an intractable problem (Leme et al., 2012).

Some additional notation is needed. Let $[a : b] = \{a, a + 1, \ldots, b\}$ and $[b] = [1 : b]$, where a, b are the integers. Let $K_j = [j + 1 : \min\{j + k, n\}]$ denote the lookahead set for job j, where $|K_j| \leq k$. Let $\bar{L}_0$ denote an initial vector of machine loads before the game, and $M(\bar{L}_0, \emptyset)$ its makespan. More generally, $\bar{L}$ denotes a vector of current loads on the machines. This definition provides a baseline for calculating the increase in makespan at any point during the playing of the game. Let $L_i(\bar{L}, J)$ denote the load of machine i after the set of players $J \subseteq N$ has played, and $M(\bar{L}, J) = \max_{i \in M}\{L_i(\bar{L}, J)\}$ the resulting makespan.

Considering any possible initial load $\bar{L}_0 \in \mathbb{R}_+^m$, we define

$$\Delta L(J) = \sup_{\bar{L} \in \mathbb{R}_+^m} \{M(\bar{L}, J) - M(\bar{L}_0, \emptyset)\}.$$

Here, $\Delta L(J)$ is used to bound the increase in makespan as a result of scheduling the set of jobs J, relative to any initial load. This amount in turn can be used to bound the SPoA, as shown below.

Consider the general case where each player j has k-lookahead ability, $j = 1 \leq k \leq n - j$. Chen and Xu (2020) prove the following preliminary result.

Lemma 9.9 $\Delta L([j : n]) \leq \Delta L([j + 1 : n]) + p_j^* + \Delta L(K_j), \ j = 1, \ldots, n.$

This result bounds the amount that each job can contribute to the makespan, and enables the main result that follows. Let $OPT(N)$ denote the value of a socially optimal solution that minimizes the makespan.

Theorem 9.17 *For the sequential scheduling game where players have k-lookahead ability, the sequential price of anarchy for the makespan is at most $O(k^2)$ for the two unrelated machines environment R_2, and at most $O(2^k \min\{mk, n\})$ for the m unrelated machines environment R_m.*

9.3 Enhanced Complete Information Games

Proof From Lemma 9.9,

$$\Delta L(N) \leq \Delta L([2:n]) + p_1^* + \Delta L(K_1) \leq \cdots \leq \sum_{j=1}^{n} p_j^* + \sum_{j=1}^{n} \Delta L(K_j). \quad (9.32)$$

First, consider the case of two unrelated machines. From (Chen et al., 2016, Theorem 4),

$$\Delta L(K_j) \leq (k-1) \sum_{i \in K_j} p_i^*. \quad (9.33)$$

This gives

$$\Delta L(N) \leq \sum_{j=1}^{n} p_j^* + \sum_{j=1}^{n} \Delta L(K_j), \quad \text{from (9.32)}$$

$$\leq \sum_{j=1}^{n} p_j^* + (k-1)\left[\sum_{j \in K_1} p_j^* + \sum_{j \in K_2} p_j^* + \cdots + \sum_{j \in K_n} p_j^* \right], \quad \text{from (9.33)}$$

$$\leq \sum_{j=1}^{n} p_j^* + k(k-1) \sum_{j=1}^{n} p_j^*$$

$$= (k^2 - k + 1) \sum_{j=1}^{n} p_j^*.$$

Therefore, it follows that

$$SPoA \leq \frac{\Delta L(N)}{OPT(N)}$$

$$\leq \frac{(k^2 - k + 1) \sum_{j=1}^{n} p_j^*}{\sum_{j=1}^{n} p_j^*/2}$$

$$= 2(k^2 - k + 1)$$

$$= O(k^2).$$

Second, consider the case of m unrelated machines. Leme et al. (2012, Theorem 4) and Bilò et al. (2016, Theorem 5) provide upper bounds for $\Delta L(K_j)$:

$$\Delta L(K_j) \le 2^k \sum_{j \in K_j} p_j^*, \text{ and} \tag{9.34}$$

$$\Delta L(K_j) \le 2^k \max_{j \in K_j}\{p_j^*\}. \tag{9.35}$$

These bounds are now used in turn to estimate the SPoA.

Using $OPT(N) \ge \sum_{j \in N} p_j^*/m$, we obtain

$$
\begin{aligned}
SPoA &\le \frac{\Delta L(N)}{OPT(N)} \\
&\le \frac{\sum_{j \in N} p_j^* + \sum_{j \in N} \Delta L(K_j)}{\sum_{j \in N} p_j/m}, \quad \text{from (9.32)} \\
&\le \frac{\sum_{j \in N} p_j^* + k2^k \sum_{j \in N} p_j^*}{\sum_{j \in N} p_j^*/m}, \quad \text{from (9.34)} \\
&= m + mk2^k \\
&= O(mk2^k). \tag{9.36}
\end{aligned}
$$

Using $OPT(N) \ge \max_{j \in N}\{p_j^*\}$, we obtain

$$
\begin{aligned}
SPoA &\le \frac{\Delta L(N)}{OPT(N)} \\
&\le \frac{\sum_{j \in N} p_j^* + \sum_{j \in N} \Delta L(K_j)}{OPT(N)}, \quad \text{from (9.32)} \\
&\le \frac{\sum_{j \in N} p_j^*}{OPT(N)} + \frac{n2^k \max_{j \in N}\{p_j\}}{OPT(N)}, \quad \text{from (9.35)} \\
&\le \frac{\sum_{j \in N} p_j^*}{\sum_{j \in N} p_j^*/m} + \frac{n2^k \max_{j \in N}\{p_j^*\}}{\max_{j \in N}\{p_j^*\}} \\
&= m + n2^k \\
&= O(n2^k). \tag{9.37}
\end{aligned}
$$

Combining (9.36) and (9.37) gives $SPoA = O(2^k \min\{mk, n\})$. $\qquad\square$

Table 9.3 summarizes results for the sequential price of anarchy from the literature, including from Chen and Xu (2020).

These results illustrate why Chen and Xu (2020) use the term "curse of rationality" in the title of their work.

Chen and Xu (2020) also study the case of simple-minded players, who select a machine with minimum anticipated load, under the assumption that all subsequent

9.3 Enhanced Complete Information Games 597

Table 9.3 Sequential price of anarchy results for makespan on unrelated machines

Machines	Two machines	m machines
Online	2	m
1-lookahead	2	$O(m)$
k-lookahead	$O(k^2)$	$O(2^k \min\{mk, n\})$
n-lookahead	$\Theta(n)$	$O(2^n)$

players choose machines with minimum processing time. They show that, in this case, the SPoA is exactly m, the number of machines. Noncooperative supply chain scheduling games with limited lookahead ability are an important subject for further research (see Sect. 9.6).

9.3.2 Leader–Follower Games

This section discusses two games with leaders and followers. While these games are sequential in nature, we distinguish them from the games considered in Sect. 9.3.1 by the fact that either the objectives of the leaders and followers are different, or their range of control is different. The sequential games studied above consist of homogeneous players making the same decisions with the same self-interested perspective. A further distinction is that the number of decision making stages here is only two.

In the first game we describe, the leader is motivated by optimization of social welfare, whereas the followers are self-interested. In the second game studied, the self-interested leader makes a decision about price, whereas the self-interested follower makes a decision about how much work to subcontract.

A *Stackelberg game* (Fudenberg & Tirole, 1993, Chapter 3) is a complete information game in which one or more players, i.e., leaders, move first, and then one or more other players, i.e., followers, react to the decisions of the leaders. A Stackelberg game contains several structural assumptions. First, the leaders know before they make their decisions that the followers will observe those decisions. Further, the leaders know the best response of the followers to their decisions and are therefore able to determine both their outcome and the overall outcome of the system from their own decisions. Solution of a Stackelberg game model is typically achieved by backward induction, i.e., by considering the followers' best responses as a function of the leaders' decisions and then optimizing over the latter. Solution of the game finds a Stackelberg equilibrium, i.e., a subgame perfect equilibrium that is a combination of sequential strategies that best serve each player, given the strategies of the other players. Then, every player is at a Nash equilibrium in every subgame. Regarding applications, many Stackelberg games model the leaders and followers as two groups of self-interested players who are either responsible for different decisions or distinguished from the other groups by order of decision making. An example of this in a supply chain is a supplier or subcontractor that makes pricing decisions before a manufacturer does. The work of Qi (2012) discussed below in this section provides an example.

An alternative perspective offered by Roughgarden (2004) defines a game where a central planner solves part of a planning problem, and self-interested players react to this partial solution and solve the remainder of the problem. In this game, the central planner is the leader and is responsible for allocating a fraction of the total available work to machines. The central planner has complete information about how the other players will react to any strategy which it adopts. The objective of the central planner is to minimize the total cost of the machines. In this role, the central planner has limited power but can partially control the solution determined by the following self-interested players.

This process results in a Nash equilibrium; however, the social cost of that equilibrium can vary considerably based on the leader's strategy. It is therefore useful to evaluate, for any central planner's strategy, the ratio of social cost given by the Stackelberg equilibrium to the optimal social cost. A further challenge is to identify the leader's strategy that minimizes this ratio at the induced Stackelberg equilibrium. These challenges fall within the study of Stackelberg games.

Consider a set $M = \{1, \ldots, m\}$ of machines. Machine i has a latency function $c(\cdot)$ that measures the load-dependent time required to complete work. Each latency function is assumed to be a nonnegative, continuous, nondecreasing, and convex function of its argument. The following players choose machines to minimize the latency of their jobs. There is a known, finite, positive, and constant rate r of arriving jobs that need to be processed by the machines. The central planner controls a fraction α of the arriving jobs, which defines an arrival rate of αr jobs to the central planner. The central planner allocates these jobs to the machines. The remaining work, with an arrival rate of $(1 - \alpha)\tau$, is assigned to the machines by the choices of the selfish, independent following players who represent the work not allocated by the central planner. An instance (M, r, α) of the Stackelberg game is defined by the set of machines M, the arrival rate of jobs r, and the fraction α of those jobs that are controlled by the decision maker. If there are no centrally controlled jobs, and hence all decisions are made by the self-interested players, then an instance is denoted as (M, r).

The following definition clarifies the role of the central planner and the other players:

Definition 9.8

(i) A *strategy* $s = (s_1, \ldots, s_m)$ for the Stackelberg instance (M, r, α) is an assignment of work αr to machines by the leader that is feasible for the game instance $(M, \alpha r)$.

(ii) An *equilibrium induced by strategy* s is an assignment t at Nash equilibrium for the instance $(M, (1 - \alpha)r)$ with respect to latency functions $f_i(\cdot), i \in M$.

(iii) Then, $s + t$ is an *assignment induced by* s for the original Stackelberg game instance (M, r, α), where s describes the leader's strategy, and t describes the decisions of the selfish players in reacting to the leader's strategy.

9.3 Enhanced Complete Information Games

To elaborate on Definition 9.8, (i) defines the only role of the central planner as assigning part of the arriving work among the machines. However, this is done with an understanding of how the remaining work will be allocated. Also, (ii) describes the situation after the jobs not allocated by the central planner have selfishly chosen their machines. Finally, (iii) describes the complete solution by both the central planner and the selfish followers.

An *assignment* of the jobs to the machines is an m-vector $x \in \mathbb{R}_+^M$, such that $\sum_{i \in M} x_i = r$, i.e., both the centrally controlled work and the remaining work have been allocated to the machines. The performance of the system, as viewed by the central planner, is measured by minimization of its total latency $C(x) = \sum_{i=1}^m x_i f_i(x_i)$, where $f_i(x_i)$ measures the performance of machine i given workload x_i. In general, the latency function varies among the machines, as is the case in many supply chain scheduling applications that employ resources of varying age and quality.

Each player minimizes his job's latency by choosing a machine on which it is to be processed. This perspective is similar to that in the congestion game of Feldman and Tamir (2012) in Sect. 9.2.2.5. All jobs assigned to the same machine experience the same latency. This assumption is consistent with the modeling of congested systems where a particular allocation of resources represents a "steady-state solution" with jobs arriving continuously over time.

The development of a good strategy by the central planner is key to obtaining good overall system performance. Roughgarden (2004) applies the intuition that a good strategy by the central planner, i.e., one that balances workload among the machines, should give more work to the machines that are least appealing to the following selfish users, i.e., machines with relatively high latency. This motivates the following strategy.

Algorithm Largest Latency First (LLF)

1. Compute an optimal assignment x^* for problem (M, r) in polynomial time, using the mathematical model:

$$\min \quad \sum_{i \in M} x_i f_i(x_i)$$

$$\text{s.t.} \quad \sum_{i \in M} x_i = r$$

$$x_i \geq 0, \quad i \in M.$$

2. Index the machines of M such that $f_1(x_1^*) \leq \cdots \leq f_m(x_m^*)$.
3. Define $k = \min\{i \leq m \mid \sum_{h=i+1}^m x_h^* \leq \alpha r\}$.
4. Set $s_i = \begin{cases} x_i^*, & i > k \\ \alpha r - \sum_{i=k+1}^m x_i^*, & i = k \\ 0, & i < k. \end{cases}$

We provide an example of Algorithm LLF.

Example 9.15 (Application of Algorithm LLF) Let $M = \{1, 2, 3\}$ denote a set of machines, and let $\tau = 10$ denote the arrival rate of work. Let $\alpha = 0.9$; hence, the central authority can assign the total work of $\alpha\tau = 9$. Consider the latency functions $l_1(x_1) = 2x_1 + 1, l_2(x_2) = x_2$, and $l_3(x_3) = 4$. The assignment problem in Step 1 is

$$\min \quad 2x_1^2 + x_1 + x_2^2 + 4x_3$$

$$\text{s.t.} \quad x_1 + x_2 + x_3 = 10$$

$$x_1, x_2, x_3 \geq 0,$$

with optimal solution $x_1^* = 0, x_2^* = 2, x_3^* = 8$.

In Step 2, we have $l_1(x_1^*) = 1, l_2(x_2^*) = 2$, and $l_3(x_3^*) = 4$, i.e., $l_1(x_1^*) \leq l_2(x_2^*) \leq l_3(x_3^*)$, and hence, the machines are correctly indexed. In Step 3, we have $k = 2$. In Step 4, since $\alpha\tau = 9$, we have $s_3 = 8, s_2 = 1$. The remaining work of 1 remains to be assigned among the three machines by the selfish players.

Under the assumption that the latency function $l_i(x_i)$ of each machine i is convex, Roughgarden (2004) shows that Step 1 involves the minimization of a convex function over a convex set that is the polytope of possible assignments, and can therefore be computed in polynomial time using convex programming techniques. As a special case, if the latency functions are linear, then Step 1 requires $O(m^2)$ time. The LLF strategy fills the machines one by one up to their x^* level, in order from the largest latency with respect to x^* to the smallest, until there is no unallocated work remaining, and thus clearly runs in polynomial time.

Next, the performance of the LLF strategy is evaluated. Roughgarden and Tardos (2002) show that a Nash equilibrium in this problem can be arbitrarily bad if there is no central planner; hence, the gains achieved under central planning are potentially significant. Roughgarden (2004) proves the following preliminary results that are needed for analysis of the problem. Let t_i denote the amount of work assigned to machine $i \in M$ by the following players.

Lemma 9.10 *Let M_1 denote the machines $i \in M$ for which $t_i = 0$ and M_2 denote the machines $i \in M$ for which $t_i > 0$. For $i = 1, 2$, let α_i denote the amount of centrally controlled jobs assigned to machines in M_i, and C_i the cost incurred by the induced assignment $s + t$ on machines in M_i, where $\alpha_1 + \alpha_2 = \alpha$. Then, every machine i with $t_i > 0$ has the same latency, which we denote by L. Moreover, $C_2 = (1 - \alpha_1)L$ and $C_1 \geq \alpha_1 L$.*

Lemma 9.10 is used to prove the next result.

Lemma 9.11 *Let (M, r, α) denote a Stackelberg instance with optimal assignment x^* from Step 1 of Algorithm LLF and index the machines of M such that $f_m(x_m^*) \geq f_i(x_i^*), i = 1, \ldots, m - 1$. Then:*

(i) $f_m(x_m^*) \geq L$.

9.3 Enhanced Complete Information Games   601

(ii) *If s is a strategy from Step 4 of Algorithm LLF with $s_m = x_m^*$, then there exists an equilibrium induced by s where $t_m = 0$.*

Part (ii) of Lemma 9.11 states that if the LLF strategy fills the mth machine up to x_m^*, then some induced equilibrium assigns all work to the first $m - 1$ machines and none to machine m.

These properties enable the main result for the performance of an LLF-induced strategy.

Theorem 9.18 *Let (M, r, α) denote a Stackelberg game instance:*

(i) *If s is an LLF central planner's strategy for this game instance that induces equilibrium t and x^* is an optimal assignment for this instance, then $C(s + t) \leq C(x^*)/\alpha$.*

(ii) *The ratio bound of $1/\alpha$ is best possible under Stackelberg strategies.*

Proof (i) The proof proceeds by induction on m, the number of machines. For each fixed m, the theorem is proved for arbitrary latency functions $f(\cdot)$, r and α. The case of $m = 1$ machine is trivial. Hence, we assume $m \geq 2$.

Consider a Stackelberg instance (M, r, α) with $m \geq 2$. Let x^* denote an optimal assignment to the instance (M, r) and s the corresponding LLF strategy that induced x^*. Index the machines such that $f_1(x_1^*) \leq \cdots \leq f_m(x_m^*)$. Rescale the total workflow to 1. Let $L = f_m(s_m + t_m) = f_m(x_m^* + t_m)$ denote the common latency with respect to $s + t$ of every machine $i \in M_2$ with $t_i > 0$ as defined in Lemma 9.10.

Case 1. Suppose $t_k = 0$ for some machine k. Let $M_1 = \{i \in M \mid t_i = 0\}$ and $M_2 = M \setminus M_1$, where $M_1, M_2 \neq \emptyset$. From Lemma 9.10, $C_2 = (1 - \alpha_1)L$ and $C_1 \geq \alpha_1 L$. Further, since x^* restricted to M_2 is an optimal assignment for $(M_2, 1 - \alpha_1, 1)$, the strategy s restricted to M_2 is an LLF strategy for the instance $(M_2, 1 - \alpha_1, \alpha_2/(1 - \alpha_1))$.
From the induction hypothesis and the fact that $x_i^* \geq s_i = s_i + t_i, i \in M_1$, we have

$$C(x^*) \geq C_1 + \alpha_2 C_2/(1 - \alpha_1).$$

Proving that $C(s + t) \leq C(x^*)/\alpha$ thus reduces to showing that

$$\alpha(C_1 + C_2) \leq C_1 + \alpha_2 C_2/(1 - \alpha_1). \tag{9.38}$$

Since $\alpha \leq 1$ and $C_1 \geq \alpha_1 L$, it suffices to prove (9.38) with C_1 replaced by $\alpha_1 L$, i.e.,

$$\alpha(\alpha_1 L + C_2) \leq \alpha_1 L + \alpha_2 C_2/(1 - \alpha_1). \tag{9.39}$$

Now, setting $C_2 = (1 - \alpha_1)L$, both sides of (9.39) reduce to αL.

602   9 Noncooperative Supply Chain Scheduling

Case 2. Suppose $t_i > 0$ for every machine i; hence, $C(s + t) = L$. If the LLF strategy has $s_m \geq x_m^*$, then from part (ii) of Lemma 9.11, the argument of Case 1 applies. Hence, we assume $\alpha < x_m^*$, as is the case in Example 9.15. Further, from part (i) of Lemma 9.11, $f_m(x_m^*) \geq L$, else $l_i(x_i^*) < L, i = 1, \ldots, m$, in which case x^* and $s + t$ do not deliver the same total load. Then,

$$C(x^*) \geq x_m^* f_m(x_m^*)$$

$$\geq \alpha L$$

$$= \alpha C(s + t).$$

(ii) The following example shows that the ratio bound of $1/\alpha$ is the best possible result under Stackelberg strategies.

$\square$

Example 9.16 (Worst-Case Instance of an LLF Strategy in a Stackelberg Game) Consider an example with $m = 2$ machines, $\alpha = 1/2$, and latency functions $f_1(x_1) = 1$ and $f_2(x_2) = 2^k x_2^k$, where k is a positive integer. For this example, any Stackelberg strategy induces the assignment $(1/2, 1/2)$ with the total cost 1. However, an optimal assignment is $(1/2 + \delta_k, 1/2 - \delta_k)$ with the total cost $1/2 + \epsilon_k$, where $\delta_k, \epsilon_k \to 0$ as $k \to \infty$. Thus, the best induced assignment may be (arbitrarily close to) twice as costly as the optimal assignment. Similar examples can be developed for any $\alpha, 0 < \alpha < 1$.

For the natural case of linear latency functions, Roughgarden (2004) proves a stronger ratio bound of $4/(3 + \alpha)$. He also shows that, even for this special case, the problem of computing an optimal Stackelberg strategy is binary NP-hard.

Having presented the above theoretical background to Stackelberg games, we now discuss an interesting application that provides different intuition. Qi (2012) describes a two-stage Stackelberg game for a manufacturer and a subcontractor whose decisions collectively form a supply chain scheduling problem. The self-interested manufacturer needs to process a set of jobs, and outsourcing some or all of them to a subcontractor can reduce its tardiness cost that is incurred when a customer deadline is not met. In the first stage of the game, the self-interested subcontractor (i.e., leader) sets a unit price, and in the second stage the manufacturer (i.e., follower) uses this information to decide which jobs to subcontract and also how to schedule the jobs on both its and the subcontractor's resources. It is assumed that the subcontractor accepts the manufacturer's schedule for outsourced work, based on the manufacturer's due date priorities, as part of the subcontract. The subcontractor knows the response of the manufacturer, i.e., the amount of work that is subcontracted, to whatever pricing decision it makes.

Consider a manufacturer with n jobs to schedule. Each job j has a processing time p_j, a due date d_j where $d_1 \leq \cdots \leq d_n \equiv D$, and a fixed tardiness cost w_j if it completes at time C_j where $C_j > d_j$. A cost c_m per unit time is incurred for in-house processing; hence, the cost of processing job j is $c_m p_j$ if it is not

9.3 Enhanced Complete Information Games

outsourced. If job j is outsourced, it requires p'_j time at the subcontractor, where in general $p'_j \neq p_j$. Let $P = \sum_{j=1}^{n} p_j$, and $P' = \sum_{j=1}^{n} p'_j$. The subcontractor's capacity is P', and therefore not a binding constraint; in practice, this is justified by the possibility of further subcontracting by the subcontractor. The subcontractor determines a price x per unit time for work received, which is therefore xp'_j for processing job j. The subcontractor's cost of processing per unit time is c_s. Naturally, the manufacturer incurs the tardiness cost w_j if it is tardy, even if a job is outsourced. Each job is scheduled either entirely in-house or entirely outsourced and in both cases is processed nonpreemptively.

The manufacturer minimizes its total cost, which includes processing, outsourcing, and tardiness costs. The subcontractor maximizes its net profit, which is its revenue from the manufacturer, less its processing cost.

Given a price x set by the subcontractor, consider the manufacturer's problem of determining which of its jobs to outsource and whether it is worth the increased outsourcing cost of scheduling them in order that they be delivered on time. This problem can be solved using the following dynamic program.

Algorithm SC

Preprocessing
Index the jobs in EDD order, i.e., such that $d_1 \leq \cdots \leq d_n \equiv D$.

Value Function
Let $f_j(a, b)$ denote the minimum total in-house processing, subcontracting, and tardiness cost, for scheduling jobs $1, \ldots, j$, where the total processing time of the on-time in-house jobs is a and the total processing time of the on-time outsourced jobs is b.

Boundary Condition
$f_0(0, 0) = 0$.

Recurrence Relation
$$f_j(a, b) = \min \begin{cases} f_{j-1}(a, b) + c_m p_j + w_j \\ f_{j-1}(a, b) + xp'_j + w_j \\ v_j(a, b) \\ y_j(a, b), \end{cases}$$

where

$$v_j(a, b) = \min \begin{cases} f_{j-1}(a - p_j, b) + c_m p_j, & \text{if } a \leq d_j \\ \infty, & \text{if } a > d_j, \end{cases}$$

$$y_j(a, b) = \min \begin{cases} f_{j-1}(a, b - p'_j) + xp'_j, & \text{if } b \leq d_j \\ \infty, & \text{if } b > d_j. \end{cases}$$

Optimal Solution Value
$h(x) \equiv \min_{0 \leq a \leq P, \, 0 \leq b \leq P'} \{f_n(a, b)\}$.

604   9 Noncooperative Supply Chain Scheduling

The recurrence relation includes four alternatives. In the first two alternatives, job j is tardy. In the first alternative, it is processed in-house, whereas in the second alternative it is subcontracted. The third and fourth alternatives attempt to schedule job j on time. However, this is only possible by in-house processing in the third alternative if $a \leq d_j$, and it is only possible by subcontracting in the fourth alternative if $b \leq d_j$. Finally, $h(x)$ represents the minimal total cost of the manufacturer, given the subcontractor's choice of x as the price.

Theorem 9.19 *For a given subcontractor's price x, Algorithm SC finds an optimal selection of jobs to outsource in $O(nPP')$ time.*

Proof Since an EDD sequence is optimal for on-time jobs on each machine (Lawler & Moore, 1969) for the classical scheduling problem $P_2 || \sum w_j U_j$, the algorithm compares the cost of all possible schedules of in-house and outsourced jobs and therefore finds a minimum cost solution. Regarding the computation time, $1 \leq j \leq n$, $0 \leq a \leq P$, $0 \leq b \leq P'$, and each application of the recurrence relation requires constant time.   □

Qi (2012) proves the following preliminary result.

Lemma 9.12 *The manufacturer's minimum cost function $h(x)$ is a piecewise linear concave increasing function of the unit subcontracting price, x.*

The next result provides a path to computationally efficient solution of the overall problem of the manufacturer and subcontractor.

Theorem 9.20

(i) *The manufacturer's optimal total subcontracting time $b^*(x)$ is a stepwise nonincreasing function of the unit subcontracting price x and has the same breakpoints as the manufacturer's minimum cost function, $h(x)$.*
(ii) *The subcontractor needs to consider only the same breakpoints as the manufacturer in setting its optimal price.*

Proof

(i) The result follows from Lemma 9.12.
(ii) Observe that the manufacturer does not change its schedule, and therefore, the subcontractor's revenue does not change between two price breakpoints. Therefore, the subcontractor's optimal price is found by comparing its profit at each of the manufacturer's breakpoints.

                                                                □

Qi (2012) provides a simple algorithm for finding all the breakpoints of $h(x)$, which from Theorem 9.20 is sufficient to enable the manufacturer to evaluate and compare its cost under any given price x, and moreover is sufficient to define the set of candidate prices that the subcontractor needs to consider.

Remark 9.4 The availability of complete information and sequential decision making help to identify an equilibrium solution in this game. While the subcontractor

9.3 Enhanced Complete Information Games

plays first by setting the price, it is able to predict with certainty the manufacturer's reaction to that price, as specified by the total amount of time subcontracted, and therefore its own revenue and cost. Moreover, the subcontractor needs only to optimize over the price breakpoints that correspond to prices where the manufacturer's subcontracting decision changes.

The equilibrium solution found by the above analysis is in general not optimal for the system as a whole. Further investigation of this point requires the following definition.

Definition 9.9

(i) The *total system cost* equals the manufacturer's processing cost, plus the subcontractor's processing cost, plus the tardiness cost.
(ii) The system is *coordinated* if the pricing decision of the subcontractor and the outsourcing decision of the manufacturer are aligned such that the total system cost is minimized.

Qi (2012) describes a coordinating contract that contains a quantity discount. In such a contract, which is defined by a triple (q, x_1, x_2), the subcontractor announces a threshold q for the amount of time subcontracted and two unit prices x_1 and x_2, where $x_1 > x_2$. The unit price paid by the manufacturer depends on the total subcontracting time, i.e.,

$$
x = \begin{cases} x_1, & \text{if } b < q \\ x_2, & \text{if } b \geq q. \end{cases}
$$

Thus, the manufacturer enjoys a discounted unit price if and only if it subcontracts a sufficient amount of work. Let $b^*(c_s)$ denote the optimal amount subcontracted by the manufacturer if the subcontractor's price is c_s. Further, let $g(b)$ denote the manufacturer's minimum cost, excluding subcontracting cost, if the total amount of time subcontracted is b. The following result (Qi, 2012) specifies the design of such a coordinating contract.

Theorem 9.21 *A quantity discount contract (q^*, x_1^*, x_2^*) where*
$q^* = b^*(c_s)$,
$x_1^* = 1 + c_m + \min_{j \in N}\{w_j/p_j\}$, *and*
$x_2^* = c_s + [g(0) - g(b^*(c_s)) - c_s b^*(c_s)]/b^*(c_s)$
coordinates the system.

Proof It suffices to prove that:

(i) The optimal subcontracting time for the manufacturer is q^*.
(ii) The subcontractor cannot reduce its cost by changing x_1^* and x_2^*.

To prove (i), if the manufacturer outsources a quantity smaller than q^*, the unit price which it pays is $1 + c_m + \min_{j \in N}\{w_j/p_j\}$, which exceeds any possible in-house production cost, including tardiness penalties.

Hence, the amount of time subcontracted by the manufacturer is at least q^*. If it is exactly q^*, the profit of the subcontractor is $(x_2^* - c_s)b^*(c_s)$, and hence, the total system cost is $g(b^*(c_s)) + c_s b^*(c_s)$, which is the minimum system cost.

If the amount of time subcontracted exceeds q^*, the subcontractor's profit is strictly greater than $(x_2^* - c_s)b^*(c_s)$. Since the total system cost is bounded below by $g(b^*(c_s)) + c_s b^*(c_s)$, the manufacturer's costs must be strictly greater than if it subcontracted exactly q^* jobs. Consequently, the manufacturer will choose not to subcontract this much. This completes the proof of (i).

To prove (ii), the profit of the subcontractor under the proposed contract is $(x_2^* - c_s)b^*(c_s)$, which equals the total system saving relative to no subcontracting. Hence, the subcontractor cannot increase its profit without incentivizing the manufacturer to avoid subcontracting entirely, which in turn will reduce the subcontractor's profit.

□

This widely observed outsourcing application, where a subcontractor sets a price first and then the manufacturer reacts to it in a way that the subcontractor can predict, provides valuable intuition about Stackelberg games. For discussions of subcontracting problems in a centralized supply chain scheduling environment, we refer the reader to Chap. 6.

9.3.3 Altruistic Games

Most classical game theory models assume that players are both rational and selfish. The players therefore focus on optimizing their utility, for example by minimizing their personal delay in a routing or congestion game. However, this assumption has been repeatedly questioned by economists and psychologists. In experiments, it has been observed that participants' behavior can be quite complex and contradictory to selfishness (Ledyard, 1997; Levine, 1998). Further motivation for altruistic behavior arises from Internet behavior, such as Wikipedia, open-source software development, or Web 2.0 applications, which explicitly rely on voluntary participation and contributions toward a joint project without direct personal benefit. These environments demonstrate forms of altruism in which players accept certain personal burdens (e.g., by investing time, attention, and money) to improve a common outcome. We consider two games that involve different ways of modeling altruistic behavior. In Sect. 9.3.3.1, we consider a congestion game where the players are all pure egoists or pure altruists. In Sect. 9.3.3.2, each player has an objective that is a weighted combination of egoistic and altruistic cost measures.

9.3.3.1 Egoists and Altruists

Motivated by the substantial evidence of altruism discussed above, Hoefer and Skopalik (2013) consider congestion games where the players, although rational,

9.3 Enhanced Complete Information Games

are altruistic. These games model supply chain scheduling problems in a horizontal supply chain, as studied by Li (2002). Each player i is assumed to be partly selfish and partly altruistic, and his objective is to optimize a linear combination of personal cost and social cost, where the latter is defined as the total cost of all players. The strength of altruism of each player i is captured by his *altruism level* $\beta_i \in [0, 1]$, where $\beta_i = 0$ implies purely egoist behavior and $\beta_i = 1$ implies pure altruism.

A *congestion game* contains a set of players $N = \{1, \ldots, n\}$. This is a supply chain scheduling problem where each player owns one or more jobs that must be assigned to a resource. Available to the players is a set E of resources or facilities that we henceforth refer to as machines for consistency with the scheduling literature. Each player i makes a choice about what subset S_i of the available machines to use. We describe this as a *strategy* $S_i \subseteq 2^E$. A *joint strategy* of all the players is denoted by $s \in S_1 \times \cdots \times S_n$. Given s, let $x_e(s)$ denote the number of players who choose machine $e \in E$. These choices result in delays that are described by delay functions $d_e : N \to \mathbb{R}_+$. This delay is experienced by all the players who use machine e, since it is a congestion effect that affects them all equally. Given s, the objective of player i is to minimize his total cost $c_i(s) = \sum_{e \in S_i} d_e(x_e(s))$. The social cost is the total cost of all the players.

Various classes of congestion games are available:

Definition 9.10

(i) If each player is allowed to select only a single machine, then the game is a *singleton game*.
(ii) If each player has the same set of available strategies, then the game is *symmetric*.

We consider symmetric singleton congestion games, where each player $i \in N$ is either a pure egoist ($\beta_i = 0$) or a pure altruist ($\beta_i = 1$). A vector of strategies $s = (S_1, \ldots, S_n)$ chosen by the players defines a state. Let $d_i(n_i)$ denote the delay experienced by each of n_i players who choose machine i, which is a nondecreasing function of n_i. The following example shows that in a symmetric singleton congestion game there may be no pure Nash equilibrium, even if the game contains only pure egoists and pure altruists.

Example 9.17 (Nonexistence of a Pure NE in an Altruistic Congestion Game) Consider a symmetric singleton congestion game with two machines a and b, three pure egoists, and one pure altruist. The delay functions are $d_a(x) = d_b(x)$ with $d_a(1) = 4, d_a(2) = 8, d_a(3) = 9$, and $d_a(4) = 11$. If either all three egoists or two egoists and the altruist choose the same machine, then one of the egoists can reduce his cost from 9 or more to 8 or less by moving to the other machine. Hence, in equilibrium, each machine must be chosen by exactly two players. However, in this case, the social cost is $2(8) + 2(8) = 32$, as a result of which the altruist is motivated to change machine so that the resulting social cost is $1(4) + 3(9) = 31$. In that event, the previous situation applies. Hence, no pure Nash equilibrium exists.

608 9 Noncooperative Supply Chain Scheduling

In view of Example 9.17, it is valuable to develop a methodology to determine in polynomial time, for a given instance of a symmetric singleton congestion game, whether it has a Nash equilibrium. We also show how to compute a Nash equilibrium with minimum and maximum social costs, if such an equilibrium exists.

Let n_e denote the number of egoists and n_a the number of altruists in an arbitrary symmetric singleton game. Hoefer and Skopalik (2013) provide the following result that simplifies the game into one with only egoists.

Lemma 9.13 *An altruist can be modeled as an egoist with a transformed cost function.*

Proof An altruist moves from strategy S_i to strategy S_i' if and only if the decrease in the total delay on the machines $e \in S_i \setminus S_i'$ from which it is leaving exceeds the increase in the total delay on the machines $e \in S_i' \setminus S_i$ which it is joining. Consequently, for the purposes of computing a Nash equilibrium, an altruist can be modeled as a selfish player i with a transformed cost function $c_i(s) = \sum_{e \in S_i} d_e'(n_e)$, where $d_e'(n_e) = n_e d_e(n_e) - (n_e - 1)d_e(n_e - 1)$, for $n_e > 0$. □

We provide some additional notation. For a given state s, let E_e (respectively, E_a) denote the set of machines chosen by at least one egoist (resp., altruist). Let the maximum delay of any machine chosen by an egoist be denoted by $d_e^{\max} = \max_{i \in E_e} d_i(n_i)$ and the minimum delay of any machine if an additional player is added be denoted by $d_e^{\min +} = \min_{i \in E_e} d_i(n_i + 1)$. Similarly, let the maximum altruistic delay of any machine chosen by an altruist be denoted by $d_a^{\max} = \max_{i \in E_a} d_i'(n_i)$ and the minimum altruistic delay of any machine if an additional player is added be denoted by $d_a^{\min +} = \min_{i \in E_a} d_i'(n_i + 1)$.

Given this notation, the following result by Hoefer and Skopalik (2013) characterizes a Nash equilibrium in a symmetric singleton congestion game.

Lemma 9.14 *Necessary and sufficient conditions for a Nash equilibrium are that*

$$d_e^{\max} \leq d_e^{\min +} \text{ and } d_a^{\max} \leq d_a^{\min +}. \tag{9.40}$$

Proof Let N_e denote the set of egoists where $n_e = |N_e|$, and let N_a denote the set of altruists where $n_a = n - n_e = |N_a|$. Thus, $E_e = \cup_{i \in N_e} S_i$ and $E_a = \cup_{i \in N_a} S_i$. Observe that, if and only if the first inequality in (9.40) is not satisfied, then an egoist can move from one machine to another and reduce his cost. Further, if and only if the second inequality in (9.40) is not satisfied, then an altruist can move similarly. □

Hoefer and Skopalik (2013) use Lemma 9.14 to prove the following result:

Theorem 9.22

(i) *Given an instance of the symmetric singleton congestion game described above with only pure altruists and egoists, there is an algorithm that determines if a pure Nash equilibrium exists in $O(n_e^3 n_a^3 m^5)$ time.*

9.3 Enhanced Complete Information Games

609

(ii) The same algorithm can be modified to compute the lowest and highest social cost Nash equilibrium with the same running time.

Proof

(i) Fix values of $d_e^{\max}$, $d_e^{\min +}$, $d_a^{\max}$, and $d_a^{\min +}$. The following procedure tests for the existence of a Nash equilibrium with exactly those four values.

Index the machines in arbitrary order. For machines 1 and 2, find a combination of egoists and altruists that satisfies the conditions in (9.40). Now, add machines i one at a time and test the number of egoists and altruists who could be assigned to i while sustaining a Nash equilibrium. By doing so, bounds are obtained on the feasible numbers of altruists and egoists remaining unassigned for later machines.

To implement this procedure, maintain a binary matrix $R = \{r_{hj}\}$ of dimension $(n_e + 1) \times (n_a + 1)$, where $r_{hj} = 1$ if and only if there is a feasible assignment of $n_e - h$ egoists and $n_a - j$ altruists to the previously considered machines. Now, consider a new machine i. For this machine, we test all possible combinations of y_e egoists and y_a altruists that could be allocated to i such that conditions (9.40) remain satisfied. If so, the matrix entry $r_{h - y_e, j - y_a}$ is set to 1. If, when the last machine has been added, the matrix entry $r_{00} = 1$, this means that all players have been assigned and a Nash equilibrium exists for the given values of $d_e^{\max}$, $d_e^{\min +}$, $d_a^{\max}$, and $d_a^{\min +}$. If so, this is sufficient to terminate the process. Otherwise, another combination of the values of $d_e^{\max}$, $d_e^{\min +}$, $d_a^{\max}$, and $d_a^{\min +}$ is tested. Failure to find a Nash equilibrium for any such combination determines that no Nash equilibrium exists.

Regarding the running time of the above procedure, observe that $d_e^{\max}, d_e^{\min +} \leq (n_e + 1)m$, and $d_a^{\max}, d_a^{\min +} \leq (n_a + 1)m$; hence, there are $O(n_e^2 n_a^2 m^4)$ iterations of the process. Each iteration tests $O(n_e n_a)$ combinations for the numbers of egoists and altruists to add, at each of m stages corresponding to the number of machines being tested. Hence, the overall running time of the algorithm is $O(n_e^3 n_a^3 m^5)$.

(ii) Lemma 9.14 can also be used to find the lowest and highest social cost Nash equilibrium. To accomplish this for the best Nash equilibrium, the procedure for identifying feasibility with an entry r_{ij} is modified to store the lowest social cost of a feasible assignment. Similarly, the worst Nash equilibrium can be found by storing the highest social cost of a feasible solution. The decisions that provide the highest and lowest costs can be found by retracing the solution.

□

Finally, consider the problem faced by a central planner who wishes to convince as many players as necessary to become altruists, in order to achieve a Nash equilibrium that is socially optimal. In this context, a natural question is how many altruists are required to stabilize a social optimum. Intuitively, the more altruists and fewer egoists are present in the game, the easier it is to establish a Nash equilibrium that is socially optimal. The investigation of this issue requires the definition of two performance measures for the game:

(a) An *optimal stability threshold*, which is the minimum number of altruists such that there exists an optimal Nash equilibrium.
(b) An *optimal anarchy threshold*, which is the minimum number of altruists such that every Nash equilibrium is optimal.

For symmetric singleton congestion games, Hoefer and Skopalik (2013) adapt the procedure described in the proof of Theorem 9.22 above for computing Nash equilibria to determine both thresholds. The main result of this analysis now follows. We provide an outline of the proof and refer the reader to their work for details.

Theorem 9.23 *The optimal stability threshold and optimal anarchy threshold of symmetric singleton congestion games with only pure altruists and egoists can be computed in polynomial time.*

Proof By iteratively applying the polynomial time algorithm that is described in the proof of Theorem 9.22 for different numbers of altruists, for any given number of altruists, compare the cost of the best or worst Nash equilibrium with the cost of the social optimum. □

Hoefer and Skopalik (2013) also show the limits to analysis of the type described above by proving that, for symmetric but nonsingleton congestion games with quadratic delay functions, it is unary *NP*-complete to determine whether a singleton congestion game with only pure egoists and pure altruists has a pure Nash equilibrium.

9.3.3.2 Common Altruistic Preference

Apt and Schäfer (2014) provide a perspective on altruistic games that is different from that of Hoefer and Skopalik as discussed in Sect. 9.3.3.1. In their version of such games, each player's payoff is modified by adding a positive fraction α of the social welfare realized by a joint strategy of all the players to the individual player's payoff. Hence, each player is partly but not completely altruistic, and to the same extent.

The *selfishness level of a game*, which is formally defined below, is the infimum over all values of $\alpha \geq 0$ that results in a social optimum being realized at a pure Nash equilibrium. Intuitively, the selfishness level of a game can be viewed as a measure of the players' unwillingness to cooperate. A low selfishness level, i.e., a low value of α, indicates that the players are easily incentivized to align their interests with those of the society, whereas a high selfishness level suggests that the players are reluctant to cooperate in this way. Since it is a measure of unwillingness to cooperate, the selfishness level is not directly comparable with the price of anarchy, hence using it provides different insights about noncooperative games. We first discuss a general model of these altruistic games and then demonstrate how this model can be applied to a linear congestion game.

An altruistic cost game $G = (N, \{S_i, i \in N\}, \{c_i, i \in N\})$ is defined by a set $N = \{1, \ldots, n\}$ of players, a nonempty set of strategies S_i for every player $i \in N$,

9.3 Enhanced Complete Information Games

and a scheduling cost function c_i for every player $i \in N$ where $c_i : S_1 \times \cdots \times S_n \to \mathbb{R}$. The players choose their strategies simultaneously, and every player $i \in N$ aims at choosing a strategy $s_i \in S_i$ so as to minimize his individual cost $c_i(s) = c_i(s_1, \ldots, s_n)$. We define $s \in S_1 \times \cdots \times S_n$ as a *joint strategy* with ith element s_i. Let $s_{-i} = (s_1, \ldots, s_{i-1}, s_{i+1}, \ldots, s_n)$ and $S_{-i} = (S_1, \ldots, S_{i-1}, S_{i+1}, \ldots, S_n)$. The social objective is the minimization of the social cost of the game, which is defined as

$$SC(s) \equiv \sum_{i=1}^{n} c_i(s).$$

Now, define an altruistic cost game instance $G(\alpha) = (N, \{S_i, i \in N\}, \{c_i, i \in N\}, \alpha \geq 0)$. The objective of each player i is to minimize his partly altruistic cost $\tau_i = c_i + \alpha SC(s)$. If, for some $\alpha \geq 0$, a pure Nash equilibrium of $G(\alpha)$ is also a social optimum, then $G(\alpha)$ is said to be α-selfish. Then, the selfishness level of $G(\alpha)$ is

$$\inf\{\alpha \in \mathbb{R}^+ \mid G(\alpha) \text{ is } \alpha\text{--}selfish.\}.$$

The motivation for studying the selfishness level of $G(\alpha)$ is that it provides an indication of how much altruism for all players would be needed to ensure that a socially optimal solution is stable. Then practical measures, for example direct appeals to the players or public service announcements, can be undertaken to induce that level.

A social optimum s is *stable* if, for all $i \in N$ and alternative strategies $s_i' \in S_i$,

$$c_i(s_i, s_{-i}) \leq c_i(s_i', s_{-i}),$$

i.e., no player is better off by unilaterally deviating to another social optimum. Finally, we define the *appeal factor* $AF(\cdot, \cdot)$ of strategy s_i' of player i, given the social optimum s, as

$$AF_i(s_i', s) = \frac{c_i(s_i, s_{-i}) - c_i(s_i', s_{-i})}{SC(s_i', s_{-i}) - SC(s_i, s_{-i})}. \tag{9.41}$$

The numerator in (9.41) represents the reduction in cost experienced individually by player i in changing his strategy from s_i to s_i', whereas the denominator represents the increase in social cost that results. Hence, if the numerator is large but the denominator is small, this change of strategy is appealing to player i. The selfishness level of a game G can be characterized by bounds on the appeal factors of possible deviations from a stable social optimum. First, Apt and Schäfer (2014) prove the following result about the properties of social optima.

Lemma 9.15 *Consider a noncooperative game $G(\alpha) = (N, \{S_i, i \in N\}, \{c_i, i \in N\}, \alpha \geq 0)$:*

(i) If s is both a Nash equilibrium of $G(\alpha)$ and a social optimum of G, then s is a stable social optimum of $G(\alpha)$.

(ii) If s is a stable social optimum of G, then s is a Nash equilibrium of $G(\alpha)$ if and only if, for all $i \in N$ and $s_i' \in U_i(s)$, $AF_i(s_i', s) \leq \alpha$, where

$$U_i(s) = \{s_i', i \in S_i \mid c_i(s_i', s_{-i}) < c_i(s_i, s_{-i})\}. \tag{9.42}$$

The set $U_i(s)$ in (9.42) contains players who could reduce their individual cost by moving from their current strategy s_i to an alternative strategy s_i' and indeed would do so if $\alpha = 0$. Also, to interpret part (ii) of Lemma 9.15, we may think of α as a minimum threshold for the appeal factor at which any possible change of strategy from s_i to s_i' is not appealing to any player $i \in N$. Lemma 9.15 enables the main result for general games that follows.

Theorem 9.24 *Consider a game $G(\alpha)$ as defined above.*

(i) The selfishness level of $G(\alpha)$ is finite if and only if a stable social optimum s exists for which $\alpha(s) \equiv \sup_{i \in N, s_i' \in U_i(s)} \{AF_i(s_i', s)\}$ is finite.

(ii) If the selfishness level of $G(\alpha)$ is finite, then it equals the minimum value of $\alpha(s)$ over all stable socially optimal solutions.

(iii) If $G(\alpha)$ is finite, then its selfishness level is finite if and only if it has a stable social optimum. In particular, if $G(\alpha)$ has a unique social optimum, then its selfishness level is finite.

(iv) If $\beta > \alpha \geq 0$ and $G(\alpha)$ is α-selfish, then $G(\alpha)$ is β-selfish.

Proof Part (i) follows from Lemma 9.15. Part (ii) follows from part (i) and Lemma 9.15. Part (iii) follows from part (i). Part (iv) follows from part (ii) of Lemma 9.15. □

We provide some intuition about Theorem 9.24. In part (i), if there exists a player in $U_i(s)$ with current strategy s_i and an infinite appeal factor $\alpha(s)$ for another s_i', then no finite value of α will ensure that the game is stable. Part (ii) recognizes that since different socially optimal solutions may have different values of $\alpha(s)$, the selfishness level is defined by the most stable of those solutions. Part (iii) is useful in establishing a property of a unique social optimum. Part (iv) makes the point that a game that is selfish under a given value of α is also selfish under a higher value of α, which follows from (9.42).

We apply the above results for general games to a symmetric singleton congestion game, as discussed by Hoefer and Skopalik (2013) in Sect. 9.3.3.1. However, we add an extra condition that the game is linear, i.e., the delay function of every machine $e \in E$ is of the form $d_e(x_e) = a_e x_e + b_e$, where x_e is the load on machine e under a given strategy s of all the players. This defines a *linear symmetric singleton congestion game*. Let s be a stable social optimum. We write x_e in place of $x_e(s)$ for conciseness. Let the *discrepancy* between two machines e and e' be defined as

9.3 Enhanced Complete Information Games

$$\delta(x_e, x_{e'}) = \frac{2a_e x_e + b_e}{a_e + a_{e'}} - \frac{2a_e x_{e'} + b_{e'}}{a_e + a_{e'}}. \tag{9.43}$$

Further, let

$$\delta_{\max}(s) = \max_{e, e' \in E} \{\delta(x_e, x_{e'}) \mid a_e + a_{e'} > 0, \ \delta(x_e, x_{e'}) < 1\}.$$

Then, $\delta_{\max}$ is the maximum discrepancy over all stable social optima. Further, let $\Delta_{\max} = \max_{e \in E}\{a_e + b_e\}$ and $\Delta_{\min} = \min_{e \in E}\{a_e + b_e\}$. Finally, let $a_{\min} = \min_{e \in E}\{a_e \mid a_e > 0\}$.

Apt and Schäfer (2014) prove the following preliminary result.

Lemma 9.16 *Consider the linear symmetric singleton congestion game defined above. Let s be a social optimum and $e, e' \in E$ be two machines with $a_e + a_{e'} > 0$. Then the discrepancy between e and e' under s satisfies $\delta(x_e, x_{e'}) \in [-1, 1]$.*

The main result for congestion games can now be stated.

Theorem 9.25 *The selfishness level of a symmetric singleton linear congestion game is at most*

$$\max\left\{0, \frac{\Delta_{\max} - \Delta_{\min}}{2(1 - \delta_{\max})a_{\min}} - \frac{1}{2}\right\}.$$

Moreover, this bound is tight.

Proof Let s be a stable social optimum that exists from Theorem 9.24, parts (ii) and (iii). If $U_i(s) = \emptyset, i \in N$, then the selfishness level is 0, from Theorem 9.24, part (ii). Now, consider some player $i \in N$ with $U_i(s) \neq \emptyset$. Let $s' = (s_i', s_{-i})$ for some $s_i' \in U_i(s)$. Let x_e and x_e' refer to $x_e(s)$ and $x_e(s')$, for $e \in E$, respectively. For every $e \in E$,

$$x_e' = \begin{cases} x_e + 1, & \text{if } e \in s_i' \setminus s_i, \\ x_e - 1, & \text{if } e \in s_i \setminus s_i' \\ x_e, & \text{otherwise.} \end{cases} \tag{9.44}$$

Let $s_i = \{e\}$ and $s_i' = \{e'\}$ be the sets of resources chosen by player i in s and s', respectively. From (9.44), we have

$$c_i(s_i, s_{-i}) - c_i(s_i', s_{-i}) = a_e x_e + b_e - a_{e'}(x_{e'} + 1) - b_{e'}. \tag{9.45}$$

Also,

$$SC(s_i', s_{-i}) - SC(s_i, s_{-i}) = a_{e'}(2x_{e'} + 1) + b_{e'} - a_e(2x_e - 1) - b_e. \tag{9.46}$$

Now, the left-hand side of (9.45) must be strictly positive, since $s_i \in U_i(s)$. Also, the left-hand side of (9.46) must be strictly positive, since s is a stable equilibrium and $s_i \in U_i(s)$. Hence, $a_e + a_{e'} > 0$, to avoid a contradiction between (9.45) and (9.46).

Further, using the definition of δ in (9.44), the left-hand side of (9.46) evaluates to $(1 - \delta)(a_e + a_{e'}) > 0$, which implies that $\delta \neq 1$. Then, from Lemma 9.16, we have $\delta < 1$. As a result,

$$
\begin{aligned}
AF_i(s_i', s) &= \frac{(a_e + a_{e'})\delta + b_e - b_{e'} - 2a_{e'}}{2(1 - \delta)(a_e + a_{e'})} \\
&= \frac{(a_e + b_e) - (a_{e'} + b_{e'})}{2(1 - \delta)(a_e + a_{e'})} - \frac{1}{2} \\
&\leq \frac{\Delta_{\max} - \Delta_{\min}}{2(1 - \delta_{\max})a_{\min}} - \frac{1}{2},
\end{aligned}
$$

where the inequality follows from the definitions of $\Delta_{\max}$, $\Delta_{\min}$, $\delta_{\max}$, and $a_{\min}$.

The result now follows from Theorem 9.24, part(ii).

The following example shows that this bound is tight, even for $n = 2$ players and two resources.

Example 9.18 (Instance of an Altruistic Game with Maximum Selfishness Level) Let $N = \{1, 2\}$, $E = \{e, e'\}$, and $S_1 = S_2 = \{\{e\}, \{e'\}\}$. Suppose we are given $\delta \in [0, 1)$ and $a_{e'} \in \mathbb{R}^+$. Let $d_e(x) = (2+\delta)a_{e'}$ and $d_{e'}(x) = a_{e'}x$. The joint strategy $s = (\{e\}, \{e'\})$ is the unique social optimum with $SC(s) = (3 + \delta)a_{e'}$. Further, $c_1(s) = (2 + \delta)a_{e'}$ and $c_2(s) = a_{e'}$. Now, suppose player 1 deviates to $s_1' = \{e'\}$, then $SC(s_1', s_2) = 4a_{e'}$ and $c_1(s_1', s_2) = 2a_{e'}$. Thus, $AF_i(s_1', s) = \delta/(1 - \delta)$, which matches the upper bound in the theorem statement. The case of $\delta \in [-1, 0]$ is similar. $\qquad\square$

The two works on altruistic games discussed in this section provide valuable insights about how variations in the motivations of players can influence the outcomes of noncooperative supply chain scheduling games. The study of altruistic supply chain scheduling games offers considerable potential for future research, and we refer the reader to Sect. 9.6 for a related discussion.

9.3.4 Central Authority Manipulation

Balcan (2011) discusses methods to improve a Nash equilibrium solution with a high social cost into another Nash equilibrium with a lower social cost. Recall the definitions of Price of Anarchy (PoA) in Definition 9.3 and Price of Stability (PoS) in Definition 9.4. There are many practical noncooperative games where the PoA (which evaluates the quality of the highest cost Nash equilibrium) is large, while the PoS (which evaluates the quality of the lowest cost Nash equilibrium) is small.

9.3 Enhanced Complete Information Games 615

For example, as shown below, in job scheduling on unrelated machines, the PoA is unbounded, while there is a Nash equilibrium that is socially optimal and hence the PoS is 1.

Example 9.19 (Noncooperative Game with PoS of 1 and Unbounded PoA) Consider the classical scheduling problem $R_m||C_{\max}$ and a supply chain scheduling instance where $m = n = 2$. The social objective is the minimization of makespan. Each player, represented by a job, minimizes the completion time of his job. Let p_{ij} denote the processing time of job j on machine M_i, where $p_{11} = p_{22} = 1$ and $p_{12} = p_{21} = 1/\delta$, for some $0 < \delta < 1$. Then, a solution with job 1 on machine M_1 and job 2 on machine M_2 is a Nash equilibrium and has $C_{\max} = 1$. This solution is socially optimal, and hence, the PoS is 1. However, a solution with job 1 on machine M_2 and job 2 on machine M_1 is also a Nash equilibrium, since if either player changes their decision, their cost increases from $1/\delta$ to $1 + 1/\delta$. This solution has $C_{\max} = 1/\delta$, and hence, the PoA is unbounded as $\delta \to 0$.

In situations where there are both high cost and low cost Nash equilibria, it is potentially valuable for a central authority—for example, a government agency or another regulator—to try to "nudge" decisions that are currently stuck at a high cost equilibrium into a low cost one, for example by running a public service advertising campaign that promotes socially better decisions.

However, it is in practice too optimistic to hope that everyone will follow any given piece of advice, even if the recommended behavior is optimal if everyone else follows it. A more realistic assumption is that following a public service announcement, some fraction $0 < \alpha < 1$ of players will follow it, whereas other players will continue to behave selfishly. For any such game, an important question is what can be achieved in this situation. More specifically, Balcan (2011) asks, "Is affecting a small constant fraction α of players sufficient to cause the rest to head toward a low-cost equilibrium, or on the other hand, is even a small constant fraction [of the players] not paying attention enough to cause the whole thing to unravel?" This question can be generalized to consider situations where the fraction of players who follow the advice from the central authority changes over time, for example as a result of the information becoming viral through social media.

There are two models (Balcan et al., 2009) by which it is possible for players to learn toward an improved cost Nash equilibrium solution. The first is a simple advertising model, under which the central authority first suggests to each player a proposed action, and each player accepts the proposal with some probability. The players that accept the new action stay with it until the other players, conditioned on that response, converge to a Nash equilibrium. The goal of the central authority is to design its advertising in such a way that the process converges to a Nash equilibrium with a low social cost. Here, it is easy to see that tradeoffs emerge in this design. For example, the more draconian the advice offered in the advertising message, the more effective it may be for those who follow it, but the smaller the proportion α of players who do so. Similarities may be observed in reactions to public service messages related to the global public health emergency in 2020–2021. The second approach uses adaptive learning, where each player individually decides, in each round, between following the advertised strategy or acting in a best response manner with some probability. Players may adjust their probabilities over time using some learning rule of their choosing. The goal again is to show that (in expectation, or with high probability) this process results in a low cost Nash equilibrium solution, under conditions that are as mild as possible on the learning rules used by the individual players.

Regrettably, based on currently existing research, supply chain scheduling games seem to be less amenable to these types of learning than others. Balcan et al. (2009) describe a negative result in this context. Consider the unrelated parallel-machine problem $R_m||C_{max}$. In this case, even for $m = n$, and allowing the central authority to convince $n - 2$ of the players to follow its advertising, there is still a possibility of reaching a pure Nash equilibrium with unbounded PoA. Even for $m = 2$ machines, the same result holds if no more than $n/2 - 1$ jobs follow the recommended behavior. Nonetheless, there are intriguing questions here for future research (see Sect. 9.6).

9.4 Private Information: Mechanisms Without Payments

This section studies supply chain scheduling games where part of a player's information is private. This information may be misreported to a central authority and to other players. Achieving good system performance in this situation requires the design of mechanisms that induce truthful reporting of private information. In general, a mechanism includes (a) an algorithm for converting reported information from the players into an output, which in the supply chain scheduling context is typically a schedule for the system, and (b) a payment scheme that defines a vector of payments to or from the players. However, the mechanisms discussed in this section rely only on an algorithm, which in some cases includes randomization steps, and do not require the use of payments either to or from the players to ensure truthfulness. Within social choice settings generally, there are various situations where payment is ethically or legally problematic (Schummer & Vohra, 2007). Within supply chain scheduling, similarly problematic issues are most likely to arise from antitrust concerns.

In Sect. 9.4.1, we describe the main concepts necessary to design mechanisms and provide a generic description of one. An important concept explored here is different types of truthfulness, including deterministic truthfulness, universal truthfulness, and truthfulness in expectation. Each of these has its own characteristics regarding when it can be used and what it enables for a particular supply chain scheduling application. In Sect. 9.4.2, we describe an application of deterministic truthfulness without payments. Section 9.4.3 demonstrates the power of randomization in designing truthful mechanisms for two supply chain scheduling applications without payments. The design of mechanisms that include both an algorithm and a payment scheme is deferred to Sect. 9.5.

9.4 Private Information: Mechanisms Without Payments

9.4.1 Design Concepts

In this section, we describe several design concepts that are important for the study of private information settings where payments are not used. In Sect. 9.4.1.1, we describe the steps in a generic mechanism design process. In Sect. 9.4.1.2, we describe three different levels of truthfulness that can be implemented through mechanism design.

9.4.1.1 A Mechanism

Consider a situation where a *principal*, or central authority, wants to achieve a good overall performance for a system that includes multiple self-interested players. A mechanism is a decision structure to elicit truthful reporting by the players who otherwise may have an incentive to provide false information in the hope of improving their outcome. The central authority designs a mechanism to collect truthful information and then uses it to determine a good or even optimal solution for the system. A mechanism has two parts. The first part is an algorithm implemented by the central authority to generate an outcome that defines a value for all the players. In the present context, an outcome is a schedule of jobs owned by the players. The value received by a player may be, for example, the cost determined by the completion time of his job in that schedule. In introducing the concept of a mechanism in Sect. 9.1, we refer to this as a truthful mechanism if it induces each player to report his private information truthfully. The second part of a mechanism is a payment between the central authority and the players, which needs to be based on the value they have received. Examples of payment schemes, along with supporting design concepts, are provided in Sect. 9.5.

We now summarize the steps of a generic mechanism.

Mechanism Any

1. The central authority announces a mechanism to the players. (For example, it may announce that all jobs submitted by the players will be processed in order of nonincreasing waiting cost and a scheme for how payments will be transacted with each player based on the reported waiting costs of the players.)
2. The players report information about their private data to the central authority, in the form of a "report," "announcement," or "bid." (For example, the players may report their waiting costs to the central authority. The submitted information may be false, if the submitting player believes that false reporting will improve his outcome. However, a well designed mechanism should disincentivize false reporting.)
3. Using the reported information, the central authority applies an algorithm to compute and possibly implement an outcome that specifies a value for each player. (For example, the outcome could be a schedule of all the submitted jobs, which defines a completion time for each job $i \in N$ and a resulting value for

each player, such as how long he needs to wait for his job to start in the computed schedule.)

4. Based on the announced payment scheme and the outcome generated, the central authority transacts a payment with each player. (For example, each player may receive compensation based on the start time of his job, which can be viewed as the inconvenience he incurs through waiting.)

As mentioned above, this section discusses the use of mechanisms without payment. Hence, for the current discussion, Step 1 does not include the announcement of a payment scheme, and Step 4 is not needed. The full version of a mechanism that includes payments is discussed in Sect. 9.5.

We complete this brief introduction to mechanism design with several important definitions. Let O denote a set of possible outcomes that could be chosen by an algorithm α that is part of a mechanism. For example, O could represent the set of all permutations of jobs $N = \{1, \ldots, n\}$, each of which represents a schedule. Each job $i \in N$ is represented by a player with true but private information t_i. Let $o \in O$ denote a particular outcome, for example, a well defined schedule of the jobs. Then, for $i \in N$, let $v_i(o \mid t_i)$ denote the value received by player i in schedule o, given his true information. Let π_i denote a payment specified by the mechanism that player $i \in N$ must pay to the central authority.

Definition 9.11 If the utility of player i can be written as $v_i(o|t_i) - \pi_i, i \in N$, then we say that the players have *quasilinear preferences*.

In common with much of the mechanism design literature, we assume quasilinear preferences.

9.4.1.2 Levels of Truthfulness

In this section, we define three concepts of truthfulness that guide the subsequent discussion and examples in this section and also in Sect. 9.5. Before doing so, however, we need some perspective on why truthfulness is important. The reason for an insistence on truthful reporting of private data by players is not immediately obvious. In this context, a reasonable question to consider is:

Q1: *Might allowing some strategic false reporting by players be less costly to an overall system solution than imposing constraints to ensure that they report truthfully?*

This question can be answered in the negative, as explained below.

A related issue is what type of actions should we expect a player to take as part of a mechanism. One possible answer is provided by the following definition.

Definition 9.12 A *direct revelation mechanism* is a mechanism where the only action that a player is required to take is reporting his type.

We observe that not all mechanisms are direct; examples of indirect mechanisms include some auctions. In a traditional or English auction, each bidder has to answer multiple binary questions about whether to participate at different bid levels. The

9.4 Private Information: Mechanisms Without Payments

literature of mechanism design focuses largely on the design of direct revelation mechanisms, and it is reasonable to wonder why that is the case. Hence, it is reasonable to ask another question:

Q2: *Might a more elaborate mechanism, for example one that requires multiple responses over time, produce a better outcome?*

This question can also be answered in the negative.

The reason for the two negative answers to Q1 and Q2 above lies in the *Revelation Principle* (Myerson, 1981; Vazirani et al., 2007, pp.224–225). This important principle states that every available truthful equilibrium can be replicated within the class of direct revelation mechanisms. Therefore, there is no loss implied by insisting on truthfulness, nor is there any loss implied by restricting the search for a suitable mechanism to the class of direct revelation mechanisms. As a result, a mechanism designer who wants to implement some outcome or property can restrict his search to mechanisms where the players reveal their private information truthfully and directly to the mechanism designer.

The above discussion enables us to summarize the three main levels of truthfulness used in the algorithmic mechanism design literature:

Definition 9.13

(i) Under *deterministic truthfulness*, a player always maximizes his utility by reporting his private data truthfully. There is no randomization involved in the process.

The following definitions (ii) and (iii) both belong to the category of *randomized mechanism design*.

(ii) Under *universal truthfulness*, the mechanism is a probability distribution over deterministically truthful mechanisms. The mechanism remains truthful even after the realization of the random numbers that are used to specify individual choices, for example which machine processes a job.

(iii) Under *truthfulness in expectation*, a player always maximizes his expected utility by reporting truthfully. However, once he sees the realized outcome, he may realize that his ex-post utility has not been maximized.

The three concepts of truthfulness introduced in Definition 9.13 define a hierarchy of strength. Deterministic truthfulness implies truthfulness in expectation; however, the converse is not true. Relaxing the truthfulness requirement provides more flexibility to achieve stronger performance results, for example, better performance guarantees for an approximation algorithm where an underlying scheduling problem is intractable. In other cases, there may be mathematical problems in establishing deterministic truthfulness, whereas truthfulness can be established using one of the two randomized concepts.

The two definitions of truthfulness that fall within randomized mechanism design have important differences. First, since universal truthfulness is the result of a randomization over deterministic mechanisms, the use of randomization in this case cannot improve truthfulness; it can only improve other aspects of the mechanism such as an approximation bound (see Nisan & Ronen, 2001 in Sect. 9.5.3). However, truthfulness in expectation may be achievable in cases where universal truthfulness is not. Second, the use of universal truthfulness makes no assumptions about a player's attitude to risk. This makes it significantly stronger in practice than truthfulness in expectation, for which reporting the truth is only provably the best strategy for players who are risk neutral.

The majority of the literature on mechanism design for supply chain scheduling problems without the use of payments falls into either the first or third category of truthfulness described above. Section 9.4.2 explores the design of algorithms that achieve deterministic truthfulness without the need for payments. Section 9.4.3 shows how randomized mechanisms can be used to establish truthfulness in expectation, also without using payments. Section 9.5 allows the use of payments to support algorithms within mechanism design, which enables the presentation of examples of all three types of truthfulness.

9.4.2 Deterministic Truthfulness

We describe an application that uses a deterministically truthful mechanism without the need for a payment. This discussion shows how to design an algorithm that is both truthful and achieves a socially optimal solution. This requires that the equivalent scheduling problem under centralized decision making is efficiently solvable.

Angel et al. (2016) describe a truthful algorithm that is also optimal for a noncooperative game defined over the classical scheduling problem of minimizing the total weighted completion time on a single machine, or problem $1||\sum w_j C_j$. The centralized decision making version of this problem is solved by scheduling the jobs in shortest weighted processing time order, i.e., $w_1/p_1 \geq \cdots \geq w_n/p_n$ (Smith, 1956).

Consider a set of jobs $N = \{1, \ldots, n\}$ and a single machine for processing them nonpreemptively. To clarify the following discussion, while processing of each job is eventually nonpreemptive for feasibility, it may be necessary, as a device to ensure truthful reporting of private information, to threaten preemption in order to discourage false reporting.

Each player i is the owner of a single job i, and he alone knows the job length p_i. The job weight w_i is public information. The player reports to a central scheduler his job length as bid b_i, which is not necessarily equal to p_i. Let $B = \{b_1, \ldots, b_n\}$ denote the set of all bids. The central scheduler uses the information B to create an output schedule $o(B)$. Under the assumptions of the *strong model of execution* assumed here, once job i starts to be executed, it is executed for p_i time units, irrespective of the value of b_i. Either $p_i < b_i$ or $p_i \geq b_i$ is possible; in the first case, the processing of job i finishes sooner than the scheduler expects, whereas in the latter case the scheduler allows the job to continue to completion.

A mechanism for this problem is an algorithm A that determines an output $o(B)$. For every job i, let S_i denote the set of jobs scheduled before i in the output schedule

9.4 Private Information: Mechanisms Without Payments

$o(B)$, and let $T_i = \{p_j \mid j \in S_i\}$, i.e., the set of true lengths of the jobs that precede i in $o(B)$. Each player plays selfishly to maximize his utility $u_i(p_i, o(B), B, T_i) = -C_i(p_i, o(B), B, T_i)$, i.e., minimize his job's completion time. The objective of the mechanism is to determine a schedule of the jobs that minimizes the sum of weighted completion times $\sum_{i=1}^n w_i C_i(p_i, o(B), B, T_i)$ or equivalently maximizes the social welfare.

The designer needs to propose a truthful mechanism, i.e., a mechanism that incentivizes the players to declare their true processing times, and moreover delivers a socially optimal solution. The following definition formalizes the concept of truthfulness for this purpose.

Definition 9.14 A mechanism is *truthful* if and only if, for every player i, $1 \leq i \leq n$, and every bid b_j, $j \neq i$, the utility u_i of job i is maximized when player i bids $b_i = p_i$. Thus, a mechanism is truthful if truth-telling is the best strategy for a player i, regardless of the strategies adopted by the other players.

The truthful algorithm described below makes use of the procedure that is now defined. Recall that player i has reported the bid b_i as the job length of job i. While the scheduler does not know the true length p_i of job i until the job completes processing, he does know that it is at least equal to the total amount of processing of that job that has occurred at any point in time. Based on this information, it is possible to know when $p_i > b_i$ and implement the following scheduling rule.

Definition 9.15 An algorithm uses *preventive preemption* if it constructs a schedule in which a job i is preempted after it has been processed for b_i time units and (if not completed) resumed later, if and only if $p_i > b_i$.

Remark 9.5 The intuition behind preventive preemption is that whenever a player bids a length smaller than its real length, the scheduler preempts his job at the *end of the bid processing time* and resumes it later, in fact potentially much later. This is essentially a threat that discourages untruthful bidding. This device enables a simple optimal truthful algorithm with no payments for the problem considered here.

A preemptive schedule on a single machine can be defined as a vector $\sigma = (\rho_1, \ldots, \rho_n)$, where for every job i, $1 \leq i \leq n$, ρ_i corresponds to the set of k time intervals during which job i is executed, i.e., $\rho_i = \cup_{j=1}^k [l_i^j, r_i^j)$, where $l_i^1 < r_i^1 < l_i^2 < r_i^2 < \cdots < l_i^k < r_i^k$ and $\sum_{j=1}^k (r_i^j - l_i^j) = p_i$, which is the true length of job i. Also, for $i, j \in N$, $\rho_i \cap \rho_j = \emptyset$. Thus, in schedule σ, job i is potentially processed in the interval $[l_i^1, r_i^1]$, then preempted, then processed in the interval $[l_i^2, r_i^2]$, again preempted, and so on, until it completes processing at time r_i^k.

Clearly, for the objective of minimizing the sum of weighted completion times, any schedule where at least one job is preempted is not better than the optimal nonpreemptive schedule. Hence, given that we are interested in obtaining a truthful algorithm that outputs an optimal outcome, we need to design an algorithm that preempts the execution of a job only when the job bids a false value of its length.

The algorithm proposed by Angel et al. (2016), named SWPT-PP and now described, uses the sequencing rule of Smith (1956), i.e., schedules the jobs following the increasing order of the ratio of the job's reported length to its publicly known weight, and uses preventive preemption. It executes each job i during b_i units of time in the time interval $[l_i^1, l_i^1 + b_i)$, as specified in Step 2 below. Whenever the real length of a job is greater than its declared length, the job is preempted at $l_i^1 + b_i$ and restarted after time $\sum_{i \in N} b_i$, following a round robin policy of rotating through the jobs if more than one job has been preempted. However, if the length of job i is reported truthfully, it completes processing by time $l_i + b_i$ without being preempted.

Algorithm SWPT-PP

1. Sort the jobs in shortest weighted processing time order based on their bid lengths, i.e., such that $w_1/b_1 \geq \cdots \geq w_n/b_n$.
2. Schedule the first interval $[l_i^1, r_i^1)$ of every job i such that $l_i^1 = \sum_{j=1}^{i-1} b_j$ and $r_i^1 = l_i^1 + b_i$, where $l_1^1 = 0$.
3. From time $t = \sum_{j=1}^{n} b_j$, schedule the jobs that are not yet completed using a round robin policy, i.e., by rotation over job index i among the preempted jobs. For each $x = 2, 3, \ldots, n$, the scheduler checks whether job i still has uncompleted work at time $\sum_{j=1}^{n} b_j + n(x-2) + i - 1$. If so, this job is scheduled in its dedicated time interval $[l_i^x, r_i^x)$, where $l_i^x = \sum_{j=1}^{n} b_j + n(x-2) + i - 1$ and $r_i^x = \sum_{j=1}^{n} b_j + n(x-2) + i$. Stop.

Remark 9.6 Observe that Step 3 of Algorithm SWPT-PP sets aside dedicated unit size intervals of time for each preempted job independently. Therefore, the timing of the preempted part of job i does not depend on the reporting decisions of the other jobs. This is the reason why the reporting decisions of the other players do not affect the incentive for an individual player to report truthfully, as required by Definition 9.14.

The schedule produced by Algorithm SWPT-PP could in theory include some periods of idle time if there is false reporting such as $b_i > p_i$. However, this possibility does not affect the reporting decision of job i, where a job does not use its setaside preemption intervals because it was not preempted. Also, observe that the preemption rule in Step 3 of Algorithm SWPT-PP is quite penal, in that a job that has not been completed is sent to the back of the schedule. However, this is not unreasonable, in that this only happens if the job has failed to complete processing in the time that it bid.

The main result that follows analyzes the performance of Algorithm SWPT-PP.

Theorem 9.26 *Algorithm SWPT-PP is a polynomial time, optimal, and truthful algorithm for the single machine problem where the private data of every job is its length and the social welfare is the weighted sum of completion times.*

Proof There are two cases:

Case 1. If job i bids $b_i > p_i$, then from Steps 1 and 2 of SWPT-PP, it will not start earlier than if it bids $b_i = p_i$ and hence there is no reduction in completion time from reporting falsely.

9.4 Private Information: Mechanisms Without Payments

Case 2. If job i bids $b_i < p_i$, then from Step 3 of SWPT-PP, it will be preempted b_i units of time after its starting time and its remaining processing time ($p_i - b_i$) will be continued after time $\sum_{j=1}^{n} b_j$. As a result, its completion time is at least $(p_i - b_i) + \sum_{j=1}^{n} b_j = p_i + \sum_{j=1, j \neq i}^{n} b_j$. However, if job i reports truthfully, it will not be preempted. Then, since no job j is allowed more than b_j processing time within the interval $[0, \sum b_j]$, its completion time will be at most $p_i + \sum_{j=1|j \neq i}^{n} b_j = \sum_{j=1}^{n} b_j$.

From the consideration of both cases, job i has no incentive to report falsely, and hence, Algorithm SWPT-PP is truthful. Thus, the obtained schedule is non-preemptive, as in the classical SWPT algorithm. From the optimality of the nonpreemptive SWPT algorithm for problem $1||\sum w_j C_j$ (Smith, 1956), it follows that Algorithm SWPT-PP is also optimal. $\qquad \square$

Angel et al. (2016) further demonstrate the power of preventive preemption by showing that, for the unweighted version of the game, there is no optimal truthful mechanism without preventive preemption, even if payments are allowed.

They also study the problem of minimizing the sum of completion times on identical parallel machines, or $P_m||\sum C_j$. The centralized version of this problem is polynomially solvable (Smith, 1956). They consider a game defined on this problem, where the private data is the processing time of the jobs, and the social objective is minimization of the total completion time. They prove that an algorithm similar to SWPT-PP is truthful and optimal for this game.

9.4.3 Randomized Mechanisms

We provide two examples of the use of randomized mechanisms without payments. The first example in Sect. 9.4.3.1 is an application of truthfulness in expectation for a problem where the players represent unrelated parallel machines that report their processing times for jobs, perhaps falsely, as they attempt to minimize their individual expected cost. In Sect. 9.4.3.2, a second example shows how an approximation algorithm for a centralized scheduling problem on uniform parallel machines can be extended, through the use of a randomized mechanism, to provide an approximation algorithm that is truthful in expectation for a decentralized version of that problem under private information.

9.4.3.1 Unrelated Parallel Machines

For the first example, we consider a simple scheduling game with job set $N = \{1, \ldots, n\}$ and available machines $M = \{1, \ldots, m\}$, as studied by Koutsoupias (2014). In this game, each machine acts as a selfish player. The game proceeds as follows. A central scheduler announces a mechanism that specifies the probabilities that jobs are assigned to the various machines, based on the not yet reported processing times for the jobs. Machine i requires time p_{ij} to process job j, but this information is private. Every machine i reports its private information, perhaps untruthfully, to the central scheduler as a bid b_{ij}, where b_{-ij} denotes the bids of all machines except i for job j. If $b_{ij} > p_{ij}$, then its actual processing time is b_{ij}. A practical explanation for this assumption is that, as a result of the reported processing time, an equivalent block of capacity is set aside. In the other case where $b_{ij} < p_{ij}$, the actual processing time is p_{ij}. Combining the two cases, the actual processing time of job j on machine i is $\max\{p_{ij}, b_{ij}\}$. This is known as a *weak model of execution*, as also used by Angel et al. (2009) and discussed in the second example below in this section. We observe that it is not in the interests of a machine to bid an extremely large processing time for a job in order to reduce the probability of having that job assigned to it, since it may nonetheless have that job assigned to it, which would commit it to the large processing time that it had bid.

Let $x_{ij} = 1$ if job j is assigned to machine i, and $x_{ij} = 0$ otherwise. The social objective is to minimize either the total actual cost of the players $\sum_{i \in M} \sum_{j \in N} \max\{p_{ij}, b_{ij}\} x_{ij}$, or the actual makespan $\max_{i \in M} \sum_{j \in N} \max\{p_{ij}, b_{ij}\}$ x_{ij}. For reference below, we note that, in the case of a single job, the total completion time and makespan objectives are equivalent.

The mechanism determined by the central scheduler specifies a probability function $\phi_{ij}(b_{ij}, b_{-ij})$ that, for any job $j \in N$, defines the probability that it is assigned to machine $i \in M$ based on its own bid and those of all the other machines. The central scheduler implements this probabilistic assignment using random numbers. A player makes a decision about bidding his reported time for each job but after bidding makes no further decisions, accepts the assignment of jobs randomly assigned by the central scheduler, and schedules them. The objective of player $i \in M$ is to minimize his expected cost $c_i = \sum_{j \in N} \phi_{ij}(b_{ij}, b_{-ij}) \max\{b_{ij}, p_{ij}\}$.

While we present results for general values of m and n, we first develop intuition by considering the case of $n = 1$, i.e., one job. Since there is only one job, we omit the second subscript on b_{ij}, p_{ij}, and ϕ_{ij}. Hence, we let $\phi_i(b_i, b_{-i})$ denote the probability that the single job is allocated to machine $i, i \in M$, where this probability depends on its reported processing time or *bid* b_i, and those of other machines b_{-i}, through a mechanism that is described below. We describe a mechanism that is truthful in expectation, i.e., one where each player minimizes his expected cost by reporting truthfully, as well as delivering a schedule that provides a close approximation in cost to a socially optimal schedule.

The following result by Koutsoupias (2014) provides intuition about the reporting process.

Theorem 9.27 *Consider an instance of the one job scheduling game with $m \geq 2$ machines. We define the following conditions: for all $i \in M$ and b_{-i},*

(i) $\phi_i(b_i, b_{-i})b_i$ is nondecreasing in b_i.

(ii) $\phi_i(b_i, b_{-i})$ is nonincreasing in b_i.

9.4 Private Information: Mechanisms Without Payments

Then, conditions (i) and (ii) are sufficient and necessary for an algorithm to be truthful in expectation for the game.

Proof We first prove sufficiency. Suppose $b_i \geq p_i$, then from (i), the cost $c_i = \phi_i(b_i, b_{-i}) \max\{p_i, b_i\} = \phi_i(b_i, b_{-i})b_i$ is minimized at $b_i = p_i$. Alternatively, if $b_i \leq p_i$, then from (ii), $c_i = \phi_i(b_i, b_{-i}) \max\{p_i, b_i\} = \phi_i(b_i, b_{-i})p_i$ is also minimized at $b_i = p_i$.

Conditions (i) and (ii) are also both necessary. We consider each condition in turn and show that its contradiction leads to false reporting. First, assume there exist some $\bar{b}$ and $\tilde{b}$ such that $\bar{b} < \tilde{b}$ and $\phi_i(\tilde{b}, b_{-i})\tilde{b} < \phi_i(\bar{b}, b_{-i})\bar{b}$, which contradicts condition (i), where $p_i = \bar{b}$. Then, in both cases $b_i \geq p_i$ and $b_i < p_i$, player i can directly reduce his cost by falsely reporting $b_i = \tilde{b}$. Alternatively, assume there exist some $\bar{b}$ and $\tilde{b}$ such that $\bar{b} > \tilde{b}$ and $\phi_i(\bar{b}, b_{-i}) > \phi_i(\tilde{b}, b_{-i})$, which contradicts condition (ii), where $p_i = \bar{b}$. Then, player i can reduce both his probability of being assigned the task, and his cost if that occurs, by bidding $b_i = \tilde{b}$. $\qquad \square$

To develop further intuition, we consider the case of $m = 2$, i.e., two machines, and still assume one job, i.e., $n = 1$. For this case, we can immediately present the main result for this problem.

Theorem 9.28 *The central scheduler indexes the machines based on the bids received, such that $b_1 \leq b_2$. Then, the mechanism defined by the following probabilities of assigning the single job to the two machines is*

$$\phi_1(b_1, b_2) = 1 - (b_1/2b_2) \text{ and } \phi_2(b_1, b_2) = b_1/2b_2 \qquad (9.47)$$

(a) is truthful in expectation
(b) has an approximation ratio with the optimal cost of 3/2

Proof

(a) We first consider player 1. Observe that player 1 does not know b_2. Therefore, while he knows the two probability formulas announced by the central scheduler in (9.47), he does not know which formula applies to him. Hence, he needs to consider his bid in the two cases $b_1 \leq b_2$ and $b_1 > b_2$.
Case 1a: Suppose $b_1 \leq b_2$ and $b_1 \leq p_1$. Then, since $\phi_1(b_1, b_2)$ is nonincreasing in b_1, it follows that $c_1 = \phi_1(p_1, b_2)p_1 \leq \phi_1(b_1, b_2)p_1$, and the processing time does not change if he bids $b_1 = p_1$, player 1 does not benefit from bidding $b_1 < p_1$.
Case 1b: Suppose $b_1 \leq b_2$ and $b_1 > p_1$. Then, since $c_1 = \phi_1(b_1, b_2)b_1 = b_1 - b_1 b_1/2b_2 = (2b_1 b_2 - b_1^2)/2b_2$ is increasing in b_1 for $b_1 < b_2$, player 1 does not benefit from bidding $b_1 > p_1$.
Case 2a: Suppose $b_1 > b_2$ and $b_1 \leq p_1$. In this case, the order of the values changes, and the probability of being assigned the task is $\phi_1(b_2, b_1) = b_2/2b_1$, giving an expected cost of $c_1 = \phi_1(b_2, b_1)p_1 = (b_2/2b_1)p_1$, which is decreasing in b_1. Thus, if he alternatively bids $b_1 = p_1$, the probability of being

626   9 Noncooperative Supply Chain Scheduling

assigned the job decreases, and the processing time of the job does not change. Therefore, he bids $b_1 = p_1$ to minimize his expected cost.

Case 2b: Suppose $b_1 > b_2$ and $b_1 > p_1$. In this case, $c_1 = \phi_1(b_2, b_1)b_1 = (b_2/2b_1)b_1 = b_2/2$, which is unchanged if he bids $b_1 = p_1$.

The analysis for the second player is similar. Hence, based on the reporting decisions of the two players to minimize their expected costs, both report their true values, and the mechanism is truthful in expectation.

(b) The social cost of the mechanism described above, under truthful reporting, is

$$\phi_1(p_1, p_2)p_1 + \phi_2(p_1, p_2)p_2 = \left(1 - \frac{p_1}{2p_2}\right)p_1 + \left(\frac{p_1}{2p_2}\right)p_2$$

$$= p_1 - \frac{p_1^2}{2p_2} + \frac{p_1}{2}$$

$$= \frac{3p_1}{2} - \frac{p_1^2}{2p_2}$$

$$\leq \frac{3p_1}{2}.$$

Therefore, the approximation ratio is always less than 3/2 and tends to 3/2 as $p_2 \to \infty$.

$\square$

Koutsoupias (2014) extends the above analysis to consider a general number of players representing m machines, for the one job case. For this case, the following mechanism is proposed. Let $b = (b_1, \ldots, b_m)$, where we assume $b_1 \leq \cdots \leq b_m$.

$$\phi_1(b) = \frac{1}{b_1} \int_0^{b_1} \prod_{i=2}^m \left(1 - \frac{y}{b_i}\right) dy, \text{ and} \tag{9.48}$$

$$\phi_k(b) = \frac{1}{b_1 b_k} \int_0^{b_1} \int_0^y \prod_{i=2,\ldots,m,i \neq k} \left(1 - \frac{x}{b_i}\right) dx\, dy, \quad k = 2, \ldots, m. \tag{9.49}$$

It is easy to show that (9.48) and (9.49) define (9.47) for the special case $m = 2$. The main result of this analysis is as follows:

Theorem 9.29

(i) *The mechanism defined by (9.48) and (9.49) provides a truthful in expectation mechanism without payments for the problem of scheduling one job on m unrelated machines with an approximation ratio $(m + 1)/2$ for both total cost and makespan.*

(ii) *No other truthful mechanism has a better approximation ratio.*

We refer the reader to Koutsoupias (2014) for details of the proof.

9.4 Private Information: Mechanisms Without Payments

Koutsoupias (2014) generalizes the above results to $m \geq 2$ machines and $n \geq 1$ jobs, by allowing the mechanism defined by (9.48) and (9.49) to run independently for each task, for which it still achieves truthfulness in expectation. This results in the same approximation bound of $(m + 1)/2$ for the total cost problem and $m(m + 1)/2$ for the makespan problem. This result for the total cost problem is known to be the best possible approximation, as a direct corollary of part (ii) of Theorem 9.29. However, it is an open question whether this result for the makespan problem can be improved by an alternative mechanism that is truthful in expectation.

9.4.3.2 Uniform Parallel Machines

In our second example of randomized mechanism design, the scheduling problem under centralized decision making is an intractable one, and hence, the result achieved is an approximate, rather than optimal, algorithm. Angel et al. (2009) consider the classical problem of scheduling n tasks on m uniform parallel machines with the objective of minimizing makespan, or problem $Q_m||C_{max}$. In the noncooperative supply chain scheduling game which they define over this problem, each task is owned by a selfish but rational player who alone knows the length of his task. There is a central scheduler who works with information reported by the players. Initially, the players report the lengths of their tasks, and then given this information, the scheduler allocates the tasks to the machines. The objective of the central scheduler is to minimize the makespan, i.e., the time at which the last task finishes its execution. The objective of each player is to minimize his task's completion time, and a player may misreport the length of his task in order to achieve this.

We are given machines $M_1, \ldots, M_m$ with speeds $s_1, \ldots, s_m$, respectively. This information is public. Without loss of generality, let $s_1 \leq \cdots \leq s_m$, and denote by $r = s_m/s_1 \geq 1$ the ratio between the largest and smallest machine speed. We are given a set of tasks $N = \{T_1, \ldots, T_n\}$. Let p_i denote the actual length of task i. If task T_i is scheduled on machine M_j, its processing time is p_i/s_j. Let $C(T_j)$ denote the completion time of task j in a given schedule. The goal of the analysis below is to design a scheduling algorithm that (a) ensures that all the players report the true values of their jobs' lengths and (b) approximately minimizes the makespan $\max_{j \in N}\{C(T_j)\}$ with bounded performance error.

Each player bids a (not necessarily true) length for his task to the algorithm. In a *weak model* of execution, if a task T_i with true length p_i bids a length p_i', then its length in the implemented schedule is $\max\{p_i, p_i'\}$. In particular, we consider the w-*weak* model, i.e., the weak model without shrinkage, under which $p_i' \geq p_i, i \in N$. That is, no player can bid a length for his job that is shorter than its true length.

Before describing a truthful mechanism for problem $Q_m||C_{max}$, some additional notation is required. Let A be an approximation algorithm for the equivalent identical parallel-machine problem, $P_m||C_{max}$, with a worst-case performance ratio of c. Let N denote a set of tasks in a given instance. Then, $A_i(N)$ denotes the set of tasks scheduled on machine M_i by Algorithm A, and $L_i(N) = \sum_{j \in A_i(N)} p_j$, denotes the load of machine M_i, for $1 \le i \le m$. Let $C_{\max}(N) = \max_{1 \le i \le m}\{L_i(N)\}$ denote the maximum load of any machine, i.e., the makespan. Consider the following Procedure $T(A)$ that takes as input a set of tasks N, the number of machines m, and the algorithm A. The output of this procedure is a schedule for problem $Q||C_{\max}$.

Procedure $T(A)$
1. Suppose that the machines all have the same fastest speed s_m, and apply Algorithm A for the tasks of N. Let $L_i(N), i = 1, \ldots, m$ denote the load on machine M_i in this solution. Let $\bar{C}_{\max}(N)$ denote the makespan of the resulting schedule for problem $P_m||C_{\max}$.
2. Add to machine M_i a dummy task of length $\bar{C}_{\max}(N) - L_i(N)$, for $i = 1, \ldots, m$. Let S_i denote the sets of jobs, including dummy jobs, scheduled on machine M_i.
3. Randomly assign the set of tasks S_i to the set of machines $M_1, \ldots, M_m$ using a uniform distribution, i.e., each set of tasks has an equal probability of being completely assigned to any machine. Let machine M_i have the original speed s_i, for $i = 1, \ldots, m$. The result is a new schedule with makespan $C_{\max}(N) \le r\bar{C}_{\max}(N)$ for problem $Q||C_{\max}$.
4. On each machine, schedule the assigned tasks in random sequence, where the execution of the dummy task corresponds to idle time on its machine. Output this schedule for problem $Q||C_{\max}$.

We define a concept that is needed for the analysis that follows.

Definition 9.16 Let $N = \{T_1, \ldots, T_n\}$ and $N' = \{T'_1, \ldots, T'_n\}$ denote two sets of jobs that are both in nonincreasing order of processing times, which we denote by p_i and p'_i, respectively, $i = 1, \ldots, n$. If $p'_i \ge p_i, 1 \le i \le n$, we say that N' *dominates* N, which is denoted by $N' \prec N$. Then, an Algorithm A is *increasing* if, given two sets of jobs N_1 and N_2 where $N_2 \prec N_1$, it returns a schedule that satisfies $C_{\max}(N_2) \ge C_{\max}(N_1)$.

Next, we present the following preliminary result that is due to Koutsoupias and Papadimitriou (1999).

Lemma 9.17 *If jobs* $T_1, \ldots, T_k$ *of lengths* $p_1, \ldots, p_k$ *are scheduled in a sequence that is randomly chosen from a uniform distribution where each set of tasks has an equal probability of being completely assigned to any machine, then the expected completion time of task* T_i *is* $p_i + \sum_{j=1, j \neq i}^{k} p_j/2$.

We can now analyze the truthfulness of Algorithm $T(A)$.

Theorem 9.30 *If A is an increasing scheduling algorithm for $P||C_{\max}$, then Procedure $T(A)$ is a truthful algorithm for problem $Q_m||C_{\max}$ in the w-weak model of execution.*

Proof Let H denote an instance where tasks $T_1, \ldots, T_{i-1}, T_{i+1}, \ldots, T_n$ bid $p'_1, \ldots, p'_{i-1}, p'_{i+1}, \ldots, p'_n$, respectively. We compare the expected completion

9.4 Private Information: Mechanisms Without Payments

time of task T_i under its two options for the w-weak model of execution, i.e., to bid its true value p_i or a false value $p_i' > p_i$.

From Lemma 9.17, if task T_i is scheduled on machine M_j with $k - 1$ other tasks from instance H, its expected completion time is $[(p_i' + \sum_{j=1, j \neq i}^{k} p_j')/2]/s_j$.

On each machine, the sum of the tasks' lengths is equal to $\bar{C}_{\max}(N)$ due to the dummy task added at Step 2. Moreover, task T_i is scheduled on machine $M_j, j \in \{1, \ldots, m\}$ with a probability equal to $1/m$. The expected completion time of this task is thus equal to

$$\sum_{j=1}^{m} \left[p_i' + \frac{\bar{C}_{\max}(N) - p_i'}{2} \right] / (ms_j) = \left[p_i' + \bar{C}_{\max}(N) \right] \frac{1}{2m} \sum_{j=1}^{m} \frac{1}{s_j}.$$

Let H_{true} be an instance where task T_i bids p_i and each other task T_j bids p_j', and H_{false} be a similar instance where task T_i bids $p_i' > p_i$. Since by assumption A is an increasing algorithm, $\bar{C}_{\max}(H_{true}) \leq \bar{C}_{\max}(H_{false})$, where $\bar{C}_{\max}(I)$ is the makespan of the schedule found by Algorithm A for instance I. Consequently, the expected completion time of task T_i is larger if it bids p_i' than if it bids the true length p_i. □

The result in Theorem 9.30 becomes most valuable when supported by the analysis of the accuracy of Procedure $T(A)$ in the following result.

Theorem 9.31 *Let $r = s_m/s_1$. If A is a c approximation algorithm for problem $P_m||C_{\max}$, then Procedure $T(A)$ is a truthful $(r \cdot c)$ approximation algorithm for problem $Q_m||C_{\max}$ in the w-weak model of execution.*

Proof Let N be an instance of problem $Q_m||C_{\max}$. Let $C1_{\max}^*$ (respectively, $C2_{\max}^*$) be the makespan of an optimal solution of the problem that schedules the jobs of N on machines with the actual speeds $s_1, \ldots, s_m$ (resp., with all speeds s_m). Then, $C1_{\max}^* \geq C2_{\max}^*$. Since A is a c approximation algorithm, the makespan of the schedule returned at Step 2 is no larger than $c \cdot C2_{\max}^*$. At Steps 3 and 4 of Procedure $T(A)$, since each set of tasks S_i is scheduled on a machine that is at most r times slower than the original machine that has a speed of s_m, the makespan of the schedule is no larger than $r \cdot c \cdot C2_{\max}^*$. Since $C1_{\max}^* \geq C2_{\max}^*$, this schedule is therefore $(r \cdot c)$ approximate. □

Angel et al. (2009) also discuss the use of Procedure $T(A)$ for online problems, where jobs arrive during processing and their data is unknown until they arrive.

Remark 9.7 Lavi and Swamy (2009) study a noncooperative game defined over the makespan minimization problem on unrelated parallel machines, i.e., problem $R_m||C_{\max}$. In the special case they study, the processing time of each job has only two possible values, which are designated as "low" or "high." For this special case, they describe a technique that converts any α-approximation algorithm into a 3α-approximation mechanism that is truthful in expectation.

9.5 Private Information: Mechanisms with Payments

This section focuses on algorithmic mechanism design for noncooperative supply chain scheduling games with private information. The definition of a mechanism used here includes both an allocation algorithm and a payment scheme. There is a large body of literature on such mechanisms. Nisan et al. (2007) provide a comprehensive introduction to algorithmic mechanism design. Section 9.5.1 provides an introduction to the environment, objectives, and solution concepts, of mechanism design with payments. Section 9.5.2 provides an example of deterministic truthfulness with payments, applied to an online supply chain scheduling problem. Section 9.5.3 provides an example of universally truthful mechanism design, with an application to a supply chain scheduling problem on unrelated parallel machines. Section 9.5.4 provides an example of a mechanism design that delivers truthfulness in expectation. Finally, Sect. 9.5.5 considers situations where private information is not completely unknown to other players. Here, all players and a central authority share prior probabilistic beliefs about the private information. For such situations, alternative solution concepts are available, and in Sect. 9.5.5, we illustrate them using a supply chain scheduling game with the social objective of minimizing expected total cost.

9.5.1 Design Concepts

This section provides an introduction to the environment, objectives, and solution concepts, of mechanism design, as well as several examples of their application. In Sect. 9.5.1.1, we introduce the fundamental concept of monotonicity, which establishes conditions for implementability, i.e., the potential to find an equilibrium, of a truthful mechanism. Section 9.5.1.2 introduces the concept of dominant strategy incentive compatibility, which is used to describe the strongest type of equilibrium available within mechanism design. A widely applied payment scheme for implementing a truthful algorithm is discussed in Sect. 9.5.1.3. Finally, the important concept of weak monotonicity, which provides conditions for ensuring truthful reporting, is discussed in Sect. 9.5.1.4.

We first provide two alternative, but equivalent, conceptualizations of an algorithmic mechanism design problem. The first is more intuitive but more abstract. Suppose there are n players and k outcomes. Then, the problem is defined by a real-valued $n \times k$ matrix by which each player values every possible outcome. There is an overall social choice function that is analogous to an objective function in the case of a centralized optimization problem. Each player knows the values of his own row of the valuation matrix; this is private information known only to that player. In a direct revelation mechanism (see Definition 9.12), each player declares his valuations of all possible outcomes; however, these declarations are not necessarily truthful. The value declarations of the players collectively form a new $n \times k$ matrix. One task

9.5 Private Information: Mechanisms with Payments

of the mechanism designer is to take as input the matrix of reported valuations and use a suitably chosen algorithm to compute a specific outcome from the finite set of possible outcomes. In the supply chain scheduling context, this finite set would typically be the set of all feasible schedules, and the outcome would be one of them. At the same time, the designer computes a payment scheme that defines a payment that will be required from each player. The payment scheme is a mapping from an n vector of reported valuations at the chosen outcome into an n vector of specific amounts payable. The utility received by each player is his true valuation of the chosen outcome, minus the payment required. There are two performance criteria for the mechanism design. First, the choice of outcome must be desirable, as measured by the social choice function. Second, the payments must be designed such that the players announce their values in a way that leads to desirable outcomes. The mechanism is called *truthful* when the algorithm and the payment functions ensure that, for a given set of reported values by the other players, the objective of each individual player is maximized when he reports his valuations for all possible outcomes truthfully.

An appealing introduction to mechanism design for decentralized scheduling problems is provided by Heydenreich et al. (2007). The definitions and basic results presented here follow their discussion. A description of a mechanism design problem that is more concrete than the one in the previous paragraph now follows. A mechanism $\mu = (\alpha, \pi)$ consists of an allocation algorithm α and a payment scheme π. The allocation algorithm takes as input any known public information, as well as reported but not necessarily true, information provided by the players, and computes an outcome, i.e., a schedule. The allocation algorithm and payment scheme jointly need to ensure that all players report their private information truthfully, leading to a good, ideally optimal, social outcome.

The following notation is used to describe a generic mechanism design problem. Consider a set of players $N = \{1, \ldots, n\}$. The data for player k is referred to as *type* k and denoted by t_k. The type of player k includes both private and public information. For player k, a strategy s_k is a mapping from a type t_k to action a_k. For the strategies, types, and actions of all players other than k, we use the notation s_{-k}, t_{-k}, and a_{-k}, respectively. Referring similarly to all the players, we use the notation $s_{(k,-k)}, t_{(k,-k)}$, and $a_{(k,-k)}$, respectively.

We provide some examples of the notation introduced in the previous paragraph. In a supply chain scheduling game, a player could represent a machine and his type could represent the time or cost to process each job. Alternatively, if a player represents a job, then his type could be the value of that job, or its waiting cost. Given his type, a player's strategy determines his actions. An action could be a machine deciding to report its speed falsely or a job determining on which machine to be processed. The outcome of the game depends on the actions of all the players and also on an allocation algorithm that uses those actions as input.

9.5.1.1 Monotonicity

In this section, we consider necessary and sufficient conditions for the implementability of a truthful mechanism. More specifically, we focus on mechanisms where only a single parameter of each player is private. An example of such a parameter is a job's cost of waiting. Myerson (1981) proves the following fundamental result for this situation, formulated for an auction setting.

Theorem 9.32 *If players' values can be described with a single parameter, a social choice function is truthfully implementable if and only if it is* monotone. *That is, a player's winnings can only increase when his bid increases, assuming that the bids of other players remain unchanged.*

We may interpret "implementable" as meaning that it can form an equilibrium. As an illustration of Theorem 9.32, consider a single-item auction that awards the item to the highest bidder. If a player is the winner, and then raises his bid, keeping all other bids constant, then he is still the winner. However, a similar auction where the item is awarded to the second highest bidder is not monotone, since a winning player who raises his bid may lose. Closer to the supply chain scheduling domain, the outcome of the mechanism is determined by an allocation algorithm rather than an auction. Suppose the players are waiting for service from a common server and need to report their cost of waiting. Further suppose that a player reports a higher waiting cost, and the reported costs of all other players remain unchanged. Then, if the result of reporting the higher waiting cost is service that is either earlier or at the same time, the allocation algorithm is monotone. However, if the allocation algorithm that defines a schedule is heuristic, then it may happen that the service time is later as a result of the higher reported waiting cost. This situation is discussed further in Sect. 9.5.1.4 below. The following remark provides some perspective.

Remark 9.8 In a truthful mechanism, the following must hold:

(i) For a fixed outcome, i.e., schedule, the payment of a player cannot depend on his own private valuation; however, it may depend on the valuations of the other players.
(ii) Also, the schedule must maximize the player's utility as a function of the payments and the player's valuation.

An example of Remark 9.8, part (i), within a scheduling context, occurs where the players represent machines to which the mechanism is assigning jobs. In this case, the payment received by a machine cannot depend on its reported valuation, rather it can only depend on the jobs assigned to it and the other player's reported valuations. This point is quite intuitive, since it suggests that the payment to a machine derives from the influence of that machine on the utilities of the other players. See Example 9.22 below for a numerical example that supports this intuition.

The next section establishes a standard for an equilibrium in this context.

9.5.1.2 Dominant Strategy Incentive Compatibility

For games with private information, we describe an equilibrium concept that is strong, in the sense that it incentivizes truthful reporting by an individual player without requiring any assumptions about the truthfulness of the reporting of other players. We first define some notation. The allocation algorithm α maps the actions of the players, i.e., $(a_1, \ldots, a_n)$ or equivalently (a_k, a_{-k}) if we wish to distinguish player k, into an *outcome*. In our context, this outcome is a schedule, which in turn determines a value that is defined as $v_j(\alpha(a_j, a_{-j}))$ for each player $j \in N$. As an example of player k's value, the schedule might place his job k sixth among the jobs scheduled on a single machine. Then, if the value of the job is defined by (the negative of) its completion time, it would equal (the negative of) the total processing time of the first six jobs in the schedule. However, since it is possible that player k submitted an action that was not based on his true type t_k, the true value gained by player k needs to be evaluated using his true type, i.e., his job's actual data. Thus, it can be written as

$$v_k(\alpha(a_k, a_{-k}) \mid t_k), \quad k \in N, \tag{9.50}$$

where "$\mid t_k$" can be read as "given that player k's true type is t_k." As mentioned above, a mechanism also contains a payment scheme that specifies a payment to each player. Since this scheme is based solely on actions that may be misleading, it is independent of the true type t_k and can be written as

$$\pi_k(a_k, a_{-k}), \quad k \in N. \tag{9.51}$$

Finally, we apply the concept of a strategy, defined above as a mapping from a true type t_k into an action a_k. This enables us to replace a_k by $s_k(t_k)$ in (9.50) and (9.51) for the case where player k reports his type truthfully. The objective of a player k is to maximize his utility, which we define as his value from the outcome, minus his payment to the system. This motivates the following definition that establishes a benchmark for algorithmic mechanism design.

Definition 9.17 A strategy vector s is a *dominant strategy equilibrium*, if for all players k, for all types t_k of player k, for all actions a_{-k} of the other players, and all alternative actions a'_k of player k,

$$v_k(\alpha(s_k(t_k), a_{-k}) \mid t_k) - \pi_k(s_k(t_k), a_{-k}) \geq v_k(\alpha(a'_k, a_{-k}) \mid t_k) - \pi_k(s_k(a'_k), a_{-k}).$$

Thus, a dominant strategy equilibrium describes a situation where, *independent of the actions of the other players*, it never benefits any player k to deviate from the action $s_k(t_k)$ based on his true type t_k and adopt some alternative action a'_k. The strength of this result lies in the emphasized condition which implies that player k need not know the strategy with respect to truth-telling or otherwise of the other players in order to benefit from truth-telling.

Recall that the Revelation Principle (see Sect. 9.4.1.2) effectively narrows the search for a direct revelation mechanism that can provide an equilibrium solution. We now apply that discussion using the following definitions:

Definition 9.18

(i) A direct revelation mechanism $\mu = (\alpha, \pi)$ is *dominant strategy incentive compatible* if the strategy vector s in which each player truthfully reports his type is a dominant strategy equilibrium.
(ii) An allocation algorithm is *truthfully implementable* if there exists a payment rule π such that the mechanism $\mu = (\alpha, \pi)$ is dominant strategy incentive compatible.

Definition 9.18 (i) provides a sufficient condition for a mechanism to be dominant strategy incentive compatible. Definition 9.18 (ii) defines a requirement for a mechanism to allow, which in practice means also to specify, a payment scheme that coordinates effectively with the allocation algorithm α. The following sections describe how this can be achieved.

9.5.1.3 Vickrey–Clarke–Groves Mechanism

We describe a general method for implementing a truthful equilibrium in mechanism design that applies to several supply chain scheduling problems. The most widely applicable general mechanism is the Vickrey-Clarke–Groves (VCG) payment scheme. This scheme was originally developed for a special case by Vickrey (1961) and then established more generally by Clarke (1971), Groves (1973), and Roberts (1979).

A formal explanation of the VCG mechanism requires additional notation. Let Y denote the set of all possible outcomes, i.e., feasible schedules. We start with a useful definition.

Definition 9.19 Given n players, their types $t_1, \ldots, t_n$, valuation functions $v_1, \ldots, v_n$, strictly positive weights $\gamma_1, \ldots, \gamma_n$, and constants $\beta_y, y \in Y$, an allocation algorithm α is an *affine maximizer* if it finds a schedule $y \in Y$ that maximizes $\beta_y + \sum_{j=1}^{n} \gamma_j v_j(y \mid t_j)$.

While it may appear complex when stated formally, the content of Definition 9.19 is quite simple. Observe that the weights $\gamma_i, i \in N$ and the constants $\beta_y, y \in Y$ do not depend on the players' valuations. Consider an objective function that maps any schedule into a real number, where this number consists of a constant that is unique to that schedule plus a total value from that schedule to the players. Then an affine maximizer optimizes this objective, given the reported information. We provide an example.

Example 9.20 (An Affine Maximizer) Consider a scheduling problem with job set $N = \{1, 2\}$ and processing times $p_1 = 2, p_2 = 5$. The jobs need to be scheduled on a single machine. The value of each job is (the negative of) its completion time

9.5 Private Information: Mechanisms with Payments   635

in a given schedule. The social objective is defined by relative weights γ for the jobs and costs β for all possible schedules. We assume $\gamma_1 = 2, \gamma_2 = 1$, for the two jobs. There are two possible schedules: $\sigma_{12} = (1, 2)$ and $\sigma_{21} = (2, 1)$. Associated with these schedules are costs $\beta_{12} = -6$ and $\beta_{21} = -2$. These costs are most likely to arise from resource costs for processing particular jobs at particular times. Then, the value of $\sigma_{12} = -6 + 2(-2) + 1(-2 - 5) = -17$, and the value of $\sigma_{21} = -2 + 1(-5) + 2(-5 - 2) = -21$. An allocation algorithm is an affine maximizer if, given all the γ and β values and the information reported by the players, it finds an optimal schedule, in this case σ_{12}.

The focus on affine maximizers follows from the work of Roberts (1979), which shows that, in a game with three or more possible outcomes, and where the players' valuations are arbitrary or "unrestricted," only affine maximizers are implementable. While the characterization of VCG payments in the following theorem is presented in this full generality, it should be noted that in most scheduling problems valuations are not unrestricted. For example, a player representing a job typically cares only about the cost of his job, not the costs of other jobs. However, it has proved difficult to establish general results for payment schemes under less restrictive but still practical conditions for players' valuations. Dobzinski and Sundararajan (2008) provide an interesting discussion of this issue.

The following theorem defines the payments needed to ensure that a mechanism is truthful. The VCG payment scheme shown here is a general one that allows for flexibility in the total amount of payment. A particular commonly used implementation of this scheme is discussed in Remark 9.9 following the theorem.

Theorem 9.33 *Let an allocation algorithm α be an affine maximizer, and t denote a vector of reported types of the players. Let $\alpha(t)$ denote an outcome found by algorithm α, given t. For every player k, let h_k be an arbitrary function mapping reports of type t_{-k} of the other players to real numbers. Then, the mechanism $\mu = (\alpha, \pi)$ is truthful if the payments required from player $k, k = 1, \ldots, n$ satisfy*

$$\pi_k(t) = h_k(t_{-k}) - \beta_{\alpha(t)}/\gamma_k - \sum_{j \neq k} \gamma_j v_j(\alpha(t) \mid t_j)/\gamma_k. \tag{9.52}$$

Proof Suppose player k reports false information $\hat{t}_k$ instead of his true information t_k, and let $\hat{t} = (\hat{t}_k, t_{-k})$. Since α is an affine maximizer, then

$$\beta_{\alpha(t)} + \sum_j \gamma_j v_j(\alpha(t)|t_j) \geq \beta_{\alpha(\hat{t})} + \sum_j \gamma_j v_j(\alpha(\hat{t})|t_j)$$

$$\Rightarrow v_k(\alpha(t)|t_k) + \frac{\beta_{\alpha(t)}}{\gamma_k} + \frac{\sum_{j \neq k} \gamma_j v_j(\alpha(t)|t_j)}{\gamma_k}$$

$$\geq v_k(\alpha(\hat{t})|t_k) + \frac{\beta_{\alpha(\hat{t})}}{\gamma_k} + \frac{\sum_{j \neq k} \gamma_j v_j(\alpha(\hat{t})|t_j)}{\gamma_k}$$

$$\Rightarrow v_k(\alpha(t)|t_k) + \frac{\beta_{\alpha(t)}}{\gamma_k} + \frac{\sum_{j\neq k} \gamma_j v_j(\alpha(t)|t_j)}{\gamma_k} - h_k(t_{-k})$$

$$\geq v_k(\alpha(\hat{t})|t_k) + \frac{\beta_{\alpha(\hat{t})}}{\gamma_k} + \frac{\sum_{j\neq k} \gamma_j v_j(\alpha(\hat{t})|t_j)}{\gamma_k} - h_k(t_{-k})$$

$$\Rightarrow v_k(\alpha(t)|t_k) - \pi_k(t)$$

$$\geq v_k(\alpha(\hat{t})|t_k) - \pi_k(\hat{t}).$$

The first inequality holds because if player k reports true information and algorithm α optimizes over it, then greater utility (when correctly evaluated using true information) cannot be achieved by applying α to false information. The left-hand side of the last inequality is the utility of player k for making a truthful declaration, and the right-hand side is his utility for making a false declaration. Hence, each player has an incentive to report his information truthfully. □

The following discussion provides guidance about the flexibility that is available within the VCG payment scheme.

Remark 9.9 The payment scheme in (9.52) includes an arbitrary function $h_k(t_{-k})$, which maps reports of the other players into a real number. This function does not affect the incentive of player k for truthful reporting, since it depends only on the reports of the other players and appears on both sides of the second last line of the proof of Theorem 9.33. It thus offers considerable flexibility in the design of a mechanism. On the other hand, if extreme values are used for $h_k(t_{-k})$, then it may not be individually rational for the players to participate, or in the opposite case, the system may be bankrupted by paying the players to participate when they also receive value.

In practical usage, a common implementation of the general payment scheme in (9.52) is to set $h_k(t_{-k})$ equal to the total value or cost of the other players if player k does not participate in the game. Then, the payment is the total value which the other players could achieve in that smaller game, minus the total value of the other players in the n player game. This implementation has the following natural interpretations:

(i) Consider a game with n players, where the players gain value by participating and then have to make a payment to a central authority in exchange. In this case, the utility of a player k is the total value of all n players in an optimal solution to the game, minus the total value of the other $(n-1)$ players in an optimal solution to a game in which only they participate. This utility equals player k's marginal value to the game.

(ii) Alternatively, consider a game with n players, where a player incurs costs by participating and receives a payment from a central authority in exchange. In this case, the utility of a player k is the total cost of all n players in an optimal solution to the game, minus the total cost incurred by the other $(n-1)$ players in

9.5 Private Information: Mechanisms with Payments   637

an optimal solution to a game in which only they participate. This utility equals player k's marginal cost to the game.

Finally, we observe that the use of optimal solutions to enable these computations suggests that if an optimal solution is difficult to find, then it may become challenging to implement the VCG payment scheme correctly. This is indeed the case, as discussed in Sect. 9.5.1.4 below.

We now provide an example of the VCG payment scheme described in Remark 9.9.

Example 9.21 (Application of a Common VCG Payment Scheme) Consider a game with a set of players $N = \{A, B, C\}$. With reference to (9.52), let $\beta_y = 0$, $y \in Y$, and $\gamma_i = 1$, $i \in N$. The values which the players receive from participating in the game are as follows: A 57, B 48, C 35. The total value of the game is 140. Further, consider two player games among the three players. If A and B play, the total value is 106; if A and C play, the total value is 97; and if B and C play, the total value is 84. Based on this given information, we now calculate the VCG payments due from the three players.

Player A has received value 57 directly from participating. Against this, he must make a payment of $84 - (48 + 35) = 1$. Here, 84 comes from the first term, and $(48 + 35)$ comes from the last term, in the right-hand side expression in (9.52). Therefore, the utility of A is $57 - 1 = 56$.

Similarly, player B has received a value 48 directly and makes a payment of $97 - (57 + 35) = 5$. Thus, the utility of B is $48 - 5 = 43$.

Similarly, player C has received value 35 directly and makes a payment of $106 - (57 + 48) = 1$. Thus, the utility of C is $35 - 1 = 34$.

As a result, each player ends up with the marginal value he adds by participating in the game: player A receives $140 - 84 = 56$, B receives $140 - 97 = 43$, and C receives $140 - 106 = 34$.

An example that demonstrates the calculation of payments under the VCG scheme to a supply chain scheduling game now follows.

Example 9.22 (Application of VCG Payment Scheme in a Scheduling Game) Consider an instance of the classical scheduling problem $1||\sum w_j C_j$, with job set $N = \{1, 2, 3\}$, where publicly known processing times are $p = (1, 2, 4)$ and private weights are $w = (6, 4, 2)$. The payoff valuation of a player is the negative of its weighted completion time, which makes the players payoff maximizers rather than cost minimizers. Hence, they will need to make a payment to the system. The set of all possible schedules is denoted by Y. We let $\beta_y = 0$, $y \in Y$, and $\gamma_i = 1$, $i \in N$, in this example. Let $C_k(t)$ denote the completion time of job k in the optimal schedule of the instance with all three jobs. Let $C_j(t_{-k})$ denote the completion time of job j in the optimal solution of an instance in which job k is removed, $j \in N \setminus \{k\}$.

We initially assume that reporting is truthful. An affine maximizer is an optimal algorithm α that minimizes the weighted sum of completion times. From Smith

638   9   Noncooperative Supply Chain Scheduling

(1956), the allocation algorithm α schedules the jobs in SWPT order, i.e., $(1, 2, 3)$, and is an affine maximizer.

The payment specified by (9.52) is $\sum_{j=1}^{3} w_j C_j$ if we set $h_k(t_{-k}) = 0$. However, following the discussion in Remark 9.9, we choose to set $h_k(t_{-k}) = \sum_{j \neq k} w_j C_j(t_{-k})$, which is the total value of the other jobs if job k does not participate. This information is as follows: $C_1(t) = C_1(t_{-2}) = C_1(t_{-3}) = 1$; $C_2(t) = 3$, $C_2(t_{-1}) = 2$, $C_2(t_{-3}) = 3$; and $C_3(t) = 7$, $C_3(t_{-1}) = 6$, $C_3(t_{-2}) = 5$.

We now compute the VCG payments, from (9.52). However, the signs are reversed because a job's value is the negative of its weighted completion time, i.e., player j receives a value of $-C_j$, $j \in N$. These payments, computed from the publicly known processing times p_j and the truthfully reported job weights w_j, are as follows:

$$\pi_k(t) = -\sum_{j \neq k} w_j C_j(t_{-k}) + \sum_{j \neq k} w_j C_j(t)$$

$$= \sum_{j \neq k} w_j [C_j(t) - C_j(t_{-k})]$$

$$= \sum_{j \,|\, w_j/p_j < w_k/p_k} w_j p_k.$$

Thus, $\pi_1(t) = p_1(w_2 + w_3) = 1(4 + 2) = 6$, $\pi_2(t) = p_2 w_3 = 2(2) = 4$, and $\pi_3(t) = 0$. Intuitively, each job k pays for its marginal cost to the game, i.e., the total increase in cost which it causes for all the other players.

We now consider the possibility of false reporting of the job weights. In the schedule from truthful reporting above, the value of job 3 is $w_3 C_3 = -(2)(7) = -14$, and it makes no payment. Now suppose that job 3 exaggerates its private weight, in order to obtain an earlier completion time, by reporting a false type $\hat{w}_3 = 8 + \epsilon$, where $\epsilon > 0$ and small. Then, $\hat{w}_3/p_3 = (8 + \epsilon)/4 > 2 = w_2/p_2$. Since the allocation algorithm α schedules the jobs in SWPT order based on their reported weights, job 3 obtains the second position in the schedule and a completion time of 5 instead of 7. Hence, its new value is $-2(1 + 4) = -10$; therefore, its increase in value directly from the game is $-10 - (-14) = 4$. However, it must now make a new payment of $w_2 p_3 = 4(4) = 16 > 4$, which is clearly not worthwhile.

To provide some further intuition, we consider an alternative situation where $w_3 = 8$. In this case, $w_2/p_2 = w_3/p_3 = 2$. Then, job 3 can be scheduled second rather than third by falsely reporting $w_3 = 8 + \epsilon$, where $\epsilon > 0$ and small. Here, the increase in value for job 3 is $8(-5) - (8)(-7) = 16$, while the new payment is 16 as in the previous example. Thus, no advantage is gained by submitting the false report, even where the extent of the deception is arbitrarily small.

The success of the VCG payment scheme in truthfully optimizing the game in Example 9.22 relies on the fact that the allocation algorithm α used, namely SWPT,

9.5 Private Information: Mechanisms with Payments   639

is optimal for the scheduling problem $1 \| \sum w_j C_j$. Hence, the algorithm is an affine maximizer, as in Definition 9.19.

9.5.1.4 Weak Monotonicity

This section is motivated by two considerations. The first consideration is that we may wish to consider private data with more than one type. For example, a supply chain scheduling problem may have jobs where both their processing times and their waiting costs are private. In this more general situation, the analysis underlying Myerson's (1981) proof of Theorem 9.32 does not generate a simple monotonicity requirement. Instead, it generates a requirement for *cyclic monotonicity*, as proved by Rochet (1987). However, cyclic monotonicity is difficult to interpret and apply. As a result, it is commonly represented by a weaker but more intuitive and implementable condition, *weak monotonicity*, as defined below. As explained by Bikhchandani et al. (2006), the distinction between the two conditions is as follows. Cyclic monotonicity is a requirement on every finite selection of type vectors from the domain, whereas weak monotonicity is only a requirement on every pair of type vectors. However, in some applications, the two conditions are equivalent, and we refer the reader to Bikhchandani et al. (2006) for more discussion of this issue.

The second consideration is that, only when the scheduling problem underlying a supply chain scheduling game is efficiently solvable, is it generally possible to find an efficient optimal allocation algorithm for mechanism design. In this case, VCG payments (see Sect. 9.5.1.3) are sufficient to ensure deterministically truthful reporting. On the other hand, if the underlying scheduling problem is *NP*-hard, then the only available allocation algorithm may be heuristic. If it is heuristic, then it is not an affine maximizer. In such a case, VCG payments do not in general ensure truthful declaration of private information. However, there are alternative paths, which typically rely on a combination of weak monotonicity and problem-specific properties, to the development of truthful mechanisms.

The following discussion (Heydenreich et al., 2007) provides helpful guidance. Let $\alpha(t_k, t_{-k})$ be an outcome computed by allocation algorithm α, where player k reports its type t_k and players $1, \ldots, k-1, k+1, \ldots, n$ report their types $t_1, \ldots, t_{k-1}, t_{k+1}, \ldots, t_n$, respectively. Observe that this definition is identical to (9.50), where the action required by player k is simply the reporting of its type. Further, let $v(\alpha(t_k, t_{-k}) \mid t_k)$ denote the value gained by player k from this outcome, given that its true type is t_k.

Definition 9.20 An allocation algorithm α satisfies *weak monotonicity* if, for all players k, for all given types t_k, other types $\hat{t}_k$, and any fixed types t_{-k} of all other players,

$$v(\alpha(\hat{t}_k, t_{-k}) \mid t_k) - v(\alpha(t_k, t_{-k}) \mid t_k) \le v(\alpha(\hat{t}_k, t_{-k}) \mid \hat{t}_k) - v(\alpha(t_k, t_{-k}) \mid \hat{t}_k).$$

640   9 Noncooperative Supply Chain Scheduling

A less formal but more intuitive explanation of weak monotonicity is as follows. Suppose a player k's true type changes from t_k to $\hat{t}_k$ and doing so changes the outcome, i.e., the schedule, given by the allocation algorithm. Then, the difference in the total valuation of all the players between the original and new outcomes, evaluated at the new type, must be at least as much as that difference evaluated at the original type. Equivalently, if the outcome changes when a single player changes his valuation, then this must be because that player increased his value of the new outcome relative to his value of the old outcome.

The next result establishes a connection between weak monotonicity and truthful implementability.

Theorem 9.34 *Weak monotonicity is a necessary condition for a deterministically truthful implementation of an allocation algorithm.*

Proof Assume that truthful payments exist. Then, we have

$$\text{(a)} \quad v(\alpha(t_k, t_{-k})|t_k) - \pi(t_k, t_{-k}) \geq v(\alpha(\hat{t}_k, t_{-k})|t_k) - \pi(\hat{t}_k, t_{-k})$$

$$\Rightarrow v(\alpha(t_k, t_{-k})|t_k) - v(\alpha(\hat{t}_k, t_{-k})|t_k) \geq \pi(t_k, t_{-k}) - \pi(\hat{t}_k, t_{-k}), \quad \text{and} \quad (9.53)$$

$$\text{(b)} \quad v(\alpha(\hat{t}_k, t_{-k})|\hat{t}_k) - \pi(\hat{t}_k, t_{-k}) \geq v(\alpha(t_k, t_{-k})|\hat{t}_k) - \pi(t_k, t_{-k})$$

$$\Rightarrow \pi(t_k, t_{-k}) - \pi(\hat{t}_k, t_{-k}) \geq v(\alpha(t_k, t_{-k})|\hat{t}_k) - v(\alpha(\hat{t}_k, t_{-k})|\hat{t}_k),$$

$$\text{then} \quad (9.54)$$

$$v(\alpha(\hat{t}_k, t_{-k})|t_k) - v(\alpha(t_k, t_{-k})|t_k) \leq v(\alpha(\hat{t}_k, t_{-k})|\hat{t}_k) - v(\alpha(t_k, t_{-k})|\hat{t}_k),$$

$$\text{from (9.53) and (9.54)},$$

i.e., weak monotonicity is established.   □

Nonetheless, in some environments, weak monotonicity may also be sufficient for deterministically truthful implementation. An important result regarding this issue is due to Saks and Yu (2005), who show that, on any convex domain, weak monotonicity is both necessary and sufficient.

However, in many applications, insistence on a truthful mechanism is incompatible with finding a socially optimal outcome. Consider a noncooperative game defined over the classical scheduling problem of minimizing the makespan on m unrelated parallel machines, or problem $R_m||C_{\max}$. In this game, the players are the machines, and their private information is their processing times of all the jobs. The following result is due to Nisan and Ronen (2001).

Theorem 9.35 *There does not exist a deterministically truthful mechanism that minimizes the makespan in the unrelated parallel-machine scheduling game.*

Proof Recall that Theorem 9.34 shows that satisfying weak monotonicity is a necessary condition for truthfulness. Now, consider the following example (Heydenreich et al., 2007).

9.5 Private Information: Mechanisms with Payments

Example 9.23 (Nonexistence of Weak Monotonicity in a Scheduling Game) Consider an instance with $m = 2$ and $n = 4$. Let the private processing times on machine M_2 be $(1, 1, 1, 1)$. Initially, let the private processing times on machine M_1 be $p = (1, 1, 1, 1)$. Assume without loss of generality that the allocation algorithm assigns jobs 1 and 2 to machine M_1. That is, for type $p = (1, 1, 1, 1)$, the set $T = \{1, 2\}$ of jobs is assigned to machine 1. Consider an alternative reported set of processing times on machine M_1, $p' = (\epsilon, \epsilon, 1 + \epsilon, 1 + \epsilon)$, where $\epsilon > 0$ is small. Now, an optimal allocation algorithm must assign jobs 1, 2 and either 3 or 4 to machine M_1 and the remaining job to machine M_2. Without loss of generality, we assume that $\{1, 2, 3\}$ is the set of jobs assigned to machine M_1, represented by $T' = \{1, 2, 3\}$. Then, weak monotonicity implies

$$v_1(T' \mid p') - v_1(T' \mid p) + v_1(T \mid p) - v_1(T \mid p') \geq 0$$

$$\Leftrightarrow -\sum_{j \in T'} p'_j + \sum_{j \in T'} p_j - \sum_{j \in T} p_j + \sum_{j \in T} p'_j \geq 0$$

$$\Leftrightarrow \sum_{j \in T \setminus T'} (p'_j - p_j) + \sum_{j \in T' \setminus T} (p_j - p'_j) \geq 0.$$

Evaluating the left-hand side of the last inequality for this example gives $p_3 - p'_3 = 1 - (1 + \epsilon) = -\epsilon < 0$. Hence, weak monotonicity is not satisfied and, from Theorem 9.34, the mechanism is not truthful. □

In fact, Nisan and Ronen (2001) establish the stronger but less concisely proved result that there does not exist a deterministically truthful mechanism that approximates the makespan for the unrelated parallel-machine scheduling problem with an error ratio bound strictly less than two. From a practical perspective, when truthfulness and finding a socially optimal solution are incompatible, a central authority needs to understand the sensitivity of the social cost function to false reporting.

9.5.2 Deterministic Truthfulness

This section studies the application of deterministically truthful mechanism design with payments to games defined over online supply chain scheduling problems. In practice, many manufacturing and service processes are online, since customers have the option to submit orders at any time. The use of Internet platforms for placing orders increases the practical relevance of this environment. In an online scheduling problem, jobs arrive during the execution of the schedule, and some or even all information about those jobs is unknown until they arrive. Pruhs et al. (2004) provide a comprehensive introduction to online scheduling problems.

Chen et al. (2016) consider an online scheduling environment with a central scheduler, which owns a machine that the players use to have their jobs processed

642   9 Noncooperative Supply Chain Scheduling

for a payment. Each job has a release date, a due date, a processing time, and a value if it is completed by its due date. None of the parameters of a job are known until it is released. Each job is owned by a separate, self-interested player. When a job arrives, it is released to the player who owns it. The player then has several options: it can decide when to pass the job to the central scheduler who owns the machine, it can falsely report the processing time, and it can declare an arbitrary value and due date. In this problem, jobs are preemptive under either preempt-restart or preempt-resume mode. In the former mode, a job that is preempted must restart its processing from the beginning, whereas in the latter mode processing restarts from the exact point where it left off previously.

Assume an infinite time period T. There is a single machine that processes at most one job at any given time. A set J of jobs arrives over time. Each job $i \in J$ is owned by a self-interested player i and characterized by a type $\theta_i = (r_i, d_i, p_i, v_i)$, representing its release date, deadline, processing time, and value, respectively. All this information is private to the owner of the job. The value of a job is earned if and only if it completes by its deadline. However, a player reports the details of its job as $\hat{\theta}_i = (\hat{r}_i, \hat{d}_i, \hat{p}_i, \hat{v}_i)$, perhaps falsely. The details $\hat{\theta}_i$ reported for job i, whether truthfully or falsely, are collectively described as its *bid*. Let $\hat{\theta}_{-i}$ denote the reported information of all jobs except i.

Remark 9.10 Some options for false reporting can be eliminated straightforwardly. First, if the job processing time is underreported, i.e., $\hat{p}_i < p_i$, then even if job i is scheduled, it cannot be completed. It would also be problematic to overreport a due date, i.e., $\hat{d}_i > d_i$, since the job could be late when it was returned to the player. Finally, in this online problem, a player i has no knowledge of his job until its release date r_i, hence it is not possible to report $\hat{r}_i < r_i$. We therefore assume for the following analysis that $\hat{p}_i \geq p_i, \hat{d}_i \leq d_i, \hat{r}_i \geq r_i, i \in J$. Observe that the reporting options $\hat{v}_i < v_i$ and $\hat{v}_i > v_i$ remain available at this point.

Let $\kappa = \max_{i,j \in J, i \neq j} \{p_i / p_j\}$, i.e., the maximum ratio of the processing times of any two jobs. To normalize the data, we assume without loss of generality that $p_j \in [1, \kappa], j \in J$. The objective of each player is to maximize his utility, which is the value of his job, less the payment required by the central planner. More formally, the utility of player j is $u_j(g(\hat{\theta}), \theta_i) = q_j(\hat{\theta}, d_j)v_j - \pi_j(\hat{\theta})$, where $q_j(\hat{\theta}, d_j) = 1$ if job j is completed on time, and 0 otherwise, since no payment is required if a job is not completed on time. The objective of the central planner is to maximize the total value of jobs that are delivered on time.

Let $e_j(\hat{\theta}, t)$ denote the amount of processing of job j that is completed by time t when the job sequence results from each player i submitting a bid $\hat{\theta}_i, i \in J$. We now describe the proposed mechanism.

Mechanism Γ

(i) When the machine becomes available, i.e., when either an existing job is completed or a new job arrives, the next job is chosen for processing. This choice is based on the priority score for every job j, which is $\hat{v}_j \cdot \beta^{\hat{p}_j - e_j(\hat{\theta}, t)}$, where $0 < \beta < 1$, and the highest priority score feasible job is processed next.

9.5 Private Information: Mechanisms with Payments

(ii) The payment is equal to the minimum bid that the players have to make in order for the job to be completed, i.e., $\pi_j(\hat{\theta}) = \min\{v'_j \mid q_j(((\hat{r}_j, \hat{d}_j, \hat{p}_j, v'_j), \hat{\theta}_{-j}), \hat{d}_j) = 1\}$.

We provide some intuition about Mechanism Γ. In either the preempt-restart or the preempt-resume mode, processing is preemptive, and the job currently in process can be preempted at any time if another job has a higher priority score, from (i). The priority rule in (i) models the intuition that a job with higher value has higher priority, and a job with larger remaining processing time has lower priority. The value of β can be adjusted for the analysis of approximation bounds, but for the purposes of defining Mechanism Γ and establishing truthfulness any $0 < \beta < 1$ suffices. If a job j is completed by its deadline d_j, then the mechanism requires a payment from job j of $\pi_j(\hat{\theta})$ based on the reported information of all the jobs, from (ii).

Both the allocation rule and the payment rule can be implemented efficiently. The allocation rule is only applied when a job arrives or a job is completed. Since the set of critical time points $t \in [r_j, d_j)$ has polynomial size, the payment for each player can be computed in polynomial time. From the payment rule, it is clear that mechanism Γ is individually rational. The remaining issue to consider is incentive compatibility.

Suppose that job j has been executed $k > 0$ times when truthfully declared but eventually abandoned. Let t_i^s and t_i^p denote the ith time at which job j starts execution and is preempted, respectively, where $i = 1, \ldots, k$, and let $t^a = \arg\inf_t(e_j(t) + \hat{d}_j - t < \hat{p}_j)$ be the time at which job j is abandoned. Also, within the interval $[r_j, t^a]$, let the *executing period A* and the *pending period P* of job j be defined according to those times. Thus, for job j, $A = [t_1^s, t_1^p) \cup [t_2^s, t_2^p) \cup \ldots \cup [t_k^s, t_k^p)$ and $P = [r_j, t_1^s) \cup [t_1^p, t_2^s) \cup \ldots \cup [t_k^p, t^a)$.

Chen et al. (2016) prove the following preliminary result.

Lemma 9.18 *Let $\mathcal{J}$ (respectively, $\mathcal{J}'$) denote the jobs that are executed during period P when θ_j is truthfully (resp., falsely) declared. Let $\mathcal{I}$ (respectively, $\mathcal{I}'$) denote the jobs that are pending during A when θ_j is truthfully (resp., falsely) declared. Then:*

(i). $\mathcal{I} \cap \mathcal{J} = \emptyset$.
(ii). $\mathcal{I} \cap \mathcal{J}' = \emptyset$.
(iii). $\mathcal{J} = \mathcal{J}'$.

We refer the reader to Chen et al. (2016) for a proof. In Lemma 9.18, (i) means that, if θ_j is declared truthfully, job $i \in \mathcal{I}$ with lower priority than job j in period $A \cup P$ cannot be executed in period P, since job j with higher priority than i is pending in that period. Also, (ii) means that, if θ_j is declared falsely, then job i cannot be executed in period P either. Finally, (iii) means that, regardless of whether θ_j is declared truthfully or not, the jobs that are executed in period P are the same.

Theorem 9.36 *Mechanism Γ is dominant strategy incentive compatible, in both the preempt-restart model and the preempt-resume model.*

Proof We first interpret monotonicity (see Theorem 9.32) for the problem at hand. An allocation rule within a mechanism is monotone if, given that a job with truthfully reported type $\theta_j = (r_j, d_j, p_j, v_j)$ cannot be completed, then if it reports $\hat{r}_j \geq r_j, \hat{d}_j \leq d_j, \hat{p}_j \geq p_j$ and $\hat{v}_j \leq v_j$, it still cannot be completed. From Theorem 9.32, a sufficient condition for the truthfulness of a mechanism is the monotonicity of its allocation rule. Hence, we prove the monotonicity of the allocation rule of mechanism Γ. Observe that this is a composite rule that incorporates the reported job value $\hat{v}_j$ and reported processing time $\hat{p}_j$ explicitly into the choice of the next job to process. Moreover, the reported ready time $\hat{r}_j$ and reported due date $\hat{d}_j$ are implicitly incorporated through the definition of feasibility.

We first recall the restrictions on the possibilities for false reporting discussed in Remark 9.10. Next, consider monotonicity with regard to $\hat{r}_j$ only. For feasibility, $\hat{r}_j \in [r_j, t^a] = P \cup A$. If player j reports falsely, a necessary condition for job j to be completed is that it should be executed sometime in the period P. We show that this condition cannot be met. Consider a job $i \in \mathscr{I}$ that has lower priority than job j in period $A \cup P$. We first show that job i cannot be executed in period P, regardless of how job j reports. There are two cases:

Case 1. Job j reports truthfully. Then, Lemma 9.18, part (i), implies that job i cannot be executed in period P, since job j that has higher priority is pending in period P.

Case 2. Job j reports falsely. Then, Lemma 9.18, part (ii), implies that again job i cannot be executed in period P.

The two cases above show that job i cannot be executed in period P. Then, Lemma 9.18, part (iii), implies that job j cannot be executed in P either. Hence, declaring $\hat{r}_j \geq r_j$ cannot cause job j to be completed if it is not completed under true reporting. A similar argument applies to $\hat{d}_j, \hat{p}_j$, and $\hat{v}_j$. As is intuitive, declaring $\hat{d}_j \leq d_j, \hat{p}_j \geq p_j$, or $\hat{v}_j \leq v_j$ does not improve job j's priority from the composite allocation rule and cannot cause it to be completed. Hence, the allocation rule of Γ is monotone, and from Theorem 9.32, it admits a truthful payment scheme.

The one remaining opportunity for false reporting is $\hat{v}_i > v_i$, which potentially provides job i with more chance of being scheduled. However, the payment rule of Mechanism Γ implies that such false reporting would increase the amount payable by the player to the central scheduler. Hence, the payment rule is truthful, and Mechanism Γ is incentive compatible. $\qquad\square$

The following competitive ratio results are achieved by Chen et al. (2016), under the above assumptions about private data:

(i). In the preempt-restart model with private job lengths, Mechanism Γ achieves the optimal competitive ratio of 5 for equal-length jobs and a near optimal ratio of $[\frac{1}{(1-\epsilon)^2} + o(1)]\kappa / \ln \kappa$ for unequal-length jobs, where $0 < \epsilon < 1$.

(ii). In the preempt-resume model with private job lengths, Mechanism Γ achieves the best possible competitive ratio of 5 for equal-length jobs and a competitive ratio within a factor of 2 for unequal-length jobs.

9.5 Private Information: Mechanisms with Payments

In earlier work, Porter (2004) derives deterministic truthfulness and approximability results for a similar online problem. It is interesting to compare the results of Porter (2004) and Chen et al. (2016), based on the different models of preemption assumed and the use of different parameters to evaluate the competitive ratios, in their respective works.

9.5.3 Universal Truthfulness

We provide an example of the use of randomized mechanism design to establish universal truthfulness, as defined in Sect. 9.4.1.2. Nisan and Ronen (2001) introduce randomized mechanism design in their study of a game defined over the problem of minimizing the makespan on two unrelated parallel machines, or problem $R_2||C_{\max}$. There is a set of jobs $N = \{1, \ldots, n\}$. These jobs require nonpreemptive processing on the machines. In this game, the players represent the two machines. Each player or machine has private information, which is the time it takes for it to process each of the jobs. If machine i processes job j, the processing time is p_{ij}, but this information is known only to player i. Each player maximizes its utility, which is defined as its payment received based on which jobs it has processed, less its processing load. In order to improve its utility, player i may report processing times that are false, i.e., $\hat{p}_{ij}$ instead of p_{ij}. The time for which a job is processed is its privately known processing time, independent of the time bid for it. The social objective is the minimization of the makespan.

As a benchmark for mechanism design for this problem, we first consider the following deterministic mechanism due to Nisan and Ronen (2001). We assume that this mechanism is implemented by a central authority. The mechanism contains both an algorithm for assigning the jobs to the machines and a payment for compensating the machines for processing the allocated jobs.

Mechanism MinWork
1. Each player reports a *bid*, i.e., its processing time for each job.
2. Each job is assigned to the machine where it has smaller reported processing time, with ties broken arbitrarily.
3. Each machine receives, for each job that it processes, a payment that equals the second smallest reported processing time for that job.

The following result specifies the performance of Mechanism MinWork relative to the social objective of makespan minimization.

Theorem 9.37 *Mechanism MinWork is truthful, i.e., the players report the processing times of all jobs truthfully, and provides a 2-approximation for problem* $R_2||C_{\max}$.

We refer the reader to Nisan and Ronen (2001) for a proof.

In order to improve on the ratio bound of 2 in Theorem 9.37, it is necessary to use a randomized mechanism. Let $o_{m_i}(a)$, $i \in F$ denote the output, i.e., in this context

646   9 Noncooperative Supply Chain Scheduling

the schedule, obtained by applying Mechanism m_i in a family F of mechanisms to a set a of strategies, i.e., reported bids, of the players, given their true types t. Then, let $f(o_{m_i}(a), t)$ denote the centralized objective value achieved in that case. A formal definition of a randomized mechanism now follows.

Definition 9.21 A *randomized mechanism* is a probability distribution over a family $\{m_i \mid i \in F\}$ of mechanisms each having the same sets of strategies and possible outputs. The *outcome* of such a mechanism is a probability distribution over outputs and payments. For optimization problems, the objective function over such a distribution is the expected objective value, $E_{i \in F}[f(o_{m_i}(a), t)]$.

To clarify, the use of expectation in Definition 9.21 does not imply that the resulting mechanism is only truthful in expectation. In fact, the mechanism described below is universally truthful, which means truthful for any realization of the random process, since it is a randomization over deterministically truthful mechanisms.

For problem $R_2||C_{\max}$, consider the following mechanism. The *bias parameter* δ introduced in Step 2 is used to control the balance of load between the two machines. The mechanism is a probability distribution over biased MinWork mechanisms.

Mechanism Randomly Biased MinWork
1. Each player reports his processing time for each job.
2. Define a constant $\delta = 4/3$.
3. Consider the jobs in arbitrary order, $j = 1, \ldots, n$, and for each:
   Generate a random integer s uniformly from $s \in \{1, 2\}$.
   If $\hat{p}_{sj} \leq \delta \hat{p}_{3-s,j}$:
       Job j is assigned to machine s.
       Machine s receives a payment of $\delta \hat{p}_{3-s,j}$.
   Otherwise:
       Job j is assigned to Machine $3 - s$.
       Machine $3 - s$ receives a payment of $\hat{p}_{s,j}/\delta$.

The main result for this mechanism can now be stated. We provide a brief outline of the proof. For full details of the proof, we refer the reader to Nisan and Ronen (2001).

Theorem 9.38 *Mechanism Randomly Biased MinWork is a polynomial time universally truthful mechanism that provides a 7/4-approximation for problem $R_2||C_{\max}$.*

Proof Observe that the overall utility of each player, i.e., machine, is the sum of the utilities of the jobs assigned to it at each job allocation; hence, it is sufficient to consider the case of a single job. The single job case is equivalent to a weighted VCG mechanism, as in (9.52) with weights $\gamma_1 = 1, \gamma_2 = \delta$ or $\gamma_1 = \delta, \gamma_2 = 1$, depending on the random value of s. Therefore, it is a randomization over deterministically truthful VCG algorithms. This establishes universal truthfulness.

To prove the approximation bound, the jobs are divided into "balanced" jobs where the ratio of larger to smaller processing times between the two machines

9.5 Private Information: Mechanisms with Payments 647

does not exceed δ, and the remaining jobs that are described as "unbalanced." Then, the worst-case outcome is shown to exist with exactly four jobs, two balanced and two unbalanced. Moreover, each of the machines schedules one balanced and one unbalanced job. This leaves three cases to consider, based on the relative processing times of the four jobs. In each case, the approximation bound of 7/4 is established.

$\square$

The work of Nisan and Ronen (2001) has motivated a substantial research literature on randomized mechanism design.

9.5.4 Truthfulness in Expectation

We illustrate the application of truthfulness in expectation with the use of payments. Archer and Tardos (2001) study a supply chain scheduling game defined over a scheduling problem on an arbitrary number of uniform parallel machines. The set of jobs is $N = \{1, \ldots, n\}$. There are players $M = \{1, \ldots, m\}$, each of whom represents a machine. Each player has private data $t_i \in \mathbb{R}$, which represents the cost per unit time of the machine. The machines accept and process work that is assigned to them by a mechanism, the details of which are discussed below. The reported value of t_i by player i is denoted as b_i, for $i = 1, \ldots, m$.

Let O denote a set of allowable outcomes, i.e., feasible schedules. Given a vector b of reported costs by the players, an algorithm within the mechanism computes an output function $o(b) \in O$, i.e., a schedule that defines a cost for all players. Each player incurs a cost $c_i(t_i, o)$ for processing the work that is assigned to it but receives a payment $\pi_i(b)$ from the mechanism as compensation. Consider a special form of the player's cost, i.e., $c_i(t_i, o) = t_i w_i(o)$. In this case, a player's cost is its private cost per unit of work times the amount of work $w_i(o)$ assigned to it. Then, each player i is self-interested and maximizes its utility, $\pi_i(b) - t_i w_i(o)$. The social objective is minimization of a function $g(o, b)$.

For this problem, Archer and Tardos (2001) describe a necessary and sufficient condition for truthfulness, that is based on "decreasing work curves," using the following definition.

Definition 9.22 Assume that the bids of all other players are fixed at b_{-i}, consider the workload of player i as a function $w_i(b_{-i}, b_i)$. This is the *work curve* of player i. If $w_i(b_{-i}, b_i)$ is a decreasing function of b_i for all i and b_{-i}, then the *work curve is decreasing*. That is, a machine that reports a higher cost receives less work.

The following result shows that these definitions are important in establishing truthfulness.

Recall that an algorithmic mechanism consists of an output function $o(b)$ and a payment scheme that need to be mutually compatible to ensure truthful reporting of costs by the players. The following result specifies conditions for this compatibility.

648   9 Noncooperative Supply Chain Scheduling

Theorem 9.39 *The output function $o(b)$ is implementable by a truthful payment scheme, i.e., one that incentivizes the players to report their costs truthfully, if and only if it is decreasing. In this case, the mechanism is truthful if and only if the payments $\pi_i(b_{-i}, b_i), i \in M$, are of the form*

$$h_i(b_{-i}) + b_i w_i(b_{-i}, b_i) - \int_0^{b_i} w_i(b_{-i}, u)du, \tag{9.55}$$

where the h_i functions are arbitrary.

We refer the reader to Archer and Tardos (2001) for the proof of Theorem 9.39. As discussed in Remark 9.9, the functions $h_i(\cdot)$ are useful for maintaining individual rationality and preventing overpayment. We relate the general problem description above to the supply chain scheduling problem $Q||C_{\max}$, i.e., the minimization of makespan on uniform parallel machines, by setting $t_i = 1/s_i$, where s_i represents the privately known speed of machine i. Then, if machine i has the total work $w_i(o)$ assigned to it, it requires time $t_i w_i(o) = w_i(o)/s_i$ to complete it. The social objective is the minimization of the makespan $C_{\max} = \max_{i \in M}\{w_i(o)/s_i\}$.

Observe that the uniform parallel-machine problem $Q||C_{\max}$ is equivalent to bin packing with bins of unequal sizes that represent the processing speeds of the machines. A mechanism that allows the jobs to be split between bins is now described. In the following, bin i represents machine i, and b_i represents the bid of machine i about its cost, or equivalently, the reciprocal of its speed.

Algorithm Greedy
1. Number the bins from largest to smallest bid of the corresponding machine, i.e., $b_1 \geq \cdots \geq b_m$ and similarly number of the jobs $p_1 \geq \cdots \geq p_n$.
2. Assign jobs $1, \ldots, k-1$ to bin 1, where k is the first job that would cause the bin to overflow.
3. Further, assign to bin 1 a piece of job k exactly as large as the remaining capacity in bin 1.
4. Continue by assigning jobs to bin 2, starting with the remaining part of job k. Repeat for the remaining jobs.

Problematically, Algorithm Greedy does not yield decreasing work curves. Hence, from Theorem 9.39, it does not admit a truthful payment scheme. Randomization is now introduced in order to obtain a monotone work curve.

Randomization Step
Starting from Step 4 of Algorithm Greedy, job j is assigned to machine i with a probability that is equal to the proportion of j that is fractionally assigned to bin i.

The main result requires the following preliminary calculation of a lower bound T_{LB} on the optimal value of $C_{\max}$.

9.5 Private Information: Mechanisms with Payments

649

Lemma 9.19

$$T_{LB} \geq \max_j \min_i \max \left\{ b_i p_j, \frac{\sum_{k=1}^{j} p_k}{\sum_{l=1}^{i} 1/b_l} \right\}. \tag{9.56}$$

Proof For each job j, let $i(j)$ denote the last bin that is at least as large as job j. Observe that, for job j, the value of $i(j)$ is at least as large as the value of j that is minimum for job j in (9.56). Then, the greedy assignment is valid if and only if, for each j, the total capacity of the first $i(j)$ bins is at least the total size of the first j jobs. So, if the greedy assignment is valid and i is the last bin to which job j is partially assigned, then $T_{LB} \geq \max\{b_i p_j, \frac{\sum_{k=1}^{j} p_k}{\sum_{l=1}^{i} 1/b_l}\}$. $\qquad\square$

The main result can now be stated.

Theorem 9.40 *The Greedy Algorithm with Randomization Step admits a truthful payment scheme satisfying voluntary participation and deterministically provides a polynomial time 3-approximation mechanism for problem $Q||C_{\max}$.*

Proof The approximation bound is easy to prove. Observe from Steps 2 through 4 of the Greedy Algorithm that each bin is assigned at most two fractional jobs. If the fractions of these two jobs are increased to full size, the amount of work added is not more than that of two jobs. Hence, each bin is not more than 300% full deterministically, i.e., regardless of how the Randomization Step realizes.

From Theorem 9.39, a sufficient condition for truthfulness is that the expected load on each machine i decreases as i increases its bid, which is equivalent to claiming to be slower. Now, the expected load is the load from the randomized greedy assignment. For full bins this is $T_{LB} = b_i$, for the (at most one) partially full bin it is the work left over from the full bins, and for the empty bins it is 0. Suppose some machine claims to be slower, replacing its bid b_i with αb_i, for some $\alpha > 1$. This would provide a new lower bound $T'_{LB} \geq T_{LB}$ from (9.56). However, we also have $T'_{LB} \leq \alpha T_{LB}$, since shrinking bin i by a factor of α and then expanding all bins by a factor of $\alpha > 1$ would allow for a valid fractional assignment. Thus, the overall effect of increasing i's bid is to enlarge the other bins while shrinking bin i, so the greedy fractional assignment gives machine i less work. This satisfies the condition in Theorem 9.39.

To compute the payments requires the computation of $w_i(b_{-i})$ and the integral $\int_{b_i}^{\infty} w_i(b_{-i}, x)dx$. This reduces to computing an integral with a closed form expression over a polynomial number of intervals, which is an overall polynomial-time computation. $\qquad\square$

Archer and Tardos (2001) extend their results for the makespan objective to develop a truthful mechanism for the problem of minimizing total completion time on uniform machines, or $Q||\sum C_j$.

Dhangwatnotai et al. (2011) present a monotone randomized polynomial-time approximation scheme (PTAS, see Section 2.3.4.2 for definitions) for problem $Q||C_{\max}$. This gives a polynomial time, truthful in expectation mechanism whose approximation guarantee attains the best possible one for all polynomial-time algorithms, if $P \neq NP$. We provide a brief description of their approximation scheme. First, jobs with processing time sizes that differ by a factor of not more than $1 + \epsilon$ are grouped together. Temporarily assume that every job in a group has a processing time equal to the average processing time in its group. The jobs are assigned to the machines, allowing fractional assignments. Randomized rounding is used to obtain an integer schedule. Finally, the processing times of the jobs are restored to their original values. We refer the reader to that work for additional details.

9.5.5 Bayes–Nash Incentive Compatibility

The assumption about private information made in all the previous sections is that players other than the owner of that information have no knowledge whatsoever about the information. However, it is easy to think of applications where, for example, one company would be able to estimate—perhaps not perfectly, but with reasonable accuracy—the costs of another company in the same industry. Such estimates might be available in the form of prior probabilities over a discrete set of reasonable values. In principle, it would be valuable to incorporate this information into mechanisms that ensure truthfulness in reporting and good performance of an overall system. This can be accomplished using a *Bayes–Nash equilibrium* and related concepts, as now defined.

Definition 9.23

(i) A Bayes–Nash equilibrium is a strategy profile that maximizes the *expected utility* of each player, given their beliefs and the strategies played by other players.

(ii) In a mechanism that is Bayes–Nash incentive compatible, if all the other players report truthfully, then any given player is *at least not worse off in expectation* by reporting his type truthfully.

We observe that the additional condition in Definition 9.23 (ii) that all the other players are acting truthfully makes Bayes–Nash incentive compatibility weaker than dominant strategy incentive compatibility. See Definition 9.17 for comparison. In addition, the use of expected utility makes an implicit assumption that the players are risk neutral.

We describe an application of Bayes–Nash incentive compatibility. Duives et al. (2015) consider a single machine setting where the players represent jobs that require compensation for waiting, where each job's waiting cost is private information. Each job must be processed nonpreemptively. Let $N = \{1, \ldots, n\}$ denote the set of jobs with publicly known processing times p_j and private weights w_j. The other players, however, know a set of possible discrete types of job j, i.e., possible values for w_j. This set is denoted by T_j, where $m_j = |T_j|$. Then,

9.5 Private Information: Mechanisms with Payments

$w_j^i, i = 1, \ldots, m_j$, are possible values of w_j with positive and commonly known probabilities which we denote by $\phi_j(w_j^i)$. A vector of payments, computed from the reported weights of all the jobs, compensates the jobs for waiting. Based on reported information about the possible types of all the jobs and prior beliefs, the mechanism designer uses an allocation rule f to compute a schedule, which is a sequence of the jobs on the single machine. In a given schedule, let S_j denote the waiting time of job j, i.e., the time at which it starts processing. The expected utility of a job is its expected payment from the system for waiting, less the cost of its expected waiting time.

Since the waiting cost of each job is private, the player who is represented by that job may report a higher than true waiting cost, in the hope that doing so will generate higher compensation payments for waiting. The optimal mechanism design problem is then to find a scheduling rule and a payment scheme under which the jobs are incentivized both to participate and to report their private information truthfully, while at the same time minimizing the total expected payments π that are made to the jobs.

The following definition is needed.

Definition 9.24 A mechanism $\mu = (\alpha, \pi)$, consisting of an allocation algorithm α and a payment scheme π, is *Bayes–Nash incentive compatible* for the supply chain scheduling game if truth-telling is a weakly dominant strategy in expectation, so for every job j and every two types $w_j^j, w_j^k \in T_j$, where w_j^j is the true type,

$$E\pi_j(w_j^j) - w_j^j ES_j(\alpha, w_j^j) \geq E\pi_j(w_j^k) - w_j^j ES_j(\alpha, w_j^k). \tag{9.57}$$

In (9.57), the left-hand side represents the expected compensation received by job j less its expected cost if it reports true type $w_j^j \in T_j$, and the right-hand side is a similar calculation if it reports false type $w_j^k \in T_j$. This expectation assumes that all jobs other than j report their type truthfully. If a given allocation algorithm α admits a payment scheme π such that the mechanism $\mu = (\alpha, \pi)$ is Bayes–Nash incentive compatible, then α is *Bayes–Nash implementable* and the *payment scheme is incentive compatible*.

Besides incentive compatibility, the other constraint that is required in a Bayes–Nash equilibrium is *individual rationality*, which ensures that each job is interested in participating. While this may seem unnecessary in the current problem setting where all jobs must be scheduled, it can be motivated in practice as ensuring "reasonable cooperation" by the job with the mechanism designer, for example timely provision of the report about the private waiting cost and timely submission of the job when scheduled. Individual rationality is now defined for truthful jobs.

Definition 9.25 A mechanism $\mu(\alpha, \pi)$ is *individually rational* if, for every player j and every true type $w_j^j \in T_j$,

$$E\pi_j(w_j^j) - w_j^j ES_j(\alpha, w_j^j) \geq 0, \quad w_j^j \in T_j. \tag{9.58}$$

Observe that this condition is stated only for truthful jobs. The following definition is also needed to define the Bayes–Nash implementability of an allocation rule.

Definition 9.26 An allocation algorithm α satisfies *monotonicity with respect to weights* if, for every job j, $w^i_j < w^k_j$ implies that $ES_j(\alpha, w^i_j) \geq ES_j(\alpha, w^k_j)$.

Definition 9.26 is intuitive. It states that the reporting of a smaller waiting cost w_j cannot decrease the expected start time of a job. Duives et al. (2015) apply this definition to establish the following result.

Theorem 9.41 *An allocation algorithm α is Bayes–Nash implementable if and only if it satisfies monotonicity with respect to weights.*

The proof relies on construction of a complete directed *type graph* for each job j, where nodes represent all possible types and arc lengths between them represent the gain in expected valuation for reporting one type over another. The Bayes–Nash implementability of f is equivalent to there being no negative length directed cycles in this graph. We refer the reader to Duives et al. (2015) for a detailed proof. The concept of a type graph is explored further below.

We provide an example to demonstrate the use of these concepts.

Example 9.24 (Application of Bayes–Nash Implementability) Consider the following instance of the problem: $n = 2$, $p_1 = 1$, $w_1 = 1$, or $w_1 = 2$, both with probability 0.5; $p_2 = 3$, and $w_2 = 4$ deterministically.

We define the allocation rule to be the indexing rule of Smith (1956), where the jobs are sequenced in nonincreasing order of w_j/p_j. As an illustration of Theorem 9.41, this rule satisfies monotonicity, since if the weight of a job increases, its start time cannot increase. Now, if $w_1 = 2$, job 1 is scheduled first, $S_1 = 0$ and $S_2 = 1$; whereas if $w_1 = 1$, job 2 is scheduled first, $S_1 = 3$ and $S_2 = 0$. Thus, since job 1 is truthful, $ES_2 = 1(0.5) + 0(0.5) = 0.5$.

For job 1, Bayes–Nash incentive compatibility (9.57) implies

$$E(\pi_1 \mid w_1 = 1) - 1 \cdot E(S_1 \mid w_1 = 1) \geq E(\pi_1 \mid w_1 = 2) - 1 \cdot E(S_1 \mid w_1 = 2)$$
$$\Rightarrow E(\pi_1 \mid w_1 = 1) - E(\pi_1 \mid w_1 = 2) \geq 1(3) - 1(0) = 3, \quad \text{and}$$

$$E(\pi_1 \mid w_1 = 2) - 2 \cdot E(S_1 \mid w_1 = 2) \geq E(\pi_1 \mid w_1 = 1) - 2 \cdot E(S_1 \mid w_1 = 1)$$
$$\Rightarrow E(\pi_1 \mid w_1 = 2) - E(\pi_1 \mid w_1 = 1) \geq 2(0) - 2(3) = -6.$$

The individual rationality constraints (9.58) for job 1 are

$$E(\pi_1 \mid w_1 = 1) - 1 \cdot E(S_1 \mid w_1 = 1) \geq 0$$
$$\Rightarrow E(\pi_1 \mid w_1 = 1) \geq 1(3) = 3, \quad \text{and}$$

$$E(\pi_1 \mid w_1 = 2) - 2 \cdot E(S_1 \mid w_1 = 2) \geq 0$$
$$\Rightarrow E(\pi_1 \mid w_1 = 2) \geq 2(0) = 0.$$

9.5 Private Information: Mechanisms with Payments

653

Observe that, for the above incentive compatibility constraints, the first condition applies to the case $w_1 = 1$, and the second condition applies to the case $w_1 = 2$. The individual rationality constraints follow the same format.

Solving the above inequalities, we observe that the payment scheme $E(\pi_1 \mid w_1 = 1) = 3$ and $E(\pi_1 \mid w_1 = 2) = 0$ is both Bayes–Nash incentive compatible and individually rational for job 1.

Since job 2 has only one type, it has no private information, and no incentive compatibility constraints arise. However, individual rationality (9.58) implies

$$E\pi_2 - w_2 E S_2 \geq 0$$

$$\Rightarrow E\pi_2 \geq 4[0.5(0) + 0.5(1)] = 2.$$

For example, $\pi_2 = 2$ in both cases $w_1 = 1$ and $w_1 = 2$ suffices.

However, the solution shown above for Example 9.24 is only one implementable payment scheme π. It is also valuable to compute the *minimal* payment scheme that is incentive compatible and individually rational. This is indeed possible, by computing shortest path lengths in the graph now described, which is justified by the absence of negative length directed cycles.

Definition 9.27 Given an allocation algorithm α, the *type graph* $G_j(\alpha)$ for job j is a complete directed graph with node set $W_j = \{w_j^1, \ldots, w_j^{m_j}\}$, which describes the type space of job j and an arc from any node w_j^i to any node w_j^k of length

$$l_{ik} = w_j^i \left[ES_j\left(\alpha, w_j^k\right) - ES_j\left(\alpha, w_j^i\right) \right],$$

which is the gain in expected waiting cost for player j from reporting its true type w_j^i instead of a false type w_i^k. We add a dummy end node $m_j + 1$ to $G_j(\alpha)$.

This definition enables the main result that follows.

Theorem 9.42 *For a Bayes–Nash implementable allocation algorithm α, the payment scheme defined by $\pi_j(w_j^{m_j+1}) = 0$, and*

$$\pi_j\left(w_j^i\right) = \sum_{k=i}^{m_j} w_j^k \left[ES_j\left(\alpha, w_j^k\right) - ES_j\left(\alpha, w_j^{k+1}\right) \right], \qquad (9.59)$$

for $i = 1, \ldots, m_j$, is incentive compatible, individually rational, and also minimizes the expected total payment made to the jobs.

Proof Since α is Bayes–Nash implementable, $T_j(\alpha)$ satisfies the nonnegative cycle property. Consequently, we can compute shortest paths in $T_j(\alpha)$. Let $P = (w_j^i = a_0, a_1, \ldots, a_m = w_j^{m_j+1})$ denote a directed path from w_j^i to a dummy node $w_j^{m_j+1}$ in the type graph for job j, and $L(P) = L(a_0, a_m)$ its length. Let $\Delta(w_j^i, w_j^{m_j+1})$

denote the length of a shortest path from node w_j^i to node $w_j^{m_j+1}$ in the type graph for job j. Adding the incentive compatibility constraints obtained from (9.57),

$$E\pi_j(a_i) \le E\pi_j(a_{i-1}) + a_{i-1}[ES_j(\alpha, a_i) - ES_j(\alpha, a_{i-1})]$$
$$= E\pi_j(a_{i-1}) + L(a_{i-1}, a_i),$$

for $i = 1, \ldots, m_i$, gives

$$E\pi_j\left(w_j^{m_j+1}\right) \le E\pi_j\left(w_j^i\right) + L(P) = E\pi_j\left(w_j^i\right) + \Delta\left(w_j^i, w_j^{m_j+1}\right). \qquad (9.60)$$

Now, since $E\pi_j(w_j^{m_j+1}) = 0$ by definition, (9.60) implies $-\Delta(w_j^i, w_j^{m_j+1}) \le E\pi_j(w_j^i)$.

Hence, $-\Delta(w_j^i, w_j^{m_j+1})$ is a lower bound on the expected payment for reporting w_j^i.

Further, observe that for any two types w_j^i and w_j^k,

$$\Delta\left(w_j^i, w_j^{m_j+1}\right) \le L(i, k) + \Delta\left(w_j^k, w_j^{m_j+1}\right)$$
$$\Rightarrow -\Delta\left(w_j^k, w_j^{m_j+1}\right) \le -\Delta\left(w_j^i, w_j^{m_j+1}\right) + L(i, k).$$

Consequently, setting the expected payment to every job for any reported type

$$\pi_j\left(w_j^i\right) = -\Delta\left(w_j^i, w_j^{m_j+1}\right)$$

yields a Bayes–Nash incentive compatible payment scheme that minimizes the expected payment to every job for any reported type of the player.

It is easy to show that if $i < k < l$, then $L(i, k) + L(k, l) \le L(i, l)$ and $L(l, k) + L(k, i) \le L(l, i)$, a property that Duives et al. (2015) name *decomposition monotonicity*. Hence, a shortest path from w_j^i to $w_j^{m_j+1}$ is exactly the path that includes $w_j^i, \ldots, w_j^{m_j}$. Finally, we observe that $\Delta(w_j^{m_j+1}, w_j^{m_j+1}) = 0$ and

$$-\Delta\left(w_j^i, w_j^{m_j+1}\right) = \sum_{k=i}^{m_j} w_j^k\left[ES_j(\alpha, w_j^k) - ES_j(\alpha, w_j^{k+1})\right],$$

for $w_j^i \in \{w_j^1, \ldots, w_j^{m_j}\}$. This establishes the result. $\qquad \square$

We refer the reader to Duives et al. (2015) for an efficiently computable closed form expression for the minimal expected total payment.

Duives et al. (2015) also show by example that, even for a problem with two symmetric jobs, each having two equal probability weights, the use of the VCG mechanism can result in payments that are 50% greater than those required by their mechanism described above.

In related work, Hoeksma and Uetz (2016) consider a supply chain scheduling problem where the processing times and weights of jobs are both private information. To model this problem, they construct a linear programming problem that represents the problem of designing a Bayes–Nash incentive compatible mechanism. The main result is a polynomial-time solution procedure for the mechanism design problem. The methodology presented also allows for the possibility of correlation across the types of different jobs.

9.6 Future Research

We provide an overview of several promising directions for future research, following the organization of the chapter into complete information games, enhanced complete information games, mechanisms without payments, and algorithmic mechanism design.

For supply chain scheduling games with complete information, relevant topics include the following:

- Lee et al. (2012) study coordination mechanisms for parallel-machine scheduling problems. Each player with a job acts selfishly to minimize his own disutility, for example, the congestion time or completion time of the job on the machine that processes it. The machines announce a common sequencing rule for the jobs assigned to them. Of particular interest is extending this work to allow for the practical generalization that each machine announces a different local sequencing rule, and analyzing the PoA and APoA in that more general environment. The work of Vijayalakshmi et al. (2021) discussed in Sect. 9.2.2.4 is an example. Classical machine scheduling generalizations such as the presence of release dates should also be considered.
- Glazer et al. (2018) study a game that involves timing the arrivals of jobs to minimize a function of job earliness and tardiness around a common due date. Various generalizations are possible, for example considering multiple servers, or considering a common due date that is restrictively early. In addition, also adding practicality to the problem, it would be valuable to study groups of customers with due dates that are common within the group and different but not widely separated across groups. An interesting question related to this problem is under what conditions all jobs in a group arrive consecutively in a Nash equilibrium.
- Vairaktarakis (2013) studies a problem including a set of manufacturers, all of which may subcontract part or all of their work to a third party that prioritizes smaller workloads, and develops Nash equilibria under three different production protocols. For possible extensions, it would be valuable to consider different scheduling environments such as flowshops, different objectives of the players

such as the completion times of multiple jobs, and different priority rules specified by the third party.

- Bukchin and Hanany (2007) consider an environment where decentralized decision makers compete for limited resources. They study the decentralization cost, which is the ratio between the cost of the solution reached when decision makers make their decisions independently while taking into account the decisions of others and the cost of a centrally optimized decision that in general is not a Nash equilibrium. While they consider minimization of the total completion time, several other objectives are also relevant.
- Agnetis et al. (2015) study a project scheduling game where multiple players have the option to crash, or expedite, their tasks and share a reward for doing so from the project client in fixed and known proportions. This presents a tradeoff with the cost of crashing. While the paper focuses on finding a Nash equilibrium solution, it would also be valuable to identify Pareto optimal strategies. For a given strategy, Nash equilibrium and Pareto optimality are independent concepts in this context, i.e., neither implies the other. Also of interest is the consideration of this problem in a private information setting.
- Vijayalakshmi et al. (2021) study supply chain scheduling problems where every machine has an independent priority list for the jobs that are assigned to it. This problem raises interesting issues as a variant of a classical scheduling problem where each machine defines a separate sequencing rule. Since their game may not have a Nash equilibrium, it would be interesting to study the existence of α-approximate Nash equilibria, under which no job changes strategy unless it can achieve a cost reduction of at least α. This problem is motivated by the cost and inconvenience of changing strategy. A further natural generalization is the consideration of games in which jobs have an arbitrary strategy space, and the cost of a job is the sum of the cost for the resources used, where each resource has its own priority list.
- Feldman and Tamir (2012) study conflicting congestion effects in resource allocation games with supply chain scheduling applications. A resource activation cost is divided between the users of that resource, whereas many users of the same resource generate congestion effects; hence, an interesting tradeoff arises. It would be valuable to generalize their results to other job scheduling settings with different machine models, different sharing rules, different cost structures, and different social choice functions. Valuable insights could also be gained from providing a characterization of initial states from which best response dynamics are guaranteed to converge to a Nash equilibrium. Additional notions of equilibria are also relevant here, for example strong equilibrium where stability is guaranteed against coalitional deviations.

For enhanced games with complete information, the following topics are relevant for future research.

- In their discussion of the benefits of sequential, rather than simultaneous, decision making, Leme et al. (2012) motivate similar studies of a broader class of games. Of particular interest is identifying classes of games where the subgame perfect equilibrium of the sequential version is a pure Nash equilibrium of the simultaneous version. They observe that where the subgame perfect equilibrium solution does not depend on the ordering of the players' decisions, then this result should apply.

- Chen and Xu (2020) investigate the interesting issue of bounded rationality, which is modeled either by limiting the number of lookahead steps that a player can use or by limiting the complexity of calculations they can perform. Such limitations apparently offer the potential for significant improvement in the price of anarchy. Their work focuses on unrelated parallel-machine scheduling games; however, their ideas can be applied more generally. They also consider games with single-minded players who always choose machines on which their jobs have minimum processing time, and such games deserve further investigation.
- Roughgarden (2004) considers scheduling strategies in Stackelberg games where the leader maximizes social welfare. He suggests extensions to consider problems without jobs of negligible size, which is not only more practical but may improve the results obtained. In addition, various practical conditions can be imposed on the machine latency functions. More generally, there are many possible extensions of Stackelberg games to different supply chain scheduling applications.
- In work that is closely related to a specific application, Qi (2012) analyzes a Stackelberg game for a manufacturer and a subcontractor. Possible extensions can include multiple manufacturers who share a common subcontractor, to address the issue of how the subcontractor may use pricing as a decision variable. An alternative direction is the consideration of multiple subcontractors who may compete with each other for the business of the manufacturer or alternatively form a coalition to negotiate more effectively with the manufacturer. Hall and Liu (2010) analyze a related problem in a cooperative game context.
- Hoefer and Skopalik (2013) study altruism in atomic congestion games, a class that includes several supply chain scheduling games. They study the existence of pure Nash equilibria and the convergence of better response dynamics in games with the total social cost. The most natural open problems include analysis of models for other relevant social functions, such as the makespan on parallel machines. Further research issues include understanding the convergence of best response dynamics in games with altruistic players. It is also of interest to consider the effect of altruism in Stackelberg games for supply chain scheduling.
- Apt and Schäfer (2014) study the effect on several strategic games of the selfishness level, which they define to be the smallest fraction of social welfare that needs to be offered to each player such that a social optimum is realized in a pure Nash equilibrium, i.e., such that the price of stability is 1. A natural extension of their work is to study a similar question for mixed, rather than pure, Nash equilibria, for which they provide an example outside the scope of supply chain scheduling games. There are also two alternative definitions of selfishness that are valuable to investigate. First, it would be interesting to study how to find the smallest value of the selfishness level such that the price of stability is 1. Second, the same question can be asked for the price of anarchy to be 1, i.e., such that all Nash equilibria are socially optimal.

- Balcan (2011) describes two models by which a central authority can influence players to move from a poor quality Nash equilibrium to a better one. However, there is an unexplored tradeoff in this idea. As a result of trying to induce a better solution, the price of stability may change if the best available Nash equilibrium solution becomes unstable. Thus, starting from a good equilibrium, it is important to investigate whether a small shock to the system can produce a bad state from which natural dynamics cannot recover (Balcan et al., 2009).

    For mechanisms without payments, we discuss three works.
- Angel et al. (2016) develop truthful and socially optimal algorithms for supply chain scheduling problems. They suggest extensions to multiple machine problems, using randomized truthful approximation algorithms.
- Koutsoupias (2014) develops a truthful in expectation mechanism for an m makespan problem with an approximation bound of $m(m + 1)/2$, and it is an open question whether any such mechanism can provide a better approximation. Also, the question remains whether there exists a non-truthful mechanism that provides a better approximation.
- Angel et al. (2009) discuss tradeoffs that arise if the requirement that an algorithm is truthful is relaxed. They mention a case where a given approximation ratio is still achievable, even if the algorithm is not truthful. This raises the interesting and more philosophical question as to what is the value of truthfulness if the real objective is the optimization of social welfare.

    For algorithmic mechanism design including payments, relevant topics for future research include the following.
- From a general perspective, Heydenreich et al. (2007) emphasize the importance of considering other criteria besides efficiency and truthfulness. They mention various definitions of fairness, as in the discussion of matching markets by Roth et al. (2004). Connections with combinatorial auctions (Cramton et al., 2006) are also relevant, especially when the allocation rule involves assigning and timing resources, as in supply chain scheduling.
- Kress et al. (2018a) provide a comprehensive overview of the literature of mechanism design for scheduling problems, as well as identifying many open research problems. We refer the reader to their work for many details. A significant and general question is how to achieve a better understanding of the tradeoff between truthfulness on one hand and computational complexity and approximation on the other hand. There also remain many open research questions with respect to supply chain scheduling games defined over classical machine scheduling settings. The literature they review focuses on parallel-machine settings, and it is also of interest to analyze games defined over flowshop, openshop, or jobshop problems. Furthermore, the literature rarely considers general and practical job characteristics such as job release dates or precedence relations. There are also various research opportunities related to emerging applications; interesting ones are described by Kovalyov and Pesch (2014). The topic of risk aversion among the players also presents interesting problems.
- A topic that includes several open problems is mechanism design in the presence of multi-dimensional private types. Lavi and Swamy (2009) obtain some initial

9.6 Future Research

results of this type. More recently, Kress et al. (2018b) show how to take advantage of problem structure to simplify the conditions of cycle monotonicity. They suggest the use of their results with heuristics for intractable supply chain scheduling problems to construct truthful polynomial-time mechanisms. Another possible research direction is considering players who are risk averse or risk seeking.

- Vairaktarakis (2013), as discussed above under complete information settings, also identifies several research issues for supply chain scheduling games with private information. It is unclear under what conditions it would be worthwhile for players to report falsely, since doing so may expose them to considerable risk. In this case, players may respond with strategies that hedge against poor outcomes.
- Chen et al. (2016) develop a mechanism for online supply chain scheduling problems with preempt-restart and preempt-resume modes. They mention several possible extensions of their work. One is a study of a hybrid model where some of the jobs are preempt-restart and others are preempt-resume. Strategic issues also arise, for example whether a preempt-resume job can benefit by presenting itself as a preempt-restart job. Finally, motivated by the increasing use of cloud computing, it would be valuable to study supply chain scheduling problems with multiple heterogeneous machines.
- Duives et al. (2015) study both one- and two-dimensional private information in a single machine scheduling environment. In the one-dimensional environment, an efficiently computable closed form expression exists for an optimal mechanism design. For the two-dimensional case, an optimal randomized mechanism can be computed in polynomial time (Hoeksma & Uetz, 2016), but the computational complexity of doing so for an optimal deterministic mechanism remains an open problem.

To conclude this chapter, the research area of noncooperative supply chain scheduling is very active, with many challenging questions remaining to be solved. Moreover, the economic insights gained from this analysis are in many cases highly valuable for a diverse range of supply chain scheduling applications.

References

Aarts, E., & Lenstra, J. K. (2003). *Local search in combinatorial optimization*. Princeton, NJ: Princeton University Press.

Adiri, I., & Amit, N. (1984). Openshop and flowshop scheduling to minimize sum of completion times. *Computers & Operations Research, 11*, 275–284.

Adiri, I., Bruno, J., Frostig, E., & Rinnooy Kan, A. H. G. (1989) Single machine flow-time scheduling with a single breakdown. *Acta Informatica, 26*, 679–696.

Agnetis, A., Aloulou, M. A., & Fu, L.-L. (2014a) Coordination of production and interstage batch delivery with outsourced distribution. *European Journal of Operational Research, 238*, 130–142.

Agnetis, A., Billaut, J.-C., Gawiejnowicz, S., Pacciarelli, D., & Soukhal, A. (2014b). *Multiagent scheduling: models and algorithms*. Berlin, Germany: Springer.

Agnetis, A., Briand, C., Billaut, J.-C., & Šucha, P. (2015). Nash equilibria for the multi-agent project scheduling problems with controllable processing times. *Journal of Scheduling, 18*, 15–27.

Agnetis, A., Detti, P., Meloni, C., & Pacciarelli, D. (2001). Set-up coordination between two stages of a supply chain. *Annals of Operations Research, 107*, 15–32.

Agnetis, A., Hall, N. G., & Pacciarelli, D. (2006). Supply chain scheduling: Sequence coordination. *Discrete Applied Mathematics, 154*, 2044–2063.

Agrawal, V., & Seshadri, S. (2000). *Joint determination of allocation & the timing of inventories in a supply chain*. Working paper, Stern School of Business, New York University.

Ahmadi, J. H., Ahmadi, R. H., Dasu, S., & Tang, C. S. (1992). Batching and scheduling jobs on batch and discrete processors. *Operations Research, 40*, 750–763.

Albers, S., & Brucker, P. (1993). The complexity of one-machine batching problems. *Discrete Applied Mathematics, 47*, 87–107.

Alidaee, B., & Ahmadian, A. (1993). Two parallel machine sequencing problems involving controllable job processing times. *European Journal of Operational Research, 70*, 335–341.

Allahverdi, A., Ng, C. T., Cheng, T. C. E., & Kovalyov, M. (2008). A survey of scheduling problems with setup times or costs. *European Journal of Operational Research, 187*(3), 985–1032.

Anderson, E., & Simester, D. (2003). Effects of $9 price endings on retail sales: Evidence from field experiments. *Quantitative Marketing and Economics, 1*(1), 93–110.

Angel, E., Bampis, E., Pascual, F., Tchetgnia, A.-A. (2009). On truthfulness and approximation for scheduling selfish tasks. *Journal of Scheduling, 12*, 437–445.

© Springer Nature Switzerland AG 2022
Z.-L. Chen, N. G. Hall, *Supply Chain Scheduling*, International Series
in Operations Research & Management Science 323,
https://doi.org/10.1007/978-3-030-90374-9

Angel, E., Bampis, E., Pascual, F., & Thibault, N. (2016). Truthfulness for the sum of weighted completion times. In *Computing and Combinatorics (COCOON 2016)*, Lecture Notes in Computer Science (Vol. 9797, pp. 15–26).

Anshlevich, E., Dasgupta, A., Kleinberg, J. M., Tardos, É., Wexler, T., & Roughgarden, T. (2004). The price of stability for network design and fair cost allocation. In *45th Symposium on Foundations of Computer Science* (FOCS 2004) (pp. 285–304).

Apt, K. R., & Schäfer, G. (2014). Selfishness level of strategic games. *Journal of Artificial Intelligence Research, 49*, 207–240.

Archer, A., & Tardos, É. (2001). Truthful mechanisms for one-parameter agents. In *Proceedings of the 42nd IEEE Symposium on Foundations of Computer Science* (FOCS'01).

Arkin, E. M., & Silverberg, E. B. (1987). Scheduling jobs with fixed start and end times. *Discrete Applied Mathematics, 18*, 1–8.

Armstrong, R., Gao, S., & Lei, L. (2008). A zero-inventory production and distribution problem with a fixed customer sequence. *Annals of Operations Research, 159*, 395–414.

Atay, A., Calleja, P., & Soteras, S. (2019). *Open shop scheduling games*. Working paper, Hungarian Academy of Sciences, July.

Averbakh, I. (2010). On-line integrated production-distribution scheduling problems with capacitated deliveries. *European Journal of Operational Research, 200*, 377–384.

Averbakh, I., & Baysan, M. (2012). Semi-online two-level supply chain scheduling problems. *Journal of Scheduling, 15*, 381–390.

Averbakh, I., & Baysan, M. (2013). Batching and delivery in semi-online distribution systems. *Discrete Applied Mathematics, 161*, 28–42.

Aydinliyim, T., & Vairaktarakis, G. L. (2010). Coordination of outsourced operations to minimize weighted flow time and capacity booking costs. *Manufacturing & Service Operations Management, 12*(2), 236–255.

Aydinliyim, T., & Vairaktarakis, G. L. (2011). Sequencing strategies and coordination issues in outsourcing and contracting operations. Section 12 In K. Kempf, P. Keskinocak, & R. Uzsoy (Eds.), *Planning production and inventories in the extended enterprise*. International Series in Operations Research and Management Science (Vol. 151, pp. 269–319). New York: Springer.

Aydinliyim, T., & Vairaktarakis, G. L. (2013). A cooperative savings game approach to a time sensitive capacity allocation and scheduling problem. *Decision Sciences, 44*(2), 357–376.

Bagchi, T. P., Gupta, J. N. D., & Sriskandarajah, C. (2006). A review of TSP based approaches for flowshop scheduling. *European Journal of Operational Research, 169*, 816–854.

Balcan, M.-F. (2011). Leading dynamics to good behavior. *CM SIGecom Exchanges, 10*(1), 19–22.

Balcan, M.-F., Blum, A., & Mansour, Y. (2009). Improved equilibria via public service advertising. In *Proceedings of ACM-SIAM Symposium on Discrete Algorithms* (pp. 728–737).

Barnhart, C., Johnson, E. L., Nemhauser, G. L., Savelsbergh, M. W., & Vance, P. H. (1998). Branch-and-price: Column generation for solving huge integer programs. *Operations Research, 46*(3), 316–329.

Bazaraa, M. S., Sherali, H. D., & Shetty, C. M. (2013). *Nonlinear programming: Theory and algorithms* (2nd ed.). Hoboken: Wiley.

Bazinet, C. G., Kahn, S. A., & Smith, S. J. (1998). Measuring the value of outsourcing. *Best's Review, 99*, 85–88.

Bean, J. C. G., Birge, J. R., Mittenthal, J., & Noon, C. E. (1991). Matchup scheduling with multiple resources, release dates and disruptions. *Operations Research, 39*, 470–483.

Bergantiños, G., Valencia-Toledo, A., & Vidal-Puga, J. (2018). Hart and Mas-Colell consistency in PERT problems. *Discrete Applied Mathematics, 243*, 11–20.

Berghman, L., & Spieksma, F. C. R. (2015). Valid inequalities for a time-indexed formulation. *Operations Research Letters, 43*, 268–272.

Berghman, L., Spieksma, F. C. R., & t'Kindt, V. (2021). Solving a time-indexed formulation for an unrelated parallel machine scheduling problem by preprocessing and cutting planes. *RAIRO-Operations Research, 55*, S1747–S1765.

Bertrand, J. W. M., & Sridharan, V. (2001). A study of simple rules for subcontracting in make-to-order manufacturing. *European Journal of Operational Research, 128*, 509–531.

References

Bikhchandani, S., Chatterji, S., Lavi, R., Mu'alem, A., Nisan, N., & Sen, A. (2006). Weak monotonicity characterizes deterministic dominant-strategy implementation. *Econometrica, 74*(4), 1109–1132.

Bilgen, B., & Ozkarahan, I. (2004). Strategic tactical and operational production-distribution models: A review. *International Journal of Technology Management, 28*, 151–171.

Bilò, V., Flammini, M., Monaco, G., & Moscardelli, L. (2016). Some anomalies of farsighted strategic behavior. *Theoretical Computer Science, 56*(1), 156–180.

Bish, E. K., Muriel, A., & Biller, S. (2005). Managing flexible capacity in a make-to-order environment. *Management Science, 51*, 167–180.

Blumenfeld, D. E., Burns, L. D., & Daganzo, C. F. (1991). Synchronizing production and transportation schedules. *Transportation Research, Part B, 25*, 23–37.

Bondareva, O. N. (1963). Some applications of linear programming methods to the theory of cooperative games. Published in Russian. *Problemy Kybernetiki, 10*, 119–139.

Borm, P., Fiestras-Janeiro, G., Hamers, H., Sánchez, E., & Voorneveld, M. (2002). On the convexity of sequencing games with due dates. *European Journal of Operational Research, 136*, 616–634.

Boysen, N., Bock, S., & Fliedner, M. (2013). Scheduling of inventory releasing jobs to satisfy time-varying demand: an analysis of complexity. *Journal of Scheduling, 16*, 185–198.

Boysen, N., Scholl, A., & Wopperer, N. (2012). Resequencing of mixed-model assembly lines: Survey and research agenda. *European Journal of Operational Research, 216*, 594–604.

Brănzei, R., Ferrari, G., Fragnelli, V., & Tijs, S. (2002). Two approaches to the problem of sharing delay costs in joint projects. *Annals of Operations Research, 109*, 359–374.

Brucker, P. (2013). *Scheduling algorithms* (4th Ed.). Springer.

Bruno, J., Coffman Jr., E. G., & R. Sethi. (1974). Scheduling independent tasks to reduce mean finishing time. *Communications of the ACM, 17*, 383–387.

Bruno, J., & Downey, P. (1978). Complexity of task sequencing with deadlines, set-up times and changeover costs. *SIAM Journal on Computing, 7*, 393–404.

Bukchin, Y., & Hanany, E. (2007). Decentralization cost in scheduling: A game-theoretic approach. *Manufaturing & Service Operations Management, 9*(3), 263–275.

Cachon, G. P. (2003). Supply chain coordination with contracts. In A. G. de Kok, & S. C. Graves (Eds.), *Supply chain management: Design, coordination, and operation* (Vol. 11, pp. 229–339).

Cachon, G. P., & Lariviere, M. A. (1999). Capacity choice and allocation: Strategic behavior and supply chain performance. *Management Science, 45*, 1091–1108.

Cai, X., & Vairaktarakis, G. L. (2012). Coordination of outsourced operations at a third-party facility subject to booking, overtime and tardiness costs. *Operations Research, 60*(6), 1436–1450.

Calleja, P., Borm, P., Hamers, H., Klin, F., & Slikker, M. (2002). On a new class of parallel sequencing situations and related games. *Annals of Operations Research, 109*, 265–277.

Calma, A., Ho, W., Shao, L., & Li, H. (2021). *Operations Research*: Topics, impact, and trends from 1952–2019. *Operations Research*, to appear.

Carr, S., & Duenyas, I. (2000). Optimal admission control and sequencing in a make-to-stock/make-to-order production system. *Operations Research, 48*, 709–720.

Castro, J., Gómez, D., & Tejada, J. (2007). A project game for PERT networks. *Operations Research Letters, 35*(6), 791–798.

Celik, S., & Maglaras, C. (2008). Dynamic pricing and lead-time quotation for a multiclass make-to-order queue. *Management Science, 54*(6), 1132–1146.

Chand, S., & Schneeberger, H. (1988). Single machine scheduling to minimize weighted earliness subject to no tardy jobs. *European Journal of Operational Research, 34*, 221–230.

Chang, Y.-C., & Lee, C.-Y. (2004). Machine scheduling with job delivery coordination. *European Journal of Operational Research, 158*, 470–487.

Charnsirisakskul, K., Griffin, P.M., & Keskinocak, P. (2006). Pricing and scheduling decisions with leadtime flexibility. *European Journal of Operational Research, 171*(1) 153–169.

Chen, B., & Vestjens, A. P. A. (1997). Scheduling on identical machines: How good is LPT in an on-line setting? *Operations Research Letters, 21* 165–169.

Chen, C., & Xu, Y. (2020). *The curse of rationality in sequential scheduling games.* Working paper arXix:2009:03634v2 (September 2020).

Chen, F. (2003). Information sharing and supply chain coordination. In A. G. de Kok, & S. C. Graves (Eds.), *Supply chain management: Design, coordination, and operation* (Vol. 11 pp. 341–421).

Chen, M., & Chen, Z.-L. (2015). Recent developments in dynamic pricing research: multiple products, competition, and limited demand information. *Production and Operations Management, 24*(5), 704–731.

Chen, M., & Chen, Z.-L. (2018). Robust dynamic pricing with two substitutable products. *Manufacturing & Service Operations Management, 20* 249–268.

Chen, X., Hu, X., Liu, T.-Y., Ma, W., Qin, T., Tang, P., Wang, C., & Zheng, B. (2016). Efficient mechanism design for online scheduling. *Journal of Artificial Intelligence Research, 56* 429–461.

Chen, X., & Simchi-Levi, D. (2012) Pricing and inventory management. In Ö. Özer, R. Phillips (Eds.) *The Oxford handbook of pricing management* (pp. 784–824).

Chen, Z.-L. (2004). Integrated production and distribution operations: Taxonomy, models, and review. In D. Simchi-Levi, S. D. Wu, & Z.-J. Shen (Eds.), *Handbook of quantitative supply chain analysis: Modeling in the E-business era.* Kluwer Academic Publishers.

Chen, Z.-L. (2010). Integrated production and outbound distribution scheduling: Review and extensions. *Operations Research, 58*, 130–148.

Chen, Z.-L., & Hall, N. G. (2007). Supply chain scheduling: Conflict and cooperation in assembly systems. *Operations Research, 55*, 1072–1089.

Chen, Z.-L., & Hall, N. G. (2010). The coordination of pricing and scheduling decisions. *Manufacturing & Service Operations Management, 12*(1), 77–92.

Chen, Z.-L., & Li, C.-L. (2005). *Scheduling with subcontracting options.* Working Paper. University of Maryland, College Park, MD 20742.

Chen, Z.-L., & Li, C.-L. (2008). Scheduling with subcontracting options. *IIE Transactions, 40*(12), 1171–1184.

Chen, Z.-L., & Powell, W. B. (1999a). A column generation based decomposition algorithm for a parallel machine just-in-time scheduling problem. *European Journal of Operational Research, 116*(1), 220–232.

Chen, Z.-L., & Powell, W. B. (1999b). Solving parallel machine scheduling problems by column generation. *INFORMS Journal on Computing, 11*, 78–94.

Chen, Z.-L., & Pundoor, G. (2006). Order assignment and scheduling in a supply chain. *Operations Research, 54*(3), 555–572.

Chen, Z.-L., & Pundoor, G. (2009). Integrated order scheduling and packing. *Production and Operations Management, 18*(6), 672–692.

Chen, Z.-L., & Vairaktarakis, G. L. (2005). Integrated scheduling of production and distribution operations. *Management Science, 51*, 614–628.

Cheng, T. C. E., & Kahlbacher, H. G. (1993). Scheduling with delivery and earliness penalties. *Asia-Pacific Journal of Operational Research, 10*, 145–152.

Cheng, T. C. E., & Liu, Z. (2004). Parallel machine scheduling to minimize the sum of quadratic completion times. *IIE Transactions, 36*(1), 11–17.

Chou, M. C., Queyranne, M., & Simchi-Levi, D. (2006). The asymptotic performance ratio of an on-line algorithm for uniform parallel machine scheduling with release dates. *Mathematical Programming, 106*(1), 137–157.

Chung, D., Lee, K., Shin, K., & Park, J. (2005). A new approach to job shop scheduling problems with due date constraints considering operation subcontracts. *International Journal of Production Economics, 98*, 238–250.

Chvátal, V. (1979). A greedy heuristic for the set covering problem. *Mathematics of Operations Research, 4*(3), 233–235.

Çiftçi, B., Borm, P., & Hamers, H. (2013). Batch sequencing and cooperation. *Journal of Scheduling, 16*, 405–413.

References

Claassen, G. D. H., Gerdessen, J. C., Hendrix, E. M. T., & van der Vorst, J. G. A. J. (2016). On production planning and scheduling in food processing industry: Modelling non-triangular setups and product decay. *Computers & Operations Research, 76*, 167–182.

Clarke, E. H. (1971). Multipart pricing of public goods. *Public Choice, 11*, 17–33.

Coffman, E. G., Jr., & Lueker, G. S. (1991). *Probabilistic analysis of packing and partitioning algorithms*. John Wiley & Sons Ltd.

Cole, R., Correa, J. R., Gkatzelis, V., Mirrokni, V., & Olver, N. (2011). Inner product spaces for minsum coordination mechanisms, In L. Fortnow, & S. P. Vadhan (Eds.), *Proceedings of the 43rd ACM Symposium on Theory of Computing* (pp. 539–548).

Corfman, K. P., & Lehman, D. R. (1993). The importance of others' welfare in evaluating bargaining outcomes. *Journal of Consumer Research, 14*, 1–13.

Cramton, P., Shoham, Y., & Steinberg, R. (2006). *Combinatorial auctions*. Cambridge, MA: MIT Press.

Craumer, M. (2002). How to think strategically about outsourcing. *Harvard Management Update, 7*, 4–6.

Curiel, I. (2010). Multi-stage sequencing situations. *International Journal of Game Theory, 39*, 151–162.

Curiel, I. (2011). Project management games. *International Journal of Game Theory, 13*(3), 281–300.

Curiel, I. (2015). Compensation rules for multi-stage sequencing games. *Annals of Operations Research, 225*, 65–82.

Curiel, I., Pederzoli, G., & Tijs, S. (1989). Sequencing games. *European Journal of Operational Research, 40*, 344–351.

Curiel, I., Potters, J., Prasad, R., Tijs, S., & Veltman, B. (1994). Sequencing and cooperation. *Operations Research, 42*(3), 566–568.

Curiel, I., Potters, J., Tijs, V. R., Prasad., S., & Veltman, B. (1993). Cooperation in one-machine scheduling. *Zeitschrift für Operations Research, 38*, 113–129.

Daniels, R.L., & Kouvelis, P. (1995). Robust scheduling to hedge against processing time uncertainty in single-stage production. *Management Science, 41*(2), 363–376.

Dantzig, G.B., & Wolfe, P. (1960). Decomposition principle for linear programs. *Operations Research, 8*, 101–111.

Dawande, M., Geismar, H. N., Hall, N. G., & Sriskandarajah, C. (2006). Supply chain scheduling: Distribution systems. *Production and Operations Management, 15*, 243–261.

de Kok, A. G., & Graves, S. C. (Eds.) (2003). *Supply chain management: Design, coordination and operation*. Handbooks in Operations Research and Management Science (Vol. 11). Elsevier.

Desaulniers, G., Desrosiers, J., & Solomon, M. M. (2010). *Column generation*. Springer.

Dhangwatnotai, P., Dobzinski, S., Gughmi, S., & Roughgarden, T. (2011). Truthful approximation schemes for single-parameter agents. *SIAM Journal on Computing, 40*(3), 915–933.

Dobzinski, S., & Sundararajan, M. (2008). On characterizations of truthful mechanisms for combinatorial auctions and scheduling. In *Proceedings of the 9th ACM Conference on Electronic Commerce*, Chicago, IL, July.

Dragan, I. (2013). Scheduling jobs with a common due date via cooperative game theory. *American Journal of Operational Research, 3*, 439–443.

Driessen, T., Tijs, S. H. (1985). The τ-value, the core and seminconvex games. *International Journal of Game Theory, 14*, 229–247.

Du, J., & Leung, J. Y.-T. (1990). Minimizing total tardiness on one machine is NP-hard. *Mathematics of Operations Research, 15*(3), 483–495.

Duives, J., Heydenreich, B., Mishra, D., Müller, R., & Uetz, M. (2015). On optimal mechanism design for a sequencing problem. *Journal of Scheduling, 18*, 45–59.

Durango-Cohen, E. J., & Yano, C. A. (2006). Supplier commitment and production decisions under a forecast-commitment contract. *Management Science, 52*(1), 54–67.

Eliashberg, J., & Steinberg, R. (1993). Marketing-production joint decision making. In *Handbooks in operations research and management science* (Vol. 5, pp. 827–880). Amsterdam, Netherlands: Elsevier Science Publishers.

Elmaghraby, W., & Keskinocak, P. (2003). Dynamic pricing in the presence of inventory considerations: Research overview, current practices, and future directions. *Management Science, 49*(10), 1287–1309.

Engels, D. W., Karger, D. R., Kolliopoulos, S. G., Sengupta, S., Uma, R. N., & Wein, J. (2003). Techniques for scheduling with rejection. *Journal of Algorithms, 49*, 175–191.

Erengüç, Ş. S., Simpson, N. C., & Vakharia, A. J. (1999). Integrated production/distribution planning in supply chains. *European Journal of Operational Research, 115*, 219–236.

Estévez-Fernández, A. (2012). A game theoretical approach to sharing penalties and rewards in projects. *European Journal of Operational Research, 216*(3), 647–657.

Estévez-Fernández, A., Borm, P., & Hamers, H. (2007). Project games. *International Journal of Game Theory, 36*, 149–176.

Estévez-Fernández, A., Mosquera, M. A., Borm, P., & Hamers, H. (2008). Proportionate flow shop games. *Journal of Scheduling, 11*, 433–447.

Fang, Q., Zhu, S., Cai, M., & Deng, X. (2002). On computational complexity of membership test in flow games and linear production games. *International Journal of Game Theory, 31*, 39–45.

Farahani, P., Grunow, M., & Günther, H.-O. (2012). Integrated production and distribution planning for perishable food products. *Flexible Services and Manufacturing Journal, 24*, 28–51.

Feldman, M., & Tamir, T. (2012). Conflicting congestion effects in resource allocation games. *Operations Research, 60*(3), 529–540.

Feng, X., Cheng, Y., Zheng, F., & Xu, Y. (2016). Online integrated production-distribution scheduling problems without preemption. *Journal of Combinatorial Optimization, 31*, 1569–1585.

Fisher, M. L. (1997). What is the right supply chain for your product? *Harvard Business Review, 75*, 105–117.

Fotakis, D., Mavronicolas, M., Kontogiannis, S., & Spiraklis, P. (2002). The structure and complexity of Nash equilibria for a selfish routing game. In: *International Colloquium on Automata, Languages, and Programming (ICALP)* (pp. 510–519). Berlin: Springer.

Frank, R. H., & Parker, I. C. (2004). *Microeconomics and behavior* (2nd ed.) Boston, MA: McGraw-Hill.

Fudenberg, D., & Tirole, J. (1993). *Game theory.* Cambridge, MA: MIT Press.

Garcia, J. M., & Lozano, S. (2004a). Production and delivery scheduling problem with time windows. *Computers & Industrial Engineering, 48*, 733–742.

Garcia, J. M., & Lozano, S. (2004b). Production and vehicle scheduling for ready-mix operations. *Computers & Industrial Engineering, 46*, 803–816.

Garey, M. R., & Johnson, D. S. (1978). "Strong" NP-completeness results: Motivation, examples, and implications. *Journal of the ACM, 25*(3), 499–508.

Garey, M. R., & Johnson, D. S. (1979). *Computers and intractability: A guide to the theory of NP-completeness.* San Francisco, CA: Freeman.

Garey, M. R., Johnson, D. S., & Sethi, R. (1976). The complexity of flowshop and jobshop scheduling. *Mathematics of Operations Research, 1*, 117–129.

Geismar, H. N., Laporte, G., Lei, L., & Sriskandarajah, C. (2008). The integrated production and transportation scheduling problem for a product with a short lifespan. *INFORMS Journal on Computing, 20*(1), 21–33.

Geismar, H. N., & Murthy, N. M. (2015). Balancing production and distribution in paper manufacturing. *Production and Operations Management, 24*(7), 1164–1178.

Gerichhausen, M., & Hamers, H. (2009). Partitioning sequencing situations and games. *European Journal of Operational Research, 196*, 207–216.

Gharbi, A., & Haouari, M. (2002). Minimizing makespan on parallel machines subject to release dates and delivery times. *Journal of Scheduling, 5*, 329–355.

Gilbert, S. M. (2000). Coordination of pricing and multiple-period production across multiple constant priced goods. *Management Science, 46*(12), 1602–1616.

Gilmore, P. C., & Gomory, R. E. (1964). Sequencing a one state-variable machine: A solvable case of the traveling salesman problem. *Operations Research, 12*, 655–679.

References

Glazer, A., Hassin, R., & Ravner, L. (2018). A strategic model of job assignment to a single machine with earliness and tardiness penalties. *IISE Transactions, 50*(4), 265–278.

Goetschalckx, M., Vidal, C. J., & Dogan, K. (2002). Modeling and design of global logistics systems: A review of integrated strategic and tactical models and design algorithms. *European Journal of Operational Research, 143*, 1–18.

Goldfarb, D., & Liu, S. (1993). An $O(n^3 L)$ primal-dual potential reduction algorithm for solving convex quadratic programs. *Mathematical Programming, 61*, 161–170.

Graham, R. L. (1969). Bounds on multiprocessor timing anomalies. *SIAM Journal on Applied Mathematics, 17*(2), 263–269.

Graham, R. L., Lawler, E. L., Lenstra, J. K., & Rinnooy Kan, A. H. G. (1979). Optimization and approximation in deterministic sequencing and scheduling: a survey. *Annals of Discrete Mathematics, 5*, 287–326.

Granot, D., & Huberman, G. (1982). The relationship between convex games and minimal cost spanning tree games: A case for permutationally convex games. *SIAM Journal of Algebraic and Discrete Methods, 3*, 288–292.

Grieco, J. (1988). Realist theory and the problem of international cooperation: Analysis with an amended prisoner's dilemma model. *Journal of Politics, 50*, 600–625.

Grosvenor, F., & Austin, T. A. (2001). Cisco's eHub initiative. *Supply Chain Management Review* July/August 28–35.

Groves, T. (1973). Incentives in teams. *Econometrica, 41*, 617–631.

Grundel, S., Çiftçi, B., Borm, P., & Hamers, H. (2013). Family sequencing and cooperation. *European Journal of Operational Research, 226*, 414–424.

Hall, L. A., & Shmoys, D. B. (1989). Approximation algorithms for constrained scheduling problems. In *Proceedings of the 30th Annual Symposium on Foundations of Computer Science* (pp. 134–140).

Hall, L. A., & Shmoys, D. B. (1992). Jackson's rule for single-machine scheduling: making a good heuristic better. *Mathematics of Operations Research, 17*, 22–35.

Hall, N. G. (1986). Single and multiple processor models for minimizing completion time variance. *Naval Research Logistics Quarterly, 33*, 49–54 (1986).

Hall, N. G. (2016). Research and teaching opportunities in project management. In *INFORMS Tutorials in Operations Research*, November, 329–388. Available at: https://doi.org/10.1287/educ.2016.0146

Hall, N. G., Kubiak, W., & Sethi, S. P. (1991). Earliness-tardiness scheduling problems, II: deviation of completion times about a restrictive common due date. *Operations Research, 39*, 847–856.

Hall, N. G., 'Lesaoana, M. A., & Potts, C. N. (2001). Scheduling with fixed delivery dates. *Operations Research, 49*, 134–144.

Hall, N. G., & Liu, Z. (2010). Capacity allocation and scheduling in supply chains. *Operations Research, 58*(6), 1711–1725.

Hall, N. G., & Liu, Z. (2016). Capacity allocation games without an initial sequence. *Operations Research Letters, 44*(6), 747–749.

Hall, N. G., Liu, Z., & Potts, C. N. (2007). Rescheduling for multiple new orders. *INFORMS Journal on Computing, 19*(4), 633–645.

Hall, N. G., & Posner, M. E. (1991). Earliness-tardiness scheduling problems, I: Weighted deviation of completion times about a common due date. *Operations Research, 39*(5), 836–846.

Hall, N. G., & Posner, M. E. (2001). Generating experimental data for computational testing with machine scheduling applications. *Operations Research, 49*(6), 854–865.

Hall, N. G., Posner, M. E., & Potts, C. N. (2009). Online scheduling with known arrival times. *Mathematics of Operations Research, 34*(1), 92–102.

Hall, N. G., & Potts, C. N. (2003). Supply chain scheduling: batching and delivery. *Operations Research, 51*, 566–584.

Hall, N. G., & Potts, C. N. (2004). Rescheduling for new orders. *Operations Research, 52*(3), 440–453.

Hall, N. G., & Potts, C. N. (2005). The coordination of scheduling and batch deliveries. *Annals of Operations Research, 135*, 41–64.

Hall, N. G., & Potts, C. N. (2010). Rescheduling for job unavailability. *Operations Research, 58*(3), 746–755.

Hall, N. G., & Sriskandarajah, C. (1996). A survey of machine scheduling problems with blocking and no-wait in process. *Operations Research, 44*, 510–525.

Hamers, H., Borm, P., & Tijs, S. (1995). On games corresponding to sequencing situations with ready times. *Mathematical Programming, 70*, 1–13.

Hamers, H., Klijn, F., & Suijs, J. (1999). On the balancedness of multimachine sequencing games. *European Journal of Operational Research, 119*, 678–691.

Hamers, H., Klijn, F., & van Velzen, B. (2002). *On the convexity of precedence sequencing games.* CentER Discussion Paper 2002–112, Tilburg University, Netherlands.

Hamers, H., Suijs, J., Tijs, S., & Borm, P. (1996). The split core for sequencing games. *Games and Economics Behavior, 15*, 165–176.

Han, B., Zhang, W., Lu, X., & Lin, Y. (2015). On-line supply chain scheduling for single-machine and parallel-machine configurations with a single customer: minimizing the makespan and delivery cost. *European Journal of Operational Research, 244*, 704–714.

Harsanyi, J. C. (1981). *Solutions for some bargaining games under the Harsanyi-Selten solution theory, part II: analysis of specific bargaining games.* Working paper CP-432, Center for Research in Management Sciences, University of California, Berkeley, CA.

He, Y., Zhong, W., & Gu, H. (2006). Improved algorithms for two single machine scheduling problems. *Theoretical Computer Science, 363*, 257–265.

Hernandez, A. (1989). *Just-in-time manufacturing: A practical approach.* Englewood Cliffs, NJ: Prentice-Hall.

Heydenreich, B., Müller, R., & Uetz, M. (2007). Games and mechanism design in machine scheduling - An introduction. *Production and Operations Management, 16*(4), 437–454.

Hochbaum, D. S. (Ed.) (1996). *Approximation algorithms for NP-hard problems.* Boston, MA: PWS Publishing Company.

Hochbaum, D. S., & Landy, D. (1997). Scheduling semiconductor burn-in operations to minimize total flowtime. *Operations Research, 45*, 874–885.

Hoefer, M., & Skopalik, A. (2013). Altruism in atomic congestion games. *ACM Transactions on Economics and Computation, 1*(4), Article 21.

Hoeksma, R., & Uetz, M. (2016). Optimal mechanism design for a sequencing problem with two-dimensional types. *Operations Research, 64*(6), 1438–1450.

Hoogeveen, J. A., & van de Velde, S. L. (1995). Minimizing total completion-time and maximum cost simultaneously is solvable in polynomial-time. *Operations Research Letters, 17*, 205–208.

Hoogeveen, J. A., & Vestjens, A. P. A. (1996). Optimal on-line algorithms for single-machine scheduling. *Lecture Notes in Computer Science, 1084*, 404–414.

Hoogeveen, J. A., & Vestjens, A. P. A. (2000). A best possible deterministic on-line algorithm for minimizing maximum delivery time on a single machine. *SIAM Journal on Discrete Mathematics, 13*, 56–63.

Hopp, W. J., & Spearman, M. L. (2000). *Factory physics*(2nd ed.). New York: Irwin McGraw-Hill.

Hu, X., Cui, N., & Demeulemeester, E. (2015). Effective expediting to improve project due date and cost performance through buffer management. *International Journal of Production Research, 53*(5), 1460–1471.

Hurter, A. P., & van Buer, M. G. (1996). The newspaper production/distribution problem. *Journal of Business Logistics, 17*, 85–107.

Hurter, A. P., & van Buer, M. G. (1999). Solving the medium newspaper production/distribution problem. *European Journal of Operational Research, 115*, 237–253.

Ibarra, O., & Kim, C. (1977). Heuristic algorithms for scheduling independent tasks on nonidentical processors. *Journal of the ACM, 24*(2), 280–289.

Immorlica, N., Li, L., Mirrokni, V. S., & Schulz, A. (2005). Coordination mechanisms for selfish scheduling. In X. Deng, & Y. Ye (Eds.), *Internet and network economics.* Lecture Notes in Computer Science (Vol. 3828, pp. 55–69). Berlin, Germany: Springer.

References

Iñarra, E., Serrano, R., & Shimomura, K.-I. (2019). *The nuclelolus, the kernel and the bargaining set: An update*. Working paper series II, 113/19, Departamento de Fundamentos del Análisis Económico, University of the Basque Country, Spain.

İnkaya, T., & Akansel, M. (2017). Coordinated scheduling of the transfer lots in an assembly-type supply chain: a genetic algorithm approach. *Journal of Intelligent Manufacturing, 28*, 1005–1015.

Ivanov, D., Sokolov, B., & Dolgui, A. (2014). Multi-stage supply chain scheduling with non-preemptive continuous operations and execution control. *International Journal of Production Research, 52*(13), 4059–4077.

Iyer, A. V., Deshpande, V., & Wu, Z. (2003). A postponement model for demand management. *Management Science, 49*(8), 983–1002.

Jackson, J. R. (1955). *Scheduling a production line to minimize maximum tardiness*. Research Report 43, Management Science Research Project, University of California, Los Angeles.

Ji, M., He, Y., & Cheng, T. C. E. (2007). Batch delivery scheduling with batch delivery cost on a single machine. *European Journal of Operational Research, 176*, 745–755.

Johnson, S. M. (1954). Optimal two and three-stage production schedules with setup times included. *Naval Research Logistics Quarterly, 1*, 61–67.

Kaminsky, P. (2003). The effectiveness of the longest delivery time rule for the flow shop delivery time problem. *Naval Research Logistics, 50*(3), 257–272.

Kaminsky, P., & Kaya, O. (2008). Scheduling and due-date quotation in a make-to-order supply chain. *Naval Research Logistics, 55*(5), 444–458.

Kaminsky, P., & Simchi-Levi, D. (1998). Probabilistic analysis and practical algorithms for the flow shop weighted completion time problem. *Operations Research, 46*(6), 872–882.

Kanet, J. J. (1981). Minimizing the average deviation of job completion times about a common due date. *Naval Research Logistics Quarterly, 28*(4), 643–652.

Kann, V. (1991). Maximum bounded 3-dimensional matching is MAX SNP-complete. *Information Processing Letters, 37*(1), 27–35.

Karp, R. M. (1972). Reducibility among combinatorial problems. In R. E. Miller, & J. W. Thatcher (Eds.), *Complexity of computer computations* (pp. 85–103). New York: Plenum Press.

Kellerer, H., Pferschy, U., & Pisinger, D. (2004). *Knapsack problems*. Berlin: Springer.

Kelley Jr., & Walker, M. R. (1959). Critical-path planning and scheduling. In *Proceedings of the Eastern Joint Computer Conference*. National Joint Computer Committee (pp. 160–173). New York: ACM.

Kergosien, Y., Gendreau, M., & Billaut, J.-C. (2017). A Benders decomposition-based heuristic for a production and outbound distribution scheduling problem with strict delivery constraints. *European Journal of Operational Research, 262*, 287–298.

Kerzner, H. R. (2013). *Project management: A systems approach to planning, scheduling, and controlling* (11th ed.). Hoboken, NJ: Wiley.

Kise, H., Ibaraki, T., & Mine, H. (1979). Performance analysis of six approximation algorithms for the one-machine maximum lateness scheduling problem with ready times. *Journal of the Operations Research Society of Japan, 22*(3), 205–224.

Klastorin, T. D. (2012). *Project management: Tools and trade-offs* (3rd Pearson, ed.). Upper Saddle River, NJ: Pearson Learning Solutions.

Kleinberg, J., & Tardos, É. (2006). *Algorithm design*. Pearson Education.

Klijn, F., & Sánchez, E. (2006). Sequencing games without initial order. *Mathematical Methods of Operations Research, 63*, 53–62.

Kolawa, A. (2004). Outsourcing is not the enemy. *Wall Street Journal*, Feb. 24, 2004, page B2.

Koulamas, C. (2010). The single-machine total tardiness scheduling problem: Review and extensions. *European Journal of Operational Research, 202*, 1–7.

Koulamas, C., Antony, S. R., & Jaen, R. (1994). A survey of simulated annealing applications to operations research problems. *Omega, 22*, 41–56.

Koutsoupias, E. (2014). Scheduling without payments. *Theory of Computer Systems, 54*, 375–387.

Koutsoupias, E., & Papadimitriou, C. (1999). Worst-case equilibria. In C. Meinel, & S. Tison (Eds.), *STAC 1999, 16th Annual Symposium on Theoretical Aspects of Computer Science*. Lecture Notes in Computer Science (Vol. 1563, pp. 404–413). Berlin, Germany: Springer.

Kovalyov, M. Y., & Pesch, E. (2014). A game mechanism for single machine sequencing with zero risk. *Omega, 44*, 104–110.

Kreipl, S., & Pinedo, M. (2004). Planning and scheduling in supply chains: An overview of issues in practice. *Production and Operations Management, 13*(1), 77–92.

Kress, D., Meiswinkel, S., & Pesch, E. (2018a). Mechanism design for machine scheduling problems: Classification and literature overview. *OR Spectrum, 40*, 583–611.

Kress, D., Meiswinkel, S., & Pesch, E. (2018b). Incentive compatible mechanisms for scheduling two-parameter jobs on parallel identical machines to minimize the weighted number of late jobs. *Discrete Applied Mathematics, 242*, 89–101.

Kroon, L. G., Salomon, M., & Van Wassenhove, L. N. (1995). Exact and approximation algorithms for the operational fixed interval scheduling problem. *European Journal of Operational Research, 82*, 190–205.

Kunreuther, H., & Schrage, L. (1973). Joint pricing and inventory decisions for constant priced items. *Management Science, 19*(7), 732–738.

Laffont, J. J. (1988). *Fundamentals of public economics*. Cambridge, MA: The MIT Press.

Lane, D. E., & Sidney, J. B. (1993). Batching and scheduling in FMS hubs: flow time considerations. *Operations Research, 41*, 1091–1103.

Lavi, R., & Swamy, C. (2009). Truthful mechanism design for multidimensional scheduling via cycle monotonicity. *Games and Economic Behavior, 67*(1), 94–124.

Lawler, E. L. (1977). A 'pseudopolynomial' time algorithm for sequencing jobs to minimize total tardiness. *Annals of Discrete Mathematics, 1*, 331–342.

Lawler, E. L., & Moore, J. M. (1969). A functional equation and its application to resource allocation and sequencing problems. *Management Science, 16*(1), 77–84.

Le Breton, M., Owen, G., & Weber, S. (1992). Strongly balanced cooperative games. *International Journal of Game Theory, 20*, 419–427.

Ledyard, J. (1997). Public goods: A survey of experimental research. In J. Kagel, & A. Roth (Eds.), *Handbook of experimental economics* (pp. 111–194). Princeton University Press.

Lee, C.-Y., & Chen, Z.-L. (2001). Machine scheduling with transportation considerations. *Journal of Scheduling, 4*, 3–24.

Lee, C.-Y., Cheng, T. C. E., & Lin, B. M. T. (1993). Minimizing the makespan in the 3-machine assembly-type flowshop scheduling problem. *Management Science, 39*, 616–625.

Lee, C.-Y., & Uzsoy, R. (1999). Minimizing makespan on a single batch processing machine with dynamic job arrivals. *International Journal of Production Research, 37*, 219–236.

Lee, C.-Y., Uzsoy, R., & Martin-Vega, L. A. (1992). Efficient algorithms for scheduling semiconductor burn-in operations. *Operations Research, 40*(4), 764–775.

Lee, H. L., Padmanabhan, V., Taylor, T. A., & Wang, S. (2000). Price protection in the personal computer industry. *Management Science, 46*, 467–482.

Lee, H. L., Padmanabhan, V., & Whang, S. J. (1997). Information distortion in a supply chain: The bullwhip effect. *Management Science, 43*, 546–558.

Lee, I. S., & Sung, C. S. (2008a). Minimizing due date related measures for a single machine scheduling problem with outsourcing allowed. *European Journal of Operational Research, 186*, 931–952.

Lee, I. S., & Sung, C. S. (2008b). Single machine scheduling with outsourcing allowed. *International Journal of Production Economics, 101*, 623–634.

Lee, K., & Choi, B.-C. (2011). Two-stage production scheduling with an outsourcing option. *European Journal of Operational Research, 213*, 489–497.

Lee, K., Leung, J.Y.-T., & Pinedo, M. L. (2012). Coordination mechanisms for parallel machine scheduling. *European Journal of Operational Research, 220*, 305–313.

Lee, K. C., & Tse, C. S. (1992). *Inventory control at Procter and Gamble, Inc. Undergraduate Thesis*, Department of Mechanical and Industrial Engineering, University of Toronto.

References 671

Lehman, D. (2001). The impact of altruism and envy on competitive behavior and satisfaction. *International Journal of Research in Marketing, 18*, 5–17.

Lei, L., Ruszcynski, A., Park, S., & Lui, S. (2006). On the integrated production, inventory and distribution routing problem. *IIE Transactions, 38*, 955–970.

Lejeune, M. (2008). *A unified approach for cycle service levels.* Technical Report TR-2008-19, The Institute for Integrating Statistics in Decision Sciences, The George Washington University, Washington, DC.

Leme, R. P., Syrgkanis, V., & Tardos, É. (2012). The curse of simultaneity. In *Proceedings of the 3rd Innovations in Theoretical Computer Science Conference* (pp. 60–67).

Leng, M., & Parlar, M. (2010). Analytic solution for the nucleolus of a three-player cooperative game. *Naval Research Logistics, 57*, 667–672.

Lenstra, J. K., Rinnooy Kan, A. H. G., & Brucker, P. (1977). Complexity of machine scheduling problems. *Annals of Discrete Mathematics, 1*, 343–362.

Leung, J. Y.-T., & Anderson, J. H. (Eds.) (2004). *Handbook of scheduling: Algorithms, models and performance analysis.* Chapman & Hall/CRC Press.

Leung, J. Y.-T., & Chen, Z.-L. (2013). Integrated production and distribution with fixed delivery departure dates. *Operations Research Letters, 41*(3), 290–293.

Levine, D. (1998). Modeling altruism and spitefulness in experiments. *Review of Economic Dynamics, 1*, 593–622.

Li, C.-L., Vairaktarakis, G., & Lee, C.-Y. (2005a). Machine scheduling with deliveries to multiple customer locations. *European Journal of Operational Research, 164*, 39–51.

Li, F., Chen, Z.-L., & Tang, L. (2017). Integrated production, inventory and delivery problems: Complexity and algorithms. *INFORMS Journal on Computing, 29*(2), 232–250.

Li, K. P., Ganesan, V. K., & Sivakumar, A. I. (2005b). Synchronized scheduling of assembly and multi-destination air-transportation in a consumer electronics supply chain. *International Journal of Production Research, 43*(13), 2671–2685.

Li, K. P., Ganesan, V. K., & Sivakumar, A. I. (2006). Scheduling of single stage assembly with air transportation in a consumer electronics supply chain. *Computers & Industrial Engineering, 51*, 264–278.

Li, K. P., Sivakumar, A. I., & Ganesan, V. K. (2008). Analysis and algorithms for coordinated scheduling of parallel machine manufacturing and 3PL transportation. *International Journal of Production Economics, 115*(2), 482–491.

Li, L. (2002). Information sharing in a supply chain with horizontal competition. *Management Science, 48*(9), 1196–1212.

Liu, L., Qi, X., & Xu, Z. (2018a). Simultaneous penalization and subsidization for stabilizing grand cooperation. *Operations Research, 66*(5), 1362–1375.

Liu, M., Chu, C., Xu, Y., & Zheng, F. (2010). An optimal online algorithm for single machine scheduling with bounded delivery times. *European Journal of Operational Research, 201*, 693–700.

Liu, P., & Lu, X. (2015). Online scheduling on two parallel machines with release dates and delivery times. *Journal of Combinatorial Optimization, 30*, 347–359.

Liu, Z., Lu, L., & Qi, X. (2012). Simultaneous and sequential price quotations for uncertain order inquiries with production scheduling cost. *IIE Transactions, 44*, 820–833.

Liu, Z., Lu, L., & Qi, X. (2018b). Cost allocation in rescheduling with machine unavailable period. *European Journal of Operational Research, 266*, 16–28.

Liu, Z., Lu, L., & Qi, X. (2020). Price quotation for orders with different due dates. *International Journal of Production Economics, 220*, 107448.

Lu, L., Liu, Z., & Qi, X. (2013). Coordinated price quotation and production scheduling for uncertain order inquiries. *IIE Transactions, 45*, 1293–1308.

Lu, L., Yuan, J., & Zhang, L. (2008). Single machine scheduling with release dates and job delivery to minimize the makespan. *Theoretical Computer Science, 393*, 102–108.

Lu, L., Zhang, L., & Ou, J. (2021). In-house production and outsourcing under different discount schemes on the total outsourcing cost. *Annals of Operations Research, 298*, 361–374.

Lu, X., Sitters, R. A., & Stougie, L. (2003). A class of on-line scheduling algorithms to minimize total completion time. *Operations Research Letters, 31*, 232–236.

Mahajan, M., Rama, R., & Sundarrajan, V. (2003). On sorting by 3-bounded transpositions. *Electronic Notes in Discrete Mathematics, 15*, 117–120.

Maniquet, F. (2003). A characterization of the Shapley value in queueing problems. *Journal of Economic Theory, 109*, 90–103.

Manoj, U. V., Gupta, J. N. D., Gupta, S. K., & Sriskandarajah, C. (2008). Supply chain scheduling: Just-in-time environment. *Annals of Operations Research, 161*, 53–86.

Manoj, U. V., Sriskandarajah, C., & Wagneur, E. (2012). Coordination in a two-stage production system: Complexity, conflict and cooperation. *Computers & Operations Research, 39*, 1245–1256.

Mastrolilli, M. (2003). Efficient approximation schemes for scheduling problems with release dates and delivery times. *Journal of Scheduling, 6*, 521–531.

Melo, R. A., & Wolsey, L. A. (2010). Optimizing production and transportation in a commit-to-delivery business mode. *European Journal of Operational Research, 203*, 614–618.

Mishra, D., & Rangarajan, B. (2007). Cost sharing in a job scheduling problem. *Social Choice and Welfare, 29*, 369–382.

Monma, C. L., & Potts, C. N. (1989). On the complexity of scheduling with batch set-up times. *Operations Research, 37*, 798–804.

Moore, J. M. (1968). A n job, one machine sequencing algorithm for minimizing the number of late jobs. *Management Science, 15*, 102–109.

Moore, S., & Gray, K. (2011). GPOs and buying consortiums must be on the radar for 2011–2012. Available online at: https://spendmatters.com/pdf/GPOperspectivespaper.pdf

Moses, M., & Seshadri, S. (2000). Policy mechanisms for supply chain coordination. *IIE Transactions, 32*, 245–262.

Munson, C. L., & Jackson, J. (2015). Quantity discounts: an overview and practical guide for buyers and sellers. *Foundations and Trends in Technology, Information and Operations Management, 8*(12), 1–130.

Musegaas, M., Borm, P. E. M., & Quant, M. (2015). Step out-step in sequencing games. *European Journal of Operational Research, 246*, 894–906.

Muto, S., Nakayama, M., Potters, J., & Tijs, S. H. (1988). On big boss games. *Economic Studies Quarterly, 39*, 302–321.

Myerson, R. B. (1981). Optimal auction design. *Mathematics of Operations Research, 6*(1), 58–73.

Myerson, R. B. (1997). *Game theory: Analysis of conflict*. Cambridge, Massachusetts: Harvard University Press.

Nash, J. F. (1950). The bargaining problem. *Econometrica, 18*, 155–162.

Nash, J. F. (1951). Non-cooperative games. *The Annals of Mathematics, 54*(2), 286–295.

Nash J. F. (1953). Two-person cooperative games. *Econometrica, 21*, 128–140.

Naso, D., Surico, M., Turchiano, B., & Kaymak, U. (2007). Genetic algorithms for supply-chain scheduling: A case study in the distribution of ready-mixed concrete. *European Journal of Operational Research, 177*, 2069–2099.

Nellemann, D. O., & Smith, L. F. (1982). Just-in-time *vs.* just-in-case production systems borrowed back from Japan. *Production and Inventory Management, 23*, 12–21.

Nemhauser, G. L., & Wolsey, L. A. (1988). *Integer programming and combinatorial optimization*. Chichester: Wiley.

Ng, C. T., Cheng, T. C. E., & Kovalyov, M. Y. (2003). Batch scheduling with controllable setup and processing times to minimize total completion time. *Journal of the Operational Research Society, 54*, 499–506.

Ng, C. T., & Lu, L. (2012). On-line integrated production and outbound distribution scheduling to minimize the maximum delivery completion time. *Journal of Scheduling, 15*, 391–398.

Ng, C. T., & Lu, L. (2020). Private communication. December 2020.

Ng, C. T. (2021). Private communication. August 2021.

Nisan, N., & Ronen, A. (2001). Algorithmic mechanism design. *Games and Economic Behavior, 35*, 166–196.

References

673

Nisan, N., Roughgarden, T., Tardos, É. Vazirani, V. (Eds.) (2007). *Algorithmic game theory.* Cambridge, U.K.: Cambridge University Press.

Ohno, T. (1988). *Toyota production system: Beyond large-scale production.* Shelton, CT: Productivity Press, Productivity .

Oron, D. (2014). Scheduling controllable processing time jobs in a deteriorating environment. *Journal of the Operational Research Society, 65*(1), 49–56.

Osborne, M. J. (2004). *An introduction to game theory.* Oxford, U.K.: Oxford University Press.

Ouchi, W. G. (1980). Markets, bureaucracies and clans. *Administrative Science Quarterly, 25,* 129–142.

Owen, G. (1975). On the core of linear production games. *Mathematical Programming, 9,* 358–370.

Özer, Ö., & Wei, W. (2006). Strategic commitments for an optimal capacity decision under asymmetric forecast information. *Management Science, 52*(8), 1238–1257.

Panwalkar, S. S., Smith, M. L., & Seidmann, A. (1982). Common due date assignment to minimize total penalty for the one machine scheduling problem. *Operations Research, 30*(2), 391–399.

Papadimitriou, C. H., & Steiglitz, K. (1998). *Combinatorial optimization: Algorithms and complexity.* North Chelmsford, U.K.: Courier Corporation.

Parlar, M., & Weng, Z. K. (1997). Designing a firm's coordinated manufacturing and supply decisions with short product life cycles. *Management Science, 43,* 1329–1344.

Peleg, B., & Sudhölter, P. (2007). *Introduction to the theory of cooperative games.* Springer.

Perakis, G., & Roels, G. (2008). Regret in the newsvendor model with partial information. *Operations Research, 56*(1), 188–203.

Pereira, V., & Costa, H. G. (2015). A literature review on lot size with quantity discounts: 1995–2013. *Journal of Modelling in Management, 10*(3), 341–359.

Pinedo, M. L. (2016). *Scheduling: Theory, algorithms, and systems* (5th ed.). Springer.

Pinedo, M. L., & Chao, X. L. (1999). *Operations scheduling with applications in manufacturing and services* (1st ed.). Irwin McGraw-Hill.

Porter, R. (2004). Mechanism design for online real-time scheduling. In *Proceedings of the 5th ACM Conference on Electronic Commerce* (pp. 61–70).

Potts, C. N. (1980). Analysis of a heuristic for one machine sequencing with release dates and delivery times. *Operations Research, 28,* 1436–1441.

Potts, C. N., & Kovalyov, M. (2000). Scheduling with batching: a review. *European Journal of Operational Research, 120*(2), 228–249.

Potts, C. N., Sevast'janov, S. V., Strusevich, V. A., Van Wassenhove, L. N., & Zwaneveld, C. M. (1995). The two-stage assembly scheduling problem: complexity and approximation. *Operations Research, 43,* 346–355.

Project Management Institute (2019). *Practice Standard for Scheduling* (3rd ed.).

Project Management Institute (2021). What is project management? Available at: https://www.pmi.org/about/learn-about-pmi/what-is-project-management, last accessed April 14, 2021.

Pruhs, K., Sgall, J., & Torng, E. (2004). Online scheduling. In J.Y.-T. Leung (Ed.), *Handbook of scheduling: Algorithms, models, and performance analysis*, Chapter 15. Boca Raton: CRC Press.

Pundoor, G., & Chen, Z.-L. (2005). Scheduling a production-distribution system to optimize the tradeoff between delivery tardiness and total distribution cost. *Naval Research Logistics, 52,* 571–589.

Qi, X. (2008). Coordinated logistics scheduling for in-house production and outsourcing. *IEEE Transactions on Automation Science and Engineering, 5,* 188–192.

Qi, X. (2011). Outsourcing and production scheduling for a two-stage flowshop. *International Journal of Production Economics, 129,* 43–50.

Qi, X. (2012). Production scheduling with subcontracting: the subcontractor's pricing game. *Journal of Scheduling, 15,* 773–781.

Rajagopalan, S., & Malhotra, A. (2001). Have U.S. manufacturing inventories really decreased? An empirical study. *Manufacturing & Service Operations Management, 3,* 14–24.

674 References

Rebollo, M., Julian, V., Carrascosa, C., & Botti, V. (2000). A multi-agent system for the automation of a port container terminal. In *Proceedings, Agents 2000 Workshop*.

Ren, J., Du, D., & Xu, D. (2013). The complexity of two supply chain scheduling problems. *Information Processing Letters, 113*, 609–612.

Respício, A., & Captivo, M. E. (2008). Marketing-production interface through an integrated DSS. *Journal of Decision Systems, 17*, 119–132.

Roberts, K. (1979). The characterization of implementable choice rules. In J.-J. Laffont (Ed.), *Aggregation and revelation of preferences*. North-Holland, Amsterdam, Netherlands.

Rochet, J.C. (1987). A necessary and sufficient condition for rationalizability in a quasilinear context. *Journal of Mathematical Economics, 16*, 191–200.

Ross, S. (1998). *A first course in probability* (5th ed.). Prentice Hall.

Roth, A., Sotomayor, M. A. O., & Chesher, A. (Eds.) (2004). *Two-sided matching: A study in game theoretic modeling and analysis*. Cambridge, MA: Cambridge University Press.

Roughgarden, T. (2004). Stackelberg scheduling strategies. *SIAM Journal on Computing, 33*(2), 332–350.

Roughgarden, T., & Tardos, É. (2002). How bad is selfish routing? *Journal of the ACM, 49*(2), 236–259.

Sahin, F., & Robinson, E. P. (2002). Flow coordination and information sharing in supply chains: review, implications, and directions for future research. *Decision Sciences, 33*(4), 505–536.

Saks, M., & Yu, L. (2005). Weak monotonicity suffices for truthfulness on convex domains. In *Proceedings of the 6th ACM Conference on Electronic Commerce* (pp. 286–293). New York: ACM.

Santos, C., & Magazine, M. (1985). Batching in single operation manufacturing systems. *Operations Research Letters, 4*, 99–103.

Sarmiento, A. M., & Nagi, R. (1999). A review of integrated analysis of production-distribution systems. *IIE Transactions, 31*, 1061–1074.

Sawik, T. (2009). Coordinated supply chain scheduling. *International Journal of Production Economics, 120*, 437–451.

Schmeidler, D. (1969). The nucleolus of a characteristic function game. *SIAM Journal on Applied Mathematics, 17*(6), 1163–1170.

Schönhage, A., Paterson, M., & Pippenger, N. (1976). Finding the median. *Journal of Computer and System Sciences, 13*, 184–199.

Schrage, L. (1968). A proof of the optimality of the shortest remaining processing time discipline. *Operations Research, 16*, 687–690.

Schubert, D., Scholz, A., & Wäscher, G. (2018). Integrated order picking and vehicle routing with due dates. *OR Spectrum, 40*, 1109–1139.

Schulz, A. S., & Uhan, N. A. (2010). Sharing supermodular costs. *Operations Research, 58*(4), 1051–1056.

Schummer, J., & Vohra, R. V. (2007). Mechanism design without payment. Chapter 10 In N. Nisan, T. Roughgarden, É. Tardos, & V. Vazirani (Eds.), *Algorithmic game theory*. Cambridge, U.K.: Cambridge University Press.

Schuurman, P., & Woeginger, G. J. (2011). Approximation schemes–a tutorial. In R. H. Möhring, C. N. Potts, A. S. Schulz, G. J. Woeginger, & L. A. Wolsey (Eds.), *Lectures on scheduling*.

Shabtay, D., & Steiner, G. (2007). A survey of scheduling with controllable processing times. *Discrete Applied Mathematics, 155*(13), 1643–1666.

Shakhlevich, N., Hoogeveen, H., & Pinedo, M. (1998). Minimizing total weighted completion time in a proportionate flow shop. *Journal of Scheduling, 1*(3), 157–168.

Shapley, L. S. (1953). A value for n-person games. In *Contributions to the theory of games (AM-28)* (Vol. 11, pp. 307–318). Princeton University Press.

Shapley, L. S. (1967). On balanced sets and cores. *Naval Research Logistics Quarterly, 14*(4), 453–460.

Shapley, L. S. (1971). Cores of convex games. *International Journal of Game Theory, 1*(1), 11–26.

Shapley, L. S., & Shubik, M. (1972). The assignment game, I: The core. *International Journal of Game Theory, 1*(1), 111–130.

References

Simchi-Levi, D., Chen, X., & Bramel, J. (2013). *The logic of logistics: Theory, algorithms, and applications for logistics management* (3rd ed.). Springer.

Simchi-Levi, D., Kaminsky, P., & Simchi-Levi, E. (2008). *Designing & managing the supply chain: Concepts, strategies and case studies* (3rd ed.). McGraw-Hill Book Company.

Simchi-Levi, D., Wu, S. D., & Shen, Z.-J. (2004). *Handbook of quantitative supply chain analysis: Modeling in the E-business era.* Kluwer Academic Publishers.

Simon, H. A. (1955). A behavioral model of rational choice. *The Quarterly Journal of Economics, 69*(1), 99–118.

Slikker, M. (2006). Relaxed sequencing games have a nonempty core. *Naval Research Logistics, 53*, 235–242.

Smith, W. E. (1956). Various optimizers for single stage production. *Naval Research Logistics Quarterly, 3*, 59–66.

So, K. C., & Song, J. S. (1998). Price, delivery time guarantees and capacity selection. *European Journal of Operational Research, 111*(1), 28–49.

Sokolov, B., Ivanov, D., & Dolgui, A. (Eds.) (2020). *Scheduling in industry 4.0 and cloud manufacturing.* Springer.

Sousa, J. P., & Wolsey, L. A. (1992). A time indexed formulation of non-preemptive single machine scheduling problems. *Mathematical Programming, 54*, 353–367.

Sriskandarajah, C., & Ladet, P. (1986). Some no-wait shops scheduling problems: Complexity aspects. *European Journal of Operational Research, 24*, 424–438.

Statista (2021). *Global market size of outsourced services from 2000 to 2019.* Available at: https://www.statista.com/statistics/189788/global-outsourcing-market-size/

Stecke, K. E., & Zhao, X. (2007). Production and transportation integration for a make-to-order manufacturing company with a commit-to-delivery business mode. *Manufacturing & Service Operations Management, 9*(2), 206–224.

Stein, T., & Sweat, J. (1998). Killer supply chains. *Information Week.*

Talluri, K. T., & Van Ryzin, G. (2004). *The theory and practice of revenue management.* Boston: Kluwer Academic Publishers.

Tan, Z., & Zhang, A. (2013). Online and semi-online scheduling. In P. M. Pardalos, D.-Z. Du, & R. L. Graham (Eds.), *Handbook of combinatorial optimization* (pp. 2192–2252). New York: Springer Press.

Tang, C. S. (2010). A review of marketing-operations interface models: From co-existence to coordination and collaboration. *International Journal of Production Economics, 1*, 22–40.

Tang, L., & Gong, H. (2008). A hybrid two-stage transportation and batch scheduling problem. *Applied Mathematical Modeling, 52*, 2467–2479.

Tang, L., Li, F., & Chen, Z.-L. (2019). Integrated scheduling of production and two-stage delivery of make-to-order products: offline and online algorithms. *INFORMS Journal on Computing, 31*(3), 493–514.

Tayur, S., Ganeshan, R., & Magazine, M. (Eds.) (1999). *Quantitative models for supply chain management.* Kluwer Academic Publishers.

The Economist (2001). A long march to mass customisation. The Economist **360**(8230), 63.

The Standish Group (2020). *CHAOS Report.* Available at: https://www.standishgroup.com/news/45

Thomas, D. J., & Griffin, P. M. (1996). Coordinated supply chain management. *European Journal of Operational Research, 94*, 1–15.

Tian, J., Cheng, T. C. E., Ng, C. T., & Yuan, J. (2012). An improved on-line algorithm for single parallel-batch machine scheduling with delivery times. *Discrete Applied Mathematics, 160*, 1191–1210.

Tian, J., Fu, R., & Yuan, J. (2008). A best on-line algorithm for single machine scheduling with small delivery times. *Theoretical Computer Science, 393*, 287–293.

Tian, J., Fu, R., & Yuan, J. (2011). An on-line algorithm for the single machine unbounded parallel-batching scheduling with large delivery times. *Information Processing Letters, 111*, 1048–1053.

Tijs, S. (1981). Bounds for the core of a game and the τ-value. In O. Moeschlin, & D. Pallaschke, *Game theory and mathematical economics* (pp. 123–132). North-Holland.

Tijs, S. H., Parasarathy, T., Potters, J. A. M., & Prasad, V. R. (1984). Permutation games: Another class of totally balanced games. *OR Spektrum, 6*, 119–123.

Toptal, A., Koc, U., & Sabuncuoglu, I. (2014). A joint production and transportation planning problem with heterogeneous vehicles. *Journal of the Operational Research Society, 65*, 180–196.

Trietsch, D., & Baker, K. R. (1993). Basic techniques for lot streaming. *Operations Research, 41*, 1065–1076.

Tsai, L.-H. (1992). Asymptotic analysis of an algorithm for balanced parallel processor scheduling. *SIAM Journal on Computing, 21*(1), 59–64.

Ullrich, C. A., & Herrmann, J. (2013). *The cost cutting potential of supply chain scheduling.* Working paper, Department of Business Administration and Economics, Bielefeld University, Germany, February. Available at: https://papers.ssrn.com/sol3/papers.cfm?abstract_id=1829138

Vairaktarakis, G. L. (2013). Noncooperative games for subcontracting operations. *Manufacturing & Service Operations Management, 15*(1), 148–158.

Van Dal, R., van der Veen, J. A. A., & Sierksma, G. (1993). Small and large TSP: Two polynomially solvable cases of the traveling salesman problem. *European Journal of Operational Research, 69*, 107–120.

Van den Akker, J. M., Hoogeveen, J. A., & Van de Velde, S.L. (1999). Parallel machine scheduling by column generation. *Operations Research, 47*, 862–872.

Van den Akker, J. M., Hurkens, C. A., & Savelsbergh, M. W. (2000). Time-indexed formulations for machine scheduling problems: Column generation. *INFORMS Journal on Computing, 12*(2), 111–124.

Van den Nouweland, A., Krabbenborg, M., & Potters, J. (1992). Flowshops with a dominant machine. *European Journal of Operational Research, 62*, 38–46.

van Velzen, B. (2006). Sequencing games with controllable processing times. *European Journal of Operational Research, 172*, 64–85.

Vazirani, V. V. (2001). *Approximation algorithms.* New York: Springer.

Vazirani, V. V., Nisan, N., Roughgarden, T., & Tardos, É. (2007). *Algorithmic game theory.* Cambridge, U.K.: Cambridge University Press.

Vestjens, A. P. A. (1997). *Online machine scheduling.* PhD. Thesis, Department of Mathematics and Computing Science, Eindhoven University of Technology, Eindhoven, The Netherlands.

Vickrey, W. (1961). Counterspeculation, auctions, and competitive sealed tenders. *Journal of Finance, 16*, 8–37.

Vickson, R. G. (1980). Choosing the job sequence and processing times to minimize total processing plus flow cost on a single machine. *Operations Research, 28*(5), 1155–1167.

Vijayalakshmi, V. R., Schröder, M., & Tamir, T. (2021). *Theoretical Computer Science, 855*, 90–103.

Voss, S., Martello, S., Osman, I. H., & Roucairol, C. (Eds.) (1999). *Meta-heuristics: Advances and trends in local search paradigms for optimization.* Springer.

Walts, A. (2020). *How inventory reduction actually helps you make more money.* Available at: https://www.skuvault.com/blog/how-inventory-reduction-actually-helps-you-make-more-money/

Wan, G., Vakati, S. R., Leung, J. Y.-T., & Pinedo, M. (2010). Scheduling two agents with controllable processing times. *European Journal of Operational Research, 205*(3), 528–539.

Wang, D.-Y., Grunder, O., & El Moundni, A. (2015). Integrated scheduling of production and distribution operations: A review. *International Journal of Industrial and Systems Engineering, 19*(1), 94–122.

Wang, Q., Batta, R., & Szczerba, R. J. (2005). Sequencing the processing of incoming mail to match an outbound truck delivery schedule. *Computers & Operations Research, 32*, 1777–1791.

References 677

Wang, S., & Wang, X. (2019). Parallel machine scheduling with pricing and rejection. In *16th International Conference on Service Systems and Service Management (ICSSSM)* (pp. 1–5). IEEE.

Weng, Z. K. (1995). Channel coordination and quantity discounts. *Management Science, 41,* 1509–1522.

Williamson, O. E. (1975). *Markets and hierarchies.* New York: Free Press.

Woeginger, G. J. (1994). Heuristics for parallel machine scheduling with delivery times. *Acta Informatica, 31,* 503–512.

Woeginger, G. J. (2000). When does a dynamic programming formulation guarantee the existence of a fully polynomial time approximation scheme (FPTAS)? *INFORMS Journal on Computing, 12*(1), 57–74.

Wu, S. D., Storer, R. H., & Chang, P.-C. (1993). Robust deterministic scheduling in stochastic environments: The method of capacity hedge points. *International Journal of Production Research, 35,* 369–379.

Yang, S., Peng, D., Meng, T., Wu, F., Chen, G., Tang, S., Li, Z., & Luo, T. (2019). On designing distributed auction mechanisms for wireless spectrum allocation. *IEEE Transactions on Mobile Computing, 18*(9), 2129–2146.

Yang, X. (2000). Scheduling with generalized batch delivery dates and earliness penalties. *IIE Transactions, 32,* 735–741.

Yano, C. A., & Gilbert, S. M. (2004). Coordinated pricing and production / procurement decisions: A review. In A. Chakravarty, & J. Eliashberg (Eds.), *Managing business interfaces: Marketing, engineering and manufacturing perspectives.* Kluwer Academic Publishers.

Yeung, W.-K., Choi, T.-M., & Cheng, T. C. E. (2011). Supply chain scheduling and coordination with dual delivery modes and inventory storage cost. *International Journal of Production Economics, 132,* 223–229.

Yuan, J., Li, S., Tian, J., & Fu, R. (2009). A best possible on-line algorithm for the single machine parallel-batch scheduling with restricted delivery times. *Journal of Combinatorial Optimization, 17,* 206–213.

Yue, Q., Chen, Z.-L., & Wan, G. (2019). Integrated pricing and production scheduling of multiple customized products with a common base product. *IISE Transactions, 51*(12), 1383–1401.

Zhang, J., Liu, F., Tang, J., & Li, Y. (2019). The online integrated order picking and delivery considering pickers' learning effects for an O2O community supermarket. *Transportation Research Part E: Logistics and Transportation Review, 123,* 180–199.

Zhang, L., Lu, L., & Yuan, J. (2009). Single machine scheduling with release dates and rejection. *European Journal of Operational Research, 198,* 975–978.

Zhang, J., Wang, X., & Huang, K. (2018). On-line scheduling of order picking and delivery with multiple zones and limited vehicle capacity. *Omega, 79,* 104–115.

Zhong, W., Chen, Z.-L., & Chen, M. (2010). Integrated production and distribution scheduling with committed delivery dates. *Operations Research Letters, 38*(2), 133–138.

Zhong, W., Dosa, G., & Tan, Z. (2007). On the machine scheduling problem with job delivery coordination. *European Journal of Operational Research, 182,* 1057–1072.

Index

A

Absolute price of anarchy, 550, 552, 554, 561–563

Activation, 564, 585–590, 656

Activity, 1, 32, 55, 443, 446, 456, 503, 505, 506, 509, 512, 514–519, 547, 578–582, 589

Activity-on-arcs, 505, 578, 580

Admissibility, 432, 434, 436, 442, 456, 457, 459, 461, 463, 464, 470, 477, 480, 487, 490, 538, 547

Admissible sequence, 44, 458, 465, 467

Affine maximizer, 634, 635, 637–639

Agent, 1, 3, 19–23, 43, 48, 336, 338, 434, 438, 549

Aggregate planning, 20, 185, 186

Algorithmic mechanism, 22, 551, 619, 630, 633, 647, 655, 658

Allocation algorithm, 523–525, 553, 630–635, 638–643, 651–653

Allocation rule, 46, 449, 450, 460, 480–482, 485, 492, 514, 518, 520, 522, 543, 643, 644, 651, 652, 658

Allowable prices, 187, 188, 205–207, 210–220, 222, 223, 227–229, 231, 238

Almost surely, 41, 42, 264, 351, 352, 376

Alternating schedule, 558

Altruist, 607, 608

Altruistic, 22, 550, 589, 606–608, 610–614, 657

Altruistic game, 606–614

Apparel, 12, 19

Appeal factor (AF), 611

Appliance manufacturers, 10

Approximability, 585, 645

Approximation algorithm, 22, 39, 149, 233–236, 619, 623, 627, 629, 658

Approximation ratio, 625, 626, 658

Artificial initial sequence, 432, 490–497

Assembly, 8, 10, 13, 18, 22, 125, 138, 303–305, 307, 335–377, 420, 428, 430

Assignment, 19, 118–122, 124, 386, 388, 395, 399, 400, 443, 444, 470, 583, 584, 586, 587, 598–602, 609, 624, 649, 650

Asymmetric information, 428, 429, 545, 548

Asymmetry, 6

Asymptotic, 41, 264, 266, 267, 308, 343, 348, 354

Asymptotically optimal, 41, 71, 79, 84, 89, 95, 122, 125, 131, 134, 256, 260, 264–266, 362, 365

Asymptotic analysis, 13, 243, 263, 341, 346, 350, 352

Asymptotic competitive ratio, 43, 152, 154, 183

Asymptotic performance, 11, 40, 41, 43, 82, 243, 255, 256

Asymptotic probabilistic analysis, 41

Auction, 19, 547, 618, 632, 658

Automated storage and retrieval system, 18

Automobile plants, 18

Auxiliary problem, 75–77, 80–83, 93–98, 248, 250, 296–298

Average-case performance, 41

Index

B

Balanced game, 441, 495, 504
Bargaining, 6, 113, 114, 334–336, 354, 360, 362, 378, 428, 522, 523
Base product, 12, 188, 220–223, 234
Batch delivery, 21, 22, 54, 60, 88, 135, 175, 308, 313, 317, 322, 325, 427
Batch delivery by direct shipping, 58–60, 88
Batch delivery to a single customer, 54, 60, 72–88, 135, 140, 147–168
Batch delivery to multiple customers, 54, 55, 60, 88–102, 135, 140, 168–175
Batch delivery with routing, 59, 88
Bayes-Nash, 552, 650–655
Benefit of cooperation, 304, 306, 308, 331–334, 382, 386, 397–403, 426, 428
Best possible algorithm, 43, 141
Best response, 555, 576, 577, 583, 584, 597, 616, 656, 657
β-rule, 454, 455, 462
Bid, 19, 506, 617, 618, 620–622, 624, 625, 627–629, 632, 642, 643, 645–649
Big boss game, 504, 510–512
Binary NP-hard, 27, 428, 461, 496, 499, 525, 532, 536, 588, 602
Block family, 382, 384–386, 389–391, 398
Bottleneck, 13, 71, 340, 376, 382, 470, 501
Bounded rationality, 594, 657
Branch-and-bound, 29, 31–33, 39, 40, 71, 240, 271, 276
Breakpoint, 503, 546, 604, 605
Buffer, 4, 7, 18, 307, 308, 320, 404–412, 415, 416, 419–425, 429, 430
Burn-in, 144, 467

C

Capacity allocation, 5, 15–16, 22, 24, 433, 434, 493–496, 520–536, 545, 547
Capacity planning, 2, 3, 12, 17
Catering, 8, 9
Central authority, 550–553, 556, 589, 600, 614–618, 630, 636, 641, 645, 658
Centralized agent, 1, 3
Centralized decision maker, ix, 2, 3, 241
Centralized supply chain, ix, 5–7, 23, 241, 537, 554, 569, 606
Central planner, 19, 301, 499, 550, 551, 553, 589, 598–601, 609, 642
Central scheduler, 551, 553, 620, 623–625, 627, 641, 642, 644

Changeover, 306, 307, 404, 488
Characteristic function, 44–46, 443, 447, 448, 458, 461, 463, 477, 490, 491, 494, 516, 517, 542, 543
Chemical, 7, 8, 20, 378, 404, 480
Cloud computing, 659
Coalition, x, 14, 15, 44–46, 432, 433, 435–445, 447–448, 451, 452, 454–471, 473–475, 477, 478, 480, 481, 484, 485, 487, 489–491, 493–497, 499–502, 505–511, 513, 515, 516, 519, 521, 525–535, 538–543, 546, 549, 657
Coalitional rationality, 437, 449, 500, 539
Column generation, 33, 35–40
Combinatorial auction, 658
Commit-to-deliver, 106, 107
Commit-to-ship, 107
Common due date, 57, 434, 435, 564, 655
Common sequence, 307, 345, 348, 350, 358, 362, 366
Compensation, 44, 362, 367, 399, 403, 433, 481, 482, 484–485, 504, 513, 543, 546, 618, 647, 650, 651
Competition, x, 3, 46, 53, 113, 131, 138, 433, 513
Competitive analysis, 42–43, 146, 158–160, 176, 182, 183
Competitive ratio, 43, 138, 140, 141, 143–145, 149, 150, 152, 154, 157–164, 173, 176, 178, 179, 181, 183, 644, 645
Complete information, 22, 47, 182, 550–616, 655, 656, 659
Completion time, 13, 24, 56, 145, 186, 244, 312, 442, 556
Computational complexity, ix, 5, 25–28, 117, 243, 309, 582, 585, 658, 659
Computer assemblies, 10
Concave cost game, 491
Concession, 441, 442
Concrete, 7, 631
Conflict, x, 4, 6, 12, 15, 18, 22, 303–430, 572
Congestion, 338, 552, 564, 585–589, 599, 606–608, 610, 612, 613, 655–657
Connected component, 447, 448, 455, 457–459, 463, 471, 472, 477, 479
Consistency, 23, 314, 315, 320, 322, 324, 460, 607
Consistent quotation, 217, 220
Consumer electronics, 6, 138
Container port, 19

Controllable processing time, 486–489, 577

Convex combination, 397, 399, 452, 453

Convex game, 16, 45, 46, 439, 448, 452, 495, 511

1-Convex game, 504, 507, 508, 510

Convex hull, 452, 453, 519

Cooperative game, x, 15, 16, 29, 43–46, 303, 431–447, 455, 457, 459, 461, 472, 477, 487, 490, 493, 497, 499, 504, 505, 507, 513, 514, 520, 525, 537, 538, 541–543, 545, 547, 549, 657

Cooperative game theory, 15, 29, 43–46, 303, 431, 433, 434, 436, 438, 439, 504, 525

Coordinated pricing and production scheduling (CPPS), 12, 186, 220, 239, 240

Coordinated problem, 12, 203

Coordination, ix, x, 3–4, 6, 7, 9, 11–17, 22, 48, 203, 204, 207–209, 303, 305, 306, 308, 332, 335, 377, 378, 427–429, 527, 534–536, 545, 547, 551, 575–577, 655

Core, 45, 46, 242, 432, 437–, 440, 442, 445, 449, 451–453, 455, 462, 463, 465–469, 473, 477, 478, 482, 484–486, 488–490, 492–500, 504–507, 516, 518–520, 526–536, 539–540, 542, 543, 547, 642, 643

Core allocation, 45, 46, 455, 478, 484, 485, 494, 496, 542, 543

Core emptiness test, 496, 531, 535, 536

Core membership test, 527–529, 535

Core solution, 438, 445, 449, 451–453, 462, 468, 477, 484–486, 489, 490, 492, 499, 519, 520, 527, 542, 543

Cost allocation scheme, 437

Cost game, 45, 491, 492, 504, 515, 516, 518, 520, 610, 611

Cost of conflict, x, 15, 304, 306, 308, 354, 381–388, 390–392, 396, 397, 429

Cost saving, 15–17, 43–46, 306, 336, 367, 370–376, 378, 400, 403, 430, 432, 436, 437, 441, 443, 445, 449, 451, 454, 455, 457, 458, 461–465, 468, 473, 475–477, 481, 482, 487, 490, 536, 538–540, 543

Cost sharing mechanism, 493, 514–516, 518

Crashing, 486, 487, 509, 512, 513, 578–581, 656

Critical sequence, 62–64

Curse of rationality, 596

Customer service, 14, 53, 113, 221, 239, 306, 338, 521

Customization, 9, 221, 222

Cutting plane, 501

Cycle time, 393

Cyclic, 381, 393, 639

D

Deadlines, 24, 56, 57, 75–77, 105, 107, 108, 110, 112, 182, 184, 210, 244, 307, 335, 366, 488, 602, 642, 643

Decentralized agent, 1, 3, 23, 549

Decentralized decision maker, ix, x, 3, 656

Decentralized supply chain, 6, 14, 23, 243, 303, 304, 433, 549, 552

Decreasing work curve, 647, 648

Delay, 10, 12, 13, 138, 163–167, 173–179, 181, 276, 284, 291, 333, 362, 408, 409, 432, 504, 513–516, 519, 520, 548, 575, 606–608, 610, 612

Delivery characteristics, 57, 58, 125

Delivery date, 10, 21, 107, 506

Delivery deadline, 56, 107, 182

Delivery lead time, 9, 25, 118, 138, 186, 222, 223, 243, 244, 246, 257, 259

Delivery schedule, 6, 20, 22, 37, 54, 56, 67, 79, 87, 100, 108, 119, 121, 122, 133, 153, 161, 165, 170, 172, 242, 289, 303, 312, 325, 386, 387

Delivery sequence, 381, 393

Delivery vehicle, 54, 56, 58, 60, 61, 66, 69, 85, 102, 104, 116, 135, 136, 140, 147, 157, 160, 182, 183

Demand gap, 208

Deterministic truthfulness, 552, 616, 619–623, 630, 641–645

Direct revelation, 618, 619, 630, 634

Direct-revelation mechanism, 618, 619, 630, 634

Direct-sell, 138

Direct shipping, 55, 58–60, 88–96, 99–102, 139, 147, 184

Discount scheme, 242, 292–298

Distributors' game, 520, 526–528, 535, 536

Dominant decision maker, 378, 389

Dominant power, 370, 390, 395

Dominant strategy equilibrium, 633, 634

Dominant strategy incentive compatible, 633–634, 643

Due date, 2, 24, 56, 184, 185, 244, 307, 435, 553

Dynamic pricing, 188, 221, 238–240

Dynamic program, 72, 198–202, 204, 213, 235, 247, 317, 319, 322, 324, 327, 330, 502, 603

682 Index

Dynamic programming, 14, 28–31, 33, 40, 42, 71, 75, 79, 87, 89, 92, 94, 97, 101, 104, 120, 121, 129, 133, 161, 190, 192, 197, 198, 200, 204, 208, 212, 213, 217, 225–228, 234, 236, 240, 246, 270, 271, 273, 274, 279, 285, 290, 291, 296, 316, 317, 319, 320, 322, 325, 326, 328, 411, 415, 461, 528, 531, 538

E

Earliest due date (EDD), 10, 26, 74, 75, 77, 92, 93, 95, 108, 109, 116, 190–192, 204, 273–275, 286–287, 314, 315, 317–319, 322, 324, 325, 327, 328, 330, 337, 350, 351, 373, 383, 384, 389, 391, 538, 561, 562, 603, 604

Earliest Latest Eligible-Departure-Time first (ELEDT), 116, 117

Earliness, 116, 435, 436, 438, 547, 552, 563–569, 655

Earned value management, 514

EDD-LPT, 109

Efficiency, 2, 6, 19, 185, 305, 430, 437, 439–441, 449, 451, 454, 458, 460, 462, 511, 540, 546, 658

Egoist, 606–610

Electronics, 6, 12, 125, 138, 305

Equal gain splitting (EGS), 46, 449–451, 454, 481, 482

Equilibrium, x, 18, 22, 550–551, 554–556, 563–590, 593, 597, 598, 601, 604, 605, 607, 608, 614, 615, 619, 630, 632–634, 656, 658

ERT rule, 296

Expected cost, 556, 566–568, 623–626, 651

Expected net profit, 211

Expected total profit, 210, 214, 218, 219

Expected utility, 48, 555, 556, 619, 650, 651

Expedition, 504, 514–519

Exponential-time algorithm, 26, 39

F

Fair cost allocation, 590, 591

False reporting, 540, 617, 618, 620, 622, 625, 638, 641, 642, 644

Family ordered, 489

Family sequencing, 488–489

Fertilizer, 404

Finished goods inventory, 7, 11

First-come first-served (FCFS), 16, 46, 537, 541, 545, 564

Five-field notation, 57, 107, 114, 139

Fixed delivery departure date, 54, 59, 60, 102–117, 136, 184

Fixed delivery time, 57, 59, 71

Fixed interval scheduling, 8, 71

Flowshop, 2, 22, 24, 25, 57, 59, 66, 69, 186, 188–193, 196–198, 200, 201, 204, 208, 209, 242, 243, 276–284, 289–292, 325, 337, 376, 405, 434, 442, 446, 470–476, 546, 655, 658

Flow time, 162, 311, 312, 316–317, 320–322, 325–327

Follower, 22, 288, 543, 550, 552, 589, 597, 599, 602

Food, 7–9

Food processing, 8, 378

Full batch, 157, 159, 163, 170, 467

Fully coordinated, 12, 207

Fully polynomial time approximation scheme (FPTAS), 42, 188, 190, 197–203, 224, 233–236, 298, 461

G

Gantt chart, 2

General quotation, 217, 218, 220

Genetic algorithm, 8, 40, 428

Glass, 523

Grand coalition, 44, 437–439, 441, 448, 452, 454, 490, 493, 496, 497, 499, 500, 507–510, 516, 521, 526, 528, 529, 531–535, 546, 549

Greedy, 591, 594, 648, 649

H

Hessian matrix, 215, 216

Heterogeneous vehicles, 55, 58, 102, 106–117

Heuristic, 2, 39, 62, 140, 190, 243, 304, 488, 634

Holding cost, 11, 17, 24, 306, 308, 312, 333, 378, 381, 386–388, 393–395, 400, 521, 547

Home textile, 8

Homogeneous vehicles, 55, 56, 102–106, 126

Horizontal supply chain, x, 3, 377

Household cleaners, 377

I

Identical parallel machines, 24, 86, 125, 244, 245, 248, 249, 501, 554, 558, 561, 585, 587, 590, 627

Imperfect information, 428, 429

Index

683

Incentive, 2, 3, 6, 14, 18, 45, 47, 209, 210, 304, 305, 333–335, 354, 356, 357, 360, 361, 367, 403, 405, 429, 452, 493, 494, 505, 507, 514, 552, 554, 573–575, 584, 617, 622, 623, 630, 633–634, 636, 643, 644, 650–654

Incremental discount, 243, 293–298

Individual and immediate delivery, 54, 55, 58–73, 139–147

Individual rationality, 437, 438, 440, 441, 449, 651–653

Industrial chemicals, 8, 378

In-house facility, 242, 264, 284, 285, 289, 291, 574–577

In-house machine, 243, 244, 248, 250–255, 262, 269, 270, 273, 277, 284–289, 299, 575

In-house plant, 242, 244, 276, 284, 286

In-house production, 12, 241, 245, 246, 253, 257, 258, 289, 299

Integer programming, 29, 33–39, 95, 109, 247, 428

Integrated production and outbound distribution scheduling, ix, 53–184

Interchange cost, 307, 308, 404, 407–412, 416, 421–424, 426

Interference job, 62–65

Intractability, 8, 11, 22, 306–309, 314, 362, 427–429, 495, 497

Inventory, 3, 7–11, 13, 17, 24, 53, 107, 113–115, 185, 186, 190, 221, 292, 305, 306, 334, 338, 377, 378, 380, 381, 386–388, 393–395, 400, 403, 420, 428, 429, 480, 521, 547, 564

J

Job, 1, 23, 54, 137, 239, 241, 304, 431, 551

Jobshop, 2, 24, 239, 546, 658

Johnson's Rule, 191, 192, 201, 204, 277–280, 282, 283, 290, 291

Joint strategy, 607, 610, 611, 614

Joint subcontracting and scheduling, 241–300

Just-in-time, 15, 19, 113–114, 306

K

k–lookahead, 594, 597

Kitchen furniture, 18

Knapsack problem, 228, 531

L

Latency, 598–602, 657

Lateness, 16, 25, 57, 61, 75–77, 89–96, 105, 106, 184, 188–192, 195–198, 204, 208, 209, 243, 285, 286, 337, 338, 348–354, 366, 373–376, 379, 383–385, 389–392, 397, 398, 403, 547

Laundry, 381

Laws of large numbers, 341, 347

Leader, 22, 288, 403, 548, 550, 552, 589, 597–606, 657

Leader-follower game, 552, 589, 597–606

Lead time, 8, 9, 18, 22, 25, 55, 118–120, 138, 186, 222, 223, 242–260, 269, 272, 298, 299, 338, 362

Least core, 438, 493, 497–500

Limited number of vehicles, 21, 55, 66–70, 74, 85–89, 99–102

Linear allocation (LA), 246, 522

Linear decomposition, 36, 446, 469

Linear programming game, 526

Liquid crystal display, 13

Local sequencing rule, 552, 582–585

Logistics, 1, 10, 11, 58, 59, 102, 107, 114, 305, 334, 335, 427, 428, 486, 505

Longest processing time (LPT), 80, 81, 109, 133, 144, 153, 158, 159, 179, 181, 220, 274, 502, 586–588

Lookahead, 594, 597, 657

Lot splitting, 521

Lot streaming, 428

Lower bound, 8, 9, 11, 32, 33, 36, 37, 40, 41, 77, 81, 95, 120–123, 125, 198, 199, 234, 256, 258, 261, 267, 268, 342–344, 347–349, 352, 354, 356, 358, 370–375, 413, 557, 559, 560, 562, 572, 581, 648, 649, 654

LP relaxation, 32, 33, 36–38, 95, 122–124, 247, 248, 257, 260

LP-relaxation problem, 248, 257, 260

LTT rule, 168–171

M

Mail, 7, 16, 20, 490

Makespan, 13, 24, 56, 188, 244, 305, 504, 556

Make-to-order, 5, 9–12, 51, 54, 106, 107, 113, 118, 125, 185, 186, 220, 239, 381, 453

Manufacturers' game, 539

Manufacturing cost, 12, 381

Marginal cost, 437, 491, 637, 638

Marginal value, 437, 438, 441, 442, 452, 507, 636

Marginal vector, 452, 486–489
Matching, 557, 562, 583, 584, 658
Materials requirements planning, 2
Maximum delivery time, 54–56, 61–70,
122–127, 131–134, 140–145, 147–160,
168–173
Maximum lateness, 25, 57, 61, 75–77, 89–96,
105, 243, 285, 286, 337, 348–354, 375,
379, 383–385, 389, 390, 403
Maximum tardiness, 9, 243, 269, 273–274, 561
Mechanism, 4, 47, 289, 304, 493, 551
Medication, 9
Metaheuristic, 8
Misreporting, 403
Mixed integer program, 246, 388, 428
Mixed-model, 18, 430
Mixed strategy, 47, 48, 555, 556, 566
Mixed strategy Nash equilibrium, 47, 555, 556
Modular pricing, 188, 221
Monotonicity, 437, 439, 547, 630, 632,
639–641, 644, 652, 654, 659
Multi-agent, 20
Multi-period problem, 187, 217, 220–239
Multiple decision makers, x, 6, 14, 18
Multiple plants, 55, 60, 117–125, 136
Multiple stages, 136, 186, 240, 305, 429
Multi-stage, 18, 20, 217, 428, 434, 443,
480–485, 546

N
Nash equilibrium, 47–49, 333, 551, 552,
554–564, 569–573, 575–591, 597, 598,
600, 607–612, 614–616, 650, 651,
655–658
Negotiating power, 397, 403
Negotiation, 335, 403, 428, 429, 438
Net profit, 12, 189, 191, 192, 194–202,
205–209, 211, 227, 523, 524, 578, 579,
603
New product development, 333
Newspapers, 7, 16, 377–379, 382, 397
Nonbottleneck, 335–337
Noncooperative, ix–xi, 5, 7, 14, 22, 29, 43,
46–48, 243, 301, 303, 549–659
Noncooperative game theory, x, ix, 5, 7, 14,
29, 46–49
Nonpreemptive, 10, 21, 152–156, 161,
164–168, 171, 222, 336, 379, 383, 461,
464, 480, 490, 497, 553, 569, 571, 573,
574, 592, 603, 620, 621, 623, 645, 650
Non-preemptive problem, 140, 152–156,
164–168, 171
No-wait, 57, 66, 69, 424, 425

No-wait flow shop, 66
NP-complete, 194, 245, 316, 317, 319, 320,
322, 324, 325, 328, 357, 366, 376,
527–529, 535, 564, 580, 583, 610
NP-hard, 26, 61, 140, 188, 243, 379, 461, 588
Nucleolus, 439, 440, 442, 505, 508, 509, 512
Number of late jobs, 56, 243, 285–287, 312,
317–320, 323, 325, 327–330, 428

O
Offline algorithm, 42, 43, 139, 181–183
Offline counterpart, 140, 147–149, 157
Online, 10, 24, 54, 138, 214, 299, 453, 594
Online algorithm, 42, 43, 51, 138, 140–142,
144, 145, 147, 149, 150, 152, 157, 158,
160–164, 168, 169, 171, 173, 175, 176,
179, 182–184
On-time, 6, 16, 53, 74, 91, 191, 204, 221,
286–288, 311, 312, 314, 315, 317, 319,
322–325, 328, 330, 332, 513, 519, 538,
568, 603, 604, 642
On-time job, 312, 323, 328, 330, 568
Openshop, 24, 434, 442, 476–478, 658
Optimal anarchy threshold, 610
Optimal basic solution, 124, 248, 260
Optimal offline solution, 150–152, 154, 165,
174, 175, 182
Optimal online algorithm, 43
Optimal schedule, 34, 63, 64, 141, 191, 253,
306, 434, 557
Optimal sequence, 447, 449, 451, 454, 456,
466, 473, 481, 482, 490, 491, 497, 539
Optimal stability threshold, 610
Optimization, x, ix, 4, 5, 15, 21, 22, 25, 28,
31, 35, 40, 78, 239, 243, 301, 303–432,
434, 456, 460, 520, 529, 549, 565, 572,
597, 630, 646, 658
Order based problem, 187, 210–220
Order inquiry, 210–212
Ordinarily NP-hard, 27–29, 37, 42, 70, 79, 89,
96, 117, 122, 135, 190, 194–196, 212,
229, 230, 245, 258, 275, 277, 278, 281,
282, 286, 289, 291, 294, 296, 461
Outbound distribution, ix, 7, 21, 53–134,
137–184
Outsourcing, 3, 5, 13, 17, 22, 434, 537–545,
547, 570–573, 602, 603, 605, 606
Overtime, 16, 386, 397, 537, 538

P
Paper manufacturing, 429
Parallel batching, 144

Parallel machines, 2, 23–25, 29, 36, 47, 48, 55, 59, 66, 79–85, 96–99, 125, 127, 128, 130, 131, 133, 136, 140, 145–147, 156, 157, 175, 176, 180, 239, 244, 245, 248, 249, 256, 263, 286, 289, 427, 435, 501, 546, 554, 558, 561, 582, 585, 587, 590–593, 616, 623–630, 640, 641, 645, 647, 648, 655, 657, 658
Pareto optimal, 21, 245, 359, 360, 545, 656
Partial batch, 104, 157, 159, 170, 174, 175
Partially coordinated, 12, 203, 207
Partial order, 8, 108, 334, 521–531, 534–536
Partition, 31, 33, 36, 38, 78–80, 98, 192, 194–197, 201, 229, 234, 278, 317, 320, 328, 340, 341, 357, 363, 366, 455–463, 471, 496, 529, 530, 532, 533, 546, 580–582, 588, 589
Partition equal gain sharing (PEGS), 457–459
Partition problem, 36, 38, 193, 194, 229, 278
Partition sequencing, 456–460, 546
Parts suppliers, 22, 303, 428
Payment scheme, 22, 437–440, 449, 551, 552, 616–618, 630, 631, 633–638, 646–649, 651, 653, 654
Payoff vector, 495, 496, 527–530, 532, 533, 535, 536
z-Penalized optimal cost allocation, 500
Penalty, 10, 16, 56, 116, 184, 222–224, 226, 231, 232, 295, 432, 434, 438, 453, 490, 497–504, 506, 513, 514, 520, 538, 540, 546, 558, 564, 575, 577, 607
Penalty-subsidy function, 500, 501, 503, 546
Perishable product, 7, 16, 185, 306, 377
Permutational convexity, 487
Permutation game, 434, 443–444, 465, 486, 546
Permutation schedule, 314, 325, 471, 472
Pessimistic, 491–493, 515, 516
Placement probability, 211–216, 218, 219
Planning system, 13, 14
Player, 43, 304, 432, 551
Polynomially reducible, 27, 74
Polynomially solvable, 26–28, 100, 117, 243, 281–282, 294, 395, 501, 623
Polynomial time, 26, 65, 148, 188, 246, 308, 461, 564
Polynomial-time algorithm, 26–28, 42, 67, 75, 100, 106, 148, 248, 308, 314, 531, 532, 610, 650
Polynomial time approximation scheme, 42, 65, 188, 190, 197–203, 461, 649
Pool point, 11, 125–134, 176–181
Positional penalty, 502, 558, 575, 577

Precedence constraints, 64, 65, 299, 485, 509, 512
Preemption, 147, 160–162, 165, 167, 168, 171, 173, 494, 521, 569, 574, 620–623, 645
Preemptive, 140, 149–152, 162–164, 175, 379, 569–571, 621, 642, 643
Preemptive problem, 140, 149–152, 162–164
Preempt-restart, 642–644, 659
Preempt-resume, 642–644, 659
Preventive preemption, 621–623
Price of anarchy, 48, 550–552, 554, 556–563, 589–594, 596, 597, 610, 614, 657
Price of stability, 561, 614, 657, 658
Price quotation, 12, 186, 210, 211, 214, 217–219, 240
Pricing, ix, 3–5, 11–12, 21, 24, 28, 51, 185–240, 547, 597, 602, 605, 657
Pricing-scheduling coordination, 203
Priority rule, 541, 570–574, 643, 656
Priority score, 642, 643
Private information, x, 4, 22, 47, 301, 540, 541, 547, 550–552, 616–656, 659
Probabilistic analysis, 41
Probabilistic assignment, 624
Probabilistic initial sequence, 493–497
Process industry, 378, 404
Product based problem, 187–210
Production planning, 2, 3, 11, 185
Production schedule, 6, 9, 13, 17, 22, 29, 30, 107, 115, 133, 134, 155, 165–167, 170, 174, 221, 223, 244, 303, 305, 379, 400, 429
Profile, 47, 48, 192, 193, 199–201, 407–410, 420–423, 578, 580, 582, 583, 650
Profit gap, 208, 209
Project, 2, 113, 432, 552
Proportional allocation, 522–524
Proportional sharing rule, 586, 588
Proportionate flowshop, 243, 278, 282–284, 442, 446, 471–476
Pseudo polynomial time, 26–29, 37, 42, 190, 194–196, 204, 212, 224–226, 229, 230, 246, 270, 273, 274, 277, 279, 281, 282, 286, 290, 291, 300, 316, 319, 325, 461, 528, 529, 532, 564
Pseudo-polynomial-time algorithm, 26, 27, 190, 194–196, 224, 226, 229, 230, 277, 281, 282, 286, 300, 316
Public information, 578, 590, 620, 631
Pure strategy, 47, 48, 554, 555, 557, 558, 560, 561, 566, 570, 572, 577, 582, 583, 586
Pure strategy Nash equilibrium, 47, 48, 554, 557, 570, 572, 586

Q

Quadratic program, 215, 216
Quantity discount, 242, 243, 292, 293, 605
Quasilinear, 618

R

Radio spectrum, 19
Railcar distribution, 429
Randomization, 551, 616, 619, 648, 649
Randomized mechanism, 552, 619, 620, 623–629, 647, 659
Randomized rounding, 652
Regular cost, 434, 442, 446, 447, 453–456
Relative error, , 197, 260, 339, 341, 343–346, 348–350, 352–354
Relaxed sequencing game, 444, 463–467
Release date, 2, 56, 57, 61, 308, 311–314, 319–321, 331, 546, 553, 642, 655
Rescheduling game, 446, 456–463
Rescheduling problem, 456, 538, 546
Resequencing, 18, 306, 307, 320, 404–427, 429–432, 454, 455, 457, 465, 468, 473, 477, 490, 538, 545
Reservation, 15, 17, 433, 537, 538, 547, 574
Resource allocation, 446, 585
Retailer, 3, 6, 10, 12, 118, 137, 138, 333, 377, 378, 380, 381, 386–388, 393, 429, 480
Revelation principle, 619, 636
Revenue, 6, 12, 28, 54, 56, 57, 59, 71, 72, 186, 188–190, 192, 197, 203–206, 209, 211, 212, 214, 215, 217–219, 221–228, 231–233, 235, 521–523, 525, 535, 536, 570, 589, 603, 604
Reward, 20, 432, 504, 505, 513–519, 547, 563, 577–581
Risk aversion, 660
Rolling horizon, 21, 138, 140, 181, 182, 184, 429
Rule S, 63, 64, 140, 141

S

Saturated batch, 164, 166
Scheduling game, 5, 16, 22, 432–434, 437, 438, 461, 467, 468, 478, 489–503, 545, 546, 550–554, 556, 563, 564, 567, 569, 578, 582, 583, 585, 589–591, 593, 594, 597, 614, 616, 623, 624, 627, 632, 633, 639, 640, 649, 653, 657–661
Scheduling situation, 444, 486, 553, 593
SEDD, 93–96

Self-interested, ix, 5, 14, 20, 22, 48, 304, 404, 553, 585, 589, 597, 598, 602, 617, 642, 649
Selfish, 550, 551, 589, 590, 598–600, 606, 608, 611, 612, 623, 627
Selfishness level, 610–614, 659
Semiconductor, 15, 144, 433, 537
Semi-online, 184
Sensitivity analysis, 208, 261, 267, 536
Separation problem, 501, 502
SEQC, 217–220
SEQG, 217–220
Sequence-dependent, 488, 538
Sequence-independent, 38, 488, 523, 529
Sequencing, 2, 24, 71, 190, 307, 432, 553
Sequential game, 48, 49, 589–597
Sequential quotation, 12, 188, 210, 214, 217–220
Sequencing game, 16, 22, 44, 46, 431–434, 442–490, 497, 545, 546
Service, 1, 6, 8, 14, 16, 19, 20, 22, 53, 59, 102, 113, 185, 186, 221, 239, 242, 258, 299, 306, 338, 432, 443, 444, 446, 480, 503, 513, 521, 537, 550, 564–566, 569, 611, 615, 634, 641
Set covering, 591
Setup, 6, 13, 18–19, 22, 185, 292, 299, 303, 306, 307, 377–382, 384–386, 388, 390–392, 395–400, 403, 427, 488, 538
Shapley value, 46, 438, 439, 442, 445, 452, 453, 459, 460, 462, 463, 468–470, 474–476, 481, 489, 492, 493, 499, 505, 512, 542
Shifted shortest processing time (SSPT) rule, 161, 162, 164, 175–177
Shipping due date, 93, 95
Shipping with fixed delivery departure dates, 59
Shortest processing time (SPT), 39, 47, 74, 79, 81, 85–87, 97, 99–101, 103, 104, 119–121, 127, 128, 131, 152, 181, 216, 220, 225, 226, 270–272, 285, 314–316, 320, 322, 325, 327, 337, 339, 342, 347, 351, 371, 373, 456, 502, 541, 553–555, 558–560, 570–572, 575–577, 592
Shortest weighted processing time (SWPT), 190, 191, 198, 204, 205, 211, 212, 215, 225, 234, 447, 450, 461, 473, 492, 494, 495, 523–525, 621–623, 638, 640
Short lead time, 8, 18
Short shelf-life, 5, 7–9, 19, 54
σ_0-component additive, 455, 468, 470, 472, 477, 486, 487, 489

Index

Simulated annealing, 40, 371, 372
Simultaneous game, 48, 591, 593
Simultaneous quotation, 188, 210, 214–216, 220
Single decision maker, x, ix, 4, 5, 20, 21, 43, 554
Single machine, 2, 23, 59, 156, 189, 245, 309, 434, 566
Single-period problem, 187, 217, 239
Smallest counterexample, 143
Socially optimal, 551, 554, 561, 565, 567, 569, 575, 577, 580, 590, 609, 611, 612, 615, 620, 621, 624, 640, 641, 659, 660
Social optimum, 568, 589, 609–614, 659
Social welfare, 550, 597, 610, 621, 622, 659, 660
Split job, 249–253, 260
Splittable delivery, 59, 114, 115
SRPT rule, 148–151, 161–163, 165, 166, 174, 175
s-shipment, 127, 131, 177, 178
Stability, x, 15, 331, 431–433, 480, 500, 504, 507, 547, 561, 580, 610, 614, 658–660
Stable coalition, 534
Stable equilibrium, 614
Stable game, 16, 45, 480, 481, 551, 611
Stackelberg, 288, 403, 548, 550, 597, 598, 600–602, 606, 659
State space trimming, 197, 234
Steel, 11, 13, 113–115, 125
Storage, 7, 10, 18, 29, 113, 114, 307, 308, 320, 404, 406, 407, 411–424, 426, 427
Strategic behavior, 545, 547
Strong law of large numbers, 42
Strongly *NP*-hard, 26–28, 33, 37, 39, 42, 61, 62, 69, 70, 77, 78, 96, 100, 116, 117, 119, 127, 135, 136, 140, 149, 157, 161, 168, 173, 239, 245, 497, 501
Strongly polynomial-time algorithm, 26, 248
Strong model of execution, 620
Subcontracting, ix, 4–6, 12–13, 17–18, 22, 24, 241–300, 541, 542, 545, 547, 552, 563, 569–577, 603–606
Subcontracting budget, 243, 269–276
Subcontracting cost, 13, 242–245, 248, 251, 253, 258, 262, 269, 270, 272, 273, 275, 277, 282, 283, 289, 291–299, 605
Subcontractor, 13, 242–247, 250–252, 256–259, 261, 262, 264–269, 272, 284–292, 298, 299, 432, 504, 545, 546, 563, 570, 574–576, 597, 602–606, 659
Subgame perfect equilibrium, 49, 590–594, 597, 658, 659

Submodular, 45
Submodularity, 45
Subset sum, 89, 230, 245, 258
Subsidy, 432, 434, 497, 499–503, 546
Sufficient number of vehicles, 55, 58, 59, 61, 73, 76, 85, 183
Sum of weighted completion times, 621
Superadditive, 454, 455, 468, 472, 477, 487, 539
Supermodular, 45, 490, 497, 499
Supermodularity, 45
Supplier, x, 3, 6, 14, 17–19, 22, 113, 114, 303–316, 319, 320, 324–326, 328, 331–343, 345–352, 354–357, 359–362, 364, 366–373, 376, 377, 404–413, 416, 419–426, 428–430, 433, 493, 494, 569, 597
Suppliers' game, 431, 433, 435, 438
Supply chain, 1, 23, 53, 54, 137, 185, 241, 303, 431, 549
Supply chain performance, 1, 19, 22, 304
Surplus sharing mechanism, 516, 518
Symmetric singleton congestion game, 607, 608, 610, 612, 613
Symmetric strategy, 566, 567
Symmetry, 394, 425, 437, 439–441, 460, 547
System cost, 6, 16, 305, 312, 324, 332, 334, 357, 371, 378, 397, 400, 405, 429, 550, 556, 561, 564, 576, 577, 606

T

Tabu search, 11, 40
Tail game, 434, 490–493
Tardiness, 9, 25, 26, 56, 57, 184, 188, 222–227, 230–232, 236, 239, 243, 269, 270, 273–276, 338, 379, 428, 429, 453, 537, 538, 552, 561–569, 602, 603, 605, 657
Task, 470, 497, 504, 513, 514, 516, 578, 579, 581, 625, 627–629
Taxation game, 516, 520
Terminal management, 19
Textile company, 19
Third party, 10, 11, 15, 17, 58, 59, 107, 114, 335, 427, 433, 434, 537–541, 545, 547, 569, 657, 658
Third-party logistics (3PL), 10, 11, 58, 59, 107, 335, 427
Three-field notation, 25
Time-indexed formulation, 33–35
Time window, 11, 19, 56, 71, 113, 114, 538
Total delay time, 163–167, 174–179
Total delivery cost, 82, 157, 164, 165, 167, 291

Total delivery time, 30, 34, 35, 55, 59, 79–85, 87, 88, 96–99, 101, 119–122, 126, 127, 129–131, 160–168, 173–175
Total tardiness, 26, 184, 222, 224, 226, 227, 231, 243, 269, 270, 274–276, 338, 379, 428, 453, 561, 562
Transportation cost, 34, 35, 37, 54, 56, 57, 59, 73–85, 96–99, 105–107, 113, 118–123, 126, 127, 131, 156–160, 162, 168–174, 176, 242, 284, 285
Transportation time, 30, 34, 37, 56, 58, 60–62, 66, 69, 73, 81, 89, 103, 124, 126, 141–145, 150, 153, 155, 168, 169, 176, 184, 284, 289, 291, 337, 346, 376, 405
Truckload, 379–381
Truthful algorithm, 47, 551, 620–622, 628, 632
Truthful mechanism, 551, 616, 617, 619–621, 623, 626, 627, 632, 634, 639–641, 648, 651, 660
Truthfulness in expectation, 552, 616, 619, 620, 623, 627, 632, 649–652
Truthful payment scheme, 644, 650
Truthful reporting, 4, 22, 540, 551, 616–618, 620, 626, 632, 635, 638–640, 649
Two-stage flowshop, 243, 276, 282, 284, 289–292
Two stages of job delivery, 60

U
Unanimity game, 434, 443–446, 458, 459, 468, 469, 474, 475, 486
Unary NP-hard, 27, 428
Uncertainty sequencing situation, 490
Uniform parallel machines, 558, 582, 627–632, 649, 650
Uniform sharing rule, 585, 586, 590
Unit sequencing game, 464, 465
Universal truthfulness, 552, 619, 620, 647–649
Unrelated parallel machines, 558, 592, 616, 623–627, 630, 640, 641, 659
Unsaturated batch, 163, 166
Upper bound, 40, 41, 77, 120, 130, 145, 198, 202, 227, 228, 261–263, 299, 342, 347, 366, 369–371, 526, 557, 559, 562, 579, 580, 595, 614
Upstream, 307, 335, 404

Utility, 46–48, 435, 440, 553–556, 590, 606, 618, 619, 621, 633–635, 638, 639, 642, 647–649, 652, 653, 657
Utilization, 138, 308, 569, 571, 572

V
τ-value, 441, 442, 452, 453, 505, 508, 509, 511, 512
Value of coordination, x, 12, 15, 203, 208, 306
Value of integration, 98, 99
Value of partial coordination, 208
Value of subcontracting, 22, 51, 242, 243, 260–269
Vehicle capacity, 56, 58, 75, 77, 79, 81, 89, 92, 95, 99, 135, 136, 150, 153, 155, 169, 377
Vehicle routing, 3, 8, 14, 59, 85, 88, 89, 99, 135, 136, 377
Vertical supply chain, 3
Vickrey–Clarke–Groves (VCG), 636–639, 648, 656
Volume discount, 22
v-shipment, 82, 87, 126–134, 176–180

W
Waiting strategy, 141, 149
Weak model of execution, 627–629
Weak monotonicity, 632, 639–641
Weight, 2, 24, 56, 58, 107, 115, 189, 190, 211, 213, 216, 222, 229, 310, 319, 324, 400, 447, 461, 464, 467, 486, 490, 494–497, 500, 521, 553, 620, 622, 640, 654
Work-in-process, 5, 24, 186, 190, 312, 338, 428, 521, 535, 536
Work-in-process inventory, 24, 190, 428, 521
Worst case, 13, 25, 26, 40–43, 48, 51, 62, 64, 65, 79, 82, 83, 97, 109, 112, 124, 125, 131, 140, 146, 149, 182, 240, 243, 255, 260, 277, 294, 296–298, 305, 338, 398, 494, 556, 589, 591, 593, 602, 627, 649
Worst-case analysis, 13, 240, 243
Worst-case performance, 40, 43, 48, 51, 62, 64, 65, 83, 97, 109, 112, 125, 131, 140, 149, 260, 294, 296, 627